PRENTICE HALL WRITING COACH

Grade Six

This work is protected by United States copyright laws and is provided *solely for the use of teachers and administrators* in teaching courses and assessing student learning in their classes and schools. Dissemination or sale of any part of this work (including on the World Wide Web) will destroy the integrity of the work and is *not* permitted.

Acknowledgments appear on page TR55, which constitute an extension of this copyright page.

Copyright © 2012 Pearson Education, Inc., or its affiliates. All Rights Reserved. Printed in the United States of America. This publication is protected by copyright, and permission should be obtained from the publisher prior to any prohibited reproduction, storage in a retrieval system, or transmission in any form or by any means, electronic, mechanical, photocopying, recording, or likewise. For information regarding permissions, write to Pearson Curriculum Group Rights & Permissions, One Lake Street, Upper Saddle River, New Jersey 07458.

Pearson, Prentice Hall, and Pearson Prentice Hall are trademarks, in the U.S. and/or other countries, of Pearson Education, Inc., or its affiliates.

ExamView® is a registered trademark of eInstruction Corporation. The DimensionL logo and tradename, the reflective "L" orb, the "Play!" button, the "Literacy. Get in the Game." tagline and all game name, logos and game graphics, including characters and backgrounds are the property of Tabula Digita, Inc. All rights reserved. ©2010 Tabula Digita, Incorporated.

ISBN-13: 978-0-13-253720-9
ISBN-10: 0-13-253720-6
7 8 9 10 V3NL 14 13

PEARSON

Upper Saddle River, New Jersey   Boston, Massachusetts   Chandler, Arizona   Glenview, Illinois

WELCOME TO
Writing COACH

Seven Great Reasons to Learn to Write Well

> *The bottom line is, students need to feel and experience what writing can do to enhance their lives and thinking.*
> —**Jeff Anderson**

1 Writing is hard, but hard is **rewarding**.

2 Writing helps you **sort things out**.

3 Writing helps you **persuade** others.

4 Writing makes you a **better reader**.

5 Writing makes you **smarter**.

6 Writing helps you get into and through **college**.

7 Writing **prepares you** for the world of work.

> *Writing doesn't just allow you to write what you already know. Sometimes writing generates ideas you didn't know you had.*
> —**Kelly Gallagher**

AUTHORS

The contributing authors guided the direction and philosophy of *Prentice Hall Writing Coach*. Working with the development team, they helped to build the pedagogical integrity of the program and to ensure its relevance for today's teachers and students.

Program Authors

Jeff Anderson

Jeff Anderson has worked with struggling writers and readers for almost 20 years. His works integrate grammar and editing instruction into the processes of reading and writing. Anderson has written articles in NCTE's *Voices from the Middle, English Journal*, and *Educational Leadership.* Anderson won the NCTE Paul and Kate Farmer Award for his *English Journal* article on teaching grammar in context. He has published two books, *Mechanically Inclined: Building Grammar, Usage, and Style into Writer's Workshop* and *Everyday Editing: Inviting Students to Develop Skill and Craft in Writer's Workshop* as well as a DVD, *The Craft of Grammar.*

Grammar gives me a powerful lens through which to look at my writing. It gives me the freedom to say things exactly the way I want to say them.

Kelly Gallagher

Kelly Gallagher is a full-time English teacher at Magnolia High School in Anaheim, California. He is the former co-director of the South Basin Writing Project at California State University, Long Beach. Gallagher is the author of *Reading Reasons: Motivational Mini-Lessons for the Middle and High School, Deeper Reading: Comprehending Challenging Texts 4–12, Teaching Adolescent Writers,* and *Readicide.* He is also featured in the video series, *Building Adolescent Readers.* With a focus on adolescent literacy, Gallagher provides training to educators on a local, national and international level. Gallagher was awarded the Secondary Award of Classroom Excellence from the California Association of Teachers of English—the state's top English teacher honor.

The best swimmers swim the most; the best writers write the most. There's only one way to become a good writer: write!

Thanks to the wisdom and classroom experience of Jeff Anderson and Kelly Gallagher, *Writing Coach* is a program that is approachable for students and teachers.

Jeff Anderson's commitment to finding ways to make grammar instruction a positive experience for students was key in the development of *Writing Coach.* He authored instruction for *Mentor Texts,* the *What Do You Notice?* feature, the *Grammar Game Plan Find It/Fix It* guide to the 20 most common student errors, and the *Grammar Mini-Lessons.*

Kelly Gallagher's commitment to the need for daily practice in writing was key to the development of *Writing Coach.* Kelly authored instruction for *Mentor Texts,* the *Reader's Eye* and *Writer's Eye, Revision RADaR, the ABCDs of On-Demand Writing,* and *Coach's Corner.*

At www.phwritingcoach.com, videos featuring both Anderson and Gallagher provide you and your students with powerful strategies for revising and editing.

Contributing Authors

Evelyn Arroyo

Evelyn Arroyo is the author of **A+RISE**,
Research-based Instructional Strategies for ELLs
(English Language Learners). Her work focuses on
closing the achievement gap for minority students
and English language learners. Through her
publications and presentations, Arroyo provides
advice, encouragement, and practical success
strategies to help teachers reach their ELL students.

> Your rich, colorful cultural life experiences are unique and can easily be painted through words. These experiences define who you are today, and writing is one way to begin capturing your history. Become a risk-taker and fall in love with yourself through your own words.

> When you're learning a new language, writing in that language takes effort. The effort pays off big time, though. Writing helps us generate ideas, solve problems, figure out how the language works, and, above all, allows us to express ourselves.

Jim Cummins, Ph.D.

Jim Cummins is a Professor in the Modern Language
Centre at the University of Toronto. A well-known
educator, lecturer, and author, Cummins focuses his
research on bilingual education and the academic
achievement of culturally diverse students. He is the
author of numerous publications, including **Negotiating
Identities: Education for Empowerment in a Diverse
Society.**

Grant Wiggins, Ed.D.

Grant Wiggins is the President of Authentic Education.
He earned his Ed.D. from Harvard University. Grant
consults with schools, districts, and state education
departments; organizes conferences and workshops;
and develops resources on curricular change. He is
the co-author, with Jay McTighe, of **Understanding By
Design,** the award-winning text published by ASCD.

> I hated writing as a student—and my grades showed it. I grew up to be a writer, though. What changed? I began to think I had something to say. That's ultimately why you write: to find out what you are really thinking, really feeling, really believing.

> Concepts of grammar can sharpen your reading, communication, and even your reasoning, so I have championed its practice in my classes and in my businesses. Even adults are quick to recognize that a refresher in grammar makes them keener— and more marketable.

Gary Forlini

Gary Forlini is managing partner of the School Growth
initiative **Brinkman—Forlini—Williams,** which trains
school administrators and teachers in Classroom
Instruction and Management. His recent works include
the book **Help Teachers Engage Students** and the data
system **ObserverTab** for district administrators, **Class
Acts: Every Teacher's Guide To Activate Learning,** and
the initiative's workshop **Grammar for Teachers.**

A well-rounded team of authors means a strong, cohesive program.

Evelyn Arroyo works to ensure that students at all levels find instructional materials accessible. She
contributed strategies for reaching English Language Learners.

Jim Cummins is committed to empowering culturally diverse learners. He authored strategies for
teaching English Language Learners and reaching students from all cultures.

Grant Wiggins champions instruction focused on essential and thought-provoking ideas that ensure
knowledge transfer and application. He authored the Big Questions for each chapter, including the
Why write? strand, which addresses essential ideas about writing.

Gary Forlini, a nationally known education consultant, is a grammar expert. He was a key
contributor to the grammar scope, sequence, and pedagogy presented in Prentice Hall *Writing Coach*.

Print and Online Components

Writing Coach offers a full writing and grammar program in formats that fit your teaching style, whether you choose print, digital, or a combination of both. All print materials are available online as eTexts. The centerpiece of the online program is the Interactive Writing Coach™ which provides personalized writing support and feedback for students at all ability levels.

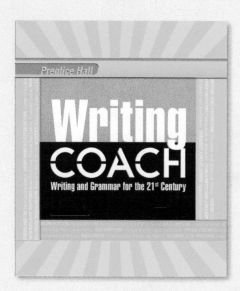

Student Edition

- In-depth 5-stage writing process lessons
- Professional Mentor Texts and Student Models
- 21st Century Skills and writing for multimedia
- Comprehensive grammar, usage, and mechanics instruction and practice
- Test prep review and practice

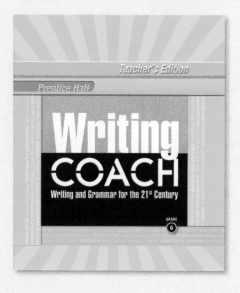

Teacher's Edition

- Annotated lessons for writing and grammar
- Flexible lesson planning and pacing
- Differentiated instruction for students at all levels
- Support for integration of writing and grammar into the language arts curriculum

WRITING COACH

Online

www.phwritingcoach.com

For the Student

- Student Edition eText
- Video Library
- Graphic Organizers
- Grammar Tutorials
- Spanish Resources
- Sentence Diagraming

WRITING

Interactive Writing Coach™ Paragraph Feedback and Essay Scoring provide personalized writing support.

Interactive Graphic Organizers Leveled support helps students plan and develop their writing.

Interactive Model Mentor Texts and Student Models provide exemplary models of writing.

Interactive Online Journal Students record and save all their assignments and writing.

Resources Links to online resources help students research and plan multimedia projects.

Videos Program authors provide point-of-use revising and editing tips.

For the Teacher

- Student Edition eText
- Teacher Edition eText
- Lesson Planner
- Video Library
- Graphic Organizers
- Grammar Tutorials
- Sentence Diagraming

GRAMMAR

Diagnostic and Practice Diagnostic tests assess skills and automatically assign instruction and practice.

Grammar Tutorials Point-of-use videos reinforce key grammar skills.

ExamView Assessment Suite (diagnostic and assessment) Electronic test generator allows teachers to customize assessment.

Tabula Digita: DimensionL
www.pearsonschool.com/dimensionL Students hone their grammar skills with this fast-paced, multiplayer video game.

CONTENTS IN BRIEF

WRITING

The **Writing Game Plan** sets the stage for students to get into the "game" of writing.

Writing without grammar only goes so far. Grammar and writing work together. To write well, grammar skills give me great tools.

The **Core Writing Chapters** provide opportunities for using the writing process while focusing on specific genres in featured assignments.

CORE WRITING CHAPTERS

WRITING COACH
Online
www.phwritingcoach.com

Interactive Writing Coach™

Interactive Graphic Organizer

Interactive Model

Online Journal

Resources

Video

vi

Writing Coach Online provides tools and resources for personalizing instruction. Students and teachers know what to use, and when, via these six easily recognizable icons found throughout the program.

GRAMMAR

GRAMMAR GAME PLAN

 **Major Grammatical Errors and How to Fix Them**

Grammar without writing is only a collection of rules, but when these rules are put into action as I write, the puzzle comes together.

The ***Grammar Game Plan*** focuses on the 20 most common grammatical errors.

CORE GRAMMAR CHAPTERS

Core Grammar Chapters provide in-depth instruction in grammar, usage, and mechanics.

STUDENT RESOURCES

Handbooks

Glossaries

WRITING COACH
Online
www.phwritingcoach.com

- Grammar Tutorials
- Grammar Practice
- Grammar Games

Students can easily access ***Writing Coach Online*** support as they apply and practice their grammar skills.

vii

Contents

The why's, what's, and how's of writing get students comfortable with the idea that "there's a writer in all of us."

An introduction to the various types of writing helps set the stage for the chapters to come, each of which focuses on a particular genre.

WRITING

WRITING GAME PLAN

An overview of the five-stage **Writing Process** provides the foundation for the core writing chapters.

An overview of the basics of writing sentences and paragraphs also provides an introduction to the *Interactive Writing Coach* and how it is integrated into the program.

WRITING COACH

Online

www.phwritingcoach.com

All content available online

- Interactive Writing Coach™
- Interactive Graphic Organizer
- Interactive Models
- Online Journal
- Resources
- Video

Contents xv

Contents

Each writing chapter focuses on a *Feature Assignment*—a particular form within the genre.

The *Connect to the Big Questions* feature encourages students to make connections among ideas and to apply their thoughts to their understanding of writing.

Connect to the Big Questions

• **What do you think?**
Which experiences shape our sense of ourselves?

• **Why write?**
What should we put in and leave out to be accurate and honest?

Instruction in the five key stages of the **writing process** provides a predictable routine for students' writing. Steps are color-coded for ease of use.

Connect to the Big Questions

- **What do you think?**
  What can we learn from playing games?

- **Why write?**
  What can fiction do better than nonfiction?

WRITING COACH
Online
www.phwritingcoach.com

All content available online
- Interactive Writing Coach™
- Interactive Graphic Organizer
- Interactive Models
- Online Journal
- Resources
- Video

Writing Coach Online offers a full digital program that stands alone or supports the print-based approach.

The ***Interactive Writing Coach*™** provides personalized feedback and support to students as they write.

Contents

Connect to the Big Questions

- **What do you think?**
  How can we communicate what we see?

- **Why write?**
  How does one best convey feelings through words on a page?

Make Your Writing Count assignments provide opportunities to write with 21st Century learning in mind. Rubrics help you assess students' learning.

CHAPTER 8 **Exposition** **144**

Feature Assignment: Compare-and-Contrast Essay

Mentor Texts provide exemplary professional models for writing.

Student Models show students writing done by peers.

Writing for Media assignments provide opportunities for short writing assignments that use 21st Century Skills.

Revision RADaR techniques in *Revising* provide students with a simple, effective way to improve their drafts.

Connect to the Big Questions

- **What do you think?**
  What can we learn from similarities and differences?

- **Why write?**
  What should we tell and what should we describe to make information clear?

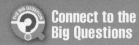

WRITING COACH

www.phwritingcoach.com

All content available online
- Interactive Writing Coach™
- Interactive Graphic Organizer
- Interactive Models
- Online Journal
- Resources
- Video

Contents

Connect to the Big Questions

- **What do you think?**
  Which responsibilities are most important?

- **Why write?**
  What is your point of view? How will you know if you've convinced others?

CHAPTER 10 Response to Literature 196

Grammar Mini-Lessons and *What Do You Notice?* features let you integrate grammar instruction into writing.

Connect to the Big Questions

- **What do you think?**
  How does literature shape who we become?

- **Why write?**
  What should you write about to make others interested in a text?

WRITING COACH
Online
www.phwritingcoach.com

All content available online
- Interactive Writing Coach™
- Interactive Graphic Organizer
- Interactive Models
- Online Journal
- Resources
- Video

Contents

Connect to the Big Questions

• **What do you think?**
What is the best way
to find important
information about
a topic?

• **Why write?**
Do you understand a
subject well enough
to write about it? How
will you find out what
the facts are?

Workplace Writing includes non-academic forms that students will need to succeed in their lives and careers.

Connect to the Big Questions

- **What do you think?**
  When is it most important to communicate clearly with teammates?

- **Why write?**
  What do daily workplace communications require of format, content, and style?

www.phwritingcoach.com

All content available online
- Interactive Writing Coach™
- Interactive Graphic Organizer
- Interactive Models
- Online Journal
- Resources
- Video

ABCDs of On-Demand Writing in *Writing for Assessment* offer a helpful memory aid to success with timed writing assignments.

Contents

GRAMMAR

What Do You Notice? features introduce students to an element of grammar in a real-life context.

WRITING COACH

Online

www.phwritingcoach.com

All content available online
- Grammar Tutorials
- Grammar Practice
- Grammar Games

Comprehensive instruction and practice activities along with speaking and writing applications ensure mastery of grammar concepts.

Contents

Chapters focus on specific and manageable topics in grammar, usage and mechanics.

WRITING COACH
Online
www.phwritingcoach.com

All content available online
- Grammar Tutorials
- Grammar Practice
- Grammar Games

Contents

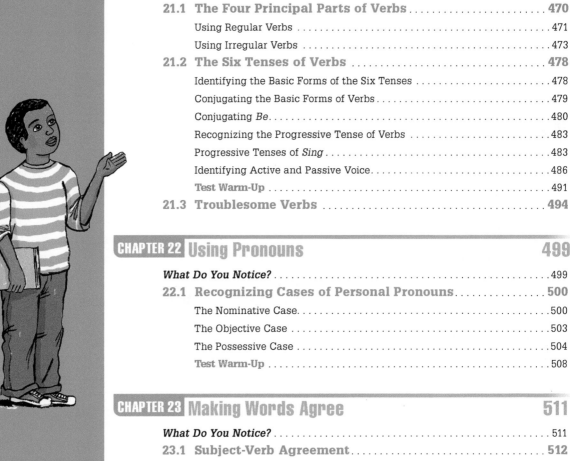

GRAMMAR
USAGE

Test Warm-Ups give students practice in the format of the Revising and Editing portion of the English Language Arts exam.

MECHANICS

A ***Cumulative Review*** ends each major section of the grammar materials— grammar, usage, and mechanics. Use it to assess your students' progress and tailor remediation.

WRITING COACH

Online

www.phwritingcoach.com

All content available online
- Grammar Tutorials
- Grammar Practice
- Grammar Games

Additional grammar instruction and practice in ***Writing Coach Online*** engages students and personalizes instruction.

GRAMMAR

WRITING COACH

Online

www.phwritingcoach.com

All content available online
- Grammar Tutorials
- Grammar Practice
- Grammar Games

xxx   Contents

STUDENT RESOURCES •———

> *Student Resources* include important information on writing for media and the workplace, graphic organizers, glossaries—and more!

xxxi

1 How Do I Differentiate Instruction?

Prentice Hall *Writing Coach* offers many opportunities for differentiated instruction.

Student Edition

Use **Student Edition** features like **Word Bank** and **Partner Talk** to reach struggling students. **Extension** opportunities in **Mentor Texts** and **Writing for Media** help you meet the needs of advanced students.

Teacher's Edition

Differentiated Instruction features in the **Teacher's Edition** include strategies for providing targeted instruction and enrichment to reach all students.

Differentiated Instruction

Differentiated Instruction Boxes in this Teacher's Edition address these student populations:

- **Below-Level Students**
- **Gifted and Talented Students**
- **English Language Learners**
- **Above-Level Students**
- **Special Needs Students**
- **Spanish Speaking Students**

In addition, for further enrichment, see the Extension features.

Writing Coach Online

Interactive Writing Coach™   Interactive Graphic Organizers   Grammar Instruction

www.phwritingcoach.com

 Interactive Writing Coach™: Use Paragraph Feedback and Essay Scorer to provide personalized and targeted support and feedback to individual students.

 Interactive Graphic Organizers: Scaffolded graphic organizers help tailor the prewriting experience to your students' ability levels.

Grammar Instruction: Based on the results of online diagnostics, students are automatically assigned targeted instruction and practice.

2 How Do I Meet the Individual Needs of ELL Students?

**Prentice Hall *Writing Coach* provides the tools and strategies you
need to support and challenge English Language Learners in your classroom.**

Student Edition

Scaffolded opportunities for language production and reception appear throughout
the **Student Edition**. To facilitate language production, use these features: ▶

- **Word Bank**
- **Listening and Speaking**
- **Partner Talk**
- **Speaking Application**

Teacher's Edition

The **Working with ELLs** notes offer strategies tailored for four proficiency levels. Centering on a common skill and topic, the notes make it easy to adapt and differentiate instruction across levels, however diverse your class. At the same time, each note is built around a single core concept, skill, text, or topic, allowing students to share in common learning experiences and helping you build coherent, efficient differentiated lessons.

Working with ELLs **ELL** Sheltered Instruction: Cognitive

Have students listen to, derive meaning from, and respond orally to information presented in a wide variety of print, electronic, and audiovisual media to build and reinforce language attainment. Find a recording of a rhyming poem or make one yourself of the poem on page 123.

Beginning Play the recording, providing support by acting out ideas. Build and reinforce language attainment by having students respond orally to simple questions, such as: *Which words rhyme?*

Intermediate Play the recording, helping students understand the imagery. Have them respond orally, discussing the poem's topic and images. Have them build language attainment by orally completing sentence frames, like: *The poem has rhyming words like _____.*

Advanced Play the recording and discuss the topic of the poem. To build language attainment, have partners define unfamiliar words and compare lists with another pair.

Advanced High Have partners complete the Advanced activity, then have students orally respond to the *Try It!* questions on page 123.

3 How Can I Reach Spanish-Speaking Students?

**To help Spanish-speaking students, use program resources that provide
teaching suggestions.**

Teacher's Edition

To help Spanish speakers master key ideas in writing and grammar, use differentiated instruction notes that provide targeted support for language transfer issues.

For an overview of the language transfer issues that Spanish speakers may encounter, see the section on Spanish speakers in this frontmatter (pp. W 34–W 35), which includes a linguistic contrastive analysis chart to help you target pronunciation practice.

Differentiated Instruction

RTI **Strategy for Special Needs Students**
Remind students that ballads are usually meant to be sung. Play recordings of musical ballads for students. Have them listen carefully and then summarize the story one ballad tells and identify the words in the refrain. Help students identify the use of figurative language and sound devices in the ballad. Then, encourage students who choose to write a ballad to create or borrow a tune to which it could be sung.

Strategy for Spanish Speakers Students whose home language is Spanish may encounter difficulties using assonance due to the phonetic spelling of vowel sounds in Spanish. Remind students that vowel sounds may have multiple spellings in English. Review spellings of different vowel sounds. For example, elicit spellings for the long and $\bar{e}$ sound such as *e, ea, ee,* and *y*. Then have students give examples for each, such as *even, speak, tree,* and *icy*.

4 What Digital Resources Can Help Me Personalize Instruction?

Prentice Hall *Writing Coach* has an online program—
***Writing Coach Online*—that is integrally linked to the print text.**
References to *Writing Coach Online* appear throughout the Student Edition.

Writing Coach Online

 The key component of *Writing Coach Online* is **Interactive Writing Coach™**, which functions like a personal writing tutor for students, giving them personalized feedback on their work. It not only helps you with grading papers but also gives you information to tailor instruction and assignments for your students individually. The **Interactive Writing Coach™** has two parts:

Paragraph Feedback Only Prentice Hall *Writing Coach* provides this tool, which analyzes student work at the paragraph level. It assesses the ideas and topic support for work submitted one paragraph at a time.

Essay Scorer Essay Scorer gives specific feedback on the traits of writing in a composition. It also features model essays at each score point to show students examples of how to improve their writing. Suggestions are focused on these traits of good writing:

- Ideas
- Organization
- Voice
- Word Choice
- Sentence Fluency
- Conventions

WRITING COACH
Online
www.phwritingcoach.com

WRITING	GRAMMAR
Interactive Graphic Organizers Leveled support helps students plan and develop their writing.	• **Grammar Diagnostic** Online diagnostics automatically assign targeted instruction and practice.
Interactive Model Audio recordings let students listen to **Mentor Texts** and **Student Models** at their own pace.	• **Grammar Tutorials** For reinforcement, motivation, or engagement, animated videos teach key grammar concepts.
Interactive Online Journal Point-of-use format lets students record responses, ideas, and drafts.	• **Grammar Practice** Additional grammar activities help students develop mastery.
Resources A variety of resources provide tools including support for 21st Century learning and an audio glossary in English and Spanish.	• **DimensionL** Fast-paced interactive video games test grammar skills.
Video Program authors Jeff Anderson and Kelly Gallagher teach strategies for effective writing.	

5 How Do I Monitor Student Progress?

**Prentice Hall *Writing Coach* makes progress monitoring easy
with frequent opportunities to evaluate student progress and
to reteach material.**

Monitoring Writing Progress

To provide support for writing and to monitor students' progress, use:

- **Interactive Writing Coach™**, including Paragraph Feedback and Essay Scorer
- Rubrics in the **Student Edition**
- Teacher feedback and conferencing notes in the **Teacher's Edition**

Personalized Assessment

	Ongoing Assessment	Formal Assessment of Feature Assignment	Progress Monitoring at End-of-Chapter
Interactive Writing Coach™	Use Paragraph Feedback and Essay Scorer as a revision tool.	Use Essay Scorer to score students' Feature Assignment papers.	Use Essay Scorer to score students' papers. Students' learner profiles can be adjusted based on their scores.
Teacher Conferencing	Use rubrics in the Student Edition as a revision tool. Conference with students to review their work and provide personalized support.	Use rubrics in the Student Edition to score students' Feature Assignment papers.	Review each student's work to plan targeted resources for the next writing assignment.

Monitoring Grammar Progress

Writing Coach provides a number of resources to monitor student progress
in grammar, including diagnostic tests, end-of-chapter tests, and Cumulative Reviews.

Grammar Assessment

Grammar Coach:	Diagnostic Assessment	End-of-Chapter Assessment	Progress Monitoring
Personalized Instruction	Students take grammar diagnostic test online and are automatically assigned instruction and practice in areas where they need support.	Teacher uses **ExamView** to administer end-of-chapter assessment and remediation. Teachers may customize **ExamView** tests or use the ones provided.	Teachers may use the **Test Warm-Ups** and the **Cumulative Reviews** in the student book or eText to check students' mastery of grammar skills.
Teacher-Directed Instruction	Teacher administers the diagnostic test and determines focus of instruction and practice.		Students may also play **DimensionL** grammar video games to test their grammar skills.

Preparing Students for Tests

To help get your students ready for high-stakes tests, use these built-in
test-prep features:

- **Writing for Assessment** in the writing section
- **Test Warm-Up** in the grammar section

6 How Does the Program Address 21st Century Learning Skills?

Prentice Hall *Writing Coach* fosters 21st Century Learning skills. Activities in several features are flexible enough to meet any technology capabilities—they can be completed with or without technology.

Make Your Writing Count

Assign your students these real-world activities that have impact beyond the classroom. Projects include multimedia presentations, debates, movie trailers, and news broadcasts. Features let you:

- Extend the mode of writing.
- Provide practice in collaboration, communication, planning, and presenting.

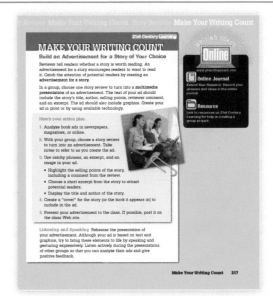

Writing for Media

Expose your students to new forms of content delivery. These individual short writing assignments incorporate non-print media and technology. Projects include webpages, scripts, consumer reports, and travel blogs. Features let you:

- Explore mentor examples.
- Reinforce writing process stages.

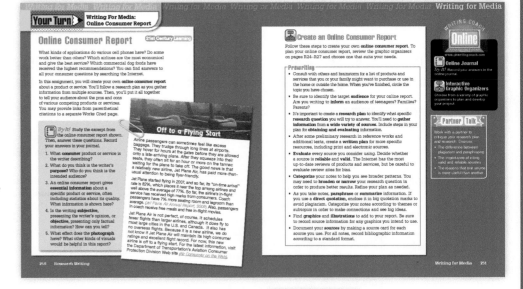

Rubrics for 21st Century Skills

Teachers Edition support includes rubrics to help you evaluate students' performance against 21st Century Learning criteria.

21st Century Learning	
Skills Rubric	Rating
Analyze Media: Look at how media can influence beliefs and behaviors.	1 2 3
Create Media Products: Use the most appropriate expressions in diverse environments.	1 2 3
Think Creatively: Elaborate, refine, analyze, and evaluate ideas in order to improve and maximize creative efforts.	1 2 3
Work Creatively With Others: Be original and inventive and understand limits to idea adoption.	1 2 3

7 How Does the Program Help Me Develop as a Teacher?

The Teacher's Edition of Prentice Hall *Writing Coach* provides built-in professional development features.

Step-by-Step Teaching Guidance

Margin notes provide strategies, tips, and examples for teaching skills. Instructional support includes special features such as:

- **Think Aloud** Specific, scripted guidance for you to walk students through content and activate their metacognitive and critical thinking skills

- **Teacher Tip** Point-of-use notes to help you focus on a particular aspect of a lesson or extend the lesson

- **Personalized Support: Teacher or Peer Feedback** Targeted suggestions and specific questions to use in Teacher or Peer Conferencing on students' writing assignments

- **Personalized Support: Interactive Writing Coach™** Guidance for using Interactive Writing Coach with all levels of students

- **Coach's Corner** Suggestions to help you model the writing process alongside your students

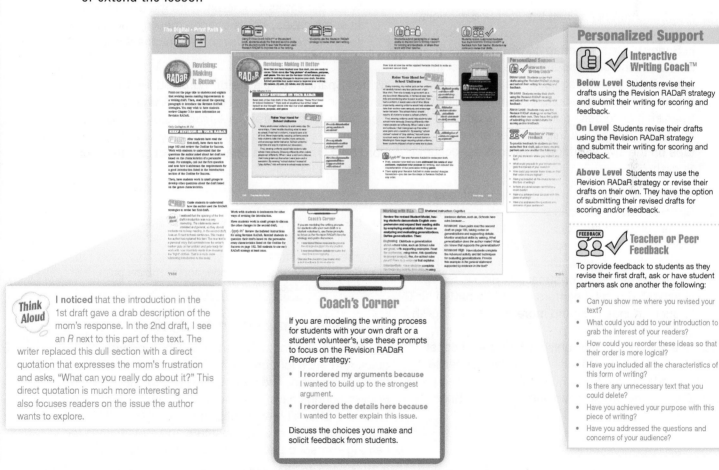

In-Depth Professional Development

 Online support including Professional Development from our authors helps you learn more about teaching writing and grammar.

Spanish Speakers

Reaching Spanish Speakers with *Writing Coach*

Spanish is the second most widely spoken language in the world. There are more than 400 million native Spanish speakers in more than 20 countries on three continents. Spanish vocabulary and pronunciation differ from country to country. While most dialect differences in English are in vowel sounds, Spanish dialects differ in their consonants.

Spoken Language

Spanish sounds are similar to those found in English, so there is a strong foundation for the native Spanish speaker learning English. However, there are three key differences between English and Spanish consonants:

1. Most of the alveolar sounds in English, such as /t/, /d/, and /n/, are produced farther forward in the mouth in Spanish. Instead of the tongue touching the alveolar ridge as in English, in Spanish it touches the back of the teeth.

2. Another difference is that the /r/ sound in English is not found in Spanish. There are two /r/ sounds in Spanish. One is the tap /ɾ/, which occurs in English as the quick sound in the middle of the name *Betty.* Psychologically, this tap sound is a kind of /t/ or /d/ sound in English, while in Spanish it is perceived as an /r/. The other /r/ sound in Spanish is a trill, or series of tongue taps on the alveolar ridge. This does not occur in English.

3. The third key difference between English and Spanish can be found in the English production of the voiceless stops /p/, /t/, and /k/. In English these sounds are aspirated, with an extra puff of air at the end, when the sound occurs at the beginning of a word or stressed syllable. So, /p/ is aspirated in *pit.* Learners can add a puff of air to such sounds to sound more like native English speakers.

There are five vowels in Spanish, which are a subset of the English vowels. Spanish vowels include tense vowel sounds /a/, /e/, /i/, /o/, and /u/. Lax vowel sounds in English are the problematic ones for native Spanish speakers.

Culture Clues

The Spanish language covers many countries, dialects, and cultures. Always encourage students to share special things about their culture, such as foods, festivals, or social customs.

Written Language

Like English, written Spanish uses the Roman alphabet, so both writing systems are similar. There are a few orthographic differences to note, however:

- The letter *h* in Spanish is silent, but the sound /h/ is written as *j* or *g*.

- A single letter *r* in Spanish represents a tap, while the double *rr* represents a trill.

- Accents are used to show the stress on a syllable when the stress is different from the usual rules. In some cases, words change meaning according to the accents. For example, *el* means *the* while *él* means *he.*

Written Spanish vowels are pronounced like the symbols in the International Phonetic Alphabet (IPA). (*See "Linguistic Contrastive Analysis" below.*) So, the Spanish "i" is pronounced with the long ē as in the word *beat.* The IPA and Spanish symbol for this letter is the same: /i/.

Grammar Hot Spots

- Double negatives are part of standard grammar in Spanish. Stress the single negative construction in English.

- English prepositions are a common stumbling point for Spanish speakers.

Linguistic Contrastive Analysis

The Linguistic Contrastive Analysis Chart provides a quick reference for comparing English sounds with those of Spanish. The chart allows you to check which English sounds have equivalents in Spanish. For those sounds that don't have equivalents, you can find the closest sound used as a substitute and suggestions for helping someone gain a native English articulation.

In these charts, the sounds are notated using the International Phonetic Alphabet (IPA), the most widely used standard for representing speech sounds in any language. Each sound is represented by one symbol, and each symbol represents only one sound.

Linguistic Contrastive Analysis Chart

IPA	English		Spanish	
		THE CONSONANTS OF ENGLISH		
p	*p*it	Aspirated at the start of a word or stressed syllable	*p*ato (duck)	Never aspirated
b	*b*it		*b*arco (boat)	Substitute voiced bilabial fricative/ᵦ/ in between vowels
m	*m*an		*m*undo (world)	
w	*w*in		a*gu*a (water)	
f	*f*un		*f*lor (flower)	
v	*v*ery		**NO EQUIVALENT**	Learners can use correct sound.
θ	*th*ing	The tongue should stick out between the teeth.	**NO EQUIVALENT**	Learners can use correct sound.
ð	*th*ere	When done correctly, the tongue will stick out between the teeth.	ca*d*a (every)	Sound exists in Spanish only between vowels; sometimes substitute voiceless /θ/.
t	*t*ime	English tongue-touch is a little farther back in the mouth than in other languages.	*t*ocar (touch)	Never aspirated
d	*d*ime	English tongue-touch is a little farther back in the mouth than in other languages.	*d*os (two)	
n	*n*ame	English tongue-touch is a little farther back in the mouth than in other languages.	*n*ube (cloud)	
s	*s*oy		*s*eco (dry)	
z	*z*eal		**NO EQUIVALENT**	Learners can use correct sound.
ɾ	but*t*er	Written 't' and 'd' are pronounced with a quick tongue-tip tap.	*r*ana (toad)	Written as single *r* and thought of as an /r/ sound.
l	*l*oop	At the ends of syllables, the /l/ bunches up the back of the tongue, becoming velarized /ɫ/ or dark-l as in the word *ball*.	*l*ibro (book)	
ɹ	*r*ed	Rare sound in world languages. Includes lip-rounding.	**NO EQUIVALENT**	Substitute /r/ sound such as the tap /ɾ/ or the trilled /r/
ʃ	*sh*allow	Often said with lip-rounding	**NO EQUIVALENT**	Substitute /s/ or /tʃ/
ʒ	vi*si*on	Rare sound in English	**NO EQUIVALENT**	Substitute /z/ or /dʒ/
tʃ	*ch*irp		*ch*ico (boy)	
dʒ	*j*oy		**NO EQUIVALENT**	Sometimes substituted with /ʃ/ sound. Some dialects have this sound for the *ll* spelling, as in *llamar*.
j	*y*ou		c*i*elo (sky)	Often substitute /dʒ/
k	*k*ite	Aspirated at the start of a word or stressed syllable	*c*asa (house)	Never aspirated
g	*g*oat		*g*ato (cat)	
ŋ	ki*ng*		ma*ng*o (mango)	
h	*h*ope		*g*ente (people)	Sometimes substitute sound with friction higher in the vocal tract as velar /x/ or uvular /χ/

IPA	English		Spanish	
		THE VOWELS OF ENGLISH		
i	b*ea*t		h*i*jo (son)	
ɪ	b*i*t	Usually confused with /i/ (*meat* vs. *mit*)	**NO EQUIVALENT**	Substitute /i/
e	b*ai*t	End of vowel diphthongized—tongue moves up to /i/ or /ɪ/ position	*e*co (echo)	
ɛ	b*e*t	Learners may have difficulty distinguishing /e/ and /ɛ/: pain vs. pen.	**NO EQUIVALENT**	Substitute /e/
æ	b*a*t	Learners may have trouble getting the tongue farther forward in the mouth	**NO EQUIVALENT**	Substitute mid central /ʌ/ or low front tense /a/
u	b*oo*t		*u*va (grape)	
ʊ	c*ou*ld	Learners may have difficulty distinguishing /u/ and /ʊ/; *wooed* vs. *wood*.	**NO EQUIVALENT**	Substitute /ù/
o	b*oa*t	End of vowel diphthongized – tongue moves up to /u/ or /ʊ/ position	*o*jo (eye)	
ɔ	l*aw*		**NO EQUIVALENT**	Substitute /o/ or /ɑ/. Substituting /o/ will cause confusion (*low* vs. *law*); substituting /ɑ/ will not.
ɑ	h*o*t		m*a*l (bad)	
a ʊ	h*ou*se	Diphthong starts /ɑ/ and moves to /ʊ/.	p*au*ta	
ɔ ɪ	b*oy*	Diphthong starts at /ɔ/ and moves to /ɪ/.	h*oy* (today)	
ɑ ɪ	b*i*te	Diphthong starts at /ɑ/ and moves to /ɪ/.	b*ai*le (dance)	
ə	*a*bout	Most common vowel in English; only in unstressed syllables. Learners may have difficulty keeping it very short.	**NO EQUIVALENT**	Substitute /ʌ/ or the full vowel from the word's spelling
ʌ	c*u*t	Very similar to schwa /ə/	**NO EQUIVALENT**	Substitute /a/
ɝ	b*ir*d	English Learners must bunch the tongue and constrict the throat.	**NO EQUIVALENT**	Substitute /ʌ/ or /er/ with trill

Writing COACH

How to Use This Program

This program is organized into two distinct sections: one for WRITING and one for GRAMMAR.

In the **WRITING** section, you'll learn strategies, traits, and skills that will help you become a better writer.

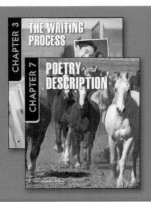

In the **GRAMMAR** section, you'll learn the rules and conventions of grammar, usage, and mechanics.

What DIGITAL writing and grammar resources are available?

The Writing Coach Online boxes will indicate opportunities to use online tools.

In **Writing,** use the **Interactive Writing Coach™** in two ways to get personalized guidance and support for your writing.

- Paragraph Feedback and
- Essay Scorer

WRITING COACH

Online

www.phwritingcoach.com

Interactive Writing Coach™

- **Choosing from the Topic Bank** gives you access to the Interactive Writing Coach™.
- **Submit your writing** and receive instant personalized feedback and guidance as you draft, revise, and edit your writing.

WRITING COACH

Online

www.phwritingcoach.com

Grammar Tutorials

Brush up on your grammar skills with these animated videos.

Grammar Practice

Practice your grammar skills with Writing Coach Online.

Grammar Games

Test your knowledge of grammar in this fast-paced interactive video game.

In **Grammar,** view grammar tutorials, practice your grammar skills, and play grammar video games.

What will you find in the WRITING section?

Writing Genre

Each chapter introduces a different **writing genre.**

Learn about the key characteristics of the **genre** before you start writing.

Focus on a single form of the genre with the **Feature Assignment**.

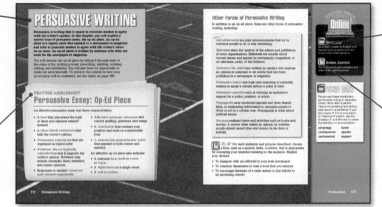

Writing Coach Online

- View the **Word Bank** words in the eText glossary, and hear them pronounced in both English and Spanish.

- Use your **Online Journal** to record your answers and ideas as you respond to **Try It!** activities.

Mentor Text and Student Model

The **Mentor Text** and **Student Model** provide examples of the genre featured in each chapter.

Writing Coach Online

- Use the **Interactive Model** to mark the text with Reader's and Writer's Response Symbols.

- Listen to an audio recording of the **Mentor Text** or **Student Model.**

Use the **Mentor Text** to see how a professional crafted a piece of writing.

Review the **Student Model** as a guide for composing your own piece.

ix

The **Topic Bank** provides prompts for the **Feature Assignment.**

Choose from a bank of topics, or follow steps to find an idea of your own.

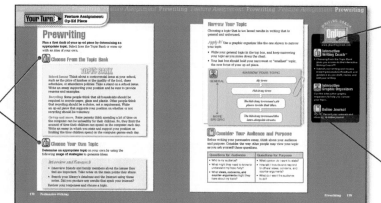

Writing Coach Online

- As you narrow your topic, get the right type of support! You'll find three different forms of graphic organizers— one model, one with step-by-step guidance, and one that is blank for you to complete.

- Use *Try It!* ideas to practice new skills. Use *Apply It!* activities as you work on your own writing.

Whether you are working on your essay drafts online or with a pen and paper, an **Outline for Success** can get you started.

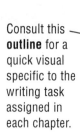

Consult this **outline** for a quick visual specific to the writing task assigned in each chapter.

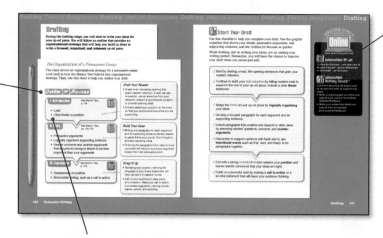

Writing Coach Online

- Start with just a paragraph and build up to your essay draft, or if you are ready, go straight to submitting your essay. The choice is yours!

Follow the bulleted suggestions for each part of your draft, and you'll be on your way to success.

x

Revision RADaR

You can use the **Revision RADaR** strategy as a guide for making changes to improve your draft.

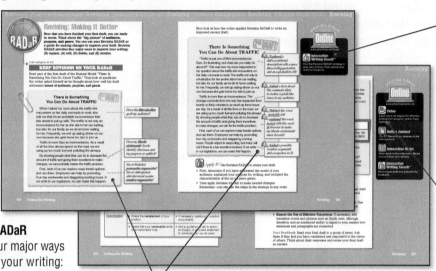

Revision RADaR

provides four major ways to improve your writing:

- **R**eplace
- **A**dd
- **D**elete
- **R**eorder

Check out these example drafts to see how to apply **Revision RADaR**.

Writing Coach Online

- With **Interactive Writing Coach™**, submit your paragraphs and essays multiple times. View your progress in your online writing portfolio. Feel confident that your work is ready to be shared in peer review or teacher conferencing.

- View **videos** with strategies for writing from program author **Kelly Gallagher**.

What Do You Notice?

In the editing stage, **What Do You Notice?** and **Mentor Text** help you zoom in on powerful sentences.

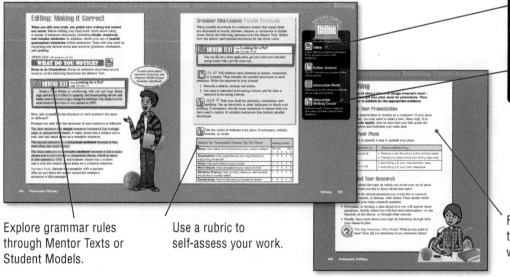

Writing Coach Online

- View **videos** with strategies for writing from program author **Jeff Anderson**.

- Submit your essay for feedback and a score.

Explore grammar rules through Mentor Texts or Student Models.

Use a rubric to self-assess your work.

Find the best way to share your writing with others.

xi

How do end-of-chapter features help you apply what you've learned?

21st Century Learning

In **Make Your Writing Count** and **Writing for Media** you will work on innovative assignments that involve the 21st Century life and career skills you'll need for communicating successfully.

Make Your Writing Count

Work collaboratively on project-based assignments and share what you have learned with others. Projects include:

• Debates
• TV Talk Shows
• News Reports

Writing for Media

Complete an assignment on your own by exploring media forms, and then developing your own content. Projects include:

• Blogs
• Documentary Scripts
• Storyboards
• Multimedia Presentations

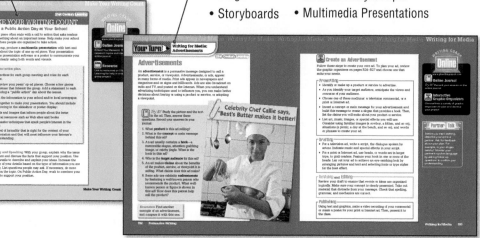

Test Prep

The **Writing for Assessment** pages help you prepare for important standardized tests.

Notice these icons that emphasize the types of writing you'll find on high-stakes tests.

Use **The ABCDs of On-Demand Writing** for a quick, memorable strategy for success.

Writing Coach Online
Submit your essay for feedback and a score.

What will you find in the GRAMMAR section?

Grammar Game Plan

The **Find It/Fix It** reference guide helps you fix the **20** most common errors in student writing.

Study each of the 20 common errors and their corrections, which are clearly explained on each page.

Follow cross-references to more instruction in the grammar chapters.

Review the **Check It** features for strategies to help you avoid these errors.

Grammar Chapters

Each grammar chapter begins with a **What Do You Notice?** feature and **Mentor Text.**

Use the **Mentor Text** to help you zoom in on powerful sentences. It showcases the correct use of written language conventions.

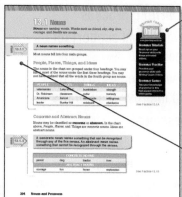

Writing Coach Online
The **Writing Coach Online** digital experience for Grammar helps you focus on just the lessons and practice you need.

Use the grammar section as a quick reference handbook. Each **grammar rule** is highlighted and numbered.

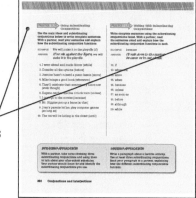

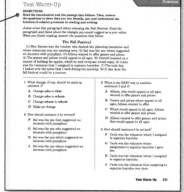

Try **Practice** pages and **Test Warm-Ups** to help you check your progress.

xiii

Supporting an Integrated English Language Arts Curriculum

Prentice Hall *Writing Coach* is perfect as a writing and grammar companion to a literature anthology or a novel-based curriculum. Reach for it to help you meet these goals:

- ✔ Reinforce instruction
- ✔ Extend key points
- ✔ Remediate
- ✔ Provide more practice
- ✔ Reteach
- ✔ Provide more writing prompts

Using *Writing Coach* with Your Integrated English Language Arts Curriculum

Use *Writing Coach* to support writing assignments linked to literature. Writing chapters include:

- **In-depth coverage** to introduce the key elements of genres
- **Mentor Texts** to help you teach from exemplary writing
- Step-by-step support of the **writing process**
- **Outline for Success** to provide visual support for organizing drafts in all key genres
- **Revision RADaR** strategies with models to guide students as they analyze and improve their drafts
- **Rubrics** to support self-assessment

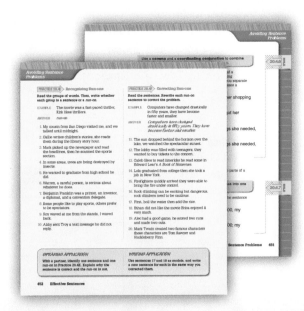

Use online tools to personalize instruction, including paragraph scoring, essay scoring, interactive graphic organizers, and instructional videos.

www.phwritingcoach.com

Use *Writing Coach* to strengthen instruction in conventions. Grammar chapters provide:

- **Thorough instruction** on all aspects of grammar, usage, and mechanics to teach key ideas
- **Practice items** to reinforce concepts and build competence
- **Speaking and Listening activities** to ensure application
- **Diagnostic** and **Chapter tests** to assess mastery

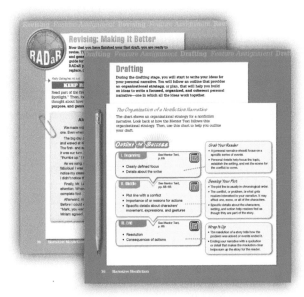

Use online resources to target instruction for each student.

www.phwritingcoach.com

Using *Writing Coach* with Prentice Hall *Literature*

Opportunities to Extend Integrated Language Skills

Leveled Selection choices include integrated language arts skills lessons:

- From **Grammar** lessons in *Literature*, use the *Writing Coach* grammar chapters to further develop concepts.

- From **Writing** lessons in *Literature*, consult the *Writing Coach* writing chapters to expand coverage of prewriting, drafting, revising, and editing.

- From **Listening and Speaking** and **Research and Technology** activities, see *Writing Coach* unit features to support student extension.

- **Make Your Writing Count** provides step-by-step direction for projects.

- **Writing for Media** offers extended instruction in new forms of content delivery.

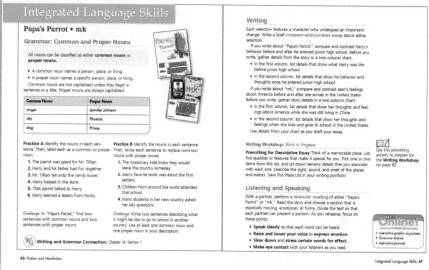

Springboards to Support Writing Workshops

Two Writing Workshops in each *Literature* unit provide detailed instruction in major writing forms.

From **Writing Workshops** in *Literature*, use these features in *Writing Coach*:

- The **Mentor Text** and **Student Models** support deeper exploration of the mode.

- More instruction in prewriting, drafting, revising, and editing helps students strengthen their writing skills.

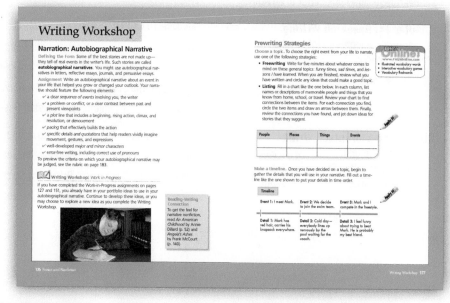

Prentice Hall *Writing Coach*/
Prentice Hall *Literature* Alignment

Use models in Prentice Hall *Literature* to support the teaching of writing.

Prentice Hall *Literature* supports *Writing Coach* with works from noted authors, Mentor Texts, Student Models, and examples of research sources, as shown in the following chart.

Writing Coach	Prentice Hall *Literature*
Chapter 5, Nonfiction Narration Feature Assignment: Personal Narrative Writing for Media: Biographical Narrative	"My Papa, Mark Twain," Susy Clemens (biography), page 96 "Names/Nombres," Julia Alvarez (personal narrative), page 114 "A Backwoods Boy," Russell Freedman (biography), page 448
Chapter 6, Fiction Narration Feature Assignment: Realistic Short Story Writing for Media: Audio Script	"Greyling," Jane Yolen (short story), page 9 "Stray," Cynthia Rylant (short story), page 24 "The Homecoming," Laurence Yep (short story), page 32 *The Phantom Tollbooth*, Act I, Susan Nanus (dramatic script), page 708 *The Phantom Tollbooth*, Act II, Susan Nanus (dramatic script), page 748
Chapter 7, Poetry and Description Feature Assignment: Rhyming Poem and Haiku Writing for Media: Descriptive Essay	"Adventures of Isabel," Ogden Nash (rhyming poem), page 564 "Dust of Snow," Robert Frost (rhyming poem), page 612 Haiku, Matsuo Bashō (haiku), page 624 Haiku, Musō Soseki (haiku), page 630 "Parade," Rachel Field (rhyming poem), page 643 "Childhood and Poetry," Pablo Neruda (descriptive writing), page 662
Chapter 8, Exposition Feature Assignment: Compare-and-Contrast Essay Writing for Media: Consumer Comparison	"Race to the End of the Earth," William G. Scheller (compare-and-contrast essay), page 335
Chapter 9, Persuasion Feature Assignment: Persuasive Essay	"Preserving a Great American Symbol," Richard Durbin (persuasive speech), page 439 "Jake Wood Baseball is the Start of Something Special," Reginald T. Dogan (persuasive essay), page 441
Chapter 10, Response to Literature Feature Assignment: Letter to an Author	"Happiness Is a Charming Charlie Brown at Orlando Rep," Matthew MacDermid (review), page 796
Chapter 11, Research Writing Feature Assignment: Informational Research Report Writing for Media: I-Search Report	"Ice Ages," Elizabeth Cleary (Writing Workshop Student Model: research report), page 994 "The Caribbean" (research source: atlas entry), page 135 "The Seven Wonders of the World," Infoplease (research source: online almanac), page 245 "Gold Rush: The Journey by Land," *The Sacramento Bee* (research source: news article), page 339 "NASA Finally Goes Metric," *SPACE* staff (research source: online news article), page 783
Chapter 12, Workplace Writing Feature Assignments: How-To Essay, Thank-You Letter, Friendly Letter Writing for Media: E-mail Message	"Letter to Scottie," F. Scott Fitzgerald (friendly letter), page 522 "Origami: Apatosaurus," Rachel Katz (how-to instructions), page 603 "How to Read a Road Map," *Britannica Student Encyclopedia* (how-to encyclopedia entry), page 959

Prentice Hall *Literature* Writing Workshops/*Writing Coach* Alignment

When you teach the writing workshops in Prentice Hall *Literature*, look to Prentice Hall *Writing Coach* for more in-depth instruction.

Users of Prentice Hall *Literature* Writing Workshops can find additional support in *Writing Coach*, including Mentor Texts, Student Models, writing process strategies, grammar applications, and connected assignments, as shown in the following chart.

Prentice Hall *Literature*	Writing Coach
Unit 1, Mid-Unit Writing Workshop **Description: Descriptive Essay,** page 86	**Chapter 7, Poetry and Description,** page 118 Writing for Media: Descriptive Essay, page 140
Unit 1, End-of-Unit Writing Workshop **Narration: Autobiographical Narrative,** page 154	**Chapter 5, Nonfiction Narration,** page 64 Feature Assignment: Personal Narrative
Unit 2, Mid-Unit Writing Workshop **Response to Literature: Review,** page 264	**Chapter 10, Response to Literature,** page 196 Other Forms of Interpretative Response, page 199
Unit 2, End-of-Unit Writing Workshop **Narration: Short Story,** page 354	**Chapter 6, Fiction Narration,** page 90 Feature Assignment: Realistic Short Story Other Forms of Fiction, page 93
Unit 3, Mid-Unit Writing Workshop **Exposition: How-to Essay,** page 462	**Chapter 12, Workplace Writing,** page 256 Feature Assignment: How-to Essay
Unit 3, End-of-Unit Writing Workshop **Exposition: Persuasive Essay,** page 526	**Chapter 9, Persuasion,** page 170 Feature Assignment: Persuasive Essay
Unit 4, Mid-Unit Writing Workshop **Exposition: Problem-and-Solution Essay,** page 614	**Chapter 8, Exposition,** page 144 Other Forms of Expository Writing, page 147
Unit 4, End-of-Unit Writing Workshop **Exposition: Comparison-Contrast Essay,** page 668	**Chapter 8, Exposition,** page 144 Feature Assignment: Compare-and-Contrast Essay
Unit 5, Mid-Unit Writing Workshop **Response to Literature: Letter,** page 738	**Chapter 10, Response to Literature,** page 196 Feature Assignment: Letter to an Author
Unit 5, End-of-Unit Writing Workshop **Exposition: Cause-and-Effect Essay,** page 800	**Chapter 8, Exposition,** page 144 Other Forms of Expository Writing, page 147
Unit 6, Mid-Unit Writing Workshop **Research: Multimedia Report,** page 906	**Chapter 11, Research Writing,** page 222 Feature Assignment: Informational Research Report
Unit 6, End-of-Unit Writing Workshop **Research: Research Report,** page 988	**Chapter 11, Research Writing,** page 222 Feature Assignment: Informational Research Report

Your Writing Coach . . .
Jeff Anderson

MENTOR TEXTS

What can we do about students' declining editing and writing skills? Should we just do more of the same practices? Fight error with more error? Fight lack of correctness with even more correction? For today's students, this focus on the negative isn't working. Yet, simply ignoring errors and hoping they will repair themselves isn't a solution either.

Doing What Works

The recent research report Writing Next (2007) calls for teachers to search out "alternate methods" to teach grammar and editing skills. This research report, focused on improving writing instruction for adolescent writers, recommends we teach using many methods to improve student writing, including:

- Study of models
- Sentence combining
- Inquiry activities

Prentice Hall *Writing Coach* provides Mentor Texts throughout both the writing and grammar sections. These texts model effective and interesting writing, using the conventions of language—punctuation, usage, and grammar—to communicate their messages and entertain readers.

Invite Students to Read Like Writers

In addition to integrating the traits of writing into the writing lessons in this book to help improve student writing, **Prentice Hall** *Writing Coach* also provides multiple opportunities to zoom in on powerful sentences and burn correctness and beauty into students' minds. You can use these models to encourage students to try new structures and patterns. Once students get in the habit of reading like writers, the style of their own writing can truly benefit.

> ❝ *For today's students, this focus on the negative isn't working.* ❞
>
> Jeff Anderson

Jeff Anderson has worked with struggling writers and readers for almost 20 years. He is known for his work with integrating reading, writing, and grammar instruction through the use of mentor texts. He has written two books, *Mechanically Inclined: Building Grammar, Usage, and Style into Writer's Workshop* and *Everyday Editing: Inviting Students to Develop Skill and Craft in Writer's Workshop.* His work has appeared in *The English Journal,* and he won the NCTE Paul and Kate Farmer Award for his *English Journal* article on teaching grammar in context.

See Jeff Anderson's professional development videos at www.phwritingcoach.com.

Your Writing Coach . . .

Kelly Gallagher

KEYS TO TEACHING WRITING

Anyone can write a first draft, but revision is the place where good papers emerge. Revision is the "make or break" moment for the paper. *Re* means "again" and *vision* means "to see"; we want our students to see their first drafts again in a new light. If a first draft has any chance to become strong, it must be "moved" to a better place. This is where good writing emerges.

Revision Is Not Editing

During the revision stage, students should work to make their papers better. This should not be confused with editing—working to make their papers correct. The "stuff" of the paper must be improved before editing comes into play. Who cares if a paper is edited properly if the first draft is so bad no one wants to read it? For a young writer, revising the paper should come before editing the paper. In **Prentice Hall *Writing Coach,*** four concrete *RADaR revision* strategies help students manage this critical stage of the writing process:

Replace
Add
Delete
 and
Reorder

The Importance of Modeling

Students benefit immensely from having real-world models in front of them. If you want your students to write an effective persuasive essay, give them an effective persuasive essay to dissect beforehand. We must move students beyond recognizing what the author says, and start having them focus on how it is said. Using professional writing as road maps is beneficial to almost all young writers. **Prentice Hall *Writing Coach*** provides Mentor Texts and Student Models to support this key stage of writing study.

Practice, Practice, Practice

Writing, like swimming, is a skill. The only way to noticeably improve is to practice a lot. If you only swim once in a while, you will not become a better swimmer. The same holds true with writing. To produce competent writers, our students need to write a lot—in many cases much more than they are currently writing. Students should write way more than the teacher can grade. Otherwise, they are not writing enough.

Kelly Gallagher is a full-time English teacher at Magnolia High School in Anaheim, California, where he has taught for 23 years. He is the author of several books:

- *Reading Reasons: Motivational Mini-Lessons for The Middle and High School*

- *Deeper Reading: Comprehending Challenging Texts*

- *Teaching Adolescent Writers*

- *Readicide*

See Kelly Gallagher's professional development videos at www.phwritingcoach.com.

> ❝ *Writing is a threshold skill for both employment and promotion, particularly for salaried employees.* ❞
>
> Kelly Gallagher

NFICTION NARRATION *Personal Narrative* **FICTION NARRATION** *Re*
trast Essay **PERSUASION** *Persuasive Essay* **RESPONSE TO LITERATUR**
v-To Essay, Thank You Letter, Friendly Letter **NONFICTION NARRATIO**
m and Haiku **EXPOSITION** *Compare-and-Contrast Essay* **PERSUASION**
al Research Report **WORKPLACE WRITING** *How-To Essay, Thank You Lett*
N Realistic Short Story **POETRY** *Rhyming Poem and Haiku* **EXPOSITION**
RE Letter to an Author **RESEARCH** *Informational Research Report* **WORKPL**
N Personal Narrative **FICTION NARRATION** *Realistic Short Story* **POE**
N Persuasive Essay **RESPONSE TO LITERATURE** *Letter to an Author* **RES**

Writing

Interactive Writing Coach™   Online Journal

Use the Online Lesson Planner at www.phwritingcoach.com to customize your instructional plan for an integrated Language Arts curriculum.

DAY 1

CHAPTER 1: YOU, THE WRITER

 ONLINE

- Why and What Do You Write?
- How Can You Find and Keep Track of Ideas?
- How Can You Get Started?
- How Do You Work With Others?
- Where Can You Keep Your Finished Work?
- Reflect on Your Writing

DAY 2

CHAPTER 2: TYPES OF WRITING

 ONLINE

- Genres and Forms
- Nonfiction Narration
- Fiction Narration
- Poetry and Description
- Exposition
- Persuasion

DAY 3

CHAPTER 2: TYPES OF WRITING *(cont'd)*

ONLINE

- Responses to Literature
- Research Writing
- Workplace Writing
- Writing for Media
- Creating Multimedia Projects
- Reflect on Your Writing

DAY 6

CHAPTER 3: THE WRITING PROCESS *(cont'd)*

 ONLINE

- Revising: Making It Better

DAY 7

CHAPTER 3: THE WRITING PROCESS *(cont'd)*

ONLINE

- Editing: Making It Correct
- Publishing
- Reflect on Your Writing

DAY 8

CHAPTER 4: SENTENCES, PARAGRAPHS, AND COMPOSITIONS

 ONLINE

- Writing Strong Sentences
- Writing Strong Paragraphs
- Composing Your Piece

Links to Prentice Hall *LITERATURE*

Featured Authors on Writing Genres and Writing Process

Jane Yolen
- What Are Fiction and Nonfiction?, p. 4
- "Greyling" (fiction), p. 9
- "My Heart Is in the Highlands" (speech), p. 17
- On Writing Narratives (Writing Workshop), p. 157

Jean Craighead George
- What Is a Short Story?, p. 178
- "The Wounded Wolf" (short story), p. 183
- On Revising a Story (Writing Workshop), p. 357

Zlata Filipović
- What Is Nonfiction?, p. 378
- from *Zlata's Diary* (excerpt from a diary), p. 383
- On Writing Persuasively (Writing Workshop), p. 529

Gary Soto
- What Is Poetry?, p. 550
- "Oranges" (poem), p. 555
- "Ode to Family Photographs" (poem), p. 557
- On Revising a Comparison (Writing Workshop), p. 671

Joseph Bruchac
- What Is a Drama?, p. 692
- *Gluskabe and Old Man Winter* (play), p. 697
- On Showing Causes and Effects (Writing Workshop), p. 803

Julius Lester
- What Is the Oral Tradition?, p. 824
- *Black Cowboy, Wild Horses* (historical fiction), p. 829
- On Writing Vivid Descriptions (Writing Workshop), p. 991
- *From the Author's Desk* Videos: Featured authors discuss writing.

Differentiated Instruction

Differentiated Instruction Boxes in this Teacher's Edition address these student populations:

- Below-Level Students
- Above-Level Students
- Gifted and Talented Students
- Special Needs Students
- English Language Learners
- Spanish Speaking Students

In addition, for further enrichment, see the **Extension** features.

LESSON OBJECTIVES

- To reflect on reasons for writing.
- To learn the genres and forms of writing.
- To review strategies for generating and recording ideas, preparing to write, working with others, and maintaining a portfolio.
- To review the traits of effective writing and to review how to use a rubric.
- To review the stages of the writing process and consider why it is important to follow the process.
- To review strategies for developing strong sentences, paragraphs, and compositions.
- To learn how to use Interactive Writing Coach online for guidance.

DAY 4

CHAPTER 3: THE WRITING PROCESS

ONLINE

- Writing Traits Rubrics and How to Use Them
- What Is the Writing Process?
- Why Use the Writing Process?

DAY 5

CHAPTER 3: THE WRITING PROCESS *(cont'd)*

ONLINE

- Prewriting
- Drafting

DAY 9

CHAPTER 4: SENTENCES, PARAGRAPHS, AND COMPOSITIONS *(cont'd)*

ONLINE

- Rhetorical and Literary Devices
- Using Writing Traits To Develop an Effective Composition

DAY 10

CHAPTER 4: SENTENCES, PARAGRAPHS, AND COMPOSITIONS *(cont'd)*

ONLINE

- Using Interactive Writing Coach
- Interactive Writing Coach and the Writing Process
- Paragraph Feedback With Interactive Writing Coach
- Essay Scoring With Interactive Writing Coach

> *Most good writing starts with bad writing. No one becomes a good writer without regular, intensive writing practice, and rarely, if even, does good writing happen without focused revision.*
>
> —Kelly Gallagher

> *Inviting students to write is where the rubber meets the road. We want to inspire their words to flow. Words can also preserve the things we may forget.*
>
> —Jeff Anderson

Alternate Pacing Suggestions

- **Block Scheduling** Each day on the Lesson Planner represents a 40–50 minute block. Teachers using block scheduling may combine days to revise pacing to meet their classroom needs.

- **Accelerated Lesson Planning** Combine instructional days, focusing on strategies for revising and for building strong sentences, paragraphs, and compositions.

- **Integrated Language Arts Curriculum** For targeted instruction that covers the essential components of the lesson use either a 3- or a 5-day plan.

3 day plan
DAY 1: Chapters 1 and 2
DAY 2: Chapter 3
DAY 3: Chapter 4

5 day plan
DAY 1: Chapters 1 and 2
DAYS 2/3: Chapter 3
DAYS 4/5: Chapter 4

CHAPTER 1

YOU, THE WRITER

Why Do You Write?

Writing well is one of the most important life skills you can develop. Being a good writer can help you achieve success in school and beyond. Most likely, you write for many reasons. You write:

To Share

You probably often write to **share** your experiences with others. Writing can be an easy way to **reach out** to people and connect with them.

To Persuade People

Writing can also be an effective way to **persuade** people to consider your opinions. For example, you may find it's easier to convince someone of your point of view when you've effectively organized your thoughts in an essay or a letter.

To Inform

Another reason to write is to **inform.** Perhaps you want to tell an audience how you built your computer network or how you finally got your e-mail to function properly.

To Enjoy

Personal fullfillment is another important motivation for writing, since writing enables you **to express** your thoughts and feelings. In addition, writing can also help you recall an event, or let you escape from everyday life.

Fortunately, writing well is a skill you can learn and one that you can continue to improve and polish. This program will help you improve your writing skills and give you useful information about the many types of writing.

2

What Do You Write?

Writing is already an important part of your everyday life. Each day is full of opportunities to write, allowing you to capture, express, think through and share your thoughts and feelings, and demonstrate what you know. Here are some ways you might write.

- Recording thoughts in a journal
- Texting friends or posting on social networking sites
- E-mailing thank-you notes to relatives
- Creating lists of things to do or things you like
- Writing research reports, nonfiction accounts, fiction stories, and essays in school

How Can You Find Ideas?

The good news is that ideas are all around you. You just need to be aware of the rich resources that are available.

By Observing

Observing is a good way to start to find ideas. Did you see anything interesting on your way to school? Was there something unusual about the video game you played last night?

By Reading

Reading is another useful option—look through newspaper articles and editorials, magazines, blogs, and Web sites. Perhaps you read something that surprised you or really made you feel concerned. Those are exactly the subjects that can lead to the ideas you want to write about.

By Watching

Watching is another way to get ideas—watch online videos or television programs, for example.

WRITING COACH

Online

www.phwritingcoach.com

Online Journal

Try It! Record your notes, answers, and ideas in the online journal. You can also record and save your answers and ideas on pop-up sticky notes in the eText.

« Writer to Writer »

I write when I want to be heard or connect. Writing lets me be a vital part of my community and reach outside it as well. All the while, I get to be me—my unique self.

—Jeff Anderson

You, the Writer   3

READ AND APPLY

Before students read page 3, ask:

- What kinds of writing do you do in school? At home? In your leisure time?

- Do you ever write lists, notes, or letters? Do you write or text your friends? Do you write on a social networking site?

- How do you find ideas about which to write?

Write all student responses on the board.

Then, have students read the text. Hold a class discussion about the similarities and differences between student responses and the information provided.

Differentiated Instruction

RTI Strategy for Below-Level Students

Students may benefit from previewing the heads on pages 2 and 3 after engaging in the Motivate and Engage activity on page 2 and the Read and Apply activity on page 3. Remind students that previewing the heads in a textbook is a helpful way to figure out the content that lies ahead. Ask students to summarize what they think will be covered on the two pages of text.

Enrichment for Gifted/Talented Students

For students who enjoy creative writing, assign the freewriting strategy to elaborate on where or how they find their best writing ideas and what makes an idea "a good idea" in their minds. Give students a fixed amount of time—five or ten minutes—to write whatever comes to mind. Then, when students have finished the freewrite, suggest that they read their work to determine how they get their best ideas.

How Can You Keep Track of Ideas?

You may sometimes think of great writing ideas in the middle of the night or on the way to math class. These strategies can help you remember those ideas.

Start an Idea Notebook or a Digital Idea File

Reserving a small **notebook** to record ideas can be very valuable. Just writing the essence of an idea, as it comes to you, can later help you develop a topic or essay. A **digital idea file** is exactly the same thing—but it's recorded on your computer, cell phone, or other electronic device.

Keep a Personal Journal

Many people find that keeping a **journal** of their thoughts is helpful. Then, when it's time to select an idea, they can flip through their journal and pick up on the best gems they wrote—sometimes from long ago.

Maintain a Learning Log

A **learning log** is just what it sounds like—a place to record information you have learned, which could be anything from methods of solving equations to computer shortcuts. Writing about something in a learning log might later inspire you to conduct further research on the same topic.

Free Write

Some individuals find that if they just let go and write whatever comes to mind, they eventually produce excellent ideas.

Free writing requires being relaxed and unstructured. This kind of writing does not require complete sentences, correct spelling, or proper grammar. Whatever ends up on the paper or on the computer screen is fine. Later, the writer can go back and tease out the best ideas.

4   You, the Writer

How Can You Get Started?

Every writer is different, so it makes sense that all writers should try out techniques that might work well for them. Regardless of your writing style, these suggestions should help you get started.

Get Comfortable

It's important to find and create an environment that encourages your writing process. Choose a spot where you'll find it easy to concentrate. Some writers prefer quiet. Others prefer to work in a room with music playing softly.

Have Your Materials Ready

Before starting to write, gather all the background materials you need to get started, including your notes, free writing, reader's journal, and portfolio. Make sure you also have writing tools, such as a pen and paper or a computer.

Spend Time Wisely

Budgeting your available writing time is a wise strategy. Depending on your writing goal, you may want to sketch out your time on a calendar, estimating how long to devote to each stage of the writing process. Then, you can assign deadlines to each part. If you find a particular stage takes longer than you estimated, simply adjust your schedule to ensure that you finish on time.

SUNDAY	MONDAY	TUESDAY	WEDNESDAY	THURSDAY	FRIDAY	SATURDAY
		1 Start Research	2 Finish Research	3 Write Outline	4	5
6	7	8 Finish First Draft	9 Finish Revising	10 Finish Proof-reading	11	12
13	14 DUE DATE	15	16	17	18	19
20	21	22	23	24	25	26
27	28	29	30	31		

◄ October ►

You, the Writer 5

Intermediate Pair students with fluent readers. Read aloud the calendar text on page 5. To enhance and confirm understanding, have partners take notes on unfamiliar words and look them up in a dictionary.

Advanced Group students, and read the Spend Time Wisely section. To enhance and confirm students' understanding, direct them to look up unfamiliar words in a dictionary. Then, have them create a model calendar of their own, based on their past writing experience.

Advanced High Have students complete the Advanced activity and report additional information they found in the dictionary, such as other forms of the words.

How Do You Work With Others?

If you think of writing as a solitary activity, think again. Working with others can be a key part of the writing process.

Brainstorming

Brainstorming works when everyone in a group feels free to suggest ideas, whether they seem commonplace or brilliant.

Cooperative Writing

Cooperative writing is a process in which each member of a group concentrates on a different part of an assignment. Then, the group members come together to discuss their ideas and write drafts.

Peer Feedback

Peer feedback comes from classmates who have read your writing and offered suggestions for improvements. When commenting, it's important to provide constructive, or helpful, criticism.

21st Century Learning

Collaborate and Discuss

In **collaborative writing,** each group member takes a role on a writing project. The goal is to work and rework the writing until all members feel they have produced the best result.

Possible Roles in a Collaborative Writing Project

LEADER	**FACILITATOR**	**COMPROMISER**	**LISTENER**
Initiates the discussion by clearly expressing group goals and moderates discussions	Works to move the discussion forward and clarify ideas	Works to find practical solutions to differences of opinion	Actively listens and serves to recall details that were discussed

---

Using Technology

Technology allows collaboration to occur in ways that were previously unthinkable.

- By working together on the Internet, students around the world have infinite opportunities to collaborate online on a wide-range of projects.

- Collaboration can range from projects that foster community cooperation, such as how to improve debates during local elections, to those that increase global awareness, such as focusing on how to encourage more recycling.

- Being able to log in and to contribute to media, such as journals, blogs, and social networks, allows you to connect globally, express your views in writing, and join a world-wide conversation.

Where Can You Keep Your Finished Work?

A **portfolio,** or growing collection of your work, is valuable for many reasons. It can serve as a research bank of ideas and as a record of how your writing is improving. You can create a portfolio on a computer or in a folder or notebook. You'll learn more about managing a portfolio in chapter 3.

A **Reader's Journal,** in which you record quotes and ideas from your reading, can also be used to store original ideas. Your journal can be housed on a computer or in a notebook.

Reflect on Your Writing

Analyzing, making inferences, and drawing conclusions about how you find ideas can help you become a better, more effective writer. Find out more about how you write by asking yourself questions like these:

- Which strategies have I found most effective for finding good ideas for writing?

- What pieces of writing represent my best work and my weakest work? What do the pieces in each group have in common?

Partner Talk

With a partner, talk about your collaborative writing experiences. Be sure to share your responses to such questions as these: What project did you work on as a collaborative effort? What did you learn that you might not have discovered if you were developing a writing project by yourself?

COLLABORATE AND DISCUSS

Have students read the Collaborate and Discuss feature on page 6. Ask students to quickwrite about collaborative writing groups. Tell students to write about either (1) their prior experiences with collaborative writing, including successes and challenges, or (2) their preferred roles in a group and why. Invite volunteers to share their quickwrites and hold a class discussion about the pros and cons of working in groups.

Differentiated Instruction

RTI Strategy for Special Needs Students

Work with students to create flashcards for each method of collaboration. On one side, write the method: brainstorming, cooperative writing, peer feedback, technology. On the other side, write a brief description of the ways students work together to accomplish the goal. Use the flashcards to reinforce the concepts, and suggest that students keep the cards for future reference.

Strategy for Spanish Speakers

Students whose home language is Spanish may reflect on their writing by asking themselves what language difficulties they may have when writing. For example, some students may forget to use subject pronouns or use the wrong word order. Encourage them to improve by asking them to make a personal checklist of these areas and refer to it when editing and revising their writing.

CHAPTER 2

TYPES *of* WRITING

Genres and Forms

Genres are types, or categories, of writing.

- Each genre has a specific **purpose,** or goal. For example, the purpose of persuasive writing is to convince readers to agree with the writer's point of view.
- Each genre has specific **characteristics.** Short stories, for example, have characters, a setting, and a plot.

In this chapter, you will be introduced to several genres: nonfiction narratives, fiction narratives, poetry and descriptive writing, expository writing, persuasive writing, responses to literature, and workplace writing.

Forms are subcategories of genres that contain all the characteristics of the genre plus some unique characteristics of their own. For example, a mystery is a form of short story. In addition to plot, characters, and setting, it has a mystery to be solved.

Selecting Genres

In some writing situations, you may need to select the correct genre for conveying your intended meaning.

- To **entertain,** you may choose to write a short story or a humorous essay.
- To **describe** an emotion, writing a poem may be best.
- To **persuade** someone to your point of view, you may want to write a persuasive essay or editorial.

Each genre has unique strengths and weaknesses, and your specific goals will help you decide which is best.

8

Working with ELLs　　**ELL** Sheltered Instruction: Cognitive

As students study types of nonfiction narration, guide them to demonstrate English comprehension by employing basic reading skills, including summarizing and comparing and contrasting. Have them use graphic organizers to expand these skills.

Beginning Write simple sentences that might appear in a personal narrative. Read

them aloud as students follow along, and lead students in recording key words in a cluster diagram. Guide them in using the diagram to summarize what they read.

Intermediate Pair students with fluent speakers and have them read an excerpt from a biography, taking notes in a main idea and details chart. Then, have partners write a summary based on their charts.

Nonfiction Narration

Nonfiction narratives are any kind of literary text that tells a story about real people, events, and ideas. This genre of writing can take a number of different forms but includes well-developed conflict and resolution, interesting and believable characters, and a range of literary strategies, such as dialogue and suspense. Examples include Gary Soto's "The Drive-In Movies"; Avi's "Superpatriot."

CHAPTER 5
NONFICTION NARRATION

Personal Narratives

Personal narratives tell true stories about events in a writer's life. These types of writing are also called **autobiographical essays.** The stories may tell about an experience or relationship that is important to the writer, who is the main character. They have a clearly defined focus and communicate the reasons for actions and consequences.

Biographical Narratives

In a **biographical narrative,** the writer shares facts about someone else's life. The writer may describe an important period, experience, or relationship in that other person's life, but presents the information from his or her own perspective.

Blogs

Blogs are online journals that may include autobiographical narratives, reflections, opinions, and other types of comments. They may also reflect genres other than nonfiction such as expository writing, and they may include other media, such as photos, music, or video.

WRITING COACH

Online

www.phwritingcoach.com

Online Journal
Try It! Record your notes, answers, and ideas in the online journal. You can also record and save your answers and ideas on pop-up sticky notes in the eText.

MOTIVATE AND ENGAGE

Before students read page 9 and 10, ask:

- **What is nonfiction writing?**
- **What are some forms of nonfiction?**

Have students work in pairs to answer the questions. Then, have pairs read the text and revise their answers as necessary. Invite volunteers to share their responses.

Nonfiction Narration   9

Advanced Have students preview page 9, filling in a K-W-L chart with what they know about nonfiction narration and what they want to learn. Have them read page 9 and complete the chart with what they learned. Have them use the chart to write a paragraph describing the similarities and differences among personal narratives, biographical narratives, and blogs.

Advanced High Have students complete the Advanced activity. Then, have them exchange paragraphs with partners and summarize each other's work.

COLLABORATE AND DISCUSS

Extend the *Try It!* activity by having small groups come up with one writing topic and two ideas about the topic for each form of nonfiction listed on pages 9 and 10. Remind students to assign roles to group members, such as facilitator, scribe or secretary, timekeeper, and presenter. Then, have each group present its examples for the class.

Diary and Journal Entries

Writers record their personal thoughts, feelings, and experiences in **diaries** or **journals.** Writers sometimes keep diaries and journals for many years and then analyze how they reacted to various events over time.

Eyewitness Accounts

Eyewitness accounts are nonfiction writing that focus on historical or other important events. The writer is the narrator and shares his or her thoughts about the event. However, the writer is not the main focus of the writing.

Memoirs

Memoirs usually focus on meaningful scenes from writers' lives. These scenes often reflect on moments of a significant decision or personal discovery. For example, many modern U.S. presidents have written memoirs after they have left office. These memoirs help the public gain a better understanding of the decisions they made while in office.

Reflective Essays

Reflective essays present personal experiences, either events that happened to the writers themselves or that they learned about from others. They generally focus on sharing observations and insights they had while thinking about those experiences. Reflective essays often appear as features in magazines and newspapers.

Try It! With a small group, discuss which of the narrative nonfiction forms would be the best choice for each of these purposes. For each, identify two ideas you would expect the writing to address. Discuss your ideas and report your decisions.

- To tell about seeing a championship kite-flying tournament
- To write about one of the first astronauts to walk in space
- To record personal thoughts about a favorite teacher

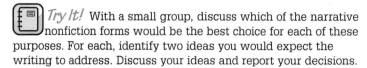

Working with ELLs   **ELL** Sheltered Instruction: Cognitive

As students read about fictional narratives, help them narrate events, describe places, people, or things, and explain situations with increasing specificity and detail in writing.

Beginning Meet with students and provide simple prompts to facilitate writing. Help students supply words and phrases in response to the following prompt, and write

them on the board: *the day school closed.* Then, help students create a story by using the phrases to narrate events, describe characters and setting, and explain a situation with specificity and detail. Finally, read the finished story aloud as students copy it down.

Intermediate Distribute story maps to groups of students. Have them use the maps

Fiction Narration

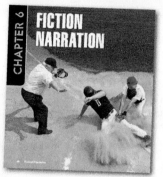

Fiction narratives are literary texts that tell a story about imagined people, events, and ideas. They contain elements such as characters, a setting, a sequence of events, and often, a theme. As with nonfiction narratives, this genre can take many different forms, but most forms include well-developed **conflict** and **resolution.** They also include **interesting and believable elements** and a range of **literary strategies,** such as dialogue and suspense. Examples include Cynthia Rylant's "Stray"; Laurence Yep's "The Homecoming"

Realistic Fiction

Realistic fiction portrays invented characters and events in everyday situations. Because the focus is on everyday life, realistic fiction often presents problems that many people face and solutions they devise to solve them.

Fantasy Stories

Fantasy stories stretch the imagination and take readers to unreal worlds. Animals may talk, people may fly, or characters may have superhuman powers. Good fantasy stories manage to keep the fantastic elements believable.

Historical Fiction

Historical fiction is about imaginary people living in real places and times in history. Usually, the main characters are fictional people who know and interact with famous people and participate in important historical events.

Mystery Stories

Mystery stories present unexplained or strange events that characters try to solve. These stories are often packed full of suspense and surprises. Some characters in mystery stories, such as Sherlock Holmes, have become so famous that many people think of them as real people.

Fiction Narration   11

MOTIVATE AND ENGAGE

Before students read pages 11 and 12, ask:

- **What is fiction?**

- **What are some elements of fiction?**

Pair students to answer the questions. Then, have students read pages 11 and 12, and revise their answers as necessary. As a class, discuss the various forms of fiction and make a list of elements the forms might share, such as characters, setting, and conflict.

to plan and write a story. As they draft, ask questions to encourage them to narrate events, describe places, people, or things, and explain situations with greater specificity and detail. Call on groups to read their stories.

Advanced Have partners write a short story about a day at school, narrating events, describing places, people, or

things, and explaining situations with specificity and detail.

Advanced High Have students complete the Advanced activity. Then, have them revise their stories, incorporating peer feedback.

Myths and Legends

Myths and **legends** are traditional stories, told in cultures around the world. They were created to explain natural events that people could not otherwise explain or understand. They may, for example, tell about the origin of fire or thunder. Many myths and legends include gods, goddesses, and heroes who perform superhuman actions.

Science Fiction

Science fiction stories tell about real and imagined developments in science and technology and their effects on the way people think and live. Space travel, robots, and life in the future are popular topics in science fiction.

Tall Tales

You can tell a **tall tale** from other story types because it tells about larger-than-life characters in realistic settings. These characters can perform amazing acts of strength and bravery. One very famous hero of tall tales is Pecos Bill, who could ride just about anything—even a tornado!

Try It! Think about what you've read about narrative fiction and narrative nonfiction genres. Then, discuss in a group which **genre** would be best if you were planning a first draft and had these purposes in mind. Select the correct genre for conveying your intended meaning to your audiences. Then, identify two or three ideas that you would expect to include in a first draft. Be sure to explain your choices.

- To tell about a Texas rancher who can lasso lightning
- To share a true story about a famous person
- To tell the story of your most exciting day at school

Poetry and Description

Poetry and other kinds of descriptive literature express ideas and feelings about real or imagined people, events, and ideas. They use rhythm, rhyme, precise language, and sensory details—words that appeal to the senses—to create vivid images. In addition, they use figurative language—writing that means something beyond what the words actually say—to express ideas in new, fresh, and interesting ways.

Structural elements, such as line length and stanzas, also help the poet express ideas and set a mood. Some examples of poetry include Lewis Carroll's "The Walrus and the Carpenter"; Langston Hughes's "April Rain Song."

Ballad

A **ballad** is a form of lyric poetry that expresses the poet's emotions toward someone or something. Ballads rhyme, and some have refrains that repeat after each stanza, which makes them easy to translate into songs.

In many places, traditional folk ballads were passed down as oral poems or songs and then later written. Some ballads tell about cultural heroes. Other ballads tell sad stories or make fun of certain events.

Free Verse

Free verse is poetry that has no regular rhyme, rhythm, or form. Instead, a free verse poem captures the patterns of natural speech. The poet writes in whatever form seems to fit the ideas best. A free verse poem can have almost anything as its subject.

> ❝ **Writer to Writer** ❞
>
> Writing fiction and poetry sharpens your creativity—a skill valued by universities and employers.
>
> —Kelly Gallagher

Partner Talk

Think about an example of fiction that you've especially enjoyed reading. Then, choose a partner and report your choices to each other. Be sure to explain what made the fiction piece so enjoyable, interesting, or exciting.

MOTIVATE AND ENGAGE

Write these questions on the board: *What forms of poetry are familiar to you? What forms of poetry have you written in the past?* Tell students to use these questions to spark a quickwrite about poetry. Encourage volunteers to share their responses.

After students have read the text on pages 13 and 14, have a class discussion about what they learned from the text and what kind of poetry they would like to write.

Poetry and Description **13**

Differentiated Instruction

RTI Strategy for Below-Level Students
Students may benefit from listening to or reading poetry. Examples of some of the forms on pages 13 and 14 can be found on pages 122 and 123. Give students copies of the latter pages. Go through the examples and help students identify the differences between the different forms.

Strategy for Spanish Speakers
Students whose home language is Spanish may have difficulty distinguishing between ballads and free verse because they need help identifying rhyming words in English. Give pairs examples of ballads and free verse poems and have them identify the ballads. Then, have them identify the rhyming words in the ballads. Review the spelling variations in rhyming words, as these often differ in Spanish.

Prose Poem

A **prose poem** shares many of the features of other poetry, but it takes the form of prose, or non-verse writing. Therefore, a prose poem may look like a short story on a page.

Sonnet

The **sonnet** is a form of rhyming lyric poetry with set rules. It is 14 lines long and usually follows a rhythm scheme called iambic pentameter. Each line has ten syllables and every other syllable is accented.

Haiku

Haiku is a form of non-rhyming poetry that was first developed in Japan hundreds of years ago. Typically, the first line has seven syllables, the second line has five syllables, and the third line has seven syllables. Haiku poets often write about nature and use vivid visual images.

Other Descriptive Writing

Descriptive writing includes descriptive essays, travel writing, and definition essays.

- **Descriptive essays** often use words that involve the senses to create a clear picture of a subject.
- A **travel essay** uses sensory words to describe a place.
- A **definition essay** can draw on a writer's emotional experience to describe something abstract, like friendship or happiness.

  Description can be used in other types of writing. For example, a short story may include strong description.

Try It! Now that you've learned more about poetry and description, discuss which specific **genre** would be best for each of these purposes. Select the correct genre for conveying your intended meaning to your audiences. Then, identify two or three types of information that you would want to include in a first draft. Be ready to explain your thinking.

- To tell about a trip to a beach in Mexico
- To describe a drop of rain
- To tell the story of a character who lives in the wilderness

READ AND APPLY

After students have read pages 13 and 14, have pairs complete the *Try It!* activity. Emphasize that descriptive words will be important in all of the genres students might choose. Ask:

- **What specific things would you be describing in each topic?**
- **What words might you use in your descriptions?**

Encourage volunteers to share their responses. Have a discussion on ways to enhance descriptive details.

Working with ELLs — ELL Sheltered Instruction: Cognitive

As students learn about descriptive writing, help them orally narrate events, describe places, people, or things, and explain situations with increasing specificity and detail.

Beginning Display a word bank of basic words that might be used to narrate a shopping trip. Review the words, miming as appropriate. Provide sentence starters about shopping, such as *At the store I saw a* ________ . Have students complete them orally to narrate events, describe people or things, and explain situations.

Intermediate Pair students with fluent partners, and distribute cluster diagrams. Have pairs fill in the diagrams with ideas for a story, including descriptions of characters and settings, narration of events, and

Exposition

Exposition is writing that seeks to communicate ideas and information. It relies on facts to inform or explain.

- Effective expository writing includes effective introductory paragraphs, body paragraphs, and concluding paragraphs.
- In addition, good expository writing uses a variety of sentence structures and rhetorical devices—deliberate uses of language for specific effects.

Examples of expository writing include "Destructive Scratching in Cats"; William Scheller's "Race to the End of the Earth"

Analytical Essay

An **analytical essay** explores a topic by supplying relevant information in the form of facts, examples, reasons, and valid inferences to support the writer's claims.

- An **introductory paragraph** presents a thesis statement, the main point to be developed.
- The **body of the essay** provides facts about the topic, using a variety of sentence structures and transitions.
- The **concluding paragraph** sums up ideas.

Compare-and-Contrast Essay

A **compare-and-contrast** essay explores similarities and differences between two or more things for a specific purpose. As with other expository essays, the compare-and-contrast essay offers clear, factual details about the subject.

Cause-and-Effect Essay

A **cause-and-effect essay** traces the results of an event or describes the reasons an event happened. It is clearly organized and gives precise examples that support the relationship between the cause and effect.

66 Writer to Writer 99

Expository forms can shape my thinking and help my writing gel. I find the expository patterns clarifying my thoughts and filling in gaps that I may have otherwise missed.

—Jeff Anderson

Partner Talk

Choose a different partner this time. Discuss a poem that you've read in class. Share your thoughts about the poem and describe what made the piece successful.

MOTIVATE AND ENGAGE

Before students read pages 15–17, have a discussion about their perceptions of expository writing. Elicit from students that expository writing explains or informs.

Have students quickwrite about different forms of exposition. Provide one or two examples, such as cause-and-effect and compare-and-contrast essays, to get students started. Ask students to write about expository writing they have done, explaining successes and challenges as well as purpose and audience. Then, discuss student responses.

explanations of situations. Then, have partners practice telling their stories. Call on pairs to tell their stories to the class.

Advanced Have students brainstorm and record ideas for a story. Then, have them use their notes to relate the story to a partner. As they practice storytelling, ensure they narrate events, describe places, people, or things, and explain

situations with increasing specificity and detail.

Advanced High Have students complete the Advanced activity. To challenge students, have them orally summarize their partners' stories.

Classification Essay

In a **classification essay,** a writer organizes a subject into categories and explains the category into which an item falls.

- An effective classification essay **sorts** its subjects—things or ideas—into several categories.
- It then offers **examples** that fall into each category. For example, a classification essay about video games might discuss three types of video games—action, adventure, and arcade.
- The essay might conclude with a statement about how the items classified are different or about how they are similar.

Problem-Solution Essay

A **problem-solution essay** presents a problem and then offers solutions to that problem. This type of essay may contain opinions, like a persuasive essay, but it is meant to explain rather than persuade.

- An effective problem-solution essay presents a clear statement of the problem, including a summary of its causes and effects.
- Then, it proposes at least one realistic solution and uses facts, statistics, or expert testimony to support the solution.
- The essay should be clearly organized, so that the relationship between the problem and the solution is obvious.

Pro-Con Essay

A **pro-con essay** examines arguments for and against an idea or topic.

- It has a topic that has two sides or points of view. For example, you might choose the following as a topic: Is it right to keep animals in zoos?
- Then, you would develop an essay that tells why it's good to keep animals in zoos, as well as why it's harmful to keep animals in zoos.
- It's important to be sure to give a clear analysis of the topic.

Newspaper and Magazine Articles

Newspaper and **magazine articles** offer information about news and events. They are typically factual and do not include the writer's opinions. They often provide an analysis of events and give readers background information on a topic. Some articles may also reflect genres other than the analytical essay, such as an editorial that aims to persuade.

Internet Articles

Articles on the **Internet** can supply relevant information about a topic.

- They are often like newspaper or magazine articles but may include shorter sentences and paragraphs. In addition, they include more visuals, such as charts and bulleted lists. They may also reflect genres other than analytical essays.
- It's always wise to consider the source when reading Internet articles because only the most reputable sources should be trusted to present correct facts.

On-Demand Writing

Because essay questions often appear on school tests, knowing how to write to **test prompts**, especially under time limits, is an important skill.

Test prompts provide a clear topic with directions about what should be addressed. The effective response to an essay demonstrates not only an understanding of academic content but also good writing skills.

Try It! Think about what you've learned about expository writing and consider the other genres you've discussed. Then, discuss in a group which **genre** would be best if you were planning a first draft with these purposes in mind. Select the correct genre for conveying your intended meaning to your audiences. Then, identify two or three key ideas that you would want to include in a first draft. Be sure to explain your choices.

- To weigh the benefits of two kinds of pets
- To imagine what life would be like on the moon

> **Partner Talk**
>
> Share your experiences with writing expository essays with a partner. Talk about strategies that worked well for you, as well as those that weren't as successful. Be sure to include your analysis of why certain strategies worked better than others.

READ AND APPLY

Before students attempt the *Try It!* activity, review some of the characteristics of good expository writing. Ask:

- **Which is more important in expository writing, clarity or imaginative description?**
- **Is expository writing better for comparing things and ideas or for developing a character?**

Explain that asking these questions will help them to effectively focus their writing.

Exposition   17

Differentiated Instruction

RTI Strategy for Below-Level Students
Preteach these vocabulary words *exposition, analytical, classification, on-demand writing*. Have students make flashcards, writing the term and the definition on either side. Then, show them the term and ask them to give you the definition. Finally, brainstorm with students for examples of expository essays. Ask, can you give me an example of a book report?

PRE-AP Enrichment for Above-Level Students Provide students with this test prompt: Write an essay in which you discuss the similarities and differences between your daily routine during the school year and during your summer vacation. Then, challenge students to write an introduction to this essay with a thesis statement.

Persuasion

CHAPTER 9
PERSUASION

Persuasive writing aims to influence the attitudes or actions of a specific audience on specific issues. A strong persuasive text is logically organized and clearly describes the issue. It also provides precise and relevant evidence that supports a clear thesis statement. Persuasive writing may contain diagrams, graphs, or charts. These visuals can help to convince the reader. Examples include Richard Durbin's "Preserving a Great American Symbol"; Krystin Oliphant's "Astros Welcome Instant Replay."

Persuasive Essays or Argumentative Essays

A **persuasive essay** or **argumentative essay** uses logic and reasoning to persuade readers to adopt a certain point of view or to take action. A strong persuasive essay starts with a clear thesis statement and provides supporting arguments based on evidence. It also anticipates readers' counter-arguments and responds to them as well.

Persuasive Speeches

Persuasive speeches are presented aloud and aim to win an audience's support for a policy, position, or action. These speeches often appeal to emotion and reason to convince an audience. Speakers sometimes change their script in order to address each specific audience's concerns.

Editorials

Editorials state the opinion of the editors and publishers of news organizations. Editorials usually present an opinion about a current issue, starting with a clear thesis statement and then offering strong supporting evidence.

Op-Ed Pieces

An **op-ed, or opposite-editorial, piece** is an essay that tries to convince readers to agree with the writer's views on an issue. The writer may not work for the publication and is often an expert on the issue or has an interesting point of view.

18   **Types of Writing**

Letters to the Editor

Readers write **letters to editors** at print and Internet publications to express opinions in response to previously published articles. A good letter to the editor gives an accurate and honest representation of the writer's views.

Reviews

Reviews evaluate items and activities, such as books, movies, plays, and music, from the writer's point of view. A review often states opinions on the quality of an item or activity and supports those opinions with examples, facts, and other evidence.

Advertisements

Advertisements in all media—from print to online sites to highway billboards—are paid announcements that try to convince people to buy something or do something. Good advertisements use a hook to grab your attention and support their claims. They contain vivid, persuasive language and multimedia techniques, such as music, to appeal to a specific audience.

Propaganda

Propaganda uses emotional appeals and often biased, false, or misleading information to persuade people to think or act in a certain way. Propaganda may tap into people's strongest emotions by generating fear or attacking their ideas of loyalty or patriotism. Because propaganda appears to be objective, it is wise to be aware of the ways it can manipulate people's opinions and actions.

Try It! Think about what you have learned about exposition, description, and persuasion. Form a group to discuss and draw conclusions about which **genres** would be best if you were planning a first draft with each of these intentions in mind. Select the correct genre for conveying your intended meaning to your audiences. Then, identify two or three types of information that you would want to include in a first draft.

- To explain how an event happened
- To describe a beautiful landscape
- To encourage teens to buy teeth-whitening toothpaste

Partner Talk

Share your experiences with various types of persuasive texts with a partner. Talk about the types of persuasive text that you think are most effective, honest, and fair. Be sure to explain your thinking.

READ AND APPLY

After students have read the text on pages 18 and 19, ask:

- What are the common elements of persuasive writing? What elements are unique to each form?

- What types of information would be used in different types of writing?

- Would you use facts in an expository essay, metaphors in a poem, and statistics in a persuasive essay?

Tell students to complete the *Try It!* activity on page 19.

Persuasion   19

RTI Strategy for Special Needs Students
Have students preview the heads on pages 18 and 19 with you. Ask students to identify words that are unfamiliar or challenging. Work with students to define each word. Have students look through a newspaper and find as many examples of the different forms of persuasive writing as they can.

Enrichment for Gifted/Talented Students
Have students choose one of the forms of persuasive writing listed on pages 18 and 19 and write a brief persuasive piece, in which they make their argument and persuade their audience to agree or to act. Invite volunteers to read their persuasive piece to the class, and to identify their purpose and intended audience.

Responses to Literature

Responses to literature analyze and interpret an author's work. They use clear **thesis statements** and **evidence from the text using embedded quotations to support the writer's ideas.** They also evaluate how well authors have accomplished their goals. Effective responses to literature extend beyond literal analysis to evaluate and discuss how and why the text is effective or not effective.

Critical Reviews

Critical reviews evaluate books, plays, poetry, and other literary works. Reviews present the writer's opinions and support them with specific examples. The responses may analyze the aesthetic effects of an author's use of language in addition to responding to the content of the writing.

Compare-and-Contrast Essays

Compare-and-contrast essays explore similarities and differences between two or more works of literature. These essays provide relevant evidence to support the writer's opinions.

Letters to Authors

Readers write **letters to authors** to share their feelings and thoughts about a work of literature directly.

Blog Comments

Blog comments on an author's Web site or book retailer pages let readers share their ideas about a work. Readers express their opinions and give interpretations of what an author's work means.

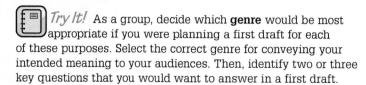 *Try It!* As a group, decide which **genre** would be most appropriate if you were planning a first draft for each of these purposes. Select the correct genre for conveying your intended meaning to your audiences. Then, identify two or three key questions that you would want to answer in a first draft.

- To tell an author why you think her book is excellent
- To write an opinion about a newspaper article
- To imagine how a certain landform came to be

> **Partner Talk**
>
> Interview your partner about his or her experiences writing interpretative responses. Be sure to ask questions such as these:
>
> - How did you support your opinion of the author's work?
> - How did you choose evidence, such as quotes, to support your analysis or opinion?

Research Writing

Research writing is based on factual information from outside sources. Research reports organize and present ideas and information. They present evidence in support of a clear thesis statement.

Research Reports and Documented Essays

Research reports and **documented essays** present information and analysis about a topic that the writer has studied. Start with a clear thesis statement. Research reports often include graphics and illustrations. Documented essays are less formal research writing that show the source of every fact, quote, or borrowed idea in parentheses.

Experiment Journals and Lab Reports

Experiment journals and **lab reports** focus on the purposes, procedures, and results of a lab experiment. They often follow a strict format that includes dates and specific observation notes.

Statistical Analysis Reports

A **statistical analysis report** presents numerical data. Writers of this type of report must explain how they gathered their information, analyze their data, tell what significance the findings may have, and explain how these findings support their thesis.

Annotated Bibliographies

An **annotated bibliography** lists the research sources a writer used. It includes the title, author, publication date, publisher, and brief notes that describe and evaluate the source.

Try It! Discuss which kinds of reports you might write if you were planning a first draft for these purposes. **Select the correct form** for conveying your intended meaning to your audiences. Then, identify two or three key questions that you would want to answer in a first draft. Explain your choices.

- To accompany a project you plan to enter in a science fair
- To write about a poll taken to predict the results of an election

Partner Talk

Share with a partner the kinds of research writing you've done in school. Explain which projects you've enjoyed and why.

MOTIVATE AND ENGAGE

Before students read the text on page 21, ask students to write responses to these questions that you write on the board:

- **Have you ever done research writing?**
- **Where did you find information about your topic?**
- **What challenges did you encounter?**
- **What did you like/ dislike about research writing?**

Invite volunteers to share their responses, and have a class discussion on the forms of research writing.

Differentiated Instruction

RTI **Strategy for Below-Level Students**
Have students work with a partner or with you to make flashcards for the response-to-literature writing and research-writing forms. To ensure comprehension, show student pairs how to test each other using the cards.

PRE-AP **Enrichment for Above-Level Students** Have students choose one form of response-to-literature writing. Ask students to write a brief response to a work of literature they have read recently using the form of their choice. You may wish to provide the work of literature, such as a poem or a short story. Invite volunteers to share their writing with the class.

Workplace Writing

Workplace writing is writing done on the job or as part of a job, often in an office setting. It usually communicates details about a particular job or work project. This type of writing features organized and accurately conveyed information and should include reader-friendly formatting techniques, such as clearly defined sections and enough blank space for easy reading.

Business Letters and Friendly Letters

A **business letter** is a formal letter written to, from, or within a business. It can be written to make requests or to express concerns or approval. For example, you might write to a company to ask about job opportunities. Business letters follow a specific format that includes an address, date, formal greeting, and closing.

In contrast, a **friendly letter** is a form of correspondence written to communicate between family, friends, or acquaintances. For example, you might write a thank-you note for a gift.

Memos

Memos are short documents usually written from one member of an organization to another or to a group. They are an important means of communicating information within an organization.

E-mails

E-mail is an abbreviation for "electronic mail" and is a form of electronic memo. Because it can be transmitted quickly allowing for instant long-distance communication, e-mail is a very common form of communication that uses a computer and software to send messages.

Forms

Forms are types of workplace writing that ask for specific information to be completed in a particular format. Examples include applications, emergency contact information forms, and tax forms.

Working with ELLs   **ELL** Sheltered Instruction: Cognitive

To help students internalize and build proficiency with new grade-level academic vocabulary, have them use and reuse the vocabulary in a speaking activity. Focus on these academic words from Partner Talk: *partner, procedural, challenge.*

Beginning Explain the academic words *partner* and *challenge*, using visuals and mime. Help students create a **Concept Illustration** for each word, drawing

a humorous caricature with words or symbols. Help students orally present their cards, using and reusing the vocabulary to complete sentence starters such as *Running twenty miles is … .*

Intermediate Have students work with fluent partners to complete **Concept Illustration** cards for the academic words, as described in the Beginning activity. Have them use the words in oral

Instructions

Instructions are used to explain how to complete a task or procedure. They provide clear, step-by-step guidelines. For example, recipes and user manuals are forms of instructions.

Project Plans

Project plans are short documents usually written from one member of an organization to another. They outline a project's goals and objectives and may include specific details about how certain steps of a project should be achieved.

Résumés

A **résumé** is an overview of a person's experience and qualifications for a job. This document lists a person's job skills and work history. Résumés can also feature information about a person's education.

College Applications

College applications are documents that ask for personal information and details about someone's educational background. College administrators use this information to decide whether or not to accept a student.

Job Applications

Job applications are similar to résumés in that they require a person to list work experience and educational background. Most employers will require a completed job application as part of the hiring process.

Try It! As a group, discuss which form of workplace writing would be best for each of these purposes. Select the correct form for conveying your intended meaning to your audiences. Identify two or three types of information you would expect to include in a first draft.

- To inform the company that made your cell phone that it does not work properly
- To prepare information about your qualifications for a job search
- To create a plan for your group assignment in science class

Partner Talk

Share with a partner your experience with workplace and procedural writing. For example, have you ever written instructions, created a résumé, or completed a job application? What do you find are particular challenges with this type of writing?

COLLABORATE AND DISCUSS

After students read pages 22 and 23, have them work in small groups to discuss scenarios where they might use the different forms of workplace writing.

Have groups assign roles, such as facilitator, timekeeper, and scribe. Tell groups each scenario should be as detailed as possible (e.g., an architect creates a project plan to build a new school; a car dealer writes an email to her employees about the new model coming out.)

Workplace Writing   23

sentences describing their cards and then reuse the words in answers to questions you ask about their illustrations.

Advanced To help students build vocabulary proficiency, use the **Cloze Method** by writing sentences on the board with the academic words omitted. Have volunteers orally state the missing words. Have students then reuse the words in oral sentences of their own.

Advanced High After students complete the Partner Talk, have them orally summarize the activity, using the academic words in context. Have them reuse the words as they meet with Intermediate students to create Concept Illustration cards.

Writing for Media

The world of communication has changed significantly in recent years. In addition to writing for print media such as magazines and books, writers also write for a variety of other **media,** in forms such as:

- Scripts for screenplays, video games, and documentaries
- Storyboards for graphic novels and advertisements
- Packaging for every kind of product
- Web sites and blogs

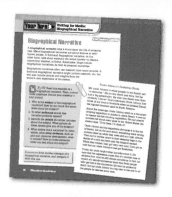

Scripts

Scripts are written for various media, such as documentaries, theater productions, speeches, and audio programs. Movies, television shows, and video games also have scripts.

- A good script focuses on a clearly expressed or implied **theme** and has a specific **purpose.**
- It also contains interesting details, which contribute to a definite **mood or tone.**
- A good script also includes a clear **setting,** **dialogue,** and well-developed **action.**

Blogs

Blogs address just about every purpose and interest. For example, there are blogs about local issues, pets, or food.

Advertisements

Advertisements are designed to persuade someone to buy a product or service. Advertisements use images, words, and music to support their message. Writers write the content of advertisements. In addition, they may help create music and design the sound and the images in the ad.

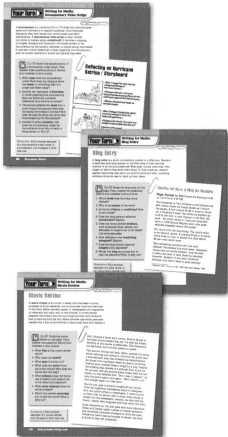

Working with ELLs   **ELL** Sheltered Instruction: Cognitive

Have students ask for and give information in situations ranging from basic communication to extended speaking assignments. Help them to monitor their oral language production and employ the self-corrective technique of watching listeners' reactions to see if they detect confusion and restating their ideas as necessary. Guide students as they use both high- frequency, concrete vocabulary and content-based words.

Beginning Review the content-based vocabulary term *Web site*. Guide students in asking for and giving information using questions and sentence frames featuring the term, such as *What is your favorite Web site? My favorite site is* _____. Remind students to use the self-corrective technique.

Creating Multimedia Projects

A **multimedia project** or presentation uses sound, video, and other media to convey a point or entertain an audience. No matter what type of project you choose as your own multimedia project, it is important to follow these steps:

- Decide on the project's **purpose** and your target **audience.**
- Choose **media** that will effectively convey your **message.**
- **Plan** your presentation. Will you work alone or with a partner or group? If you work with others, how you will assign the tasks?
- What **equipment** will you need? Will you produce artwork, record audio, and take photographs? Should you produce a storyboard to show the sequence of details in your presentation? Be sure to allow enough time to produce the text and all the other elements in your project.
- Keep the **writing process** in mind. There should be working and reworking along the way.
- **Assess** the progress of the project as you work. Ask questions, such as: Does my project incorporate appropriate writing genres? Will the presentation interest my audience? Have I kept my purpose in mind?
- **Rehearse!** Before presenting your project, be sure to do several "practice runs" to weed out and correct any errors.
- Keep an electronic record of your presentation for future reference.
- After your presentation, have others assess the project. Their critique will help you to do an even better job next time!

Reflect on Your Writing

Learning more about the different types of writing can help you focus on the characteristics of each type so you can keep improving your own writing. Think about what you've learned in Chapter 2 as you answer these questions:

- What type of writing most interests you?
- What type of writing do you think is most useful? Why?

Partner Talk

Share with a partner your experience with writing for media or multimedia projects. Have you created a Web site or contributed to one? Have you had to complete multimedia projects for a class assignment or for a personal project on which you worked? Talk about how writing for media presents different challenges from more traditional writing and how you have dealt with those challenges.

CHAPTER 3

THE WRITING PROCESS

Writing Traits

Good writing has specific qualities, or traits. In this chapter you will learn about these traits and how to use rubrics to evaluate them. You will also learn how to apply traits during the stages of the writing process.

Ideas

Good writing sends a strong message or presents a clear "angle" or point of view on a subject. It is also informative. The ideas are well developed, or explained with examples and other details.

Organization

A well-organized paper has an obvious plan. You will want to make sure that your ideas move from sentence to sentence and paragraph to paragraph in a logical way. For example, events in a story often appear in the order in which they occurred.

Voice

Voice is the combination of word choice and personal writing style that makes your writing unique. Voice connects a reader to the writer. It can show your personality or "take" on a story.

26

Word Choice

Your choice of words can help you achieve your purpose. Precise word choice means choosing the word that says exactly what you mean to say. Vivid word choice involves choosing words that create pictures for readers, describing how a subject looks, sounds, smells, and so on.

Sentence Fluency

Good writing is like a song—it has fluency, or a rhythm and a flow. By varying sentence patterns, writers ensure that the rhythm of their writing stays interesting.

Conventions

By following the rules of spelling, capitalization, punctuation, grammar, and usage, you help readers understand your ideas.

Overview of Writing Traits	
Ideas	• Significant ideas and informative details • Thorough development of ideas • Unique perspective or strong message
Organization	• Obvious plan • Clear sequence • Strong transitions
Voice	• Effective word choice • Attention to style
Word Choice	• Precise, not vague, words • Vivid, not dull, words • Word choices suited to audience and purpose
Sentence Fluency	• Varied sentence beginnings, lengths, and structures • Smooth sentence rhythms
Conventions	• Proper spelling and capitalization • Correct punctuation, grammar, usage, and sentence structure

WRITING COACH
Online
www.phwritingcoach.com

Online Journal

Try It! Record your answers and ideas in the online journal. You can also record and save your answers and ideas on pop-up sticky notes in the eText.

" Writer to Writer "

Good writing is a symphony of traits—all coming together to make the paper sing.

—Kelly Gallagher

COLLABORATE AND DISCUSS

Ask:

- **What qualities does good writing have?**

Write all student responses on the board.

Then, have students study the chart on page 27. Explain to students that the items in the first column are qualities of good writing. Have a class discussion on the similarities and differences between student responses and the qualities listed in the chart.

Differentiated Instruction

RTI Strategy for Below-Level Students
Before reading the Organization section on page 26, students may benefit from a brief review of the different types of writing: descriptive, expository, persuasive, and narrative. First, ask students to describe each type to establish prior knowledge. Help students generate descriptors for each type of writing as needed.

PRE-AP Enrichment for Above-Level Students Challenge students to explore ways to create a strong voice in their writing. Have students write a brief paragraph on a topic. Then, ask them to examine their word choice and use of active voice to create a livelier tone. Also, suggest that they use a hook to grab their readers' attention. Invite students to share their paragraphs with a partner or with the class.

Rubrics and How To Use Them

You can use rubrics to evaluate the traits of your writing. A rubric allows you to score your writing on a scale in different categories. You will use a six-point rubric like this to help evaluate your writing in chapters 5–12.

Writing Traits	Rating Scale					
Ideas: How interesting, significant, or original are the ideas you present? How well do you develop ideas?	Not very 1	2	3	4	5	Very 6
Organization: How logically is your piece organized? Do your transitions, or movements from idea to idea, make sense?	1	2	3	4	5	6
Voice: How authentic and original is your voice?	1	2	3	4	5	6
Word Choice: How precise and vivid are the words you use? To what extent does your word choice help achieve your purpose?	1	2	3	4	5	6
Sentence Fluency: How well do your sentences flow? How strong and varied is the rhythm they create?	1	2	3	4	5	6
Conventions: How correct is your punctuation? Your capitalization? Your spelling?	1	2	3	4	5	6

Each trait appears in the first column. The rating scale appears in the second column. The higher your score for a trait, the better your writing exhibits that trait.

Using a Rubric on Your Own

A rubric can be a big help in assessing your writing while it is still in process. Imagine you've just started writing a piece of narrative fiction. You know that narrative fiction should have characters, a setting, and a conflict and resolution. You can check the rubric as you write to make sure you are on track. For example, you may use the rubric and decide that you have not developed the conflict well. You can revise to improve your writing and get a better score.

Narrative Fiction Elements	Rating Scale					
	Not very				Very	
Interesting characters	1	2	3	4	5	6
Believable setting	1	2	3	4	5	6
Literary strategies	1	2	3	4	5	6
Well-developed conflict	1	2	3	4	5	6
Well-developed resolution	1	2	3	4	5	6

 Try It! If you checked your story against the rubric and rated yourself mostly 1s and 2s, what actions might you want to take next?

Using a Rubric With a Partner

In some cases, building your own rubric can help you ensure that your writing will meet your expectations. For example, if your class has an assignment to write a poem, you and a partner might decide to construct a rubric to check one another's work. A rubric like the one shown here can help point out whether you should make any changes. Extra lines allow room for you to add other criteria.

Poetry Elements	Rating Scale					
	Not very				Very	
Good sensory details	1	2	3	4	5	6
Colorful adjectives	1	2	3	4	5	6
	1	2	3	4	5	6
	1	2	3	4	5	6
	1	2	3	4	5	6

Try It! What other elements might you add to the rubric?

Using a Rubric in a Group

It is also helpful to use a rubric in a group. That way you can get input on your writing from many people at the same time. If the group members' ratings of your piece are similar, you will probably have an easy time deciding whether to make changes. If the responses vary significantly, you might want to discuss the results with the group. Then, analyze what led to the differing opinions and make careful judgments about what changes you will make.

WRITING COACH

Online

www.phwritingcoach.com

Online Journal
Try It! Record your answers and ideas in the online journal. You can also record and save your answers and ideas on pop-up sticky notes in the eText.

COLLABORATE AND DISCUSS

Discuss with students the benefits and drawbacks of peer evaluations. Students may say that a writer's popularity with group members might lead to a positive (or negative) review regardless of the quality of the writing. Suggest to students that the names of writers should not be disclosed to ensure a more objective review. Have students make other suggestions for ensuring objective reviews.

Differentiated Instruction

RTI Strategy for Below-Level Students
Students may benefit from working with a partner or with you to create rubric items. Explain to students that many school writing assignments explain what is expected of students, and are therefore good guides for creating a rubric. Provide students with a writing assignment, and work with them to change the instructions into questions for a rubric.

PRE-AP Enrichment for Above-Level Students Have students create rubrics for a persuasive essay and for an expository essay. Allow students to work in pairs or small groups. Tell students to use the writing traits rubric on page 28 as a starting point, but to add specific items for each type of writing. Invite students to present their rubrics to the class and to discuss why some items in the persuasive rubric differ from those in the expository rubric.

What Is the Writing Process?

The five steps in the writing process are prewriting, drafting, revising, editing, and publishing. Writing is a process because your idea goes through a series of changes or stages before the product is finished.

Study the diagram to see how moving through the writing process can work. Remember, you can go back to a stage in the process. It does not always have to occur in order.

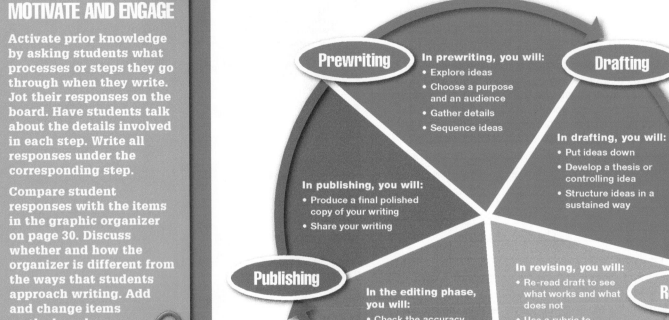

Prewriting

In prewriting, you will:
- Explore ideas
- Choose a purpose and an audience
- Gather details
- Sequence ideas

Drafting

In drafting, you will:
- Put ideas down
- Develop a thesis or controlling idea
- Structure ideas in a sustained way

Revising

In revising, you will:
- Re-read draft to see what works and what does not
- Use a rubric to evaluate
- Analyze what you want to change or improve
- Make changes

Editing

In the editing phase, you will:
- Check the accuracy of facts
- Correct errors in spelling, grammar, usage, and mechanics

Publishing

In publishing, you will:
- Produce a final polished copy of your writing
- Share your writing

Why Use the Writing Process?

Writing involves careful thinking, which means you will make changes as you write. Even professional writers don't just write their thoughts and call it a finished work of art. They use a process. For example, some writers keep going back to the revising stage many times, while others feel they can do the revision in just one step. It is up to each writer to develop the style that works best to produce the best results.

You might find that the writing process works best for you when you keep these tips in mind:

- Remember that the five steps in the writing process are equally important.
- Think about your audience as you plan your paper and develop your writing.
- Make sure you remember your topic and stick to your specific purpose as you write.
- Give your writing some time to "rest." Sometimes it can be good to work on a piece, walk away, and look at it later, with a fresh eye and mind.

The following pages will describe in more detail how to use each stage of the writing process to improve your writing.

WRITING COACH

Online

www.phwritingcoach.com

Online Journal

Try It! Record your answers and ideas in the online journal. You can also record and save your answers and ideas on pop-up sticky notes in the eText.

❝ Writer to Writer ❞

Writing process gives us the freedom to write like mad, tinker like an engineer, evaluate like a judge—playing different roles at different stages. Most importantly it gives us the freedom to get our words out of our heads and into the world.

—Jeff Anderson

READ AND APPLY

Have students read the text on page 31 silently. Tell students to answer these questions in their writing journals or notebooks.

- Which bulleted point on the page did you find most helpful? Why?
- Reflect on your own writing process. What process has worked best for you in the past? Why?
- What process has not worked? Why?

Invite volunteers to share their responses with the class.

What Is the Writing Process? 31

Differentiated Instruction

RTI Strategy for Special Needs Students
Work with students to create flashcards for each stage of the writing process. On one side, write the name of the stage (prewriting, drafting, and so on). On the other side, write one bulleted step in the stage. Have students organize the cards according to the stages. Use the flashcards to review the writing process with students. When students are ready, shuffle the cards. Read a step, and ask students to identify the stage.

RTI Strategy for Below-Level Students To reinforce the writing process terminology for students, have them come up with a familiar cue word for each stage. For example, for prewriting, they may use the word *planning*. For drafting, they may use the word *writing*; for revising *fixing* or *rewriting;* for editing *correcting;* and for publishing *sharing.* This strategy may help students remember the purpose of each stage.

Prewriting

Prewriting
Drafting
Revising
Editing
Publishing

No matter what kind of writing you do, planning during the prewriting stage is crucial. During prewriting, you determine the topic of your writing, its purpose, and its specific audience. Then, you narrow the topic and gather details.

Determining the Purpose and Audience

What Is Your Purpose?

To be sure your writing communicates your ideas clearly, it is important to clarify why you are writing. Consider what you want your audience to take away from your writing. You may want to entertain them, or you may want to warn them about something. Even when you write an entry in a private journal, you're writing for an audience—you!

Who Is Your Audience?

Think about the people who will read your work and consider what they may already know about your topic. Being able to identify this group and their needs will let you be sure you are providing the right level of information.

Choosing a Topic

Here are just a few of the many techniques you can use to determine an appropriate topic.

- **Brainstorm**
  You can brainstorm by yourself, with a partner, or with a group. Just jot down ideas as they arise, and don't rule out anything. When brainstorming in a group, one person's idea often "piggy-backs" on another.

- **Make a Mind Map**
  A mind map is a quick drawing you sketch as ideas come to you. The mind map can take any form. The important thing is to write quick notes as they come to you and then to draw lines to connect relationships among the ideas.

- **Interview**
  A fun way to find a writing topic is to conduct an interview. You might start by writing interview questions for yourself or someone else. Questions that start with *what, when, why, how,* and *who* are most effective. For example, you might ask, "When was the last time you laughed really hard?" "What made you laugh?" Then, conduct the interview and discover the answers.

- **Review Resources and Discuss Ideas**
  You can review resources, such as books, magazines, newspapers, and digital articles, to get ideas. Discussing your initial ideas with a partner can spark even more ideas.

Narrowing Your Topic

Once you have settled on a topic idea you really like, it may seem too broad to tackle. How can you narrow your topic?

- **Use Graphic Organizers**
  A graphic organizer can help narrow a topic that's too broad. For example, you might choose "Animals" as a topic. You might make your topics smaller and smaller until you narrow the topic to "The Habitat of Emperor Penguins."

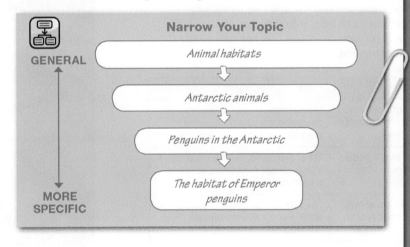

Narrow Your Topic

GENERAL

Animal habitats

Antarctic animals

Penguins in the Antarctic

The habitat of Emperor penguins

MORE SPECIFIC

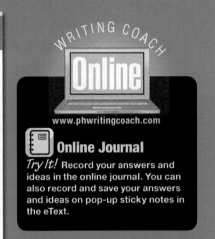

WRITING COACH

Online
www.phwritingcoach.com

Online Journal
Try It! Record your answers and ideas in the online journal. You can also record and save your answers and ideas on pop-up sticky notes in the eText.

"Writer to Writer"

Put something down. Anything. Then, magic will happen.

—Jeff Anderson

READ AND APPLY

You may wish to model narrowing a topic by using the graphic organizer on page 33. Then, narrow the general topic *School Clothes* to *School Uniforms: Pro or Con* using the chart.

As you complete the chart, engage students in the process. Ask:

- What do I want to focus on in my report?

- How can my topic be narrowed further?

- Is my final topic appropriate for a research report? Why or why not?

- Can I find enough information on the topic?

Differentiated Instruction

RTI Strategy for Special Needs Students
Work with students to read and apply the different strategies for choosing a topic. Brainstorm for ideas with the students, jotting down all of their ideas on a topic. Model how to make a mind map, allowing students to draw lines to connect related ideas. Have students interview you briefly. Show students examples of resources, such as newspapers, magazines, and digital articles.

Strategy for Spanish Speakers
Students whose home language is Spanish may reverse the subject-verb order when writing questions with the *wh-* words (*When you are going?* versus *When are you going?*). Write or say different *Wh-* questions with correct and incorrect subject-verb order. Have students indicate correct or incorrect usage with a "thumbs up" or "thumbs down" sign. Have volunteers write new questions using the *wh-* words.

Prewriting (continued)

Prewriting
Drafting
Revising
Editing
Publishing

- **Use Resource Materials**
  The resource materials you use to find information can also help you narrow a broad topic. Look up your subject online in an encyclopedia or newspaper archive. Scan the resources as you look for specific subtopics to pursue.

Gather Details

After you decide on a topic, you will want to explore and develop your ideas. You might start by looking through online resources again, talking with people who are knowledgeable about your topic, and writing everything you already know about the topic. It will be helpful to gather a variety of details. Look at these types:

- Facts
- Statistics
- Personal observations
- Expert opinions

- Examples
- Descriptions
- Quotations
- Opposing viewpoints

After you have narrowed your topic and gathered details, you will begin to plan your piece. During this part of prewriting, you will develop your essay's thesis or controlling idea—its main point.

As you plan your piece, you can use a graphic organizer. Specific kinds of graphic organizers can help structure specific kinds of writing. For example, a pro-con chart like this one can clarify the reasons for and against an idea.

Pro	Con
Adding funds to the school music budget would allow more students to learn to play instruments.	Giving more money to the music department would mean other programs would get less money.
Research shows that music helps the brain become more flexible.	Other programs, such as sports, are important in keeping students physically healthy.
Band members could stop selling gift-wrap materials at holiday time.	The school board has already approved the current budget allocations.

READ AND APPLY

Model creating a pro-con chart for the topic explored in Motivate and Engage on page 32. Some possible examples of the pros and cons of school uniforms might be:

- **Pros: students don't have to worry about what to wear**

- **Cons: students can't express their individuality**

Discuss your choices and elicit other suggestions from students. Write student suggestions in the appropriate column in the chart.

Working with ELLs   **ELL** Sheltered Instruction: Cognitive

As students study the drafting process, help them narrate events, describe places, people, or things, and explain situations in writing with increasing specificity and detail.

Beginning Facilitate writing by using prompts to elicit words from students and scribing them on the board. For example, write the prompts *I found a large box. It was. . . . The next thing I did was …* Guide students in responding, and then lead them to narrate the events, describe the people, and explain the situation of the story. Have students write the story as you generate it.

Intermediate Have students complete the Beginning activity. Then, have them revise the written story with fluent partners, narrating, describing, and explaining with increasing specificity and detail.

Drafting

In the drafting stage, you get your ideas down. You may consult an outline or your prewriting notes as you build your first draft.

Prewriting

Drafting

Revising

Editing

Publishing

WRITING COACH

Online

www.phwritingcoach.com

Online Journal

Try It! Record your answers and ideas in the online journal. You can also record and save your answers and ideas on pop-up sticky notes in the eText.

The Introduction

Most genres should have a strong introduction that immediately grabs the reader's attention and includes the thesis. Even stories and poems need a "hook" to grab interest.

Try It! Which of these first sentences are strong openers? Read these examples of first sentences. Decide which ones are most interesting to you. Explain why they grab your attention. Then, explain why the others are weak.

- Have you ever wondered what it would be like to wake up one morning to find you're someone else?
- There are many ways to paint a room.
- Autumn is a beautiful season.
- On Sunday, we went to the store.
- When I woke up that morning, I had no idea that it would be the best day of my life.

The Body

The body of a paper develops the main idea and details that elaborate on and support the thesis. These details may include interesting facts, examples, statistics, anecdotes or stories, quotations, personal feelings, and sensory descriptions.

The Conclusion

The conclusion typically restates the thesis and summarizes the most important concepts of a paper.

Advanced Have partners choose an opening sentence from page 35 and use it to write the first paragraph of a short story, narrating events, describing people and places, and explaining situations in detail. Have them meet in small groups to share their paragraphs.

Advanced High Have individuals complete the Advanced activity. Challenge them to revise their paragraphs with increasing specificity and detail and then to share them aloud.

Revising: Making It Better

Prewriting
Drafting
Revising
Editing
Publishing

No one gets every single thing right in a first draft. In fact, most people require more than two drafts to achieve their best writing and thinking. When you have finished your first draft, you're ready to revise.

Revising means "re-seeing." In revising, you look again to see if you can find ways to improve style, word choice, figurative language, sentence variety, and subtlety of meaning. As always, check how well you've addressed the issues of purpose, audience, and genre. Carefully analyze what you'd want to change and then go ahead and do it. Here are some helpful hints on starting the revision stage of the writing process.

Take a Break

Do not begin to revise immediately after you finish a draft. Take some time away from your paper. Get a glass of water, take a walk, or listen to some music. You may even want to wait a day to look at what you've written. When you come back, you will be better able to assess the strengths and weaknesses of your work.

Put Yourself in the Place of the Reader

Take off your writer's hat and put on your reader's hat. Do your best to pretend that you're reading someone else's work and see how it looks to that other person. Look for ideas that might be confusing and consider the questions that a reader might have. By reading the piece with an objective eye, you may find items you'd want to fix and improve.

Read Aloud to Yourself

It may feel strange to read aloud to yourself, but it can be an effective technique. It allows you to hear the flow of words, find errors, and hear where you might improve the work by smoothing out transitions between paragraphs or sections. Of course, if you're more comfortable reading your work aloud to someone else, that works, too.

MOTIVATE AND ENGAGE

Take a poll and find out how many students in the class revise their work. Have students that do revise explain their revision processes. Write them on the board.

Compare and contrast students' revision strategies to the strategies on pages 36 and 37. Have students change the chart on page 27 into a checklist or rubric. Model by changing the first bullet into the question: *Is my topic focused?*

Working with ELLs   ELL Sheltered Instruction: Cognitive

As students learn about revising, help them distinguish intonation patterns of English with increasing ease. On the board, write three columns, with examples underneath: (1) *Yes/No Questions;* (2) *Declarative Statements;* (3) *Exclamatory Sentences Showing Surprise.* Read the examples, modeling appropriate intonation: (1) raise your voice at the end; (2) use a falling voice at the end; and (3) use a rising pitch.

Beginning Pair students with English-proficient speakers. Have proficient speakers read the example sentences as students distinguish sentence types based on intonation.

Intermediate Have proficient speakers read aloud the example sentences as students distinguish sentence types based on intonation. Then, have partners complete a **Partner Fluency Check:**

Share Your Work to Get Feedback

Your friends or family members can help you by reading and reacting to your writing. Ask them whether you've clearly expressed your ideas. Encourage them to tell you which parts were most and least interesting and why. Try to find out if they have any questions about your topic that were not answered. Then, evaluate their input and decide what will make your writing better.

Use a Rubric

A rubric might be just what you need to pinpoint weaknesses in your work. You may want to think about the core parts of the work and rate them on a scale. If you come up short, you'll have a better idea about the kinds of things to improve. You might also use a rubric to invite peer review and input.

21st Century Learning

Collaborate and Discuss

When presenting and sharing drafts in the revision stage with a small group, it may be wise to set some ground rules. That way, the group is more likely to help each other analyze their work and make thoughtful changes that result in true improvements.

Here are some suggestions for reviewing drafts as a group:

- Cover the names on papers the group will review to keep the work anonymous.
- Print out copies for everyone in the group.
- Show respect for all group members and their writing.
- Be sure all critiques include positive comments.
- While it is fine to suggest ways to improve the work, present comments in a positive, helpful way. No insults are allowed!
- Plan for a second reading with additional input after the writer has followed selected suggestions.

WRITING COACH

Online

www.phwritingcoach.com

Online Journal

Try It! Record your answers and ideas in the online journal. You can also record and save your answers and ideas on pop-up sticky notes in the eText.

Partner Talk

After a group revision session, talk with a partner to analyze each other's feelings on how the session went. Discuss such issues as these: Did the group adhere to the ground rules? What suggestions could you and your partner make to improve the next session?

COLLABORATE AND DISCUSS

Before students share and present their drafts ask them to assign specific roles to group members to help the group stay focused. Some important roles include:

- **moderator,** who keeps the conversation on topic and ensures equal participation
- **note-taker,** who captures the ideas of the meeting

Students may come up with their own roles as they learn more about the process of receiving and providing feedback.

Revising **37**

Provide a chart with columns labeled *Reading 1, Reading 2,* and so on and a single row labeled *Number Correct;* have partners complete the chart, monitoring speakers' increasing ease in distinguishing intonation patterns after repeated readings.

Advanced Have students write another sentence of each type. Have partners take turns reading their work aloud, using the

correct intonation, as the listener distinguishes sentence types based on intonation.

Advanced High Assign a grade-level text for students to read aloud as partners conduct a **Partner Fluency Check** for correct intonation.

Revision RADaR

Prewriting

Drafting

Revising

Editing

Publishing

The Revision RADaR strategy, which you will use throughout this book, is an effective tool in helping you conduct a focused revision of your work.

You can use your Revision RADaR to revise your writing. The letters **R**, **A**, **D**, and **R** will help you remember to **r**eplace, **a**dd, **d**elete, and **r**eorder.

To understand more about the Revision RADaR strategy, study the following chart.

R Replace . . .	A Add . . .	D and Delete . . .	R Reorder . . .
• Words that are not specific • Words that are overused • Sentences that are unclear	• New information • Descriptive adjectives and adverbs • Rhetorical or literary devices	• Unrelated ideas • Sentences that sound good, but do not make sense • Repeated words or phrases • Unnecessary details	• So most important points are last • To make better sense or to flow better • So details support main ideas

R Replace

You can strengthen a text by replacing words that are not specific, words that are overused, and sentences that are unclear. Take a look at this before and after model.

BEFORE
I kicked the soccer ball hard into the goal.

AFTER
With amazing power, I slammed the soccer ball into the goal.

Apply It! **How did the writer replace the overused word** *kicked*? **What other replacement do you see? How did it improve the text?**

MOTIVATE AND ENGAGE

To help students understand the RADaR acronym, ask: What does it mean to keep something on your "radar"?

Students may say that it means you are paying extra attention to or are on the lookout for something. Ask students why they think the acronym is used here. Write their responses on the board and explain that the RADaR strategy helps writers remember the purpose and goals of revising.

Add

You can add new information, descriptive adjectives and adverbs, and rhetorical or literary devices to make your piece more powerful. Study this before and after model.

BEFORE
I was happy when I won the award.

AFTER
I was beyond thrilled when I won the Science Fair award.

Apply It! **How did the second sentence make you feel, compared with the first? Explain. What information was added to the second sentence?**

 Delete

Sometimes taking words out of a text can improve clarity. Analyze this before and after model.

BEFORE
I knew the test would be difficult, so I should have studied harder for the test before the test day.

AFTER
I knew the test would be difficult, so I should have studied harder for it.

Apply It! **Describe the revision you see. How did taking out unnecessary repetition of the word *test* help the sentences flow more naturally?**

 Reorder

When you reorder, you can make sentences flow more logically.

BEFORE
Today, I have band practice, but yesterday I didn't.

AFTER
I didn't have band practice yesterday, but today I do.

Apply It! **Which of the models flows more logically? Why?**

WRITING COACH

Online

www.phwritingcoach.com

Online Journal

Try It! Record your answers and ideas in the online journal. You can also record and save your answers and ideas on pop-up sticky notes in the eText.

USING TECHNOLOGY

Most word processing programs have a built-in thesaurus tool. You can use the thesaurus to find descriptive words that can often substitute for weaker, overused words.

READ AND APPLY

Have students apply the RADaR strategy to their own writing. With a partner, have students write two or three sentences and then work together to revise them according to each step in the RADaR strategy. Invite students to share their work with the class and explain how they employed the specific strategy in the revision.

Differentiated Instruction

RTI Strategy for Below-Level Students
Students may benefit from working with you or with a partner to complete the *Apply It!* questions. Have students write the Before and After sentences on a sheet of paper. Then, encourage them to highlight the words of each sentence that have changed before answering the *Apply It!* question. If necessary, read the question aloud as students study the sentences they have copied and highlighted.

Strategy for Spanish Speakers
Students whose home language is Spanish may place adjectives after nouns and add an –s to adjectives if the noun is plural, due to Spanish rules of adjective placement and agreement. Elicit nouns with adjectives and write them in two separate columns. Have pairs write a sentence using both words. Have partners check each other's sentences for grammar and meaning.

T39

Revision RADaR (continued)

Prewriting

Drafting

Revising

Editing

Publishing

Read the first draft of the Student Model—a review of the novel *End Game*. Think about how you might use your Revision RADaR to improve the text in a second draft.

Kelly Gallagher, M. Ed.

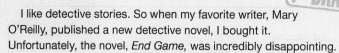

KEEP REVISION ON YOUR RADaR

End Game Fails to Thrill 1ST DRAFT

I like detective stories. So when my favorite writer, Mary O'Reilly, published a new detective novel, I bought it. Unfortunately, the novel, *End Game,* was incredibly disappointing.

In the story, an online video gamer disappears. A detective, Katherine, tries to track down the missing man through gaming Web sites. But here's where O'Reilly really messed up. It's clear that she didn't research the technology involved in online gaming. For example: "Katherine waited while her dial-up modem connected her to the virtual world."

The cheesy and ridiculous dialogue made my reading experience even worse. The errors in the book were bad enough! For example, the suspect says to Katherine, "I'm gonna get you, copper!" Now, this is the year 2010. A modern-day criminal would never use such outdated, silly lines. Instead of making the story exciting, the dialogue made it laughably bad.

O'Reilly has written many great books. My favorites were *On the High Seas* and *Danger in Denver.* They were great. I loved them! But I think it's time for O'Reilly to put down her pen. She clearly doesn't have what it takes any more to be a great writer. And as for *End Game*...don't waste your money!

Is my introduction interesting? Does it grab my readers' attention?

Have I fully analyzed and explained my examples from the text?

Is my information logically ordered?

Is my information relevant to the thesis? Have I included only necessary information?

After writing a draft, the student asked questions like these:

- What could I **replace**?
- What could I **add**?
- What words might I **delete**?
- Should I **reorder** anything?

READ AND APPLY

You may wish to model for students how to evaluate the first draft of the book review, *"End Game* Fails to Thrill,*"* by answering the first two bulleted questions on page 40. Write your responses on the board. Then, elicit answers to the last two questions from volunteers. Write all responses on the board. Then, have students read the second draft with the suggested revisions in mind.

The student writer created this second draft.

End Game Fails to Thrill

The suspense and high-paced action in detective stories are so thrilling! I simply can't get enough of these books. So when my favorite writer, Mary O'Reilly, published a new detective novel, I ran to the store to buy my copy. Unfortunately, the novel, *End Game,* was incredibly disappointing.

In the story, an online video gamer disappears. A detective, Katherine, tries to track down the missing man through gaming Web sites. But here's where O'Reilly really messed up. It's clear that she didn't research the technology involved in online gaming. For example: "Katherine waited while her dial-up modem connected her to the virtual world." Dial-up modems aren't fast enough to do serious online gaming!

Although the errors in the book were bad enough, the cheesy and ridiculous dialogue made my reading experience even worse. For example, the suspect says to Katherine, "I'm gonna get you, copper!" Now, this is the year 2010. A modern-day criminal would never use such outdated, silly lines. Instead of making the story exciting, the dialogue made it laughably bad.

I think it's time for O'Reilly to put down her pen. She clearly doesn't have what it takes any more to be a great writer. And as for *End Game*...don't waste your money!

R *Replaced dull first line with a more engaging opening.*

A *Added a sentence to better explain to my audience why the information from the text was incorrect.*

R *Reordered text so that the information about the errors connected the ideas in the second and third paragraphs.*

D *Deleted unnecessary information.*

Try It! What other words did the writer replace? Add? Delete? Reorder?

WRITING COACH

Online

www.phwritingcoach.com

Online Journal

Try It! Record your answers and ideas in the online journal. You can also record and save your answers and ideas on pop-up sticky notes in the eText.

Partner Talk

Work with a partner to come up with a list of words that describe detective stories. For example, you might use "high-paced action" or "thrilling." Then discuss the value of using more specific words in your writing.

COLLABORATE AND DISCUSS

Have students read both drafts silently, noting the changes the writer made in the revision. Then, have students work in small groups to discuss the changes. Ask each group to answer these questions:

- How did the RADaR strategy help this writer improve the book review?

- What could still be improved?

- How would these changes make the review better?

Invite groups to share their responses with the class.

Differentiated Instruction

RTI Strategy for Below-Level Students

Students may benefit from working with a partner to complete the *Try It!* activity. Make a copy of each draft for the students to mark up as they read. Suggest they use a highlighter to note words that have been replaced, added, or deleted and to place brackets around sentences that have been reordered. Remind them to use the same techniques when they evaluate their own writing.

PRE-AP Enrichment for Above-Level Students

Challenge students to write a critique of the revised review. Ask students to describe three ways in which the second draft improved the ideas in the first draft. Also have them suggest three more ways to further improve the review. Finally, have them write a final draft, using the RADaR strategy and incorporating the suggestions they made.

Editing: Making It Correct

Editing is the process of checking the accuracy of facts and correcting errors in spelling, grammar, usage, and mechanics. Using a checklist like the one shown here can help ensure you've done a thorough job of editing.

Prewriting

Drafting

Revising

Editing

Publishing

Editing Checklist

Task	Ask Yourself
Check your facts and spelling	❏ Have I checked that my facts are correct? ❏ Have I used spell check or a dictionary to check any words I'm not sure are spelled correctly?
Check your grammar	❏ Have I written any run-on sentences? ❏ Have I used the correct verbs and verb tenses? ❏ Do my pronouns match their antecedents, or nouns they replace?
Check your usage	❏ Have I used the correct form of irregular verbs? ❏ Have I used object pronouns, such as *me*, *him*, *her*, *us*, and *them* only after verbs or prepositions? ❏ Have I used subject pronouns, such as *I*, *he*, *she*, *we*, and *they* correctly—usually as subjects?
Check for proper use of mechanics	❏ Have I used correct punctuation? ❏ Does each sentence have the correct end mark? ❏ Have I used apostrophes in nouns but not in pronouns to show possession? ❏ Have I used quotation marks around words from another source? ❏ Have I used correct capitalization? ❏ Does each sentence begin with a capital letter? ❏ Do the names of specific people and places begin with a capital letter?

MOTIVATE AND ENGAGE

Activate students' prior knowledge of editing by asking them what the difference is between revising and editing. Tell students that revising is fixing the communication of the ideas while editing is fixing errors in spelling, grammar, usage, mechanics, and facts.

After students have reviewed the checklist, ask:

▪ **Why is it beneficial to wait until you have finished revising to edit your work?**

▪ **How is the checklist helpful while editing your writing?**

Working with ELLs   **ELL** Sheltered Instruction: Cognitive

Help students monitor and edit their writing for pronoun-antecedent agreement, using self-corrective techniques. Remind students of rules about pronoun-antecedent agreement. Then:

Beginning Write on the board a sentence with incorrect pronoun-antecedent agreement and have students copy it: for example, *The horse walked to their stable.*

Model this self-corrective technique: Circle *their* and underline *horse.* Explain that *horse* is the antecedent. Ask *How many?* of each word (*one, more than one*). Guide students in correcting the sentence, and read it with students.

Intermediate Have students complete the Beginning activity. Then, have them write two short sentences with a pronoun and antecedent. Have groups edit their work

Using Proofreading Marks

Professional editors use a set of proofreading marks to indicate changes in a text. Here is a chart of some of the more common proofreading marks.

Proofreader's Marks

Mark	Meaning
(b.f.)	boldface
⌐	break text|start new line
(caps)	capital letter
⌒	clos̮e up
ℓ	delete̮s
⌢/	insert ⋀word
⋌/	insert⋀comma
=/	insert⋀hyphen
+/	insert let̮ter
⊙/	insert period⋀
(ital)	italic type
(stet)	let stand as̮ is
(l.f.)	**lightface**
(l.c.)	⫽ower case letter
⌐	[move left
⌐	] move right
¶	new paragraph
(rom)	*roman type*
	run text up
(sp)	spell out whole word
	transpo(es)

Online

www.phwritingcoach.com

Online Journal

Try It! Record your answers and ideas in the online journal. You can also record and save your answers and ideas on pop-up sticky notes in the eText.

USING TECHNOLOGY

Many word processing programs have automatic spelling and grammar checks. While these tools can be helpful, be sure to pay attention to any suggestions they offer. That's because sometimes inappropriate substitutes are inserted automatically!

READ AND APPLY

On the board, write several sentences that contain obvious errors in spelling, punctuation, and mechanics. Then, use the proofreader's marks in the chart to correct the first sentences. Invite volunteers to fix the remaining errors. You may also wish to provide copies of the proofreader's marks for students to keep in their writing journals or notebooks.

together by employing the self-corrective technique of circling the pronouns and underlining the antecedents, checking for agreement.

Advanced Have partners write a short paragraph using pronouns. Then, have partners employ the self-corrective technique of circling the pronouns and underlining the antecedents, checking for agreement and editing as necessary.

Advanced High Have students complete the Advanced activity. Challenge them to edit their writing for vague and unclear antecedents as well.

Editing: Making It Correct (continued)

Prewriting
Drafting
Revising
Editing
Publishing

WRITE GUY *Jeff Anderson, M. Ed.*

WHAT DO YOU NOTICE?

Using an editing checklist is a great way to check for correct grammar. However, using a checklist is not enough to make your writing grammatically correct. A checklist tells you what to look for, but not how to correct mistakes you find. To do that, you need to develop and apply your knowledge of grammar.

Looking closely at good writing is one way to expand your grammar know-how. The *What Do You Notice?* feature that appears throughout this book will help you zoom in on passages that use grammar correctly and effectively.

As you read this passage, from "Jobs for Kids," zoom in on the sentences in the passage.

> I have a paper route. After school, I deliver newspapers on my bike to my neighbors. I love this job because I get exercise, and I get to be outside.

Now, ask yourself: *What do you notice about the sentences in this passage?*

Maybe you noticed that the writer uses sentences of varying lengths and with different structures.

After asking a question that draws your attention to the grammar in the passage, the *What Do You Notice?* feature provides information on a particular grammar topic. For example, following the passage and question, you might read about simple and complex sentences, which are both used in the passage.

The *What Do You Notice?* feature will show you how grammar works in actual writing. It will help you learn how to make your writing correct.

READ AND APPLY

Have students read the What Do You Notice? feature. Explain to students that they will see this feature throughout the book. Ask: What is the purpose of this feature? How will it help you to edit your work and improve your own grammar? What strategies does the writer of this essay use that you could incorporate in your own writing?

Working with ELLs   **ELL** Sheltered Instruction: Cognitive

Help students monitor and edit their writing for appropriate verb tenses, using self-corrective techniques. Review with students the rules of verb tenses. Then:

Beginning Display the sentence *The dog barked when he gets the ball.* Read the sentence, using gestures for clarity, and have students copy it. Help students employ self-corrective techniques by

modeling these steps: Circle the verbs *barked* and *gets*. Ask *When?* of each word (*before now* / *now*). Work with students to replace *gets* with *got*. Read the corrected sentence with students.

Intermediate Have students complete the Beginning activity. Then, distribute additional sentences with incorrect verb tenses for students to edit with fluent

Jobs for Kids

I like having my own money. That way, I can buy things I want and can also save money for my future. But here's the problem: How can we, as kids, make money? There are many types of jobs for kids, but each job has pluses and minuses.

I have a paper route. After school, I deliver newspapers on my bike to my neighbors. I love this job because I get exercise, and I get to be outside. This job isn't for everyone, though. Some kids have a lot of after-school activities, so they don't go straight home. Because papers have to be delivered on time, this can be challenging.

A friend of mine babysits because she has fun with and loves taking care of children. To be a babysitter, you have to find out if your state has a law about how old you have to be before you can babysit. You also have to be a patient, responsible person who is good with children. Finally, it helps to know first-aid, just in case a child gets injured.

My brother does yard work for neighbors. He rakes leaves, weeds gardens, and mows lawns. He loves to be outside and doesn't mind getting dirty. However, there are certain safety issues involved. For example, you have to know how to handle a lawnmower properly and wear protective gear.

What type of job is right for you? What are your interests? Get creative, and start making some money!

Try It! Read "Jobs for Kids." Then, zoom in on two more passages. Write a response to each question in your journal.

1. What do you notice about the pronouns (*you, he*) in the fourth paragraph?

2. How does the writer use transitions, such as the word *finally*, to connect ideas in the third paragraph?

WRITING COACH

Online
www.phwritingcoach.com

Online Journal
Try It! Record your answers and ideas in the online journal. You can also record and save your answers and ideas on pop-up sticky notes in the eText.

❝ Writer to Writer ❞

If I wonder how to write any kind of writing, I look at models— well-written examples of the kind of writing I want to do. Models are the greatest how-to lesson I have ever discovered.

—Jeff Anderson

COLLABORATE AND DISCUSS

Have students read "Jobs for Kids." Then, have students work in pairs to answer the *Try It!* questions. Also, ask pairs to answer these questions:

- What are the strongest elements of this essay? Give two examples.

- What have you learned from reading this essay that you can use in your own writing?

Invite pairs to share their responses with the class.

Editing   45

partners, using the same self-corrective technique.

Advanced Have partners write short paragraphs about a series of events. Partners should use the self-corrective technique of circling all verbs and identifying the tense of each, editing for consistent tense as necessary.

Advanced High Have students complete the Advanced activity. Challenge them to explain when a shift in tense might be appropriate and when it is not.

Prewriting

Drafting

Revising

Editing

Publishing

Publishing

When you publish, you produce a final copy of your work and present it to an audience. When publishing you'll need to decide which form will best reach your audience, exhibit your ideas, show your creativity, and accomplish your main purpose.

To start assessing the optimal way to publish your work, you might ask yourself these questions:

- What do I hope to accomplish by sharing my work with others?
- Should I publish in print form? Give an oral presentation? Publish in print form and give an oral presentation?
- Should I publish online, in traditional print, or both?
- What specific forms are available to choose from?

The answers to most of these questions will most likely link to your purpose for writing and your audience. Some choices seem obvious. For example, if you've written a piece to contribute to a blog, you'll definitely want to send it electronically.

Each publishing form will present different challenges and opportunities and each will demand different forms of preparation. For example, you may need to prepare presentation slides for a speech, or you may want to select music and images if you will be posting a video podcast online.

Ways to Publish

There are many ways to publish your writing. This chart shows some of several opportunities you can pursue to publish your work.

Genre	Publishing Opportunities	
Narration: Nonfiction	• Blogs • Book manuscript • Audio recording	• Private diary or journal entries • Electronic slide show
Narration: Fiction	• Book manuscript • Film	• Audio recording • Oral reading to a group
Poetry and Description	• Bound collection • Visual display	• Audio recording • Oral reading to a group
Exposition and Persuasion	• Print or online article • Web site • Slide show • Visual display	• Film • Audio recording • Oral reading or speech
Response to Literature	• Print or online letters • Visual displays	• Blogs • Slide show
Research Writing	• Traditional paper • Print and online experiment journals	• Multimedia presentation

Reflect on Your Writing

Think about what you learned in Chapter 3 as you answer these questions:

- What did you learn about the writing process?
- What steps in the writing process do you already use in your writing?
- Which stage do you think is the most fun? Which one may be most challenging for you? Explain.

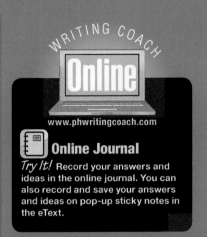

WRITING COACH

Online

www.phwritingcoach.com

Online Journal

Try It! Record your answers and ideas in the online journal. You can also record and save your answers and ideas on pop-up sticky notes in the eText.

> **Partner Talk**
>
> Discuss the chart on this page with a partner. If there are ways to publish that neither of you has ever tried, talk about how you might go about experimenting with those forms.

COLLABORATE AND DISCUSS

Have students work in small groups to share their responses to the Reflect on Your Writing questions. Extend the discussion by having group members help each other think of strategies for the stage of the writing process they find most challenging. See last question.) Invite groups to share their strategies with the class. You may wish to offer your own strategies as well.

Differentiated Instruction

RTI **Strategy for Special Needs Students**

Students may need reinforcement about the different ways to publish their work. Place the class in small groups and have each group choose a genre and one of the publishing opportunities listed next to it in the chart. Have groups create, act out, or find an example of the chosen publishing opportunity for the class. For example, for poetry, a group could find or create a short poem and read it to the class as an "Oral reading to a group."

PRE-AP **Enrichment for Above-Level Students**

Have students write a brief report or give an oral presentation on one of the media listed in the chart and why it provides publishing options for the type of writing in the genre column. Tell students to discuss how that particular form of media addresses the purpose and needs of a specific audience. Invite students to present their work to the class.

CHAPTER 4:

SENTENCES, PARAGRAPHS, and COMPOSITIONS

Good writers know that strong sentences and paragraphs help to construct effective compositions. Chapter 4 will help you use these building blocks to structure and style excellent writing. It will also present ways to use rhetorical and literary devices and online tools to strengthen your writing.

The Building Blocks: Sentences and Paragraphs

A **sentence** is a group of words with two main parts: a subject and a predicate. Together, these parts express a complete thought.

A **paragraph** is built from a group of sentences that share a common idea and work together to express that idea clearly. The start of a new paragraph has visual clues—either an indent of several spaces in the first line or an extra line of space above it.

In a good piece of writing, each paragraph supports, develops, or explains the main idea of the whole work. Of course, the traits of effective writing—ideas, organization, voice, word choice, sentence fluency, and conventions—appear in each paragraph as well.

48

Writing Strong Sentences

To write strong paragraphs, you need strong sentences. While it may be your habit to write using a single style of sentences, adding variety will help make your writing more interesting. Combining sentences, using compound elements, forming compound sentences, and using subordination all may help you make your sentences stronger, clearer, or more varied.

Combine Sentences

Putting information from one sentence into another can make a more powerful sentence.

BEFORE	Basketball is a fun game. It takes a lot of skill and practice.
AFTER	Basketball, which takes a lot of skill and practice, is a fun game.

Use Compound Elements

You can form compound subjects, verbs, or objects to help the flow.

BEFORE	Students enjoy many different hobbies. Some play sports. Some write poetry. Some paint.
AFTER	Students enjoy many different hobbies, such as playing sports, writing poetry, and painting.

Form Compound Sentences

You can combine two sentences into a compound sentence.

BEFORE	Some people enjoy skateboarding. It can be a dangerous hobby.
AFTER	Some people enjoy skateboarding, but it can be a dangerous hobby.

Use Subordination

Combine two related sentences by rewriting the less important one as a subordinate clause.

BEFORE	Horseback riding allows you to be outside in the fresh air. That is good for you.
AFTER	Horseback riding allows you be outside in the fresh air, which is good for you.

WRITING COACH

Online

www.phwritingcoach.com

Online Journal

Try It! Record your answers and ideas in the online journal. You can also record and save your answers on pop-up sticky notes in the eText.

LEARN MORE

For more on sentence combining see Chapter 20.

COLLABORATE AND DISCUSS

After students read page 49, ask:

- What are the different types of sentences?

Write all student responses on the board.

Then, have volunteers read aloud each Before and After sentence. Ask volunteers to explain how the sentences differ and why the revision is an improvement.

Intermediate Repeat portions of the instruction using accessible language. Give small groups sentence starters, such as *Strong writing makes reading...* to help them summarize and restate the general meaning, main points, and important details of your presentation.

Advanced Have partners create an outline summarizing the general meaning,

main points, and important details of your presentation.

Advanced High Have partners complete the Advanced activity, and then write a brief paragraph explaining how one of the techniques discussed makes writing stronger.

Writing Strong Paragraphs

If all the sentences in a paragraph reflect the main idea and work together to express that idea clearly, the result will be a strong paragraph.

Express Your Main Idea With a Clear Topic Sentence

A **topic sentence** summarizes the main idea of a paragraph. It may appear at the beginning, middle, or end of a paragraph. It may even be unstated. When the topic sentence comes at the beginning of a paragraph, it introduces the main idea and leads the reader naturally to the sentences that follow it. When it appears at the end of a paragraph, it can draw a conclusion or summarize what came before it. If the topic sentence is unstated, the rest of the paragraph must be very clearly developed, so the reader can understand the main idea from the other sentences.

Think about the topic sentence as you read this paragraph.

> There is no question that computer skills are necessary to have today. Without these skills, it will be difficult to get a college degree and find a good job. Most assignments in college must be done on a computer. Much research in college is done on the Internet, and many libraries have switched from a paper card catalog to a digital catalog. In addition, many companies won't hire someone who has no computer skills. After all, if you can't send e-mails and create important documents in word processing programs, how will you be able to properly do many jobs?

 Try It! Look back at the sample paragraph to answer these questions.

1. What is the topic sentence?
2. Does the topic sentence introduce the main idea or draw a final conclusion? Explain.
3. What makes this topic sentence strong?

Write Effective Supporting Sentences

A clear topic sentence is a good start, but it needs to be accompanied by good details that support the paragraph's main idea. Your supporting sentences might tell interesting facts, describe events, or give examples. In addition, the supporting sentences should also provide a smooth transition, so that the paragraph reads clearly and logically.

Think about the topic sentences and supporting details as you read this paragraph.

> Owning a dog can be hard work, but it is well worth it! A dog owner must be very responsible and take good care of her pet. She has to feed and walk the dog every day and bathe it regularly. Every dog also needs a lot of play time with its owner! All of this takes a great deal of time and energy. However, a dog can be your best friend. It will love you and protect you, and sometimes make you laugh! Plus, what could be better than snuggling up with a sweet, loving dog?

 Try It! Look at the paragraph and answer these questions.

1. What is the topic sentence of the paragraph?
2. Do you think it's an effective topic sentence? Why or why not?
3. What supporting details does the writer provide?
4. If you were the writer, what other supporting details might you add to strengthen the paragraph?

www.phwritingcoach.com

Online Journal

Try It! Record your answers and ideas in the online journal. You can also record and save your answers on pop-up sticky notes in the eText.

READ AND APPLY

Have students read pages 50 and 51. Then, ask:

- The example on page 50 is about computer skills, but what is the topic sentence?
- What are some details the writer includes in the supporting sentences?
- The topic of the second example is pet ownership, but what is the topic sentence?
- What are some details the writer includes in the supporting sentences?

Writing Strong Paragraphs   51

Intermediate Provide students with prompts using the words, such as *What do you feed dogs? How do you feed dogs?* Have partners take turns responding to the prompts, using and reusing the vocabulary words.

Advanced Have partners complete the *Try It!* activity, using and reusing the vocabulary. As one partner answers the

questions orally, the other should monitor his or her use of the words.

Advanced High After partners complete the Advanced activity, have students ask Intermediate partners simple interview-style questions reusing the words.

Include a Variety of Sentence Lengths, Structures, and Beginnings

To be interesting, a paragraph should include sentences of different lengths, types, and beginnings. Similarly, if every sentence has the same structure—for example, article, adjective, noun, verb—the paragraph may sound boring or dry.

21st Century Learning

Collaborate and Discuss

With a group, study this writing sample.

> On the night of the school concert, I didn't think I'd survive my stage fright. My hands felt cold and clammy, and a lump was stuck in my throat. A trickle of sweat slipped between my shoulder blades and down my back. I was so nervous! As the band began playing the opening notes of the first song and I stepped up to the microphone, the glare of the bright lights blinded me. I closed my eyes, took a deep breath, and belted out the song without even thinking. When the song was over, the audience responded with deafening applause. I had done it!

Discuss these questions about the paragraph.

1. What is the topic sentence? How does it draw in the reader?
2. What details support the topic sentence in each paragraph?
3. Point out some examples of varying sentence lengths and beginnings.
4. What examples can you find of sentences with a variety of sentence structures?

Composing Your Piece

You've learned that the building blocks of writing are strong sentences and paragraphs. Now it's time to use those building blocks to construct a composition. While the types of writing vary, most types have a definite structure with clearly defined parts.

The Parts of a Composition

Writers put together and arrange sentences and paragraphs to develop ideas in the clearest way possible in a composition. Some types of writing, such as poetry and advertisements, follow unique rules and may not have sentences and paragraphs that follow a standard structure. However, as you learned in Chapter 3, most compositions have three main sections: an introduction, a body, and a conclusion.

I. Introduction

The introduction of a composition introduces the focus of the composition, usually in a thesis statement. The introduction should engage the reader's interest, with such elements as a question, an unusual fact, or a surprising scene.

II. Body

Just as supporting statements develop the ideas of a topic sentence, the body of a composition develops the thesis statement and main idea. It provides details that help expand on the thesis statement. The paragraphs in the body are arranged in a logical order.

III. Conclusion

As the word implies, the conclusion of a composition concludes or ends a piece of writing. A good way to ensure the reader will remember your thesis statement is to restate it or summarize it in the conclusion. When restating the thesis, it's usually most effective to recast it in other words. Quotations and recommendations are other ways to conclude a composition with memorable impact. The conclusion should provide a parting insight or reinforce the importance of the main idea.

" Writer to Writer "

Strong, varied sentences and unified paragraphs are the building blocks of effective writing.

—Kelly Gallagher

MOTIVATE AND ENGAGE

Before students read the text on page 53, have them quickwrite about compositions or essays. Ask students to think about these questions as they write.

- **What kinds of compositions have I written?**
- **What were the easiest and most difficult parts of writing a particular composition?**

When students are finished, invite volunteers to share their responses. Review the parts of compositions: introduction, body, and conclusion.

Intermediate Provide small groups with a main idea web. Instruct them to record your general meaning in the center circle and add main points and important details in the outer circles. Invite groups to discuss their webs, linking familiar to unfamiliar language.

Advanced Provide pairs with a cluster diagram in which to record the general meaning, main points, and important details

of your description. Encourage students to use the familiar and unfamiliar language in their diagrams.

Advanced High Have students complete the Advanced activity. Then, have them use language from your presentation in oral context sentences with less-fluent partners.

Rhetorical and Literary Devices

Like any builders, good writers have a set of tools, or devices, at their fingertips to make their writing interesting, engaging, and effective. Writers can use the rhetorical devices of language and their effects to strengthen the power of their style. This section presents some tools you can store in your own writing toolbox to develop effective compositions.

Sound Devices

Sound devices, which create a musical or emotional effect, are most often used in poetry. The most common sound devices include these:

- **Alliteration** is the repetition of consonant sounds at the beginning of words that are close to one another.

  Example: The sweet sound of singing swam in the breeze.

- **Assonance** is the repetition of vowel sounds in words that are close to one another.

  Example: We see shells on the beach, by the sea.

- **Consonance** is the repetition of consonants within or at the end of words.

  Example: The doctor checked the sick patient at three o'clock.

Structural Devices

Structural devices determine the way a piece of writing is organized. Rhyme and meter are most often used to structure poetry, as are stanzas and many other structural devices.

- **Rhyme** is the repetition of sounds at the ends of words. Certain poetry forms have specific rhyme schemes.
- **Meter** is the rhythmical pattern of a poem, determined by the stressed syllables in a line.
- **Visual elements,** such as stanzas, line breaks, line length, fonts, readability, and white space, help determine how a piece of writing is read and interpreted. These elements can also affect the emotional response to a piece.

54   **Sentences, Paragraphs, and Compositions**

Other Major Devices

You can use these devices in many forms of writing. They help writers express ideas clearly and engage their readers.

Device	Example
Figurative language is writing that means something beyond what the words actually say. Common forms of figurative language include these: • A **simile** compares two things using the words *like* or *as*. • A **metaphor** compares two things by mentioning one thing as if it is something else. It does not use *like* or *as*. • **Personification** gives human characteristics to a non-human object.	*His voice sounded like nails on a chalkboard.* *The trapeze artist was a bird in flight.* *The sun smiled down on us.*
Hyperbole is exaggeration used for effect.	*I felt stronger than a superhero!*
Irony is a contradiction between what happens and what is expected.	In a famous story, a wife cuts her hair to buy her husband a watch fob, and he sells his watch to buy her a brush.
Paradox is a statement that contains elements that seem contradictory, but could be true.	Mother Teresa said, "…if you love until it hurts, there can be no more hurt, only more love."
An **oxymoron** is word or phrase that seems to contradict itself.	The movie was seriously funny!
Symbolism is an object that stands for something else.	The American flag is often considered a symbol of freedom.
An **allegory** is a narrative that has a meaning other than what literally appears.	Some say the story of the sinking ship is an allegory for the effects of pride.
Repetition (or tautology) occurs when content is repeated, sometimes needlessly—for effect.	The band's song was loud, loud and far too long.

WRITING COACH

Online

www.phwritingcoach.com

Online Journal

Try It! Record your answers and ideas in the online journal. You can also record and save your answers on pop-up sticky notes in the eText.

USING TECHNOLOGY

Most word processing programs have a built-in thesaurus tool. You can use the thesaurus to find descriptive words that can often substitute for weaker, overused words.

Partner Talk

There are many online tools that can help you strengthen your writing. For example, you can search for examples of figurative language and sound devices. Then you can model your own writing after the samples. Just be sure that you don't plagiarize or copy the written work of others.

READ AND APPLY

Have students read the text on page 54 and review the chart on page 55. Ask:

- What word that begins with *s* could replace *breeze* in the first example on page 54?

- What is one way we personify the moon?

Then, pair students to create examples for as many structural devices as they can. Ask volunteers to share their examples with the class.

Intermediate Echo read the figurative language entry, and provide pictures in support, as in the Beginning activity. Then, have students work in groups to retell the definitions and examples of figurative language, using and reusing the words.

Advanced Have partners read the figurative language entry, and provide pictures in support, as in the Beginning activity. Then,

have partners retell the definitions and examples of figurative language, using and reusing the words.

Advanced High After students complete the Advanced activity, have them read and retell the definitions and examples of irony.

Using Writing Traits to Develop an Effective Composition

You read about rubrics and traits in Chapter 3. Now it's time to look at how they function in good writing.

Ideas

A good writer clearly presents and develops important information, a strong message, and original ideas.

As you read the sample, think about the ideas it presents.

Achoo!

Achoo! The common cold can be a major downer. Who wants to be home with a runny nose and sore throat? It happens more often than you might think, though. According to the Mayo Clinic, students can get as many as six to ten colds a year! If you understand the causes of the common cold and take precautions, you can successfully avoid catching a cold.

A common cold is caused by a virus. Many different viruses could be responsible for your runny nose, but all of them have one thing in common: they're very contagious. A common-cold virus can spread in the air when a sick person coughs, sneezes, or even talks.

Once you know how colds spread, you can see that avoiding a cold is fairly easy, if you follow some simple rules. Wash your hands often. Keep doorknobs and countertops clean. Don't share drinking glasses or silverware. Most importantly, avoid being around sick people. If you do happen to catch a cold, sneeze or cough into your elbow to help keep your cold from spreading to others. No one likes to be sick!

Try It! Think about ideas in the writing sample as you answer this question.

What is the writer's message? List three details that clearly convey or give support for this message.

MOTIVATE AND ENGAGE

Remind students of the writing traits introduced in Chapter 3. Ask: What is each trait? How does each trait contribute to an effective composition? Then, have them quickwrite responses to your questions.

When students have finished, invite volunteers to share their responses. Write them on the board, and refer back to them as the class covers pages 56–59. Finally, remind students to look back at the Overview of Writing Traits on page 27.

Organization

A well-organized composition flows easily from sentence to sentence and paragraph to paragraph. It clearly shows relationships between ideas. The paper also avoids needless repetition.

Think about organization as you reread "Achoo!" on page 56.

 Try It! Answer the questions about the writing sample on page 56.

1. Which sentence introduces the topic of the piece?
2. Why must the second paragraph appear before the third?
3. List three details in the third paragraph. Explain how each supports the first sentence in the paragraph.

Voice

Voice is the individual "sound" of a writer's writing, reflecting the writer's personality or perspective. A successful paper has a definite voice expressing the writer's individuality.

Read the writing sample. Think about voice as you read.

> I'll never forget the day my parents got home with 4-month-old Liang. I was sitting on the couch, waiting for them. My stomach was doing flip-flops. Then Mom and Dad walked through the door, carrying this little bundle wrapped in a blanket. Mom sat on the couch with me and introduced me to my new brother. I expected him to totally freak out—to scream and cry. Instead, he just looked up at me with his big, brown eyes and smiled. His tiny hand reached out and grabbed my finger. He had a pretty strong grip!
>
> I found out that while babies are sometimes loud, smelly, and drooly, all of that stuff didn't matter. I loved my little brother, and I couldn't wait till he grew up, so I could teach him how to use that strong grip to hold a football!

 Try It! Consider the writer's voice as you answer this question.

Which words and phrases give you a clear sense of the writer's personality and perspective? Explain.

WRITING COACH

Online

www.phwritingcoach.com

Online Journal

Try It! Record your answers and ideas in the online journal. You can also record and save your answers on pop-up sticky notes in the eText.

Partner Talk

Analyze the composition about colds on page 56 with a partner. Discuss how well it might score on the traits of ideas and organization—from ineffective (1), to somewhat effective (2), to fairly effective (3), to effective (4), to highly effective in parts (5), to highly effective throughout (6).

COLLABORATE AND DISCUSS

Have students work in small groups to complete the *Try It!* activities on pages 56 and 57.

Next, have groups use the rubric on page 28 to score "Achoo!" on page 56 for ideas, organization, and voice. As a class, discuss each group's assessment. For each trait, discuss whether improvements could be made to raise the score. If so, what are they? If not, why not?

Using Writing Traits 57

Differentiated Instruction

RTI Strategy for Below-Level Students

Students may benefit from a review of the Writing Traits (page 27) and scoring rubric (page 28) in Chapter 3. Go over the first three categories in both charts with students before having them complete the Collaborate and Discuss activity on this page. Encourage students to keep copies of each chart in their writing journal or folder for easy reference.

Strategy for Spanish Speakers

Students whose home language is Spanish may have a more limited range of words and phrases for connecting ideas. Help students identify the connections in the sample text and elicit the Spanish equivalent. Encourage students to keep a list of connecting words and phrases in English and Spanish. Remind students to use the list to incorporate the words and phrases in their own writing.

Word Choice

By choosing words with precision, good writers give their writing energy and help readers picture exactly what they are talking about. Think about word choice as you read these two drafts:

> Bob got into Ted's car. As he sat down, he realized he was hearing something familiar. "That's right," Ted said. "I finally put our stuff on CD. It sounds so nice on this system!"

> Bob climbed over chrome fittings into Ted's customized SUV. As Bob eased into the leather-upholstered seat, he recognized the crunching guitar chords that came crashing through the car stereo's speakers. "That's right," Ted said. "I finally mixed our band's songs down to a CD. They sound so crisp on this system!"

 Try It! Answer these questions about the two drafts.

1. List two vague or imprecise words in the first draft.
2. What do the precise words in the second draft help you understand?

Sentence Fluency

In the best writing, sentences have rhythm. They flow smoothly when read aloud, rather than sounding awkward. To control rhythm, good writers use a variety of sentence structures. Think about the rhythm of the writer's sentences as you read this draft:

> After six years of weekly lessons, I can say I have done my best to master the cello. I may not have been good enough for the All-County Orchestra last year, but this year will be different. This year, my dedication will pay off!

 Try It! Respond to this prompt about the draft.

Describe the rhythm of the sentences in the passage.

COLLABORATE AND DISCUSS

Continue the Collaborate and Discuss activity from page 57. Have groups use the rubric on page 28 to score each sample on page 58 for voice, word choice, and sentence fluency. As a class, discuss the groups' scores and whether improvements could have been made.

Then, have students read the second sample on page 59. Discuss the difference in word choice between the second draft of the story about Bob and Ted and the description of the action movie.

Working with ELLs   **ELL** Sheltered Instruction: Cognitive

Help students comprehend language structures used routinely in written classroom materials. Compare correctly capitalized geographical names with lowercase common nouns, explaining that common nouns may also be capitalized when used as titles or labels. Provide students with copies of a simple geographical map. Then:

Beginning Review entries on the map. Guide students in identifying nouns spelled with capital letters and nouns not spelled with capital letters. Clarify the meaning of each, identifying the language structure it represents (place name, common noun).

Intermediate Have students work in groups to list nouns on the map that are capitalized and nouns that are not and to identify the

Conventions

If a piece of writing reflects a good command of spelling, capitalization, punctuation, grammar, usage, and sentence structure, it is much more likely to communicate clearly to readers.

Pay attention to spelling, capitalization, punctuation, grammar, usage, and sentence structure as you read this first draft.

WRITING COACH
Online
www.phwritingcoach.com

Online Journal

Try It! Record your answers and ideas in the online journal. You can also record and save your answers on pop-up sticky notes in the eText.

1ST DRAFT

If your an action-movie fan, you have to run—not walk—to see *Welcome to Mars!* This movie is non-stop action, from start to finish. Me and my friend were blown away by the battle scenes, special effects, and suspense.

The movie has a great message, too: Understanding can lead to peace. In one very tense moment, the lead scientist on Mars is captured by aliens. I was so sure they would kill her! Instead, she stayed with them learning their language and to learn, their ways of life. This led to peace between the humans and the aliens.

Now, read this section of the reviewer's second draft.

2ND DRAFT

If you're an action-movie fan, you have to run—not walk—to see *Welcome to Mars!* This movie is non-stop action, from start to finish. My friend and I were blown away by the battle scenes, special effects, and suspense.

The movie has a great message, too: Understanding can lead to peace. In one very tense moment, the lead scientist on Mars is captured by aliens. I was so sure they would kill her! Instead, she stayed with them, learning their language and their ways of life. This led to peace between the humans and the aliens.

Try It! Answer these questions about both drafts.

1. What errors in convention did the writer correct in the second draft?
2. Why is the next-to-last sentence easier to read in the second draft?

READ AND APPLY

Discuss the importance of using conventions correctly in writing. Ask: What might happen if your writing has errors in grammar, spelling, punctuation, or capitalization? Students may say that readers will become distracted or have difficulty understanding the meaning.

Next, have students rewrite three sentences from the sample first draft. Then, have them exchange papers with a partner and check each other's work for errors in conventions.

---

language structure that each represents (place name, common noun). Then, guide them to write two facts derived from the map, using correct capitalization.

Advanced Have partners list nouns on the map and identify the language structure (place name, common noun) that each represents. Have them write directions from one place on the map to another, using correct capitalization.

Advanced High Have partners complete the Advanced activity. Then, have them use the examples to write rules for capitalizing place names and post their rules in the classroom.

Using Interactive Writing Coach

As you learned in Chapter 3, you can use rubrics and your Revision RADaR to check how well your paragraphs and essays read. With Writing Coach, you also have another tool available to evaluate your work: the Interactive Writing Coach.

The Interactive Writing Coach is a program that you can use anywhere that you have Internet access. Interactive Writing Coach functions like your own personal writing tutor. It gives you personalized feedback on your work.

The Interactive Writing Coach has two parts: **Paragraph Feedback** and **Essay Scorer**.

- Paragraph Feedback gives you feedback on individual paragraphs as you write. It looks at the structure of sentences and paragraphs and gives you information about specific details, such as sentence variety and length.

- Essay Scorer looks at your whole essay and gives you a score and feedback on your entire piece of writing. It will tell you how well your essay reflects the traits of good writing.

This chart shows just a few questions that Paragraph Feedback and Essay Scorer will answer about your writing. The following pages explain Paragraph Feedback and Essay Scorer in more detail.

Sentences	• Are sentences varied in length? • Do sentences have varied beginnings? • Which sentences have too many ideas? • Are adjectives clear and precise? • Is the sentence grammatically correct? • Is all spelling correct in the sentence?
Paragraphs	• Does the paragraph support its topic? • Does the paragraph use transitions? • Does the paragraph contain the right amount of ideas and information?
Compositions	• Does the essay reflect characteristics of the genre? • Does it demonstrate the traits of good writing? • Is the main idea clear? • Is the main idea well supported? • Is the essay cohesive—does it hold together?

Interactive Writing Coach and the Writing Process

You can begin to use Essay Scorer during the drafting section of the writing process. It is best to complete a full draft of your essay before submitting to Essay Scorer. (While you are drafting individual paragraphs, you may want to use Paragraph Feedback.) Keep in mind, however, that your draft does not need to be perfect or polished before you submit to Essay Scorer. You will be able to use feedback from Essay Scorer to revise your draft many times. This chart shows how you might use the Interactive Writing Coach and incorporate Essay Scorer into your writing process.

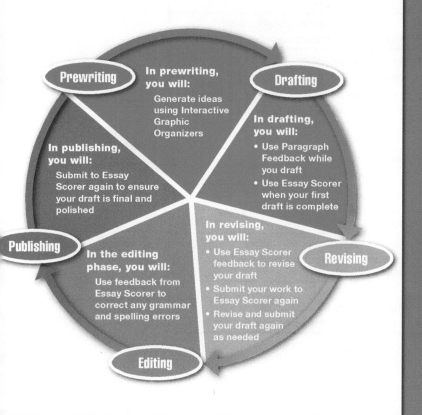

Prewriting

In prewriting, you will:
Generate ideas using Interactive Graphic Organizers

Drafting

In drafting, you will:
• Use Paragraph Feedback while you draft
• Use Essay Scorer when your first draft is complete

In publishing, you will:
Submit to Essay Scorer again to ensure your draft is final and polished

Publishing

In the editing phase, you will:
Use feedback from Essay Scorer to correct any grammar and spelling errors

In revising, you will:
• Use Essay Scorer feedback to revise your draft
• Submit your work to Essay Scorer again
• Revise and submit your draft again as needed

Revising

Editing

MOTIVATE AND ENGAGE

Ask:

▪ **What types of errors do you struggle with as a writer?**

▪ **What part of writing do you find the most difficult?**

▪ **In what ways might the Interactive Writing Coach help you to fix your errors or make writing easier?**

Invite volunteers to share their responses. Answer questions from students about the types of errors the Interactive Writing Coach addresses and problems the program might not address.

Differentiated Instruction

RTI Strategy for Below-Level Students
Students may benefit from working with you to review the information about the Interactive Writing Coach. Go through each item in the chart on page 60. Ask if students have questions about the types of errors the program will address. If possible, have students use Paragraph Feedback to see how it works on their writing. Review the feedback with students and suggest a plan for revision.

RTI Strategy for Special Needs Students
Students may benefit from watching you model how to use Paragraph Feedback on a piece of writing. Sit with students to show them how the tool works on a paragraph you have either written yourself or one that they have chosen from their writing portfolio. Review the feedback with students and suggest a plan for revision.

Paragraph Feedback With Interactive Writing Coach

Paragraph Feedback assesses the ideas and topic support for each paragraph you write. You can enter your work into Paragraph Feedback one paragraph at a time. This makes it easy to work on individual paragraphs and get new feedback as you revise each one. Here are some things that Paragraph Feedback will be able to tell you.

Overall Paragraph Support	• Does the paragraph support the main idea? • Which sentences do not support the main idea?
Transitions	• Which sentences contain transition words? • Which words are transition words?
Ideas	• How well are ideas presented? • Which sentences have too many ideas?
Sentence Length and Variety	• Which sentences are short, medium, and long? • Which sentences could be longer or shorter for better sense or variety? • Are sentences varied?
Sentence Beginnings	• How do sentences begin? • Are sentence beginnings varied?
Sentence Structure	• Are sentence structures varied? • Are there too many sentences with similar structures?
Vague Adjectives	• Are any adjectives vague or unclear? • Where are adjectives in sentences and paragraphs?
Language Variety	• Are words repeated? • Where are repeated words located? • How can word choice be improved?

Before students read page 62, have them quickwrite about their favorite writers and what good writing means to them. Ask: How does reading examples of good writing help you to improve your writing?

Have students tell you the components necessary to a good paragraph. Write students' responses on the board. Then, compare these responses with the chart on page 62. Discuss what was missing from the board and why it is important.

Essay Scoring With Interactive Writing Coach

Essay Scorer assesses your essay. It looks at the essay as a whole, and it also evaluates individual paragraphs, sentences, and words. Essay Scorer will help you evaluate the following traits.

Ideas	• Are the ideas significant or original? Is a clear message or unique perspective presented? • Is the main idea clearly stated? • Is the main idea supported by informative details?
Organization	• Is the organization logical? • Is the introduction clear? Is the conclusion clear? • What transitions are used, and are they effective?
Voice	• Does the writing have a unique, individual "sound" showing the personality or perspective of the writer? • Does the tone match the audience and purpose?
Word Choice	• Are precise words used? • Are vivid words used? • Do the word choices suit the purpose and audience?
Sentence Fluency	• Are sentence beginnings, lengths, and structures varied? • Do the sentences flow smoothly?
Conventions	• Is spelling correct? • Is capitalization used properly? • Is all punctuation (ending, internal, apostrophes) accurate? • Do subjects and verbs agree? • Are pronouns used correctly? • Are adjectives and adverbs used correctly? • Are plurals formed correctly? • Are commonly confused words used correctly?

Whenever you see the Interactive Writing Coach icon, you can go to Writing Coach Online and submit your writing, either paragraph by paragraph or as a complete draft, for personalized feedback and scoring.

www.phwritingcoach.com

Interactive Writing Coach™

Interactive Writing Coach provides support and guidance to help you improve your writing skills.
• Select a topic to write about from the Topic Bank.
• Use the interactive graphic organizers to narrow your topic.
• Go to Writing Coach Online and submit your work, paragraph by paragraph or as a complete draft.
• Receive immediate, personalized feedback as you write, revise, and edit your work.

MOTIVATE AND ENGAGE

Have a class discussion about the differences between a single paragraph and a full essay. Ask:

- What must an essay convey that a paragraph might not?

- What different kinds of feedback would you need for an essay versus a single paragraph?

- Would you get the same result feeding an essay paragraph by paragraph into Paragraph Feedback as you would using the Essay Scorer? Why, or why not?

Differentiated Instruction

RTI Strategy for Below-Level Students
Students may benefit from seeing the Essay Scorer in action. Sit with students and show them how the Essay Scorer works. Use a draft of an essay in this chapter, such as the one on page 56, or one that the students have in their writing portfolio. Review the feedback and the score, and discuss a plan for revision.

PRE-AP Enrichment for Above-Level Students Have students use the Essay Scorer to evaluate a piece of writing they have completed. Ask students to critique the tool. Ask: What errors did it find? How did the feedback help you to improve your writing? Do you think the score was fair? Next, have students incorporate the feedback in a new draft and use the tool again. Ask: Did your score improve? Why or why not?

Interactive Writing Coach™ Interactive Graphic Organizers Interactive Models

Online Journal Resources Video

Use the Online Lesson Planner at www.phwritingcoach.com to customize your instructional plan for an integrated Language Arts curriculum.

DAY 1

CHAPTER OPENER/ GENRE INTRODUCTION

ONLINE

- What Do You Remember?
- What's Ahead
- Connect to the Big Questions
- **Feature Assignment: Narrative Nonfiction: Personal Narrative**
- Other Forms of Narrative Nonfiction
- Word Bank

DAY 2

MENTOR TEXT/ STUDENT MODEL

ONLINE

- **Mentor Text: Personal Narrative**
- Learn From Experience
- **Student Model: Personal Narrative**
- Reader's Eye and Writer's Eye

DAY 3

Prewriting

ONLINE

- Choose From the Topic Bank
- Choose Your Own Topic
- Narrow Your Topic
- Consider Your Audience and Purpose

DAY 6

Revising

ONLINE

- Keep Revision on Your RADaR
- Look at the Big Picture
- Focus on Craft
- Fine-Tune Your Draft

DAY 7

For additional grammar support, see Grammar Game Plan, Error 12, p. 284.

Editing

ONLINE

- What Do You Notice?/ Grammar Mini-Lesson
  Rubric for Nonfiction Narration: Biographical Narrative

Publishing

- Publish Your Piece
- Reflect on Your Writing

DAY 8

21st Century Learning

ONLINE

MAKE YOUR WRITING COUNT

- **Create a Storyboard for a Personal Narrative**
- Here's Your Action Plan
- Listening and Speaking

Alternate Pacing Suggestions

- **Block Scheduling** Each day on the Lesson Planner represents a 40–50 minute block. Teachers using block scheduling may combine days to revise pacing to meet their classroom needs.

- **Accelerated Lesson Planning** Combine instructional days by aiding students in choosing a topic and then focusing on two core stages of the writing process, outlining for success (Day 5) and RADaR revision (Day 6).

- **Integrated Language Arts Curriculum** For targeted instruction that covers the essential components of the lesson use either a 3- or a 5-day plan.

3 day plan

DAY 1: Introduction to the Genre, Mentor Text, Student Model
DAY 2: Prewriting/Drafting
DAY 3: Revising/Editing/ Publishing

5 day plan

Use 3-day plan, and add:

DAY 4: Make Your Writing Count
DAY 5: Writing for Assessment

Links to Prentice Hall *LITERATURE*

Featured Author: Jane Yolen

- What Are Fiction and Nonfiction?, p. 4
- "Greyling" (fiction), p. 9
- "My Heart Is in the Highlands" (speech), p. 17
- On Writing Narratives (Writing Workshop), p. 157
- *From the Author's Desk* Videos: Jane Yolen

Additional Mentor Text:

- "Water" (autobiography), Helen Keller, p. 398

Differentiated Instruction

Differentiated Instruction Boxes in this Teacher's Edition address these student populations:

- Below-Level Students
- Above-Level Students
- Gifted and Talented Students
- Special Needs Students
- English Language Learners
- Spanish Speaking Students

In addition, for further enrichment, see the **Extension** features.

LESSON OBJECTIVES

- To learn the forms and defining characteristics of nonfiction narration.
- To learn the elements of a successful personal narrative, the chapter Feature Assignment.
- To read a Mentor Text in the genre, analyzing its use of the elements of effective nonfiction narration.
- To read a Student Model of a personal narrative, analyzing it from the perspective of a reader and from the perspective of a writer.
- To apply prewriting strategies in developing a personal narrative, including strategies for choosing and narrowing a topic, planning writing, and gathering details, as well as tips for considering audience and purpose.
- To apply drafting strategies in developing a personal narrative.
- To apply RADaR revision strategies to a draft personal narrative.
- To learn about the Focus on Craft topic, sentence variety, and apply what is learned to a draft personal narrative.
- To edit the draft, zooming in on verb tenses and focusing on maintaining consistent tense.
- To complete the Make Your Writing Count assignment, developing and presenting a storyboard for a personal narrative.
- To complete the Writing for Media assignment, developing a biographical narrative.
- To practice writing for assessment.

DAY 4

Prewriting

- Plan Your Piece
- Gather Details

ONLINE

DAY 5

Drafting

- Outline for Success
- Start Your Draft

ONLINE

DAY 9

WRITING FOR MEDIA

- **Biographical Narrative**
- Create a Biographical Narrative

ONLINE

DAY 10

WRITING FOR ASSESSMENT

- Narrative Nonfiction Prompt
- The ABCDs of On-Demand Writing
- More Prompts for Practice
- More Strategies for Writing Assessment

ONLINE

Personalized Assessment

	Ongoing Assessment	Formal Assessment of Feature Assignment	Progress Monitoring at End-of-Chapter
Interactive Writing Coach™	Use Paragraph Feedback and Essay Scorer as a revision tool.	Use Essay Scorer to score students' Feature Assignment papers.	Use Essay Scorer to score students' papers. Students' learner profiles can be adjusted based on their scores.
FEEDBACK **Teacher Conferencing**	Use rubrics in the Student Edition as a revision tool. Conference with students to review their work and provide personalized support.	Use rubrics in the Student Edition to score students' Feature Assignment papers.	Review each student's work to plan targeted resources for the next writing assignment.

The Digital • Print Path ▶

1  ▶ Using **Writing Coach Online™** or the student book, students discuss the photograph in the chapter opener as it relates to the writing genre.

2 📔 ▶ Students record their ideas and responses in their online journals or notebooks. They may also record and save their responses on pop-up sticky notes in **Writing Coach Online™**.

Chapter Objectives

1. Write a personal narrative by planning, drafting, revising, editing, and publishing individual work.

2. Produce a storyboard.

3. Use the five-step writing process to write a biographical narrative.

4. Write a personal narrative in response to a prompt.

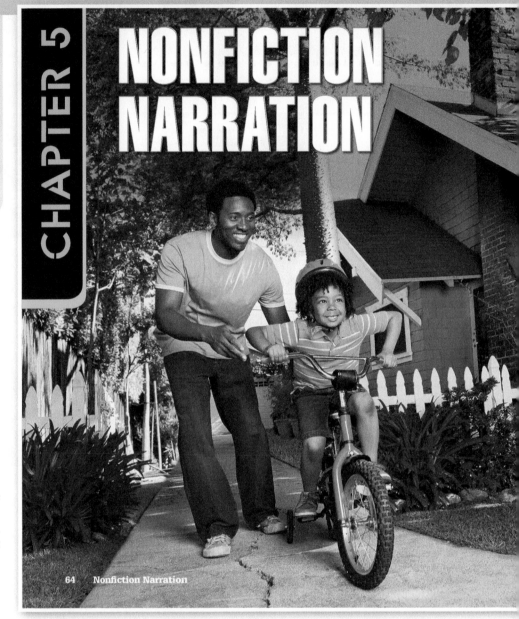

CHAPTER 5
NONFICTION NARRATION

64   Nonfiction Narration

NONFICTION NARRATION

What Do You Remember?

Activate Prior Knowledge Tell students that the purpose of narrative nonfiction is to tell a true story about real people. Explain to students that they will use what they know about important experiences and memories to analyze the photo on page 64. Then, guide students in analyzing the photo.

 Think Aloud When we analyze something, we look at it and think about what it means. For example, in the photo **I see** a father teaching his child how to ride a bicycle. They are smiling and enjoying themselves. I think they will both have a happy memory of this important childhood experience.

Work with students to share their memories about learning to ride a bicycle or some other significant accomplishment. Begin by sharing your own memory of an important event, including how you felt about the experience.

Try It! **Have students** work individually to develop responses to the questions. Check that students have generated sufficient details, including their feelings, about a favorite memory.

Possible responses: I saw the ocean for the first time. My family and I went to Florida and stayed at a motel on the beach. The sand was sugar white, and it squeaked when I walked on it. The water was many shades of blue and warm like bathwater. The roaring waves tried to knock me down. It was exciting, and I loved it.

Connect to the Big Questions

Have students use their experience to discuss the Big Questions. Explain that they will revisit **Why write?** at the end of this chapter. Tell students to consider these points during their discussion:

1. Our sense of self is based on the things that we consider most important about us, including our relationships, abilities, and character traits.

2. Daily life is full of details too small and insignificant to be remembered, yet they can make our lives—and our narratives—interesting.

What's Ahead

Have students preview the Mentor Text and Student Model on pages 68–71. Tell students that they will write their own personal narrative using the five-step writing process: prewriting, drafting, revising, editing, and publishing.

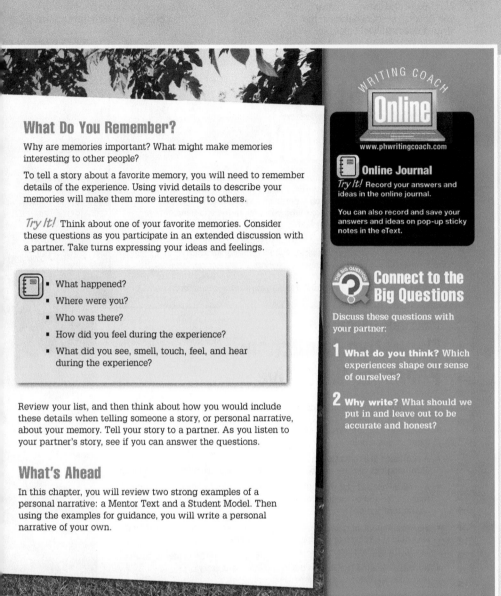

What Do You Remember?

Why are memories important? What might make memories interesting to other people?

To tell a story about a favorite memory, you will need to remember details of the experience. Using vivid details to describe your memories will make them more interesting to others.

Try It! Think about one of your favorite memories. Consider these questions as you participate in an extended discussion with a partner. Take turns expressing your ideas and feelings.

- What happened?
- Where were you?
- Who was there?
- How did you feel during the experience?
- What did you see, smell, touch, feel, and hear during the experience?

Review your list, and then think about how you would include these details when telling someone a story, or personal narrative, about your memory. Tell your story to a partner. As you listen to your partner's story, see if you can answer the questions.

What's Ahead

In this chapter, you will review two strong examples of a personal narrative: a Mentor Text and a Student Model. Then using the examples for guidance, you will write a personal narrative of your own.

WRITING COACH

Online

www.phwritingcoach.com

Online Journal

Try It! Record your answers and ideas in the online journal.

You can also record and save your answers and ideas on pop-up sticky notes in the eText.

Connect to the Big Questions

Discuss these questions with your partner:

1 What do you think? Which experiences shape our sense of ourselves?

2 Why write? What should we put in and leave out to be accurate and honest?

Personalized Support

FEEDBACK Teacher or Peer Feedback

To encourage students in their discussion of the photograph as it relates to the writing genre, ask the following questions:

- What is the first thing you think of when you look at this photo?
- How does it relate to your life?
- How does it relate to things you've learned in other subjects?
- What questions come to mind when you look at this photograph?
- How does your response to the photograph compare to those of your classmates?

Working with ELLs ELL Sheltered Instruction: Metacognitive

Have students demonstrate listening comprehension of increasingly complex spoken English by following the *Try It!* activity directions after you read them aloud.

Beginning Write the *Try It!* directions as statements in a sequence chart. Read them aloud, pointing to the steps in the chart. Ask yes/no questions to help students monitor comprehension, reminding them to seek clarification as needed. Guide them in following directions.

Intermediate Read aloud the *Try It!* directions. Have students listen and write the steps in sequence charts to monitor

understanding. Have them seek clarification as necessary. Guide them in following directions.

Advanced Read aloud the *Try It!* directions and have students take notes. Have them follow the directions to complete the activity, encouraging them to monitor comprehension and seek clarification as needed.

Advanced High Have partners take turns reading aloud the *Try It!* directions and taking notes. They should review notes to monitor comprehension. Have partners follow the directions to complete the activity, seeking clarification as needed.

1  STUDENT BOOK ▶

Students learn vocabulary from the Word Bank and listen to English and Spanish pronunciations in the *Writing Coach Online™* glossary.

2  Writing Journal ▶

Students record answers to questions about forms of writing in their online journals or notebooks.

NARRATIVE NONFICTION

To introduce this chapter's writing form, discuss the opening paragraphs with students. Make sure students understand that a personal narrative is a form of narrative nonfiction. Explain that good writers use a step-by step process to develop their work. Then, have students preview the rubric on page 83.

Narrative Nonfiction: Personal Narrative

Ask volunteers to read aloud the feature assignment characteristics. Tell students that they will identify these characteristics in a Mentor Text and a Student Model. Then, they will use the characteristics to guide the writing of their own personal narrative.

Other Forms of Narrative Nonfiction

Guide students to understand the main purpose, or reason for writing, for each form of narrative nonfiction.

Say: I notice that there are several forms of narrative nonfiction. If I note the main purpose, or reason, for writing each one, I can more easily remember them all. For example, the main purpose of a biographical narrative is to tell a story about someone else's life.

Ask: How are these forms of narrative nonfiction alike? (They all tell a true story.) How do they differ? (Each form has a different purpose.)

Have students brainstorm for appropriate topics for each form of narrative nonfiction.

Try It! Remind students that the audience is the people who will read their writing. The purpose is the author's reason for writing. Have students record their responses in their journal.

Possible responses: diary entry, because the topic is very personal; blog, because the topic is of current interest and it invites readers'

responses; biographical narrative, because the topic is about someone else's life story

Word Bank

To assist English Language Learners and struggling readers, echo read each word or have students log on to Writing Coach Online to listen to the pronunciations. Then, have partners take turns using each word in a sentence. Ask volunteers to share one of their sentences with the class.

NARRATIVE NONFICTION

In this chapter, you will explore a special type of narrative nonfiction: the personal narrative. In a personal narrative, you tell a story about YOU. By sharing a personal experience, you can let readers know something about who you are, and you can encourage them to look inside themselves, too.

You will develop the personal narrative by taking it through each of the steps of the writing process: prewriting, drafting, revising, editing, and publishing. You will also have an opportunity to use your personal narrative to create a biographical narrative. To preview the criteria for how your personal narrative will be evaluated, see the rubric on page 83.

FEATURE ASSIGNMENT
Narrative Nonfiction: Personal Narrative

An effective narrative nonfiction essay has these characteristics:

- An interesting story with a clear focus, or main point
- A sequence of events told in chronological, or time, order
- A well-developed plot that tells the reasons for and consequences of characters' actions
- Sensory details, or details that appeal to the senses of sight, sound, touch, smell, and taste
- Narrative devices to enhance the plot, such as dialogue and suspense

- Effective sentence structure and correct spelling, grammar, and usage

A personal narrative also includes:

- Specific details about your personal experiences
- Strong descriptions of characters, who are real people, including yourself
- A way for the reader to connect to your story

66   Narrative Nonfiction

Teacher Tip

To extend students' understanding, have pairs quiz each other orally about the different forms of narrative nonfiction. Have one partner read the description of the form and the other name the correct form. Then, have them switch roles.

Other Forms of Narrative Nonfiction

In addition to personal narratives, there are other forms of narrative nonfiction, including:

Biographical narratives are stories that share facts about someone else's life. These stories can include the writer's ideas and feelings about the subject of the narrative.

Blogs, or comments that writers share in online forums, may include autobiographical narratives (short or long), reflections, opinions, and other types of comments. Blogs often invite responses, and they usually are not considered a "permanent" form of writing.

Diary entries, which are highly personal, include experiences, thoughts, and feelings—but the audience is private, unless writers choose to share the entries.

Memoirs contain a writer's reflections on an important person or event from his or her own life. Book-length memoirs by famous people often are quite popular.

Narrative essays use one or more biographical or autobiographical narratives to illustrate or prove a point (the main idea).

Reflective essays present personal experiences (either events that happened to the writers themselves or that they learned about from others), but they focus more on sharing the observations and insights that writers had while thinking about those experiences. Reflective essays often appear as features in magazines and newspapers.

Try It! For each audience and purpose described, choose a form, such as a diary entry, blog, or biographical narrative, that is appropriate for conveying your intended meaning to the audience. Explain your choices.

- To express your feelings about a family situation
- To comment about your experiences volunteering at the local food bank and invite community members' responses
- To tell the story of the life of the person you most admire

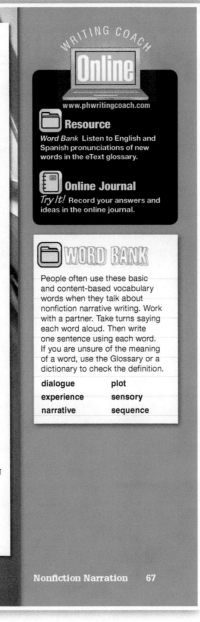

WRITING COACH

Online

www.phwritingcoach.com

Resource
Word Bank Listen to English and Spanish pronunciations of new words in the eText glossary.

Online Journal
Try It! Record your answers and ideas in the online journal.

WORD BANK

People often use these basic and content-based vocabulary words when they talk about nonfiction narrative writing. Work with a partner. Take turns saying each word aloud. Then write one sentence using each word. If you are unsure of the meaning of a word, use the Glossary or a dictionary to check the definition.

dialogue	plot
experience	sensory
narrative	sequence

Nonfiction Narration   67

Personalized Support

FEEDBACK
Teacher or Peer Feedback

To help students understand the characteristics of the writing form, ask or have student partners ask one another the following questions:

- What are the main characteristics of narrative nonfiction?
- What makes this form of writing different from other forms?
- Who are the likely readers or audience for this form of writing?
- What kind of organization could be used for this form of writing?
- What kind of voice would be most effective for this form of writing?

Working with ELLs   **ELL** Sheltered Instruction: Cognitive

Have students use accessible language and strategic learning techniques, such as comparing and contrasting meanings, to acquire new essential language, including basic and grade-level vocabulary. Pair the vocabulary in the Word Bank with accessible synonyms, such as *narrative/story,* and provide these pairs to students.

Beginning Help students compare and contrast the words in each pair to acquire new vocabulary, then speak each word in a context sentence.

Intermediate Have students write two sentences using accessible synonyms and exchange with a partner. Have them read the sentences aloud, replace the synonyms with the new vocabulary, and read again. Have partners answer questions, such as *When might you use the word [plot]?*

Advanced Have students complete the Intermediate activity. Have partners exchange sentences and compare and contrast the meaning of the words and their synonyms in context.

Advanced High Have students complete the Advanced activity. Have them write a paragraph using all six words from the Word Bank.

Using Writing Coach Online™ or the student book, students read and listen to an audio recording of the Mentor Text. As they complete their writing assignments they can refer back to the Mentor Text for support whenever they need it.

MENTOR TEXT

About the Selection The selection is a personal narrative. The author tells about the time his brother tried to sell him his own shirt. The author uses this experience to describe the kind of person his brother is.

Learn From Experience

After students have read the text, point out that the numbered notes refer to the characteristics of a personal narrative introduced on page 66.

Try It! Guide students to understand how the genre characteristics shape the text.

Say: The second *Try It!* question asks about the author's use of chronological order in relating the events in the narrative. The question is, "What does the author do first?" **I read** until I come to his first action: The author, Jon, digs through a pile of clothes looking for a shirt to wear. This is my answer.

Ask: The second part of the *Try It!* question asks, "What does his brother do next?" How can you answer this question? (I read on until I see what the author's brother, Jim, does: He takes out a clean shirt and offers it to Jon—for a price.)

Have students reply to the *Try It!* questions in their journals. If students have difficulty responding to a particular question, model a response, as with Question 2.

Check the accuracy and completeness of student responses.

1. The focus of the narrative is the occasion on which Jim tries to sell Jon's own shirt to Jon.

2. First, the author discovers he has no clean shirts. Then, his brother offers to sell the author a shirt.

3. Jim is persuasive, confident, smooth, and somewhat devious.

4. The dark blue shirt smells "like two-week-old socks." The description helps readers imagine just how awful the shirt smells and why the author can't wear it.

Personal Narrative **Mentor Text** Personal Narrative **Mentor**

MENTOR TEXT | Personal Narrative

Learn From Experience

 After reading the personal narrative on pages 68–69, read the numbered notes in the margins to learn about how the author presented his ideas.

Answer the *Try It!* questions online or in your notebook.

---

❶ Here, the general topic, Jim, is narrowed to a clearly defined **focus**. That focus is a specific situation involving Jim.

> *Try It!* What situation is the focus of the narrative? Describe it in your own words.

❷ The author uses **chronological order** to describe what he and his brother did. That means events are given in the order in which they actually happened.

> *Try It!* What does the author do first? What does his brother do next?

❸ The author uses **dialogue** to help tell his story and let you know what his brother was like.

> *Try It!* What does this dialogue tell you about Jim?

❹ The author uses vivid **sensory details** to help readers imagine how things looked and even **smelled.**

> *Try It!* What does the dark blue shirt smell like? How does this description help you imagine the scene?

68 Narrative Nonfiction

Roommates

by Jon Scieszka

❶ Jim was a pretty good roommate because he was neat and not too much of a pain in the neck like the little brothers. But man, could Jim talk.

5 I think Jim knew from the time he was four that he was going to be a lawyer. He was always trying to win an argument or make a case why you should agree with him. Jim would talk and talk and then talk some more.

His best pitch ever was the time he tried to sell me my own shirt.

10 ❷ I was looking for a clean shirt to wear. Most of my clothes were in a pile on the floor of my closet. I was digging through the pile, sniffing for one that was not too smelly.

Jim pulled a clean, folded, short-sleeved shirt out of his dresser drawer.

15 "I really should save this shirt, Jon. But because you need it, I'm going to give you a deal," said Jim.

I found a shirt with only a couple of grass stains on the elbows. "What's that?" I said.

❸ "This is an excellent shirt, a clean shirt, a lightweight
20 shirt, a short-sleeved shirt," said Jim. "But because you need it, I'm going to give it to you for a bargain price."

I held up a pretty good-looking dark blue shirt. ❹ It smelled like the two-week-old socks still hanging on it.

"Look at this shirt. It's a great shirt. Probably the best
25 shirt," said Jim. "And I'm going to let you have it, while I wear my same old shirt, for only fifty cents."

I looked at the shirt. It was a great shirt.

"It's perfectly clean," said Jim.

He was right. It was perfectly clean.
30 I checked my pockets.

"I've only got twenty-five cents," I said.

Jim put the shirt back in his drawer.

---

5. Responses should be supported by a reasonable explanation for the ending's effect on the reader.

Extension Lead a discussion in which students compare and contrast how their additional personal narrative examples use the genre characteristics. Use the *Try It!* questions as a guide.

Teacher Tip

Quick Write Have students write a short scene to add before the ending of the Mentor Text. Ask them to imagine that a parent interrupts the brothers' wrestling match. Remind students to use dialogue and sensory details in their scene and to make sure that it still leads into the surprise ending.

2 [Writing Journal icon]

Students record their answers to questions about the Mentor Text in their online journals or notebooks.

onal Narrative **Mentor Text** *Personal Narrative* **Mentor Text**

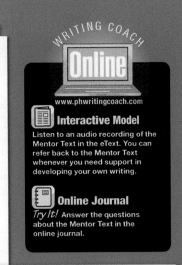

"I'm afraid I can't go any lower than forty cents. It's my only clean shirt. I'm going to need it soon. I was going to do you a favor, but I can see it's not going to work out."

35 I tried on a brown shirt. It smelled even worse than the green shirt.

"Maybe I can get twenty-five cents off Tom," I said. "Let me see the shirt."

40 Jim handed it over. I tried it on. It fit perfectly. It was so clean. It was so . . . familiar.

"Hey," I said. "This is my shirt."

"It was in my drawer," said Jim. "You owe me fifty cents."

45 "I do not."

"You do too."

"Do not."

"Take it off."

"Make me."

50 Our legal debate quickly turned into a wrestling match. Jim jumped on me. I got him in a choke hold. We rolled around on the bedroom floor.

❺ So I think it was really me who made Jim a better, stronger lawyer.

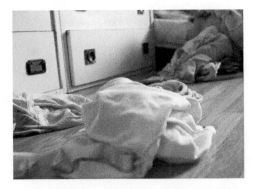

WRITING COACH

Online

www.phwritingcoach.com

Interactive Model
Listen to an audio recording of the Mentor Text in the eText. You can refer back to the Mentor Text whenever you need support in developing your own writing.

Online Journal
Try It! Answer the questions about the Mentor Text in the online journal.

❺ The surprise ending is a **narrative device** that makes the story more interesting.

Try It! Did the ending surprise you? Explain why or why not.

Extension Find another example of a personal narrative from classical or contemporary literature and compare it with this one. How are their structures and themes similar and different?

Mentor Text 69

Personalized Support

[FEEDBACK] **Teacher or Peer Feedback**

To provide feedback to students on their responses to the Mentor Text and their answers to the *Try It!* questions, ask or have student partners ask one another the following:

- What is the thesis or controlling idea of the Mentor Text?
- How does the Mentor Text illustrate the characteristics of narrative nonfiction?
- How did you answer this *Try It!* question? How could you use your answer to help you plan your piece of writing?

Working with ELLs [ELL] Sheltered Instruction: Cognitive

Have students listen to, derive meaning from, and respond orally to information presented in a wide variety of print, electronic, and audiovisual media to build and reinforce concept attainment. Provide a recording of a dialogue about a problem. Play the recording, and build and reinforce attainment of the concept of dialogue.

Beginning Pause frequently and clarify. Provide concept-related words such as *dialogue, speaker, statement, first,* and *last.* Review the words, and have students use them in responding orally to questions, such as, *Who is the first speaker?*

Intermediate During playback, have students seek clarification as needed. Then, have them discuss the conversation. To build concept attainment, provide sentence frames for responses, like, *The last speaker said ____.*

Advanced Have groups discuss the dialogue, identifying the problem and offering solutions in sentence frames like, *The two speakers can resolve ____ by ____.*

Advanced High Have students complete the Advanced activity. Have them summarize the dialogue.

The Digital · Print Path ▶

1  STUDENT BOOK ▶

Using *Writing Coach Online*™ or the student book, students read and listen to an audio recording of the Student Model.

STUDENT MODEL

Tell students that good writers react to what they read in ways that show their understanding of the text. Explain that students will react to the Student Model by placing two sets of symbols in the text. Then, distribute printed copies of the Student Model or have students log on to Writing Coach Online.

Use a Reader's Eye

Read aloud the instruction for using the Reader's Response Symbols and the meaning of each symbol. Then, guide students through their use.

 Think Aloud

I think that the writer presented many interesting details in his narrative. For example, in lines 32–36 he writes, "I could see a huge canyon stretching out in front of us. And across that canyon was a narrow bridge, suspended by what looked like little wires." Details such as "huge canyon," "narrow bridge," and "little wires" help me imagine how scary that suspension bridge must have looked. I'll place an exclamation point next to that part of the text.

Work with students to identify other parts of the text that they found interesting or unusual.

Have students read and respond to the Student Model, using each Reader's Response Symbol at least once.

Partner Talk

After partners have shared their thoughts about the theme, have each student pair summarize their thoughts for the class.

Use a Writer's Eye

Read aloud the instructions for using the Writer's Response Symbols and the meaning of each symbol. Then, guide students through their use.

STUDENT MODEL — Personal Narrative

With a small group, take turns reading this Student Model aloud. As you read, practice newly acquired vocabulary by correctly producing the word's sound. Notice how the writer mixes action with thoughts and dialogue. Also notice how the story unfolds and holds your interest. Afterward, write down a few notes that describe what you learned about yourself, others, or the world from the reading.

 Use a Reader's Eye

Now, reread the Student Model. On your copy of the Student Model, use the Reader's Response Symbols to react to what you read.

Reader's Response Symbols

+ I like where this is going.

– This isn't clear to me.

? What will happen next?

! Wow! That is really cool/weird/interesting!

 **Partner Talk**

Discuss the theme of the Student Model with a partner, and express your opinions, ideas, and feelings about it. Note and discuss responses that were the same for both of you, as well as responses that were different.

70   Narrative Nonfiction

The BRIDGE

by Thomas Waylan

What are you afraid of? Spiders? Dogs? Writing essays? I have always been afraid of heights. I never slid down the tallest slide, climbed a tree, or went off the high diving
5   board. Or at least I didn't before last summer.

Last summer, my family drove to Canyon State Park. Now, canyons tend to involve cliffs, otherwise known as heights, and I'm afraid of heights. On the last day, my dad told
10   us, "This morning, we're going on a special, guided hike. It's called the 'Bridge Hike.'"

"What kind of bridge?" I asked, already sensing that I wasn't going to like it.

"A suspension bridge, over the spectacular
15   Vista Canyon. It's going to be great."

"No way," I said. "I'll stay here and hold down the fort." I gestured to our little campsite.

My mom shook her head. "Honey, you can't stay here by yourself."

20   So, there I was an hour later, following our guide, Alejandro, through some of the most beautiful forest I've ever seen. Sunlight fell through the branches as Alejandro pointed out hawks overhead and coyote tracks along the trail.

25   "So, tell me about this bridge we're going to cross," I said to Alejandro.

"Don't worry," he said, with a Spanish accent, looking me straight in the eye. "You can walk with

1

Say: I noticed that the writer created several believable characters. For example, in lines 14–15 the father encouragingly describes the bridge as being located over "the spectacular Vista Canyon." He adds, "It's going to be great." His son, who is afraid of heights, responds, "No way. I'll stay here and hold down the fort." I can imagine a father and son speaking exactly that way in that situation. I'll write B.C. next to that part of the text for believable characters.

Ask: Where else does the writer use dialogue to create believable characters? (lines 18–19, the mother's response to her son; lines 27–30, the guide's response to the son)

Have students read and respond to the Student Model, using each Writer's Response Symbol at least once.

2  **STUDENT BOOK** ▶

First, students respond to the Student Model as a reader, using symbols to mark the text. They can mark the text using pop-up sticky notes in *Writing Coach Online*™ or they can mark a printed copy of the Student Model.

3 WRITING COACH **Online** **STUDENT BOOK** ▶

Then, students respond to the Student Model as a writer, using different symbols to mark the text. They can use either *Writing Coach Online*™ or a printed copy of the Student Model.

arrative **Student Model** *Personal Narrative* **Student Model**

me. Just hold your head up, instead of looking
30 down. Trust me—you'll love it. The vista is beautiful!"

Yeah, right, I thought.

At last we came out of the forest, and I could see a huge canyon stretching out in front of us. And across that canyon was a narrow
35 bridge, suspended by what looked like little wires. I stopped in my tracks. I felt sick and weak in the knees just looking at the bridge, but somehow I knew that I had to do it.

"You ready, son?" my dad asked.

40 I let out a big sigh and nodded. "Let's go," I said, walking straight toward the bridge, holding my head high as Alejandro had suggested.

When I stepped out onto the bridge I could feel it swing slightly beneath me, but I kept going. With
45 each step, there was a slight bounce. I didn't look down. I looked straight ahead, looking at the colors of the canyon wall—oranges and reds—against the bright blue of the sky. I put one foot in front of the other, and then I was across. I had done it!

50 Ever since then, I've known that my fear of heights would never stop me again. It wouldn't stop me from climbing a tree or going off the high dive.

2

Student Model 71

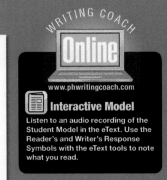

WRITING COACH
Online
www.phwritingcoach.com

Interactive Model

Listen to an audio recording of the Student Model in the eText. Use the Reader's and Writer's Response Symbols with the eText tools to note what you read.

Use a Writer's Eye

Now evaluate the piece as a writer. On your copy of the Student Model, use the Writer's Response Symbols to react to what you read. Identify places where the student writer uses characteristics of an effective personal narrative.

Writer's Response Symbols	
E.S.	**Engaging story**
C.R.	**Clear, well-developed conflict and resolution**
B.C.	**Believable characters**
S.D.	**Specific and vivid details**

Personalized Support

FEEDBACK **Teacher or Peer Feedback**

To provide feedback to students on their responses to the Student Model, ask or have student partners ask one another the following:

- What is the thesis or controlling idea of the Student Model?
- How does the Student Model illustrate the characteristics of a personal narrative?
- Which feature or characteristic of the Student Model might you use in your own piece of writing?
- How could you alter or adapt this feature to make it your own?

Working with ELLs **ELL** Sheltered Instruction: Cognitive

Help students learn basic vocabulary heard during classroom instruction and interactions. Write the words *author*, *sentence*, *school*, and *example* on the board and read them aloud. Use students' prior experiences to help them understand the words' meanings in English.

Beginning Say *I read books by my favorite author*, miming reading a book. Help students use their prior experiences with books to determine that an *author* is someone who writes books.

Intermediate Have pairs create **T-Charts** for the words using words or phrases

describing prior experiences related to the meaning of each word. For example: *Yesterday, I wrote five sentences in class.*

Advanced Have students complete the Intermediate activity. Have them meet in groups to use the words in oral sentences that illustrate each word's meaning. Instruct groups to monitor that the words are used correctly.

Advanced High Have students use the words in a paragraph describing their prior experiences. Have them read their paragraph aloud in groups. Instruct groups to make sure each member uses the words properly.

The Digital • Print Path ▶

1  Students select or are assigned a topic for their personal narrative from the Topic Bank, or they may choose a topic of their own.

2 Students complete online or printed graphic organizers to narrow the topic for their personal narrative.

Prewriting

Explain that the first task students need to complete as they plan their personal narrative is to determine an appropriate topic.

Choose From the Topic Bank

Read aloud each topic and then ask volunteers to describe them in their own words. If you are assigning topics to students, you may wish to do so now. Encourage students to ask questions about their topic.

Choose Your Own Topic

Introduce and discuss the Talk and Reflect strategies. If students were not assigned writing topics, have them use the strategies to brainstorm for topics for their essays.

Extension Have each student choose one of the strategies. Then, have them write an action plan that outlines the resources and steps they will use to develop their topic.

Narrow Your Topic

Tell students that they will use a Narrow Your Topic graphic organizer to determine an appropriate topic for their narrative. Then, distribute printed copies or have students log on to Writing Coach Online.

Apply It! Guide students through the instructions for completing the graphic organizer. Have students complete the exercise based on their topic.

Consider Your Audience and Purpose

Guide students to consider the audience and purpose for their personal narrative.

Feature Assignment **Prewriting** *Feature Assignment* **Prewri**

Your Turn ▶ **Feature Assignment: Personal Narrative**

Prewriting

Plan a first draft of your personal narrative **by determining an appropriate topic.** You may select from the Topic Bank or come up with an idea of your own.

 Choose From the Topic Bank

TOPIC BANK

What Are You Going to Wear? Clothing can be associated with particular events or circumstances, such as a lucky hat or a sweatshirt you always bring on a family trip. Identify a piece of clothing you associate with a special event in your life. In an autobiographical narrative, tell the story of what makes this piece of clothing special.

Gifted Think of a gift that you have been given that has special meaning for you. Write a personal narrative in which you describe the gift and why it is so important to you.

WOW! Think about an exciting experience you had. Write a personal narrative that describes your experience and explains why it was so exciting.

 Choose Your Own Topic

Determine an appropriate topic on your own by using the following **range of strategies** to generate ideas.

Talk and Reflect

- Talk to some friends about things that have happened in your life. Then, ask your friends which experience they feel is the most interesting. Monitor their spoken language by asking follow-up questions to confirm your understanding.
- If you post to social networking sites, review what you have posted lately. Could you develop a post into a story starring you?

Review your responses and choose a topic.

Say: I see that the questions in the first column of the chart ask about my possible audience, or the people who will read my work. If I choose the second topic from the Topic Bank, about a gift, my audience might be my friends and family, or people who are interested in the important events in my life.

Ask: Based on your topic, who is most likely to read your personal narrative? Who would you most like to read it? **(Responses will vary.)**

Have students with similar topics work in small groups to discuss and respond to the remaining questions.

Coach's Corner

You may wish to model prewriting activities for students by brainstorming for your own writing topic. Use these prompts to model your thought process:

- **I am interested in** gifts, so that could be my general topic.
- **I can narrow my topic by** focusing on a gift I received on a special birthday.

Discuss the choices you make and solicit feedback from students.

3 Writing Journal

Students record their answers to questions about audience and purpose in their online journals or notebooks.

Narrow Your Topic

Narrowing your topic will help ensure that your personal narrative has a clearly defined focus, or main point.

Apply It! Use a graphic organizer like the one shown to narrow your topic.

- Record your general topic—your broadest story idea—in the top box; then narrow your topic as you move down the chart.
- Your final box should hold your narrowest story idea, the new focus of your personal narrative.

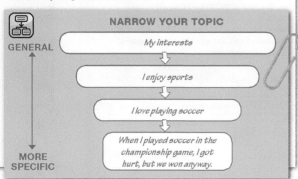

NARROW YOUR TOPIC

GENERAL

My interests

I enjoy sports

I love playing soccer

When I played soccer in the championship game, I got hurt, but we won anyway.

MORE SPECIFIC

Consider Your Audience and Purpose

Before writing, think about your audience and purpose. Consider how your narrative will convey the intended meaning to this audience. Consider the views of others as you ask these questions.

Questions for Audience	Questions for Purpose
• Who are the people in my audience?	• What is my purpose? Do I want my writing to be humorous, thought-provoking, or something else?
• What might the audience want to know about me—and why?	
• How can I communicate the importance of my experience?	• How much about myself do I want to share?

Record your answers in your writing journal.

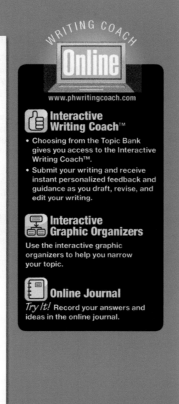

Online

www.phwritingcoach.com

Interactive Writing Coach™

- Choosing from the Topic Bank gives you access to the Interactive Writing Coach™.
- Submit your writing and receive instant personalized feedback and guidance as you draft, revise, and edit your writing.

Interactive Graphic Organizers

Use the interactive graphic organizers to help you narrow your topic.

Online Journal

Try It! Record your answers and ideas in the online journal.

Personalized Support

Interactive Writing Coach™

Below Level Teachers select a topic from the topic bank for below-level students. Students submit their writing to the **Interactive Writing Coach™** for feedback paragraph by paragraph or as a complete draft. It is recommended that below-level students submit their writing one paragraph at a time.

On Level Students may select a topic from the Topic Bank. They may submit their writing for feedback paragraph by paragraph or as a complete draft.

Above Level Students may select from the Topic Bank or come up with their own topic. Above-level students should submit their writing as a complete draft.

Interactive Graphic Organizer

Below Level Students complete three graphic organizers that provide models and scaffolded support.

On Level Students complete one, two, or three graphic organizers, depending on how much support they need.

Above Level Students complete the least scaffolded graphic organizer or narrow their topic without the help of a graphic organizer.

Differentiated Instruction

RTI Strategy for Below-Level Students
Tell students that one way to use the graphic organizer is to ask *Who? What? When? Where? Why?* or *How?* for each step in the narrowing process. For example, if they wrote *Gifts* in the top oval, they could ask, *What is a special gift I received?* They could then answer: *a watch from my grandmother.* They could then ask, *Why was it so special?* answering: *I had lost my watch and needed a new one,* and so on.

PRE-AP Enrichment for Above-Level Students Encourage students to think more deeply about the topic, audience, and purpose for their personal narrative by analyzing the Student Model on pages 70–71. Have them consider the following questions: *What is the clearly defined topic, or main point, expressed in the first paragraph? Based on the narrative, who is the intended audience? Why? What was the intended purpose? Why?* Students should then apply their analysis of the Student Model to the writing of their own personal narrative.

The Digital · Print Path ▶

1

Using *Writing Coach Online*™ or the student book, students read and discuss the model graphic organizer.

2

Students complete online or printed graphic organizers to develop their ideas and gather details.

Plan Your Piece

Explain that writers use graphic organizers to develop their ideas and show relationships between different parts of the text. Then, point out the Plan Your Story graphic organizer on page 74. Tell students that they will use this organizer to outline their personal narrative. Then, distribute printed copies or have students log on to Writing Coach Online.

Introduce the graphic organizer by explaining that the first column lists the different parts of a personal narrative. The second column lists the writer's specific ideas for each part.

Develop Your Focus Guide students to notice that the information about Characters and Setting in the example organizer is based on the narrowed topic from page 73. Have students develop the focus of their narrative by entering information about their topic's characters and setting on their graphic organizer.

Map Out Your Story Remind students that the plot of their narrative should involve a problem. Ask students to identify the information in the organizer's first column about how the problem is developed in each part of the narrative. Then, have students enter events for each part of their plot on their graphic organizer.

Gather Details

Remind students that personal narratives depend on concrete details to make the story come alive. Ask volunteers to read aloud each kind of detail and its example. Then, guide students to place the details in the example graphic organizer.

Say: I notice that the Plan Your Story organizer has space for events and details that happen in the beginning, middle, and end. The details on page 75 supply this information. For example, the Sensory Detail example says, "A shooting pain raced up my leg, and I crumpled to the ground." This detail shows the problem getting worse, so I'll record that in the Middle section of the organizer.

Ask: Where should the Actions and Their Consequencs example be placed in the organizer? (End)

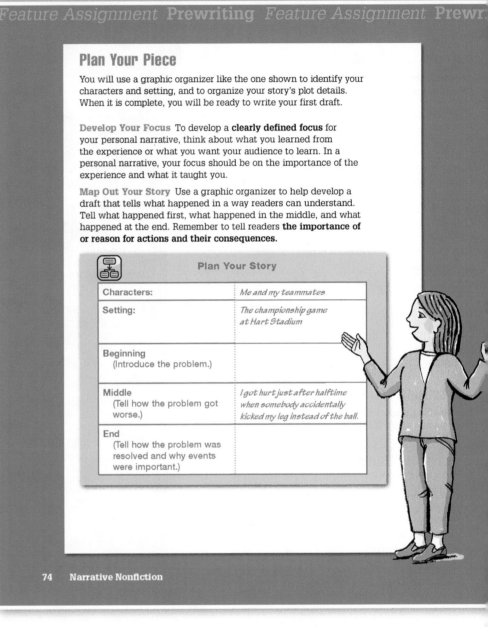

Plan Your Piece

You will use a graphic organizer like the one shown to identify your characters and setting, and to organize your story's plot details. When it is complete, you will be ready to write your first draft.

Develop Your Focus To develop a **clearly defined focus** for your personal narrative, think about what you learned from the experience or what you want your audience to learn. In a personal narrative, your focus should be on the importance of the experience and what it taught you.

Map Out Your Story Use a graphic organizer to help develop a draft that tells what happened in a way readers can understand. Tell what happened first, what happened in the middle, and what happened at the end. Remember to tell readers **the importance of or reason for actions and their consequences.**

Plan Your Story

Characters:	*Me and my teammates*
Setting:	*The championship game at Hart Stadium*
Beginning (Introduce the problem.)	
Middle (Tell how the problem got worse.)	*I got hurt just after halftime when somebody accidentally kicked my leg instead of the ball.*
End (Tell how the problem was resolved and why events were important.)	

Have students work in small groups to place the remaining details on the example graphic organizer.

Try It! Guide students to understand that the passage discusses the writer's fear of heights generally, and then focuses on a specific event about that fear.

Apply It! Read aloud the bulleted instructions. Then, have students add appropriate details to each section of their graphic organizer.

Writer's Block

IF students can't identify appropriate details for their personal narrative . . .

THEN have them turn to the Student Model on pages 70–71. Discuss the details that the student writer used in his personal narrative.

Students refer back to the Mentor Text or the
Student Model as they plan their writing.

e Assignment **Prewriting** *Feature Assignment* **Prewriting**

Gather Details

To develop their ideas in a personal narrative, writers use some of
the kinds of details shown in these examples.

- **Actions and Their Consequences:** *I thought that my teammates
  depended on me to win. I felt a lot of pressure, so I played more
  aggressively than usual. This might have led to my injury.*
- **Sensory Details:** *A shooting pain raced up my leg, and I
  crumpled to the ground.*
- **Dialogue:** *Coach said, "Lupita, you can't play on that leg. You're
  going to have to sit out the rest of the game."*
- **Suspense:** *The other team was still four points ahead. Could we
  catch up before the game ended?*

Good writers use a variety of strategies to engage readers and to
tell their stories.

Try It! Read the Student Model excerpt and identify how the
author's opening engages the readers' interest and defines the focus.

 **STUDENT MODEL** | from **The Bridge**
page 70; lines 1–5

> What are you afraid of? Spiders? Dogs? Writing essays?
> I have always been afraid of heights. I never slid down
> the tallest slide, climbed a tree, or went off the high
> diving board. Or at least I didn't before last summer.

Apply It! Review the kinds of details that writers of
personal narratives often use. Then identify at least one
detail for the beginning, middle, and end of your story. Be sure to
also identify details to describe the characters and setting of your
personal narrative.

- Decide which details help you to show the focus of your
  narrative. They will be details that help to show the importance
  of the story's events.
- Add these details to your graphic organizer, matching each
  detail to the right part of the story.
- Determine which narrative devices, such as suspense and
  dialogue, you will use to enhance the plot, or make it stronger.

WRITING COACH
Online
www.phwritingcoach.com

**Interactive
Graphic Organizers**
Use the interactive graphic
organizers to help you create a
plan for your writing.

Interactive Model
Refer back to the Interactive Model
in the eText as you plan your writing.

Prewriting **75**

Personalized Support

 **Interactive
Graphic Organizer**

Below Level Students complete three
graphic organizers that provide models
and scaffolded support.

On Level Students complete one, two,
or three graphic organizers, depending on
how much support they need.

Above Level Students complete the least
scaffolded graphic organizer or narrow
their topic without the help of a graphic
organizer.

FEEDBACK **Teacher or Peer
Feedback**

To provide feedback to students as they
plan their first draft, ask or have student
partners ask one another the following:

- What do you want your audience to know
  about the topic?
- What questions or concerns will your
  audience have about the topic?
- What details have you identified for your
  piece? How do these details support your
  thesis or controlling idea?
- Are your details varied? Will they interest
  your readers? Explain.

Differentiated Instruction

RTI Strategy for Below-Level Students

Students may have trouble seeing how all
the parts of the organizer work together
as a plan for a personal narrative. Use the
Student Model on pages 70–71 to review
each part of an effective narrative: the
clearly defined focus in the first paragraph;
the characters; the setting; and the
beginning, middle, and end. Ask students
to identify the details that the writer used
to develop each part of the narrative.

Enrichment for Gifted/Talented Students

Encourage students to plan different
engaging introductions for their personal
narrative. Point out to them that skilled
writers do not always put the focus, or
main point, at the very beginning of an
essay. It may appear after an introduction
that grabs the reader with exciting details, a
vivid setting, or an emotional situation. As
they write their introductions, have them
experiment with various placements of their
focus statement for maximum effect.

The Digital · Print Path ▶

1 WRITING COACH Online STUDENT BOOK ▶

Using *Writing Coach Online*™ or the student book, students read and discuss the Outline for Success for narrative nonfiction.

2 WRITING COACH Online STUDENT BOOK ▶

Students discuss how the Mentor Text illustrates the characteristics of narrative nonfiction.

Drafting

Outline for Success

Explain that the Outline for Success shows an organizational strategy for narrative nonfiction. Students will use the Outline to write a focused, organized, and coherent draft of their personal narrative.

I. Beginning

Link the Outline to a specific personal narrative by having students turn to the Mentor Text on pages 68–69. Ask a volunteer to read aloud the introduction (lines 1–9). Then, guide students to understand how the author has created an interesting opening and introduced a focus, or main idea.

Say: I see that the author has written an interesting opening by giving details about his roommate Jim. In lines 1–3, the author tells us that Jim "was neat and not too much of a pain in the neck." Then he says, "But man, could Jim talk." These interesting details fill in our understanding of Jim bit by bit. As a reader, I want to keep reading to find out more about their relationship.

Ask: Which sentence introduces the focus of the narrative? (lines 8–9, "His best pitch ever was the time he tried to sell me my own shirt.")

Have students work with a partner to discuss how they will create an effective introduction.

II. Middle

Lead a discussion about how the body paragraphs of the Mentor Text reflect the characteristics of a personal narrative.

- Events in chronological order (lines 10, 13–14, 19–21, 30–32, 36–41, 50–52)
- Development of setting (lines 10–14) and characters (lines 1–7, 10–12)
- Suspense (lines 15–16) and dialogue (throughout)
- Sensory details (lines 11–12, 13–14, 17–18, 22–23, 36–37, 40–41)

Drafting Feature Assignment Drafting Feature Assignment

Drafting

During the drafting stage, you will start to write your ideas for your personal narrative. You will follow an outline that provides an **organizational strategy** that will help you build on ideas to write a **focused, organized, and coherent** personal narrative.

The Organization of a Personal Narrative

The chart shows an organizational strategy for a personal narrative. Look back at how the Mentor Text follows this organizational strategy. Then, use this chart to help you outline your draft.

Outline for Success

I. Beginning — See Mentor Text, p. 68.
- Interesting opening
- Introduce focus, or main idea

Grab Your Reader
- An interesting opening, such as a question or a vivid detail, will catch the reader's attention.
- A personal narrative should have a clear focus. The focus suggests why the story you are going to tell is important.

II. Middle — See Mentor Text, pp. 68–69.
- Sequence of events in chronological order, or time order
- Development of interesting plot, setting, and characters
- Narrative devices, including suspense and dialogue
- Details that appeal to the senses of sight, touch, hearing, and smell

Develop Your Plot
- Readers will be better able to understand your story if events are presented in chronological order. In this section, readers get to experience why characters do things and what the consequences of those actions are. Narrative devices, such as suspense, will help to further develop the plot.
- Readers are better able to identify with characters if dialogue to make the characters true to life is included.
- Vivid sensory details—about the characters, setting, and action—help readers feel a part of the story. These details strengthen the focus of your narrative.

III. Conclusion — See Mentor Text, p. 69.
- Resolution
- Ending that reflects the focus

Wrap It Up
- The resolution shows how the problem was solved.
- The ending shows the importance of the events that took place in the story and how those events affected you.

76 **Narrative Nonfiction**

III. Conclusion

Have small groups discuss how the Mentor Text conclusion reflects the characteristics of a personal narrative (lines 50–54).

Start Your Draft

Have small groups read aloud and discuss the boxed instructions for drafting. Direct students to work individually on their first draft.

Coach's Corner

If you are modeling the writing process for students with your own topic or a student volunteer's, you may wish to use these prompts to guide your drafting and discussion:

- **To capture readers' attention, my introduction will** ask questions and include a clearly defined focus.
- **I will organize my body paragraphs** to create an interesting plot with suspense.

Discuss the choices you make and solicit feedback from students.

3  Students begin writing their personal narrative online or in their notebooks.

4 Students submit paragraphs or complete drafts to the Interactive Writing Coach™ for scoring and feedback, or share their work with their teacher.

5 Students receive customized feedback from the Interactive Writing Coach™, or feedback from their teacher. Students may continue to work on their drafts.

Feature Assignment **Drafting** *Feature Assignment* **Drafting**

Start Your Draft

Use the checklist below to help complete your draft. Use the graphic organizer that shows your characters, setting, and plot outline, and the Outline for Success as guides.

While drafting, aim at writing your ideas, not on making your writing perfect. Remember, you will have the chance to improve your draft when you revise and edit.

- √ Start by drafting an attention-getting **opening** sentence.
- √ Continue your **beginning** by giving details that introduce the **focus** of your narrative and make the story interesting. Make your readers want to read on!

- √ Develop the **middle** of your personal narrative. Introduce interesting, believable characters and develop the conflict.
- √ Present specific actions and events in **chronological** order.
- √ Show the **reasons** for each action—and the consequences. Sharpen the focus of the narrative by suggesting why events are important.
- √ Use narrative **devices,** such as suspense and dialogue, and include plenty of sensory details to describe actions, setting, and characters.

- √ At the **end** of your narrative, show the **resolution** of the conflict, or how the events worked out.
- √ Finish by reflecting on why the experience was important—the **focus** of your personal narrative.

WRITING COACH

Online
www.phwritingcoach.com

Interactive Model

Outline for Success View pop-ups of Mentor Text selections referenced in the Outline for Success.

Interactive Writing Coach™

Use the Interactive Writing Coach to receive the level of support you need:
- Write one paragraph at a time and submit each one for immediate, detailed feedback.
- Write your entire first draft and submit it for immediate, personalized feedback.

Drafting 77

Personalized Support

 Interactive Writing Coach™

Below Level Students complete the drafting process in small steps by submitting each paragraph for scoring and feedback.

On Level Depending on the support they need, students submit their writing paragraph by paragraph or as a complete draft for scoring and feedback.

Above Level Students may write their drafts on their own but have the option of submitting them for scoring and/or feedback.

 Teacher or Peer Feedback

To provide feedback to students on their first draft, ask or have student partners ask one another the following:

- Can you explain how you organized your ideas in this piece?
- Why did you include this information here?
- Why did you choose this beginning? Does it grab your reader and identify your thesis or controlling idea?
- What supporting details could you add here?
- Why did you choose this conclusion? How does it add to your piece?
- Can you show me a place where I can hear your unique voice?
- Can you show me a place where you used vivid language?

Working with ELLs **ELL** Sheltered Instruction: Cognitive

Have students write using and reusing newly acquired basic vocabulary. Encourage them to incorporate the vocabulary in their drafts.

Beginning Introduce the words *first, next,* and *last.* Mime a series of actions, such as eating, drinking, and writing, providing a verb for each. Repeat the mime, and help students use and reuse the words to complete sentences such as *First, [he/she] [ate/drank/wrote]. Next, [he/she] [ate/drank/wrote].*

Intermediate Write *first, next, finally, before, suddenly,* and *after a while.* Help students use the **Frayer Model** for each word by having them fill in four sections

of a card, one for a definition, one for characteristics, one for examples, and one for non-examples. Have students use and reuse each word in a written sentence.

Advanced Review basic words that indicate chronological order. Have students use and reuse them in sentences about an event. Each partner should write a sentence using an appropriate word to indicate sequence.

Advanced High Help students create a **Word Bank** of basic words indicating sequence. Have students use and reuse the vocabulary in a paragraph.

The Digital · Print Path ▶

WRITING COACH
Online
STUDENT BOOK

1  WRITING COACH Online STUDENT BOOK ▶
Using **Writing Coach Online**™ or the student book, students study the first and second drafts of the student model to see how the writer used Revision RADaR to improve his or her writing.

2 WRITING COACH Online Writing Journal ▶
Students use the Revision RADaR strategy to revise their own writing.

Revising: Making It Better

Point out the page title to students and explain that revising means making improvements to a writing draft. Then, read aloud the opening paragraph to introduce the Revision RADaR strategies. You may wish to have students review Chapter 3 for more information on Revision RADaR.

Kelly Gallagher, M. Ed.

KEEP REVISION ON YOUR RADaR

 After students have read the first draft, have them turn to page 76 and review the Outline for Success. Work with students to understand that the questions the author asked about the draft are based on the characteristics of a personal narrative. For example, call out the first two questions and note how they address the concerns listed in the Beginning section of the Outline for Success.

Then, have students work in small groups to develop other questions about the draft based on the genre characteristics.

  Guide students to understand how the author used the RADaR strategies to revise the first draft.

Think Aloud I noticed that the beginning of the 1st draft didn't grab my attention. It also didn't include specific details introducing a clearly defined focus. In the 2nd draft, though, I see an *A* next to the introduction, meaning that the writer has added some text. The new text consists of questions that grab my attention. In the 2nd draft, I also see an *R* next to the introduction, meaning that the writer has replaced some text. The replacement text contains interesting, detailed information that introduces a clearly defined focus, or main point. Now the beginning is very effective.

Revising: Making It Better

Now that you have finished your first draft, you are ready to revise. Think about the "big picture" of **audience, purpose, and genre.** You can use the Revision RADaR strategy as a guide for making changes to improve your draft. Revision RADaR provides four major ways to improve your writing: (R) replace, (A) add, (D) delete, and (R) reorder.

Kelly Gallagher, M. Ed.

KEEP REVISION ON YOUR RADaR

Read part of the first draft of the Student Model, "The Bridge." Then look at questions the writer asked himself as he thought about how well his draft addressed issues of **audience, purpose, and genre.**

The Bridge   1ST DRAFT

I have always been afraid of heights. I really don't like them. They scare me. Or at least they did before last summer.

Last summer my family drove to Canyon State Park. Now, canyons tend to involve cliffs, otherwise known as heights, and I am afraid of heights. I like camping and sleeping in a tent, but I wished that there were some video games to play. Until the last day when my dad told us, "This morning, we're going on a special, guided hike. It's called the 'Bridge Hike.'"

Bridges are usually very high up from the ground. I was terrified! I told my parents that there was no way I was going to go. I wanted to stay at our campsite, but they wouldn't let me.

So, there I was an hour later, following our guide, Alejandro, through some of the most beautiful forest I've ever seen.

> *Have I grabbed my audience's attention?*

> *Have I included details that introduce a clearly defined focus for my personal narrative?*

> *Have I kept the focus of my narrative sharp?*

> *Have I included enough narrative devices to keep the story interesting?*

78   Narrative Nonfiction

Work with students to brainstorm for other ways to revise the introduction.

Have students work in small groups to discuss the other changes in the 2nd draft.

Apply It! Review the bulleted instructions for using Revision RADaR. Remind students to question their drafts based on the genre characteristics listed on the Outline for Success on page 76. Tell students to use each RADaR strategy at least once.

Coach's Corner

If you are modeling the writing process for students with your own draft or a student volunteer's, use these prompts to focus on the Revision RADaR *Add* strategy:

- **I added suspense here because** I wanted to develop the plot further.

- **I added dialogue here because** I wanted to create believable characters the readers could identify with.

Discuss the choices you make and solicit feedback from students.

3 Students submit paragraphs or revised drafts to the Interactive Writing Coach™ for scoring and feedback, or share their work with their teacher.

4 Students receive customized feedback from the Interactive Writing Coach™, or feedback from their teacher. Students may continue to revise their drafts.

Feature Assignment **Revising** *Feature Assignment* **Revising**

Now look at how the writer applied Revision RADaR to write an improved second draft.

The BRIDGE
2ND DRAFT

What are you afraid of? Spiders? Dogs? Writing essays? I have always been afraid of heights. I never slid down the tallest slide, climbed a tree, or went off the high diving board. Or at least I didn't before last summer.

> **A** Added questions to grab the audience

Last summer, my family drove to Canyon State Park. Now, canyons tend to involve cliffs, otherwise known as heights, and I'm afraid of heights. On the last day, my dad told us, "This morning, we're going on a special, guided hike. It's called the 'Bridge Hike.'"

> **R** Replaced general information with specific details

"What kind of bridge?" I asked, already sensing that I wasn't going to like it.

> **D** Deleted details that didn't directly relate to the focus

"A suspension bridge, over the spectacular Vista Canyon. It's going to be great."

"No way," I said. "I'll stay here and hold down the fort." I gestured to our little campsite.

> **A** Added dialogue to develop characters and build suspense

My mom shook her head. "Honey, you can't stay here by yourself."

So, there I was an hour later, following our guide, Alejandro, through some of the most beautiful forest I've ever seen.

 Apply It! Use your Revision RADaR to revise your draft.

- First, make sure you have included a clearly defined focus and have communicated the importance of your story's events.
- Then, apply the Revision RADaR strategy to make needed changes. Remember—you can use the steps in any order.

Revising 79

WRITING COACH

Online
www.phwritingcoach.com

 Interactive Writing Coach™

Use the Revision RADaR strategy in your own writing. Then submit your paragraph or draft for feedback.

Personalized Support

 Interactive Writing Coach™

Below Level Students revise their drafts using the Revision RADaR strategy and submit their writing for scoring and feedback.

On Level Students revise their drafts using the Revision RADaR strategy and submit their writing for scoring and feedback.

Above Level Students may use the Revision RADaR strategy or revise their drafts on their own. They have the option of submitting their revised drafts for scoring and/or feedback.

 Teacher or Peer Feedback

To provide feedback to students as they revise their first draft, ask or have student partners ask one another the following:

- Can you show me where you revised your text?
- What could you add to your beginning to grab the interest of your readers?
- How could you reorder these ideas so that their order is more logical?
- Have you included all the characteristics of this form of writing?
- Is there any unnecessary text that you could delete?
- Have you achieved your purpose with this piece of writing?
- Have you addressed the questions and concerns of your audience?

Working with ELLs **ELL** Sheltered Instruction: Cognitive

As you review the revised Student Model, have students demonstrate English comprehension and expand their reading skills by employing the analytical skill of evaluating written information.

Beginning Write on the board: *I am afraid of bugs. They are bad./ I am afraid of spiders. They are creepy.* Use visuals to ensure that students understand. Help them evaluate which statement offers more detail.

Intermediate Distribute the sentences from the Beginning activity to groups. Have them read and compare the sentences. Monitor their ability to evaluate written

information by having them complete sentence starters, such as, *The [first/second] pair of sentences is clearer than the [first/second] pair because . . . .*

Advanced Have pairs read the second draft on page 79, taking notes on audience, purpose, and genre. Monitor their analytical skills by asking, *Who is the audience for this piece? What is the genre? How well does the piece fit its audience? Its genre?*

Advanced High Have students complete the Advanced activity individually. Have students compare their evaluations.

T79

The Digital · Print Path ▶

1  ▶
Using Writing Coach Online™ or the student book, students study and discuss the revision chart.

2 ▶
In a video by program author Kelly Gallagher, students learn more strategies for effective writing.

Revising: Making It Better

Look at the Big Picture

Introduce the revision chart to students. Explain that the Section column identifies the three main parts of a personal narrative. The Evaluate column identifies the characteristics found in each section and explains how to assess them. The Revise column presents specific strategies for revising each characteristic.

Then, have students draw lines between and label the three sections of their drafts. Direct students to work individually to evaluate and revise their draft, using the chart to guide their work.

Focus on Craft: Sentence Variety

Have students read the introductory text. Guide students to understand that using simple and compound sentences in their writing can help them create rhythm and emphasize ideas.

Say: I notice that the first sentence of the Student Model is short. This sentence emphasizes that the writer is scared. The second sentence is long. It creates a rhythm that seems to pull the writer ahead—to get him to walk across the bridge.

Ask: Is the third sentence long or short? (long) What effect does this sentence have? (Like the second sentence, it moves the writer across the bridge.)

Have students work with a partner to discuss the length and effect of the last sentence in the Student Model.

Try It! Have students discuss the questions and record responses in their journals. Follow up with students to check that their responses reflect an understanding of how using simple and compound sentences in their writing can create rhythm and emphasize ideas.

Revising Feature Assignment Revising Feature Assignment

Look at the Big Picture

Use the chart and your analytical skills to evaluate how well each section of your personal narrative addresses **purpose, audience, and genre.** When necessary, use the suggestions in the chart to revise your narrative.

Section	Evaluate	Revise
Beginning	• Decide whether your **opening** sentence is interesting, making your audience want to read on.	• Add a question or vivid detail that engages readers' curiosity.
	• Make sure that your **focus** is clearly defined. Readers should know why you're writing about this experience.	• Add a sentence and/or details that introduce and explain the focus of your narrative.
Middle	• Review the **plot** of your narrative. Are the events clearly presented in chronological order? Have you used narrative devices, such as suspense?	• Rearrange events to ensure chronological, or time, order. Add, change, or even take out details to keep readers in suspense about the outcome.
	• Underline details that show your characters in action in one or more settings. Do **sensory details** make the characters and settings interesting and believable?	• To help readers identify with your characters and settings, add sensory details about both. Also consider adding or revising dialogue to make the characters more real.
	• Look at the middle as a whole and evaluate whether you have shown the reasons for **actions** and their consequences and importance.	• Add details and sentences that clarify meaning, showing why things happen and why they are important.
End	• Check for a well-developed **resolution**—one that clearly illustrates the focus of the narrative.	• Add or revise details to show how the problem was solved and why events were important to you.
	• Evaluate your **closing** to see if it reflects the beginning and brings the narrative full circle.	• Add or substitute language that reminds readers of the problem and shows how it was solved.

80   **Narrative Nonfiction**

Fine-Tune Your Draft

Apply It! Ask volunteers to read aloud the instructions for fine-tuning their drafts. Then, have students work in pairs to edit their writing to include a variety of sentence lengths.

Teacher Feedback Have students identify Mentor Text examples of the characteristics that were marked for improvement. Use the Mentor Text references on page T76 to guide students to appropriate examples.

Teacher Tip

Quick Write Have students re-read their narratives and add transitional words as needed. Then, have them meet with a partner and explain how the transitional words show the sequence of events or the relationship among events.

---

3 ▶ STUDENT BOOK ▶

Using *Writing Coach Online™* or the student book, students refer back to the Mentor Text or Student Model for examples of writer's craft.

4 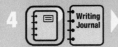 ▶ Writing Journal ▶

Students record answers to questions about writer's craft in their online journals or notebooks.

5  ▶

Students submit revised drafts to the *Interactive Writing Coach™* for scoring and feedback, or share their work with their teacher.

6 FEEDBACK ✓ ▶

Students receive customized feedback from the *Interactive Writing Coach™*, or feedback from their teacher.

Feature Assignment **Revising** *Feature Assignment* **Revising**

Focus on Craft: Sentence Variety

Think about **sentence variety** when you write. Sentences should have different lengths. A paragraph or essay composed of all short, simple sentences will be choppy. Using too many long, compound sentences will make your essay difficult to follow. Try to vary sentences by including both simple and compound sentences to create a rhythm and emphasize important points.

Think about variety in sentence length as you read the following sentences from the Student Model.

 STUDENT MODEL from **The Bridge,** page 71; lines 45–49

> I didn't look down. I looked straight ahead, looking at the colors of the canyon wall—oranges and reds—against the bright blue of the sky. I put one foot in front of the other, and then I was across. I had done it!

 *Try It!* Now, ask yourself these questions:

- Are the sentences in this passage different lengths? Does the rhythm of the sentences reflect the rhythm of the actions described?
- What is the impact of a short sentence followed by a long one?

Fine-Tune Your Draft

Apply It! Use the revision suggestions to prepare your final draft **after rethinking how well questions of purpose, audience, and genre have been addressed.**

- **Ensure Sentence Variety** Raise the interest level by including both long, compound sentences with two main clauses with their own subjects and verbs and short, simple sentences with only one clause.
- **Clarify Meaning** Add words and phrases that clarify meaning by adding transition words that show the sequence of events and the relationship among them, such as *first, later,* and *on the other hand*.

Teacher Feedback Show your final draft to your teacher. Ask for his or her feedback and revise as necessary.

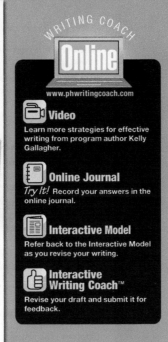

WRITING COACH

Online

www.phwritingcoach.com

 Video
Learn more strategies for effective writing from program author Kelly Gallagher.

 Online Journal
Try It! Record your answers in the online journal.

Interactive Model
Refer back to the Interactive Model as you revise your writing.

Interactive Writing Coach™
Revise your draft and submit it for feedback.

Revising 81

Personalized Support

  Interactive Writing Coach™

Below Level Students complete the revising process by submitting their writing for scoring and feedback.

On Level Students complete the revising process by submitting their writing for scoring and feedback.

Above Level Students finish revising their drafts. They have the option of submitting their revised drafts for scoring and/or feedback.

FEEDBACK ✓ **Teacher or Peer Feedback**

To provide feedback to students as they continue to revise their first draft, ask or have student partners ask one another the following:

- What are you trying to say here? What part of the text could you replace to make your meaning clearer?
- Is there a more precise word you could use here?
- How does the rhythm of these sentences sound to you? Could you make the length and structure of these sentences more varied?
- How could you include transitional words and phrases here to help your reader understand these ideas?
- Are there details you could add here to make this part come alive?

Working with ELLs ELL Sheltered Instruction: Social/Affective

Have students demonstrate listening comprehension of increasingly complex spoken English by collaborating with peers as they share information in cooperative learning interactions. Read the Student Model excerpt aloud as students follow along, defining any key words, and discuss it. Have students close their books. Then:

Beginning Read the paragraph aloud again slowly, using images or gestures to aid comprehension. Have partners discuss the paragraph and collaborate, sharing information to answer recall questions you provide.

Intermediate Read the paragraph aloud again, having students monitor their comprehension and seek clarification. Have groups share information about what they heard and collaborate in answering recall questions you provide.

Advanced Read the paragraph aloud again, and have pairs write a short retelling to share information with another pair.

Advanced High Have students complete the Advanced activity and then collaborate with a peer on a comparison of the two drafts.

The Digital · Print Path ▶

  STUDENT BOOK

1 ▶

In a video by program author Jeff Anderson, students learn effective editing techniques.

2  ▶

Students record answers to questions about writer's craft in their online journals or notebooks.

Editing: Making It Correct

Discuss the opening paragraph with students. Explain that they will edit their drafts for proper grammar, mechanics, and spelling, including use of a consistent verb tense.

WRITE GUY *Jeff Anderson, M.Ed.*
WHAT DO YOU NOTICE?

Introduce students to consistent verb tense by reading aloud the Mentor Text excerpt and discussing responses to the "ask yourself" question that follows. Then, have students read the explanation of past and past progressive tense verbs.

To monitor students' comprehension, guide them to identify and use verb tenses consistently.

 Think Aloud **I notice** that one sentence in the Mentor Text example uses a past tense verb and the other uses a past progressive tense verb, yet the verb tenses are still consistent because both sentences tell about past actions. The only difference is that the second action was happening for a while.

Work with students to identify the verb tenses in the sentences in lines 34–37 of the Mentor Text on page 69 and discuss reasons for any shift, or change, in tense.

Have students write several sentences that have verbs in the same tense, exchange sentences with a partner, and rewrite the sentences using a different tense.

Grammar Mini-Lesson: Consistent Tenses

Discuss the paragraph and the Student Model excerpt on page 83 with students. Guide them to understand that the writer uses past tense forms for all three verbs in the sentence in order to keep the verb tense consistent.

Try It! Have students work with a partner to rewrite the sentences.

Editing Feature Assignment Editing Feature Assignment

Editing: Making It Correct

When you edit your work, you polish your writing and correct errors.

Before you edit, make sure that you have used a **consistent verb tense,** and have not included multiple verb tenses without a reason. Then edit your draft by correcting any errors in **grammar, mechanics, and spelling.**

WRITE GUY *Jeff Anderson, M. Ed.*
WHAT DO YOU NOTICE?

Zoom in on Conventions Focus on verb tenses as you zoom in on these lines from the Mentor Text.

> 📄 **MENTOR TEXT** from **Roommates** pages 68–69, lines 10–12
>
> Most of my clothes were in a pile on the floor of my closet. I was digging through the pile, sniffing for one that was not too smelly.

Now, ask yourself: *When did the events in each sentence occur?*

Perhaps you said that both sentences show actions that happened in the past. You probably noticed right away that the verb *were* in the first sentence is the past tense of the verb *are*. The verb *was digging* in the second sentence is a little more unusual.

A **progressive tense** verb shows that an action is or was happening for a period of time. Progressive tense verbs consist of a form of the helping verb *be*, such as *is, are, was,* or *were,* with the present participle of the main verb, which ends in *-ing*. The past progressive tense "was digging" shows the action the author was completing for a period of time.

Partner Talk Discuss this question with a partner: *Why do you think the author used a progressive tense verb in this passage?*

82 **Narrative Nonfiction**

To learn more about consistent verb tense, see Chapter 14 of your Grammar Handbook.

---

1. Lightning frightens me, but it's thunder that scares my dog!

2. Bowling sounded like a fun activity for the birthday party, but we went last week.

Apply It! Remind students to look closely for use of a consistent verb tense as they edit.

Use the Rubric Explain to students they will rate how well their draft addresses the elements of a personal narrative on a scale of 1 to 6, with 6 being the best score.

Then, have students use the rubric to evaluate their drafts and revise necessary.

Writer's Block

IF students have difficulty evaluating whether they used verb tenses consistently in their drafts . . .

THEN have them circle and compare the verb forms to see whether they used the same tense throughout, making changes only when they have a good reason, for example, in dialogue or to clarify sequence.

3  Using Writing Coach Online™ or the student book, students refer back to the Mentor Text or Student Model as they edit their writing.

4  Using Writing Coach Online™ or the student book, students evaluate their writing using the rubrics.

5  Students submit edited drafts to the Interactive Writing Coach™ for scoring and feedback, or share their work with their teacher.

6   Students receive personalized feedback from the Interactive Writing Coach™ or feedback from their teacher.

 Feature Assignment **Editing** Feature Assignment **Editing**

Grammar Mini-Lesson: Consistent Tenses

Usually, you should use one verb tense for consistency. Sometimes, though, you must change tense to show the sequence of events. For example, a writer may use the past tense when the narrator discusses events, but change to the present tense when characters speak in dialogue. **Consistent verb tense** is especially important in sentences that have more than one action and more than one clause. "She *went* to Africa, and she *will go* to India." Notice how the past tense is used consistently in the Student Model.

To learn more, see page 284.

STUDENT MODEL from **The Bridge**
page 70; lines 3–5

I never <u>slid</u> down the tallest slide, <u>climbed</u> a tree, or <u>went</u> off the high diving board.

Try It! Rewrite these sentences so that they use **verb tenses consistently**, and shift tenses only to make the sequence clear. Write the answers in your journal.

1. Lightning frightens me, but it's thunder that scared my dog!
2. Bowling sounds like a fun activity for the birthday party, but we went last week.

Apply It! Edit your draft for grammar, mechanics, and spelling. Check that you have used verb tenses correctly and consistently.

Use the rubric to evaluate your piece. If necessary, rethink, rewrite, or revise.

Rubric for Nonfiction Narration: Personal Narrative	Rating Scale					
	Not very				Very	
Ideas: How focused is your narrative on a single, important event?	1	2	3	4	5	6
Organization: How logical is your sequence of events?	1	2	3	4	5	6
Voice: How authentic and engaging is your voice?	1	2	3	4	5	6
Word Choice: How vivid is your word choice?	1	2	3	4	5	6
Sentence Fluency: How varied are your sentence beginnings?	1	2	3	4	5	6
Conventions: How correct is your usage of verb tenses?	1	2	3	4	5	6

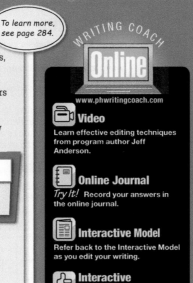

WRITING COACH
Online
www.phwritingcoach.com

Video
Learn effective editing techniques from program author Jeff Anderson.

Online Journal
Try It! Record your answers in the online journal.

Interactive Model
Refer back to the Interactive Model as you edit your writing.

Interactive Writing Coach™
Edit your draft. Check it against the rubric and then submit it for feedback.

Editing **83**

Personalized Support

 Interactive Writing Coach™

Below Level Students complete the editing process by submitting their writing for scoring and feedback.

On Level Students complete the editing process by submitting their writing for scoring and feedback.

Above Level Students finish editing their drafts. They have the option of submitting their final drafts for scoring and/or feedback.

 Teacher or Peer Feedback

To provide feedback to students as they edit their draft, ask or have student partners ask one another the following:

- Have you looked for mistakes that you tend to make?
- Have you read your piece aloud to yourself or to a partner? What kind of errors did you find?
- Can you show me something you changed through editing?
- What resources have you used to look for possible spelling errors?
- Read this sentence aloud. Does the grammar sound correct to you?
- Read this sentence aloud. Does the punctuation accurately convey your meaning?

Working with ELLs   **ELL** Sheltered Instruction: Social/Affective

Have students demonstrate listening comprehension of increasingly complex spoken English by collaborating with peers as they share information in cooperative learning interactions. Read the Student Model excerpt aloud as students follow along, defining any key words, and discuss it. Have students close their books. Then:

Beginning Read the paragraph aloud again slowly, using images or gestures to aid comprehension. Have partners discuss the paragraph and collaborate, sharing information to answer recall questions you provide.

Intermediate Read the paragraph aloud again, having students monitor their comprehension and seek clarification. Have groups share information about what they heard and collaborate in answering recall questions you provide.

Advanced Read the paragraph aloud again, and have pairs write a short retelling to share information with another pair.

Advanced High Have students complete the Advanced activity and then collaborate with a peer on a comparison of the two drafts.

The Digital · Print Path ▶

 **1** Using **Writing Coach Online™** or the student book, students complete the writing process by deciding the best way to publish their writing for their intended audience.

 **2** Students record their answers to Reflect on Your Writing in their online journals or notebooks.

Publishing

Wrap Up Your Presentation

Remind students who handwrote their work to use proper margins. For students who wrote their work on a computer, display some easy-to-read computer fonts.

Publish Your Piece

Explain to students that the final step in the writing process is to decide which form of publication will present their work most effectively. Then, tell students the chart shows how specific audiences can be reached using different media.

Have students whose narratives address similar audiences work in small groups to discuss appropriate ways to publish their work.

Reflect On Your Writing

Have students discuss the questions with a partner, including the Big Question, and record responses in their journal.

Extension Have students develop a research plan for learning more about their topic. Students should identify what they want to learn, which resources they will use, and how this information could be used to improve or embellish their personal narrative.

Manage Your Portfolio You may wish to have students include development materials such as graphic organizers and drafts.

MAKE YOUR WRITING COUNT

Introduce the movie storyboard activity by discussing the opening paragraphs with students. Make sure students understand that the project may be produced electronically or by hand. Then, guide students through each step in the action plan.

Publishing *Feature Assignment* **Publishing** *Feature Assignm*

Publishing

Share your experiences by publishing your personal narrative. First, get your narrative ready for presentation. Then, choose ways to **publish it for appropriate audiences**.

Wrap Up Your Presentation

Is your personal narrative handwritten or written on a computer? If your narrative is handwritten, you may need to make a new, clean copy. If so, be sure to **write legibly**. Also, be sure the title to your narrative grabs the reader's attention.

Publish Your Piece

Use the chart to identify ways to publish your personal narrative for appropriate audiences.

If your audience is...	...then publish it by...
Classmates and teachers at school	• Reading it aloud • Submitting it to the school newspaper or Web site
People in your town or around the world that you may never meet	• Posting it to a blog for people who share your interests • Submitting it to a print or online magazine that publishes first-person, true-life accounts

 Reflect on Your Writing

Now that you are done with your personal narrative, read it over and use your writing journal to answer the following questions. Use specific details to describe and explain your reflections. Increase the specificity of your details based on the type of information requested.

- Does your final product accurately express your emotions?
- Are any parts weak—dull, for example, or unrealistic? If so, what can you focus on in your next writing assignment?
- In what ways did your narrative work well? How can you apply these strengths in future writing assignments?

 The Big Question: Why Write? What did you decide to put in or leave out to be accurate and honest?

Manage Your Portfolio You may wish to include your published personal narrative in your writing portfolio. If so, consider what your narrative reveals about your writing and your growth as a writer.

84 Narrative Nonfiction

Resources You may wish to have students use these graphic organizers: Meeting Agenda, Meeting Notes, and Flow Chart/Series of Events. Distribute printed copies or have students log on to Writing Coach Online.

Use the 21ˢᵗ Century Skills Rubric to evaluate each group's process and final product on a scale of 1 to 3, indicating weak, moderate, or strong use of the skill. ▶

Listening and Speaking Monitor students as they use feedback to refine their presentations.

21st Century Learning	
Skills Rubric	Rating
Work Creatively With Others: Incorporate group input and feedback into the work.	1 2 3
Communicate Clearly: Use media, and know how to judge their effectiveness and impact.	1 2 3
Apply Technology Effectively: Use technology as a tool to research, organize, evaluate, and communicate information.	1 2 3
Interact Effectively With Others: Respond open-mindedly to different ideas and values.	1 2 3

3 Students use a variety of graphic organizers, either online or in print, to help them work together to create a multimedia group project.

4 Through *Writing Coach Online™* students link to resources on 21st Century Learning for help in creating a multimedia group project.

rative Make Your Writing Count *Personal Narrative* Make Your Writing Count

MAKE YOUR WRITING COUNT

Create a Storyboard for a Personal Narrative

Personal narratives can take many forms. True-life stories are often compelling enough to transfer to the movie screen. Plan a movie version of a personal narrative written by one of your peers.

Create a **storyboard**, which is a drafting tool used by filmmakers as they plan a movie. A storyboard is a series of sketches containing the elements of each scene to be filmed. Your storyboard should have a clear focus and details that communicate the importance of the event.

Your storyboard can be created with pen and ink. Present each frame on a large poster or scan each frame into presentation software.

Here's your action plan.

1. Choose group roles, such as illustrator, dialogue writer, and a producer who puts the final storyboard together.

2. Working with your group to evaluate your personal narratives, choose one that you would like to make into a movie. Consider the narrative's action, characters, dialogue, and ending.

3. Create the storyboard to tell the story visually, scene by scene.

   - Find example storyboards online.
   - Make a separate frame for each scene. Include the characters, setting, and action, as well as text that describes the action and the dialogue.
   - Place the frames in the correct sequence.

4. Present the storyboard to the class, either as a series of posters or as a set of slides in a presentation software application.

Listening and Speaking Work as a team to present the storyboard in a dynamic way. For example, act out dialogue and include music and sound effects for each scene. Explain the creative process and the solid reasoning behind each scene. Afterward, ask the audience for feedback about improving the storyboard's flow.

WRITING COACH
Online
www.phwritingcoach.com

Online Journal
Reflect on Your Writing Record your answers and ideas in the online journal.

Resource
Link to resources on 21st Century Learning for help in creating a group project.

All About Me

Make Your Writing Count 85

Personalized Support

FEEDBACK Teacher or Peer Feedback

To provide feedback to students on their published writing, ask or have student partners ask one another the following:

- How did you go about writing this piece? What was your process?

- What did you learn from the writing model that you used in this piece?

- What surprised you the most as you wrote this piece?

- Did you try anything new as you worked on this piece?

- What did you learn from this piece of writing that you would like to remember and reuse?

- What do you think you do best as a writer right now?

Differentiated Instruction

RTI Strategy for Special Needs Students
For students who are going to publish their narrative by reading it aloud, have them practice reading it aloud a few times with a partner. Encourage them to read their narrative several times until they can read it smoothly. Have partners give each other feedback on their reading.

PRE-AP Enrichment for Above-Level Students For students who are going to publish their narrative by submitting it to a print or online magazine, have them work with a partner to research appropriate magazines and the requirements for submission. Have them write out the submission requirements and make any necessary adjustments to their narrative, for example to length. Be sure they get permission from their parents or guardian before submitting their narrative.

The Digital • Print Path ▶

WRITING COACH Online | STUDENT BOOK

1  WRITING COACH Online | STUDENT BOOK ▶

Students use Writing Coach Online™ or their student books to analyze and discuss the Writing for Media topic.

 **Writing for Media: Biographical Narrative**

Biographical Narrative

Discuss the opening paragraph with students. Be sure students understand the difference between a biographical narrative and a personal narrative.

Try It! Guide students to understand the structure and content of the biographical narrative.

Say: The first *Try It!* question asks about the subject of the biographical narrative. The first sentence mentions the writer's uncle Johnny, so **I know** that the biographical narrative will be about Johnny.

Ask: How does the writer feel about his Uncle Johnny? (He likes and admires him.) How do you know? (At the end he says Uncle Johnny "is a big hero to me.")

Have students discuss the remaining questions in small groups and record individual responses in their journals.

Extension Have students bring in other examples of biographical narratives. Lead a media discussion about the examples, using the *Try It!* questions as a guide.

Create a Biographical Narrative

Tell students that they will create a biographical narrative using the five-step writing process. Then, preview the writing process instructions on page 87.

> **Resources** You may wish to have students use the Timeline graphic organizer. Distribute printed copies or have students log on to Writing Coach Online.

For each step in the writing process, have partners read aloud and discuss the list of tasks. Then, have them work individually. Once both partners have completed the tasks, have them evaluate each other's work before moving to the next step.

Your Turn ▶ **Writing for Media: Biographical Narrative**

Writing for Media   Writing for Media   Writing for Media   Wri

Biographical Narrative

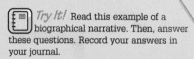 21st Century Learning

A **biographical narrative** tells a story about the life of someone else. Many biographical narratives are about famous or well-known people. A firsthand biographical narrative, on the other hand, tells about someone the writer knows—a relative, community member, or friend. Sometimes, blogs include biographical narratives, as well as personal narratives.

Biographical narratives often use research from many sources. A firsthand biographical narrative might include research, too, but will also include details and insights from the writer's own experience of the person.

> *Try It!* Read this example of a biographical narrative. Then, answer these questions. Record your answers in your journal.
>
> 1. Who is the **subject** of the biographical narrative? How do you think the writer feels about the subject?
> 2. To what **audiences** would this narrative probably appeal?
> 3. Identify the **details** the writer includes about the subject. What picture do these details give you of the subject?
> 4. What makes this a narrative? In other words, what **story elements**, such as plot and character development, does it include? How do these elements make you feel about the subject?

> **Extension** Find another example of a biographical narrative, and compare it with this one.

86   Narrative Nonfiction

Uncle Johnny's Amazing Climb

My uncle Johnny is what people in my family call "a character." He is very short and wiry, but he has a big personality. He also has fewer toes than anybody I know! That's because Uncle Johnny lost three of his toes to frostbite when he climbed Denali, the highest mountain peak in North America.

About five years ago, Uncle Johnny went on a mountain-climbing expedition in Alaska to climb Denali. It was by no means his first climbing expedition. He had already climbed just about every peak in the United States. He always says, "If it's there, I'll climb it!"

Uncle Johnny and the expedition did make it to the top of Denali, but on the way down, something went wrong. A storm blew up while they were still at a high altitude. They had to hunker down in their sleeping bags in the shelter of a rock and wait until the blizzard cleared. While they waited, they got very, very cold. They got so cold that my uncle Johnny's toes got frostbitten.

Today, my uncle laughs when he talks about it. He says that the experience cured him of a terrible case of athlete's foot. And he still climbs mountains. In fact, he is part of a search-and-rescue team that finds people who get lost in the mountains. He may be physically small, but my uncle Johnny is a big hero to me and to all the people he rescues every year.

Use the 21st Century Skills Rubric to evaluate each student's process and final product on a scale of 1 to 3, indicating weak, moderate, or strong use of the skill. ▶

Partner Talk

Remind students to point out elements of the narrative that work well in addition to elements that need improvement.

21st Century Learning

Skills Rubric	Rating
Communicate Clearly: Articulate thoughts and ideas using oral, written, and nonverbal communication skills.	1 2 3
Create Media Products: Understand and utilize the most appropriate media creation tools, characteristics, and conventions.	1 2 3
Be Flexible: Incorporate feedback effectively.	1 2 3
Manage Goals and Time: Utilize time and manage workload effectively.	1 2 3

2 Writing Journal ▶

Students learn about the characteristics of a biographical narrative by answering questions about the model. Students record their answers to the *Try It!* questions in their online journals or notebooks.

3 STUDENT BOOK ▶

Students follow the five-step writing process to write their own biographical narrative. Students may select online or printed graphic organizers to help them plan and develop their writing.

dia *Writing for Media* *Writing for Media* *Writing for Media* **Writing for Media**

 ## Create a Biographical Narrative

Follow these steps to create your own biographical narrative. To plan your biographical narrative, review the graphic organizers on pages R24–R27 and choose one that suits your needs.

Prewriting

- Choose a subject. Take a few minutes to note the names of people you know who are interesting or have qualities you admire.
- Review your list and choose the person you find most interesting or whom you think your audience would find most interesting.
- Decide what aspect of the person's life you would like to focus on and write an outline for your narrative. Jot down key events, traits, and details.

Drafting

- As you begin to draft, write a sentence that states your main idea about your subject—the focus of your essay.
- Look at the outline you made and write your narrative, organizing events and details in a logical order, such as chronological, or time order.
- Use specific details to write your ideas and feelings.

Revising and Editing

- Make sure you have identified the subject of your biography and clearly expressed your thoughts about the subject.
- Check to see if your ideas are organized in a way that makes sense so that readers can follow your narrative.
- Check that spelling, grammar, and mechanics are correct.

Publishing

- Add photographs or illustrations to your biographical narrative and create a booklet to share with others who are interested in your subject or with the subject him- or herself.
- You might also want to publish your biographical narrative as a multimedia presentation that includes text, video, and pictures of your subject. Your presentation would make a wonderful tribute to your subject.

WRITING COACH

Online

www.phwritingcoach.com

Online Journal
Try It! Record your answers in the online journal.

Interactive Graphic Organizers
Choose from a variety of graphic organizers to plan and develop your project.

Partner Talk

Before you start drafting, describe and explain the details of your biographical narrative to a partner and ask for feedback. What does your partner want to know more about?

Personalized Support

 **FEEDBACK** ## Teacher or Peer Feedback

To provide feedback to students as they write for media, ask or have student partners ask one another the following:

- What are the main characteristics of this form of writing?
- Have you included most or all of these characteristics in your piece of writing?
- What is your purpose for writing this piece?
- Who is your audience?
- How did you organize your ideas in this piece of writing?
- How did you go about revising the piece? Editing it?
- How do you plan on publishing your piece?
- What other publishing options also might work?

Working with ELLs ELL Sheltered Instruction: Cognitive

Orally present the sample biographical narrative on page 86 and help students demonstrate an understanding of the general meaning, main points, and important details of spoken language on topics ranging from familiar to unfamiliar. Discuss a familiar topic, camping, and use the discussion to aid students' comprehension of the unfamiliar topic of mountain climbing. Then:

Beginning Reread the first paragraph aloud, clarifying meaning. Ask questions to elicit the general meaning, main points, and important details of the paragraph. Have students draw to demonstrate understanding.

Intermediate Provide groups with a **Spider-Web Diagram**. Have them record the general meaning of the narrative in the center circle and add main points and important details in the outer circles. Have groups discuss their webs.

Advanced Provide pairs with a **Spider-Web Diagram** and have them record the general meaning, main points, and important details of the narrative.

Advanced High Have students complete the Advanced activity independently. Have partners describe a biography they enjoyed.

The Digital · Print Path ▶

1 Before they write, students use the ABCDs of On-Demand Writing to analyze and plan how to respond to each prompt. They can use either their online journals or notebooks to take notes.

2 Students submit their writing paragraph by paragraph or as a complete draft to t Interactive Writing Coach™ for feedback share their writing with their teacher.

Writing for Assessment

Read aloud or have a student read aloud the introductory text. Then, tell students that they will learn and practice a technique for writing in response to a test prompt.

Try It! Read the Narrative Nonfiction Prompt aloud and then have volunteers read aloud the Format and Academic Vocabulary boxes. Tell students that they will use the ABCD method to respond to the prompt.

The ABCDs of On-Demand Writing

Have students identify the words associated with the ABCD method. (attack, brainstorm, choose, detect) Then, guide students through their use.

Think Aloud I'll **attack the prompt** by circling the verbs *write* and *describe*. These verbs remind me that I need to write a personal narrative in which I describe the events of a special day and why the day was so special. I can rewrite the prompt to state that clearly: "Write a personal narrative that explains the order of events on an important day and describes why the day was special."

Work with students to brainstorm for an appropriate graphic organizer for a personal narrative, such as a timeline.

Have students write their drafts individually and then work with a partner to detect errors.

More Prompts for Practice

Apply It! **Test Prep** Have students apply the ABCD method to the two practice prompts.

Prompt 1 Have partners attack the prompt and brainstorm for possible answers. Then, have each pair swap their information with another group to evaluate whether the teams

---

ssment **Writing for Assessment** *Writing for Assessment* *Writing for Assessment* *Wr:*

Writing for Assessment

Many standardized tests include a prompt that asks you to write an essay about a personal experience. Respond using the characteristics of a personal narrative. (See page 66.)

Try It! Read the **narrative nonfiction** prompt and the information on format and academic vocabulary. Use the ABCDs of On-Demand Writing to help you plan and write your essay.

Format
The prompt directs you to write a *personal narrative*. A beginning sets the scene; a middle narrates a sequence of events; and an end tells why the events were important.

Narrative Nonfiction Prompt
We all have special days we will never forget. Write a personal narrative about a day you shared with a favorite family member or friend. Describe the sequence of events and why the day was so special.

Academic Vocabulary
Remember to include a *sequence of events*, a series of related events told in chronological order, or the order in which they happened in time. Your personal narrative should include a sequence of events.

The ABCDs of On-Demand Writing

Use the following ABCDs to help you respond to the prompt.

Before you write your draft:

Attack the prompt [1 MINUTE]

- Circle or highlight important verbs in the prompt. Draw a line from the verb to what it refers to.
- Rewrite the prompt in your own words.

Brainstorm possible answers [4 MINUTES]

- Create a graphic organizer to generate ideas.
- Use one for each part of the prompt if necessary.

Choose the order of your response [1 MINUTE]

- Think about the best way to organize your ideas.
- Number your ideas in the order you will write about them. Cross out ideas you will not be using.

After you write your draft:

Detect errors before turning in the draft [1 MINUTE]

- Carefully reread your writing.
- Make sure that your response makes sense and is complete.
- Look for spelling, punctuation, and grammar errors.

88 **Narrative Nonfiction**

---

have developed personal narratives that have a clearly defined focus.

Prompt 2 Have students work individually to attack the prompt and brainstorm for possible answers. Then, have students work in small groups to evaluate their work before writing their drafts.

More Strategies for Writing for Assessment

Review the strategies with students. Then, have students brainstorm for their own strategies for responding to a prompt. Record student responses on the board and discuss which of these strategies the class should adopt for its next prompt-based writing assignment.

3 Students receive personalized feedback from the **Interactive Writing Coach™**, or feedback from their teacher.

 **More Prompts for Practice**

Apply It! Respond to Prompts 1 and 2 by writing **personal narratives** that each have a **clearly defined focus** and that **communicate the importance of or reason for actions and/or consequences.** As you write, be sure to:

- Identify an appropriate audience for your intended purpose
- Organize the sequence of events in chronological order
- Fully develop the plot, setting, and characters
- Include narrative devices, such as suspense and dialogue
- Include sensory details

> **Prompt 1** Write a personal narrative about a family celebration. It could be a special holiday, family dinner, or trip to the park. Tell what happened and why this event was meaningful or important.

> **Prompt 2** What day stands out as the best day in your life so far? Why? Write a personal narrative about that day. Tell what happened and what made it so great. Include sensory details and your thoughts about the day.

More Strategies for Writing for Assessment

- Consider several possible topics and quickly list details that you might use in your response. Then, choose the topic for which you have the strongest ideas.
- If you do not understand any words in the prompt, use context clues to help you determine the meaning.
- Be sure to follow the ABCDs of writing to a prompt. Planning is an important part of writing. Don't just start writing right away.
- Make sure to reread your piece after you have completed it. This will give you time to find and correct errors. If you are in a timed situation, be sure to leave enough time for this step.

WRITING COACH
Online
www.phwritingcoach.com

 Interactive Writing Coach™

Plan your response to the prompt. If you are using the prompt for practice, write one paragraph at a time or your entire draft and then submit it for feedback. If you are using the prompt as a timed test, write your entire draft and then submit it for feedback.

Remember **ABCD**

A ttack the prompt
B rainstorm possible answers
C hoose the order of your response
D etect errors before turning in the draft

Writing for Assessment 89

Personalized Support

 Assessment/Monitor Progress

For timed writing practice, assign students a prompt to be completed in a timed setting. For Prompts 1 and 2, have students submit their writing to **Interactive Writing Coach™** to get immediate feedback.

For a formal writing assessment, assign the Assessment writing prompt for this chapter in **Writing Coach Online™**. Then, have students submit their writing to **Interactive Writing Coach™** to be assessed. Use the results to assess student progress and skill levels. **Interactive Writing Coach™** will update student levels to ensure that students get the appropriate support.

 Teacher Feedback

To create an assessment environment, have students use a prompt in a timed setting. Grade papers using the appropriate rubric and use the results to assess student progress and skill levels. In the next writing assignment, ensure that students get the appropriate level of support.

If you conference with students, use these questions to guide your discussion:

- What form of writing did the prompt call for? Does your response include most or all of the characteristics of that form?
- How did you organize your ideas?
- Did you make good use of your time as you planned and wrote your response?
- What did you learn that you can use when responding to a prompt during a timed test?

Differentiated Instruction

RTI Strategy for Below-Level Students
Use the Evaluate column in the chart on page 80 and the Student Model on pages 70–71 to review the characteristics of a personal narrative with students. Ask students to name the parts that are the most difficult for them. Have students give more attention to those parts during peer review.

Strategy for Spanish Speakers
Students whose home language is Spanish may encounter additional difficulties in understanding words in a writing prompt. Encourage students to look for cognates in the prompt in addition to using context clues to help them determine the meaning. Point out cognates in Prompt 1 on page 89 such as *personal, celebration,* and *event* and have students provide Spanish equivalents.

CHAPTER 6 LESSON PLANNER
Fiction Narration

Interactive Writing Coach™

Interactive Graphic Organizers

Interactive Models

Online Journal

Resources

Video

Use the Online Lesson Planner at www.phwritingcoach.com to customize your instructional plan for an integrated Language Arts curriculum.

DAY 1

CHAPTER OPENER/ GENRE INTRODUCTION
- What's the Story?
- What's Ahead
- Connect to the Big Questions
- **Feature Assignment: Short Story: Realistic Short Story**
- Other Forms of Fiction
- Word Bank

ONLINE

DAY 2

MENTOR TEXT/ STUDENT MODEL
- **Mentor Text: Realistic Short Story**
- Learn From Experience
- **Student Model: Realistic Short Story**
- Reader's Eye and Writer's Eye

ONLINE

DAY 3

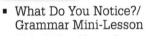 **Prewriting**
- Choose From the Topic Bank
- Choose Your Own Topic
- Narrow Your Topic
- Consider Your Audience and Purpose

ONLINE

DAY 6

 Revising
- Keep Revision on Your RADaR
- Look at the Big Picture
- Focus on Craft
- Fine-Tune Your Draft

ONLINE

DAY 7
For additional grammar support, see Section 19.1, p. 402.

 **Editing**
- What Do You Notice?/ Grammar Mini-Lesson
- **Rubric for Short Story: Realistic Short Story**

Publishing
- Publish Your Piece
- Reflect on Your Writing

ONLINE

DAY 8

 **21st Century Learning**

MAKE YOUR WRITING COUNT
- **Give a Dramatic Reading of a Realistic Story**
- Here's Your Action Plan
- Listening and Speaking

ONLINE

Alternate Pacing Suggestions

- **Block Scheduling** Each day on the Lesson Planner represents a 40–50 minute block. Teachers using block scheduling may combine days to revise pacing to meet their classroom needs.

- **Accelerated Lesson Planning** Combine instructional days by aiding students in choosing a topic and then focusing on two core stages of the writing process, outlining for success (Day 5) and RADaR revision (Day 6).

- **Integrated Language Arts Curriculum** For targeted instruction that covers the essential components of the lesson use either a 3- or a 5-day plan.

3 day plan
DAY 1: Introduction to the Genre, Mentor Text, Student Model
DAY 2: Prewriting/Drafting
DAY 3: Revising/Editing/ Publishing

5 day plan
Use 3-day plan, and add:
DAY 4: Make Your Writing Count
DAY 5: Writing for Assessment

Links to Prentice Hall *LITERATURE*

Featured Author: Jean Craighead George
- What Is a Short Story?, p. 178
- "The Wounded Wolf" (short story), p. 183
- On Revising a Story (Writing Workshop), p. 357
- *From the Author's Desk* Videos: Jean Craighead George

Additional Mentor Text:
- "Zlateh the Goat" (short story), Isaac Bashevis Singer, p. 222

Differentiated Instruction

Differentiated Instruction Boxes in this Teacher's Edition address these student populations:

- Below-Level Students
- Above-Level Students
- Gifted and Talented Students
- Special Needs Students
- English Language Learners
- Spanish Speaking Students

In addition, for further enrichment, see the **Extension** features.

LESSON OBJECTIVES

- To learn the forms and defining characteristics of fictional narratives.
- To learn the elements of a successful realistic short story, the chapter Feature Assignment.
- To read a Mentor Text in the genre, analyzing its use of the elements of an effective fictional narrative.
- To read a Student Model of a realistic short story, analyzing it from the perspective of a reader and from the perspective of a writer.
- To apply prewriting strategies in developing a realistic short story, including strategies for choosing and narrowing a topic, planning writing, and gathering details, as well as tips for considering audience and purpose.
- To apply drafting strategies in developing a realistic short story.
- To apply RADaR revision strategies to a draft realistic short story.
- To learn about the Focus on Craft topic, improving transitions, and apply what is learned to a draft realistic short story.
- To edit the draft, zooming in on prepositional phrases and focusing on using prepositional phrases as transitions.
- To complete the Make Your Writing Count assignment, developing and presenting a dramatic reading of a realistic short story.
- To complete the Writing for Media assignment, developing an audio script.
- To practice writing for assessment.

DAY 4

Prewriting

- Plan Your Piece
- Gather Details

ONLINE

DAY 5

Drafting

- Outline for Success
- Start Your Draft

ONLINE

DAY 9

WRITING FOR MEDIA

- **Audio Script**
- Create an Audio Script

ONLINE

DAY 10

WRITING FOR ASSESSMENT

- Short Story Prompt
- The ABCDs of On-Demand Writing
- More Prompts for Practice Spiral Review: Narrative

ONLINE

Personalized Assessment

FEEDBACK

Teacher Conferencing

	Ongoing Assessment	Formal Assessment of Feature Assignment	Progress Monitoring at End-of-Chapter
	Use rubrics in the Student Edition as a revision tool. Conference with students to review their work and provide personalized support.	Use rubrics in the Student Edition to score students' Feature Assignment papers.	Review each student's work to plan targeted resources for the next writing assignment.

The Digital · Print Path ▶

1 Using *Writing Coach Online*™ or the student book, students discuss the photograph in the chapter opener as it relates to the writing genre.

2 Students record their ideas and responses in their online journals or notebooks. They may also record and save their responses on pop-up sticky notes in *Writing Coach Online*™.

Chapter Objectives

1. Write a realistic short story by planning, drafting, revising, editing, and publishing individual work.

2. Produce a dramatic reading of a realistic story.

3. Use the five-step writing process to write an audio script.

4. Write a realistic short story and a personal narrative in response to a prompt.

FICTION NARRATION

What's the Story?

Activate Prior Knowledge Tell students that the purpose of fiction is to entertain. Explain to students that they will use what they know about baseball to analyze the photo on page 90. Then, guide the students in analyzing the photo.

 Think Aloud To analyze something means to study the relationships among its parts. Sometimes you need to analyze a story to understand literary elements, such as plot. For example, in the photo **I see** a baseball player sliding in a cloud of dust. The umpire has a tense look on his face as he signals "safe." I can tell by this interaction that a suspenseful part of the plot has just been resolved.

Work with students to brainstorm for other literary elements based on their analysis of the photo. Record students' responses on the board.

Try It! **Have students** work individually to develop responses to the questions. Then, have them tell a story based on their responses, using details from the photograph and their own imaginations.

Possible responses: Details: a baseball field, home plate; Conflict: Is the runner safe as he slides into home plate? The catcher has not tagged him in time, and the umpire calls the play "safe." Characters: An umpire, a determined runner, and a catcher.

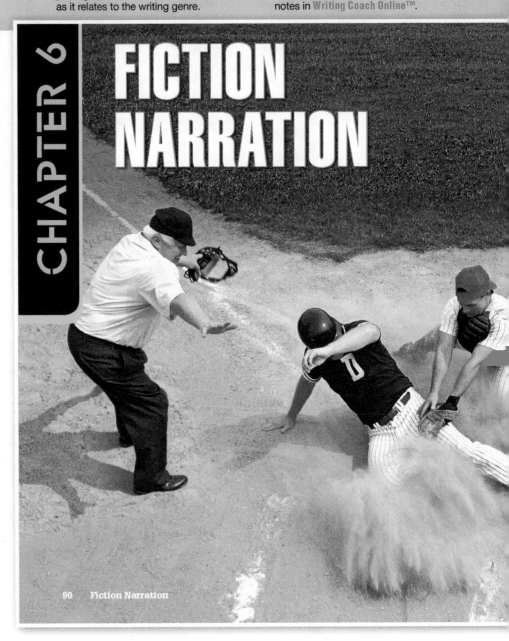

CHAPTER 6

FICTION NARRATION

90   Fiction Narration

Connect to the Big Questions

Have students use their experience to discuss the Big Questions. Explain that they will revisit **Why write?** at the end of this chapter. Tell students to consider these points during their discussion:

1. Think of how a particularly challenging game makes you feel. Simple games can help us push beyond our perceived limits.

2. Why do you think many people have a stronger emotional connection to fiction than nonfiction?

What's Ahead

Have students preview the Mentor Text and Student Model on pages 94–99. Tell students that they will write their own realistic short story using the five-step writing process: prewriting, drafting, revising, editing, and publishing.

What's the Story?

What is happening in the baseball game? What story can you tell about what happened shortly before this photograph was taken?

Many stories have realistic settings. Believable details about setting, such as the weather or specifics about the baseball field, help get the reader interested and add to the story. Conflict is also important. It is the central problem of the story.

Try It! Think about how each of the people in the photograph reacted in the moments before the photograph was taken. Write notes about each of their reactions.

Consider these questions as you participate in an extended discussion with a partner. Take turns expressing your ideas and feelings.

- What details can you tell about the setting of the game?
- What is the conflict during this part of the game?
- Who are the characters here and what are they like?

Review your notes. Use your notes to tell a story about how each player reacted to the situation. Be sure to use details to make your story believable.

What's Ahead

In this chapter, you will review two strong examples of a short story: a Mentor Text and a Student Model. Then, using the examples as guidance, you will write a short story of your own.

WRITING COACH
Online
www.phwritingcoach.com

Online Journal
Try It! Record your answers and ideas in the online journal.

You can also record and save your answers and ideas on pop-up sticky notes in the eText.

Connect to the Big Questions

Discuss these questions with your partner:

1 **What do you think?** What can we learn from playing games?

2 **Why write?** What can fiction do better than nonfiction?

91

Personalized Support

FEEDBACK
Teacher or Peer Feedback

To encourage students in their discussion of the photograph as it relates to the writing genre, ask the following questions:

- What is the first thing you think of when you look at this photo?
- How does it relate to your life?
- How does it relate to things you've learned in other subjects?
- What questions come to mind when you look at this photograph?
- How does your response to the photograph compare to those of your classmates?

Working with ELLs **ELL** Sheltered Instruction: Cognitive

Help students learn new expressions heard during classroom instruction and interactions. Discuss the image on page 90 and tell an anecdote using the following idiomatic expressions related to sports: *drop the ball, keep your eye on the ball, make a homerun.* Then:

Beginning Explain the literal and figurative meaning of the expressions, using examples. Have students make **Puzzle Cards**, writing each expression on one half of a card, an illustration of it on the other, and cutting the card in two. Have them hold up the correct image when you say each expression.

Intermediate Define each new idiomatic expression and use each in a new sentence. Have groups demonstrate understanding by using each expression in their own sentences.

Advanced Have students find the definition of each new expression in a dictionary or online and use them in a partner discussion.

Advanced High Have students use context clues to infer the meaning of each new idiomatic expression. Confirm understanding by having them use each expression in a partner discussion.

The Digital · Print Path ▶

1

Students learn vocabulary from the Word Bank and listen to English and Spanish pronunciations in the **Writing Coach Online™** glossary.

2

Students record answers to questions about forms of writing in their online journals or notebooks.

SHORT STORY

To introduce this chapter's writing form, discuss the opening paragraphs with students. Make sure students understand that a short story is a type of fiction. Explain that good writers use a step-by-step process to develop their work. Then, have students preview the rubric on page 111.

Short Story: Realistic Short Story

Ask volunteers to read aloud the feature assignment characteristics. Tell students that they will identify these characteristics in a Mentor Text and a Student Model. Then, they will use the characteristics to guide the writing of their own realistic short story.

Other Forms of Fiction

Guide students to understand how the forms of fiction are alike and different.

Say: I notice that there are several types of fiction and that most have unique types of characters. For example, historical fiction often includes famous people from history, while myths and legends may include supernatural characters.

Ask: What are some other differences among the types of fiction? (setting, plot, degree of fantasy versus realism)

Have students work in small groups to discuss examples of each type of fiction they have read.

Try It! Remind students that the audience is the people who will read their writing. The purpose is the author's reason for writing. Have students record their responses in their journal.

Possible responses: historical fiction, because it is set in a real historical time and place; science fiction, because it may explore space travel; realistic fiction, because it involves characters and events from everyday life

---

SHORT STORY

A short story is a brief work of fiction that presents characters in a conflict that is first developed and then resolved. In this chapter, you will explore a special type of short story, realistic fiction. Like other kinds of fiction, realistic fiction is untrue. However, the characters, setting, and conflict should all feel true to life. Realistic fiction closely resembles real life and often takes place in the present.

You will develop a realistic short story by taking it through each of the steps of the writing process: prewriting, drafting, revising, editing, and publishing. You will also have an opportunity to create an audio script. To preview the criteria for how your realistic short story will be evaluated, see the rubric on page 111.

FEATURE ASSIGNMENT

Short Story: Realistic Short Story

An effective short story has these characteristics:

- **Characters** who are well-developed and interesting. Well-developed characters have realistic thoughts and actions.

- A believable **setting**, or the time and place in which a story takes place, created using **sensory details**. Sensory details use the five senses to help readers experience the story.

- A clearly defined **focus**, or main idea, and **plot**, or events in the story centered on a **conflict**, or problem

- A definite **point of view**, or perspective from which the story is told. Stories usually use the first-person or third-person point of view.

- **Dialogue** that develops the story and moves the action along

- **Effective sentence structure** and correct spelling, grammar, and usage

A realistic short story also includes:

- Characters, setting, and dialogue that seem real and a plot that could actually happen

- A contemporary **setting** that most readers will recognize

92 Short Story

Word Bank

To assist English Language Learners and struggling readers, echo read each word or have students log on to Writing Coach Online to listen to the pronunciations. Then, have partners take turns using each word in a sentence. Ask volunteers to share one of their sentences with the class.

Teacher Tip

Help students extend their understanding by asking volunteers to orally summarize a work of one type of fiction without telling what form they are summarizing. Then, ask the class to identify the type of fiction summarized and its traits.

Other Forms of Fiction

In addition to realistic short stories, there are other forms of fiction, including:

Fantasy stories stretch the imagination and take readers to unreal worlds. Animals may talk, people may fly, or characters may have superhuman powers.

Historical fiction tells about imaginary people living in real places and times in history. Usually, the main characters are fictional people who know and interact with famous people in history and participate in important historical events.

Mystery stories focus on unexplained or strange events that one of the characters tries to solve. These stories are often full of suspense and surprises.

Myths and legends are traditional stories that different cultures have told to explain natural events, human nature, or the origins of things. They often include gods and goddesses from ancient times and heroes who do superhuman things.

Science fiction stories focus on real or imagined developments in science and technology and their effects on the way people think and live. Space travel, robots, and life in the future are popular topics for science fiction.

Try It! For each audience and purpose described, choose a form, such as historical fiction, science fiction, or fantasy, that is appropriate for conveying your intended meaning to the audience. Explain your choices.

- To tell your social studies classmates the events of a significant historical event
- To show your science classmates what life on the moon is like
- To tell how a teenager might handle moving to a new community

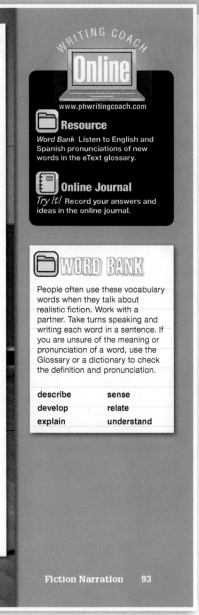

WRITING COACH Online
www.phwritingcoach.com

Resource
Word Bank Listen to English and Spanish pronunciations of new words in the eText glossary.

Online Journal
Try It! Record your answers and ideas in the online journal.

WORD BANK

People often use these vocabulary words when they talk about realistic fiction. Work with a partner. Take turns speaking and writing each word in a sentence. If you are unsure of the meaning or pronunciation of a word, use the Glossary or a dictionary to check the definition and pronunciation.

describe	sense
develop	relate
explain	understand

Fiction Narration   93

Personalized Support

 FEEDBACK Teacher or Peer Feedback

To help students understand the characteristics of the writing form, ask or have student partners ask one another the following questions:

- What are the main characteristics of a short story?
- What makes this form of writing different from other forms?
- Who are the likely readers or audiences for this form of writing?
- What kind of organization could be used for this form of writing?
- What kind of voice would be most effective for this form of writing?

Working with ELLs   **ELL** Sheltered Instruction: Cognitive

To help students learn and use basic routine language, such as *understand*, to expand and internalize initial English vocabulary, have them use and reuse the Word Bank vocabulary in a speaking activity.

Beginning Write *describe* on the board. Pick up a pencil and say, "I will describe this pencil. It is long and yellow." Have students turn to a partner, choose an item, and orally complete this sentence: "Please describe this _____." Give students sentences they can repeat orally to use and reuse the other vocabulary words in the Word Bank.

Intermediate Help students define each word. Have them repeat a sentence that uses each word. Have them reuse the vocabulary words in their own spoken sentences.

Advanced Have students find definitions of the Word Bank words in a dictionary and then use and reuse each word in a question-and-answer session with a partner.

Advanced High Have partners use the words to discuss a story they have read recently. Have students reuse the vocabulary words by asking other pairs questions about the stories they discussed.

The Digital · Print Path ▶

1

Using Writing Coach Online™ or the student book, students read and listen to an audio recording of the Mentor Text. As they complete their writing assignments, they can refer back to the Mentor Text for support whenever they need it.

MENTOR TEXT

About the Selection The selection is a realistic short story about one family's relationship to a piece of land and the mother's plan to keep it. The narrator describes her late grandfather's farm and the positive effect it has on her brother. A loophole in an agreement between the mother and the new landowner allows the family to live at the farm for many years to come.

Learn From Experience

After students have read the text, point out that the numbered notes refer to the characteristics of a realistic short story introduced on page 92.

Try It! Guide students to understand how the genre characteristics shape the text.

Say: The first *Try It!* question asks you to summarize what happened to the family before the story began and answer why the mother is busy tidying up the farm. **I read** in the first three lines that the narrator's grandfather had died and her mother was left in charge of selling his property. She is tidying the farm to sell it.

Ask: What other event happened before the story began? (The mother told a doctor he could buy the farm.)

Have students reply to the *Try It!* questions in their journals. If students have difficulty responding to a particular question, model a response, as with Question 1.

Check the accuracy and completeness of student responses.

1. The narrator's grandfather has died. Her mother is busy tidying the farm because she has been left with the responsibility of selling it.

2. The story is told in the first-person point of view. I know because the narrator uses *I*, *we*, and *my*.

3. Responses will vary. The brother was lazy or uninterested in life before coming to the farm. Now he is happy and engaged.

4. The mother agrees to give over the land after she is allowed to plant and harvest one crop. The agreement suggests that people in this area are generous and honorable.

---

istic Short Story   Mentor Text   Realistic Short Story   Mentor Te

MENTOR TEXT   Realistic Short Story

Learn From Experience

 Read the realistic short story on pages 94–97. As you read, take notes to develop your understanding of basic sight and English vocabulary. Then, read the numbered notes in the margins to learn about how the author presented her ideas.

Answer the *Try It!* questions online or in your notebook.

---

❶ This **clearly defined focus** tells what has happened and how it affects the characters. The focus sparks interest in reading more and makes it easier to understand the story.

Try It! Sum up what happened before the story began. Why is the mother busy tidying up the farm?

❷ Throughout the story, the narrator, or voice telling the story, is the daughter of a family living on a farm. The narrator tells what happens from her **point of view.**

Try It! Is the story told in the first-person point of view or the third-person point of view? How can you tell?

Extension Find another example of a realistic short story, and compare it with this one. Analyze what the selections tell you about the cultural contexts in which they were written.

94   Short Story

From A Gentleman's Agreement

by Elizabeth Jolley

❶ Grandpa was an old man and though his death was expected it was unexpected really and it was a shock to Mother to find she suddenly had eighty-seven acres to sell. And there was the house too. She had a terrible lot
5 to do as she decided to sell the property herself and, at the same time, she did not want to let down the people at South Heights. There was a man interested to buy the land, Mother had kept him up her sleeve for years, ever since he had stopped once by the bottom paddock to ask if it was for
10 sale. At the time Mother would have given her right arm to be able to sell it and she promised he should have first refusal if it ever came on the market.

We all three, Mother and myself and my brother, went out at the weekend to tidy things up. We lost my brother
15 and then we suddenly saw him running and running and shouting, his voice lifting up in the wind as he raced up the slope of the valley.

"I do believe he's laughing! He's happy!" Mother just stared at him and she looked so happy too.
20 ❷ I don't think I ever saw the country look so lovely before.

The tenant was standing by the shed. The big tractor had crawled to the doorway like a sick animal and had stopped there, but in no time my brother had it going.

Extension Lead a discussion in which students compare and contrast how their additional realistic short stories use the genre characteristics. Use the *Try It!* questions as a guide.

Teacher Tip

Help students extend their understanding by having students orally summarize the Mentor Text to partners. Remind them to identify the literary elements of a realistic short story in their summaries.

2 Students record their answers to questions about the Mentor Text in their online journals or notebooks.

ic Short Story **Mentor Text** *Realistic Short Story* **Mentor Text**

25 ❸ It seemed there was nothing my brother couldn't do. Suddenly after doing nothing in his life he was driving the tractor and making fire breaks, he started to paint the sheds and he told Mother what fencing posts and wire to order. All these things had to be done before the sale could go
30 through. We all had a wonderful time in the country. I kept wishing we could live in the house, all at once it seemed lovely there at the top of the sunlit meadow. But I knew that however many acres you have they aren't any use unless you have money too. I think we were all thinking this but
35 no one said· anything though Mother kept looking at my brother and the change in him.

There was no problem about the price of the land, this man, he was a doctor, really wanted it and Mother really needed the money.

40 "You might as well come with me," Mother said to me on the day of the sale. "You can learn how business is done." So we sat in this lawyer's comfortable room and he read out from various papers and the doctor signed things and Mother signed. Suddenly she said to them, "You know my
45 father really loved his farm but he only managed to have it late in life and then he was never able to live there because of his illness." The two men looked at her.

❹ "I'm sure you will understand," she said to the doctor, "with your great love of the land, my father's love for his
50 valley. I feel if I could live there just to plant one crop and stay while it matures, my father would rest easier in his grave."

"Well I don't see why not." The doctor was really a kind man. The lawyer began to protest, he seemed quite angry.

"It's not in the agreement," he began to say. But the
55 doctor silenced him, he got up and came round to Mother's side of the table.

"I think you should live there and plant your one crop and stay while it matures," he said to her. "It's a gentleman's agreement," he said.

WRITING COACH
Online
www.phwritingcoach.com

📖 Interactive Model
Listen to an audio recording of the Mentor Text in the eText. You can refer back to the Mentor Text whenever you need support in developing your own writing.

📓 Online Journal
Try It! Answer the questions about the Mentor Text in the online journal.

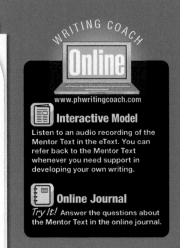

❸ The author focuses on the **character** of the brother in this passage. Both the narrator and her mother notice a change in him.

Try It! What was the brother like in the past? What is he like now?

❹ In a gentleman's agreement, people promise to keep an agreement out of a sense of honor. This **dialogue** about the agreement introduces a twist in the plot.

Try It! What deal does the mother work out in the agreement? What does the agreement suggest about the culture, or traditions, of the people in the story?

Mentor Text 95

Working with ELLs 🔲ELL Sheltered Instruction: Cognitive

Help students develop and expand their repertoire of learning strategies by drawing conclusions from a text. Explain that when we draw conclusions, we use what we've read and what we know to make educated guesses. Model drawing a conclusion, using real-world examples. Then:

Beginning Choral read the first paragraph on page 94, supporting comprehension with mime. Ask: "What happened to Grandpa?" and "What does Mother have to do?" Help students reuse the strategy to draw another conclusion: "What conclusion can you draw about the land?" *(It belonged to Grandpa.)*

Intermediate Have groups read the first paragraph and answer the questions in the Beginning activity. Have them reuse the strategy by drawing another conclusion.

Advanced Have pairs apply the strategy to answer question 3 (page 95), drawing a conclusion about the brother.

Advanced High Have students apply the strategy by drawing two conclusions from the first two pages of the story, identifying details in support. Have them expand their skills by checking a partner's work.

The Digital • Print Path ▶

1

Using Writing Coach Online™ or the student book, students read and listen to an audio recording of the Mentor Text. As they complete their writing assignments, they can refer back to the Mentor Text for support whenever they need it.

MENTOR TEXT

Try It! Continue to guide students to understand how the genre characteristics shape the text.

Check the accuracy and completeness of students' responses.

5. Mother gets much-needed money and the doctor gains the farm. The family can live on the farm, and the doctor can visit his land.

6. Responses will vary. The story is set in a rural area, in a cottage. Details that describe the boxes of seedlings: "unfasten the hessian coverings"; "little plastic containers."

7. The mother plants jarrah forest seedlings because they take many years to mature, allowing her family to stay at the farm for a long time.

8. The narrator thinks the doctor will be sad yet patient, looking over the land he cannot have yet.

9. Responses will vary. This story has a twist at the end, like the stories I have read by O. Henry. The doctor is the "gentleman" because he did not trick anybody to get what he wanted.

Realistic Short Story Mentor Text *Realistic Short Story* Mentor Text

❺ The **plot line,** or sequence of events in the story, seems to move toward a happy ending here, but the story is not over yet.

Try It! Why is each person who is part of the agreement satisfied with it?

❻ The author uses **sensory details** in this paragraph to help readers picture the **setting,** or where the story takes place.

Try It! Describe where the story takes place. Then give two specific details that describe the boxes of seedlings.

❼ The **plot** moves toward the climax, or moment of highest tension, when the mother explains what she plans to plant.

Try It! Why has the mother chosen to plant jarrah forest seedlings?

---

60 "That's the best sort," Mother smiled up at him and they shook hands.

"I wish your crop well," the doctor said, still shaking her hand.

❺ The doctor made the lawyer write out a special clause
65 which they all signed. And then we left, everyone satisfied. Mother had never had so much money and the doctor had the valley at last but it was the gentleman's agreement that was the best part.

My brother was impatient to get on with improvements.
70 "There's no rush," Mother said.

"Well one crop isn't very long," he said.

"It's long enough," she said.

❻ So we moved out to the valley and the little weatherboard cottage seemed to come to life very quickly
75 with the pretty things we chose for the rooms.

"It's nice whichever way you look out from these little windows," Mother was saying and just then her crop arrived. The carter set down the boxes along the edge of the verandah and, when he had gone, my brother began
80 to unfasten the hessian coverings. Inside were hundreds of seedlings in little plastic containers.

"What are they?" he asked.

"Our crop," Mother said.

❼ "Yes I know, but what is the crop? What are these?"
85 "Them," said Mother, she seemed unconcerned, "oh they're a jarrah forest," she said.

"But that will take years and years to mature," he said.

"I know," Mother said. "We'll start planting tomorrow. We'll pick the best places and clear and plant as we
90 go along."

2 Writing Journal ▶

Students record their answers to questions about the Mentor Text in their online journals or notebooks.

Short Story **Mentor Text** *Realistic Short Story* **Mentor Text**

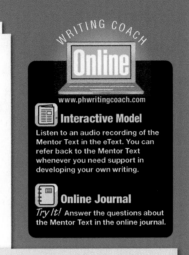

WRITING COACH

Online

www.phwritingcoach.com

Interactive Model
Listen to an audio recording of the Mentor Text in the eText. You can refer back to the Mentor Text whenever you need support in developing your own writing.

Online Journal
Try It! Answer the questions about the Mentor Text in the online journal.

8 The author returns to the **character** of the doctor in this paragraph as the narrator imagines how he might respond to the mother's clever trick.

Try It! How does the narrator imagine the doctor will respond?

9 The story ends with a twist as the final outcome is revealed in the **resolution**.

Try It! How does the ending of this story compare to that of other stories you have read? Who is the true "gentleman" in the agreement: the mother or the doctor? Explain.

"But what about the doctor?" I said. **8** Somehow I could picture him pale and patient by his car out on the lonely road which went through his valley. I seemed to see him looking with longing at his paddocks and his meadows and at his
95 slopes of scrub and bush.
9 "Well he can come on his land whenever he wants to and have a look at us," Mother said. "There's nothing in the gentleman's agreement to say he can't."

Mentor Text   97

Personalized Support

FEEDBACK Teacher or Peer Feedback

To provide feedback to students on their responses to the Mentor Text and their answers to the *Try It!* questions, ask or have student partners ask one another the following:

- What is the thesis or controlling idea of the Mentor Text?
- How does the Mentor Text illustrate the characteristics of a realistic short story?
- How did you answer this *Try It!* question? How could you use your answer to help you plan your piece of writing?

Working with ELLs   ELL Sheltered Instruction: Metacognitive

Have students demonstrate listening comprehension of increasingly complex spoken English by retelling or summarizing spoken messages. Read the Mentor Text aloud as students follow along, defining key words and discussing it with students. Have students close their books. Then:

Beginning Read aloud the final two paragraphs slowly, stopping to have students monitor comprehension and seek clarification. Use images or gestures to aid comprehension. Ask students recall questions to help them retell what they heard.

Intermediate Read aloud the final two paragraphs, reminding students to monitor comprehension and seek clarification. Have groups retell what they heard.

Advanced Read aloud the final two paragraphs, and have pairs write a short retelling to share with another pair. Have partners monitor comprehension and seek clarification.

Advanced High Challenge students by reading a longer section of the story aloud; have students monitor comprehension and seek clarification as you read. Have them retell the section in their own words to a peer.

The Digital • Print Path ▶

1

STUDENT BOOK ▶

Using *Writing Coach Online™* or the student book, students read and listen to an audio recording of the Student Model.

STUDENT MODEL

Tell students that good writers react to what they read in ways that show their understanding of the text. Explain that students will react to the Student Model by placing two sets of symbols in the text. Then, distribute printed copies of the Student Model or have students log on to Writing Coach Online.

Use a Reader's Eye

Read aloud the instructions for using the Reader's Response Symbols and the meaning of each symbol. Then, guide students through their use.

Think Aloud After reading the first three paragraphs, **I wondered** what would happen next. The writer has created interesting, realistic characters. The plot is based on the conflict between Lara and her teammates Tony and Suze. At this point in the story, I wonder how the conflict will be resolved, or worked out. I'll place a question mark next to the third paragraph.

Work with students to identify other places in the text where the writer makes them wonder what will happen next.

Have students read and respond to the Student Model, using each Reader's Response Symbol at least once.

Partner Talk

During their discussion, have partners identify places where the writer uses suspense to make readers wonder what will happen next.

Use a Writer's Eye

Read aloud the instructions for using the Writer's Response Symbols and the meaning of each symbol. Then, guide students through their use.

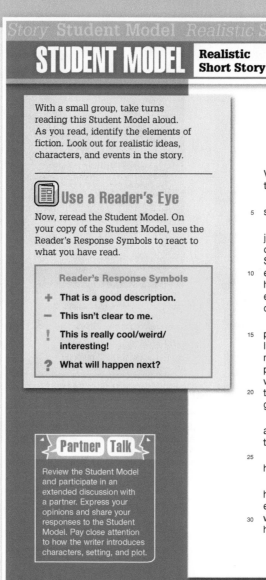

STUDENT MODEL | Realistic Short Story

With a small group, take turns reading this Student Model aloud. As you read, identify the elements of fiction. Look out for realistic ideas, characters, and events in the story.

📖 Use a Reader's Eye

Now, reread the Student Model. On your copy of the Student Model, use the Reader's Response Symbols to react to what you have read.

Reader's Response Symbols

+ **That is a good description.**

− **This isn't clear to me.**

! **This is really cool/weird/interesting!**

? **What will happen next?**

⟨ Partner Talk ⟩

Review the Student Model and participate in an extended discussion with a partner. Express your opinions and share your responses to the Student Model. Pay close attention to how the writer introduces characters, setting, and plot.

98 **Short Story**

Playing to Win

by Monica LaRocque

"Wow, Lara. For someone who won the Most Valuable Player Award last year, you sure blew it today," said Tony, pulling off his sweaty mitt.

5 "Yeah. Thanks for helping us lose the game, Lara," said Suze, as she stomped off the hot, dusty field.

"Geez! I'm the best player on this team. I was just having an off day," Lara mumbled. "What crummy friends! They don't have to be so rude." Sure, Tony had called the fly ball, but going after 10 everything was what made Lara the best. If Tony hadn't been in the way, they wouldn't have run into each other and Lara would have made a really great catch. And they had the nerve to be mad at *her!*

Later that day, Lara and her little brother were 15 playing Total Athlete 3 in their cozy and sunny living room. The smell of their dad's famous meatballs came from the kitchen. They had already passed the track-and-field level and were now working together to beat the game at doubles 20 tennis. They were losing pretty badly. Gary kept going for the balls in Lara's part of the court.

"Gary, cut it out! You can't play your position and my position," Lara snapped. "We have to play together. You have to trust that I'll cover my zone!"

25 "Geez, Lara!" Gary replied. "I was just having fun trying to get to all the balls."

Lara looked at Gary, and suddenly it hit her: She had been the one at fault at the baseball game earlier in the day. She had been the one who 30 was showing off. And she had been the one who hadn't trusted her teammate to make the catch.

1

Say: I found an example of vivid sensory details in paragraph 4, lines 16–17. The writer describes the smell of meatballs in the kitchen. This detail appeals to my sense of smell and helps me imagine being in the house with the characters. I'll write S.D. next to this part of the text for vivid sensory details.

Ask: What vivid sensory details do you find in paragraph 8? To what sense do the details appeal? ("sweltering afternoon sun," "trickle of sweat dripping down her back"; "touch")

Have students read and respond to the Student Model, using each Writer's Response Symbol at least once.

2 First, students respond to the Student Model as a reader, using symbols to mark the text. They can mark the text using pop-up sticky notes in *Writing Coach Online™* or they can mark a printed copy of the Student Model.

3 Then, students respond to the Student Model as a writer, using different symbols to mark the text. They can use either *Writing Coach Online™* or a printed copy of the Student Model.

rt Story Student Model *Realistic Short Story* **Student Model**

At the game the following week, Lara stood in the outfield in the sweltering afternoon sun, a trickle of sweat dripping down her back. At the top of the
35 ninth with two outs, Lara caught a line drive deep in left field. She threw the ball to Suze at shortstop. Suze made a great throw to the catcher and got an out at home plate to win the game. The crowd roared, and Suze and Tony ran over to Lara.

40 "I thought for sure you were going to try to make that throw to home plate yourself!" exclaimed Tony.

"Nah," Lara said, a little embarrassed. "Great play, Suze. And look, Tony, I'm really sorry about the other day. I was way out of line. Thanks for not
45 holding it against me."

"Of course not!" Tony said.

At the exact same time, Suze said, "We're teammates, aren't we?"

They all laughed as they walked back across
50 the field.

2

WRITING COACH

Online
www.phwritingcoach.com

Interactive Model

Listen to an audio recording of the Student Model in the eText. Use the Reader's and Writer's Response Symbols with the eText tools to note what you read.

Use a Writer's Eye

Now, evaluate the piece as a writer. On your copy of the Student Model, use the Writer's Response Symbols to react to what you have read. Identify places where the student writer uses characteristics of an effective realistic short story.

Writer's Response Symbols

R.D. Realistic and believable dialogue

S.D. Vivid sensory details that create and suggest mood

W.C. Well-developed, interesting characters

E.S. Engaging story

Student Model **99**

Personalized Support

FEEDBACK **Teacher or Peer Feedback**

To provide feedback to students on their responses to the Student Model, ask or have student partners ask one another the following:

• What is the thesis or controlling idea of the Student Model?

• How does the Student Model illustrate the characteristics of a realistic short story?

• Which feature or characteristic of the Student Model might you use in your own piece of writing?

• How could you alter or adapt this feature to make it your own?

Working with ELLs **ELL** Sheltered Instruction: Cognitive

To provide students with prereading supports to enhance comprehension of written texts, pre-teach key vocabulary, defining it in advance or directing students to make predictions about it. Read the Student Model title aloud and discuss what the topic of the story might be. Then:

Beginning Write, say, and define these words and phrases from the passage: *Most Valuable Player, fly ball, great catch, home plate.* Help students read the model, guiding them to use their knowledge of the words to enhance comprehension.

Intermediate Review the terms in the Beginning activity. Have groups look up any unfamiliar idioms: *stomped off, had the nerve, cut it out, suddenly it hit her.* Before reading, have students share with Beginning students.

Advanced Give students a **Vocabulary Prediction Chart** with words from the Beginning and Intermediate activities. Have pairs guess the meanings before reading, watch for context clues while reading, and confirm the meanings after reading.

Advanced High Have students complete the Advanced activity independently.

The Digital • Print Path ▶

1  STUDENT BOOK ▶

Students select or are assigned a topic for their realistic short story from the Topic Bank, or they may choose a topic of their own.

2 STUDENT BOOK ▶

Students complete online or printed graphic organizers to narrow the topic for their realistic short story.

Prewriting

Explain that the first task students need to complete as they plan their realistic short story is to determine an appropriate topic.

Choose From the Topic Bank

Read aloud each topic and then ask volunteers to describe them in their own words. If you are assigning topics to students, you may wish to do so now. Encourage students to ask questions about their topic.

Choose Your Own Topic

Introduce and discuss the List and Discuss strategies. If students were not assigned writing topics, have them use the strategies to brainstorm for topics for their short stories.

Extension Have each student choose one of the strategies. Then, have them write an action plan that outlines the resources and steps they will use to develop their topic.

Narrow Your Topic

Tell students that they will use a Narrow Your Topic graphic organizer to focus their topic on necessary characters and events. Then, distribute printed copies or have students log on to Writing Coach Online.

Apply It! Guide students through the instructions for completing the graphic organizer. Have students complete the exercise based on their topic.

Consider Your Audience and Purpose

Guide students to consider the audience and purpose for their realistic short story.

Your Turn ▶ **Feature Assignment: Realistic Short Story**

Prewriting

Plan a first draft of your realistic short story by **determining an appropriate topic.** You can select from the Topic Bank or come up with an idea of your own.

Choose From the Topic Bank

TOPIC BANK

Achieving a Goal Think about all the hard work that goes into achieving a goal. Write a realistic short story about a character who accomplishes a goal in the face of many problems.

A Misunderstanding Even friends misunderstand one another. Sometimes people cannot see eye to eye. Write a realistic short story about two friends who have a misunderstanding.

Learning a Lesson Lessons are not always learned in school. They can be learned in very unlikely places. Sometimes surprising lessons are the best ones. Write a realistic short story about a character who learns a lesson he or she was not expecting.

Choose Your Own Topic

Determine an appropriate topic on your own by using the following **range of strategies** to generate ideas.

List and Discuss

- Jot down notes about some of the best stories you have read. What were they about? What were some of the problems the characters in the stories had to face?
- Write a list of some of the funny, sad, or exciting things you have experienced. How did those experiences change you?
- With a group of classmates, talk about ideas, events, and characters you would like to see in a story.

Review your responses and choose a topic.

100   Short Story

Say: The third question on the left-hand side of the chart asks what background information my audience will need to understand my realistic fiction story. If **I choose** the first topic from the Topic Bank, about someone who accomplishes a goal in a specific field, such as dancing or sailing, my audience will need background information about the field.

Ask: What background information will your audience need to understand your realistic fiction story? (Responses will vary.)

Have students with similar topics work in small groups to discuss and respond to the remaining questions.

Coach's Corner

You may wish to model prewriting activities for students by brainstorming for your own writing topic. Use these prompts to model your thought process:

- **I am interested in** sailing, so that could be my general topic.
- **I can narrow my topic by** focusing on a person who learns a lesson while sailing around the world.

Discuss the choices you make and solicit feedback from students.

3

Students record their answers to questions about audience and purpose in their online journals or notebooks.

Narrow Your Topic

It is important that the topic of your story be focused. A focused topic will help you choose only necessary characters and events.

Apply It! Use a graphic organizer like the one shown to narrow your topic.

- Write your general topic in the top box, and keep narrowing your topic as you move down the chart.
- Your last box should hold your narrowest or "smallest" topic, the new focus of your story.

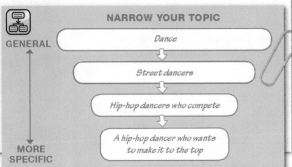
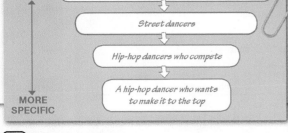

NARROW YOUR TOPIC

GENERAL

Dance

Street dancers

Hip-hop dancers who compete

A hip-hop dancer who wants to make it to the top

MORE SPECIFIC

WRITING COACH

Online

www.phwritingcoach.com

Interactive Graphic Organizers

Use the interactive graphic organizers to help you narrow your topic.

Online Journal

Try It! Record your answers and ideas in the online journal.

Consider Your Audience and Purpose

Before writing, think about your audience and purpose. Ask yourself what your audience needs and wants to know about your realistic short story.

Questions for Audience	Questions for Purpose
• Who will read my story? • What kinds of story lines will my audience find realistic? • What background information will my audience need to understand my realistic fiction story?	• Why am I writing this story? What do I want my audience to question, notice, or learn? • How can I keep my audience's attention? • What point of view is best for this story?

Record your answers in your writing journal.

Personalized Support

Interactive Graphic Organizer

Below Level Students complete three graphic organizers that provide models and scaffolded support.

On Level Students complete one, two, or three graphic organizers, depending on how much support they need.

Above Level Students complete the least scaffolded graphic organizer or narrow their topic without the help of a graphic organizer.

Working with ELLs **ELL** Sheltered Instruction: Cognitive

As students choose a topic, help them narrate events; describe people, places, or things; and explain situations with increasing specificity and detail. Write *What Happened?, Who Was There?, What Was It Like?,* **and** *Why Did It Happen?* **on the board. Then:**

Beginning Help students narrate, describe, and explain. Brainstorm ideas about an event, and answer the questions on the board. Help students write short sentences narrating what happened. Help them write two descriptive and two explanatory sentences about the event.

Intermediate Have groups use the questions to write sentences narrating, describing, and explaining an event. Have students be creative and share their writing.

Advanced Have pairs write sentences answering the questions by narrating, describing, and explaining an event. Have students be specific and swap writing with another pair for feedback.

Advanced High Have students write sentences narrating, describing, and explaining an event. Tell them they can use their writing to begin their short story.

The Digital • Print Path ▶

1  ▶

Using **Writing Coach Online**™ or the student book, students read and discuss the model graphic organizer.

2 ▶

Students complete online or printed graphic organizers to develop their ideas and gather details.

Plan Your Piece

Explain that writers use graphic organizers to develop their ideas and show relationships between different parts of the text. Then, point out the Develop Your Realistic Story graphic organizer on page 102. Tell students that they will use this organizer to outline their realistic short story. Then, distribute printed copies or have students log on to Writing Coach Online.

Introduce the graphic organizer by explaining that the column on the left lists the information to be entered in the column on the right. The first row defines the main character and conflict, while the next three rows identify the three main parts of a story plot.

Outline Your Story Guide students to use the graphic organizer to map out the events in their plot.

Say: I notice that the organizer has helped the writer develop the main character and her conflict and the events that will happen at the end of the story. For example, the character starts a hip-hop dance class at her ballet school and wins the top competition with her new friends. These events happen after the character resolves her conflict.

Ask: What events might happen to this character in the middle of the story before her conflict is resolved? **(Responses will vary.)** In what order would you place these events in the graphic organizer? **(Responses will vary.)**

Have students work individually to brainstorm for the events that will happen to their character in the beginning, middle, and end of the story and then record them on their graphic organizers.

Develop Characters and Setting Guide students to understand that the main character's traits are shown by the actions he or she performs. The setting is dependent on the characters and their actions. Have students add details about their characters and setting that are based on the events in their story.

Gather Details

Remind students that vivid details in a short story create interesting characters and realistic

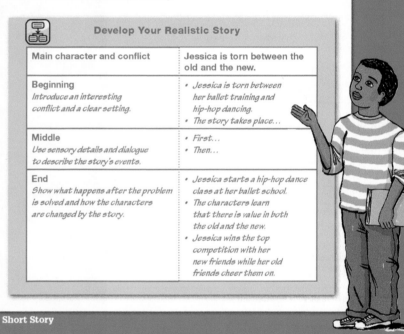

Plan Your Piece

You will use a graphic organizer like the one shown to establish a setting, characters, and plot events for your imaginative story. When it is complete, you will be ready to write your first draft.

Outline Your Story Use a graphic organizer like this one to map out an interesting story with a clearly defined **focus, plot, and point of view**. The plot or action should move toward an ending that makes sense. Be sure to decide the **point of view** for your story. Will the main character be the narrator, or will the narrator be a voice outside of the story? Look at these examples:

First-person point of view: I had always wanted to dance.

Third-person point of view: She had always loved to dance.

Develop Characters and Setting Leave space on your outline to plan for realistic characters. Write down the **sensory details** you will use to create a **believable setting**.

Develop Your Realistic Story

Main character and conflict	Jessica is torn between the old and the new.
Beginning *Introduce an interesting conflict and a clear setting.*	• *Jessica is torn between her ballet training and hip-hop dancing.* • *The story takes place...*
Middle *Use sensory details and dialogue to describe the story's events.*	• *First...* • *Then...*
End *Show what happens after the problem is solved and how the characters are changed by the story.*	• *Jessica starts a hip-hop dance class at her ballet school.* • *The characters learn that there is value in both the old and the new.* • *Jessica wins the top competition with her new friends while her old friends cheer them on.*

102   **Short Story**

settings. Ask volunteers to read aloud each literary device and sensory detail and its example. Challenge students to provide new examples for each kind of detail.

Try It! Guide students to understand how dialogue and descriptions are used. The descriptions use the senses of touch and sight.

Apply It! Read aloud the bulleted instructions for using sensory details and dialogue. Then, have students develop vivid details and dialogue for their story and enter them on their graphic organizer. Remind students to use a variety of details to develop their story.

Writer's Block

IF students' stories do not have a clearly defined plot with a beginning, middle, and end . . .

THEN ask students to identify the most important scenes in their story. Guide them to place the scenes in the proper order.

3 **STUDENT BOOK** ▶

Students refer back to the Mentor Text or the
Student Model as they plan their writing.

re Assignment **Prewriting** *Feature Assignment* **Prewriting**

Gather Details

Writers use a variety of different literary devices to enhance their
short stories. Look at these examples.

- **Dialogue:** *"Jess, I can't believe what you're saying to me," Callie
  whispered. "I know, Cal. I can hardly believe it myself."*
- **Interesting Comparisons:** *Jessica felt a thousand butterflies
  fluttering in her stomach, and she wished they would settle down.*
- **Descriptions:** *The tiny community center was nothing like the
  academy's high-tech studios.*

Sensory details help readers feel like they are "in the story." Look
at these examples.

- **Sight:** *She squinted her eyes against the bright sun.*
- **Smell:** *Kate wrinkled her nose at the stench of the garbage.*
- **Sound:** *The constant tap, tap, tapping made his brain rattle.*
- **Taste:** *Julio thought of home and cinnamon peach pie.*
- **Touch:** *The fabric was so rough that it felt like sandpaper.*

Try It! Read the Student Model excerpt and identify which kinds
of details the author uses.

STUDENT MODEL from **Playing to Win**
page 98; lines 1–5

> "Wow, Lara. For someone who won the Most Valuable Player
> Award last year, you sure blew it today," said Tony, pulling off his
> sweaty mitt.
>
> "Yeah. Thanks for helping us lose the game, Lara," said Suze,
> as she stomped off the hot, dusty field.

Apply It! Review the types of details a short story writer
can use. Then use **sensory details** and **dialogue,** as well as
other literary devices, to develop each section of your story.

- Use these elements to create a **clear focus, plot,** and **point of
  view** and to **develop the story** through the beginning, middle,
  and end of the story.
- Then add these details to your graphic organizer. Be sure to **use
  sensory details to help create a specific and believable setting**
  and interesting characters.

Prewriting **103**

**Interactive
Graphic Organizers**
Use the interactive graphic
organizers to help you create
a plan for your writing.

Interactive Model
Refer back to the Interactive Model
in the eText as you plan your writing.

The Digital · Print Path ▶

1 Using *Writing Coach Online*™ or the student book, students read and discuss the Outline for Success for a realistic short story. ▶

2 Students discuss how the Mentor Text illustrates the characteristics of a realistic short story.

Drafting

Outline for Success

Explain that the Outline for Success shows an organizational strategy for a short story. Students will use the Outline to write a focused, organized, and coherent draft of their realistic short story.

I. Beginning

Link the Outline to a specific realistic short story by having students turn to the Mentor Text on pages 94–97. Ask a volunteer to read aloud the first paragraph. Then, guide students to understand how the setting influences the characters and sets the plot in motion.

Say: I **notice** that the author introduces the conflict and the main character in the first sentence. The conflict in the story will concern the sale of the eighty-seven acres of land. The central character in this story is Mother. The first paragraph gives us important details about her life.

Ask: What is the story's point of view? (first person) How does the writer make the point of view clear? (She uses the first person pronouns *I* and *we* throughout the story.)

Have students work with a partner to evaluate the details they entered next to Beginning on their graphic organizers.

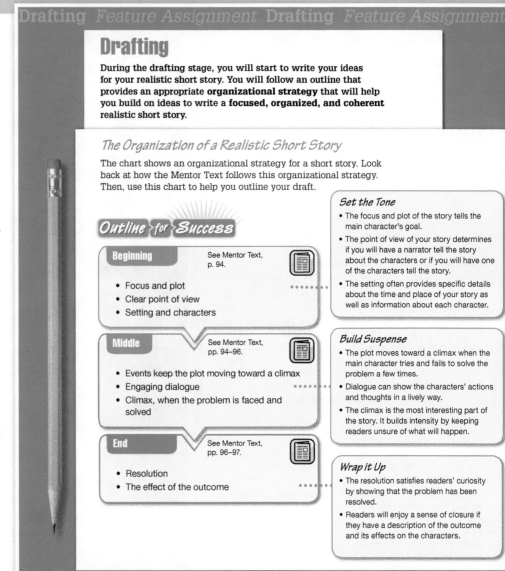

Drafting Feature Assignment Drafting Feature Assignment

Drafting

During the drafting stage, you will start to write your ideas for your realistic short story. You will follow an outline that provides an appropriate **organizational strategy** that will help you build on ideas to write a **focused, organized, and coherent** realistic short story.

The Organization of a Realistic Short Story

The chart shows an organizational strategy for a short story. Look back at how the Mentor Text follows this organizational strategy. Then, use this chart to help you outline your draft.

Outline for Success

Beginning See Mentor Text, p. 94.
- Focus and plot
- Clear point of view
- Setting and characters

Middle See Mentor Text, pp. 94–96.
- Events keep the plot moving toward a climax
- Engaging dialogue
- Climax, when the problem is faced and solved

End See Mentor Text, pp. 96–97.
- Resolution
- The effect of the outcome

Set the Tone
- The focus and plot of the story tells the main character's goal.
- The point of view of your story determines if you will have a narrator tell the story about the characters or if you will have one of the characters tell the story.
- The setting often provides specific details about the time and place of your story as well as information about each character.

Build Suspense
- The plot moves toward a climax when the main character tries and fails to solve the problem a few times.
- Dialogue can show the characters' actions and thoughts in a lively way.
- The climax is the most interesting part of the story. It builds intensity by keeping readers unsure of what will happen.

Wrap it Up
- The resolution satisfies readers' curiosity by showing that the problem has been resolved.
- Readers will enjoy a sense of closure if they have a description of the outcome and its effects on the characters.

104 Short Story

II. Middle

Lead a discussion about how the middle paragraphs of the Mentor Text reflect the characteristics of a realistic short story.

- Events that keep the plot moving (lines 13–14, 40–44, 64–65, 73–75)

- Engaging dialogue (lines 18, 40–41, 44–47, 48–52, 54, 57–62, 70–72, 76–77, 82–90)

- Climax (lines 84–90)

III. End

Have small groups discuss how the end of the Mentor Text reflects the characteristics of a realistic short story (lines 91–98).

Start Your Draft

Have small groups read aloud and discuss the boxed instructions for drafting. Direct students to work individually on their first draft.

Coach's Corner

If you are modeling the writing process for students with your own topic or a student volunteer's, you may wish to use these prompts to guide your drafting and discussion:

- **To introduce my story's plot, my beginning will** tell the main character's problem or goal.

- **I will organize the plot events** so they move toward a climax.

Discuss the choices you make and solicit feedback from students.

3  Students begin writing their realistic short story online or in their notebooks.

4 Students share their work with their teacher.

5  Students receive feedback from their teacher. Students may continue to work on their drafts.

Feature Assignment **Drafting** *Feature Assignment* **Drafting**

Start Your Draft

Use the checklist to help you complete your draft. Use the graphic organizer that shows the plot and setting, and the Outline for Success as guides.

While drafting, aim at writing your ideas, not on making your writing perfect. Remember, you will have the chance to improve your draft when you revise and edit.

√ Start drafting with the **beginning** of your realistic short story. Decide on a topic and a perspective from which to tell the story in order to clearly define the focus and **point of view.**

√ Use sensory details to create a specific and **believable setting** and characters.

√ Introduce the character's **goal** and problem.

√ Create a well-defined **plot** in the **middle.** Build suspense by dropping hints about what will happen next. As you draft, use realistic details to help readers feel like they are "in the story."

√ Use literary devices such as **dialogue** to develop the story and keep the reader interested.

√ Keep the action moving with events that are linked to solving the **problem** in the story. Make the reader feel the importance of finding a solution to the problem.

√ Make the **climax** emotional.

√ **End** by showing what happens after the problem has been **solved.**

√ Describe how the characters' **decisions** and actions have taught them something or changed their lives.

WRITING COACH

Online

www.phwritingcoach.com

Interactive Model

Refer back to Mentor Text in the eText as you write your draft.

Drafting 105

Personalized Support

FEEDBACK ✓ **Teacher or Peer Feedback**

To provide feedback to students on their first draft, ask or have student partners ask one another the following:

- Can you explain how you organized your ideas in this piece?
- Why did you include this information here?
- Why did you choose this beginning? Does it grab your reader and identify your thesis or controlling idea?
- What supporting details could you add here?
- Why did you choose this conclusion? How does it add to your piece?
- Can you show me a place where I can hear your unique voice?
- Can you show me a place where you used vivid language?

Working with ELLs   **ELL** Sheltered Instruction: Cognitive

Help students in the drafting process by having them narrate events, describe people, and explain situations aloud with increasing specificity and detail. Tell students that including specific details will help them communicate clearly. Then:

Beginning Have students take turns narrating aloud events that took place after school, describing at least two people or things involved and explaining what the situation was like. Model, and then help them complete sentence starters: *After school I ____. I saw ____. The events made me feel ____.*

Intermediate Have groups complete the Beginning activity aloud. Have listeners provide constructive feedback about students' use of specific details.

Advanced Have partners narrate aloud the events of a day they remember, describing the people involved and explaining why the day was memorable. Have listeners ask questions that evoke specific details.

Advanced High Have students complete the Advanced activity and incorporate their listener's feedback into a new oral telling.

1 Using *Writing Coach Online™* or the student book, students study the first and second drafts of the student model to see how the writer used Revision RADaR to improve his or her writing.

2 Students use the Revision RADaR strategy to revise their own writing.

Revising: Making It Better

Point out the page title to students and explain that revising means making improvements to a writing draft. Then, read aloud the opening paragraph to introduce the Revision RADaR strategies. You may wish to have students review Chapter 3 for more information on Revision RADaR.

Kelly Gallagher, M. Ed.

KEEP REVISION ON YOUR RADAR

1ST DRAFT After students have read the first draft, have them turn to page 104 and review the Outline for Success. Work with students to understand that the questions the author asked about the draft are based on the characteristics of a realistic short story. For example, call out the first question and note how it addresses the concerns listed in the Beginning section in the Outline for Success.

Then, have students work in small groups to develop other questions about the draft based on the genre characteristics.

2ND DRAFT Guide students to understand how the author used the RADaR strategies to revise the first draft.

Think Aloud I noticed that the first paragraph, about Lara and her brother playing the game, doesn't show a believable setting. In the 2nd draft, though, I see an *A* next to the paragraph, meaning that the author has added sensory details, such as "cozy and sunny living room." Now the paragraph does show readers an interesting, believable setting.

Work with students to brainstorm for other ways of revising details about the story's setting.

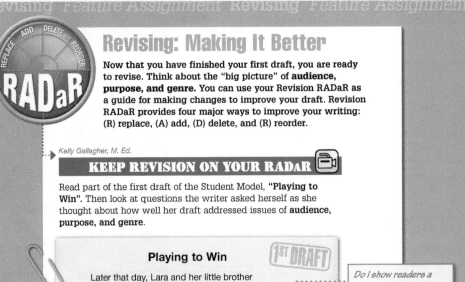

Revising: Making It Better

Now that you have finished your first draft, you are ready to revise. Think about the "big picture" of **audience, purpose, and genre**. You can use your Revision RADaR as a guide for making changes to improve your draft. Revision RADaR provides four major ways to improve your writing: (R) replace, (A) add, (D) delete, and (R) reorder.

Kelly Gallagher, M. Ed.

KEEP REVISION ON YOUR RADAR

Read part of the first draft of the Student Model, **"Playing to Win"**. Then look at questions the writer asked herself as she thought about how well her draft addressed issues of **audience, purpose, and genre**.

Playing to Win — 1ST DRAFT

Later that day, Lara and her little brother were playing Total Athlete 3. They had already passed the track-and-field level and were now working together to beat the game at doubles tennis. They were losing pretty badly. Gary kept going for the balls in her part of the court.

Gary was really annoying Lara. He was playing all the positions and hogging the ball.

"Geez, Lara!" Gary replied. "I was just having fun trying to get to all the balls."

Lara looked at Gary, and suddenly it hit her: She had been the one at fault at the baseball game earlier in the day. I had been the one who was showing off. And I had been the one who hadn't trusted my teammate to make the catch. I didn't believe he could do it without me.

Do I show readers a believable setting?

Can I use dialogue here to help move the story forward?

Is my point of view clear?

106   Short Story

Have students work in small groups to discuss the other changes in the 2nd draft.

Apply It! Review the bulleted instructions for using Revision RADaR. Remind students to question their drafts based on the realistic short story characteristics listed on the Outline for Success on page 104. Tell students to use each RADaR strategy at least once.

Coach's Corner

If you are modeling the writing process for students with your own draft or a student volunteer's, use these prompts to focus on the Revision RADaR *Replace* strategy:

- I **replaced narration with dialogue here** to advance the plot.
- I **replaced third-person pronouns with the first-person pronoun *I*** to make the point of view consistent.

Discuss the choices you make and solicit feedback from students.

3 Students share their work with their teacher.

4 FEEDBACK Students receive feedback from their teacher. Students may continue to revise their drafts.

Feature Assignment **Revising** Feature Assignment **Revising**

Now, look at how the writer applied Revision RADaR to write an improved second draft.

Playing to Win

2ND DRAFT

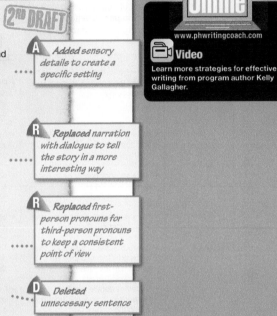

Later that day, Lara and her little brother were playing Total Athlete 3 in their cozy and sunny living room. The smell of their dad's famous meatballs came from the kitchen. They had already passed the track-and-field level and were now working together to beat the game at doubles tennis. They were losing pretty badly. Gary kept going for the balls in her part of the court.

"Gary, cut it out! You can't play your position and my position," Lara snapped. "We have to play together. You have to trust that I'll cover my zone!"

"Geez, Lara!" Gary replied. "I was just having fun trying to get to all the balls."

Lara looked at Gary, and suddenly it hit her: She had been the one at fault at the baseball game earlier in the day. She had been the one who was showing off. And she had been the one who hadn't trusted her teammate to make the catch.

A Added sensory details to create a specific setting

R Replaced narration with dialogue to tell the story in a more interesting way

R Replaced first-person pronouns for third-person pronouns to keep a consistent point of view

D Deleted unnecessary sentence

Apply It! Use your Revision RADaR to revise your draft.

- First, determine if you have established a clearly defined focus, plot, and point of view.
- Check that you have built a specific setting through sensory details. Look for places to strengthen your story with dialogue.
- Then, apply the Revision RADaR strategy to make needed changes. Remember—you can use the steps in the strategy in any order.

Revising   107

WRITING COACH
Online
www.phwritingcoach.com

Video Learn more strategies for effective writing from program author Kelly Gallagher.

Working with ELLs **ELL** Sheltered Instruction: Cognitive

Students should show an increasing ability to distinguish between formal and informal English and an increasing knowledge of when to use each. Have them adapt spoken language appropriately for informal purposes. Help them identify if these situations call for formal or informal language, and put each in a T-chart labeled *Formal* and *Informal*: a friendly talk, a speech, etc.

Beginning Say sentences ("What's new?") and have students say, "formal" or "informal." If a sentence is formal, assist students in adapting it appropriately for informal purposes.

Intermediate Say formal and informal sentences aloud, and ask a volunteer to identify the sentence as "informal" or adapt the sentence orally for informal purposes.

Advanced Have pairs take turns reading aloud the sentences from the Intermediate activity. Listeners should identify each sentence as formal or informal and adapt the formal language for informal purposes.

Advanced High Have students complete the Advanced activity. Have individuals say their own formal and informal sentences. Have partners check each other's sentences.

The Digital · Print Path ▶

1

Using *Writing Coach Online*™ or the student book, students study and discuss the revision chart.

2

In a video by program author Kelly Gallagher, students learn more strategies for effective writing.

Revising: Making It Better

Look at the Big Picture

Introduce the revision chart to students. Explain that the Section column identifies the three main parts of a realistic short story. The Evaluate column identifies the characteristics found in each section and explains how to assess them. The Revise column presents specific strategies for revising each characteristic.

Then, have students draw lines between and label the three sections of their drafts. Direct students to work individually to evaluate and revise their draft, using the chart to guide their work.

Focus on Craft: Improve Transitions

Have students read the introductory text. Guide students to understand that transitions are essential in a short story to tell the events in order and make connections clear.

Say: I notice that, in the first line of the Student Model, the writer uses the phrase "later that day." This phrase is a transition that helps make the order of the events of the story clear.

Ask: What other words or phrases in the Student Model are transitions? (*already, now*)

Have students work with a partner to discuss how the transitions improve the clarity of the passage.

Try It! Have students discuss the questions in small groups and record responses in their journals. Follow up with students to check that their responses reflect an understanding of how the use of transitions helps organize a story and tell the events in order.

Revising Feature Assignment Revising Feature Assignment

Look at the Big Picture

Use the chart and your analytical skills to evaluate how well each section of your realistic short story addresses **purpose, audience, and genre.** When necessary, use the suggestions in the chart to revise your piece.

Section	Evaluate	Revise
Beginning	• Check the opening. Is the story's **focus** clear?	• Rewrite sentences to create a clearly defined focus. Use strong nouns and verbs to describe the problem and main character.
	• Is the **point of view** both clear and consistent?	• Avoid confusing your reader—make sure that you are using only one point of view throughout the story.
	• Have sensory details been used to establish the **setting**?	• Add descriptive language to create a specific, believable setting that will engage the reader's interest.
	• Have well-developed **characters** been introduced?	• Introduce interesting characters that are realistic and believable.
Middle	• Check that the **action** is related to the problem and creates emotion in the reader.	• To strengthen your plot, show the character struggling to make a decision.
	• Underline details that build **suspense**. Draw a line from each one to the climax.	• Rearrange details and events to keep your reader interested and guessing. Take out or replace details that don't help build up to the climax.
	• Use **dialogue** and other literary devices that develop the story.	• Delete scenes or dialogue that do not move the story forward. Replace dull narration with dialogue.
End	• Check that the **problem** has been solved.	• Wrap up loose ends by explaining the result of what the character did.
	• Make sure you described how the character's actions have affected the **resolution**.	• Answer questions such as *Has the character been changed in some way? What has he or she learned from the experience?*

108   **Short Story**

Fine-Tune Your Draft

Apply It! Ask volunteers to read aloud the instructions for fine-tuning their drafts. Then, have students work in pairs to improve the transitions and enhance the style of their drafts.

Peer Feedback Have students identify Mentor Text examples of the characteristics that were marked for improvement. Use the Mentor Text references on page T104 to guide students to appropriate examples.

Teacher Tip

Have students tell their stories aloud to a partner. They can then write the events of the story in list form and work with their partners to arrange them in the most effective order.

3 Using *Writing Coach Online*™ or the student book, students refer back to the Mentor Text or Student Model for examples of writer's craft.

4  Students record answers to questions about writer's craft in their online journals or notebooks.

5 Students share their work with their teacher.

6 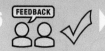 Students receive feedback from their teacher.

Feature Assignment **Revising**

Focus on Craft: Improve Transitions

Clear **transitions**, or changes, from one idea to another allow readers to follow the plot line. Transition words like *first, after,* and *before* are like signals that tell the reader what kind of information is coming. Transitions help with the organization of a story and telling events in order. Look at these examples:

- The word *next* signals to readers that something is about to happen.
- The word *or* signals a choice.

Transitions can connect ideas within a sentence or paragraph, between sentences or paragraphs, or between sections of a story.

 STUDENT MODEL from **Playing to Win** page 98; lines 14–20

> Later that day, Lara and her little brother were playing Total Athlete 3 in their cozy and sunny living room. They had already passed the track-and-field level and were now working together to beat the game at doubles tennis. They were losing pretty badly.

Try It! Read the passage. Then, ask yourself these questions. Record your answers in your journal.

- What do the words *later, already,* and *now* signal to readers?
- How would the reader's understanding change if the last sentence was moved to the beginning of the passage?

Fine-Tune Your Draft

Apply It! Use the revision suggestions to prepare your final draft after rethinking how well questions of **purpose, audience, and genre** have been addressed.

- **Improve Transitions** Use transitions to organize your imaginative story. Add, delete, combine, or rearrange sentences or paragraphs to improve transitions.
- **Enhance Style** Your style is the unique way you communicate. Improve the style of your writing by adding interesting comparisons or sentence patterns.

Peer Feedback Read your final draft to a group of peers. Ask them to comment on your plot and characters. Think about their responses and revise your final draft as needed.

WRITING COACH Online

www.phwritingcoach.com

Online Journal
Try It! Record your answers in the online journal.

Interactive Model
Refer back to the Interactive Model as you revise your writing.

Personalized Support

FEEDBACK ✓ Teacher or Peer Feedback

To provide feedback to students as they continue to revise their first draft, ask or have student partners ask one another the following:

- What are you trying to say here? What part of the text could you replace to make your meaning clearer?
- Is there a more precise word you could use here?
- How does the rhythm of these sentences sound to you? Could you make the length and structure of these sentences more varied?
- How could you include transitional words and phrases here to help your reader understand these ideas?
- Are there details you could add here to make this part come alive?

Differentiated Instruction

RTI Strategy for Special Needs Students
Write the transitions *first, then, next, before, after,* and *finally* on flash cards. Tell students to think about the steps involved in making a peanut butter-and-jelly sandwich. Hold up the cards one at a time in the order listed above. Ask students to state a step in making the sandwich using the word on the flash card. Help students use each transition word correctly.

PRE-AP Enrichment for Above-Level Students Have students add sensory details to the descriptions in their stories. Ask students to write a descriptive detail that appeals to each of the following senses: sight, sound, touch, taste, and smell. Encourage them to use vivid nouns, verbs, and adjectives to make the descriptions create a specific mood. Have students share their details with a partner and decide which ones to use in their final drafts.

The Digital • Print Path ▶

  STUDENT BOOK

1 ▶

In a video by program author Jeff Anderson, students learn effective editing techniques.

2  ▶

Students record answers to questions about writer's craft in their online journals or notebooks.

Editing: Making It Correct

Discuss the opening paragraph with students. Explain that they will edit their drafts for proper grammar, mechanics, and spelling, including prepositional phrases.

WRITE GUY *Jeff Anderson, M.Ed.*
WHAT DO YOU NOTICE?

Introduce students to prepositional phrases by reading aloud the Mentor Text excerpt and discussing responses to the "Ask yourself" question that follows. Then, have students read the explanation of prepositional phrases.

To monitor students' comprehension, guide them to identify and use prepositional phrases.

 Think Aloud **I know** that *on* is a preposition. In this sentence, *on* links me to information about the setting, specifically the time of the action. I can use the preposition to locate a prepositional phrase. "On the day of the sale" is a prepositional phrase.

Work with students to write an original sentence that uses prepositional phrases and tell the function of each phrase.

Have students reread a portion of the Mentor Text and locate another prepositional phrase. Have them describe the purpose of the prepositional phrase in context.

Grammar Mini-Lesson:
Prepositional Phrases

Discuss the paragraph and the Student Model excerpt on page 111 with students. Guide them to understand that the introductory prepositional phrase is used as a transition between ideas.

Try It! Have students work with a partner to identify the prepositional phrases and correctly add commas to the sentences.

Editing: Making It Correct

Editing means polishing your writing. It can be helpful to read your draft out loud to listen for places where the writing needs correction.

Before you edit, think about using **prepositional phrases to convey location, time, and direction or to provide details.** They can also be used as **transitions**. Then correct any errors in **grammar, mechanics, and spelling.**

WRITE GUY *Jeff Anderson, M. Ed.*
WHAT DO YOU NOTICE?

Zoom in on Conventions Focus on prepositional phrases as you zoom in on this sentence from the Mentor Text.

> **MENTOR TEXT** from **A Gentleman's Agreement** page 95; lines 40–41
>
> "You might as well come with me," Mother said to me on the day of the sale.

Now ask yourself: *Which of the phrases in the sentence expresses time?*

Perhaps you said that *on the day* shows time.

In this sentence, *on* is a **preposition.** A preposition relates one word to another in a sentence in order to convey, or express, information about location, time, or direction or provide details.

A **prepositional phrase** contains a preposition and a noun or pronoun that is the object of the preposition, plus its modifiers. The prepositional phrases in the Mentor Text are *with me, to me, on the day,* and *of the sale.* The phrases *with me* and *to me* convey direction, *on the day* conveys time, and *of the sale* provides a detail.

Partner Talk Discuss this question with a partner: *How might an author use prepositions to describe the setting of a short story?*

To learn more about prepositional phrases, see Chapter 19 of your Grammar Handbook.

110   **Short Story**

1. <u>In the meantime,</u> a new game had started in Field Park.

2. <u>Since the season ended,</u> the players have more time for other activities.

Apply It! Remind students to look closely for prepositional phrases as they edit their drafts.

Use the Rubric Explain to students that they will rate how well their draft addresses the elements of a short story on a scale of 1 to 6, with 6 being the best score.

Then, have students use the rubric to evaluate their drafts and revise as necessary.

Writer's Block

IF students need to add transitions to make their writing smoother . . .

THEN have them work with a partner to note places where they can add prepositional phrases to connect ideas. Remind them to add a comma after each introductory phrase.

2 Students share their writing with their teacher.

3  Students receive personalized feedback from the **Interactive Writing Coach™** or feedback from their teacher.

essment *Writing for Assessment* **Writing for Assessment**

More Prompts for Practice

Apply It! Respond to Prompts 1 and 2 by writing imaginative **short stories** with engaging story lines that keep the reader's interest.

- Create a **specific, believable setting** through the use of **sensory details**.
- Create **characters** that are realistic and interesting.
- Decide on a single **point of view**.
- Determine a topic to define the **focus** and **plot**.
- Show the **results** of the characters' actions.
- Include **dialogue** that develops the action of the story.

Prompt 1 Write a short story about something that happens in a park. Be sure to include the following fiction elements: believable setting and characters, clear point of view and focus, engaging plot, and dialogue. Use sensory details to bring your story to life.

Prompt 2 Write a short story about a family vacation. Make sure your setting and characters are interesting and believable and that your plot is engaging. Include a problem and solution in your story and use sensory details to define the focus.

 Spiral Review: Narrative Respond to Prompt 3 by writing a **personal narrative**. Make sure it reflects all of the characteristics described on page 66. Your essay should include these elements:

- A **clearly defined focus**
- The **importance of or reasons for actions and/or consequences**

Prompt 3 Write a personal narrative about a time you took part in a competition. Think about the reasons for decisions you made and how you acted. Discuss the importance of the consequences, or the outcome of your choices.

WRITING COACH

Online

www.phwritingcoach.com

 Interactive Writing Coach™

Plan your response to the prompt. If you are using the prompt for practice, write one paragraph at a time or your entire draft and then submit it for feedback. If you are using the prompt as a timed test, write your entire draft and then submit it for feedback.

Remember **ABCD**

- **A**ttack the prompt
- **B**rainstorm possible answers
- **C**hoose the order of your response
- **D**etect errors before turning in the draft

Personalized Support

Assessment/Monitor Progress

For timed writing practice, assign students a prompt to be completed in a timed setting. For Prompt 3, have students submit their writing to **Interactive Writing Coach™** to get immediate feedback.

For a formal writing assessment, assign the Assessment writing prompt for this chapter in **Writing Coach Online™**. Then, have students submit their writing to **Interactive Writing Coach™** to be assessed. Use the results to assess student progress and skill levels. **Interactive Writing Coach™** will update student levels to ensure that students get the appropriate support.

Teacher Feedback

To create an assessment environment, have students use a prompt in a timed setting. Grade papers using the appropriate rubric and use the results to assess student progress and skill levels. In the next writing assignment, ensure that students get the appropriate level of support.

If you conference with students, use these questions to guide your discussion:

- What form of writing did the prompt call for? Does your response include most or all of the characteristics of that form?
- How did you organize your ideas?
- Did you make good use of your time as you planned and wrote your response?
- What did you learn that you can use when responding to a prompt during a timed test?

Working with ELLs   **ELL** Sheltered Instruction: Cognitive

Help respond to creative writing prompts by having them orally narrate the events, describe the characters, and explain the outcome of a fictional event with increasing specificity and detail. Read aloud the Short Story Prompt, ensuring comprehension. Have students warm up for the prompt by orally telling a story about a lottery winner.

Beginning Provide sentence starters to narrate events (e.g., *The man saw his ticket and ____*), describe character(s) (e.g., *The man's eyes were ____*), and explain the outcome (e.g., *The man bought a ____*).

Intermediate Have groups tell a story aloud, taking turns narrating the events, describing the characters, and explaining the outcome. Monitor progress and provide feedback about the use of specific details.

Advanced Have partners take turns telling the story aloud, narrating events, describing characters, and explaining the outcome. Encourage the use of specific details.

Advanced High Have students complete the Advanced activity and tell their story to the class.

CHAPTER 7 LESSON PLANNER
Poetry and Description

Interactive Writing Coach™   **Interactive Graphic Organizers**   **Interactive Models**

Online Journal   **Resources**   **Video**

Use the Online Lesson Planner at www.phwritingcoach.com to customize your instructional plan for an integrated Language Arts curriculum.

DAY 1

CHAPTER OPENER/ GENRE INTRODUCTION

- What Do You See?
- What's Ahead
- Connect to the Big Questions
- **Feature Assignment: Poem**
- Other Forms of Poetry and Description
- Word Bank

ONLINE

DAY 2

MENTOR TEXT/ STUDENT MODEL

- **Mentor Text: Rhyming Poem and Haiku**
- Learn From Experience
- **Student Model: Rhyming Poem and Haiku**
- Reader's Eye and Writer's Eye

ONLINE

DAY 3

Prewriting

- Choose From the Topic Bank
- Choose Your Own Topic
- Narrow Your Topic
- Consider Your Audience and Purpose

ONLINE

DAY 6

Revising

- Keep Revision on Your RADaR
- Look at the Big Picture
- Focus on Craft
- Fine-Tune Your Draft

ONLINE

DAY 7
For additional grammar support, see Section 24.1, p. 534.

Editing

- What Do You Notice?/ Grammar Mini-Lesson
- **Rubric for Poetry: Rhyming Poem or Haiku**

Publishing

- Publish Your Piece
- Reflect on Your Writing

ONLINE

DAY 8

21st Century Learning

MAKE YOUR WRITING COUNT

- **Share the Vision of Your Poetry Using Multimedia**
- Here's Your Action Plan
- Listening and Speaking

ONLINE

Alternate Pacing Suggestions

- **Block Scheduling** Each day on the Lesson Planner represents a 40–50 minute block. Teachers using block scheduling may combine days to revise pacing to meet their classroom needs.

- **Accelerated Lesson Planning** Combine instructional days by aiding students in choosing a topic and then focusing on two core stages of the writing process, outlining for success (Day 5) and RADaR revision (Day 6).

- **Integrated Language Arts Curriculum** For targeted instruction that covers the essential components of the lesson use either a 3- or a 5-day plan.

3 day plan

DAY 1: Introduction to the Genre, Mentor Text, Student Model

DAY 2: Prewriting/Drafting

DAY 3: Revising/Editing/ Publishing

5 day plan

Use 3-day plan, and add:

DAY 4: Make Your Writing Count

DAY 5: Writing for Assessment

Links to Prentice Hall *LITERATURE*

Featured Author: Gary Soto

- What Is Poetry?, p. 550
- "Oranges" (poem), p. 555
- "Ode to Family Photographs" (poem), p. 557
- On Revising a Comparison (Writing Workshop), p. 671
- *From the Author's Desk* Videos: Gary Soto

Additional Mentor Text:

- Haiku (poem), Matsuo Bashō, p. 624

Differentiated Instruction

Differentiated Instruction Boxes in this Teacher's Edition address these student populations:

- Below-Level Students
- Above-Level Students
- Gifted and Talented Students
- Special Needs Students
- English Language Learners
- Spanish Speaking Students

In addition, for further enrichment, see the **Extension** features.

LESSON OBJECTIVES

- To learn the forms and defining characteristics of poetry and description.
- To learn the elements of a successful rhyming poem and a successful haiku, the chapter feature assignments.
- To read mentor texts in the genre, analyzing their use of the elements of effective poetry.
- To read student models of a rhyming poem and a haiku, analyzing them from the perspective of a reader and from the perspective of a writer.
- To apply prewriting strategies in developing a rhyming poem or a haiku, including strategies for choosing and narrowing a topic, planning writing, and using poetic devices, as well as tips for considering audience and purpose.
- To apply drafting strategies in developing a rhyming poem or a haiku.
- To apply RADaR revision strategies to a rhyming poem or a haiku.
- To learn about the Focus on Craft topic, enhancing style, and apply what is learned to a draft rhyming poem or haiku.
- To edit the draft, zooming in on adjectives and focusing on forms of adjectives.
- To complete the Make Your Writing Count assignment, developing and presenting a multimedia presentation of poetry.
- To complete the Writing for Media assignment, developing a descriptive essay.
- To practice writing for assessment.

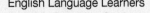

DAY 4

Prewriting

ONLINE

- Plan Your Piece
- Poet's Toolbox

DAY 5

Drafting

ONLINE

- Drafting a Rhyming Poem or Haiku
- Start Your Draft

DAY 9

WRITING FOR MEDIA

ONLINE

- **Descriptive Essays**
- Create a Descriptive Essay

DAY 10

WRITING FOR ASSESSMENT

ONLINE

- Poetry Prompt
- The ABCDs of On-Demand Writing
- More Prompts for Practice
  Test Prep Spiral Review: Narrative
  Test Prep Spiral Review: Short Story

Personalized Assessment

FEEDBACK

Teacher Conferencing

	Ongoing Assessment	Formal Assessment of Feature Assignment	Progress Monitoring at End-of-Chapter
	Use rubrics in the Student Edition as a revision tool. Conference with students to review their work and provide personalized support.	Use rubrics in the Student Edition to score students' Feature Assignment papers.	Review each student's work to plan targeted resources for the next writing assignment.

The Digital · Print Path ▸

1  ▸

Using Writing Coach Online™ or the student book, students discuss the photograph in the chapter opener as it relates to the writing genre.

2 ▸

Students record their ideas and responses in their online journals or notebooks. They may also record and save their responses on pop-up sticky notes in Writing Coach Online™.

Chapter Objectives

1. Write a poem by planning, drafting, revising, editing, and publishing individual work.

2. Produce a multimedia poetry presentation.

3. Use the five-step writing process to write a descriptive essay.

4. Write a poem and a personal narrative or short story in response to a prompt.

POETRY and DESCRIPTION

What Do You See?

Activate Prior Knowledge Tell students that the purpose of poetry is to express ideas and feelings through imaginative language and description. Explain to students that they will use what they know about fireworks to analyze the photo on page 118. Then, guide students in analyzing the photo.

Think Aloud When **I analyze** this photo, I look at it closely and think about what it means. I see fireworks in the sky over a city. I think about why there are fireworks. We have fireworks on the Fourth of July, so the city may be celebrating that holiday. I also think about how the photo makes me feel. I am amazed because the fireworks seem to be coming off the tops of the buildings!

Work with students to brainstorm for things they see, think about, or feel as they analyze the photo. Record their responses on the board.

Try It! **Have students** work individually to develop responses to the questions. Check that students have thought about what the fireworks mean to them.

Possible responses: I see many fireworks exploding above a city. The photo makes me feel happy because I like fireworks. If I were near these fireworks, I would be pleased and excited. To me, fireworks mean celebrations, and celebrations are fun.

CHAPTER 7

POETRY and DESCRIPTION

118   Poetry and Description

Connect to the Big Questions

Have students use their experience to discuss the Big Questions. Explain that they will revisit **Why write?** at the end of this chapter. Tell students to consider these points during their discussion:

1. When we communicate, we give or exchange information, thoughts, and ideas.

2. Words can be arranged on a page in an almost infinite number of ways to express unique feelings and experiences.

What's Ahead

Have students preview the Mentor Text and Student Model on pages 122–125. Tell students that they will write their own poem using the five-step writing process: prewriting, drafting, revising, editing, and publishing.

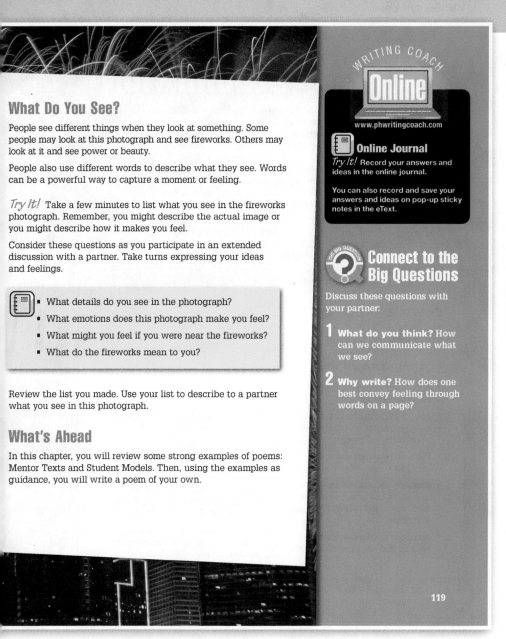

What Do You See?

People see different things when they look at something. Some people may look at this photograph and see fireworks. Others may look at it and see power or beauty.

People also use different words to describe what they see. Words can be a powerful way to capture a moment or feeling.

Try It! Take a few minutes to list what you see in the fireworks photograph. Remember, you might describe the actual image or you might describe how it makes you feel.

Consider these questions as you participate in an extended discussion with a partner. Take turns expressing your ideas and feelings.

- What details do you see in the photograph?
- What emotions does this photograph make you feel?
- What might you feel if you were near the fireworks?
- What do the fireworks mean to you?

Review the list you made. Use your list to describe to a partner what you see in this photograph.

What's Ahead

In this chapter, you will review some strong examples of poems: Mentor Texts and Student Models. Then, using the examples as guidance, you will write a poem of your own.

WRITING COACH
Online
www.phwritingcoach.com

Online Journal
Try It! Record your answers and ideas in the online journal.

You can also record and save your answers and ideas on pop-up sticky notes in the eText.

Connect to the Big Questions

Discuss these questions with your partner:

1 What do you think? How can we communicate what we see?

2 Why write? How does one best convey feeling through words on a page?

119

Personalized Support

FEEDBACK Teacher or Peer Feedback

To encourage students in their discussion of the photograph as it relates to the writing genre, ask the following questions:

- What is the first thing you think of when you look at this photo?
- How does it relate to your life?
- How does it relate to things you've learned in other subjects?
- What questions come to mind when you look at this photograph?
- How does your response to the photograph compare to those of your classmates?

The Digital · Print Path ▶

1 STUDENT BOOK ▶

Students learn vocabulary from the Word Bank and listen to English and Spanish pronunciations in the **Writing Coach Online™** glossary.

2  Writing Journal ▶

Students record answers to questions about forms of writing in their online journals or notebooks.

POETRY AND DESCRIPTION

To introduce this chapter's writing forms, discuss the opening paragraphs with students. Make sure students understand that a rhyming poem and a haiku are types of poetry. Explain that poets often use a step-by-step process to develop their work. Then, have students preview the rubric on page 137.

Poem

Ask volunteers to read aloud the feature assignment characteristics. Tell students that they will identify these characteristics in Mentor Texts and Student Models. Then, they will use the characteristics to guide the writing of their own rhyming poem or haiku.

Forms of Poetry and Description

Guide students to understand how the forms of poetry and description are alike and different.

Say: I notice that most of the forms on the list are poems, but one form is an essay. Poems and essays are different kinds of writing. I wonder why these forms are on a list together.

Ask: How are all the forms on the list alike? (All of them contain poetic conventions, such as sensory details, figurative language, and imagery.) How are the forms different? (The poetry forms have different purposes and characteristics. Prose poems and descriptive essays are in prose form.)

Have students work in small groups to make a chart showing the purposes and characteristics of each writing form.

Try It! Remind students that the audience is the people who will read their writing. The purpose is the poet's reason for writing. Have students record their responses in their journal.

Possible responses: descriptive essay, helps readers imagine a place; lyric poem, expresses feelings about a person; ballad, has regular meter and rhyme

Word Bank

To assist English Language Learners and struggling readers, echo read each word or have students log on to Writing Coach Online to listen to the pronunciations. Then, have partners take turns using each word in a sentence. Ask volunteers to share one of their sentences with the class.

POETRY AND DESCRIPTION

In this chapter, you will focus on writing a poem. Poetry is different from other kinds of writing. Rather than using sentences and paragraphs, poets write in lines and stanzas to convey their emotions and ideas. Because poems tend to be short, poets must choose their words carefully, using language that is vivid, precise, and pleasing to the ear. They may use rhythm and rhyme to add a musical quality to the work. Most writing includes description, but this type of language is especially important in poetry. Poets use sensory details to help readers imagine how things look, smell, sound, feel, and taste.

You will develop a poem by taking it through each stage of the writing process: prewriting, drafting, revising, editing, and publishing. To preview the criteria for how your poem will be evaluated, see the rubric on page 137. You will also have an opportunity to use your descriptive writing skills in an essay about a place you have visited.

FEATURE ASSIGNMENT
Poem

An effective poem has these characteristics:

- A clear **focus, topic, theme,** or **controlling idea**

- **Poetic techniques** that create a musical quality, emphasize words, or enhance the rhythm

- **Figurative language** that expresses ideas imaginatively

- **Sensory details** and **imagery** that allow the reader to see, smell, hear, taste, and feel what the poet describes

- Attention to **graphic elements,** such as line length or capital letters

A **rhyming poem** also has these characteristics (see pages 129–130):

- **Rhyming words** that fall within or at the ends of lines

- A strong, regular **rhythm**

A **haiku** also has these characteristics (see pages 129–130):

- A set **structure** of 17 syllables arranged in three lines of 5, 7, and 5 syllables

- A clear **image,** often of nature, that creates an emotional response in the reader

120   **Poetry and Description**

Teacher Tip

Provide examples of the forms of poetry and description on the list. Have volunteers read aloud the examples without identifying the forms. Ask the class to identify the forms and explain their reasoning.

Forms of Poetry and Description

There are many forms of poetry and description, including:

Ballads are poems that tell a story and are usually meant to be sung. Ballads often contain repetition and have a simple, regular rhyme pattern and meter, or "beat."

Descriptive essays use imagery and vivid details to help readers imagine a person, place, thing, or event. Like all essays, they are made up of an introduction, body, and conclusion.

Free verse is poetry that imitates the rhythms of everyday speech. It has no set rhythm and rhyme patterns and uses poetic devices to convey ideas and feelings.

Haiku are three-line poems that originated in Japan. In a haiku, the first and last lines consist of five syllables, and the middle line consists of seven syllables.

Lyric poems express a speaker's feelings about a particular person, place, thing, or event. Unlike ballads, lyric poems usually do not tell a story.

Prose poems look like prose, or regular text you might find in a story or essay, but use poetic techniques to create a memorable description of a person, place, thing, or event.

Sonnets are 14-line poems written in a regular meter and pattern of rhyme. One kind of sonnet has three four-line stanzas and a final couplet, or two rhyming lines. In each stanza, alternating lines usually rhyme.

 Try It! For each audience and purpose described, choose a form, such as a sonnet, descriptive essay, or lyric poem, that is appropriate for conveying your intended meaning to the audience. Explain your choices.

- To describe a special trip to classmates
- To express feelings about a beloved pet
- To impress your reader with your use of regular meter and rhyme

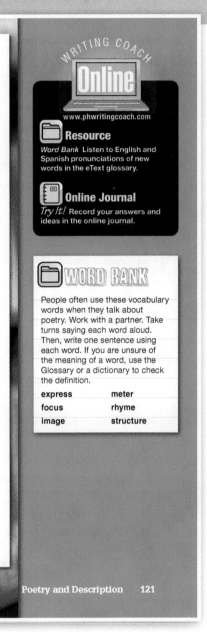

WRITING COACH

Online

www.phwritingcoach.com

📁 **Resource**

Word Bank Listen to English and Spanish pronunciations of new words in the eText glossary.

📓 **Online Journal**

Try It! Record your answers and ideas in the online journal.

📁 WORD BANK

People often use these vocabulary words when they talk about poetry. Work with a partner. Take turns saying each word aloud. Then, write one sentence using each word. If you are unsure of the meaning of a word, use the Glossary or a dictionary to check the definition.

express	**meter**
focus	**rhyme**
image	**structure**

Personalized Support

FEEDBACK 👥 **Teacher or Peer Feedback**

To help students understand the characteristics of the writing form, ask or have student partners ask one another the following questions:

- What are the main characteristics of poetry and description?
- What makes this form of writing different from other forms?
- Who are the likely readers or audiences for this form of writing?
- What kind of organization could be used for this form of writing?
- What kind of voice would be most effective for this form of writing?

Working with ELLs   **ELL** Sheltered Instruction: Cognitive

Have students use strategic learning techniques, such as reviewing, to acquire basic and grade-level vocabulary from the page, including *express, image,* **and** *rhyme* **in the Word Bank and** *person, event, ideas,* **and** *feelings* **from the text. Help students use accessible language to learn this new and essential language.**

Beginning Use accessible language to explain the vocabulary. Have students review the words, repeating your explanations. Help students complete sentences, such as Hand *and* sand *are words that* _____.

Intermediate Have partners make **Puzzle Cards** to review vocabulary. Have them write words on the left half and accessible definitions on the right, then cut the cards, mix them up, and match them again.

Advanced Have partners review the words, using accessible language and a dictionary as needed. Have partners use each word in a sentence about a work the class has read.

Advanced High Have partners review the vocabulary, using accessible language to define it. Have pairs use the vocabulary to discuss the forms explained on page 121.

T121

The Digital • Print Path ▶

WRITING COACH
Online

STUDENT
BOOK

1  STUDENT BOOK ▶

Using **Writing Coach Online™** or the student book, students read and listen to an audio recording of the Mentor Texts. As they complete their writing assignments, they can refer back to the Mentor Text for support whenever they need it.

MENTOR TEXT

About the Selection The first selection is a rhyming poem in which the poet humorously describes a baby in computer terms. The other selections are three haiku that present images of a snail on the move, falling snow, and a sunrise.

Learn From Experience

After students have read the text, point out that the numbered notes refer to the characteristics of rhyming poems and haiku introduced on page 120.

Try It! Guide students to understand how the genre characteristics shape the text.

Say: The first *Try It!* question asks me to write a sentence about the focus of the poem, or what the poem is about. After reading the first stanza, **I can state** what the focus is: "After eating a microchip, a baby starts acting like a computer." I can also tell that the poet is writing a funny poem.

Ask: How can you tell what the focus of a poem is? (by reading the poem, thinking about its words, and picturing its images)

Have students reply to the *Try It!* questions in their journals. If students have difficulty responding to a particular question, model a response, as with Question 1.

Check the accuracy and completeness of student responses.

1. Responses will vary but should be complete sentences and show an understanding of the poem's topic.

2. the word *beep* in line 3

3. *thrives/drives, fits/bits, fights/bytes, ruthless/toothless*

4. The snow can play music. Responses will vary but might say that the language makes the reader feel calm and contented.

5. Responses will vary but might note that the short length may make a haiku easy to read because it has so few words to interpret.

Text *Poem* Mentor Text *Poem* Mentor Text *Poem* Ment

MENTOR TEXT Rhyming Poem and Haiku

Learn From Experience

 Read the rhyming poem and haiku on pages 122–123. As you read, take notes to develop your understanding of basic sight and English vocabulary. Then, read the numbered notes in the margins to learn about how the poets presented their ideas.

Answer the *Try It!* questions online or in your notebook.

❶ There is a **clear focus** to the poem from the start. Knowing what the poem will be about helps readers understand it.

Try It! Write a sentence that tells what the focus is.

❷ The poet uses **onomatopoeia**, or words that imitate sounds, to make the poem more vivid and funny.

Try It! Which word imitates a sound made by a computer?

❸ Regular **rhyme** creates pleasing sounds when the poem is read aloud and supports the humor in the poem.

Try It! Which words rhyme in lines 9–12?

Baby Ate a Microchip
by Neal Levin

❶ Baby ate a microchip,
Then grabbed a bottle, took a sip.
❷ He swallowed it and made a beep,
And now he's thinking pretty deep.

5 He's downloading his ABCs
And calculating 1-2-3s.
He's memorizing useless facts
While doing Daddy's income tax.

❸ He's processing, and now he thrives
10 On feeding his internal drives.
He's throwing fits, and now he fights
With ruthless bits and toothless bytes.

He must be feeling very smug.
But hold on, Baby caught a bug.
15 Attempting to reboot in haste,
He accidentally got erased!

122   Poetry and Description

Extension Lead a discussion in which students compare and contrast how their additional poetry examples use the genre characteristics. Use the *Try It!* questions as a guide.

Teacher Tip

Quick Write Ask students to write a short, non-rhyming poem or description about the snail in the photo on page 123 or another small animal. Encourage students to review the characteristics of poetry on page 120 as well as the examples of haiku on page 123.

2 Writing Journal ▶

Students record their answers to questions about the Mentor Texts in their online journals or notebooks.

Poem **Mentor Text** Poem **Mentor Text** Poem **Mentor Text**

Three Haiku

by Julienne Marlaire

The Journey

Snail inches across
The garden, never stopping.
Where is he going?

Nighttime in Winter

❹ Falling snow blankets,
Making silent, still music—
A sweet lullaby.

Sunrise

❺ Sunlight floods the land,
Glistening on dewy grass.
A new day begins!

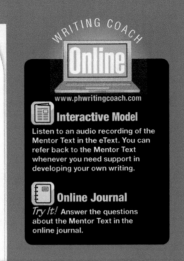

WRITING COACH Online

www.phwritingcoach.com

Interactive Model
Listen to an audio recording of the Mentor Text in the eText. You can refer back to the Mentor Text whenever you need support in developing your own writing.

Online Journal
Try It! Answer the questions about the Mentor Text in the online journal.

❹ The poet uses **personification** when she describes the falling snow. This helps readers picture snow in a fresh, new way.

Try It! Which human characteristics or actions does she give to the snow? How did this figurative language make you feel when you read the poem? Explain.

❺ The poems follow the traditional haiku structure of **three lines** made up of words that total 17 syllables.

Try It! How does the length of the poem affect you as a reader? Explain.

Mentor Text 123

Personalized Support

FEEDBACK Teacher or Peer Feedback

To provide feedback to students on their responses to the Mentor Texts and their answers to the *Try It!* questions, ask or have student partners ask one another the following:

• What is the thesis or controlling idea of the Mentor Texts?

• How do the Mentor Texts illustrate the characteristics of a rhyming poem and haiku?

• How did you answer this *Try It!* question? How could you use your answer to help you plan your piece of writing?

The Digital • Print Path ▶

1

Using Writing Coach Online™ or the student book, students read and listen to an audio recording of the Student Models.

STUDENT MODEL

Tell students that good writers react to what they read in ways that show their understanding of the text. Explain that students will react to the Student Models by placing two sets of symbols in each text. Then, distribute printed copies of the Student Models or have students log on to Writing Coach Online.

Use a Reader's Eye

Read aloud the instructions for using the Reader's Response Symbols and the meaning of each symbol. Then, guide students through their use.

Think Aloud
I see that the student writer begins the poem "The Game" with a simile that creates a strong image. The line "like lions on the prowl" helps me clearly picture in my mind the basketball players moving swiftly and skillfully around the court, looking for opportunities to score. I'll place a plus sign next to these lines to show I can picture what the poet is describing.

Work with students to find other examples of strong images in the poem.

Have students read and respond to the Student Models, using each Reader's Response Symbol at least once.

Partner Talk

After partners have finished discussing the poems, have each pair point out images and poetic language that support their opinions, feelings, and ideas about the poems.

Use a Writer's Eye

Read aloud the instructions for using the Writer's Response Symbols and the meaning

---

STUDENT MODEL — Rhyming Poem and Haiku

With a small group, take turns reading each Student Model aloud. As you read, note the structure and elements of the poems. You may want to take a look at the Poet's Toolbox on page 129. Ask yourself how the images and poetic language affect your emotions.

Use a Reader's Eye

Now, reread the Student Models. On your copies of the Student Models, use the Reader's Response Symbols to react to what you read.

Reader's Response Symbols

+ **I can picture this.**

– **This image could be stronger.**

? **I wonder what this means.**

! **This is cool!**

Partner Talk

Participate in an extended discussion with a partner. Express your opinions and share your responses to the Student Model. About what do you agree? How do your feelings about the poems differ?

124   Poetry and Description

The Game

A Rhyming Poem by Justine Margolis

Players maneuver in and out
Like lions on the prowl.
Pass, run, shoot, and shout,
Never fumble, never foul.

5 Guard and block, assist, rebound,
The team works all as one.
Fans create a wall of sound
As the other team comes undone.

Grace in action, strength, and power
10 So much more than play.
Fighting to the final hour,
We'll win this game today.

1

---

of each symbol. Then, guide students through their use.

Say: While reading the haiku "Autumn," **I noticed** that the second line uses the long *i* sound in the words *fire, climbing,* and *sky.* This repeated sound helps link the fire to the sky. I'll write S.D. next to this line for its effective use of sound devices.

Ask: What sound device do you notice in the first line of the poem "Changing Seasons"? (repeated use of long *e* and final *s* in *tree's* and *leaves*)

Have students read and respond to the Student Models, using each Writer's Response Symbol at least once.

2 First, students respond to the Student Model as a reader, using symbols to mark the text. They can mark the text using pop-up sticky notes in *Writing Coach Online™* or they can mark a printed copy of the Student Models.

3 Then, students respond to the Student Models as a writer, using different symbols to mark the text. They can use either *Writing Coach Online™* or a printed copy of the Student Model.

Student Model *Poem* Student Model *Poem* **Student Model**

Changing Seasons

A Haiku by Renee Baker

The summer tree's leaves
are greener than autumn's, but
spring's are the greenest.

Autumn

A Haiku by Renee Baker

Red and yellow leaves
Like fire climbing in the sky
Flaunt autumn's beauty.

2

Student Model   125

WRITING COACH

Online
www.phwritingcoach.com

Interactive Model
Listen to an audio recording of the Student Models in the eText. Use the Reader's and Writer's Response Symbols with the eText tools to note what you read.

Use a Writer's Eye

Now, evaluate the poems as a writer. On your copies of the Student Models, use the Writer's Response Symbols to react to what you read. Identify places where the student writers use characteristics of an effective rhyming poem or haiku.

Writer's Response Symbols

R.R.   Rhythm or rhyme, if present, fits poem's form

S.D.   Effective use of sound devices

F.L.   Figurative language conveys a mood

I.D.   Images and details appeal to the senses

Personalized Support

Teacher or Peer Feedback

To provide feedback to students on their responses to the Student Models, ask or have student partners ask one another the following:

- What is the thesis or controlling idea of the Student Models?
- How do the Student Models illustrate the characteristics of a rhyming poem and haiku?
- Which feature or characteristic of the Student Models might you use in your own piece of writing?
- How could you alter or adapt this feature to make it your own?

Help students use and reuse new basic language in speaking activities and expand and internalize initial English vocabulary by retelling basic information supported by pictures. Preteach these basic vocabulary words from pages 124–125: *players, shoot, team, win,* **and** *leaves.* **Help students read the poems. Then:**

Beginning Help students use the vocabulary by orally completing sentence frames about the photographs, such as *He [shoots] the ball; The leaves are [red] and [yellow].* Help them reuse these words in retelling information from the poems.

Intermediate Have groups use the vocabulary when discussing the photographs. Have students reuse the vocabulary to retell information from the poems.

Advanced Have partners use the vocabulary as they retell the information from the poems, using the pictures for support. Have students reuse the vocabulary by discussing how the pictures relate to images in the poems.

Advanced High Have students complete the Advanced activity, then share their retellings.

The Digital • Print Path ▶

1 ▶ Students select or are assigned a topic for their poem from the Topic Bank, or they may choose a topic of their own.

2 ▶ Students complete online or printed graphic organizers to narrow the topic for their poem.

Prewriting

Explain that the first task students need to complete as they plan their poem is to determine an appropriate topic.

Choose From the Topic Bank

Read aloud each topic, and then ask volunteers to describe it in their own words. If you are assigning topics to students, you may wish to do so now. Encourage students to ask questions about their topic.

Choose Your Own Topic

Introduce and discuss the Observe and Discuss strategies. If students were not assigned writing topics, have them use the strategies to brainstorm topics for their poems.

Extension Have each student choose one of the strategies. Then, have students write an action plan that outlines the resources and steps they will use to develop their topic.

Narrow Your Topic

Tell students that they will use a Narrow Your Topic graphic organizer to reduce their poem's topic to a focused subject. Then, distribute printed copies or have students log on to Writing Coach Online.

Apply It! Guide students through the instructions for completing the graphic organizer. Have students complete the exercise based on their topic.

Consider Your Audience and Purpose

Guide students to consider the audience and purpose for their poem.

Your Turn ▶ Feature Assignment: Rhyming Poem or Haiku

Prewriting

Plan a first draft of your poem by **determining an appropriate topic.** First, decide which form of poetry you will write—a rhyming poem, haiku, or other form of poetry. Then, select a topic from the Topic Bank or come up with an idea of your own.

Choose From the Topic Bank

TOPIC BANK

Memorable Day Think of a day that was memorable because of the weather, such as a day with a summer thunderstorm. In a poem, describe the weather and the mood the weather created.

Hero Write a poem about one of your personal heroes, such as your favorite author, singer, or leader. Be sure to be specific and detailed in your explanation about what makes the person heroic to you.

Special Place Write a poem about a place you go to have fun or relax. Describe the place so that readers can picture it in their minds.

Choose Your Own Topic

Determine an appropriate topic of your own by using the following **range of strategies** to generate ideas.

Observe and Discuss

- Walk through your neighborhood, a local park, or an area of natural beauty. What images catch your eye?
- Look through photos of the people and events of your life. What ideas do they spark?
- List ideas you gathered through observation and discuss them with a partner. Circle the topic that is the most interesting.

Review your responses and choose a topic.

126   Poetry and Description

Say: The first question in the first column asks who might enjoy my poem and suggests several possible audiences. If **I choose** the second topic from the Topic Bank, about my personal hero, I think my audience would be anyone interested in knowing about my ideas, such as readers of the school paper and online friends.

Ask: Based on your topic, who is most likely to enjoy reading your poem? Who would you most like to read it? (**Responses will vary.**)

Have students with similar topics work in small groups to discuss and respond to the remaining questions.

Coach's Corner

You may wish to model prewriting activities for students by brainstorming for your own writing topic. Use these prompts to model your thought process:

- **My broad topic is** family and friends.
- **I can narrow my topic by** focusing on a kind act by someone who cares for me.

Discuss the choices you make and solicit feedback from students.

3 Writing Journal ▶

Students record their answers to questions about audience and purpose in their online journals or notebooks.

ture Assignment **Prewriting** *Feature Assignment* **Prewriting**

Narrow Your Topic

Choosing a topic that is too broad may result in a poem that lacks focus.

Apply It! Use a graphic organizer like the one shown to narrow your topic.

- Write your general topic in the top box, and keep narrowing your topic as you move down the chart.
- Your last box should hold your narrowest or "smallest" topic, the new focus or central image of your poem.

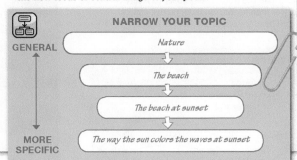

NARROW YOUR TOPIC

GENERAL → Nature → The beach → The beach at sunset → The way the sun colors the waves at sunset ← MORE SPECIFIC

Consider Your Audience and Purpose

Before writing, think about your audience and purpose. Think about how others may see things as you ask yourself these questions.

Questions for Audience	Questions for Purpose
• Who might enjoy my poem? My teacher? Readers of the school paper? My online friends?	• Do I want to entertain my audience, make them feel emotions, or something else?
• What form of poetry would best convey my meaning to my audience?	• What kinds of poetic techniques will help me fulfill my purpose?
• How will I help readers visualize my images?	• What figurative language and graphic elements will help me fulfill my purpose?

Record your answers in your writing journal.

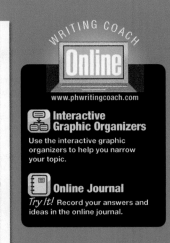

WRITING COACH

Online

www.phwritingcoach.com

Interactive Graphic Organizers

Use the interactive graphic organizers to help you narrow your topic.

Online Journal

Try It! Record your answers and ideas in the online journal.

Prewriting 127

Personalized Support

Interactive Graphic Organizer

Below Level Students complete three graphic organizers that provide models and scaffolded support.

On Level Students complete one, two, or three graphic organizers, depending on how much support they need.

Above Level Students complete the least scaffolded graphic organizer or narrow their topic without the help of a graphic organizer.

Differentiated Instruction

RTI Strategy for Special Needs Students
Find several pictures of people, places, or objects, making sure each picture shows one strong, clear image. For example, a picture might show a vase of colorful flowers or a bird feeding its babies in a nest. Show each picture to students and ask them to describe what they see in the picture in their own words. Record their responses in lists on the board. Create one list for each picture.

Ask each student to choose one of the pictures to use as the topic for his or her poem. Suggest that students use the responses in the list for their picture to help them as they write. Encourage them to focus on describing their picture using figurative language that helps readers visualize the image. Then, remind students of the other characteristics of a rhyming poem and haiku.

The Digital • Print Path ▶

1 Using **Writing Coach Online**™ or the student book, students read and discuss the model graphic organizer.

2 Students complete online or printed graphic organizers to develop their ideas and gather details.

Plan Your Piece

Explain that writers use graphic organizers to develop their ideas and show relationships between different parts of the text. Then, point out the Develop Your Ideas graphic organizer on page 128. Tell students that they will use this organizer to develop details for their poem. Then, distribute printed copies or have students log on to Writing Coach Online.

Introduce the graphic organizer by explaining that the center circle contains the poem's topic, theme, or controlling idea. The other circles identify ideas, feelings, and sensory details related to the central idea.

Develop a Topic, Theme, or Controlling Idea Guide students to notice that the topic in the example organizer is based on the narrowed topic from page 127. Have students write a sentence or phrase that expresses their topic, theme, or controlling idea and record it on their graphic organizer.

Develop Ideas and Details Ask students to identify the kinds of details recorded in each supporting circle. Remind students that each detail should be related to their topic, theme, or controlling idea. Then, have students work in pairs to discuss and record details for their poems on their graphic organizers.

Poet's Toolbox

Remind students that poets express their ideas in a variety of ways. Then, guide students to use the techniques in the Poet's Toolbox to express the ideas in the example graphic organizer.

Say: I notice that the Sights circle on the Develop Your Ideas graphic organizer contains the detail "sparkles on the surface." The Poet's Toolbox shows how this detail can be expressed using the sound device of alliteration: "Sunshine sparkles on the sea."

Ask: How could you use a simile, or a comparison using *like* or *as,* to convey the idea of "soft wind" from the graphic organizer's Touch circle? (**Possible response:** The wind on my skin feels as soft as a kitten's fur.)

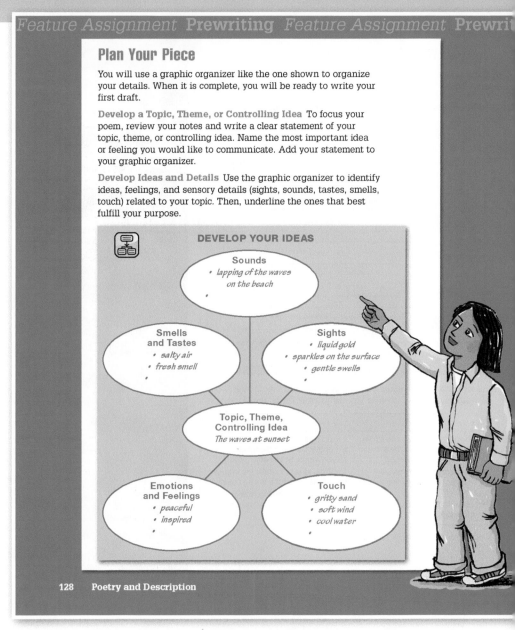

Plan Your Piece

You will use a graphic organizer like the one shown to organize your details. When it is complete, you will be ready to write your first draft.

Develop a Topic, Theme, or Controlling Idea To focus your poem, review your notes and write a clear statement of your topic, theme, or controlling idea. Name the most important idea or feeling you would like to communicate. Add your statement to your graphic organizer.

Develop Ideas and Details Use the graphic organizer to identify ideas, feelings, and sensory details (sights, sounds, tastes, smells, touch) related to your topic. Then, underline the ones that best fulfill your purpose.

DEVELOP YOUR IDEAS

Sounds
• lapping of the waves on the beach

Smells and Tastes
• salty air
• fresh smell

Sights
• liquid gold
• sparkles on the surface
• gentle swells

Topic, Theme, Controlling Idea
The waves at sunset

Emotions and Feelings
• peaceful
• inspired

Touch
• gritty sand
• soft wind
• cool water

128   Poetry and Description

Have students work in small groups to apply other poetic techniques to the details in the Develop Your Ideas organizer on page 128.

Try It! Read aloud the instructions for reviewing students' graphic organizers. Then, have students work in small groups to discuss the poetic techniques they would like to use in their poems. Remind students to use a variety of techniques and sensory details to express their ideas and feelings.

Writer's Block

IF students have difficulty understanding any of the poetic techniques or literary devices in the Poet's Toolbox . . .

THEN help them find other examples of the techniques in the Student Model poems or provide additional examples for them to study.

Students refer back to the Mentor Texts or the Student Models as they plan their writing.

re Assignment **Prewriting** Feature Assignment **Prewriting**

Poet's Toolbox

Writers use a variety of poetic techniques and literary devices to convey ideas, create images, and appeal to readers' emotions. Here are some techniques you might use in your poem.

Figurative language is writing that means something beyond what the words actually say.	
Simile: comparison using *like* or *as*	*The waves are like gentle hills, rolling in the distance.*
Metaphor: comparison made by saying that one thing is something else	*The beach is my home.*
Personification: human characteristics applied to non-human objects	*The wind whispers quietly.*
Symbols add depth and insight to poetry.	
An object that stands for something else	*The gulls soaring overhead might be symbols of freedom.*
Sound Devices create a musical or emotional effect.	
Alliteration: repetition of consonant sounds at the beginning of nearby words	*Sunshine sparkles on the sea.*
Assonance: repetition of vowel sounds in nearby words	*Winds blow and waves grow in an endless flow.*
Consonance: repetition of consonants in the middle or at the end of words	*I watch as each beached wave reaches out to me.*
Structural Elements help build the framework for poetic language.	
Rhyme: repetition of sounds at the ends of lines of poetry	*"Sunshine sparkles on the sea* *As the wind whispers quietly."*
Meter: rhythmical pattern of a poem. It is determined by stressed syllables in a line. Some forms of poetry have specific patterns of stressed syllables.	*Sunshine sparkles on the sea* (Stressed syllables in poetry are marked with a ´, while unstressed syllables are marked with a ˘.)
Graphic Elements position the words on the page.	
Arrangement of words on a page	capital letters, line spacing, and line breaks

 Apply It! Review the ideas and details you added to your prewriting graphic organizer.

- First, confirm the poetic form you will develop.
- Then, decide what techniques from the Poet's Toolbox you would like to use in your poem. Keep in mind that some poetic techniques must be used in specific forms, while other techniques are optional.

WRITING COACH
Online
www.phwritingcoach.com

 Interactive Graphic Organizers
Use the interactive graphic organizers to help you create a plan for your writing.

Interactive Model
Refer back to the Interactive Model in the eText as you plan your writing.

Personalized Support

 Interactive Graphic Organizer

Below Level Students complete three graphic organizers that provide models and scaffolded support.

On Level Students complete one, two, or three graphic organizers, depending on how much support they need.

Above Level Students complete the least scaffolded graphic organizer or narrow their topic without the help of a graphic organizer.

FEEDBACK **Teacher or Peer Feedback**

To provide feedback to students as they plan their first draft, ask or have student partners ask one another the following:

- What do you want your audience to know about the topic?
- What questions or concerns will your audience have about the topic?
- What details have you identified for your piece? How do these details support your thesis or controlling idea?
- Are your details varied? Will they interest your readers? Explain.

Differentiated Instruction

Strategy for Spanish Speakers
Students whose home language is Spanish may encounter difficulties using assonance due to the phonetic spelling of vowel sounds in Spanish. Remind students that some vowel sounds may have multiple spellings in English. Review common spellings of different vowel sounds. For example, elicit spellings for the long ō sound such as *o, o* with silent *e, oa,* and *ow.* Then have students give examples for each, such as *go, mope, boat,* and *snow.*

PRE-AP **Enrichment for Above-Level Students** Challenge students to use at least one poetic technique or literary device from each group shown in the Poet's Toolbox in their poem. Students would include at least one kind of figurative language, one symbol, one sound device, one structural element, and one graphic element. Remind them to keep in mind which are required for their chosen poetic form and which are optional.

The Digital • Print Path ▶

1 WRITING COACH Online | STUDENT BOOK ▶

Using *Writing Coach Online™* or the student book, students read and discuss the charts of poetry characteristics.

2 WRITING COACH Online | STUDENT BOOK ▶

Students discuss how the Mentor Texts illustrate the characteristics of a rhyming poem and haiku.

Drafting

Tell students that they will use the charts on page 130 to help them develop drafts of their poems. Explain that the first column of each chart lists the characteristics of a specific poetic form. The second column contains questions that will help guide students' work.

Drafting a Rhyming Poem or Haiku

Link the charts to specific poetic forms by having students turn to the Mentor Texts on pages 122–123. Then, guide students to respond to the chart questions.

Say: I see that the rhyming poem chart asks which words I will rhyme in each stanza. The rhyming poem "Baby Ate a Microchip" shows one way I might rhyme words in stanzas. In the first stanza, the ends of the first and second lines rhyme *(microchip/sip),* and the ends of the third and fourth lines rhyme *(beep/deep).*

Ask: Do the other stanzas in this poem have the same pattern of rhyme? Describe it. (Yes, other stanzas also have an AABB rhyme scheme.)

Have students who are writing the same kind of poem work with a partner to respond to the chart questions. You may wish to direct students writing rhyming poems to these characteristics in the Mentor Text on p. 122:

- Poetic techniques used (lines 3, 11–12)
- Vivid descriptions (lines 5–8, 15–16)

Direct students writing a haiku to these characteristics in the Mentor Texts on p. 123:

- One central image, often from nature (all three haiku, line 1)
- Figurative language ("Nightime in Winter," lines 1–3; "Sunrise," line 1)

Drafting Feature Assignment Drafting Feature Assignment

Drafting

During the drafting stage, you will start to write your ideas for your rhyming poem, haiku, or other poetic form you chose. First, **choose an appropriate organizational strategy,** based on the form of poem you choose to write. Then, **build on the ideas** you developed in your graphic organizer to **write a focused, organized, and coherent** poem.

Drafting a Rhyming Poem or Haiku

Each poetic form has specific characteristics. You will write your poem using these characteristics, the techniques from the Poet's Toolbox, and the ideas, feelings, and sensory details you developed in your graphic organizer. The charts show the characteristics of each form. Review the characteristics. Then, answer the questions in the right column as you draft your poem.

Rhyming Poem Characteristics	Questions to Answer While Drafting
• Varied number of lines • Varied number of stanzas • Rhyme at the ends of lines • Poetic techniques used • Figurative language likely used • Vivid descriptions	• How long will my poem be? • How will I break the lines into stanzas? **Tip:** Stanzas should focus on a single idea or image. • Will each stanza have the same number of lines? • What words will I rhyme in each stanza? **Tip:** Consult a rhyming dictionary. • What poetic techniques will I use? • How can I use figurative language? • How will I make my descriptions vivid?

Haiku Characteristics	Questions to Answer While Drafting
• One central image, often from nature • 3 lines of 5, 7, and 5 syllables each • Feeling or emotion conveyed • Precise wording • Typically does not include rhyme • Figurative language may be used • Poetic techniques may be used	• What image will I choose? • How can I choose the best words with the correct number of syllables? **Tip:** Consult a thesaurus. • What feelings or emotions will I express? • What figurative language or poetic techniques will I use?

130   **Poetry and Description**

Start Your Draft

For each stage of the drafting process, have small groups read aloud and discuss the boxed instructions. Then, direct students to work individually on their first draft.

Coach's Corner

If you are modeling the writing process for students with your own topic or a student volunteer's, you may wish to use these prompts to guide your drafting and discussion:

- I will **organize my ideas** into lines and stanzas.
- I will use **vivid descriptions** to express my ideas and feelings.

Discuss the choices you make and solicit feedback from students.

3  Using *Writing Coach Online™* or the student book, students refer back to the Mentor Text or Student Model as they edit their writing.

4  Using *Writing Coach Online™* or the student book, students evaluate their writing using the rubrics.

5 Students submit edited drafts to their teacher.

6  Students receive personalized feedback from their teacher.

Feature Assignment **Editing** Feature Assignment **Editing**

Grammar Mini-Lesson:
Prepositional Phrases

To learn more, see Chapter 19.

Prepositional phrases can also be used as **transitions** between ideas. A transition appears at the beginning of a sentence and is followed by a comma. Notice how the Student Model author uses a prepositional phrase as a transition.

 **STUDENT MODEL** from **Playing to Win** page 99; lines 32–34

At the game the following week, Lara stood in the outfield in the sweltering afternoon sun, a trickle of sweat dripping down her back.

Try It! Copy each sentence into your journal. Underline the prepositional phrases in each sentence, and then place a comma after each phrase used as a transition.

In the meantime a new game had started in Field Park.

Since the season ended the players have more time for other activities.

Apply It! Edit your draft for grammar, mechanics, and spelling. If necessary, rewrite some sentences to ensure that you have used prepositional phrases as transitions to organize your writing.

Use the rubric to evaluate your piece. If necessary, rethink, rewrite, or revise.

Rubric for Short Story: Realistic Short Story	Rating Scale
Ideas: How well have you developed your characters and plot?	Not very Very 1 2 3 4 5 6
Organization: How clearly organized are the events in your story?	1 2 3 4 5 6
Voice: How well does your style engage the reader?	1 2 3 4 5 6
Word Choice: How effective is your word choice in creating setting and characters?	1 2 3 4 5 6
Sentence Fluency: How well have you used transitions to help readers follow the plot?	1 2 3 4 5 6
Conventions: How correct are your prepositional phrases?	1 2 3 4 5 6

WRITING COACH

Online
www.phwritingcoach.com

Video
Learn effective editing techniques from program author Jeff Anderson.

Online Journal
Try It! Record your answers in the online journal.

Interactive Model
Refer back to the Interactive Model as you edit your writing.

Personalized Support

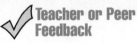 **FEEDBACK** **Teacher or Peer Feedback**

To provide feedback to students as they edit their draft, ask or have student partners ask one another the following:

- Have you looked for mistakes that you tend to make?
- Have you read your piece aloud to yourself or to a partner? What kind of errors did you find?
- Can you show me something you changed through editing?
- What resources have you used to look for possible spelling errors?
- Read this sentence aloud. Does the grammar sound correct to you?
- Read this sentence aloud. Does the punctuation accurately convey your meaning?

Working with ELLs   **ELL** Sheltered Instruction: Metacognitive

As they revise, students should monitor and edit writing for pronoun-antecedent agreement, using self-corrective techniques. Review rules of pronoun-antecedent agreement by thinking aloud as you revise the example sentence *The table and chairs had crumbs on it.* Then:

Beginning Write a list of pronouns or have students refer to a list in their books. Help students use the self-corrective technique of highlighting pronouns and circling antecedents to check for agreement.

Intermediate Have students review their writing with an Advanced High student, using the self-corrective technique of highlighting pronouns and circling antecedents.

Advanced Have students use the self-corrective technique of highlighting the pronouns and circling the antecedents to check for agreement in their drafts. Have students swap stories and double-check pronoun-antecedent agreement.

Advanced High Have students complete the Advanced activity and work with an Intermediate student to help check for pronoun-antecedent agreement. Have students provide specific, helpful feedback.

The Digital • Print Path ▶

1 Using Writing Coach Online™ or the student book, students complete the writing process by deciding the best way to publish their writing for their intended audience.

2 Students record their answers to Reflect on Your Writing in their online journals or notebooks.

Publishing

Wrap Up Your Presentation

Remind students who handwrote their work to use proper margins. For students who wrote their work on a computer, display some easy-to-read computer fonts. Make sure students know how to find them on the computer.

Publish Your Piece

Explain to students that the final step in the writing process is to decide which form of publication will present their work most effectively. Then, introduce students to the chart. Explain that the chart shows how specific audiences can be reached using different kinds of media.

Have students whose short stories address similar audiences work in small groups to discuss appropriate ways to publish their work.

Reflect On Your Writing

Have students discuss the questions with a partner, including the Big Question, and record responses in their journal.

Extension Have students develop a research plan for learning more about their topic. Students should identify what they want to learn, which resources they will use, and how this information could be used to improve or embellish their realistic short story.

Manage Your Portfolio You may wish to have students include development materials such as graphic organizers and drafts.

MAKE YOUR WRITING COUNT

Introduce the dramatic reading activity by discussing the opening paragraphs with students. Make sure students understand that the project may be produced electronically or by hand. Then, guide students through each step in the action plan.

Publishing Feature Assignment Publishing Feature Assignm

Publishing

Share your realistic story with others by publishing it. First, get the story ready to present. Then choose a way to **publish your work for an appropriate audience**.

Wrap Up Your Presentation

Is your short story handwritten or written on a computer? If you use a computer, be sure to choose a readable font. Even though a font can be used to communicate style, the purpose in publishing is to share your writing with readers. That means you must choose a plain, easy-to-read font.

Publish Your Piece

Use this chart to identify a way to publish your written work.

If your audience is...	...then publish it by...
Family or friends	• Presenting it as an audio or video recording of a drama • Reading it aloud at a family and friend gathering
Students or adults in your school	• Posting it to a literary blog and allowing peer and teacher responses • Creating a class Web site of realistic stories for the school library

 Reflect on Your Writing

Now that you are done with your short story, read it over and use your writing journal to answer these questions. Use specific details to describe and explain your reflections. Increase the specificity of your details based on the type of information requested.

- What did you most enjoy about writing a realistic short story? Why?
- What did you find to be the most difficult? Why?

The Big Question: Why Write? What can fiction do better than non-fiction?

Manage Your Portfolio You may wish to include your published realistic short story in your writing portfolio. If so, consider what this piece reveals about your writing and your growth as a writer.

Resources You may wish to have students use these graphic organizers: Meeting Agenda, Meeting Notes, and Flow Chart/Series of Events. Distribute printed copies or have students log on to Writing Coach Online.

Use the 21st Century Skills Rubric to evaluate each group's process and final product on a scale of 1 to 3, indicating weak, moderate, or strong use of the skill.

Listening and Speaking Monitor students as they use feedback to refine their presentations.

21st Century Learning

Skills Rubric	Rating
Work Creatively With Others: Demonstrate originality and inventiveness in work.	1 2 3
Apply Technology Effectively: Use technology as a tool to research and communicate information.	1 2 3
Communicate Clearly: Articulate ideas effectively through oral, written, and nonverbal communication skills.	1 2 3
Collaborate With Others: Make compromises in order to achieve a common goal.	1 2 3

3 Students use a variety of graphic organizers, either online or in print, to help them work together to create a multimedia group project.

4 Through Writing Coach Online™ students link to resources on 21st Century Learning for help in creating a multimedia group project.

21st Century Learning

MAKE YOUR WRITING COUNT

Give a Dramatic Reading of a Realistic Story

Realistic fiction often tells dramatic stories about life in the modern world. Bring the world of a short story to life for classmates by performing a **dramatic reading** of realistic fiction.

Working as team, choose a realistic short story to perform in a dramatic reading for your classmates. During the planning, rehearsal, and performance, be open to each group member's perspective, ideas, and input. Perform your dramatic reading live, or record it as an audiobook.

Here's your action plan.

1. Choose roles, such as editor, director, narrator, and actors.

2. With your group, review your peers' short stories. Choose one with multiple characters and plenty of dialogue.

3. Analyze the story. Your group must understand it in order to perform it well.

4. Search online for audio clips of dramatic readings to use as models for your own performance.

5. Mark up the story text to show where to pause, emphasize words, and change speakers. Then, practice reading the story in a group.

   - Make your voice express appropriate emotions.
   - Pause when a character or narrator would pause.
   - Use louder voices to indicate the climax.

6. Perform your reading for the class. You may wish to record your performance, and make it available online for students to download.

Listening and Speaking Work as a team to rehearse for your presentation. Ask group members to listen critically during rehearsal. Take notes to help you improve your performance. During your dramatic reading for the class, use your notes. Speak clearly and in the appropriate tones. After the performance, listen for reactions from your classmates.

WRITING COACH

Online

www.phwritingcoach.com

Online Journal

Reflect on Your Writing Record your answers and ideas in the online journal.

Resource

Link to resources on 21st Century Learning for help in creating a group project.

Personalized Support

FEEDBACK Teacher or Peer Feedback

To provide feedback to students on their published writing, ask or have student partners ask one another the following:

- How did you go about writing this piece? What was your process?

- What did you learn from the writing model that you used in this piece?

- What surprised you the most as you wrote this piece?

- Did you try anything new as you worked on this piece?

- What did you learn from this piece of writing that you would like to remember and reuse?

- What do you think you do best as a writer right now?

Working with ELLs   **ELL** Sheltered Instruction: Cognitive

To help students internalize and build proficiency with new grade-level academic vocabulary, have them use and reuse the vocabulary in contextual speaking activities. Write and say these academic vocabulary words and have students repeat: *accurate, conclusion, consequently, demonstrate, detect.*

Beginning Provide context sentences for the vocabulary, such as *I dropped a glass. Consequently, it broke,* and have students repeat. Help students reuse the vocabulary with oral sentence starters, such as *I missed the end of the film and did not see the _____.*

Intermediate Define each word and have students use it in a sentence. Have students reuse the words to discuss a story they have read.

Advanced Have partners look up each word in a dictionary and each say a sentence using the word correctly. Have them reuse each word in a discussion about a story they have read.

Advanced High Have students complete the Advanced activity and then use each word as they give feedback on classmates' Dramatic Reading of a Realistic Story.

The Digital · Print Path ▶

1

Students use *Writing Coach Online*™ or their student books to analyze and discuss the Writing for Media topic.

Your Turn ▶ Writing for Media: Audio Script

Audio Script

Discuss the opening paragraph with students. As a class, discuss examples of audio scripts that students have listened to and examples of stories or television programs that might be effective as audio programs.

Try It! Guide students to understand the structure of the sample audio script, helping students identify the dialogue and stage directions.

Say: I notice that the first *Try It!* question asks about the drama's focus. The stage direction says that the scene is a county fairground, and the stage direction mentions livestock and judging animals. So I know the drama's focus is the animal competition at a county fair.

Ask: What other details help you get a sense of the drama's focus? (the loudspeaker's announcement and the stage direction describing animal sounds)

Have students discuss the remaining questions in small groups and record individual responses in their journals.

Extension Have students bring in other examples of audio scripts. Lead a media discussion about the examples, using the *Try It!* questions as a guide.

Create an Audio Script

Tell students that they will create an audio script using the five-step writing process. Then, preview the writing process instructions on page 115.

> **Resources** You may wish to have students use the Flow Chart/Series of Events graphic organizer. Distribute printed copies or have students log on to Writing Coach Online.

For each step in the writing process, have partners read aloud and discuss the list of tasks. Then, have them work individually. Once both partners have completed the tasks,

---

Writing for Media Writing for Media Writing for Media Writ

Your Turn ▶ Writing for Media: Audio Script

21st Century Learning

Audio Script

An **audio script** is a piece of writing that is made especially for radio, podcast, or online listening. Just like a film or stage script, it has a plot, lines for characters, settings, and directions. However, an audio script depends on dialogue with sensory details, music, and sound effects because its audience will not be able to see the characters and setting or read about them on a page. Like other stories, audio script drama have a focus, point of view, plot, setting, and characters.

 Try It! Study the script. Then, answer these questions in your journal.

1. Which details help you to get a sense of the drama's **focus**?
2. What evidence of a **problem** do you see?
3. How would you describe the **characters**?
4. Which **sensory details** add to the description?
5. Do you think the **setting** is realistic? Explain.
6. Identify **sound effects** and **directions** used in the script. How do they support the story?

Extension Find another example of a radio drama or audio script and compare it with this one.

114   **Short Story**

Maribelle Strikes Again!

[Scene: A county fairground. JEFF and his sister CAITLYN are walking through the carnival grounds on the way to one of the livestock barns. The sounds of footsteps as well as carnival music can be heard in the background.]

LOUDSPEAKER. The judges will be in the livestock barns in 15 minutes to judge the animals.

JEFF. I didn't realize it was so late, Caitlyn! Hurry!

[Sound of running footsteps and heavy breathing]

CAITLYN. [Out of breath] Do you think Maribelle will win?

JEFF. [Out of breath] Yes. [pause] Whew! We made it.

[Sounds of footsteps slow to a walk. Various animal sounds are in the background—goats and sheep.]

JEFF. [Gasps] Oh no! Where's Maribelle? Caitlyn, she's not in her pen! Why would someone steal Maribelle?!

CAITLYN. I don't see her, Jeff! I bet she escaped again. How does she do it? [chuckles] Let's go see if we can find her, but I bet we won't be able to find her in time for the judges.

[Sound of judges' discussions in the distance.]

JEFF. How much do you want to bet...? Let's go!

[Sound of running footsteps]

WOMAN. [Shrieking] Where did this goat come from? It's eating my prize-winning pie!

CAITLYN. [Calmly] Ma'am, I'm really very sorry. Okay, Maribelle. Let's go, you little escape artist!

CAITLYN. I bet we still have time to get her back to her pen for the judging. Let's go, Jeff!

---

have them evaluate each other's work before moving to the next step.

Use the 21st Century Skills Rubric to evaluate each student's process and final product on a scale of 1 to 3, indicating weak, moderate, or strong use of the skill. ▶

Partner Talk

Remind students to keep in mind the traits of a radio drama and carefully consider whether their partner's idea will be effective in this form.

21st Century Learning

Skills Rubric	Rating
Think Creatively: Use a wide range of idea creation techniques.	1 2 3
Communicate Clearly: Utilize multiple media and technologies and know how to judge their effectiveness.	1 2 3
Create Media Products: Understand and use the most appropriate media creation tools.	1 2 3
Manage Projects: Prioritize, plan, and manage work to achieve the intended result.	1 2 3

2  **Writing Journal**

Students learn about the characteristics of an audio script by answering questions about the model. Students record their answers to the *Try It!* questions in their online journals or notebooks.

3 **STUDENT BOOK**

Students follow the five-step writing process to write their own audio script. Students may select online or printed graphic organizers to help them plan and develop their writing.

dia Writing for Media Writing for Media **Writing for Media**

 ## Create an Audio Script

Follow these steps to create your own audio script. To plan your script, review the graphic organizers on pages R24–R27 and choose one that suits your needs.

Prewriting

- Write a list of possible ideas for your audio script and select the one that would suit a play best.
- Identify the focus of the script and its point of view. For example, will your play be funny, serious, scary, or something else? Will you use third- or first-person narration?
- Decide the setting. Remember, you will have to use dialogue with sensory details to help listeners imagine the setting.
- Write descriptions of the script's characters.
- Before you draft, summarize the events of the script. Be sure to tell a full narrative. Introduce a conflict and then resolve it.

Drafting

- Use language that reflects who the characters are. Think about their backgrounds as you create dialogue.
- Make sure the conflict and resolution are well-developed.
- Be sure to provide helpful directions to the performers. Keep in mind that your audio script is meant for actors.

Revising and Editing

- Review your draft to make sure events are organized logically. Make sure the problem and the outcome of the story are clear.
- Use the Revision RADaR strategy to improve your draft.
- Check that spelling, grammar, and mechanics are correct.

Publishing

- Make an audio recording of your script. Use a music player and sound effects to create more realistic scenes. Make posters to advertise your script.
- Perform your audio script for the class. Create a division in the classroom that prevents your classmates from seeing you and allows them to just listen.

WRITING COACH
Online
www.phwritingcoach.com

Online Journal
Try It! Record your answers in the online journal.

Interactive Graphic Organizers
Choose from a variety of graphic organizers to plan and develop your project.

> **Partner Talk**
>
> Before you start drafting, use specific details to describe and explain the theme of your audio script to a partner. Ask for feedback about your theme. For example, will your story sustain reader interest?

Personalized Support

FEEDBACK ## Teacher or Peer Feedback

To provide feedback to students as they write for media, ask or have student partners ask one another the following:

- What are the main characteristics of this form of writing?
- Have you included most or all of these characteristics in your piece of writing?
- What is your purpose for writing this piece?
- Who is your audience?
- How did you organize your ideas in this piece of writing?
- How did you go about revising the piece? Editing it?
- How do you plan on publishing your piece?
- What other publishing options also might work?

Working with ELLs   **ELL** Sheltered Instruction: Cognitive

Help students understand the general meaning, main points, and important details in spoken language ranging from the familiar to the unfamiliar. Relate a narrative to students, such as a scene in a movie, with language ranging from familiar, like *man*, to unfamiliar, like *character*. Then:

Beginning Help students understand your summary using visuals. Help students identify your general meaning, main points, and important details. Help them use familiar language, such as *people*, to understand unfamiliar language, such as *characters*.

Intermediate Have groups restate the general meaning, main points, and important details of your summary. Help them use familiar language, such as *story*, to understand unfamiliar language, such as *drama*.

Advanced Have partners restate the general meaning, main points, and important details of your summary to each other, then identify unfamiliar words in your description and find their meaning using familiar words as context.

Advanced High Have students complete the Advanced activity, then present a summary of a movie as partners take notes.

STUDENT BOOK

Before they write, students use the ABCDs of On-Demand Writing to analyze and plan how to respond to each prompt. They can use either their online journals or notebooks to take notes.

Writing for Assessment

Read aloud or have a student read aloud the introductory text. Then, tell students that they will learn and practice a technique for writing in response to a prompt.

Try It! Read aloud the Short Story Prompt, then have volunteers read aloud the Format and Academic Vocabulary boxes. Tell students that they will use the ABCD method to respond to the prompt.

The ABCDs of On-Demand Writing

Have students identify the words associated with the ABCD method. (attack, brainstorm, choose, detect) Then, guide students through their use.

Think Aloud   **I'll attack the prompt** by circling the words *describe, establish,* and *use.* These words remind me to use sensory details and to make every part of the story believable. I can rewrite the prompt to state that clearly: "Write a story using sensory details and dialogue to make every part of the story believable."

Work with students to brainstorm for an appropriate graphic organizer for a short story, such as a story chart.

Have students write their drafts individually and then work with a partner to detect errors.

More Prompts for Practice

Apply It! **Test Prep** Have students apply the ABCD method to the two practice prompts.

Prompt 1 Have partners attack the prompt and brainstorm for possible answers. Then, have each pair swap their information with

another group to evaluate whether the teams have developed a focused and believable short story.

Prompt 2 Have students work individually to attack the prompt and brainstorm for possible answers. Then, have students work in small groups to evaluate their work before writing their drafts.

Test Prep Spiral Review: Narrative Read aloud the instructions and the prompt. Then, have students review the personal narrative characteristics on page 66.

Prompt 3 Remind students to use the ABCD method to write their personal narrative.

---

ssment **Writing for Assessment** *Writing for Assessment* Wr

Writing for Assessment

You may have to write to a prompt that asks you to write creatively. Use the prompts on these pages to practice. Respond using the characteristics of your realistic short story. (See page 92.)

Try It! To begin, read the realistic **short story** prompt and the information on format and academic vocabulary. Use the ABCDs of On-Demand Writing to help you plan and write your short story.

Format
The prompt directs you to write a *short story.* Start with a beginning that introduces the conflict. Include a middle that develops the problem. Finish by showing what happens after the climax.

Short Story Prompt
Write a **short story** about a character who wins the lottery. Describe the events of the story using sensory details. Establish a believable setting, interesting characters, and events that move toward a solution. Use **dialogue** to develop your story.

Academic Vocabulary
Remember that *dialogue* is the conversation between two or more characters.

The ABCDs of On-Demand Writing

Use the following ABCDs to help you respond to the prompt.

Before you write your draft:

Attack the prompt [1 MINUTE]
- Circle or highlight important verbs in the prompt. Draw a line from the verb to what it refers to.
- Rewrite the prompt in your own words.

Brainstorm possible answers [4 MINUTES]
- Create a graphic organizer to generate ideas.
- Use one for each part of the prompt if necessary.

Choose the order of your response [1 MINUTE]
- Think about the best way to organize your ideas.
- Number your ideas in the order you will write about them. Cross out ideas you will not be using.

After you write your draft:

Detect errors before turning in the draft [1 MINUTE]
- Carefully reread your writing.
- Make sure that your response makes sense and is complete.
- Look for spelling, punctuation, and grammar errors.

116   **Short Story**

Differentiated Instruction Boxes in this Teacher's Edition address these student populations:
- Below-Level Students
- Gifted and Talented Students
- English Language Learners
- Above-Level Students
- Special Needs Students
- Spanish Speaking Students

In addition, for further enrichment, see the **Extension** features.

LESSON OBJECTIVES

- To learn the forms and defining characteristics of exposition.
- To learn the elements of a successful compare-and-contrast essay, the chapter Feature Assignment.
- To read a Mentor Text in the genre, analyzing its use of the elements of an effective expository essay.
- To read a Student Model of a compare-and-contrast essay, analyzing it from the perspective of a reader and from the perspective of a writer.
- To apply prewriting strategies in developing a compare-and-contrast essay, including strategies for choosing and narrowing a topic, planning writing, and gathering details, as well as tips for considering audience and purpose.
- To apply drafting strategies in developing a compare-and-contrast essay.
- To apply RADaR revision strategies to a draft compare-and-contrast essay.
- To learn about the Focus on Craft topic, improving transitions, and apply what is learned to a draft compare-and-contrast essay.
- To edit the draft, zooming in on subordinating conjunctions and focusing on using commas with subordinate clauses.
- To complete the Make Your Writing Count assignment, developing a survey and presenting the survey results.
- To complete the Writing for Media assignment, developing a consumer comparison.
- To practice writing for assessment.

DAY 4

Prewriting
- Plan Your Piece
- Gather Details

ONLINE

DAY 5

Drafting
- Outline for Success
- Start Your Draft

ONLINE

DAY 9

WRITING FOR MEDIA
- **Consumer Comparison**
- Create a Consumer Comparison

ONLINE

DAY 10

WRITING FOR ASSESSMENT
- Compare-and-Contrast Prompt
- The ABCDs of On-Demand Writing
- More Prompts for Practice
- Spiral Review: Poetry

ONLINE

Personalized Assessment

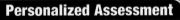

	Ongoing Assessment	Formal Assessment of Feature Assignment	Progress Monitoring at End-of-Chapter
Interactive Writing Coach™	Use Paragraph Feedback and Essay Scorer as a revision tool.	Use Essay Scorer to score students' Feature Assignment papers.	Use Essay Scorer to score students' papers. Students' learner profiles can be adjusted based on their scores.
FEEDBACK **Teacher Conferencing**	Use rubrics in the Student Edition as a revision tool. Conference with students to review their work and provide personalized support.	Use rubrics in the Student Edition to score students' Feature Assignment papers.	Review each student's work to plan targeted resources for the next writing assignment.

The Digital • Print Path ▶

1  ▶

Using *Writing Coach Online*™ or the student book, students discuss the photograph in the chapter opener as it relates to the writing genre.

2  ▶

Students record their ideas and responses in their online journals or notebooks. They may also record and save their responses on pop-up sticky notes in *Writing Coach Online*™.

Chapter Objectives

1. Write an expository essay by planning, drafting, revising, editing, and publishing individual work.

2. Produce a survey.

3. Use the five-step writing process to write a consumer comparison.

4. Write a compare-and-contrast essay and a poem in response to a prompt.

EXPOSITION

How Can You Explain This?

Activate Prior Knowledge Tell students that the purpose of expository writing is to explain an idea or ideas. Tell students that they will use what they know about dogs to explain the photo on page 144. Then, guide the students in analyzing the photo.

 Think Aloud To write an expository essay means to explain a topic or idea. Sometimes you may explain a topic by showing how two things are alike and different. For example, in this photo **I see** two animals. They appear to have many differences. One is very large and one is very small.

Work with students to brainstorm for another difference based on their analysis of the photo.

Try It! **Have students** work individually to develop responses to the questions. Check that students have identified similarities and differences.

Possible responses: The dogs are similar in that they are both the same species of animal, with four legs and similarly shaped bodies. They are different in that one is very large and one is very small, and one is dark and one is golden. Details that could be used to describe the dogs include color; length of fur; size of head, ears, and tail; and length of legs.

CHAPTER 8

EXPOSITION

144   Exposition

Connect to the Big Questions

Have students use their experience to discuss the Big Questions. Explain that they will revisit **Why write?** at the end of this chapter. Tell students to consider these points during their discussion:

1. What have you learned from friends who are similar to you? From friends who are different from you?

2. Considering how two things are similar and different is only useful if the two things have one or more fundamental similarities.

What's Ahead

Have students preview the Mentor Text and Student Model on pages 148–151. Tell students that they will write their own compare-and-contrast essay using the five-step writing process: prewriting, drafting, revising, editing, and publishing.

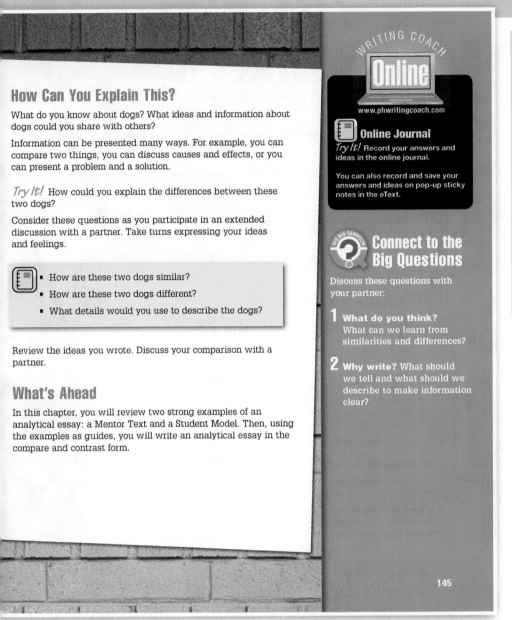

How Can You Explain This?

What do you know about dogs? What ideas and information about dogs could you share with others?

Information can be presented many ways. For example, you can compare two things, you can discuss causes and effects, or you can present a problem and a solution.

Try It! How could you explain the differences between these two dogs?

Consider these questions as you participate in an extended discussion with a partner. Take turns expressing your ideas and feelings.

- How are these two dogs similar?
- How are these two dogs different?
- What details would you use to describe the dogs?

Review the ideas you wrote. Discuss your comparison with a partner.

What's Ahead

In this chapter, you will review two strong examples of an analytical essay: a Mentor Text and a Student Model. Then, using the examples as guides, you will write an analytical essay in the compare and contrast form.

WRITING COACH

Online
www.phwritingcoach.com

Online Journal
Try It! Record your answers and ideas in the online journal.

You can also record and save your answers and ideas on pop-up sticky notes in the eText.

Connect to the Big Questions

Discuss these questions with your partner:

1 **What do you think?** What can we learn from similarities and differences?

2 **Why write?** What should we tell and what should we describe to make information clear?

145

The Digital • Print Path ▶

WRITING COACH Online

STUDENT BOOK

1

STUDENT BOOK

Students learn vocabulary from the Word Bank and listen to English and Spanish pronunciations in the **Writing Coach Online™** glossary.

2

Writing Journal

Students record answers to questions about forms of writing in their online journals or notebooks.

EXPOSITORY ESSAY

To introduce this chapter's writing form, discuss the opening paragraphs with students. Make sure students understand that a compare-and-contrast essay is a type of expository essay. Explain that good writers use a step-by-step process to develop their work. Then, have students preview the rubric on page 163.

Expository Essay: Compare-and-Contrast Essay

Ask volunteers to read aloud the feature assignment characteristics. Tell students that they will identify these characteristics in a Mentor Text and a Student Model. Then, they will use the characteristics to guide the writing of their own compare-and-contrast essay.

Other Forms of Expository Writing

Guide students to understand how the forms of expository essays are alike and different.

Say: I notice that there are many forms of expository writing, some of which I read more often than others. For example, I've read many newspaper and magazine articles, both in print and on the Internet. However, I read classification essays less often.

Ask: How are expository essays alike? (They all provide information or explain something.) How are they different? (Each form has a different purpose and organizational structure.)

Have students brainstorm for appropriate topics for each writing form.

Try It! **Remind students** that the audience is the people who will read their writing. The purpose is the author's reason for writing. **Have students** record their responses in their journal.

Possible responses: Pro/con essay tells reasons for and against an action or decision; problem/solution essay explores a problem and presents one or more solutions; cause-and-effect essay traces the results of an event

EXPOSITORY ESSAY

An expository essay gives readers information about a topic. In this chapter, you will learn to write a type of expository essay known as a compare-and-contrast essay. A compare-and-contrast essay organizes this information by showing similarities and differences. Compare-and-contrast essays often present different points of view on an issue or information about many products.

You will develop the compare-and-contrast essay by taking it through each of the steps of the writing process: prewriting, drafting, revising, editing, and publishing. You will also have an opportunity to develop a consumer report, which provides information about products. To preview the criteria for how your compare-and-contrast essay will be evaluated, see the rubric on page 163.

FEATURE ASSIGNMENT

Expository Essay: Compare-and-Contrast Essay

An effective expository essay has these characteristics:

- Detailed **information** and **explanations** about a specific topic to guide and inform the reader's understanding of key ideas and evidence
- An effective **introduction** that states the main idea and **conclusion** that wraps up the essay
- An **organized structure** that logically follows the writer's points
- A **variety of sentence structures** to keep readers interested and **transitions** to connect ideas

- **Effective sentence structure** and correct spelling, grammar, and usage

A compare-and-contrast essay also includes:

- A **thesis** statement that sets up the compare/contrast points
- Specific **facts, details,** and **examples** to support the thesis

146   Expository Essay

Word Bank

To assist English Language Learners and struggling readers, echo read each word or have students log on to Writing Coach Online to listen to the pronunciations. Then, have partners take turns using each word in a sentence. Ask volunteers to share one of their sentences with the class.

Teacher Tip

Have student pairs quiz each other on the types of expository essays. Have one student read either the type of essay or its description. The other student responds by stating the missing information.

Other Forms of Expository Writing

In addition to compare-and-contrast essays, there are other forms of expository writing, including:

Cause-and-effect essays trace the results of an event or the reasons an event happened.

Classification essays organize a subject into categories or explain the category into which an item falls.

Newspaper and magazine articles that are printed or published on the Internet supply relevant information about a particular topic by analyzing the topic's elements. They may also reflect genres other than analytical essays—for example, persuasive writing, or narrative nonfiction writing.

Pro/con essays examine the arguments for and against a particular action or decision.

Problem/solution essays explore a particular problem and present one or more possible solutions to it. They may address concerns related to personal issues; businesses or consumers; or the local, national, or global community.

 Try It! For each audience and purpose described, choose a form, such as a speech, essay, or review, that is appropriate for conveying your intended meaning to the audience. Explain your choices.

- To tell your friends the reasons for and against buying a particular video game
- To inform your community about ways to fix a local pollution problem
- To inform classmates about a new scientific discovery

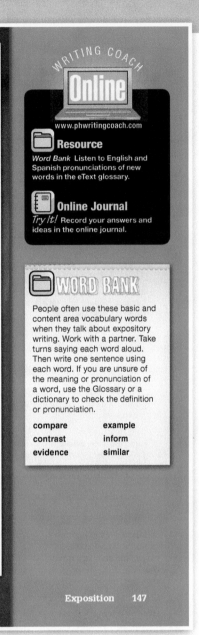

WRITING COACH

Online

www.phwritingcoach.com

📁 **Resource**

Word Bank Listen to English and Spanish pronunciations of new words in the eText glossary.

📓 **Online Journal**

Try It! Record your answers and ideas in the online journal.

📁 WORD BANK

People often use these basic and content area vocabulary words when they talk about expository writing. Work with a partner. Take turns saying each word aloud. Then write one sentence using each word. If you are unsure of the meaning or pronunciation of a word, use the Glossary or a dictionary to check the definition or pronunciation.

compare	example
contrast	inform
evidence	similar

Personalized Support

FEEDBACK Teacher or Peer Feedback

To help students understand the characteristics of the writing form, ask or have student partners ask one another the following questions:

- What are the main characteristics of an expository essay?
- What makes this form of writing different from other forms?
- Who are the likely readers or audiences for this form of writing?
- What kind of organization could be used for this form of writing?
- What kind of voice would be most effective for this form of writing?

Working with ELLs   ELL Sheltered Instruction: Cognitive

Using the first *Try It!* activity, have students expand and internalize initial English vocabulary, learning, using, and reusing basic, high-frequency words to orally identify and describe objects. List these high-frequency words on the board: *great, well, different, change, power,* **and** *machine.*

Beginning Use the words in phrases that list reasons for and against buying a particular game. Help students use and reuse the words as they say the phrases aloud.

Intermediate Help students use the vocabulary to orally complete sentences

about whether or not to buy the game. Provide corrective feedback, helping students use and reuse the vocabulary.

Advanced Provide additional high-frequency words, such as *produce, building, carefully, decide,* and *finally.* Have students use and reuse each of the words on the expanded list as they talk about reasons to buy a certain game.

Advanced High Have partners complete the Advanced activity. Extend by having listeners note and discuss any unfamiliar words used by their partners.

The Digital · Print Path ▶

1

Using **Writing Coach Online™** or the student book, students read and listen to an audio recording of the Mentor Text. As they complete their writing assignments, they can refer back to the Mentor Text for support whenever they need it.

MENTOR TEXT

About the Selection The selection is an expository essay about teen volunteers. It explains specific reasons why teens choose to volunteer. Then, it profiles three teens who have participated in three different types of volunteer work: building homes for Habitat for Humanity, caring for penguins at a city zoo, and raising money to end child hunger.

Learn From Experience

After students have read the text, point out that the numbered notes refer to the characteristics of an expository essay introduced on page 146.

Try It! Guide students to understand how the genre characteristics shape the text.

Say: The first *Try It!* question asks what you think the essay will be about. **I notice** that the second sentence describes teens volunteering. This sentence suggests that the essay will be about teens improving the lives of others.

Ask: What does the title suggest about the content of the essay? (It suggests the essay will include profiles of teens who volunteer.)

Have students reply to the *Try It!* questions in their journals. If students have difficulty responding to a particular question, model a response, as with Question 1.

Check the accuracy and completeness of student responses.

1. Responses will vary. The description of teens doing volunteer work in the second sentence indicates that this is a main topic.

2. Responses will vary. People have different motivations for volunteering.

3. Responses will vary. Students may note that the statistic that 61% of young people feel responsible for improving the world best supports the controlling idea—teens want to help.

4. Responses will vary. Leena Patel learned to identify with other people by helping build houses; Kaleigh Gerlich got work experience by volunteering at the zoo; Daniel Feldman inspires others with his fight against hunger.

MENTOR TEXT — Expository Essay

Learn From Experience

After reading the expository essay on pages 148–149, read the numbered notes in the margins to learn about how the author presented ideas. Later you will read a Student Model, which shares these characteristics and also has the characteristics of a compare-and-contrast essay.

Answer the *Try It!* questions online or in your notebook.

---

❶ The **introduction** describes teen activities, including volunteer jobs. Specific details like these **grab readers' interest** and let readers know the topic of the essay.

Try It! What do you think the essay will be about, and why do you think so?

❷ The author states her **controlling idea** here.

Try It! What is the controlling, or main, idea of the essay? Put it in your own words.

❸ Specific **facts**, **details**, and **quotations** from experts **support** the controlling idea.

Try It! Which fact, detail, or quotation do you think most strongly supports the author's thesis? Why?

Extension Find another example of an expository essay, and compare it with this one.

148 Expository Essay

Profiles in Caring

by Kirsten Weir

❶ Between school, sports, clubs, and friends, today's teens have plenty to keep them busy. But that doesn't stop many young people from adding volunteer jobs to their to-do lists.

❷ There are many reasons to volunteer. Young people
5 involved in community service are more likely to get good grades, graduate from high school, and go to college, says Steve Culbertson, president of Youth Service America (YSA). They also gain valuable skills that help them shine in paid jobs down the line.
10 ❸ Notably, 61 percent of 13- to 25-year-olds feel personally responsible for making a difference in the world, according to a study by the companies Cone Inc. and AMP Insights. Eighty-one percent of those surveyed had volunteered within the past year. "In the last two decades," Culbertson says, "the
15 number of teenagers volunteering has doubled in the United States. Kids [today] are exposed much more to the problems of the world and [are] more likely to help."

Volunteering is rewarding in its own right. But donating your time can also give you a head start down your future
20 career path. Volunteers discover new talents, learn new skills, build real-world experience, and test potential career fields. Read on for stories of three teens who make community service part of their routines. As they have learned, volunteering is fun and loaded with benefits—for
25 the community as well as the volunteer.

All the teens had different reasons for volunteering; this supports the author's thesis.

5. Daniel's advice about volunteering supports the thesis that teen volunteerism is worthwhile for many reasons.

Extension Lead a discussion in which students compare and contrast how their additional expository essay examples use the genre characteristics. Use the *Try It!* questions as a guide.

Teacher Tip

Quick Write Ask students to think of an additional example of a young person who volunteers. Then, have students write a description of the person's work that could be added to the Mentor Text.

T148

2 | Writing Journal ▶

Students record their answers to questions about the Mentor Text in their online journals or notebooks.

❹ Community Building

In the summer of 2006, Arizona native Leena Patel, now 17, traveled to North Carolina for a 13-day volunteer mission. As part of a team of 14 teens, Leena helped build homes through Habitat for Humanity, an organization that serves families who need safe, affordable housing.

Working eight hours every day, Leena's team built homes for four families. "I had never done construction before," Leena says. She quickly learned to install doors and windows, attach baseboards, and put up vinyl siding. After all her hard work, the biggest reward was meeting the families who would live in the homes. "They were so genuine and so thankful," she says. "I didn't expect them to be just like me."

❹ Birds on the Brain

Kaleigh Gerlich has a cool volunteer job—literally. She's a penguin keeper's assistant at the Denver Zoo. The 18-year-old has volunteered at the zoo for three years. "People always think it's crazy; they say the penguins smell like fish," she says. "But they're just so much fun. They have the greatest personalities."

Gerlich worked at the zoo every Sunday throughout high school. In the summers, she spent even more time there. Last summer, she logged 150 volunteer hours cleaning the penguin enclosures and preparing food for penguins and other birds. As a teen leader, Gerlich also helped coordinate other teen volunteers and pitched in with office work.

❹ Bake a Difference

Daniel Feldman, 17, of Linwood, N.J., has a big goal: ending child hunger in the United States. It's not far-fetched for someone who practically grew up volunteering. Since age 7, Daniel has worked with Peer Partners, a youth volunteer organization his sister founded. Daniel started his own organization, Kids Feeding Kids. The group holds bake sales, plant sales, and other community fundraisers to fight child hunger. In the past four years, Kids Feeding Kids has raised nearly $40,000, as well as "pounds upon pounds of food for the local food bank," he says.

Daniel hopes that his success will inspire others. ❺ "Find a cause you think is worthy, and go for it," he says. "The smallest things can make the biggest difference."

WRITING COACH
Online
www.phwritingcoach.com

Interactive Model
Listen to an audio recording of the mentor text in the eText. You can refer back to the mentor text whenever you need support in developing your own writing.

Online Journal
Try It! Answer the questions about the Mentor Text in the online journal.

❹ The essay has a **clear, logical organization.** Headings set off the three supporting **examples,** marking the **transition** from one teen's story to the next.

Try It! How does each teen's story support the author's thesis? Write a sentence or two comparing the experiences of the teen volunteers.

❺ In the conclusion, the author **quotes** the last student's words to wrap up the essay.

Try It! How do the last quotations support the controlling idea of the essay?

Mentor Text   149

The Digital • Print Path ▶

1 STUDENT BOOK ▶

Using *Writing Coach Online*™ or the student book, students read and listen to an audio recording of the Student Model.

STUDENT MODEL

Tell students that good writers react to what they read in ways that show their understanding of the text. Explain that students will react to the Student Model by placing two sets of symbols in the text. Then, distribute printed copies of the Student Model or have students log on to Writing Coach Online.

Use a Reader's Eye

Read aloud the instructions for using the Reader's Response Symbols and the meaning of each symbol. Then, guide students through their use.

 Think Aloud While reading the text, **I noticed** that the student writer states clearly what he is going to compare. He also makes some good points about both e-mail and face-to-face communication. However, **I'm not sure I agree** with his point in line 23 about e-mail stressing out people. Does he have evidence to support this statement? I'll place a question mark here.

Work with students to identify other places in the text where they have questions.

Have students read and respond to the Student Model, using each Reader's Response Symbol at least once.

Partner Talk

After students have discussed the text, have each pair identify how the writer presents the points being compared.

Use a Writer's Eye

Read aloud the instructions for using the Writer's Response Symbols and the meaning of each symbol. Then, guide students through their use.

STUDENT MODEL — Compare-and-Contrast Essay

With a small group, take turns reading this Student Model aloud. As you read, practice newly acquired vocabulary by correctly producing the word's sound. Think about the author's purpose and main ideas. Look for evidence, such as facts and details, in the text.

 Use a Reader's Eye

Now, reread the Student Model. On your copy of the Student Model, use the Reader's Response Symbols to react to what you read.

Reader's Response Symbols

+ **Aha! That makes sense to me.**

− **This isn't clear to me.**

? **I have a question about this.**

! **Wow! That is cool/weird/interesting.**

Partner Talk

Take turns reading the Student Model aloud to a partner. Then discuss how the writer organizes the three points of comparison. Decide how this organization helps the author identify main ideas and achieve a purpose.

150 **Expository Essay**

Do We Still Need to Talk FACE-TO-FACE?

by Travis Barry

I just read an awesome science fiction story in which people live below ground and rarely meet face-to-face. Instead, they communicate through a machine. Could humans really live that way?
5 The story made me think about why we need both e-mail and face-to-face communication.

E-mail is a great way to keep in touch. It's fast, it connects people around the world, and it makes it easy to share information. For example, my uncle
10 lived in Japan for two years. When I had to do a report on Japanese art, he asked an artist he knew if I could e-mail him some questions. The artist agreed. I sent the questions and got his answers the next day. Doing an e-mail interview this way
15 was much faster than if I'd had to travel all the way to Japan to do the interview face-to-face. I was also able to contact the artist immediately and directly, even though I didn't know him.

Although e-mail is so fast and easy that people
20 send over 200 billion e-mails every day, talking face-to-face is sometimes better. For one thing, e-mail is so fast that it can make people feel they have to reply quickly, which can stress out some people. Although getting together can be slower,
25 it gives people time to think. Another problem is that although connecting by e-mail is easy, it can be hard to build trust. When we meet face-to-face, we can use smiles and gestures to show how we

1

Say: I see the writer's thesis in lines 5–6, where he states, "We need both e-mail and face-to-face communication." I'll write C.T. next to that sentence, because it clearly states that the essay will present differences between these two means of communication.

Ask: Why does the writer place the thesis sentence in the first paragraph? (The thesis sentence introduces readers to the main idea that will be developed in the rest of the essay.)

Have students read and respond to the Student Model, using each Writer's Response Symbol at least once.

2 First, students respond to the Student Model as a reader, using symbols to mark the text. They can mark the text using pop-up sticky notes in *Writing Coach Online*™ or they can mark a printed copy of the Student Model.

3 Then, students respond to the Student Model as a writer, using different symbols to mark the text. They can use either *Writing Coach Online*™ or a printed copy of the Student Model.

Student Model *Compare-and-Contrast Essay* **Student Model**

feel about what we say. When we read an e-mail,
30 we can't see the sender's face or hear a voice.
So it's easy to misunderstand a joke or to think
someone who is just slightly annoyed is really angry.

If you want to end a disagreement or share
bad news, do it face-to-face. On the other hand,
35 if you need to send information to someone far
away, use e-mail. E-mail is fast and convenient,
but it can send the wrong message about how
someone feels. That's why e-mail will never
completely replace face-to-face communication.

2

www.phwritingcoach.com

Interactive Model

Listen to an audio recording of the Student Model in the eText. Use the Reader's and Writer's Response Symbols with the eText tools to note what you read.

Use a Writer's Eye

Now evaluate the piece as a writer. On your copy of the Student Model, use the Writer's Response Symbols to react to what you read. Identify places where the student writer uses characteristics of an effective **compare-and-contrast essay**.

Writer's Response Symbols	
C.T.	**Clearly stated thesis**
I.C.	**Effective introduction and conclusion**
T.W.	**Transition words show how ideas are alike or different**
S.E.	**Effective supporting evidence**

Student Model 151

Personalized Support

FEEDBACK Teacher or Peer Feedback

To provide feedback to students on their responses to the Student Model, ask or have student partners ask one another the following:

• What is the thesis or controlling idea of the Student Model?

• How does the Student Model illustrate the characteristics of a compare-and-contrast essay?

• Which feature or characteristic of the Student Model might you use in your own piece of writing?

• How could you alter or adapt this feature to make it your own?

The Digital • Print Path ▶

1  Students select or are assigned a topic for their compare-and-contrast essay from the Topic Bank, or they may choose a topic of their own.

2 Students complete online or printed graphic organizers to narrow the topic for their compare-and-contrast essay.

Prewriting

Explain that the first task students need to complete as they plan their compare-and-contrast essay is to determine an appropriate topic.

Choose From the Topic Bank

Read aloud each topic and then ask volunteers to describe them in their own words. If you are assigning topics to students, you may wish to do so now. Encourage students to ask questions about their topic.

Choose Your Own Topic

Introduce and discuss the Make Comparisons and Organize strategies. If students were not assigned writing topics, have them use the strategies to brainstorm for topics for their essays.

Extension Have each student choose one of the strategies. Then, have them write an action plan that outlines the resources and steps they will use to develop their topic.

Narrow Your Topic

Tell students that they will use a Narrow Your Topic graphic organizer to identify two items to compare and contrast. Then, distribute printed copies or have students log on to Writing Coach Online.

Apply It! Guide students through the instructions for completing the graphic organizer. Have students complete the exercise based on their topic.

Consider Your Audience and Purpose

Guide students to consider the audience and purpose for their essay.

Say: The first question in the first column asks about who my audience is. If **I compare** ethnic foods, the first topic from the Topic Bank, my audience might be someone who hasn't eaten

---

Feature Assignment Prewriting Feature Assignment Prewrit

Your Turn ▶ Feature Assignment: Compare-and-Contrast Essay

Prewriting

Plan a first draft of your compare-and-contrast essay. Select from the Topic Bank or think of an idea of your own.

 Choose From the Topic Bank

TOPIC BANK

Ethnic Foods All nationalities have special foods. Burritos and tacos are two popular Mexican foods. Ravioli and lasagna are famous Italian dishes. Compare any two international food favorites and describe the ingredients, appearance, and taste.

Rules Think about the rules you have at home and at school. They may be rules about helping with household chores or about bedtimes. They may be rules about being quiet while your teacher is talking or about running in the hallways. Write an essay in which you compare and contrast the rules you have to follow at home with the rules you have to follow at school.

Buildings Choose two buildings in your city or town. Think about how they are alike and how they are different. Think about the way they look, their age, how they are used, and who uses them. Write an essay in which you compare and contrast these two buildings.

Choose Your Own Topic

Generate your own ideas or topics with these strategies.

Make Comparisons and Organize

- Write a list of five people, things, or activities you know well. Then, next to each, list a different type of related thing or activity. For example, you could write *soccer* and *football*.
- Next, draw two circles that overlap. Label each circle with your two related points.

Review your responses and choose a topic.

152   **Expository Essay**

---

these foods and is interested in trying something new.

Ask: Based on your topic, who is most likely to read your compare-and-contrast essay? Who would you most like to read it? (**Responses will vary.**)

Have students who are comparing similar subjects work in small groups to discuss and respond to the remaining questions.

Coach's Corner

You may wish to model prewriting activities for students by brainstorming for your own writing topic. Use these prompts to model your thought process:

- **I am interested in** sports, so that could be my general topic.
- **I can narrow my topic by** comparing basketball and soccer.

Discuss the choices you make and solicit feedback from students.

3

Students record their answers to questions about audience and purpose in their online journals or notebooks.

Narrow Your Topic

Choosing a topic that is too broad will make it hard to find similarities and differences to compare and contrast.

Apply It! Use a graphic organizer like the one shown to narrow your topic.

- Write a category in the top box.
- Use the next box to list interesting people, things, or ideas in that category.
- Finally, choose two items from the list to compare and contrast.

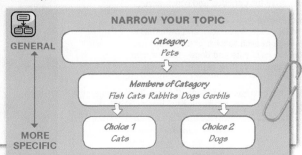

NARROW YOUR TOPIC

GENERAL

Category
Pets

Members of Category
Fish Cats Rabbits Dogs Gerbils

MORE SPECIFIC

Choice 1
Cats

Choice 2
Dogs

Consider Your Audience and Purpose

Before writing, think about your audience and purpose. Ask yourself what your audience needs and wants to know about your compare-and-contrast essay.

Questions for Audience	Questions for Purpose
• Who is my audience? • What does my audience already know about what I'm comparing and contrasting? • What kinds of ideas will grab and keep my audience's attention?	• Which people, things, or ideas do I want to compare and contrast? • Which similarities and differences do I want to include in my essay? What evidence will I need? • What do I want people to learn through this comparison and contrast?

Record your answers in your writing journal.

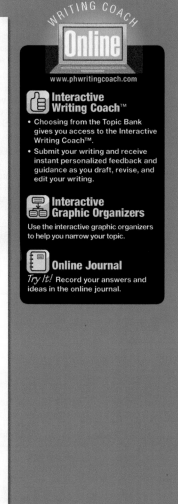

WRITING COACH

Online

www.phwritingcoach.com

Interactive Writing Coach™
- Choosing from the Topic Bank gives you access to the Interactive Writing Coach™.
- Submit your writing and receive instant personalized feedback and guidance as you draft, revise, and edit your writing.

Interactive Graphic Organizers
Use the interactive graphic organizers to help you narrow your topic.

Online Journal
Try It! Record your answers and ideas in the online journal.

Personalized Support

Interactive Writing Coach™

Below Level Teachers select a topic from the topic bank for below-level students. Students submit their writing to the **Interactive Writing Coach™** for feedback paragraph by paragraph or as a complete draft. It is recommended that below-level students submit their writing one paragraph at a time.

On Level Students may select a topic from the Topic Bank. They may submit their writing for feedback paragraph by paragraph or as a complete draft.

Above Level Students may select from the Topic Bank or come up with their own topic. Above-level students should submit their writing as a complete draft.

Interactive Graphic Organizer

Below Level Students complete three graphic organizers that provide models and scaffolded support.

On Level Students complete one, two, or three graphic organizers, depending on how much support they need.

Above Level Students complete the least scaffolded graphic organizer or narrow their topic without the help of a graphic organizer.

Differentiated Instruction

RTI Strategy for Below-Level Students
Work with students to brainstorm for a list of possible audiences for their essays: in school, at home, and in the community. Then, work with them to further narrow their audience. For example, a school audience might be a specific class or school athletes. List these audiences on the board and discuss their common traits. Understanding their audience will help students choose the best points of comparison and supporting details to present their thesis.

Enrichment for Gifted and Talented Students Encourage students to draw on their areas of talent when developing their topics. For example, students skilled in music might select two musical forms, such as a sonata and a symphony, to compare and contrast, while students talented in the visual arts could compare and contrast art forms such as painting and collage. Encourage students to think beyond superficial similarities of form to the topics' common purpose, such as evoking emotion or expressing inner conflict.

The Digital • Print Path ▶  ▶ Using **Writing Coach Online™** or the student book, students read and discuss the model graphic organizer.

2 ▶ Students complete online or printed graphic organizers to develop their ideas and gather details.

Plan Your Piece

Explain that writers use graphic organizers to develop their ideas and show relationships between different parts of the text. Then, point out the Develop Your Points of Comparison/Contrast graphic organizer on page 154. Tell students that they will use this organizer to outline their compare-and-contrast essay. Then, distribute printed copies or have students log on to Writing Coach Online.

Introduce the graphic organizer by explaining that the column on the left lists the information to be entered in the column on the right. Each row identifies a different part of a compare-and-contrast essay.

Develop a Clear Thesis Guide students to notice that the thesis in the example organizer is based on the narrowed topic from page 153. Then, have students write a thesis sentence that clearly states what they will compare and contrast and record it on their graphic organizer.

Logically Organize Your Points Explain to students that the example organizer shows a point-by-point style of organization. Explain that each paragraph in an essay written in this way will have one or two sentences about dogs and one or two sentences about cats. With block organization, each paragraph would focus only on cats or only on dogs. Have students work with a partner to decide which style is best for their essays.

Gather Details

Remind students that they should use details to support each point of comparison and contrast in their essay. Ask volunteers to read aloud each kind of detail and its example. Then, guide students to place the details in the example graphic organizer.

Say: I notice that the graphic organizer has space to record Supporting Evidence/Details for each point of comparison/contrast. Some of the details on page 155 can be added to the organizer. For example, the Examples detail—"Cats quickly learn to use a litter box"—supports the first point, "Cats are easier to care for than dogs." I'll record that detail in the proper place.

Plan Your Piece

You will use a graphic organizer like this one to state your thesis, organize your arguments, and identify details. When it is complete, you will be ready to write your first draft.

Develop a Clear Thesis List similarities and differences between what you're comparing. These are your points of comparison and contrast. For example, you could compare dogs and cats according to levels of care, sociability, and trainability. Use these points to **develop your thesis**. Then, think about how you will use the information from your thesis to create an **effective introduction and conclusion**.

Logically Organize Your Points You can use **point-by-point organization** as in the model—care, sociability, and trainability, discussing both cats and dogs in each section. You can also use **block organization** for the topics of cats and dogs—first explain cats' care, sociability, and trainability; then explain the same elements about dogs.

Develop Your Points of Comparison/Contrast

Clear Thesis	*Both cats and dogs can make great pets, but there are many differences between the two.*
First Point of Comparison/Contrast	*Cats are easier to care for than dogs.*
Supporting Evidence/Details	
Second Point of Comparison/Contrast	*Cats tend to be less sociable than dogs.*
Supporting Evidence/Details	
Third Point of Comparison/Contrast	*Dogs can be trained more easily than cats.*
Supporting Evidence/Details	
Conclusion	*Knowing the differences between cats and dogs will help you choose the right pet.*

154 **Expository Essay**

Ask: Which point does the Expert Opinion support? (Second Point of Comparison/Contrast: Cats tend to be less sociable.)

Have students work in small groups to place the remaining relevant details on the example graphic organizer.

Try It! Lead students to see that the paragraph contains an example with a personal observation.

Apply It! Read aloud the bulleted instructions for gathering details. Then, have students develop relevant supporting details for their points of comparison/contrast and enter them

on the graphic organizer. Remind students to use a variety of details to support their ideas.

Writer's Block

IF students are not balancing points of similarity or difference . . .

THEN have them turn to the Student Model on pages 150–151 and identify information that would be entered in each part of the graphic organizer.

3 STUDENT BOOK ▶

Students refer back to the Mentor Text or the Student Model as they plan their writing.

ure Assignment **Prewriting** *Feature Assignment* **Prewriting**

Gather Details

To provide supporting evidence for their points, writers use these kinds of details. Look at these examples.

- **Facts:** *With American pet owners dogs are slightly more popular than cats.*
- **Examples:** *Cats quickly learn to use a litter box.*
- **Expert Opinions:** *Our veterinarian says that dogs are pack animals, so they are very sociable.*
- **Personal Observations:** *When we moved, our dog quickly made friends with the neighbors. Our cat was more interested in exploring her new home.*

Try It! Read the excerpt from the Student Model and identify which types of details the author used to support his points.

 **STUDENT MODEL** | from **Do We Still Need to Talk Face-to-Face?** page 150; lines 7–14

E-mail is a great way to keep in touch. It's fast, it connects people around the world, and it makes it easy to share information. For example, my uncle lived in Japan for two years. When I had to do a report on Japanese art, he asked an artist he knew if I could e-mail him some questions. The artist agreed. I sent the questions and got his answers the next day.

Apply It! Review the types of support the writer of a compare-and-contrast essay can use. Then, identify at least one supporting detail for each of your points. Evaluate each detail and determine if it will support your thesis.

- Make sure your evidence includes **specific facts, details, and examples.** Review your details to decide which ones will be best to **guide and inform your reader's understanding of the key ideas and evidence.**
- Then, add these details to your graphic organizer. Match each detail to the right point of comparison/contrast to create an **appropriately organized structure.**

WRITING COACH **Online**
www.phwritingcoach.com

Interactive Graphic Organizers
Use the interactive graphic organizers to help you create a plan for your writing.

Interactive Model
Refer back to the Interactive Model in the eText as you plan your writing.

Prewriting **155**

Personalized Support

Interactive Graphic Organizer

Below Level Students complete three graphic organizers that provide models and scaffolded support.

On Level Students complete one, two, or three graphic organizers, depending on how much support they need.

Above Level Students complete the least scaffolded graphic organizer or narrow their topic without the help of a graphic organizer.

FEEDBACK Teacher or Peer Feedback

To provide feedback to students as they plan their first draft, ask or have student partners ask one another the following:

- What do you want your audience to know about the topic?
- What questions or concerns will your audience have about the topic?
- What details have you identified for your piece? How do these details support your thesis or controlling idea?
- Are your details varied? Will they interest your readers? Explain.

Differentiated Instruction

RTI Strategy for Below-Level Students
Help students develop supporting evidence for their thesis. First, direct students to make a four-column chart on a piece of paper and label each column at the top with one of the following types of supporting details: *Facts, Examples, Expert Opinions,* and *Personal Observations.* Then, have them brainstorm for ideas for each column of this chart, either individually or with a partner.

Strategy for Spanish Speakers
Students whose home language is Spanish may encounter difficulties determining when to use the comparative and superlative -er and -est endings, and when to use the *more + adjective* construction. Point out adjectives in the Student Model on page 155: *great, fast,* and *easy.* Elicit additional one-, two-, and three-syllable adjectives. Have students write a list of the comparative and superlative forms of each adjective and use them in a sentence.

T155

The Digital • Print Path ▶

WRITING COACH Online | STUDENT BOOK

1 WRITING COACH Online | STUDENT BOOK ▶

Using *Writing Coach Online™* or the student book, students read and discuss the Outline for Success for an expository essay.

2 WRITING COACH Online | STUDENT BOOK ▶

Students discuss how the Mentor Text illustrates the characteristics of an expository essay.

Drafting

Outline for Success

Explain that the Outline for Success shows an organizational strategy for a compare-and-contrast essay. Students will use the Outline to write a focused, organized, and coherent draft of their compare-and-contrast essay.

I. Introduction

Link the Outline with a specific compare-and-contrast essay by having students turn to the Mentor Text on pages 148–149. Ask a volunteer to identify and read aloud the thesis statement (lines 23–25). Then, guide students to understand how the thesis statement identifies points of comparison and contrast.

Think Aloud — **I noticed** that the author's thesis statement does not occur until the end of paragraph 4. However, this sentence does clearly state the author's main point: volunteering benefits "the community as well as the volunteer."

Work with students to identify how the author's unique style of introduction grabs reader interest.

Have students work with a partner to discuss how they will grab reader interest and clearly state the thesis in the introduction of their compare-and-contrast essays.

II. Body

Lead a discussion about how the body paragraphs of the Mentor Text reflect the characteristics of a compare-and-contrast essay.

- Points of comparison or contrast (lines 14–17, 23–25)
- Block organization of points (lines 25–37, 38–49, 50–60)

III. Conclusion

Have small groups discuss how the conclusion of the Mentor Text restates the thesis (lines 61–63).

Start Your Draft

Have small groups read aloud and discuss the boxed instructions for drafting. Direct students to work individually on their first draft.

Drafting *Feature Assignment* Drafting *Feature Assignment*

Drafting

During the drafting stage, you will start to write your ideas for your compare-and-contrast essay. You will follow an outline that provides an **organizational strategy** that will help you build on ideas to write a **focused, organized, and coherent** compare-and-contrast essay.

The Organization of a Compare-and-Contrast Essay

The chart shows an organizational strategy for a compare-and-contrast essay. Look back at how the Mentor Text follows this organizational strategy. Then use this chart to help you outline your draft.

Outline for Success

I. Introduction — See Mentor Text, p. 148.
- Interesting opening to grab readers' interest
- Clear thesis

II. Body — See Mentor Text, pp. 148–149.
- Points of comparison and contrast
- Logical organization of points

Point-by-Point	Block Organization
• Point 1: Topic A and B	• Topic A: Points 1, 2, and 3
• Point 2: Topic A and B	• Topic B: Points 1, 2, and 3
• Point 3: Topic A and B	

III. Conclusion — See Mentor Text, p. 149.
- Restatement of thesis
- Ending that shows why this topic matters

Grab Your Reader
- An interesting opening can ask a question, use an anecdote, or use a strong detail.
- A clear thesis, or the main point you are making, states what you are comparing or contrasting.

Compare and contrast
- Full development of each point of comparison and contrast provides supporting evidence that explains the main point and informs your readers.
- The organizational strategy—point-by-point (see page 154) or block organization—helps readers follow your ideas more easily. Block organization works best if you have only one or two points of comparison, otherwise use point-by-point.

Wrap It Up
- Restating your thesis reinforces your main points and briefly summarizes your points of comparison and contrast.
- A powerful sentence at the end of your essay leaves readers thinking that your main point matters.

Coach's Corner

If you are modeling the writing process for students with your own topic or a student volunteer's, you may wish to use these prompts to guide your drafting and discussion:

- **To capture readers' attention, my introduction will** ask a startling question.
- **I will organize my body paragraphs** point by point.

Discuss the choices you make and solicit feedback from students.

3  **Writing Journal** ▶

Students begin writing their compare-and-contrast essay online or in their notebooks.

4  ▶

Students submit paragraphs or complete drafts to the Interactive Writing Coach™ for scoring and feedback, or share their work with their teacher.

5 ▶

Students receive customized feedback from the Interactive Writing Coach™ or feedback from their teacher. Students may continue to work on their drafts.

Feature Assignment **Drafting** *Feature Assignment* **Drafting**

Start Your Draft

Use the checklist to help complete your draft. Use the graphic organizer that shows your thesis, points of comparison and contrast, and supporting details, and the Outline for Success as guides.

While drafting, aim at writing your ideas down, not on making your writing perfect. Remember, you will have the chance to improve your draft when you revise and edit.

√ Identify your **topics** of comparison and contrast.

√ Create an **effective introduction** by beginning with an interesting opening and your thesis statement.

√ Shape the **body** of your essay by using an appropriate organizational strategy for comparing and contrasting, such as **point-by-point** or **block organization**.

√ Include **evidence** such as specific facts, details, and examples to inform your reader's understanding of your key ideas.

√ Use both long and short sentences. A **variety of sentence structures** keeps your writing interesting and lively.

√ Use **transitions** such as *however, in contrast, similarly,* or *in the same way* to connect and build on ideas between sentences and paragraphs. This will help you be sure that your essay is focused, organized, and coherent.

√ End with an **effective conclusion** that summarizes your main points.

√ Help readers to remember your ideas by ending with a **powerful thought**.

WRITING COACH

Online

www.phwritingcoach.com

Interactive Model

Outline for Success View pop-ups of Mentor Text selections referenced in the Outline for Success.

Interactive Writing Coach™

Use the Interactive Writing Coach to receive the level of support you need:
• Write one paragraph at a time and submit each one for immediate, detailed feedback.
• Write your entire first draft and submit it for immediate, personalized feedback.

Drafting 157

Personalized Support

 ### Interactive Writing Coach™

Below Level Students complete the drafting process in small steps by submitting each paragraph for scoring and feedback.

On Level Depending on the support they need, students submit their writing paragraph by paragraph or as a complete draft for scoring and feedback.

Above Level Students may write their drafts on their own but have the option of submitting them for scoring and/or feedback.

Teacher or Peer Feedback

To provide feedback to students on their first draft, ask or have student partners ask one another the following:

• Can you explain how you organized your ideas in this piece?

• Why did you include this information here?

• Why did you choose this introduction? Does it grab your reader and identify your thesis or controlling idea?

• What supporting details could you add here?

• Why did you choose this conclusion? How does it add to your piece?

• Can you show me a place where I can hear your unique voice?

• Can you show me a place where you used vivid language?

The Digital · Print Path ▶

STUDENT BOOK

1  STUDENT BOOK ▶

Using **Writing Coach Online™** or the student book, students study the first and second drafts of the student model to see how the writer used Revision RADaR to improve his or her writing.

2  Writing Journal ▶

Students use the Revision RADaR strategy to revise their own writing.

Revising: Making It Better

Point out the page title to students and explain that revising means making improvements to a writing draft. Then, read aloud the opening paragraph to introduce the Revision RADaR strategies. You may wish to have students review Chapter 3 for more information on Revision RADaR.

Kelly Gallagher, M. Ed.

KEEP REVISION ON YOUR RADaR

 After students have read the 1st draft, have them turn to page 156 and review the Outline for Success. Work with students to understand that the questions the author asked about the draft are based on the characteristics of a compare-and-contrast essay. For example, call out the second question and note how it addresses the first concern listed in the Body section in the Outline for Success.

Then, have students work in small groups to develop other questions about the draft based on the genre characteristics.

 Guide students to understand how the author used the RADaR strategies to revise his draft.

Think Aloud **I thought** that the body paragraphs in the first draft didn't flow as well as they could. In the second draft, I see the letter *A* in three places. The writer has added two transitions to show relationships: *for example,* in the first body paragraph, and *although,* in the second body paragraph. The writer also added several sentences to more fully explain the first point. Now, the body paragraphs are more developed and read more smoothly.

Work with students to brainstorm for other ways of revising the body paragraphs.

Revising: Making It Better

Now that you have finished your first draft, you are ready to revise. Think about the "big picture" of **audience, purpose, and genre.** You can use the Revision RADaR strategy as a guide for making changes to improve your draft. Revision RADaR provides four major ways to improve your writing: (R) replace, (A) add, (D) delete, and (R) reorder.

Kelly Gallagher, M. Ed.

KEEP REVISION ON YOUR RADaR

Read part of the first draft of the Student Model "Do We Still Need to Talk Face-to-Face?" Then look at questions the writer asked himself as he thought about how well his draft **addressed issues of audience, purpose, and genre.**

Do We Still Need to Talk Face-to-Face? [1ST DRAFT]

E-mail is a great way to keep in touch. It's fast. It connects people around the world. It makes it easy to share information. My uncle lived in Japan for two years. When I had to do a report on Japanese art, he asked an artist he knew if I could e-mail some questions. The artist agreed. I sent the questions and got his answers the next day.

E-mail is so fast and easy that people send many e-mails every day. Talking face-to-face is sometimes better. For one thing, e-mail is so fast that it can make people feel they have to reply quickly, which can stress out some people. Although getting together can be slower, it gives people time to think. Another problem is that although connecting by e-mail is easy, it can be hard to build trust. When we meet face to face, we can use smiles and gestures to show how we feel...

*Have I used a variety of **sentence structures?** Have I included **transitions** to connect ideas?*

*Have I explained my points to help guide and inform my **readers?***

*Have I used **transitions** between paragraphs to link ideas and set up comparisons and contrasts? Have I included specific **facts, details, and examples?***

158   **Expository Essay**

Have students work in small groups to discuss other changes in the second draft.

Apply It! Review the bulleted instructions for using Revision RADaR. Remind students to question their drafts based on the genre characteristics listed on the Outline for Success on page 156. Tell students to use each RADaR strategy at least once.

Coach's Corner

If you are modeling the writing process for students with your own draft or a student volunteer's, use these prompts to focus on the Revision RADaR *Add* strategy:

• **I added a transition here to** make clear the similarity between the two items.

• **I added another point of comparison because** I thought my points of contrast were not balanced.

Discuss the choices you make and solicit feedback from students.

3
Students submit paragraphs or revised drafts to the Interactive Writing Coach™ for scoring and feedback, or share their work with their teacher.

4
Students receive customized feedback from the Interactive Writing Coach™, or feedback from their teacher. Students may continue to revise their drafts.

Feature Assignment **Revising** *Feature Assignment* **Revising**

Now, look at how the writer applied Revision RADaR to write an improved second draft.

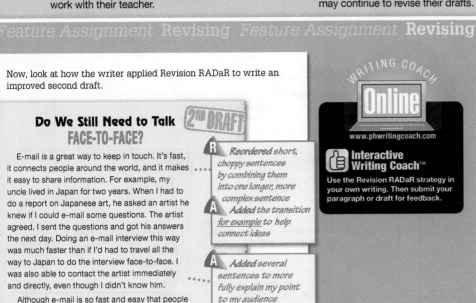

Do We Still Need to Talk FACE-TO-FACE? **2ND DRAFT**

E-mail is a great way to keep in touch. It's fast, it connects people around the world, and it makes it easy to share information. For example, my uncle lived in Japan for two years. When I had to do a report on Japanese art, he asked an artist he knew if I could e-mail some questions. The artist agreed. I sent the questions and got his answers the next day. Doing an e-mail interview this way was much faster than if I'd had to travel all the way to Japan to do the interview face-to-face. I was also able to contact the artist immediately and directly, even though I didn't know him.

Although e-mail is so fast and easy that people send over 200 billion e-mails every day, talking face-to-face is sometimes better. For one thing, e-mail is so fast that it can make people feel they have to reply quickly, which can stress out some people. Although getting together can be slower, it gives people time to think. Another problem is that although connecting by e-mail is easy, it can be hard to build trust. When we meet face to face, we can use smiles and gestures to show how we feel…

R Reordered short, choppy sentences by combining them into one longer, more complex sentence
A Added the transition *for example* to help connect ideas

A Added several sentences to more fully explain my point to my audience

A Added the transition *Although* to connect ideas between paragraphs and to set up a contrast between e-mailing and face-to-face communication
R Replaced the general word *many* with a fact

 Apply It! Use your Revision RADaR to revise your draft.

- First, determine if you have organized your points of comparison and contrast clearly, provided supporting evidence for each point, and used transitions to link ideas between sentences and paragraphs.
- Then, apply Revision RADaR to make needed changes. Remember—you can use the steps in the strategy in any order.

Revising **159**

WRITING COACH
Online
www.phwritingcoach.com
Interactive Writing Coach™
Use the Revision RADaR strategy in your own writing. Then submit your paragraph or draft for feedback.

Personalized Support

 Interactive Writing Coach™

Below Level Students revise their drafts using the Revision RADaR strategy and submit their writing for scoring and feedback.

On Level Students revise their drafts using the Revision RADaR strategy and submit their writing for scoring and feedback.

Above Level Students may use the Revision RADaR strategy or revise their drafts on their own. They have the option of submitting their revised drafts for scoring and/or feedback.

 Teacher or Peer Feedback

To provide feedback to students as they revise their first draft, ask or have student partners ask one another the following:

- Can you show me where you revised your text?
- What could you add to your introduction to grab the interest of your readers?
- How could you reorder these ideas so that their order is more logical?
- Have you included all the characteristics of this form of writing?
- Is there any unnecessary text that you could delete?
- Have you achieved your purpose with this piece of writing?
- Have you addressed the questions and concerns of your audience?

Working with ELLs **ELL** Sheltered Instruction: Cognitive

Review the Student Draft, having students demonstrate English comprehension and expand reading skills by employing the inferential skill of finding supporting text evidence. Define *inference*. Then:

Beginning Have students **Echo Read** the third sentence of the draft. Explain how you infer that the uncle does not live in Japan now with supporting evidence. (*He lived in Japan for two years.*) Help students create a chart of the inference and evidence.

Intermediate Have students read along as you read the first paragraph aloud. Model making an inference based on this

sentence: "He lived in Japan for two years." Have students make an inference based on the uncle's connection to the artist (e.g., *They spoke a language in common*). Have students identify their supporting evidence.

Advanced Have students individually read the student draft. Have students make two inferences about the uncle, identifying the supporting evidence. Have partners review their answers together.

Advanced High Expand the Advanced activity by having students make inferences about the uncle and the student-writer.

The Digital · Print Path ▶

1 ▶ Using *Writing Coach Online™* or the student book, students study and discuss the revision chart.

2 ▶ In a video by program author Kelly Gallagher, students learn more strategies for effective writing.

Revising: Making It Better

Look at the Big Picture

Introduce the revision chart to students. Explain that the Section column identifies the three main parts of a compare-and-contrast essay. The Evaluate column identifies the characteristics found in each section and explains how to assess them. The Revise column presents specific strategies for revising each characteristic.

Then, have students draw lines between and label the three sections of their drafts. Direct students to work individually to evaluate and revise their draft, using the chart to guide their work.

Focus on Craft: Improve Transitions

Have students read the introductory text. Guide students to understand that transitions help make an essay coherent by showing the relationship between ideas and leading readers from one idea to next.

Say: I **notice** that the Student Model describes two situations. To show the relationship between them, the writer uses the transition *on the other hand,* indicating that the second situation contrasts with the first.

Ask: What are some other transitions the writer might have used to show this contrast? (*however, but*)

Have students work with a partner to substitute different transitions in the Student Model, evaluate the effect of each, and decide which is most effective.

Try It! Have students discuss the questions in small groups and record responses in their journals. Follow up with students to check that their responses reflect an understanding of the role and effectiveness of transitions in an essay.

Revising Feature Assignment Revising Feature Assignment

Look at the Big Picture

Use the chart and your analytical skills to evaluate how well each section of your compare-and-contrast essay addresses **purpose, audience, and genre**. When necessary, use the suggestions in the chart to revise your piece.

Section	Evaluate	Revise
Introduction	• Check the **opening** sentence. Will it grab readers' attention and make them want to read more?	• Make your introduction more interesting by adding a question, anecdote, quotation, or strong detail.
	• Does the thesis identify the topics I'm comparing and contrasting to create an effective **introduction?**	• To check your thesis sentence, circle each topic and underline the point you're making about them. Add or delete information as needed.
Body	• Check that you have **organized** your essay in an easy-to-follow way.	• Make sure you have used either a point-by-point or block organization consistently.
	• Underline specific facts, details, and **examples** that provide support and help to guide and inform the reader's understanding of your key ideas and evidence.	• Rearrange a detail that is not in the same paragraph as the point it supports. When necessary, add or take out details.
	• Place a check mark by each **transition** you have used.	• If necessary, add words such as *in contrast* and *similarly* to show how your ideas are related.
	• Make sure you have a mixture of simple and compound **sentences.**	• Avoid too many of the same type of sentences. Rearrange words to include a variety of structures.
Conclusion	• Check that you have restated your thesis and provided a brief **summary** of your main points.	• If necessary, restate your thesis more clearly to create an **effective conclusion**.
	• Make sure you have ended your essay in a way that helps readers understand your **points**.	• Add a quotation or a forceful statement to conclude your essay on a memorable point. It is not enough to show comparison and contrast—tell readers why it matters.

Fine-Tune Your Draft

Apply It! Ask volunteers to read aloud the instructions for fine-tuning their drafts. Then, have students work in pairs to improve their drafts' sentence structure and use of transitions.

Peer Feedback Have students identify Mentor Text examples of the characteristics that you marked for improvement. Use the Mentor Text references on page T156 to guide students to appropriate examples.

> *Teacher Tip*
>
> Have students make a chart listing transitions for comparing and contrasting. Then, post this chart in the classroom for student reference.

3  ► Using **Writing Coach Online™** or the student book, students refer back to the Mentor Text or Student Model for examples of writer's craft.

4 ► Students record answers to questions about writer's craft in their online journals or notebooks.

5 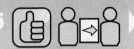 ► Students submit revised drafts to the **Interactive Writing Coach™** for scoring and feedback, or share their work with their teacher.

6   ► Students receive customized feedback from the **Interactive Writing Coach™** or feedback from their teacher.

Feature Assignment **Revising** *Feature Assignment* **Revising**

Focus on Craft: Improve Transitions

In a compare-and-contrast essay, you show both similarities and differences. The information can get confusing for readers unless you use transitions. **Transitions** are signal words that show how ideas are related. They link ideas between sentences and paragraphs. To show similarities, you can use transitions such as *in the same way*, *similarly*, or *likewise*. To show differences, you can use transitions such as *on the other hand*, *but*, or *however*.

Think about transitions as you read the following sentences from the Student Model.

 **STUDENT MODEL** from **Do We Still Need to Talk Face to Face?** page 151; lines 33–36

> If you want to end a disagreement or share bad news, do it face-to-face. On the other hand, if you need to send information quickly to someone far away, use e-mail.

 Try It! Now, ask yourself these questions:

- What transition is used to show contrast?
- Would the second sentence be more or less effective if there were no transition? Explain.

Fine-Tune Your Draft

Apply It! Use the revision suggestions to prepare your final draft **after rethinking how well questions of purpose, audience, and genre have been addressed.**

- **Improve Transitions** Make the transitions that link ideas and paragraphs stronger by adding, deleting, combining, and rearranging sentences.
- **Improve Sentences** Simple sentences include only a main clause—a subject, a verb, and their objects and modifiers. Avoid too many short, simple sentences.

Peer Feedback Read your final draft to a group of peers. Ask classmates to tell you about your comparisons and contrasts. Think about their responses and revise your final draft as needed.

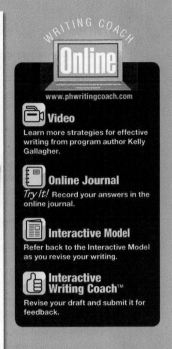

WRITING COACH

Online

www.phwritingcoach.com

Video
Learn more strategies for effective writing from program author Kelly Gallagher.

Online Journal
Try It! Record your answers in the online journal.

Interactive Model
Refer back to the Interactive Model as you revise your writing.

Interactive Writing Coach™
Revise your draft and submit it for feedback.

Personalized Support

 Interactive Writing Coach™

Below Level Students complete the revising process by submitting their writing for scoring and feedback.

On Level Students complete the revising process by submitting their writing for scoring and feedback.

Above Level Students finish revising their drafts. They have the option of submitting their revised drafts for scoring and/or feedback.

Teacher or Peer Feedback

To provide feedback to students as they continue to revise their first draft, ask or have student partners ask one another the following:

- What are you trying to say here? What part of the text could you replace to make your meaning clearer?
- Is there a more precise word you could use here?
- How does the rhythm of these sentences sound to you? Could you make the length and structure of these sentences more varied?
- How could you include transitional words and phrases here to help your reader understand these ideas?

Working with ELLs | **ELL** Sheltered Instruction: Cognitive

As students read, help them use support from peers and from you to enhance and confirm understanding and to develop their grasp of language structures, such as transitions, needed to comprehend increasingly challenging language. Read the Focus on Craft box with students, and create a list of transitions. Then:

Beginning Write, *My friend plays baseball. Similarly, I play baseball.* Choral read with students, using gestures as support. Help students identify the transition *similarly* and the transition in the Student Model excerpt.

Intermediate Discuss transitions with students, and have groups identify the transition in the Student Model excerpt and complete the *Try It!*.

Advanced Have partners use the **KIM Strategy**, writing a key word, information, and a memory clue about the terms *transition, contrast,* and *similarity.* Have them read the Student Model excerpt, identifying the transition and completing the *Try It!*.

Advanced High Have partners complete the Advanced activity then add a new sentence to the excerpt with a transition.

The Digital • Print Path ▶

WRITING COACH Online

STUDENT BOOK

1 ▶
In a video by program author Jeff Anderson, students learn effective editing techniques.

2  ▶ Writing Journal
Students record answers to questions about writer's craft in their online journals or notebooks.

Editing: Making It Correct

Discuss the opening paragraph with students. Explain that they will edit their drafts for proper grammar, mechanics, and spelling, including the use of subordinating conjunctions.

WRITE GUY *Jeff Anderson, M.Ed.*
WHAT DO YOU NOTICE?

Introduce students to subordinating conjunctions by reading aloud the Student Model excerpt and discussing responses to the "Ask yourself" question that follows. Then, have students read the explanation of connecting ideas with subordinating conjunctions.

Guide them to identify and use subordinating conjunctions.

 Think Aloud

I notice that the Student Model uses the subordinating conjunction *even though* to join ideas. The Mentor Text uses a subordinating conjunction in the last sentence of the first page: "As they have learned, volunteering is fun and loaded with benefits..." I can use a subordinating conjunction to summarize the Mentor Text: *Since* young people care about the world, they volunteer.

Work with students to use subordinating conjunctions to make additional statements about the Mentor Text.

Have students use a subordinating conjunction to join two sentences in their essays. You may also wish to have students turn to Chapter 17 of the Grammar Handbook to learn more about conjunctions.

Grammar Mini-Lesson:
Commas With Clauses

Discuss the paragraph and the Student Model excerpt on page 163 with students. Guide them to understand that the writer placed a comma after the subordinating clause because it is at the beginning of the sentence.

Editing: Making It Correct

Once you have your final draft the way you want it, spend a few minutes doing a careful edit. Read your draft sentence by sentence to check it thoroughly.

When editing your final draft, think about using **subordinating conjunctions**. These elements of writing will connect your ideas and improve the flow of your essay. Then edit your final draft for factual errors and errors in **grammar, mechanics, and spelling**.

 WRITE GUY *Jeff Anderson, M. Ed.*
WHAT DO YOU NOTICE?

Zoom In On Conventions Focus on words that connect ideas as you zoom in on this sentence from the Student Model.

> **STUDENT MODEL** from **Do We Still Need to Talk Face-to-Face?** page 150; lines 16-18
>
> I was also able to contact the artist immediately and directly, even though I didn't know him.

Now, ask yourself: *Which words connect different ideas in the sentence?*

Perhaps you said that *even though* connects different ideas.

Even though is a subordinating conjunction. A **subordinating conjunction** connects two ideas by making one idea dependent on the other. Common subordinating conjunctions include *after, even though, if, since, until,* and *when.*

The ideas that subordinating conjunctions connect are expressed in clauses. A clause is a group of words with its own subject and verb. A main clause can stand by itself as a sentence, but a subordinate clause cannot. In the Student Model, the subordinate clause is *even though I didn't know him.*

Partner Talk Discuss this question with a partner: *Why do you think the author chooses to connect ideas using subordinating conjunctions instead of writing separate sentences?*

> To learn more about subordinating conjunctions, see Chapter 17 of your Grammar Handbook.

162   **Expository Writing**

Try It! Have students work with a partner to identify each subordinating clause and tell whether a comma is needed.

1. *until;* no comma

2. *After;* comma after *phone*

Apply It! Remind students to look closely for introductory subordinate clauses that require commas as they edit their drafts.

Use the Rubric Explain to students that they will rate how well their draft addresses the elements of a compare-contrast essay on a scale of 1 to 6, with 6 being the best score.

Then, have students use the rubric to evaluate their drafts and revise as necessary.

Writer's Block

> **IF** students have difficulty identifying introductory subordinate clauses in their drafts . . .

> **THEN** have them circle all subordinating conjunctions and decide whether they are a part of a clause that comes at the beginning of a sentence.

3  ▶ Using *Writing Coach Online™* or the student book, students refer back to the Mentor Text or Student Model as they edit their writing.

4  ▶ Using *Writing Coach Online™* or the student book, students evaluate their writing using the rubrics.

5  ▶ Students submit edited drafts to the *Interactive Writing Coach™* for scoring and feedback, or share their work with their teacher.

6   ▶ Students receive personalized feedback from the *Interactive Writing Coach™*, or feedback from their teacher.

Feature Assignment Editing *Feature Assignment* **Editing**

Grammar Mini-Lesson: Commas With Clauses

To learn more, see Chapter 25.

If a subordinate clause occurs at the beginning of the sentence, place a comma at the end of the clause. If a subordinate clause occurs at the end of the sentence, a comma may or may not be placed before the main and subordinate clause. Notice how the author of the Student Text placed a comma after an introductory subordinate clause.

 STUDENT MODEL from **Do We Still Need to Talk Face-to-Face?** page 151; lines 29–30

> When we read an e-mail, we can't see the sender's face or hear a voice.

Try It! Identify the subordinating clause in each sentence. Then tell if a comma is needed and where it should go. Write the answers in your journal.

1. Mia stood at the bus stop until it began to rain.
2. After Jill hung up the phone she sat patiently and waited for her friend to arrive.

Apply It! Edit your draft for grammar, mechanics, and spelling. If necessary, rewrite sentences to include **subordinating conjunctions.** Place commas before or after subordinate clauses as needed.

Use the rubric to evaluate your piece. If necessary, rethink, rewrite, or revise.

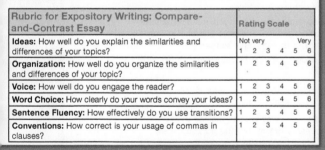

Rubric for Expository Writing: Compare-and-Contrast Essay	Rating Scale					
	Not very					Very
Ideas: How well do you explain the similarities and differences of your topics?	1	2	3	4	5	6
Organization: How well do you organize the similarities and differences of your topic?	1	2	3	4	5	6
Voice: How well do you engage the reader?	1	2	3	4	5	6
Word Choice: How clearly do your words convey your ideas?	1	2	3	4	5	6
Sentence Fluency: How effectively do you use transitions?	1	2	3	4	5	6
Conventions: How correct is your usage of commas in clauses?	1	2	3	4	5	6

WRITING COACH

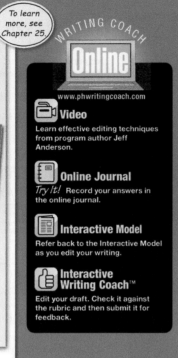

Online

www.phwritingcoach.com

 Video
Learn effective editing techniques from program author Jeff Anderson.

Online Journal
Try It! Record your answers in the online journal.

Interactive Model
Refer back to the Interactive Model as you edit your writing.

Interactive Writing Coach™
Edit your draft. Check it against the rubric and then submit it for feedback.

Editing   163

Personalized Support

 **Interactive Writing Coach™**

Below Level Students complete the editing process by submitting their writing for scoring and feedback.

On Level Students complete the editing process by submitting their writing for scoring and feedback.

Above Level Students finish editing their drafts. They have the option of submitting their final drafts for scoring and/or feedback.

Teacher or Peer Feedback

To provide feedback to students as they edit their draft, ask or have student partners ask one another the following:

- Have you looked for mistakes that you tend to make?
- Have you read your piece aloud to yourself or to a partner? What kind of errors did you find?
- Can you show me something you changed through editing?
- What resources have you used to look for possible spelling errors?
- Read this sentence aloud. Does the grammar sound correct to you?
- Read this sentence aloud. Does the punctuation accurately convey your meaning?

Working with ELLs   **ELL** Sheltered Instruction: Metacognitive

Use *Apply It!* to help students monitor and edit their writing for subject-verb agreement. Review the rules of subject-verb agreement, and have students use the following self-corrective techniques:

Beginning Review the forms of a verb students have been studying, writing appropriate singular and plural subjects for each form. Have students write sentences using the verbs. Help them use this self-corrective technique: circle subjects and underline verbs and compare them with those on the board. Help them make any needed corrections.

Intermediate Have partners circle four verbs in each other's drafts. Have them underline the subject for each verb. Have them check to ensure that they have chosen the correct verb form for each subject.

Advanced Have students put a transparency over their drafts and use a marker to circle the verbs and check for subject-verb agreement.

Advanced High Have students complete the Advanced activity, then exchange papers with a partner and check each other's agreement.

The Digital • Print Path ▶

1 Using *Writing Coach Online*™ or the student book, students complete the writing process by deciding the best way to publish their writing for their intended audience.

2 Students record their answers and ideas to Extend Your Research in their online journals or notebooks.

Publishing *Feature Assignment* Publishing *Feature Assignm*

Publishing

Wrap Up Your Presentation

Lead a class discussion about the kinds of images that students might use to illustrate their compare-and-contrast essays, such as photographs or charts. Then, have students find or create at least one image to illustrate their essays.

Publish Your Piece

Explain to students that the final step in the writing process is to decide which form of publication will present their work most effectively. Then, tell students that the chart shows how specific audiences can be reached using different media.

Have students whose essays address similar audiences work in small groups to discuss appropriate ways to publish their work.

Extend Your Research

Extension Tell students that their thinking about their topic does not have to end with its final publication. Then, guide students through the instructions for extending their research.

Big Question Have students respond to the question in their journals.

Manage Your Portfolio You may wish to have students include development materials such as graphic organizers and drafts.

MAKE YOUR WRITING COUNT

Introduce the survey activity by discussing the opening paragraphs with students. Make sure students understand that the project may be produced electronically or by hand. Then, guide students through the action plan.

Publishing

Share your ideas with a wider audience. Get your essay ready for presentation. Then, choose a way to **publish it for the appropriate audiences.**

Wrap Up Your Presentation

Adding images to your expository essay can provide readers with visual support to illustrate the evidence you presented. Think of some images you can include to bring your compare-and-contrast essay to life.

Publish Your Piece

Use the chart to find a way to publish your essay.

If your audience is...	...then publish it by...
Students or adults at school	• Reading it aloud during a writer's workshop • Posting your essay online and inviting responses
Your local community	• Submitting it to a local newspaper • Posting it on a community Web site

Extend Your Research

Think more about the topic on which you wrote your compare-and-contrast essay. What else would you like to know about this topic?

• Brainstorm for several questions that you would like to research and then consult, or discuss, with others. Then, decide which question is your major research question.

• Formulate, or develop, a plan about how you will answer these questions. Decide where you will find more information—on the Internet, at the library, or through other sources.

• Finally, learn more about your topic by following through with your research plan.

The Big Question: Why Write? What should we tell and what should we describe to make information clear?

Manage Your Portfolio You may wish to include your published compare-and-contrast essay in your writing portfolio. If so, consider what this piece reveals about your writing.

Use the 21st Century Skills Rubric to evaluate each group's process and final product on a scale of 1 to 3, indicating weak, moderate, or strong use of the skill. ▶

Listening and Speaking Monitor students' oral communication and active listening as they collaborate in groups.

21st Century Learning

Skills Rubric	Rating
Make Judgments and Decisions: Interpret information and draw conclusions based on the best analysis.	1 2 3
Work Creatively With Others: Develop and communicate new ideas to others effectively.	1 2 3
Communicate Clearly: Articulate thoughts and ideas effectively.	1 2 3
Apply Technology Effectively: Use technology as a tool to research, organize, and evaluate.	1 2 3

3 STUDENT BOOK ▶

Students use a variety of graphic organizers, either online or in print, to help them work together to create a multimedia group project.

4 STUDENT BOOK ▶

Through *Writing Coach Online*™ students link to resources on 21st Century Learning for help in creating a multimedia group project.

21st Century Learning

MAKE YOUR WRITING COUNT

Write and Present the Results of a Survey

Compare-and-contrast essays identify and explain similarities and differences between people, things, or issues. Identify your classmates' preferences by using a **survey** to determine what people, things, or issues are important to them.

With a group, create a paper or electronic survey for students at your school. The goal of the survey is to evaluate what your peers consider to be important. Then, present the results in a **multimedia presentation** including text and graphics. Present the results orally to a group. Support your presentations with charts and graphs made using available technology or with handmade posters.

Here's your action plan.

1. Choose roles, such as writer and graphics creator.

2. Review your compare-contrast essays for topics. Choose appropriate people, things, or issues to present in your survey.

3. Look at sample surveys online. Then, prepare a brief survey following these guidelines:
   - Ask questions that can be answered with yes or no, or ask multiple-choice questions.
   - Write your questions legibly or type them.
   - Distribute copies by hand or electronically.

4. Analyze the completed surveys. Create a graph of the results by hand or with software.

5. Produce a multimedia presentation that includes the survey, a verbal summary of the results, and a graph showing the results visually. Share it with the school.

Listening and Speaking After you collect the results, work in a group together to discuss conclusions you can draw about the answers. Listen for disagreements about the data and resolve them. Then, rehearse your group oral presentation. Make sure your graphics will be clearly visible to the audience. During your presentation, sum up the overall meaning of your survey results.

WRITING COACH

Online

www.phwritingcoach.com

Online Journal

Extend Your Research Record your answers and ideas in the online journal.

Resource

Link to resources on 21st Century Learning for help in creating a group project.

Make Your Writing Count 165

Personalized Support

FEEDBACK **Teacher or Peer Feedback**

To provide feedback to students on their published writing, ask or have student partners ask one another the following:

- How did you go about writing this piece? What was your process?

- What did you learn from the writing model that you used in this piece?

- What surprised you the most as you wrote this piece?

- Did you try anything new as you worked on this piece?

- What did you learn from this piece of writing that you would like to remember and reuse?

- What do you think you do best as a writer right now?

Differentiated Instruction

RTI **Strategy for Below-Level Students**
Guide students to devise yes-or-no and multiple-choice questions for their survey. First, share with students an example of a yes-or-no question, such as: *Should the lunch period be moved from noon to 11:30 a.m.?* Then, give an example of a multiple-choice question: *Which sport do you like best? a) baseball, b) basketball, c) football* Have students brainstorm for examples of both types of questions. Then, direct students to create survey questions based on their topics.

PRE-AP **Enrichment for Above-Level Students** Challenge students to classify the responses from the class surveys. Have them devise categories for the topics revealed in the survey and sort the topics into the appropriate categories. Then, hold a discussion in which you ask them to draw conclusions about the results and perhaps speculate on the reasons for the results.

The Digital • Print Path ▶

1  ▶

Students use *Writing Coach Online*™ or their student books to analyze and discuss the Writing for Media topic.

 **Writing for Media: Consumer Comparison**

Consumer Comparison

Discuss the opening paragraph with students. As a class, brainstorm for places where consumers might find such comparisons and the purpose of these comparisons.

Try It! Guide students to understand the purpose and content of a consumer comparison.

Say: The second *Try It!* question asks about the purpose of this comparison. As **I scan** the table, it looks to me as if the writer is providing information to help readers choose the right restaurant for their needs.

Explain that an effective consumer comparison is based on facts, not the writer's personal preference. **Ask:** What facts does the writer provide to help consumers make a decision? (price, atmosphere, and food quality)

Have students discuss the remaining questions in small groups and record individual responses in their journals.

Extension Have students bring in other examples of consumer comparisons. Lead a media discussion about the examples, using the *Try It!* questions as a guide.

Create a Consumer Comparison

Tell students that they will create a consumer comparison using the five-step writing process. Then, preview the writing process instructions on page 167.

> **Resources** You may wish to have students use the Cluster Diagram graphic organizer. Distribute printed copies or have students log on to Writing Coach Online.

For each step in the writing process, have partners read aloud and discuss the list of tasks. Then, have them work individually. Once both partners have completed the tasks, have them evaluate each other's work before moving to the next step.

Your Turn **Writing for Media: Consumer Comparison**

Consumer Comparison
21st Century Learning

A **consumer comparison** is a review intended to help people choose the best product. Some reviews are based on formal tests and are published in magazines. Others are more informal—they are posted on Web sites by people who have purchased a product and want to let others know how they liked it. When you write a consumer comparison, you choose criteria you will use to compare and contrast products. You also provide supporting details to show whether a product meets each criterion.

Try It! Study the table on this page. Then, answer these questions. Record the answers in your journal.

1. What two things are being compared and contrasted?
2. What is the **purpose** of this consumer comparison?
3. Who is the target **audience** for this comparison?
4. Will the points of comparison and contrast chosen help the **audience** choose the best product?
5. How do the **supporting details** help readers make the right choice?
6. Are there enough **supporting details** to write a fair and balanced comparison? Why or why not?
7. How does the **organization** of the table make it easier to understand how the restaurants are alike and different?

Extension Find another example of a consumer comparison, and compare it with this one.

Report on: Taco Shack and Gourmet Garden
Date of visit: Nov. 10
Observations:

- Long line moved quickly at the Taco Shack
- Gourmet Garden ran out of what I wanted, so they gave me a free dessert.

Points of Comparison/ Contrast	Taco Shack	Gourmet Garden
Price	• From $.99 to $5.99 • Generous portions	• From $15.99 to $35.99 • Small portions
Atmosphere	• Typical strip mall • Casual • Family friendly	• Upscale • Formal • Not family friendly
Food quality	• Mexican fast food • Fresh ingredients • Many items • Consistent quality	• Dishes from all over the world • Fresh ingredients • Only a few specials • Inconsistent quality

166   **Expository Essay**

Use the 21st Century Skills Rubric to evaluate each student's process and final product on a scale of 1 to 3, indicating weak, moderate, or strong use of the skill.

Partner Talk

Remind students to listen closely to their partners and give them their full attention when sharing information.

21st Century Learning

Skills Rubric	Rating
Reason Effectively: Use various types of reasoning as appropriate to the situation.	1 2 3
Communicate Clearly: Articulate thoughts and ideas effectively using oral and written communication.	1 2 3
Use and Manage Information: Use information accurately for the purpose at hand.	1 2 3
Apply Technology Effectively: Use technology as a tool to communicate information.	1 2 3

2  Writing Journal ▶

Students learn about the characteristics of a consumer comparison by answering questions about the model. Students record their answers to the *Try It!* questions in their online journals or notebooks.

3 STUDENT BOOK ▶

Students follow the five-step writing process to write their own consumer comparison. Students may select online or printed graphic organizers to help them plan and develop their writing.

edia Writing for Media Writing for Media **Writing for Media**

 ## Create a Consumer Comparison

Follow these steps to create your own consumer comparison. To plan your consumer report, review the graphic organizers on pages R24–R27 and choose one that suits your needs.

Prewriting

- Choose a topic for your review. Consider stores, video games, restaurants, or any other product or service you often use.
- Identify your target audience. How are they likely to use this comparison? What will they want to know about the product?
- Determine your points of comparison and contrast. If you review two restaurants, you might compare price, atmosphere, and quality of food.
- List supporting details for each point of comparison and contrast.

Drafting

- Decide whether you are going to organize your review with a point-by-point or block organization. For example, you could start by comparing prices at both restaurants. Another approach would be to discuss the price, atmosphere, and food at one restaurant, then address each of these points at the other.
- Consider organizing your information into a table to make it easier to read.

Revising and Editing

- Review your draft to ensure that your points of comparison and contrast are organized logically.
- Consider whether your comparison is fair. Do you support your opinion with accurate details? Also check that you have included the same amount of detail for each topic. Remove any biased points.
- Check that spelling, grammar, and mechanics are correct.

Publishing

- Submit your comparison to your student newspaper.
- Turn your comparison into a multimedia presentation. In a slideshow, make an opening that includes text titles, and add music and images to help support your ideas.

WRITING COACH
Online
www.phwritingcoach.com

Online Journal
Try It! Record your answers in the online journal.

Interactive Graphic Organizers
Choose from a variety of graphic organizers to plan and develop your project.

Partner Talk

Explain your review to a partner. While explaining, increase the specificity of your details based on the type of information you are discussing. Describe your main points and ask whether your consumer report is clear and fair. Consider your partner's responses when you revise your report.

 ## Personalized Support

FEEDBACK
Teacher or Peer Feedback

To provide feedback to students as they write for media, ask or have student partners ask one another the following:

- What are the main characteristics of this form of writing?
- Have you included most or all of these characteristics in your piece of writing?
- What is your purpose for writing this piece?
- Who is your audience?
- How did you organize your ideas in this piece of writing?
- How did you go about revising the piece? Editing it?
- How do you plan on publishing your piece?
- What other publishing options also might work?

Working with ELLs **ELL** Sheltered Instruction: Social/Affective

As students prepare to write a consumer comparison, help them orally express opinions, ideas, and feelings in contexts ranging from communicating in single words to participating in extended discussions. If they have trouble expressing an idea, help them use learning strategies such as using nonverbal cues and synonyms.

Beginning Write: *I feel ___, I think ___, I like ___.* Help students express their opinions, ideas, and feelings about a local store as they orally complete these sentences. Have them use nonverbal cues, such as gestures, to express meaning when they lack a word.

Intermediate Help students brainstorm ideas about a consumer product. Have groups discuss their opinions, ideas, and feelings about the product. Have students use nonverbal cues and synonyms.

Advanced Have partners discuss their opinions, ideas, and feelings about a consumer product. If they do not know a word, have them use synonyms as they ask each other for help.

Advanced High Have students share their opinions, ideas, and feelings about a consumer product using synonyms.

The Digital · Print Path ▶

1

Before they write, students use the ABCDs of On-Demand Writing to analyze and plan how to respond to each prompt. They can use either their online journals or notebooks to take notes.

2

Students submit their writing paragraph by paragraph or as a complete draft to the Interactive Writing Coach™ for feedback, or share their writing with their teacher.

Writing for Assessment

Read aloud or have a student read aloud the introductory text. Then, tell students that they will learn and practice a technique for writing in response to a test prompt.

Try It! Read aloud the Compare-and-Contrast Prompt and then have volunteers read aloud the Format and Academic Vocabulary boxes. Tell students that they will use the ABCD method to respond to the prompt.

The ABCDs of On-Demand Writing

Have students identify the words associated with the ABCD method. (attack, brainstorm, choose, detect) Then, guide students through their use.

Think Aloud I'll **attack the prompt** by circling the verbs *choose* and *use* and identifying what they refer to. I see that I must choose two celebrities and two points of comparison. I also have to use either point-by-point or block organization. I can rewrite the prompt to state that clearly: "Write an essay that compares and contrasts at least two attributes of two celebrities."

Work with students to identify an appropriate graphic organizer to help them brainstorm for ideas, such as a Venn Diagram. Then, remind them to decide on an organizational structure before they begin to write.

Have students write their drafts individually and then work with a partner to detect errors.

More Prompts for Practice

Apply It! **Test Prep** Have students apply the ABCD method to the two practice prompts.

Writing for Assessment *Writing for Assessment* Writing for Assessment *Writing for Assessment* Writ

Writing for Assessment

Many tests include a prompt that asks you to compare and contrast. Respond using the characteristics of an effective compare-and-contrast essay. (See page 146.)

Try It! To begin, read the **expository** prompt and the information on format and academic vocabulary. Use the ABCDs of On-Demand Writing to help you plan and write your essay.

Format
The prompt directs you to write a *compare-and-contrast essay*. Be sure to include an introduction that identifies who you are comparing, a body with supporting evidence, and a conclusion that restates your main ideas.

Compare-and-Contrast Prompt
Choose two celebrities and write a compare-and-contrast essay about how they are alike and different. Choose at least two points of comparison/contrast. Use an organized structure that's easy for readers to follow.

Academic Vocabulary
Each similarity or difference you write about is *a point of comparison/contrast.* An *organized structure* is the way you organize your points—such as point-by-point or block organization.

The ABCDs of On-Demand Writing

Use the following ABCDs to help you respond to the prompt.

Before you write your draft:

A ttack the prompt [1 MINUTE]

- Circle or highlight important verbs in the prompt. Draw a line from the verb to what it refers to.
- Rewrite the prompt in your own words.

B rainstorm possible answers [4 MINUTES]

- Create a graphic organizer to generate ideas.
- Use one for each part of the prompt if necessary.

C hoose the order of your response [1 MINUTE]

- Think about the best way to organize your ideas.
- Number your ideas in the order you will write about them. Cross out ideas you will not be using.

After you write your draft:

D etect errors before turning in the draft [1 MINUTE]

- Carefully reread your writing.
- Make sure that your response makes sense and is complete.
- Look for spelling, punctuation, and grammar errors.

168 Expository Essay

Prompt 1 Have partners attack the prompt and brainstorm for possible answers. Then, have each pair swap their information with another group to evaluate whether the teams have developed a detailed, balanced, and effective compare-and-contrast essay.

Prompt 2 Have students work individually to attack the prompt and brainstorm for possible answers. Then, have students work in small groups to evaluate their work before writing their drafts.

Spiral Review: Poetry Read aloud the instructions and the prompt. Then, have students review the poetry characteristics on page 120.

Prompt 3 Remind students to use the ABCD method to write their poem.

3 Students receive personalized feedback from the Interactive Writing Coach™, or feedback from their teacher.

More Prompts for Practice

Apply It! Respond to Prompts 1 and 2 by writing **compare-and-contrast essays** that convey information about your topics. As you write, be sure to:

- Include effective **introduction** and **conclusion** paragraphs.
- Include specific **facts, details,** and **examples** to support your ideas.
- Establish points of comparison and contrast.
- Include **explanations** that will guide and inform your reader's understanding of your key ideas and evidence.
- Use an **organizing structure** appropriate for comparing and contrasting.
- Vary your **sentence structure.**
- Use **transitions** to link paragraphs.

Prompt 1 Many different beautiful places in nature exist all over the world. Write a composition that compares and contrasts two places in nature. Make sure that you use facts and details that will guide and inform your reader's understanding of your key ideas.

Prompt 2 Life in the country can be very different from life in a city. Write a composition that compares and contrasts an urban place and a rural place. Remember to think about ways these places are similar and different so that you can find a basis for comparison.

Spiral Review: Poetry Respond to Prompt 3 by writing a **poem**. Make sure your poem reflects all of the characteristics described on page 120. Include **poetic techniques** such as rhythm and rhyme. Also, consider including **figurative language** such as similes and metaphors to bring the language to life. Your poem should also make use of **graphic elements,** such as line length.

Prompt 3 Think about your school. What are your favorite things about your school? What are the best things that have happened here? Write a poem expressing your ideas and feelings about your school.

Interactive Writing Coach™

Plan your response to the prompt. If you are using the prompt for practice, write one paragraph at a time or your entire draft and then submit it for feedback. If you are using the prompt as a timed test, write your entire draft and then submit it for feedback.

Remember **ABCD**

Attack the prompt

Brainstorm possible answers

Choose the order of your response

Detect errors before turning in the draft

Personalized Support

  Assessment/Monitor Progress

For timed writing practice, assign students a prompt to be completed in a timed setting. For Prompts 1 and 2, have students submit their writing Interactive Writing Coach™ to get immediate feedback.

For a formal writing assessment, assign the Assessment writing prompt for this chapter in Writing Coach Online™. Then, have students submit their writing to Interactive Writing Coach™ to be assessed. Use the results to assess student progress and skill levels. Interactive Writing Coach™ will update student levels to ensure that students get the appropriate support.

FEEDBACK ✓ **Teacher Feedback**

To create an assessment environment, have students use a prompt in a timed setting. Grade papers using the appropriate rubric and use the results to assess student progress and skill levels. In the next writing assignment, ensure that students get the appropriate level of support.

If you conference with students, use these questions to guide your discussion:

- What writing form did the prompt call for?
- How did you organize your ideas?
- Did you make good use of your time?

Differentiated Instruction

RTI Strategy for Special Needs Students
Completing an essay within a tight time frame may be a challenge for special needs students. Before they attempt a prompt-based writing exercise, review the ABCD strategy, emphasizing the number of minutes allotted to each step. Then, have students look again at the Outline for Success on page 156. Allot a specific number of minutes for writing each part of the essay—the introduction, the body, and the conclusion—that accounts for the total time allotment.

As students work on the essay, be sure they can see a clock to check the time spent on each ABCD step and on each part of the essay. Or, as they write, you might monitor their time, moving them along from one step to the next at the appropriate intervals so that they complete the essay within the specified time.

T169

Interactive Writing Coach™ **Interactive Graphic Organizers** **Interactive Models**

Online Journal **Resources** **Video**

Use the Online Lesson Planner at www.phwritingcoach.com to customize your instructional plan for an integrated Language Arts curriculum.

DAY 1

CHAPTER OPENER/ GENRE INTRODUCTION

ONLINE

- What Do You Think?
- What's Ahead
- Connect to the Big Questions
- **Feature Assignment: Persuasive Essay**
- Other Forms of Persuasive Writing
- Word Bank

DAY 2

MENTOR TEXT/ STUDENT MODEL

ONLINE

- **Mentor Text: Persuasive Essay**
- Learn From Experience
- **Student Model: Persuasive Essay**
- Reader's Eye and Writer's Eye

DAY 3

Prewriting

ONLINE

- Choose From the Topic Bank
- Choose Your Own Topic
- Narrow Your Topic
- Consider Your Audience and Purpose

DAY 6

Revising

ONLINE

- Keep Revision on Your RADaR
- Look at the Big Picture
- Focus on Craft
- Fine-Tune Your Draft

DAY 7

For additional grammar support, see Grammar Game Plan, Error 4, p. 276.

Editing

ONLINE

- What Do You Notice?/ Grammar Mini-Lesson **Rubric for Persuasive Essay**

Publishing

- Publish Your Piece
- Extend Your Research

DAY 8

21st Century Learning

MAKE YOUR WRITING COUNT

ONLINE

- **Debate an Issue**
- Here's Your Action Plan
- Listening and Speaking

Alternate Pacing Suggestions

- **Block Scheduling** Each day on the Lesson Planner represents a 40–50 minute block. Teachers using block scheduling may combine days to revise pacing to meet their classroom needs.

- **Accelerated Lesson Planning** Combine instructional days by aiding students in choosing a topic and then focusing on two core stages of the writing process, outlining for success (Day 5) and RADaR revision (Day 6).

- **Integrated Language Arts Curriculum** For targeted instruction that covers the essential components of the lesson use either a 3- or a 5-day plan.

3 day plan
DAY 1: Introduction to the Genre, Mentor Text, Student Model
DAY 2: Prewriting/Drafting
DAY 3: Revising/Editing/ Publishing

5 day plan
Use 3-day plan, and add:
DAY 4: Make Your Writing Count
DAY 5: Writing for Assessment

Links to Prentice Hall *LITERATURE*

Featured Author: Zlata Filipović
- What Is Nonfiction?, p. 378
- from *Zlata's Diary* (excerpt from a diary), p. 383
- On Writing Persuasively (Writing Workshop), p. 529
- *From the Author's Desk* Videos: Zlata Filipović

Additional Mentor Text:
- "Jake Wood Baseball is the start of something special" (editorial), Reginald T. Dogan, p. 441

LESSON OBJECTIVES

- To learn the forms and defining characteristics of persuasion.

- To learn the elements of a successful persuasive essay, the chapter Feature Assignment.

- To read a Mentor Text in the genre, analyzing its use of the elements of effective persuasion.

- To read a Student Model of a persuasive essay, analyzing it from the perspective of a reader and from the perspective of a writer.

- To apply prewriting strategies in developing a persuasive essay, including strategies for choosing and narrowing a topic, planning writing, and gathering details, as well as tips for considering audience and purpose.

- To apply drafting strategies in developing a persuasive essay.

- To apply RADaR revision strategies to a draft persuasive essay.

- To learn about the Focus on Craft topic, enhancing style, and apply what is learned to a draft persuasive essay.

- To edit the draft, focusing on vague pronoun reference.

- To complete the Make Your Writing Count assignment, preparing for and holding a debate.

- To complete the Writing for Media assignment, developing a magazine cover.

- To practice writing for assessment.

DAY 4

Prewriting

ONLINE

- Plan Your Piece
- Gather Details

DAY 5

Drafting

ONLINE

- Outline for Success
- Start Your Draft

DAY 9

WRITING FOR MEDIA

ONLINE

- **Magazine Covers**
- Create a Magazine Cover

DAY 10

WRITING FOR ASSESSMENT

ONLINE

- Persuasive Prompt
- The ABCDs of On-Demand Writing
- More Prompts for Practice
- **Test Prep** Spiral Review: Expository

Personalized Assessment

	Ongoing Assessment	Formal Assessment of Feature Assignment	Progress Monitoring at End-of-Chapter
Interactive Writing Coach™	Use Paragraph Feedback and Essay Scorer as a revision tool.	Use Essay Scorer to score students' Feature Assignment papers.	Use Essay Scorer to score students' papers. Students' learner profiles can be adjusted based on their scores.
FEEDBACK **Teacher Conferencing**	Use rubrics in the Student Edition as a revision tool. Conference with students to review their work and provide personalized support.	Use rubrics in the Student Edition to score students' Feature Assignment papers.	Review each student's work to plan targeted resources for the next writing assignment.

The Digital · Print Path ▶

 Using **Writing Coach Online™** or the student book, students discuss the photograph in the chapter opener as it relates to the writing genre.

Chapter Objectives

1. Write a persuasive essay by planning, drafting, revising, editing, and publishing individual work.

2. Participate in a debate.

3. Use the five-step writing process to write and lay out a magazine cover.

4. Write a persuasive essay and a compare-and-contrast expository essay in response to a prompt.

PERSUASION

What Do You Think?

Activate Prior Knowledge Tell students that the purpose of persuasive writing is to convince readers to agree with an opinion or to take an action. Explain to students that they will use what they know about farm chores to analyze the photo on page 170. Then, guide the students in analyzing the photo.

Think Aloud

I see that the girl in the photo is brushing a horse. Grooming the horse may be one of her daily jobs on the family farm. She must be a responsible person, or her family would not have given her the job. In addition, her family must believe that children should have chores to do. How might the girl's family have decided that she was ready for this responsibility?

Work with students to brainstorm for a list of actions that show responsibility.

Try It! **Have students** work individually to develop responses to the questions. Check that students have explored a range of pros and cons about home chores.

Possible responses: Teens show responsibility by following rules at home and doing their best in school. When everyone cooperates to do essential tasks, homes function well and kids learn life skills. Too many chores take away time for play, schoolwork, and social growth.

CHAPTER 9

PERSUASION

170 · Persuasion

Connect to the Big Questions

Have students use their experience to discuss the Big Questions. Explain that they will revisit **Why write?** at the end of this chapter. Tell students to consider these points during their discussion:

1. Students should list the responsibilities and evaluate and rank them in order of importance.

2. Explain that position statements should briefly state an opinion and at least one reason that supports it. A successful argument is based on logic and convincing evidence.

What's Ahead

Have students preview the Mentor Text and Student Model on pages 174–177. Tell students that they will write their own persuasive essay using the five-step writing process: prewriting, drafting, revising, editing, and publishing.

2 Writing Journal ▶

Students record their ideas and responses in their online journals or notebooks. They may also record and save their responses on pop-up sticky notes in Writing Coach Online™.

What Do You Think?

Some teenagers have responsibilities around their homes. For example, this girl brushes the horse on her family farm. Should teenagers have to show responsibility by doing chores? Or is working on homework and going to school responsibility enough?

What is your opinion about this topic? Once you have your opinion, you may want to convince someone to share it. When you use words to convince people to think or act in a certain way, you are using persuasion.

Try It! List reasons why teenagers should and should not have to do household chores to show they can handle responsibilities.

Consider these questions as you participate in an extended discussion with a partner. Take turns expressing your ideas and feelings.

- What are some ways teenagers can show responsibility?
- What are the benefits of doing household chores?
- What are some of the reasons why teenagers should not have to do household chores?

Review the list you made. Choose a position on the issue by deciding which side to take. Write a sentence that states which position, or side, you will take. Then, take turns talking about your ideas and positions with a partner.

What's Ahead

In this chapter, you will review two strong examples of a persuasive essay: a Mentor Text and a Student Model. Then, using the examples as guidance, you will write a persuasive essay of your own.

WRITING COACH
Online
www.phwritingcoach.com

Online Journal
Try It! Record your answers and ideas in the online journal.

You can also record and save your answers and ideas on pop-up sticky notes in the eText.

Connect to the Big Questions

Discuss these questions with your partner:

1 What do you think? Which responsibilities are most important?

2 Why write? What is your point of view? How will you know if you've convinced others?

171

Personalized Support

FEEDBACK
Teacher or Peer Feedback

To encourage students in their discussion of the photograph as it relates to the writing genre, ask the following questions:

- What is the first thing you think of when you look at this photo?
- How does it relate to your life?
- How does it relate to things you've learned in other subjects?
- What questions come to mind when you look at this photograph?
- How does your response to the photograph compare to those of your classmates?

Have students demonstrate listening comprehension of increasingly complex spoken English by following the directions for the *Try It!* after you read them aloud.

Beginning Reread the first sentence of the *Try It!* directions aloud. Using mime, clarify the meaning of *list, teenagers, chores,* and *show responsibility*. Ask yes/no questions to help students monitor understanding and seek clarification as needed. Help them follow directions.

Intermediate Read aloud the *Try It!* directions. Have students write the steps in flow charts to monitor understanding. Have

them seek clarification when necessary. Then, help them follow directions.

Advanced As you read aloud the *Try It!* directions, have students take notes. Have them monitor comprehension and seek clarification as needed. Have them follow directions to complete the activity.

Advanced High Have partners take turns reading aloud the directions in the *Try It!* activity and taking notes. They should review notes to monitor comprehension, seeking clarification as needed, then partners follow directions to complete the activity.

The Digital • Print Path ▶

WRITING COACH Online
STUDENT BOOK

1 **STUDENT BOOK** ▶

Students learn vocabulary from the Word Bank and listen to English and Spanish pronunciations in the *Writing Coach Online™* glossary.

2 **Writing Journal** ▶

Students record answers to questions about forms of writing in their online journals or notebooks.

PERSUASIVE ESSAY

To introduce this chapter's writing form, discuss the opening paragraphs with students. Make sure students understand that a persuasive essay is a type of persuasive writing. Explain that good writers use a step-by-step process to develop their work. Then, have students preview the rubric on page 189.

Persuasive Essay

Ask volunteers to read aloud the feature assignment characteristics. Tell students that they will identify these characteristics in a Mentor Text and a Student Model. Then, they will use the characteristics to guide the writing of their own persuasive essay.

Other Forms of Persuasive Writing

Guide students to understand how the forms of persuasive writing are alike and different.

Say: I see several common forms of persuasive writing fairly often. For example, I read many persuasive essays in print and digital newspapers in the form of reviews, letters to the editor, and advertisements.

Ask: How are editorials and advertisements alike? (They try to convince readers to believe something or take some action.) How are they different? (Advertisements often appeal to emotion, while editorials use logic and evidence.)

Have students brainstorm for appropriate topics for each form of persuasive writing.

Try It! Remind students that the audience is the people who will read their writing. The purpose is the author's reason for writing. Have students record their responses in their journal.

Possible responses: letter to the editor, to express an opinion in response to an article; review, to state an opinion about attending an activity; persuasive speech, to win an audience's support for a policy or action

Word Bank

To assist English Language Learners and struggling readers, echo read each word or have students log on to Writing Coach Online to listen to the pronunciations. Then, have partners take turns using each word in a sentence. Ask volunteers to share one of their sentences with the class.

PERSUASIVE ESSAY

In this chapter, you will explore a type of persuasive writing called the persuasive essay. The writer of a persuasive essay presents his or her view on an issue. Then the writer tries to persuade the reader to agree with that view. The writer supports his or her position with detailed evidence. Using sound reasoning, the writer shows why his or her point of view is stronger than other points of view.

You will develop the persuasive essay by taking it through each of the steps of the writing process: prewriting, drafting, revising, editing, and publishing. You will also have an opportunity to create a magazine cover. To preview the criteria for how your persuasive essay will be evaluated, see the rubric on page 189.

FEATURE ASSIGNMENT
Persuasive Essay

An effective persuasive essay has these characteristics:

- A **clear thesis** to **establish a position** on an issue that has at least two sides
- **Sound reasoning** to establish a position and create a convincing argument
- **Powerful language** to appeal to the emotion and reason of an appropriate audience
- **Detailed and relevant evidence,** such as facts and examples
- Consideration of **alternatives and counter-arguments,** or the ideas of people who do not share your opinions
- **Clear organization,** including an introduction, a body, and a conclusion
- A **conclusion** that restates your view and provides a memorable ending
- **Effective sentence structure** and correct spelling, grammar, and usage
- **Other types of evidence,** such as quotes from an expert on the topic

---

Teacher Tip

Have students monitor their understanding by selecting an example of each form of persuasive writing and explaining its purpose and persuasive techniques to a partner.

Other Forms of Persuasive Writing

In addition to the persuasive essay, there are other forms of persuasive writing, including:

Advertisements are paid announcements that try to convince people to do or buy something.

Editorials state the opinion of the editors and publishers of news organizations. Editorials are usually about current issues. They appear in newspapers and magazines, or on television, radio, or the Internet.

Letters to the editor are written by readers of a newspaper or magazine. The letters express an opinion in response to an article in the newspaper or magazine.

Op-ed pieces, or opinion editorials, try to persuade readers of a newspaper or magazine to agree with the writer's views on an issue. Op-eds differ from editorials in two ways. Op-eds are signed, while editorials are usually unsigned. Op-ed pieces are often written by people who do not work for the newspaper or magazine.

Persuasive speeches aim at winning an audience's support for a policy, position, or action.

Propaganda tries to persuade people to think or act in a certain way. This type of persuasive writing uses emotional appeals and often biased, false, or misleading information. Propaganda is often about political issues.

Reviews evaluate items and activities, such as books and movies. A review often states an opinion on whether people should spend time and money on the item or activity.

Try It! For each audience and purpose described, choose a form, such as an advertisement, a letter, or a review, that is appropriate for conveying your intended meaning to the audience. Explain your choices.

- To express your support for an editorial in your local newspaper
- To encourage your friends and family to go see the school play
- To convince people to donate money or to volunteer for an important cause

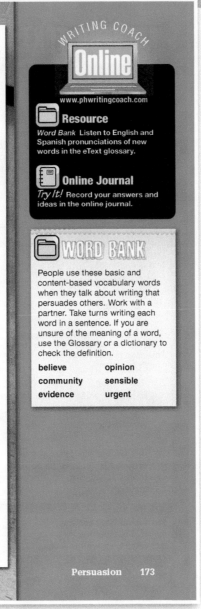

WRITING COACH
Online
www.phwritingcoach.com

Resource
Word Bank Listen to English and Spanish pronunciations of new words in the eText glossary.

Online Journal
Try It! Record your answers and ideas in the online journal.

WORD BANK

People use these basic and content-based vocabulary words when they talk about writing that persuades others. Work with a partner. Take turns writing each word in a sentence. If you are unsure of the meaning of a word, use the Glossary or a dictionary to check the definition.

believe	opinion
community	sensible
evidence	urgent

The Digital • Print Path ▶

1  STUDENT BOOK ▶

Using Writing Coach Online™ or the student book, students read and listen to an audio recording of the Mentor Text. As they complete their writing assignments they can refer back to the Mentor Text for support whenever they need it.

MENTOR TEXT

About the Selection This persuasive essay takes the position that each person can and should make a difference in keeping one's community clean. The writer describes the satisfaction of cleaning up one area, points out that all actions are taken by individuals, and states that we are all responsible for taking care of our communities.

Learn From Experience

After students have read the text, point out that the numbered notes refer to the characteristics of a persuasive essay introduced on page 172.

Try It! Guide students to understand how the genre characteristics shape the text.

Say: The first *Try It!* question asks which description I found most effective. I like the way the writer described the way the grass was covered with "the belch of brown cardboard and silver aluminum." Her description was unexpected and vivid.

Ask: What effect did the author's use of vivid language have on you as you read? (**Possible responses:** The language made me pay attention because it was unexpected and vivid. It made me think differently about garbage.)

Have students reply to the *Try It!* questions in their journals. If students have difficulty responding to a particular question, model a response, as with Question 1.

Check the accuracy and completeness of student responses.

1. Responses will vary but should mention the description of the "belch of brown cardboard and silver aluminum" or the "eyesore" caused by the trash.

2. The list emphasizes the amount and variety of garbage, and thus the extent of the problem.

3. Responses will vary. Possible thesis: *Every person should take responsibility for keeping public areas clean.* The purpose is to convince people to stop littering and to pick up trash. She is addressing any citizen, especially those who live in her area.

Text *Persuasive Essay* Mentor Text *Persuasive Essay* Me

MENTOR TEXT — Persuasive Essay

Learn From Experience

Read the persuasive essay on pages 174–175. As you read, take notes to develop your understanding of basic sight and English vocabulary. Then, read the numbered notes in the margins to learn about how the author presented her ideas.

Answer the *Try It!* questions online or in your notebook.

---

① **Vivid language** in the **introduction** helps get readers' attention and make readers aware of the litter problem.

Try It! In your opinion, which descriptions of littering are the most vivid in the introduction?

② The author gives specific **examples** of litter that she found on the ground. These examples support her position that litter is ruining a city park.

Try It! What is the effect of listing so many specific examples of litter?

③ In the **thesis**, the author makes her position clear.

Try It! Put the thesis in your own words. What is the purpose of the essay? Who do you think is the audience?

Extension Find another example of a persuasive essay, and compare it with this one.

174 Persuasive Writing

Individuals Can Make a Difference

by Martha M. Everett

① Two weeks ago, I cleaned up a city block along a fir old city park, the edge of which has become a forgotten n man's land. It's in my neighborhood, and I pass it by car c on foot nearly every day. It is littered with trash, its qui green grass dotted with the belch of brown cardboard an silver aluminum. What should be an oasis among the city brick and asphalt had become an eyesore the city doesn clean. I couldn't stand it any longer. I put on latex gloves an took a lawn bag to the spot on Loughborough Avenue. Wit cars speeding past spewing carbon monoxide, I bent an hauled and scraped up everything I could. In 90 minute the huge green bag was filled with trash.

② There was an empty medicine vial, a cut-up cred card (why bother to cut it up if you're going to throw on the street?), an Xbox game case, pieces of broken CDs ribbons of cassette tape, pennies, plastic bottles, a rippe up photo of a young woman, . . . and lots of things I cou not (or preferred to not) identify or decipher.

For a few days, it was lovely. I passed the area an enjoyed the view. But within a week, the block once agai was littered with garbage. I felt defeated and powerless.

During the time I spent bent over retrieving what othe had discarded, I had ample time to think. And I starte thinking about that phrase people say so often: One perso can't make a difference. I don't know if they believe that c if it's just a convenient excuse to not take action, but the lir kept ringing in my head. And the more trash I picked u the more ridiculous the statement seemed to me.

③ Of course an individual can make a difference. A simplistic as it sounds, the world is made up of individuals

---

4. The author's examples of historic, powerful individuals show that an individual can make a difference. The example of her own effort shows that an ordinary citizen can make a difference, too.

5. Responses will vary. Phrases such as "shared treasures" and "tend our own garden" may stimulate emotional responses.

Extension Lead a discussion in which students compare and contrast how their additional persuasive essay examples use the genre characteristics. Use the *Try It!* questions as a guide.

Teacher Tip

Quick Write Ask students to recall a time when they cleaned up litter or made a choice not to litter. Then, have students write a new introduction to the Mentor Text based on this experience. Remind students to use vivid language to grab readers' attention.

---

2 Writing Journal

Students record their answers to questions about the Mentor Text in their online journals or notebooks.

Wednesday, February 20   **14**

❹ The CEO of a multimillion-dollar corporation is an individual, as are the people on its board of directors. Presidents are individuals. The Founding Fathers were individuals, and look what they accomplished.

What I was doing—as an individual—was making a difference; it's just that the effect of it was temporary. If every individual who tosses waste on the street chose not to do so, collectively they would make a lasting difference. And if those people were the ones along this block of my South St. Louis neighborhood, they would make a true, permanent difference. And the area would thrive.

I'm not the most dedicated environmentalist. I recycle when I can, although the city doesn't make it convenient. And I try to conserve water and plant trees.

❺ Public areas are shared treasures. As Voltaire's Candide said, we must tend our own garden. The Earth is our garden. On a list of sins against the planet, littering may not rank high, but littering certainly is not tending.

Maintaining our garden is an individual responsibility for the good of the whole. And as individuals, we can make a difference.

WRITING COACH

Online

www.phwritingcoach.com

Interactive Model
Listen to an audio recording of the Mentor Text in the eText. You can refer back to the Mentor Text whenever you need support in developing your own writing.

Online Journal
Try It! Answer the questions about the Mentor Text in the online journal.

❹ The author supports her position with **sound reasoning** and **examples.**

Try It! Do you think the reasoning and examples are persuasive? Explain.

❺ The **conclusion** contains **language that appeals to both emotion and reason.**

Try It! Quote a sentence that stirs your emotions, or feelings. Which statement or statements seem especially reasonable to you?

Mentor Text   175

Personalized Support

FEEDBACK 👥 **Teacher or Peer Feedback**

To provide feedback to students on their responses to the Mentor Text and their answers to the *Try It!* questions, ask or have student partners ask one another the following:

• What is the thesis or controlling idea of the Mentor Text?

• How does the Mentor Text illustrate the characteristics of a persuasive essay?

• How did you answer this *Try It!* question? How could you use your answer to help you plan your piece of writing?

Working with ELLs   **ELL** Sheltered Instruction: Cognitive

Help students develop and expand their repertoire of learning strategies by looking for patterns in language and analyzing their significance. Read aloud the first paragraph of the conclusion on page 175. Then:

Beginning Model looking for the language pattern of repeated words (*garden, tend/tending,* and *littering*). Explain that repeated words help readers think about key terms. Ask yes/no questions to help students analyze the importance of the repeated words to the text.

Intermediate Have students complete the Beginning activity in groups, then expand the strategy by completing sentence starters about the language pattern, focusing on the effect of repetition.

Advanced Have pairs read the highlighted text, looking for the language pattern of repeated words and keeping a list. Have them use their lists to explain how repeated words create an emotional response.

Advanced High Have students complete the Advanced activity. Have them find a language pattern in another paragraph, analyze its effect, and compare their findings with a partner.

The Digital • Print Path ▶

1 ▶

Using Writing Coach Online™ or the student book, students read and listen to an audio recording of the Student Model.

STUDENT MODEL

Tell students that good writers react to what they read in ways that show their understanding of the text. Explain that students will react to the Student Model by placing two sets of symbols in the text. Then, distribute printed copies of the Student Model or have students log on to Writing Coach Online.

Use a Reader's Eye

Read aloud the instruction for using the Reader's Response Symbols and the meaning of each symbol. Then, guide students through their use.

Think Aloud The student writer has clearly stated her reasons for supporting school uniforms. However, **I have questions** about some of the reasons for her position. For example, in paragraph 2, lines 13–16, to prove that uniforms cause students to take school more seriously she says, "When I wear a skirt and a blouse, I feel more grown-up." Is feeling grown-up really more important than feeling comfortable? I'll place a question mark next to this part of the text.

Work with students to identify and develop other questions about the text.

Have students read and respond to the Student Model, using each Reader's Response Symbol at least once.

Partner Talk

After partners have shared their opinions about the text, have each student pair present their opinions and reasons for a different paragraph to the class.

Use a Writer's Eye

Read aloud the instructions for using the Writer's Response Symbols and the meaning of each symbol. Then, guide students through their use.

STUDENT MODEL — Persuasive Essay

With a small group, take turns reading this Student Model aloud. Ask yourself if you find the author's arguments convincing.

 Use a Reader's Eye

Now, reread the Student Model. On your copy of the Student Model, use the Reader's Response Symbols to react to what you read.

Reader's Response Symbols

+ I strongly agree with this.

− I strongly disagree with this.

? I have a question about this.

! Wow! That is cool/weird/interesting.

⬗ Partner Talk ⬖

Participate in an extended discussion with a partner. Express your opinions and share your responses to the Student Model. Take notes and discuss responses that were the same for both of you, and that were different.

176 Persuasive Essay

Raise Your Hand for School Uniforms

by Jane Scott

Every morning, my mother puts on her uniform of carefully ironed navy blue pants and a light blue shirt. Then she is ready to go to work as a city bus driver. Meanwhile, in homes all over town, 5 kids are wondering what to wear to school. If we had a uniform, it would save a lot of time. More importantly, wearing uniforms would help students take their studies more seriously and encourage better behavior. The school district should 10 require all students to wear a school uniform.

First, wearing uniforms could help students take school more seriously. Dressing differently often makes people act differently. When I wear a skirt and a blouse, I feel more grown-up than when I 15 wear jeans and a sweatshirt. By wearing "school clothes" instead of "play clothes," kids will come to school ready to learn. When a school district in Washington State began requiring school uniforms, fewer students skipped school or were late to class.

20 Despite the evidence that uniforms can help students, some people don't want a uniform policy. They say that uniforms are too expensive for families. However, uniforms are sold at much lower prices than trendy clothes. The school district could also 25 help those families that are unable to afford uniforms.

Another reason to promote school uniforms is to encourage good behavior. Clothes can be a major distraction in school. Some kids like to gossip about people's outfits. Students who can't afford trendy 30 clothes sometimes get teased. If everyone wore the

1

Say: I found an example of a good response to a counter-argument. In lines 34–37, the writer notes that many kids think uniforms stifle their creativity. In lines 37–39, she responds that art, writing, and thinking are more important creative outlets. I'll write C.A. next to this part of the text for good response to readers' counter-arguments.

Ask: How does the author respond to the counter-argument presented in line 22? (She argues that uniforms are cheaper than trendy clothes and that the school district could help families that cannot afford uniforms.)

Have students read and respond to the Student Model, using each Writer's Response Symbol at least once.

2

First, students respond to the Student Model as a reader, using symbols to mark the text. They can mark the text using pop-up sticky notes in *Writing Coach Online™* or they can mark a printed copy of the Student Model.

3

Then, students respond to the Student Model as a writer, using different symbols to mark the text. They can use either *Writing Coach Online™* or a printed copy of the Student Model.

e Essay Student Model *Persuasive Essay* **Student Model**

same clothes, fashion and cost would matter much less. Kids would get along better. We could focus on what's on the inside instead of the outside.

35 However, many kids like thinking about what's on the outside. They believe that choosing their outfits is a form of creativity. These students don't want the school to limit their self-expression. But school offers many more important ways for students to express themselves: through their art, writing, and thinking.

40 School uniforms can have positive effects on learning and behavior. One year after students began wearing uniforms in a school district in California, the district had 36 percent less school crime. If you are in favor of a school uniform policy,

45 write to the school board. Let's help schools focus on what's important: education, not fashion.

2

WRITING COACH
Online
www.phwritingcoach.com

Interactive Model

Listen to an audio recording of the Student Model in the eText. Use the Reader's and Writer's Response Symbols with the eText tools to note what you read.

Use a Writer's Eye

Now, evaluate the piece as a writer. On your copy of the Student Model, use the Writer's Response Symbols to react to what you read. Identify places where the student writer uses characteristics of an effective persuasive essay.

Writer's Response Symbols	
C.T.	**Clearly stated thesis**
P.A.	**Good persuasive arguments**
S.E.	**Effective supporting evidence**
C.A.	**Good responses to readers' counter-arguments**

Student Model 177

Personalized Support

FEEDBACK
Teacher or Peer Feedback

To provide feedback to students on their responses to the Student Model, ask or have student partners ask one another the following:

- What is the thesis or controlling idea of the Student Model?
- How does the Student Model illustrate the characteristics of a persuasive essay?
- Which feature or characteristic of the Student Model might you use in your own piece of writing?
- How could you alter or adapt this feature to make it your own?

Working with ELLs ELL Sheltered Instruction: Cognitive

Help students learn basic vocabulary heard during classroom instruction, drawing on prior experiences. Write the words *school* and *year* from the Student Model on the board, as well as *friend*, *o'clock*, *morning*, and *today*. Read the words aloud. Then:

Beginning Display a calendar. Say *The year is (date)*. Have students complete statements using the word *year*, drawing on prior experiences of a school year, such as, *I started sixth grade in the year (date)*. Use gestures to reinforce meanings.

Intermediate Have pairs create **Spider-Web Diagrams** for the words, writing

phrases describing prior experiences related to each. Have students share their diagrams.

Advanced Have students complete the Intermediate activity. Have groups use the words in oral sentences, monitoring each other's use of the words.

Advanced High Have students use the words in a paragraph, describing prior experiences that clarify the meaning of each word. Have them read their paragraphs aloud in groups. Instruct groups to monitor one another's use of the words.

The Digital • Print Path ▶

1  STUDENT BOOK ▶
Students select or are assigned a topic for their persuasive essay from the Topic Bank, or they may choose a topic of their own.

2 STUDENT BOOK ▶
Students complete online or printed graphic organizers to narrow the topic for their persuasive essay.

Prewriting

Explain that the first task students need to complete as they plan their persuasive essay is to determine an appropriate topic.

Choose From the Topic Bank

Read aloud each topic and then ask volunteers to describe them in their own words. If you are assigning topics to students, you may wish to do so now. Encourage students to ask questions about their topic.

Choose Your Own Topic

Introduce and discuss the Discussion and Research strategies. If students were not assigned writing topics, have them use the strategies to brainstorm for topics for their essays.

Extension Have each student choose one of the strategies. Then, have them write an action plan that outlines the resources and steps they will use to develop their topic.

Narrow Your Topic

Tell students that they will use a Narrow Your Topic graphic organizer to reduce their topic to a specific position. Then, distribute printed copies or have students log on to Writing Coach Online.

Apply It! Guide students through the instructions for completing the graphic organizer. Have students complete the exercise based on their topic.

Consider Your Audience and Purpose

Guide students to consider the audience and purpose for their persuasive essay.

Say: The first question in the chart asks about my audience, or the people who will read my essay. For example, if **I choose** the third topic

 **Your Turn** ▶ **Feature Assignment: Persuasive Essay**

Prewriting

Plan a first draft of your persuasive essay by determining an appropriate topic. You can select from the Topic Bank or come up with an idea of your own.

Choose From the Topic Bank

 **TOPIC BANK**

Pets Anyone who has ever owned a pet has an opinion on which animal makes the best pet. Take a stand on which kind of animal makes the best pet. Write an essay using reasons and examples to support your choice.

Community Issues Think about issues affecting your community, such as littering or the use of cell phones while driving. Choose the issue that you feel is the most important. Write a persuasive essay in which you state and explain your opinion on the issue.

Persuade Your Parents Think of an item that you would like to buy or an activity you would like to do. Write an essay in which you identify the item or activity and persuade your parent or caregiver to give his or her permission.

Choose Your Own Topic

To determine an appropriate topic on your own, use the following **range of strategies** to generate ideas before you plan a first draft.

Discussion and Research

- With your friends and family, discuss the issues that interest you. Ask about their views. Take notes on your conversations.
- Review your notes. Circle key words and phrases that describe the issues you want to learn more about.
- Search your library's database and the Web for the key words and phrases from your notes. Keep records of any sources you may use.

Review your responses and choose a topic.

178 **Persuasive Essay**

from the Topic Bank, about persuading parents to give permission, then my audience will be my parents or caregivers.

Ask: Based on the topic you have chosen, who is most likely to read your persuasive essay? Whom would you most like to read it? (Responses will vary.)

Have students who have chosen the same or similar topics work in small groups to discuss and respond to the remaining questions.

Coach's Corner

You may wish to model prewriting activities for students by brainstorming for your own writing topic. Use these prompts to guide your work and discussion.

- **I am interested in** our town's empty land.
- **I can narrow my topic by** focusing on building parks.

Discuss the choices you make and solicit feedback from students.

Students record their answers to questions about audience and purpose in their online journals or notebooks.

Assignment **Prewriting** *Feature Assignment* **Prewriting**

Narrow Your Topic

If your topic is too broad, your essay will be vague. A narrow topic helps you write a clear thesis statement and build a strong argument.

Apply It! Use a graphic organizer like the one shown to narrow your topic.

- Write your general topic in the top box. Make your topic more specific as you move down the chart.
- Use the last box to establish a position on your chosen issue. This is the topic for your persuasive essay.

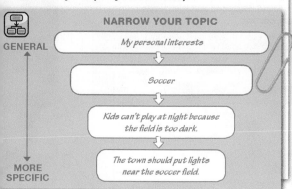

NARROW YOUR TOPIC

GENERAL

My personal interests

↓

Soccer

↓

Kids can't play at night because the field is too dark.

↓

The town should put lights near the soccer field.

MORE SPECIFIC

Consider Your Audience and Purpose

Before writing, think about your audience and purpose. Consider the views of others and **alternatives to your position** as you ask yourself these questions.

Questions for Audience	Questions for Purpose
• Who is in my audience, and what do they need to know to understand my topic?	• What is my **position** on my chosen issue?
• What counter-arguments might they have? How will I respond to those arguments?	• What do I want the audience to do?

Record your answers in your writing journal.

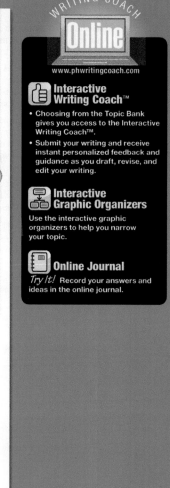

WRITING COACH

Online

www.phwritingcoach.com

Interactive Writing Coach™

- Choosing from the Topic Bank gives you access to the Interactive Writing Coach™.
- Submit your writing and receive instant personalized feedback and guidance as you draft, revise, and edit your writing.

Interactive Graphic Organizers

Use the interactive graphic organizers to help you narrow your topic.

Online Journal

Try It! Record your answers and ideas in the online journal.

Prewriting **179**

Personalized Support

Interactive Writing Coach™

Below Level Teachers select a topic from the topic bank for below-level students. Students submit their writing to the **Interactive Writing Coach™** for feedback paragraph by paragraph or as a complete draft. It is recommended that below-level students submit their writing one paragraph at a time.

On Level Students may select a topic from the Topic Bank. They may submit their writing for feedback paragraph by paragraph or as a complete draft.

Above Level Students may select from the Topic Bank or come up with their own topic. Above-level students should submit their writing as a complete draft.

Interactive Graphic Organizer

Below Level Students complete three graphic organizers that provide models and scaffolded support.

On Level Students complete one, two, or three graphic organizers, depending on how much support they need.

Above Level Students complete the least scaffolded graphic organizer or narrow their topic without the help of a graphic organizer.

Differentiated Instruction

RTI **Strategy for Special Needs Students**
Explain that a persuasive essay topic is the writer's opinion. Model developing a topic by writing *I think that . . .* on the board. Have students state opinions based on their experience. Then, explain that a persuasive essay also states what the writer wants readers to do, in the form of a statement that contains the words *should* or *should not*. For example, *My parents should increase my allowance by $1 per week.*

RTI **Strategy for Below-Level Students**
Challenge students to make their position specific and clear. Have them use the Cluster Diagram graphic organizer and place their general essay topic in the center oval. Then, have them write specific facts and ideas they have about the topic in the surrounding ovals. After they consider these details, have students write a statement that tells exactly what they think should be done to correct the issue or accomplish the goal.

The Digital • Print Path ▶

1   ▶

Using *Writing Coach Online*™ or the student book, students read and discuss the model graphic organizer.

2 ▶

Students complete online or printed graphic organizers to develop their ideas and gather details.

Plan Your Piece

Explain that writers use graphic organizers to develop their ideas and show relationships between different parts of the text. Then, point out the Develop Your Persuasive Arguments graphic organizer on page 180. Tell students that they will use this organizer to outline their persuasive essay. Then, distribute printed copies or have students log on to Writing Coach Online.

Introduce the graphic organizer by explaining that the column on the left lists the elements of a persuasive essay, and the column on the right lists the information for an example essay.

Develop a Clear Thesis Guide students to notice that the thesis in the example organizer is based on the narrowed topic from page 179. Have students write a thesis sentence that clearly states their issue and record it on their graphic organizer.

Organize Your Arguments Point out that the graphic organizer has helped the writer clarify the arguments or reasons for taking the action recommended in the thesis. Have students work in pairs to brainstorm for persuasive arguments to support their thesis and record them on their graphic organizer.

Gather Details

Remind students that arguments in persuasive essays are supported by relevant evidence. Ask volunteers to read aloud each kind of support and its example. Then, guide the students to place the details in the example organizer.

Say: I notice that the Develop Your Persuasive Argument organizer has spaces to list supporting evidence and details for each persuasive argument. The details on page 181 supply this information. For instance, the Expert Opinion example, in which a police chief says that lights would reduce crime, supports the First Persuasive Argument, which says that lights would make the park safer.

Ask: Which persuasive argument is supported by the Sound Reasoning evidence? (Second Persuasive Argument: Lights would allow more kids to participate in soccer.)

Plan Your Piece

You will use the graphic organizer to state your thesis, organize your arguments, and identify details. When it is complete, you will be ready to write your first draft.

Develop a Clear Thesis Make sure the audience knows which side of the issue you support. Write a **thesis statement**—one sentence in which you **establish a position** on the issue. Add your thesis statement to a graphic organizer like the one shown.

Organize Your Arguments Fill in the graphic organizer to arrange your arguments from least to most important. Make sure each argument is based on **sound reasoning** and is supported with **detailed and relevant evidence**.

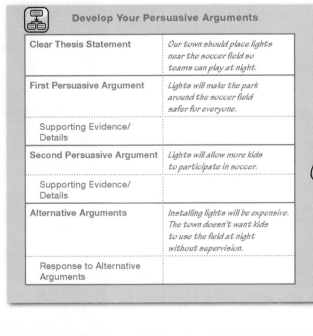

Develop Your Persuasive Arguments	
Clear Thesis Statement	*Our town should place lights near the soccer field so teams can play at night.*
First Persuasive Argument	*Lights will make the park around the soccer field safer for everyone.*
Supporting Evidence/ Details	
Second Persuasive Argument	*Lights will allow more kids to participate in soccer.*
Supporting Evidence/ Details	
Alternative Arguments	*Installing lights will be expensive. The town doesn't want kids to use the field at night without supervision.*
Response to Alternative Arguments	

180   **Persuasive Essay**

Have students work in small groups to place the remaining details on the example graphic organizer.

Try It! Guide students to understand that school uniforms can encourage good behavior because fashion can be a cause of distraction and social and emotional conflict.

Apply It! Read aloud the bulleted instruction for gathering details. Then, have students develop supporting details for their persuasive essay and enter them on their graphic organizer. Remind students to use a variety of types of details to support their position.

Writer's Block

IF students are not developing strong arguments for their position or supporting them adequately . . .

THEN have them review the Student Model on pages 176–177. Discuss the logic of each argument and the effectiveness of the supporting details.

3 STUDENT BOOK ▶

Students refer back to the Mentor Text or the Student Model as they plan their writing.

Gather Details

To support their arguments, writers gather information that is relevant, or important, to their topic. Look at these examples of types of information:

- **Sound Reasoning:** There are not enough daylight hours to allow the participation of all the kids who want to play soccer. Lights on the soccer field would increase the number of hours in which games could be played. Therefore, we could form more teams and allow more kids to play.

- **Facts:** Kids who play sports are healthier on average than kids who do not.

- **Examples:** Since lighting its sports fields, a nearby town no longer has a waiting list to join soccer teams.

- **Expert Opinions:** Police Chief Reyes says that lights on the soccer field would also reduce crime in the area around the field.

Try It! Read the Student Model excerpt and identify which details the author used to support her argument.

STUDENT MODEL | from **Raise Your Hand for School Uniforms** pages 176–177; lines 26–33

> Another reason to promote school uniforms is to encourage good behavior. Clothes can be a major distraction in school. Some kids like to gossip about people's outfits. Students who can't afford trendy clothes sometimes get teased. If everyone wore the same clothes, fashion and cost would matter much less. Kids would get along better. We could focus on what's on the inside instead of the outside.

Apply It! Review the types of support a persuasive writer can use. Then identify at least one detail for each of your arguments.

- Remember to find evidence to use in your **consideration of alternatives,** where you address the views of people who disagree with you.

- Then add these details to your graphic organizer. Reread your arguments and supporting details to check that they support your thesis.

WRITING COACH

Online

www.phwritingcoach.com

Interactive Graphic Organizers

Use the interactive graphic organizers to help you create a plan for your writing.

Interactive Model

Refer back to the Interactive Model in the eText as you plan your writing.

Personalized Support

Interactive Graphic Organizer

Below Level Students complete three graphic organizers that provide models and scaffolded support.

On Level Students complete one, two, or three graphic organizers, depending on how much support they need.

Above Level Students complete the least scaffolded graphic organizer or narrow their topic without the help of a graphic organizer.

FEEDBACK Teacher or Peer Feedback

To provide feedback to students as they plan their first draft, ask or have student partners ask one another the following:

- What do you want your audience to know about the topic?

- What questions or concerns will your audience have about the topic?

- What details have you identified for your piece? How do these details support your thesis or controlling idea?

- Are your details varied? Will they interest your readers? Explain.

Differentiated Instruction

RTI Strategy for Below-Level Students

Help students analyze their arguments to be sure they have not repeated the same idea in different words. Have writers look for repeated words, phrases, or synonyms in their organizer. Then, have them rephrase each reason and compare the new wording to other arguments. Also have them note whether different arguments call for the same supporting details. Writers should replace repeated arguments until they have three distinct reasons to support.

RTI Strategy for Special Needs Students

Work with students to understand the concept of cause and effect. Explain that just because one event comes before another does not mean it caused the second event. Use the Cause and Effect graphic organizer to show how causes and effects are related to each other. Point out that if a student drops her pencil and then another student sneezes, those two events are not related by cause and effect. But if a student drops her pencil and the pencil breaks, these two events do have a cause-and-effect relationship.

The Digital · Print Path ▶

1  Using **Writing Coach Online™** or the student book, students read and discuss the Outline for Success for a persuasive essay.

2 Students discuss how the Mentor Text illustrates the characteristics of a persuasive essay.

Drafting

Outline for Success

Explain that the Outline for Success shows an organizational strategy for a persuasive essay. Students will use the Outline to write a focused, organized, and coherent draft of their persuasive essay.

I. Introduction

Link the Outline to a specific persuasive essay by having students turn to the Mentor Text on pages 174–175. Ask a volunteer to read aloud the thesis statement (line 29). Then, guide students to see how the writer has created interest and stated the thesis clearly.

Say: I notice that the writer has taken her time to introduce her topic by creating a vivid scene. She captures my attention by describing her efforts to clean up her trash-filled neighborhood. Her writing makes me care about her efforts and raises my curiosity about what will happen next. By the time she states her thesis in line 29, I am already on her side.

Ask: How does the introduction support the thesis? (It shows a single person taking action to make a difference.) Why does the author say that she felt "defeated and powerless" in line 21? (She wanted to suggest that her essay would tell readers how she changed her mind.)

Have students work with partners to evaluate the interest of their introduction and effectiveness of their theses.

II. Body

Lead a discussion about how the body paragraphs of the Mentor Text reflect the characteristics of a persuasive essay.

- Logical organization (lines 22–25)
- Relevant evidence (lines 13–18, 31–34)
- Consideration of alternatives (lines 26–28, 42–43)

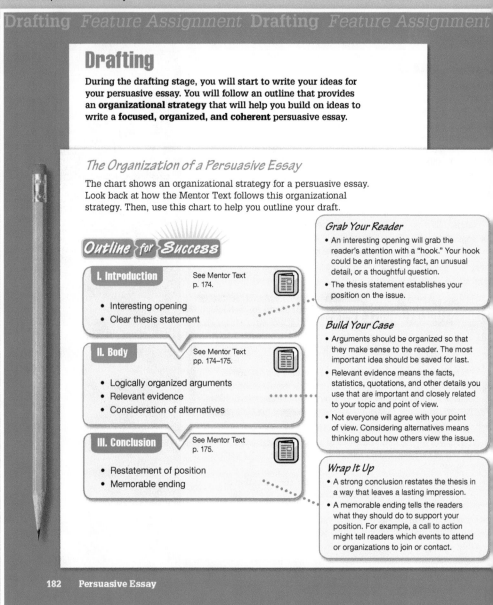

Drafting

During the drafting stage, you will start to write your ideas for your persuasive essay. You will follow an outline that provides an **organizational strategy** that will help you build on ideas to write a **focused, organized, and coherent** persuasive essay.

The Organization of a Persuasive Essay

The chart shows an organizational strategy for a persuasive essay. Look back at how the Mentor Text follows this organizational strategy. Then, use this chart to help you outline your draft.

Outline for Success

I. Introduction — See Mentor Text p. 174.
- Interesting opening
- Clear thesis statement

II. Body — See Mentor Text pp. 174–175.
- Logically organized arguments
- Relevant evidence
- Consideration of alternatives

III. Conclusion — See Mentor Text p. 175.
- Restatement of position
- Memorable ending

Grab Your Reader
- An interesting opening will grab the reader's attention with a "hook." Your hook could be an interesting fact, an unusual detail, or a thoughtful question.
- The thesis statement establishes your position on the issue.

Build Your Case
- Arguments should be organized so that they make sense to the reader. The most important idea should be saved for last.
- Relevant evidence means the facts, statistics, quotations, and other details you use that are important and closely related to your topic and point of view.
- Not everyone will agree with your point of view. Considering alternatives means thinking about how others view the issue.

Wrap It Up
- A strong conclusion restates the thesis in a way that leaves a lasting impression.
- A memorable ending tells the readers what they should do to support your position. For example, a call to action might tell readers which events to attend or organizations to join or contact.

182   Persuasive Essay

III. Conclusion

Have small groups discuss how the Mentor Text conclusion wraps up the essay arguments and restates the thesis (lines 45–51).

Start Your Draft

Have small groups read aloud and discuss the boxed instructions for drafting. Direct students to work individually on their first draft.

Coach's Corner

If you are modeling the writing process for students with your own topic or a student volunteer's, you may wish to use these prompts to guide your drafting and discussion:

- **To capture readers' attention,** my introduction will list some surprising facts about my topic.

- **I will organize my body paragraphs** by building up to the most important and convincing support for each argument.

Discuss the choices you make and solicit feedback from students.

3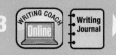

Students begin writing their persuasive essay online or in their notebooks.

4

Students submit paragraphs or complete drafts to the Interactive Writing Coach™ for scoring and feedback, or share their work with their teacher.

5

Students receive customized feedback from the Interactive Writing Coach™ or feedback from their teacher. Students may continue to work on their drafts.

Feature Assignment **Drafting** *Feature Assignment* **Drafting**

Start Your Draft

Use the checklist below to help complete your draft. Use the graphic organizer that shows your thesis, persuasive arguments, and supporting evidence, and the Outline for Success as guides.

While drafting, aim at writing your ideas, not on making your writing perfect. Remember, you will have the chance to improve your draft when you revise and edit.

√ First, draft your **opening** sentences. These first few sentences should interest your audience and make them want to keep reading.

√ Continue your **introduction** by summarizing your most important arguments. Establish your position in your thesis statement.

√ Shape the **body** of your persuasive essay.

√ Write one paragraph for each argument. Organize your **arguments** logically. Start with the second-strongest argument and end with the strongest argument.

√ Use detailed and relevant **evidence** and sound reasoning to support each argument.

√ Address counter-arguments. Use evidence to explain why readers should agree with your point of view instead of the **alternative views**.

√ Use **transition** words, such as *first, next,* and *finally* to connect ideas and help readers follow your arguments.

√ End with a strong **conclusion** that restates your position.

√ Call your readers to **action** by telling them what you want them to do or think about the issue.

WRITING COACH
Online
www.phwritingcoach.com

Interactive Model
Outline for Success View pop-ups of Mentor Text selections referenced in the Outline for Success.

Interactive Writing Coach™
Use the Interactive Writing Coach to receive the level of support you need:
• Write one paragraph at a time and submit each one for immediate, detailed feedback.
• Write your entire first draft and submit it for immediate, personalized feedback.

Drafting   183

Personalized Support

Interactive Writing Coach™

Below Level Students complete the drafting process in small steps by submitting each paragraph for scoring and feedback.

On Level Depending on the support they need, students submit their writing paragraph by paragraph or as a complete draft for scoring and feedback.

Above Level Students may write their drafts on their own but have the option of submitting them for scoring and/or feedback.

FEEDBACK
Teacher or Peer Feedback

To provide feedback to students on their first draft, ask or have student partners ask one another the following:

• Can you explain how you organized your ideas in this piece?

• Why did you include this information here?

• Why did you choose this introduction? Does it grab your reader and identify your thesis or controlling idea?

• What supporting details could you add here?

• Why did you choose this conclusion? How does it add to your piece?

• Can you show me a place where I can hear your unique voice?

• Can you show me a place where you used vivid language?

Working with ELLs   ELL Sheltered Instruction: Cognitive

Point out these content-based academic words from Start Your Draft: *transition* and *evidence*. **Help students internalize this new academic language by using and reusing the words in writing activities.**

Beginning Write and mime the word *transition* and sentences describing a sequence of events using the words *first* and *second*. Circle *first* and *second* and say, *These words show a transition, or passing of one event to another.* Help students write *transition* on a card then use and reuse it in written sentences about the words *first* and *second*.

Intermediate Have students write the two terms on cards. Work through examples of each, then have students write two example sentences reusing each word on the back of its card.

Advanced Have students write two sets of three related events, out of order, for partners to sequence. Have partners write to explain their answers, using and reusing the words *transition* and *evidence*.

Advanced High After students complete the Advanced activity, have them write definitions of *transition* and *evidence*.

The Digital • Print Path ▶

  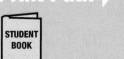

1  ▶

Using *Writing Coach Online™* or the student book, students study the first and second drafts of the student model to see how the writer used Revision RADaR to improve his or her writing.

2 ▶

Students use the Revision RADaR strategy to revise their own writing.

Revising: Making It Better

Point out the page title to students and explain that revising means making improvements to a writing draft. Then, read aloud the opening paragraph to introduce the Revision RADaR strategies. You may wish to have students review Chapter 3 for more information on Revision RADaR.

Kelly Gallagher, M. Ed.

KEEP REVISION ON YOUR RADaR

 After students have read the first draft, have them turn to page 182 and review the Outline for Success. Work with students to understand that the questions the author asked about her draft are based on the characteristics of a persuasive essay. For example, call out the first question and note how it addresses the requirements for a good introduction listed in the Introduction section of the Outline for Success.

Then, have students work in small groups to develop other questions about the draft based on the genre characteristics.

 2ND DRAFT Guide students to understand how the author used the RADaR strategies to revise her first draft.

Think Aloud I **noticed** that the opening of the first draft introduction was not very interesting. The statements seem unrelated and general, so they do not motivate me to keep reading. In the second draft, I see an *R* next to these sentences. This means the author has replaced this text. The new text is a personal story that contrasts how the writer's mother puts on her uniform and gets ready for work with how most kids waste time choosing the "right" clothes. That is a much more interesting introduction to the essay.

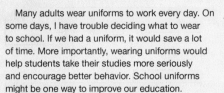

Revising: Making It Better

Now that you have finished your first draft, you are ready to revise. Think about **the "big picture" of audience, purpose, and genre.** You can use the Revision RADaR strategy as a guide for making changes to improve your draft. Revision RADaR provides four major ways to improve your writing: (R) replace, (A) add, (D) delete, and (R) reorder.

Kelly Gallagher, M. Ed.

KEEP REVISION ON YOUR RADaR

Read part of the first draft of the Student Model "Raise Your Hand for School Uniforms." Then look at questions the writer asked herself as she thought about how well her draft **addressed issues of audience, purpose, and genre**.

Raise Your Hand for School Uniforms

1ST DRAFT

Many adults wear uniforms to work every day. On some days, I have trouble deciding what to wear to school. If we had a uniform, it would save a lot of time. More importantly, wearing uniforms would help students take their studies more seriously and encourage better behavior. School uniforms might be one way to improve our education.

First, wearing uniforms could help students take school more seriously. Dressing differently often makes people act differently. When I wear a skirt and a blouse, I feel more grown-up than when I wear jeans and a sweatshirt. By wearing "school clothes" instead of "play clothes," kids will come to school ready to learn.

*Does the **introduction** get my audience's attention?*

*Does my **thesis statement** establish a clear position?*

*Have I used **persuasive arguments**? Have I supported them with evidence?*

184   **Persuasive Essay**

Work with students to brainstorm for other ways of revising the introduction.

Have students work in small groups to discuss the other changes in the second draft.

Apply It! Review the bulleted instructions for using Revision RADaR. Remind students to question their drafts based on the persuasive essay characteristics listed on the Outline for Success on page 182. Tell students to use each RADaR strategy at least once.

Coach's Corner

If you are modeling the writing process for students with your own draft or a student volunteer's, use these prompts to focus on the Revision RADaR *Reorder* strategy and guide discussion.

- **I reordered these reasons to** provide the strongest support for my position.

- **I reordered these details to** make the ideas flow more logically.

Discuss the choices you make and solicit feedback from students.

3
Students submit paragraphs or revised drafts to the Interactive Writing Coach™ for scoring and feedback, or share their work with their teacher.

4
Students receive customized feedback from the Interactive Writing Coach™ or feedback from their teacher. Students may continue to revise their drafts.

Feature Assignment **Revising** *Feature Assignment* **Revising**

Now look at how the writer applied Revision RADaR to write an improved second draft.

Raise Your Hand for School Uniforms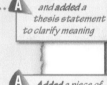

Every morning, my mother puts on her uniform of carefully ironed navy blue pants and a light blue shirt. Then she is ready to go to work as a city bus driver. Meanwhile, in homes all over town, kids are wondering what to wear to school. If we had a uniform, it would save a lot of time. More importantly, wearing uniforms would help students take their studies more seriously and encourage better behavior. The school district should require all students to wear a school uniform.

First, wearing uniforms could help students take school more seriously. Dressing differently often makes people act differently. When I wear a skirt and a blouse, I feel more grown-up than when I wear jeans and a sweatshirt. By wearing "school clothes" instead of "play clothes," kids will come to school ready to learn. When a school district in Washington State began requiring school uniforms, fewer students skipped school or were late to class.

R *Replaced opening sentences with a personal story to add interest*

D *Deleted an unclear sentence*
A *and added a thesis statement to clarify meaning*

A *Added a piece of evidence to support my argument*

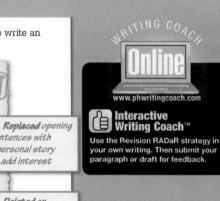
Online
www.phwritingcoach.com
Interactive Writing Coach™
Use the Revision RADaR strategy in your own writing. Then submit your paragraph or draft for feedback.

 Apply It! Use your Revision RADaR to revise your draft.

- First, consider how well you have **addressed the needs of your audience, explained your purpose** for writing, and included the characteristics of the persuasive writing **genre**.
- Then apply your Revision RADaR to make needed changes. Remember—you can use the steps in Revision RADaR in any order.

Revising 185

Below Level Students revise their drafts using the Revision RADaR strategy and submit their writing for scoring and feedback.

On Level Students revise their drafts using the Revision RADaR strategy and submit their writing for scoring and feedback.

Above Level Students may use the Revision RADaR strategy or revise their drafts on their own. They have the option of submitting their revised drafts for scoring and/or feedback.

 Teacher or Peer Feedback

To provide feedback to students as they revise their first draft, ask or have student partners ask one another the following:

- Can you show me where you revised your text?
- What could you add to your introduction to grab the interest of your readers?
- How could you reorder these ideas so that their order is more logical?
- Have you included all the characteristics of this form of writing?
- Is there any unnecessary text that you could delete?
- Have you achieved your purpose with this piece of writing?
- Have you addressed the questions and concerns of your audience?

Working with ELLs **ELL** Sheltered Instruction: Cognitive

Review the revised Student Model, having students demonstrate English comprehension and expand their reading skills by employing analytical skills. Focus on analyzing and evaluating *generalizations*. Define *generalization*. Then:

Beginning Distribute a generalization about school rules, such as *School rules are good,* with supporting examples. Read the sentences, using mime. Ask questions to prompt analysis, like, *Are school rules good?* Point to a sentence that explains.

Intermediate Have students complete the Beginning activity, then analyze using sentence starters, such as, *Schools have rules because …*

Advanced Have pairs read the second draft on page 185, taking notes on generalizations and supporting details. Monitor analytical skills by asking, *What generalization does the author make? What do I know that supports the generalization?*

Advanced High Have students complete the Advanced activity and list techniques for evaluating generalizations. Provide this example: *Is the general statement supported by evidence in the text?*

The Digital · Print Path ▶

1 ▶ Using *Writing Coach Online*™ or the student book, students study and discuss the revision chart.

2 ▶ In a video by program author Kelly Gallagher, students learn more strategies for effective writing.

Revising: Making It Better

Look at the Big Picture

Introduce the revision chart to students. Explain that the Section column identifies the three main parts of a persuasive essay. The Evaluate column identifies the characteristics found in each section and explains how to assess them. The Revise column presents specific strategies for revising each characteristic.

Then, have students draw lines between and label the three sections of their drafts. Direct students to work individually to evaluate and revise their draft, using the chart to guide their work.

Focus on Craft: Enhance Style

Have students read the introductory text. Guide students to understand how specific, concrete language makes writing vivid and appealing.

Say: I notice that the first sentence of the Student Model passage uses concrete nouns such as *skirt, blouse, jeans,* and *sweatshirt* to paint a very specific picture of two ways of dressing.

Ask: What other details in the Student Model make it vivid and persuasive? (school clothes, play clothes)

Have students work with partners to rewrite sentences from the Student Model using more specific, vivid language.

Try It! Have students discuss the questions and record responses in their journals. Follow up with students to check that their responses reflect an understanding of the effectiveness of clear, specific word choices in creating persuasive text.

Look at the Big Picture

Use the chart and your analytical skills to evaluate how well each section of your persuasive essay addresses **purpose, audience, and genre**. When necessary, use the suggestions in the chart to revise your piece.

Section	Evaluate	Revise
Introduction	• Check the **introduction.** Will it draw your readers in and keep them reading?	• To make your introduction more interesting, add a question, personal story, or strong statement.
	• Does the thesis clearly establish your **position** on the issue?	• Replace weak language with more forceful language to express your opinion strongly.
Body	• Check that the organization of your persuasive **arguments** makes the strongest case for your view.	• Reorder your paragraphs to support strong reasoning. Put your second-strongest argument first, the weaker arguments in the middle, and the strongest argument last.
	• Make sure that your supporting evidence is detailed and **relevant.** Draw a line from each detail to the argument it supports.	• Delete evidence that is not relevant. Delete any detail that is not in the same paragraph as the argument it supports.
	• Review **alternatives** and counter-arguments. Be certain that you have answered each one.	• Add information to prove that alternative views are less strong than your view.
Conclusion	• Check your **thesis** restatement.	• Restate the important points of your thesis using slightly different words, and make sure the meaning is clear.
	• Make sure that your essay has a memorable **ending.**	• Add a call to action, question, or prediction to strengthen your conclusion.

186 **Persuasive Essay**

Fine-Tune Your Draft

Apply It! Ask volunteers to read aloud the instructions for fine-tuning their drafts. Then, have students work in pairs to enhance the style, clarify the meaning, and improve the transitions in their draft.

Peer Feedback Have students identify Mentor Text examples of the characteristics that were marked for improvement. Use the Mentor Text references on page T182 to guide students to appropriate examples.

Teacher Tip

Have students practice identifying general words and replacing them with more specific ones using dictionaries and thesauruses. Have them read aloud the revised sentences to a partner to receive feedback.

T186

3 ▶

Using *Writing Coach Online*™ or the student book, students refer back to the Mentor Text or Student Model for examples of writer's craft.

4  ▶

Students record answers to questions about writer's craft in their online journals or notebooks.

5 ▶

Students submit revised drafts to the *Interactive Writing Coach*™ for scoring and feedback, or share their work with their teacher.

6  ▶

Students receive customized feedback from the *Interactive Writing Coach*™ or feedback from their teacher.

Feature Assignment **Revising** *Feature Assignment* **Revising**

Focus on Craft: Enhance Style

Style is the way a writer chooses to use language. In order to convince readers, your language should be interesting and persuasive. Vivid language helps persuade your audience to agree with you. By using language more effectively, you will draw the reader to your purpose. Think about style as you read the following sentences from the Student Model.

 STUDENT MODEL from **Raise Your Hand for School Uniforms** page 176; lines 13–17

> When I wear a skirt and a blouse, I feel more grown-up than when I wear jeans and a sweatshirt. By wearing "school clothes" instead of "play clothes," kids will come to school ready to learn.

Try It! Now, ask yourself these questions. Record your answers in your journal.

- What is the main idea of this passage? Does the writer have a casual or formal attitude about the subject? Explain.
- Would the last sentence be more or less convincing if it read *By wearing uniforms instead of casual clothes, kids will come to school ready to learn*? Explain.

Fine-Tune Your Draft

Apply It! First, **rethink how well questions of purpose, audience, and genre have been addressed** in your essay. Then use the ideas for revision to prepare your final draft.

- **Enhance Style** Add language that is more vivid and appealing.
- **Clarify Meaning** Look for confusing sentences and add explanations as needed.
- **Improve Transitions** To connect ideas, add, delete, combine, or rearrange sentences by using words like *next* and *in contrast*.

Peer Feedback Read your final draft to a group of peers. Ask if you have **considered and answered alternative viewpoints**. Think about your group's responses and revise your draft as needed.

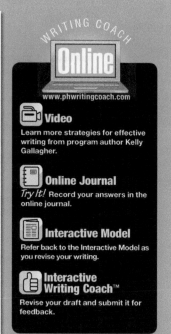

WRITING COACH Online

www.phwritingcoach.com

Video
Learn more strategies for effective writing from program author Kelly Gallagher.

Online Journal
Try It! Record your answers in the online journal.

Interactive Model
Refer back to the Interactive Model as you revise your writing.

Interactive Writing Coach™
Revise your draft and submit it for feedback.

Revising **187**

Personalized Support

 Interactive Writing Coach™

Below Level Students complete the revising process by submitting their writing for scoring and feedback.

On Level Students complete the revising process by submitting their writing for scoring and feedback.

Above Level Students finish revising their drafts. They have the option of submitting their revised drafts for scoring and/or feedback.

Teacher or Peer Feedback

To provide feedback to students as they continue to revise their first draft, ask or have student partners ask one another the following:

- What are you trying to say here? What part of the text could you replace to make your meaning clearer?
- Is there a more precise word you could use here?
- How does the rhythm of these sentences sound to you? Could you make the length and structure of these sentences more varied?
- How could you include transitional words and phrases here to help your reader understand these ideas?
- Are there details you could add here to make this part come alive?

Working with ELLs **ELL** Sheltered Instruction: Social/Affective

As students read, help them use support from peers and you to enhance and confirm understanding and to develop their grasp of language structures needed to comprehend increasingly challenging language. Review the terms *complex sentence, dependent clause, and independent clause.* **List words that often begin dependent clauses, like** *when.* **Then:**

Beginning Write, *After she puts on her coat, she goes outside.* Choral read, using gestures to support comprehension. Help students identify *after* as the word that begins the dependent clause. Repeat with the first sentence in the Student Model excerpt.

Intermediate Discuss complex sentences, helping students read the examples in the Beginning activity. Ask partners to paraphrase each example.

Advanced Have partners use the KIM Strategy, writing key words, information, and memory clues for *complex sentence, dependent clause,* and *independent clause.* Have them read the Student Model excerpt, restating the complex sentence.

Advanced High Have partners complete the Advanced activity and discuss the effectiveness of the writer's complex sentence.

The Digital • Print Path ▶

1 ▶

In a video by program author Jeff Anderson, students learn effective editing techniques.

2 [Writing Journal] ▶

Students record answers to questions about writer's craft in their online journals or notebooks.

Editing: Making It Correct

Explain that students will edit their drafts for proper grammar, mechanics, and spelling, including vague, or unclear, pronoun references.

WRITE GUY *Jeff Anderson, M.Ed.*

WHAT DO YOU NOTICE?

Introduce students to vague pronoun references by reading aloud the Student Model excerpt and discussing responses to the "ask yourself" question that follows. Then, guide students to identify and correct vague pronoun references.

 Think Aloud

I notice that the Student Model contains an example of a pronoun that refers clearly to an antecedent. The first sentence identifies the writer's mother. In the second sentence, *she* clearly refers to the mother. The third sentence identifies kids, but the fourth sentence uses *we*. The pronoun *we* refers to the writer and someone else, not to *kids*, so this pronoun reference is vague.

Work with students to correct unclear pronoun references in sentences you provide.

Have students work with a partner to find pronoun referents in a familiar text. Ask them to pair each pronoun with its antecedent.

Editing *Feature Assignment* Editing *Feature Assignmen*

Editing: Making It Correct

To edit your work, read your draft carefully to correct errors in spelling and grammar.

Review pronouns you have used in your writing. Each **pronoun** must have a clear **antecedent**, or a clearly stated person, place, or thing that the pronoun later replaces. Look at these sentences:

Karen and Walter missed the bus. They were late for school.
(The pronoun *they* clearly refers to Karen and Walter.)

I am going away for the weekend with my family. It should be fun.
(The antecedent for *it* is unclear. The second sentence could be corrected this way: *The trip should be fun.*)

WRITE GUY *Jeff Anderson, M. Ed.*

WHAT DO YOU NOTICE?

Zoom in on Conventions Focus on the use of pronouns as you read these lines from the Student Model.

> [📰] **STUDENT MODEL** from **Raise Your Hand for School Uniforms** page 176; lines 1–6
>
> Every morning, my mother puts on her uniform of carefully ironed navy blue pants and a light blue shirt. Then she is ready to go to work as a city bus driver. Meanwhile, in homes all over town, kids are wondering what to wear to school. If we had a uniform, it would save a lot of time.

Now, ask yourself: *Which pair of sentences contains a vague pronoun reference?*

Perhaps you chose the second pair of sentences, which contains a vague pronoun reference. The antecedent of the pronoun *we* is unclear. To correct this vague pronoun reference, the sentences would read: *Meanwhile, in homes all over town, kids like my friends and me are wondering what to wear to school. If we had a uniform, it would save a lot of time.*

The first pair of sentences has correct pronoun-antecedent usage. Since only one woman, *my mother*, is mentioned in the first sentence, the pronoun *she* clearly takes the place of that antecedent. There is no way that the pronoun could refer to any other person.

188 Persuasive Essay

To learn more about pronoun-antecedent agreement see Chapter 23 of your Grammar Handbook.

Grammar Mini-Lesson: Vague Pronoun References

Discuss the bulleted text and the Student Model excerpt on page 189 with students. Guide them to understand that, in the second sentence, the writer correctly uses the pronoun *they* to refer to *kids* in the previous sentence.

Try It! Have students find and correct vague pronoun references.

1. Clear reference. *She* refers to Kari.

2. At the games, Kari loves to watch the soccer teams play.

Apply It! Remind students to look closely for vague pronoun references as they edit their drafts.

Use the Rubric Explain to students that the rubric lists six important elements of a persuasive essay. Tell students that they will rate how well their draft addresses each element on a scale of 1 to 6, with 6 being the best score. Then, have students use the rubric to evaluate their drafts and revise as necessary.

Writer's Block

IF students have difficulty identifying vague pronoun references . . .

THEN have partners read their writing aloud to each other, identify pronouns, and locate the antecedent of each.

3  ▶ Using Writing Coach Online™ or the student book, students refer back to the Mentor Text or Student Model as they edit their writing.

4  ▶ Using Writing Coach Online™ or the student book, students evaluate their writing using the rubrics.

5  ▶ Students submit edited drafts to the Interactive Writing Coach™ for scoring and feedback, or share their work with their teacher.

6 ▶ Students receive personalized feedback from the Interactive Writing Coach™ or feedback from their teacher.

Feature Assignment **Editing** *Feature Assignment* **Editing**

Grammar Mini-Lesson: Vague Pronoun References

To learn more, see page 276.

Look at these other examples of vague pronoun references and their corrections:

Vague: *When we got to the stadium, they showed us to our seats.*
Correct: *When we got to the stadium, the ushers showed us to our seats.*
Vague: *My favorite player made a goal. It was great!*
Correct: *My favorite player made a goal. His kick was great!*

Notice how the pronoun *they* in these lines from the Student Model has a clear antecedent.

STUDENT MODEL from **Raise Your Hand for School Uniforms** page 177; lines 34–36

However, many kids like thinking about what's on the outside. They believe that choosing their outfits is a form of creativity.

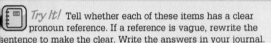

Try It! Tell whether each of these items has a clear pronoun reference. If a reference is vague, rewrite the sentence to make the clear. Write the answers in your journal.

1. Kari is a huge soccer fan, so she never misses a game.
2. At the games, Kari loves to watch them play.

Apply It! Edit your draft for **grammar, mechanics, and spelling.** Be sure to check each pronoun reference to make sure that its antecedent is clear. Revise sentences, if necessary.

Use the rubric to evaluate your piece. If necessary, rethink, rewrite, or revise.

Rubric for Persuasive Essay	Rating Scale					
	Not very					Very
Ideas: How clearly are the issue and your position stated?	1	2	3	4	5	6
Organization: How organized are your arguments and supporting evidence?	1	2	3	4	5	6
Voice: How authoritative is your voice?	1	2	3	4	5	6
Word Choice: How persuasive is your word choice?	1	2	3	4	5	6
Sentence Fluency: How smooth are your transitions?	1	2	3	4	5	6
Conventions: How clear are your pronoun references?	1	2	3	4	5	6

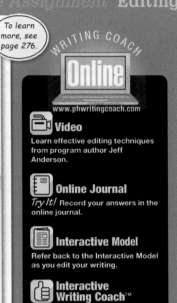

WRITING COACH

Online

www.phwritingcoach.com

Video
Learn effective editing techniques from program author Jeff Anderson.

Online Journal
Try It! Record your answers in the online journal.

Interactive Model
Refer back to the Interactive Model as you edit your writing.

Interactive Writing Coach™
Edit your draft. Check it against the rubric and then submit it for feedback.

Editing **189**

Personalized Support

 Interactive Writing Coach™

Below Level Students complete the editing process by submitting their writing for scoring and feedback.

On Level Students complete the editing process by submitting their writing for scoring and feedback.

Above Level Students finish editing their drafts. They have the option of submitting their final drafts for scoring and/or feedback.

 Teacher or Peer Feedback

To provide feedback to students as they edit their draft, ask or have student partners ask one another the following:

- Have you looked for mistakes that you tend to make?
- Have you read your piece aloud to yourself or to a partner? What kind of errors did you find?
- Can you show me something you changed through editing?
- What resources have you used to look for possible spelling errors?
- Read this sentence aloud. Does the grammar sound correct to you?
- Read this sentence aloud. Does the punctuation accurately convey your meaning?

Working with ELLs   ELL Sheltered Instruction: Metacognitive

As students revise for vague pronoun references, they should also monitor and edit writing for pronoun-antecedent agreement, employing self-corrective techniques as they review their writing. Review the meaning of *pronoun-antecedent agreement*. Then:

Beginning Help students complete sentence frames, using pronouns from a word bank you provide. For example: *The girl reads (her) book.* Help students edit their sentences and employ the self-corrective technique of highlighting pronouns and circling antecedents to check agreement.

Intermediate Have pairs complete the Beginning activity and apply the self-corrective technique as they review their sentences.

Advanced Have pairs find sentences with pronouns in their drafts and check for correct agreement by employing the self-corrective technique from the Beginning activity.

Advanced High Have partners complete the Advanced activity and present other self-corrective techniques students can use while editing for pronoun agreement.

The Digital · Print Path ▶

1  Using *Writing Coach Online*™ or the student book, students complete the writing process by deciding the best way to publish their writing for their intended audience.

2 Students record their answers and ideas to Extend Your Research in their online journals or notebooks.

Publishing

Wrap Up Your Presentation

Remind students who hand-wrote their work to use proper margins. For students who wrote their work on a computer, display some easy-to-read computer fonts. Make sure students know how to find them on a computer.

Publish Your Piece

Explain to students that the final step in the writing process is to decide which form of publication will present their work most effectively. Then, introduce students to the chart. Explain that the chart shows how specific audiences can be reached using different kinds of media.

Have students whose persuasive essays address similar audiences work in small groups to discuss appropriate ways to publish their work. Encourage students to think of other publishing opportunities not listed on the chart, such as sending the essay to an elected official.

Extend Your Research

Extension Tell students that their thinking about their topic does not have to end with its final publication. Then, guide students through the bulleted instructions for extending their research.

Big Question Have students respond to the question in their journal.

MAKE YOUR WRITING COUNT

Introduce the debate activity by discussing the opening paragraphs with students. Make sure students understand that the project may be produced electronically or by hand. Then, guide students through each step in the action plan.

Publishing *Feature Assignment* Publishing *Feature Assign*

Publishing

Give your persuasive essay a chance to influence someone—publish it! First, get your essay ready for presentation. Then, choose a way to **publish it for the appropriate audience**.

Wrap Up Your Presentation

Is your persuasive essay handwritten or written on a computer? If your essay is handwritten, you may need to make a new, clean copy. If so, be sure to **write legibly**.

Publish Your Piece

Use the chart to identify a way to publish your persuasive essay for the appropriate audience.

If your audience is...	...then publish it by...
Students or adults at school	• Submitting it to your school newspaper • Posting it on your school's Web site and asking for responses
People in your city	• Submitting it to your local newspaper • Recording it and submitting it to a local radio station

 Extend Your Research

Think more about the topic on which you wrote your persuasive essay. What else would you like to know about this topic?

- Brainstorm for several questions you would like to research and then consult, or discuss, with others. Then decide which question is your major research question.
- Formulate, or develop, a plan about how you will answer these questions. Decide where you will find more information—on the Internet, at the library, or through other sources.
- Finally, learn more about your topic by following through with your research plan.

The Big Question: Why Write? What is your point of view? How did you determine if you convinced others?

190   **Persuasive Essay**

Resources You may wish to have students use these graphic organizers: Meeting Agenda, Meeting Notes, and Main Idea and Details Web. Distribute printed copies or have students log on to Writing Coach Online.

Use the 21st Century Skills Rubric to evaluate each group's process and final product on a scale of 1 to 3, indicating weak, moderate, or strong use of the skill. ▶

Listening and Speaking Monitor students as they use feedback to refine their presentations.

21st Century Learning

Skills Rubric	Rating
Communicate Clearly: Listen and articulate ideas effectively using oral communication.	1 2 3
Work Creatively With Others: Develop, implement, and communicate new ideas to others.	1 2 3
Collaborate With Others: Work responsibly and respectfully with teams.	1 2 3
Apply Technology Effectively: Use technology as a tool to organize and communicate information.	1 2 3

3 STUDENT BOOK ▶
Students use a variety of graphic organizers, either online or in print, to help them work together to create a multimedia group project.

4 STUDENT BOOK ▶
Through *Writing Coach Online*™, students link to resources on 21st Century Learning for help in creating a multimedia group project.

Make Your Writing Count Persuasive Essay **Make Your Writing Count**

21st Century Learning

MAKE YOUR WRITING COUNT

Debate an Issue

When you write persuasively, you try to convince your audience to agree with you or to act upon an issue. When you speak persuasively, you have the same goal. Take a side on an issue and **debate** the topic.

With a group, choose the topic of one persuasive essay to debate. Your group will present both sides of an issue to clearly communicate opposing points of view. Hold the debate for your class or video-record it to share with others.

Here's your action plan.

1. With your group, choose one persuasive essay to use in the debate. Pick an essay whose topic will interest most students.

2. Divide into two smaller groups and assign each small group a side of the argument.
   - Meet with your smaller group to work on your argument and supporting details.
   - Think about the other side's argument, and find details that weaken it.
   - Consider the tone of a debate—the style and content of your language should be formal, and your attitude will influence your listener's understanding.

3. Figure out how much time you will have to debate. Be sure you can make your important points within the timeframe.

4. Hold your debate, and have the class vote for the winner.

5. If you are video-recording the debate, watch it afterward.

Listening and Speaking When working with your small group, actively listen to group members' ideas for making a strong argument. During the debate, keep your group's feedback in mind. Speak slowly and clearly. Listen actively and jot notes while your opponent is speaking. This will help you to adjust your presentation and plan your response.

WRITING COACH

Online
www.phwritingcoach.com

Online Journal
Extend Your Research Record your answers and ideas in the online journal.

Resource
Link to resources on 21st Century Learning for help in creating a group project.

Make Your Writing Count 191

Personalized Support

FEEDBACK Teacher or Peer Feedback

To provide feedback to students on their published writing, ask or have student partners ask one another the following:

- How did you go about writing this piece? What was your process?
- What did you learn from the writing model that you used in this piece?
- What surprised you the most as you wrote this piece?
- Did you try anything new as you worked on this piece?
- What did you learn from this piece of writing that you would like to remember and reuse?
- What do you think you do best as a writer right now?

Differentiated Instruction

RTI Strategy for Below-Level Students

Students may find it helpful to work in pairs, so that one partner can give feedback for practice readings or presentations and then record the final reading or presentation. If the students are filming their debates, remind the recorder/filmer to monitor equipment to be sure volume, light, and other factors are appropriate to the set.

Enrichment for Gifted/Talented Students

In debates, challenge students who are interested in dramatic performance to listen actively and think "on their feet" in order to rebut opponents' arguments. While preparing for debates, have students list and think of answers for probable arguments their opponents will make. Their rebuttals should use appropriate tone and gesture to point out some way that the opposing argument is illogical, misleading, or unproved.

The Digital • Print Path ▸

1  ▸ Students use **Writing Coach Online™** or their student books to analyze and discuss the Writing for Media topic.

2  ▸ Students learn about the characteristics of a maga cover by answering questions about the model. St record their answers to the *Try It!* questions in their journals or notebooks.

 **Writing for Media: Magazine Covers**

Magazine Covers

Discuss the opening paragraph with students. As a class, analyze the cover of a teen or youth magazine and discuss the images and headlines that grab the students' attention.

Try It! Guide students to understand how the elements in the example cover try to persuade viewers to buy the magazine.

Say: The first *Try It!* question asks about the magazine title. **I think** that *Discovery Girls* suggests a magazine aimed at active girls who are curious about the world. The second question talks about *layout*, or arrangement of elements. The image and words are laid out on the page in a bold and appealing way.

Ask: What feeling does the layout of the cover create? (The image emphasizes style and confidence. The headlines focus on events in which girls shine as winners.)

Have students discuss the remaining questions in small groups and record individual responses in their journals.

Extension At this point you may wish to have students bring in other examples of magazine covers. If so, lead a media discussion about the examples, using the *Try It!* questions as a guide.

Create a Magazine Cover

Tell students that they will create a magazine cover using the five-step writing process. Then, preview the writing process instructions on page 193. Have students select a printed graphic organizer or log on to Writing Coach Online.

> **Resources** You may wish to have students use the Cluster Diagram graphic organizer. Distribute printed copies or have students log on to Writing Coach Online.

For each step in the writing process, have partners read aloud and discuss the list of tasks. Then, have them work individually. Once both partners have completed the tasks,

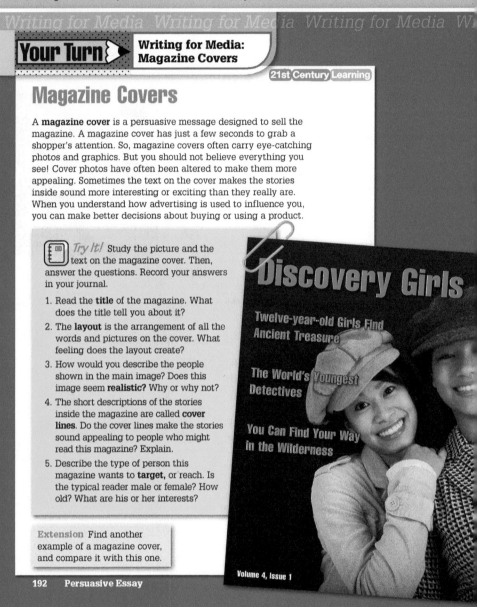

have them evaluate each other's work before moving to the next step.

Use the 21st Century Skills Rubric to evaluate each student's process and final product on a scale of 1 to 3, indicating weak, moderate, or strong use of the skill. ▸

Partner Talk

Remind students to listen actively to their partners and ask for clarification of wording and images if they are not clearly explained.

21st Century Learning

Skills Rubric	Rating
Think Creatively: Elaborate and refine your own ideas to improve creative effort.	1 2 3
Use Systems Thinking: Analyze how parts of a whole interact with each other to produce overall effects.	1 2 3
Create Media Products: Understand and effectively use expressions and interpretations.	1 2 3
Analyze Media: Understand how media messages are constructed, and for what purpose.	1 2 3

3 ▶

Students follow the five-step writing process to create their own magazine cover. Students may select online or printed graphic organizers to help them plan and develop their writing.

Create a Magazine Cover

Follow these steps to create your own magazine cover.

Prewriting

- Think about what type of magazine your cover will advertise. For example, you could choose news, sports, or fashion.
- Establish a position on your magazine's topic. For example, you could create the cover for a cooking magazine. Then think of an appropriate title for the magazine.
- Identify your target audience. Decide if your readers are male or female or both, and how old they are, along with other traits.
- Decide what types of stories and images are appropriate for your target audience.
- Brainstorm a list of articles that will be in your magazine and a list of images you might use on the cover.

Drafting

- Write the cover lines for your stories. Brainstorm several cover lines for each story. Then, consider the alternatives you have developed and choose the most interesting one.
- Choose one or more images that will grab readers' attention.
- Lay out your cover. Decide where the title, the image(s), and the cover lines will go, and how large each will be. Choose fonts or type styles for the title and cover lines. Try different layouts to achieve an eye-catching look.

Revising and Editing

- Review your draft. Make sure that your cover lines and pictures are relevant to your target audience. Check that the most important and appealing elements are the largest.
- Check that spelling, grammar, and mechanics are correct.

Publishing

- Make a multimedia version of your magazine cover. Include both your text **and graphics** to enhance the main ideas.
- Present your multimedia cover to the class.

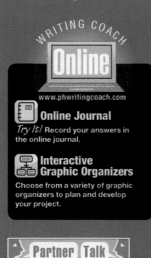

WRITING COACH

Online

www.phwritingcoach.com

Online Journal
Try It! Record your answers in the online journal.

Interactive Graphic Organizers
Choose from a variety of graphic organizers to plan and develop your project.

Partner Talk

Before you start drafting, describe your magazine cover to a partner. Use specific details to describe and explain your ideas. Increase the specificty of your details based on the type of information you are discussing. Ask for feedback about your plan. For example, will your cover lines appeal to your target audience?

Personalized Support

FEEDBACK Teacher or Peer Feedback

To provide feedback to students as they write for media, ask or have student partners ask one another the following:

- What are the main characteristics of this form of writing?
- Have you included most or all of these characteristics in your piece of writing?
- What is your purpose for writing this piece?
- Who is your audience?
- How did you organize your ideas in this piece of writing?
- How did you go about revising the piece? Editing it?
- How do you plan on publishing your piece?
- What other publishing options also might work?

Working with ELLs   **ELL** Sheltered Instruction: Cognitive

Have students respond orally to information presented in a wide variety of print, electronic, audio, and visual media to build and reinforce language attainment. Provide a bank of magazine terms (including words from page 192), such as *article, image, title, cover lines*, and *layout*. Display a magazine cover and discuss its features.

Beginning Review the vocabulary, having students use the words to respond orally to questions like, *What word names the picture on the cover? What does the image show?*

Intermediate As you discuss magazines, have students take notes in a cluster

diagram. Have them respond orally to the cover. Provide sentence frames: for example, *The cover shows _____ and _____.*

Advanced Distribute magazines to groups. Have them compare two magazine covers in a **Venn Diagram**. To build language attainment, have students discuss their diagrams using word bank words.

Advanced High After students complete the Advanced activity, have them write a paragraph using their notes and word bank vocabulary. Have them read the paragraphs aloud and respond orally to questions.

T193

Before they write, students use the ABCDs of On-Demand Writing to analyze and plan how to respond to each prompt. They can use either their online journals or notebooks to take notes.

Writing for Assessment

Read aloud or have a student read aloud the introductory text. Then, tell students that they will learn and practice a technique for writing in response to a timed test prompt.

Try It! Read the Persuasive Prompt aloud and then have volunteers read aloud the Format and Academic Vocabulary boxes. Tell students that they will use the ABCD method to respond to the prompt.

The ABCDs On-Demand Writing

Have students identify the words associated with the ABCD method. (attack, brainstorm, choose, detect) Then, guide students through their use.

Think Aloud I'll **attack the prompt** by circling the words *convince* and *Support,* which remind me to use convincing evidence in support of my arguments. I can rewrite the prompt to state this clearly: "Write an essay that persuades an audience that your opinion is correct by using clear reasoning and supporting details."

Work with students to brainstorm for an appropriate graphic organizer for a persuasive essay, such as a Main Idea and Details Web.

Have students write their drafts individually and then review their drafts with a small group to detect errors.

More Prompts for Practice

Apply It! Have students apply the ABCD method to the two practice prompts.

Prompt 1 Have partners attack the prompt and brainstorm for possible answers. Then, have each pair swap their information with another group to evaluate whether the teams have developed a focused persuasive argument.

Writing for Assessment

Many standardized tests include writing prompts. Use the prompts on these pages to practice. Your responses should include the same characteristics as your persuasive essay. (See page 172.)

Try It! Read the prompt and the information on format and academic vocabulary. Then write an essay using the ABCDs of On-Demand Writing.

Format
The prompt asks you to write a *persuasive essay.* Be sure to include an introduction, body paragraphs with supporting evidence, and a conclusion.

Persuasive Prompt
Some students and teachers think that the school day is too long. Write a persuasive essay to convince your principal to shorten the school day. Support your opinion with evidence.

Academic Vocabulary
Remember that an *opinion* is a personal belief about something. *Evidence* helps prove something is true. Facts and examples are often used as evidence.

The ABCDs of On-Demand Writing

Use the following ABCDs to help you respond to the prompt.

Before you write your draft:

A ttack the prompt [1 MINUTE]

- Circle or highlight important verbs in the prompt. Draw a line from the verb to what it refers to.
- Rewrite the prompt in your own words.

B rainstorm possible answers [4 MINUTES]

- Create a graphic organizer to generate ideas.
- Use one for each part of the prompt if necessary.

C hoose the order of your response [1 MINUTE]

- Think about the best way to organize your ideas.
- Number your ideas in the order you will write about them. Cross out ideas you will not be using.

After you write your draft:

D etect errors before turning in the draft [1 MINUTE]

- Carefully reread your writing.
- Make sure that your response makes sense and is complete.
- Look for spelling, punctuation, and grammar errors.

194   **Persuasive Essay**

Prompt 2 Have students work individually to attack the prompt and brainstorm for possible answers. Then, have students work in small groups to evaluate their work before writing their drafts.

Spiral Review: Expository Read aloud the instructions and the prompt. Then, have students review the expository characteristics on page 146.

Prompt 3 Remind students to use the ABCD method to write their expository essay.

2  Students submit their writing paragraph by paragraph or as a complete draft to the Interactive Writing Coach™ for feedback, or share their writing with their teacher.

3  Students receive personalized feedback from the Interactive Writing Coach™ or feedback from their teacher.

ssment *Writing for Assessment* **Writing for Assessment**

More Prompts for Practice

Apply It! Respond to Prompts 1 and 2 by writing **persuasive** **essays** that influence your readers' opinions or actions. As you write, be sure to:

- Identify an appropriate audience
- Establish a **clear position or thesis**
- Use **sound reasoning** to make your arguments convincing
- Provide **consideration of alternative arguments**
- Include **detailed and relevant evidence** to support your view

Prompt 1 Think of a place you would like to visit or an activity you would like to take part in. Imagine that on a specific occasion, you would prefer not to go to this place or do this activity alone. Write a persuasive essay to convince a friend to go with you.

Prompt 2 Do your parents or guardians have any rules that you think are unfair? Choose one rule that you would like to change. In a persuasive essay, make the case to your parents or guardians that the rule is unfair and should be changed.

Spiral Review: Expository Respond to Prompt 3 by writing a compare-and-contrast **expository essay**. Make sure your essay reflects all the characteristics described on page 146, including an **effective introduction and concluding paragraphs; specific facts, details, and examples in an appropriately organized structure; and a variety of sentence structures and transitions to link paragraphs.** Your essay should also **guide and inform the reader's understanding of key ideas and evidence.**

Prompt 3 Think about the many different kinds of workers who make your school a great place to be: teachers, cafeteria workers, the principal, and so on. Write an expository essay that compares and contrasts the jobs of two kinds of school workers.

Interactive Writing Coach™

Plan your response to the prompt. If you are using the prompt for practice, write one paragraph at a time and then submit for immediate feedback. If you are using the prompt as a timed test, write your entire draft and then submit it for feedback.

Remember **ABCD**

Ⓐ ttack the prompt
Ⓑ rainstorm possible answers
Ⓒ hoose the order of your response
Ⓓ etect errors before turning in the draft

Personalized Support

Assessment/ Monitor Progress

For timed writing practice, assign students a prompt to be completed in a timed setting. Have students submit their writing to Interactive Writing Coach™ to get immediate feedback.

For a formal writing assessment, assign the Assessment writing prompt for this chapter in Writing Coach Online™. Then, have students submit their writing to Interactive Writing Coach™ to be assessed. Use the results to assess student progress and skill levels. Interactive Writing Coach™ will update student levels to ensure that students get the appropriate support.

Teacher Feedback

To create an assessment environment, have students use a prompt in a timed setting. Grade papers using the appropriate rubric and use the results to assess student progress and skill levels. In the next writing assignment, ensure that students get the appropriate level of support.

If you conference with students, use these questions to guide your discussion:

- What form of writing did the prompt call for? Does your response include most or all of the characteristics of that form?
- How did you organize your ideas?
- Did you make good use of your time as you planned and wrote your response?
- What did you learn that you can use when responding to a prompt during a timed test?

Differentiated Instruction

Strategy for Spanish Speakers

Students whose home language is Spanish may overuse subordinate clauses when trying to persuade or convince others, due to the Spanish subjunctive constructions (*I want that you believe me.* versus *I want you to believe me.*). Read through Prompt 1 on page 195. Elicit different arguments and have students construct complex sentences using the verbs *want, need,* and *tell.* For example, *I want you to come with me because it is fun.*

PRE-AP Enrichment for Above-Level Students

Students who extend their research may enjoy searching appropriate blogs and other Web sites where their chosen topic is discussed; at some sites, students can submit questions for expert answers. When they have found complete answers to their questions, challenge students to create a Web podcast or interactive blog of their own to share what they learned and link interested users to more information.

Interactive Writing Coach™ Interactive Graphic Organizers Interactive Models

Online Journal Resources Video

Use the Online Lesson Planner at www.phwritingcoach.com to customize your instructional plan for an integrated Language Arts curriculum.

DAY 1

CHAPTER OPENER/ GENRE INTRODUCTION

ONLINE

- What Do You Think?
- What's Ahead
- Connect to the Big Questions
- **Feature Assignment: Interpretative Response: Letter to an Author**
- Other Forms of Interpretative Response

DAY 2

MENTOR TEXT/ STUDENT MODEL

ONLINE

- **Mentor Text: Book Review**
- Learn From Experience
- **Student Model: Letter to an Author**
- Reader's Eye and Writer's Eye

DAY 3

> Prewriting

ONLINE

- Choose From the Topic Bank
- Choose Your Own Topic
- Narrow Your Topic
- Consider Your Audience and Purpose

DAY 6

> Revising

ONLINE

- Keep Revision on Your RADaR
- Look at the Big Picture
- Focus on Craft
- Fine-Tune Your Draft

DAY 7

For more grammar support, see Sections 25.4 and 25.8, pp. 575 and 601.

> Editing

ONLINE

- What Do You Notice?/ Grammar Mini-Lesson
  Rubric for Interpretative Response: Letter to an Author

> Publishing

- Publish Your Piece
- Extend Your Research

DAY 8

> 21st Century Learning

MAKE YOUR WRITING COUNT

ONLINE

- **Share Letters With the School Community**
- Here's Your Action Plan
- Listening and Speaking

Alternate Pacing Suggestions

- **Block Scheduling** Each day on the Lesson Planner represents a 40–50 minute block. Teachers using block scheduling may combine days to revise pacing to meet their classroom needs.

- **Accelerated Lesson Planning** Combine instructional days by aiding students in choosing a topic and then focusing on two core stages of the writing process, outlining for success (Day 5) and RADaR revision (Day 6).

- **Integrated Language Arts Curriculum** For targeted instruction that covers the essential components of the lesson use either a 3- or a 5-day plan.

3 day plan

DAY 1: Introduction to the Genre, Mentor Text, Student Model

DAY 2: Prewriting/Drafting

DAY 3: Revising/Editing/ Publishing

5 day plan

Use 3-day plan, and add:

DAY 4: Make Your Writing Count

DAY 5: Writing for Assessment

Links to Prentice Hall *LITERATURE*

Featured Author: Zlata Filipović

- What Is Nonfiction?, p. 378
- from *Zlata's Diary* (excerpt from a diary), p. 383
- On Writing Persuasively (Writing Workshop), p. 529
- *From the Author's Desk* Videos: Zlata Filipović

Additional Mentor Text:

- "Happiness Is a Charming Charlie Brown at Orlando Rep" (drama review), Matthew MacDermid, p. 796

Differentiated Instruction

Differentiated Instruction Boxes in this Teacher's Edition address these student populations:

- Below-Level Students
- Above-Level Students
- Gifted and Talented Students
- Special Needs Students
- English Language Learners
- Spanish Speaking Students

In addition, for further enrichment, see the **Extension** features.

LESSON OBJECTIVES

- To learn the forms and defining characteristics of a response to literature.
- To learn the elements of a successful letter to an author, the chapter Feature Assignment.
- To read a Mentor Text in the genre, analyzing its use of the elements of an effective response to literature.
- To read a Student Model of a letter to an author, analyzing it from the perspective of a reader and from the perspective of a writer.
- To apply prewriting strategies in developing a letter to an author, including strategies for choosing and narrowing a topic, planning writing, and gathering details, as well as tips for considering audience and purpose.
- To apply drafting strategies in developing a letter to an author.
- To apply RADaR revision strategies to a draft letter to an author.
- To learn about the Focus on Craft topic, clarifying meaning, and apply what is learned to a draft letter to an author.
- To edit the draft, zooming in on quotation marks and focusing on editing quotations.
- To complete the Make Your Writing Count assignment, developing and presenting a plan for sharing letters with the school community.
- To complete the Writing for Media assignment, developing a blog entry.
- To practice writing for assessment.

DAY 4

Prewriting

ONLINE

- Plan Your Piece
- Gather Details

DAY 5

Drafting

ONLINE

- Outline for Success
- Start Your Draft

DAY 9

WRITING FOR MEDIA

ONLINE

- **Blog Entry**
- Create a Blog Entry

DAY 10

WRITING FOR ASSESSMENT

ONLINE

- Interpretative Response Prompt
- The ABCDs of On-Demand Writing
- More Prompts for Practice
- Spiral Review: Persuasive

Personalized Assessment

	Ongoing Assessment	Formal Assessment of Feature Assignment	Progress Monitoring at End-of-Chapter
Interactive Writing Coach™	Use Paragraph Feedback and Essay Scorer as a revision tool.	Use Essay Scorer to score students' Feature Assignment papers.	Use Essay Scorer to score students' papers. Students' learner profiles can be adjusted based on their scores.
FEEDBACK **Teacher Conferencing**	Use rubrics in the Student Edition as a revision tool. Conference with students to review their work and provide personalized support.	Use rubrics in the Student Edition to score students' Feature Assignment papers.	Review each student's work to plan targeted resources for the next writing assignment.

The Digital • Print Path ▶

  WRITING COACH Online | STUDENT BOOK

1  Online STUDENT BOOK ▶

Using **Writing Coach Online**™ or the student book, students discuss the photograph in the chapter opener as it relates to the writing genre.

2 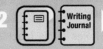 Writing Journal ▶

Students record their ideas and responses in their online journals or notebooks. They may also record and save their responses on pop-up sticky notes in **Writing Coach Online**™.

Chapter Objectives

1. Write an interpretative response essay by planning, drafting, revising, editing, and publishing individual work.

2. Produce the technology plan for sharing letters.

3. Use the five-step writing process to write a blog entry.

4. Write an interpretative response essay and a persuasive essay in response to a prompt.

RESPONSE *to* LITERATURE

What Do You Think?

Activate Prior Knowledge Tell students that the purpose of an interpretative response is to analyze an author's work. Explain to students that they will use what they know about reading to analyze the photo on page 196. Then, guide students in analyzing the photo.

 Think Aloud When we analyze something, we use what we see and what we know to figure out what it means. For example, in the photo **I see** children listening to a woman reading aloud a book. Using what I know about books being read aloud, I can figure out that this is either a teacher reading aloud to her students in a classroom or a librarian reading aloud to children at a library.

Work with students to use what they see and know to figure out other things about the photo, such as why the woman is showing the book and whether the children are enjoying it.

Try It! **Have students** work individually to develop responses to the questions. Check that students have addressed the role of the author.

Possible responses: In *The Cat in the Hat* by Dr. Seuss, a cat visits two children and makes a huge mess in their house that gets cleaned up just before their mother returns. Dr. Seuss keeps you guessing about what crazy trick the cat will do next. I loved the rhythm and rhyme, and I could recite the entire story from memory long before I learned to read it.

CHAPTER 10

RESPONSE *to* LITERATURE

196 Response to Literature

Connect to the Big Questions

Have students use their experience to discuss the Big Questions. Explain that they will revisit **Why write?** at the end of this chapter. Tell students to consider these points during their discussion:

1. In this question, the word *literature* means forms of imaginative writing, such as novels, short stories, poems, and plays.

2. People often remember for their entire lives the characters and events in stories, poems, and books they heard or read when they were young.

What's Ahead

Have students preview the Mentor Text and Student Model on pages 200–203. Tell students that they will write their own letter to an author using the five-step writing process: prewriting, drafting, revising, editing, and publishing.

What Do You Think?

Think back to your first experiences reading. Did a teacher read to you? What were your favorite books and authors? What did those authors do to interest you?

Part of being an active reader is thinking about how an author uses words and ideas to affect a reader.

Try It! Think about a book you had read to you when you were younger. Then, write notes about that book and why it was meaningful to you.

Consider these questions as you participate in an extended discussion with a partner. Take turns expressing your ideas and feelings.

- What was the book about?
- How did the author keep your interest?
- What was unique, or special, about the book?

Review your list. Then, think about other books you have read recently. What was powerful or interesting about those books?

What's Ahead

In this chapter, you will review two strong examples of an interpretative response essay: a Mentor Text and a Student Model. Then, using the examples as guides, you will write an interpretative response essay of your own.

WRITING COACH

Online

www.phwritingcoach.com

Online Journal
Try It! Record your answers and ideas in the online journal.

You can also record and save your answers and ideas on pop-up sticky notes in the eText.

Connect to the Big Questions

Discuss these questions with your partner:

1 What do you think? How does literature shape who we become?

2 Why write? What should you write about to make others interested in a text?

197

Personalized Support

FEEDBACK **Teacher or Peer Feedback**

To encourage students in their discussion of the photograph as it relates to the writing genre, ask the following questions:

- What is the first thing you think of when you look at this photo?
- How does it relate to your life?
- How does it relate to things you've learned in other subjects?
- What questions come to mind when you look at this photograph?
- How does your response to the photograph compare to those of your classmates?

Working with ELLs   ELL Sheltered Instruction: Metacognitive

Have students demonstrate listening comprehension of increasingly complex spoken English by following the *Try It!* directions after you read them aloud.

Beginning Slowly read aloud the first sentence of the *Try It!* directions and help students name a book. Read the second sentence and ask questions to help students monitor comprehension of the task. Have them seek clarification as needed. Help them as they follow the second direction.

Intermediate Read aloud the first paragraph of *Try It!* Have pairs monitor

comprehension by naming the three things they should write (name of book, notes about it, notes about why it was meaningful). Help them follow the direction, seeking clarification as needed.

Advanced Have partners take notes as you read aloud the *Try It!* directions, having them monitor understanding and seek clarification as needed. Then, have students follow directions to complete the activity.

Advanced High Have students complete the Advanced activity and then discuss other works they thought of.

The Digital • Print Path ▶

  STUDENT BOOK

1  STUDENT BOOK

Students learn vocabulary from the Word Bank and listen to English and Spanish pronunciations in the **Writing Coach Online™** glossary.

2  Writing Journal

Students record answers to questions about forms of writing in their online journals or notebooks.

INTERPRETATIVE RESPONSE

To introduce this chapter's writing form, discuss the opening paragraphs with students. Make sure students understand that a letter to an author is a type of interpretative response. Explain that good writers use a step-by-step process to develop their work. Then, have students preview the rubric on page 215.

Interpretative Response: Letter to an Author

Ask volunteers to read aloud the feature assignment characteristics. Tell students that they will identify these characteristics in a Mentor Text and a Student Model. Then, they will use the characteristics to guide the writing of their own letter to an author.

Other Forms of Interpretative Response

Guide students to understand how the forms of interpretative response are alike and different.

 Think Aloud The forms of interpretative response all look closely at a written work, but **I notice** that they address different audiences. For example, the audience for an author's blog is likely to consist of people who are familiar with the author's work. However, a critical review addresses people who may know little about the author and who wonder whether his or her work is worth reading.

Work with students to discuss possible audiences for each form of interpretative response.

Have students work in small groups to brainstorm for how the discussion of a literary work might be different in each form of interpretative response.

Try It! Remind students that the audience is the people who will read their writing. The purpose is the author's reason for writing. Have students record their responses in their journal.

INTERPRETATIVE RESPONSE

An interpretative response analyzes an author's work. In this chapter, you will explore a special kind of interpretative response, a letter to an author. In a letter to an author, you analyze that person's work and describe your reactions to it. You also share your thoughts and feelings and tell what the work meant to you. If you liked the author's style or sense of humor, for example, you might discuss that.

You will develop your letter to an author by taking it through each of the steps of the writing process: prewriting, drafting, revising, editing, and publishing. You will also have an opportunity to write a blog entry, or short commentary posted on a Web site, about one of your favorite books, poems, or stories. To preview the criteria for how your letter to an author will be evaluated, see the rubric on page 215.

FEATURE ASSIGNMENT
Interpretative Response: Letter to an Author

An effective interpretative response has these characteristics:

- A **clear thesis or controlling idea** that expresses the main idea of your response to the work
- An **analysis** of your ideas about what happens in the work, with conclusions about what the work means
- **Details and evidence from the text** that show understanding of the work
- **Personal insights and evaluations** of the meaning and quality of the work

- A discussion of how **literary elements,** such as plot, setting, and character, affect the quality and interest of the selection

A letter to an author also includes:

- A greeting and closing
- Polite and professional language
- Questions or requests

198 **Interpretative Response**

Possible responses: critical review, to evaluate a literary work; comparison essay, to explore similarities and differences between two or more works of literature; blog, to share ideas about an author's work

Word Bank

To assist English Language Learners and struggling readers, echo read each word or have students log on to Writing Coach Online to listen to the pronunciations. Then, have partners take turns using each word in a sentence. Ask volunteers to share one of their sentences with the class.

Teacher Tip

Have students deepen their understanding of an interpretative response by asking them whose opinions they listen to about books, movies, and music. Have them explain why those opinions are worth listening to.

Other Forms of Interpretative Response

In addition to a letter to an author, there are other forms of interpretative response, including these:

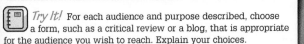

Blog comments posted on an author's Web site are a way to share ideas about an author's work. Readers express their opinions and give their interpretations of what an author's work means.

Comparison essays explore similarities and differences between two or more works of literature. For example, a comparison essay may compare how major characters in two different stories handle a similar problem.

Critical reviews discuss the quality of books, plays, poetry, and other literary works. Reviews appear in newspapers and magazines, on television and radio, and on the Internet. These works state the writer's opinions and support them with specific examples.

Response to literature essays analyze and interpret an author's work. Such essays examine what an author states and what those statements mean. Essay writers also evaluate how well an author has accomplished what he or she has set out to do.

Try It! For each audience and purpose described, choose a form, such as a critical review or a blog, that is appropriate for the audience you wish to reach. Explain your choices.

- To convince readers that a play is worth reading
- To demonstrate to a classmate how two plots are alike
- To explain to online readers why a story that seems simple actually has a deeper meaning

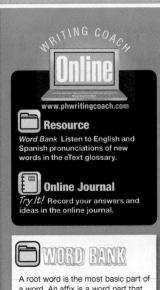

WRITING COACH Online

www.phwritingcoach.com

📁 **Resource**

Word Bank Listen to English and Spanish pronunciations of new words in the eText glossary.

📖 **Online Journal**

Try It! Record your answers and ideas in the online journal.

📁 WORD BANK

A root word is the most basic part of a word. An affix is a word part that is added to the beginning of a word, as a prefix, or at the end of a word, as a suffix. For example, the word *dance* is a root word. The word part *-er* is a suffix. Adding *-er* to *dance* makes the word *dancer*, or someone who dances.

People use these vocabulary words when they talk about interpretative responses. Work with a partner. Take turns saying each word aloud. Then, write sentences using each word. If you are unsure of the meaning of a word, use the Glossary or a dictionary to check the definition.

analyze	interpret
describe	respond
evaluate	style

The Digital • Print Path ▸

WRITING COACH Online · STUDENT BOOK

1  STUDENT BOOK ▸

Using Writing Coach Online™ or the student book, students read and listen to an audio recording of the Mentor Text. As they complete their writing assignments, they can refer back to the Mentor Text for support whenever they need it.

MENTOR TEXT

About the Selection The selection is a review of the book *Looking for Bobowicz* by Daniel Pinkwater. The reviewer gives some details about the book's characters and plot but does not reveal too much. She also states her opinion of the book and its author.

Learn From Experience

After students have read the text, point out that the numbered notes refer to the characteristics of a letter to an author introduced on page 198.

Try It! Guide students to understand how the genre characteristics shape the text.

Say: The first *Try It!* question asks whether the book review makes me want to read the book. I like that the reviewer doesn't begin with the title and author or her opinion of the book. The details about the parents show right away that the book is funny and unusual. They make me interested in finding out more about it.

Ask: Does the description of the boy's parents make you want to read the book? Why or why not? (Responses will vary.)

Have students reply to the *Try It!* questions in their journals. If students have difficulty responding to a particular question, model a response, as with Question 1.

Check the accuracy and completeness of student responses.

1. Responses will vary but should use information from the introduction to support the student's character descriptions and the opinion.

2. Responses will vary but might note that the scene in which Nick meets his friends reveals that the characters are intriguing and creative.

3. The book is *Looking for Bobowicz*; the author is Daniel Pinkwater. You can tell she likes the author's work because she says if you haven't "met" him yet, now's the time.

4. The reviewer's main message is the book is funny and offbeat, her purpose for writing is to persuade people to read the book, and her audience is children and their parents.

5. If she tells more, people will not need to read the book to find out what happens.

Extension Lead a discussion in which students compare and contrast how their additional book review examples use the genre characteristics. Use the *Try It!* questions as a guide.

MENTOR TEXT — Book Review

Review Mentor Text Book Review Mentor Text Book Review

Learn From Experience

 After reading the review on pages 200–201, read the numbered notes in the margins to learn about how the reviewer presented her ideas. Later you will read a Student Model, which shares these characteristics and also has the characteristics of a letter to an author.

Answer the *Try It!* questions online or in your notebook.

---

❶ The unusual **introduction** gives interesting details about the parents of Nick, the main **character** in the book. The reviewer does this to capture readers' attention.

Try It! From the introduction, what do you think Nick's parents are like? Do the details about the parents make you want to read the book? Explain.

❷ The reviewer gives more **details** about the **plot**, or what happens in the book.

Try It! Why do you think the reviewer chose to tell readers about this scene in the book?

❸ The reviewer **identifies the work** and its author. She also takes the **position** that the author is worth reading.

Try It! What is the title of the book being reviewed, and who wrote it? How can you tell the reviewer enjoys the author's work?

200 Response to Literature

Search for Boy and Giant Chicken Will Charm Young and Old

by Sandy Bauers

❶ They have decided Nick needs a dose of urban reality. The first day, his bicycle is stolen. His room is sweltering. Worse, . . . his father speaks with an affected British accent and calls people "old chap" and exclaims "Odds bodkins!" and the like.

His mother is the kind who says with delight, as Nick tells her he's going out to interview street bums, "Oh, another urban experience!"

("I simply tolerate these weirdnesses," Nick notes.)

❷ One day, as Nick is exploring the dark basement, he hears voices on the other side of the wall. He creeps closer and speaks through a crack: "I am Edmond Dantes and I have been unjustly imprisoned by my enemies."

A voice responds: "I am the Abbé Faria . . . also unjustly imprisoned in the Chateau d'If."

Naturally, they are kids just like Nick. And they all know the lines to Dumas' *Count of Monte Cristo* because they're fans of classic comics.

And so a friendship is born.

❸ If you haven't met author Daniel Pinkwater yet, now's the time. The comic curmudgeon, perhaps best described as a National Public Radio raconteur, turns his offbeat sights to children's books from time to time, and the story of Nick and his buddies, *Looking for Bobowicz*, is his latest.

About the name *Bobowicz*: The children find an old scrapbook with tales of a giant chicken that rampaged through Hoboken years before. It turned out to be the 266-pound pet of a boy named Arthur Bobowicz.

---

2 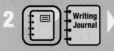 Writing Journal ▶

Students record their answers to questions about the Mentor Text in their online journals or notebooks.

Text *Book Review* Mentor Text *Book Review* Mentor Text

Well, of course, they just happen to be the very same
30 chicken and Bobowicz in Pinkwater's 1977 book, *The Great Hoboken Chicken Emergency.*

It's been getting laughs for 27 years now. Harper recorded it in 1999, and has now reissued it to go with a recording of the sequel. . . .

35 Pinkwater reads both, but his debut on *The Great Hoboken Chicken Emergency* is a disappointment. He reads too fast. And he rarely pauses. I wanted a performance, not a pell-mell gushing. But his reading on the sequel is much better.

❹ Both books are wonderfully, humorously, endearingly
40 kooky. Pinkwater is witty and mischievous to the core. Parents and children can listen together and all get a kick out of it.

Nick and his buddies decide they have to know more, of course, and they set out on a search for Bobowicz, during
45 which they spot a phantom, are aided and abetted by a librarian in a cape, and are almost asphyxiated by sauerkraut.

They also befriend the DJ of the pirate radio station WRJR (Radio Jolly Roger). His name is Vic Trola, and he plays corny oldies that go, "I gave you my heart in a
50 diamond, and you clubbed me with a spade."

❺ I don't think I'm giving anything away by revealing that they find Bobowicz. After all, it's a children's book and things pretty much have to turn out right.

But that's all I'm saying.

WRITING COACH Online

www.phwritingcoach.com

Interactive Model

Listen to an audio recording of the mentor text in the eText. You can refer back to the mentor text whenever you need support in developing your own writing.

Online Journal

Try It! Answer the questions about the Mentor Text in the online journal.

❹ This **controlling idea** sums up the reviewer's opinion of *Looking for Bobowicz* as well as *The Great Hoboken Chicken Emergency.*

Try It! What is the reviewer's main message about the book? What is her purpose for writing, and for what audience do you think she wrote the review?

❺ The reviewer **includes important information** about the book but does not tell everything that happens.

Try It! Why do you think the reviewer says she does not want to tell more about what happens in the book?

Extension Find another example of a book review, and compare it with this one.

Mentor Text   201

Personalized Support

FEEDBACK Teacher or Peer Feedback

To provide feedback to students on their responses to the Mentor Text and their answers to the *Try It!* questions, ask or have student partners ask one another the following:

- What is the thesis or controlling idea of the Mentor Text?

- How does the Mentor Text illustrate the characteristics of an interpretative response?

- How did you answer this *Try It!* question? How could you use your answer to help you plan your piece of writing?

Working with ELLs   ELL Sheltered Instruction: Metacognitive

Have students demonstrate listening comprehension of increasingly complex English by retelling or summarizing spoken messages. Read aloud the Mentor Text, pausing frequently to paraphrase or explain. Have students monitor understanding and seek clarification as needed.

Beginning Reread section 5 aloud, miming for clarity. Pause after each sentence, having students monitor understanding and seek clarification. Have students retell an idea, gesturing or drawing as needed.

Intermediate Reread section 5 aloud. Ask simple questions, helping students monitor

understanding and seek clarification. Have partners discuss and retell what you said, then share their retelling with the class.

Advanced Reread the Mentor Text aloud. Have students monitor understanding by writing questions about the spoken message. Have partners respond to each other's questions, seeking clarification as needed. Have them write summaries of the message.

Advanced High Have students complete the Advanced activity and use the *Try It!* questions to monitor their understanding, seeking clarification as needed.

1  **STUDENT BOOK** ▶

Using **Writing Coach Online**™ or the student book, students read and listen to an audio recording of the Student Model.

STUDENT MODEL

Tell students that good writers react to what they read in ways that show their understanding of the text. Explain that students will react to the Student Model by placing two sets of symbols in the text. Then, distribute printed copies of the Student Model or have students log on to Writing Coach Online.

Use a Reader's Eye

Read aloud the instruction for using the Reader's Response Symbols and the meaning of each symbol. Then, guide students through their use.

Think Aloud **I think** the student writer did a good job interpreting the story. I especially like the way she expressed some of her ideas. For example, lines 4–5 tell me very clearly that she thinks the story is about "survival and friendship." These are strong, vivid words. I'm going to put an exclamation mark next to that sentence.

Work with students to identify other places in the text where the writer expresses her ideas in a clear, compelling way.

Have students read and respond to the Student Model, using each Reader's Response Symbol at least once.

Partner Talk

After students have talked with each other about the student model, have each student pair give a two- or three-sentence summary of their discussion.

Use a Writer's Eye

Read aloud the instructions for using the Writer's Response Symbols and the meaning of each symbol. Then, guide students through their use.

STUDENT MODEL | **Letter to an Author**

ent Model Book Review Student Model Book Review Stud

With a small group, take turns reading this Student Model aloud. As you read, practice newly acquired vocabulary by correctly producing the word's sound. Together, determine which elements make it a strong letter to an author. Look for evidence in the text, such as facts and details, that supports your conclusions.

Use a Reader's Eye

Now, reread the Student Model. On your copy of the Student Model, use the Reader's Response Symbols to react to what you read.

Reader's Response Symbols

+ **I agree with this point.**

− **This isn't clear to me**

? **I have a question about this.**

! **Well said!**

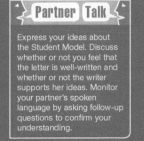

Partner Talk

Express your ideas about the Student Model. Discuss whether or not you feel that the letter is well-written and whether or not the writer supports her ideas. Monitor your partner's spoken language by asking follow-up questions to confirm your understanding.

202 Interpretative Response

I. B. Singer's "Zlateh the Goat"

Dear Mr. Singer:

    I really liked reading your story "Zlateh the Goat." At first, it seemed like a very simple tale about a boy and a goat caught in a storm. Then, I realized it was
5 really a great story about survival and friendship.

    The description of how Zlateh and Aaron begin their adventure really got me interested in what was going to happen. When you wrote that Zlateh was going to be sold because she was
10 not producing milk anymore, I felt sorry for her, especially because she trusted the family: "She knew that they always fed her and never did her any harm." I also felt bad for the family because I could tell that it wasn't an easy decision to send
15 Zlateh away. For example, the mother and the little sisters all shed tears for Zlateh. I was glad you told us that they had cared for Zlateh for twelve years and were having a hard time making money from the fur business because of the weather. This
20 information helped me to understand the family and their choice better. I liked this beginning because it made me think about the relationship people have with animals. Animals can help feed us and give us clothes, but they can also be our friends.
25   The middle of the story is my favorite part because it is so suspenseful and shows good survival thinking. I really liked how the storm was so unexpected. When Aaron and Zlateh start their trip, the day is sunny. The sudden change
30 in the weather made things exciting because I knew Aaron wasn't prepared for a storm like this. You tell us that Aaron had "never experienced a snow like this one." I also like the way you show

1

Say: I like the way this student gave evidence for her idea in lines 10–13. She says that the goat trusted the family and supports that idea with a quote from the story: "She knew that they always fed her and never did her any harm." The quote shows clearly that her interpretation is based on a close reading of the text. I'll write S.E. next to this for effective supporting evidence. I'm also going to write E.Q. for effective quotation.

Ask: In lines 32–39, what evidence does the writer give to support her statement that Aaron makes good decisions? (He looks for shelter, digs a warm cave in the haystack, and makes a hole for air.)

Have students read and respond to the Student Model, using each Writer's Response Symbol at least once.

2 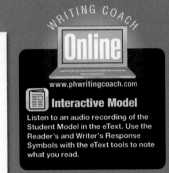 WRITING COACH Online ▸ STUDENT BOOK ▸

First, students respond to the Student Model as a reader, using symbols to mark the text. They can mark the text using pop-up sticky notes in *Writing Coach Online™* or they can mark a printed copy of the Student Model.

3 WRITING COACH Online ▸ STUDENT BOOK ▸

Then, students respond to the Student Model as a writer, using different symbols to mark the text. They can use either *Writing Coach Online™* or a printed copy of the Student Model.

Book Review   Student Model   *Book Review*   **Student Model**

35 Aaron making good decisions. First, he looks for shelter and finds the haystack, and then, he digs a warm cave. He even remembers to make a large enough air hole so he and Zlateh can breathe. Each problem and solution kept me interested in reading to see what would happen next.

40 This part of the story is also a good example of how animals help humans. During the storm, Zlateh made milk, even though she wasn't supposed to be able to anymore. Aaron was able to survive off of it. Zlateh also keeps him warm and from

45 feeling too alone. I was relieved that in the end of the story Zlateh was saved and loved by the family for the rest of her life. She had definitely shown that she was more than a working animal.

This story really showed how danger can be

50 avoided through smart thinking and teamwork. The boy and the goat both needed and helped each other. Neither of them would have survived the blizzard without each other.

Thank you for writing this story. It really made

55 me think about making smart choices and how I treat animals. I will read it many more times.

Sincerely,
Denise Jenkins

2

Student Model   203

Online
www.phwritingcoach.com

Interactive Model
Listen to an audio recording of the Student Model in the eText. Use the Reader's and Writer's Response Symbols with the eText tools to note what you read.

Use a Writer's Eye

Now, evaluate the piece as a writer. On your copy of the Student Model, use the Writer's Response Symbols to react to what you read. Identify places where the student writer uses characteristics of an effective letter to an author.

Writer's Response Symbols	
C.T.	Clearly stated thesis
I.A.	In-depth analysis
S.E.	Effective supporting evidence
E.Q.	Effective quotations

Personalized Support

FEEDBACK Teacher or Peer Feedback

To provide feedback to students on their responses to the Student Model, ask or have student partners ask one another the following:

- What is the thesis or controlling idea of the Student Model?
- How does the Student Model illustrate the characteristics of a letter to an author?
- Which feature or characteristic of the Student Model might you use in your own piece of writing?
- How could you alter or adapt this feature to make it your own?

Working with ELLs   ELL Sheltered Instruction: Cognitive

Help students use and reuse new basic language in speaking activities and expand and internalize initial English vocabulary by retelling basic information supported by pictures. Preteach these basic vocabulary words from the Student Model: *boy, goat, story, sold, trusted, cared,* **and** *choice.* **Help them read the Student Model. Then:**

Beginning Help students use the basic vocabulary to orally complete sentence frames about the photograph, like *It shows ___ and ___,* and reuse the words to retell simple information from the Student Model.

Intermediate Have groups use the basic vocabulary when discussing the photograph and reuse the vocabulary to retell simple information from the Student Model.

Advanced Have partners use the basic vocabulary to retell the information in the Student Model, referring to the picture for support. Have them reuse the vocabulary in describing the relationship between the picture and what happens in the story.

Advanced High Have students complete the Advanced activity, then share their retelling.

The Digital • Print Path ▶

 **1** ▶ Students select or are assigned a topic for their letter to an author from the Topic Bank, or they may choose a topic of their own.

2 ▶ Students complete online or printed graph organizers to narrow the topic for their lett to an author.

Prewriting

Explain that the first task students need to complete as they plan their letter to an author is to determine an appropriate topic.

Choose From the Topic Bank

Read aloud each topic and then ask volunteers to describe them in their own words. If you are assigning topics to students, you may wish to do so now. Encourage students to ask questions about their topic.

Choose Your Own Topic

Introduce and discuss the Discussion and Personal Interests strategies. If students were not assigned writing topics, have them use the strategies to brainstorm for topics for their essays.

Extension Have each student choose one of the strategies. Then, have them write an action plan that outlines the resources and steps they will use to develop their topic.

Narrow Your Topic

Tell students that they will use a Narrow Your Topic graphic organizer to focus their topic. Then, distribute printed copies or have students log on to Writing Coach Online.

Apply It! Guide students through the instructions for completing the graphic organizer. Have students complete the exercise based on their topic.

Consider Your Audience and Purpose

Guide students to consider the audience and purpose for their letter to an author.

 **Your Turn** ▶ **Feature Assignment: Letter to an Author**

Prewriting

Plan a first draft of your letter to an author **by determining an appropriate topic.** You can select from the Topic Bank or come up with an idea of your own.

 Choose From the Topic Bank

TOPIC BANK

Review of a Short Story Write an entry for a reader's response journal for "Greyling" by Jane Yolen. The entry should focus on whether you liked or disliked the story. Include specific examples from the literature to back up your opinions.

Response to a Plot Think about a book or short story you enjoyed reading. Write a letter to the author explaining why you enjoyed the plot of the book or short story.

Response to a Mentor Text Read "Roommates" by John Scieszka on page 68. Write a letter to the author telling how you felt about the the two main characters.

 Choose Your Own Topic

Determine an appropriate topic on your own by using the following **range of strategies** to generate ideas.

Discussion and Personal Interests

- Think about your favorite work by an author. Discuss with a partner reasons why this work has special meaning for you.
- Consider questions that you had about an author's work. Think about whether the answers to these questions are directly stated or just hinted at in the work. Brainstorm for ideas.

Review your responses and choose a topic.

 Think Aloud **I see** that the first question in the first column asks who the audience is for my letter. I know that the audience would seem to include only the author to whom the letter is addressed, but the question points out that other people may read it, too. This reminds me that the letter should be written so that someone who may not have read the work can still understand my ideas.

Work with students to discuss the possible audiences for their letter to an author.

Have students with similar topics work in small groups to discuss and respond to the remaining questions.

Coach's Corner

You may wish to model prewriting activities for students by brainstorming for your own writing topic. Use these prompts to model your thought process:

- **I am interested in** the author O. Henry, so that could be my general topic.
- **I can narrow my topic by** focusing on the short story "The Gift of the Magi."

Discuss the choices you make and solicit feedback from students.

Students record their answers to questions about audience and purpose in their online journals or notebooks.

Narrow Your Topic

Choosing a topic that is too broad results in writing that is too general and unfocused.

Apply It! Use a graphic organizer like the one shown to narrow your topic.

- Write your general topic in the top box, and keep narrowing your topic as you move down the chart.
- Your last box should hold your narrowest or "smallest" topic, the focus of your letter to the author.

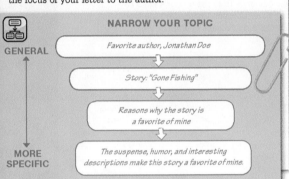

NARROW YOUR TOPIC

GENERAL — Favorite author, Jonathan Doe

Story: "Gone Fishing"

Reasons why the story is a favorite of mine

MORE SPECIFIC — The suspense, humor, and interesting descriptions make this story a favorite of mine.

Consider Your Audience and Purpose

Before writing, think about your audience and purpose. Consider the views of others as you ask yourself these questions.

Questions for Audience	Questions for Purpose
• Who will read my letter: My teacher? Classmates? The author? All of them? • What will make my reaction to the work interesting and convincing?	• What do I want my readers to know about the work? • What thoughts and feelings do I want to share in my letter? • What response do I want to get from readers?

Record your answers in your writing journal.

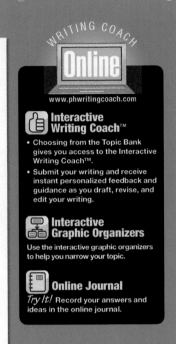

WRITING COACH

Online

www.phwritingcoach.com

Interactive Writing Coach™
- Choosing from the Topic Bank gives you access to the Interactive Writing Coach™.
- Submit your writing and receive instant personalized feedback and guidance as you draft, revise, and edit your writing.

Interactive Graphic Organizers

Use the interactive graphic organizers to help you narrow your topic.

Online Journal

Try It! Record your answers and ideas in the online journal.

Personalized Support

Interactive Writing Coach™

Below Level Teachers select a topic from the topic bank for below-level students. Students submit their writing to the Interactive Writing Coach™ for feedback paragraph by paragraph or as a complete draft. It is recommended that below-level students submit their writing one paragraph at a time.

On Level Students may select a topic from the Topic Bank. They may submit their writing for feedback paragraph by paragraph or as a complete draft.

Above Level Students may select from the Topic Bank or come up with their own topic. Above-level students should submit their writing as a complete draft.

Interactive Graphic Organizer

Below Level Students complete three graphic organizers that provide models and scaffolded support.

On Level Students complete one, two, or three graphic organizers, depending on how much support they need.

Above Level Students complete the least scaffolded graphic organizer or narrow their topic without the help of a graphic organizer.

Differentiated Instruction

RTI Strategy for Below-Level Students Students may find it helpful to talk to a partner about why they like the story they have chosen. Ask students to take notes as their partners talk. For example, students might write *funny* or *likes main character*. Students may then use the notes to help organize their thoughts and fill in the Narrow Your Topic organizer.

PRE-AP Enrichment for Above-Level Students Encourage students to do a deeper analysis of their chosen short stories. Ask them to think about the theme of their story and whether it relates to their own experience and understanding of life. Have them consider the setting of the story and how it affects both plot and character development in the story.

The Digital · Print Path ▶

 ▶

1 Using Writing Coach Online™ or the student book, students read and discuss the model graphic organizer.

 ▶

2 Students complete online or printed graphic organizers to develop their ideas and gather details.

Plan Your Piece

Explain that writers use graphic organizers to develop their ideas and show relationships between different parts of the text. Then, point out the Develop Your Response graphic organizer on page 206. Tell students that they will use this organizer to outline their letter to an author. Then, distribute printed copies or have students log on to Writing Coach Online.

Introduce the graphic organizer by explaining that the center circle contains the thesis of their letter and the outer circles will contain evidence, or support, for that thesis.

Develop a Clear Thesis Guide students to develop a clear thesis, using the notes they have made on the Narrow Your Topic graphic organizer from page 205. Have them write their thesis statements in the center circle of the organizer.

Organize Your Supporting Evidence Have students read aloud the three Evidence circles. Explain that the evidence in each circle is related to the interpretation stated in the thesis. For example, the thesis mentions the story's humor, and evidence for this idea appears in the upper left circle.

Gather Details

Remind students that an interpretative response must be supported by details. Ask volunteers to read aloud each kind of detail and its example. Then, guide students to place the details in the example organizer.

Say: I notice that the Evidence circles include incomplete lines. The details on page 207 supply some of this information. For example, the Descriptive Details example about the cabin could be included in the lower circle, about the story descriptions. I'll record that detail in that circle.

Ask: In which Evidence circle would you place the Example detail? (upper right circle, about suspense)

Have students work in small groups to place the remaining details in the example organizer.

Feature Assignment **Prewriting** *Feature Assignment* **Prew**

Plan Your Piece

You will use a graphic organizer like the one shown to state your thesis and organize your evidence. When it is complete, you will be ready to write your first draft.

Develop a Clear Thesis Think about your reaction to the author's work. Then state your feelings and thoughts in a **clear thesis**. Add your thesis to a graphic organizer like this one.

Organize Your Supporting Evidence Use a graphic organizer to help you logically organize evidence from the author's work to support your response and to show that you understand the work. Evidence from the text can include quotations, examples, and other specific details from the work.

Develop Your Response

Title: Gone Fishing
Author: Jonathan Doe

Evidence
• The story has humor: For example, when Carl says, "Hang in there, Eva." She answers, "I am... by my pinky finger!"
• Another funny part is . . .

Evidence
• The suspense starts when Eva's usual fishing spot dries up.
• The suspense builds when . . .

Thesis
• Full of suspense, humor, and interesting descriptions, "Gone Fishing" is a favorite story of mine.

Evidence
• I enjoyed this description: "It was an old and battered row boat from her grandfather's day. The paint was chipped and peeling and about twenty coats deep. To Eva, it was beautiful. It was peace."
• I also liked this description . . .

206   Interpretative Response

Try It! Help students understand how the quotation from the story supports the writer's statement that Zlateh trusts the family.

Apply It! Read aloud the bulleted instructions for gathering details. Then, have students select story details that support their thesis and enter them on their graphic organizers. Remind students to use a variety of details to support their ideas.

Writer's Block

IF students have difficulty finding relevant evidence . . .

THEN have them identify a section of their story that they most enjoyed and look there for a quotation that relates to their thesis.

3

Students refer back to the Mentor Text or the
Student Model as they plan their writing.

Gather Details

To support their ideas, writers provide evidence from the text.
Look at these examples:

- **Quotations:** *"I don't understand it," Eva said. "My family has
  been fishing here for generations."*
- **Examples:** *A scary situation occurs when Eva and Carl realize
  that they are the only people around for miles and miles.*
- **Descriptive Details:** *In the cabin, "he noticed that there
  wouldn't be enough food to live off of if they couldn't count on
  fish as a food source."*
- **Personal Observations:** *What makes the story so interesting is
  that you expect the characters to behave one way but they act
  another way.*

Try It! Read the Student Model excerpt and identify the evidence
that the author uses to support her ideas.

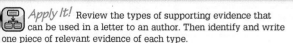

STUDENT MODEL from I. B. Singer's "Zlateh the Goat"
page 202; lines 8–13

When you wrote that Zlateh was going to be sold because
she was not producing milk anymore, I felt sorry for her,
especially because she trusted the family: "She knew
that they always fed her and never did her any harm."

Apply It! Review the types of supporting evidence that
can be used in a letter to an author. Then identify and write
one piece of relevant evidence of each type.

- Review your evidence to make sure it supports your thesis. Be
  sure to include one or more pieces of each kind of **evidence
  from the text to demonstrate your understanding.**
- Add your supporting evidence to your graphic organizer.

WRITING COACH Online
www.phwritingcoach.com

**Interactive
Graphic Organizers**

Use the interactive graphic
organizers to help you create
a plan for your writing.

Interactive Model

Refer back to the Mentor Text in the
eText as you plan your writing.

Personalized Support

Interactive Graphic Organizer

Below Level Students complete three
graphic organizers that provide models
and scaffolded support.

On Level Students complete one, two,
or three graphic organizers, depending on
how much support they need.

Above Level Students complete the least
scaffolded graphic organizer or narrow
their topic without the help of a graphic
organizer.

FEEDBACK Teacher or Peer Feedback

To provide feedback to students as they
plan their first draft, ask or have student
partners ask one another the following:

- What do you want your audience to know
  about the topic?
- What questions or concerns will your
  audience have about the topic?
- What details have you identified for your
  piece? How do these details support your
  thesis or controlling idea?
- Are your details varied? Will they interest
  your readers? Explain.

Differentiated Instruction

RTI Strategy for Below-Level Students

When students are developing their thesis
statements, suggest that they begin with
all the things they like about the story.
Then, have them read through their stories
to decide which points have the most
supporting evidence. The points with the
most evidence to support them should
be included in the thesis. This will help
students focus their theses and gather
evidence for their letters.

RTI Strategy for Special Needs Students

Help students grasp the idea of providing
supporting evidence for their opinions by
asking questions about their stories in a
variety of ways, such as: *Why do you think
the story is funny? What is funny about
the story? Do the characters say or do
funny things? Can you show me something
specific in the story, such as a quotation or
a detail, that is funny to you?*

The Digital · Print Path ▶

WRITING COACH Online / STUDENT BOOK

1 WRITING COACH Online / STUDENT BOOK ▶
Using **Writing Coach Online**™ or the student book, students read and discuss the Outline for Success for a letter to an author.

2 WRITING COACH Online / STUDENT BOOK ▶
Students discuss how the Mentor Text illustrates the characteristics of a letter to an author.

Drafting

Outline for Success

Explain that the Outline for Success shows an organizational strategy for an interpretative response. Students will use the Outline to write a focused, organized, and coherent draft of their letter to an author.

I. Introduction

Link the Outline to a specific interpretative response by having students turn to the Mentor Text on pages 200–201. Then, guide students to identify and understand the characteristics of a strong introduction.

Say: I noticed that the Mentor Text introduction is in an unusual place. It doesn't occur until lines 20–24 of the text. However, the introduction does include an interesting opening statement and a clear thesis in lines 20–21: "If you haven't met author Daniel Pinkwater yet, now's the time." This statement tells me the author enjoyed the book, and does so in an interesting way.

Ask: What is the name of the book being reviewed, and where is that information found? (*Looking for Bobowicz*, line 24)

Have students work with a partner to evaluate the thesis they entered on their organizers.

II. Body

Lead a discussion about how the Mentor Text reflects the characteristics of an interpretative response.

- Thoughtful analysis and interpretation (lines 6–8, 35–38)
- Details and evidence from the text (lines 2–18, 43–50)
- Logically organized statements (lines 10, 14, 19)

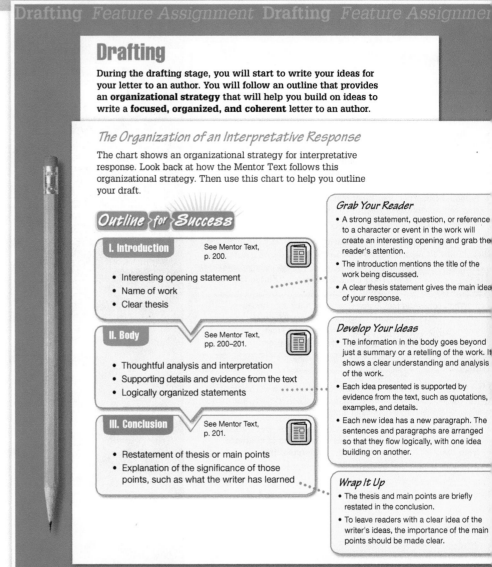

Drafting *Feature Assignment* **Drafting** *Feature Assignment*

Drafting

During the drafting stage, you will start to write your ideas for your letter to an author. You will follow an outline that provides an **organizational strategy** that will help you build on ideas to write a **focused, organized, and coherent** letter to an author.

The Organization of an Interpretative Response

The chart shows an organizational strategy for interpretative response. Look back at how the Mentor Text follows this organizational strategy. Then use this chart to help you outline your draft.

Outline for Success

I. Introduction See Mentor Text, p. 200.
- Interesting opening statement
- Name of work
- Clear thesis

II. Body See Mentor Text, pp. 200–201.
- Thoughtful analysis and interpretation
- Supporting details and evidence from the text
- Logically organized statements

III. Conclusion See Mentor Text, p. 201.
- Restatement of thesis or main points
- Explanation of the significance of those points, such as what the writer has learned

Grab Your Reader
- A strong statement, question, or reference to a character or event in the work will create an interesting opening and grab the reader's attention.
- The introduction mentions the title of the work being discussed.
- A clear thesis statement gives the main idea of your response.

Develop Your Ideas
- The information in the body goes beyond just a summary or a retelling of the work. It shows a clear understanding and analysis of the work.
- Each idea presented is supported by evidence from the text, such as quotations, examples, and details.
- Each new idea has a new paragraph. The sentences and paragraphs are arranged so that they flow logically, with one idea building on another.

Wrap It Up
- The thesis and main points are briefly restated in the conclusion.
- To leave readers with a clear idea of the writer's ideas, the importance of the main points should be made clear.

208 Interpretative Response

III. Conclusion

Have small groups discuss how the Mentor Text reflects the characteristics of an interpretative response (lines 51–54).

Start Your Draft

Have small groups read aloud and discuss the boxed instructions for drafting. Direct students to work independently on their first draft.

Coach's Corner

If you are modeling the writing process for students with your own topic or a student volunteer's, you may wish to use these prompts to guide your drafting and discussion:

- **To capture readers' attention, my introduction will** ask an interesting question.

- **I will organize my body paragraphs by** showing how the characters answer that question.

Discuss the choices you make and solicit feedback from students.

3  ▶ Students begin writing their letter to an author online or in their notebooks.

4 ▶ Students submit paragraphs or complete drafts to the Interactive Writing Coach™ for scoring and feedback, or share their work with their teacher.

5 ▶ Students receive customized feedback from the Interactive Writing Coach™ or feedback from their teacher. Students may continue to work on their drafts.

ature Assignment **Drafting** *Feature Assignment* **Drafting**

tart Your Draft

e this checklist to help you complete your draft. Use the graphic ganizer that shows your thesis and evidence from the text, and e Outline for Success as guides.

hile drafting, aim at writing your ideas, not on making your iting perfect. Remember, you will improve the draft when you vise and edit.

√ A **salutation** to the author, such as "Dear Ms. Barnes," should start your letter.

√ Your **introduction** should identify the work about which you're writing.

√ Present your thesis statement.

√ Use the **body** of your letter to develop your ideas. Write a response that explains your understanding of the work and how the author's work affected you.

√ To create a focused and **organized** letter to an author, choose an appropriate organizational strategy that builds on ideas in a logical way.

√ Include only information that is related to your thesis. Make sure your letter is **coherent**—it should flow well, and all the details should support your main idea.

√ Support your ideas with specific **evidence** from the text, including examples and quotations, to demonstrate your understanding of the text. Provide specific and detailed explanations to show how the evidence supports your ideas.

√ In your **conclusion**, restate or summarize your thesis.

√ Include a memorable **final statement** that clearly tells your opinions.

√ End your letter with a **closing,** such as "Sincerely," and sign your name.

WRITING COACH
Online
www.phwritingcoach.com

Interactive Model
Outline for Success View pop-ups of Mentor Text selections referenced in the Outline for Success.

Interactive Writing Coach™
Use the Interactive Writing Coach to receive the level of support you need:
• Write one paragraph at a time and submit each one for immediate, detailed feedback.
• Write your entire first draft and submit it for immediate, personalized feedback.

Drafting 209

Personalized Support

 Interactive Writing Coach™

Below Level Students complete the drafting process in small steps by submitting each paragraph for scoring and feedback.

On Level Depending on the support they need, students submit their writing paragraph by paragraph or as a complete draft for scoring and feedback.

Above Level Students may write their drafts on their own but have the option of submitting them for scoring and/or feedback.

 Teacher or Peer Feedback

To provide feedback to students on their first draft, ask or have student partners ask one another the following:

• Can you explain how you organized your ideas in this piece?
• Why did you include this information here?
• Why did you choose this introduction? Does it grab your reader and identify your thesis or controlling idea?
• What supporting details could you add here?
• Why did you choose this conclusion? How does it add to your piece?
• Can you show me a place where I can hear your unique voice?
• Can you show me a place where you used vivid language?

Working with ELLs Sheltered Instruction: Cognitive

Present these content-based grade-level academic words from Start Your Draft: *draft, evidence, thesis,* **and** *conclusion.* **Help students internalize this new academic language by using and reusing it in writing activities.**

Beginning Write a definition of *thesis* and read it aloud. Have students use and reuse the word in writing activities by helping them complete sentence frames, such as *The thesis of the Student Model is _____.*

Intermediate Discuss the words with students. Have partners use and reuse the words by writing a brief definition of each

and then writing two sentences using each word.

Advanced Have students use the **KIM Strategy.** In a three-column chart, they should write *Key Word, Information,* and *Memory Cue* and write the word, a definition, and an example or illustration. Have them use and reuse the words in written sentences about their draft.

Advanced High Have students use and reuse the words in written comments about a partner's draft, such as *The thesis is clearly stated in the first paragraph.*

The Digital · Print Path ▶

WRITING COACH Online | STUDENT BOOK

1 WRITING COACH Online | STUDENT BOOK ▶

Using *Writing Coach Online*™ or the student book, students study the first and second drafts of the student model to see how the writer used Revision RADaR to improve his or her writing.

2 WRITING COACH Online | Writing Journal ▶

Students use the Revision RADaR strategy to revise their own writing.

Revising: Making It Better

Point out the page title to students and explain that revising means making improvements to a writing draft. Then, read aloud the opening paragraph to introduce the Revision RADaR strategies. You may wish to have students review Chapter 3 for more information on Revision RADaR.

Kelly Gallagher, M. Ed.

KEEP REVISION ON YOUR RADaR

1ST DRAFT After students have read the first draft, have them turn to page 208 and review the Outline for Success. Work with students to understand that the questions the author asked about the draft are based on the characteristics of an interpretative response. For example, call out the first question and note how it addresses concerns listed in the Introduction section in the Outline for Success.

Then, have students work in small groups to develop other questions about the draft based on the genre characteristics.

2ND DRAFT Guide students to understand how the author used the RADaR strategies to revise her draft.

Think Aloud When **I read** the introduction in the first draft, it didn't seem very interesting to me. All the writer said is that "Zlateh the Goat" is a "great story." In the second draft, though, I see the letter *A* next to the first paragraph, which tells me the writer added some information to more clearly express her thesis. Now the thesis says that the story "is about survival and friendship," as well as being a great story.

Work with students to think of other ways to revise the introduction.

Revising Feature Assignment Revising Feature Assignme...

Revising: Making It Better

Now that you have finished your first draft, you are ready to revise. Think about the "big picture" of **audience, purpose,** and **genre**. You can use your Revision RADaR as a guide for making changes to improve your draft. Revision RADaR provides four major ways to improve your writing: (R) replace, (A) add, (D) delete, and (R) reorder.

Kelly Gallagher, M. Ed.

KEEP REVISION ON YOUR RADaR

Read part of the first draft of the Student Model "I. B. Singer's 'Zlateh the Goat.'" Then look at questions the writer asked herself as she thought about how well her draft **addressed issues of audience, purpose, and genre**.

I. B. Singer's "Zlateh the Goat"

1ST DRAFT

I read your story "Zlateh the Goat." It was a great story of how a goat saved a boy's life.

The description of how Zlateh and Aaron begin their adventure really got me interested in what was going to happen. When you wrote that Zlateh was going to be sold because she was not producing milk for the family anymore I felt sorry for her. I also felt bad for the family because I could tell that it wasn't an easy decision to send Zlateh away. For example, the mother and the little sisters all shed tears for Zlateh. Aaron's dad is a furrier. This winter is a very dry season and people are not buying furs. If no one buys furs, Aaron's family needs to get money from somewhere else like selling Zlateh. Animals can help feed us and give us clothes, but they can also be our friends.

*Does the **introduction** grab my reader's attention? Does my **thesis statement** clearly express my overall response?*

*Have I included relevant **evidence**, such as quotations, to support my opinions?*

*Have I included an **analysis** of the work that is not simply a summary or a retelling?*

210 Interpretative Response

Have students work in groups to discuss the other changes in the second draft.

Apply It! Review the bulleted instructions for using Revision RADaR. Remind students to question their drafts based on the genre characteristics listed on the Outline for Success on page 208. Tell students to use each RADaR strategy at least once.

Coach's Corner

If you are modeling the writing process for students with your own draft or a student volunteer's, use these prompts to focus on the Revision RADaR *Add* strategy:

- **I added information to my thesis because** I wanted to clearly state my interpretation.

- **I added a quotation from the story here because** I wanted to provide evidence for my ideas.

Discuss the choices you make and solicit feedback from students.

3

Students submit paragraphs or revised drafts to the **Interactive Writing Coach™** for scoring and feedback, or share their work with their teacher.

4

Students receive customized feedback from the **Interactive Writing Coach™** or feedback from their teacher. Students may continue to revise their drafts.

Feature Assignment **Revising** *Feature Assignment* **Revising**

Now look at how the writer applied Revision RADaR to write an improved second draft.

I. B. Singer's "Zlateh the Goat" **2ND DRAFT**

At first it seemed like a very simple tale about a boy and a goat caught in a storm. Then I realized it was really a great story about survival and friendship.

The description of how Zlateh and Aaron begin their adventure really got me interested in what was going to happen. When you wrote that Zlateh was going to be sold because she was not producing milk anymore, I felt sorry for her, especially because she trusted the family: "She knew that they always fed her and never did her any harm." I also felt bad for the family because I could tell that it wasn't an easy decision to send Zlateh away. For example, the mother and the little sisters all shed tears for Zlateh. I was glad you told us that they had cared for Zlateh for twelve years and were having a hard time making money from the fur business because of the weather. This information helped me to understand the family and their choice better. I liked this beginning because it made me think about the relationship people have with animals. Animals can help feed us and give us clothes, but they can also be our friends.

A *Added specific information so that the opening is more interesting and the thesis statement more clearly expresses my main idea*

A *Added a quotation to support my idea with evidence from the work*

D *Deleted a simple retelling of the events of the story*

R *Replaced it with personal insights*

WRITING COACH

Online

www.phwritingcoach.com

 Interactive Writing Coach™

Use the Revision RADaR strategy in your own writing. Then submit your paragraph or draft for feedback.

 Apply It! Now, revise your draft after rethinking how well questions of **purpose, audience,** and **genre** have been addressed.

- First, determine if you have clearly stated your ideas and supported them with **evidence** from the text to show your understanding.
- Then, apply your Revision RADaR to make needed changes. Focus especially on working to **clarify your meaning** to your audience. You can use the steps in RADaR in any order.

Revising 211

Personalized Support

 Interactive Writing Coach™

Below Level Students revise their drafts using the Revision RADaR strategy and submit their writing for scoring and feedback.

On Level Students revise their drafts using the Revision RADaR strategy and submit their writing for scoring and feedback.

Above Level Students may use the Revision RADaR strategy or revise their drafts on their own. They have the option of submitting their revised drafts for scoring and/or feedback.

FEEDBACK **Teacher or Peer Feedback**

To provide feedback to students as they revise their first draft, ask or have student partners ask one another the following:

- Can you show me where you revised your text?
- What could you add to your introduction to grab the interest of your readers?
- How could you reorder these ideas so that their order is more logical?
- Have you included all the characteristics of this form of writing?
- Is there any unnecessary text that you could delete?
- Have you achieved your purpose with this piece of writing?
- Have you addressed the questions and concerns of your audience?

Working with ELLs **ELL** Sheltered Instruction: Cognitive

Help students demonstrate comprehension and expand reading skills by employing inferential skills such as drawing inferences from text and finding supporting text evidence. Review the revised draft. Then:

Beginning Choral read the first paragraph of the draft, pausing to clarify drawing an inference based on supporting text evidence by saying, *The phrase* at first *tells me that something changes later.* Help students draw an inference about the writer's feelings (*She likes it*) and identify evidence in the text ("*a great story*").

Intermediate Have groups discuss the draft and respond to inferential questions such as *Did the student like the story?*, supporting answers with text evidence.

Advanced Have partners review the draft and discuss the writer's feelings about the story, using text evidence as support. Have them draw other inferences and share their ideas.

Advanced High Have students complete the Advanced activity and write a paragraph explaining their inferences and the supporting text evidence.

The Digital • Print Path ▶

1
Using Writing Coach Online™ or the student book, students study and discuss the revision chart.

2
In a video by program author Kelly Gallagher, students learn more strategies for effective writing.

Revising: Making It Better

Look at the Big Picture

Introduce the revision chart to students. Explain that the Section column identifies the three main parts of a letter to an author. The Evaluate column identifies the characteristics found in each section and explains how to assess them. The Revise column presents specific strategies for revising each characteristic.

Then, have students draw lines between and label the three sections of their drafts. Direct students to work individually to evaluate and revise their draft, using the chart to guide their work.

Focus on Craft: Clarify Meaning

Have students read the introductory text. Guide students to understand how simple, direct language helps clarify meaning.

Think Aloud I noticed that the first sentence of the excerpt says, "Danger can be avoided through smart thinking and teamwork." This simple, direct language clearly communicates the writer's interpretation of the story.

Work with students to identify other examples of simple, direct language in the excerpt or complete Student Model text.

Have students work with a partner to find sentences in the Student Model that could be clearer and then rewrite them.

Try It! Have students discuss the questions and record responses in their journals. Follow up with students to check that their responses reflect an understanding of how clarifying meaning increases the effectiveness of a letter to an author.

Look at the Big Picture

Use the chart and your analytical skills to evaluate how well each section of your letter to an author **addresses purpose, audience, and genre**. When necessary, use the suggestions in the chart to revise your letter.

Section	Evaluate	Revise
Introduction	• Check the **opening.** It should grab readers' attention and make them want to read on.	• Make your opening more interesting by writing a strong first sentence or asking a question.
	• Make sure the **thesis** clearly expresses the main idea of your response.	• Ask yourself if you have made important points that are not covered in the thesis. If so, rewrite the thesis to cover all your points.
Body	• Check that you have presented **evidence** from the text to support your ideas and to demonstrate your understanding.	• Skim the story to find and add more examples and quotations that explain and support your ideas.
	• Make sure your **analysis** goes beyond summarizing and retelling.	• Don't just tell what happens in the story. Also describe, specifically and with detail, why it happens or what you think it means.
	• Check your letter's **coherence**—be sure that you have ordered sentences and paragraphs so that they flow logically.	• Reorder text as needed to improve flow. You can add, delete, combine, or reorder sentences to make them sound better.
	• Check that you have developed an **analysis** —make sure you have analyzed specific elements of the work.	• Identify something that you think the author did especially well. Then, tell how that "something" makes the work enjoyable.
Conclusion	• Check the restatement of your **thesis.**	• If necessary, discuss your restatement with a classmate and ask for suggestions.
	• Check that your conclusion leaves readers with a new **insight** and a clear understanding of your feelings.	• Add a final statement that sums up how you feel about the work or why it is important to you.

212   **Interpretative Response**

Fine-Tune Your Draft

Apply It! Ask volunteers to read aloud the instructions for fine-tuning their drafts. Then, have students work in pairs to clarify the meaning in their drafts.

Teacher Feedback Have students identify Mentor Text examples of the characteristics that you marked for improvement. Use the Mentor Text references on page T208 to guide students to appropriate examples.

T212

3 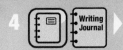 Using Writing Coach Online™ or the student book, students refer back to the Mentor Text or Student Model for examples of writer's craft.

4  Students record answers to questions about writer's craft in their online journals or notebooks.

5 Students submit revised drafts to the Interactive Writing Coach™ for scoring and feedback, or share their work with their teacher.

6 Students receive customized feedback from the Interactive Writing Coach™ or feedback from their teacher.

Feature Assignment **Revising** Feature Assignment **Revising**

Focus on Craft: Clarify Meaning

When writing, it is important to **clarify your meaning**, or to clearly state your views. Simple, direct language without unnecessary repetition is a good way to communicate meaning to readers. Using precise words and transitions such as *then* and *next* will help you to state your ideas in a logical, clear way.

Think about clarifying meaning as you read the following sentences from the Student Model.

 STUDENT MODEL from **I. B. Singer's "Zlateh the Goat"**
page 203; lines 49-53

> This story really showed how danger can be avoided through smart thinking and teamwork. The boy and the goat both needed and helped each other. Neither of them would have survived the blizzard without each other.

Try It! Now, ask yourself these questions:

- How does the following version of the text differ from the example? *This story is a tale about how teamwork and working together to overcome the odds can be achieved through smart thinking about good decisions.*
- Which version is simpler and more interesting to read? Explain.

 Fine-Tune Your Draft

Apply It! Use the revision suggestions to prepare your final draft after again rethinking how well questions of **purpose, audience,** and **genre** have been addressed.

- **Clarify Meaning** Use simple language and avoid unnecessarily repeating ideas. Cut words that are not needed, and make sure to say exactly what you mean.
- **Improve Transitions** You can improve your transitions from one idea to another by adding, deleting, combining, and rearranging sentences or larger units of text.

Teacher Feedback Submit your final draft to your teacher and revise it based on his or her feedback.

WRITING COACH
Online
www.phwritingcoach.com

 Video
Learn more strategies for effective writing from program author Kelly Gallagher.

Online Journal
Try It! Record your answers in the online journal.

Interactive Model
Refer back to the Interactive Model as you revise your writing.

 Interactive Writing Coach™
Revise your draft and submit it for feedback.

Revising **213**

Personalized Support

 Interactive Writing Coach™

Below Level Students complete the revising process by submitting their writing for scoring and feedback.

On Level Students complete the revising process by submitting their writing for scoring and feedback.

Above Level Students finish revising their drafts. They have the option of submitting their revised drafts for scoring and/or feedback.

Teacher or Peer Feedback

To provide feedback to students as they continue to revise their first draft, ask or have student partners ask one another the following:

- What are you trying to say here? What part of the text could you replace to make your meaning clearer?
- Is there a more precise word you could use here?
- How does the rhythm of these sentences sound to you? Could you make the length and structure of these sentences more varied?
- How could you include transitional words and phrases here to help your reader understand these ideas?
- Are there details you could add here to make this part come alive?

Differentiated Instruction

RTI Strategy for Below-Level Students
If students need to revise simple retellings in order to include analysis, ask them some of these questions: *What do the character's actions tell you about the character? How does that action make you feel? How would the story be different if the character made a different choice here?*

Enrichment for Gifted/Talented Students
Remind students who are interested in creative writing that specific word choices usually are more effective than more general statements. Have students go through the Student Model to find opportunities to use more specific words and then do the same with their own drafts.

The Digital · Print Path ▶

  STUDENT BOOK

1 ▶

In a video by program author Jeff Anderson, students learn effective editing techniques.

2 ▶

Students record answers to questions about writer's craft in their online journals or notebooks.

Editing: Making It Correct

Discuss the opening paragraph with students. Explain that they will edit their drafts for proper grammar, mechanics, and spelling, including proper punctuation and spacing for quotations.

WRITE GUY *Jeff Anderson, M.Ed.*

WHAT DO YOU NOTICE?

Introduce students to quotation marks by reading aloud the Mentor Text excerpt and discussing responses to the "Ask yourself" question. Then, have students read the explanation of quotation marks. Guide them to use quotation marks correctly.

 Think Aloud **I notice** in the Mentor Text example that quotation marks are used in pairs, one before and one after the exact words the voice says. If the voice had started with "Who is that?" and ended with "Help me!" the opening quotation marks would go before the word *Who* and the closing quotation marks would go after the exclamation point.

Work with students to write and punctuate quotations using the Mentor Text on pages 200–201. For example, the first sentence might become this: *They said, "You need a dose of urban reality, Nick."*

Have students find uses of quotation marks in a favorite book and explain them to the class. You may also wish to have students turn to Chapter 25 of the Grammar Handbook to learn more about quotations.

Grammar Mini-Lesson:
Editing Quotations

Discuss the paragraph and the Mentor Text excerpt on page 215 with students. Guide them to understand that the writer used ellipses, parentheses, and brackets correctly when editing the Mentor Text.

Editing: Making It Correct

Editing means checking your draft for errors in spelling, grammar, and punctuation.

When editing your draft, make sure you use **proper punctuation and spacing for quotations.** Also, use **parentheses, brackets, and ellipses to indicate missing text, interruptions, or incomplete statements.** Then correct any other errors in **grammar, mechanics, and spelling.**

WRITE GUY *Jeff Anderson, M. Ed.*

WHAT DO YOU NOTICE?

Zoom in on Conventions Focus on the quotation marks as you zoom in on this sentence from the Mentor Text.

> **MENTOR TEXT** from **Search for Boy and Giant Chicken Will Charm Young and Old** page 200; lines 14–15
>
> A voice responds: "I am the Abbé Faria… also unjustly imprisoned in the Chateau d'If."

Now ask yourself: *How does the use of quotation marks help make the writer's meaning clear?*

Perhaps you said that **quotation marks** help make it clear exactly what the voice is responding to and what the writer has quoted directly from the text.

When using quotations, place quotation marks before the first word of the quote and after the last word. The end punctuation, such as a period, goes inside the quotation marks. A comma or a colon is usually used to set off the direct quotation from the rest of the sentence. When the quotation cannot stand alone, it is not set off by a comma.

If you are quoting a passage of more than four lines, set it off in a block of its own. Add a line of **spacing** above and below it. Indent the whole passage, but don't use quotation marks.

To learn more about quotations, see Chapter 25 of your Grammar Handbook.

214 **Interpretative Response**

Try It! Have students work with a partner to rewrite the sentences.

Possible response: "It was a very bad year for [Paul]…," the story states. (It was for many others, too.)

Apply It! Remind students to look closely at their quotations as they edit.

Use the Rubric Explain to students that the rubric lists six important elements of a letter to an author. Tell students that they will rate how well their draft addresses each element on a scale of 1 to 6, with 6 being the best score.

Then, have students use the rubric to evaluate their drafts and revise as necessary.

Writer's Block

> **IF** students have difficulty remembering how to use ellipses, parentheses, and brackets . . .

> **THEN** have them make a three-column chart in their notebooks showing the punctuation marks, their uses, and example sentences.

Using *Writing Coach Online™* or the student book, students refer back to the Mentor Text or Student Model as they edit their writing.

Using *Writing Coach Online™* or the student book, students evaluate their writing using the rubrics.

Students submit edited drafts to the *Interactive Writing Coach™* for scoring and feedback, or share their work with their teacher.

Students receive personalized feedback from the *Interactive Writing Coach™* or feedback from their teacher.

Feature Assignment Editing Feature Assignment Editing

Grammar Mini-Lesson: Editing Quotations

Use **ellipses**, a series of three or four periods, to show omitted, incomplete, or interrupted text. Use **parentheses** to set off closely related information. Use **brackets** to show explanations, replacements for pronouns, or changes to capitalization and punctuation. Notice the edits to the Mentor Text.

> To learn more, see Chapter 25.

 **MENTOR TEXT** from **Search for Boy and Giant Chicken Will Charm Young and Old** page 200; lines 6–7

> [Nick's] mother is the kind who says... "Oh, another urban experience!"
>
> ("I simply tolerate these weirdnesses," Nick notes.)

Try It! Rewrite the sentences, using ellipses to shorten the quotation and brackets to identify the furrier's name as Paul. Enclose the second sentence in parentheses.

It was a very bad year for a furrier such as him," the story states. It was for many others, too.

Apply It! Edit your draft for grammar, mechanics, and spelling. Use proper punctuation and spacing for quotations. Use parentheses, brackets, and ellipses to show omitted, missing, or interrupted text.

Use the rubric to evaluate your piece. If necessary, rethink, rewrite, or revise.

Rubric for Interpretative Response: Letter to an Author	Rating Scale					
	Not very					Very
Ideas: How well does your response present a focused statement about the work?	1	2	3	4	5	6
Organization: How clearly organized is your analysis?	1	2	3	4	5	6
Voice: How well have you engaged the reader and sustained his or her interest?	1	2	3	4	5	6
Word Choice: How clearly do your words state your views?	1	2	3	4	5	6
Sentence Fluency: How well have you used transitions to improve the flow of your writing?	1	2	3	4	5	6
Conventions: How correct is your punctuation for quotations?	1	2	3	4	5	6

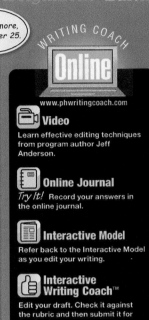

WRITING COACH Online
www.phwritingcoach.com

Video
Learn effective editing techniques from program author Jeff Anderson.

Online Journal
Try It! Record your answers in the online journal.

Interactive Model
Refer back to the Interactive Model as you edit your writing.

Interactive Writing Coach™
Edit your draft. Check it against the rubric and then submit it for feedback.

Editing 215

Personalized Support

Interactive Writing Coach™

Below Level Students complete the editing process by submitting their writing for scoring and feedback.

On Level Students complete the editing process by submitting their writing for scoring and feedback.

Above Level Students finish editing their drafts. They have the option of submitting their final drafts for scoring and/or feedback.

Teacher or Peer Feedback

To provide feedback to students as they edit their draft, ask or have student partners ask one another the following:

- Have you looked for mistakes that you tend to make?
- Have you read your piece aloud to yourself or to a partner? What kind of errors did you find?
- Can you show me something you changed through editing?
- What resources have you used to look for possible spelling errors?
- Read this sentence aloud. Does the grammar sound correct to you?
- Read this sentence aloud. Does the punctuation accurately convey your meaning?

Working with ELLs   ELL Sheltered Instruction: Metacognitive

As students edit drafts during the *Apply It!*, help them monitor and edit writing for appropriate verb tense using self-corrective techniques. Remind students of rules for verb tense by thinking aloud as you revise example sentences on the board. Then:

Beginning Read this sentence aloud as students copy from the board: *The cat walked across and jumps on the table.* As a self-corrective technique, have students underline the verbs and ask themselves *When?* of each (*before now, now*). Help them see the shift in tenses, and lead volunteers in writing corrected sentences on the board.

Intermediate Have students complete the Beginning activity. Provide other pairs of sentences and have groups apply the self-corrective technique to them, editing for appropriate verb tense.

Advanced Have pairs apply the self-corrective technique in the Beginning activity to their drafts to edit for appropriate verb tense.

Advanced High Have partners use the self-corrective technique of reading their draft aloud to monitor for appropriate verb tense, editing as needed.

The Digital · Print Path ▶

1  Using *Writing Coach Online™* or the student book, students complete the writing process by deciding the best way to publish their writing for their intended audience.

2 Students record their answers and ideas to Extend Your Research in their online journals or notebooks.

Publishing

Wrap Up Your Presentation

Have students check for the parts of a formal letter and be sure that they have included all parts, especially if they have written to a living author and will be sending the letter.

Publish Your Piece

Explain to students that the final step in the writing process is to decide which form of publication will present their work most effectively. Then, introduce students to the chart. Explain that the chart shows how specific audiences can be reached using different kinds of media.

Have students work in small groups to discuss appropriate ways to publish their work.

Extend Your Research

Extension Tell students that their thinking about their topic does not have to end with its final publication. Then, guide students through the bulleted instructions for extending their research.

Big Question Have students respond to the question in their journals.

Publishing

Share the feelings and thoughts expressed in your letter to an author—publish it! First, get your letter ready for presentation. Then, choose a way to **publish it for the appropriate audience.**

Wrap Up Your Presentation

Now that you have finished your draft, add the final details. Make a final draft that is neat and is easy for others to read. Be sure to include page numbers on each page of your letter.

Publish Your Piece

Use the chart to identify a way to publish your letter for the appropriate audience.

If your audience is...	...then publish it by...
A living author	• Mailing or e-mailing it to the author through his or her publishing company • Submitting it to the author's Web site
Students at school	• Reading it aloud in English class • Submitting it to your school newspaper • Posting your piece online and inviting responses

 ### Extend Your Research

Think more about the topic on which you wrote your letter to an author. What else would you like to know about this topic?

- Brainstorm several questions that you would like to research and then consult, or discuss, with others. Then, decide which question is your major research question.
- Formulate, or develop, a plan about how you will answer these questions. Decide where you will find more information—on the Internet, at the library, or through other sources.
- Finally, learn more about your topic by following through with your research plan.

The Big Question: Why Write? What should you write about to make others interested in a text?

MAKE YOUR WRITING COUNT

Introduce the letter sharing activity by discussing the opening paragraphs with students. Make sure students understand that the project may be produced electronically or by hand. Then, guide students through each step in the action plan.

Resources You may wish to have students use these Graphic Organizers: Meeting Agenda, Meeting Notes, and Outline. Distribute printed copies or have students log on to Writing Coach Online.

Use the 21ˢᵗ Century Skills Rubric to evaluate each group's process and final product on a scale of 1 to 3, indicating weak, moderate, or strong use of the skill. ▶

Listening and Speaking Monitor students' feedback as they brainstorm for ideas.

21st Century Learning

Skills Rubric	Rating
Apply Technology Effectively: Use digital technologies to access, manage, integrate, evaluate, and create information.	1 2 3
Work Creatively With Others: Develop, implement, and communicate new ideas to others.	1 2 3
Communicate Clearly: Articulate ideas using oral and written communication skills.	1 2 3
Interact Effectively With Others: Know when it is appropriate to listen and when to speak.	1 2 3

3 ▸ Students use a variety of graphic organizers, either online or in print, to help them work together to create a multimedia group project.

4 ▸ Through *Writing Coach Online™* students link to resources on 21st Century Learning for help in creating a multimedia group project.

21st Century Learning

MAKE YOUR WRITING COUNT

Share Letters With the School Community

The mail is just one of the many ways you can share a letter with others, such as an author. For example, newspapers and magazines have a Letters to the Editor page and blogs and Web sites have places to post your ideas and opinions. What ways can you think of to share your letters with other students in your school or elsewhere?

With a group, decide on a way to use technology to publish the letters for your audience, in this case other students and teachers in the school. Your group will come up with a plan and present it to the teacher or principal to explain how it can be done. If possible, publish the letters applying the chosen technology.

Here's your action plan.

1. With your group, identify roles such as leader and notetaker.

2. With your group, brainstorm for different ways to use technology, such as a Web site, group e-mail, or a blog, to publish and share your letters.

3. Use the Internet to research additional technology options for sharing letters.

4. Review the ideas you have brainstormed, and vote for the best one.

5. Create a plan that explains how you will use the technology to share the letters.

   ▪ Use poster paper or a bulletin board to display a flowchart illustrating the process.

   ▪ Include an explanation of the technology in your plan.

6. If possible, use your plan to publish your letters.

Listening and Speaking Come to your group's brainstorming session with an open mind. Listen actively and effectively to your group members' ideas and offer your own ideas as part of the discussion, as well. As you plan your presentation, consult with others to ask for advice on ways to improve your plan. Incorporate this advice and feedback as you give your presentation.

WRITING COACH

Online
www.phwritingcoach.com

Online Journal
Extend Your Research Record your answers and ideas in the online journal.

Resource
Link to resources on 21st Century Learning for help in creating a group project.

Make Your Writing Count 217

Personalized Support

FEEDBACK Teacher or Peer Feedback

To provide feedback to students on their published writing, ask or have student partners ask one another the following:

- How did you go about writing this piece? What was your process?
- What did you learn from the writing model that you used in this piece?
- What surprised you the most as you wrote this piece?
- Did you try anything new as you worked on this piece?
- What did you learn from this piece of writing that you would like to remember and reuse?
- What do you think you do best as a writer right now?

Differentiated Instruction

RTI Strategy for Below-Level Students
As a way of extending their research, have students read another story by the same author to whom they wrote a letter. Alternatively, have students read another story that has a similar setting or main character. Have students work with partners and explain the similarities and differences between the stories and which one they liked better.

RTI Strategy for Special Needs Students
Have students create a class bulletin board or scrapbook of letters as a means for publication that could be less intimidating than a more public forum. Suggest that students might also illustrate the project with their own drawings or with copies of illustrations from the books that contained the stories.

The Digital · Print Path ▶

1  Students use Writing Coach Online™ or their student books to analyze and discuss the Writing for Media topic.

2 Students learn about the characteristics of a blog entry by answering questions about the model. Students record their answers to the *Try It!* questions in their online journals or notebooks.

 **Writing for Media: Blog Entry**

Blog Entry

Discuss the opening paragraph with students. As a class, discuss any blogs students may have read.

Try It! Guide students to understand the content and structure of the sample blog entry.

Say: The first *Try It!* question asks which work the blog entry discusses. I see the answer in the first sentence. It is the novel *Honus and Me*. The answer to the second question is in the same sentence. The author is Dan Gutman.

Ask: How do you know that this book is a work of fiction? (The first sentence calls the book a novel.)

Have students discuss the remaining questions in small groups and record individual responses in their journals.

Extension Have students bring in other examples of blogs. Lead a media discussion about the examples, using the *Try It!* questions as a guide.

Create a Blog Entry

Tell students that they will create a blog entry using the five-step writing process. Then, preview the writing process instructions on page 219.

> **Resources** You may wish to have students use the Outline graphic organizer. Distribute printed copies or have students log on to Writing Coach Online.

For each step in the writing process, have partners read aloud and discuss the list of tasks. Then, have them work individually. Once both partners have completed the tasks, have them evaluate each other's work before moving to the next step.

Your Turn **Writing for Media: Blog Entry**

21st Century Learning

Blog Entry

A **blog entry** is a short commentary posted on a Web site. Readers sometimes post blog entries on the Web sites of their favorite authors or on online bookstores' Web sites. Others have their own pages on which they write their blogs. In their postings, readers explain what they like about an author's work and why, including evidence from the text to back up their ideas.

Try It! Study the blog entry on this page. Then, answer the questions. Record your answers in your journal.

1. Which **work** does this blog entry discuss?
2. Who is the **author** of the work?
3. Is the book **fiction** or **nonfiction?** How do you know?
4. Does the blog have an effective **introduction**? Explain.
5. Does the writer provide **evidence**, such as specific facts, details, and examples, to support his or her ideas? List some examples.
6. How effective is the **concluding paragraph**? Explain.
7. Does the blog contain personal **insights** and judgments?
8. Would this **blog** encourage you to read the selection? Why or why not?

Extension Find another example of a blog entry, or an online book review and compare it with this one.

Stories for Now: A Blog for Readers

Page Turner to Try Posted by Reading Dude on 12/17/12 at 5:35 PM

The suspense in Dan Gutman's novel *Honus and Me*[1] almost made my hands shake as I turned the pages. A boy named Stosh is hired to throw out a neighbor's trash. But when he gathers up junk in her attic, a card flutters to the floor. He says. "No doubt about it. I had just stumbled upon a T-206 Honus Wagner card—*the most valuable baseball card in the world.*"

But that's only the beginning. The card's value is far beyond money. It enables Stosh to actually travel back in time, to attend the 1909 World Series—and much more.

The interesting storyline isn't the only element that makes this story great. Gutman's characters are totally realistic, and his style is clear and easy to read. Here's a warning, however: Beware! If you don't finish by bedtime; you won't want to stop reading!

[1] Gutman, Dan. *Honus and Me.* New York: Avon Books, 1997.

218   Interpretative Response

Use the 21st Century Skills Rubric to evaluate each student's process and final product on a scale of 1 to 3, indicating weak, moderate, or strong use of the skill. ▶

Partner Talk

Remind students to listen carefully and respond politely to their partners.

21st Century Learning

Skills Rubric	Rating
Work Creatively With Others: Be open to new perspectives.	1 2 3
Make Judgments and Decisions: Interpret information and draw conclusions based on the best analysis.	1 2 3
Collaborate With Others: Value contributions made by each team member.	1 2 3
Analyze Media: Understand how and why media messages are constructed, and for what purposes.	1 2 3

3

Students follow the five-step writing process to write their own blog entry. Students may select online or printed graphic organizers to help them plan and develop their writing.

 Create a Blog Entry

Follow these steps to create your own blog entry. Review the graphic organizers on pages R24–R27 and choose one that suits your needs.

Prewriting

- Choose a book that you have recently read and enjoyed. Then, think about which readers are sure to like the book as well as which readers *might* enjoy it.
- Think about how best to grab readers' attention. For example, you might begin with a question or start with an exciting passage.
- Jot down ideas about the author's style, the selection's message, and what quotations or details you might include.
- Review your notes and decide the main insight you'd like to convey about the work.

Drafting

- Begin with a strong opening statement to grab your reader's attention. Then, write a brief summary that makes the book sound appealing to the target audience. Take your writing further by adding the insight you will develop.
- Provide evidence from the text to demonstrate your understanding of it and to support your ideas. Use this evidence to persuade others to read the book.
- Describe the author's style and tell why it is effective.

Revising and **Editing**

Review your draft to ensure that your ideas flow logically and that you have presented them in a persuasive way. Be sure that you have used a positive tone and done all you can to "sell" the book and the author. Edit your draft for errors in grammar, mechanics, and spelling.

Publishing

Post your blog entry on a school Web site, and invite your classmates to read and respond to the entry.

WRITING COACH

Online

www.phwritingcoach.com

Online Journal
Try It! Record your answers in the online journal.

Interactive Graphic Organizers

Choose from a variety of graphic organizers to plan and develop your project.

Partner Talk

Before you start drafting, describe and fully explain your ideas for your planned blog entry to a partner. Be specific and detailed, and ask your partner for feedback. For example, you might ask whether your blog entry ideas are persuasive enough or if you have included enough evidence to support your ideas.

Writing for Media 219

Personalized Support

FEEDBACK  **Teacher or Peer Feedback**

To provide feedback to students as they write for media, ask or have student partners ask one another the following:

- What are the main characteristics of this form of writing?
- Have you included most or all of these characteristics in your piece of writing?
- What is your purpose for writing this piece?
- Who is your audience?
- How did you organize your ideas in this piece of writing?
- How did you go about revising the piece? Editing it?
- How do you plan on publishing your piece?
- What other publishing options also might work?

Working with ELLs **Sheltered Instruction:** Cognitive

Help students demonstrate an understanding of the general meaning, main points, and important details of spoken language on topics ranging from familiar to unfamiliar. Discuss a familiar topic, baseball, and aid comprehension by relating the discussion to the unfamiliar topic in the blog entry on page 218, expensive baseball cards. Then:

Beginning Write a **Word Bank** based on your discussion, explaining with mime. Help students identify your general meaning, main points, and important details by using the words to respond to questions.

Intermediate Have groups note key words as you speak and use them to retell the general meaning, main points, and important details of your description.

Advanced Have students take notes as you speak. Have partners write summaries of your general meaning, main points, and important details. Have partners share their summaries with another pair.

Advanced High Have students take notes as you speak and work individually to summarize the general meaning, main points, and important details.

T219

Writing for Assessment

Read aloud or have a student read aloud the introductory text. Then, tell students that they will learn and practice a technique for writing in response to a prompt.

Try It! Read aloud the Interpretative Response Prompt, then have volunteers read aloud the Format and Academic Vocabulary boxes. Tell students that they will use the ABCD method to respond to the prompt.

The ABCDs of On-Demand Writing

Have students identify the words associated with the ABCD method. (attack, brainstorm, choose, detect) Then, guide students through their use.

Think Aloud I'll **attack the prompt** by circling the words *analyze, evaluate,* and *support.* These words tell me that I will have to give evidence for my interpretation. I can rewrite the prompt to say, "Use evidence to support your ideas about a literary work."

Work with students to brainstorm for an appropriate organizer for an interpretative response, such as a Cluster Diagram.

Have students write their drafts individually and then work with a partner to detect errors.

More Prompts for Practice

Apply It! Have students use the ABCD method to respond to the practice prompts.

Prompt 1 Have partners attack the prompt and brainstorm for possible answers. Then, have each group swap their information with another group and evaluate whether the team has developed a focused interpretative response.

---

ssment **Writing for Assessment** *Writing for Assessment* V

Writing for Assessment

You may see a prompt that asks you to write an essay in which you respond to literature. Use these prompts to practice. Respond using the characteristics in your letter to an author. (See page 198.)

Try It! To begin, read the **interpretative response** prompt and the information on format and academic vocabulary. Use the ABCDs of On-Demand Writing to help you plan and write your essay.

Format
The prompt directs you to write a *critical review* of a story, book, or poem. Your introduction should include a clear thesis. The body of your essay should provide supporting evidence from the text. The conclusion should strongly support your thesis.

Interpretative Response Prompt
Write an essay that is a critical review of a short story, book, or poem you have read. Analyze and evaluate the work. Support your analysis and opinions with specific details, such as examples and quotations from the work. [30 minutes]

Academic Vocabulary
When you *analyze* a story, book, or poem, you study and respond to its elements. When you *evaluate* a work of literature, you state and support your opinion about its strengths and weaknesses.

The ABCDs of On-Demand Writing

Use the following ABCDs to help you respond to the prompt.

Before you write your draft:

Attack the prompt [1 MINUTE]

- Circle or highlight important verbs in the prompt. Draw a line from the verb to what it refers to.
- Rewrite the prompt in your own words.

Brainstorm possible answers [4 MINUTES]

- Create a graphic organizer to generate ideas.
- Use one for each part of the prompt if necessary.

Choose the order of your response [1 MINUTE]

- Think about the best way to organize your ideas.
- Number your ideas in the order you will write about them. Cross out ideas you will not be using.

After you write your draft:

Detect errors before turning in the draft [1 MINUTE]

- Carefully reread your writing.
- Make sure that your response makes sense and is complete.
- Look for spelling, punctuation, and grammar errors.

220 **Interpretative Response**

Prompt 2 Have students work individually to attack the prompt and brainstorm for possible answers. Then, have students work in small groups to evaluate their work before writing their drafts.

Spiral Review: Persuasive Read aloud the instructions and the prompt. Then, have students review the persuasive essay characteristics on page 172.

Prompt 3 Remind students to use the ABCD method to write their persuasive essay.

2 Students submit their writing paragraph by paragraph or as a complete draft to the Interactive Writing Coach™ for feedback, or share their writing with their teacher.

3 Students receive personalized feedback from the Interactive Writing Coach™ or feedback from their teacher.

More Prompts for Practice

Try It! Respond to Prompts 1 and 2 by writing **interpretative** responses. As you write, be sure to:

- Express the main idea of your response in a clear thesis statement
- Include effective introductory and concluding paragraphs
- Include supporting details and **evidence from the text**
- Go beyond a simple retelling to include a careful analysis of the work
- **Demonstrate your understanding of the text** and what it means to you
- Clearly convey meaning through an appropriately organized structure

Prompt 1 Write an interpretative essay comparing and contrasting two characters from two different books or short stories. Support your ideas and opinions with specific details and examples from the texts.

Prompt 2 Write an essay interpreting a theme or central insight in a short story, book, or poem you have read. Analyze how well the author demonstrates the theme and discuss what the theme means to you.

Spiral Review: Persuasive Respond to Prompt 3 by writing a **persuasive essay** for appropriate audiences. Make sure your persuasive essay reflects all of the characteristics described on page 172, including:

- **establish a clear position**
- **demonstrate sound reasoning**
- **provide detailed and relevant evidence**
- **include a consideration of alternative views**

Prompt 3 Write an essay to persuade the mayor of your town to start a new community program, such as a recycling program or an after-school program at a local community center.

WRITING COACH

Online

www.phwritingcoach.com

Interactive Writing Coach™

Plan your response to the prompt. If you are using the prompt for practice, write one paragraph at a time or your entire draft and then submit it for feedback. If you are using the prompt as a timed test, write your entire draft and then submit it for feedback.

Remember **ABCD**

Attack the prompt
Brainstorm possible answers
Choose the order of your response
Detect errors before turning in the draft

Personalized Support

 Assessment/Monitor Progress

For timed writing practice, assign students a prompt to be completed in a timed setting. Have students submit their writing to Interactive Writing Coach™ to get immediate feedback.

For a formal writing assessment, assign the Assessment writing prompt for this chapter in Writing Coach Online™. Then, have students submit their writing to Interactive Writing Coach™ to be assessed. Use the results to assess student progress and skill levels. Interactive Writing Coach™ will update student levels to ensure that students get the appropriate support.

 Teacher Feedback

To create an assessment environment, have students use a prompt in a timed setting. Grade papers using the appropriate rubric and use the results to assess student progress and skill levels. In the next writing assignment, ensure that students get the appropriate level of support.

If you conference with students, use these questions to guide your discussion:

- What writing form did the prompt call for? Does your response include most or all of the characteristics of that form?
- How did you organize your ideas?
- Did you make good use of your time as you planned and wrote your response?
- What did you learn that you can use when responding to a prompt during a timed test?

Differentiated Instruction

RTI Strategy for Special Needs Students Guide the students through the ABCD method using Prompt 1. Discuss together what words in the prompt are most significant and should be attacked. Then, rewrite the prompt until all students agree that they understand what is being asked of them. Do the brainstorming step as a group. Use graphic organizers as necessary. Write possible answers on the chalkboard.

Strategy for Spanish Speakers Students whose home language is Spanish might omit the serial comma in a list of three or more items, as the serial comma is not used in Spanish. Write *and* and *or* on the board. Provide examples of two- and three-item lists and elicit punctuation from students. In their persuasive essay to the mayor, have students write at least one sentence with a list of three reasons. Have partners check each other's punctuation.

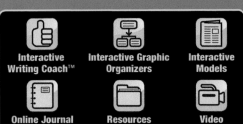

| Interactive Writing Coach™ | Interactive Graphic Organizers | Interactive Models |
| Online Journal | Resources | Video |

Use the Online Lesson Planner at www.phwritingcoach.com to customize your instructional plan for an integrated Language Arts curriculum.

DAY 1

CHAPTER OPENER/ GENRE INTRODUCTION

- What Do You Want to Know?
- What's Ahead
- 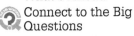 Connect to the Big Questions
- **Feature Assignment: Informational Research Report**
- Other Forms of Research Writing
- Word Bank

ONLINE

DAY 2

STUDENT MODEL

- **Student Model: Informational Research Report**
- Learn From Experience
- Reader's Eye and Writer's Eye

ONLINE

DAYS 3–4

Prewriting

- Choose Your Topic
- Formulate Your Research Question
- Consider Your Audience and Purpose
- Make a Research Plan

ONLINE

DAYS 9–10

Revising

- Keep Revision on Your RADaR
- Look at the Big Picture
- Focus on Craft
- Fine-Tune Your Draft

ONLINE

DAY 11

For additional grammar support, see Section 25.4, p. 575.

Editing

- What Do You Notice?/ Grammar Mini-Lesson **Rubric for Research Writing**

Publishing

- Publish Your Piece
- Reflect on Your Writing

ONLINE

DAY 12

21st Century Learning

MAKE YOUR WRITING COUNT

- **Get Your Message Out in a Magazine or eZine**
- Here's Your Action Plan
- Listening and Speaking

ONLINE

Alternate Pacing Suggestions

- **Block Scheduling** Each day on the Lesson Planner represents a 40–50 minute block. Teachers using block scheduling may combine days to revise pacing to meet their classroom needs.

- **Accelerated Lesson Planning** Combine days by focusing on core stages of the writing process: choosing a topic (Days 3–4), outline for success (Days 7–8), and RADaR revision (Days 9–10).

- **Integrated Language Arts Curriculum** For targeted instruction that covers the essential components of the lesson use either a 3- or a 5-day plan.

  3 day plan
  DAY 1: Introduction to the Genre, Student Model
  DAY 2: Prewriting/Drafting
  DAY 3: Revising/Editing/ Publishing

  5 day plan
  Use 3-day plan, and add:
  DAY 4: Make Your Writing Count
  DAY 5: Writing for Assessment

Links to Prentice Hall *LITERATURE*

Expand and deepen students' knowledge of research sources using the Informational Texts features, which include excerpts from an atlas, a Web site, an online almanac, and other research sources.

Differentiated Instruction

Differentiated Instruction Boxes in this Teacher's Edition address these student populations:

- Below-Level Students
- Above-Level Students
- Gifted and Talented Students
- Special Needs Students
- English Language Learners
- Spanish Speaking Students

In addition, for further enrichment, see the **Extension** features.

LESSON OBJECTIVES

- To learn the forms and defining characteristics of research writing.
- To learn the elements of a successful informational research report, the chapter Feature Assignment.
- To read a Student Model of an informational research report, analyzing it from the perspective of a reader and from the perspective of a writer.
- To apply prewriting strategies in developing an informational research report, including strategies for choosing a topic, formulating a research question, planning research, gathering details, and documenting sources, as well as tips for considering audience and purpose.
- To apply drafting strategies in developing an informational research report.
- To apply RADaR revision strategies to a draft informational research report.
- To learn about the Focus on Craft topic, sentence variety, and apply what is learned to a draft informational research report.
- To edit the draft, focusing on integrating and punctuating quotations.
- To complete the Make Your Writing Count assignment, developing and presenting a magazine or eZine.
- To complete the Writing for Media assignment, developing an I-search report.
- To practice writing for assessment.

DAYS 5–6

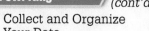 **Prewriting** *(cont'd)* **ONLINE**

- Collect and Organize Your Data
- Avoid Plagiarism
- Document Your Sources

DAYS 7–8

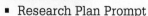 **Drafting** **ONLINE**

- Outline for Success
- Provide and Document Evidence
- Use Graphics and Illustrations

DAYS 13–14

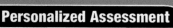 **WRITING FOR MEDIA** **ONLINE**

- I-Search Report
- Create an I-Search Report

DAY 15

WRITING FOR ASSESSMENT **ONLINE**

- Research Plan Prompt
- The ABCDs of On-Demand Writing
- More Prompts for Practice
  Test Prep Spiral Review: Narrative
- Spiral Review: Response to Literature

Personalized Assessment

	Ongoing Assessment	Formal Assessment of Feature Assignment	Progress Monitoring at End-of-Chapter
Interactive Writing Coach™	Use Paragraph Feedback and Essay Scorer as a revision tool.	Use Essay Scorer to score students' Feature Assignment papers.	Use Essay Scorer to score students' papers. Students' learner profiles can be adjusted based on their scores.
FEEDBACK Teacher Conferencing	Use rubrics in the Student Edition as a revision tool. Conference with students to review their work and provide personalized support.	Use rubrics in the Student Edition to score students' Feature Assignment papers.	Review each student's work to plan targeted resources for the next writing assignment.

The Digital • Print Path ▶

WRITING COACH Online   STUDENT BOOK

1 WRITING COACH Online   STUDENT BOOK ▶

Using *Writing Coach Online*™ or the student book, students discuss the photograph in the chapter opener as it relates to the writing genre.

2 Writing Journal ▶

Students record their ideas and responses in their online journals or notebooks. They may also record and save their responses on pop-up sticky notes in *Writing Coach Online*™.

Chapter Objectives

1. Write an informational research report by planning, drafting, revising, editing, and publishing individual work.

2. Produce a magazine.

3. Use the five-step writing process to write an I-search report.

4. Write a research plan, research plan critique, personal narrative, and response to literature in response to prompts.

RESEARCH WRITING

What Do You Want to Know?

Activate Prior Knowledge Tell students that the purpose of a research report is to gather, organize, and present information about a specific topic. Explain to students that they will use what they know about jellyfish to analyze the photo on page 222. Then, guide students in analyzing the photo.

 Think Aloud When **I look** at the photo, first I think about what I already know about jellyfish. They live in the ocean. They can sting you if you touch them. Then I think about what I would like to know about jellyfish. Why are they called jellyfish? What do they eat, and how? I can find the answers to these questions by looking up information about this animal.

Work with students to list in two columns on the board things they already know about jellyfish and other aquatic creatures and things they would like to know.

Try It! **Have students** work individually to develop responses to the questions. Check that students have listed several things they want to know about jellyfish.

Possible responses: I want to know, among other things, whether jellyfish live in all oceans, what their bodies are made of, and what enemies they have. I can look in books in the library to find information about jellyfish.

CHAPTER 11

RESEARCH WRITING

222   Research Writing

Connect to the Big Questions

Have students use their experience to discuss the Big Questions. Explain that they will revisit **Why write?** at the end of this chapter. Tell students to consider these points during their discussion:

1. Information can include text, images, art works and other forms of communication and expression.

2. Have students discuss what they know, what they don't know, and how they could

find more information about a topic familiar to them, such as a favorite sport or hobby.

What's Ahead

Have students preview the Student Model on pages 226–229. Tell students that they will write their own research report using the five-step writing process: prewriting, drafting, revising, editing, and publishing.

What Do You Want To Know?

How do people find out more information about interesting topics? They do research. Research writing is a way to gather, organize, and present information in a report that others can read.

One of the first steps of research is to identify a topic that interests you and then develop research questions. For example, if you want to find out more about jellyfish, like the kind shown in the photograph, you would first decide what you want to know about them.

Try It! Take a few minutes to brainstorm for some things you want to know about jellyfish. Write them in a list.

Consider these questions as you participate in an extended discussion with a partner. Take turns expressing your ideas.

- What do you want to know about where jellyfish live?
- What do you want to know about their bodies?
- What do you want to know about how jellyfish survive?
- Where could you find information about jellyfish?

Review your list of questions with your partner. Compare your lists to determine if any ideas overlap or how you might build off each other's ideas. Then, discuss where you would go to research answers to your questions.

What's Ahead

In this chapter, you will review a strong example of an informational research report. Then, using the examples as guidance, you will develop a research plan and write your own informational research report.

WRITING COACH
Online
www.phwritingcoach.com

Online Journal
Try It! Record your answers and ideas in the online journal.

You can also record and save your answers and ideas on pop-up sticky notes in the eText.

Connect to the Big Questions

Discuss these questions with your partner:

1 What do you think? What is the best way to find important information about a topic?

2 Why write? Do you understand a subject well enough to write about it? How will you find out what the facts are?

223

Personalized Support

FEEDBACK
Teacher or Peer Feedback

To encourage students in their discussion of the photograph as it relates to the writing genre, ask the following questions:

- What is the first thing you think of when you look at this photo?
- How does it relate to your life?
- How does it relate to things you've learned in other subjects?
- What questions come to mind when you look at this photograph?
- How does your response to the photograph compare to those of your classmates?

Working with ELLs   ELL Sheltered Instruction: Cognitive

Support students in learning new expressions heard during classroom instruction and interactions. Use idiomatic expressions as you discuss the picture on page 222, such as *caught my eye, can't make heads or tails out of it, out of this world,* and *got a kick out of it*. Then:

Beginning Model *caught my eye* in a sentence, gesturing for support and providing an explanation. Have students use the expression by completing the sentence frame *That _____ caught my eye.*

Intermediate Repeat the expressions, explain them, and model using them in sentences. Have partners make **Concept**

Illustrations, drawing a picture illustrating the idiomatic meaning of one expression and then demonstrate their understanding by using it in a sentence. Have pairs share their work.

Advanced Repeat the expressions. Have partners look up their meanings in an idiom dictionary. Have pairs demonstrate that they have learned the expressions by using each in a sentence. Have pairs share their sentences.

Advanced High Have students complete the Advanced activity then rewrite each sentence, substituting other words for the idioms.

The Digital · Print Path ▶

1 STUDENT BOOK ▶

Students learn vocabulary from the Word Bank and listen to English and Spanish pronunciations in the Writing Coach Online™ glossary.

2  Writing Journal ▶

Students record answers to questions about forms of writing in their online journals or notebooks.

RESEARCH WRITING

To introduce this chapter's writing form, discuss the opening paragraphs with students. Make sure students understand that an informational research report is a type of research writing. Explain that good writers use a step-by-step process to develop their work. Then, have students preview the rubric on page 247.

Research Writing: Informational Research Report

Ask volunteers to read aloud the feature assignment characteristics. Tell students that they will identify these characteristics in a Student Model. Then, they will use the characteristics to guide the writing of their own informational research report.

Other Forms of Research Writing

Guide students to understand how the forms of research writing are alike and different.

Say: I notice that all the forms of research writing involve gathering and using information about real people, places, events, or things. This means they are all forms of nonfiction writing.

Ask: How are biographical profiles, health reports, historical reports, and scientific reports alike? (They all provide information.) How are they different? (They focus on different subject areas.)

Have students discuss other similarities and differences among research writing forms.

Try It! Remind students that the audience is the people who will read their writing. The purpose is the author's reason for writing. Have students record their responses in their journal.

Possible responses: Topic: local political leader; Question: How has our mayor improved our community? Topic: the effects of various fertilizers on plant growth; Question: Which fertilizer helps plants grow the most? Topic: the

Civil War years; Question: How did the Civil War affect our state?

Word Bank

To assist English Language Learners and struggling readers, echo read each word or have students log on to Writing Coach Online to listen to the pronunciations. Then, have partners take turns using each word in a sentence. Ask volunteers to share one of their sentences with the class.

RESEARCH WRITING

Research writing is a way to gather information, and then synthesize, or combine, that information into a report for others to read. In this chapter, you will write an informational research report. Your report will provide information about a topic that interests you. Before you write, you will search for information about your topic in different kinds of sources. You will decide which facts and details to use in your report, and organize your ideas clearly for your audience.

You will develop your informational research report by taking it through each of the steps of the writing process: prewriting, drafting, revising, editing, and publishing. You will also have an opportunity to use your informational research report in an oral or multimedia presentation that uses text and graphics to share what you have learned. To preview the criteria for how your research report will be evaluated, see the rubric on page 247.

FEATURE ASSIGNMENT

Research Writing: Informational Research Report

An effective informational research report has these characteristics:

- A specific **topic sentence** or thesis statement that identifies a major research topic

- Information from a variety of **reliable, accurate, and relevant sources** to support the main ideas

- Information that is compiled from **multiple sources** and that is **accurate, relevant, valid, and current**

- **Evidence,** including facts, details, examples, quotations, and explanations, that supports conclusions

- Clear presentation that **summarizes findings**

- A **bibliography with citations** to credit others for their work according to a standard format

- **Effective sentence structure** and correct spelling, grammar, and usage

224   **Research Writing**

Teacher Tip

Have students extend their understanding by relating each form of research writing to the medium in which that form might appear. For example, biographical profiles might appear in newspapers or magazines or on news or entertainment television shows.

Other Forms of Research Writing

In addition to an informational research report, there are other forms of research writing, including:

Biographical profiles give specific details about the life and work of a real person. The person may be living or dead, someone famous, or someone familiar to the writer.

Documentaries are filmed reports that focus on a specific topic. These multimedia presentations use spoken and written text as well as photographs, videos, music, and other sound effects.

Health reports present the latest information, data, and research about a specific disease or health-related issues.

Historical reports give in-depth information about a past event. These kinds of reports focus on a narrow topic and may discuss causes and effects.

I-Search reports blend informational and personal writing. In an I-search report, you tell the story of your research and investigations, including the dead-ends and small victories, in addition to presenting the results of your research.

Scientific reports analyze information and data concerning a scientific issue or problem. A **lab report** describes a scientific experiment, including observations and conclusions.

 Try It! For each research report described, brainstorm for possible topics with other students. Then, consult with one another to choose a major research topic for each report and write a research question for each topic. As you write, keep your audience and purpose in mind.

- A biographical profile of an important member of your community
- A lab report about the results of a scientific experiment
- A historical report about an event in the history of your state

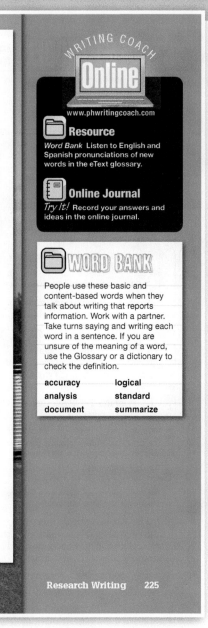

WRITING COACH

Online

www.phwritingcoach.com

Resource
Word Bank Listen to English and Spanish pronunciations of new words in the eText glossary.

Online Journal
Try It! Record your answers and ideas in the online journal.

WORD BANK

People use these basic and content-based words when they talk about writing that reports information. Work with a partner. Take turns saying and writing each word in a sentence. If you are unsure of the meaning of a word, use the Glossary or a dictionary to check the definition.

accuracy	logical
analysis	standard
document	summarize

Personalized Support

 Teacher or Peer Feedback

To help students understand the characteristics of the writing form, ask or have student partners ask one another the following questions:

- What are the main characteristics of an informational research report?
- What makes this form of writing different from other forms?
- Who are the likely readers or audiences for this form of writing?
- What kind of organization could be used for this form of writing?
- What kind of voice would be most effective for this form of writing?

Working with ELLs   **ELL** Sheltered Instruction: Cognitive

To help students with the *Try It!*, work with them to expand and internalize initial English vocabulary. Help them learn, use, and reuse basic, high-frequency words in speaking to identify and describe people related to the research report topics.

Beginning Use a word web to identify and describe people in the community. Model statements using high-frequency words from the web like *teacher, doctor, mayor, help, lead,* and *build.* Use illustrations for support. Have students repeat your statements and reuse the words orally in sentence frames.

Intermediate List the Beginning activity high-frequency words and review their

meanings. Have students use and reuse the words when responding to questions, such as *What does a mayor do?*

Advanced Provide high-frequency words related to people in the community, such as *person, building, job,* and *leader.* Have partners use and reuse the words in spoken sentences about people in the community.

Advanced High Provide the Advanced activity words. Have students use and reuse the words in a group discussion identifying and describing people in the community.

The Digital • Print Path ▶

STUDENT BOOK

1  **STUDENT BOOK** ▶

Using **Writing Coach Online™** or the student book, students read and listen to an audio recording of the Student Model. As they complete their writing assignments, they can refer back to the Student Model for support whenever they need it.

STUDENT MODEL

Tell students that good writers react to what they read in ways that show their understanding of the text. Explain that students will react to the Student Model by using two sets of symbols in the text and responding to questions about what they have read. Then, distribute printed copies of the Student Model or have students log on to Writing Coach Online.

Use a Reader's Eye

Read aloud the instructions for using the Reader's Response Symbols and the meaning of each symbol. Then, have students read and respond to the Student Model, using each Reader's Response Symbol at least once.

Learn From Experience

Point out that the numbered notes refer to the characteristics of an informational research report introduced on page 224.

Try It! Guide students to understand how the genre characteristics shape the text.

Say: The first *Try It!* question asks about the major research topic of the report, or what the report is about. I see that the writer states his major research topic in the topic sentence, in lines 6–8: The report is about how understanding certain science basics can help those who climb Mount Everest stay safe.

Ask: What open-ended questions might the writer have asked about the research topic as he wrote his report? (Responses will vary.)

Have students respond to the *Try It!* questions in their journals. Then, check the accuracy and completeness of their responses.

3. Responses will vary. Possible open-ended questions include: What dangers do climbers face? What kinds of equipment can help climbers? Does proper training play a role? If so, how?

5. Responses will vary but should indicate that using a variety of sources strengthens the writer's ideas and arguments.

6. Sentences 2, 3, 4, 5, and 6 contain facts. Sentence 1 includes an opinion.

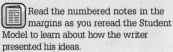

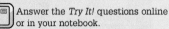

STUDENT MODEL | Informational Research Report

Use a Reader's Eye

Read the Student Model on pages 226–229. Then, use the symbols to react to what you've read.

Reader's Response Symbols

√ **OK. I understand this. It's very clearly explained.**

? **I don't follow what the writer is saying here.**

+ **I think the writer needs more details here.**

− **This information doesn't seem relevant.**

! **Wow! That is cool/weird/interesting.**

Learn From Experience

Read the numbered notes in the margins as you reread the Student Model to learn about how the writer presented his ideas.

Answer the *Try It!* questions online or in your notebook.

---

❶ The writer uses **proper formatting** for heads and pagination according to a style manual.

❷ The **topic sentence** identifies the major research topic and gives the main ideas.

❸ The writer uses a **quotation** from an expert as **evidence** to explain an important idea.

Try It! What is the major research topic of the report? What open-ended questions might this writer have asked about this topic as he was creating his report?

226   **Research Writing**

---

❶ Butler 1

❶ John Butler
Mrs. Harker
English 101
21 December 2009

❶ Big Mountain, Big Challenge

When you reach the summit of Mount Everest, you stand on top of the world. At 29,035 feet tall, the mountain is the highest point on earth ("Everest, Mount"). Everest has fascinated many climbers. Between 2000 and 2006, 4,886 people attempted
5 the climb, and 38 climbers died ("Everest Expedition"). ❷ While climbing Mount Everest can be dangerous, an understanding of science basics such as altitude, air pressure, and simple machines can help climbers stay safe.

Everest is at a very high altitude. The word *altitude*
10 means how far above sea level something is. The higher up you go, the less oxygen there is (Platt 12). Because people need oxygen to breathe, they may get altitude sickness as they climb to higher altitudes. ❸ "Because of the lack of oxygen," explains British mountaineer Graham Ratcliffe,
15 "you get nausea and bad headaches and suffer from loss of appetite" ("Double Feat"). These are the most common symptoms of altitude sickness.

To lessen altitude sickness, climbers go up the mountain in stages (see figure 1) ("Everest, Mount"). Climbers spend
20 about a month adjusting to higher altitudes before trying to reach the top. But it is impossible to avoid altitude sickness completely. At 25,000 feet begins the "death zone." Here, the level of oxygen in the air drops sharply. To make it through the death zone to the summit, almost all climbers
25 carry containers of oxygen to help them breathe (Leahy).

Climbers spend about four weeks acclimatizing, or getting used to the altitude, before trying to reach the top. At first, they stay in Base Camp. Then, they carry supplies to Camp I

Teacher Tip

Discuss with students the ways in which graphics such as photos, maps, charts, diagrams, and timelines can help readers when they read research writing. Then, ask students to explain how the graphic on page 227 helped them when they read the Student Model.

2 Students record their answers to questions about the Student Model in their online journals or notebooks.

3 First, students respond to the Student Model as a reader, using symbols to mark the text. They can mark the text using pop-up sticky notes in **Writing Coach Online™** or they can mark a printed copy of the Student Model.

4 Then, students respond to the Student Model as a writer, using different symbols to mark the text. They can use either **Writing Coach Online™** or a printed copy of the Student Model.

Student Model *Informational Research Report* **Student Model**

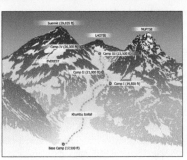

Butler 2

4 Figure 1. Southern Climbing Route; based on information from Jean Ricard, "About Everest," *Everest for Kids,* (Everest for Kids: 2007). Web. 15 Dec. 2009.

and return to Base Camp to sleep, then climb to Camp II and
30 return to Base Camp, and so on ("Everest, Mount").

5 One symptom of severe altitude sickness is confused thinking (Platt 12). Climbers may hallucinate—see or feel things that are not really there. Frozen climbers have been found on Everest without their coats or gloves. They removed
35 their protective clothing after hallucinating that they were in a warm place (Viesturs). Climbers know that if they become too sick, they must descend to a lower altitude where there is more oxygen ("Everest, Mount").

Another danger of climbing Everest is the evil weather,
40 which includes storms and high winds. **6** Storms are caused by changes in air pressure. Air moves to an area of lower pressure near Earth's surface, and the air rises and cools. If there is enough moisture in the air, snow can fall (Williams, "What's Happening"). Differences in air pressure also cause
45 wind. Air flows from an area of high pressure to an area of low pressure (Williams, "Pressure Differences").

Forecasting storms and winds on Everest is difficult. The mountain's vast size affects different weather patterns. Therefore, precautions must be taken. First, climbers schedule
50 climbs in the spring and fall, when the weather is best (Platt 17). They also receive frequent weather forecasts. Forecasters take information on air pressure and other conditions from satellites and computer models. They

WRITING COACH

Online

www.phwritingcoach.com

Interactive Model

Listen to an audio recording of the Student Model in the eText. You can refer back to the Student Model whenever you need support in developing your own writing.

Online Journal

Try It! Record your answers and ideas in the online journal.

4 This **graphic** is relevant to the written explanation of how climbers lessen altitude sickness.

5 The writer compiles relevant information from **multiple sources** to support the main ideas.

Try It! How does using information from a variety of sources make research writing stronger?

6 Facts are pieces of information that can be proven. Facts like this one are an important type of **evidence** in a research report.

Try It! Which sentence(s) in this paragraph contain facts? Which include a statement or opinion that cannot be proven true?

Student Model 227

Personalized Support

FEEDBACK ### Teacher or Peer Feedback

To provide feedback to students on their responses to the Student Model and their answers to the *Try It!* questions, ask or have student partners ask one another the following:

- What is the thesis or controlling idea of the Student Model?
- How does the Student Model illustrate the characteristics of a research report?
- Which characteristics of the Student Model could you use in your own writing?
- How did you answer this *Try It!* question? How could you use your answer to help you plan your piece of writing?

Working with ELLs   **ELL** Sheltered Instruction: Cognitive

Help students learn basic vocabulary heard during classroom instruction and interactions. Prepare an oral presentation based on the Student Model basic vocabulary words: *climbed, mountain, cold, clothes, learn,* and *explain*. Help students use their prior experiences with high places such as hills and mountains to understand the words' meanings in English.

Beginning Review the words, using images and gestures for support and eliciting students' related prior experiences. Have students complete sentences containing basic vocabulary, like *A ___ is tall and rocky.* Allow them to draw or gesture as needed.

Intermediate Have students respond to questions containing basic vocabulary, like *What did you learn about the mountain?* using prior experiences to understand meanings.

Advanced Provide the words and have students use the **KIM Strategy,** writing the word, information about it, and a memory clue. Have students use the words in sentences, drawing on prior experiences.

Advanced High Have students use each word in a paragraph, drawing on prior experiences. Have partners share their work.

The Digital · Print Path ▶

1  Using Writing Coach Online™ or the student book, students read and listen to an audio recording of the Student Model. As they complete their writing assignments, they can refer back to the Student Model for support whenever they need it.

2 Students record their answers to questions about the Student Model in their online journals or notebooks.

Learn From Experience (continued)

Check the accuracy and completeness of student responses to the *Try It!* questions.

7. **Possible response:** Yes, the quote contains many first-hand details that support the idea that the weather on Everest can change without warning.

8. Figure references include captions that help identify the ideas, people, or objects being pictured, as well as the image's source.

9. Responses will vary but should indicate that the data from valid, reliable sources can be trusted while weak sources may have inaccurate, outdated data.

10. The information is from the writer's own ideas; it does not have a citation and states an opinion about the motivations of people who climb Everest.

11. Alphabetization helps readers find references more easily.

Extension Ask volunteers to share their synopses with the class and explain their source's main idea and most important details.

Use a Writer's Eye

Read aloud the instructions for using the Writer's Response Symbols and the meaning of each symbol. Then, guide students through their use.

 Think Aloud The writer says that understanding simple machines can help climbers. I **found** supporting evidence for this idea on page 228, lines 78–82. The writer explains how an ice axe is a simple machine and how it can help climbers stay safe. I'll write S.E. next to those lines for supporting evidence.

Work with students to find places in the text where the writer uses strong evidence to support his ideas.

Have students read and respond to the Student Model, using each Writer's Response Symbol at least once.

STUDENT MODEL | Informational Research Report *(continued)*

Butler 2

7 A long **quotation** of 4 lines or more is set off from the rest of the text, indented without quotation marks.

> *Try It!* Is this quotation a strong piece of supporting evidence? Why or why not?

8 This **photo** helps the reader picture the tool discussed in the text.

> *Try It!* How does the figure reference to a graphic help you locate information you need?

9 Throughout the report, the writer cites, or gives credit to, the source of his data.

> *Try It!* Why is it important to use and cite a valid and reliable source? What are the dangers of using weak sources?

10 The report ends with a conclusion and a final thought on the topic.

> *Try It!* Is this information from research or the writer's own ideas? How do you know?

11 The Works Cited list provides proper **documentation** by listing publication information for each source. The **formatting** of the list follows an appropriate style.

> *Try It!* Study the Works Cited list. Why is it helpful to readers to list sources in alphabetical order?

Extension Locate one of the sources from the Works Cited page, and write a brief synopsis of it in your own words.

228 Research Writing

---

combine this data with their experience from years of watching the weather on the mountain.

But no forecaster can be one hundred percent right. The weather can change quickly. For example, the morning of May 10, 1996, was clear. A large number of Everest climbers decided to try for the top. Famous American climber Ed Viesturs was on the mountain. He described what he could and could not see of the summit from his location:

7 That day dawned perfect, so there was no reason for them not to go. We had a telescope in camp with us to monitor the climbers' progress…. Then, the big storm rolled in. The summit disappeared, the clouds lowered swallowing up more and more of the upper mountain until finally our visibility was cut off…. It wasn't until 10 p.m. that we got any news. Paula radioed up to us and said, "Only half the people who left the South Col this morning have made it back." … By May 12 five climbers from the two teams were dead.

To cope with conditions on the mountain, climbers need the right equipment. Simple machines are the basis of some important climbing tools. One example is the ice axe (see figure 2). The slopes of Everest are covered in glaciers. A glacier is a mass of ice that exists year-round. The ice axe has a pick on one end. A pick is a kind of wedge. When the climber swings the axe, the inclined planes of the pick split the ice, driving the point deep inside (Tomecek). Climbers use the pick to stop themselves if they begin to fall down the glacier (Platt 39).

8 Figure 2. Ice axe is a wedge. Courtesy of Jupiter Images.

9 Over time, glaciers move. Cracks form in the ice. Deep cracks are called crevasses (Platt 11). Crevasses are very dangerous for climbers. Another simple machine called a pulley can help if a person falls into a crevasse. Other climbers can use a pulley system to get the stranded person out. Pulley

3  ▶

First, students respond to the Student Model as a reader, using symbols to mark the text. They can mark the text using pop-up sticky notes in *Writing Coach Online™* or they can mark a printed copy of the Student Model.

4  ▶

Then, students respond to the Student Model as a writer, using different symbols to mark the text. They can use either *Writing Coach Online™* or a printed copy of the Student Model.

dent Model *Informational Research Report* Student Model

Butler 4

multiply the force applied to a rope ("How Pulleys Work"). The climbers attach a rope to the stranded person. With the advantage provided by the pulleys, the other climbers—who may be weak and tired themselves—can lift the stranded person to safety (Tyson and Clelland 130).

In 1923, British climber George Mallory was asked why he wanted to climb Everest. Mallory said, "Because it's there" (Golden 72). Mallory died on the mountain. No one knows if he reached the summit (Platt 19). The conditions on Everest mean that climbing this mountain will never be completely free of danger. However, increased understanding of altitude, air pressure, and simple machines makes climbing Everest safer today than it was in Mallory's time. ⑩ Perhaps only one thing is certain: As long as there are those who, like Mallory, want to test their limits, people will climb Everest.

⑪ Works Cited

"Double Feat Proved the Peak of Achievement." *Evening Chronicle*, [Newcastle, UK], 21 May 2003, ed. 1, sec. 01A: 28. Print.

"Everest Expedition Statistics 2000–2006." *AdventureStats.com*. ExplorersWeb, n.d. Web. 17 Dec. 2009.

"Everest, Mount." *Encyclopaedia Britannica Online Library Edition*. Encyclopaedia Britannica, 2009. Web. 17 Dec. 2009.

Golden, Frederic. "Who Got There First?" *Time* 17 May 1999: 72+. Print.

"How Pulleys Work." *NASA's Our World*. NASA, n.d. Web. 19 Dec. 2009.

Leahy, Michael. "The Dark Side of the Mountain." *Washington Post* 28 Nov. 2004, final ed.: W12. Print.

Platt, Richard. *Everest: Reaching the World's Highest Peak*. New York: Dorling Kindersley, 2000. Print.

Tomecek, Steve. "Simple Machines: The Wedge." *Dirtmeisters's Science Reporters*. Scholastic, n.d. Web. 19 Dec. 2009.

Tyson, Andy and Mike Clelland. *Glacier Mountaineering: An Illustrated Guide to Glacier Travel and Crevasse Rescue*. Helena, Montana: Falcon, 2009. Print.

Viesturs, Ed. "Ed Viesturs on 1996: Turn Around, Guys!" *National Geographic Online*. National Geographic, n.d. Web. 17 Dec. 2009.

Williams, Jack. "Pressure Differences Get the Wind Going." *USATODAY.com*. USA Today. 20 May 2005. Web. 15 Dec. 2009.

—. "What's Happening Inside Highs and Lows." *USATODAY.com*. USA Today, n.d. Web. 15 Dec. 2009.

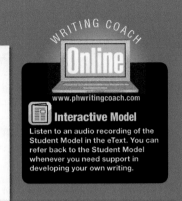

WRITING COACH

Online

www.phwritingcoach.com

Interactive Model

Listen to an audio recording of the Student Model in the eText. You can refer back to the Student Model whenever you need support in developing your own writing.

 Use a Writer's Eye

Now go back to the beginning of the Student Model and evaluate the piece as a writer. On your copy of the Student Model, use the Writer's Response Symbols to react to what you read. Identify places where the student writer uses characteristics of an effective informational research report.

Writer's Response Symbols

T.S.	Clear topic sentence
S.E.	Supporting evidence
R.G.	Relevant graphic
D.S.	Proper documentation of sources

Student Model **229**

Personalized Support

 FEEDBACK **Teacher or Peer Feedback**

To provide feedback to students on their responses to the Student Model, ask or have student partners ask one another the following:

- Where did the writer get the information used in the report?
- What kinds of facts and evidence does the writer use to support the research topic?
- Where would you look for information to answer your research question?
- How would you organize your information?

Working with ELLs **ELL** Sheltered Instruction: Metacognitive

Have students demonstrate listening comprehension of increasingly complex spoken English by responding to oral questions and requests. Remind them to monitor their comprehension and seek clarification as necessary. Read aloud lines 72–94 of the Student Model. Then:

Beginning Reread the paragraph aloud, gesturing for support. Have students monitor comprehension and seek clarification by raising their hands. Help them respond to oral questions, like *What tools do climbers use?*

Intermediate Give students a web graphic organizer, and reread the selection aloud. To

monitor comprehension, have them fill in the organizer as you read, seeking clarification as needed. Have them respond to oral questions, like *What tools help climbers? How?*

Advanced Have students take notes to monitor comprehension as your read, seeking clarification of unfamiliar ideas. Ask questions like *What information does this paragraph give?* Have partners share their response.

Advanced High Have individuals complete the Advanced activity and share their work with a partner. Have pairs ask and answer questions about their descriptions.

The Digital • Print Path ▶

1  Students select or are assigned a topic for their research report from the Topic Bank, or they may choose a topic of their own.

2 Students complete online or printed graphic organizers to formulate a research question.

Prewriting

Explain that the first task students need to complete as they plan their research report is to determine an appropriate topic.

Choose From the Topic Bank

Read aloud each topic and then ask volunteers to describe it in their own words. If you are assigning topics to students, you may wish to do so now. Encourage students to ask questions about their topic.

Choose Your Own Topic

Introduce and discuss the Brainstorm and Browse strategies. If students were not assigned writing topics, have them use the strategies to brainstorm for topics for their reports.

Extension Have each student choose one of the strategies. Then, have students write an action plan that outlines the resources and steps they will use to develop their topic.

Formulate Your Research Question

Tell students that they will use a Formulate a Research Question graphic organizer to develop their research question. Then, distribute printed copies or have students log on to Writing Coach Online.

Apply It! Guide students through the instructions for completing the graphic organizer. Have students complete the exercise based on their topic.

Consider Your Audience and Purpose

Guide students to consider the audience and purpose for their research report.

Say: The first question in the right column asks about my purpose, or reason, for writing this report. Since it is an informational research report, my main purpose is to inform my audience. But if **I choose** a topic such as the first one in the Topic Bank, ways people can conserve energy, then my purpose might also be to persuade people to use my ideas.

Ask: Based on your topic, what is the main purpose for your report? Is there another purpose? If so, what is it? (**Responses will vary.**)

Have students with similar research questions work in small groups to discuss and respond to the remaining questions.

Your Turn ▶ **Feature Assignment: Informational Research Report**

Prewriting

Begin to plan a first draft by **choosing an appropriate topic**. You can select from the Topic Bank or come up with an idea of your own.

 Choose From the Topic Bank

TOPIC BANK

Conservation Counts Research ways that you can help conserve energy at home and reasons why your efforts matter. How do small steps add up to big savings?

How Did It Happen? What causes a natural disaster such as an earthquake, tsunami, or cyclone? Research the science behind one of these events: the 2004 Sri Lankan tsunami, the Great Tangshan Earthquake of 1976, or the 1970 Bhola cyclone in Bangladesh. Also, find out how the disaster affected safety measures and ways people prepare for emergencies in the country where it took place.

Special Delivery—Music Technology has changed the music industry in the past 20 years. What changes have occurred in the ways in which music is delivered? How has listening to music changed? Which technologies have had the greatest impact on the industry?

Choose Your Own Topic

Determine a topic of your own by using these strategies.

Brainstorm and Browse

- **Consult** with a partner to **brainstorm** for a list of topics.
- **Formulate open-ended questions** about your topics. Circle key words in your questions. Use your key words to browse your library's research resources.
- Search the Internet, using the same key words. Work with your partner to decide which topic provides results that interest you.
- Review your work and choose a topic.

230   **Research Writing**

Coach's Corner

You may wish to model prewriting activities for students by brainstorming for your own research question. Use these prompts to model your thought process:

- **I am interested in** earthquakes, so that could be my general topic.
- **I can narrow my topic by** focusing on the largest, most destructive, or most recent earthquake and reasons it happened.

Discuss the choices you make and solicit feedback from students.

3 · **Writing Journal** ▶

Students record their answers to questions about audience and purpose in their online journals or notebooks.

Formulate Your Research Question

A topic that is too broad is almost impossible to research well. It also makes writing a report more difficult. Plan to do some research to help narrow your topic and then formulate your research question.

Apply It! Use a printed or online graphic organizer like the one shown to narrow your topic.

- Write your general topic in the top box, and keep narrowing your topic by **refining** your **research questions**. You may need to develop a secondary set of questions to guide you as you move down the chart.

- Your last box should hold your narrowest or most refined research question. This will be the focus of your report.

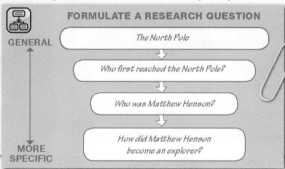

FORMULATE A RESEARCH QUESTION

GENERAL

The North Pole

Who first reached the North Pole?

Who was Matthew Henson?

How did Matthew Henson become an explorer?

MORE SPECIFIC

Consider Your Audience and Purpose

Before researching for your informational research report, think about your audience and purpose. Ask yourself these questions. Then, think about the kinds of information you'll look for in order to meet your audience's needs and your purpose.

Questions About Audience	Questions About Purpose
• Who is my audience: My teacher? My classmates? Someone else? • What does my audience need and want to know about my topic? • What vocabulary will I need to explain to my audience?	• Why am I writing the report: To inform? To make my audience want to learn more about the topic? Something else? • How do I want my audience to react as they read my report?

Record your answers in your writing journal.

Prewriting **231**

WRITING COACH

Online

www.phwritingcoach.com

Interactive Writing Coach™

- Choosing from the Topic Bank gives you access to the Interactive Writing Coach™.
- Submit your writing paragraph by paragraph and receive detailed feedback and guidance as you draft, revise, and edit your writing.

Interactive Graphic Organizers

Use the interactive graphic organizers to help you narrow your topic.

Online Journal

Record your answers and ideas in the online journal.

Personalized Support

Interactive Graphic Organizer

Below Level Students complete three graphic organizers that provide models and scaffolded support.

On Level Students complete one, two, or three graphic organizers depending on how much support they need.

Above Level Students complete the least scaffolded graphic organizer or narrow their topic without the help of a graphic organizer.

Differentiated Instruction

RTI Strategy for Below-Level Students
Help students better visualize the process of narrowing their topic by using circles of different sizes. Write the most general topic in the largest circle and ask students how they can make the topic "smaller." Write their idea in the next-largest circle and place it on top of the first circle. Continue in the same way until the topic is specific enough.

PRE-AP Enrichment for Above-Level Students Ask students to help classmates who are having difficulty narrowing the topic for their report. Have students plan a lesson for teaching the process that goes beyond the steps and graphic organizer in the Student Book. Remind them that graphic aids are an important part of any lesson. After students have prepared their lessons, have them present them to the class.

The Digital · Print Path ▶

1 Using Writing Coach Online™ or the student book, students use a variety of resources to make a research plan.

2 Students take notes, gather information, and record their ideas in their online journals or notebooks.

Make a Research Plan

Tell students that they will create a research plan for finding and evaluating the sources they need to create an effective informational research report. Explain to students that this is a large, long-term project, but they will have many opportunities to receive your direction, feedback, and other support.

Find Multiple Relevant Sources Introduce the four kinds of resources listed in the chart. Then, guide students to identify appropriate resources for their topics.

Say: I see that there are several kinds of resources I can use to research a topic. For example, if my topic is the formation of Mount Everest, I could use electronic or online resources such as the Web sites of a well-known science magazine or a public television documentary to find information on my topic.

Ask: What electronic or online resources could you use to research your topic? (**Responses will vary.**)

Have students work with a partner to discuss which types of resources will be most useful for their topics.

Evaluate Your Sources Have volunteers read aloud the Checklist for Evaluating Sources. Define unfamiliar or difficult words, or have students look them up in the Glossary. You may wish to refer back to works cited on page 229 to model using the checklist to evaluate the relevance and validity of sources.

Differentiate Between Types of Sources Introduce students to primary and secondary sources and discuss the strengths and weaknesses of each. For example, a primary source may be written by an eyewitness, but a secondary source may be written by an expert on the issue or event. Then, have students brainstorm for possible examples of each kind of source for their topics.

Apply It! Guide students through the instructions for creating a research plan and explain that you will provide support for each step. Encourage students to gather the notes and information they need to complete their research plan in a single place, such as a computer folder or a research portfolio.

Feature Assignment **Prewriting** *Feature Assignment* **Prewr**

Make a Research Plan

Once you have written your major research question, you are ready to make a research plan. As part of your plan, you will create a timeline for finishing your report. You will also find and evaluate sources of information.

Find Multiple Relevant Sources For your report, you will need to collect data, or gather information. You should **compile**, or gather, important information from a range of print and electronic resources, including expert interviews and multimedia resources. Follow these guidelines:

Print Resources
- Find print resources in libraries and bookstores.
- Use encyclopedias, magazines, newspapers, and textbooks.
- Search for print resources using electronic databases or with help from a reference librarian.

Electronic Resources
- Find electronic resources using search engines on the Internet.
- Choose only authoritative reliable sites, such as those ending in:
  .edu (educational institution)
  .gov (government group)
  .org (not-for-profit organization; these may be biased toward a specific purpose)
- If you are not sure that a site is reliable and unbiased, do not use it.

Interviews with Experts
- Ask questions of an expert on your topic.
- Set up a short in-person, e-mail, or telephone interview.
- Record the interview and take good notes.

Multimedia Resources
- Watch movies about your topic.
- Listen to podcasts or seminars related to the topic.
- Search for relevant photos, diagrams, charts, and graphs.

Evaluate Your Sources Do not assume that all sources of information on your topic are useful or trustworthy. Use the checklist to evaluate sources of information you find. The more questions that you can answer with a yes, the more likely you should use the source.

232 **Research Writing**

Change Your Plan If Necessary Tell students that a research plan outlines a process that may change over time. Remind them that their research question or sources may change as they discover more information about their topic, but their vigorous approach to gathering and evaluating their sources will not.

Teacher Tip

Quick Write Find the text of a brief speech to deliver to the class. After you have given the speech, have students write a summary of what they heard. Then, use the text of the speech and students' summaries to discuss the differences between primary and secondary sources and the validity of each.

3 STUDENT BOOK ▶

Students can refer back to the Student Model as they plan their writing.

e Assignment **Prewriting** Feature Assignment **Prewriting**

Checklist for Evaluating Sources

Does the source of information:

☐ Contain **relevant** information that answers your research question?

☐ Give facts and details at a level you can understand?

☐ Tell all sides of a story, including opposing viewpoints, so that it is **unbiased**?

☐ Provide **valid and reliable** information written or gathered by experts?

☐ Have a **recent** publication date, indicating that it provides current information?

Differentiate Between Types of Sources As you research, you will discover two kinds of sources: primary sources and secondary sources. Your teacher may require that you use both kinds.

▪ **A primary source** is an original document that provides direct, firsthand knowledge. Examples of primary sources include speeches such as Abraham Lincoln's *Gettysburg Address* and journals such as *The Diary of Anne Frank*.

▪ **A secondary source** is a source that gives indirect or secondhand understanding of a subject. For example, a book about the Gettysburg Address is a secondary source. In a secondary source, the writer may include his or her opinion about the subject.

Apply It! Generate a **research plan** and timeline for finishing your report, and list at least four print and electronic sources of information, including expert and multimedia resources, that you plan to use.

▪ Work with your teacher to determine the dates by which you need to finish your research, your drafting, and your final report.

▪ For each source you plan to use, give full publication information.

▪ Tell whether each source is primary or secondary.

▪ **Evaluate the relevance and reliability** of each source by using the Checklist for Evaluating Sources. For each source, explain why you answered yes or no.

Change Your Plan If Necessary After you begin to follow your research plan and collect data, you may find that you need to refine, or change, your research question. If you cannot find answers to a research question, you may decide to change the focus of your topic.

WRITING COACH
Online
www.phwritingcoach.com
📓 **Online Journal**
Record your answers and ideas in the online journal.

Prewriting   233

Personalized Support

FEEDBACK 👥 **Teacher or Peer Feedback**

To provide feedback to students as they make a research plan, ask or have student partners ask one another the following:

● What do you want your audience to know about your topic?

● Which resources are best for your topic and purpose?

● What sources have you found on your topic? Are they relevant?

● Will you use primary as well as secondary sources?

Working with ELLs **ELL** Sheltered Instruction: Cognitive

Have students use visual and contextual support as they read to enhance and confirm understanding and to develop background knowledge needed to comprehend increasingly challenging language. Use primary and secondary sources as visual and contextual support: *The Diary of Anne Frank*, a speech by Abraham Lincoln, and a book about Frank. Elicit and develop students' background knowledge of the sources as they read Differentiate Between Types of Sources.

Beginning Read the section, using the examples for support. Hold up a source.

Help students complete the sentence *This is a [primary/secondary] source.*

Intermediate Review the text with the sources. Have pairs complete frames, like *The speech is a _____ source because _____.*

Advanced Support with the example sources. Have pairs read the section and draw a **T-Chart** with *Primary* and *Secondary* columns. List various sources as students categorize them and explain.

Advanced High Have students complete the Advanced activity. Have them identify two sources of each type.

The Digital · Print Path ▶

1 Using *Writing Coach Online*™ or the student book, students learn to collect and organize data and the rules regarding plagiarism.

2 Students take notes, gather information, and record their ideas in their online journals or notebooks.

Feature Assignment **Prewriting** *Feature Assignment* **Prev**

Collect and Organize Your Data

Tell students that they will use a computer or handwritten notes to record information about their topic from multiple sources.

Keep Track of Multiple Sources Have students turn to page 229 and identify the range of sources in the Works Cited section of the Student Model. Tell students that they can learn more about proper citation styles on pages 236 and R16.

Take Notes Guide students through the bulleted instructions for taking notes. Explain that notes should include complete information but do not have to include complete sentences, unless the note is a direct quotation. Conclude by asking students to identify the heading and details on the example note.

Apply It! Have students begin collecting and organizing data for their research reports using proper source tracking and note-taking techniques.

Avoid Plagiarism

Read aloud the introductory paragraph, pointing out the definition of plagiarism. At this time, you may wish to explain to students the consequences of plagiarism in your class.

Careful Note-taking Matters Emphasize to students the importance of careful note-taking during the research process. Then, guide students to identify the plagiarized material in the example note.

Say: I notice that the Notes From Source 3 contain many of the same important phrases as the original source. For example, the phrases *new materials* and *safer and lighter* occur in both versions of the source material.

Ask: What other important phrases are repeated in the source material and the note?
("the modern ice axe," "the shape of the axe has changed")

Have students read and discuss the strategies for avoiding plagiarism in the chart. You may wish to present examples of each strategy to the class.

Collect and Organize Your Data

For your informational research report, you will need to use **multiple** sources of information. Notes will help you **record data** and see the **relationships between ideas.** Notes will also help you keep track of the sources of your information. There are different forms of notes from which you can choose. You can keep handwritten notes on note cards, or utilize available **technology** such as **word processors** to keep electronic notes on a computer.

Keep Track of Multiple Sources A good way to stay organized is to create a source card for each one of your sources. Give each source its own number. Then, note the full publishing information for the source, including the author, title, city of publication, publisher, and copyright date. Here is a source card that the writer of the Student Model made. Notice that he recorded the information in the same MLA style he used on his Works Cited page.

Take Notes When you take notes on a source, follow these guidelines.

- Note only facts and details you might use.
- Organize the notes using headings that sum up the main ideas of each group of notes.
- Be very careful to use your own words. You can also use abbreviations.
- If you want to quote someone, enclose the exact words in large quotation marks. They will remind you that these are someone else's words—not your own.

Apply It! Take written notes to record data that is relevant to your research question. As you work, effectively organize the information on note cards or on the computer.

- Group related information together and consider using software or graph paper to turn your notes into a chart, graph, or map. These techniques will help you see the **relationships** between ideas.
- Paraphrase or summarize the information in your own words. Convert data from charts, diagrams, or timelines into your own words. If you want to quote, carefully copy the original and enclose the quotation in quotation marks. **Identify each source** you use and record its bibliographic information according to a standard.

> **Source 1**
>
> Platt, Richard. *Everest: Reaching the World's Highest Peak.* New York: Dorling Kindersley, 2000. Print.

> **Notes From Source 1**
>
> *Diagram of human body: effects of altitude sickness p. 12*
> - *Shows all systems of body and how affected by altitude*
> - *Brain: Altitude makes person dizzy, trouble concentrating/thinking/ sleeping, can lead to person becoming unconscious*

234   **Research Writing**

Try It! Have students work with a partner to identify the plagiarized material and write an appropriate paraphrase.

Partner Talk

Remind students to be active listeners when discussing the note-taking process.

Writer's Block

> **IF** students have difficulty paraphrasing source material…

> **THEN** have partners practice orally paraphrasing passages from the Student Model. One student paraphrases a passage without looking at the text, while the other student checks the paraphrase against the original text. Have students discuss how the paraphrase is like and unlike the original passage.

3  Students begin writing their report online or in their notebooks.

4  Students submit their work paragraph by paragraph to the Interactive Writing Coach™ for scoring and feedback or share their work with their teacher.

5  Students receive personalized feedback from the Interactive Writing Coach™ or feedback from their teacher. Students may continue to work on their drafts.

ature Assignment Drafting *Feature Assignment* **Drafting**

Start Your Draft

e the checklist below to help complete your draft. Use the aphic organizer that shows your topic sentence; the outline that ows the order of your ideas and evidence, your graphics; and e Outline for Success as guides.

hile drafting, aim at writing your ideas, not on making your iting perfect. Remember, you will have the chance to improve ir draft when you revise and edit.

√ Start your **introduction** by drafting an attention-getting sentence.

√ End the introduction with a clearly worded **topic sentence** that is based on your research question. Your topic sentence, or thesis statement, should be the roadmap for your report.

√ Develop the **body** one paragraph at a time.

√ Start by drafting the first sentence of each paragraph. This sentence states the main idea.

√ Then, write the rest of the paragraph, using only the best **evidence**, including quotations, to support the main idea and your conclusions. **Compile** important supporting information from multiple sources.

√ Use an appropriate form of documentation, such as parenthetical references, to **acknowledge your sources** and give credit to others' ideas.

√ Draft a **conclusion** that **summarizes** your findings and adds a final thought.

WRITING COACH
Online
www.phwritingcoach.com

 Interactive Model
Outline for Success View pop-ups of Student Model selections referenced in the Outline for Success.

 Interactive Writing Coach™
Submit your draft one paragraph at a time and receive immediate, detailed feedback.

Drafting 239

Personalized Support

Interactive Writing Coach™

Students submit their research reports paragraph by paragraph for personalized feedback and scores.

Teacher or Peer Feedback

To provide feedback to students on their first draft, ask or have student partners ask one another the following:

- Can you explain how you organized your ideas in this piece?
- Why did you choose this introduction? Does it grab your reader and identify your thesis or controlling idea?
- What supporting evidence have you included?
- How does your conclusion add to your report?

Working with ELLs   ELL Sheltered Instruction: Cognitive

Have students develop and demonstrate an increasing ability to distinguish formal from informal English and knowledge of when to use each. Have them adapt spoken language appropriately for formal purposes. Present a variety of situations, like a friendly chat or a speech, and have all students determine if each situation calls for formal or informal language. Then:

Beginning Model an informal greeting: *Hey guys!* Have students repeat and identify it as ormal or informal, then orally adapt it for a ormal purpose: *Good afternoon, everyone!*

Intermediate Say formal and informal sentences. Have partners identify each as formal or informal and orally adapt informal language for a formal purpose.

Advanced Have partners read aloud written examples of formal and informal sentences. Listeners should identify each sentence as formal or informal and adapt informal sentences for a formal purpose.

Advanced High Have students complete the Advanced activity. Have students say their own formal and informal sentences.

The Digital · Print Path ▶

1  ▶

Using *Writing Coach Online*™ or the student book, students identify different forms of supporting evidence.

2 ▶

Students refer back to the Student Model for examples of supporting evidence.

Provide and Document Evidence

Tell students that the evidence they present can take several forms. Then, read and discuss how to use each form of evidence to support their claims, using Student Model examples to guide the discussion:

- **Facts and statistics** (lines 2–5, 31–36)
- **Examples** (lines 39–40, 57–58, 74–75)
- **Explanations** (lines 9–13, 76–78)
- **Quotations** (lines 13–16, 62–71)

Apply It! Read aloud the instructions. Then, have students draft a paragraph that shows an understanding of how to use and cite evidence to support a paragraph's main idea.

Use Graphics and Illustrations

Tell students that graphics help readers to understand or visualize complex information. Remind students that they must cite sources both for borrowed graphics and graphics they created from borrowed information.

Then, have students read and discuss the information about each type of graphic. Guide students to understand how the example table organizes information.

Say: I notice that the caption above the table and the title in the first row both tell what the table is about. Below the title, the table has two columns and eight rows. The headings *Equipment* and *Purpose* tell what information is in each column. Each row names a piece of equipment and tells how it is used.

Ask: What equipment helps prevent falls? (ice axe, ropes and pulleys)

Have students work with a partner to discuss where they would place the example table in the Student Model text on pages 226–229.

Try It! Have students respond to the prompt in their journals. Then, check that student responses show an understanding of how to interpret and evaluate a diagram.

Provide and Document Evidence

While you are drafting, you will compile **evidence** to support your conclusions about your topic. Your evidence may include facts, examples, explanations, and quotations. Evidence must come from multiple valid and reliable sources. **Document** other people's words and ideas when you provide evidence.

Give Facts and Statistics Facts are convincing because they can be proven true. Statistics, or facts stated in numbers, are also convincing when they come from reliable and current sources. Be sure to give the source of facts that are not common knowledge.

Give Examples Make complicated ideas clear by providing examples. You do not need to document examples from personal experience, but you do need to document examples from a particular source.

Give Explanations Complex ideas may require you to describe how they work. For example, you can help your reader understand a process, system, or technology by explaining it. Document any information that doesn't come from your knowledge or experience.

Use Quotations Direct quotations from experts are also convincing evidence. Make sure a quotation fits smoothly into your paragraph, and use your own words to identify the expert.

 **STUDENT MODEL** from **"Big Mountain, Big Challenge"** page 229; lines 95–96

In 1923, British climber George Mallory was asked why he wanted to climb Everest. Mallory said, "Because it's there" (Golden 72).

Remember to follow these guidelines:
- Do not quote if paraphrasing is just as clear.
- Separate and inset a quote of four lines or more.
- Identify who wrote the quote and why that person is an expert.
- Be sure to punctuate quotes correctly. (See page 247.)
- Follow quotes with a proper parenthetical citation.

Apply It! Draft a paragraph for your research report. Develop a clear topic sentence. Your paragraph should:
- **Compile information** from multiple sources
- **Summarize** the main ideas of your findings
- Use evidence, including at least one fact and one **direct quotation**, to support the main idea and your conclusions
- Use in-text citations to **acknowledge sources** of information

240   Research Writing

Apply It! Guide students through the instructions for brainstorming for visual elements. Then, have students with similar topics work as partners to discuss and develop appropriate graphics. Have students share their ideas about effective graphics with the class.

Extension Have students bring in examples of each kind of graphic for their topic. Lead a discussion about how each graphic conveys information to the viewer.

Partner Talk

Role play using constructive language when providing feedback on a partner's ideas.

Coach's Corner

If you are modeling the writing process for students with your own draft or a student volunteer's, use these prompts to model using evidence and graphics:

- **I will place statistics here because I** want to provide convincing evidence.
- **I will place a diagram here so** my audience can better visualize and understand this information.

Discuss the choices you make and solicit feedback from students.

3

Students continue writing their report online or in their notebooks.

4

Students may resubmit their work paragraph by paragraph to the Interactive Writing Coach™ for scoring and feedback or share their work with their teacher.

5

Students receive personalized feedback from the Interactive Writing Coach™ or feedback from their teacher.

Feature Assignment **Drafting** Feature Assignment **Drafting**

Use Graphics and Illustrations

Some ideas are more easily explained by a graphic than by a written account. For example, the diagram on page 227 in the Student Model helps the reader understand a climber's route up the mountain. While drafting, consider how you can present evidence in a diagram or type of graphic. If you copy an existing graphic, you will need permission from the copyright holder if you publish your work for use outside school. Always label your visuals with a figure or table number, caption, and source information. Number the tables or figures in numerical order and refer to it in your text.

- **Photographs** Use a photograph to show your audience how something looks. For example, a photo of a tool could help the reader understand how it works. If you use a photograph, include a caption, or brief sentence explaining what the photo shows.
- **Charts, Tables, and Graphs** Create a chart, table, or graph to provide information in a more visual or organized way. Give each a title. Include a citation for the source of information you used to create it. Put the citation below after the word Source and a colon.

Table 1. Typical gear needed for mountain climbing.

Mountain Climbing Gear	
Equipment	Purpose
Backpack	Carries equipment and food
Clothing (climbing suit, gloves, boots)	Prevents climber from freezing
Crampons	Attach to boots to provide grip on ice
Ice axe	Assists in climbing; prevents falls
Oxygen tank and mask	Lessens altitude sickness
Radio	Allows climbers to stay in touch with each other and base camp
Ropes and pulleys	Prevent falls; used for rescue

Source: Steve Jenkins, *The Top of the World: Climbing Mount Everest.* Boston: Houghton Mifflin Company, 1999. Print.

- **Maps** A map can show where a place is or where an event occurred. Always include a legend and a compass with your map, in addition to the figure number, caption, and source.

Try It! Study the diagram of the Mount Everest climbing route on page 227. Then, write in your own words all of the information that the diagram conveys. Evaluate the diagram for its clarity and usefulness. Could the diagram be improved? Explain.

Apply It! Brainstorm for two graphics that you might use in your informational research report. Be sure to identify the type of information each graphic would explain. Give your graphics titles, and document your sources.

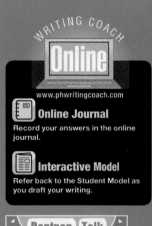

WRITING COACH

Online

www.phwritingcoach.com

Online Journal
Record your answers in the online journal.

Interactive Model
Refer back to the Student Model as you draft your writing.

 Partner Talk

With a partner, discuss the paragraph you wrote for the *Try It!* Use the information on page 240 to evaluate your writing. Ask and answer these questions:

- Does the paragraph have a topic sentence that states the main idea?
- Is the main idea supported by at least one fact and one direct quotation?
- Is the quotation introduced and punctuated correctly?
- Are sources of information properly documented?

Drafting 241

Personalized Support

 Interactive Writing Coach™

Students submit their research reports paragraph by paragraph for personalized feedback and scores.

 **Teacher or Peer Feedback**

To provide feedback to students as they continue drafting, ask or have student partners ask one another the following:

- Have you checked your facts and statistics to make sure they are correct?
- Have you provided all the information you need to cover your topic?
- What kinds of visuals or graphics are you including?
- How do they support your topic?
- What more do you need to do?

Differentiated Instruction

RTI Strategy for Below-Level Students
Display a variety of graphics, including diagrams, charts, graphs, timelines, and maps, in books and magazines. Have students identify each graphic and then discuss what it shows and why the author included it with the text. Make sure students understand that a graphic always supports or adds to the information in the text. Arrange the graphics by type and encourage students to review them when drafting their reports.

PRE-AP Enrichment for Above-Level Students Explain to students that using different types of evidence makes a report more interesting to read. Have students devise a system for categorizing their evidence as facts/statistics, examples, explanations, or quotations. For example, they might use a combination of abbreviations and numbers placed on their notes. Their system can help them monitor and adjust the types of evidence they gather and use.

The Digital • Print Path ▶

1 STUDENT BOOK ▶

Using **Writing Coach Online™** or the student book, students study the first and second drafts of the Student Model to see how the writer used Revision RADaR to improve his or her writing.

2  Writing Journal ▶

Students use the Revision RADaR strategy to revise their own writing.

Revising: Making It Better

Point out the page title to students and explain that revising means making improvements to a writing draft. Then, read aloud the opening paragraph to introduce the Revision RADaR strategies. You may wish to have students review Chapter 3 for more information on Revision RADaR.

Kelly Gallagher, M. Ed.

KEEP REVISION ON YOUR RADaR

1ST DRAFT After students have read the first draft, have them turn to page 238 and review the Outline for Success. Work with students to understand that the questions the author asked about the draft are based on the characteristics of a research report. For example, call out the second question and note how it addresses the first bullet in the Introduction section in the Outline for Success.

Then, have students work in small groups to develop other questions about the draft based on the genre characteristics.

2ND DRAFT Guide students to understand how the author used the RADaR strategies to revise the first draft.

Say: I **noticed** that the topic sentence in the 1st draft was weak. It didn't really tell me what the report would be about. In the 2nd draft, however, I see an *R* next to the topic sentence, which means the author has replaced that text. The new topic sentence has more specific details that make the topic of the report much clearer.

Ask: What else does the new topic sentence provide? (**Possible responses:** a structure for the upcoming body paragraphs; a hint to readers about what to expect as they read on)

Revising: Making It Better

Now that you have finished your draft, you are ready to revise. Think about the "big picture" of **audience, purpose, and genre.** You can use the Revision RADaR strategy as a guide for making changes to improve your draft. Revision RADaR provides four major ways to improve your writing: (R) replace, (A) add, (D) delete, and (R) reorder.

Kelly Gallagher, M. Ed.

KEEP REVISION ON YOUR RADaR

Read part of the first draft of the Student Model "Big Mountain, Big Challenge." Then, look at questions the writer asked himself as he thought about how well his draft addressed issues of audience, purpose, and genre.

Big Mountain, Big Challenge · 1ST DRAFT

When you reach the summit of Mount Everest, you stand on top of the world. At 29,035 feet tall, the mountain is the highest point on earth ("Everest, Mount"). Everest has fascinated many climbers. Between 2000 and 2006, 4,886 people attempted the climb ("Everest Expedition Statistics"). This undertaking can be dangerous. An understanding of science is important for climbers on Mount Everest.

The higher up you go on the mountain, the less oxygen there is. Everest is at a very high *altitude*. The word *altitude* means how far above sea level something is. People need oxygen to breathe. The lack of oxygen on Everest causes altitude sickness. "Because of the lack of oxygen," explains British mountaineer Graham Ratcliffe, "you get nausea and bad headaches and suffer from loss of appetite" ("Double Feat"). If you experience altitude sickness, you may feel like you have a case of the flu and have trouble sleeping ("Altitude Sickness Cure").

Have I used evidence to support my conclusions?

Have I developed my topic sentence effectively?

Is information well organized?

Have I properly evaluated the relevance and reliability of my sources?

Have students work in small groups to discuss other changes to the draft.

Apply It! Review the bulleted instructions for using Revision RADaR. Remind students to question their drafts based on the genre characteristics listed on the Outline for Success on page 238. Tell students to use each RADaR strategy at least once.

Coach's Corner

If you are modeling the writing process for students with your own draft or a student volunteer's, use these prompts to focus on the Revision RADaR *Reorder* strategy and guide discussion:

- **I reordered these words because I** wanted them to match the order of the explanations in the body paragraphs.

- **I reordered these details because I** wanted to put the strongest detail last.

Discuss the choices you make and solicit feedback from students.

3  Students submit their writing paragraph by paragraph to the Interactive Writing Coach™ for scoring and feedback or share their work with their teacher.

4  Students receive customized feedback from the Interactive Writing Coach™ or feedback from their teacher. Students may continue to revise their drafts.

Feature Assignment **Revising** *Feature Assignment* **Revising**

Now look at how the writer applied Revision RADaR to write an improved second draft.

Big Mountain, Big Challenge

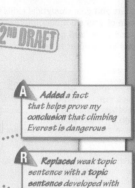

When you reach the summit of Mount Everest, you stand on top of the world. At 29,035 feet tall, the mountain is the highest point on Earth ("Everest, Mount"). Everest has fascinated many climbers. Between 2000 and 2006, 4,886 people attempted the climb. This undertaking can be dangerous—38 climbers died ("Everest Expedition Statistics"). While climbing Mount Everest can be dangerous, an understanding of science basics such as altitude, air pressure, and simple machines can help climbers stay safe.

Everest is at a very high altitude. The word *altitude* means how far above sea level something is. The higher up you go, the less oxygen there is (Platt 26). Because people need oxygen to breathe, they may get altitude sickness as they climb to higher altitudes. "Because of the lack of oxygen," explains British mountaineer Graham Ratcliffe, "You get nausea and bad headaches and suffer from loss of appetite" ("Double Feat"). These are the most common symptoms of altitude sickness.

A *Added a fact that helps prove my conclusion that climbing Everest is dangerous*

R *Replaced weak topic sentence with a topic sentence developed with more specific details*

R *Reordered a detail, moving it further down to where it supports the main idea, which is now the first sentence of the paragraph*

D *Deleted the sentence with information from an unreliable source (a Web site selling a product)*

R *Replaced it with a concluding sentence that summarizes my findings*

WRITING COACH

Online
www.phwritingcoach.com

 Video
Learn more strategies for effective writing from program author Kelly Gallagher

 Interactive Writing Coach™
Use the Revision RADaR strategy in your own writing. Then, submit your draft paragraph by paragraph for feedback.

 Apply It! Use your Revision RADaR to revise your draft.

- First, ask yourself if you have addressed the needs of your audience, explained your ideas clearly and logically, and included the characteristics of an informational research report. If necessary, make changes to **clarify meaning** in your report.
- Then, apply Revision RADaR to make needed changes. Remember—you can use the steps in the strategy in any order.

Revising   243

Personalized Support

 Interactive Writing Coach™

Students submit their research reports paragraph by paragraph for personalized feedback and scores.

FEEDBACK **Teacher or Peer Feedback**

To provide feedback to students as they revise their first draft, ask or have student partners ask one another the following:

- Can you show me how you revised your text?
- How could you reorder these ideas so that their order is more logical?
- Is there any unnecessary text that you could delete?
- Have you achieved your purpose with this piece of writing?
- Have you addressed the questions and concerns of your audience?

Working with ELLs   **ELL** Sheltered Instruction: Cognitive

Help students read the revised draft, using visual and contextual support to enhance and confirm understanding and to develop background knowledge needed to comprehend increasingly challenging language. To elicit and develop students' background knowledge (including previous discussion of the Student Model), show images of icy mountain peaks, climbers with oxygen masks, etc. Discuss what the pictures show about high altitude. Then:

Beginning Refer to the visual support while helping students read the second paragraph of the revised draft. Help them complete

sentences like *There is [more/less] oxygen at the top of a mountain than at the bottom.*

Intermediate Have groups use the visual support as they read the second draft and retell the dangers of high altitude climbing.

Advanced Review the visual support. Have partners read the second draft, summarize the text, then conduct research about mountain climbing and present their findings.

Advanced High Have students complete the Advanced activity, then decide if all the claims in the second draft are supported by evidence.

The Digital • Print Path ▶

STUDENT BOOK

1
STUDENT BOOK ▶

Using **Writing Coach Online™** or the student book, students study and discuss the revision chart.

2 ▶

In a video by program author Kelly Gallagher, students learn more strategies for effective writing.

Revising: Making It Better

Look at the Big Picture

Introduce the revision chart to students. Explain that the Section column identifies the three main parts of a research report. The Evaluate column identifies the characteristics found in each section and explains how to assess them. The Revise column presents specific strategies for revising each characteristic.

Then, have students draw lines between and label the four sections of their drafts. Direct students to work individually to evaluate and revise their drafts, using the chart to guide their work.

Focus on Craft: Sentence Variety

Have students read the introductory text. Guide students to understand that sentence variety not only makes writing more interesting to read but also makes it flow more smoothly.

Say: I notice that the second sentence of the Student Model is a simple sentence. To create variety, the writer could add a phrase that explains what air pressure is.

Ask: What kinds of sentences are the other sentences in the Student Model excerpt? (Complex, compound) How is the simple sentence different from the first sentence? (The simple sentence does not have a dependent clause.)

Have students work with a partner to rewrite the sentences in the Student Model as simple sentences and then add their own dependent clause to each.

Try It! Have students discuss the questions and record responses in their journals. Follow up with students to check that their responses reflect an understanding of how sentence variety affects writing.

Revising *Feature Assignment* **Revising** *Feature Assignmer*

Look at the Big Picture

Use the chart and your analytical skills to evaluate how well each section of your informational research report addresses **purpose, audience, and genre.** When necessary, use the suggestions in the chart to revise your piece.

Section	Evaluate	Revise
Introduction	• Check that the opening paragraph grabs your reader's attention. It should make the reader want to learn the answers to your **research question.**	• Add an interesting fact, anecdote, brief story, or quotation.
	• Make sure you have a well-developed **topic sentence,** or thesis statement, that identifies the major ideas your report will explore.	• Clarify your topic sentence, or thesis statement. Rearrange your introduction so that the topic sentence comes at the end.
Body	• Make sure each body paragraph clearly develops one **main idea.** Present your findings in a consistent format.	• Add a sentence to the beginning of each paragraph that states the main idea. Use a style manual to check your report's formatting.
	• Check that the information in each paragraph is **well organized,** and that the body of the report presents your ideas in the most effective order.	• Reorder words, sentences, and paragraphs to communicate information and ideas in a logical manner.
	• Make sure you have given enough **evidence** to support your conclusions.	• Use quotations and information compiled from multiple sources to support important points.
	• Make sure quotations and facts that are not common knowledge are **documented** and presented according to a style manual.	• Identify the source of each quotation. Add parenthetical citations, following the style specified in a style manual. Set off long quotes.
Conclusion	• Check that your conclusion **summarizes** your findings.	• Briefly restate the main points from the body of your report.
	• Make sure your research report leaves the reader with a **final thought.**	• Add a quotation or fact, or restate your topic sentence, to create a satisfying conclusion.
Works Cited/ Bibliography	• Make sure your Works Cited page or Bibliography is complete and uses **an appropriate style.**	• Add any missing sources, and format your list according to the correct style manual. • Add parenthetical citations that are missing.

244   **Research Writing**

Fine Tune Your Draft

Apply It! Ask volunteers to read aloud the instructions for fine-tuning their drafts. Then, have students work in pairs to improve their drafts' sentence variety and clarity by using different types of sentences.

Teacher and Family Feedback Have students identify Student Model examples of the characteristics that were marked for improvement. Use the Student Model references on page T238 to guide students to appropriate examples.

Teacher Tip

Encourage students to check sentence variety in their reports by marking the sentences in their drafts with *S* for "simple" and *C* for "compound." This will help them see places where they have too many of one kind and plan how to combine or divide sentences.

---

3 ▶ Using *Writing Coach Online*™ or the student book, students refer back to the Student Model for examples of writer's craft.

4 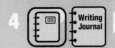 ▶ Students record answers to questions about writer's craft in their online journals or notebooks.

5  ▶ Students submit revised drafts to the *Interactive Writing Coach*™ for scoring and feedback, or share their work with their teacher.

6 ▶ Students receive customized feedback from the *Interactive Writing Coach*™ or feedback from their teacher.

Feature Assignment **Revising** Feature Assignment **Revising**

Focus on Craft: Sentence Variety

A simple sentence has only one independent clause (group of words that can stand on its own). A compound sentence has two or more independent clauses. However, compound sentences may also contain one or more dependent clauses. Using a variety of simple and compound sentences will add interest to your writing. It will also help to create a pleasing rhythm for the reader. Think about sentence variety as you read these sentences from the Student Model.

 **STUDENT MODEL** from **"Big Mountain, Big Challenge"** page 227; lines 39–43

> Another danger of climbing Everest is the evil weather, which includes storms and high winds. Storms are caused by changes in air pressure. Air moves to an area of lower pressure near Earth's surface, and the air rises and cools.

 Try It! Now, ask yourself these questions:

- The second sentence is a simple sentence. How could the writer create variety in this sentence?
- Divide the last sentence, which is compound, into two simple sentences. How does this change the effect of the writing?

Fine-Tune Your Draft

Apply It! Use the revision suggestions to prepare your final draft. Make sure you keep your audience, purpose, and genre in mind as you focus on making your report read smoothly.

- **Focus on Sentence Variety** Review your draft for passages that sound choppy or dull. Vary sentence types to include simple and compound sentences and make your writing livelier.

- **Use the Best Sentence Structure** Think about the purpose of and audience for your research report. Then, revise sentence structures to clarify meaning. For example, you might connect two related simple sentences with a conjunction to make a compound sentence.

Teacher and Family Feedback Share your draft with your teacher or a family member. Carefully review the comments you receive and revise your final draft as needed.

WRITING COACH

Online

www.phwritingcoach.com

Online Journal
Try It! Record your answers in the online journal.

Interactive Model
Refer back to the Interactive Model as you edit your writing.

Interactive Writing Coach™
Revise your draft and submit it paragraph by paragraph for feedback.

Revising 245

Personalized Support

 Interactive Writing Coach™

Students submit their research reports paragraph by paragraph for personalized feedback and scores.

 Teacher or Peer Feedback

To provide feedback to students as they continue to revise their first draft, ask or have student partners ask one another the following:

- What are you trying to say here? What part of the text could you replace to make your meaning clearer?

- Is there a more precise word you could use here?

- How does the rhythm of these sentences sound to you? Could you make the length and structure of these sentences more varied?

- How could you include transitional words and phrases here to help your reader understand these ideas?

Differentiated Instruction

RTI Strategy for Special Needs Students Choose a simple or compound sentence from the Student Model on pages 226–229 and write it on the board. Draw one line under the independent clause(s) and two lines under any dependent clauses. Circle the main subject(s) and verb(s). Name and label these parts. Ask students to identify the kind of sentence and to explain their answer using the markup and labels. Continue the process with other sentences.

Strategy for Spanish Speakers Students whose home language is Spanish may overuse complex sentences with multiple subordinate clauses, due to sentence structure in Spanish. Write on the board a complex sentence with multiple subordinate clauses about climbing Mount Everest. Have students work in pairs to break the sentence into simple sentences. Have volunteers share their sentences with the class. Then have students do the same for the last sentence in the Student Model on page 245.

The Digital · Print Path ▶   1 ▶

In a video by program author Jeff Anderson, students learn effective editing techniques.

2  ▶

Students record answers to questions about writer's craft in their online journals or notebooks.

Editing: Making It Correct

Discuss the opening paragraph with students. Explain that they will edit their drafts for proper grammar, mechanics, and spelling, including formatting quotations and citations.

WRITE GUY *Jeff Anderson, M.Ed.*

WHAT DO YOU NOTICE?

Introduce students to quotations by reading aloud the Student Model excerpt and discussing responses to the "Ask yourself" question. Then, have students read the explanation of how to use long quotations. Guide them to identify and use a block quotation.

To monitor students' comprehension, guide them to identify the techniques used to surround a quotation.

Say: I notice that the writer did not place quotation marks around this quotation. Instead, he used a block quotation, because he wanted to quote more than two lines of text. This type of quotation begins on the next line, and each line is indented. This format sets off the quotation from the rest of the text and makes it easy to identify.

Ask: Where is the citation placed in a block quotation? (after the quotation, following the end punctuation)

Have students work in small groups to examine other quotations in the Student Model and identify how they are formatted.

Partner Talk Ask students to consider how they would create a block quotation in handwritten text and on a computer.

Grammar Mini-Lesson: Punctuation

Discuss the paragraph and the Student Model excerpt on page 247 with students. Guide them to understand that the writer punctuated the quotation and its citation correctly.

Editing: Making It Correct

Before editing your final draft, think about how you have **paraphrased, summarized, quoted,** and **cited** all researched information. Then, edit your draft using a **style manual,** such as *MLA Handbook for Writers of Research Papers,* to accurately **document sources** and format the materials, including quotations. Finally, edit your final draft for errors in **grammar, mechanics,** and **spelling.**

WRITE GUY *Jeff Anderson, M. Ed.*

WHAT DO YOU NOTICE?

Zoom in on Conventions Focus on quotations as you zoom in on these lines from the Student Model.

> 📖 **STUDENT MODEL** from **"Big Mountain, Big Challenge"** page 228; lines 59–71
>
> Famous American climber Ed Viesturs was on the mountain. He described what he could and could not see of the summit from his location:
>
> > That day dawned perfect. . . . Then, the big storm rolled in. The summit disappeared, the clouds lowered, swallowing up more and more of the upper mountain until finally our visibility was cut off. . . .
> > It wasn't until 10 p.m. that we got any news. Paula radioed up to us and said, "Only half the people who left the South Col this morning have made it back." ... In all, five climbers would die as a result of the storm that day.

To learn more about integrating quotations see Grammar Game Plc Error 18, page 290.

Now, ask yourself this question: *How well has the writer worked the long quotation into his report?*

Perhaps you noted the writer used these helpful techniques to surround the quotation. The writer:

- Provides a lead-in to the quotation
- Tells us whom he is quoting
- Uses ellipses to let us know when he has left out irrelevant information
- Omits quotation marks and insets the quotation per MLA style for extended quotes

Partner Talk Discuss this question with a partner: *Why is it particularly easy to figure out which words from the Student Model are the student's and which words are not the student's?*

246   Research Writing

Try It! Students should note that the second sentence has a comma after *said* and a period outside the citation.

Apply It Remind students to look closely at the punctuation of quotations as they edit.

Use the Rubric Explain to students that they will rate how well their draft addresses the elements of a research report on a scale of 1 to 6, with 6 being the best score. Then, have students use the rubric to evaluate their drafts and edit as necessary.

Writer's Block

IF students have difficulty deciding how to punctuate their quotations and citations. . .

THEN review the appropriate examples in the MLA handbook or the style manual you are using, noting in particular the placement of punctuation marks.

3  ▶ Using Writing Coach Online™ or the student book, students refer back to the Student Model as they edit their writing.

4  ▶ Using Writing Coach Online™ or the student book, students evaluate their writing using the rubrics.

5 ▶ Students submit edited drafts to the Interactive Writing Coach™ for scoring and feedback or share their work with their teacher.

6   ▶ Students receive customized feedback from the Interactive Writing Coach™ or feedback from their teacher.

Feature Assignment **Editing** *Feature Assignment* **Editing**

Grammar Mini-Lesson: Punctuation

To learn more, see Chapter 25.

Punctuating Quotations With Citations Quotations follow specific punctuation rules. Study this sentence from the Student Model. Notice how the writer punctuated the quotation and the information about its source. Parenthetical citations occur after the quote but before the period.

 **STUDENT MODEL** from **"Big Mountain, Big Challenge"** page 229; lines 95–97

In 1923, British climber George Mallory was asked why he wanted to climb Everest. Mallory said, "Because it's there" (Golden 72).

Try It! Which of these sentences uses correct punctuation for the quotation and for the citation in the parentheses? Write the answers in your journal.

1. Ken Burns and Stephen Ives, the filmmakers, have said "America without the West is unthinkable now." *(New Perspectives on the West.)*

2. Ken Burns and Stephen Ives, the filmmakers, have said, "America without the West is unthinkable now" *(New Perspectives on the West).*

Apply It! Edit your draft for grammar, mechanics, and spelling. If necessary, rewrite sentences so that quotations work well next to your own words. Also correctly punctuate and acknowledge sources.

Use the rubric to evaluate your piece. If necessary, rethink, rewrite, or revise.

Rubric for Informational Research Report	Rating Scale					
	Not very					Very
Ideas: How focused and supported is your thesis statement?	1	2	3	4	5	6
Organization: How logical is the progression of your ideas?	1	2	3	4	5	6
Voice: How clearly is your personal point of view expressed?	1	2	3	4	5	6
Word Choice: How effectively does your word choice explain your thesis statement?	1	2	3	4	5	6
Sentence Fluency: How well have you varied the sentence types in your report?	1	2	3	4	5	6
Conventions: How correctly are your sources formatted?	1	2	3	4	5	6

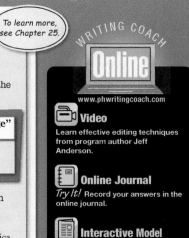

WRITING COACH

Online

www.phwritingcoach.com

Video
Learn effective editing techniques from program author Jeff Anderson.

Online Journal
Try It! Record your answers in the online journal.

Interactive Model
Refer to the Student Model as you edit your writing.

Interactive Writing Coach™
Edit your draft and check it against the rubric. Submit it paragraph by paragraph for feedback.

Editing 247

Personalized Support

 Interactive Writing Coach™

Students complete the editing process by submitting their writing for scoring and feedback.

Teacher or Peer Feedback

To provide feedback to students as they edit their drafts, ask or have student partners ask one another the following:

- Have you read your piece aloud to yourself or to a partner? What kinds of errors did you find?
- Have you included correct and complete citations for your sources?
- Have you titled and identified the source for photographs, graphics, and other visuals?
- Can you show me something you changed through editing?
- What resources have you used to look for possible spelling errors?
- Read this sentence aloud. Does the grammar sound correct to you?

Working with ELLs 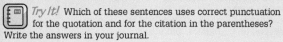 ELL Sheltered Instruction: Metacognitive

Use topics on page 247 to help students monitor and edit their writing for subject-verb agreement, using self-corrective techniques. Review subject-verb agreement and the meanings of *plural* and *singular*. Then introduce the self-corrective technique of underlining subjects, circling verbs, and asking themselves *How many?* to check agreement.

Beginning Write: *George Mallory were a British climber.* Have students copy the sentence, and help them correct it using the self-corrective technique.

Intermediate Have students complete the Beginning activity. Provide a list of

irregular verbs and have students write four sentences with them, using the self-corrective technique.

Advanced Have pairs complete *Apply It!*. As they revise their work, have them use the self-corrective technique. Have partners double-check agreement in each other's draft.

Advanced High Have students complete the Advanced activity independently, asking partners to check their work. Then, have each work with an Intermediate student to help check for subject-verb agreement. Have students provide specific, helpful feedback.

The Digital · Print Path ▶

1

Using **Writing Coach Online™** or the student book, students complete the writing process by deciding the best way to publish their writing for their intended purpose and audience.

2

Students record their answers to Reflect on Your Writing in their online journals or notebooks.

Publishing

Wrap Up Your Presentation

To prepare for more formal academic presentations, you may require students to produce their work using word processing software and a digital printer.

Publish Your Piece

Explain to students that the final step in the writing process is to decide which form of publication will present their work most effectively. Then, tell students that the chart shows how specific audiences can be reached using different media.

Have students whose research reports address similar audiences work in small groups to discuss appropriate ways to publish their work.

Reflect on Your Writing

Have students discuss the questions with a partner, including the Big Question, and record responses in their journal.

Manage Your Portfolio You may wish to have students include development materials such as graphic organizers and drafts.

MAKE YOUR WRITING COUNT

Introduce the magazine project by discussing the opening paragraphs with students. Make sure students understand that the project may be produced electronically or by hand. Then, guide students through each step in the action plan.

> **Resources** You may wish to have students use these graphic organizers: Meeting Agenda, Meeting Notes, and Outline. Distribute printed copies or have students log on to Writing Coach Online.

Publishing *Feature Assignment* **Publishing** *Feature Assign*

Publishing

Share your knowledge! When you're happy with the final draft of your research report, **publish** it **for an appropriate audience.**

Wrap Up Your Presentation

Your teacher may require that you provide a typed final draft of your paper. Prepare a cover sheet, and number the pages according to your style manual. Also be sure to add a title that indicates what your report is about.

Publish Your Piece

Use the chart to identify a way to publish your informational research report for the appropriate audience. You might publish a written report. You could also present your report as an oral or **multimedia presentation** that uses **text, graphics, and sound.**

If your audience is...	...then publish it by...
Students or adults at school	• Displaying your written report in the school library, along with books about your topic • Recording a podcast of your report and posting it on a school Web site where others can download it
A local group with a special interest in your topic	• Presenting a multimedia report at a group meeting and answering questions about your research • Posting your written report on the group's Web site and inviting comments

 Reflect on Your Writing

Now that you are done with your informational research report, read it over and use your writing journal to answer these questions.

- Which parts of your research report are you proudest of? Which parts do you think are weak?
- What will you do differently the next time you are assigned a research report?

The Big Question : Why Write? Do you understand a subject well enough to write about it? How did you find out what the facts were?

Manage Your Portfolio You may include your published informational research report in your writing portfolio. If so, consider what this piece reveals about your writing and your growth as a writer.

248   **Research Writing**

Use the 21st Century Skills Rubric to evaluate each group's process and final product on a scale of 1 to 3, indicating weak, moderate, or strong use of the skill. ▶

Listening and Speaking Monitor students as they give and receive feedback.

21st Century Learning

Skills Rubric	Rating
Create Media Products: Understand and utilize the most appropriate media creation tools.	1 2 3
Access and Evaluate Information: Access information effectively and evaluate it critically.	1 2 3
Work Creatively With Others: Incorporate group input and feedback into the work.	1 2 3
Interact Effectively With Others: Conduct themselves in a professional manner.	1 2 3

3 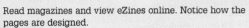 STUDENT BOOK ▶ Students use a variety of graphic organizers, either online or in print, to help them work together to create a multimedia group project.

4 STUDENT BOOK ▶ Through *Writing Coach Online*™ students link to resources on 21st Century Learning for help in creating a multimedia group project.

Make Your Writing Count

21st Century Learning

MAKE YOUR WRITING COUNT

Get Your Message Out in a Magazine or eZine

Research reports answer questions about how the world works. Share information with your classmates by creating a **magazine**.

A magazine is a regularly published group of articles based on a theme, such as news, sports, or current research. An eZine is a magazine published on the Web. (The *e* stands for *electronic*.) Both use text and images to share information. eZines also use graphics, audio, and video. Create articles based on your research reports. Then, organize them into a print or electronic magazine. Share your work in a **multimedia presentation**.

Here's your action plan.

1. With your group, set goals and choose roles, such as writer, editor, image finder, and page designer.

2. Review your research reports. Assign topics. Write short articles reporting on each other's research. Each article should answer the *5Ws and an H* questions.

3. Read magazines and view eZines online. Notice how the pages are designed.

4. Edit and arrange your articles. Create or find visuals and graphics. Name your magazine.

5. Your magazine should include:
   - Several informative articles
   - Text, images, and graphics arranged in an eye-catching way
   - Audio or visual links, if possible

6. Rehearse your multimedia presentation, highlighting each medium you used. Then, present your work to the class.

Listening and Speaking Meet with your group to discuss how to present your magazine to the class. Consider making a poster of your magazine pages or showing a Web site. Then, practice your presentation. Ask listeners for feedback on volume, pacing, and word choice. Keep their responses in mind as you present your magazine.

WRITING COACH

Online

www.phwritingcoach.com

Online Journal
Reflect on Your Writing Record your answers and ideas in the online journal.

Resource
Link to resources on 21st Century Learning for help in creating a group project.

Personalized Support

FEEDBACK Teacher or Peer Feedback

To provide feedback to students on their published writing, ask or have student partners ask one another the following:

- How did you go about writing this piece? What was your process?
- What did you learn from the writing model that you used in this piece?
- What surprised you the most as you wrote this piece?
- Did you try anything new as you worked on this piece?
- What did you learn from this piece of writing that you would like to remember and reuse?
- What do you think you do best as a writer right now?

Differentiated Instruction

RTI Strategy for Below-Level Students

Review the *5Ws and an H* questions with students. Remind them that the *5 Ws* are *Who, What, When, Where,* and *Why;* the *H* is *How*; and the answers to these six questions will be found in any nonfiction article, usually at the beginning. Read aloud the opening paragraph of a newspaper or magazine article, ask each of the six questions, and have students answer them.

Enrichment for Gifted/Talented Students

Students who are artistically inclined might be interested in taking photographs or drawing illustrations to accompany their group's articles. Point out that a mix of created and chosen artwork will add variety to the magazine. Also, explain that, as in real magazine publishing, all artwork will need to be approved by others in the group before it can appear in the magazine.

The Digital • Print Path ▶

1 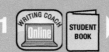 STUDENT BOOK ▶
Students use Writing Coach Online™ or their student books to analyze and discuss the Writing for Media topic.

2 Writing Journal ▶
Students learn about the characteristics of I-search report by answering questions abo model. Students record their answers to th questions in their online journals or notebo

I-Search Report

Discuss the opening paragraph with students. As a class, discuss the similarities and differences between an informational research report and an I-search report.

Try It! Guide students to understand the purpose, content, and structure of the sample I-search report outline.

Say: The first *Try It!* question asks about the writer's purpose. The outline contains many facts about grizzly bears as well as details about what the writer did. **I think** the writer wrote this outline to inform readers about the topic and the writing process for his or her report.

Ask: Who do you think is the writer's audience? Whom does the writer want to read the outline? (Responses will vary but might include people who are interested in conserving wildlife.)

Have students discuss the remaining questions in small groups and record individual responses in their journals. Later, address any questions students may have.

Create an I-Search Report

Tell students that they will create an I-search report using the five-step writing process. Then, preview the writing process instructions on pages 251–253.

> **Resources** You may wish to have students use the Outline graphic organizer. Distribute printed copies or have students log on to Writing Coach Online.

Introduce students to the Prewriting stage of the I-search report activity. Have students read aloud and discuss the list of tasks, noting how they addressed the requirements for that stage in the chapter's feature assignment, the informational research report.

Your Turn ▶ Writing for Media: I-Search Report

Writing for Media Writing for Media Writing for Media W

I-Search Report

21st Century Learning

In an **I-search report**, writers examine and tell their readers about their research process as well as their findings about their topic. There are four main steps to writing an I-search report:

1) Choose a topic by thinking about your interests, brainstorming, and browsing resources.
2) Research by creating questions, finding sources (usually including an interview), and keeping a log of your research process.
3) Analyze the information in your sources and take notes.
4) Create a final product that includes the six parts shown in the model.

Try It! Study the excerpt from the I-search report outline shown on this page. Then, answer these questions. Record your answers in your journal.

1. What do you think is the writer's **purpose?** Who do you think is the intended **audience?**
2. What information does this writer provide about the research process?
3. How do the writer's **sources** provide evidence that answers the research questions? Why is it important to cite valid and reliable sources?
4. What types of **visuals** do you think would enhance the writer's I-search report on this topic? Explain.

250 Research Writing

Protecting Grizzly Bears

I. Why I Chose My Topic
I saw a grizzly bear when I visited Yellowstone National Park. It was cool!

II. What I Already Know/What I Want to Learn
A park ranger told me that the government is trying to increase the number of bears in the United States. I wonder why. I wonder where else grizzlies live. What do they eat? How long do they live?

III. The Search: Steps I Took/The Interview
I started my search online. At first I found a lot of information on sports teams named the Grizzlies. I found better information when I used "grizzly bear" as a search term. My interview with zookeepe Rob Singer gave me great information.

IV. What I Learned
I learned that the grizzly bear is a threatened species in the United States. This means that grizzly bears could become an endangered species if they are not protected. That's why the government is trying to increase the number of grizzlies (U.S. Fish and Wildlife Service). I also learned that this type of brown bear lives mainly in western North America, although a few are still found in Europe and Asia (Singer).

V. Conclusion/Reflection
People need to work to protect grizzlies. It would be too bad if people who went to national parks could no longer see this fierce yet beautiful animal.

VI. References
"Grizzly Bear Recovery." *Endangered Species*. U.S. Fish and Wildlife Service. n.d. Web. 5 Jan. 2010.
Singer, Rob. Personal interview. 1 Jan. 2010.

Then, ask students to predict how these tasks might differ for an I-search report. For example, students may have to take different kinds of notes for an I-search report.

Following the discussion, have students begin working through each Prewriting task individually. Once they have completed a task, have them work in groups to evaluate their work before moving to the next task.

Partner Talk

Remind students to listen to their partner's feedback and ask questions to clarify if necessary.

You may wish to have students review this chapter's information about gathering and evaluating source material.

- Gathering data, pages 232–234
- Evaluating sources, 232–233

Students may select online or printed graphic organizers to help them plan their writing.

 Create an I-Search Report

Follow these steps to create your own **I-search report**. Review the graphic organizers on R24–R27 and choose one that suits your needs.

Prewriting

- Consult your peers to brainstorm for a list of topics. When you've finished, circle the topic you have decided to use.

- Be sure to identify the target **audience** and your purpose for your online report. Are you writing to **inform** an audience of students? Families with children? Older adults?

- It's important to generate a **research plan** for gathering sources and information. To guide your research, choose an open-ended **research question** related to your topic that your report will try to answer. Then, follow your plan.

- You'll need to get information from a range of **print and electronic sources**, including data and quotations from experts on your topic.

- **Evaluate** every source you consider using. Before using it, evaluate the source to make sure it is **relevant** and **reliable**. Remember, as you gather data you should reflect on what you're learning and **refine the research question** as needed to get better search results.

- To identify the source of your notes, record information on note cards, in a learning log, or through an online application. Make a source card for each source. Record bibliographic information according to a standard format and note whether it's a **primary or secondary source.**

- As you take notes, look for similarities and differences in how the multiple texts present information. Be sure to **summarize** information. Take written notes on graphic and visual sources as well. If you use a **direct quotation,** enclose it in big quotation marks to remind you to cite it later.

- Check your notes to make sure you have paraphrased or quoted but not **plagiarized.**

- Use graph paper or technology to record your data as graphs or charts. This can help you to better see the relationships between certain ideas.

- Think of **audio-visual support** you can add to your report. Be sure to record source information for any you intend to use.

WRITING COACH

Online

www.phwritingcoach.com

Online Journal

Try It! Record your answers in the online journal.

Interactive Graphic Organizers

Choose from a variety of graphic organizers to plan and develop your project.

Partner Talk

Summarize your findings for a partner. Ask for feedback on your research plan. Did you gather enough data? Did you cite valid and reliable sources? Discuss why this is important and make adjustments as needed.

Personalized Support

FEEDBACK **Teacher or Peer Feedback**

To provide feedback to students as they write for media, ask or have student partners ask one another the following:

- What are the main characteristics of this form of writing?

- What is your purpose for writing this piece? Who is your audience?

- Have you created a research plan?

- Where will you find information for your topic?

- Will you include photographs, graphics, and charts in your report?

Working with ELLs **ELL** Sheltered Instruction: Social/Affective

As students prepare to write an I-Search Report, help them orally express their opinions, ideas, and feelings in contexts ranging from communicating with single words to participating in extended discussions. Have them speak using learning strategies, such as nonverbal cues or circumlocution, if they lack a word.

Beginning Discuss a research topic. Help students orally express their opinions, ideas, and feelings about the topic. If students lack a word, have them use the learning strategy of using nonverbal cues, such as gestures.

Intermediate Have groups list and discuss topics for an Internet search,

orally presenting their opinions, ideas, and feelings. Have them use the learning strategy of circumlocution, giving descriptions of nouns they do not know.

Advanced Have partners choose a topic and orally express their opinions, ideas, and feelings about it, using the learning strategy of requesting assistance if they lack a word.

Advanced High Have partners talk about various topics and audiences for their writing. Have them orally express their opinions, ideas, and feelings on the topics, using learning strategies like circumlocution, as needed.

The Digital • Print Path ▶

1  ▶

Students follow the five-step writing process to create an I-search report.

2 STUDENT BOOK ▶

Students may select online or printed graphic organizers to help them develop their writing.

 **Writing for Media: Create an I-Search Report**

Create an I-Search Report (continued)

Guide students to use their experience writing the chapter feature assignment, an informational research report, to understand the drafting process for the I-search report activity.

Say: I notice that the last bullet in the Drafting instructions asks you to acknowledge your sources. We did something similar when we worked on our research reports in this chapter. You placed citations after sentences in the main text that included borrowed words or ideas and then listed those sources in a Works Cited section at the end of your report.

Ask: How will you acknowledge your sources in your I-search report? (Students will list sources in a References or Credits section at the end of the report.)

Have students begin working through the remaining stages of the writing process. You may wish to direct students who need extra support to the writing process overview in Chapter 3:

- Prewriting, pages 32–34
- Drafting, page 35
- Revising, pages 36–41
- Editing, pages 42–45
- Publishing, pages 46–47

When students have completed their I-search report, use the 21st Century Skills Rubric to evaluate each student's process and final product on a scale of 1 to 3, indicating weak, moderate, or strong use of the skill.

Extension Have students bring in other examples of I-search reports. Lead a media discussion about the examples, using the *Try It!* questions as a guide.

Your Turn **Writing for Media: I-Search Report** *(continued)*

21st Century Learning

Drafting

- Create an I-Search outline to help you organize your information. Think about an introduction, decide what main ideas you will cover in the body, and consider how you will conclude the report.
- Once you know the main ideas of your report, develop a topic **sentence** for each paragraph.
- **Compile** your notes from all of your sources and organize the information according to your outline. Then, start writing.
- Think about why someone would want to read or hear your report. Use your ideas to begin your report with an attention-grabbing opening.
- Choose **important information** and **evidence**, such as facts or quotations, to **support** your main ideas and conclusions. Summarize complex ideas and findings so that your audience can understand them.
- Remember, presenting someone else's words or ideas as your own is plagiarism. Use your own words, or enclose direct quotations in quotation marks.
- Think about how to include visuals and sound in your multimedia report. You might want to project a screen from your computer during your presentation, so write text that would make that work smoothly.
- **Acknowledge** your **sources** as needed in context or in a credits section.

Revising

Use Revision RADaR techniques as you review your draft carefully.

- **Replace** general terms with vivid details and unclear explanations with precise ideas.
- **Add** specific details or missing information to support your argument. **Delete** information that does not support your thesis or develop your argument.
- **Reorder** sentences and paragraphs to present ideas clearly and logically.
- Read aloud your report to make sure it reads smoothly and presents your findings in a consistent format.

252 **Research Writing**

Partner Talk

Tell students to discuss parts of the project that they found especially difficult, so their partners can look especially closely for those errors.

21st Century Learning

Skills Rubric	Rating
Make Judgments and Decisions: Effectively analyze and evaluate evidence.	1 2 3
Use and Manage Information: Manage the flow of information from a wide variety of sources.	1 2 3
Work Independently: Monitor, define, and complete tasks without direct oversight.	1 2 3
Manage Projects: Prioritize, plan, and manage work to achieve the intended result.	1 2 3

iting

w take the time to check your I-search report carefully before a present it to the class. Focus on each sentence and then on ch word. Look for these common kinds of errors:

Errors in subject-verb agreement

Errors in pronoun usage

Run-on sentences and sentence fragments

Spelling and capitalization mistakes

Omitted punctuation marks

Problems with appropriate documentation and quotations

blishing

Give your report to other classes or community groups who might be interested in learning more about Internet research.

Turn your report into a slide presentation and post it on your school's Web site so that other students can view it.

Post the text of your I-search report as a blog entry. Search for a Web site that allows users to create a free blog.

With your classmates, compile your I-search reports into a complete guide to Internet searching. Print it for classroom display or for your school library.

WRITING COACH

Online

www.phwritingcoach.com

Online Journal
Record your answers in the online journal.

Interactive Graphic Organizers
Choose from a variety of graphic organizers to plan and develop your project.

> **Partner Talk**
>
> Before you present your I-search report to the class, practice with a partner. Critique each other's presentations. Think about the speed of the presentation and how well it uses media.

Extension Find another example of an I-Search report and compare it with the one you are writing.

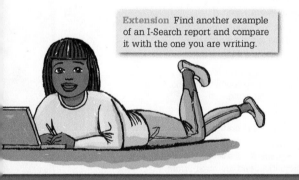

Personalized Support

FEEDBACK **Teacher or Peer Feedback**

To provide feedback to students as they write for media, ask or have student partners ask one another the following:

- Have you included most or all of the characteristics of an I-search report in your piece of writing?
- How did you organize your ideas in this piece of writing?
- Have you correctly and completely cited your sources of information?
- How did you go about revising the piece? Editing it?
- How do you plan on publishing your report?

Differentiated Instruction

RTI **Strategy for Below-Level Students**

Explain to students that editing is like the final polish that makes a piece of writing shine. Editing removes the mistakes that detract from the writing. Suggest students try these editing strategies:

- Place a ruler or the edge of a sheet of paper under each line of text as they proofread. This will help them concentrate on just one line at a time.

- Read backwards. This will help them spot spelling errors because it makes them look at each word on its own.

- Check for one kind of error at a time. Look for grammar errors, then punctuation errors, and finally spelling errors.

- Keep a dictionary close by. Check the spelling of any word of which they aren't completely sure.

The Digital • Print Path ▶

1

Before they write, students use the ABCDs of On-Demand Writing to analyze and plan how to respond to each prompt. They can use either their online journals or notebooks to take notes.

2

Students submit their writing paragra by paragraph or as a complete draft Interactive Writing Coach™ for feedb share their writing with their teacher.

Writing for Assessment

Read aloud or have a student read aloud the introductory text. Then tell students that they will learn and practice a technique for writing in response to an assessment prompt.

Try It! Read the Research Plan Prompt aloud and then have volunteers read aloud the Format and Academic Vocabulary boxes. Tell students that they will use the ABCD method to respond to the prompt.

The ABCDs of On-Demand Writing

Have students identify the words associated with the ABCD method. (attack, brainstorm, choose, detect) Then, guide students through their use.

Think Aloud **I'll attack the prompt** by circling the words *ask* and *tell*. These verbs remind me that, in my research plan, I will ask questions and I will tell steps. I can rewrite the prompt to state that clearly: "Write a research plan about a Civil War topic. Ask questions about the topic. Choose one question to research. Tell how you will research it. List steps and sources."

Work with students to fill out an Outline graphic organizer with information related to the prompt.

Have students write their drafts individually and then work with a partner to look for errors and check for sense.

More Prompts for Practice

Apply It! Have students apply the ABCD method to the practice prompts.

Prompt 1 Have partners attack the prompt and brainstorm for possible answers. Then, have each pair swap their information with another group to evaluate whether the teams have included ideas for graphics and sources in their plans.

Spiral Review: Narrative Read aloud the instructions and prompt. Then, have students review the nonfiction narrative characteristics on page 66.

Prompt 2 Remind students to use the ABCD method to write their personal narrative.

Spiral Review: Response to Literature Read aloud the instructions and prompt. Then, have

students review the response to literature characteristics on page 198.

Prompt 3 Remind students to use the ABCD method to write their response to literature.

Writing for Assessment

Many tests include a prompt that asks you to write or critique a research plan. Use these prompts to practice. Respond using the characteristics of your Internet-research report. (See page 224.)

Try It! Read the prompt and create a **research plan.** Use the ABCDs of On-Demand Writing to help you plan and write your research plan.

Format
Write your *research plan* in the form of an outline. List all the steps you would follow. Put the steps in the order you would do them. Under some main headings, you may have subheadings.

Research Plan Prompt
Write a research plan about a person, battle, or event related to the Civil War. First, ask open-ended questions about the topic to help you decide on a major research question. Then, tell how you will go about researching your question. What kinds of primary and secondary sources will you use? What other steps will you take before you start drafting your report? [30 minutes]

Academic Vocabulary
Primary sources are first-hand accounts from people who experienced the events they are telling about. *Secondary sources* provide analysis of primary sources. As you list possible sources of information, consider whether the information in them will be relevant (directly related to your research question) and valid (true).

The ABCDs of On-Demand Writing

Use these ABCDs to help you respond to the prompt.

Before you write your draft:

Attack the prompt [1 MINUTE]
- Circle or highlight important verbs in the prompt. Draw a line from the verb to what it refers to.
- Rewrite the prompt in your own words.

Brainstorm for possible answers [4 MINUTES]
- Create a graphic organizer to generate ideas.
- Use one for each part of the prompt if necessary.

Choose the order of your response [1 MINUTE]
- Think about the best way to organize your ideas.
- Number your ideas in the order you will write about them. Cross out ideas you will not be using.

After you write your draft:

Detect errors before turning in the draft [1 MINUTE]
- Carefully reread your writing.
- Make sure that your response makes sense and is complete.
- Look for spelling, punctuation, and grammar errors.

254   Research Writing

3

FEEDBACK

Students receive personalized feedback from the **Interactive Writing Coach**™ or feedback from their teacher.

ssment *Writing for Assessment* **Writing for Assessment**

More Prompts for Practice

Apply It! Work with a partner to **critique the research plan** n Prompt 1. In a written response, make specific suggestions to mprove the plan.

- Has the research plan covered all of the Prewriting steps?
- Is there a limited topic appropriate for the audience and purpose?
- Is the writer planning to find enough sources? Are they varied?
- Does the writer plan to include graphics?
- Does the research plan say anything about evaluating sources?

Prompt 1 Alana wrote this research plan. Explain what she did well and what needs improvement.

> *My Topic:* My research question is, *Can people ride on zebras, and why or why not?*
>
> *My Research:* I'm going to search the Internet and the databases at the library. I'll also look for print sources there. I'll interview a zookeeper who works with zebras.
>
> *My Writing:* I'll start writing when I find the perfect book.

piral Review: Narrative If you choose to respond to rompt 2, write a **personal narrative**. Make sure your story eflects the characteristics described on page 66.

rompt 2 Write a personal narrative about a time you went omeplace you had never been to before. Include details about ow you felt and what you heard and saw. Were there surprises? isappointments? Would you recommend that someone else go ere as well?

piral Review: Response to Literature If you choose to write **response to literature** in response to Prompt 3, make sure it eflects all of the characteristics on page 198. Your interpretative esponse essay should provide **evidence from the text** to support our ideas and show your **understanding of the work**.

rompt 3 People in life, as well as characters in literary texts, often ce tasks that require great courage. Write a response to a literary xt or an expository or nonfiction text that describes such a situation. rovide evidence from the text to demonstrate your understanding.

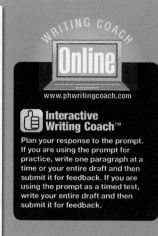

WRITING COACH

Online

www.phwritingcoach.com

Interactive Writing Coach™

Plan your response to the prompt. If you are using the prompt for practice, write one paragraph at a time or your entire draft and then submit it for feedback. If you are using the prompt as a timed test, write your entire draft and then submit it for feedback.

Remember **ABCD**

A ttack the prompt

B rainstorm for possible answers

C hoose the order of your response

D etect errors before turning in the draft

Personalized Support

Assessment/Monitor Progress

For timed writing practice, assign students a prompt to be completed in a timed setting. For Prompts 2 and 3, have students submit their writing to **Interactive Writing Coach**™ to get immediate feedback.

For a formal writing assessment, assign the Assessment writing prompt for this chapter in **Writing Coach Online**™. Then, have students submit their writing to **Interactive Writing Coach**™ to be assessed. Use the results to assess student progress and skill levels. **Interactive Writing Coach**™ will update student levels to ensure that students get the appropriate support.

FEEDBACK

Teacher Feedback

To create an assessment environment, have students use a prompt in a timed setting. Grade papers using the appropriate rubric and use the results to assess student progress and skill levels. In the next writing assignment, ensure that students get the appropriate level of support.

If you conference with students, use these questions to guide your discussion:

- What writing form did the prompt call for?
- How did you organize your ideas?
- Did you make good use of your time?

Working with ELLs **ELL** Sheltered Instruction: Cognitive

Use Prompt 1 to help students develop and demonstrate an increasing ability to distinguish between formal and informal English and knowledge of when to use each. Have them adapt spoken language appropriately for formal purposes. Describe various situations, like a friendly question and a job interview, and help all students determine if each calls for formal or informal language. Then:

Beginning Model a friendly question: *What's the coolest animal?* Help students repeat, then orally adapt it for a formal interview with a zookeeper: *What animals do you find interesting?* Discuss when

each question is appropriate. Repeat with additional examples.

Intermediate Ask questions, as partners identify them as formal or informal and adapt informal language for a formal purpose.

Advanced Have partners read aloud written versions of the Intermediate questions. Listeners should identify each as formal or informal and adapt informal sentences for a formal interview.

Advanced High Have students complete the Advanced activity. Have them present their own formal interview questions.

Interactive Writing Coach™ **Interactive Graphic Organizers** **Interactive Models**

Online Journal **Resources** **Video**

Use the Online Lesson Planner at www.phwritingcoach.com to customize your instructional plan for an integrated Language Arts curriculum.

DAY 1

CHAPTER OPENER/ GENRE INTRODUCTION

- What's Ahead
- Characteristics of Writing
- Forms of Writing
- Connect to the Big Questions
- Word Bank

ONLINE

DAY 2

FEATURE ASSIGNMENT: HOW-TO ESSAY

- Student Model
- Learn From Experience
- Choose from the Topic Bank
- Prewriting

ONLINE

DAY 3

FEATURE ASSIGNMENT: HOW-TO ESSAY *(cont'd)*

- Drafting
- Revising
- Editing
- Publishing

ONLINE

DAY 6

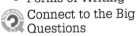 **21st Century Learning**

MAKE YOUR WRITING COUNT

- Present a Research Report on Making Connections
- Action Plan

ONLINE

DAY 7

21st Century Learning

MAKE YOUR WRITING COUNT *(cont'd)*

- Present a Research Report on Making Connections
- Action Plan

ONLINE

DAY 8

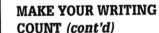 **21st Century Learning**
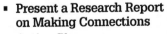

MAKE YOUR WRITING COUNT *(cont'd)*

- Present a Research Report on Making Connections
- Action Plan

ONLINE

Alternate Pacing Suggestions

- **Block Scheduling** Each day on the Lesson Planner represents a 40–50 minute block. Teachers using block scheduling may combine days to revise pacing to meet their classroom needs.

- **Accelerated Lesson Planning** Combine instructional days, choosing one of the Feature Assignments to focus on.

- **Integrated Language Arts Curriculum** For targeted instruction that covers the essential components of the lesson, use either a 3- or a 5-day plan.

3 day plan

DAY 1: Introduction to the Genre How-to Essay

DAY 2: Thank-You Letter

DAY 3: Friendly Letter

5 day plan

Use 3-day plan, and add

DAY 4: Make Your Writing Count

DAY 5: Writing for Assessment

Links to Prentice Hall *LITERATURE*

Additional Mentor Text:
"Origami: Apatosaurus" (instructions), Rachel Katz, p. 603

Differentiated Instruction

Differentiated Instruction Boxes in this Teacher's Edition address these student populations:

- Below-Level Students
- Above-Level Students
- Gifted and Talented Students
- Special Needs Students
- English Language Learners
- Spanish Speaking Students

In addition, for further enrichment, see the **Extension** features.

LESSON OBJECTIVES

- To learn the forms and defining characteristics of workplace writing.
- To learn the elements of successful how-to essays, thank-you letters, and friendly letters, the chapter feature assignments.
- To read student models of a how-to essay, a thank-you letter, and a friendly letter.
- To apply prewriting strategies in developing a how-to essay, a thank-you letter, and a friendly letter, including strategies for gathering details.
- To apply drafting strategies in developing a how-to essay, a thank-you letter, and a friendly letter.
- To apply strategies for revising and editing a how-to essay, a thank-you letter, and a friendly letter.
- To complete the Make Your Writing Count assignment, developing and presenting a research report on making connections.
- To complete the Writing for Media assignment, developing an e-mail message.
- To practice writing for assessment.

DAY 4

FEATURE ASSIGNMENT: THANK-YOU LETTER

ONLINE

- Student Model
- Choose from the Topic Bank
- Prewriting – Publishing

DAY 5

FEATURE ASSIGNMENT: FRIENDLY LETTER

ONLINE

- Student Model
- Choose from the Topic Bank
- Prewriting – Publishing

DAY 9

WRITING FOR MEDIA

ONLINE

- E-Mail Message
- Create an E-Mail Message

DAY 10

WRITING FOR ASSESSMENT

ONLINE

- Procedural Text Prompt
- The ABCDs of On-Demand Writing
- More Prompts for Practice
  Test Prep Spiral Review: Expository
- Spiral Review: Research Plan

> **❝** *Writing is a threshold skill for employment and promotion.* **❞**
>
> —**Kelly Gallagher**

Personalized Assessment

	Ongoing Assessment	Formal Assessment of Feature Assignment	Progress Monitoring at End-of-Chapter
Interactive Writing Coach™	Use Paragraph Feedback and Essay Scorer as a revision tool.	Use Essay Scorer to score students' Feature Assignment papers.	Use Essay Scorer to score students' papers. Students' learner profiles can be adjusted based on their scores.
FEEDBACK **Teacher Conferencing**	Use rubrics in the Student Edition as a revision tool. Conference with students to review their work and provide personalized support.	Use rubrics in the Student Edition to score students' Feature Assignment papers.	Review each student's work to plan targeted resources for the next writing assignment.

The Digital • Print Path

 **1** Using Writing Coach Online™ or the student book, students discuss the photograph in the chapter opener as it relates to the writing genre.

 **2** Students record their ideas and responses in their online journals or notebooks. They may also record and save their responses on pop-up sticky notes in Writing Coach Online™.

Chapter Objectives

1. Write a how-to essay, thank-you letter, and friendly letter by planning, drafting, revising, editing, and publishing individual work.

2. Produce a research report.

3. Use the five-step writing process to create an e-mail message.

4. Write a procedural text, a compare-and-contrast expository essay, and a critique of a research plan in response to a prompt.

WORKPLACE WRITING

What's Ahead

Guide students in understanding what constitutes workplace and procedural documents. Preview the Student Models on pages 258–263. Tell students that they will write their own documents using the five-step writing process.

Activate Prior Knowledge Using the photo on page 256, guide students to understand the purposes of workplace writing.

 Think Aloud In this photo, **I see** the players grouped around the coach while they all look at a diagram on a clipboard. I know the information on the clipboard is important so that each player understands what to do on the basketball court. It is important that the information is well-organized and easily understood.

Work with students to brainstorm for possible problems that might occur if the diagram does not clearly show each player's position on the clipboard.

Have students brainstorm for other situations where well-organized information is critical for success.

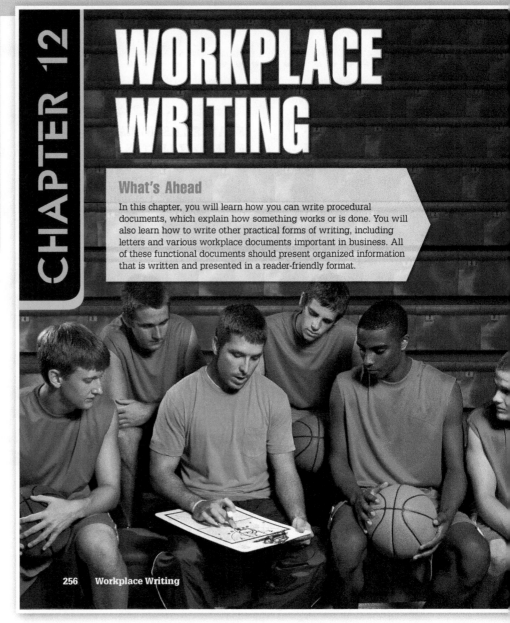

256 Workplace Writing

CHAPTER 12
WORKPLACE WRITING

What's Ahead

In this chapter, you will learn how you can write procedural documents, which explain how something works or is done. You will also learn how to write other practical forms of writing, including letters and various workplace documents important in business. All of these functional documents should present organized information that is written and presented in a reader-friendly format.

Characteristics of Writing

Ask volunteers to read aloud the characteristics of workplace and procedural writing. Explain that academic writing forms, such as research papers, also use formal language and standard formats for presenting information. Then, have students identify academic writing forms that share these characteristics.

Forms of Writing

Discuss the forms and purposes of workplace writing.

Try It! Have students record their responses in their journal.

Possible responses: thank-you letter, expresses gratitude; business letter, expresses concerns or approval to a business; how-to essay, explains a process

3 STUDENT BOOK ▶

Students learn vocabulary from the Word Bank
and listen to English and Spanish pronunciations
in the Writing Coach Online glossary™.

Characteristics of Writing

Effective workplace and practical writing has these characteristics:

- **Information** that is well-organized and accurate
- A clear **purpose** and intended audience
- **Formal, polite** language
- **Reader-friendly formatting techniques,** such as sufficient white or blank space and clearly defined sections
- Correct **grammar, punctuation,** and **spelling** appropriate to the form of writing

Forms of Writing

Forms of workplace writing include:

How-to essays are used to explain how something works or how to do something. These essays are written in a step-by-step format.

Thank-you letters are formal or informal correspondence written to express gratitude.

Business letters are formal correspondence written to, from, or within a business. They can be written for various reasons, including to make requests and to express concerns or approval.

Memos are short documents usually written from one member of a group to another, or to another group. They assume some background knowledge of the topic.

Other forms of practical writing include:

Friendly letters are informal letters written to a friend or acquaintance. They can be written for various reasons, including to ask how someone is doing or just to say hello.

Try It! For each audience and purpose described, select the appropriate form of writing such as a thank-you letter, friendly letter, how-to essay, or business letter. Explain your choices.

- To thank a relative for a birthday gift
- To explain how to order supplies

WRITING COACH

Online

www.phwritingcoach.com

📁 **Resource**
Word Bank Use the eText glossary to learn more about these words.

📰 **Online Journal**
Try It! Record your answers and ideas in the online journal.

❓ **Connect to the Big Questions**

Discuss these questions:

1 **What do you think?** When is it most important to communicate clearly with teammates?

2 **Why write?** What do daily workplace communications require of format, content, and style?

📁 **WORD BANK**

These vocabulary words are often used with workplace writing. Use the Glossary or a dictionary to check the definitions.

| communicate | instructions |
| document | technical |

257

Personalized Support

FEEDBACK 👥 **Teacher or Peer Feedback**

To encourage students in their discussion of the photograph and the characteristics of workplace writing, ask the following questions:

- What is the first thing you think of when you look at this photo?
- What kind of communication might be important in this setting?
- How is workplace writing different from other kinds of writing?
- Who is the most likely audience for this form of writing?
- What kind of voice would be most effective for this form of writing?

❓ Connect to the Big Questions

Have students use their experience to discuss the Big Questions. Explain that they will revisit **Why write?** at the end of this chapter. Tell students to consider these points during their discussion:

1. Ask students to recall and discuss times when clear communication was important to work effectively with teammates.

2. Ask students to compare the differences in format, content, and style between a thank-you letter and a business letter.

Word Bank

To assist English Language Learners and struggling readers, echo read each word or have students log on to Writing Coach Online to listen to the pronunciations. Then, have partners take turns using each word in a sentence. Ask volunteers to share one of their sentences with the class.

Working with ELLs   ELL Sheltered Instruction: Cognitive

Have students use prior knowledge to understand and learn the meanings of English academic vocabulary heard during classroom instruction and interactions. Review academic vocabulary from the Word Bank: *communicate; document; instructions; technical.* **Discuss each word, modeling the use of prior academic knowledge, like:** *I remember the word document from when we discussed memos.* **Document** *must mean "a piece of writing for work or public purposes."*

Beginning Review the vocabulary using gestures. Help students refer to their prior knowledge with cloze sentences, like *When*

I assign homework, I give you ____ so you know what to do.

Intermediate Complete the Beginning activity with students. Then, have groups draw on prior knowledge to use the vocabulary words in context sentences.

Advanced Have partners review the vocabulary, drawing on prior assignments, then use it to orally retell the lesson.

Advanced High Have students complete the Advanced activity, then use the words with other academic vocabulary, like *procedure.*

The Digital · Print Path ▶

1  ▶

Using **Writing Coach Online™** or the student book, students read and listen to an audio recording of the Student Model. As they complete their writing assignments they can refer back to the Student Model for support whenever they need it.

2 ▶

Students record answers to questions about the Student Model in their online journals or notebooks.

STUDENT MODEL

Learn From Experience

After students have read the text, point out that the numbered notes refer to the characteristics of a how-to essay.

Try It! Guide students to understand how the genre characteristics shape the text. For example, use instruction as shown below, which refers to the first *Try It!* question.

Say: While reading the text, **I see** that Jimmy Dixon, the writer, begins his how-to essay by clearly stating his purpose. Even though Jimmy titles his essay "How to Write an E-mail," it is also important for Jimmy to explain why someone should learn how to use e-mail.

Ask: Why is it important to clearly identify the purpose of a how-to essay? **(Possible response: so readers will know you have important information they can use)**

Have students reply to the *Try It!* questions in their journals. If students have difficulty responding to a particular question, model a response, as with the first question.

Check the accuracy and completeness of student responses.

- Stating the purpose helps the readers know what they will be reading about.
- *Then, next, now, after, finally*
- Responses will vary, but should recognize that the essay presents all relevant information for writing an e-mail.

Create a How-To Essay

Tell students that they will create a how-to essay using the five-step writing process. Then, preview the writing process instructions.

For each step in the writing process, have partners read aloud and discuss the list of tasks. Then, have them work individually. Once both partners have completed the tasks, have them evaluate each other's work before moving to the next step.

STUDENT MODEL — How-To Essay

Learn From Experience

 After reading the how-to essay on this page, read the numbered notes in the margin to learn about how the writer presented his ideas. As you read, practice newly acquired vocabulary by correctly producing the word's sound.

Try It! Record your answers and ideas in the online journal.

① In the first paragraph, the writer makes the **audience** and **purpose** clear.

② **Transition words** like *first* and *second* help the reader understand what to do first, next, and so on.

③ **Sentences in the body,** or main part of the essay, **explain important information.** Notice that the writer explains how to avoid a possible problem.

④ The last paragraph **brings the essay to a logical end** by explaining the last step in the process.

Try It!

- Why is it helpful to state the purpose of a work-related document, such as a how-to-essay?
- What transition words besides *first* and *second* are used in the essay?
- Do you think the essay clearly explains how to write an e-mail? Explain.

258   Workplace Writing

How To Write an E-mail

by Jimmy Dixon

① E-mail is an easy way to send messages over the Internet. If you are new to e-mail, follow these steps to write a message.

② First, open your e-mail program, and click on the command for writing mail. It will be "New Mail," "Write," or something similar to that. After you click, you will get a blank e-mail.

② Second, fill in the "To" field, or blank, at the top of the e-mail. Type the e-mail address of the person who will receive your message. **③** Then, read the address to make sure it is right. Even one little mistake will keep your e-mail from being sent.

Next, fill in the "Subject" field. Think of a short, clear way to say why you are writing, and type that in the blank. Now, write your message. Type it in the blank space below the "To" and "Subject" fields. Keep it short and clear. After you have typed your message, read it to make sure your message is clear and to see if you made any mistakes. If you did, fix them.

④ Finally, click on "Send." Away your e-mail goes! It really is that easy to write and send an e-mail!

Partner Talk

After partners edit each other's how-to essay for a clear purpose and a step-by-step process, have each student retell the steps of the partner's how-to-essay.

Writer's Block

IF the organization of a student's text does not help to lead a reader through it logically...

THEN talk through the steps using a graphic organizer and/or a model text.

3 ▶ Students begin planning their how-to essay by selecting a topic. Then, they write their first draft online or in their notebooks.

4 ▶ Students watch videos from program authors Jeff Anderson and Kelly Gallagher to learn effective strategies for revising and editing their writing.

5  ▶ Students submit their essays paragraph by paragraph to the Interactive Writing Coach™ for scoring and feedback, or share their work with their teacher.

6 ▶ Students receive personalized feedback from the Interactive Writing Coach™, or feedback from their teacher.

Feature Assignment *How-To Essay* **Feature Assignment**

 **Feature Assignment: How-To Essay**

Prewriting

- Plan a first draft of your **how-to essay**. You can select from the Topic Bank or come up with an idea of your own.

TOPIC BANK

Hobby Time Many people have hobbies. Choose a hobby, such as skateboarding or collecting baseball cards. Write an essay explaining how to get started in this hobby.

Hit the Books Think about the ways that students can successfully study and review material before a test. Explain one of your favorite ways to prepare for a test.

- Brainstorm for a list of ideas for your how-to essay. Sketch out the steps of the process you will include in your explanation.

- Read your step-by-step list aloud to a partner. Ask your partner to help you identify any steps you may have left out.

Drafting

- Use reader-friendly formatting techniques, including all the features of a how-to essay. Use an **active voice** when writing out the steps. For example, write *Hammer three nails* instead of *Three nails should be hammered*.

- Include the **important information** so that the purpose is clearly stated early in the essay and so that each step is clearly explained.

- Accurately **convey ideas** by using logical steps in your essay.

Revising and Editing

- Before you revise, review your draft to ensure that information is presented accurately and concisely.

- After rethinking purpose and audience, revise the draft to use appropriate conventions, such as spelling, capitalization, and bullets.

Publishing

- Print your essay and share it with a partner or the whole class.

- Post your essay to a Web site or blog on a similar topic.

WRITING COACH
Online
www.phwritingcoach.com

Interactive Model
Listen to an audio recording of the Student Model.

Online Journal
Try It! Record your answers and ideas in the online journal.

Interactive Writing Coach
Submit your writing and receive personalized feedback and support as you draft, revise, and edit.

Video
Learn strategies for effective revising and editing from program authors Jeff Anderson and Kelly Gallagher.

Partner Talk
Work with a partner to edit your how-to essay. Read your draft to your partner. Then, ask him or her to retell the steps of the process to you. Decide whether or not you need to include more steps.

How-To Essay **259**

Personalized Support

Teacher or Peer Feedback

To provide feedback to students as they plan and write their how-to essays, ask or have student partners ask one another the following questions:

- Which characteristics of a how-to essay have you included? Are you missing any?

- What is your purpose for writing? Is it clearly stated?

- How have you organized your ideas?

- Are your language and tone appropriate for the audience you are addressing?

- What details have you included to make your writing clear?

- How did you revise your draft?

- Have you checked your grammar and spelling?

Working with ELLs   Sheltered Instruction: Cognitive

Help students expand and internalize their initial English vocabulary by learning basic routine language needed for classroom communication and use and reuse this new basic language in speaking activities.

Beginning Display the basic routine word *organize*. Act out organizing several pencils by length. Say *I organize the pencils.* Have students repeat to use the word, then complete oral cloze sentences to reuse it.

Intermediate Review basic routine words from the Topic Bank: *plan, first, study, review, material, explain, prepare.* For each, have pairs create a **Mental**

Connections Card: On a card, have them write a word and make a mental connection illustrating the word. On the other, have them make a cluster diagram of related words. Have them use and reuse the words as they discuss their cards.

Advanced Have partners orally review the Intermediate activity words, then reuse the words in oral sentences about their hobbies.

Advanced High Have pairs use the Intermediate activity words to discuss their hobbies. Then, have students reuse the words to tell what they learned about their partner.

The Digital · Print Path ▶

1 **STUDENT BOOK** ▶

Using Writing Coach Online™ or the student book, students read and listen to an audio recording of the Student Model. As they complete their writing assignments they can refer back to the Student Model for support whenever they need it.

2 **Writing Journal** ▶

Students record answers to questions about the Student Model in their online journals or notebooks.

STUDENT MODEL

Learn From Experience

After students have read the text, point out that the numbered notes refer to the characteristics of a thank-you letter.

Try It! Guide students to understand how the genre characteristics shape the text. For example, use Think Alouds like the one below, which refers to the first *Try It!* question.

 Think Aloud I am going to look at each of the numbered sections of this e-mail and see if I can describe the tone, or "feel" of the language. First, **I notice** the greeting, *Dear Auntie Amita*. I think that *Dear* is friendly and polite; this kind of language could be used in business writing or personal writing. Using the word *Auntie* seems informal, or casual. When I look at the purpose, I see the phrase *big birthday surprise*, which gives me a clue about the excitement the writer feels.

Work with students to complete the review of each of the called-out features and how they contribute to the tone of the letter. Point out that this letter differs somewhat from the characteristics of workplace writing listed at the top of the chapter: Instead of a formal, friendly tone, this letter has an informal, or casual, friendly tone because Farah is writing to a family member.

Have students reply to the *Try It!* questions in their journals. If students have difficulty responding to a particular question, model a response, as shown above.

Check the accuracy and completeness of student responses.

- The tone of letter is friendly, polite, excited.
- Responses will vary possibilities include: *Auntie, so happy, so much fun, exciting, best of all, never forget, Love.*
- Yes, the tone is appropriate for the audience. Because Farah is writing to a family member, her tone should be friendly and casual.

STUDENT MODEL — Thank-You Letter

Learn From Experience

 After reading the thank-you letter on this page, read the numbered notes in the margin to learn about how the writer presented her ideas.

Try It! Record your answers and ideas in the online journal.

---

① The writer begins with the date and a salutation, or **greeting,** that is appropriate for the recipient. The greeting is followed by a comma.

② In the first paragraph, the writer makes the **purpose** of the letter clear.

③ Here and elsewhere in the **body** of the letter, the writer fulfills the purpose by **developing ideas.** Notice that she gives an example of something she especially enjoyed.

④ The writer ends the letter with an appropriate **closing.** She might use a more formal closing, like *Sincerely,* if the letter were for a teacher or someone else outside her family.

Try It!

- How would you describe the tone, or "sound," of the thank-you letter? Friendly? Informal? Happy? Something else?
- Which words help create that tone?
- Is the tone appropriate for the audience and purpose of the letter? Explain.

---

① May 21, 2010

Dear Auntie Amita,

② I am writing to thank you for the big birthday surprise. I was so happy to see you last Saturday. I did not know you were planning to make the trip all the way from Michigan.

How did you know that a day at the amusement park was exactly what I wanted? **③** I had so much fun on the rides. I especially liked the roller coaster. It was so exciting!

The surprise waiting for me at home was the best of all. I never guessed that you got me out of the house so Mom could set up a party for me. I was shocked when I walked in the house and saw all my friends.

Everyone had a great time. Thanks to you, I will never forget my 12th birthday.

④ Love,

Farah

Create a Thank-You Letter

Tell students that they will create a thank-you letter using the five-step writing process. Then, preview the writing process instructions.

For each step in the writing process, have partners read aloud and discuss the list of tasks. Then, have them work together to complete each task. Once they have completed the tasks, have them exchange work with another paired team to evaluate each other's work before moving to the next step.

Partner Talk

After partners work to revise the thank-you letters, have them review each other's letter for proper tone (i.e., friendly language that is either formal or informal) in relation to their audience.

Writer's Block

IF the student is having difficulty incorporating the characteristics of the genre...

THEN discuss how the student can use the Student Model example to plan his or her own piece.

3

Students begin planning their thank-you letters by selecting a topic. Then, they write their first draft online or in their notebooks.

4

Students watch videos from program authors Jeff Anderson and Kelly Gallagher to learn effective strategies for revising and editing their writing.

5

Students submit their thank-you letters paragraph by paragraph to the Interactive Writing Coach™ for scoring and feedback, or share their work with their teacher.

6

Students receive personalized feedback from the Interactive Writing Coach™, or feedback from their teacher.

Feature Assignment *Feature Assignment* Feature Assignment

 **Feature Assignment: Thank-You Letter**

Prewriting

- Plan a first draft of your **thank-you letter.** You can select from the Topic Bank or come up with an idea of your own.

TOPIC BANK

School Spirit Write to your student council thanking them for something they have done for your school in the past year.

Class Act Write to your favorite teacher thanking him or her for teaching or sharing something interesting or important with the class.

- Brainstorm for a list of things that your letter's recipient will need to know about you and your purpose for writing the letter.
- Use a telephone directory or online resources to find the accurate contact information for the letter's recipient.

Drafting

- Use reader-friendly formatting techniques, including all the **conventions** of an informal letter.
- Use a salutation that matches your relationship with the recipient.
- Include the **important information** so that the purpose of your letter is clearly stated.
- Demonstrate a sense of **closure** in your final paragraph by summing up the purpose of your letter.

Revising and Editing

As you revise, review your draft to ensure that your ideas are conveyed accurately and concisely. Ask yourself if the **purpose and audience** for your letter are clearly identified and addressed. After rethinking purpose and audience, revise to clarify meaning, and edit for appropriate use of conventions.

Publishing

- If you plan to mail the letter, print the letter or write it neatly on paper or stationery suitable for the recipient.
- If you plan to e-mail the letter, confirm the correct e-mail address and attach your letter to a message as a Portable Document Format (PDF).

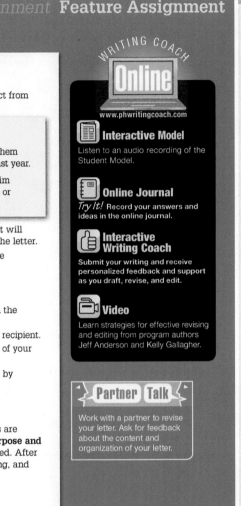

WRITING COACH
Online
www.phwritingcoach.com

Interactive Model
Listen to an audio recording of the Student Model.

Online Journal
Try It! Record your answers and ideas in the online journal.

Interactive Writing Coach
Submit your writing and receive personalized feedback and support as you draft, revise, and edit.

Video
Learn strategies for effective revising and editing from program authors Jeff Anderson and Kelly Gallagher.

Partner Talk
Work with a partner to revise your letter. Ask for feedback about the content and organization of your letter.

Personalized Support

 Teacher or Peer Feedback

To provide feedback to students as they plan and write their thank-you letters, ask or have student partners ask one another the following questions:

- Which characteristics of a thank-you letter have you included? Are you missing any?
- What is your purpose for writing? Is it clearly stated?
- How have you organized your ideas?
- Are your language and tone appropriate for the audience you are addressing?
- What details have you included to make your writing clear?
- How did you revise your draft?
- Have your checked your grammar and spelling?

Working with ELLs ELL Sheltered Instruction: Cognitive

Have students listen to, derive meaning from, and respond orally to information presented in a wide variety of print, electronic, and audiovisual media to build and reinforce language attainment. Record a conversation, based on the first Topic Bank prompt, about your school's student council. Play it for students.

Beginning Pause the recording often to clarify meaning. To build language attainment, provide a bank with words like *student council, school, thanks,* and *work.* Introduce the words using visuals. Have students use them to respond orally to

questions on the recording, like, *Why should we thank the student council?*

Intermediate Have groups respond orally to the recording. To build language attainment, provide them with sentence frames for responses: for example, *The student council helped the school by ___.*

Advanced Have partners orally discuss the recording. To build language attainment, provide sentence frames for responses, like: *I agree the student council ___ because ___.*

Advanced High Have students complete the Advanced activity and identify a cause-effect relationship in the recording.

The Digital · Print Path ▶

1 Using *Writing Coach Online*™ or the student book, students read and listen to an audio recording of the Student Model. As they complete their writing assignments they can refer back to the Student Model for support whenever they need it.

2   Students record answers to questions about the Student Model in their online journals or notebooks.

STUDENT MODEL

Learn From Experience

After students have read the text, point out that the numbered notes refer to the characteristics of a friendly letter.

Try It! Guide students to understand how the genre characteristics shape the text. For example, use instruction as shown below, which refers to the *Try It!* question.

Say: This letter starts with the proper features of a letter, the date (day, month, and year) and a salutation, or greeting, followed by a comma. **I see** the purpose of the letter in the first paragraph. In this case, the purpose is to welcome the Mallari family to the neighborhood and invite them to the annual block party.

Ask: Why is it important to state the purpose of the letter in the first paragraph? How do you think putting the purpose right up front is a kind of reader-friendly formatting technique? (**Possible response:** It's important so the reader knows exactly what the purpose of the letter is right away. This makes it easier for the reader to understand the rest of the letter.)

Have students reply to the *Try It!* question in their journals. If students have difficulty responding to the question, model a response, as with the instruction above.

Check the accuracy and completeness of student responses.

- Responses will vary, but should include the possibility that if a letter is not well-organized, people might not read the entire thing or understand it.

Extension Lead a discussion in which students outline the ways their response letters are well-organized and reader friendly, according to the arrangement of information shown in the Student Model. Use the *Try It!* question as a guide.

STUDENT MODEL Friendly Letter

Learn From Experience

 After reading the friendly letter on this page, read the numbered notes in the margin to learn about how the writer presented his ideas. As you read, take notes to develop your understanding of basic sight and English vocabulary.

Try It! Record your answers and ideas in the online journal.

❶ The writer includes the proper informal letter features:
- Date including day, month, and year
- Salutation followed by a comma
- A closing followed by a comma and a signature

❷ In the first paragraph, the writer sets a **friendly tone** and **conveys the purpose** of the letter.

❸ Here and elsewhere in the **body** of the letter, the writer **conveys ideas** that help fulfill the letter's purpose.

❹ The writer signs his letter. It is important to include your **signature** when you write a letter on paper.

Try It! Why is it important for an informal letter to be well-organized and reader friendly?

Extension Play the role of the recipient of the letter and write a response to the sender.

262 Workplace Writing

---

❶ June 15, 2010

❶ Dear Mallari Family,

❷ Welcome to the neighborhood! Now that you are settled in, we'd like to invite you to our annual block party.

❸ The party will take place on Nightingale Street on Sunday, July 4, from 11 a.m. to 7 p.m. Each family brings its own picnic lunch and one extra snack or dessert to share. The Nightingale Block Party Committee sets up picnic tables on the street for everyone to use.

❸ In the afternoon, there will be games and races for the younger children, and a baseball game for the older kids. The party breaks up in the evening so that families can get ready for the fireworks show in Elmtown Park.

❸ We hope that you can join us for the celebration. Everyone is looking forward to getting to know you! Please let me know by June 25 if you will be able to attend. My telephone number is (690) 555-1011. Or, leave me a note if you prefer.

Sincerely,

❹ *Vito Santos*

Vito Santos

Create a Friendly Letter

Tell students that they will create a friendly letter using the five-step writing process. Then, preview the writing process instructions.

For each step in the writing process, have partners read aloud and discuss the list of tasks. Then, have them work individually. Once both partners have completed the tasks, have them evaluate each other's work before moving to the next step.

Partner Talk

Have partners read their letters aloud to each other. As one partner reads, the other should listen for clear purpose and appropriate tone.

Writer's Block

IF the student does not attend to word choice or parts of speech are imprecise or general...

THEN refer the student to a model text that uses precise language.

3 Students begin planning their friendly letters by selecting a topic. Then, they write their first draft online or in their notebooks.

4 Students watch videos from program authors Jeff Anderson and Kelly Gallagher to learn effective strategies for revising and editing their writing.

5  Students submit their friendly letters paragraph by paragraph to the Interactive Writing Coach™ for scoring and feedback, or share their work with their teacher.

6   Students receive personalized feedback from the Interactive Writing Coach™, or feedback from their teacher.

Op-Ed Piece **Student Model** *Op-Ed Piece* **Student Model**

 **Feature Assignment: Friendly Letter**

Prewriting

- Plan a first draft of your **friendly letter**. You can select from the Topic Bank or come up with an idea of your own.
- Make a list of the ideas you want to include in your letter.
- Use a telephone directory or online resources to find the accurate contact information for the letter's recipient.

TOPIC BANK

Camp Days Imagine that you've just spent a week at a summer camp. Write a friendly letter to your grandparents or another relative telling them about your experiences at camp.

Far and Away Write a friendly letter to a pen pal in another country. Start by identifying the place where your imaginary pen pal lives. What will you share with your pen pal about life in the United States?

Drafting

- Use reader-friendly formatting techniques, including all the **conventions** of an informal letter.
- Use a greeting that matches your relationship with the recipient.
- Include **important information** so that the purpose is clearly stated.
- **Demonstrate a sense of closure** in your final paragraph by summing up the purpose of your letter.

Revising and Editing

As you revise, review your draft to ensure that information is concisely and **accurately conveyed**. Then, revise the draft according to teacher and peer feedback.

Publishing

- If you plan to mail the letter, print the letter or write it neatly on paper or stationery suitable for the recipient.
- If you plan to e-mail the letter, confirm the correct e-mail address and attach your letter to a message as a PDF.

WRITING COACH Online

www.phwritingcoach.com

Interactive Model
Listen to an audio recording of the Student Model.

Online Journal
Try It! Record your answers and ideas in the online journal.

Interactive Writing Coach
Submit your writing and receive personalized feedback and support as you draft, revise, and edit.

Video
Learn strategies for effective revising and editing from program authors Jeff Anderson and Kelly Gallagher.

Partner Talk
Read your final draft to a partner. Ask your partner to listen for correct grammar and usage. Revise your final draft as needed.

Friendly Letter 263

Personalized Support

 Teacher or Peer Feedback

To provide feedback to students as they plan and write their friendly letters, ask or have student partners ask one another the following questions:

- Which characteristics of a friendly letter have you included? Are you missing any?
- What is your purpose for writing? Is it clearly stated?
- How have you organized your ideas?
- Are your language and tone appropriate for the audience you are addressing?
- What details have you included to make your writing clear?
- How did you revise your draft?
- Have your checked your grammar and spelling?

Differentiated Instruction

PRE-AP Enrichment for Above-Level Students Have students compose a friendly letter in which bad news is delivered. For example, the student could write a letter to a friend to say that a visit has to be canceled. The combination between friendly, familiar language and the formal language that may be necessary when delivering negative news will challenge advanced students to set an appropriate tone. For a further challenge have students write another letter to a friend or relative asking for a favor.

Strategy for Spanish Speakers
Students whose home language is Spanish might use overly formal greetings and language toward different speakers, due to the formality distinction in both pronouns and verb forms in Spanish. Elicit and record a list of different relationships on the board (parents, siblings, friends, teacher, grandfather, pen pal, and so on). Then, provide different English expressions for greetings and closings in letter-writing that match the formality and social context of each relationship. Elicit Spanish language equivalents.

The Digital · Print Path ▶

WRITING COACH Online STUDENT BOOK

1  STUDENT BOOK ▶
Using Writing Coach Online™ or the student book, students create a research plan, collect and organize data, and document sources for an informational research report.

2 STUDENT BOOK ▶
Students use a variety of graphic organizers, either online or in print, to help them work together as a group to research and write their report.

Make Your Writing Count

Present a Research Report

Introduce the research report activity by having students read page 264. Make sure students understand that they will work in teams to produce their research report. Then, guide students to formulate a research question for their topic.

Say: I know I want to write a research report on how to make connections with family overseas. I think this will help a lot of people stay in touch with family in the military. I think that is where I will start my research because I bet the military has things in place for staying in touch, like video phone calls. I will collect that information so my readers will have the information they need. But lots of people overseas are not in the military.

Ask: Can you think of any ways to stay in touch with family overseas? **(Possible response: e-mail)** What about sharing video and other files that are too big for e-mail? I think I will narrow my topic to: In what ways, besides e-mail, can people use the Internet to stay in touch?

Have students work in their groups to narrow their topics and formulate a focused research question.

Action Plan

Guide students through each step in the action plan. For additional support, you may wish to direct students to related research report information in Chapter 11:

- Make a Research Plan, page 232
- Collect and Organize Your Data, page 234
- Avoid Plagiarism, page 235
- Document Your Sources, page 236
- Critique Your Research Process, page 237
- Provide and Document Evidence, page 240
- Use Graphics and Illustrations, page 241

21st Century Learning

MAKE YOUR WRITING COUNT

Present a Research Report on Making Connections

How-to essays communicate important information to specific audiences. These workplace documents may involve ideas or activities that could be further developed by research. Write a **research report** and presentation about ideas for ways to connect with family, friends, and community.

With a group, **brainstorm for** topics from among your work in this chapter that you can explore further. Have a discussion with others to **decide upon a topic** that will be helpful to someone thinking about making connections with other people. Work together to **formulate an open-ended research question** that will help you produce a research report about the topic.

Consider topics like planning a family reunion, having a neighborhood block party, or starting an annual day-in-the park event in your town.

Group members should **consult** one another and **critique the process** as you work. Be prepared to **refine** the research question and adjust the plan as needed. Remember that a research report should:

- Include a specific thesis statement or topic sentence
- Meet the needs of audience and purpose
- Express a clear point of view
- Provide supporting evidence
- Present ideas in a logical way
- Document sources using correct formatting

Then, present your research results to students in your school. Your report should be a **multimedia presentation** that uses text and graphics. You may use posters or presentation software.

264 **Workplace Writing**

Resources You may wish to have students use these graphic organizers: Meeting Agenda, Meeting Notes, and Outline. Distribute printed copies or have students log on to Writing Coach Online.

Use the 21st Century Skills Rubric to evaluate each group's process and final product on a scale of 1 to 3, indicating weak, moderate, or strong use of the skill. ▶

Listening and Speaking Have students present their reports to the class. Monitor whether students speak clearly and confidently.

21st Century Learning

Skills Rubric	Rating
Access and Evaluate Information: Access information efficiently and effectively.	1 2 3
Communicate Clearly: Use communication for a range of purposes (e.g., to inform and instruct).	1 2 3
Interact Effectively With Others: Know when to listen and when to speak.	1 2 3
Create Media Products: Understand and use appropriate media creation tools, characteristics, and conventions.	1 2 3

3 Students take notes, create a research plan, collect and organize data, document sources and write a first draft of a report in their online journals or notebooks.

4 Through *Writing Coach Online*™ students link to resources on 21st Century Learning for help in creating a multimedia group project.

Make Your Writing Count

21st Century Learning

ere's your action plan.

Research takes time. In a group, make a plan for several group meetings. Set objectives and choose roles for each member.

Work together to create a **research plan** that includes:

- Locating and exploring **print and electronic resources**, data from experts, and **quotations**
- Using **software** or graph paper to turn data into graphs or charts in order to make connections and see big ideas
- Interpreting visuals by recording their data as **written notes**
- Checking that your sources are **reliable and relevant**
- Collecting supporting evidence and **documenting sources** appropriately. Record **bibliographic information** according to a standard format.
- Noting whether a source is **primary** (firsthand account) or **secondary** (interpretation of events or data)

Discuss your findings. **Evaluate the sources,** discussing the importance of citing valid and relevant sources. Reject weak sources. Work together to create a clear thesis statement or **topic sentence** that conveys the main idea of the research.

Outline the content of the report. Assign sections of the outline to each group member. Be sure to **summarize** your findings, and cite sources.

Work together to write a rough draft by **compiling** collected information. As a group, discuss the difference between **plagiarism** and **paraphrasing**. Remember to use citations to acknowledge all sources.

Revise and edit to ensure the thesis statement and conclusions are well-supported by evidence and that the findings are presented in a **consistent format.**

Add appropriate audio and visuals to support the topic.

Present your report to students, counselors, and teachers.

Listening and Speaking Practice the presentation in front of another group or each other. Listen to feedback to help you make improvements. When you present, speak clearly and confidently.

WRITING COACH

Online

www.phwritingcoach.com

Online Journal
Record your answers and ideas in the online journal.

Resource
Link to resources on 21st Century Learning for help in creating a group project.

Personalized Support

FEEDBACK

Teacher or Peer Feedback

To provide feedback to students as they work together to develop a research report, ask or have student partners ask one another the following:

- How is the group organized and how are tasks assigned?
- What is your purpose for writing this piece? Who is your audience?
- How did you record information and document your sources?
- How did you decide what information to include in your report?
- How did you go about revising the piece? Editing it?
- In what ways did the group work effectively together? What could have been improved?
- What did you learn from the process and the final product that you could use in future writing projects?

Differentiated Instruction

RTI Strategy for Special Needs Students Special needs students may have difficulty narrowing their topic because of the wealth of information available. Help them to articulate how they might narrow their topics by having them state their topics as questions. Using the example on p. 264, they might ask: How can I find out more about contacting my relatives in the military? What methods of communication would I use? Where can I get current information from the military?

Then, help them identify one or two brief sources (such as current Internet or magazine articles) for their research. As students work, provide appropriate graphic organizers. For the Making Connections research project, the Steps in a Process organizer will help students itemize each task needed to complete the research paper.

The Digital • Print Path ▶

1

Students use Writing Coach Online™ or their student books to analyze and discuss the Writing for Media topic.

2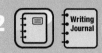

Students learn about the characteristics of an e-mail message by answering questions about the model. Students record their answers to the *Try It!* questions in their online journals or notebooks.

 Writing for Media: E-mail Message

E-mail Message

Discuss the opening paragraph with students. As a class, discuss how e-mails can be formal or informal, depending on the purpose of the message and the recipient.

Try It! Guide students to understand what form the e-mail should be written in depending on the audience and the purpose of the message.

 Think Aloud When I read this subject line, **I see** what the e-mail will be about. Then, when I read the first paragraph, I see the purpose of the e-mail is to praise the magazine for publishing the article.

Work with students to help them see that the purpose of an e-mail is often more specific than the subject of the e-mail.

Have students discuss the remaining *Try It!* questions in small groups and record individual responses in their journals.

At this point, you may wish to have students bring in other examples of e-mails. If so, lead a media discussion about the examples, using the *Try It!* questions as a guide.

Extension Lead a discussion in which students compare and contrast the format of the letters shown earlier in the chapter with the format of the e-mail.

Your Turn Writing for Media: E-mail Message

21st Century Learning

E-mail Message

An **e-mail message** can be formal or informal, depending on the relationship of the writer and recipient and the purpose of the message. For example, an e-mail message from a student to the editor of a school magazine may be informal.

Magazines frequently feature a "Letters to the Editor" page or a "Letters from our Readers" page. This section is devoted to letters from readers who have sent messages—either by mail or by e-mail—to the magazine about a story it published. The **Letters section of a magazine** is the place where readers can see their opinions published for all to read.

Try It! Read the e-mail message on this page. Then, answer these questions. Record your answers in your journal.

1. How does the **subject line** help the reader know what the e-mail will be about?
2. What is the **purpose** of this e-mail message? How does the writer introduce the purpose?
3. Who is the intended **audience** for this e-mail? How does the writer address the audience?
4. Is the writer of the **e-mail message** in favor of or critical of the article he discussed? What **details** in the message support your response?

Extension Look at the formatting of this e-mail. How is it the same or different from that of a friendly letter?

266 Workplace Writing

To: MagazineEditor@example.com
From: BenNorth@example.com
Subject: Letter to the Editor on Skateboarding Article
Date: October 5, 2011

Dear Editor,

Thanks for your article about the popularity of skateboarding! Your coverage of famous boarders was the best I've read in our school's magazine.

I also enjoyed the feature "Best Places to Board." I was especially excited to see our town on the map. It also gave me good ideas for other places in our area to board.

The school magazine has changed for the better by including stories that truly interest the students. Thanks for listening to us, and keep up the good work.

Sincerely,
Ben North

Create an E-mail Message

Tell students that they will create an e-mail using the five-step writing process. Then, preview the writing process instructions on page 267.

Resources You may wish to have students use the **Steps in a Process** graphic organizer. Distribute printed copies or have students log on to Writing Coach Online.

For each step in the writing process, have partners read aloud and discuss the list of tasks. Then, have them work individually. Once both partners have completed the tasks, have them evaluate each other's work before moving to the next step.

Use the 21st Century Skills Rubric to evaluate each student's process and final product on a scale of 1 to 3, indicating weak, moderate, or strong use of the skill. ▶

Partner Talk

Have partners exchange e-mails. Have students identify whom the e-mail is for and identify the purpose of the partner's message.

Skills Rubric	Rating
Access and Evaluate Information: Access information efficiently and effectively.	1 2 3
Communicate Clearly: Articulate thoughts and ideas effectively in writing.	1 2 3
Create Media Products: Effectively utilize appropriate expressions.	1 2 3
Apply Technology Effectively: Use technology as a tool to communicate.	1 2 3

3 STUDENT BOOK

Students use a graphic organizer, either online or printed, to help them plan and develop their writing. Students follow the five-step writing process to write their own e-mail messages.

Writing for Media Writing for Media Writing for Media **Writing for Media**

Create an E-mail Message

Follow these steps to create your own informal **e-mail message** to the editor of a school publication, such as the school newspaper or magazine. Review the graphic organizers on R24–R27 and choose one that suits your needs.

Prewriting
- Brainstorm for a list of school publications you like to read. Include details about some recent stories you have read.
- Choose one story to which you would like to respond.
- Consider the needs of your specific audience. What would you say to the editor of this magazine in your e-mail message?

Drafting
- Organize your ideas and include **important information,** so that the purpose is clearly stated early in the e-mail message and so that each paragraph has a clear purpose.
- Use reader-friendly formatting techniques, including all the **conventions** of an e-mail message, such as a clear subject line.
- Accurately **convey ideas** by double-checking your ideas.

Revising and **Editing**
- As you revise, review your draft to ensure that information is presented accurately and concisely and that the message has a sense of **closure.**
- Ask yourself if the purpose and audience for your e-mail message are clearly identified and addressed.
- After rethinking purpose and audience, revise the draft to improve your style.

Publishing
- Type the message in an e-mail program. Be sure to include a subject in the subject line.
- Confirm that you have the recipient's correct e-mail address.
- Send the e-mail message. Check your "sent messages" list to confirm the message was sent successfully.

WRITING COACH
Online
www.phwritingcoach.com

Online Journal
Try It! Record your answers and ideas in the online journal.

Interactive Graphic Organizers
Use the graphic organizers to plan your e-mail message.

Partner Talk

Exchange e-mail messages with a partner. Have your partner answer these questions: Whom is this e-mail message for? What is the purpose of the message? Monitor your partner's spoken language by asking follow-up questions to confirm your understanding.

Writing for Media 267

Personalized Support

FEEDBACK **Teacher or Peer Feedback**

To provide feedback to students as they write for media, ask or have student partners ask one another the following:

- What are the main characteristics of this form of writing?
- Have you included most or all of these characteristics in your piece of writing?
- What is your purpose for writing this piece? Who is your audience?
- How did you organize your ideas in this piece of writing?
- How did you go about revising the piece? Editing it?
- How do you plan on publishing your piece? What other publishing options also might work?

Working with ELLs **ELL** Sheltered Instruction: Cognitive

Help students demonstrate understanding of the general meaning, main points, and important details of spoken language in contexts ranging from familiar to unfamiliar. Orally present the instruction on page 267. Discuss informal e-mail messages in a familiar context—e-mailing friends. Then, relate the discussion to an unfamiliar context—writing e-mails to government officials. Discuss how students' language would change in each situation.

Beginning Review your presentation. Help students restate the general meaning, main points, and important details using sentence

frames like *E-mails to friends are (friendly/ formal). E-mails to people in government are (chatty/polite).*

Intermediate Have groups complete sentence frames summarizing your presentation's general meaning, main points, and important details.

Advanced Have partners create an outline summarizing your presentation's general meaning, main points, and important details.

Advanced High After partners complete the Advanced activity, have them write a brief comparison of formal and informal e-mails.

T267

The Digital · Print Path ▶

1 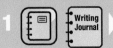 ▶

Before they write, students use the ABCDs of On-Demand Writing to analyze and plan how to respond to each prompt. They can use either their online journals or notebooks to take notes.

2 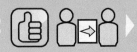 ▶

Students submit their writing paragraph by paragraph or as a complete draft to the Interactive Writing Coach™ for feedback, or share their writing with their teacher.

Writing for Assessment

Read aloud or have a student read aloud the introductory text. Then, tell students that they will learn and practice a technique for writing in response to a test prompt.

Try It! Read the Procedural Text Prompt aloud and then have volunteers read aloud the Format and Academic Vocabulary boxes. Tell students that they will use the ABCD method to respond to the prompt.

The ABCDs of On-Demand Writing

Have students identify the words associated with the ABCD method. (attack, brainstorm, choose, detect) Then, guide students through their use.

Think Aloud I'll **attack the prompt** by circling the words *wants to learn and how to operate.* These words explain why and what I am writing. I can paraphrase the task: "Write instructions to teach a friend how to use an MP3 player."

Work with students to brainstorm for an appropriate graphic organizer for a procedural text, such as a Steps in a Process chart.

Have students write their drafts individually and then work with a partner to detect errors.

More Prompts for Practice

Apply It! Have students apply the ABDC method to the practice prompts.

Prompt 1 Have partners attack the prompt and brainstorm for possible answers. Then, have each pair swap their information with another pair to evaluate whether the teams have developed clear step-by-step instructions.

Writing for Assessment

Many tests include a prompt that asks you to write a procedural text. Your responses should include most of the same characteristics as your **how-to-essay.** (See pages 258–259.)

Try It! Read the procedural text prompt and the information on format and academic vocabulary. Use the ABCDs of On-Demand Writing to help you plan and write your response.

Format
The prompt directs you to write a *procedural text.* Describe the purpose of the text in the first section. Be sure to include steps with organized information such as a numbered list or materials list.

Procedural Text Prompt
Your friend wants to learn to use an MP3 player. He would like to read written instructions. Write a procedural text that includes stepped-out instructions on how to operate an MP3 player. [30 minutes]

Academic Vocabulary
A procedural text is a kind of text that tells somebody how to perform a task. *Stepped-out instructions* have numbered lists that provide details in the order they are used.

The ABCDs of On-Demand Writing

Use the following ABCDs to help you respond to the prompt.

Before you write your draft:

Attack the prompt [1 MINUTE]
- Circle or highlight important verbs in the prompt. Draw a line from the verb to what it refers to.
- Rewrite the prompt in your own words.

Brainstorm possible answers [4 MINUTES]
- Create a graphic organizer to generate ideas.
- Use one for each part of the prompt if necessary.

Choose the order of your response [1 MINUTE]
- Think about the best way to organize your ideas.
- Number your ideas in the order you will write about them. Cross out ideas you will not be using.

After you write your draft:

Detect errors before turning in the draft [1 MINUTE]
- Carefully reread your writing.
- Make sure that your response makes sense and is complete.
- Look for spelling, punctuation, and grammar errors.

268   Workplace Writing

Test Prep Spiral Review: Expository Read aloud the instructions and prompt. Then, have students review the characteristics for a compare-and-contrast expository essay on page 146.

Prompt 2 Remind students to use the ABCD method to write their expository essay.

Spiral Review: Research Plan Read aloud the instructions and prompt. Then, have students review the research plan characteristics on page 224.

Prompt 3 Remind students to use the ABCD method to write their critique.

Students receive personalized feedback from the **Interactive Writing Coach™**, or feedback from their teacher.

More Prompts for Practice

Apply It! Respond to Prompt 1 by writing a **procedural text**. As you write, be sure to:

Consider what your **audience** knows and needs to know

Organize **information** into steps or paragraphs

Define any **terms** that your audience may not know

Prompt 1 You are writing a cookbook. Choose your favorite sandwich and write a procedural text for the cookbook. Include stepped-out instructions for making your favorite sandwich.

Spiral Review: Expository If you choose to respond to Prompt 2, write a compare-and-contrast **expository essay**. Make sure your essay reflects the characteristics described on page 146.

Prompt 2 In some communities you are required to reduce, reuse, or recycle certain materials. Write an expository essay that compares and contrasts two ways to conserve the same item or material.

Spiral Review: Research Plan If you choose to respond to prompt 3, write a **critique of the research plan**. Make sure your critique evaluates all of the characteristics described on page 224. Your critique should determine if the research plan:

Contains a **narrowed topic**, and is appropriate for the **audience**

Includes enough **primary** and **secondary sources**, and says something about **evaluating** sources

Prompt 3 Juana wrote the following research plan. Explain what she did well and what needs improvement.
My Topic: Altitude sickness.
My Research: I'm going to search the Internet, talk to the reference librarian, and look for print sources. I know that Mount Everest is at a very high altitude, so I'll look for articles and stories about people who have climbed it.
My Drafting: After a week of research, I will use my notes to write my draft. Then, I'll show my teacher before revising it.

WRITING COACH

Online
www.phwritingcoach.com

Interactive Writing Coach™

Plan your response to the prompt. If you are writing the prompt for practice, write one paragraph at a time or your entire draft and submit it for feedback. If you are using the prompt for a timed test, write your entire draft and submit it for feedback.

Remember **ABCD**

Attack the prompt

Brainstorm possible answers

Choose the order of your response

Detect errors before turning in the draft

Personalized Support

 Assessment/Monitor Progress

For timed writing practice, assign students a prompt to be completed in a timed setting. For Prompts 1 and 2, have students submit their writing to **Interactive Writing Coach™** to get immediate feedback.

For a formal writing assessment, assign the Assessment writing prompt for this chapter in **Writing Coach Online™**. Then, have students submit their writing to **Interactive Writing Coach™** to be assessed. Use the results to assess student progress and skill levels. **Interactive Writing Coach™** will update student levels to ensure that students get the appropriate support.

 Teacher or Peer Feedback

To create an assessment environment, have students use a prompt in a timed setting. Grade papers using the appropriate rubric and use the results to assess student progress and skill levels. In the next writing assignment, ensure that students get the appropriate level of support.

If you conference with students, use these questions to guide your discussion:

- What writing form did the prompt call for?
- How did you organize your ideas?
- Did you make good use of your time?

Working with ELLs **ELL** Sheltered Instruction: Cognitive

Have students demonstrate an **increasing ability to distinguish between formal and informal English and an increasing knowledge of when to use each. Have them adapt spoken language appropriately for formal purposes. Model various situations, like a family talk, a presentation, or friendly phone call. Help all students identify if each calls for formal or informal language. Then:**

Beginning Speak short statements, like *Recycling is super easy.* Help students label the statements as formal or informal and adapt the informal ones for a formal purpose.

Intermediate Speak sentences about reusing paper. Have students identify each as formal or informal, then adapt the informal sentences for a formal purpose.

Advanced Provide written versions of the Intermediate activity sentences, and have pairs take turns reading them aloud, identifying each as formal or informal, and adapting the informal language for formal purposes.

Advanced High After students complete the Advanced activity, have them orally state rules of when to speak formally.

OUNS AND PRONOUNS *Concrete and Abstract Nouns* VERBS *Transitive*

Adverb? CONJUNCTIONS AND INTERJECTIONS *Subordinating Conju*

sitive Phrases EFFECTIVE SENTENCES *Combining Sentence Parts* PUN

rbs ADJECTIVES AND ADVERBS *Interrogative Adjectives* PREPOSITI

ctions BASIC SENTENCE PARTS *Subjects and Predicates* PHRASES AN

NCTUATION NOUNS AND PRONOUNS *Concrete and Abstract Nouns*

ONS *Preposition or Adverb?* CONJUNCTIONS AND INTERJECTIONS *Su*

D CLAUSES *Appositive Phrases* EFFECTIVE SENTENCES *Combining Se*

RBS *Transitive Verbs* ADJECTIVES AND ADVERBS *Interrogative Adjec*

Grammar

The 20 Errors

Find It FIX IT

Grammar Game Plan

This handy guide will help you find and fix errors in your writing!

20 Major Grammatical Errors and How to Fix Them

ABOUT THE GRAMMAR GAME PLAN

The twenty errors in the Grammar Game Plan represent the most common errors in student writing as determined by a research study conducted by Andrea Lunsford and Karen Lunsford in 2006. Their study of college freshman writers was published by the National Council of Teachers of English in the June 2008 issue of *College Composition and Communication.*

GAME PLAN Use the right words to make your writing clear. Make sure your words say exactly what you mean them to say.

CLARIFY MEANING Do not confuse the meanings of words with similar spellings. Also, words with similar definitions can have important shades of meaning. Check that words you found in a thesaurus are used correctly.

Do you know the ~~affect~~ effect of skipping breakfast?

The bookstore was having a book sale for the whole ~~weak~~ week.

SPELL-CHECK ERRORS Computer spell-checkers often correct a misspelling with a different, similarly spelled word. Be sure to proofread your work carefully to catch these errors. In each of the following examples, the word with a strikethrough represents an inappropriate spell-checker correction.

Sally asked if he ~~sent~~ went to the movie.

The teacher chose Emilio to be the class helper for the ~~say~~ day.

✓ **Check It**

Use a current or completed draft of your work to practice using words correctly.

✓ **READ carefully.** Take the time to read your draft closely. For a double-check, have someone else read your work.
✓ **IDENTIFY possible mistakes.** Mark any difficult or commonly misused words in your draft.
✓ **USE a dictionary.** If you are not sure of a word's meaning, look it up in a dictionary.

Find It/FIX IT

1

Using the Wrong Word

Tech Tip

Be your own "spell-checker"! Proofread! Your computer's spell-checker will not identify every misspelling or incorrectly used word.

LEARN MORE
- See Chapter 20, Effective Sentences, pages 461–465
- See Writing Coach Online

HOW TO USE THE GRAMMAR GAME PLAN

This resource will help students identify and correct common errors in writing conventions. Encourage students to refer to the Grammar Game Plan during the editing stage of the writing process. Cross-references to the Grammar Game Plan are provided within the grammar chapters.

Point out that each page of the Grammar Game Plan gives helpful tips to correct a single common error in grammar, spelling, punctuation, or source citation.

Inside TRACK

1. Tell students to be particularly careful when they use a new word. Remind them that a new word they've heard or read may not mean exactly what they think it means. New words may also be spelled differently than they expect.

2. Emphasize the importance of reading word for word in the editing and proofreading stage to catch spell-check errors.

✓ **Check It**

Encourage students to use the *Check It* strategies when editing. If used consistently, these strategies become good habits. Each *Check It* includes steps to improve students' drafts.

Read, Scan, Review. Guides students to look over their drafts to find specific errors.

Identify. Suggests that students highlight or circle errors that they find

Use, Revise. Guides students to use a dictionary or another resource to correct their errors or to revise their writing to eliminate the error

Find It/FIX IT

2

Missing Comma After Introductory Element

Tech Tip

Remember to add commas to introductory elements that you cut and paste from different parts of a sentence or paragraph.

LEARN MORE
• See Chapter 25, Punctuation, pages 561, 564
• See Writing Coach Online

GAME PLAN Place a comma after the following introductory elements in your work.

WORDS Place a comma after introductory words.

Dana, would you like some help with that?

Yes, please carry the boxes for me.

PHRASES Place a comma after introductory prepositional phrases. If the prepositional phrase has only two words, a comma is not necessary.

From top to bottom, your outfit looks great.

Upon arriving on our street, you need to turn left.

Before bed we turn off the lights.

CLAUSES Introductory adverbial clauses should be followed by a comma.

Because she missed the bus, she was late for school.

Whenever her friend is in town, she meets her for dinner.

✓ *Check It*

Use a current or completed draft of your work to practice placing commas after introductory clauses.

✓ **SCAN your draft.** Look for introductory words, phrases, and clauses.

✓ **IDENTIFY missing commas.** Mark sentence starters that might need a comma.

✓ **USE your textbook.** Check the grammar section of your textbook if you are not sure whether or not to use a comma.

274   **Grammar Game Plan**

Differentiated Instruction

RTI Strategy for Below-Level Students
Invite students to create a chart of the types of introductory elements that require commas. Have students create a three-column chart with *Words, Phrases,* and *Clauses* as column headers. Then, have students find sentences in their own drafts with each type of introductory element and add them to their charts. Check students' work for correct use of commas.

PRE-AP Enrichment for Above-Level Students Remind students that strong writing contains a variety of sentence types, including sentences with introductory elements. Have students work in pairs to construct three original sentences for each type of introductory element: word, phrase, and clause. Invite student pairs to exchange papers with others to check for accuracy and correct use of commas.

GAME PLAN Provide complete citations for borrowed words and ideas. Use the citation style (such as MLA) that your teacher recommends.

MISSING CITATIONS Cite sources of direct quotes and statistics. Remember—when in doubt, cite the source.

The scientist said, "This animal was unusual in many ways" ∧(Gaspard 8).

Mr. Cleaver identified twelve new species of plant life ∧(Brooks 24).

INCOMPLETE CITATIONS Make sure your citations include complete source information. This information will vary depending on the source and the citation style. It often includes the author's name, the source's title, and the page numbers. You may use the shortened version you see here if your paper includes a bibliography where the reader can get the title of the source and the author's first name.

The author's newest book has been called "a terrific read" (∧Cho 25).

A 12 percent drop in sales was reported in January (Alberts ∧31).

✔ *Check It*

Use a current or completed draft of your work to practice documenting your sources.

✔ **REVIEW your notes.** Look for introductory words, phrases, and clauses.

✔ **USE a style guide.** Check the correct format for your citations in the style guide your teacher recommends.

Find It/FIX IT

3

Incomplete or Missing Documentation

Tech Tip

When researching for an assignment on the Internet, be sure to use only reputable sources that cite their information. Then, use the correct citation style for Internet sources, which often includes the Web site URL and date visited.

LEARN MORE
- See Chapter 11, Research Writing, pages 234–237
- See Writing Coach Online

Inside TRACK

Explain that in certain kinds of writing students will need to prove their points as well as give credit where it is due. That means the reader needs to be able to find *exactly* where students found their information.

1. Give students tips on how to keep track of their sources as they write a paper, such as maintaining a "Source Sheet" as they research.

2. Tell students that when in doubt they should include more information in a citation not less.

Find It/FIX IT

4

Vague Pronoun Reference

LEARN MORE
- See Chapter 5, Nonfiction Narration, pages 82–83
- See Writing Coach Online

GAME PLAN Create clear pronoun-antecedent relationships to make your writing more accurate and powerful.

VAGUE IDEA Pronouns such as *which, this, that*, and *these* should refer to a specific idea. To avoid a vague reference, try changing a pronoun to an adjective that modifies a specific noun.

Amaya bought new running shoes for her upcoming races. These ∧shoes will be important for many months.

UNCLEAR USE OF *IT, THEY,* AND *YOU* Be sure that the pronouns *it, they*, and *you* have a clearly stated antecedent. Replacing the personal pronoun with a specific noun can make a sentence clearer.

My best friend's dad drove us to the baseball game yesterday. I̶t̶ ∧The game was a lot of fun.

The teachers asked the students i̶f̶ ̶t̶h̶e̶y̶ ̶c̶o̶u̶l̶d̶ ∧to help with plans for the class play.

Every morning y̶o̶u̶ ∧students should get to class on time.

✓ *Check It*

Use a current or completed draft of your work to practice identifying vague pronoun references.

✓ **READ** carefully. Read your draft slowly to locate pronouns.

✓ **IDENTIFY** possible errors. Mark any vague pronoun references.

✓ **REVISE** your draft. Rewrite sentences with vague pronoun-antecedent relationships.

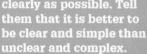

Inside TRACK

Writers sometimes falsely assume that readers will understand intended meanings. Remind students that it is their job as writers to state what they mean as clearly as possible. Tell them that it is better to be clear and simple than unclear and complex.

Have students do a word search in their papers for pronouns and confirm that each pronoun they use has a clear antecedent.

Working with ELLs **Sheltered Instruction: Metacognitive**

As students work on correcting vague pronoun references, remind them to monitor and edit their writing for pronoun-antecedent agreement, using self-corrective techniques. Remind students of rules of pronoun-antecedent agreement by reviewing the meanings of the words *singular* and *plural*. Then:

Beginning Have two volunteers stand in front of the class. Say *Two students stand.* On the board, write *He stands* and *They stand.* Ask students to copy down the correct sentence and then use the self-corrective strategy of circling the pronoun and comparing it to the antecedent, asking themselves *How many?* about each *(one/more than one)*.

GAME PLAN Spelling errors can change the meaning of a sentence. Proofread your work after spell-checking to be sure you have used the correct words.

SPELL-CHECK ERRORS Computer spell-checkers often replace misspelled words with others close in spelling but different in meaning. Proofread your work carefully to correct these errors.

 When we go camping, my dad likes to make a ~~tire~~ fire to cook our food.

Nicolas took us on a ~~talk~~ walk to the local forest preserve.

HOMOPHONES Words that are pronounced the same but have different spellings and meanings are called homophones. Check that you have used the correct homophones to convey your meaning.

 Hiroshi ~~red~~ read to his younger brother yesterday.

We want to go ~~their~~ there for vacation.

Check It

Use a current or completed draft of your work to practice spelling words correctly.

✓ **READ** carefully. Read your draft word by word looking for spelling errors.

✓ **IDENTIFY** possible mistakes. Mark any incorrect words or words that are misspelled.

✓ **USE** a dictionary. If you are not certain how to spell a word or think a homophone has been used incorrectly, check a dictionary.

Find It / FIX IT

5

Spelling Error

Tech Tip
Proper nouns are not checked by a computer spell-checker. Proofread to make sure that you have spelled people's names correctly.

LEARN MORE
- See Chapter 20, Effective Sentences, pages 461–465
- See Writing Coach Online

Inside TRACK

Tell students that running spell-check is not a guarantee that all their spelling errors will be fixed. (For example, if they left the *e* off the end of *spine*, the spell-check would not have a problem with *spin*.)

1. Explain that reading one's work out loud is often the best way to bring spell-check errors to light.

2. Encourage students to ask a peer or adult to read their draft for misused homophones.

Intermediate Have students write two short sentences using pronouns. Then, help them apply the self-corrective technique of writing an *s* above singular pronouns and antecedents and a *p* above plural pronouns and antecedents and checking that they match.

Advanced Have students write a brief paragraph on a topic of their choice using

pronouns. Then, have them apply the self-corrective technique from the Intermediate activity.

Advanced High Challenge students to complete the Advanced activity and then to explain to the class any difficult cases they found and how they resolved them.

Find It/FIX IT

6

Punctuation Error With a Quotation

GAME PLAN Quotation marks are used to identify direct quotations. Correct punctuation helps to identify quotations and relate them to your work.

DIRECT AND INDIRECT QUOTATIONS A direct quotation is enclosed in quotation marks. Indirect quotations do not need quotation marks.

"How short do you want your hair cut?" the barber asked.

The barber asked me how short I wanted my haircut.

QUOTATION MARKS WITH OTHER PUNCTUATION When commas or periods end a quotation, the punctuation goes inside the quotation marks. Question marks and exclamation marks go either inside or outside the quotation marks, depending on the sentence structure.

The park ranger said, "To your left, you'll see redwood trees."

"The trees are so tall!" Jules exclaimed.

Did he just say, "The trees are so small"?

Check It

Use a current or completed draft of your work to practice punctuating quotations correctly.

✓ **READ** carefully. If you used indirect quotations, make sure you did not put them in quotation marks.

✓ **IDENTIFY** direct quotations. Mark each direct quotation in your work. Is each quotation punctuated correctly?

✓ **REVISE** your sentences. Correct all punctuation errors in your quotations.

Inside TRACK

1. Remind students that they must use quotation marks when using a source's exact words. Have students explain the difference between a direct quotation and an indirect quotation.

2. Explain that the key to punctuating sentences with quotations is to consider the *entire* sentence. If the sentence (not the quote) asks a question or makes an exclamation, the end mark belongs *outside* the quotation marks.

Tech Tip

If you cut and paste quotations, remember to copy the taglines to make sure you have included all of the correct punctuation marks with direct quotations.

LEARN MORE

- See Chapter 25, Punctuation, pages 579–583
- See Writing Coach Online

278   **Grammar Game Plan**

Differentiated Instruction

PRE-AP Enrichment for Above-Level Students Students may find it helpful to create a quick list of rules for punctuating sentences with quotations to keep in their notebooks. Have students write the rule(s) for commas and periods, question marks and exclamation marks, and colons and semicolons. Then, work with students to create an original example for each rule.

Enrichment for Gifted/Talented Students Gifted/Talented students may do a great deal of informational research writing in their coursework. Have students research a topic of interest and write a paragraph that contains at least two quotations from expert sources. Elicit from students how and why they punctuated sentences with quotations the way they did.

Find It/FIX IT

7

Unnecessary Comma

GAME PLAN Before you insert a comma, think about how your ideas relate to one another. Make sure the comma is necessary.

APPOSITIVES If an appositive is essential to the meaning of a sentence, it is *not* set off by commas.

My neighbor Mrs. Romero knows a lot about nature.

PARTICIPIAL PHRASES If a participial phrase is essential to the meaning of a sentence, it should *not* be set off by commas.

The student studying trees for her research paper asked if Mrs. Romero knew anything about maple trees.

ADJECTIVAL CLAUSES Essential adjectival clauses should *not* be set off by commas.

The tree that gives us maple syrup is the maple tree!

✓ Check It

Use a current or completed draft of your work to practice correctly punctuating essential elements.

✓ **SCAN** Mentor Texts. Notice how professional writers use commas.

✓ **IDENTIFY** essential elements. Did you incorrectly use commas to indicate these elements?

✓ **REVISE** your sentences. Delete any commas that set off essential elements.

Tech Tip

Remember to add or delete commas as needed when you cut and paste and move text.

LEARN MORE

• See Chapter 25, Punctuation, pages 563, 565
• See Writing Coach Online

Inside TRACK

Students may need the most help identifying the elements.

1. Remind students that an appositive restates a noun.

2. Explain that participles are verbs acting as adjectives that end in *–ing* or *–ed* (e.g., *The girl walking to school is late.*) Point out that if the participle is with a helping verb, it might be acting as the verb in a sentence (e.g., *She was walking to school*).

3. Point out that adjectival clauses have a subject and a verb. Review relative pronouns and adverbs.

Find It/FIX IT

8

Unnecessary or Missing Capitalization

LEARN MORE
- See Chapter 26, Capitalization, pages 608–627
- See Writing Coach Online

GAME PLAN Follow the rules of capitalization. For example, capitalize proper nouns, the first word of a sentence, and titles of works of art.

PROPER NOUNS Names, geographical locations, organizations, abbreviations, and acronyms are examples of nouns that should be capitalized.

Abby showed her friends all of the badges she received from the Girl Scouts.

Micha lives in Texas near the Rio Grande.

There are many shows on TV about the FBI.

TITLES OF WORKS OF ART The first word and all other key words in the titles of books, poems, stories, plays, paintings, and other works of art are capitalized.

Have you read any of the poems in Shel Silverstein's book *Where the Sidewalk Ends*?

The book *The Polar Express* was made into a movie.

 Check It

Use a current or completed draft of your work to practice correctly capitalizing words.

✓ **SCAN** your draft. Look for words that are capitalized.

✓ **IDENTIFY** errors in capitalization. Mark words that might be capitalized incorrectly.

✓ **USE** your textbook. Check the grammar section of your textbook if you are not sure if a word should be capitalized.

Find It/FIX IT

9

Missing Word

GAME PLAN Make sure there are no missing words in a text so that your ideas flow smoothly and are clear to readers.

ARTICLES To make sure that ideas flow smoothly, you must proofread your work. A missing word, even a missing article (*a, an, the*), can confuse a reader.

After we went ice-skating, I wanted ∧a warm drink.

KEY IDEAS When copying and pasting text, you might miss moving a word in a sentence. If that word is part of the main idea of the sentence, your meaning could be lost.

Isabelle told her teacher that she ∧was moving to Florida.

When asked why she had to move, she said her ∧dad got a new job in Florida.

✓ Check It

Use a current or completed draft of your work to practice proofreading.

- ✓ **READ** carefully. Read your draft word by word to make sure that you did not leave out a word.
- ✓ **IDENTIFY** unclear sentences. Mark any sentences you find that do not make sense. Are they unclear because of a missing word?
- ✓ **REVISE** your sentences. Add words to your sentences to make the meaning clear.

Tech Tip

When cutting and pasting sentences, you may use the same word twice by mistake. Proofread to be sure your sentences read correctly.

LEARN MORE
- See Editing sections in the writing chapters
- See Writing Coach Online

Inside TRACK

1. Tell students that it is easy to mentally insert small words such as articles when we are proofreading our own work, even when the words aren't there. That is why reading out loud, slowly, and word for word is such a good way to catch these types of small errors.

2. Point out that anyone can leave out important words when one is writing quickly. Copying and pasting is also a time when words can be lost.

Grammar Game Plan   281

Differentiated Instruction

RTI Strategy for Special Needs Students
Students may find it helpful to review the uses of the articles *a, an,* and *the*. Explain that *a* and *an* are used to refer to general nouns, e.g., a dog, an animal, while *the* refers to a specific noun, e.g. *the* dog who ran into the woods. Encourage students to create their own example for each article, and to write the rules and examples in their notebooks for reference.

Strategy for Spanish Speakers
Students whose home language is Spanish may transfer the use of the definite article to English when making generalizations. (*The peace is a universal goal* versus *Peace is a universal goal*.) Write several sentences that use the definite article correctly and incorrectly in generalizations. Have students correct the incorrect sentences by rewriting them.

Find It/FIX IT

10

Faulty Sentence Structure

Tech Tip

Be careful when you cut one part of a sentence and paste it in another. Check that the new sentence structure is correct.

LEARN MORE

- See Chapter 20, Effective Sentences, pages 438–442
- See Writing Coach Online

GAME PLAN Sentences should express complex ideas clearly. Combine two main clauses with similar ideas to form a compound sentence.

JOINING CLAUSES When you have two sentences that express a similar idea, you can join them using a comma and a coordinating conjunction (e.g., *and, or, but, nor, yet, so*). Make sure that the ideas expressed are expressed in a similar way.

The county fair has rides that are scary, and it has rides that are tame.

The Ferris wheel was fun, yet the rollercoaster was scary.

My sister is bringing a friend, but I am bringing a cousin.

✓ Check It

Use a current or corrected draft of your work to practice joining clauses expressing similar ideas.

- ✓ **SCAN** Mentor Texts. Notice how professional writers present complex ideas.
- ✓ **READ** your draft. Mark any clauses that can be joined.
- ✓ **REVISE** your sentences. Rewrite any clauses that can be joined to form a compound sentence.

Differentiated Instruction

RTI Strategy for Below-Level Students
To reinforce the concepts of faulty parallelism and coordination, students may benefit from working with you individually to edit their drafts. Encourage students to use a highlighter to mark sentences that they think contain faulty sentence structures. Work with students to correct a few errors before encouraging them to edit the rest independently or with a partner.

PRE-AP Enrichment for Above-Level Students Remind students that high-level writing often contains complex ideas. Have students work in pairs to construct three original sentences with parallel grammatical structures and three sentences with ideas of unequal importance. Invite student pairs to exchange papers with others to check for faulty parallelism or faulty coordination and to correct errors.

Find It/FIX IT

11

Missing Comma With a Nonessential Element

GAME PLAN Use commas to set off nonessential elements of sentences.

APPOSITIVE If an appositive is not essential to the meaning of a sentence, it should be set off by commas.

The town picnic, a big event, has been held at the park for the past 30 years.

PARTICIPIAL PHRASE A participial phrase not essential to the meaning of a sentence is set off by commas.

I waited for my friend, running late again, at the park entrance.

ADJECTIVAL CLAUSE Use commas to set off an adjectival clause if it is not essential to the meaning of a sentence.

My home town, which has been around for 120 years, has a population of 2,000.

✔ Check It

Use a current or completed draft of your work to practice using commas correctly with nonessential elements.

✔ **SCAN** Mentor Texts. Notice how professional writers use commas to set off nonessential elements.

✔ **IDENTIFY** nonessential elements. Did you use commas to indicate these words, phrases, or clauses?

✔ **REVISE** your sentences. Use commas to set off nonessential elements.

Tech Tip

When you cut part of a sentence and paste it to another, be sure to include the correct punctuation. Proofread these sentences carefully.

LEARN MORE

- See Chapter 25, Punctuation, pages 563–565
- See Writing Coach Online

Inside TRACK

Tell students that when they are in doubt about whether a word, phrase, or clause is essential or nonessential to a sentence, they should take the words in question out of the sentence. Does the sentence still make sense? If so, then the information is not essential and should be separated by commas.

Another test is to add the words *by the way* before the word, phrase, or clause. If the sentence still makes sense then the phrase or clause is probably nonessential.

Find It/FIX IT

12

Unnecessary Shift in Verb Tense

Tech Tip

When you cut text from one section to paste to another, the new sentence may have verbs that are not consistent in tense. Proofread revised sentences to make sure they use consistent tenses.

LEARN MORE
- See Chapter 9, Persuasion, pages 188–189
- See Writing Coach Online

GAME PLAN Use consistent verb tenses in your work. Shift tenses only to show that one event comes before or after another.

ACTIONS OCCURRING AT THE SAME TIME Use consistent tenses to show actions that occur at the same time.

I walked to the beach, and I ~~play~~ ∧played in the sand.

I see my best friend in the hall, and I ~~tried~~ ∧try to get her attention.

ACTIONS OCCURRING AT DIFFERENT TIMES If actions occur at different times, you can switch from one tense to another. You may use a time word or phrase to show the shift in tense.

Yesterday, Sarah visted relatives in California; today she ~~flew~~∧flies home.

A few hours ago Jeffrey saw a raccoon in his yard; now he ~~saw~~∧sees a rabbit.

✔ *Check It*

Use a current or completed draft of your work to practice using consistent tenses.

✔ **SCAN** Mentor Text. Notice how professional writers use consistent tenses within a sentence.

✔ **IDENTIFY** possible mistakes. Mark any unnecessary shift in verb tense within a sentence.

✔ **USE** your textbook. Consult the grammar section of your textbook if you are not sure you have used consistent tenses.

Inside TRACK

1. Use a timeline to help students see that actions that happen at the same time should have the same tense.

2. Explain that sentences that contain a shift in time should also have a shift in verb tense (e.g., "The teacher *told* us that we *will have* a test on Friday.") Tell students that time words such as *today, tomorrow, yesterday. first, next,* and *then* can help them indicate a sequence of events.

Working with ELLs **ELL** Sheltered Instruction: Metacognitive

Have students monitor and edit their writing to correct unnecessary shifts in verb tense, using self-corrective techniques. Review verb tenses.

Beginning Have students copy these sentences from the board: *I walked to class. Now I sit down.* Read the sentences aloud, miming for support. Then, guide them in using the self-corrective technique of circling the verbs and asking themselves

When? about each *(before now / now / later)* to help them edit for tense.

Intermediate Have students copy the sentences from the Beginning activity. Have them use a self-corrective technique by writing each verb in the past, present, and future tenses, comparing these forms to the verbs in the sentences, and editing as necessary to avoid a tense shift.

GAME PLAN Use a comma before a coordinating conjunction to separate two or more main clauses in a compound sentence.

13

Missing Comma in a Compound Sentence

MAIN CLAUSES Place a comma before a coordinating conjunction (e.g. *and, but, or, nor, yet, so, for*) in a compound sentence.

My cousin Charlotte is starting college this year, and she wants to study Italian.

Reba's uncle was supposed to arrive at her house tonight, but his flight was canceled.

BRIEF CLAUSES The main clauses in some compound sentences are brief and do not need a comma if the meaning is clear.

Rita is tall and Keiko is short.

SINGLE WORDS Commas should *not* be used to separate single words that are joined by a conjunction.

We bought red and yellow paint.

He took the baseballs and bats to practice.

Check It

Use a current or completed draft of your work to practice using commas in compound sentences.

✓ **SCAN** your draft. Look for compound sentences.

✓ **IDENTIFY** missing commas. Mark any compound sentences that should be punctuated with a comma.

✓ **REVISE** your sentences. Add commas before coordinating conjunctions to separate main clauses.

Tech Tip
Be careful when you create a compound sentence by cutting and pasting from different parts of a sentence or paragraph. Remember to include a comma to separate the main clauses.

LEARN MORE
- See Chapter 25, Punctuation, pages 556, 559
- See Writing Coach Online

Inside TRACK

Students may confuse compound sentences and compound subjects and verbs.

1. Remind students that a compound sentence contains two main clauses connected by *and*, *or*, or *but*. Tell them to read each clause by itself to determine if it sounds like a complete thought.

2. Explain that "brief main clauses" are usually just a simple subject and predicate.

3. Reinforce the fact that commas are not used every time a conjunction is used.

Advanced Have pairs of students write brief paragraphs on a topic of their choice and then use the self-corrective technique described in the Intermediate activity on page 284. Have students exchange papers and check each other's work.

Advanced High Have students independently complete the Advanced activity. Then, challenge them to write a sentence using a correct shift in tense (for example, *Yesterday, I went to school, but today is Saturday*).

Find It/FIX IT

14
Unnecessary or Missing Apostrophe

Tech Tip

Proofread your draft carefully. Not all computer grammar checkers will point out incorrect uses of apostrophes.

LEARN MORE
• See Chapter 22, Using Pronouns, pages 504, 507
• See Chapter 25, Punctuation, pages 593–597
• See Writing Coach Online

Inside TRACK

Help students identify when a word is possessive.

1. Teach students to check if an *s* is possessive by using the word *of*, as in, *Susan's hat* reworked as *the hat of Susan.*

2. For plural possessives tell students to mentally say the additional *s.*

3. Remind students of the technique of replacing *its* with the phrase *it is* or *it has* in order to determine whether the word needs an apostrophe. If the replacement makes sense, the word should be inserted as *it's*; if the phrase doesn't make sense, insert *its.*

GAME PLAN Use apostrophes correctly to show possession.

SINGULAR NOUNS To show the possessive case of most singular nouns, add an apostrophe and -*s*.

 Adara's figure skating routine was the best one they saw.

PLURAL NOUNS Add an apostrophe to show the possessive case for most plural nouns ending in -*s* or -*es*. For plural nouns that do not end in -*s* or -*es*, add an apostrophe and -*s*.

 The ducks' quacks could be heard across the pond.

The workmen's tools were all stored in the shed.

POSSESSIVE PRONOUNS Possessive pronouns (e.g., *his, hers, its, our, their*) show possession without the use of an apostrophe. Do not confuse *its* and *it's*. The word *its* shows possession, but the word *it's* means "it is."

 You can tell by it's its name that his his store sells books.

 Check It

Use a current or completed draft of your work to practice showing possession.

✓ **SCAN** Mentor Texts. Notice when professional writers use apostrophes to indicate possession.

✓ **IDENTIFY** possible mistakes. Mark each apostrophe in your draft. Did you use them correctly to show possession?

✓ **REVISE** your sentences. Make sure to delete any apostrophes you used with possessive pronouns.

Differentiated Instruction

Strategy for Spanish Speakers
Students whose home language is Spanish may have difficulty with possessive pronouns because in Spanish possessive pronouns agree with the gender of the object possessed. Prepare one set of pictures of people and another set of pictures of objects. Hold up a picture from each set and ask students to use the correct possessive pronoun (*their jacket, his book,* and so on).

RTI Strategy for Special Needs Students
Refer students to page 287 and Find It/FIX IT 15. Help students understand the correct punctuation to avoid run-on sentences. Write the following: *The boy's dog ran down the street a man grabbed the leash he brought the dog back.* Have students correct the sentence: *The boy's dog ran down the street. A man grabbed the leash. He brought the dog back.* Ask students to explain why they made their corrections.

Find It/FIX IT

15

Run-on Sentence

GAME PLAN Use correct punctuation to avoid run-on sentences. A run-on sentence is two or more sentences punctuated as if they were a single sentence.

FUSED SENTENCE A fused sentence contains two or more sentences joined with no punctuation. To correct a fused sentence, place a period or an end mark between the main clauses.

He wanted to be a part of the musical, but he couldn't ~~sing the~~ sing. The drama teacher suggested that he be part of the stage crew.

Why did Jan try out for the volleyball ~~team she~~ team? She wanted to play basketball.

RUN-ON SENTENCE Place a comma and a coordinating conjunction between main clauses to avoid run-on sentences.

Raj was excited to go skateboarding, but he was also nervous because he had never tried it before.

Check It

Use a current or completed draft of your work to practice correcting run-on sentences.

✔ **SCAN** your draft. Look for run-on sentences.

✔ **IDENTIFY** missing punctuation. Mark sentences that might need a period or another end mark to separate main clauses.

✔ **REVISE** your sentences. When correcting fused sentences, vary your sentence structure.

Tech Tip

Remember to proofread your work. Not all grammar checkers identify run-on sentences.

LEARN MORE
- See Chapter 20, Effective Sentences, pages 451–455
- See Writing Coach Online

Inside TRACK

Students often create fused and run-on sentences by forgetting to link two or more independent clauses with punctuation or connecting words. Remind students to use a comma and a coordinating conjunction to form a compound sentence or a period and proper capitalization to form two separate sentences.

Find It/FIX IT

16

Comma Splice

Tech Tip

Some grammar checkers will not catch comma splices. Proofread your work carefully to avoid comma splices.

---LEARN MORE---
- See Chapter 20, Effective Sentences, pages 451–455
- See Chapter 25, Punctuation, pages 556–557
- See Writing Coach Online

GAME PLAN Use correct punctuation to avoid comma splices. A comma splice happens when two or more complete sentences are joined only with a comma.

PERIOD Replace the comma with a period (and capitalize the following word) to separate two complete thoughts.

 I read the book three times,̶ ₍.₎ I learned something new each time.

SEMICOLON Replace the comma with a semicolon if the ideas are similar.

 Tara made baked apples for dessert, ₍;₎ her family loved them.

COORDINATING CONJUNCTION A comma splice can be corrected by placing a coordinating conjunction (e.g., *and, or, but, yet, nor*) after the comma.

 I wanted to go with them, ₍yet₎ something was holding me back.

✓ *Check It*

Use a current or completed draft of your work to practice correcting comma splices.

✓ **READ** carefully. Take time to read your draft carefully. Have someone else read your work for a double-check.

✓ **IDENTIFY** possible mistakes. Mark any comma splices you find.

✓ **REVISE** your sentences. Fix comma splices in different ways to vary your sentence structure.

Differentiated Instruction

RTI Strategy for Below-Level Students
Students may benefit from working with a partner to review their draft for comma splices. Have partners review each draft and highlight examples of comma splices. Then, work with partners to determine the best strategy for correcting each error: using a comma and coordinating conjunction, using a semicolon, or creating two separate sentences.

PRE-AP Enrichment for Above-Level Students Challenge students to write a paragraph with related independent clauses. Have them avoid comma splices by using each strategy for separating independent clauses: using a comma and coordinating conjunction, using a semicolon, or creating two separate sentences.

GAME PLAN Check that pronouns agree with their antecedents in number, person, and gender. When the gender is not specified, the pronoun must still agree in number.

GENDER NEUTRAL ANTECEDENTS When gender is not specific, use *his or her* to refer to the singular antecedent.

Each teammate must return ~~their~~ his or her uniform after the game.

OR, NOR, AND When two or more singular antecedents are joined by *or* or *nor*, use a singular personal pronoun. Use a plural personal pronoun when two or more antecedents are joined by *and*.

Ren or Dara will finish ~~their~~ her history paper first.

Brian and Yoshi will ride together to ~~his~~ their basketball game.

INDEFINITE PRONOUNS A plural personal pronoun must agree with a plural indefinite pronoun. A singular personal pronoun must agree with a singular indefinite pronoun.

Both of the boys want to go somewhere warm for ~~his~~ their vacation.

One of the hostesses was late for ~~their~~ her shift.

✓ Check It

Use a current or completed draft of your work to practice pronoun-antecedent agreement.

✔ **READ** carefully. Take time to read your draft carefully. For a double-check, have someone else read your work.

✔ **IDENTIFY** possible mistakes. Mark any pronouns that do not agree with their antecedents in a sentence.

✔ **USE** your textbook. Check the grammar section of your textbook if you are not sure whether your pronouns and antecedents agree.

Tech Tip

Be careful when you cut and paste text from one sentence to another. Check that the pronouns agree with the antecedents in the new sentences you create.

LEARN MORE
- See Chapter 23, Making Words Agree, pages 529–532
- See Writing Coach Online

Inside TRACK

1. Remind students that many gender neutral antecedents are singular and require a singular pronoun.

2. Tell students that *or* and *nor* means one or the other, not both. *And*, on the other hand, means "both" which is more than one. Words joined by *and* use a plural pronoun.

3. Have students consider number when using indefinite pronouns.

Find It/FIX IT

18

Poorly Integrated Quotation

Tech Tip

Sometimes you might cut a quote from one sentence and paste it in another. Remember to revise the surrounding sentence to integrate the quote into the text.

LEARN MORE
- See Chapter 25, Punctuation, pages 575–583
- See Writing Coach Online

Inside TRACK

Students often sprinkle their research reports with quotes without considering how or whether these quotes flow with the rest of their ideas. Tell students that the extra step of framing the quotation can help strengthen the quality of their writing.

Remind students that they must tell readers who said a quote and link the quote to the main points of the report or essay. Explain that an introduction to a quotation can be an independent clause followed by a colon or a brief phrase followed by a comma.

GAME PLAN Quotations should flow smoothly into the sentence that surrounds them. Add information to explain and link quotes to the rest of your work.

QUOTE IN A SENTENCE Prepare the reader for the information contained in the quote by introducing the quote's idea.

 Find It FIX IT

The critic_∧spoke about the film's success: "Never before have I seen so much excitement about a movie" (Rico 8).

Jeremiah says_∧the play was not rehearsed: "The characters did not seem to know their lines."

QUOTE AS A SENTENCE Place an introductory phrase before or after a quotation that stands alone. In most cases, this phrase should identify the quote's author or speaker.

 Find It FIX IT

_∧According to Ms. Feldman, "The donation drive covered the expenses for the school's addition" (Kahn 19).

 Check It

Use a current or completed draft of your work to practice integrating quotations.

✓ **SCAN Mentor Texts.** Notice how professional writers integrate quotations into their work.

✓ **IDENTIFY quotes.** Mark each quote in your work. Does each quote flow smoothly with the surrounding sentence?

✓ **REVISE your sentences.** Add information as needed to explain and introduce quotes.

Differentiated Instruction

RTI Strategy for Below-Level Students
Have students work with a partner to review their drafts for abrupt uses of quotations. Have partners highlight all quotations. Then, work with partners to determine the best strategy for connecting each quote to the surrounding ideas: using an introductory clause with a colon for a quote in a sentence or using an introductory phrase and a comma for a quote that is a sentence.

PRE-AP Enrichment for Above-Level Students Have students choose a quotation to incorporate into a paragraph. Ask students to introduce the quotation using one of the two strategies presented: using an introductory clause with a colon for a quote in a sentence or using an introductory phrase and a comma for a quote that is a sentence. Invite students to share their paragraphs with classmates.

GAME PLAN Use hyphens correctly in your writing, including with compound words and compound adjectives.

COMPOUND WORDS Hyphens can connect two or more words that are used as one compound word. Some compound words do not require a hyphen. Check a current dictionary if you are not sure about hyphenating a word.

The ~~ten year old~~ ten-year-old boy asked for a ~~basket-ball~~ basketball.

Her ~~soninlaw~~ son-in-law is taking his daughter to the ~~play-ground~~ playground.

COMPOUND ADJECTIVES A compound adjective that appears before a noun should be hyphenated. Remember, do not hyphenate a compound proper noun acting as an adjective. Also, do not hyphenate a compound adjective that has a word ending in -ly.

The ~~right handed~~ right-handed pitcher is the best on the softball team.

I prefer ~~Central-American~~ Central American cuisine.

The ~~happily-smiling~~ happily smiling student just made the basketball team.

✔ *Check It*

Use a current or completed draft of your work to practice hyphenating words.

✔ **IDENTIFY** possible errors. Mark any compound adjectives before a noun that are not hyphenated.

✔ **REVISE** your sentences. Add a hyphen to words that should be hyphenated.

✔ **USE** a dictionary. Check a dictionary if you are not sure if a word should be hyphenated.

Find It/FIX IT

19

Unnecessary or Missing Hyphen

Tech Tip

The automatic hyphenation setting in word processors causes words at the end of a line of text to hyphenate automatically. Be sure that this setting is turned off when you are writing an essay.

LEARN MORE
- See Chapter 25, Punctuation, pages 587–592
- See Writing Coach Online

Inside TRACK

1. Remind students that the best way to check the use of hyphens in compound words is to use a dictionary.

2. Explain to students that a verb with more than one word is *only* hyphenated when it is used as an adjective (i.e., *the filled-up tank*) not when it is acting as the verb (i.e., *they filled up the tank*).

Find It/FIX IT

20

Sentence Fragment

GAME PLAN Use complete sentences when writing. Make sure you have a subject and a complete verb in each and that each sentence expresses a complete thought.

LACKING A SUBJECT OR VERB A complete sentence must have a subject and a complete verb.

His dog always barks at squirrels. ~~And~~ ˄The dog tries to chase them, too!

Miguel ˄is turning 12 this month.

SUBORDINATE CLAUSE A subordinate clause cannot stand on its own as a complete sentence because it does not express a complete thought.

Another baseball was hit over the fence. ~~After~~ ˄after we had already lost three baseballs behind it!

Zane asked his teacher if he could borrow the book. ~~Because~~ ˄because he wanted to read it at home.

✓ Check It

Use a current or completed draft of your work to practice writing complete sentences.

✓ **SCAN** your draft. Look for incomplete sentences.

✓ **IDENTIFY** missing words. Mark sentences that have missing subjects or verbs.

✓ **REVISE** your sentences. Rewrite any sentences that are missing subjects or verbs, or are subordinate clauses standing on their own.

Inside TRACK

1. Remind students that the best way to check for use of complete sentences is to read their drafts aloud. Better yet, have a classmate or family member read while the student writer listens for missing words.

2. Students often mistake subordinate clauses, especially lengthy ones, for complete sentences. Again, having someone else read their drafts aloud, pausing after periods, is a good strategy for catching these errors.

Tech Tip

Sometimes, when you cut text from a sentence and paste it to another, you may miss cutting the whole sentence. Make sure you have both a subject and a verb in the new sentences.

LEARN MORE
- See Chapter 20, Effective Sentences, pages 446–450
- See Writing Coach Online

---

292   Grammar Game Plan

Differentiated Instruction

RTI Strategy for Below-Level Students Have students work in pairs and read their drafts aloud to each other. Tell the readers to pause for a long moment at every period, but not unless they actually see a period. Have partners tell each other when they hear a sentence fragment or run-on sentence. Have pairs work together to correct the missing words or sentence fragments in their work.

Enrichment for Gifted/Talented Students Strong writers may think it is acceptable to use sentence fragments in their writing, either to create a certain tone or to express the writer's voice. Explain to students that sentence fragments may distract the reader and create confusion. Invite students to find examples of their written work that contain sentence fragments. Encourage students to defend a decision to keep a fragment or revise the text to correct the fragments.

Use the Online Lesson Planner at www.phwritingcoach.com to customize your instructional plan for an integrated Language Arts curriculum.

DAY 1 13.1 Nouns

"What Do You Notice?" **Objectives:** Identify, use, and understand nouns, including • as people, places, and things • concrete and abstract nouns • collective nouns • count and non-count nouns	**INSTRUCTION AND PRACTICE** Student Edition pp. 293–298 Test Warm-Up p. 299

DAY 2 13.1 Nouns *(continued)*

Objectives: Identify, use, and understand nouns, including • compound nouns • common and proper nouns	**INSTRUCTION AND PRACTICE** Student Edition pp. 300–301

DAY 3 13.2 Pronouns

Objectives: Identify, use, and understand pronouns, including • antecedents of pronouns	**INSTRUCTION AND PRACTICE** Student Edition pp. 302–304

DAY 4 13.2 Pronouns *(continued)*

Objectives: Identify, use, and understand pronouns, including • personal pronouns • reflexive and intensive pronouns	**INSTRUCTION AND PRACTICE** Student Edition pp. 305–307

Alternate Pacing Plans

• **Block Scheduling** Each day in the Lesson Planner represents a 40–50 minute block. Teachers using block scheduling may combine days to revise pacing to meet their classroom needs.

• **Accelerated Lesson Planning** Combine instructional days, focusing on concepts called out by students' diagnostic test results.

• **Integrated Language Arts Curriculum** Use the instruction and practice in this chapter to provide reinforcement, remediation, or extension of grammar concepts taught in your literature curriculum.

Links to Prentice Hall *LITERATURE*

• **Unit 1** Common and Proper Nouns, p. 40; Singular and Plural Nouns, p. 62; Personal and Possessive Pronouns, p. 108; Interrogative and Indefinite Pronouns, p. 130

WRITING COACH

Online

www.phwritingcoach.com

Grammar Assessment

Grammar Coach:	Diagnostic Assessment	End-of-Chapter Assessment	Progress Monitoring
Personalized Instruction	Students take grammar diagnostic test online and are automatically assigned instruction and practice in areas where they need support.	Teacher uses **ExamView** to administer end-of-chapter assessment and remediation. Teachers may customize **ExamView** tests or use the ones provided.	Teachers may use the **Test Warm-Ups** and the **Cumulative Reviews** in the student book or eText to check students' mastery of grammar skills. Students may also play **DimensionL** grammar video games to test their grammar skills.
Teacher-Directed Instruction	Teacher administers the diagnostic test and determines focus of instruction and practice.		

Grammar Assessment and Practice

Chapter diagnostic tests assess students' skills and assign instruction and practice.

DimensionL Video Games

Fast-paced interactive video games challenge students' mastery of grammar.

Lesson Planner continues on next page →

DAY 5 13.2 Pronouns *(continued)*

Objectives: Identify, use, and understand pronouns, including
- demonstrative pronouns
- relative pronouns
- interrogative pronouns
- indefinite pronouns

INSTRUCTION AND PRACTICE

Student Edition pp. 308–313

Test Warm-Up p. 314

" *Nouns are the stuff of writing. In terms of writer's craft, the well-chosen noun can be all the difference between bug and cockroach, or a writer saying "stuff" instead of a list of items that reveal something about a character or setting. Naming names gives a reader an exact image on which to focus.* **"**

—Jeff Anderson

Differentiated Instruction

Differentiated Instruction Boxes in this Teacher's Edition address these student populations:
- Below-Level Students
- Gifted and Talented Students
- English Language Learners
- Above-Level Students
- Special Needs Students
- Spanish Speaking Students

In addition, for further enrichment, see the **Extension** features.

Grammar Ground Rule: Keep It Clear!

Model with Students

In this chapter, keeping it clear means using pronouns correctly. For example, explain to students that personal pronouns, such as *I, he, she,* and *it,* usually have antecedents. In other words, they stand in for specific nouns or noun phrases.

Say: It's great to use pronouns to keep your writing from being repetitive and boring, but you need to keep clear to what each pronoun refers. Here's an example from someone who didn't. *She told her sister that she was not the neatest person in the world. They decided that her clothes would go only in the dresser and closet near the door and they could be messy if she wanted.* Who was not the neatest person in the world? Whose clothes would go in the dresser near the door? What could be messy? Here's how the sentences sound with clear antecedents. *She told her sister, "You're not the neatest person in the world." They decided that the sister's clothes would go only in the dresser and closet near the door. Then the clothes could be messy if she wanted.*

Small Group Activity – Finding Pronouns and Antecedents

Have students form groups to search articles on the internet or in magazines to find examples of pronouns and their antecedents. Have the groups discuss what they found. Their discussion should answer these questions:

- What is the antecedent of sentence?
- Is the antecedent clear to the reader?

Have a member of each group present their findings to the class with at least one example, and explain why the group thought the pronoun followed this grammar ground rule: Keep it clear.

Grammar Ground Rules

1. Keep it clear.
2. Make them agree.
3. Make it specific.
4. Dot your *i*'s and cross your *t*'s
5. Make it active.

NOUNS *and* PRONOUNS

ell-chosen nouns can help your readers picture the people, ces, things, and ideas in your writing.

WRITE GUY *Jeff Anderson, M.Ed.*

WHAT DO YOU NOTICE?

Search for the nouns as you zoom in on these sentences from the story "Stray" by Cynthia Rylant.

MENTOR TEXT

> The puppy stopped in the road, wagging its tail timidly, trembling with shyness and cold.
> Doris trudged through the yard, went up the shoveled drive and met the dog.

Now, ask yourself the following questions:

- Which nouns name people, which nouns name places, and which nouns name things in these sentences?
- How can you decide whether the word *shyness* is an abstract or a concrete noun?

Doris is a noun that names a person. The words *road, yard,* and *drive* are all nouns that name places. The words *puppy, tail,* and *dog* are all nouns that name things. *Shyness* is an abstract noun because you can't recognize it through your five senses. It is a noun that names an idea.

Grammar for Writers Nouns are a powerful tool writers use to tell what they have observed or what they are thinking. Choose the right noun to exactly describe people, places, things, and ideas in your writing.

What's a noun that begins with the letter L?

Lunch! Now that's a noun I can sink my teeth into.

293

CHAPTER 13

NOUNS *and* PRONOUNS

As students progress in their writing skills, it will be important for them to be able to apply the rules of grammar, usage, and mechanics to their own drafts. Use the *What Do You Notice?* feature to help them see effective conventions in the work of professional writers. Encourage students to incorporate proper voice, tense, and syntax as they edit their own writing.

Remind students that common nouns name general types of items and proper nouns name specific people, places, or things. Tell them that concrete nouns name things that you can recognize through the five senses. Abstract nouns name ideas. Then, tell them how important it is to distinguish between types of nouns in their writing. Point out that proper nouns are capitalized but common nouns are not.

WRITE GUY *Jeff Anderson, M. Ed.*

WHAT DO YOU NOTICE?

When students have read the Mentor Text, **say:** How would the meaning of the text change if the abstract nouns *shyness* and *cold* were changed to concrete nouns and the end of the sentence read: *trembling with a collar around its neck and a leash on the ground.* (**Possible response:** The text would not describe the emotion the puppy was feeling. It would describe only how the puppy looked.)

Have students read the rest of the page. **Ask:** Why is it important for writers to use nouns that name people and places as well as abstract nouns that name ideas in their writing? (**Possible response:** It helps readers to not only picture what the writer is describing but also to know what characters might be feeling or thinking.)

Grammar for Writers: Syntax

Explain to students that understanding the functions of nouns and pronouns helps writers to use them effectively. The rules and activities on these pages will help students define, identify, and use nouns and pronouns correctly.

T293

Lesson Objectives

1. Define, identify, and distinguish among four main noun groups.

2. Use various types of nouns correctly.

RULE 13.1.1 Read aloud the rule and then have students repeat the line with you.

People, Places, Things, and Ideas

Talk with the class about the importance of using names and labels—*nouns*—to identify the people they know, the places they visit, the things they see, and the ideas they have. Explain that nouns allow them to talk about their experiences and feelings, too.

Concrete and Abstract Nouns

RULE 13.1.2 Read aloud the rule and then have students repeat the lines with you.

Have students use their senses to determine whether a noun is concrete or abstract. If they come across the word *rain* in a sentence, they should ask themselves if they can see, hear, or touch it. Because rain can be touched, it is a noun. But nouns that are ideas can be difficult to identify. Words like *happiness* name a quality that you might think about or a feeling you might have. They're also nouns, even though you can't touch, see, or hear them.

13.1 Nouns

Nouns are naming words. Words such as *friend, sky, dog, love, courage,* and *Seattle* are nouns.

 RULE 13.1.1

> A **noun** names something.

Most nouns fall into four main groups.

People, Places, Things, and Ideas

The nouns in the chart are grouped under four headings. You may know most of the nouns under the first three headings. You may not have realized that all the words in the fourth group are nouns.

PEOPLE	PLACES	THINGS	IDEAS
veterinarian	Lake Mead	bumblebee	strength
Dr. Robinson	classroom	collar	honesty
Americans	kennel	motorcycle	willingness
leader	Bunker Hill	notebook	obedience

 RULE 13.1.2

Concrete and Abstract Nouns

Nouns may be classified as **concrete** or **abstract.** In the chart above, *People, Places,* and *Things* are concrete nouns. *Ideas* are abstract nouns.

> A **concrete noun** names something that can be recognized through any of the five senses. An **abstract noun** names something that cannot be recognized through the senses.

CONCRETE NOUNS			
pencil	dog	tractor	river
ABSTRACT NOUNS			
courage	fun	honor	exploration

See Practice 13.1A

See Practice 13.1B

Collective Nouns

A few nouns name groups of people or things. A *pack*, for example, is "a group of dogs or other animals that travel together." These nouns are called **collective nouns**.

> A **collective noun** names a group of people or things.

RULE 13.1.3

COLLECTIVE NOUNS		
club	herd	army
troop	orchestra	committee
class	team	group

Practice 13.1C

Count and Non-count Nouns

Nouns can be grouped as **count** or **non-count** nouns.

> **Count nouns** name things that can be counted. **Non-count nouns** name things that cannot be counted.

RULE 13.1.4

COUNT NOUNS	NON-COUNT NOUNS
orange	thunder
bench	rice
street	grass

Practice 13.1D
Practice 13.1E
Practice 13.1F

Count nouns can take an article and can be plural.

EXAMPLE   an orange   the orange   three oranges

Non-count nouns do not take an indefinite article (*a* or *an*) and cannot be plural:

EXAMPLES   We heard thunder last night.
(*not* We heard *a* thunder last night.)

He needs clothing for the camping trip.
(*not* He needs clothing*s* for the camping trip.)

Teacher Tip

If identifying nouns is difficult for students, give them an index card with the Noun Test printed on it: 1. Can I hold, see, hear, or touch this word? 2. Can I visit this word? 3. Can I "think" this word or visit it with my mind? Explain that if they answer yes to any of these questions, the word is a noun. Encourage students to continually refer to the Noun Test.

Collective Nouns

Explain that collective nouns, such as *team*, refer to a collection or group of people or things.

RULE 13.1.3   Read aloud the rule and then have students repeat the line with you.

Use a Think Aloud as part of a gradual release progression.

Think Aloud   **Say:** It sometimes makes more sense to call a group of people or things by one name. A good example of this is the word *audience.* It makes more sense to use this word than to say *the people watching the play.* Think about how long it would take me to call out your names one by one. Instead, **I can just say,** "Class, please take out your books." *Class* and *audience* are collective nouns. Each has many members, but each has one name.

Work with students to help them understand collective nouns by having them form small groups and brainstorm for collective nouns related to professional sports teams or cast members of familiar television programs.

Count and Non-count Nouns

Direct students' attention to the definitions of count and non-count nouns. Have them discuss the "clues" given by the names *Count* and *Non-count.* Point out to students that an example of a non-count noun is *milk.* You can measure milk, but you can't count it. But *toe* is a count noun because you can count toes individually.

RULE 13.1.4   Read aloud the rule and then have students repeat the lines with you.

Have students brainstorm for and list five count and five non-count nouns (without labeling them). Then, partner students and have them exchange lists. Ask students to categorize each other's words.

1. Borneo, islands, world
2. zoo, place, animals
3. neighbors, dogs, turtle
4. Australia, land, parrots
5. winter, sun, days
6. planes, wings, tail
7. bird, sticks, string, leaves, rocks, nest
8. clouds, droplets, water
9. spring, bees, plants, farms
10. trees, leaves, autumn

PRACTICE 13.1B

11. students—concrete (c); futures—abstract (a)
12. story (c); paper (c)
13. actors (c); imaginations (a)
14. carnival (c); excitement (a); school (c)
15. animals (c); climate (a)
16. people (c); election (c)
17. exercise (a); activity (a); children (c); adults (c)
18. Engineers (c); enjoyment (a); problems (c)
19. people (c); fear (a); speaking (c)
20. Firefighters (c); courage (a); building (c)

SPEAKING APPLICATION

Have each group explain how it decided that a noun was an abstract noun.

WRITING APPLICATION

Have students identify the abstract nouns and explain how they distinguished them from the concrete nouns.

PRACTICE 13.1A Finding Nouns

Read the sentences. Then, write the nouns in each sentence.

EXAMPLE   An ostrich is a type of bird.

ANSWER   *ostrich, type, bird*

1. Borneo is one of the largest islands in the world.
2. The zoo is a good place to learn about animals.
3. One of our neighbors has two dogs and a turtle.
4. Australia is sometimes called the land of parrots.
5. In winter, the sun sets earlier and days are shorter.
6. All planes have wings and a tail.
7. A bird may collect sticks, string, leaves, or rocks to build a nest.
8. Clouds are formed from droplets of water.
9. Each spring, bees pollinate the plants on many farms.
10. Many trees lose their leaves in the autumn.

PRACTICE 13.1B Identifying Concrete and Abstract Nouns

Read the sentences. Then, write the nouns in each sentence and label each one *concrete* or *abstract*.

EXAMPLE   The nurse used humor to cheer her patients.

ANSWER   *nurse* — concrete
humor — abstract
patients — concrete

11. The eager students wanted to learn about their futures.
12. His story was written on lined paper.
13. Actors must have active imaginations.
14. The carnival caused excitement throughout the school.
15. Some animals cannot live in a cold climate.
16. Many young people voted in the election.
17. Exercise is an important activity for both children and adults.
18. Engineers often find enjoyment in solving math problems.
19. Most people have a fear of public speaking.
20. Firefighters show amazing courage when they race into a burning building.

SPEAKING APPLICATION

In a small group, brainstorm a short list of abstract nouns (two or three more nouns than group members). Then, have each person choose one of the nouns and use it in a sentence.

WRITING APPLICATION

Write two sentences and include one concrete and one abstract noun in each sentence.

PRACTICE 13.1C Finding Collective Nouns

Read the pairs of nouns. Each pair includes one collective noun. Write the collective noun.

EXAMPLE   child, family

ANSWER   *family*

1. elephant, herd
2. student, class
3. employee, staff
4. team, player
5. coin, collection
6. Senate, Senator
7. panel, juror
8. soprano, choir
9. faculty, teacher
10. club, member

PRACTICE 13.1D Identifying Count and Non-count Nouns

Read the sentences. Then, list the count and non-count nouns. One sentence has only count nouns.

EXAMPLE   We crammed our luggage into the car.

ANSWER   count noun — *car*
non-count noun — *luggage*

11. We heard thunder before the storm began.
12. My little sister began to play hockey when she was ten years old.
13. All living things need oxygen.
14. There is too much furniture to fit into the room.
15. If you like to dance, you will love our neighborhood's block parties.
16. Has the mail come yet?
17. When they saw a skunk on the grass by the sidewalk, they waited to leave the house.
18. Traffic on the highway is always heavy on weekends.
19. Honesty is the best policy.
20. Everyone in the city lost electricity during the blackout.

SPEAKING APPLICATION

With a partner, take turns telling about a game you watched recently. Your partner should listen for and name two collective nouns, two count nouns, and two non-count nouns you used.

WRITING APPLICATION

Write three sentences and include one of the following in each: a collective noun, a count noun, and a non-count noun. Read your sentences out loud to a partner. Have your partner name the non-count nouns you used.

Practice   297

PRACTICE 13.1C

1. herd
2. class
3. staff
4. team
5. collection
6. Senate
7. panel
8. choir
9. faculty
10. club

PRACTICE 13.1D

11. non-count noun (n-c) thunder; count noun (c) storm
12. (c) sister; (n-c) hockey; (c) years
13. (c) things; (n-c) oxygen
14. (n-c) furniture; (c) room
15. (c) neighborhood; (c) parties
16. (n-c) mail
17. (c) skunk; (n-c) grass; (c) sidewalk; (c) house
18. (n-c) traffic; (c) highway; (c) weekends
19. (n-c) honesty; (c) policy
20. (c) city; (n-c) electricity; (c) blackout

SPEAKING APPLICATION

Have partners identify the collective nouns and explain how they recognized them to show that they can use and understand the function of nouns.

WRITING APPLICATION

Have students share their sentences with the class, pointing out the collective nouns, count nouns, and non-count nouns to show that they can use and understand the function of nouns.

Working with ELLs   ELL Sheltered Instruction: Cognitive

As students complete Practice 13.1B (on page 296), help them use prior knowledge to understand and learn academic vocabulary heard during classroom instruction. Write *noun, concrete,* and *abstract* on the board and orally review their meaning.

Beginning Partner students with more fluent peers to provide home language equivalents for the nouns in sentences 17 and 20 (on page 296), using prior knowledge. Guide them in learning the academic words with simple questions like: *Is courage a concrete noun?*

Intermediate Have groups of students use prior knowledge to discuss the academic vocabulary and review the nouns in Practice 13.1B (on page 296).

Have them use the words in these cloze sentences: _____ *is a concrete noun. It names a thing.* _____ *is an abstract noun. It names an idea.*

Advanced Direct students to use the **KIM strategy** as they listen to you explain the academic vocabulary. Have them create a three-column chart labeled *Key Word, Information,* and *Memory Cue,* filling in the first column with the vocabulary and using prior knowledge to complete the chart.

Advanced High Have students complete the Advanced activity. Then, have them write a compare-and-contrast paragraph about concrete and abstract nouns, drawing on prior knowledge.

PRACTICE 13.1E

1. equipment
2. soccer
3. fruit
4. lemonade
5. jewelry
6. art
7. paint
8. information
9. knowledge
10. rice

PRACTICE 13.1F

Answers will vary. Sample answers:

11. strength—She showed her strength when she went climbing.
12. paper—I bought paper for my printer.
13. software—The software is old.
14. volleyball—Our team plays volleyball on the beach.
15. dust—The old piano is collecting dust.
16. sadness—We felt sadness when Julio moved last year.
17. rice—I like rice with my beans.
18. music—The band played some of the girl's favorite music.
19. salt—The recipe called for salt.
20. production—The production of laptop computers is increasing.

SPEAKING APPLICATION

Students should demonstrate they understand non-count nouns by explaining how they recognized the non-count nouns.

WRITING APPLICATION

Students' sentences should demonstrate that students can use non-count nouns in writing.

PRACTICE 13.1E Using Non-count Nouns

Read the sentence and the two word choices that follow it. Write the sentence using the word that is a non-count noun.

EXAMPLE   We are having _____ with the sauce. (pasta, steak)

ANSWER   *We are having pasta with the sauce.*

1. The school is replacing the _____ in the media center. (copiers, equipment)
2. We will play _____ on the field on Saturday. (soccer, games)
3. Danica needs to get some _____ from the store. (bananas, fruit)
4. At her party, my sister served _____. (lemonade, sandwiches)
5. Some _____ will be displayed at the art fair. (earrings, jewelry)
6. The museum has many pieces of fine _____. (art, paintings)
7. I found _____ in the attic. (toys, paint)
8. The test will cover the _____ we learned in the chapter. (information, facts)
9. Max has jazz band _____. (knowledge, instruments)
10. The dish was served on a bed of _____. (peas, rice)

PRACTICE 13.1F Recognizing Non-count Nouns

Read the sentence. Find and write the non-cou noun. Then, write a sentence using that noun

EXAMPLE   Jamie heard your laughter in the room down the hall.

ANSWER   *laughter— His jokes always bri laughter.*

11. Arturo has been lifting weights to build h strength.
12. We re-use shopping bags to save paper.
13. Marissa needs to install new software on computer.
14. My brother plays volleyball every week.
15. The table is covered with a layer of dust.
16. Sometimes it is impossible to hide tears of sadness.
17. If you cook rice too long, it gets sticky.
18. All night long, music blared through the o window.
19. It is not good to use too much salt when y cook.
20. The company stopped production because one was buying the car.

SPEAKING APPLICATION

In a small group, talk about different sports. Choose a recorder to take notes. Review the notes and identify non-count nouns. Then, each person writes two sentences using non-count nouns and reads the sentences to the group.

WRITING APPLICATION

Think about your favorite foods. Write three sentences about food. Include a non-count nou in each one. Read your sentences to a partner, who should identify your non-count nouns.

298   Nouns and Pronouns

Test Warm-Up

Test Warm-Up

1. **B** Change *a* to **the**
2. **G** James offered to go for tacos while his sister, Tamara, promised to watch the luggage.
3. **C** Dad gave James ten dollars and asked for cheddar cheese on his taco.
4. **H** Change *foods* to **food**

Reteach

If students have not mastered these skills, review the content in Section 13.1.4 Count and Non-count Nouns.

Test Tip

Many students answer some questions incorrectly because they have misread the directions for the section or misunderstood what individual questions have asked them to do. Encourage students to read carefully all instructions for a section before beginning the section. Remind students to read each question stem slowly and carefully, making sure that they don't miss any key words in the stem, such as *not, always, never, first, second, before,* or *after.*

DIRECTIONS

Read the introduction and the passage that follows. Then, answer the questions to show that you can use and understand the function of non-count nouns in reading and writing.

This paragraph tells what happens when James offers to get food. Read the paragraph and think about the changes you would suggest as a peer editor. When you finish reading, answer the questions that follow.

James Almost Meets Disaster

(1) Because of a bad weather, flights were delayed, and people were milling around the airport waiting for information. (2) James offered to go for tacos. (3) His sister, Tamara, promised to watch the luggages. (4) Dad gave James ten dollar and asked for cheddar cheeses on his taco. (5) James went to the food stand and ordered. (6) Then, he remembered milk for his baby brother. (7) Finally, balancing a full tray, James searched the crowd for his family and nearly knocked over a garbage can. (8) What a big mess that would have been with foods flying everywhere!

1 What change, if any, should be made in sentence 1?

A Change *weather* to **weathers**
B Change *a* to **the**
C Change *information* to **informations**
D Make no change

2 What is the BEST way to combine sentences 2 and 3?

F James offered to go for tacos, his sister, Tamara, promised to watch the luggages.
G James offered to go for tacos while his sister, Tamara, promised to watch the luggage.
H James offered to go for taco, because his sister, Tamara, promised to watch the luggage.
J James offered to go for tacos because his sister, Tamara, promised to watch the luggages.

3 How should sentence 4 be revised?

A Dad gave James ten dollars and asked for cheddar cheeses on his taco.
B Dad gave James moneys and asked for cheddar cheeses on his taco.
C Dad gave James ten dollars and asked for cheddar cheese on his taco.
D Dad gave James ten dollar and asked for cheddar cheese on his taco.

4 What change, if any, should be made to sentence 8?

F Change *mess* to **messes**
G Change *big* to **bigs**
H Change *foods* to **food**
J Make no change

Recognizing Compound Nouns

Discuss with students the fact that compound nouns consist of two separate nouns.

RULE 13.1.5 Read aloud the rule and then have students repeat the lines with you.

Use an index card or sheet of paper to cover up one half of several compound nouns. Show students how a compound noun consists of two separate words. **Say:** Some nouns are created by combining two or more words. The new noun, called a compound noun, uses the definitions of two different words to create a new meaning. **Ask:** Can someone tell me the two words that make up the compound noun *toothpaste*?

Separate these compound nouns into their word parts and list them on the board: *grandfather, schoolhouse, doorbell, nowhere, railroad.*

Work with students to combine the single words to create compound words.

Have student pairs brainstorm for and write three or more compound words. Ask students to share their words with the class.

Using Common and Proper Nouns

Point out to students that proper nouns name a particular person, place, or thing. For example, the *Atlantic Ocean* and *Harriet Tubman* are proper nouns. On the other hand, a common noun can bring to mind many different people, places, or things. The word *woman* can be used to describe billions of different people.

RULE 13.1.6 Read aloud the rule and then have students repeat the lines with you.

Have students identify these nouns as proper or common: *firefighter, Mt. McKinley, David, food, determination.* Ask students to explain whether or not each noun should be capitalized.

Teacher Tip

For some students, remembering the many categories of nouns will be a daunting task. Create a worksheet that lists each noun category. Define the noun category and list several examples. Allow students to refer to the sheet when necessary.

Recognizing Compound Nouns

Some nouns are made up of two or more words. *Classroom* is a **compound noun** made up of *class* and *room*.

> A **compound noun** is one noun made by joining two or more words.

Compound nouns are written in three different ways: as single words, as hyphenated words, and as two or more separate words.

COMPOUND NOUNS		
SINGLE WORDS	HYPHENATED WORDS	SEPARATE WORDS
crossbar	by-product	dinner jacket
firefighter	right-hander	pole vault
thunderstorm	middle-distance	pen pal
classroom	mother-in-law	chief justice

See Practice 13.1G

Using Common and Proper Nouns

All nouns can be divided into two large groups: **common nouns** and **proper nouns.**

> A **common noun** names any one of a class of people, places, things, or ideas. A **proper noun** names a specific person, place, thing, or idea.

Common nouns are not capitalized. Proper nouns are always capitalized.

COMMON NOUNS	PROPER NOUNS
inventor	Alexander Graham Bell
village	Tarrytown
story	"The Tell-Tale Heart"
organization	American Red Cross
idea	Germ Theory of Disease

See Practice 13.1H

300   **Nouns and Pronouns**

Differentiated Instruction

RTI Strategy for Special Needs Students

Have students touch and see a variety of "nouns," such as windows, doors, and desks. To demonstrate place, have students visit the cafeteria or use a wall map to point out places they've been. Have students record the nouns in a chart labeled *People, Places, Things,* and *Ideas.* After students have completed the first three columns of their charts, have them complete column 4—*Ideas,* or feelings, concepts, or things that students can "visit in their minds." Write these on the board: *justice, honesty, courage, patience, friendship.* Talk about how these concepts are named by nouns.

Strategy for Spanish Speakers

Students whose home language is Spanish may erroneously transfer Spanish capitalization rules to English nouns. On the board, write a list of proper nouns in English. Include days of the week, months of the year, names of languages, and personal titles. Have students translate the words into Spanish and explain whether the words should be capitalized. (None are capitalized except abbreviations for personal titles, such as *Sr.* and *Sra.*) Write the Spanish words next to their English equivalents, and summarize the differences in capitalization.

PRACTICE 13.1G ▷ Identifying Compound Nouns

Read the sentences. Then, write the compound nouns, and draw a line between the words that make up each compound noun.

EXAMPLE   We have a doghouse in the yard.

ANSWER   *dog | house*

1. We built our campsite on the hilltop.
2. In high school we will study more science.
3. Wildflowers covered the countryside.
4. Always wear your seat belt when in a car.
5. Fireflies flickered in the moonlight.
6. Many children start day care at an early age.
7. Mr. Nguyen's brother-in-law is a firefighter.
8. Tomorrow we'll slide our homemade rowboat into the lake.
9. My grandfather used to play basketball.
10. All you need for this trip are a fishing pole and sunglasses.

PRACTICE 13.1H ▷ Using Common and Proper Nouns

Read the sentences. Then, rewrite them, replacing the underlined words with proper nouns.

EXAMPLE   My class took a trip to the city last month.

ANSWER   *My class took a trip to Atlanta last April.*

11. He pointed to an ocean on the classroom globe.
12. We saw a planet through the telescope.
13. Yesterday, I heard someone speaking a foreign language.
14. That store is my favorite store at the mall.
15. We went to the zoo.
16. When I started school, I met the teacher.
17. In class, we studied a country.
18. I would love to see a game at the sports stadium.
19. I walked slowly along the street, which is near my house.
20. I really enjoyed reading a book.

SPEAKING APPLICATION

With a partner, name as many things as you can related to your classroom and school that are compound nouns. Take turns saying how the parts create meaning. For example, *wastebasket* is a basket for waste.

WRITING APPLICATION

Write two or three sentences about places in and around your town. Use proper nouns to name places (streets, stores, parks, and so on) that you know or visit.

Practice   301

PRACTICE 13.1G ▷

1. camp | site, hill | top
2. high | school
3. wild | flowers, country | side
4. seat | belt
5. fire | flies, moon | light
6. day | care
7. brother- | in- | law, fire | fighter
8. home | made, row | boat
9. grand | father, basket | ball
10. fishing | pole, sun | glasses

PRACTICE 13.1H ▷

Answers will vary. Sample answers:

11. . . . Pacific Ocean . . .
12. . . . Mars . . .
13. . . . French.
14. The Shirt Shop . . .
15. . . . Bronx Zoo.
16. . . . Mrs. Martinez.
17. . . . Russia.
18. . . . Yankee Stadium.
19. . . . Greenway Street . . .
20. . . . *The Story of Doctor Dolittle.*

SPEAKING APPLICATION

Have partners take turns using the compound nouns they named in sentences.

WRITING APPLICATION

Have students read their sentences aloud to a partner. Partners should identify the proper nouns in the sentences.

Working with ELLs   ELL Sheltered Instruction: Cognitive

As students study nouns, guide them to learn the relationships between sounds and letters of the English language. Using words from the Practice activities (on page 301), reinforce their ability to decode words by recognizing sound-letter relationships in affixes.

Beginning Write the word *imagination* on the board, using visuals to aid comprehension. Help students decode the first four syllables using sound-letter relationships: /im/ /a/ /ji/ /nā /. Then, explain they will read the suffix *-tion* at the end of many nouns, and that it is pronounced /shen/. Have them write *imagination* as you sound it out. Repeatedly choral read the word.

Intermediate Say the *words actor, firefighter,* and *imagination* and write them on the board. Help students decode each word using sound-letter relationships. Focus on the word parts in each word. Tell them that recognizing familiar suffixes like *-or, -er,* and *-tion* can help them read many nouns.

Advanced Have students complete the Intermediate activity. Then, have them decode *droplets, pollinate, engineer, climate,* and *amazing.*

Advanced High Have students complete the Advanced activity. Have partners create flash cards to test their reading and spelling of the words.

Lesson Objectives

1. Identify and distinguish between various types of pronouns.

2. Use a variety of complete sentences (simple, compound, complex) that include correctly identified antecedents.

3. Identify, use, and understand the function of relative pronouns such as *whose, that,* and *which.*

Discuss how pronouns eliminate redundancy and contribute to the "flow" of a sentence.

RULE 13.2.1 Read aloud the rule and then have students repeat the lines with you.

Use a Think Aloud as part of a gradual release progression.

Think Aloud

Say: Pronouns are far more useful than you might think. While they tend to be short words such as *her* and *it*, they pack a lot of power. Let's try to have a conversation without using any pronouns.

Work with students to help them understand the function of pronouns. Conduct a conversation with a student without using any pronouns. Remind the student to respond without using pronouns. *[Student], what is [student]'s favorite sport? Be sure to tell [teacher] why [student] likes [student]'s favorite sport.*

Have small groups of students repeat the same activity. Have them discuss how pronouns helped the flow of the second conversation.

13.2 Pronouns

Pronouns are words that take the place of nouns. They are used rather than repeating a noun again and again. Pronouns make sentences clearer and more interesting.

 RULE 13.2.1

A pronoun is a word that takes the place of a noun or a group of words acting as a noun.

Imagine, for example, that you are writing about Aunt Jenny. If you were using only nouns, you might write the following sentence:

WITH NOUNS   Aunt Jenny was late because **Aunt Jenny** had waited for **Aunt Jenny's** computer technician.

WITH PRONOUNS   Aunt Jenny was late because **she** had waited for **her** computer technician.

Sometimes a pronoun takes the place of a noun in the same sentence.

EXAMPLES   My father opened **his** files first.
pronoun

Many people say exercise has helped **them**.
pronoun

A pronoun can also take the place of a noun used in an earlier sentence.

EXAMPLES   My father opened his e-mail first. **He** couldn't wait any longer.
pronoun

Students must take a science class. **They** can choose biology or ecology.
pronoun

A pronoun may take the place of an entire group of words.

EXAMPLE   Trying to make the team is hard work. **It** takes hours of practice every day.
pronoun

Grammar Tutorials
Brush up on your Grammar skills with these animated videos.

Grammar Practice
Practice your grammar skills with Writing Coach Online.

Grammar Games
Test your knowledge of grammar in this fast-paced interactive video game.

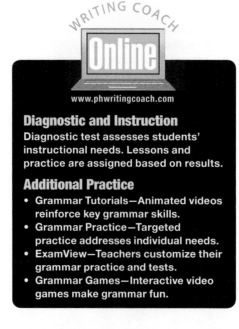

WRITING COACH
Online
www.phwritingcoach.com

Diagnostic and Instruction
Diagnostic test assesses students' instructional needs. Lessons and practice are assigned based on results.

Additional Practice
- **Grammar Tutorials**—Animated videos reinforce key grammar skills.
- **Grammar Practice**—Targeted practice addresses individual needs.
- **ExamView**—Teachers customize their grammar practice and tests.
- **Grammar Games**—Interactive video games make grammar fun.

Antecedents of Pronouns

The word or group of words that a pronoun replaces or refers to is called an **antecedent.**

> An **antecedent** is the noun (or group of words acting as a noun) to which a pronoun refers.

13.2.2 RULE

EXAMPLES   The **firefighters** described how **they** did **their** jobs.
antecedent   pronoun   pronoun

Finally, the **rescue worker** reappeared. **She** seemed to be unharmed.
antecedent   pronoun

How Kim was rescued is amazing. **It** is a story that will be told often.
antecedent   pronoun

Although **he** was known as an expert software
pronoun
developer, **Darryl** enjoyed selling computers.
antecedent

See Practice 13.2A

Some kinds of pronouns do not have any antecedent.

EXAMPLES   **Everyone** knows what the truth is.
indefinite pronoun

Who will represent the class at the town-wide
interrogative pronoun
school meeting?

The pronouns *everyone* and *who* do not have a specific antecedent because their meaning is clear without one.

See Practice 13.2B

Antecedents of Pronouns

Remind students that pronouns almost always have antecedents, or words to which they refer. Antecedents are often easy to identify by asking *to whom or what does the pronoun refer?*

RULE 13.2.2 Read aloud the rule and then have students repeat the lines with you.

Write on the board several sentences with pronouns and antecedents. Demonstrate for students the process for identifying the antecedents in each. First, place a box around any pronouns. Then, draw an arrow connecting the pronouns to their antecedents. As you do this, ask questions such as *Who is him?* or *What is it?*

Next, have students create and say aloud several complete sentences that include pronouns and antecedents. Have students identify each pronoun and its antecedent. Then, write the following list of pronouns on the board: *it, his, they, she.* Have students write a short paragraph using these pronouns and clear antecedents. Then, have partners review each other's paragraphs, drawing an arrow from each pronoun to its antecedent.

Extension

To help students synthesize and apply what they have learned about pronouns, have them find pronouns and their antecedents in a story or book you have studied in class. Select a passage of at least 100 words, making sure it has pronouns. Have students copy the passage. Then, ask them to work in pairs or small groups to underline each pronoun and draw an arrow to its antecedent, if any. When students are finished, call for a volunteer to read the passage to the class, pausing to point out every pronoun and antecedent.

Teacher Tip

Anticipate student concern over what constitutes an indefinite pronoun by listing some. Point out indefinite pronouns such as *another, each,* and *either.* Then, have students come up with others. Tell students that words such as *plenty* (*I've had plenty.*) and *enough* (*The children have seen enough.*) are indefinite pronouns, too.

Differentiated Instruction

RTI Strategy for Below-Level Students
It may be helpful to have struggling students create a reference sheet that lists several common pronouns. This way, they can begin to memorize the most frequent ones while working with them. Have students fold a sheet of paper in half. On one side they should list common pronouns. On the second side they should write sentences using the pronouns. Provide highlighters and have students highlight the pronouns throughout the reference sheet.

PRE-AP Enrichment for Above-Level Students Have students write a short story about a topic of their choice. In the story, students should include these types of sentences:

1. Two sentences in which a pronoun takes the place of a noun in the same sentence
2. Two sentences in which a pronoun takes the place of a noun used in an earlier sentence
3. Two sentences in which a pronoun takes the place of an entire group of words

T303

PRACTICE 13.2A

1. they, children

2. he, Dad

3. she, Lianna

4. its, car

5. their, people

6. her, teacher

7. it, squirrel

8. his, mayor

9. hers, mother

10. they, students

PRACTICE 13.2B

11. I like reading <u>books</u>. They always give me new ideas.

12. If I left the <u>cupboard</u> open, could you close it for me?

13. <u>Farmer Johnson</u> discovered that he liked organic farming.

14. <u>Ahmed and Sepida</u> went to their rooms to do homework.

15. <u>Rosa</u> wanted everyone to see her paintings.

16. <u>Washington, D.C.</u>, is famous for its great monuments.

17. My <u>mom</u> is a great cook. I wonder how she learned to cook.

18. I returned the <u>dress</u> because it didn't fit.

19. By early autumn, the <u>tree</u> had lost all its leaves.

20. <u>Billy</u> ran because he was afraid the bus would leave without him.

PRACTICE 13.2A Recognizing Pronouns and Antecedents

Read the sentences. Then, write each pronoun and its antecedent.

EXAMPLE   Many people are interested in dogs and their care.

ANSWER   *their, dogs*

1. The children wanted to play, so they grabbed the ball.

2. Dad said he would be working in the basement.

3. Lianna thought she would like to try out for the school play.

4. That car is known for its reliability.

5. Most people can remember their phone numbers.

6. The teacher asked if Joseph had seen her ruler.

7. The squirrel looked as if it couldn't find any acorns.

8. The mayor knew that his job included balancing the budget.

9. My mother said the car on television is just like hers.

10. The students understood that they needed to finish the assignment.

PRACTICE 13.2B Supplying Pronouns for Antecedents

Read the sentences. Then, write each sentence, filling in the blank with the appropriate pronoun. Correctly identify and underline the antecedent of the pronoun you supply.

EXAMPLE   Did Michael bring _____ camera?

ANSWER   *Did <u>Michael</u> bring his camera?*

11. I like reading books. _____ always give me new ideas.

12. If I left the cupboard open, could you close _____ for me?

13. Farmer Johnson discovered that _____ liked organic farming.

14. Ahmed and Sepida went to _____ rooms to do homework.

15. Rosa wanted everyone to see _____ paintings.

16. Washington, D.C., is famous for _____ great monuments.

17. My mom is a great cook. I wonder how _____ learned to cook.

18. I returned the dress because _____ didn't fit.

19. By early autumn, the tree had lost all _____ leaves.

20. Billy ran because he was afraid the bus would leave without _____.

304   Nouns and Pronouns

Recognizing Personal Pronouns

The pronouns used most often are **personal pronouns.**

> **Personal pronouns** refer to (1) the person speaking or writing, (2) the person listening or reading, or (3) the topic (person, place, thing, or idea) being discussed or written about.

RULE 13.2.3

The first-person pronouns *I, me, my, mine, we, us, our,* and *ours* refer to the person or persons speaking or writing.

EXAMPLES   **I** like the new design.

            Please give **us** an example.

The second-person pronouns *you, your,* and *yours* refer to the person or persons spoken or written to.

EXAMPLES   **You** will see the photo.

            Your friend is at the door.

The third-person pronouns *he, him, his, she, her, hers, it, its, they, them, their,* and *theirs* refer to the person, place, thing, or idea being spoken or written about.

EXAMPLES   **He** wants to listen to the radio show.

            They wrote letters to the editor.

Some personal pronouns show possession. Although they can function as adjectives, they are still identified as personal pronouns because they take the place of possessive nouns.

EXAMPLES   **Mary's** town paper comes out weekly.
                possessive noun

           Her town paper comes out weekly.
             possessive pronoun

The chart on the next page presents the personal pronouns.

Pronouns 305

Differentiated Instruction

RTI Strategy for Below-Level Students

Have students practice using personal pronouns. For those struggling to recognize personal pronouns, provide an index card with five personal pronouns written across the top. Tell students to pretend they're writing a postcard to a relative in a faraway place. Explain that their postcard must include each of the listed personal pronouns. Once students are finished, discuss the functions of the personal pronouns in each sentence.

Enrichment for Gifted/Talented Students

Have students go on a creative scavenger hunt for personal and possessive pronouns. Students can listen to a song and write the pronouns they hear or read an excerpt of a play and list as many pronouns as they can find. Once students have collected the personal and possessive pronouns, have them create a crossword puzzle using them. They should design the puzzles and create clues for each pronoun using key words that reveal its definition. Students should share the puzzles with the class.

Recognizing Personal Pronouns

Explain that it is important to understand how personal pronouns function so that we can use them correctly when we construct sentences. Read aloud the first examples and explain to whom or what the pronouns refer.

RULE 13.2.3 Read aloud the rule and then have students repeat the lines with you.

Use a Think Aloud as part of a gradual release progression.

Think Aloud   **Say:** We all use personal pronouns all the time. **I am using them** right now. Can you tell me three personal pronouns I have used just while I was talking to you? (**Response:** we, I, and you)

Sometimes, personal pronouns show possession. **Work with students** to help them understand how possessive nouns show possession. Then, illustrate how possessive pronouns that represent those nouns can also show possession. Ask students a question such as this: *Whose bag is that?* (**Possible answer:** This is my bag.) **Say:** Which word in your response shows that the object belongs to you? (Accept the correct answer.)

Have student pairs brainstorm for a list of personal pronouns. Have them write their ideas in a two-column *Personal Pronouns* chart. The first column should be called *Non-Possessive.* The second column should be called *Possessive.* Work with students to include correct choices and to exclude incorrect choices. Have students put their lists aside. (After students examine the Personal Pronouns chart on page 306, have them make adjustments as necessary.)

Reflexive and Intensive Pronouns

Explain that reflexive and intensive pronouns have similar endings—*self* or *selves*—but they do not perform the same function.

RULE 13.2.4 Read aloud the rule and then have students repeat the lines with you.

Draw students' attention to the fact that a reflexive pronoun directs the action of a verb back on the subject of that verb. Point out the importance of being able to identify the subject and verb in a sentence when trying to determine if a pronoun is reflexive. Write this sentence on the board: *Doris saw herself in the mirror.* Ask students to name the subject and the verb. (*Doris* and *saw*) Underline the subject once and the verb twice. Point to the word *herself* and ask if the word *herself* directs the action *saw* to the subject *Doris*. (Yes.) Tell students that the word *herself* is a reflexive pronoun in this sentence.

Provide several more examples for practice.

RULE 13.2.5 Read aloud the rule and then have students repeat the lines with you.

Tell students that intensive pronouns end similarly to reflexive pronouns but do not direct the verb's action back to the subject. These pronouns are kind of like decorations—they add emphasis but they are not needed. Write these sentences on the board: *I myself do not like chocolate. I do not like chocolate.* Explain that the intensive pronoun *myself* does not change the meaning of the sentence. Ask students why they think writers and speakers use intensive pronouns. (**Possible answers:** To make a point; for stylistic purposes.)

Teacher Tip

Give students a rectangular slip of paper. Tell them to place the slip over words ending with *-self* or *-selves* when they are unsure if the word is reflexive or intensive. If, when they place the slip over the word, the sentence's meaning does not change, they know they have discovered an intensive pronoun.

T306

PERSONAL PRONOUNS		
	SINGULAR	PLURAL
First person	I, me, my, mine	we, us, our, ours
Second person	you, your, yours	you, your, yours
Third person	he, him, his, she, her, hers, it, its	they, them, their, theirs

See Practice 13.2C

Reflexive and Intensive Pronouns

The ending *-self* or *-selves* can be added to some pronouns to form **reflexive** or **intensive pronouns.** These two types of pronouns look the same, but they function differently within a sentence.

REFLEXIVE AND INTENSIVE PRONOUNS		
	SINGULAR	PLURAL
First person	myself	ourselves
Second person	yourself	yourselves
Third person	himself, herself, itself	themselves

> A **reflexive pronoun** directs the action of the verb toward its subject. Reflexive pronouns point back to a noun or pronoun earlier in the sentence.

A reflexive pronoun is essential to the meaning of a sentence.

REFLEXIVE **Joy** helped **herself** to some turkey.
        noun   reflexive pronoun

        They poured **themselves** some milk.
        pronoun   reflexive pronoun

See Practice 13.2D

> An **intensive pronoun** simply adds emphasis to a noun or pronoun in the same sentence.

An intensive pronoun is not essential to the meaning of the sentence.

INTENSIVE The mayor **herself** attended the carnival.

306   **Nouns and Pronouns**

PRACTICE 13.2C Recognizing Personal
Pronouns

Read the sentences. Then, write the personal
pronouns in each sentence.

EXAMPLE   We took a trip to San Antonio, Texas,
last summer.

ANSWER   *We*

1. I like having dinner with my family.
2. The neighbors say that ours is the nicest
garden.
3. Is that T-shirt yours or mine?
4. Mom and Dad trusted us, and we didn't
disappoint them.
5. Luis asked his mother to remind him to
return the library books.
6. We forgot to bring food, but Carla and Shaun
gave us some of theirs.
7. You can put your books over there.
8. Dad and Tim handed the usher their entrance
tickets.
9. Do you want me to come along too?
10. My parents said they were going to a movie.

PRACTICE 13.2D Supplying Reflexive and
Intensive Pronouns

Read the sentences. Write the reflexive or
intensive pronoun that completes each sentence.

EXAMPLE   I painted that painting _____.

ANSWER   *myself*

11. We cooked this meal _____.
12. The coach _____ was amazed at the team's
playing.
13. Those students painted the room _____.
14. Adam called the dentist _____.
15. Kim said she could do it by _____.
16. Allow _____ enough time for research.
17. The map _____ wasn't that detailed.
18. Help _____ to the free samples.
19. The trip _____ took one week.
20. The drivers congratulated _____.

Practice   307

PRACTICE 13.2C

1. I, my
2. ours
3. yours, mine
4. us, we, them
5. his, him
6. We, us, theirs
7. You, your
8. their
9. you, me
10. my, they

PRACTICE 13.2D

11. ourselves
12. herself *or* himself
13. themselves
14. himself
15. herself
16. yourself *or* yourselves
17. itself
18. yourself *or* yourselves
19. itself
20. themselves

Working with ELLs   ELL Sheltered Instruction: Cognitive

As students learn about personal
pronouns, help them enhance and
confirm their understanding as they read.
Help students use visual and contextual
support to develop the background
knowledge and vocabulary needed to
comprehend increasingly challenging
language in Practice 13.2C.

Beginning Write these words from
Practice 13.2C on the board and provide
pictures illustrating each: *having dinner,
garden, library, usher, tickets,* and *movie.*
Read the words chorally, explaining their
meaning. Then, ask simple questions about
the pictures, helping students use the
words and replace them with pronouns:
for example, *Is the garden pretty? Yes, the
garden is pretty./Yes, it is pretty.*

Intermediate Review the words and
pictures from the Beginning activity. Have
students and more fluent partners write
sentences about each picture using the
words and personal pronouns such as
our(s), your(s), and *we.* Have partners
explain the connection between the
sentences and the pictures.

Advanced Have partners complete the
Intermediate activity, then review another
pair's work, identifying the personal pronouns.

Advanced High Have students complete
the Intermediate activity. Have them
label each pronoun by case and number,
using the pronoun charts on page 306 as
additional visual and contextual support.

Demonstrative Pronouns

Discuss with students the fact that demonstrative pronouns help speakers and writers to identify or point out specific persons, places, or things. Writers use them to distinguish one noun from another.

RULE 13.2.6 Read aloud the rule and then have students repeat the lines with you.

Refer to items in the classroom to illustrate how demonstrative pronouns function. For example, point to your desk and **say:** *This is my desk.* Then, point to a student's desk and say to the student: *That is your desk.*
Do this several times and include examples of plural demonstrative pronouns as well. Allow students to demonstrate their understanding by referring to classroom items of their choosing.

Using Relative Pronouns

RULE 13.2.7 Read aloud the rule and then have students repeat the lines with you.

Draw attention to how short the relative pronoun list is. Encourage students to memorize it so they can focus on how the words function in a sentence.

Write this sentence on the board: *She is the girl who won the spelling bee.* **Say:** Who can identify the independent clause in this sentence? If students struggle to identify it, restate the question: *Which part of this sentence can stand alone?* (She is the girl.) Draw a bridge over the word *who* as if connecting the independent clause to the subordinate clause. Explain that the relative pronoun connects the two.

> *Teacher Tip*
>
> Be prepared to review and define independent clauses and subordinate clauses. It may be helpful to prepare several examples of each to present to students who may need a refresher.

Demonstrative Pronouns

Demonstrative pronouns point to people, places, and things, much as you point to them with your finger.

> A **demonstrative pronoun** points to a specific person, place, or thing.

There are two singular and two plural demonstrative pronouns.

DEMONSTRATIVE PRONOUNS			
SINGULAR		PLURAL	
this	that	these	those

This and *these* point to what is near the speaker or writer. *That* and *those* point to what is more distant.

NEAR   **This** is the desk where I sit.

        These are my favorite books.

FAR   Is **that** the cafeteria down the hall?

        Those are my sandwiches.

See Practice 13.2E

Using Relative Pronouns

Relative pronouns are connecting words.

> A **relative pronoun** begins a subordinate clause and connects it to another idea in the same sentence.

There are five main relative pronouns.

RELATIVE PRONOUNS				
that	which	who	whom	whose

The chart on the next page gives examples of relative pronouns connecting subordinate clauses to independent clauses. (See Chapter 19 to find out more about relative pronouns and clauses.)

308   **Nouns and Pronouns**

Differentiated Instruction

RTI Strategy for Below-Level Students
Relative pronouns require a firm understanding of independent and subordinate clauses. Help students understand the difference between the two by having them play a matching game that allows them to see each type of clause both separately and together. Write a few complex sentences on sentence strips. For each sentence, include an independent clause and a subordinate clause that begins with a relative pronoun. Cut the sentence strips so that each sentence part remains intact. Have students arrange the sentences correctly. Point out each sentence part as they do.

PRE-AP Enrichment for Above-Level Students Give students a list of subordinate clauses that begin with relative pronouns. Have students write independent clauses for each. Then, have students mix and match the clauses and relative pronouns to make several new complete sentences. Have students find similar sentence patterns in a magazine.

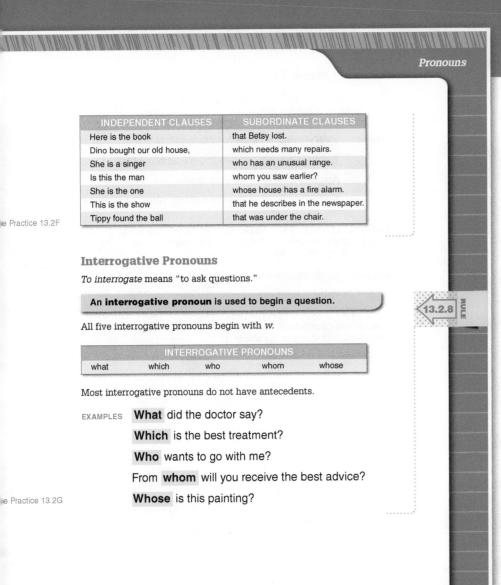

INDEPENDENT CLAUSES	SUBORDINATE CLAUSES
Here is the book	that Betsy lost.
Dino bought our old house,	which needs many repairs.
She is a singer	who has an unusual range.
Is this the man	whom you saw earlier?
She is the one	whose house has a fire alarm.
This is the show	that he describes in the newspaper.
Tippy found the ball	that was under the chair.

Practice 13.2F

Interrogative Pronouns

To interrogate means "to ask questions."

> An **interrogative pronoun** is used to begin a question.

◄ 13.2.8 RULE

All five interrogative pronouns begin with *w*.

INTERROGATIVE PRONOUNS				
what	which	who	whom	whose

Most interrogative pronouns do not have antecedents.

EXAMPLES **What** did the doctor say?

Which is the best treatment?

Who wants to go with me?

From **whom** will you receive the best advice?

Whose is this painting?

Practice 13.2G

To help students identify and understand relative pronouns, write these sentences on the board. Have students point out each relative pronoun and explain its use in the sentence.

Garry was the boy who played the tuba. (who)

That dog is the one that can swim. (that)

Nikki is the girl whose frog jumped the highest. (whose)

Interrogative Pronouns

Point out that interrogative pronouns can be easily memorized because they each begin with the letter *w* and indicate that a question will be posed.

RULE 13.2.8 Read aloud the rule and then have students repeat the line with you.

Ask for a student volunteer. In front of the class, ask the student several questions using interrogative pronouns. *What did you do after school yesterday? Who is your gym teacher?* As you do, display each pronoun on a large sheet of paper.

Explain that interrogative pronouns are used to begin sentences and that they often do not have stated antecedents.

Have student pairs brainstorm to create one question for each interrogative pronoun. Then, ask students to share their questions with the class.

Quick-Write Extension

To help students synthesize and apply what they have learned about interrogative pronouns, have students write poems about themselves. The first line must be a question that begins with an interrogative pronoun; for example, *What do I like?* The second line must answer the question; for example, *I like playing baseball in the summer.* Direct students to write at least four questions and answers, alternating questions with answers to form a poem. Challenge students to use as many different interrogatives as they can. Students should highlight or underscore each interrogative pronoun they use. Call for volunteers to read their poems aloud.

Indefinite Pronouns

Explain to students that indefinite pronouns do not refer to any particular person, place, thing, or idea. For example, in the sentence *Everyone won a prize,* the word *everyone* does not refer to any particular person. It is an indefinite pronoun.

RULE 13.2.9 Read aloud the rule and then have students repeat the lines with you.

Use a Think Aloud as part of a gradual release progression.

 Say: One of the many interesting things about the English language is that a single word can serve as several different parts of speech. Certain words, for example, can function as indefinite pronouns in some sentences, and as adjectives in other sentences. Refer to these sentences from page 310: *Both students want to be nurses. Both want to be nurses.* Explain how the word *Both* plays two different roles in the sentences.

Using the Indefinite Pronoun list on page 310, **work with students** to construct three to five sets of sentences in which a single word first serves as an adjective and then as a subject. (**Possible answers:** *Many* alligators live in the swamp. *Many* live in the swamp.)

Have pairs of students write their own sentences using a word from the chart on page 310 as an adjective and as a subject.

Indefinite Pronouns

An **indefinite pronoun** refers to a person, place, thing, or idea that is not specifically named.

EXAMPLES

Everything is ready for the field trip.

Everyone wants to see the medical center.

Anyone can learn to play tennis.

Something fell out of the cabinet when I opened it.

Among its other uses, an indefinite pronoun can function as an adjective or as the subject of a sentence. If it functions as an adjective, it is called an indefinite adjective.

ADJECTIVE **Both** students want to be nurses.

SUBJECT **Both** want to be nurses.

A few indefinite pronouns can be either singular or plural, depending on their use in the sentence.

INDEFINITE PRONOUNS			
SINGULAR		PLURAL	SINGULAR OR PLURAL
another	much	both	all
anybody	neither	few	any
anyone	nobody	many	more
anything	no one	others	most
each	nothing	several	none
either	one		some
everybody	other		
everyone	somebody		
everything	someone		
little	something		

See Practice 13.2H
See Practice 13.2I
See Practice 13.2J

Working with ELLs   EL Sheltered Instruction: Cognitive

Help students speak using a variety of grammatical structures with increasing accuracy and ease. Use the chart and examples on page 308 to allow students to practice using indefinite pronouns.

Beginning Read Rule 13.2.9 to students. Then, read the first example sentence. Explain its meaning, using visuals and mime. Then, repeat the sentence aloud, noting the indefinite pronoun in the sentence. Have students respond orally by repeating the sentence after you. Continue with other examples on the page.

Intermediate Write the example sentences on the board. Have partners take turns saying the example sentences to each other. Then, have students identify the indefinite pronoun in each sentence. Allow students to refer to the chart on page 310, as needed.

Advanced Have students write their own sentences with indefinite pronouns using the sentences on page 310 as an example. Then, have students say their sentences aloud to a partner. Partners should identify the indefinite pronoun in each sentence.

Advanced High Have students complete the Advanced activity. Then, challenge students to tell their partners if the indefinite pronoun in each sentence functions as an adjective or as the subject of the sentence.

PRACTICE 13.2E ▷ Identifying Demonstrative Pronouns

Read the sentences. Then, write the demonstrative pronoun and the noun to which it refers.

EXAMPLE   This is an old camera.

ANSWER   *This, camera*

These are the new basketball uniforms.

This is a copy of the letter.

Do you know if those are the photographs that were chosen for the yearbook?

This is my favorite meal of the week.

That was a loud noise we heard during the play.

These are the blankets for the children in the hospital.

This is an amazing biography.

That was the house where my mom lived when she was my age.

Yes, these are my boots.

I think those are the two songs from the musical that Mrs. Brennan likes the most.

PRACTICE 13.2F ▷ Supplying Relative Pronouns

Read the sentences. Then, write the correct relative pronoun for each sentence.

EXAMPLE   Rick Carson, _____ the players like, is leaving soon.

ANSWER   *whom*

11. The plumber, _____ has worked for twenty years, is scheduled for the job.

12. Players _____ like Stephanie want to join her team.

13. The team _____ they want to join hasn't won many games.

14. I met a writer _____ students adore.

15. The message, _____ Marcus is sending, will surprise everyone.

16. The driver, _____ car has a flat tire, is looking for a ride.

17. The only person _____ can solve the problem is gone.

18. Vanessa, _____ office is huge, is holding the meeting there.

19. The other horse _____ will race today is a palomino.

20. My grandmother, _____ we call every week, is coming to visit this summer.

SPEAKING APPLICATION

With a partner, take turns telling about a recent event you attended. Your partner should listen for and name two demonstrative and two relative pronouns you used.

WRITING APPLICATION

Write five sentences, including one of the following relative pronouns in each: *that, which, who, whom,* and *whose.*

Practice   311

PRACTICE 13.2E ▷

1. These, uniforms
2. This, copy
3. those, photographs
4. This, meal
5. That, noise
6. These, blankets
7. This, biography
8. That, house
9. these, boots
10. those, songs

PRACTICE 13.2F ▷

11. who
12. who
13. that
14. whom
15. which
16. whose
17. who
18. whose
19. that
20. whom

SPEAKING APPLICATION

Have partners explain how they recognized the demonstrative and relative pronouns.

WRITING APPLICATION

Have students share their paragraphs with the class and point out the relative pronouns.

PRACTICE 13.2G

1. What
2. Who
3. Which
4. Who
5. What
6. Whose
7. What
8. whom
9. Which
10. What

PRACTICE 13.2H

11. Sample answer: anything
12. Sample answer: Someone
13. Sample answer: everyone
14. Sample answer: All
15. nothing *or* something
16. Sample answer: anyone
17. something *or* nothing
18. another
19. others
20. Both

PRACTICE 13.2G Identifying Interrogative Pronouns

Read the sentences. Then, write the interrogative pronoun in each sentence.

EXAMPLE   Who invented the telephone?

ANSWER   *Who*

1. What was your sister's assignment?
2. Who will play soccer after school today?
3. Which is your dad's office?
4. Who called the fire station?
5. What were the reasons given?
6. Whose is this coat?
7. What are the answers to these questions?
8. With whom are you going to the library?
9. Which is the most interesting radio show?
10. What will happen next?

PRACTICE 13.2H Supplying Indefinite Pronouns

Read the sentences. Then, write an appropriate indefinite pronoun (e.g., *all, both, nothing, anything*) for each sentence.

EXAMPLE   Would _____ close the door, please?

ANSWER   *someone*

11. Did _____ new happen while I was gone?
12. _____ must have moved the plants.
13. I'm sure _____ will be there tonight.
14. _____ of the copies of the book I need are missing!
15. There's _____ we can do about the squeak in that wheel.
16. Can _____ join this club?
17. I think there's _____ funny going on here.
18. If the one you want is gone, then pick _____
19. Briana and Chai are here, but where are the _____?
20. _____ girls want to play shortstop, but only one of the two girls knows how to play the position.

SPEAKING APPLICATION

With a partner, take turns acting like a newspaper reporter conducting an interview. Ask at least four questions that use interrogative pronouns. Your partner should answer each of the questions, using one of the indefinite pronouns (e.g., *all, both, nothing, anything*) in each answer.

WRITING APPLICATION

Write a short paragraph about a story you have read that you think others should read. Use at least four indefinite pronouns (e.g., *all, both, nothing, anything*). Then, read your sentences aloud to a partner. Have your partner identify the indefinite pronouns you used.

312   Nouns and Pronouns

Working with ELLs   ELL Sheltered Instruction: Social/Affective

Scaffold the Speaking Application (on page 313), and provide opportunities for students to share information in cooperative learning interactions and to demonstrate listening comprehension of increasingly complex spoken English by collaborating with peers and taking notes. Coach students to incorporate relative pronouns in their discussions. Have students monitor their comprehension and seek necessary clarifications.

Beginning Pair students with fluent speakers. Describe the classroom, incorporating gestures and visuals. Have partners ask and answer simple questions to demonstrate listening comprehension, using gestures as needed.

Intermediate Describe the classroom, using simple vocabulary and the objects around you. Have small groups take turns sharing information about the classroom to demonstrate listening comprehension. Provide them with sentence starters, such as *On the wall, I see. . .*

Advanced Have partners describe the classroom to each other. Have them use a main idea and details chart to take notes as they listen. Have them orally summarize their descriptions for the class, using their notes.

Advanced High Have students describe to the class an event that has happened in the classroom. Listeners should take notes in a *who/what/where/when* chart as they listen. Then, have listeners compare charts and write brief summaries.

PRACTICE 13.2I ▷ Recognizing Indefinite Pronouns

Read the sentence. Write the indefinite pronoun. Then, write another sentence using the same indefinite pronoun.

EXAMPLE   Several of these options will work.

ANSWER   *several — Several of us are working on the neighborhood clean-up.*

1. Rob wants nothing to do with networking on the Internet.

2. Some went to the party last night.

3. Last night, somebody left the lights on downstairs.

4. Ms. Johnson wants everyone to sign up for a committee.

5. Mom said we can bring both of the dogs to the lake on Saturday.

6. I want none of your silliness right now.

7. All of the computers are in use.

8. That bike is the one I want to get.

9. Jacqueline asked if she could do anything to help.

10. Only a few are in the auditorium so far.

PRACTICE 13.2J ▷ Supplying Indefinite Pronouns

Read the sentences. Then, complete each sentence, filling in the blank with an indefinite pronoun. Identify the pronoun as singular or plural.

EXAMPLE   _____ of the students has become ill.

ANSWER   *another — singular*

11. Have you finished _____ of the leftovers?

12. _____ of the parents is coming on Friday.

13. I checked, but _____ is in the kitchen.

14. _____ of the twins are at the movies.

15. _____ of the books on the list are in the library.

16. We are ready for the presentation, so _____ remains to be done.

17. They accumulated _____ of their wealth illegally.

18. Have you done _____ about finding a summer job?

19. It took _____ hours to build that table.

20. The new girl invited _____ to her party.

SPEAKING APPLICATION

With a partner, talk about several television series. Use indefinite pronouns to explain the reasons you like certain ones. Then, write four sentences, each using one of these indefinite pronouns: *all*, *both*, *nothing*, and *anything*.

WRITING APPLICATION

Write a paragraph about music you enjoy listening to. Use the indefinite pronouns *all*, *both*, *nothing*, and *anything* in your paragraph. Then, read your paragraph to a partner. Your partner should identify the indefinite pronouns that you used.

PRACTICE 13.2I

Answers will vary. Sample answers:

1. nothing—I did nothing wrong.

2. some (used as adjective)—The shopper bought some dresses.

3. somebody—Somebody donated a bicycle to the fundraiser.

4. everyone—Everyone who went to the school play had a good time.

5. both—Both of the actors learned lines quickly.

6. none—Maria will have none of the potatoes and extra greens.

7. All—All of the parents cheered at the game.

8. one—This song is the one I like best.

9. anything—Is there anything I can bring to the dinner?

10. few (used as adjective)—A few of the students did extra homework.

PRACTICE 13.2J

Answers will vary. Sample answers:

11. all—plural

12. Neither—singular

13. no one—singular

14. both—plural

15. All—plural

16. nothing—singular

17. much—singular

18. anything—singular

19. someone—singular

20. everybody—singular

SPEAKING APPLICATION

Have students demonstrate their understanding of indefinite pronouns by reading their partners' sentences and underlining the indefinite pronouns.

WRITING APPLICATION

Have students demonstrate their understanding of indefinite pronouns by explaining how they identified the indefinite pronouns in their partners' sentences.

Test Warm-Up

1. **A** Change *nothing* to **anything**

2. **J** Make no change

3. **A** As I step up to the plate, everyone in the stands yells.

4. **G** Change *no one* to **nothing**

Reteach

If students have not mastered these skills, review the content in Section 13.2.9 Indefinite Pronouns.

Test Tip

Tell students that they may run into an unfamiliar word on a test. When that happens, they should not focus on the word unless it is a key word in the question, answer choices, or a target sentence in a passage. Instead, they should make a quick, educated guess at the meaning of the word based on context clues (the individual words, phrases, and sentences before and after the unfamiliar word), and answer the question based on their best guess.

Test Warm-Up

DIRECTIONS
Read the introduction and the passage that follows. Then, answer the questions to show that you can use and understand the function of indefinite pronouns in reading and writing.

The narrator writes about coming to bat during a close baseball game. Read the paragraph and think about the changes you would suggest as peer editor. When you finish reading, answer the questions that follow.

The Bottom of the Ninth

(1) Because nothing can happen in baseball, until the very last inning, all is not yet lost. (2) My team is at bat and behind by one point in the bottom of the ninth inning. (3) Julio picks up his bat and takes a few practice swings. (4) He grabs another bat, so something is wrong. (5) Then, he hits a grounder and beats the throw. (6) I step up to the plate. (7) Everyone in the stands yell. (8) I connect, and the ball sails the fence for a home run, proving that no one is impossible in this game.

1 What change, if any, should be made in sentence 1?

  A Change *nothing* to **anything**

  B Change *all* to **most**

  C Change *all* to **nothing**

  D Make no change

2 What change, if any, should be made in sentence 4?

  F Change *another* to **other**

  G Change *something* to **nothing**

  H Change *something* to **anything**

  J Make no change

3 What is the BEST way to combine sentences 6 and 7?

  A As I step up to the plate, everyone in the stands yells.

  B I step up to the plate all in the stands yell.

  C As I stepped up to the plate, anyone in the stands yells.

  D I stepped to the plate as both in the stands yells.

4 What change, if any, should be made in sentence 8?

  F Change *no one* to **someone**

  G Change *no one* to **nothing**

  H Change *no one* to **none**

  J Make no change

Use the Online Lesson Planner at www.phwritingcoach.com to customize your instructional plan for an integrated Language Arts curriculum.

DAY 1 14.1 Action Verbs

"What Do You Notice?"

Objectives: Identify, use, and understand verbs and action verbs, including

- transitive verbs
- intransitive verbs

INSTRUCTION AND PRACTICE

Student Edition pp. 315–318

DAY 2 14.2 Linking Verbs

Objectives: Identify, use, and understand linking verbs, including

- forms of *be*
- other linking verbs
- action or linking verb?

INSTRUCTION AND PRACTICE

Student Edition pp. 319–322

Test Warm-Up p. 323

DAY 3 14.3 Helping Verbs

- **Objectives:** Identify, use, and understand helping verbs.

INSTRUCTION AND PRACTICE

Student Edition pp. 324–326

Alternate Pacing Plans

- **Block Scheduling** Each day in the Lesson Planner represents a 40–50 minute block. Teachers using block scheduling may combine days to revise pacing to meet their classroom needs.

- **Accelerated Lesson Planning** Combine instructional days, focusing on concepts called out by students' diagnostic test results.

- **Integrated Language Arts Curriculum** Use the instruction and practice in this chapter to provide reinforcement, remediation, or extension of grammar concepts taught in your literature curriculum.

Links to Prentice Hall *LITERATURE*

Unit 2 Verbs, p. 216

> *Verbs sizzle, snap, and move. A verb may just be the most crucial word in a sentence. Without verbs, nothing would ever happen— nothing could even exist. A well-chosen verb can enliven student writing more than any other part of speech.*
>
> **—Jeff Anderson**

www.phwritingcoach.com

Grammar Assessment and Practice

Chapter diagnostic tests assess students' skills and assign instruction and practice.

DimensionL Video Games

Fast-paced interactive video games challenge students' mastery of grammar.

Grammar Assessment

Grammar Coach:	Diagnostic Assessment	End-of-Chapter Assessment	Progress Monitoring
Personalized Instruction	Students take grammar diagnostic test online and are automatically assigned instruction and practice in areas where they need support.	Teacher uses **ExamView** to administer end-of-chapter assessment and remediation. Teachers may customize **ExamView** tests or use the ones provided.	Teachers may use the **Test Warm-Ups** and the **Cumulative Reviews** in the student book or eText to check students' mastery of grammar skills.
Teacher-Directed Instruction	Teacher administers the diagnostic test and determines focus of instruction and practice.		Students may also play **DimensionL** grammar video games to test their grammar skills.

Lesson Planner continues on next page

> *Look at verbs this way: If a sentence were a car, the verb would be the engine. Strong sentences usually contain strong verbs. Take the following sentence, for example: 'The day was cloudy.' Simply improving the verb elevates the sentence: 'The clouds hung in the sky.' That's the importance of verbs.*
>
> **—Kelly Gallagher**

Differentiated Instruction

Differentiated Instruction Boxes in this Teacher's Edition address these student populations:

- Below-Level Students
- Above-Level Students
- Gifted and Talented Students
- Special Needs Students
- English Language Learners
- Spanish Speaking Students

In addition, for further enrichment, see the **Extension** features.

Grammar Ground Rule: Make It Active!

Model with Students

In this chapter, making it active means writing most of your sentences in the **active voice, or tense.** Explain to students that most sentences in English have a subject that *does* something or that *is* a certain way. It's not wrong to write a sentence in which the subject has something done *to* it, instead, but there should be a good reason for it.

> **Say:** I could tell you what I did this morning this way: *I ate my breakfast. I drove my car to school. I had a cup of coffee.* Or I could tell you this way: *My breakfast was eaten by me. My car was driven to school by me. A cup of coffee was had by me.* Which one makes me sound more active? Which one is easier to hear and understand?

Explain to students that there will be times when an active verb will just not seem right. They will usually know when that happens. For example, *John F. Kennedy was elected president in 1960* or *That chair was broken before I got here.*

Small Group Activity – Looking at Active and Passive Verbs

Have students form small groups and look at a paragraph from a history book. Have them decide which verbs in the paragraph are active and which are passive. If they find passive verbs, have them see if they can rewrite the sentences in the active voice. Have the groups discuss how the rewrite changes their sense of the event. Their discussion should answer these questions:

- Is it usually important in history to think about who performed an action?
- Does writing a sentence in the active voice help you think about that?

Have a member of each group present their findings to the class with at least one example, and explain why the group followed this grammar ground rule: Make it active.

Grammar Ground Rules

1. Keep it clear.
2. Make them agree.
3. Make it specific.
4. Dot your *i*'s and cross your *t*'s
5. Make it active.

hen you write, choose verbs that show exactly what someone
something is doing.

WRITE GUY *Jeff Anderson, M.Ed.*

WHAT DO YOU NOTICE?

Chase down some verbs as you zoom in on these sentences from the story "The Tail" by Joyce Hansen.

MENTOR TEXT

> I spotted Keisha and Yvonne walking into the playground. Junior tagged behind me and Naomi as we went to meet them.

Now, ask yourself the following questions:

- Who performs the action of the verb *spotted* in the first sentence, and who receives the action?
- Do the verbs *tagged* and *went* in the second sentence have receivers for their actions?

The narrator *I* is the one who *spotted,* and *Keisha and Yvonne* are the ones who were spotted. *Keisha and Yvonne* receive the action. *Spotted* is a transitive verb because the receivers of the action are named. The verbs *tagged* and *went* do not have receivers of their action, so they are intransitive verbs.

Grammar for Writers Think of verbs as the muscles that make your sentences move. When you use verbs that describe action, your writing is lively and interesting.

Name an action verb that you hope or expect to hear today.

Cancel! As in "Mr. Brown canceled tomorrow's test."

315

Grammar for Writers: Tense

Help students understand that interesting action verbs make writing come alive. Verbs capture all kinds of action. The rules on these pages will help students use verbs more effectively in their writing and speaking and understand when to use different verb tenses to express the time at which actions occurred.

VERBS

As students progress in their writing skills, it will be important for them to be able to apply the rules of grammar, usage, and mechanics to their own drafts. Use the *What Do You Notice?* feature to help them see effective conventions in the work of professional writers. Encourage students to incorporate effective voice, tense, and syntax as they edit their own writing.

Read the opening sentence aloud. Discuss how the use of vivid action verbs can bring writing to life. Point out that verbs can describe actions that can be seen, such as *smile,* and actions that cannot be seen, such as *think.*

WRITE GUY *Jeff Anderson, M. Ed.*

WHAT DO YOU NOTICE?

When students have read the Mentor Text, **ask:** What did the speaker actually do here? **(Response: saw, screamed, almost ran)** The words that describe these actions—*saw, screamed, ran*—are *action verbs.* Some verbs describe actions you can see, like *screamed* and *ran.* Other verbs describe actions you cannot see, like *saw.*

Have students finish reading the page. Then, **say:** Notice that some words receive the action of the verb. Verbs that have receivers are called transitive verbs. In the Mentor Text, *saw* is a transitive verb because *the thing with tentacles* receives the action of seeing. It is what the speaker saw. Verbs that do not have receivers are called intransitive verbs.

Write the verbs *screamed* and *ran* on the board. **Ask:** What would happen if we dropped all the verbs from the text? Students should see that the text would no longer be action-oriented and would not make sense. **Say:** When we write or speak, we can use action verbs to create a clear and detailed picture of what is happening. They make our writing more vivid and interesting.

Lesson Objectives

1. Recognize and identify action verbs.

2. Distinguish between transitive and intransitive verbs.

Discuss the fact that there is action all around us. People, animals, and the technology around us are always *doing* something. Verbs are the words we use to name these actions.

RULE 14.1.1 Read aloud the rule and then have students repeat the lines with you.

Use a Think Aloud as part of a gradual release progression.

Think Aloud

Say: It's easy to identify most action verbs. **I simply look** for words that describe actions, or things that can be done. For example, *talk* is an action verb. *I talk.* **Demonstrate.** *Talk* describes my action. Some action verbs are harder to identify because you cannot see them being done. Thinking and feeling are actions, though you cannot see them.

Work with students to identify the action verbs in this group: *deer, working, bean, drank.*

Have student pairs brainstorm for examples of different action verbs. Have them sort their examples into two categories: actions they can see and actions they cannot see.

Using Transitive Verbs

Explain that action verbs are transitive if the receiver of the action, or object, is named in the sentence.

RULE 14.1.2 Read aloud the rule and then have students repeat the lines with you.

Write this sentence on the board: *Al threw the football.* Ask students to identify the verb. Underline *threw.* Then, **ask:** What did Al throw? (a football) Explain that *football* is the receiver of the action. *Threw* is therefore a transitive verb.

14.1 Action Verbs

Verbs such as *walk, sailed, played, migrate, raced, crossed, learn,* and *arrive* all show some kind of action.

RULE 14.1.1

> An **action verb** tells what action someone or something is performing.

EXAMPLES   Father **carries** the ladder.

The ship **chugged** into the harbor.

I **believe** it will snow.

Sandor **remembered** to bring his puzzle.

The verb *carries* explains what Father does with the ladder. The verb *chugged* tells what the ship did. The verb *believe* explains my action about the weather. The verb *remembered* explains Sandor's action with the puzzle.

Some actions, such as *carries* or *chugged,* can be seen. Some actions, such as *believe* or *remembered,* cannot be seen.

Using Transitive Verbs

RULE 14.1.2

> An action verb is **transitive** if the receiver of the action is named in the sentence. The receiver of the action is called the **object** of the verb.

EXAMPLES   Pete **opened** the **window** with great difficulty.
            verb   object

The truck suddenly **hit** the **trashcan** .
                     verb   object

In the first example, *opened* is transitive because the object of the verb—*window*—names what Pete opened. In the second example, *hit* is transitive because the object of the verb—*trashcan*—tells what the truck hit.

Using Intransitive Verbs

> An action verb is **intransitive** if there is no receiver of the action named in the sentence. An intransitive verb does not have an object.

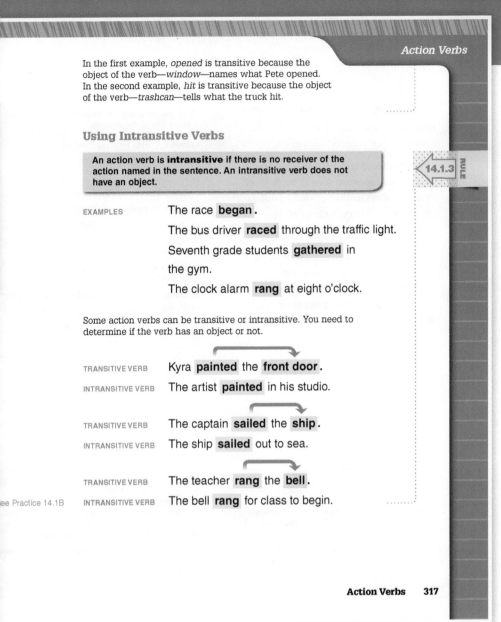

RULE 14.1.3

EXAMPLES

The race **began**.

The bus driver **raced** through the traffic light.

Seventh grade students **gathered** in the gym.

The clock alarm **rang** at eight o'clock.

Some action verbs can be transitive or intransitive. You need to determine if the verb has an object or not.

TRANSITIVE VERB   Kyra **painted** the **front door**.

INTRANSITIVE VERB   The artist **painted** in his studio.

TRANSITIVE VERB   The captain **sailed** the **ship**.

INTRANSITIVE VERB   The ship **sailed** out to sea.

TRANSITIVE VERB   The teacher **rang** the **bell**.

See Practice 14.1B   INTRANSITIVE VERB   The bell **rang** for class to begin.

Action Verbs   317

Using Intransitive Verbs

Remind students that not all verbs are transitive. Present this example to students: *Kayla sings beautifully.* Point out that the verb *sings* is transitive if the sentence is *Kayla sings beautiful songs.* Explain why.

RULE 14.1.3 Read aloud the rule and then have students repeat the lines with you.

Read aloud the example sentences on page 317. Draw students' attention to the prepositional phrase that follows the verb in the second, third, and fourth sentences. Point out that a prepositional phrase cannot be the object of a verb. Only nouns or pronouns can receive action. All the verbs in the examples are intransitive because none of them have an object. Write this sentence on the board: *The lion roars.* Ask students to identify the verb. Underline *roars*. Point out that *roars* does not take an object. *Roars* is therefore an intransitive verb.

Write this sentence on the board: *The rain fell and Mark grabbed his umbrella.* Have students identify the verbs. Underline *fell* and *grabbed*. Ask whether *fell* or *grabbed* takes an object. Circle *his umbrella*. *Grabbed* is a transitive verb. *Fell* does not take an object, so *fell* is an intransitive verb.

> *Teacher Tip*
>
> If a student has difficulty distinguishing between transitive and intransitive verbs, provide flash cards containing sample sentences such as *The flower blooms* and *Rianne swings the racket.* On the back of the card, label the verb, the object (if there is one), and the category of the verb—transitive or intransitive. Students should read the sentence aloud to a partner and identify the verb and the object (if there is an object). Partners should then discuss whether the verb is transitive or intransitive. Partners can then turn the card over and see if their answer is correct.

Working with ELLs   **ELL** Sheltered Instruction: Cognitive

Help students employ increasingly complex grammatical structures in writing by having them use correct tenses of action verbs in sentences.

Beginning Pair students with fluent speakers. Have the fluent speaker say a simple sentence that identifies an action in the present, then write the sentence one word at a time as Beginning students copy it. Have pairs repeat, changing the verb to past tense. Guide pairs in comparing the sentences.

Intermediate Write the action verbs from page 316 (e.g., *carries, chugged, believe, remembered*) on the board. Have partners write their own sentences using the verbs. Have them discuss how the tense of each verb shows when the action occurs.

Advanced Write *believe, believes, believed,* and *will believe* on the board. Have students write four sentences, each featuring one form of the verb. Then, have partners exchange sentences and identify the tense of the action verb in each.

Advanced High Have students draw a four-column chart and write ten action verbs in the first column. Partners should fill in the rest of the chart with the present, past, and future tense of the verb. Challenge students to write sentences using several action verbs in the correct tense.

PRACTICE 14.1A

1. eats
2. saw
3. slows
4. creates
5. forget
6. bloomed
7. said
8. encourage
9. arrived
10. walked

PRACTICE 14.1B

11. stands—intransitive
12. shone—intransitive
13. covered—transitive
14. came—intransitive
15. threw—transitive
16. created—transitive
17. grow—intransitive
18. protect—transitive
19. rose—intransitive
20. found—transitive

SPEAKING APPLICATION

Partners should explain how they identified the action verbs.

WRITING APPLICATION

Have partners identify the objects in the sentences that have transitive verbs. Partners should explain how they identified the objects.

PRACTICE 14.1A **Finding Action Verbs**

Read the sentences. Then, write each action verb.

EXAMPLE   I see a cocoon on that tree branch.

ANSWER   *see*

1. For breakfast, my mom usually eats cereal.
2. I saw an interesting show about Australia.
3. Traffic slows dramatically during rush hour.
4. The potter creates bowls out of clay.
5. Sometimes I forget my password for the computer.
6. Our flowers bloomed this weekend.
7. She said it would be a good movie.
8. My parents encourage my interest in music.
9. The new books arrived last week.
10. I walked the dog after dinner last night.

PRACTICE 14.1B **Identifying Transitive and Intransitive Verbs**

Read the sentences. Write each verb and label it *transitive* or *intransitive*.

EXAMPLE   Lisa rode her bike down the hill.

ANSWER   *rode — transitive*

11. The post office stands near the corner of Main Street and Hill Street.
12. The sun shone throughout the day.
13. A heavy blanket covered the bed.
14. The marathon runners came from many cities.
15. My brother threw his clothes into the washing machine.
16. I created small toys to take to the children.
17. Redwood trees grow amazingly tall.
18. Most animals protect their young.
19. The big balloon rose into the air.
20. We found the perfect place for a picnic.

SPEAKING APPLICATION

With a partner, take turns telling about something you enjoy doing on the weekend. Your partner should listen for and name three action verbs.

WRITING APPLICATION

Write two pairs of short sentences. In each pair, write one sentence using a transitive verb and one using an intransitive, in any order. For example, "I planted a flower. The flower grew."

Working with ELLs   ELL Sheltered Instruction: Cognitive

As students practice with action verbs, have them demonstrate their comprehension of increasingly complex English by retelling and summarizing.

Beginning Write three simple statements about Texas history on the board. Read them aloud, using pictures and gestures to aid comprehension. Then, have students read the sentences chorally. Help them identify the action verbs and summarize by taking notes in a word web.

Intermediate Provide students with simple written sentences about Texas history. Help them identify the action verbs in the sentences. Provide cloze prompts to help them retell what they read. For example, *At the Johnson Space Center ____.*

Advanced On a transparency, prepare paragraphs about Texas history. Provide partners with a copy of the transparency and an erasable marker. Have them circle all of the action verbs. Then, model crossing out inessential details to summarize a paragraph. Have students mark subsequent paragraphs and write a summary of the passage.

Advanced High Provide each student with a passage about Texas history. Have students complete K-W-L charts to monitor their comprehension. Then, have them write a summary about what they read, using action verbs.

14.2 Linking Verbs

Some widely used verbs do not show action. They are called **linking verbs**.

> A **linking verb** is a verb that connects a subject with a word that describes or identifies it.

14.2.1 RULE

EXAMPLES

Sheridan **was** a Union general.
subject · linking verb · predicate nominative (IDENTIFIES)

The **winners** **were** Tony and I.
subject · linking verb · predicate nominative (IDENTIFIES)

We **felt** extremely **tired** after all our running.
subject · linking verb · predicate adjective (DESCRIBES)

Recognizing Forms of *Be*

In English, the most common linking verb is *be*. This verb has many forms.

FORMS OF *BE*		
am	can be	has been
are	could be	have been
is	may be	had been
was	might be	could have been
were	must be	may have been
am being	shall be	might have been
are being	should be	must have been
is being	will be	shall have been
was being	would be	should have been
were being		will have been
		would have been

Linking Verbs   319

14.2 Linking Verbs

Lesson Objectives

1. Recognize and identify different forms of *be*.

2. Distinguish between linking verbs and action verbs.

Point out to students that not all verbs are action verbs. For example, the verbs *am, is, are, was,* and *were* do not show action, yet they are verbs. These non-action verbs are called linking verbs.

RULE 14.2.1 Read aloud the rule and then have students repeat the lines with you.

Use a Think Aloud as part of a gradual release progression.

Think Aloud

Say: I know that some verbs connect a subject with a word that identifies or describes it. These verbs are called linking verbs. Consider this sentence: *I am a teacher.* The verb *am* does not describe what I am doing. It links the subject, *I*, to a word that identifies who I am. It is a linking verb.

Work with students to identify the linking verbs in this group: *was, dream, is, charge, learn.* Help them understand why *was* and *is* are linking verbs.

Have student pairs write descriptive sentences about themselves using a form of the linking verb *be.* Invite students to use their sentences to introduce themselves to the group.

Recognizing Forms of *Be*

Discuss with students that the most common linking verb is *be. Be* has many different forms. Draw students' attention to the chart on the bottom of page 319.

T319

Using Other Linking Verbs

Point out that there are other linking verbs besides *be*. These other linking verbs function in the same way as *be*. Like *be*, they connect the subject with a word that describes or identifies it.

Have student pairs brainstorm for example sentences using the verbs listed in the chart on page 320.

Action Verb or Linking Verb?

Point out that some verbs can be action verbs or linking verbs, depending upon how they are used in sentences. Read aloud the pairs of example sentences at the bottom of page 320. Explain why *looked* and *grew* are linking verbs in the first sentence of each pair yet action verbs in the second sentence.

Then, point out that students can test whether a verb is a linking verb or an action verb by replacing the verb with *is*, *am*, or *are*. If the sentence still makes sense, then the verb is a linking verb.

Write these sentences on the board: *The cake tastes good. The cook tastes the soup.* Ask students to identify the verb. Underline *tastes*. Then, erase *tastes* and replace *tastes* with *is*. Read the revised sentences aloud. *Tastes* in the first sentence is a linking verb, but it is an action verb in the second sentence.

Teacher Tip

If students have difficulty distinguishing action verbs from linking verbs, provide them with flash cards containing sentences using verbs such as *look*, *grow*, and *taste*. Have student partners practice substituting *is*, *am*, or *are* in place of the verb to test whether the verb is an action or linking verb in the sentence. Explain that the correct answer is on the back of each flash card.

Using Other Linking Verbs

Several other verbs also function as linking verbs. They connect the parts of a sentence in the same way as the forms of *be*. In the sentence below, *calm* describes *chief*.

DESCRIBES

EXAMPLE   The **chief** **remained** **calm** during the battle.
subject   linking verb   predicate adjective

OTHER LINKING VERBS		
appear	look	sound
become	remain	stay
feel	seem	taste
grow	smell	turn

Action Verb or Linking Verb?

Some verbs can be used either as linking verbs or action verbs.

LINKING   The water **looked** polluted.
(*Looked* links *water* and *polluted*.)

ACTION   The inspectors **looked** at the water.
(The inspectors performed an action.)

LINKING   The people **grew** unhappy.
(*Grew* links *people* and *unhappy*.)

ACTION   The people **grew** poor crops.
(The people performed an action.)

To test whether a verb is a linking verb or an action verb, replace the verb with *is*, *am*, or *are*. If the sentence still makes sense, then the verb is a linking verb.

EXAMPLE   The people **are** unhappy.
linking verb

See Practice 14.2A
See Practice 14.2B
See Practice 14.2C
See Practice 14.2D

320   Verbs

Working with ELLs   **ELL** Sheltered Instruction: Cognitive

To help students write using a variety of grade-appropriate sentence lengths in increasingly accurate ways, help them use linking verbs as they review the lesson on page 320.

Beginning Read the example sentences aloud to students, having them repeat after you. Write on the board the verb in each sentence and have students copy. Guide them in writing their own sentences using the verbs.

Intermediate Have students choose *appear*, *feel*, or *look* from the table on page 320 and use it as both a linking verb and an action verb in two written sentences. Then, have partners exchange sentences and

create longer versions of each sentence by adding words or phrases.

Advanced Write on the board *remain*, *taste*, and *smell* from the table on page 320. Have students write a sentence with each one as a linking verb and as an action verb. Then, help students combine two sentences into a longer one.

Advanced High Challenge students to create their own sentences with four of the linking verbs in the table on page 320. Then, have students switch papers with a partner and write four longer sentences using their partners' linking verbs as action verbs.

PRACTICE 14.2A Identifying Action Verbs and Linking Verbs

Read the sentences. Write the verb in each sentence, and label it either *action* or *linking*. One sentence has two verbs.

EXAMPLE   The coach called to the skaters.

ANSWER   *called* — action

1. The driver was unhappy with his car.
2. Sheila waved to the neighbors.
3. The players heard the coach's voice.
4. I don't feel very well.
5. The job you did looks really professional.
6. The two boys raced to the corner.
7. The sun shone on the new snow.
8. This story is about a lost rabbit.
9. We all helped Mom with the dishes.
10. They were happy with their grades.

PRACTICE 14.2B Using *Be* and Other Linking Verbs

Read the pairs of words below. For each pair of words, write a sentence that uses a linking verb to connect them.

EXAMPLE   Patrick   busy

ANSWER   Patrick *looked* busy as he prepared for the party.

11. homework   easy
12. Sondra   puzzled
13. door   locked
14. Felipe   surprised
15. food   good
16. sweater   warm
17. idea   interesting
18. day   cloudy
19. puppy   happy
20. Alicia   careful

SPEAKING APPLICATION

With a partner, take turns telling about something you read about or saw on television. Your partner should listen for and name two linking verbs and two action verbs you used.

WRITING APPLICATION

Choose three different linking verbs, other than *be* verbs. Write three sentences, each one using a different linking verb.

Practice   321

PRACTICE 14.2A

1. was—linking
2. waved—action
3. heard—action
4. feel—linking
5. did—action
   looks—linking
6. raced—action
7. shone—action
8. is—linking
9. helped—action
10. were—linking

PRACTICE 14.2B

Answers will vary. Sample answers:

11. The math homework was easy.
12. Sondra looked puzzled.
13. The office door was locked.
14. Felipe appeared surprised by the news.
15. The food tasted good.
16. The wool sweater felt warm.
17. Your idea sounds interesting.
18. The day turned cloudy.
19. The puppy seemed happy.
20. Alicia was careful.

SPEAKING APPLICATION

Have students explain to their partners how they identified the linking verbs and action verbs.

WRITING APPLICATION

Have students share their sentences, pointing out the linking verbs.

Differentiated Instruction

Strategy for Spanish Speakers
Students whose home language is Spanish may find subject-verb agreement difficult with forms of the verb *to be*. Give students practice by writing different singular and plural subjects and subject pronouns on flashcards. Have pairs of students quiz each other on the verb forms of *to be* by having one partner hold up the flashcard and the other partner say the form of the verb that corresponds with it. Challenge students to see how quickly they can correctly respond to the flashcards. Then, have students use the flashcards to start sentences which use the verb *to be*. Remind them that the point of the exercise is to check subject-verb agreement, not to write sophisticated sentences. To extend practice, have students complete the activity with different verb tenses.

PRACTICE 14.2C

1. hiked—action
2. looks—linking
3. remains—linking
4. plunged—action
5. flew—action
6. stayed—linking
7. glimpsed—action
8. grew—linking
9. collected—action
10. tasted—linking

PRACTICE 14.2D

Answers will vary. Sample answers:

11. The students became anxious as the test neared.
12. We remain eager to hear your speech.
13. The man smelled the roses.
14. Dinner smelled spicy.
15. The greens tasted bitter.
16. The father felt the baby blanket to make sure it was soft.
17. The worker feels exhausted after a long day.
18. I thought she seemed eager.
19. She looked at all the trucks before making her choice.
20. She looked disappointed when her friend cancelled their plans.

SPEAKING APPLICATION

Have partners explain how they differentiated between action verbs and linking verbs.

WRITING APPLICATION

Have students explain how they determined when to use a linking verb and when to use an action verb.

PRACTICE 14.2C > Identifying Verbs

Read the sentences. Choose the verb in parentheses that makes sense in the sentence. Write it and label it *action* or *linking*.

EXAMPLE   A tornado _____ the town twice. (struck, was)

ANSWER   *struck*— action

1. We _____ three miles yesterday. (became, hiked)
2. The puzzle _____ easy enough. (looks, questions)
3. The location _____ a problem for us. (moves, remains)
4. The duck _____ into the water. (plunged, is)
5. The pelican _____ away with a fish in its bill. (was, flew)
6. The flowers _____ fresh for a week. (stayed, swayed)
7. We _____ the celebrity on Fifth Avenue. (are, glimpsed)
8. The crackers _____ stale. (grew, reached)
9. We _____ money to help the victims of the flood. (collected, appeared)
10. The stew _____ too salty. (swallowed, tasted)

SPEAKING APPLICATION

With a partner, take turns talking about pets. Then, write two sentences with action verbs and two sentences with linking verbs. Use action verbs for what pets do and linking verbs for their appearance. Finally, read your sentences to your partner, who will tell which verbs are action verbs and which are linking verbs.

PRACTICE 14.2D > Using Action Verbs and Linking Verbs

Read the verbs. For each verb, write a sentence using the verb as an action verb or a linking verb as indicated in parentheses.

EXAMPLE   feel (linking)

ANSWER   *Sam feels nervous about the upcoming race.*

11. become (linking)
12. remain (linking)
13. smell (action)
14. smell (linking)
15. taste (linking)
16. feel (action)
17. feels (linking)
18. seem (linking)
19. look (action)
20. look (linking)

WRITING APPLICATION

Write a short description of an imaginary animal. Use at least two action and two linking verbs. Then, exchange papers with a partner. Your partner should circle the action verbs and underline the linking verbs.

Quick-Write Extension

To help students synthesize and apply what they have learned about verbs, have them use strong action verbs to write a scene for a teleplay. Students should describe an action-oriented scene, such as a car chase. Challenge students to use vivid verbs such as *swerved, zoomed, skidded, careened.* Remind students that when writers are at a loss for words, they sometimes consult a thesaurus. After students have finished writing, have them exchange scenes, identify action verbs, and make suggestions for improvement. Have students read their teleplays to the class, or post them on a class Web site.

est Warm-Up

DIRECTIONS

ad the introduction and the passage that follows. Then,
swer the questions to show that you can use and understand
e function of action verbs and linking verbs in reading and
iting.

*e student wrote a report about a strange and comical animal. Read
paragraph and think about the changes you would suggest as a peer
tor. When you finish reading, answer the questions that follow.*

Comedians of the Animal Kingdom

1) Wildebeests are the comedians of the animal kingdom. (2) From the
nt they look like an ox, but from the back they look like a horse.
Most of the time, they are strange because they groan and make loud
ses. (4) If startled by a human, they throw back their large heads.
They kick up their heels. (6) Wildebeests are in large groups and
vel in search of food and water. (7) Many tourists are on safari enjoy
tching them.

What change, if any, should be made in
sentence 1?

A Change *are* to **sound**

B Change *are* to an action verb

C Change *are* to **look**

D Make no change

What change should be made to clarify
sentence 3?

F Change *are* to **feel**

G Change *are* to **sound**

H Change *are* to **taste**

J Change *are* to **eat**

3 What change, if any, should be made to
sentence 6?

A Change *travel* to **grow**

B Change *are* to **remain**

C Change *are* to **grow**

D Make no change

4 What is the BEST way to revise sentence 7?

F Many tourists are looking for them on
safari.

G They enjoy watching tourists on safari.

H Many wildebeest enjoy safaris and
tourists watching them.

J Many tourists on safari enjoy watching
them.

Test Warm-Up   **323**

Test Warm-Up

1. **D** Make no change

2. **G** Change *are* to **sound**

3. **B** Change *are* to **remain**

4. **J** Many tourists on safari enjoy
watching them.

Reteach

If students have not mastered these skills,
review the content in Section 14.2 Linking
Verbs.

Test Tip

Tell students that if a test question doesn't
make sense or doesn't seem to have any correct
answer, there is a strong probability that they
have skipped a key word, misread a key word,
or accidentally reversed two words in the
question stem. Encourage students to reread
the question stem, looking at every word, and
ask themselves what the question is really
asking.

Lesson Objectives

1. Recognize, identify, and use different helping verbs.

2. Recognize that helping verbs are part of verb phrases, and that verb phrases are sometimes separated by other words.

Discuss with students the fact that the verb in a sentence may be made up of several words. This type of verb is called a verb phrase.

RULE 14.3.1 Read aloud the rule and then have students repeat the lines with you.

Write these sentences on the board: *Josie read the book. Josie could have read the book. Josie will have read the book.* Point out the single verb *read* in the first sentence and the verb phrase *could have read* in the second sentence. Work with students to identify the main verb and helping verbs in the third sentence.

Recognizing Helping Verbs

Point out that forms of *be* are often used as helping verbs. Then, challenge students to make sentences using the different verb phrases in the chart on page 324.

14.3 Helping Verbs

Sometimes, a verb in a sentence is just one word. Often, however, a verb will be made up of several words. This type of verb is called a **verb phrase**.

RULE 14.3.1

Helping verbs are added before another verb to make a **verb phrase**.

Notice how these helping verbs change the meaning of the verb *run*.

EXAMPLES   run   **might have** run

had run   **should have** run

will have run   **will be** running

Recognizing Helping Verbs

Forms of *Be* Forms of *be* are often used as helping verbs.

SOME FORMS OF *BE* USED AS HELPING VERBS	
HELPING VERBS	MAIN VERBS
am	growing
has been	warned
was being	told
will be	reminded
will have been	waiting
is	opening
was being	trained
should be	written
had been	sent
might have been	played

See Practice 14.3A

324   Verbs

Differentiated Instruction

RTI **Strategy for Below-Level Students**
Help students understand that sometimes verbs can be made up of several words.

Distribute five blank index cards to each student. On each card, have students copy one form of *be* from the chart. Then, give each student an index card with a conjugated action verb written on it

(such as *waiting*, *trained*, or *played*). Have students manipulate their index cards to form different verb phrases.

Have students work in pairs to write an example sentence using one of the verb phrases created with index cards. Invite pairs to share their sentence with a group.

Other Helping Verbs Many different verb phrases can be formed using one or more of these helping verbs. The chart below shows just a few.

HELPING VERBS	MAIN VERBS	VERB PHRASES
do	remember	do remember
has	written	has written
would	hope	would hope
shall	see	shall see
can	believe	can believe
could	finish	could finish
may	attempt	may attempt
must have	thought	must have thought
should have	grown	should have grown
might	win	might win
will	jump	will jump
have	planned	have planned
does	want	does want

Sometimes the words in a verb phrase are separated by other words, such as *not* or *certainly*. The parts of the verb phrase in certain types of questions may also be separated.

WORDS SEPARATED

She **could** certainly **have come** earlier.

This **has** not **happened** before.

Marie **has** certainly not **contacted** us.

He **had** carefully **kept** all the records.

Did you ever **expect** to see an elephant?

When **will** we **open** our presents?

Can they really **build** their own home?

They **must** not **have taken** the bus.

Would you ever **want** to go skiing?

Practice 14.3B

Helping Verbs 325

Other Helping Verbs

Draw attention to the chart that lists other helping verbs. Write these sentences on the board: *She has worn that dress before. He will repair my car this afternoon. They should have practiced before the game.* Have students identify the helping verbs in each sentence. Underline *has*, *will*, and *should have*.

Have student pairs make sentences using helping verbs from the chart. Invite pairs to share their sentences with the group.

Explain that sometimes the words in a verb phrase can be separated by other words, such as *not* and *certainly*. Give this example: *We can certainly use your help.* Add that in some questions the subject separates a helping verb from the main verb. Give this example: *Would you have left your books in the car?* Have students change the question into a statement: *You would have left your books in the car.* Point out that to form the questions, the first helping verb is moved to the front of the sentence.

Have student pairs revise the sentences made earlier using helping verbs from the chart. They should use words such as *not, carefully, certainly,* and so on to separate the verbs in the verb phrase; for example: *I have not seen that sweater before.* Invite students to share their revised sentences with the group. Then, call for volunteers to change each statement into a question and identify which words, if any, separate the verbs in the verb phrase.

Working with ELLs ELL Sheltered Instruction: Cognitive

Help students use visual and contextual support as they read to enhance and confirm understanding and to develop vocabulary needed to comprehend increasingly challenging language.

Beginning Write these words from page 325 on the board and provide pictures illustrating each: *records, Maria, elephant,* and *skiing*. Read the words chorally, explaining their meaning. Then, ask simple questions, featuring helping verbs, about the pictures: for example, *Has Maria talked to us?* Finally, guide students in reading the example sentences on page 325.

Intermediate Review the words and pictures from the Beginning activity. Have students meet with more fluent partners to write sentences about each picture using the words. Finally, have them read and discuss the meaning of the example sentences on page 325.

Advanced Provide students with visual support for these words from page 325: *contacted, kept,* and *expect*. Then, have them explain what the helping verb adds to the meaning of each example sentence.

Advanced High Have students complete the Intermediate activity. Have them then rewrite each example sentence with a different appropriate helping verb, explaining the difference the new word makes in meaning.

PRACTICE 14.3A

1. helping verb
2. helping verb
3. main verb
4. helping verb
5. main verb
6. helping verb
7. main verb
8. helping verb
9. main verb
10. helping verb

PRACTICE 14.3B

Answers will vary. Sample answers:

11. She had been dancing for years.
12. Mom must have known that we were up to something.
13. I might have finished my project sooner if I hadn't gone to the game.
14. We wished they could stay longer.
15. I promise I will study harder for the next test.
16. The puppies have learned not to go into that room.
17. They did go to the party, after all.
18. The weatherman says it should rain tomorrow.
19. The flower was growing until I forgot to water it.
20. I do wonder what will happen next in the story.

SPEAKING APPLICATION

Have students explain how they distinguished between the main verbs and helping verbs.

WRITING APPLICATION

Assign partners and have students take turns identifying main verbs and helping verbs in each other's sentences.

PRACTICE 14.3A Identifying Helping and Main Verbs

Read the sentences. Write *main verb* if the underlined verb is a main verb. Write *helping verb* if it is a helping verb.

EXAMPLE   For weeks now, the weather <u>has</u> been cold and windy.

ANSWER   *helping verb*

1. The school construction <u>was</u> finished in August.
2. They must <u>have</u> believed they were doing the right thing.
3. The children had been <u>told</u> not to go there.
4. You <u>should</u> have seen their faces.
5. If I hadn't called the fire department, the house might have <u>burned</u> down.
6. I have <u>been</u> studying for three hours.
7. By the time we get home, the flowers may have <u>bloomed</u>.
8. The new sewing machine <u>does</u> work.
9. If you had missed the bus, you would have <u>been</u> late.
10. It's spring, and the birds <u>are</u> returning.

PRACTICE 14.3B Using Verb Phrases

Read the verb phrases. Use each verb phrase in an original sentence.

EXAMPLE   were going

ANSWER   We *were going* to the movies.

11. had been dancing
12. must have known
13. might have finished
14. could stay
15. will study
16. have learned
17. did go
18. should rain
19. was growing
20. do wonder

SPEAKING APPLICATION

With a partner, discuss something you've learned in history class. Use helping verbs when you talk. Your partner should listen for and name two examples of helping verbs, along with the main verbs they help.

WRITING APPLICATION

Write three sentences about how things might have been different. You may use any main verbs and any additional helping verbs, but you should choose three of the following: *would, should, could, might,* or *may*.

Quick-Write Extension

To help students synthesize and apply what they have learned about helping verbs, have them write brief biographies of a favorite character in a novel or movie. Using information from the book or film, students should describe the character's past and speculate about his or her future. Have students exchange biographies, underline all main verbs, and circle all helping verbs.

CHAPTER 15 LESSON PLANNER
Adjectives and Adverbs

Use the Online Lesson Planner at www.phwritingcoach.com to customize your instructional plan for an integrated Language Arts curriculum.

DAY 1 15.1 Adjectives

"What Do You Notice?" **Objectives:** Identify, use, and understand adjectives, including ■ articles	**INSTRUCTION AND PRACTICE** **Student Edition** pp. 327–332

DAY 2 15.1 Adjectives *(continued)*

Objectives: Identify, use, and understand adjectives, including ■ proper adjectives ■ nouns used as adjectives ■ compound adjectives	**INSTRUCTION AND PRACTICE** **Student Edition** pp. 333–335 **Test Warm-Up** p. 346

DAY 3 15.1 Adjectives *(continued)*

Objectives: Identify, use, and understand adjectives, including ■ pronouns used as adjectives ■ possessive nouns and pronouns as adjectives ■ demonstrative adjectives ■ interrogative adjectives ■ indefinite adjectives	**INSTRUCTION AND PRACTICE** **Student Edition** pp. 336–338

DAY 4 15.2 Adverbs

Objectives: Identify, use, and understand adjectives, including ■ adverbs that modify verbs ■ adverbs that modify adjectives ■ adverbs that modify other adverbs ■ finding adverbs in sentences ■ adverb or adjective?	**INSTRUCTION AND PRACTICE** **Student Edition** pp. 339–345 **Test Warm-Up** p. 346

Grammar Assessment

Grammar Coach:	Diagnostic Assessment	End-of-Chapter Assessment	Progress Monitoring
Personalized Instruction	Students take grammar diagnostic test online and are automatically assigned instruction and practice in areas where they need support.	Teacher uses **ExamView** to administer end-of-chapter assessment and remediation. Teachers may customize **ExamView** tests or use the ones provided.	Teachers may use the **Test Warm-Ups** and the **Cumulative Reviews** in the student book or eText to check students' mastery of grammar skills. Students may also play **DimensionL** grammar video games to test their grammar skills.
Teacher-Directed Instruction	Teacher administers the diagnostic test and determines focus of instruction and practice.		

Alternate Pacing Plans

- **Block Scheduling** Each day in the Lesson Planner represents a 40–50 minute block. Teachers using block scheduling may combine days to revise pacing to meet their classroom needs.

- **Accelerated Lesson Planning** Combine instructional days, focusing on concepts called out by students' diagnostic test results.

- **Integrated Language Arts Curriculum** Use the instruction and practice in this chapter to provide reinforcement, remediation, or extension of grammar concepts taught in your literature curriculum.

Links to Prentice Hall *LITERATURE*

Unit 3 Adjectives and Articles, p. 416; Adverbs, p. 486

WRITING COACH
Online
www.phwritingcoach.com

Grammar Assessment and Practice

Chapter diagnostic tests assess students' skills and assign instruction and practice.

DimensionL Video Games

Fast-paced interactive video games challenge students' mastery of grammar.

Lesson Planner continues on next page ➤

> *Much maligned by professional writers, adjectives and adverbs do have their place. A powerful verb is better than a weak one paired with an adverb. A list of features that make some thing beautiful or ugly is better than the simple adjectives. Yet, a precise adjective or a deftly used adverb sings.*
>
> **—Jeff Anderson**

Differentiated Instruction

Differentiated Instruction Boxes in this Teacher's Edition address these student populations:

- Below-Level Students
- Above-Level Students
- Gifted and Talented Students
- Special Needs Students
- English Language Learners
- Spanish Speaking Students

In addition, for further enrichment, see the Extension features.

Grammar Ground Rule: Make It Specific!

Model with Students

In this chapter, making it specific means choosing **adjectives** and **adverbs** carefully. Explain to students that sometimes they may think of modifiers as decoration for their sentences. But modifiers are really language tools that will allow them to craft sentences that express just about anything they can think.

Say: The difference between giving a piece of information and really communicating often lies with the adjectives and adverbs you choose. I could write, for example, "*The cat came into the yard.*" This sentence just gives you piece of information. Or I could write, "*The hungry cat came fearfully into my yard.*" The second sentence communicates an image and an emotion, along with the information, because it is specific.

Write this sentence on the board: *The boy ran across the grass.* Have students come up with modifiers that could make that sentence specific and say the new sentence. For example, *The joyful boy walked quickly across the soft, green grass. The sad boy walked slowly across the dry grass.*

Small Group Activity – Finding Adjectives and Adverbs

Have students form groups to find one short story or poem and one newspaper article. Ask the groups to compare the kinds of adjectives and adverbs they find in the two kinds of writing. Their discussion should answer these questions:

- Does this modifier create an image or communicate an emotion?
- Does this modifier add more information to the sentence?
- Does the modifier make the sentence more specific?

Have a member of each group present their group's conclusions to the class and give one good example of modifier usage that follows this grammar ground rule: Make it specific.

Grammar Ground Rules

1. Keep it clear.
2. Make them agree.
3. Make it specific.
4. Dot your *i*'s and cross your *t*'s.
5. Make it active.

DJECTIVES *and* ADVERBS

ke your writing more vivid by using adjectives to describe
ple, places, and things.

WRITE GUY *Jeff Anderson, M.Ed.*

WHAT DO YOU NOTICE?

ook for adjectives as you zoom in on these sentences from Russell
aker's autobiographical essay "Hard as Nails."

MENTOR TEXT

> Deems was short and plump and had curly brown hair.
> He owned a car and a light gray suit and always wore a necktie
> and a white shirt.

ow, ask yourself the following questions:

In the first sentence, which adjectives modify the proper noun
Deems, and which two adjectives in a row modify the noun *hair*?
Which adjective in the second sentence modifies the noun *suit*?

he author describes Deems using the adjectives *short* and *plump*
d uses the adjectives *curly* and *brown* to describe Deems's hair.
he adjective *gray* modifies the noun *suit*. The word
ght is an adverb, rather than an adjective, because it
odifies *gray*.

rammar for Writers An artist crafts a picture
ith paint, but a writer uses words to create a
cture in the reader's mind. Use a variety of
djectives to help bring your writing to life.

Which two adjectives best describe your book bag?

I only need one: heavy!

327

Grammar for Writers: Voice

Help students understand that adverbs and
adjectives enrich their writing by describing
and modifying other types of words. They
should be careful, however, not to overuse
adjectives or adverbs. They should also vary
how they use them. The rules on these pages
will help students use adjectives and adverbs
more effectively in their writing and speaking.

ADJECTIVES *and* ADVERBS

As students progress in their writing skills, it
will be important for them to be able to apply
the rules of grammar, usage, and mechanics to
their own drafts. Use the *What Do You Notice?*
feature to help them see effective conventions
in the work of professional writers. Encourage
students to incorporate proper voice, tense, and
syntax as they edit their own writing.

Read the opening sentence aloud. Discuss how
adjectives and adverbs make descriptions of
persons, places, and things more vivid. Explain
how adjectives and adverbs enrich writing and
provide the details that make writing come
alive for the reader.

WRITE GUY *Jeff Anderson, M. Ed.*

WHAT DO YOU NOTICE?

When students have read the Mentor Text, **say:**
As you may already know, adjectives are words
that describe nouns and pronouns. Adverbs, on the
other hand, can describe verbs, adjectives, or other
adverbs. What are some adjectives used in these
sentences? What are some adverbs? (**Accept all
correct responses.**)

Have students finish reading the page. Point
out that *short* and *plump* are adjectives that
modify *Deems*. They give us a much clearer
picture of what Deems looked like. Ask
students what adjectives describe Deems's suit
and shirt. Then point out that the passage also
contains adverbs. For example, *always* is an
adverb that modifies the verb *wore*.

Guide students in understanding how
adjectives and adverbs provide information to
the reader.

Say: Look at the noun *hair*. What adjectives
modify *hair*? (**curly and brown**) What other
adjectives could be used to modify *hair* in place
of *curly* and *brown*? (**straight, blond, thin**)

15.1 Adjectives

Lesson Objectives

1. Recognize and identify various types of adjectives.

2. Recognize and identify various types of articles.

3. Demonstrate how to use various types of adjectives and articles in writing and speaking.

Lead a discussion about the ways that people use adjectives to make nouns more specific and detailed. Adjectives make written and spoken statements clearer and more vivid.

RULE 15.1.1 Read aloud the rule and then have students repeat the line with you.

Say: Nouns by themselves are kind of plain. Think of the word *building*. What words can we use to describe *building*? (**Possible responses:** tall, old, wooden) Write all correct responses on the board. Now let's use these adjectives together to describe a building. Use student responses to create different descriptions of a building. Adjectives describe, or modify, a noun and make it more vivid and specific.

Work with students to identify the adjectives in this group: *cat, dry, ice, purple, sweater, soft*. Have students tell why each word is an adjective.

Write several nouns on the board: *tree, turtle, shirt*. Have student pairs choose a noun and brainstorm for examples of different adjectives that describe it. Then, make sentences using different adjectives. Have pairs share their examples with the group.

15.1 Adjectives

Adjectives are words that make language come alive by adding description or information.

Adjectives help make nouns more specific. For example, *car* is a general word, but a *red two-door car* is more specific. Adjectives such as *red* and *two-door* make nouns and pronouns clearer and more vivid.

RULE 15.1.1

> An **adjective** is a word that describes a noun or pronoun.

Adjectives are often called *modifiers*, because they modify, or change, the meaning of a noun or pronoun. You can use more than one adjective to modify a noun or pronoun. Notice how *game* is modified by each set of adjectives below.

EXAMPLES   **old-fashioned** game

new **video** game

children's **word** game

first **baseball** game

Adjectives answer several questions about nouns and pronouns. They tell *What kind? Which one? How many?* or *How much?* Numeral adjectives, such as *eleven*, tell exactly how many. In the chart below, notice how adjectives answer these questions.

WHAT KIND?	WHICH ONE?	HOW MANY?	HOW MUCH?
brick house	that judge	one daffodil	no time
white paper	each answer	several roses	enough raisins
serious argument	those sisters	both brothers	many hobbies
colorful shirts	this student	four books	some teams

Writing Coach Online — www.phwritingcoach.com

Grammar Tutorials
Brush up on your Grammar skills with these animated videos.

Grammar Practice
Practice your grammar skills with Writing Coach Online

Grammar Games
Test your knowledge of grammar in this fast-paced interactive video game.

WRITING COACH — Online

www.phwritingcoach.com

Diagnostic and Instruction

Diagnostic test assesses students' instructional needs. Lessons and practice are assigned based on results.

Additional Practice

- **Grammar Tutorials**—Animated videos reinforce key grammar skills.
- **Grammar Practice**—Targeted practice addresses individual needs.
- **ExamView**—Teachers customize their grammar practice and tests.
- **Grammar Games**—Interactive video games make grammar fun.

Adjective Position An adjective usually comes before the noun it modifies, as do all the adjectives in the chart on the previous page. Sometimes, however, adjectives come after the nouns they modify.

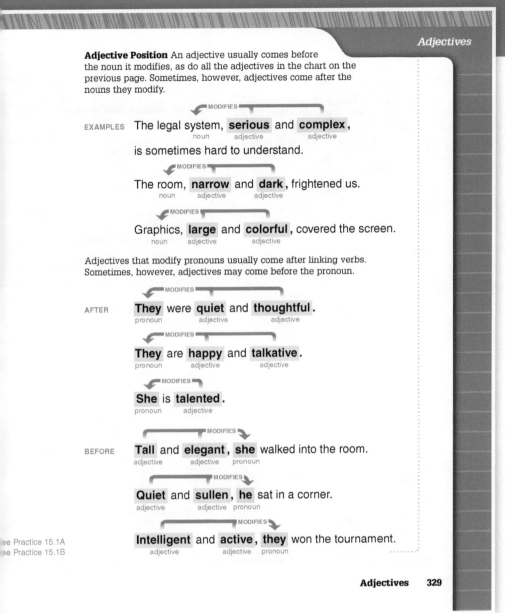

EXAMPLES
The legal system, **serious** and **complex**,
 noun   adjective   adjective
is sometimes hard to understand.

The room, **narrow** and **dark**, frightened us.
 noun   adjective   adjective

Graphics, **large** and **colorful**, covered the screen.
 noun   adjective   adjective

Adjectives that modify pronouns usually come after linking verbs. Sometimes, however, adjectives may come before the pronoun.

AFTER
They were **quiet** and **thoughtful**.
 pronoun   adjective   adjective

They are **happy** and **talkative**.
 pronoun   adjective   adjective

She is **talented**.
 pronoun   adjective

BEFORE
Tall and **elegant**, **she** walked into the room.
 adjective   adjective   pronoun

Quiet and **sullen**, **he** sat in a corner.
 adjective   adjective   pronoun

Intelligent and **active**, **they** won the tournament.
 adjective   adjective   pronoun

e Practice 15.1A
e Practice 15.1B

Adjectives 329

Write this sentence on the board and read it aloud: *He lived in a new yellow house.* Ask students to identify the adjectives in the sentence and the word they modify. Then, explain that adjectives can come before or after the noun they modify.

Write this sentence on the board: *Fog, thick and dangerous, covered the mountain.* Ask students to identify the adjectives. (*thick, dangerous*) What word do these adjectives modify? (*fog*) Explain that adjectives that describe the subject of a sentence can come before the subject, after the subject (as in the sentence above), or after a linking verb. Ask students to fill in the blank in these sentences with appropriate adjectives: *My puppy is _____. Heather's hair was _____ because she was walking in the wind.*

Point out that adjectives can describe pronouns, too. Adjectives can come before or after pronouns, just as they can with nouns.

Have student pairs write example sentences using adjectives that modify nouns and pronouns. Some sentences should feature the adjective before the noun or pronoun, and others should feature the adjective after the noun or pronoun. Invite students to read their best sentences aloud.

Teacher Tip

If students have difficulty understanding the placement of adjectives, organize several students into a small group. Assign each group member a word. One student should be a noun or pronoun. The other students should be adjectives. These students can place themselves in front of or behind the other student, depending on which placement makes the most sense. When students are satisfied with their placement, have them brainstorm for a complete sentence.

Working with ELLs **ELL** Sheltered Instruction: Cognitive

Help students demonstrate comprehension of increasingly complex English by responding to questions about a familiar text they are reading or have read. Guide them in using adjectives in their responses.

Beginning Ask students two simple questions about the selection they read. Before they answer, review adjectives they might use in their responses, such as *funny* and *sad*. Have students respond orally using the adjectives they choose.

Intermediate Write *funny, sad, exciting, several,* and *enough* on the board. Have students say each word aloud. Then, ask students questions about the selection they read and have students respond orally,

speaking in complete sentences and using one or more of the words listed on the board.

Advanced Have each student write two questions about the text he or she read using the following ideas as a base: *what kind? which one? how many?* and *how much?* Then, have partners answer the questions using adjectives, supporting their answers with details from the selection.

Advanced High Have students complete the Advanced activity. Then, challenge them to replace the adjectives in their answers with more precise synonyms, consulting a thesaurus and a dictionary.

PRACTICE 15.1A

1. several—How many? unusual—What kind?

2. clever—What kind? friendly—What kind?

3. That—Which one? music—What kind? four—How many?

4. Some—How much? bright—What kind?

5. important—What kind? all—How much?

6. Some—How much? young—What kind?

7. eight—How many? advanced—What kind? science—What kind?

8. bright—What kind? cold—What kind?

9. Those—Which one? little—What kind? five—How many?

10. red—What kind? gray—What kind?

PRACTICE 15.1B

11. sharp, fragrant, needles; tall, pines

12. long, time; huge, modern, store

13. old, dirt, rocky, bumpy, road

14. one, person; thousand, other, people

15. hollow, tree; good, place; some, birds

16. right, attitude; big, difference; many, competitions

17. cool, inviting, water; short, swim

18. long, blue, skirt; red, white, shirt

19. Most, people; safe, reliable, car

20. Five, heavy, sweaters; little, cardboard, box

SPEAKING APPLICATION

Students' descriptions should demonstrate students' understanding of and ability to use adjectives.

WRITING APPLICATION

Have students write the questions the adjectives in their sentences answer. (What kind? Which one? How many? How much?)

PRACTICE 15.1A Identifying Adjectives

Read the sentences. Then, write each adjective and list which question it answers. (What kind? Which one? How many? How much?)

EXAMPLE   Many people enjoy classical music.

ANSWER   *Many — How much?*
classical — What kind?

1. Australia is home to several unusual animals.

2. The parrot is a clever, friendly bird.

3. That music class was divided into four groups.

4. Some bright colors attract bees.

5. Nitrogen is an important chemical for all plants.

6. Some young people enjoy sports.

7. Eight advanced students went to the science museum.

8. In winter, bright days often bring cold weather.

9. Those little kittens went to five owners.

10. I think red paint will show up best on the gray wall.

PRACTICE 15.1B Identifying Adjectives and Words They Modify

Read the sentences. Then, write the adjectives and the words they modify.

EXAMPLE   Outside the dark house, the sky was blue and cloudless.

ANSWER   *dark, house*
blue, sky
cloudless, sky

11. The ground was covered with the sharp, fragrant needles from the tall pines.

12. It took a long time to build a huge, modern store.

13. The old dirt road was rocky and bumpy.

14. If one person leads, a thousand other people may follow.

15. A hollow tree makes a good place for some birds to nest.

16. The right attitude can make a big difference in many competitions.

17. The water, cool and inviting, tempted us to stop for a short swim.

18. The long blue skirt looks best with the red and white shirt.

19. Most people want a safe, reliable car.

20. Five heavy sweaters will not fit in a little cardboard box.

SPEAKING APPLICATION

With a partner, take turns describing a park near your home or school. Use adjectives to make your description more specific. Your partner should listen for and name three adjectives you used and what they modified.

WRITING APPLICATION

Write three sentences describing what you might see in a store you like. Use adjectives to help readers "see" what you are describing.

330   **Adjectives and Adverbs**

Working with ELLs   **ELL** Sheltered Instruction: Cognitive

As students study adjectives, guide them to demonstrate comprehension of increasingly complex English by taking notes. Provide students with a copy of a passage that includes many adjectives. Then:

Beginning Read the passage aloud as students follow along. Take notes in a cluster diagram about the main ideas. Include adjectives that describe events or characters. Students should copy your notes. Then, ask students simple questions about the text as they use their notes to respond.

Intermediate Have partners read the passage aloud and complete a main idea and details chart. Students should include adjectives in their notes. Have students

ask each other questions to monitor comprehension: *What is the passage mainly about? What adjectives did you use to describe the events/characters/ideas?*

Advanced Have students read the passage and complete a main idea and details chart that includes adjectives. Have students exchange charts and discuss similarities and differences in their work.

Advanced High Have students read the passage, taking notes about the adjectives used. Then, have students identify which question—*what kind, which one, how many, how much*—each adjective answers. Challenge students to use the adjectives to write a paragraph summarizing the passage.

Articles

Three frequently used adjectives are the words *a, an,* and *the.* They are called **articles.** Articles can be **definite** or **indefinite.** Both types indicate that a noun will soon follow.

> *The* is a **definite article.** It points to a specific person, place, thing, or idea. *A* and *an* are **indefinite articles.** They point to any member of a group of similar people, places, things, or ideas.

DEFINITE

Mr. Ryan is **the** man to call. (a specific person)

Go into **the** gym. (a specific place)

I want to play **the** game. (a specific thing)

INDEFINITE

I want to see **a** game. (any game)

Please take **an** apple. (any apple)

You should see **a** teacher for help. (any teacher)

A is used before consonant sounds. *An* is used before vowel sounds. You choose between *a* and *an* based on sound. Some letters are tricky. The letter *h,* a consonant, may sound like either a consonant or a vowel. The letters *o* and *u* are vowels, but they may sometimes sound like consonants.

USING *A* AND *AN*	
A WITH CONSONANT SOUNDS	*AN* WITH VOWEL SOUNDS
a blue hat	an endangered water bird
a happy time (*h* sound)	an honest person (no *h* sound)
a one-way street (*w* sound)	an old map (*o* sound)
a unicorn (*y* sound)	an uncle (*u* sound)
a taxi	an opportunity
a pineapple	an angry look
a university (*y* sound)	an eraser

See Practice 15.1C

Adjectives 331

Articles

Explain that the words *a, an,* and *the* are special kinds of adjectives called articles. There are two types of articles: definite and indefinite.

RULE 15.1.2 Read aloud the rule and then have students repeat the lines with you.

Use a Think Aloud as part of a gradual release progression.

 Say: It's easy to remember when to use *a, an,* and *the.* The first thing I ask myself is whether the article is pointing to a specific person, place, thing, or idea. If the answer is yes, then I use the definite article *the.* Consider this sentence: *I'm going to the store.* The phrase *the store* refers to a specific place—a particular store that I sometimes go to. Now, what happens if the article is not pointing to a specific person, place, thing, or idea? Consider this sentence: *The boy is going to a park. A park* in this case does not refer to a specific park, so I have used the indefinite article *a.*

Why did I use *a* instead of *an?* *Park* starts with a consonant sound. Use the indefinite article *a* with words beginning with a consonant sound. Use *an* with words beginning with a vowel sound.

Write this sentence on the board: *Would you buy me _____ apple at the store?* **Work with students** to complete the sentence using the correct definite and indefinite articles.

Have student pairs brainstorm for and construct three sentences using *a, an,* and *the.* Invite pairs to share their sentences with the group.

PRACTICE 15.1C

1. an—indefinite
   the—definite

2. The—definite
   a—indefinite
   an—indefinite

3. a—indefinite
   the—definite
   the—definite

4. An—indefinite
   a—indefinite
   the—definite

5. The—definite
   a—indefinite

6. a—indefinite
   the—definite
   a—indefinite

7. the—definite
   a—indefinite
   the—definite

8. a—indefinite
   the—definite

9. An—indefinite
   the—definite
   the—definite
   a—indefinite

10. the—definite
    the—definite
    a—indefinite

PRACTICE 15.1C > Identifying Definite and Indefinite Articles

Read the sentences. Then, write the articles, and label them *definite* or *indefinite*.

EXAMPLE   A pair of cardinals built their nest in the tree outside my bedroom window.

ANSWER   *A* — indefinite
          the — definite

1. During an average summer day in Antarctica, the temperature is around 20 degrees.

2. The children drew pictures of a waterfall they had seen in an encyclopedia.

3. Javier took a look through the telescope and saw one of the moon's craters.

4. An elephant is quite a sight in the jungles of Southeast Asia.

5. The first time I saw a shooting star, I didn't know what to think.

6. When visiting a new city for the first time, it is important to have a good map.

7. At the zoo, I hoped to see a lion or tiger, but I also wanted to visit the monkey house.

8. It is important when studying a subject like history to remember that the stories are about real people.

9. An unforgettable scene in the movie is when the hero saves a whole town from disaster.

10. After the storm, the clouds parted, and there was a beautiful rainbow.

Working with ELLs   ELL Sheltered Instruction: Metacognitive

Scaffold the Speaking Application, and have students take notes to demonstrate listening comprehension of increasingly complex spoken English by following directions. Have them monitor their comprehension and seek clarification as needed.

Beginning Describe an item using simple phrases and gestures, but do not name it. Pause occasionally to ask students whether they understand and to encourage them to seek clarification. Repeat, guiding students to take notes in a cluster diagram. Finally, lead students in guessing the item.

Intermediate Have students take notes in a prediction chart as you describe an item without naming it. Have them work with a fluent partner to review your clues and guess the item. Guide them to monitor their understanding and to ask their partners to explain unfamiliar words.

Advanced Have partners take turns as one tells about an item without naming it while the other takes notes and then guesses the item. Suggest students monitor understanding by using the self-questioning technique: *Do I understand this clue?* They should seek clarification as needed.

Advanced High Have students complete the Advanced activity. Then, have them write a list of tips on how to clarify understanding of spoken language.

Using Proper Adjectives

A **proper adjective** begins with a capital letter. There are two types of proper adjectives.

> **A proper adjective** is (1) a proper noun used as an adjective or (2) an adjective formed from a proper noun.

RULE 15.1.3

A proper noun used as an adjective does *not* change its form. It is merely placed in front of another noun.

PROPER NOUNS	USED AS PROPER ADJECTIVES
Thanksgiving	Thanksgiving dinner (*Which* dinner?)
Florida	Florida wetlands (*Which* wetlands?)
December	December weather (*What kind* of weather?)

When an adjective is formed from a proper noun, the proper noun will change its form. Notice that endings such as *-n, -ern, -ian,* or *-ese* have been added to the proper nouns in the chart below or the spelling has been changed.

PROPER NOUNS	PROPER ADJECTIVES FORMED FROM PROPER NOUNS
America	American history (*Which kind* of history?)
Japan	Japanese cities (*Which* cities?)
Norway	Norwegian legends (*Which* legends?)
Inca	Incan empire (*Which* empire?)
South	Southern hospitality (*Which* hospitality?)

See Practice 15.1D

Adjectives **333**

Adjectives

Using Proper Adjectives

Point out that proper adjectives are closely related to proper nouns. Like a proper noun, a proper adjective begins with a capital letter. Explain that there are two types of proper adjectives: proper nouns used directly as adjectives and adjectives formed from proper nouns. For example, in the chart on page 333 the proper noun *Florida* is used as an adjective to modify the noun *wetlands*. In the phrase *Norwegian legends,* the adjective is formed from the noun *Norway.*

RULE 15.1.3 Read aloud the rule and then have students repeat the lines with you.

Use a Think Aloud as part of a gradual release progression.

Think Aloud

Say: It's pretty easy to identify proper adjectives. **I just look** for adjectives that begin with capital letters. Consider this sentence: *The January snows are so beautiful.* I know that there are two adjectives in this sentence: *January* and *beautiful. January* is capitalized because it is a proper noun. In this sentence, *January* is a proper noun used as an adjective to describe *snows.* Now consider this sentence: *Oscar loves Italian cars.* I know that *Italian* is a proper adjective. It is capitalized. The last letter *-y* has been dropped and the ending *-ian* has been added to the proper noun *Italy. Italian* is an adjective formed from a proper noun.

Have student pairs construct two sentences using proper adjectives. One sentence should use a proper noun as an adjective and the other sentence should use an adjective formed from a proper noun. Invite partners to share their sentences with the group.

Differentiated Instruction

Strategy for Spanish Speakers

Students whose home language is Spanish may tend to have a proper adjective follow a noun by using a prepositional phrase—*the dances of Spain* rather than *Spanish dances.* Remind students that in English proper adjectives precede the noun, and like proper nouns, they are always capitalized. Elicit different nouns from students and have students write them on pieces of paper. Elicit possible proper adjectives from students and have them copy these words on sticky notes. Have students underline or retrace the initial capital of each proper adjective. On the board, model the placement of a proper adjective before a noun. Then, have students work in pairs to match a proper adjective with a noun by sticking it before the noun. Have pairs construct sentences with each proper adjective and noun pair.

T333

Using Nouns as Adjectives

Write these phrases on the board: *log house, model train, dog food, paper towel.* Point out to students that nouns can sometimes be used as adjectives. In these examples, *log, model, dog,* and *paper* are all nouns that are used as adjectives. A noun used as an adjective comes directly before another noun. It answers the question *What kind?* or *Which one?* With students, brainstorm for additional phrases in which a noun is used as an adjective to modify another noun. Write the phrases on the board.

Using the phrases you wrote on the board, work with students to ask the questions *What kind?* or *Which one?* to determine how the noun is being used as an adjective.

Using Compound Adjectives

Explain that compound adjectives can be two hyphenated words or one combined word.

RULE 15.1.4 Read aloud the rule and then have students repeat the line with you.

Use a Think Aloud as part of a gradual release progression.

 Think Aloud **Say: I know that** many compound adjectives are hyphenated words. A *part-time* worker, a *five-year-old* boy, and a *low-budget* movie are a few examples. But some compound adjectives are combined words, such as *childlike* voice. If I'm not sure whether a compound adjective is supposed to be hyphenated, I look it up in the dictionary to make sure.

Work with students to generate a list of compound adjectives.

Have student pairs find the words in a dictionary to check whether the words are hyphenated or combined. Invite students to make a sentence using one of the words and share it with the group.

Using Nouns as Adjectives

Nouns can sometimes be used as adjectives. A noun used as an adjective usually comes directly before another noun and answers the question *What kind?* or *Which one?*

NOUNS	USED AS ADJECTIVES
shoe	a shoe salesperson (*What kind* of salesperson?)
waterfowl	the waterfowl refuge (*Which* refuge?)
court	a court date (*What kind* of date?)
morning	a morning appointment (*What kind* of appointment?)

Using Compound Adjectives

Adjectives, like nouns, can be compound.

> A **compound adjective** is made up of more than one word.

Most **compound adjectives** are written as hyphenated words. Some are written as combined words, as in "a *runaway* horse." If you are unsure about how to write a compound adjective, look up the word in a dictionary.

HYPHENATED	COMBINED
a well-known actress	a featherweight boxer
a full-time job	a freshwater lake
snow-covered mountains	a sideways glance
one-sided opinions	heartbreaking news
so-called experts	a nearsighted witness

See Practice 15.1E

334 **Adjectives and Adverbs**

Quick-Write Extension

To help students synthesize and apply what they have learned about adjectives, have them write travel advertisements for a real or imaginary place. Working in pairs, students should use adjectives to help persuade readers to visit the destination. Students may add pictures, but they must also use adjectives to help readers create mental pictures. Have student pairs exchange advertisements and highlight or underscore the adjectives in the advertisement.

PRACTICE 15.1D > Using Proper Adjectives

Read each group of words. Then, rewrite the words to include a proper adjective before the underlined noun.

EXAMPLE a <u>shop</u> in Morocco
ANSWER *a Moroccan shop*

1. a <u>visitor</u> from Russia
2. <u>birds</u> from South America
3. an <u>invention</u> from Australia
4. <u>food</u> from Mexico
5. <u>salmon</u> from Alaska
6. the <u>flag</u> of Britain
7. a <u>castle</u> built by a German
8. <u>pepper</u> from Brazil
9. the <u>artwork</u> of China
10. <u>pyramids</u> in Egypt

PRACTICE 15.1E > Recognizing Nouns Used as Adjectives

Read the sentences. Write the noun, proper noun, or compound noun used as an adjective. Then, write the noun that the adjective modifies.

EXAMPLE He enjoyed watching the trains in the railroad yard.
ANSWER *railroad, yard*

11. December weather is usually cold.
12. The laptop computer might work.
13. We built a stone fireplace.
14. The Lincoln exhibit leaves soon.
15. It looked like a scene from a Dickens novel.
16. I need a guide to Chicago restaurants.
17. Both sides signed the cease-fire treaty.
18. Would you like to visit a South Pacific island?
19. The steel blade gleamed in the dim light.
20. The story came from a newspaper reporter.

SPEAKING APPLICATION

With a partner, take turns describing places around the world that interest you, being sure to use proper adjectives or proper nouns as adjectives. Your partner should listen for and name three or more of the adjectives.

WRITING APPLICATION

Write three sentences and include three of the following: a noun used as an adjective, a compound noun used as an adjective, a proper noun used as an adjective, or a proper adjective.

Practice   335

PRACTICE 15.1D

1. a Russian visitor
2. South American birds
3. an Australian invention
4. Mexican food
5. Alaskan salmon
6. the British flag
7. a German castle
8. Brazilian pepper
9. the Chinese artwork
10. Egyptian pyramids

PRACTICE 15.1E

11. December, weather
12. laptop, computer
13. stone, fireplace
14. Lincoln, exhibit
15. Dickens, novel
16. Chicago, restaurants
17. cease-fire, treaty
18. South Pacific, island
19. steel, blade
20. newspaper, reporter

SPEAKING APPLICATION

Have partners identify which questions the proper adjectives and nouns functioning as adjectives answer. (What kind? Which?) Discuss whether any compound adjectives were used.

WRITING APPLICATION

Assign partners, and have students circle and identify the proper adjectives and nouns used as adjectives in each other's sentences.

Working with ELLs **ELL** Sheltered Instruction: Cognitive

Scaffold the Speaking Application, and help students understand information and make inferences about implicit ideas in increasingly complex spoken language.

Beginning Using mime and visuals, describe a place that interests you. Hint at your feelings about this place without naming them. Then, ask, *Why does this place interest me?* and *How do you think I feel about taking a trip there someday?*

Intermediate Have students working in groups take turns describing a place that interests them. Group members should assist each other in expressing ideas. After each member contributes, listeners should answer these questions: *Where is this place? Based on what he/she has said, why do you think he/she would like to visit that place?*

Advanced Have student pairs take turns describing a place that interests them. Instruct them to hint at their reasons for being interested in that place without expressing them directly. Listeners should take notes, identifying proper adjectives, recording information, and making inferences about implied motives.

Advanced High Have student pairs complete the Advanced activity. To extend the activity, have them write about each other's places of interest as journal entries.

Using Pronouns as Adjectives

Explain to students that some pronouns, such as *this, which,* and *that,* can also be used as adjectives.

RULE 15.1.5 Read aloud the rule and then have students repeat the line with you.

Say: Consider these sentences: *The cats like that kind of food. Which cats have eaten already?* Which words are often used as pronouns? (**Possible responses:** *that* and *which*) What word does each of these words modify? (*That* modifies *kind; which* modifies *cats.*) In both sentences the pronoun becomes an adjective because it modifies a noun.

Using Possessive Nouns and Pronouns as Adjectives

Discuss how possessive nouns and possessive personal pronouns function as adjectives. Read aloud the examples and explanations. Then, have students use the examples as models to write their own sentences.

Have student pairs make sentences using possessive nouns and pronouns as adjectives. Students should identify whether each sentence features a possessive pronoun or possessive noun as an adjective. If the sentence uses a possessive pronoun as an adjective, have students circle the word modified by the pronoun and underline the pronoun's antecedent (if it is stated in the sentence). If the sentence uses a possessive noun as an adjective, have students circle the noun the possessive noun modifies. Invite partners to share their sentences with the group.

Using Pronouns as Adjectives

Pronouns, like nouns, can sometimes be used as adjectives.

> **A pronoun becomes an adjective if it modifies a noun.**

EXAMPLES   We see the ducklings on **this** side of the pond.

Which ducks are the males?

In the first example, the demonstrative pronoun *this* modifies *side,* and in the second example, the interrogative pronoun *which* modifies *ducks.*

Using Possessive Nouns and Pronouns as Adjectives

The following personal pronouns are often **possessive adjectives:** *my, your, her, his, its, our,* and *their.* They are adjectives because they come before nouns and answer the question *Which one?* They are pronouns because they have antecedents.

EXAMPLES   The **ducks** flapped **their** wings.
              antecedent   pronoun

The **club** wants to increase **its** membership.
     antecedent   pronoun

In the first example, *their* is an adjective because it modifies *wings.* At the same time, it is a pronoun because it refers to the antecedent *ducks.*

In the second example, *its* is an adjective because it modifies *membership.* The word *its* is also a pronoun because it refers to the antecedent *club.*

Note About Possessive Nouns Possessive nouns function as adjectives when they modify a noun.

EXAMPLES   The pond is on **Mrs. Smith's** property.

The **duck's** feathers are colorful.

See Practice 15.1F

336   **Adjectives and Adverbs**

Differentiated Instruction

RTI Strategy for Below-Level Students
A chart can help struggling students visualize and remember the different types of words that can be used as adjectives. Have students create a four-column chart and label these headings: *Pronouns as Adjectives, Nouns as Adjectives, Possessive Nouns as Adjectives, Possessive Pronouns as Adjectives.* Then, have students list at least one example of a word used as an adjective for each column. Have students use words from their chart to write example sentences and share them with others. Encourage students to keep their charts handy and refer to them when necessary.

PRE-AP Enrichment for Above-Level Students Remind students that different types of words are frequently used as adjectives. Have students create an adjectives "catalogue" that provides examples of pronouns, nouns, and possessive nouns and pronouns used as adjectives. Examples should be collected from books, magazines, or Web sites. Students can illustrate their examples with photographs clipped from magazines or line drawings. Display student catalogues in the classroom.

Using Demonstrative Adjectives

This, that, these, and *those*—the four demonstrative pronouns—can also be **demonstrative adjectives.**

PRONOUN   We saw **that** .

ADJECTIVE   **That** lake is home to many geese.

PRONOUN   What are **these** ?

ADJECTIVE   **These** gulls are searching for food.

Using Interrogative Adjectives

Which, what, and *whose*—three of the interrogative pronouns—can be **interrogative adjectives.**

PRONOUN   **Which** do you think he will choose?

ADJECTIVE   **Which** parrot do you think he will buy?

PRONOUN   **Whose** can that be?

ADJECTIVE   **Whose** macaw can that be?

Using Indefinite Adjectives

A number of indefinite pronouns—*both, few, many, each, most,* and *all,* among others—can also be used as **indefinite adjectives.**

PRONOUN   I bought one of **each** .

ADJECTIVE   **Each** judge writes an opinion.

PRONOUN   I don't want **any** .

e Practice 15.1G   ADJECTIVE   I don't want **any** help.

Adjectives   337

Using Demonstrative Adjectives

Write the four demonstrative pronouns—*this, that, these,* and *those*—on the board. Tell students that when these words are used as adjectives they are called *demonstrative adjectives.* When one of these words does not modify a noun, it is a demonstrative pronoun, as in *I like that.* When *this, that, these,* or *those* precedes a noun and modifies it, the word is a demonstrative adjective. Give this example: *Jerry owns that brand of bike, too.*

Have student pairs make two sentences. One sentence should use a demonstrative pronoun, and the other should use a demonstrative adjective. Have partners share their sentences with the group. Challenge other students to determine which sentence uses a demonstrative pronoun and which sentence uses a demonstrative adjective.

Using Interrogative Adjectives

Write *which, what,* and *whose* on the board. Explain that these interrogative pronouns can also be used as interrogative adjectives. Give this example: *What question were you going to ask?* Explain that *what* is an interrogative adjective because it modifies the noun *question.*

Call on individual students and ask them to use an interrogative pronoun or an interrogative adjective in a sentence.

Using Indefinite Adjectives

Draw students' attention to the text that states that a number of indefinite pronouns can be used as indefinite adjectives. Write the following sentence on the board: *I keep each photograph in a nice frame.* Point out that the word *each* modifies the word *photograph.* Explain that an indefinite adjective modifies a noun. Have students point to the noun modified in the example sentences in the book. Then, have students write sentences using *each* and *any* as indefinite pronouns. Have them repeat the exercise using the words as indefinite adjectives.

T337

PRACTICE 15.1F

1. Mr. Levin's
2. her
3. their
4. Mrs. Kamora's
5. your
6. John Smith's
7. his
8. our
9. Freddie Johnson's
10. my

PRACTICE 15.1G

11. Which—interrogative
12. this—demonstrative
13. That—demonstrative
14. few—indefinite
15. What—interrogative
16. Most—indefinite
17. both—indefinite
18. those—demonstrative
19. Whose—interrogative
20. many—indefinite

SPEAKING APPLICATION

Have students explain how they recognized the possessive pronouns in their partner's sentences and which nouns those pronouns modified.

WRITING APPLICATION

Have students exchange sentences. Partners should underline any possessive nouns and pronouns used as adjectives in their sentences.

PRACTICE 15.1F Recognizing Possessive Nouns and Pronouns Used as Adjectives

Read the sentences. Then, write the possessive noun or pronoun used as an adjective in each sentence.

EXAMPLE   Dad almost forgot his wallet this morning.

ANSWER   *his*

1. I walked by Mr. Levin's house.
2. Mom let me wear her bracelet.
3. The Sanchez children are going to visit their grandmother.
4. Mrs. Kamora's brownies are the best.
5. Why don't you bring your dog with you?
6. When we studied about Jamestown, I enjoyed John Smith's story.
7. Mr. Madorsky let me use his lawn mower.
8. Mrs. Cleary asked the three of us to talk about our vacations.
9. Freddie Johnson's home run tied the game.
10. Did you want me to show you my photographs?

PRACTICE 15.1G Identifying Demonstrative, Interrogative, and Indefinite Adjectives

Read the sentences. Then, write the adjective in each sentence and label it *demonstrative, interrogative,* or *indefinite.*

EXAMPLE   These shoes don't fit me anymore.

ANSWER   *These*— demonstrative

11. Which color do you think looks best on me?
12. Does this dress make me look too young?
13. That bowl will hold the fruit we bought.
14. I have only a few dollars, but I think it's enough.
15. What vegetable should I serve with fish?
16. Most doctors encourage people to eat right.
17. Call and find out if both boys are coming to dinner.
18. I wonder if those shirts will fit Johnny.
19. Whose books are those on the table?
20. Do you have many adventure movies in your collection?

SPEAKING APPLICATION

With a partner, take turns talking about something you or someone you know collects. Your partner should listen for and name two possessive pronouns.

WRITING APPLICATION

Write three or four sentences about your neighborhood. Write about people's houses, pets, and anything else that would give you an opportunity to use possessive nouns and possessive pronouns as adjectives.

15.2 Adverbs

Adverbs can modify three different parts of speech. They make the meaning of verbs, adjectives, or other adverbs more precise.

> An **adverb** modifies a verb, an adjective, or another adverb.

◁ 15.2.1 RULE

Although adverbs may modify adjectives and other adverbs, they generally modify verbs.

Using Adverbs That Modify Verbs

Adverbs that modify verbs will answer one of these four questions: *Where? When? In what way? To what extent?* These adverbs are also known as *adverbs of place, adverbs of time, adverbs of manner,* and *adverbs of degree.*

ADVERBS THAT MODIFY VERBS			
WHERE?	**WHEN?**	**IN WHAT WAY?**	**TO WHAT EXTENT?**
push upward	will leave soon	works carefully	hardly ate
fell there	comes daily	speaks well	really surprised
stay nearby	swims often	chews noisily	almost cried
go outside	exhibits yearly	acted willingly	partly finished
is here	report later	walk quietly	nearly won
jump away	come tomorrow	smiled happily	fully agree
drove down	went yesterday	moved gracefully	totally oppose

Negative adverbs, such as *not, never,* and *nowhere,* also modify verbs.

EXAMPLES   Helen **never** **arrived** at the party.
                        adverb   verb

I **could** **not** **answer** the question.
     verb adverb verb

The trail in the forest **led** **nowhere** .
                                 verb   adverb

Practice 15.2A

Adverbs   339

15.2 Adverbs

Lesson Objectives

1. Use adverbs to modify verbs, adjectives, and adverbs.

2. Distinguish between adverbs and adjectives.

Using Adverbs That Modify Verbs

Discuss the function of adverbs and how they can add detail to and enhance the meaning of verbs, adjectives, and other adverbs.

RULE 15.2.1 Read aloud the rule and then have students repeat the line with you.

Say: Adverbs that modify verbs usually answer one of these questions: *Where? When? In what way? To what extent?* To figure out which word in a sentence is an adverb, I ask myself one of these questions. Consider this sentence: *The spider climbed quickly.* I think *quickly* is the adverb. I can check this by asking myself *How did the spider climb?* or *In what way did the spider climb?* It climbed *quickly. Quickly* is an adverb that modifies the verb *climbed.*

Work with students to help them understand that negative adverbs modify verbs. Then, review the chart *Adverbs That Modify Verbs* with students. Have partners create one sentence for each of the four questions on the chart.

Differentiated Instruction

RTI Strategy for Special Needs Students
Students may have difficulty identifying adverbs and their modifiers. Make a list of verbs. Say one verb, such as *swim,* aloud and act it out in various ways (quickly, slowly, strongly, weakly). Then, ask students to describe the verb. Say the word *hum.* Hum quietly and slowly. Ask students to describe your humming. Vary your style of humming. Write their responses on the board and tell them that each response modifies, or describes, *hum.* Vary your style of humming and repeat the exercise. Then, work with students to use one or more of their adverbs in sentences.

Have students work with a partner to make a list of adverbs that modify another verb from the board. Then, have each pair write a sentence using the verb and one of the adverbs from their list.

Using Adverbs That Modify Adjectives

Point out that adverbs that modify adjectives always answer the question *To what extent?* Read aloud the first example. Discuss how *very* expresses the extent to which forests are beautiful. It answers the question *How beautiful are they?*

RULE 15.2.2 Read aloud the rule and then have students repeat the lines with you.

Write this sentence on the board: *Lenny was really happy.* **Then, ask:** How happy was Lenny? In other words, to what extent was he happy? (really happy) Have students identify the adjective (happy) and the adverb (really).

Organize students into pairs. Have one student create a sentence using an adverb to modify an adjective. Have the other student ask a question using this sentence frame: *How _____?* Then, have the student identify the adjective and adverb.

Adverbs Modifying Other Adverbs

Point out that adverbs can modify other adverbs as well as adjectives. When an adverb modifies another adverb, it answers the question *To what extent?*

Have student pairs make sentences using adverbs that modify other adverbs. Invite partners to share their best sentences with the class.

Using Adverbs That Modify Adjectives

An adverb modifying an adjective answers only one question: *To what extent?*

RULE 15.2.2

> When adverbs modify adjectives or adverbs, they answer the question *To what extent?*

ADVERBS THAT MODIFY ADJECTIVES	
very upset	extremely tall
definitely wrong	not hungry

EXAMPLE   Forests can be **very** **beautiful** .

The adverb *very* modifies the adjective *beautiful*.

EXAMPLE   The building is **extremely** **tall** .

The adverb *extremely* modifies the adjective *tall*.

Adverbs Modifying Other Adverbs

When adverbs modify other adverbs, they again answer the question *To what extent?*

ADVERBS MODIFYING ADVERBS	
traveled less slowly	move very cautiously
lost too easily	lived almost happily

EXAMPLE   The raccoon and beaver are **hardly** **ever** seen in dry areas of the forest.

The adverb *hardly* modifies the adverb *ever*.

EXAMPLE   When running, I get tired **too** **quickly** .

The adverb *too* modifies the adverb *quickly*.   See Practice 15.2B

340   Adjectives and Adverbs

Working with ELLs   EL Sheltered Instruction: Cognitive

As students learn about adverbs, guide them to develop basic sight vocabulary used routinely in written classroom materials.

Beginning Write on the board the following sight words from the Practice 15.2A directions: *where, when, what*. Read the words with students. As you use each word in an oral context sentence, call on a student to point to the word on the board. Add the words to a class list of sight words and review frequently.

Intermediate Have students read the words from the Beginning activity and review them with fluent partners. Extend by adding these sight words from the activities

on page 341: *read, then, write*. Have a fluent partner write a sentence using each word, and have the Intermediate student read each sentence aloud.

Advanced Help students develop basic sight vocabulary by instructing them to use the words from the Beginning and Intermediate activities in sentences. Call on students to read their sentences aloud.

Advanced High Have students partner with Beginning or Intermediate students. Give the pairs a list of sight words to review. Remind students to coach their partners on pronunciation and provide clear context clues as needed.

PRACTICE 15.2A Identifying How Adverbs Modify Verbs

Read the sentences. Write the adverb in each sentence and list what question it answers. (When? Where? In what way? To what extent?)

EXAMPLE   Put the table there.

ANSWER   *there — Where?*

1. I hope this friendship never ends.
2. Carnations will grow well in this garden.
3. Rhonda seemed extremely excited at the fair.
4. Yesterday, I saw a bird fly out of the library.
5. Carlos seems very upset.
6. Jeffrey did his chores carelessly.
7. Mrs. Shapiro can take us home later.
8. You should put your boots outside.
9. Celia works on her science fair project happily.
10. Bring the flowers here.

PRACTICE 15.2B Recognizing Adverbs and Words They Modify

Read the sentences. Write the word that each underlined adverb modifies. Then, write whether that word is a *verb*, an *adjective*, or an *adverb*.

EXAMPLE   In 1950, <u>very</u> few people had televisions.

ANSWER   *few — adjective*

11. By mid-afternoon, we had <u>successfully</u> completed our snow fort.
12. We washed the dishes <u>very</u> carefully.
13. The two scientists were <u>extremely</u> precise when recording their discoveries.
14. In the early days of airplane travel, flying was <u>quite</u> dangerous.
15. Some stuntmen have been injured <u>rather</u> seriously while making movies.
16. When we finally saw a gas station, the car's gas tank was <u>nearly</u> empty.
17. My grandmother returned <u>safely</u> from her first ride in a boat.
18. This book on rare animals is <u>definitely</u> interesting.
19. Did you know you can fly <u>nonstop</u> from Chicago to Beijing?
20. My sister <u>hardly</u> ever forgets to feed the dog.

SPEAKING APPLICATION

With a partner, take turns talking about activities you do regularly. Your partner should listen for three adverbs you use and say which question each adverb answers.

WRITING APPLICATION

Write three sentences about someone you admire—from your life or from history. Modify at least one verb, one adjective, and one adverb with an adverb.

Practice   341

PRACTICE 15.2A

1. never—When?
2. well—In what way?
3. extremely—To what extent?
4. Yesterday—When?
5. very—To what extent?
6. carelessly—In what way?
7. later—When?
8. outside—Where?
9. happily—In what way?
10. here—Where?

PRACTICE 15.2B

11. completed—verb
12. carefully—adverb
13. precise—adjective
14. dangerous—adjective
15. seriously—adverb
16. empty—adjective
17. returned—verb
18. interesting—adjective
19. fly—verb
20. ever—adverb

SPEAKING APPLICATION

Have students explain how they knew which question each adverb answered. Then, have them think of an adverb that answers a different question to make a new sentence.

WRITING APPLICATION

Students' sentences should demonstrate that they can recognize and use adverbs in writing.

Finding Adverbs in Sentences

Have students review the chart on page 342 which lists the different places adverbs can be located in sentences. Remind students of the questions to ask when identifying an adverb: *When? Where? In what way? To what extent?*

Organize students into seven groups. Assign each group a specific adverb location. Have each group brainstorm for and construct a sentence with an adverb located in the group's specific position. Then, have groups present their sentences aloud. Have the other students identify the adverb, note the location, and identify the part of speech of the word the adverb modifies.

Conjunctive Adverbs

Explain that certain adverbs can serve as conjunctions, or joining words, as well as adverbs. For this reason, these words are called *conjunctive adverbs.* Three common conjunctive adverbs are *consequently, however,* and *therefore.* Write this sentence on the board: *I studied hard; therefore, I got an A on my test.* Ask students to point out the conjunctive adverb. Point out the two simple sentences, or independent clauses, that *therefore* is joining. Then, explain how *therefore* suggests the cause-and-effect relationship between the two sentences. Have student pairs write three sentences using the conjunctive adverbs *consequently, however,* and *therefore.* Have each pair read one of its sentences to the class.

Extension

To help students synthesize and apply what they have learned, have them create an adverb bulletin board. You will need two note cards per student. Have students work in pairs, and assign each pair a different action verb. Each pair should then use the cards to list four adverbs that could be used with the verb. Post the action verbs on a bulletin board. Beneath each verb, post students' adverb cards in alphabetical order.

Finding Adverbs in Sentences

Adverbs can be found in different places in sentences. The chart below shows examples of possible locations for adverbs. Arrows point to the words that the adverbs modify.

LOCATION OF ADVERBS IN SENTENCES	
LOCATION	EXAMPLE
At the beginning of a sentence	Silently, she approached the ocean.
At the end of a sentence	She approached the ocean silently.
Before a verb	She silently approached the ocean.
After a verb	She tiptoed silently into the ocean.
Between parts of a verb phrase	She had silently entered the ocean.
Before an adjective	Her father was always quiet.
Before another adverb	Her father spoke rather quietly.

Conjunctive adverbs **Conjunctive adverbs** are adverbs that join independent clauses. (See Chapter 17 for more about conjunctive adverbs.)

EXAMPLES She injured her leg; **therefore** , she couldn't play in
the game.
conjunctive adverb

Ben predicted his score in the game; **however** ,
his prediction was not accurate.
conjunctive adverb

See Practice 15.2C

342   **Adjectives and Adverbs**

Adverb or Adjective?

Some words can function as adverbs or as adjectives, depending on their use in a sentence.

> If a noun or pronoun is modified by a word, that modifying word is an **adjective**. If a verb, adjective, or adverb is modified by a word, that modifying word is an **adverb**.

15.2.3 RULE

An adjective will modify a noun or pronoun and will answer one of the questions *What kind? Which one? How many?* or *How much?*

An adverb will modify a verb, an adjective, or another adverb and will answer one of the questions *Where? When? In what way?* or *To what extent?*

ADVERB MODIFYING VERB

Lumberjacks **work** **hard**.
　　　　　　verb　adverb

When the wolves reached the clearing, they **turned** **right**.
　　　　　 verb　adverb

ADJECTIVE MODIFYING NOUN

Lumberjacks accomplish **hard** **tasks**.
　　　　　　　　　　adjective　noun

The **right** **side** of the road is a good spot
　　 adjective　noun
to view the wolves safely.

While most words ending in *-ly* are adverbs, some are not. Several adjectives also end in *-ly*. These adjectives are formed by adding *-ly* to nouns.

ADJECTIVES WITH -LY ENDINGS

a **kingly** feast

a **friendly** person

Practice 15.2D
Practice 15.2E
Practice 15.2F

EXAMPLES

At the restaurant, we enjoyed a **kingly** feast.

I like Andrew; he is such a **friendly** person.

Adverbs **343**

RTI **Strategy for Below-Level Students**
Help students understand how to distinguish whether a word is functioning as an adverb or an adjective. Write these two example sentences on the board: *The mist rose gently in the forest. A gentle mist filled the forest.* Circle the words *gently* and *gentle.* Ask students to state the word modified by *gently,* and then repeat the

question with *gentle.* Guide students to understand that adverbs modify verbs, adjectives, and adverbs, while adjectives modify nouns and pronouns.

Have students create their own sentences using the same or similar words as adverbs and adjectives. Invite students to share their sentences with the group.

Adverb or Adjective?

Point out that some words can be used as either adverbs or adjectives. Explain that the difference depends on which words they modify in a sentence.

RULE 15.2.3 Read aloud the rule and then have students repeat the lines with you.

Use a Think Aloud as part of a gradual release progression.

Think Aloud

Say: So, now I know that some words can act as either an adjective or an adverb, but how do I know which is which? **I need to figure out** which word is modified. If the modified word is a noun or pronoun, then I am looking at an adjective. But if the modified word is anything other than a noun or pronoun, I am looking at an adverb. That means if the modified word is an adjective, a verb, or an adverb, then the word in question is an adverb.

Students can ask questions to determine what kind of word is being modified. Write these questions on the board: *What kind? How many? Which one? How much? Where? When? To what extent? In what way?* Then, draw a T-chart on the board and label one column *Adjective* and the other column *Adverb.* **Work with students** to sort the questions into the correct categories.

Have student pairs brainstorm for and construct several sentences using adverbs and adjectives. Then, have pairs exchange sentences with other pairs. Partners should work together to determine whether the modifier in each sentence is an adjective or an adverb.

PRACTICE 15.2C >

1. slowly, climbed
   very, steep

2. Suddenly, came
   carefully, had been
   planted

3. always, seems
   really, harsh

4. easily, defeated

5. especially, beautiful
   wonderfully, sunny

6. Eventually, learned
   quickly, had made

7. gently, placed
   directly, behind

8. Noisily, rushed
   recently, filled

9. wearily, crossed

10. often, return
    luckily, had found

PRACTICE 15.2D >

11. adjective	16. adjective
12. adverb	17. adjective
13. adverb	18. adverb
14. adjective	19. adverb
15. adverb	20. adjective

SPEAKING APPLICATION

Students should explain how they identified the adverbs in their partner's sentences and which words those adverbs modified.

WRITING APPLICATION

Students' sentences should demonstrate that students can recognize and use adjectives and adverbs.

PRACTICE 15.2C > Locating Adverbs

Read the sentences. Then, write each adverb and the word or words it modifies.

EXAMPLE   The chair was amazingly old and had almost broken when it was moved.

ANSWER   *amazingly, old*
almost, had broken

1. The hiker slowly climbed the very steep trail.

2. Suddenly, we came to a garden where flowers had been carefully planted.

3. Spring always seems nicer after a really harsh winter.

4. Our team easily defeated our rivals.

5. The mountains looked especially beautiful on that wonderfully sunny day.

6. Eventually, the boys learned that the plans they had quickly made would not work.

7. My mom gently placed the kitten directly behind my sister.

8. Noisily, the chickens rushed toward the recently filled feed bin.

9. The marathon runners crossed the finish line wearily.

10. We often return to the place where we had luckily found a good campsite.

SPEAKING APPLICATION

With a partner, take turns telling about an interesting book you recently read. Your partner should listen for and name three adverbs you used.

PRACTICE 15.2D > Recognizing Adverbs and Adjectives

Read the sentences. Then, write whether each underlined word is an *adjective* or an *adverb*.

EXAMPLE   He answered wisely.

ANSWER   *adverb*

11. The fever is gone, and the doctor says Billy well.

12. She loves ballet, and she dances well.

13. He worked hard at the math problems.

14. The farmer broke up the hard dirt.

15. Anna and Chen were there by 4:00, but Sas arrived later.

16. They decided to take a later bus.

17. There's an outside chance we'll make it to t playoffs.

18. If you want to play ball, you need to play outside.

19. He held the book close to the light.

20. That was a close race!

WRITING APPLICATION

Write two pairs of sentences, using the same word in each sentence of a pair—once as an adverb and once as an adjective.

344   **Adjectives and Adverbs**

Working with ELLs   ELL Sheltered Instruction: Metacognitive

Scaffold the Speaking Application, and have students respond to questions and requests to demonstrate listening comprehension of increasingly complex spoken English. Practice ways students can monitor their comprehension of spoken language during classroom instruction and interactions and seek clarification as needed.

Beginning Using adverbs, tell about an interesting book you recently read. Use mime and gesture to support understanding. Help students practice asking you to repeat what you have said and requesting clarification. Repeat, and then ask: *What happened? Tell me or show me.*

Intermediate Provide a list of adverbs students might use in the Speaking

Application, such as *suddenly* and *amazingly*. As students complete the activity, have listeners monitor understanding and ask partners to repeat or explain as necessary. Finally, have them answer these questions: *What happened? Why was it interesting?*

Advanced Have partners complete the Speaking Application, monitoring understanding and seeking clarification as needed. Then, have them write answers to these questions: *What happened? Why did it happen? Why was it interesting?*

Advanced High Have partners complete the Advanced activity. Then, have them suggest three other adverbs their partner might have used, explaining their choices.

PRACTICE 15.2E > Identifying Adjectives and Adverbs

Read the sentences. Write the adverb or the adjective in each sentence and label it.

EXAMPLE   He took a straight path to his friend's house.

ANSWER   *straight* — adjective

1. My answer on the test was wrong.
2. Justin reads fast when he likes the book.
3. The milk tastes sour to me.
4. He writes harshly about his childhood in the memoir.
5. There was dew on the grass in the early sunshine.
6. Arte finished entirely on his own.
7. Lilianna speaks unkindly of no one.
8. The check will go straight into the bank.
9. Ancient pieces of gold were found by the archaeologists.
10. Her necklace is beautiful.

PRACTICE 15.2F > Recognizing Adverbs and Adjectives

Read the sentences. Find at least one adverb and one adjective in each. Write the words and label them *adverb* or *adjective*.

EXAMPLE   Lee wisely stopped before spending his last dollar.

ANSWER   *wisely* — adverb
          last — adjective

11. Her mother carefully ties Kesi's long hair with ribbon.
12. The concert was really extraordinary.
13. She shouted out in a very loud voice to warn me.
14. Roz is going home early to watch her new baby sister.
15. He will never walk to school on a rainy day.
16. Early risers like to watch the sun come up slowly over the horizon.
17. This is certainly the best meal that I ever ate.
18. Ryan proudly introduced the opening act in the show.
19. The snake's skin is incredibly smooth.
20. Our school is growing more rapidly every year.

SPEAKING APPLICATION

Take turns with a partner. Describe what you do after school. Your partner will identify all the adjectives and adverbs that you use in your description.

WRITING APPLICATION

Write a brief paragraph about an experience you had recently. Use at least three adjectives and three adverbs. Exchange papers with a partner. Your partner should underline all the adjectives and circle all the adverbs in your paragraph.

Practice   345

PRACTICE 15.2E >

1. wrong—adjective
2. fast—adverb
3. sour—adjective
4. harshly—adverb
5. early—adjective
6. entirely—adverb
7. unkindly—adverb
8. straight—adverb
9. Ancient—adjective
10. beautiful—adjective

PRACTICE 15.2F >

11. carefully—adverb; long—adjective
12. really—adverb; extraordinary—adjective
13. very—adverb; loud—adjective
14. early—adverb; new—adjective; baby—adjective
15. never—adverb; rainy—adjective
16. Early—adjective; slowly—adverb
17. certainly—adverb; best—adjective; ever—adverb
18. proudly—adverb; opening—adjective
19. incredibly—adverb; smooth—adjective
20. more—adverb; rapidly—adverb; every—adjective

SPEAKING APPLICATION

Have partners point out each word that is modified and identify that word's part of speech.

WRITING APPLICATION

Students' paragraphs should demonstrate that they can use and recognize adjectives and adverbs.

Test Warm-Up

1. **B** Change *quick* to **quickly**

2. **F** Change *real* to **really**

3. **B** When I was little, she told me marvelous adventure stories.

4. **H** She has a rock collection, so I will take her an unusual rock that I found.

Reteach

If students have not mastered these skills, review the content in Sections 15.1 Adjectives and 15.2 Adverbs.

1. Adverb or Adjective? 15.2.3

2. Adverb or Adjective? 15.2.3

3. Using Nouns as Adjectives 15.1.3

4. Adverb or Adjective? 15.2.2

Test Tip

Students may have difficulty with the meaning of grammatical terms in a question. Explain to students that they can use key words to help them. For example, if a question requires students to identify a direct object in a sentence, students can use the key word *object* as a clue. They know that an object is a thing. Then, because they know a noun is the name of a person, place, or thing, students can deduce that the word they are looking for is a noun or pronoun.

Test Warm-Up

DIRECTIONS
Read the introduction and the passage that follows. Then, answer the questions to show that you can use and understand the function of adjectives and adverbs in reading and writing.

Tom wrote this paragraph about his neighbor, Ms. Flowers. Read the paragraph and think about the changes you would suggest as a peer editor. When you finish reading, answer the questions that follow.

Keeping in Touch

(1) Early Monday morning, I was walking quick because the bus usually pulled up at 7:30. (2) As I looked across the dusty road at the tiny old cottage, I wondered about its owner, Ms. Flowers. (3) It was a real long time since I had seen her. (4) When I was little, she told me marvelous stories and the stories were adventure. (5) I decided to visit her after school. (6) She has a rock collection. (7) I will take her a rock that I found, and it was unusual.

1 What change, if any, should be made in sentence 1?

  A Add a comma before *Monday*

  B Change *quick* to **quickly**

  C Change *usually* to **usual**

  D Make no change

2 What change, if any, should be made in sentence 3?

  F Change *real* to **really**

  G Add a comma before *since*

  H Change *long* to **longly**

  J Make no change

3 What is the BEST way to revise sentence 4?

  A When I was little, she told me marvelous stories and the stories were adventures.

  B When I was little, she told me marvelous adventure stories.

  C When I was little, she told me adventures that were stories.

  D When I was little she told me marvelous stories and adventures.

4 What is the BEST way to combine sentences 6 and 7?

  F She has a rock collection. I will take her an unusually rock that I found.

  G She has a rock collection, and I will take her a rock that I found, unusual.

  H She has a rock collection, so I will take her an unusual rock that I found.

  J She has a rock collection, so I will take her a rock that I found unusually.

Use the Online Lesson Planner at www.phwritingcoach.com to customize your instructional plan for an integrated Language Arts curriculum.

DAY 1　16.1　Prepositions

"What Do You Notice?" Objectives: Identify, use, and understand prepositions, including • compound prepositions	**INSTRUCTION AND PRACTICE** Student Edition pp. 347–350 Test Warm-Up p. 356

DAY 2　16.1　Prepositions *(continued)*

Objectives: Identify, use, and understand prepositions, including • prepositions used in sentences • preposition or adverb?	**INSTRUCTION AND PRACTICE** Student Edition pp. 351–355 Test Warm-Up p. 356

Alternate Pacing Plans

- **Block Scheduling** Each day in the Lesson Planner represents a 40–50 minute block. Teachers using block scheduling may combine days to revise pacing to meet their classroom needs.

- **Accelerated Lesson Planning** Combine instructional days, focusing on concepts called out by students' diagnostic test results.

- **Integrated Language Arts Curriculum** Use the instruction and practice in this chapter to provide reinforcement, remediation, or extension of grammar concepts taught in your literature curriculum.

Links to Prentice Hall *LITERATURE*

Unit 5 Prepositions and Appositives, p. 734

> *Prepositions ground us in a specific place. Without prepositional phrases, writing just floats in time and space.* The bird flies. *is indeed a sentence, but* The bird flies above an abandoned grain elevator in the fading night sky. *tells where and when.*
>
> **—Jeff Anderson**

WRITING COACH
Online
www.phwritingcoach.com

Grammar Assessment and Practice

Chapter diagnostic tests assess students' skills and assign instruction and practice.

DimensionL Video Games

Fast-paced interactive video games challenge students' mastery of grammar.

Grammar Assessment

Grammar Coach:	Diagnostic Assessment	End-of-Chapter Assessment	Progress Monitoring
Personalized Instruction	Students take grammar diagnostic test online and are automatically assigned instruction and practice in areas where they need support.	Teacher uses **ExamView** to administer end-of-chapter assessment and remediation. Teachers may customize **ExamView** tests or use the ones provided.	Teachers may use the **Test Warm-Ups** and the **Cumulative Reviews** in the student book or eText to check students' mastery of grammar skills. Students may also play **DimensionL** grammar video games to test their grammar skills.
Teacher-Directed Instruction	Teacher administers the diagnostic test and determines focus of instruction and practice.		

Lesson Planner continues on next page ▶

> " *To help students understand the value of prepositions and to encourage sentence variety, have students practice by writing sentences that begin with prepositional phrases ('Across the country, she waited for the phone to ring.' 'Under the weather, he stayed home.')* "
>
> **—Kelly Gallagher**

Differentiated Instruction

Differentiated Instruction Boxes in this Teacher's Edition address these student populations:

- Below-Level Students
- Above-Level Students
- Gifted and Talented Students
- Special Needs Students
- English Language Learners
- Spanish Speaking Students

In addition, for further enrichment, see the **Extension** features.

Grammar Ground Rule: Keep It Clear!

Model with Students

In this chapter, keep it clear means putting a prepositional phrase in just the right place in a sentence. Explain to students that prepositional phrases tell the relationship between a noun and some part of a sentence. To keep it clear, the prepositional phrase needs to be near that part of the sentence.

> **Say:** I could use a prepositional phrase to help describe a noun: *The lion with the golden mane.* Or I could use one to describe a verb: *walked around his cage.* Each prepositional phrase is right next to the thing it modifies. But what if I put those sentence parts together this way? *The lion walked around his cage with the golden mane.* One of the prepositional phrases has been moved away from the word it modifies, and the sentence doesn't make sense.

Write this sentence on the board: *The horse ran.* Ask students to think of prepositional phrases to describe either the horse or the way it ran. Have them tell you where the phrase would go in the sentence.

Small Group Activity – Finding Adjectives and Adverbs

Have students form groups to a set of directions for a simple task. Ask the groups to look for prepositional phrases in the directions. Have them discuss how moving the phrases to different places in the sentences could confuse the directions. Their discussion should answer these questions:

- What sentence part does the prepositional phrase modify?
- Is the phrase closely connected to that part?

Have a member of each group present their conclusions to the class and give one good example of prepositional phrase usage that follows this grammar ground rule: Keep it clear.

Grammar Ground Rules

1. Keep it clear.
2. Make them agree.
3. Make it specific.
4. Dot your *i*'s and cross your *t*'s .
5. Make it active.

PREPOSITIONS

e prepositions in your writing to make connections between
rds and ideas clearer.

WRITE GUY *Jeff Anderson, M.Ed.*

WHAT DO YOU NOTICE?

Look for prepositions as you zoom in on these lines from the play
The Phantom Tollbooth by Susan Nanus, based on the book by
Norton Juster.

MENTOR TEXT

> In this box are the letters of the alphabet. With them you can
> form all the words you will ever need to help you overcome the
> obstacles that may stand in your path.

Now, ask yourself the following questions:

- Which preposition shows the relationship between the letters
  and the box, and which preposition connects the word *letters* to
  the phrase *the alphabet*?
- Which preposition connects *stand* to *your path*?

The preposition *in* shows the location of the letters; they are inside
the box. The preposition *of* connects *letters* and *the alphabet*.
The preposition *in* connects *stand* and *your path* to show where
someone might stand.

Grammar for Writers Making clear connections between
words and ideas is an essential part of a writer's task. Think of
prepositions as strings you use to tie together different parts of
your writing.

*erday, my sister
me to balance a
ok in my head.*

*Wait a minute. She
meant on your head!*

347

PREPOSITIONS

As students progress in their writing skills, it
will be important for them to be able to apply
the rules of grammar, usage, and mechanics to
their own drafts. Use the *What Do You Notice?*
feature to help them see effective conventions
in the work of professional writers. Encourage
students to incorporate effective voice, tense,
and syntax as they edit their own writing.

Read aloud the opening sentence of the Mentor
Text. Discuss how prepositions are used to
connect elements in a sentence. A preposition
relates the noun or pronoun that follows it to
another word in a sentence in order to show
location, time, or direction.

WRITE GUY *Jeff Anderson, M. Ed.*

WHAT DO YOU NOTICE?

When students have read the Mentor Text, **say:**
This text has several prepositions. Prepositions
are words that introduce a phrase that adds
some detail to the sentence. Often, prepositions
tell where or when something happened. For
example, an explorer may look over a valley from
a mountaintop. The preposition *over* tells where
the explorer is looking.

Have students finish reading the page. Remind
them that prepositions and the words that
work with them may show where an event
takes place.

Then, ask: How would the text you just read
change if the prepositions and the phrases they
introduced were removed? (**Possible response:**
The sentences would not make sense. The
prepositional phrases include important
information about the subjects that the text is
discussing.)

Invite students to name some prepositions
from the text. **Ask:** Can prepositions stand
alone? Guide students in understanding that
prepositions always begin phrases.

Grammar for Writers: Syntax

Help students understand that prepositional
phrases enhance written descriptions.
Carefully chosen prepositions connect words
to phrases in text and can provide interesting
details about where and when events happen,
among other things. The rules on these pages
will help students write and correctly position
phrases to craft effective sentences.

Lesson Objectives

1. Distinguish between common and compound prepositions.

2. Identify prepositional phrases and objects of prepositions.

3. Differentiate between prepositions and adverbs.

Explain that a preposition adds detail to a word by relating it to a noun or a pronoun.

RULE 16.1.1 Read aloud the rule and then have students repeat the line with you.

Explain the function of the preposition in each example sentence on page 348. For example, **say:** In the first sentence, *on* relates the noun *surface* to the verb *floated* to explain where the duck floated. *Of* relates the noun *pond* to the noun *surface* to tell on which surface the duck floated.

www.phwritingcoach.com

Diagnostic and Instruction
Diagnostic test assesses students' instructional needs. Lessons and practice are assigned based on results.

Additional Practice
- Grammar Tutorials—Animated videos reinforce key grammar skills.
- Grammar Practice—Targeted practice addresses individual needs.
- ExamView—Teachers customize their grammar practice and tests.
- Grammar Games—Interactive video games make grammar fun.

16.1 Prepositions

Prepositions function as connectors, relating one word to another within a sentence.

They allow a speaker or writer to express the link between separate items. **Prepositions** can convey information about location, time, or direction or provide details.

RULE 16.1.1

> A **preposition** relates the noun or pronoun following it to another word in the sentence.

EXAMPLES

The duck floated **on** the surface **of** the pond.

The dog ran **across** the yard and

hid **between** the bushes.

In the first example, the duck floated where? (on the surface) It was the surface of what? (the pond) In the second example, the dog ran where? (across the yard) The dog hid where? (between the bushes)

FIFTY COMMON PREPOSITIONS				
about	behind	during	off	to
above	below	except	on	toward
across	beneath	for	onto	under
after	beside	from	opposite	underneath
against	besides	in	out	until
along	between	inside	outside	up
among	beyond	into	over	upon
around	but	like	past	with
at	by	near	since	within
before	down	of	through	without

348   Prepositions

See Practice 16.1A

Differentiated Instruction

RTI Strategy for Below-Level Students
Students may find it helpful to create a visual representation of some common prepositions. Have student pairs choose an object such as a laptop or a cell phone and draw it in the middle of a sheet of paper. Then have them write prepositions in the appropriate places, *under* the image, *over* the image, *across* the image, etc. Ask volunteers to show their illustrations to the class.

PRE-AP Enrichment for Above-Level Students Have students exercise their understanding of prepositions and their creativity by writing sentences in which both the subject and the verb are modified by prepositional phrases. Each student's first sentence should be followed by a second in which the adverb phrase in the first sentence becomes the adjective phrase. In the third sentence, the adverb phrase from the second becomes the adjective phrase.

Compound Prepositions Prepositions consisting of more than one word are called **compound prepositions.** Some of them are listed in the chart below:

COMPOUND PREPOSITIONS		
according to	by means of	instead of
ahead of	in addition to	in view of
apart from	in back of	next to
aside from	in front of	on account of
as of	in place of	on top of
because of	in spite of	out of

See Practice 16.1B

Because prepositions have different meanings, using a particular preposition will affect the way other words in a sentence relate to one another. In the first sentence, for example, notice how each preposition changes the relationship between *parade* and *City Hall.*

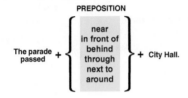

In this sentence, the preposition changes the relationship between *girls* and *gym.*

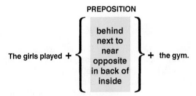

Prepositions   **349**

Compound Prepositions

Discuss the fact that some prepositions are two or three words. Draw students' attention to the chart on page 349. Explain that phrases like *in place of* and *on top of* actually perform the same job as a one-word preposition. Remind students that prepositions can be used to add many different types of details, including details about time, direction, location, or cause.

Have students brainstorm for sentences that include these compound prepositions: *ahead of, in back of, instead of, next to.*

Have students individually create sentences with compound prepositions. Then, have students trade their sentences with a partner. Partners should identify the compound prepositions and describe the relationship that the compound prepositions define.

Teacher Tip

If students have difficulty identifying the noun or pronoun to which a preposition relates, encourage them to ask *What?* after reading the preposition. (e.g., *Before what? Above what?*) The response to that question will be the noun or pronoun.

Working with ELLs   **ELL** Sheltered Instruction: Cognitive

Help students speak using a variety of connecting words with increasing accuracy and ease as they learn to use prepositions to link ideas.

Beginning Show visuals illustrating the two example sentences on page 348. Read the sentences aloud to students, emphasizing the connecting words, or prepositions. Have students repeat after you. Then, guide students in using the same prepositions to describe another visual you provide.

Intermediate Have students take turns saying sentences using the connecting words *above*, *outside*, and *down*, from the table on page 348. As students speak their sentences, write them on the board. Then,

have volunteers underline the prepositions in each.

Advanced Write several connecting words from the table on page 348 on index cards. Sit with students in a circle. Have the student to your left say a sentence that includes the word on the first card. Then, have the next student say a sentence with the word, and so on. Continue until all students have spoken a sentence with each word.

Advanced High Have partners develop a spoken dialogue featuring eight words from the table on page 348. Have them perform their dialogues for the class.

PRACTICE 16.1A

1. on—location
2. underneath—location
3. in—location
4. beside—location
5. beyond—location or direction
6. of—details
7. during—time
8. under—location
9. before—time
10. between—location

PRACTICE 16.1B

11. instead of
12. Because of
13. in front of
14. out of
15. In addition to
16. ahead of
17. next to
18. In back of
19. by means of
20. on account of

PRACTICE 16.1A Identifying Prepositions

Read the sentences. Write the preposition in each sentence. Then, write the function of the preposition (to convey *location*, *time*, or *direction*, or to provide *details*).

EXAMPLE Just tie a string around the middle.

ANSWER *around — location*

1. Some people live on islands.
2. The ball got stuck underneath the car.
3. We heard a large crash in the next room.
4. Put the wood beside the fireplace.
5. Finally, the boat disappeared beyond the horizon.
6. Have you thought of a topic?
7. We were excited to find that it had snowed during the night.
8. There are mountains, valleys, and volcanoes under the sea.
9. We left before sunrise to go fishing.
10. There was a high fence between the two yards.

PRACTICE 16.1B Identifying Compound Prepositions

Read the sentences. Then, write the compound preposition in each sentence.

EXAMPLE They worked hard and finished ahead of schedule.

ANSWER *ahead of*

11. I'll have a salad instead of the soup.
12. Because of the storm, we have to go home.
13. Put the small picture in front of the larger one.
14. Some really fabulous food comes out of my mom's kitchen.
15. In addition to herbs, we planted several vegetables.
16. Don't get too far ahead of your sister.
17. The fire extinguisher is next to the fire alarm.
18. In back of the school, there's a large playing field.
19. The coach communicated by means of hand signals.
20. The game was canceled on account of rain.

SPEAKING APPLICATION

With a partner, take turns discussing a ball game, using prepositions to describe where players are in relation to the ball, other players, or positions on the field. Your partner should listen for and name four prepositions.

WRITING APPLICATION

Choose three prepositions and three compound prepositions from the sentences in Practice 16.1A and Practice 16.1B. Write six sentences of your own, using a different preposition or compound preposition in each to convey location, time, or direction, or to provide details.

350　**Prepositions**

Extension

To help students synthesize and apply what they have learned about prepositions, have them write a class poem consisting mainly of prepositional phrases. Provide the first line of the poem: *The rain falls . . .* Then, call on volunteers to add prepositional phrases to create a poem; for example: *The rain falls / like tears, / in large, cold drops, / on the windows, / of our classroom, / at noon.* Students should use as many different prepositions as possible.

Prepositions Used in Sentences

A preposition is never used by itself in a sentence. Instead, it appears as part of a phrase containing one or more other words.

> A **preposition** in a sentence always introduces a **prepositional phrase.**

RULE 16.1.2

Prepositional Phrases

A **prepositional phrase** is a group of words that begins with a preposition and ends with a noun or pronoun. The noun or pronoun following the preposition is the **object of the preposition.**

Some prepositional phrases contain just two words—the preposition and its object. Others are longer because they contain modifiers.

EXAMPLES

in water
preposition object

from the solar **system**
preposition   object

in place of the old, broken **antenna**
        preposition   object

inside the large, modern **stadium**
  preposition   object

with us
preposition object

according to the new **coach**
        preposition   object

Prepositional phrases convey information about location, time, or direction or provide details. (See Chapter 23 to learn about prepositional phrases and their influence on subject–verb agreement.)

Practice 16.1C
Practice 16.1D
Practice 16.1E
Practice 16.1F
Practice 16.1H

Prepositions   **351**

Prepositions Used in Sentences

Point out that a preposition does not stand alone. It begins a phrase made up of two or more words; for example, *in the closet,* as in the sentence *I put the fishing rod in the closet,* and *according to,* as in the sentence *According to Aisha, the rehearsal starts at one.*

RULE 16.1.2 Read aloud the rule and then have students repeat the line with you.

Prepositional Phrases

Say: A prepositional phrase is easy to identify because it always begins with a preposition and ends with a noun or a pronoun. The noun or pronoun that ends the phrase is called the object of the preposition.

Discuss the example prepositional phrases on page 351. Point out the noun that ends each phrase other than the second-to-the-last phrase, which ends with the pronoun *us.* Then, write this sentence on the board: *I saw an eagle in the sky above the ocean.* Call for volunteers to identify the object of each preposition (sky, ocean).

With students, brainstorm for several sentences with prepositional phrases. Encourage students to use at least one compound preposition. Work with students to identify the prepositions in the sentences. Then, guide students to name the prepositional phrases and the objects of the prepositions.

Have student pairs look around the classroom to find examples of locations that can be described by using prepositional phrases (e.g, under the window, on the bookcase). Have students use prepositional phrases to describe the locations.

Working with ELLs   **ELL** Sheltered Instruction: Cognitive

To help students internalize and build proficiency with new grade-level academic vocabulary, have them use and reuse the vocabulary in a speaking activity. Focus on these key academic words from the lesson: *preposition* and *prepositional phrase.*

Beginning Write the sentence *We found the money buried in the dirt.* Read the sentence aloud and have students repeat it. Explain the meaning of the sentence. Then, point to the preposition *in* and say *preposition.* Have students repeat. Next, underline the prepositional phrase *in the dirt,* say *prepositional phrase,* and have students repeat. Repeat the activity with other simple sentences featuring prepositional phrases.

Intermediate Write several prepositions and prepositional phrases on the board. As you point to each one, have students speak a complete sentence: _____ *is a preposition.* _____ *is a prepositional phrase.*

Advanced Write several sentences featuring prepositional phrases on the board. Have volunteers orally identify the preposition and prepositional phrases in each, using these terms.

Advanced High Have students list ten prepositions and write a prepositional phrase for each. Then, have partners switch lists and orally identify each item as either a preposition or a prepositional phrase. Challenge students to use the prepositional phrases in complete sentences.

Preposition or Adverb?

Point out that some words can be used as either prepositions or adverbs. Read aloud the first two example sentences. Explain that *outside* is a preposition when it is followed by an object, but it is an adverb when it stands alone. Remind students that prepositions always begin phrases. Therefore, if a word that appears to be a preposition stands alone, the word is functioning as an adverb, not a preposition.

Tell students that they should not decide whether a word is a preposition until they see whether it begins a prepositional phrase.

Have students create sentences using the words listed in the chart on page 352. Next, have them discuss whether each word is used as an adverb or a preposition in the sentences, and how they know. Then, have students identify the prepositional phrase and the object of the preposition if the sentence includes a preposition.

Have students create sentences with prepositional phrases and adverbs and share them with a partner. Partners should explain whether a word is being used as an adverb or a preposition. Then, have the pairs create another sentence using the word in the other form.

Extension

To help students synthesize and apply what they have learned, have them create an adverb bulletin board. You will need two note cards per student. Have students work in pairs, and assign each pair a different action verb. Each pair should then use the cards to list four adverbs that could be used with the verb. Post the action verbs on a bulletin board. Beneath each verb, post students' adverb cards in alphabetical order.

Preposition or Adverb?

Some words can be used either as prepositions or as adverbs. The following chart lists some examples. When the word is used as a preposition, it begins a prepositional phrase and is followed by the object of the preposition. If the word has no object, it is probably being used as an adverb.

PREPOSITION OR ADVERB		
above	inside	outside
after	nearby	past
around	opposite	underneath
before	out	within

PREPOSITION The broken panel was **outside** the spacecraft.

ADVERB The astronauts slowly stepped **outside**.

PREPOSITION He appeared **before** the court.

ADVERB I had not realized that **before**.

PREPOSITION The ball flew **past** third base.

ADVERB The umpire ran **past** quickly.

PREPOSITION They sat **inside** the dugout.

ADVERB Please come **inside** soon.

PREPOSITION The umpire stands **behind** the catcher.

ADVERB Harry stayed **behind**.

See Practice 16.1G

PREPOSITION The team lined up **nearby** the water fountain.

ADVERB Please play **nearby**.

352　Prepositions

Differentiated Instruction

RTI Strategy for Special Needs Students Students may have difficulty distinguishing between a word that is used as a preposition and one that is used as an adverb. Have them create a mini-sentence diagram for each word that puzzles them, drawing a slanted line that turns into a horizontal line and putting the word on the slanted line. Explain that, if they cannot find a word to put on the horizontal line, they are not looking at a preposition, but an adverb.

Enrichment for Gifted and Talented Students Have students as a group create a chart of words that can fill either role—adverb or preposition—in a sentence. Then have students exercise their understanding of sentence elements and their creativity by writing two or three sentences in which a word that can be used as either an adverb or a preposition is used in both senses. Ask volunteers to present their sentences to the class.

PRACTICE 16.1C Recognizing Prepositional Phrases

[Re]ad the sentences. Write the prepositional [phr]ase in each sentence, and underline the object [of t]he preposition. Then, write the function of the [pre]positional phrase (to convey *location*, *time*, or [dir]ection, or to provide *details*).

[EXA]MPLE   I read it in the Sunday newspaper.

[AN]SWER   *in the Sunday newspaper—* *location*

During recess, we played soccer.

He parked the car in front of their house.

The teacher hung the calendar near the clock.

He saved his money to buy a new pair of shoes.

A submarine can travel beneath the water's surface.

Maria will be going in place of Jolene.

The baker turned the flour into bread.

Wildflowers had bloomed along the path.

He pushed hard against the door but found it wouldn't open.

The nature photographer hiked through the old forest.

SPEAKING APPLICATION

[W]ith a partner, take turns describing your [l]ocation. Use at least two prepositional phrases [t]o convey location. Your partner should name [t]he prepositional phrases and the prepositions.

PRACTICE 16.1D Distinguishing Prepositions and Prepositional Phrases

Read the sentences. Write the prepositional phrases. Then, underline the preposition in each phrase.

EXAMPLE   Just leave the package inside the screen door.

ANSWER   *inside the screen door*

11. He wondered if he could climb over the fence.

12. Across from the store, there's a mailbox.

13. School was canceled today because of the snow.

14. The students gathered outside the classroom.

15. In the closet, you'll find extra blankets.

16. He put a flag on top of the fort.

17. We drove toward the next town.

18. Underneath the porch, the rabbit felt safe.

19. Dad helped me look for my lost homework.

20. Is there anything interesting on television?

WRITING APPLICATION

Write three sentences about your neighborhood. Use at least one prepositional phrase in each sentence to convey location, time, or direction, or to provide details. Circle the prepositions and underline the objects of the prepositions.

Practice   353

PRACTICE 16.1C

1. During <u>recess</u>—time
2. in front of their <u>house</u>—location
3. near the <u>clock</u>—location
4. of <u>shoes</u>—details
5. beneath the water's <u>surface</u>—location
6. in place of <u>Jolene</u>—details
7. into <u>bread</u>—details
8. along the <u>path</u>—location
9. against the <u>door</u>—location
10. through the old <u>forest</u>—location

PRACTICE 16.1D

11. <u>over</u> the fence
12. <u>Across from</u> the store
13. <u>because of</u> the snow
14. <u>outside</u> the classroom
15. <u>In</u> the closet
16. <u>on top of</u> the fort
17. <u>toward</u> the next town
18. <u>Underneath</u> the porch
19. <u>for</u> my lost homework
20. <u>on</u> television

SPEAKING APPLICATION

Students' descriptions should demonstrate that they can use and understand the function of prepositional phrases.

WRITING APPLICATION

Have students explain how they identified the prepositional phrases in their sentences to show that they can use and understand the function of prepositional phrases.

Working with ELLs **ELL** Sheltered Instruction: Cognitive

As students study prepositional phrases, have them demonstrate English comprehension and expand their reading skills by employing the analytical skill of evaluating written information.

Beginning Write these two sentences on the board: *Walk down the street and turn left. / Walk down the street and turn left at the second light.* Use visuals and the assistance of a fluent student who shares the same home language to ensure that all students understand. Then, guide them to evaluate which statement gives better directions.

Intermediate Provide students with the written sample sentences from the Beginning activity. Lead students in evaluating the difference between them. Then, have

students complete the Writing Application, working with partners to revise their work. Finally, have students exchange papers and evaluate each other's work.

Advanced After students have completed the Writing Application, have them read their partners' directions for clarity. Direct them to make suggestions based on their evaluation, including suggestions for incorporating prepositional phrases.

Advanced High Have students complete the Advanced activity. Then, have them check the accuracy of their partner's directions using an online map or other reference.

1. but me
2. without
3. As of
4. in the wrong direction
5. ahead of
6. In addition
7. next to
8. At five o'clock sharp
9. inside your desks
10. between

Answers will vary. Sample answers:

11. You can find the post office across the street.
12. Our cat had three kittens during the night.
13. Today at seven o'clock is our committee meeting.
14. My little brother was hiding in the tree house last night.
15. On Wednesday, I take an exercise class at the gym.
16. The marathon is this Sunday in Boston.
17. Dad bought a new car for my older sister on her birthday.
18. Will you come to my birthday dinner next Thursday?
19. Tomorrow at noon is the final audition for the school play.
20. Dr. Freeman's office will not be open on Saturday.

SPEAKING APPLICATION

Students' spoken and written sentences should demonstrate they can use and understand the function of prepositions and prepositional phrases.

WRITING APPLICATION

Students' paragraphs should demonstrate they can use and understand the function of prepositions and prepositional phrases.

PRACTICE 16.1E Supplying Prepositions and Prepositional Phrases

Read and discuss the sentences with a partner. Choose the appropriate preposition or prepositional phrase in parentheses. Then, write the sentences.

EXAMPLE New tenants moved _____. (into the apartment, with the apartment)

ANSWER *New tenants moved into the apartment.*

1. Nobody _____ seems ready. (instead of, but me)
2. We left _____ our gear. (across, without)
3. _____ Friday, he made the team. (Next to, As of)
4. Keshia headed _____. (in the wrong direction, against the wrong direction)
5. We expect them soon, _____ the other guests. (by means of, ahead of)
6. _____, I have a meeting. (According to, In addition)
7. Our place is _____ that house. (next to, on top of)
8. _____, we are leaving. (Around five o'clock sharp, At five o'clock sharp)
9. Please put your books _____. (inside your desks, through your desks)
10. The restaurant is _____ the museum and fountain. (among, between)

SPEAKING APPLICATION

With a partner, talk about your school. Use prepositions and prepositional phrases to convey location, time, or direction, or to provide details. Then, write four sentences about your school using prepositional phrases.

PRACTICE 16.1F Adding Prepositional Phras

Read the sentences. Rewrite them adding at lea one prepositional phrase to convey location, tim or direction, or to provide details. Then, read yo sentences to a partner and discuss the function your prepositional phrase.

EXAMPLE Lunch will be served.

ANSWER *At noon, lunch will be served in the cafeteria.*

11. You can find the post office.
12. Our cat had three kittens.
13. Today is our committee meeting.
14. My little brother was hiding.
15. I take an exercise class.
16. The marathon is this Sunday.
17. Dad bought a new car.
18. Will you come?
19. Tomorrow is the final audition.
20. Dr. Freeman's office will not be open.

WRITING APPLICATION

Write a paragraph about a store. Use at least five prepositions and prepositional phrases to convey location, time, or direction, or to provide details. Have a partner underline the prepositions and prepositional phrases.

Working with ELLs EL Sheltered Instruction: Cognitive

Scaffold the Speaking Application, and help students understand information and implicit ideas in increasingly complex spoken language commensurate with grade-level learning expectations.

Beginning Using prepositions, list some features about a valuable object you have lost. Use mime and visuals as needed to ensure understanding. Then, ask, *What does the object look like?* To gauge students' understanding of implicit ideas, ask, *Is it a small object? Is the object hard to find? Why?*

Intermediate Using prepositions, describe some features of a valuable object you lost with small groups. Monitor their understanding of information and implicit

ideas by asking these questions: *What does the object look like? What would you do to find it? Why?* Then, invite group members to discuss objects they think are valuable.

Advanced Have partners complete the Speaking Application. Monitor their understanding of information and implicit ideas by having them answer these questions: *What does the object look like? Where was it lost? What does your partner think about the object? How can you tell?*

Advanced High Have partners complete the Advanced activity. To extend the activity, have partners describe what they would do in order to protect something valuable.

PRACTICE 16.1G Distinguishing Prepositions and Adverbs

Read the sentences. Label each underlined word *preposition* or *adverb*.

EXAMPLE   My excitement grew as the day of the party drew <u>near</u>.

ANSWER   *adverb*

Leticia was afraid she would be left <u>behind</u>.

Is the library <u>behind</u> the school?

I left my wet boots <u>by</u> the door.

We watched the horses race <u>by</u>.

They built a bridge <u>over</u> the stream.

If you have time, why don't you come <u>over</u>?

He wondered if he'd ever learn what was <u>inside</u> the box.

To really appreciate the house, you have to go <u>inside</u>.

Stefan asked if he could come <u>along</u>.

Be careful that you cut <u>along</u> the dotted line.

PRACTICE 16.1H Supplying Prepositions and Prepositional Phrases

Read the sentences. Then, expand each sentence by adding a prepositional phrase that begins with a preposition of your choice, or use one of these prepositions: *in, for, on, of, by, from, with, into, between, through,* or *about.*

EXAMPLE   We watched the dogs play.

ANSWER   *We watched the dogs play in the yard.*

11. There were many clouds.
12. I received a package.
13. May I bring my cat?
14. What did you find out?
15. She found her paper.
16. We saw a groundhog digging.
17. Gabriella put the book down.
18. Jeremy bought a watch.
19. I thought I would look.
20. There is a movie I want to see.

SPEAKING APPLICATION

With a partner, take turns saying a sentence. Use the sentences in Practice 16.1H as models. Have your partner repeat the sentence, adding a prepositional phrase.

WRITING APPLICATION

Use the sentences in Practice 16.1G as models, and write two pairs of sentences. Each pair should have one sentence with a preposition and one sentence in which the same word is used as an adverb.

Practice   355

PRACTICE 16.1G

1. adverb
2. preposition
3. preposition
4. adverb
5. preposition
6. adverb
7. preposition
8. adverb
9. adverb
10. preposition

PRACTICE 16.1H

Answers will vary. Sample answers:

11. There were many clouds in the sky.
12. I received a package from my grandmother.
13. May I bring my cat with me?
14. What did you find out about the test?
15. She found her paper between two books.
16. We saw a groundhog digging in the flowerbed.
17. Gabriella put the book down on the table.
18. Jeremy bought a watch for his father.
19. I thought I would look through the telescope.
20. There is a movie I want to see about a famous sports hero.

SPEAKING APPLICATION

Students should demonstrate they can use and understand the function of prepositions by explaining how the use of prepositions was effective in adding descriptive details to their sentences.

WRITING APPLICATION

Students' written sentences should demonstrate their ability to use and understand the function of prepositions.

Test Warm-Up

1. **B** Change *without* to **next to**

2. **J** Summer squash was sown between the cucumbers and the lettuce.

3. **D** Change *People said* to **According to people in the group,**

4. **F** The first shoots appeared around the beginning of April.

Reteach

If students have not mastered these skills, review the content in Section 16.1 Prepositions.

1. Prepositions Used in Sentences 16.1.2

2. Prepositions Used in Sentences 16.1.2

3. Compound Prepositions 16.1.1

4. Prepositions Used in Sentences 16.1.2

Test Tip

Tell students that, for many grammar questions, they can choose the correct answer by simply plugging the answer choices into a sentence and saying the sentence in their heads. If it sounds right it usually, but not always, is right. If students have had a difficult time with a particular grammar topic, like subjective and objective pronouns, they should not trust this test. In those cases, they should recall the rules that they have learned and apply them to the problem.

Preposition

Test Warm-Up

DIRECTIONS
Read the introduction and the passage that follows. Then, answer the questions to show that you can use and understand the function of prepositions and prepositional phrases in reading and writing.

The following paragraph describes the layout of a community garden. Read the paragraph and think about the changes you would suggest a peer editor. When you finish reading, answer the questions that follow.

The Community Garden

(1) A group of neighbors planted a garden in a vacant lot across from the fire station. (2) Before winter's end, they dug into the soil and laid out the beds. (3) They planted taller plants like corn near the back. (4) Sunflowers were planted without the tomato plants. (5) Summer squash was sown to the right of the cucumbers and to the left of the lettuce. (6) People said working in the garden was relaxing and fun. (7) The first shoots appeared on about the beginning of April.

1 What change should be made in sentence 4?

  A Change *without* to **inside**

  B Change *without* to **next to**

  C Change *planted* to **into**

  D Change *without* to **during**

2 What is the BEST way to rewrite the ideas in sentence 5?

  F Summer squash was sown without the cucumbers or the lettuce.

  G Summer squash was sown inside the cucumbers and the lettuce.

  H Summer squash was sown upon the cucumbers and the lettuce.

  J Summer squash was sown between the cucumbers and the lettuce.

3 What change should be made to clarify sentence 6?

  A Change *People said* to **People never said**

  B Change *People said* to **In spite of the snow,**

  C Change *People said* to **In view of the vegetables,**

  D Change *People said* to **According to people in the group,**

4 What is the BEST way to revise sentence

  F The first shoots appeared around the beginning of April.

  G The first shoots appeared within the beginning of April.

  H The first shoots appeared upon the beginning of April.

  J The first shoots appeared under the beginning of April.

356   **Test Warm-Up**

T356

CHAPTER 17 LESSON PLANNER
Conjunctions and Interjections

Use the Online Lesson Planner at www.phwritingcoach.com to customize your instructional plan for an integrated Language Arts curriculum.

DAY 1 17.1 Conjunctions

"What Do You Notice?" **Objectives:** Identify, use, and understand conjunctions, including • coordinating conjunctions • correlative conjunctions • subordinating conjunctions • conjunctive adverbs • punctuation with conjunctive adverbs	**INSTRUCTION AND PRACTICE** Student Edition pp. 357–365 Test Warm-Up p. 366

DAY 2 17.2 Interjections

Objectives: Identify, use, and understand interjections	**INSTRUCTION AND PRACTICE** Student Edition pp. 367–368

DAY 3 Cumulative Review

Objectives: Identify, use, and understand the parts of speech, including • nouns, pronouns, and verbs • the other parts of speech	**INSTRUCTION AND PRACTICE** Student Edition pp. 369–370

> **"** Have students practice using short interjections as a way of adding power to their writing. Do it! Now! Okay? **"**
>
> —**Kelly Gallagher**

Grammar Assessment

Grammar Coach:	Diagnostic Assessment	End-of-Chapter Assessment	Progress Monitoring
Personalized Instruction	Students take grammar diagnostic test online and are automatically assigned instruction and practice in areas where they need support.	Teacher uses **ExamView** to administer end-of-chapter assessment and remediation. Teachers may customize **ExamView** tests or use the ones provided.	Teachers may use the **Test Warm-Ups** and the **Cumulative Reviews** in the student book or eText to check students' mastery of grammar skills. Students may also play **DimensionL** grammar video games to test their grammar skills.
Teacher-Directed Instruction	Teacher administers the diagnostic test and determines focus of instruction and practice.		

Alternate Pacing Plans

- **Block Scheduling** Each day in the Lesson Planner represents a 40–50 minute block. Teachers using block scheduling may combine days to revise pacing to meet their classroom needs.

- **Accelerated Lesson Planning** Combine instructional days, focusing on concepts called out by students' diagnostic test results.

- **Integrated Language Arts Curriculum** Use the instruction and practice in this chapter to provide reinforcement, remediation, or extension of grammar concepts taught in your literature curriculum.

Links to Prentice Hall *LITERATURE*

Unit 3 Conjunctions and Interjections, p. 508

www.phwritingcoach.com

Grammar Assessment and Practice

Chapter diagnostic tests assess students' skills and assign instruction and practice.

DimensionL Video Games

Fast-paced interactive video games challenge students' mastery of grammar.

Lesson Planner continues on next page

" *Have some fun with conjunctions. I love to use mnemonics to help students feel less threatened. The coordinating conjunctions become FANBOYS, helping us quickly recall for, and, nor, but, or, yet, so. But that's just the first step—the real key to teaching conjunctions isn't memorizing them; it's learning how they function for writers and readers.* "

—Jeff Anderson

Differentiated Instruction

Differentiated Instruction Boxes in this Teacher's Edition address these student populations:

- Below-Level Students
- Above-Level Students
- Gifted and Talented Students
- Special Needs Students
- English Language Learners
- Spanish Speaking Students

In addition, for further enrichment, see the **Extension** features.

Grammar Ground Rule: Make It Specific!

Model with Students

In this chapter, making it specific means using conjunctions to say what you really mean. Explain to students that two clauses always have some kind of relationship with each other. If they don't, they shouldn't be in the same sentence. Conjunctions make that relationship clear.

> **Say:** I could say, *I lost my pen and I can't write.* Using the conjunction *and* indicates that the two things are of equal importance and just happened together. But that's not really what I mean. I mean, *Because I lost my pen, I can't write.* One thing (losing the pen) made the other thing (not being able to write) happen. Using the specific conjunction *Because* makes the sentence communicate that.

Write this sentence on the board: *The boy ate his breakfast and he went to school.* Ask students to think of a conjunction that could tell the time relationship between the boy eating his breakfast and his going to school (*before, when*).

Small Group Activity – Looking at Conjunctions

Have students form groups to find a recipe for a simple meal. If it is written in paragraph form, have students identify the subordinating conjunctions and discuss how they relate the clauses. If it is written in numbered steps, have the students turn it into a paragraph by using subordinating conjunctions, then have them discuss why they used particular conjunctions. Have a member of each group present their conclusions to the class and give one good example of conjunction usage that follows this grammar ground rule: Make it specific.

Grammar Ground Rules

1. Keep it clear.
2. Make them agree.
3. Make it specific.
4. Dot your *i*'s and cross your *t*'s.
5. Make it active.

CONJUNCTIONS _and_ INTERJECTIONS

e conjunctions to connect and highlight important ideas in
ur writing; add interjections to help create emotion.

WRITE GUY _Jeff Anderson, M.Ed._

WHAT DO YOU NOTICE?

Watch for conjunctions as you zoom in on these sentences from the
book _The Pigman & Me_ by Paul Zindel.

> MENTOR TEXT
>
> Life does that to us a lot. Just when we think something
> awful's going to happen one way, it throws you a curve and the
> something awful happens another way.

Now, ask yourself the following questions:

- Which idea does the subordinating conjunction _when_ introduce?
- Which groups of words does the coordinating conjunction _and_
  link in the second sentence?

The subordinating conjunction _when_ introduces the dependent idea
we think something awful's going to happen one way. The main
idea is _it throws you a curve and the something awful happens
another way_. The coordinating conjunction _and_ links _it throws you
a curve_ with _the something awful happens another way_.

Grammar for Writers You can add variety
to your writing by placing a
subordinating conjunction, such
as _if_, in different locations in
a sentence. _If it snows, they
will cancel school. They will
cancel school if it snows._

_I think I'll have a
conjunction for lunch._

_Okay. Are you
having the soup
and sandwich
with a salad or
vegetable?_

357

Grammar for Writers: Syntax

Help students understand that instead of
writing two or more sentences, they can use
conjunctions to compare words or ideas
within a single sentence. Good writing often
means being less wordy and condensing ideas.
Explain that the rules in this chapter will help
students use conjunctions and interjections
more effectively in their writing.

CONJUNCTIONS _and_ INTERJECTIONS

As students progress in their writing skills, it
will be important for them to be able to apply
the rules of grammar, usage, and mechanics to
their own drafts. Use the _What Do You Notice?_
feature to help them see effective conventions
in the work of professional writers. Encourage
students to incorporate proper voice, tense, and
syntax as they edit their own writing.

Read the opening sentence aloud. Discuss
how we use conjunctions to relate multiple
ideas to one another or group ideas together.
Conjunctions are common and found in all
kinds of text. Point out how interjections are
not common in writing but are frequently used
in spoken language.

WRITE GUY _Jeff Anderson, M. Ed._

WHAT DO YOU NOTICE?

When students have read the Mentor Text,
say: As you may already know, conjunctions
are used when combining words or ideas in a
sentence. A conjunction is a word or words that
connect together, compare, or contrast two words
or ideas of the same type.

Have students complete reading the page.
Explain that the words _and_ and _when_ are
some examples of conjunctions. Then, **ask:**
How do conjunctions make a writer's job easier?
(**Possible response:** They allow a writer to
compare two ideas or identify two closely
related ideas in the same sentence.)

Guide students in understanding that there are
several different types of conjunctions that can
be used in sentences.

Lesson Objectives

1. Identify and distinguish between the three types of conjunctions.

2. Identify, use, and understand the function of subordinating conjunctions and conjunctive adverbs.

3. Identify, use, and understand the function of transitions for sentence-to-sentence and paragraph-to-paragraph coherence in reading, writing, and speaking.

Explain that there are three types of conjunctions. Each type joins words and ideas in a slightly different way.

RULE 17.1.1 Read aloud the rule and then have students repeat the line with you.

Coordinating Conjunctions

Explain that coordinating conjunctions join words or groups of words of the same type, like verbs, nouns, or independent clauses. Discuss with students how the meanings of the coordinating conjunctions *and, or, but, nor, for, so,* and *yet* are different from one another.

RULE 17.1.2 Read aloud the rule and then have students repeat the line with you.

Use a Think Aloud as part of a gradual release progression.

Think Aloud

Say: I can easily recognize coordinating conjunctions while I'm reading. In the examples on page 358, there are words I use often to connect two words or groups of words of the same type and importance, like *apples* and *oranges*.

Explain that coordinating conjunctions always connect two or more of the same things. For example, they may connect two nouns or pronouns, two verbs, two prepositional phrases, or even two sentences or clauses.

Help students understand the functions of conjunctions by reading the example sentences aloud and discussing what each conjunction does in a sentence. Then, discuss how the ideas would have to be presented in separate sentences if we didn't use conjunctions to link them together.

17.1 Conjunctions

Conjunctions are like links in a chain: They help you join words and ideas.

RULE 17.1.1

> **A conjunction** connects words or groups of words.

Conjunctions fall into three groups: **Coordinating conjunctions, correlative conjunctions,** and **subordinating conjunctions.**

Coordinating Conjunctions

RULE 17.1.2

> **Coordinating conjunctions** connect words of the same kind, such as two or more nouns or verbs. They can also connect larger groups of words, such as prepositional phrases or even complete sentences.

COORDINATING CONJUNCTIONS						
and	but	for	nor	or	so	yet

In the following examples, notice the coordinating conjunctions that connect the highlighted words.

Connecting Nouns	My cousin and his wife left today for a trip to Washington, D.C.
Connecting Verbs	They printed directions but forgot to bring them.
Connecting Prepositional Phrases	Put the luggage onto the doorstep or into the garage.
Connecting Two Sentences	The flowers were blooming, yet it was still cold outside.

See Practice 17.1A

Correlative Conjunctions

Correlative conjunctions are *pairs* of words that connect similar kinds of words or groups of words.

Have student pairs create a list of three activities they have taken part in today. Have them use their lists of activities to write sentences with coordinating conjunctions.

Correlative Conjunctions

Explain that correlative conjunctions are pairs of words that are separated in a sentence but work together to connect similar words or groups of words. For example, *neither* and *nor* work together in the sentence *Neither Joel nor I went to the game.*

WRITING COACH Online

www.phwritingcoach.com

Grammar Tutorials
Brush up on your Grammar skills with these animated videos.

Grammar Practice
Practice your grammar skills with Writing Coach Online.

Grammar Games
Test your knowledge of grammar in this fast-paced interactive video game.

Diagnostic and Instruction
Diagnostic test assesses students' instructional needs. Lessons and practice are assigned based on results.

Additional Practice
- Grammar Tutorials—Animated videos reinforce key grammar skills.
- Grammar Practice—Targeted practice addresses individual needs.
- ExamView—Teachers customize their grammar practice and tests.
- Grammar Games—Interactive video games make grammar fun.

CORRELATIVE CONJUNCTIONS		
both . . . and	neither . . . nor	whether . . . or
either . . . or	not only . . . but also	

Notice the correlative conjunctions in the following examples.

Connecting Nouns	Either the van or the bus will pick us up.
Connecting Pronouns	Neither he nor she is to be blamed.
Connecting Verbs	Every morning, she both runs and swims.
Connecting Prepositional Phrases	She'll come—whether by train or by plane, I can't say.
Connecting Two Clauses	Not only do they sing, but also they dance.

See Practice 17.1B

Subordinating Conjunctions

> **Subordinating conjunctions** connect two ideas by making one idea dependent on the other.

17.1.3 RULE

FREQUENTLY USED SUBORDINATING CONJUNCTIONS				
after	as soon as	if	though	whenever
although	as though	in order that	till	where
as	because	since	unless	wherever
as if	before	so that	until	while
as long as	even though	than	when	

Conjunctions   359

With students, read the list of correlative conjunctions aloud. Have students brainstorm for sentences that use each pair of conjunctions correctly. Write them on the board and analyze together what the conjunctions are connecting.

Have partners create sentences using correlative conjunctions and explain what types of words or word groups they are connecting.

Subordinating Conjunctions

Explain that a subordinating conjunction always introduces a subordinate clause, and defines the relationship between the subordinate clause and an independent clause. For example, the conjunction might define a cause-and-effect relationship *(because, in order that)*, a time relationship *(when, before, after, until)*, or a conflicting relationship *(even though, though)*.

RULE 17.1.3 Read aloud the rule and then have students repeat the line with you.

Remind students that a subordinate clause contains a subject and a verb but cannot stand alone as a sentence. Write these sentences on the board.

Michelle worked on the paper until she was too tired to hold a pencil.

Jason arrived first because he started early.

Have students work with a partner to identify the subordinating conjunction in each sentence. Have them discuss the dependent idea each conjunction introduces.

(continued)

Working with ELLs   ELL Sheltered Instruction: Cognitive

Help students speak using a variety of connecting words with increasing accuracy and ease as they learn to use conjunctions.

Beginning Show visuals illustrating the example sentences on page 358. Read the sentences aloud, emphasizing the connecting words, or conjunctions. Have students repeat after you. Then, guide students in using one or more of the same conjunctions to describe another visual.

Intermediate Have students take turns using the connecting words *and, or,* and *but,* from the table on page 358, in sentences. As students speak their sentences, write them on the board.

Have volunteers underline the conjunction in each.

Advanced Write the coordinating conjunctions from the table on page 358 on index cards. Have the students sit in a circle. Have the student to your left say a sentence that includes the word on the first card. Then, have the next student say a sentence with the word, and so on. Continue until all students have spoken a sentence with each word.

Advanced High Have partners develop a skit with dialogue featuring all of the coordinating conjunctions. Have them perform their skits for the class.

Subordinating Conjunctions (*continued*)

Explain that, when a subordinating conjunction is used, it always comes at the beginning of a dependent idea, so locating the subordinating conjunction is a good way to identify which idea is dependent and which is independent.

Conjunctive Adverbs

Explain that conjunctive adverbs provide transitions between two independent clauses by indicating how the clauses are related. Read aloud the example on page 360. Then, discuss how *however* defines the relationship and provides a transition between the two clauses *The film was great;* and *I prefer the play.*

Help students to use conjunctive adverbs and transitions and understand their functions by writing these sentences on the board:

Maria waited for her brother; otherwise, she would have been early.

Joshua brought the bats; therefore, we can start the game.

Albert stayed home; consequently, he didn't hear about the contest.

John made the sandwiches; furthermore, he brought all the plates and cups.

Have students identify the conjunctive adverbs and explain how these words provide transitions between different ideas. Point out that conjunctive adverbs are usually set off from the rest of the sentence by a semicolon and a comma.

The Dependent Idea The subordinating conjunction always introduces the dependent idea. The subordinating conjunction connects the dependent idea to the main idea.

EXAMPLES I did the planning **after** **he made the date**.

When **he rested** , he felt better.

The examples show that the main idea can come at the beginning or at the end of the sentence. When the dependent idea comes first, it must be separated from the main idea with a comma. If the dependent idea comes second, no comma is necessary.

See Practice 17.1C
See Practice 17.1D
See Practice 17.1E

Conjunctive Adverbs

Conjunctive adverbs are used as conjunctions to connect complete ideas. They are often used as transitions, connecting different ideas by showing comparisons, contrasts, or results.

Transitional Words and Phrases The transitional words in the chart below, and transitional phrases such as *on the contrary* and *in addition*, are used in writing to provide coherence and improve organization.

CONJUNCTIVE ADVERBS			
accordingly	consequently	indeed	otherwise
again	finally	instead	then
also	furthermore	moreover	therefore
besides	however	nevertheless	thus

Notice the punctuation that is used before and after the conjunctive adverb in the following example. (See Chapter 25 for more about punctuation with conjunctive adverbs.)

EXAMPLE The film was great; **however** , I prefer the play.

See Practice 17.1F
See Practice 17.1G
See Practice 17.1H
See Practice 17.1I
See Practice 17.1J

360   **Conjunctions and Interjections**

Then, have students write three sentences using three different conjunctive adverbs to provide transitions. Have students read their sentences aloud, identifying each conjunctive adverb. Have the class discuss how the conjunctive adverbs provided transitions.

Teacher Tip

Show students how using conjunctions makes writing tighter. Read two related simple sentences aloud. Then, combine the sentences into a single sentence with a conjunction. (*He won't read this book. He does not like fantasy. He won't read this book because he does not like fantasy.*)

Quick-Write Extension

To help students synthesize and apply what they have learned, have small groups of students classify and use conjunctive adverbs. Write each of these on its own sticky note: *consequently, furthermore, however, moreover, on the other hand, otherwise, therefore.* Each group should write these headings on sheets of paper, one heading per page: *And, But, Or, So.* Groups should then place each sticky note beneath the coordinating conjunction with which it is roughly synonymous (e.g., *furthermore* and *moreover* under *And*). Have groups use their charts to write, for each category, an example compound sentence that uses a conjunctive adverb. Students should punctuate their sentences using the example on page 360 as a model.

PRACTICE 17.1A › Supplying Coordinating Conjunctions

Read the sentences. Then, write each sentence, replacing the blank with a coordinating conjunction that makes sense in the sentence.

EXAMPLE   Was Mr. Kim born in Korea _____ the United States?

ANSWER   *Was Mr. Kim born in Korea or the United States?*

1. We weren't on time for the first show, _____ we went to the second show.

2. I like mustard _____ relish on my hot dog.

3. The necklace was expensive _____ seemed worth every penny.

4. We could not score a goal, _____ could we stop our opponents from scoring.

5. You may choose a sandwich _____ a burrito.

6. Marcel wanted to see his friends, _____ he went to their house.

7. The skater showed great skill _____ obvious confidence.

8. Put the key on a chain, _____ you might lose it.

9. Serena doesn't like algebra, _____ she does like geometry.

10. Flowers need water _____ sunlight in order to grow.

PRACTICE 17.1B › Writing Sentences With Correlative Conjunctions

Write ten sentences, using each of the correlative conjunctions below.

EXAMPLE   both . . . and

ANSWER   *Both my sister and my brother went camping last weekend.*

   Both her mom and her dad attended the school conference.

11. both . . . and

12. neither . . . nor

13. not only . . . but also

14. either . . . or

15. whether . . . or

16. both . . . and

17. neither . . . nor

18. not only . . . but also

19. either . . . or

20. whether . . . or

1. so *or* but
2. and *or* or
3. but *or* yet
4. nor
5. or
6. so
7. and
8. or
9. but *or* yet
10. and

Answers will vary. Sample answers:

11. We went to both dinner and a movie.

12. Neither hot weather nor cold seems to slow him down.

13. At the mall, we not only saw nice dresses but also tried some on.

14. Bring either a jacket or a sweater.

15. Whether he comes or stays home, I want to go.

16. Both my parents and your parents talked to the teacher.

17. He liked neither the shirt nor the pants.

18. I received not only a new bicycle but also a new helmet.

19. Either he or I will call you.

20. I don't think it matters whether you write your paragraph on paper or type it on the computer.

SPEAKING APPLICATION

With a partner, take turns talking about what you do when you have free time. Your partner should listen for and name three coordinating conjunctions.

WRITING APPLICATION

Write a short paragraph about someone you admire. Use two or more coordinating conjunctions and at least one correlative conjunction in your paragraph.

Practice   361

SPEAKING APPLICATION

Have students explain what types of words or groups of words the coordinating conjunctions link.

WRITING APPLICATION

Have students read aloud their paragraphs, identifying the conjunctions.

Working with ELLs   Sheltered Instruction: Cognitive

To build and reinforce student attainment of the concept of conjunctions, provide opportunities for them to listen to, derive meaning from, and respond orally to information presented in a wide variety of print, electronic, and audiovisual media.

Beginning Write *and, but,* and *or* and read them aloud with students. Play a recording of a familiar story as students follow along. Ask them to listen for *and, but,* and *or.* Discuss the ideas that each conjunction joins.

Intermediate Meet with groups to conduct the Beginning activity. Extend by having students discuss story elements. Guide them with sentence frames featuring conjunctions, such as _____ *and* _____ *are characters in the story.*

Advanced Instruct students to take notes while listening to an advertisement on TV or on the radio. Have them record conjunctions used, noting the ideas the conjunctions join. Then, have them meet with partners to discuss how the conjunctions reinforce the persuasive message.

Advanced High Modify the Advanced activity to have students listen to two advertisements. Have them take notes in a **Venn Diagram,** comparing the use of conjunctions in each advertisement. Have them discuss their observations with partners.

1. Before
2. because
3. As soon as
4. Unless
5. while
6. wherever
7. If
8. although
9. so that
10. Whenever

PRACTICE 17.1D

Answers will vary. Sample answers:

11. I bring a book with me whenever I go to the swimming pool.
12. It's possible to see the stars if it's a clear night.
13. Coach called time out even though we were winning.
14. A car should come to a complete stop when a driver comes to a stop sign.
15. We're stuck inside until the storm passes.
16. Mrs. Dumont needed a pair of red shoes because she had bought a red dress.
17. Latrice played the song over and over again while the dancers practiced.
18. I've been depositing money into a savings account since I was ten.
19. The neighborhood kids stopped traffic so that the kittens could cross.
20. Greg got a haircut as soon as he could.

SPEAKING APPLICATION

Students' speech should demonstrate that they can use and understand subordinating conjunctions.

WRITING APPLICATION

Have students demonstrate their understanding of subordinating conjunctions by explaining what each conjunction does in their paragraph.

PRACTICE 17.1C Identifying Subordinating Conjunctions

Read the sentences. Then, write the subordinating conjunction (e.g., *while*, *because*, *although*, *if*) in each sentence.

EXAMPLE   You can go to the park after you finish your chores.

ANSWER   *after*

1. Before a plane takes off, there is a safety check.
2. I wanted to see the movie because my friends all liked it.
3. As soon as I finish this math problem, I'll help you with your homework.
4. Unless we get a little more wind, we won't be able to fly our kites today.
5. I can make the sauce while you boil the pasta.
6. My sister makes friends wherever she goes.
7. If you do that, the teacher will be upset.
8. We worked hard on the snow fort although we knew it would soon melt.
9. Put those books on the lower shelves so that younger children can reach them.
10. Whenever you need me, just call.

PRACTICE 17.1D Using Subordinating Conjunctions

Read each sentence. Then, rewrite it, using the subordinating conjunction indicated in parentheses to create a complete sentence with a dependent idea. Discuss with a partner the function of each subordinating conjunction.

EXAMPLE   Alexa won't be able to go swimming (unless)

ANSWER   *Alexa won't be able to go swimming unless she cleans her room.*

11. I bring a book with me. (whenever)
12. It's possible to see the stars. (if)
13. Coach called time out. (even though)
14. A car should come to a complete stop. (when)
15. We're stuck inside. (until)
16. Mrs. Dumont needed a pair of red shoes. (because)
17. Latrice played the song over and over again. (while)
18. I've been depositing money into a savings account. (since)
19. The neighborhood kids stopped traffic. (so that)
20. Greg got a haircut. (as soon as)

SPEAKING APPLICATION

With a partner, take turns talking about a story you read. Use two subordinating conjunctions. Your partner should listen for and name the subordinating conjunctions.

WRITING APPLICATION

Write a short paragraph about your favorite time of year. Use subordinating conjunctions in at least three of the sentences in your paragraph. Be sure to punctuate your sentences correctly.

362   **Conjunctions and Interjections**

Working with ELLs   **ELL** Sheltered Instruction: Cognitive

As students study subordinating conjunctions, guide them to demonstrate English comprehension by employing and expanding basic reading skills, including summarizing, distinguishing main idea from supporting details, and comparing and contrasting.

Beginning Write sentences featuring subordinating conjunctions about an after-school activity. Read the sentences aloud as students follow along. Repeat, instructing students to take notes in a cluster diagram. Then, have them use the diagram to orally summarize what they read.

Intermediate Pair students with fluent speakers to complete the Writing Application as a shared writing activity.

Then, have them exchange paragraphs with another pair. Have students identify subordinating conjunctions in the written paragraph. Then, have them write a sentence expressing the main idea.

Advanced Have students complete the Writing Application and exchange paragraphs with a partner. Have them read their partners' writing silently and then write a sentence expressing the main idea.

Advanced High Have students complete the Advanced activity. To extend the activity, have them use a **Venn Diagram** to compare and contrast their paragraphs with their partners'. Invite them to share their findings.

PRACTICE 17.1E › Using Subordinating Conjunctions

Read the sentences. Write a sentence combining the two sentences in each item. Use a subordinating conjunction and underline it.

EXAMPLE He worked hard. He has not finished the assignment.

ANSWER *Even though he worked hard, he has not finished the assignment.*

1. We are going to the store. What can we get for you?
2. Please come over and help us. Your guests leave.
3. It is early. We thought we would go to a movie.
4. We cannot write the paper. The research is done.
5. Your package must have arrived. We were on vacation.
6. I must send the payment. The order is filled.
7. The house is on that street. Jake can find it.
8. We needed some rest. We had a vacation.
9. The cat always tries to sneak out. We close the door immediately.
10. We have energy left. We will keep working.

PRACTICE 17.1F › Identifying Conjunctive Adverbs

Read the sentences. Then, identify the conjunctive adverb in each sentence.

EXAMPLE You must do your homework; otherwise, you cannot go.

ANSWER *otherwise*

11. Brooke cleaned her room; then, she weeded the garden.
12. Chen memorized the U.S. Constitution; consequently, he passed the test.
13. Alicia got up at six o'clock to work; also, she got to bed much later than usual.
14. Evie forgot; however, Mom remembered.
15. You have only 20 minutes; thus, you must plan your time well.
16. Check the paper for misspelled words; furthermore, proofread for commas.
17. Maia did not set her alarm; therefore, she overslept and missed the bus.
18. Humans may land on Mars some day; indeed, they may build colonies there.
19. Meteors look like a streak of light; nevertheless, they are called shooting stars.
20. We practiced every day; finally, we were ready.

SPEAKING APPLICATION

With a partner, discuss a project you enjoyed. Use subordinating conjunctions and conjunctive adverbs. Then, write two sentences based on your conversation. Use a subordinating conjunction in one and a conjunctive adverb in the other.

WRITING APPLICATION

Write a paragraph explaining how you solved a problem. Use at least two subordinating conjunctions and one conjunctive adverb. Read your paragraph to a partner. Your partner should identify the subordinating conjunctions and conjunctive adverb.

Practice   363

PRACTICE 17.1E ›

Answers will vary. Sample answers:

1. <u>Since</u> we are going to the store, what can we get for you?
2. Please come over and help us <u>after</u> your guests leave.
3. <u>Because</u> it is early, we thought we would go to a movie.
4. We cannot write the paper <u>before</u> the research is done.
5. Your package must have arrived <u>when</u> we were on vacation.
6. I must send the payment <u>before</u> the order is filled.
7. <u>Since</u> the house is on that street, Jake can find it.
8. <u>Because</u> we needed some rest, we had a vacation.
9. <u>Since</u> the cat always tries to sneak out, we close the door immediately.
10. <u>If</u> we have energy left, we will keep working.

PRACTICE 17.1F ›

11. then	16. furthermore
12. consequently	17. therefore
13. also	18. indeed
14. however	19. nevertheless
15. thus	20. finally

SPEAKING APPLICATION

Students' discussions should demonstrate that they understand and can use subordinating conjunctions and conjunctive adverbs when speaking.

WRITING APPLICATION

Have students demonstrate they can use and understand the function of subordinating conjunctions and conjunctive adverbs in writing by explaining what these components do in each sentence they write.

Differentiated Instruction

RTI Strategy for Below-Level Students
Remind students that all adverb clauses are introduced by subordinating conjunctions. Review the four **W**'s of adverbs: **W**hen, **W**here, **W**hy, and in **W**hat way. Make four columns on the board and label them with the **W**'s. Go over the most common subordinating conjunctions with students and have them help you put those conjunctions in the columns where they belong.

PRE-AP Enrichment for Above-Level Students Students can synthesize what they have learned about conjunctions by making a conjunction bookmark. Direct students to write these headings on a strip of paper: *Coordinating, Correlative, Conjunctive, Subordinating.* Under each heading, students should list conjunctions that exemplify the words in the category. Students should then use the bookmark as a reference when they write.

Answers will vary. Sample answers:

1. ; furthermore,   2. ; consequently,
3. ; therefore,   4. ; however,
5. ; therefore,   6. ; indeed,
7. ; instead,   8. ; moreover,
9. ; therefore,   10. ; finally,

PRACTICE 17.1H

Answers will vary. Sample answers:

11. consequently—I got good grades; consequently, my parents let me go to the mall.   12. moreover—We had a great time at dinner; moreover, we watched a great movie.   13. indeed—Studying for exams can be tiring; indeed, I'm exhausted.   14. however—Learning new words is difficult; however, I like having a large vocabulary.   15. finally—The game was long; finally, it was over.   16. furthermore—The lawn needs to be mowed; furthermore, the trees should be trimmed.   17. instead—I thought about taking a nap; instead, I took the dog for a walk.   18. otherwise—I have to set my alarm; otherwise, I sleep late.   19. thus—I don't like poor manners; thus, I am always polite.   20. moreover—She volunteers at the pound; moreover, she encourages her friends to volunteer.

SPEAKING APPLICATION

Students' discussions should demonstrate that they can use and understand the function of conjunctive adverbs in speaking.

WRITING APPLICATION

Students' sentences should demonstrate they can use and understand the function of conjunctive adverbs in writing.

PRACTICE 17.1G Using Conjunctive Adverbs

Read the sentences. Write the sentences, supplying a conjunctive adverb, such as *consequently*, *furthermore*, and *indeed*, and the correct punctuation.

EXAMPLE   Noah got another hit _____ he leads the league in home runs.

ANSWER   *Noah got another hit; consequently, he leads the league in home runs.*

1. William sings well _____ he has taken dancing lessons for years.
2. The construction was completed on schedule _____ the charges were not high.
3. Jessica got the flu _____ she missed the party.
4. Ella is a good swimmer _____ she is a better runner.
5. The twins like to fish _____ they are vacationing at a lake this summer.
6. Finish washing the car first _____ do not leave here until the car is spotless.
7. We decided not to go shopping _____ we are going to the game.
8. The library needs money to buy books _____ it could use a media center.
9. The company had to economize _____ it closed seven stores.
10. We waited to learn who made the team _____ the list was posted today.

SPEAKING APPLICATION

With a partner, talk about what it takes to be on a team. Use conjunctive adverbs. Then, based on your conversation, write three sentences with conjunctive adverbs.

364   Conjunctions and Interjections

PRACTICE 17.1H Identifying and Using Conjunctive Adverbs

Read the sentences. Identify the conjunctive adverbs. Then, write sentences using the conjunctive adverbs.

EXAMPLE   The paper is due Friday; furthermore, it must be neat.

ANSWER   *furthermore — The movie is my favorite; furthermore, it won an award.*

11. Taxes were increased; consequently, teache[r] could be rehired.
12. We auditioned for the talent show; moreove[r] we were chosen.
13. I do not want to move; indeed, I dread it.
14. The first section on the test was easy; however, the second was difficult.
15. The flight was long; finally, we arrived.
16. The pool needs scrubbing; furthermore, the chlorine should be tested.
17. Mom did not go to college; instead, she attended trade school.
18. I may try out for the drama club; otherwise, I will join the debate team.
19. Kofi disagrees with the policy; thus, he wro[te] a letter to the editor.
20. Saul will shop for tennis shoes; moreover, he needs socks.

WRITING APPLICATION

Write five sentences about school assignments. Use a conjunctive adverb in each one. Read your sentences aloud to a partner. Have your partner identify the conjunctive adverbs.

Working with ELLs   **ELL** Sheltered Instruction: Cognitive

Help students speak using a variety of connecting words with increasing accuracy and ease as they practice using conjunctive adverbs.

Beginning Show visuals illustrating Item 5. Read the completed sentence aloud, emphasizing the conjunctive adverb *therefore*. Have students repeat after you. Then, guide students in using the same conjunctive adverb to describe another visual.

Intermediate Have students take turns using the conjunctive adverbs *consequently, furthermore,* and *indeed* in sentences. As students speak their sentences, write them on the board. Have

volunteers underline the conjunctive adverb in each.

Advanced Write a variety of conjunctive adverbs on index cards, including those used in Practice 17.1G. Sit in a circle with the students. Have the student to your left say a sentence that includes the word on the first card. Then, have the next student say a sentence with the word, and so on. Continue until all students have spoken a sentence with each word.

Advanced High Have partners develop a skit with dialogue featuring at least five conjunctive adverbs. Have them perform their skits for the class.

PRACTICE 17.1I > Identifying Transitional Words and Phrases

Read the sentences. Then, write the transitional word or phrase in each sentence and use it in a new sentence. Read your sentences to a partner and discuss if your sentences are correct.

EXAMPLE   Besides being fun, after-school sports promote health.

ANSWER   *besides; Besides being wet, I'm also hungry.*

As a rule, caution should be used at all times.

On the contrary, uniforms help keep students focused on their studies.

First of all, scientists studied migrating birds.

As a result, many biking clubs were started.

In addition to flour, we need to add salt.

In fact, there are many ways to save money.

Therefore, we should leave immediately.

As usual, it is important to remember the source of the information.

For example, a science class might visit the local wetlands.

Moreover, trees are an important source of carbon dioxide.

SPEAKING APPLICATION

With a partner, debate the issue of global warming. Use transitional words and phrases such as *on the contrary* and *in addition to.* Make a list of the transitions you used in your debate.

PRACTICE 17.1J > Writing With Transitional Words and Phrases

Write a sentence for each of the transitional words and phrases provided. Then, read your sentences to a partner who should tell you if you have used the transitional words or phrases correctly.

EXAMPLE   as well as

ANSWER   *As well as being tasty, orange juice contains vitamin C.*

11. as a result
12. in addition to
13. therefore
14. moreover
15. for example
16. on the contrary
17. as usual
18. in order to
19. first of all
20. besides

WRITING APPLICATION

Write a paragraph explaining why you are for or against field trips during the school week. Use at least three transitional words and phrases such as *on the contrary* and *in addition to* to state the reasons for your position. Read your paragraph aloud to a partner. Your partner should identify the transitional words and phrases in your paragraph.

Practice 365

SPEAKING APPLICATION

Students should demonstrate they can use transitions and understand their functions in their debates.

WRITING APPLICATION

Students should demonstrate they can use and understand the function of transitions in writing by explaining how each transition in their paragraphs establishes a relationship between ideas.

PRACTICE 17.1I >

Answers will vary. Sample answers:

1. As a rule; As a rule, I eat breakfast before I walk the dog.

2. On the contrary; On the contrary, eating out is more expensive than bringing lunch from home.

3. First of all; First of all, Luis entered the building.

4. As a result; As a result, all students must stay at school for lunch.

5. In addition to; In addition to soup, we had bread and milk for dinner.

6. In fact; In fact, people often find swimming to be good exercise.

7. Therefore; Therefore, we should mind our own business.

8. As usual; As usual, we headed to the movies on Friday evening.

9. For example; For example, Philip paints wonderful portraits.

10. Moreover; Moreover, trees offer excellent shade.

PRACTICE 17.1J >

Answers will vary. Sample answers:

11. As a result of the month of rain, our basement flooded.

12. In addition to sauce, we added cheese to the pasta.

13. Therefore, we should get to the airport early.

14. Moreover, my old jeans had a hole in the knee.

15. For example, some people like westerns.

16. On the contrary, I prefer jogging to swimming.

17. As usual, he was late.

18. In order to arrive on time, we set our alarms ten minutes early.

19. First of all, I would like to thank everyone for coming tonight.

20. Besides, we like your sketches better than her paintings.

Test Warm-Up

1. **D** First of all, you can speak to people from different countries.

2. **G** Change *Therefore* to **Moreover**

3. **A** However, learning the grammar of a foreign language helps you understand English grammar.

4. **F** Change *For example* to **Consequently**

Reteach

If students have not mastered these skills, review the content in Section 17.1 Conjunctive Adverbs.

Test Tip

Some incorrect answer choices are very similar to the correct answer choice. When the differences between these choices are very small or subtle, students sometimes choose the first distractor that seems reasonable and move on to the next question without ever reading the remaining answer choices. Remind students that they should read all of the answers carefully before selecting one.

If two answer choices sound like they are the same to a student, then the student has missed something. He or she should carefully re-read the question and the answer choices until the difference between the two choices is clear.

Test Warm-Up

DIRECTIONS
Read the introduction and the passage that follows. Then, answer the questions to show that you can use and understand the function of transitional words and phrases in reading and writing.

Tyrell wrote this paragraph about the benefits of learning a foreign language. Read the paragraph and think about the changes you would suggest as a peer editor. When you finish reading, answer the questions that follow.

Learning a Foreign Language

(1) Learning a foreign language has many benefits. (2) You can speak to people from different countries. (3) This makes travelling more enriching. (4) Therefore, you can speak to people from different cultures in your own country. (5) This can help you make new friends. (6) Many people say that foreign language is confusing. (7) Learning the grammar of a foreign language helps you understand English grammar. (8) For example, there are many benefits to learning a foreign language.

1 How should sentence 2 be revised?

  A Otherwise, you can speak to people from different countries.

  B Besides, you can speak to people from different countries.

  C However, you can speak to people from different countries.

  D First of all, you can speak to people from different countries.

2 How should sentence 4 be clarified?

  F Change *Therefore* to **As a result**

  G Change *Therefore* to **Moreover**

  H Change *Therefore* to **Nevertheless**

  J Change *Therefore* to **As a rule**

3 How should sentence 7 be revised?

  A However, learning the grammar of a foreign language helps you understand English grammar.

  B On the contrary, learning the grammar of a foreign language helps you understand English grammar.

  C Accordingly learning the grammar of a foreign language helps you understand English grammar.

  D Furthermore, learning the grammar of a foreign language helps you understand English grammar.

4 How should sentence 8 be clarified?

  F Change *For example* to **Consequently**

  G Change *For example* to **Instead**

  H Change *For example* to **Besides**

  J Change *For example* to **As well as**

17.2 Interjections

The **interjection** is the part of speech that is used the least. Its only use is to express feelings or emotions.

Practice 17.2A
Practice 17.2B

An **interjection** expresses feeling or emotion and functions independently from the rest of a sentence.

An interjection has no grammatical relationship to any other word in a sentence. It is, therefore, set off from the rest of the sentence with a comma or an exclamation mark.

Interjections can express different feelings or emotions.

JOY	**Wow!**	I can't believe you won the race.
SURPRISE	**Oh**,	I didn't expect to hear from you.
PAIN	**Ouch!**	That hurts.
IMPATIENCE	**Hey!**	How long do they expect me to wait?
HESITATION	I, **uh**,	think we should leave now.

Interjections are used more in speech than in writing. They are informal, rather than formal, expressions. When you do see them in writing, they are often included in dialogue. The following chart lists words often used as interjections.

INTERJECTIONS			
ah	gosh	nonsense	ugh
aha	great	oh	uh
alas	heavens	oops	um
boy	hey	ouch	well
darn	huh	psst	what
eureka	hurray	shh	whew
fine	my	terrible	wonderful
golly	never	terrific	wow

Interjections 367

Lesson Objectives

1. Use and understand interjections.
2. Recognize and use punctuation marks including commas after introductory words, phrases, and clauses.

Explain that interjections express strong emotions but are grammatically independent from the rest of the sentence.

RULE 17.2.1 Read aloud the rule and then have students repeat the line with you.

Use a Think Aloud as part of a gradual release progression.

Think Aloud Say: I use interjections all the time when I speak. I sometimes say *Terrific*, *Ouch*, and other words to express emotions and feelings. I might say, *Wow, that was fun!* or *Hey, wait for me!* These interjections are separate from the rest of the sentence. They can't function as the subject, object, verb, adjective, adverb, preposition, or conjunction in a sentence.

Point out that interjections have to be separated from the rest of the sentence, usually by a comma or an exclamation point.

Work with students to compose several sentences about an exciting event, but don't use any interjections at first. Discuss the emotions evoked by each event. Then, discuss how the emotions expressed by each interjection in the table on page 367 might fit the emotions of the event. Work with students to add an interjection to each sentence and punctuate it correctly.

Have student pairs write and perform a short dialogue using as many interjections as they can.

PRACTICE 17.2A

1. Ugh—Sample answer: disgust
2. Oh—Sample answer: surprise
3. Wonderful—Sample answer: joy
4. Aha—Sample answer: discovery
5. Nonsense—Sample answer: impatience
6. Alas—Sample answer: sorrow
7. Whew—Sample answer: relief
8. Darn—Sample answer: frustration
9. Ah—Sample answer: pleasure
10. uh—Sample answer: hesitation

PRACTICE 17.2B

Answers will vary. Sample answers:

11. Darn!
12. Ouch!
13. Whew!
14. Gosh!
15. Hey!
16. Wonderful!
17. Ugh!
18. Wow!
19. Aha!
20. Nonsense!

SPEAKING APPLICATION

Have students explain what each interjection contributes to the conversation.

WRITING APPLICATION

Have students share their sentences with a partner. Have partners check each other's sentences for proper punctuation.

PRACTICE 17.2A Identifying Interjections

Read the sentences. Write the interjection in each sentence. Then, write what emotion the interjection conveys.

EXAMPLE   Hey! Get out of there now!

ANSWER   *Hey*— anger

1. Ugh! That medicine tastes awful.
2. Oh! That's not what was supposed to happen.
3. Wonderful! You got straight A's!
4. Aha, that's where you hid it.
5. Nonsense! You should not believe everything you read in the newspapers.
6. Alas, he never returned from that last voyage.
7. Whew! I didn't think we were going to make it.
8. Darn! Why didn't I remember there was a test today?
9. Ah, these boots help my feet stay warm.
10. I, uh, don't want to go to that restaurant.

PRACTICE 17.2B Supplying Interjections

Read the sentences. Rewrite each sentence, using an appropriate interjection in place of the feeling shown in parentheses. Use a comma or exclamation mark after each interjection.

EXAMPLE   (joy) Our football team won the championship.

ANSWER   *Hurray!* Our football team won the championship.

11. (impatience) I can't believe you were late again.
12. (pain) Be careful taking off the bandage.
13. (relief) I thought that test would never end.
14. (surprise) I didn't expect to see you here.
15. (anger) Get those dogs away from our picnic.
16. (pleasure) The Kramers are coming for dinner.
17. (disgust) What is that smell coming from the science lab?
18. (wonder) That was an amazing fireworks display!
19. (discovery) Now we see what you were trying to do.
20. (disbelief) I don't believe anyone would do that.

SPEAKING APPLICATION

With a partner, take turns talking about things that happen at school. Your partner should listen to each comment and respond with an interjection. For example, one person might say, "There is a test today," and the other might respond, "Ugh!"

WRITING APPLICATION

Write three sentences that include appropriate interjections. You can use interjections from Practice 17.2A and Practice 17.2B or from the list in the lesson.

368   **Conjunctions and Interjections**

Working with ELLs   **EL** Sheltered Instruction: Cognitive

As students begin using interjections, help students enhance and confirm their understanding of the increasingly complex spoken language by providing visual support.

Beginning Write the example sentence from Practice 17.2A on the board: *Hey! Get out of there now!* Read the sentence aloud, providing visual support by adopting a look of anger or by showing a photograph of a clearly angered person. Point to each part of the sentence as you say it, emphasizing the interjection. Have students repeat after you.

Intermediate Provide visual support for Practice 17.2B by creating sentence strips of the items as well as strips featuring various interjections. Have partners

identify which interjections might go with which sentences. Then, speak the correct completed sentences aloud as students use their sentence strips to match your completed sentences.

Advanced Have students complete the Intermediate activity. Then, have them create alternative answers for each item and say them to their partner. Partners should replicate the answers using the sentence strips.

Advanced High Have students complete the Intermediate activity. Extend as in the Advanced activity. Then, challenge students to write a brief dialogue featuring five interjections.

18.4 Hard-to-Find Subjects

It can be difficult to identify simple subjects in certain sentences. These sentences do not follow **normal word order** in which the subject comes before the verb. Sometimes the subject will follow the verb or part of a verb phrase. This is called **inverted word order**. Questions are often presented in inverted word order.

NORMAL WORD ORDER

The **concert** **will begin** at 8:30 P.M.
    subject   verb

INVERTED WORD ORDER

When **will** the **concert** **begin**?
     verb   subject   verb

Sometimes the subject will not actually be stated in the sentence. It will be understood to be the pronoun *you*. This is often true in sentences that express commands or requests.

The Subject of a Command or Request

When a sentence commands or requests someone to do something, the subject is often unstated.

> The subject of a command or request is understood to be the pronoun *you*.

 18.4.1 RULE

COMMANDS OR REQUESTS	HOW THE SENTENCES ARE UNDERSTOOD
Stop!	You stop!
Begin at once.	You begin at once.
Please come here.	You please come here.
Audrey, make a list.	Audrey, you make a list.
Bob, get the tickets.	Bob, you get the tickets.

Practice 18.4A

Even though a command or request may begin with the name of the person spoken to, the subject is still understood to be *you*.

Hard-to-Find Subjects   381

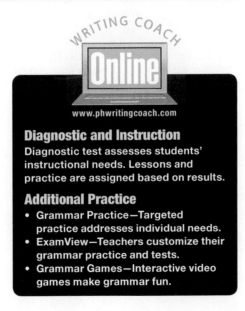

WRITING COACH

Online

www.phwritingcoach.com

Diagnostic and Instruction
Diagnostic test assesses students' instructional needs. Lessons and practice are assigned based on results.

Additional Practice
• Grammar Practice—Targeted practice addresses individual needs.
• ExamView—Teachers customize their grammar practice and tests.
• Grammar Games—Interactive video games make grammar fun.

Lesson Objectives

1. Identify the subject in sentences that do not follow normal subject-verb word order.

The Subject of a Command or Request

Write on the board the sentence *Run to home plate!* Point out that this sentence does not seem to have a subject. Explain that some sentences have a subject that is difficult to identify.

RULE 18.4.1 Read aloud the rule and then have students repeat the lines with you.

Use a Think Aloud as part of a gradual release progression.

Think Aloud

Say: When **I give** a command or make a request, I am usually telling or asking another person to do something. If I say *Run to home plate*, it is as if I am saying *You run to home plate. You* is the subject of the sentence even though it is not written or spoken.

With students, read through the examples in the chart on page 381. Make sure students notice that, even if the sentence starts with the person's name, the subject is still understood to be *you*.

Have students make a two-column graphic organizer of sentences similar to the one on page 381. First, have them write several sentences that are commands or requests and that have understood subjects. Then, have them enter their sentences in the first column, and ask them to describe how the sentences are understood in the second column. Suggest using the sentences *Forget it!* and *Don't pet the lion!* to begin their graphic organizers.

Finding Subjects in Questions

Remind students that certain types of sentences use an inverted, or reversed, word order. Questions are a good example. Often, with a question, the subject of a sentence will be in the middle or near the end of a sentence.

RULE 18.4.2 Read aloud the rule and then have students repeat the line with you.

Ask: What is the subject of the sentence *Elephants are social animals*? **(elephants)** What is the subject of the question *What kind of animal are elephants*? **(elephants)** Then, **say:** In both sentences, *elephants* is the simple subject. But you can see that in the question, the subject came at the end of the sentence.

Using the example sentences on page 382 as a guide, work with students to generate questions that begin with the words *what, which, whom, who, whose, when, where, why,* and *how*.

Have volunteers identify the subject of each sentence. Discuss whether each sentence uses inverted word order (verb-subject) or normal word order (subject-verb).

Teacher Tip

If students are having difficulty identifying the subject of a sentence, review rule 18.1.2: *The subject of a sentence is the word or group of words that names the person, place, thing, or idea that performs the action or is described. It answers the question Who? or What? before the verb.* Students can find the verb in the sentence, then think about who or what is performing that action or being described.

T382

Questions are often presented in inverted word order. You will usually find the subject in the middle of the sentence.

> In questions, the subject often follows the verb.

Some questions in inverted word order begin with the words *what, whom, when, where, why,* and *how*. Others begin with the verb itself or with a helping verb.

EXAMPLES   How **are** the **kittens** today?

Did you feed them in the morning?

Have you found homes for all of them yet?

If you ever have trouble finding the subject in a question, use this trick: Change the question into a statement. The subject will then appear in normal word order before the verb.

QUESTIONS	REWORDED AS STATEMENTS
How are the pups today?	The pups are how today.
What did the doctor say?	The doctor did say what.
Were the labels ready?	The labels were ready.
Did she bring her camera with her?	She did bring her camera with her.

Not every question is in inverted word order. Some are in normal word order, with the subject before the verb. Questions beginning with *who, whose,* or *which* often follow normal word order.

EXAMPLES   **Who has** the camera?

Whose **story won** the writing contest?

Which **painting should win** the contest?   See Practice 18.4B

382   Basic Sentence Parts

PRACTICE 18.4A Identifying Subjects in Commands or Requests

Read the sentences. Write the subject of each sentence.

EXAMPLE   Get the tools I left in the garage.

ANSWER   *you*

Get the clothes out of the washing machine.

Place the books onto the correct shelves.

Please, close the door.

Juwan, bring me that globe.

Don't forget to take an umbrella.

Come to the window so I can see you.

Jason and Keiko, put these boxes in the car.

For dessert, order whatever looks good.

Jena, get me five eggs from the refrigerator.

Bring the soup to a boil.

PRACTICE 18.4B Identifying Subjects in Questions

Read the questions. Write the subject of each question. If you have trouble finding the subject in a question, change the question into a statement.

EXAMPLE   Are the girls coming with us?

ANSWER   *girls*

11. Did you remember to lock the back door?
12. Are dogs allowed in your apartment?
13. Is it too late to buy tickets?
14. Will Daniel and Felicia be in the play?
15. Can Stefan bring his guitar?
16. Has everyone signed the petition?
17. Were the Donovans at the party?
18. Was Fernando ready for school?
19. Would your parents let you go to the dance?
20. Did the teacher explain the project to you?

SPEAKING APPLICATION

With a partner, take turns role-playing a coach or teacher getting players or students to do things. Your partner should listen for and identify commands and questions and name the subject.

WRITING APPLICATION

Write a short series of instructions for carrying out a task, such as making soup or turning on a computer. Include at least two command/request sentences.

Practice   383

PRACTICE 18.4A

1. you
2. you
3. you
4. you
5. you
6. you
7. you
8. you
9. you
10. you

PRACTICE 18.4B

11. you
12. dogs
13. it
14. Daniel and Felicia
15. Stefan
16. everyone
17. Donovans
18. Fernando
19. parents
20. teacher

SPEAKING APPLICATION

Have student pairs relate to the class at least two of the commands or questions they identified.

WRITING APPLICATION

Have students exchange instructions and identify the command/request sentences.

Working with ELLs   **ELL** Sheltered Instruction: Cognitive

To build and reinforce student attainment of the concept of a subject, help them listen, derive meaning from, and respond orally to information presented in a wide variety of print, electronic, audio, and visual media.

Beginning   Display a printout from a simple how-to Web site or magazine article. Read the directions aloud with students, incorporating gestures. Review that directions are often written as commands, and that the subject of a command is understood as *you*. Lead students in restating the commands, saying: *You …*

Intermediate   Have groups of students complete the Beginning activity. Call on volunteers to restate the commands using the word *you*.

Advanced   Distribute a magazine or newspaper article containing questions and commands to pairs of students. Have them read and discuss the article, listing any commands or questions and identifying the subject of each. Have them discuss their findings with another pair and respond orally to questions.

Advanced High   Have students complete the Advanced activity individually. Then, have them meet in groups to discuss the print media they have read. Ensure that students identify the subjects in their media.

Finding the Subject in Sentences Beginning With *There* or *Here*

Explain that like many questions, sentences that begin with *there* or *here* often use an inverted word order.

RULE 18.4.3 Read aloud the rule and then have students repeat the line with you.

Use a Think Aloud as part of a gradual release progression.

Say: When **I see that** a sentence begins with *here* or *there*, it is a clue that the subject might come after the verb. In these cases, I know that finding the verb can help me identify the subject of the sentence. In the first example sentence, I can see that *are* is the verb. Then, I can see that it is the musicians who are in the band, so *musicians* must be the simple subject.

Write this sentence on the board: *There are many tornados in the spring.* **Work with students** to reword the sentence so that the subject, *many tornados*, is before the verb, *are*. (Many tornados are in the spring.) Ask students to explain whether the subject in the second sentence is the same as the subject in the first sentence. (The subject is the same.)

Have students each write five sentences that begin with either *here* or *there*. Then, have them exchange sentences with a partner. Partners should change the order of words in the sentences so that the subject precedes the verb.

Teacher Tip

Students should usually locate the verb in a sentence before they look for the subject. Students may have difficulty, however, realizing that forms of the verb *to be* are part of many verbs. You may want to review these forms of the verb: Present tense: *I am; You are; He/she/it is; We are; You are; They are.* Past tense: *I was; You were; He/she/it was; We were; You were; They were.* Have students practice using each of these verb forms in a sentence.

Finding the Subject in Sentences Beginning With *There* or *Here*

Sentences beginning with *there* or *here* are usually in inverted word order.

 RULE 18.4.3

> ***There* or *here* is never the subject of a sentence.**

There can be used to start a sentence.

SENTENCE STARTER
There are two musicians from Texas in the band.

There or *here* can also be used as an adverb at the beginning of sentences. As adverbs, these two words point out *where* and modify the verbs.

ADVERB
There goes the famous rock star.

Here are the invitations to the party.

Be alert to sentences beginning with *there* and *here*. They are probably in inverted word order, with the verb appearing before the subject. If you cannot find the subject, reword the sentence in normal word order. If *there* is just a sentence starter, you can drop it from your reworded sentence.

SENTENCES BEGINNING WITH *THERE* OR *HERE*	REWORDED WITH SUBJECT BEFORE VERB
There is a mistake in the ad for the show.	A mistake is in the ad for the show.
Here comes the star of the show.	The star of the show comes here.

See Practice 18.4C

384   Basic Sentence Parts

Finding the Subject in Sentences Inverted for Emphasis

Sometimes a subject is intentionally put after its verb to draw attention to the subject.

> In some sentences, the subject follows the verb in order to emphasize the subject, or make it stand out.

18.4.4 RULE

In the following examples, notice how the order of the words builds suspense by leading up to the subject.

EXAMPLES

In the midst of the crowd outside the theater **stood** the **star**.
         verb   subject

Soaring high above the crowd **was** a huge
 verb   verb
bald eagle.
 subject

Hiding under the bedspread **were** my two
 verb   verb
orange **kittens**.
      subject

You can reword sentences such as these in normal word order to make it easier to find the subject.

INVERTED WORD ORDER	REWORDED WITH SUBJECT BEFORE VERB
In the midst of the crowd outside the theater stood the star.	The star stood in the midst of the crowd outside the theater.
Soaring high above the crowd was a huge bald eagle.	A huge bald eagle was soaring high above the crowd.
Hiding under the bedspread were my two orange kittens.	My two orange kittens were hiding under the bedspread.

Practice 18.4D

Differentiated Instruction

Strategy for Below-Level Students Students may need to review nouns and verbs before continuing with the chapter. Briefly go over the definitions of nouns and verbs with students and have them say several examples. Then, have students write the words *Noun* and *Verb* on index cards. Read aloud a passage from a story or an article. Have students raise the appropriate card every time you read a noun or a verb.

PRE-AP Strategy for Above-Level Students Explain that, when inverted word order is used for emphasis, the predicate often presents a situation that elicits a strong emotional reaction in order to make readers wonder who or what is involved. Then, challenge students to write a paragraph or a poem that uses inverted word order at least twice to achieve a dramatic effect and draw attention to the subject.

Finding the Subject in Sentences Inverted for Emphasis

Explain that writers often vary the normal word order of a sentence to create a specific effect. Placing the subject at the end of a sentence can sometimes draw attention to it. For example, *Here in the middle of the hot, dirty city is a lovely little garden.*

RULE 18.4.4 Read aloud the rule and then have students repeat the lines with you.

Point out that the goal of the example sentences is to keep the reader in suspense until the very end. Read the first example sentence aloud, pausing and using your voice to emphasize the suspense before arriving at the subject.

Ask students to do the same with the other two examples. Encourage students to use dramatic intonation and pauses to emphasize the subject.

Remind students that these sentences all have inverted word order. If students have difficulty locating the subject, reversing the order of the major parts of the sentence will usually make the subject easier to find.

Discuss the sentences in the chart on page 385. Then, have students use the examples as a guide in writing their own sentences. Ask them to share their sentences with a small group. Have other group members identify the subject of each sentence.

Before closing the section, review with students the most common types of sentences that use an inverted word order: questions, sentences beginning with *there* and *here*, and sentences inverted for emphasis. Have students give examples of each before moving on.

PRACTICE 18.4C

1. deliveryman
2. jacket
3. fly
4. guidebooks
5. Johnsons
6. story
7. musician
8. rain
9. mystery
10. information

PRACTICE 18.4D

11. tree
12. hurricane
13. car
14. test
15. roses
16. islands
17. reef
18. fox
19. sign
20. stew

SPEAKING APPLICATION

Have partners reword the sentences to eliminate the words *here* and *there*. Partners should identify the subjects in the new sentences.

WRITING APPLICATION

Have students exchange sentences and check each other's work, explaining why it is or is not right.

PRACTICE 18.4C Identifying Subjects in Sentences Beginning With *Here* or *There*

Read the sentences. Write the subject of each sentence.

EXAMPLE   Here is our library.

ANSWER   *library*

1. There goes the deliveryman.
2. Here is your jacket.
3. There is a fly near my soup.
4. Here are the guidebooks for our trip.
5. There were the Johnsons, in that car.
6. Here was a story to make you think.
7. There is a great musician playing on television.
8. Here comes the first rain of the month.
9. There lies the mystery behind this event.
10. Here is the information you requested.

PRACTICE 18.4D Identifying Subjects in Sentences Inverted for Emphasis

Read the sentences. Write the subject of each sentence.

EXAMPLE   At the end of the road stood a crumbling house.

ANSWER   *house*

11. On the shores of the lake grew a magnifice[nt] tree.
12. In late August came the worst hurricane.
13. Right there in the driveway was the car I liked.
14. As I had feared, on the desk lay a math tes[t]
15. In the carefully tended garden bloomed the most splendid roses.
16. In the middle of the Pacific Ocean are man[y] islands.
17. Near the east coast of Australia lies a spectacular reef.
18. Behind the hedges waits the hunting fox.
19. By the side of the road was a strange sign.
20. On the stove simmers some stew.

SPEAKING APPLICATION

With a partner, take turns talking about a movie you saw. Be sure to start two or three sentences with *there* or *here*. Your partner should listen for and identify the subjects of the sentences.

WRITING APPLICATION

Write two sentences in normal word order. You may write on any topic that interests you. Then, rewrite the sentences in inverted order.

Working with ELLs   **ELL** Sheltered Instruction: Cognitive

As students learn how to identify subjects, practice using a variety of grade-appropriate connecting words to combine phrases, clauses, and sentences in increasingly accurate ways.

Beginning Use gestures and simple words to identify things in the classroom. Incorporate the words *here* and *there* from Practice 18.4C, as in these examples: *Here are pencils. There are chairs.* Write the sentences on the board, and then combine them using the connecting word *and*. Students should copy your sentences.

Intermediate Pair students with fluent speakers. Have them write the sentences they generated during the Speaking Application. Then, have them use those sentences to write longer sentences, incorporating the connecting word *and*. Provide a model: *There was a car chase, and there was a love story.*

Advanced Have students complete the Writing Application. Then, have them rewrite their original sentences by adding a connecting word and a clause to each. Provide this example: *I went to a baseball game, and I had fun.*

Advanced High Have students complete the Advanced activity. Then, have them exchange sentences with partners and circle the connecting words in each other's sentences.

18.5 Complements

Often, a subject and verb alone can express a complete thought. For example, *Birds fly* can stand by itself as a sentence, even though it contains only two words, a subject and a verb. Other times, however, the thought begun by a subject and its verb must be completed with other words. For example, *Toni bought, The eyewitness told, Our mechanic is, Richard feels,* and *Marco seems* all contain a subject and verb, but none expresses a complete thought. All these ideas need **complements.**

A **complement** is a word or group of words that completes the meaning of a sentence.

 18.5.1 RULE

Complements are usually nouns, pronouns, or adjectives. They are located right after or very close to the verb. The complements are shown below in blue. The complements answer questions about the subject or verb in order to complete the sentence.

DIFFERENT KINDS OF COMPLEMENTS

Toni bought cars.
subject verb complement

The eyewitness told us the story.
subject verb complements

Our mechanic is a genius.
subject verb complement

Richard feels sad.
subject verb complement

Marco seems happy.
subject verb complement

This section will describe three types of complements: **direct objects, indirect objects,** and **subject complements.** All complements add information about the subjects or verbs in the sentence. They paint a clearer picture that helps the reader understand the writer's thoughts.

Complements   387

WRITING COACH

Online

www.phwritingcoach.com

Diagnostic and Instruction
Diagnostic test assesses students'
instructional needs. Lessons and
practice are assigned based on results.

Additional Practice
- Grammar Tutorials—Animated videos
  reinforce key grammar skills.
- Grammar Practice—Targeted
  practice addresses individual needs.
- ExamView—Teachers customize their
  grammar practice and tests.
- Grammar Games—Interactive video
  games make grammar fun.

Lesson Objectives

1. Identify the complements used in sentences.

2. Describe the effect of complements on the meaning of the sentence.

3. Distinguish between the various types of complements.

Explain to students that, while a sentence always has a subject and a verb, these basic parts alone are not always enough to create a sentence that makes sense.

RULE 18.5.1 Read aloud the rule and then have students repeat the lines with you.

Use a Think Aloud as part of a gradual release progression.

Think Aloud **Say: I can see that** a sentence like *Every rabbit is* does not make any sense, even though it has a subject and a verb. As a reader, I ask, *Every rabbit is what?* Is every rabbit cute, furry, a pest, or something else?

Explain that in this type of situation, the sentence needs more words to complete the thought. Read aloud the example sentences on page 387, but leave out the complement(s) in each one. Have students ask the question that the complement answers. **Say:** *Toni bought* and pause to let students ask *What did Toni buy?* Explain that these questions can be answered and complete sentences can be formed by adding complements.

Have the class brainstorm for a list of verbs that often need complements, such as *is, was, wants, wrote,* and *like.* Then, **have students work in pairs** to write four sentences using the verbs from the list.

Teacher Tip

To help students remember the function of a complement in a sentence, point out that *complement* is from the same root as *complete.* Both are related to the Latin root *complēre,* which means *to complete* or *to fill.* Make sure that students are not confusing *complement* with *compliment.*

Recognizing Direct Objects

Remind students that many verbs indicate action. The noun or pronoun that receives this action is called a direct object. Direct objects are a type of complement.

RULE 18.5.2 Read aloud the rule and then have students repeat the lines with you.

Say: In a sentence with a direct object, there will usually be at least two nouns: the subject and the direct object. Listen to this sentence: *My brother eats apples.* What is the simple subject? (brother) What is another noun in this sentence? (apples) Is this noun receiving the action of the verb *eats*? (Yes, the apples are getting eaten.) What question does the word *apple* answer? (What does my brother eat?)

Explain that questions and sentences with unstated subjects can also have direct objects. Write these sentences on the board and work with students to find the direct objects and the subjects:

Who lost the football?

Feed the dog!

Please wash the dishes.

Compound Direct Objects

Explain that there may be more than one noun or pronoun that receives the action of the verb.

Write these sentences on the board: *Keith plays the guitar. Keith plays the piano. Keith plays the flute.* **Ask:** How could I rewrite these sentences as one sentence with a compound direct object? (*Keith plays the guitar, the piano, and the flute.*)

Teacher Tip

Explain that only certain action verbs can take a direct object. If students are confused about what an action verb is, remind them that there are action verbs and linking verbs. Linking verbs link the subject to additional information about the subject. Action verbs describe an action. If students need to review these verb forms, make a list of several verbs and have students use a T-chart with the headings *Action Verbs* and *Linking Verbs* to classify them.

Recognizing Direct Objects

Direct objects follow action verbs.

> A **direct object** is a noun or pronoun that receives the action of a verb.

You can find a direct object by asking *What?* or *Whom?* after an action verb.

EXAMPLES   My older **brother** **found** a grass **snake**.
subject ‧ verb ‧ direct object

I **called** **Ricky** early in the day.
subject ‧ verb ‧ direct object

My dog **Champ** **likes** a good **scratch**
subject ‧ verb ‧ direct object
on his belly.

Snake, Ricky, and *scratch* are the direct objects of the verbs in the examples. In the first sentence, *snake* answers the question *Found what?* In the second sentence, *Ricky* answers the question *Called whom?* In the third sentence, *scratch* answers the question *Likes what?*

Compound Direct Objects
Like subjects and verbs, direct objects can be compound. That is, one verb can have two or more direct objects.

EXAMPLES   The **lizard** **eats** **crickets** and other **bugs**.
subject ‧ verb ‧ direct object ‧ direct object

The **committee** **chose** **Mrs. Franks**,
subject ‧ verb ‧ direct object

Mr. Lynch, and **Ms. Chin** to organize the
direct object ‧ direct object
reptile show.

See Practice 18.5A
See Practice 18.5B

PRACTICE 18.5A > Recognizing Direct Objects

Read the sentences. Write the direct object or the compound direct object in each sentence.

EXAMPLE   He loved building models.

ANSWER   *models*

1. Maria baked bread.
2. My friends brought gifts to the party.
3. Bears eat plants and meat.
4. The Carlisle twins raise rabbits.
5. Freddy strummed the guitar.
6. Mr. Sanchez speaks Spanish, English, and German.
7. The plant known as the Venus flytrap catches insects.
8. Sasha's older brother studied math and science.
9. The female kangaroo carries her young in a pouch.
10. We all ordered salad, chicken, and potatoes.

PRACTICE 18.5B > Adding Complements

Read the sentences. Rewrite the sentences, and fill in the blanks with appropriate direct objects. Use both nouns and pronouns.

EXAMPLE   Marcus found his _____.

ANSWER   *Marcus found his key.*

11. Chandar saw _____ at the fair.
12. Estancia played the _____.
13. Jeffrey dug a _____.
14. The two boys visited _____.
15. Carly and Selene knitted _____.
16. I carefully watered _____ each morning.
17. Frankie asked _____ for a pencil.
18. Hey, Tommy, throw me that _____.
19. Michael's dad cooked a great _____.
20. Cecily scanned the _____.

SPEAKING APPLICATION

With a partner, discuss a hobby you have or would like to have. Your partner should listen for and name two direct objects.

WRITING APPLICATION

Write a short paragraph about packing for a trip. Make sure two or more sentences contain direct objects. Underline the direct object or direct objects in each sentence.

Practice   389

PRACTICE 18.5A

1. bread
2. gifts
3. plants, meat
4. rabbits
5. guitar
6. Spanish, English, German
7. insects
8. math, science
9. young
10. salad, chicken, potatoes

PRACTICE 18.5B

Answers will vary. Sample answers:

11. Chandar saw him at the fair.
12. Estancia played the piano.
13. Jeffrey dug a hole.
14. The two boys visited us.
15. Carly and Selene knitted sweaters.
16. I carefully watered it each morning.
17. Frankie asked her for a pencil.
18. Hey, Tommy, throw me that ball.
19. Michael's dad cooked a great dinner.
20. Cecily scanned the page.

SPEAKING APPLICATION

Have partners explain how they identified the direct objects.

WRITING APPLICATION

Have students exchange sentences and check each other's work, explaining why it is or is not correct.

Working with ELLs   ELL Sheltered Instruction: Cognitive

As students learn about direct objects, help them demonstrate comprehension of increasingly complex English by responding to your questions about a text.

Beginning After students complete the Speaking Application, distribute simple sentences about a familiar hobby. Include direct objects. Read the sentences with students, using mime as needed. Then, ask questions about the text requiring brief responses, such as, *What would you need to enjoy this hobby?*

Intermediate After students complete the Speaking Application, distribute the simple sentences from the Beginning activity to small groups. Have them read the sentences and identify the direct object in each. Monitor comprehension by asking questions, such as, *Is this a hobby for one person, or a group? What is the goal of the hobby?*

Advanced Distribute copies of an encyclopedia article about a hobby. Have pairs read the sentences and circle the direct objects. Then, ask questions to monitor their comprehension, such as, *When did the hobby begin? How was it different in the past?*

Advanced High Direct students to complete the Advanced activity. Then, challenge students to list techniques for finding direct objects in sentences. Provide this example: *Does the word answer What? or Whom? after an action verb?*

Distinguishing Between Direct Objects, Adverbs, and Objects of Prepositions

Point out that other words may follow the verb in a sentence, but not all of these words are direct objects.

RULE 18.5.3 Read aloud the rule and then have students repeat the lines with you.

Use a Think Aloud as part of a gradual release progression.

Say: Rule 18.5.3 describes two things a direct object is *not*. It tells me that a direct object can't be an adverb. I **remember that** an adverb tells how, when, or where an action was done. So if a word tells me *how, when,* or *where* the action was done, I know it is *not* a direct object. A direct object is always a noun or a pronoun. The rule also tells me that if a noun is part of a prepositional phrase, it can't be a direct object. So, if I find a noun that closely follows a preposition and seems to relate to that preposition, I know it can't be a direct object. For example, in the sentence *I swam in the river,* it looks as if *river* is a direct object at first. But I know that *in* is a preposition, and *river* relates to *in,* so *river* can't be a direct object. In the sentence *I swam the river,* on the other hand, there is no preposition, so I can tell that *river* is the direct object.

Read aloud the example sentences with students and discuss why *quickly* and *through town* are not direct objects. Then, say: Joanne rode on her bike. Explain that *bike* is not a direct object here because it is at the end of a prepositional phrase.

Then, display the sentence starter *Marina rowed _____.* **Work with students** to use the example sentences to complete the sentence three ways: with a direct object, with an adverb, and with a prepositional phrase.

Display the sentence starter *Isabel played _____.* **Have pairs work together** to complete the sentence three ways: with a direct object, with an adverb, and with a prepositional phrase.

Ask pairs to read their sentences aloud to the class. Classmates may then identify whether the sentence contains a direct object.

Distinguishing Between Direct Objects, Adverbs, and Objects of Prepositions

Not all action verbs have direct objects. Be careful not to confuse a direct object with an adverb or with the object of a preposition. If you are unsure if a word or phrase is a direct object, ask yourself who or what is receiving the action of the verb.

RULE 18.5.3

> A direct object is never an adverb or the noun or pronoun at the end of a prepositional phrase.

Compare the following examples. Notice that the action verb *drove* has a direct object in only the first sentence.

EXAMPLES

Joanne **drove** her new **sports car**.
subject   verb   direct object

Joanne **drove** **quickly**.
subject   verb   adverb

Joanne **drove** **through the town**.
subject   verb   prepositional phrase

Each example shows a very common sentence type. The first consists of a subject, a verb, and a direct object. The compound noun *sports car* is the direct object of the verb *drove.*

The second example consists of a subject, a verb, and an adverb. Nothing after the verb in the sentence answers the question *What?* so there is no direct object. *Quickly* modifies the verb and tells *how* Joanne drove.

The third example consists of a subject, a verb, and a prepositional phrase. Again, no noun or pronoun answers the question *What?* after the verb. The prepositional phrase tells *where* Joanne drove.

Notice also that a single sentence can contain more than one of these three parts.

EXAMPLE

Joanne drove her new **sports car** **quickly**
direct object   adverb
through the town.
prepositional phrase

See Practice 18.5C

Differentiated Instruction

RTI Strategy for Special Needs Students
Before discussing how to find direct objects in questions, play a game of charades to review the function of a direct object in a sentence. First, show students these sentence frames:

I love _____.

I gave a _____ to my friend.

I drove the _____.

Explain that the subject of each sentence is *I.* Students will take turns writing a sentence using one of the frames and acting it out. Their classmates must identify the sentence frame, then try to guess what the "missing word" is. Explain that the missing word is the direct object.

Finding Direct Objects in Questions

In normal word order, a direct object follows a verb. In questions that are in inverted word order, however, the direct object often appears before the verb and subject.

> **A direct object in a question will sometimes be found before the verb.**

◁ 18.5.4 RULE

In the following chart, questions are paired with sentences reworded in normal word order. Direct objects are highlighted in pink, subjects are highlighted in yellow, and verbs are highlighted in orange. Compare the positions of the direct objects in each.

QUESTIONS	REWORDED IN NORMAL WORD ORDER
What did Mary play at her recital?	Mary did play what at her recital.
Which car did he drive to school today?	He did drive which car to school today.
What does a snake eat?	A snake does eat what.
Which T-shirt do you like, the purple one or the green striped one?	You do like which T-shirt, the purple one or the green striped one.
Whom did you meet in the cafeteria?	You did meet whom in the cafeteria.

In each of the five questions, the direct object appears before, rather than after, the verb. To locate the direct object in a question, put the sentence into normal word order with the subject appearing before the verb. Then, the direct object will be found in its usual position after the verb.

Practice 18.5D

Finding Direct Objects in Questions

Remind students that the word order in questions is often inverted, that is, the verb comes before the subject. This can make it difficult to identify a direct object in a question.

RULE 18.5.4 Read aloud the rule and then have students repeat the lines with you.

Read the questions and reworded sentences in the chart with students. Make sure that students understand that the subject in each reworded sentence is the same as the subject in the associated question. Then, ask students what they need to remember about the word order of questions. (It is often inverted.) Display this sentence for students: *Rowena rejected the knights.* Ask a volunteer to tell you the direct object of the sentence. (knights) Ask another volunteer to tell you what question this statement answers. (Whom did Rowena reject?) Have a third volunteer tell you the direct object of the question. (whom)

Have each student write a statement with a direct object on a small slip of paper. These statements should use normal word order. Have students fold the papers and pass them to you. Mix the papers and redistribute to students, ensuring that no one receives the same one he or she wrote. Each student should then write a question based on the statement received. Ask students to read both the statement and the related question aloud. As a class, identify the direct object in each.

Extension

To help students synthesize and apply what they have learned about objects, have them create silly sentences. Direct each student to think of the name of a famous person, living or dead. On the board, write these sentence frames: *I met (famous person) in the hallway in front of our classroom. (Famous person) e-mailed (famous person).* At random, call on students to fill in a name for each sentence frame. Write students' silly sentences on the board. Then, call for volunteers to identify the direct object in each.

PRACTICE 18.5C

1. DO
2. OP
3. DO
4. ADV
5. OP
6. ADV
7. DO
8. ADV
9. OP
10. DO

PRACTICE 18.5D

11. Whom
12. What
13. shoes
14. Whom
15. What
16. class
17. What
18. Whom
19. flavor
20. What

SPEAKING APPLICATION

Have students explain how they identified the direct objects.

WRITING APPLICATION

Have students exchange sentences and check each other's work, explaining why it is or is not correct.

PRACTICE 18.5C Distinguishing Direct Object, Adverb, and Object of a Preposition

Read the sentences. Label each underlined word *DO* for direct object, *ADV* for adverb, or *OP* for object of a preposition.

EXAMPLE Melissa walked through <u>town</u>.

ANSWER *OP*

1. The jeweler polished the <u>bracelet</u>.
2. The squirrels ran up the <u>tree</u>.
3. Pedro carried the <u>groceries</u> into the house.
4. Tonight, the girls played <u>happily</u>.
5. The farmer walked into the <u>barn</u>.
6. The painter worked <u>quickly</u>.
7. Mr. Shapiro washed his <u>dog</u> today.
8. The willow tree swayed <u>gracefully</u>.
9. The children ran across the <u>field</u>.
10. The Nguyen family opened a new <u>restaurant</u>.

PRACTICE 18.5D Finding Direct Objects in Questions

Read the questions. Write the direct object in each question.

EXAMPLE What will you wear tonight?

ANSWER *What*

11. Whom did you talk to at the bank?
12. What are you reading for your book report?
13. Which shoes should I take?
14. Whom did Dennis ask to the dance?
15. What will Kerri make for the bake sale?
16. Which class should I take first?
17. What did you throw out?
18. Whom will you be inviting to your party?
19. Which flavor do you like best?
20. What do squirrels do with the nuts they gather?

SPEAKING APPLICATION

With a partner, take turns asking questions about planning a party. Include at least two questions with direct objects. Your partner should listen for and name the direct objects.

WRITING APPLICATION

Use Practice 18.5C as a model, and write three sentences: one with a direct object following the verb, one with a prepositional phrase, and one with an adverb. As with the practice, write *DO*, *ADV*, or *OP* after each sentence.

Working with ELLs   **ELL** Sheltered Instruction: Cognitive

Have students read aloud the sentences in Practice 18.5C to give them practice speaking with increasing accuracy and ease using a variety of sentence lengths.

Beginning Read sentences 3, 4, and 5 aloud to students, having them repeat after you. Praise their efforts to speak with increased accuracy and ease. Then, use yes/no questions to help them label each underlined word as a direct object, adverb, or object of a preposition.

Intermediate Have students read the even sentences from 1–10 aloud with you several times. Coach them in speaking the sentences accurately and with ease. Work as a group to identify each underlined word as a direct object, adverb, or object of a preposition.

Advanced Have partners read sentences 1–10 aloud, coaching each other in accuracy and ease of speech. Have them work cooperatively to identify each underlined word as a direct object, adverb, or object of a preposition. Call on pairs to share their answers.

Advanced High Have students pair with Beginning students. Instruct them to read several sentences from 1–10 with their partners, providing assistance as needed. Then, have the Advanced High students work independently to identify each underlined word as a direct object, adverb, or object of a preposition. They should explain their answers to the Beginning students.

Recognizing Indirect Objects

Sentences with a direct object may also contain another kind of complement, called an **indirect object.** A sentence cannot have an indirect object unless it has a direct object.

> An **indirect object** is a noun or pronoun that comes after an action verb and before a direct object. It names the person or thing to which something is given or for which something is done.

18.5.5 RULE

An indirect object answers the questions *To* or *for whom?* or *To* or *for what?* after an action verb. To find an indirect object, find the direct object first. Then, ask the appropriate question.

EXAMPLE   Shrini's **mom told them** the **story**.
indirect object   direct object

(Told *what?* [*story*])
(Told the story *to whom?* [*them*])

Keep in mind the following pattern: *Subject + Verb + Indirect Object + Direct Object*. An indirect object will almost always come between the verb and the direct object in a sentence.

Compound Indirect Objects
Like a subject, verb, or direct object, an indirect object can be compound.

EXAMPLES   **Dave assigned** each **car and truck** a
subject   verb   compound indirect object

new **parking place**.
direct object
(Assigned *what?* [*parking place*])
(Assigned a parking place *to what?* [*car and truck*])

Mom offered my sister and me sandwiches
subject   verb   compound indirect object   compound direct object

and milk.
(Offered *what?* [*sandwiches* and *milk*])
(Offered *sandwiches to whom?* [*my sister and me*])

ee Practice 18.5E

Recognizing Indirect Objects

Explain that another type of complement is called an indirect object. Clarify that a sentence can have an indirect object only if it also has a direct object.

| RULE 18.5.5 | Read aloud the rule and then have students repeat the lines with you.

Say: Consider these sentences: *Melita gave me her scarf. I passed Jaime the ball.* In each case, there is a subject, a verb, a direct object that receives the action of the verb, and an indirect object that answers the question *To* or *for whom?* Review the first example. **Say:** Which word answers the question *To* or *for whom?* (them)

Explain that you can often identify an indirect object by placing the preposition *to* in front of it and then moving the prepositional phrase to follow the verb. If the meaning of the sentence doesn't change, the word was an indirect object. Have the class brainstorm for a variety of nouns and verbs. Work with students to use these words to write sentences that contain both direct and indirect objects.

Have pairs of students write their own sentences. Then, have volunteers share their sentences and identify the subject, verb, direct object, and indirect object.

Compound Indirect Objects

Remind students that subjects, verbs, and direct objects can all be compound. This means that there is more than one. Indirect objects can also be compound. Review the second example on the page. **Say:** Which words answer the question *To* or *for whom?* (car and truck)

Have students use the sentences they generated based on the list of nouns and verbs. Have students choose one and rewrite it so that it has a compound indirect object.

Distinguishing Between Indirect Objects and Objects of Prepositions

Remind students that an indirect object answers the questions *To or for whom?* or *To or for what?* after an action verb. Tell students an object of a preposition also answers these questions, but it always follows a preposition.

RULE 18.5.6 Read aloud the rule and then have students repeat the lines with you.

Emphasize that indirect objects and objects of prepositions often answer the same questions. The difference is in the wording.

Use a Think Aloud as part of a gradual release progression.

Say: I know that indirect objects and objects of prepositions can answer the same questions in a sentence. If I say *The trainer gave the horse a carrot,* I am using the indirect object *horse* to tell to whom or what the trainer gave a carrot. But if I say *The trainer gave a carrot to her horse,* I am using *horse* as the object of a preposition. This is true because *to* is a preposition.

Display these sentences on the board: *My brother gave Ella a bracelet. He gave a necklace to me.* **Guide students** to distinguish between the sentence that uses an indirect object and the one that uses an object of a preposition. Point out that the difference is word order and the use of the preposition *to.*

Have each student write one sentence that uses an object of a preposition. Have them switch sentences with a partner. Partners should reword the sentence into the Subject + Verb + Indirect Object + Direct Object pattern.

Teacher Tip

If students have difficulty distinguishing between direct and indirect objects, suggest they write the pattern Subject + Verb + Indirect Object + Direct Object on an index card. Have them create a mnemonic device to help remember the pattern, such as <u>S</u>ugarless <u>V</u>alentines <u>I</u>mpress <u>D</u>entists.

Distinguishing Between Indirect Objects and Objects of Prepositions

Do not confuse an indirect object with the object of a preposition.

> **An indirect object never follows the preposition *to* or *for* in a sentence.**

Compare the following examples.

EXAMPLES   Father bought **him** a **car**.
                   indirect   direct
                   object   object

                Father bought a **car** for **him**.
                        direct   object of
                        object   preposition

In the first example above, *him* is an indirect object. It comes after the verb *bought* and before the direct object *car.* In the second example, *him* is the object of the preposition *for* and follows the direct object *car.*

EXAMPLES   Paul gave **Jerome** a **sandwich**.
                   indirect object   direct object

                Paul gave a **sandwich** to **Jerome**.
                      direct object   object of
                                preposition

To find the indirect object in the first example above, you must first find the direct object. Ask yourself what Paul gave. He gave a sandwich, so *sandwich* is the direct object. Then, ask yourself to whom Paul gave the sandwich. He gave it to *Jerome,* so *Jerome* is the indirect object.

Use the same questions in the second example. Again, *sandwich* is the direct object of *gave;* however, *Jerome* is no longer the indirect object. Instead, it is the object of the preposition *to.*

See Practice 18.5F

Differentiated Instruction

Strategy for Spanish Speakers

Students whose home language is Spanish may overuse the preposition *to* with direct and indirect objects, as Spanish indirect objects are often accompanied by a prepositional phrase in the same sentence (e.g., *Le di el libro a Èl*). Spanish speakers will often insert the preposition *to* before the indirect object. For example, they may say *She wrote to him a letter. The teacher taught to him math.* Explain that in English when a pronoun is an indirect object, it never has a preposition added to it. Only if a pronoun comes after the direct object can it be the object of a preposition and be used with *to.* Write a sentence that has a direct and indirect object on the board: *He gave her the book.* Have students rewrite the sentence, but with the prepositional phrase: *He gave the book to her.* Then, write a similar type of sentence with a prepositional phrase and have students rewrite the corresponding sentence with an indirect object.

PRACTICE 18.5E > Recognizing Indirect Objects

...d the sentences. Write the indirect object ...ach sentence.

...MPLE   I brought Mom the paper.
...WER   *Mom*

...Miguel threw Charlie the ball.

...The Riveras got their dog a new collar.

...Terry brought the kittens their dinner.

...The company gave my dad a promotion.

...Sheila bought her mother flowers.

...Mom made us costumes for the play.

...gave my report a title page.

...Kelly offered me money for my old bicycle.

...The committee awarded the project a blue ...ribbon.

...The park ranger gave the tourists directions.

PRACTICE 18.5F > Distinguishing Indirect Object and Object of a Preposition

Read the sentences. Write whether the underlined word is an *indirect object* or an *object of a preposition*.

EXAMPLE   John threw the ball to <u>Ravi</u>.
ANSWER   *object of a preposition*

11. Johanna got a birthday card from her <u>grandmother</u>.
12. The baker brought <u>us</u> the bread we ordered.
13. Victoria gave the message to <u>Martina</u>.
14. Mom and I planned a party for <u>him</u>.
15. Our neighbor found <u>me</u> a job.
16. We fed the <u>seals</u> fish.
17. The artist showed her sketch to <u>me</u>.
18. Justin brought his <u>mother</u> a scarf.
19. Gina borrowed a dress from <u>me</u>.
20. My brother sent <u>me</u> a letter from camp.

SPEAKING APPLICATION

...With a partner, talk about errands you or ...family members run regularly, such as trips ...to the store or library. Be sure to use indirect ...objects at least two times. Your partner should ...listen for and name the indirect objects.

WRITING APPLICATION

Write two sentences with indirect objects. Then, rewrite the sentences so that the indirect objects become objects of prepositions. Use the sentences in Practice 18.5F to help you with ideas.

Practice   395

PRACTICE 18.5E >

1. Charlie
2. dog
3. kittens
4. dad
5. mother
6. us
7. report
8. me
9. project
10. tourists

PRACTICE 18.5F >

11. object of a preposition
12. indirect object
13. object of a preposition
14. object of a preposition
15. indirect object
16. indirect object
17. object of a preposition
18. indirect object
19. object of a preposition
20. indirect object

SPEAKING APPLICATION

Have partners explain how they identified the indirect objects.

WRITING APPLICATION

Have students explain how they changed the indirect objects into objects of prepositions.

Subject Complements

Remind students that linking verbs connect the subject of a sentence to information about the subject. When linking verbs have a complement, it is known as a subject complement.

RULE 18.5.7 Read aloud the rule and then have students repeat the lines with you.

Point out that a complement completes the thought of a sentence by giving additional information. Therefore, it makes sense that a subject complement gives information about the subject. Explain that subject complements can be nouns, pronouns, or adjectives.

Predicate Nouns and Pronouns

Confirm that students can understand and give examples of common nouns, proper nouns, and pronouns.

RULE 18.5.8 Read aloud the rule and then have students repeat the lines with you.

Read aloud the paragraph under rule 18.5.8. Explain that a predicate pronoun or noun renames or identifies the subject. Help students use the technique of substituting an equal sign for a linking verb to determine whether a word is a predicate noun or pronoun. Then, discuss the example sentences with students. Tell them that *Ronnie will be the captain of our team* could be expressed *Ronnie = captain. Captain* renames the subject *Ronnie,* so *captain* is a predicate noun.

Work with students to repeat this exercise for the remaining example sentences.

Have students write their own sentences with predicate nouns and pronouns and then express the sentences as *subject = predicate noun* or *pronoun.*

Subject Complements

Both direct objects and indirect objects are complements used with action verbs. Linking verbs, however, have a different kind of complement called a **subject complement.** Like direct and indirect objects, subject complements add information to a sentence. However, subject complements give readers more information about the subject of the sentence, not the verb.

> **A subject complement** is a noun, pronoun, or adjective that follows a linking verb and provides important details about the subject.

Predicate Nouns and Pronouns

Both nouns and pronouns are sometimes used as subject complements after linking verbs.

> **A predicate noun** or **predicate pronoun** follows a linking verb and renames or identifies the subject of the sentence.

It is easy to recognize predicate nouns and predicate pronouns. The linking verb acts much like an equal sign between the subject and the noun or pronoun that follows the verb. Both the subject and the predicate noun or pronoun refer to the same person or thing.

EXAMPLES

Ronnie will be the **captain** of our team.
subject   verb   predicate noun

(The predicate noun *captain* renames the subject *Ronnie*.)

Ford's first **car was** the **Model A**.
subject   verb   predicate noun

(The predicate noun *Model A* identifies the subject *car*.)

The two **winners are they**.
subject   verb predicate pronoun

(The predicate pronoun *they* identifies the subject *winners*.)   See Practice 18.5G

396   **Basic Sentence Parts**

Extension

To help students synthesize and apply what they have learned about complements, have them play a linking-verb completion game. Working in pairs, students should think of a famous person with whom they are familiar. One student should then list words that describe the person's physical traits, for example, *tall, dark, handsome.* The other student should list words that rename the person, for example, *an actor, a husband, a father.* Write these sentence frames on the board: *(Famous person) is (describer). (Famous person) is (renamer).* Have students complete the frames by inserting words from their lists. Call on volunteers to read their sentences to the class.

Predicate Adjectives

A **predicate adjective** can also follow a linking verb.

> **A predicate adjective** follows a linking verb and describes the subject of the sentence.

A predicate adjective is considered part of the complete predicate of a sentence because it comes after a linking verb. In spite of this, a predicate adjective does not modify the words in the predicate. Instead, it describes the noun or pronoun that serves as the subject of the linking verb.

EXAMPLES   The **flight** to Houston **was** **swift**.
            subject   *verb* *predicate adjective*

(The predicate adjective *swift* describes the subject *flight*.)

The **salesperson** **seems** very **efficient**.
    subject   *verb*   *predicate adjective*

(The predicate adjective *efficient* describes the subject *salesperson*.)

Predicate Adjectives and Their Comparative and Superlative Forms

The comparative form of the predicate adjective is used when two items are being compared. The superlative form is used when three or more items are being compared.

Use -er or *more* to form the comparative degree of most one- or two-syllable predicate adjectives. Use -est or *most* to form the superlative of most one- or two-syllable predicate adjectives. When the superlative form is used, the article *the* is often added.

EXAMPLES   The **flight** to Houston **was** **swifter** than the flight
            subject   *verb* *predicate adjective*
            to Dallas.

The **flight** to San Antonio **was** the **swiftest** of
    subject   *verb*   *predicate adjective*
the three flights.

(For adjectives ending in y, replace the y with -ier and -iest.)

Practice 18.5H

Predicate Adjectives

Explain that a predicate adjective is a subject complement that describes, but does not rename, a noun or pronoun.

RULE 18.5.9 Read aloud the rule and then have students repeat the lines with you.

Say: I use predicate adjectives all the time in my daily life. If I'm gardening and I see some red tomatoes, I'll say, "Oh, good. The tomatoes are ripe." The word *ripe* is an adjective. When it follows any form of the linking verb *is*, it is called a predicate adjective. Or, I might say, *Denise looks happy.* The verb *looks* is acting as a linking verb, so the adjective *happy* is a predicate adjective modifying the subject *Denise*.

Write on the board this sentence: *The game was exciting.* Guide students to identify *was* as the linking verb and *exciting* as the predicate adjective.

Write these sentences on the board: *Roberto seemed grumpy after a long day. The wolves in the dark forest were wild. My brown coat looked woolly.*

Have students work in pairs to identify all the adjectives used in these sentences (grumpy, long, dark, wild, brown, woolly), and then decide which ones are predicate adjectives (grumpy, wild, woolly).

Predicate Adjectives and Their Comparative and Superlative Forms

Explain that predicate adjectives are often used in comparisons. Read this sentence to students: *The kangaroo is larger than the wallaby.* **Ask:** What is the predicate adjective? Is it comparative or superlative? (larger, comparative)

Differentiated Instruction

RTI Strategy for Below-Level Students
If students are having difficulty distinguishing between predicate nouns and predicate adjectives, check to make sure they can distinguish between nouns and adjectives. Have students define *noun* and *adjective* and give examples of each. Then, explain that if a noun follows a linking verb and means the same as the subject, the noun is a predicate noun. If an adjective follows a linking verb and describes the subject, it is a predicate adjective. Point out that common linking verbs are *is, was,* and *are.*

PRE-AP Enrichment for Above-Level Students Point out to students that sentences may contain both an adjective and a predicate adjective. The sentence *The large refrigerator looked funny* is one example. Another is *The lazy day was hot and humid.* Both adjectives and predicate adjectives describe the subject. However, often more emphasis is placed on the predicate adjective because of its position in the sentence. Encourage students to try writing sentences with both multiple adjectives and a predicate adjective.

Three or More Syllables

Explain to students that predicate adjectives with three or more syllables form their comparative and superative forms with the words *more* and *most*. **Say:** It sounds awkward to say "The sky is beautifuler than ever" or "That is the effectivest way to do the job." That's the main reason that adjectives with three or more syllables don't take the *-er* and *-est* endings.

Have students look at the examples on page 398. Ask for volunteers to read the sentences as they are written and then to read them again with the usual comparative and superlative ends. **Ask:** Which way sounds better? (**Possible response: the sentences with *more* and *most*)

Compound Subject Complements

RULE 18.5.10 Read aloud the rule and then have students repeat the lines with you.

Explain that a clause can have more than one predicate noun or more than one predicate adjective. However, a clause should never have both a predicate noun and a predicate adjective. For example, *Mac is short and my best friend* is not a correct sentence.

Read this sentence to students: *The night was dark and stormy.* **Say:** This sentence includes a compound predicate adjective. What is it? (**Answer: dark and stormy)

Guide students in writing their own sentences using compound predicate nouns, pronouns, and adjectives.

Three or More Syllables

Use *more* and *most* for predicate adjectives with three or more syllables.

EXAMPLES

The Houston **airport** **seemed** more **congested** than the Dallas airport.
subject *verb* *predicate adjective*

The New York **airport** **seemed** the most **congested** of all three airports.
subject *verb* *predicate adjective*

That **oak tree** **looks** more **beautiful** than that maple tree.
subject *verb* *predicate adjective*

That **dogwood** **looks** the most **beautiful** of all three trees.
subject *verb* *predicate adjective*

This **trip** **was** more **fun** than last year's trip.
subject *verb* *predicate adjective*

The **trip** to New York **was** the most **fun** of all the trips.
subject *verb* *predicate adjective*

Compound Subject Complements

Like other sentence parts, subject complements can be compound.

RULE 18.5.10

> A **compound subject complement** consists of two or more predicate nouns, pronouns, or adjectives joined by a conjunction such as *and* or *or*.

EXAMPLES

My two best **friends** **are** **Phil and Mark**.
subject *verb* *compound predicate noun*

The **highway** **seems** **slick and icy**.
subject *verb* *compound predicate adjective*

The **dessert** **was** **apples and oranges**.
subject *verb* *compound predicate noun*

The two **dogs** **are** **wet and muddy**.
subject *verb* *compound predicate adjective*

The **caller** **might have been** **he or she**.
subject *verb* *compound predicate pronoun*

398   Complements

PRACTICE 18.5G Identifying Predicate Nouns and Predicate Pronouns

Read the sentences. Write the predicate noun or predicate pronoun in each sentence.

EXAMPLE   My mom is a psychologist.

ANSWER   *psychologist*

The Komodo dragon is the largest lizard.

A loud voice announced, "It is I."

The man in the uniform was captain of the ship.

Rome is a city with a lot of history.

My favorite fruit is a peach.

That tree is a birch.

Margo is a good singer.

The caterpillar had become a butterfly.

The winner is he.

Even after his injury, Paco remained our best player.

PRACTICE 18.5H Recognizing Comparative and Superlative Predicate Adjectives

Read the sentences. Write sentences using the comparative and superlative forms of the predicate adjective. Discuss the function of each predicate adjective in its comparative and superlative form with a partner.

EXAMPLE   The steps are slippery after the rain.

ANSWER   *The first step is more slippery than the second one.*

The top step is the most slippery of the three.

11. Miguel is particular about his appearance.

12. Kelsey seems friendly.

13. That detail is important.

14. The last lesson was valuable.

15. Leticia's eyes are blue.

16. The crossing at the stoplight had been hazardous.

17. Diamonds are hard.

18. The chicken casserole is appetizing.

19. Their house design is traditional.

20. Watermelon is juicy.

SPEAKING APPLICATION

In a small group, share memorable experiences. Use comparative and superlative predicate adjectives. Then, make a list of your adjectives and read the list. Discuss the function of these comparative or superlative forms and write a sentence for each.

WRITING APPLICATION

Write a paragraph about characters in a book. Use comparative and superlative forms of predicate adjectives. Read your paragraph to a partner. Have your partner identify the predicate adjectives and explain the forms.

Practice   399

PRACTICE 18.5G

1. lizard
2. I
3. captain
4. city
5. peach
6. birch
7. singer
8. butterfly
9. he
10. player

PRACTICE 18.5H

Answers will vary. Sample answers:

11. Miguel is more particular about his appearance than his friends are. Miguel is the most particular about his appearance of his friends.

12. Kelsey is more friendly than Sam. Kelsey is the most friendly of the chess players.

13. That detail is more important than this detail. That detail is the most important of all.

14. The last lesson was more valuable than the first. The last lesson was the most valuable of all the lessons.

15. Leticia's eyes are bluer than Sally's. Leticia's eyes are the bluest of all the girls'.

16. The crossing at the stoplight had been more hazardous than the other crossings. The crossing at the stoplight had been the most hazardous of all the crossings in town.

17. Diamonds are harder than other gems. Diamonds are the hardest gem.

18. The chicken casserole is more appetizing than the chicken pie. The chicken casserole is the most appetizing chicken dish.

19. Their house design is more traditional than their neighbors'. Their house design is the most traditional of all the houses on the street.

20. Watermelons are juicier than apples. Watermelon is the juiciest fruit.

SPEAKING APPLICATION

While speaking, students should demonstrate that they can use and understand the function of the comparative and superlative forms of predicate adjectives.

WRITING APPLICATION

Students' paragraphs should demonstrate that they can use and understand the function of the comparative and superlative forms of predicate adjectives in writing.

Test Warm-Up

1. **B** Change *most* to **more**

2. **G** No one could agree about which of the dozen treats was most delicious.

3. **A** The sandwiches were great, but the lasagna was more flavorful.

4. **H** In my opinion, the salad was most scrumptious of all.

Reteach

If students have not mastered these skills, review the content in Section 18.5.9 Predicate Adjectives and Their Comparative and Superlative Forms.

Test Tip

Explain to students that sometimes they will be asked to choose the *best answer,* or they will encounter a question for which no answer seems to be completely right. In those cases, they should try to compose a correct answer in their head, then choose the answer that is closest to the answer they have composed.

Test Warm-Up

DIRECTIONS
Read the introduction and the passage that follows. Then, answer the questions to show that you can use and understand the function of predicate adjectives and their comparative and superlative forms in reading and writing.

Morgan wrote this paragraph to describe a school celebration. Read the paragraph and think about the changes you would suggest as a peer editor. When you finish reading, answer the questions that follow.

The Best Party Ever

(1) Our school had a party to celebrate winning the trivia contest w Jefferson Middle School. (2) It was a big victory for us since the quest were most challenging than the ones in our earlier contests. (3) Every says that Andrea planned a party that became the all-time best. (4) N one could agree about which of the dozen treats was more deliciouser. (5) The sandwiches were great. (6) The lasagna was flavorfuler. (7) In opinion, the salad was more scrumptious of all.

1 What change, if any, should be made in sentence 2?

  A Add *more* before **most**

  B Change *most* to **more**

  C Add a comma after *challenging*

  D Make no change

2 What is the BEST way to revise sentence 4?

  F No one could agree about which of the dozen treats was more delicious.

  G No one could agree about which of the dozen treats was most delicious.

  H No one could agree about which of the dozen treats was more delicious of all.

  J No one could agree about which of the dozen treats was most deliciouser.

3 What is the BEST way to combine sentences 5 and 6?

  A The sandwiches were great, but the lasagna was more flavorful.

  B The sandwiches were great, the lasag was more flavorfulest.

  C The sandwiches were more great, but lasagna was more flavorful.

  D The sandwiches were more great, and lasagna was more flavorful.

4 What is the BEST way to revise sentence

  F In my opinion, the salad was more scrumptiouser of all.

  G In my opinion, the salad was most scrumptiouser of all.

  H In my opinion, the salad was most scrumptious of all.

  J In my opinion, the salad was scrumpt of all.

Use the Online Lesson Planner at www.phwritingcoach.com to customize your instructional plan for an integrated Language Arts curriculum.

DAY 1 19.1 Phrases

"What Do You Notice?"

Objectives: Identify, use, and understand phrases, including

- prepositional phrases
- appositives and appositive phrases

INSTRUCTION AND PRACTICE
Student Edition pp. 401–408

DAY 2 19.1 Phrases *(continued)*

Objectives: Identify, use, and understand verbals and verbal phrases (participles)

INSTRUCTION AND PRACTICE
Student Edition pp. 409–412

DAY 3 19.1 Phrases *(continued)*

Objectives: Identify, use, and understand verbals and verbal phrases (gerunds, infinitives)

INSTRUCTION AND PRACTICE
Student Edition pp. 413–416

DAY 4 19.2 Clauses

Objectives: Identify, use, and understand adjectival clauses

INSTRUCTION AND PRACTICE
Student Edition pp. 417–422

Alternate Pacing Plans

- **Block Scheduling** Each day in the Lesson Planner represents a 40–50 minute block. Teachers using block scheduling may combine days to revise pacing to meet their classroom needs.

- **Accelerated Lesson Planning** Combine instructional days, focusing on concepts called out by students' diagnostic test results.

- **Integrated Language Arts Curriculum** Use the instruction and practice in this chapter to provide reinforcement, remediation, or extension of grammar concepts taught in your literature curriculum.

Links to Prentice Hall *LITERATURE*

- **Unit 5** Prepositions and Appositives, p. 734; Gerunds and Gerund Phrases, p. 778

- **Unit 6** Independent and Subordinate Clauses, p. 854; Simple, Compound, and Complex Sentences, p. 874

Grammar Assessment

Grammar Coach:	Diagnostic Assessment	End-of-Chapter Assessment	Progress Monitoring
Personalized Instruction	Students take grammar diagnostic test online and are automatically assigned instruction and practice in areas where they need support.	Teacher uses **ExamView** to administer end-of-chapter assessment and remediation. Teachers may customize **ExamView** tests or use the ones provided.	Teachers may use the **Test Warm-Ups** and the **Cumulative Reviews** in the student book or eText to check students' mastery of grammar skills.
Teacher-Directed Instruction	Teacher administers the diagnostic test and determines focus of instruction and practice.		Students may also play **DimensionL** grammar video games to test their grammar skills.

WRITING COACH

Online

www.phwritingcoach.com

Grammar Assessment and Practice

Chapter diagnostic tests assess students' skills and assign instruction and practice.

DimensionL Video Games

Fast-paced interactive video games challenge students' mastery of grammar.

Lesson Planner continues on next page

DAY 5 19.2 Clauses (continued)

Objectives: Identify, use, and understand adverbial clauses	**INSTRUCTION AND PRACTICE** Student Edition pp. 423–425

DAY 6 19.3 Classifying Sentences by Structure

Objectives: Identify, use, and understand the four structures of sentences, including • simple sentences • compound sentences • complex sentences • compound-complex sentences	**INSTRUCTION AND PRACTICE** Student Edition pp. 426–431 Test Warm-Up p. 432

> **❝** *Powerful writing has a lot to do with the artful use of phrases and clauses. In these sentence parts are the potential of powerful detail. These grammatical structures, more than any other, help students paint clear pictures and establish rhythms and patterns in their writing.* **❞**
>
> **—Jeff Anderson**

> **❝** *Students like to write simple sentences, usually in the 6–10 word range. It is not until we teach them how to add branches (phrases and clauses) to their sentences that we begin to see their writing flourish. We want to move our students' sentencing past the 'palm tree' stage and into writing that exhibits multiple branching.* **❞**
>
> **—Kelly Gallagher**

Differentiated Instruction

Differentiated Instruction Boxes in this Teacher's Edition address these student populations:

• Below-Level Students

• Above-Level Students

• Gifted and Talented Students

• Special Needs Students

• English Language Learners

• Spanish Speaking Students

In addition, for further enrichment, see the Extension features.

PHRASES *and* CLAUSES

Understanding how to build sentences using phrases and clauses will help add variety to your writing.

WRITE GUY *Jeff Anderson, M.Ed.*

WHAT DO YOU NOTICE?

Look for phrases as you zoom in on sentences from the play *The Phantom Toll Booth* by Susan Nanus, based on the book by Norton Juster.

MENTOR TEXT

> This is Dictionopolis, a happy kingdom, advantageously located in the foothills of Confusion and caressed by gentle breezes from the Sea of Knowledge. Today, by royal proclamation, is Market Day.

Now, ask yourself the following questions:

- What purpose does the appositive phrase *a happy kingdom* serve in the first sentence?
- What are the prepositional phrases in the first sentence?

The appositive phrase *a happy kingdom* provides readers with more information about Dictionopolis. The five prepositional phrases in the first sentence are *in the foothills, of Confusion, by gentle breezes, from the Sea,* and *of Knowledge.*

Grammar for Writers Writers can use phrases to add more information to their sentences. Be sure to place phrases carefully in your sentences so that they modify the correct words.

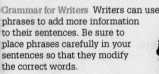

Are phrases always short?

It depends on who their parents are.

401

Grammar for Writers: Syntax

Help students understand that good writers use a variety of sentence types to keep their writing interesting. Not every sentence needs to have several phrases and clauses, but writers who can use these sentence elements correctly are better able to express their ideas. In the lessons, students will learn about different types of phrases and clauses they can use to make their writing clear, informative, and interesting.

PHRASES *and* CLAUSES

As students progress in their writing skills, it will be important for them to be able to apply the rules of grammar, usage, a1nd mechanics to their own drafts. Use the *What Do You Notice?* feature to help them see effective conventions in the work of professional writers. Encourage students to incorporate proper voice, tense, and syntax as they edit their own writing.

Read aloud the opening sentence. Remind students of the difference between phrases and clauses. A clause has a subject and a verb. A phrase may have one or the other, but it may not have both. Point out that both phrases and clauses are important to sentence structure. They are the building blocks of sentences. All types of sentences, no matter how long or complex, have at least one clause, and most have one or more phrases.

WRITE GUY *Jeff Anderson, M. Ed.*

WHAT DO YOU NOTICE?

When students have read the Mentor Text, **say:** Look again at the first sentence. Can anyone tell me the main clause of the sentence—the part that has the subject that tells what the sentence is about and the verb that goes with the subject? **(Response:** This is Dictionopolis. The subject is *This* and the verb is *is.*) Have students finish reading the page. **Say:** There are an appositive phrase and five prepositional phrases in the first sentence of the passage. **(Read the phrases aloud.) Ask:** What do the phrases add to the sentence? How would the meaning and impact of the sentence change if the phrases were omitted?

Help students see that the phrases add details that make the sentence more informative and interesting.

Lesson Objectives

1. Use and understand the function of adjectival phrases in reading, writing, and speaking.

2. Use and understand the function of adverbial phrases in reading, writing, and speaking.

3. Use and understand the function of appositive, participial, gerund, and infinitive phrases.

Prepositional Phrases

Discuss with students that one very common type of phrase is the prepositional phrase. As the name suggests, this type of phrase begins with a preposition.

RULE 19.1.1 Read aloud the rule and then have students repeat the lines with you.

Use a Think Aloud as part of a gradual release progression.

Think Aloud

Say: **I remember** that a preposition shows the relationship between a noun and another word in the sentence. So, if I say *The soup is on the stove,* I am using the preposition *on* to show the relationship between the soup and the stove. In this case, the prepositional phrase would be *on the stove.*

Explain that a prepositional phrase begins with a preposition and ends with a noun or pronoun—the *object of the preposition.* Have students name prepositions with which they are familiar, such as *in, out, above, below,* and *under.* **Work with students** to generate prepositional phrases using these prepositions or others they suggest.

Have pairs of students use these prepositional phrases to generate five original sentences. Ask pairs to share their sentences with the class.

19.1 Phrases

Sentences are usually built with more than just a subject and a verb. **Phrases** play an important role in sentences by adding more information.

RULE 19.1.1 A **phrase** is a group of words that functions in a sentence as a single part of speech. Phrases do not contain a subject and a verb.

Prepositional Phrases

A **prepositional phrase** has at least two parts, a preposition and a noun or pronoun that is the object of the preposition.

EXAMPLES

near **airports**
prep   object

around **trees**
prep   object

The object of the preposition may be modified by one or more adjectives.

EXAMPLES

near busy urban **airports**
prep adj adj   object

around lovely green **trees**
prep   adj   adj   object

The object may also be a compound, consisting of two or more objects connected by a conjunction such as *and* or *nor.*

EXAMPLES

near busy urban **highways** and **airports**
prep adj adj   object   object

around lovely green **trees** and **grass**
prep   adj   adj   object   object

In a sentence, some prepositional phrases can act as adjectives that modify a noun or pronoun. Other prepositional phrases can act as adverbs that modify a verb, adjective, or adverb.

402   Phrases and Clauses

Using Prepositional Phrases That Act as Adjectives

A prepositional phrase that acts as an adjective in a sentence is called an **adjective phrase** or **adjectival phrase**.

> An **adjective phrase** or **adjectival phrase** is a prepositional phrase that modifies a noun or pronoun by telling *what kind* or *which one*.

19.1.2 RULE

Unlike one-word adjectives, which usually come before the nouns or pronouns they modify, adjectival phrases usually come after the nouns or pronouns they modify.

ONE-WORD ADJECTIVES	ADJECTIVAL PHRASES
The asphalt roadway began there.	The roadway with two lanes began there.
The angry rancher stopped us.	The rancher with the angry face stopped us.

Adjectival phrases answer the same questions as one-word adjectives do. *What kind* of roadway began there? *Which* rancher stopped us?

USES OF ADJECTIVAL PHRASES	
Modifying a Subject	The sound of the wind scared us.
Modifying a Direct Object	It rattled windows in the room.

When two adjectival phrases appear in a row, the second phrase may modify the object of the preposition in the first phrase or both phrases may modify the same noun or pronoun.

ADJECTIVAL PHRASES IN A ROW	
Modifying the Object of a Preposition	The weather vane on the roof of the barn spun wildly.
Modifying the Same Noun	There was a smell of rain in the air.

ee Practice 19.1B

Using Prepositional Phrases That Act as Adjectives

Explain that a prepositional phrase can be used in a variety of ways in a sentence. When it is used as an adjective, it is called an adjective phrase or an adjectival phrase.

RULE 19.1.2 Read aloud the rule and then have students repeat the lines with you.

Say: Consider the sentence: *The bug in the spider's web seemed small and frail.* What is the prepositional phrase? **(in the spider's web)** Does this phrase give you more information about the verb *seemed* or the subject *bug*? **(bug)** When the phrase modifies, or gives more information about, a noun, it is acting as an adjective. This is an adjectival phrase.

On the board, write a few sentences that contain adjectival phrases. Have students identify the prepositional phrase, then decide if it modifies a noun in the sentence. Read aloud one of the sentences. Then, demonstrate how to identify the prepositional phrase. Remind students that it will always begin with a preposition and end with its object. Underline the prepositional phrase in the first sentence. Then, guide students in identifying and circling the noun the phrase modifies. You can use the questions *What kind?* and *Which one?* to help.

Working with ELLs   ELL Sheltered Instruction: Cognitive

Help students understand the general meaning, main points, and important details in spoken language in situations in which language ranges from familiar to unfamiliar. Describe a scene on a roadway incorporating two of the example sentences from the first chart on page 403.

Beginning Use visuals and mime to help students understand your description. Lead students in identifying the general meaning, main points, and important details for your description. Help them use more familiar language, such as *paved,* to understand less familiar language, such as *asphalt.*

Intermediate Have students restate the general meaning, main points, and important details of your description to a partner. Guide them in using familiar

language in your description, such as *yelled,* to understand less familiar language, such as *bellowed.*

Advanced Have students restate the general meaning, main points, and important details of your description by writing sentences using adjectival phrases. Have them identify unfamiliar words in your description and give definitions based on familiar context clues.

Advanced High Have students complete the Advanced activity. Extend by having them present their own descriptions of a roadway scene as partners take notes on general meaning, main points, and important details.

Using Prepositional Phrases That Act as Adverbs

Explain to students that prepositional phrases can also modify verbs, adjectives, and adverbs in sentences.

RULE 19.1.3 Read aloud the rule and then have students repeat the lines with you.

Use a Think Aloud as part of a gradual release progression.

Think Aloud

Say: Because an adjectival phrase is a prepositional phrase that acts as an adjective, it makes sense that an adverbial phrase is a prepositional phrase that acts as an adverb. To identify adverbial phrases, I remember that an adverb often gives information about the verb in a sentence. It can also tell more about adjectives and other adverbs.

Write on the board: *The circus practices in Florida before it tours its new show.* **Guide students** to identify the prepositional phrases. Then, show students that the phrases modify the verb *practices* by telling *when* and *where* the circus practices.

Have students read and discuss the examples of adverbial phrases on page 404 with a partner. Have students write two complete sentences using adverbial phrases and speak them aloud to a partner. Partners should identify the adbverbial phrases.

Using Prepositional Phrases That Act as Adverbs
A prepositional phrase that acts as an adverb modifies the same parts of speech as a one-word adverb does.

> An **adverbial phrase** or **adverb phrase** is a prepositional phrase that modifies a verb, an adjective, or an adverb. Adverbial phrases point out *where, when, in what way,* or *to what extent.*

Adverbial phrases are used in the same way as one-word adverbs, but they sometimes provide more precise details.

ONE-WORD ADVERBS	ADVERBIAL PHRASES
Bring your saddle here .	Bring your saddle to the barn .
The parade began early .	The parade began at exactly eleven o'clock .

Adverbial phrases can modify verbs, adjectives, and adverbs.

USES OF ADVERBIAL PHRASES	
Modifying a Verb	Raindrops fell in heavy torrents . (Fell *in what way?*)
Modifying an Adjective	The day was warm for December . (Warm *in what way?*)
Modifying an Adverb	The rain fell softly, for a monsoon storm . (Softly *in what way?*)

Adverbial phrases, unlike adjectival phrases, are not always located near the words they modify in a sentence.

MODIFIES

EXAMPLE **During the storm** , ranchers chased the herd.

Two or more adverbial phrases can also be located in different parts of the sentence and still modify the same word.

MODIFIES   MODIFIES

EXAMPLE **In an instant** , a tornado tore **through our house** . See Practice 19.1C See Practice 19.1D

Differentiated Instruction

RTI Strategy for Below-Level Students
Students may be having difficulty identifying prepositional phrases. Post a list of common prepositions in a prominent place where students may refer to it. Also, give students a "test" phrase as one way to identify a preposition. Phrases such as ____ the desk or ____ the building can be completed with prepositions: *in the desk, above the desk, under the desk.*

Enrichment for Gifted/Talented Students
Have students generate a list of interesting, concrete nouns. Show students that each noun can be used in a prepositional phrase. Brainstorm for these phrases and list them on the board. Using the list as a starting place, have students write poems or song lyrics in which each line uses an adjectival phrase. Musical students may want to compose a melody to go with their lyrics.

PRACTICE 19.1A ▸ Identifying Prepositional Phrases

Read the sentences. Then, write the prepositional phrase in each sentence and underline the object of the preposition. Then, write the function of the prepositional phrase (to convey *location, time,* or *direction,* or to provide *details*).

EXAMPLE   Stories exist in all societies.

ANSWER   *in all societies* — details

1. I found the professor in the chemistry lab.
2. Can you get my shirts from the cleaners?
3. She parked her bike in front of the store.
4. The advanced math concept was beyond his understanding.
5. They ran around the backyard.
6. The two baby girls were snug under the soft, warm, pink blanket.
7. I left the rake inside the tool shed.
8. The road runs between a forest and the river.
9. She read a history book during the first study period.
10. He backed his car into the neighbor's garage.

PRACTICE 19.1B ▸ Identifying Adjectival Phrases

Read the sentences. Then, write the adjectival phrase in each sentence. One sentence has two adjectival phrases.

EXAMPLE   The door to his office is locked.

ANSWER   *to his office*

11. The road toward the east is the one we will take.
12. Many of these books have great plots.
13. I want the one between the red and gray bicycles.
14. That's the birthday present from my grandmother.
15. The bed with the firm mattress was most comfortable.
16. The store at the corner has that magazine.
17. The sound of rushing water helped us find the waterfall.
18. I'm buying food for a friend with allergies.
19. This would be a great day for kite flying.
20. I bought a book about Booker T. Washington.

SPEAKING APPLICATION

With a partner, take turns talking about a trip to a store. Use at least four prepositional phrases (to convey *location, time,* or *direction,* or to provide *details*) including two adjectival phrases to describe something about the trip, such as where the store is, what it's like, or things you might buy there. Your partner should listen for and identify the prepositional phrases.

WRITING APPLICATION

Write a short paragraph about a trip into the country. Use prepositional phrases (to convey *location, time,* or *direction,* or to provide *details*) including adjectival phrases to describe the things you might see, hear, or experience.

Practice   **405**

PRACTICE 19.1A ▸

1. in the chemistry lab—location
2. from the cleaners—location
3. in front of the store—location
4. beyond his understanding—details
5. around the backyard—location
6. under the soft, warm, pink blanket—location
7. inside the tool shed—location
8. between a forest and the river—location
9. during the first study period—time
10. into the neighbor's garage—location

PRACTICE 19.1B ▸

11. toward the east
12. of these books
13. between the red and gray bicycles
14. from my grandmother
15. with the firm mattress
16. at the corner
17. of rushing water
18. for a friend, with allergies
19. for kite flying
20. about Booker T. Washington

SPEAKING APPLICATION

Partners should demonstrate that they understand prepositional phrases and can recognize adjectival phrases by identifying what each phrase modifies and justifying their answers.

WRITING APPLICATION

Students' sentences should demonstrate students' understanding of prepositional phrases that function as adverbs and adjectives.

Working with ELLs   **ELL** Sheltered Instruction: Cognitive

Help students use visual and contextual support to enhance and confirm understanding as they read and to develop vocabulary needed to comprehend increasingly challenging language.

Beginning Read item 1 in Practice 19.1A aloud as students track in their books. Using pictures to support your explanations, point out that *chemistry* is a field of science and review the meanings of *professor* and *lab.* Then, help students use context to determine that a *lab* might be a place to do or teach science. Clarify by providing an example.

Intermediate List these words from Practice 19.1A: *labs, cleaners, backyard, blanket,* and *forest.* Provide an image illustrating each, and have students work in small groups to match images with the words, using the context of the exercise items in which the words appear. Confirm results.

Advanced Provide an image illustrating each of these words from Practice 19.1A: *chemistry, advanced, period,* and *garage.* Have partners match images with the words, using the context of the exercise items in which the words appear. Have them confirm their conclusions in a dictionary.

Advanced High Have students complete the Advanced activity. Then, have them write a brief paragraph featuring each of the vocabulary words.

PRACTICE 19.1C

1. on a ferry
2. with a loud crash
3. in the rain
4. in hushed voices
5. on the soccer team
6. In the morning, before sunrise
7. under the table
8. in the cupboard
9. with increasing fury
10. toward the cheering crowd

PRACTICE 19.1D

Answers will vary. Sample answers:

11. Many rivers flow into the sea.
12. I would like a jacket with a hood.
13. We went swimming in the morning.
14. Jena works at the drugstore after school.
15. The bicycle with the red seat looks great.
16. The forest near our house is where we hike.
17. The football team practices on the playing field.
18. I bought a wooden box with a lock.
19. Some pieces of the puzzle are missing.
20. Before starting, we read the directions.

PRACTICE 19.1C Identifying Adverbial Phrases

Read the sentences. Then, write the adverbial phrase in each sentence. One sentence has two adverbial phrases.

EXAMPLE   Mother worried about our safety.

ANSWER   *about our safety*

1. We crossed Lake Michigan on a ferry.
2. The glasses fell with a loud crash.
3. He stood in the rain.
4. The children spoke in hushed voices.
5. Carlotta plays on the soccer team.
6. In the morning, before sunrise, my mom starts making breakfast.
7. The ball rolled under the table.
8. Put those groceries in the cupboard.
9. The rain came down with increasing fury.
10. Craig and Aaron ran toward the cheering crowd.

PRACTICE 19.1D Writing Adjectival and Adverbial Phrases

Read the sentences. Then, rewrite the sentences by adding adjectival or adverbial phrases, as directed in parentheses.

EXAMPLE   Close the door. (adjectival phrase)

ANSWER   Close the door *to the basement.*

11. Many rivers flow. (adverbial phrase)
12. I would like a jacket. (adjectival phrase)
13. We went swimming. (adverbial phrase)
14. Jena works at the drugstore. (adverbial phrase)
15. The bicycle looks great. (adjectival phrase)
16. The forest is where we hike. (adjectival phrase)
17. The football team practices. (adverbial phrase)
18. I bought a wooden box. (adjectival phrase)
19. Some pieces are missing. (adjectival phrase)
20. We read the directions. (adverbial phrase)

SPEAKING APPLICATION

With a partner, discuss the climate where you live. Use at least one adjectival phrase and one adverbial phrase to describe different types of weather you experience. Your partner should listen for and identify the adjectival and adverbial phrases.

WRITING APPLICATION

Write a short paragraph about a visit to an amusement park. Use at least one adjectival phrase and one adverbial phrase to describe what you do and what you see.

406   Phrases and Clauses

SPEAKING APPLICATION

Students should demonstrate they understand the function of adjectival and adverbial phrases in speaking by identifying what each phrase modifies and justifying their answer.

WRITING APPLICATION

Students should show they understand the function of adverbial phrases by identifying the adverbial phrase in their paragraph and explaining how it functions.

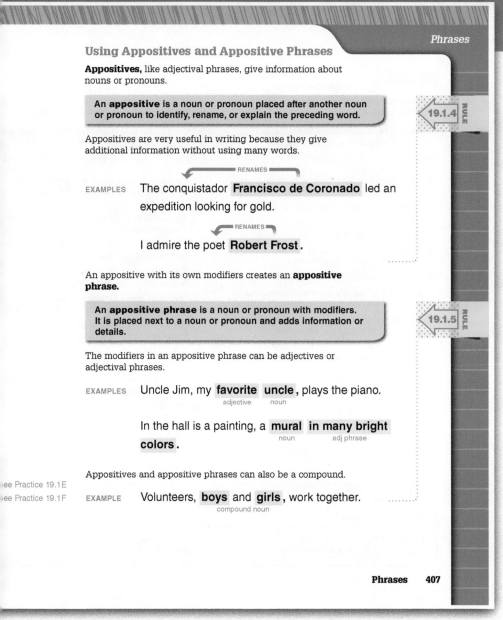

Using Appositives and Appositive Phrases

Appositives, like adjectival phrases, give information about nouns or pronouns.

> An **appositive** is a noun or pronoun placed after another noun or pronoun to identify, rename, or explain the preceding word.

19.1.4 RULE

Appositives are very useful in writing because they give additional information without using many words.

RENAMES

EXAMPLES   The conquistador **Francisco de Coronado** led an expedition looking for gold.

RENAMES

I admire the poet **Robert Frost** .

An appositive with its own modifiers creates an **appositive phrase.**

> An **appositive phrase** is a noun or pronoun with modifiers. It is placed next to a noun or pronoun and adds information or details.

19.1.5 RULE

The modifiers in an appositive phrase can be adjectives or adjectival phrases.

EXAMPLES   Uncle Jim, my **favorite uncle** , plays the piano.
                                adjective   noun

In the hall is a painting, a **mural in many bright colors** .
                                noun   adj phrase

Appositives and appositive phrases can also be a compound.

ee Practice 19.1E
ee Practice 19.1F   EXAMPLE   Volunteers, **boys** and **girls** , work together.
                                          compound noun

Using Appositives and Appositive Phrases

Explain that appositives provide information about a noun or pronoun by renaming, identifying, or explaining the noun or pronoun.

RULES 19.1.4, 19.1.5 Read aloud the rules and then have students repeat the lines with you.

Say: In the first example sentence on page 407, the name *Francisco de Coronado* is an appositive that gives us more information about the conquistador by telling us his name. An appositive comes immediately after a noun or pronoun that it modifies.

Say: You may recall that adjectives and adjectival phrases modify nouns. So an appositive, which is a noun, may be modified by an adjective or adjectival phrase. If so, the appositive and its adjective or adjectival phrase is called an appositive phrase. Consider the sentence *My brother loves to play video games.* How can I add an appositive to the sentence? (**Possible response:** My brother, Burt, loves to play video games.) How can I add an appositive phrase to the sentence? (**Possible response:** My brother, a tall, stringy kid named Burt, loves to play video games.)

Have students further demonstrate that they can identify and use appositive phrases and that they understand their function by identifying the appositive phrase in each of these sentences: *Kevin, the Ravens' captain, shouted that the team needed to work together. The sun, a golden globe, baked the dry desert.*

Help students understand implicit ideas and information in increasingly complex spoken language. Read the first half of page 407 aloud.

Beginning Guide students in restating the information about appositives that you have read. Use simple, familiar examples from the classroom, such as *Dolores, my student, sits there.* Then, help them understand the implicit idea in the second paragraph: It is often better not to use too many words in writing.

Intermediate Have students working in small groups restate the information that you have read. Then, guide them to

understand the implicit idea in the second paragraph by asking, *Why are appositives useful in writing? What does this show about good writing?*

Advanced Have partners restate the information you have read. Then, have them draw a conclusion about the qualities of good writing, based on the idea that appositives are useful in giving additional information without using many words.

Advanced High Have students complete the Advanced activity. Extend by having them write three sentences featuring appositives.

PRACTICE 19.1E

1. bicycle mechanics
2. Mozart
3. our neighbor
4. the largest state in the nation
5. Misha
6. one of Japan's three alphabets
7. the great Spanish singer
8. the 1920s
9. the great science fiction writer
10. animals that carry their young in pouches

PRACTICE 19.1F

11. Samuel Adams, an American patriot, entered Harvard at the age of 14.
12. Ancient Greeks played the lyre, a stringed instrument.
13. Thistles, the national flower of Scotland, are plants with purple flowers. *or* The thistle, a plant with purple flowers, is the national flower of Scotland.
14. Apples, members of the rose family, have white and pink flowers.
15. Sequoyah, a Cherokee, invented an alphabet for the Cherokee people.
16. The fourth Thursday in November is Thanksgiving, a national holiday.
17. A diamond, a form of pure carbon, is the hardest mineral in the world.
18. Dr. Martin Luther King Jr., a civil rights leader, was a great speaker. *or* Dr. Martin Luther King Jr., a great speaker, was a civil rights leader.
19. The pomegranate, a tart fruit, has many seeds.
20. The poem is about a gosling, a young goose.

PRACTICE 19.1E Identifying Appositives and Appositive Phrases

Read the sentences. Then, write the appositive or appositive phrase in each sentence.

EXAMPLE   My cousin, Sarah Donnelly, is a veterinarian at our local zoo.

ANSWER   *Sarah Donnelly*

1. The Wright brothers, bicycle mechanics, built the first successful airplane.
2. I enjoy music written by the composer Mozart.
3. We took flowers to Mrs. Tran, our neighbor.
4. Alaska, the largest state in the nation, covers more than 500,000 square miles.
5. My mom's cousin, Misha, will be visiting.
6. Kanji, one of Japan's three alphabets, was adapted from Chinese characters.
7. Placido Domingo, the great Spanish singer, will be performing here next week.
8. America's Jazz Age, the 1920s, saw a growing appreciation of African American art and music.
9. This story was told by Isaac Asimov, the great science fiction writer.
10. Marsupials, animals that carry their young in pouches, include kangaroos and koalas.

PRACTICE 19.1F Combining Sentences With Appositive Phrases

Read the sentences. Combine each pair of sentences by using an appositive phrase.

EXAMPLE   He won first prize. First prize is a tr to Hawaii.

ANSWER   *He won first prize, a trip to Hawa*

11. Samuel Adams was an American patriot. Samuel Adams entered Harvard at the age of 14.
12. Ancient Greeks played the lyre. The lyre is a stringed instrument.
13. Thistles are plants with purple flowers. The thistle is the national flower of Scotland.
14. Apples are members of the rose family. Apples have white and pink flowers.
15. Sequoyah was a Cherokee. Sequoyah invented an alphabet for the Cherokee peop
16. The fourth Thursday in November is Thanksgiving. It is a national holiday.
17. A diamond is the hardest mineral in the world. A diamond is a form of pure carbon.
18. Dr. Martin Luther King Jr. was a civil rights leader. Dr. King was a great speaker.
19. The pomegranate is a tart fruit. The pomegranate has many seeds.
20. The poem is about a gosling. A gosling is a young goose.

SPEAKING APPLICATION

With a partner, take turns telling about something you learned at school. Use two appositive phrases. Your partner should listen for and identify the appositive phrases.

WRITING APPLICATION

Write three sentences about a person or people you have studied. In each sentence, include an appositive phrase that adds information to the sentence.

408   Phrases and Clauses

SPEAKING APPLICATION

Have students demonstrate they can use and understand the function of appositive phrases in speaking by identifying the nouns to which the appositive phrases refer.

WRITING APPLICATION

Students' writing should demonstrate their ability to identify, use, and understand the function of appositive phrases in writing.

Using Verbals and Verbal Phrases

A **verbal** is any verb form that is used in a sentence not as a verb but as another part of speech.

Like verbs, verbals can be modified by an adverb or adverbial phrase. They can also be followed by a complement. A verbal used with a modifier or a complement is called a **verbal phrase.**

Participles
Participles are verb forms with two basic uses. When they are used with helping verbs, they are verbs. When they are used alone to modify nouns or pronouns, they become adjectives.

> **A participle** is a form of a verb that is often used as an adjective.

There are two kinds of participles, **present participles** and **past participles.** Each kind can be recognized by its ending.

All present participles end in *-ing*.

EXAMPLES   talking   doing   eating   wanting

Most past participles end either in *-ed* or in *-d*.

EXAMPLES   opened   jumped   played   moved

Other past participles end in *-n*, *-t*, *-en*, or another irregular ending.

EXAMPLES   grown   felt   bought   eaten   held

Both present and past participles can be used in sentences as adjectives. They tell *what kind* or *which one*.

PRESENT PARTICIPLES	PAST PARTICIPLES
He arranged a walking tour.	Chilled fruit tastes good.
The dancing bears were a delight.	He was, by then, a grown man.

See Practice 19.1G

Phrases   409

Help students use the sentences in Practice 19.1E on page 408 to enhance and confirm their understanding of the nouns and the appositive phrases in the sentences. Students should use support from peers and from you to read and to develop background knowledge needed to comprehend increasingly challenging language.

Beginning Prompt students to share their background knowledge about concepts such as *took, flowers,* and *neighbor* in Item 3. Have students read the words aloud with you. Then, use gestures and illustrations to act out the sentence and confirm their understanding.

Intermediate Have students read Item 1 aloud. Then, act out riding a bicycle.

Elicit background knowledge by asking questions such as *What is a person who builds machines called?* Encourage partners to share what they know about the subject.

Advanced Assign partners specific items from the Practice exercises. Have them read the sentences aloud and work together to determine meaning by sharing background knowledge. Partners can use a dictionary to confirm understanding.

Advanced High Have students complete the Advanced activity. Extend by having them create background notes for each item they worked on.

Using Verbals and Verbal Phrases

Explain that certain forms of verbs can sometimes be used as other parts of speech. When that is the case, they are called *verbals*. A verbal can be modified by an adverb, just like a regular verb, and it can have a complement.

Participles

Tell students that participles are a type of verbal.

RULE 19.1.6 Read aloud the rule and then have students repeat the lines with you.

Use a Think Aloud as part of a gradual release progression.

Think Aloud Say: I **use** verbals as adjectives all the time, such as when I say *The waddling ducks look funny* or *The wounded bird quickly got better. Waddling* and *wounded* are verb forms used to modify the nouns *ducks* and *bird*.

With students, review the examples of present participles and past participles on page 409. Then, write this sentence on the board: *The giggling girls annoyed their brother.* **Say:** Consider this sentence. What is the participle in the sentence? (**giggling**) What noun does it modify? (**girls**) How can you use *giggling* as a verb? (**Possible response:** The girls were giggling at the joke.)

Explain that participles can take either the present participle form of a verb (usually ending in *-ing*) or the past participle form (often ending in *-ed*).

Work with students to write two sentences: one using *rushing* as a verb, the other using it as a verbal. **Then, have students write their own sentences independently** using the participle *jumping*. Have students share their sentences with the class, explaining how they used participles.

Participle or Verb?

Help students understand and recognize the difference between a participle and a verb phrase.

Have students consider again the sentences *The barking dog made the man angry* and *The dog was barking.* **Then, say:** Notice that in the first sentence, *barking* describes the dog, so it functions as an adjective to modify the noun *dog*. In the second sentence, the subject of the sentence, *the dog,* is actually doing the barking, so it is part of the verb phrase *was barking*. To determine whether a verb form is used as a participle or verb, look at how it functions in the sentence.

Participial Phrases

Explain that a participle may be modified by other words. A participle with all of its modifiers is known as a participial phrase.

RULE 19.1.7 Read aloud the rule and then have students repeat the lines with you.

Write several participles on the board. Have students use them to generate sentences that include participles and participial phrases.

Participle or Verb?

Sometimes, verb phrases (verbs with helping verbs) are confused with participles. A verb phrase always begins with a helping verb. A participle used as an adjective stands by itself and modifies a noun or pronoun.

VERB PHRASES	PARTICIPLES
The car was racing around the curve.	The racing car crashed into the wall.
Early settlers may have traveled on this road.	The traveled road led to the sea.

Participial Phrases

A participle can be expanded into a participial phrase by adding a complement or modifier.

> **A participial phrase** is a present or past participle and its modifiers. The entire phrase acts as an adjective in a sentence.

Participial phrases can be formed by adding an adverb, an adverbial phrase, or a complement to a participle.

EXAMPLES   The instructor, **speaking slowly**, explained the use of skis.

The esteemed poet, **honored by the award**, expressed his thanks.

The first participial phrase contains the adverb *slowly* added to the participle *speaking*. The second includes the adverbial phrase *by the award* added to the participle *honored*.

A participial phrase can also be placed at the beginning of a sentence. The phrase is usually followed by a comma.

EXAMPLE   **Honored by the award**, the esteemed poet expressed his thanks.

See Practice 19.1H
See Practice 19.1I
See Practice 19.1J

410   **Phrases and Clauses**

Differentiated Instruction

RTI Strategy for Below-Level Students
Students may find it difficult to distinguish between verbs and participles. Write several common participles (e.g., *laughing, crying, running, traveling*) on index cards. Have students pick a card and make up a sentence that uses that word as either a verb or a participle. See if other students can identify whether the word was used as a verb or a participle in the sentence.

PRE-AP Enrichment for Above-Level Students One test students might use to help distinguish between verbs and participles is to identify another verb in the sentence. If so, the word is likely to be a participle. Post the sentence: *The babbling brook ran through the meadow.* Have students first identify the subject and verb. (brook, ran) This makes it easier to see that *babbling* is a participle.

This is a good opportunity to remind students that a word's part of speech doesn't depend on the word itself, but how it functions in the sentence.

PRACTICE 19.1G Identifying Present and Past Participles

[Rea]d the sentences. Then, write the participle in [each] sentence and label it *present participle* or [past] *participle*.

EXAMPLE   Holding onto the railing, the toddler
          went down the stairs.

[ANS]WER   *Holding — present participle*

[1.] The rabbit, hopping across the yard, saw [the] cat.

[2.] The only people allowed in the classroom are [s]tudents.

[3.] The actors, dressed in funny costumes, sprint [a]cross the stage.

[4.] Rushing down the hall, the doctor responds [t]o an emergency.

[5.] Chess is a challenging game.

[6.] The picture drawn in charcoal wins first prize [in] the art contest.

[7.] The bird hurt in the storm couldn't return to [it]s nest.

[8.] During the scavenger hunt, the best clue was [the] map hidden under the statue.

[9.] Neil's new running shoes were uncomfortable.

[10.] The laughter spreading through the audience [a]lmost brings the play to a halt.

PRACTICE 19.1H Distinguishing Verbs and Participles

Read the sentences. Then, write *verb* or *participle* for the underlined word in each sentence.

EXAMPLE   The woman standing in the corridor
          is the school principal.

ANSWER   *participle*

11. Those participating in the game were eager
    to start.

12. The airplane had landed twenty minutes
    early.

13. Dripping steadily, the leak filled the bucket in
    no time at all.

14. She was learning to play the guitar after
    school.

15. Greg showed up without any warning.

16. The plot of the mystery, taken from a recent
    news story, was familiar to everyone.

17. The trees cleared from the land were used to
    make wood for furniture.

18. The mayor is defending the new budget.

19. There were varying opinions on the success
    of the play.

20. The number of goals scored during the period
    was the highest of the season.

SPEAKING APPLICATION

With a partner, take turns describing a character in a book, movie, or television show. Use at least one present or past participle. Your partner should listen for and name the participle and tell whether it is present or past.

WRITING APPLICATION

Use sentence 13 as a model, and write one sentence with a participle. Then, use sentence 18 as a model, and write one sentence with a verb.

Practice   411

PRACTICE 19.1G

1. hopping—present participle
2. allowed—past participle
3. dressed—past participle
4. Rushing—present participle
5. challenging—present participle
6. drawn—past participle
7. hurt—past participle
8. hidden—past participle
9. running—present participle
10. spreading—present participle

PRACTICE 19.1H

11. participle
12. verb
13. participle
14. verb
15. verb
16. participle
17. participle
18. verb
19. participle
20. participle

SPEAKING APPLICATION

Students should demonstrate they can identify, use, and understand the function of participles by explaining how they know each word functions as a participle.

WRITING APPLICATION

Students' sentences should demonstrate that students can understand participles and use them in writing.

Working with ELLs   **ELL** Sheltered Instruction: Cognitive

Point out these content-based academic words from the Practice: *identify, distinguish,* and *describe.* Help students internalize new academic language by using and reusing this content-based grade-level academic vocabulary in writing activities.

Beginning Write the word *identify* and a simple sentence on the board. Circle the verb and say *I identified the verb.* Have students write *identify* on a card and draw a picture that illustrates its meaning. Then, guide them as they use and reuse the word in two written sentences of their own.

Intermediate Have students write the three terms on cards. Then, work through examples of each. On the back of each

card, have students write two example sentences using each word.

Advanced Have students use the **KIM strategy** to internalize, use, and reuse the academic terms. In a three-column chart, they should write *Key Word, Information,* and *Memory Cue* and write the word, a definition, and an example or illustration. Then, have them write two sentences using the words.

Advanced High Have students complete the Advanced activity. Then, have them complete the Practice and write sentences using the words to explain what they did.

PRACTICE 19.1I

1. <u>Told</u> around the campfire
2. <u>sent</u> by airmail
3. <u>measuring</u> up to 25 feet in length
4. <u>Originating</u> in Africa
5. <u>Heading</u> into the wind
6. <u>grown</u> in Texas
7. <u>ignoring</u> all warnings
8. <u>related</u> to the lily
9. <u>Climbing</u> the tree
10. <u>Impressed</u> by the student's interest

PRACTICE 19.1J

Answers will vary. Sample answers:

11. Growing quickly, the weeds soon overtook the small garden.
12. The students, followed by the principal, entered the auditorium.
13. Responding to the sunshine, the tulips were the first to bloom.
14. The music box, carved from wood, created a warm, rich sound.
15. Recognized by everyone, the captain could not avoid the press.
16. Emma, laughing happily, raced toward the ocean.
17. Caught by the wind, the kite swooped and dove gracefully.
18. Annoyed by the noise outside, my mom shut the window.
19. Praised by the critics, the author's first book sold well.
20. Silently watching the cheetah, Carl stood and held his breath.

PRACTICE 19.1I > **Identifying Participial Phrases**

Read the sentences. Then, write the participial phrase in each sentence. Underline the participle.

EXAMPLE   Snakes found in South America are often poisonous.

ANSWER   *found in South America*

1. Told around the campfire, the stories seemed particularly exciting.
2. Letters sent by airmail arrive faster.
3. Saltwater crocodiles, measuring up to 25 feet in length, are the largest reptiles.
4. Originating in Africa, many folktales about animals are shared around the world.
5. Heading into the wind, the geese began their flight.
6. The pecans grown in Texas are some of the best.
7. The boys, ignoring all warnings, walked onto the ice-covered pond.
8. This plant, related to the lily, is easy to grow.
9. Climbing the tree, the camper had a better view of her surroundings.
10. Impressed by the student's interest, the teacher let him use the microscope.

SPEAKING APPLICATION

With a partner, take turns talking positively about someone you know. Use two participial phrases. Your partner should listen for and identify the participial phrases.

PRACTICE 19.1J > **Combining Sentences Using Participial Phrases**

Read the sentences. Combine each pair of sentences by using a participial phrase.

EXAMPLE   Cassie was trusted by the students She was elected class president.

ANSWER   *Trusted by the students, Cassie was elected class president.*

11. The weeds were growing quickly. The weeds soon overtook the small garden.
12. The students entered the auditorium. The principal followed the students.
13. The tulips were the first to bloom. The tulips were responding to the sunshine.
14. The music box was carved from wood. The music box created a warm, rich sound.
15. Everyone recognized the captain. The captain could not avoid the press.
16. Emma was laughing happily. Emma raced toward the ocean.
17. The kite was caught by the wind. The kite swooped and dove gracefully.
18. My mom shut the window. The noise outside annoyed her.
19. The critics praised the author's first book. The book sold well.
20. Carl stood silently watching the cheetah. Carl held his breath.

WRITING APPLICATION

Write three sentences about an animal you have seen or read about. Include a participial phrase in each sentence to add information about the animal's appearance or behavior.

412   **Phrases and Clauses**

SPEAKING APPLICATION

Students should demonstrate they can use and understand the function of participles by identifying the participial phrases in their sentences, and naming the words that these phrases modify.

WRITING APPLICATION

Students should demonstrate they can use and understand the function of participles by identifying the participles in their sentences as past or present and naming the words the participles modify.

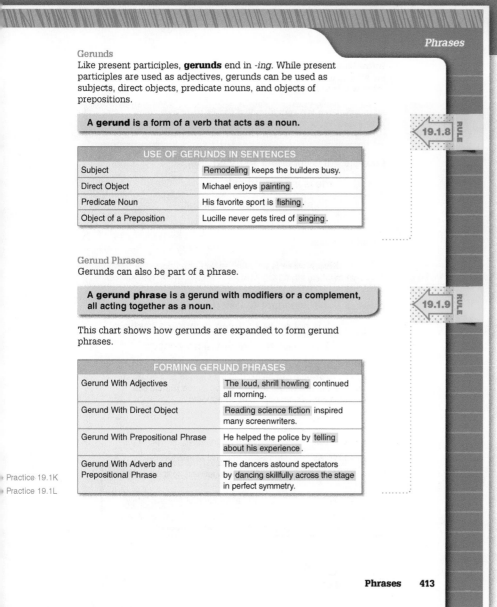

Gerunds

Like present participles, **gerunds** end in *-ing*. While present participles are used as adjectives, gerunds can be used as subjects, direct objects, predicate nouns, and objects of prepositions.

> A **gerund** is a form of a verb that acts as a noun.

19.1.8 RULE

USE OF GERUNDS IN SENTENCES	
Subject	Remodeling keeps the builders busy.
Direct Object	Michael enjoys painting .
Predicate Noun	His favorite sport is fishing .
Object of a Preposition	Lucille never gets tired of singing .

Gerund Phrases

Gerunds can also be part of a phrase.

> A **gerund phrase** is a gerund with modifiers or a complement, all acting together as a noun.

19.1.9 RULE

This chart shows how gerunds are expanded to form gerund phrases.

FORMING GERUND PHRASES	
Gerund With Adjectives	The loud, shrill howling continued all morning.
Gerund With Direct Object	Reading science fiction inspired many screenwriters.
Gerund With Prepositional Phrase	He helped the police by telling about his experience .
Gerund With Adverb and Prepositional Phrase	The dancers astound spectators by dancing skillfully across the stage in perfect symmetry.

• Practice 19.1K
• Practice 19.1L

Phrases   413

Gerunds

Explain that verbs can also be used as nouns. When these verbals end in *-ing*, they are called gerunds. For example, in the sentence *Running is good exercise,* the word *Running* is a gerund that functions as the subject of the sentence.

RULE 19.1.8   Read aloud the rule and then have students repeat the line with you.

Read aloud and discuss each example sentence. Point out that gerunds, like nouns, can function as the subject of a sentence, a direct object, a predicate noun, or the object of a preposition.

Gerund Phrases

Explain that a gerund with all of its modifiers and complements is a gerund phrase.

RULE 19.1.9   Read aloud the rule and then have students repeat the lines with you.

Use a Think Aloud as part of a gradual release progression.

Think Aloud

Say: Like other nouns, gerunds can be modified by adjectives and can become part of a prepositional phrase. **I can use** the gerund *crowing* with the adjective *loud* in the sentence *The entire farm was awakened by the loud crowing of the rooster.* Work with students to identify the preposition of which the gerund is the object (by), and the prepositional phrase that modifies the gerund (of the rooster).

Using the example sentences as a guide, **work with students to generate** sentences that include the gerunds *learning, sleeping, beeping,* and *practicing*.

Have pairs of students work together to use each of these gerunds as part of a gerund phrase in a sentence: *writing, fishing, swimming, eating, working*. Have students share their sentences with the class.

> *Teacher Tip*
>
> If students have trouble distinguishing gerunds from participles, have students start by eliminating the word as a participle. Give students this example: *Typing is difficult for me.* Have them examine the *-ing* word to see if it modifies a noun or pronoun. If it doesn't, then have them check to see if the word is part of the verb. If it is not part of the verb in the sentence, it is most likely a gerund.

Working with ELLs   **ELL** Sheltered Instruction: Cognitive

Use Practice 19.1I on page 412 to allow students to practice speaking using a variety of sentence types, including sentences featuring participial phrases. Ensure that students speak with increasing accuracy and ease.

Beginning   Read a sentence from Practice 19.1I. Then, have students echo you. Ask students to suggest an additional detail about a person or object in the sentence. Add this detail to the original sentence, and say the new sentence aloud. Have students repeat.

Intermediate   Have partners read aloud the sentences in items 8–10 from Practice 19.1I. Then, challenge students to change the information in one sentence,

such as the participle or the plant named in Item 8. Have students say their revised sentence to their partner while the partner identifies the participial phrase.

Advanced   Have partners each choose three items from Practice 19.1I and say a new sentence describing a person or object in each. Direct them to use participial phrases. For example, for Item 10 a student might say: *Spying the microscope, the student asked the teacher to let her use it.*

Advanced High   Have students complete the Advanced activity. Then, have them orally describe three objects in the classroom using participial phrases.

Infinitives

Explain that some verb forms can be used as nouns, adjectives, and adverbs. These verb forms, known as infinitives, usually begin with the word *to*.

RULE 19.1.10 Read aloud the rule and then have students repeat the lines with you.

Have students brainstorm for a list of verb forms that begin with *to,* such as *to be, to have, to say, to take.* Point out that these forms are very common and that their function as nouns is extremely versatile. Write this sentence on the board: *My brother loves to swim.* Explain that in this sentence *to swim* is an infinitive that functions as a noun—the direct object of the verb *loves.* Walk through the examples for rule 19.1.10 with students, discussing how each infinitive works in its sentence. Clarify that *to* can also be used as a preposition meaning "toward," but that is not its meaning when used as part of an infinitive. Have students brainstorm for sentences using the verbs listed above as infinitives.

Infinitive Phrases

Explain that, like gerunds, infinitives can be part of a phrase.

RULE 19.1.11 Read aloud the rule and then have students repeat the lines with you.

Review with students the uses of infinitives and example sentences in the Uses of Infinitives chart. Then, have pairs of students work together to generate sentences with infinitives and infinitive phrases. Students can write three to four sentences that use an infinitive, then switch sentences with a partner. Partners will add modifiers or a complement to the infinitive to make it an infinitive phrase. Example: *He wanted to go* can become *He wanted to go to the store.*

Infinitives

Infinitives are verb forms that are used as nouns, adjectives, and adverbs. Like participles and gerunds, they can be combined with other words to form phrases.

 RULE 19.1.10

> An **infinitive** is a verb form that can be used as a noun, an adjective, or an adverb. The word *to* usually appears before the verb.

EXAMPLES

It is important **to listen**.

He is the one **to ask**.

To stay calm can be difficult.

Infinitive Phrases

 RULE 19.1.11

> An **infinitive phrase** is an infinitive with modifiers or a complement, all acting together as a single part of speech.

EXAMPLES

It is important **to listen carefully**.

It is not polite **to listen through a keyhole**.

They want **to give you a present**.

An **infinitive phrase** can be used in a sentence as a noun, an adjective, or an adverb. As a noun, an infinitive phrase can function as a subject, an object, or an appositive.

USES OF INFINITIVES	
Used as a Subject	To speak slowly is important.
Used as an Object	She tried to speak slowly.
Used as an Appositive	His suggestion, to speak slowly, was appreciated.
Used as an Adjective	It was her goal to speak slowly.
Used as an Adverb	It isn't always easy to speak slowly when you are excited.

See Practice 19.1M
See Practice 19.1N

Differentiated Instruction

RTI Strategy for Special Needs Students
Before discussing infinitives, show students several simple present- and future-tense sentences, such as *I walk. I get a seat in the front row. He will never have a party. She is giving a speech.* Read the sentences aloud and identify the verb in each. Have a student volunteer underline the verb in each sentence as you identify it.

Write a large *To* on a sheet of paper. Read each sentence again, and then hold up the *To* sign. Rephrase the sentence using *to.* For example, *I like to walk. I will run to get a seat in the front row. He will never get to have a party. She is going to give a speech.*

Tell students that when they see *to* before a verb, it is called an **infinitive**.

PRACTICE 19.1K Identifying Gerund Phrases

[Read] the sentences. Then, write the gerund [phra]se from each sentence, and underline the [geru]nd. Remember to include all modifiers with [the p]hrase.

EXAMPLE   The constant dripping began to bother me.

ANSWER   *The constant dripping*

[M]oving gracefully is important in women's [g]ymnastics.

[H]e gained confidence from his running.

[S]tudying for the math exam took two hours.

[T]he first step is buying the right equipment.

[R]ocking the crib might get the baby to sleep.

[C]handra took off the bandages without [c]onsidering the consequences.

[S]tudying weather patterns helps scientists [f]orecast the weather.

[U]se a sharp knife when cutting the [v]egetables.

[T]he sweet, cheerful chirping of the birds told [th]e spring was coming soon.

[C]ounting your change is always a good idea.

PRACTICE 19.1L Writing Gerunds and Gerund Phrases

Read the sentences. Then, rewrite each sentence, completing it with a gerund or gerund phrase.

EXAMPLE   In the summer, I do a lot of _____.

ANSWER   *In the summer, I do a lot of swimming.*

11. I enjoy _____ for bargains.

12. _____ helped prepare me for the English test.

13. It's important to use the right tools when _____.

14. My mom regretted _____ that dress.

15. The _____ could be heard for miles.

16. When the hikers returned, they told us about _____.

17. _____ can really mess up the kitchen.

18. He gained satisfaction from _____.

19. The most fun activity in the winter is _____.

20. _____ is the first step in making soup.

Practice   415

PRACTICE 19.1K

1. <u>Moving</u> gracefully

2. his <u>running</u>

3. <u>Studying</u> for the math exam

4. <u>buying</u> the right equipment

5. <u>Rocking</u> the crib

6. <u>considering</u> the consequences

7. <u>Studying</u> weather patterns

8. <u>cutting</u> the vegetables

9. The sweet, cheerful <u>chirping</u> of the birds

10. <u>Counting</u> your change

PRACTICE 19.1L

Answers will vary. Sample answers:

11. I enjoy shopping for bargains.

12. Studying grammar helped prepare me for the English test.

13. It's important to use the right tools when fixing a watch.

14. My mom regretted buying that dress.

15. The loud ringing could be heard for miles.

16. When the hikers returned, they told us about seeing a hawk.

17. Making bread can really mess up the kitchen.

18. He gained satisfaction from playing the piano.

19. The most fun activity in the winter is building a snowman.

20. Finding the right pot is the first step in making soup.

Quick-Write Extension

To help students synthesize and apply what they have learned about gerunds, have the class write a poem in which lines begin with gerunds. Have each student list at least three gerund phrases that name activities they enjoy doing; for example, *listening to music, talking with friends, reading mysteries.* On the board, write the first line of the poem: *We enjoy.* Then, call on students at random to read aloud their list of gerund phrases. Write each phrase beneath the line *We enjoy* to create a poem; for example, *We enjoy / listening to music, / talking with friends, / reading mysteries,* and so on.

PRACTICE 19.1M

1. <u>To find</u> the solution to the puzzle—noun
2. <u>to hold</u> the baby gently—noun
3. <u>to escape</u> communism—adverb
4. <u>to write</u> before Friday—adjective
5. <u>to speak</u> in front of a large group—noun
6. <u>To see</u> our grandmother smiling—noun
7. <u>to build</u> a new house—adjective
8. <u>to buy</u> groceries—adverb
9. <u>to go</u> to the beach—noun
10. <u>to raise</u> money for hungry children—adjective

PRACTICE 19.1N

Answers will vary. Sample answers:

11. to build
12. to plant
13. To see the ocean
14. to go to college
15. to sing
16. To read the next chapter in her book
17. to finish
18. to widen the road
19. To see my dad fixing dinner
20. to travel

SPEAKING APPLICATION

Have students identify how they recognized the infinitive phrases and infinitive verbs in their partners' sentences.

WRITING APPLICATION

Have students trade sentences with a partner. Partners should identify the infinitive phrases in each other's sentences.

PRACTICE 19.1M ▶ **Identifying Infinitives and Infinitive Phrases**

Read the sentences. Then, write the infinitive phrase from each sentence, and underline the infinitive. Also write *noun*, *adjective*, or *adverb* to describe each infinitive phrase.

EXAMPLE   The easiest way to get there is through the woods.

ANSWER   *to get there* — adjective

1. To find the solution to the puzzle was Katrina's goal.
2. You can trust Miguel to hold the baby gently.
3. The Kim family came from North Korea to the United States to escape communism.
4. Sarai has a paper to write before Friday.
5. John's goal is to speak in front of a large group.
6. To see our grandmother smiling was reassuring.
7. Their plan to build a new house will be challenging.
8. My mom went to buy groceries.
9. We all wanted to go to the beach.
10. The project to raise money for hungry children was successful.

SPEAKING APPLICATION

With a partner, take turns talking about school assignments. Use the sentences in Practice 19.1M as models to help you include two infinitive phrases. Your partner should listen for and identify the infinitive phrases.

PRACTICE 19.1N ▶ **Writing Infinitives and Infinitive Phrases**

Read the sentences. Then, rewrite each senten___ completing it with an infinitive or an infinitive phrase.

EXAMPLE   Last summer we went ____ our favorite cousins.

ANSWER   *Last summer we went to visit our favorite cousins.*

11. His plan ____ was approved.
12. The class wanted ____ for Earth Day.
13. ____ is really unforgettable.
14. Marsha's dream is ____.
15. Why don't you ask your friends ____?
16. ____ was all that Clara had planned for th___ evening.
17. Don't you have a report ____?
18. The proposal ____ was put up for a vote.
19. ____ made everyone happy.
20. Grandfather wanted ____ after he retired.

WRITING APPLICATION

Use the sentences in Practice 19.1M as models, and write three sentences about everyday life that include infinitive phrases.

Working with ELLs   **ELL** Sheltered Instruction: Cognitive

Adapt the Writing Application by having students write sentences with infinitive phrases about the purpose of an everyday object. Guide students to use sentences of a variety of grade-appropriate lengths in increasingly accurate ways.

Beginning Show a pencil. Ask: *What is this? What can I use it for?* Act out using the object. Then provide the cloze sentence *I use ____ to write.* Have students complete the sentence by writing words such as *pens, pencils,* or *chalk.* Have students increase sentence length by adding words such as *sometimes* or *always.*

Intermediate Have student pairs write sentences describing the purposes of an everyday object using the sentence frame

You can use ____ to ____. Have them increase the length of their sentences by adding alternatives: *You can use ____ or ____ to ____.*

Advanced Have partners work together on a paragraph describing different uses for an everyday object, using infinitives. Have them increase sentence length by adding details.

Advanced High Have students write a paragraph that describes the uses of an everyday object using at least two infinitives. Students should check their sentences for accuracy. Then, have them combine sentences to create a variety of sentence lengths.

19.2 Clauses

Clauses are the basic structural unit of a sentence.

A **clause** is a group of words with its own subject and verb.

There are two basic kinds of clauses, **main** or **independent clauses** and **subordinate clauses.**

A **main** or **independent clause** has a subject and a verb and can stand by itself as a complete sentence.

As you can see in the examples below, a main clause can be long or short. All main clauses express a complete thought and can stand by themselves as complete sentences.

EXAMPLES   The **air vibrated**.
             subject verb

             Early in the day, **he began** playing the cello.
                               subject verb

A **subordinate clause,** also known as a dependent clause, has a subject and a verb but cannot stand by itself as a complete sentence. It is only part of a sentence.

SUBORDINATE   after **she performed** her solo
CLAUSES   subject verb

             while the **band practiced** in the garage
                        subject verb

After reading a subordinate clause, you will still need more information to have a complete sentence.

Clauses   417

Lesson Objectives

1. Differentiate between main and subordinate clauses.

2. Identify, use, and understand the function of adjectival clauses in reading, writing, and speaking.

3. Identify, use, and understand the function of adverbial clauses and subordinating conjunctions in reading, writing, and speaking.

Have students recall that the basic parts of a sentence are the subject and the verb. Unlike phrases, clauses contain both of these parts.

RULE 19.2.1 Read aloud the rule and then have students repeat the line with you.

Clarify that the terms *main clause* and *independent clause* are used interchangeably.

RULE 19.2.2 Read aloud the rule and then have students repeat the lines with you.

Use a Think Aloud as part of a gradual release progression.

Think Aloud

Say: **I know** that *independent* means that something or someone can work on its own without help. If a person is independent, it means he or she does not ask for help. So independent clauses do not need help. They can stand alone as sentences.

Write several sentences on the board and **guide students** in identifying the main clause in one or two of these. Point out that every sentence will have a main, or independent, clause.

Have students work independently to identify the main clause in the remaining sentences. Remind students that they are working *independently* to identify *independent* clauses.

RULE 19.2.3 Read aloud the rule and then have students repeat the lines with you.

Clarify that the terms *subordinate clause* and *dependent clause* are interchangeable. Discuss why the subordinate clauses on page 417 cannot stand alone as sentences.

RULE 19.2.4 Read aloud the rule and then have students repeat the lines with you.

Tell students that page 418 gives them several clues for identifying a subordinate, or dependent, clause. Point out the subordinating conjunctions and explain that many subordinate clauses begin with these types of conjunctions. Another clue is that subordinate clauses may begin with a relative pronoun. Review examples of subordinating conjunctions and relative pronouns.

Read aloud the example sentences and discuss why each clause is either a main clause or a subordinate clause.

Teacher Tip

If students are having trouble keeping the terms *independent clause*, *dependent clause*, *main clause*, and *subordinate clause* straight, clarify by drawing on their prior knowledge. For example, **say:** A subordinate is someone who works under the authority of someone else. They are not independent. They are dependent on their employer, commanding officer, or other authority figure. Encourage students to make similar connections and share them with the class.

RULE 19.2.4 ▶

> Subordinate clauses begin with **subordinating conjunctions** or **relative pronouns.**

Some subordinate clauses begin with **subordinating conjunctions,** such as *if, since, when, although, after, because,* and *while.* Others begin with **relative pronouns,** such as *who, which,* or *that.* These words are clues that the clause may not be able to stand alone. Notice how the addition of subordinating words changes the meaning of the main clauses in the examples below.

COMPARING TWO KINDS OF CLAUSES	
MAIN	SUBORDINATE
He arrives this morning.	*when* he arrives this morning
This mosque has a golden dome.	*because* the mosque has a golden dome
I planted the seeds.	the seeds *that* I planted

In order to form a complete thought, a subordinate clause must be combined with a main clause.

EXAMPLES   **After she performed her piece**, Debbie felt
                  subordinate clause   main clause
relieved.

The audience applauded **after Debbie performed**
                              main clause   subordinate clause
her piece.

It was Debbie **who was asked to perform first**.
       main clause   subordinate clause

When he arrives this morning, Tom needs to
          subordinate clause   main clause   See Practice 19.2A
go right to the nurse.   See Practice 19.2B

Working with ELLs   ELL Sheltered Instruction: Cognitive

Have students use visual and contextual support as they read the student page to enhance and confirm understanding and to develop a grasp of language structures needed to comprehend increasingly challenging language.

Beginning Read aloud the first set of examples in the chart on page 418 while students follow along in their books. Have students repeat each clause after you. Point out that both main and subordinate clauses have a subject and verb—called out by highlighting—but that only the main clause is a complete idea, indicated by the use of capital letters and periods.

Intermediate Have partners take turns reading the chart examples. Prompt them to verbally compare and contrast main and subordinate clauses, using visual support such as the highlighting and the italicized words.

Advanced Have partners review the chart and use the visual support to verbally compare and contrast main and subordinate clauses. Then, have them read the examples and explain how they can distinguish subordinate from main clauses.

Advanced High Have students complete the Advanced activity. Then, challenge them to create their own sentences with main and subordinate clauses.

PRACTICE 19.2A Identifying Main and Subordinate Clauses

Read the clauses. Then, write whether each clause is a *main clause* or a *subordinate clause*.

EXAMPLE   Because archaeology is a science.

ANSWER   *subordinate clause*

1. Where many seashells are found.
2. The rules of the game are easy.
3. After the third person walked across the hall.
4. Which meant someone had to call for help immediately.
5. Until the storm finally passed.
6. The team listened intently to the coach's words.
7. He worked hard.
8. That was hiding in plain sight on the lowest bookshelf in the library.
9. Whose paper was about to rip apart.
10. It seemed unbelievable to most listeners.

PRACTICE 19.2B Identifying and Using Main and Subordinate Clauses

Read the clauses. Write *main clause* or *subordinate clause* for each clause. Then, expand each subordinate clause into a complete sentence by adding a main clause.

EXAMPLE   Since the snowstorm ended.

ANSWER   *subordinate clause*
We have been shoveling the driveway since the snowstorm ended.

11. When you are ready.
12. Every day is a new opportunity.
13. Although it was hot and sunny outside.
14. If the trumpet solo is easy enough to learn.
15. Jumping over a hurdle is difficult.
16. All the mail arrived safely.
17. After he arrived.
18. Ambulance driving is dangerous.
19. Even babies respond to smiles.
20. Who worked every weekend for a month.

SPEAKING APPLICATION

With a partner, take turns saying a subordinate clause. Your partner should expand the subordinate clause into a complete sentence by adding a main clause.

WRITING APPLICATION

Write three complete sentences about what you did at school today. Include a main clause and a subordinate clause. Circle the main clause and underline the subordinate clause in each sentence.

Practice   419

PRACTICE 19.2A

1. subordinate clause
2. main clause
3. subordinate clause
4. subordinate clause
5. subordinate clause
6. main clause
7. main clause
8. subordinate clause
9. subordinate clause
10. main clause

PRACTICE 19.2B

11. subordinate clause
Sample answer: I'll be ready to go when you are ready.
12. main clause
13. subordinate clause
Sample answer: Although it was hot and sunny outside, Gracie was shivering.
14. subordinate clause
Sample answer: I think my sister will play in the concert if the trumpet solo is easy enough to learn.
15. main clause
16. main clause
17. subordinate clause
Sample answer: We started the tournament after he arrived.
18. main clause
19. main clause
20. subordinate clause
Sample answer: It was my mother who worked every weekend for a month.

SPEAKING APPLICATION

Have partners explain how they knew the words they added to each other's sentences were main clauses. Students' explanations should demonstrate that students can differentiate between main and subordinate clauses in speaking.

WRITING APPLICATION

Have each student read one of his or her sentences aloud and identify which clause is the main clause and which is the subordinate.

Adjectival Clauses

Tell students that we classify words and groups of words in a sentence according to the function they have in the sentence. So, a clause that is functioning as an adjective in a sentence is called an adjectival clause.

RULE 19.2.5 Read aloud the rule and then have students repeat the lines with you.

Say: Adjectives, such as *cute, yellow,* and *soft,* modify nouns, such as *chick*. When a subordinate clause modifies a noun, it is called an adjectival clause. You can use the questions *What kind?* and *Which one?* to help decide if a subordinate, or dependent, clause is adjectival.

Recognizing Adjectival Clauses

With students, review the example sentences in the "Adjectival Clauses" chart on page 420. Pay special attention to the question that each clause answers.

Post the clue words *that, which, who, whom, whose, since, where,* and *when* where students can easily refer to them.

Say: Consider the sentence, *The boy, who had run into the room, stopped and looked around.* What is the clue word that indicates the presence of an adjectival clause? **(who)** Repeat with other examples.

Adjectival Clauses

A subordinate clause will sometimes act as an adjective in a sentence. An adjectival clause or adjective clause is a dependent clause and can not stand on its own.

> An **adjectival clause** or **adjective clause** is a subordinate clause that modifies a noun or a pronoun.

Like one-word adjectives and adjectival phrases, **adjectival clauses** tell *what kind* or *which one*.

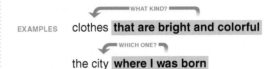

EXAMPLES   clothes **that are bright and colorful**

the city **where I was born**

Recognizing Adjectival Clauses

Most adjectival clauses begin with the words *that, which, who, whom,* and *whose*. Sometimes an adjectival clause begins with a subordinating conjunction, such as *since, where,* or *when*. In the chart below, the adjectival clauses are hightlighted in pink.

ADJECTIVAL CLAUSES
The teacher whom I asked for help stayed after school to work with me. (*Which* teacher?)
The talent show, which was advertised in the local paper, is tomorrow. (*Which* talent show?)
In the years since she started playing, Maia has become an accomplished pianist. (*Which* years?)
I hid my treasure box in the small closet where no one usually goes. (*Which* closet?)
We visited the museum that honors veterans of World War II. (*Which* museum?)
The museum whose exhibits include aircraft carriers is located in our town. (*Which* museum?)

See Practice 19.2C

Combining Sentences With Adjectival Clauses

Two sentences can be combined into one sentence by changing one of them into an adjectival clause. Sometimes you will need to add a relative pronoun or subordinating conjunction to make the sentence read correctly. In the sentences below, the adjectival clauses are highlighted in pink.

TWO SENTENCES	COMBINED WITH AN ADJECTIVAL CLAUSE
My history teacher has written books on the American Revolution. My history teacher is a famous scholar.	My history teacher, who has written books on the American Revolution, is a famous scholar.
We visited the history museum. The history museum is Tori's favorite museum.	We visited the history museum, which is Tori's favorite.
We decided to shop in Don's Grocery. We usually get the best bargains there.	We decided to shop in Don's Grocery, where we usually get the best bargains.
Paula visited her cousin last summer. Paula's cousin lives on a farm in Kansas.	Paula visited her cousin, who lives on a farm in Kansas, last summer.
Every summer, Elizabeth goes to a camp. Her camp is on a beautiful lake.	Every summer, Elizabeth goes to a camp that is on a beautiful lake.

Practice 19.2D

Combining Sentences With Adjectival Clauses

Tell students that combining two sentences into one sentence is a way to make your writing flow more gracefully. It also adds interest by clearly showing the relationship between two thoughts. In many cases, adjectival clauses can be used to join two closely related sentences.

Say: I know that when two sentences are related in some way, it can be helpful to show how they are related. The sentences *The wolves are prowling the forest* and *The wolves are very hungry* can be combined into *The wolves, which are very hungry, are prowling the forest*. The relative pronoun *which* shows the relationship between the two thoughts.

Read aloud the example sentences with students and guide them in identifying which ones use a relative pronoun and which one uses a subordinating conjunction *(. . . where we usually get the best bargains)*. Then, write these sentences on the board: *Laura makes necklaces to sell at the fair. Laura is very talented.*

Have students work together to combine the sentences by making one of them into an adjectival clause. Then, ask students to compare their sentences with a partner's sentences.

Differentiated Instruction

RTI Strategy for Below-Level Students
Combining sentences and turning one sentence into an adjectival clause may be difficult for some students. For students needing extra assistance, have them use a two-column chart modeled after the one on page 421. Students write two sentences in each cell in the first column labeled *Two Sentences*. Both sentences in a cell must *either* have the same subject *or* the second sentence must give information about the direct object of the first sentence. Partners combine the sentences to complete the second column.

PRE-AP Enrichment for Above-Level Students Have students look in books, magazines, and newspapers to find pairs of sentences that could be combined using an adjectival clause. Have students rewrite the sentences using adjectival clauses. Encourage students to improve the quality of the sentences by adding additional detail or by revising the language in the sentences. You may want to keep a running total of the "improved" sentences that each student has submitted.

PRACTICE 19.2C

1. that Sam saw at the aquarium   2. who asked if we could leave   3. whose bark is loud   4. whom she had not seen in many days   5. who will be the soloist tonight   6. whom he never met; who named him   7. that were easy to follow   8. which no one ever took   9. where the playwright was born   10. when technological innovation was the greatest

PRACTICE 19.2D

Answers will vary. Sample answers:

11. The middle school held a science fair, which was a great success.

12. The thunderstorm ruined the picnic, which was for the softball team.

13. Tarik, whose cousin was visiting from Louisiana, hosted a Fourth of July party.

14. The dentist, who examined my teeth, was happy I had no cavities.

15. A snake that was slithering in the grass startled me.

16. Babies whose mothers leave the room often start crying.

17. Adam, who is in good shape, ran his eighth marathon last year. *or* Adam, who ran his eighth marathon last year, is in good shape.

18. The firehouse, which was just rebuilt, is ready to house a new engine.

19. Talia, who did not know anyone, was the last to arrive. *or* Talia, who was the last to arrive, did not know anyone.

20. The letter that was waiting for him at home was an acceptance letter.

SPEAKING APPLICATION

Have students explain how they recognized the adjectival clause.

WRITING APPLICATION

Have students explain the process they used to combine sentences.

PRACTICE 19.2C **Identifying Adjectival Clauses**

Read the sentences. Then, write the adjectival clause in each sentence. One sentence has two adjectival clauses.

EXAMPLE   The book, which my sister lent me, was totally engrossing.

ANSWER   *which my sister lent me*

1. The fish that Sam saw at the aquarium were incredibly colorful.

2. The movie scared my cousin, who asked if we could leave.

3. Your dog, whose bark is loud, is actually a nice dog, isn't he?

4. Heather's neighbors, whom she had not seen in many days, had been away on vacation.

5. The violinist who will be the soloist tonight is originally from Poland.

6. Jerry's great-grandmother, whom he never met, was the person who named him.

7. She had a strong preference for recipes that were easy to follow.

8. The path, which no one ever took, was overgrown and almost impassable.

9. The house where the playwright was born is now a tourist site.

10. Until now, the era when technological innovation was the greatest was the Industrial Revolution.

SPEAKING APPLICATION

With a partner, take turns describing something in the classroom. Use at least one adjectival clause. Your partner should listen for and identify the adjectival clause.

PRACTICE 19.2D **Combining Sentences Using Adjectival Clauses**

Read the sentences. Combine the pairs of sentences by changing one of them into an adjectival clause.

EXAMPLE   Kyle and Marcus ran indoors. They were dying of thirst.

ANSWER   *Kyle and Marcus, who were dying of thirst, ran indoors.*

11. The middle school held a science fair. The science fair was a great success.

12. The thunderstorm ruined the picnic. The picnic was for the softball team.

13. Tarik's cousin was visiting from Louisiana. Tarik hosted a Fourth of July party.

14. The dentist examined my teeth. The dentist was happy I had no cavities.

15. A snake startled me. The snake was slithering in the grass.

16. The babies' mothers leave the room. Babies often start crying.

17. Adam ran his eighth marathon last year. Adam is in good shape.

18. The firehouse was just rebuilt. The firehouse is ready to house a new engine.

19. Talia was the last to arrive. Talia did not know anyone.

20. The letter was waiting for him at home. The letter was an acceptance letter.

WRITING APPLICATION

Use the sentences in Practice 19.2D as models, and write two pairs of sentences. Then, for each pair, combine the sentences by changing one of them into an adjectival clause.

Working with ELLs   **ELL** Sheltered Instruction: Cognitive

Help students learn the academic vocabulary term *adjectival clauses* using prior knowledge. Draw a Venn Diagram with circles labeled *adjectives* and *clauses*, and the area of overlap labeled *adjectival clauses*. Then:

Beginning Review the meaning of *adjectives* and *clauses* with students, using simple definitions, examples, and gestures as necessary. Then have students identify the *adjectives, clauses,* and *adjectival clauses* sections of the **Venn Diagram.** Discuss the meaning of the new term drawing on their prior knowledge of the other terms.

Intermediate Review the **Venn Diagram**. Have students working in groups draw

their own version and give examples of adjectives and clauses based on prior knowledge. Then, help them define *adjectival clauses*.

Advanced Have partners draw their own **Venn Diagram** with examples of adjectives and clauses. Have students use prior academic knowledge to explain the traits that adjectives and clauses share with adjectival clauses.

Advanced High Have students complete the Advanced activity and then generate sentences that include adjectival clauses.

Adverbial Clauses

Subordinate clauses can also be used as adverbs. Adverbial clauses or adverb clauses are dependent clauses.

> An **adverbial clause** or **adverb clause** is a subordinate clause that modifies a verb, an adjective, or an adverb.

19.2.6 RULE

Adverbial clauses can answer any of the following questions about the words they modify: *Where? When? In what manner? To what extent? Under what conditions?* or *Why?*

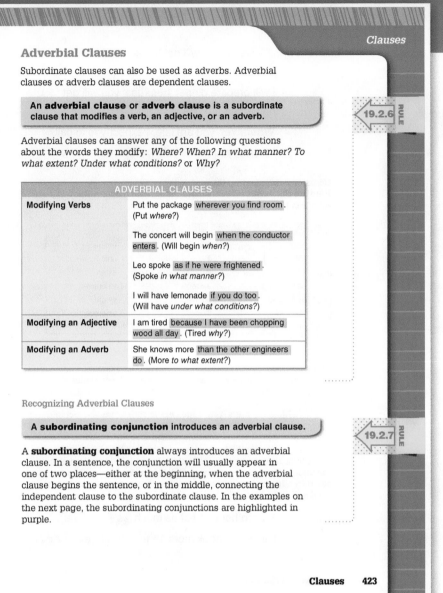

ADVERBIAL CLAUSES	
Modifying Verbs	Put the package wherever you find room. (Put *where?*)
	The concert will begin when the conductor enters. (Will begin *when?*)
	Leo spoke as if he were frightened. (Spoke *in what manner?*)
	I will have lemonade if you do too. (Will have *under what conditions?*)
Modifying an Adjective	I am tired because I have been chopping wood all day. (Tired *why?*)
Modifying an Adverb	She knows more than the other engineers do. (More *to what extent?*)

Recognizing Adverbial Clauses

> A **subordinating conjunction** introduces an adverbial clause.

19.2.7 RULE

A **subordinating conjunction** always introduces an adverbial clause. In a sentence, the conjunction will usually appear in one of two places—either at the beginning, when the adverbial clause begins the sentence, or in the middle, connecting the independent clause to the subordinate clause. In the examples on the next page, the subordinating conjunctions are highlighted in purple.

Adverbial Clauses

Explain that subordinate clauses that modify verbs, adjectives, and adverbs are called adverbial clauses.

RULE 19.2.6 Read aloud the rule and then have students repeat the lines with you.

Ask: What is the function of an adverb in a sentence? (It modifies a verb, an adjective, or an adverb.) Then, **ask:** How is the function of an adverb related to the function of an adverbial clause? (They are the same.)

Explain that adverbial clauses answer questions such as *Where? When? In what manner? To what extent? Under what conditions?* and *Why?* Review the example questions. Draw students' attention to the first word of each adverbial clause.

Recognizing Adverbial Clauses

RULE 19.2.7 Read aloud the rule and then have students repeat the line with you.

Point out that an adverbial clause *always* begins with a subordinating conjunction. Have students look back at the examples and identify the subordinating conjunctions.

Write these sentences on the board: *The race will start when the runners are ready. Helen is happy because her sister is coming to visit.*

Work with students to identify which question is being answered in each sentence. (*Start when?* and *Happy why?*) Then, have students demonstrate their understanding of adverbial clauses by explain how each adverbial clause functions in the sentence.

Read these sentences aloud: *Sit down because you are making me nervous. Joan acted as if Henry weren't there.* Have students explain how each adverbial clause functions in the sentence.

Differentiated Instruction

RTI Strategy for Below-Level Students
Help students who are having difficulty with adjectival and adverbial clauses. Play a version of a fill-in-the-blank game with students. Divide students into small groups. Have each group write a short story or news article that uses a variety of adjectival and adverbial clauses.

Next, have students identify the adverbial and adjectival clauses and rewrite the story, replacing the identified clauses with blanks. Make sure students know if each blank should be filled with an adjectival clause or an adverbial clause. (They may want to note this directly under each blank.)

Then, have them ask other students to supply adverbial and adjectival clauses *without* reading aloud the story. Have students fill these in, then read aloud the resulting story.

Common Subordinating Conjunctions

Review the list of common subordinating conjunctions with students. Work with students to create sentences with adverbial clauses that are introduced by these subordinating conjunctions. For example, *Whenever I go to the cafeteria, I get hungry. Whenever I go to the cafeteria* is an adverbial clause that answers the question: When?

Elliptical Adverbial Clauses

Remind students that an elliptical sentence is one in which some words have been left out. They are "understood" by the listener or reader. In an elliptical adverbial clause, the verb or the subject and verb have been omitted.

RULE 19.2.8 Read aloud the rule and then have students repeat the lines with you.

Point out that we encounter elliptical clauses often and automatically fill in the missing words. For example, in the sentence *Nelly wrote more carefully than Sam,* the word *wrote* has been left out.

Teacher Tip

Explain that the word *ellipsis* often refers to the three dots (. . .) that indicate missing text from a quotation. An ellipsis is often used in articles when only the significant portion of a long quotation is published.

EXAMPLES **Because** you will get home late, I will prepare dinner.

I will prepare dinner **because** you will get home late.

Whenever you are late, I expect you to call.

I expect you to call **whenever** you are late.

Common Subordinating Conjunctions
Here are the most common subordinating conjunctions. Knowing them can help you recognize adverbial clauses.

COMMON SUBORDINATING CONJUNCTIONS		
after	even though	unless
although	if	until
as	in order that	when
as if	since	whenever
as long as	so that	where
because	than	wherever
before	though	while

Elliptical Adverbial Clauses
In certain adverbial clauses, words are left out. These clauses are said to be elliptical.

> In an **elliptical adverbial clause,** the verb or the subject and verb are understood rather than stated.

Many elliptical adverbial clauses are introduced by one of two subordinating conjunctions, *as* or *than.* In the following examples, the understood words have been added in parentheses. The first elliptical adverbial clause is missing a verb; the second is missing a subject and a verb.

EXAMPLES My brother can eat as much **as I** (can eat).

I liked this book more **than** (I liked) **that one**.

See Practice 19.2E
See Practice 19.2F

424   **Phrases and Clauses**

As students read the student page, provide support from peers and from you to enhance and confirm understanding and to develop their grasp of the language structure of subordination needed to comprehend increasingly challenging language.

Beginning Read aloud the first pair of examples as students read with you. Act out the sentences. Explain that the word *because* tells a reason. Explain that the word *because* is called a subordinating conjunction.

Intermediate Discuss subordinating conjunctions, explaining the highlighted examples and the chart. Then, guide students as they read the page. Ask partners to restate the ideas in their own words to confirm understanding.

Advanced Have partners work together using the **KIM Strategy**, writing a key word, information, and a memory clue about the terms *adverbial clause* and *subordinating conjunction*. Then, have them write sentences with adverbial clauses using subordinating conjunctions from the page.

Advanced High Have partners read the page together. Ask them to discuss the meaning of each conjunction on the chart, consulting a dictionary as necessary. Then, have students print a copy of a Web-based article, highlighting adverbial clauses and circling subordinating conjunctions.

PRACTICE 19.2E Identifying Adverbial Clauses and Recognizing Elliptical Adverbial Clauses

Read the sentences. Then, write the adverbial clauses. For any of the adverbial clauses that are elliptical, add the understood words in parentheses.

EXAMPLE I enjoyed Barcelona more than Madrid.

ANSWER *than (I enjoyed) Madrid*

Not all countries have the same laws as the United States.

David wore boots so that his feet would not get wet in the rain.

Christine will not see her family again until after New Year's Day.

As long as the weather is good, we can have our picnic!

I liked this book more than that one.

China's population is larger than Japan's.

As the years go by, my aunt's eyesight worsens.

Carmen spent more time in France than in Germany.

When she arrived at the station, Sherri phoned.

Because I was tired, I didn't mind that everyone went home.

SPEAKING APPLICATION

With a partner, take turns discussing two books that you read. Use Sentence 5 as a model, and say which book you liked more than the other. Your partner should listen for and identify the adverbial clause.

PRACTICE 19.2F Combining Sentences With Adverbial Clauses

Read the sentences. Combine each pair of sentences by changing one of them into an adverbial clause. Use an appropriate subordinating conjunction, and drop or change words as necessary.

EXAMPLE I want to keep walking. My feet hurt.

ANSWER *I want to keep walking even though my feet hurt.*

11. We watched a movie. We ate dinner.

12. We stayed home. There was a blizzard.

13. Jorge put a gate across the door. His puppy could not get into the kitchen.

14. Many people celebrated. The new president was inaugurated.

15. I will do the cooking. The dishes get washed and put away.

16. This book is interesting. It describes the history of baseball.

17. The carpenter began working. The oak boards had not yet been delivered.

18. Jeremy left the meeting. It was still going on.

19. Monica recognized her uncle. She had not seen him in five years.

20. I wanted to stay. I could continue to take notes.

WRITING APPLICATION

Use the sentences in Practice 19.2F as models, and write two pairs of sentences. For each pair, combine the two sentences by changing one of them into an adverbial clause using an appropriate subordinating conjunction.

Practice 425

SPEAKING APPLICATION

Students should explain how they identified the adverbial clauses in their partners' discussions.

WRITING APPLICATION

Students' sentences should demonstrate that they can use adverbial phrases in writing.

PRACTICE 19.2E

1. as the United States (has)

2. so that his feet would not get wet in the rain

3. until (she sees them) after New Year's Day

4. As long as the weather is good

5. than (I liked) that one

6. than Japan's (population is)

7. As the years go by

8. than (she spent) in Germany

9. When she arrived at the station

10. Because I was tired

PRACTICE 19.2F

Answers will vary. Sample answers:

11. We watched a movie after we ate dinner.

12. We stayed home because there was a blizzard.

13. Jorge put a gate across the door so that his puppy could not get into the kitchen.

14. Many people celebrated when the new president was inaugurated.

15. I will do the cooking as long as the dishes get washed and put away.

16. This book is interesting because it describes the history of baseball.

17. The carpenter began working although the oak boards had not yet been delivered.

18. Jeremy left the meeting while it was still going on.

19. Monica recognized her uncle even though she had not seen him in five years.

20. I wanted to stay so that I could continue to take notes.

Lesson Objectives

1. Recognize simple, compound, complex, and compound-complex sentence structures.

2. Write complex sentences and differentiate between main and subordinate clauses.

The Simple Sentence

Remind students that an independent clause is a clause that can stand alone as a sentence. Explain that a simple sentence is composed of one and only one independent clause.

RULE 19.3.1 Read aloud the rule and then have students repeat the line with you.

Review the chart on page 426 with students. Help them understand the types of simple sentences. Point out that some examples are very long, but classifying a sentence as a simple sentence has to do with structure, not length.

Work with students to brainstorm for one of each type of sentence shown in the table on page 426. Write the sentences on the board, and identify the subject and verb in each. Then, have students work in pairs to write their own simple sentences.

All sentences can be classified according to the number and kinds of clauses they contain.

The Simple Sentence

The **simple sentence** is the most common type of sentence structure.

RULE 19.3.1

> A **simple sentence** consists of a single independent clause.

Simple sentences vary in length. Some are quite short; others can be several lines long. All simple sentences, however, contain just one subject and one verb. They may also contain adjectives, adverbs, complements, and phrases in different combinations.

Simple sentences can also have various compound parts. They can have a compound subject, a compound verb, or both. Sometimes, they will also have other compound elements, such as a compound direct object or a compound phrase.

All of the following sentences are simple sentences.

TYPES OF SIMPLE SENTENCES	
With One Subject and Verb	The rain came.
With a Compound Subject	Rain and snow are common.
With a Compound Verb	The door squeaked and rattled.
With a Compound Subject and Compound Verb	My mother and father said good-bye and left on vacation.
With a Compound Direct Object	He opened the letter and the box. direct object direct object
With a Compound Prepositional Phrase	It can rain from the east or from the west. prep phrase prep phrase

A simple sentence never has a subordinate clause, and it never has more than one main or independent clause.

Working with ELLs   **ELL** Sheltered Instruction: Cognitive

Help students learn new language structures heard during classroom instruction by providing examples of different types of simple sentences.

Beginning Remind students that a simple sentence has one main clause. Say a simple sentence as you reinforce the meaning with actions: *I pick up the pen.* Have students repeat. If students are ready, add more elements to your simple sentence, reinforcing that it is still a simple sentence.

Intermediate Read aloud the examples of simple sentences in the chart on page 426. For each example, ask students to tell you the targeted sentence part, such as a compound subject. Then, have partners say their own simple sentences using the first three types.

Advanced Have partners take turns reading aloud the examples in the chart. Then, have each partner write an example of three different types. Have students read aloud their sentences while partners identify the type of each.

Advanced High Read aloud the examples in the chart, pointing out how each sentence type adds different details. Then, have students write a paragraph with four different types of simple sentences. Have students read their paragraph to a partner, who should listen for and identify the type of each simple sentence.

The Compound Sentence

A **compound sentence** is made up of more than one simple sentence.

> A **compound sentence** consists of two or more main or independent clauses.

In most compound sentences, the main or independent clauses are joined by a comma and a coordinating conjunction (*and, but, for, nor, or, so,* or *yet*). They may also be connected with a semicolon (;) or a colon (:).

EXAMPLES   **Jamal organized** a two-day music festival **, and** eight **bands agreed** to play.

All the bands **performed** on the first day **; two were missing** the second day.

Notice in both of the preceding examples that there are two separate and complete main clauses, each with its own subject and verb. Like simple sentences, compound sentences never contain subordinate clauses.

Practice 19.3A
Practice 19.3B

The Complex Sentence

Complex sentences contain subordinate clauses, which can be either adjectival clauses or adverbial clauses.

> A **complex sentence** consists of one main or independent clause and one or more subordinate clauses.

In a complex sentence, the independent clause is often called the **main clause.** The main clause has its own subject and verb, as does each subordinate clause.

In a complex sentence, the main clause can stand alone as a simple sentence. The subordinate clause cannot stand alone as a sentence.

Classifying Sentences by Structure   **427**

The Compound Sentence

Tell students that the second type of sentence they will learn about is the compound sentence. **Ask:** Have you ever heard of something being *compound*? What parts of sentences have we learned about that can be *compound*? (compound subjects; compound verbs; lesson 18.3) What did *compound* mean in those cases? (It meant there was more than one. A compound subject had more than one subject; a compound verb had more than one verb.) **Say:** Whole sentences can be compound, too. A compound sentence is made up of more than one simple sentence. It has two or more independent clauses.

RULE 19.3.2 Read aloud the rule and then have students repeat the lines with you.

Explain that compound sentences are usually formed by combining two simple sentences with a comma and a coordinating conjunction like *and, but, or,* or *so*.

The Complex Sentence

Tell students that both simple sentences and compound sentences only contain independent clauses. Point out that a complex sentence is different because it has both an independent (main) clause and one or more subordinate clauses.

RULE 19.3.3 Read aloud the rule and then have students repeat the lines with you.

Review the method students can use to determine whether a sentence contains a subordinate clause. Remind students that a subordinate clause cannot stand on its own, but it does have a subject and a verb.

(continued)

> *Teacher Tip*
>
> Students may want to classify all short sentences as simple sentences. Show students that many short sentences can be compound or complex: *I ate, and then I played. Will he sink or will he swim? I like bread when it is warm. The dog will sleep when it is dark.*

Differentiated Instruction

Strategy for Spanish Speakers
Students whose home language is Spanish might leave out subject pronouns in clauses and sentences because in Spanish certain verb endings give enough information to identify the subject, and therefore subjects are not used. Review the structure of a clause by writing simple compound sentences on the board, such as *I go to the store, and I walk down every aisle.*

Have students identify the subject and verb in each clause. Have students suggest sentences of their own. Write students' suggestions on the board and underline the subject in each. (If students provide sentences without subjects, write those on the board too and add the subject.) Then have students write compound sentences and underline the subject in each clause.

The Complex Sentence
(continued)

Read the examples with students. Tell students that, in a complex sentence, the subordinate clause can appear at the beginning, end, or middle of the sentence.

Have students write two complex sentences with one main and one subordinate clause. Then, have students share their sentences with the class.

The Compound-Complex Sentence

Before reading about the compound-complex sentence, have students predict the sentence structure of these sentences based on what they have learned. Then, read the definition.

RULE 19.3.4 Read aloud the rule and then have students repeat the lines with you.

Walk through the examples with students. Ask them how they can identify which clauses are the main clauses, and which are the subordinate clauses.

Work together with students to write a compound-complex sentence. Use the example sentence as a model. For example, have student volunteers fill in the blanks:

When he went _____,
Hector asked _____,
and he talked _____,
who _____.

Have students brainstorm for several independent and dependent clauses, and write them on index cards. Distribute these to small groups of students. Have groups work together to assemble complex sentences using the cards. Then, have them differentiate between the main clause and the subordinate clause in each complex sentence.

EXAMPLES

January 26, 1950, is the day *(main clause)* **that India adopted** *(subordinate clause)* **its constitution** .

Because the day is so important, *(subordinate clause)* **many of the festivities are official** . *(main clause)*

In some complex sentences, the main clause is split by a subordinate clause that acts as an adjective.

EXAMPLE

Schoolchildren , **who have the day off** , **participate in an exciting parade** .

See Practice 19.3C
See Practice 19.3D
See Practice 19.3E
See Practice 19.3F

The two parts of the main clause form one main clause: *Schoolchildren participate in an exciting parade.*

The Compound-Complex Sentence

A **compound-complex sentence,** as the name indicates, contains the elements of both a compound sentence and a complex sentence.

RULE 19.3.4

> A **compound-complex sentence** consists of two or more main or independent clauses and one or more subordinate clauses.

EXAMPLE

As he was leaving for school , *(subordinate clause)* **Larry remembered to take his lunch** , but *(main clause)* **he forgot the report** *(main clause)* **that he had finished the** *(subordinate clause)* **night before** .

428 **Phrases and Clauses**

Working with ELLs **ELL** Sheltered Instruction: Cognitive

Have students use visual and contextual support to enhance and confirm understanding as they read and to develop a grasp of the language structure of complex sentences needed to comprehend increasingly challenging language.

Beginning Write this complex sentence on the board. Read it aloud while acting it out: *Before she went to bed, Martha brushed her teeth.* Repeat the sentence as students read with you. Explain that it is a complex sentence. Point out the visual and contextual clues *before* and the comma, which help to signal that the sentence is complex.

Intermediate Read aloud the examples at the top of the page while students follow along. Point out how the highlighting and

the labels help students understand the structure of a complex sentence. Then, have students identify the main and subordinate clause in the sentence from the Beginning activity.

Advanced Have students read the examples of compound and compound-complex sentences. Ask partners to describe the differences between the two, using the text highlighting to aid them. Challenge them to create their own complex sentences.

Advanced High Have students complete the Advanced activity. Then, challenge them to write three compound-complex sentences.

T428

PRACTICE 19.3A Distinguishing Simple and Compound Sentences

Read the sentences. Then, write *simple* or *compound* for each sentence.

EXAMPLE Students will perform the school musical at the end of March.

ANSWER *simple*

The parrots flew out of the forest.

The lions and tigers were in separate cages, but they ate at the same time.

My mom went on a business trip to San Francisco, so I did not see her.

The train puffed and chugged up the hill.

The Pony Express carried mail across the West.

My grandfather and my dad measured the wall, yet the refrigerator did not quite fit.

My brother mowed Mrs. Clausen's lawn and trimmed her hedges.

Last night's snowstorm kept us from going to school today, but we should be back in school tomorrow.

My sister and her friends wanted to go to a museum, so they planned a trip for next Tuesday.

The plane arrived ten minutes early.

PRACTICE 19.3B Combining Simple Sentences to Form Compound Sentences

Read the sentences. Combine the pairs of simple sentences to form compound sentences.

EXAMPLE The sun was hot. The water was cold.

ANSWER *The sun was hot, but the water was cold.*

11. Dad found a worm in the apple. He threw out the apple.

12. The snow was falling. The children were catching the snowflakes.

13. Eva cried and stamped her feet. Dad still would not let her see that movie.

14. Johnny and Carlos ran to school. The twins followed them.

15. My sister wanted to live in a warmer climate. She moved to Texas.

16. We must fix the roof. The rain will get in.

17. Latisha and Samuel finished their homework. They may go out to play.

18. The rain began to come down. I opened my umbrella.

19. We tried to get tickets for the play. The box office was closed.

20. Mrs. Baez just arrived for dinner. I heard her car door close.

SPEAKING APPLICATION

With a partner, take turns talking about chores you do around your house. Use one compound sentence. Your partner should listen for and identify two main clauses.

WRITING APPLICATION

Write three compound sentences about activities you do after school. Underline the main clauses.

Practice   429

PRACTICE 19.3A

1. simple
2. compound
3. compound
4. simple
5. simple
6. compound
7. simple
8. compound
9. compound
10. simple

PRACTICE 19.3B

Answers will vary. Sample answers:

11. Dad found a worm in the apple, so he threw out the apple.

12. The snow was falling, and the children were catching the snowflakes.

13. Eva cried and stamped her feet, but Dad still would not let her see that movie.

14. Johnny and Carlos ran to school, and the twins followed them. *or* Johnny and Carlos ran to school; the twins followed them.

15. My sister wanted to live in a warmer climate, so she moved to Texas.

16. We must fix the roof, or the rain will get in.

17. Latisha and Samuel finished their homework, so they may go out to play.

18. The rain began to come down, so I opened my umbrella.

19. We tried to get tickets for the play, but the box office was closed.

20. Mrs. Baez just arrived for dinner; I heard her car door close. *or* Mrs. Baez just arrived for dinner, and I heard her car door close.

SPEAKING APPLICATION

Students should identify each main clause in their compound sentences, and explain why neither clause is subordinate.

WRITING APPLICATION

Students' sentences should demonstrate that they can use compound sentences in writing.

1. complex
2. not complex
3. complex
4. not complex
5. complex
6. complex
7. not complex
8. complex
9. complex
10. not complex

11. compound
12. complex
13. complex
14. compound
15. complex
16. compound
17. compound
18. complex
19. complex
20. compound

SPEAKING APPLICATION

Have students explain how they recognized the subordinate clauses in their partner's conversation.

WRITING APPLICATION

Have each student read one of their complex sentences aloud and explain why it is complex.

PRACTICE 19.3C > Recognizing Complex Sentences

Read the sentences. Then, label each sentence *complex* or *not complex*.

EXAMPLE   Kim had never had a pet, so her parents gave her one for her birthday.

ANSWER   *not complex*

1. Before she entered a room, the nurse checked to see that she had everything.
2. Mom sent me to the store to buy noodles and celery.
3. Until the Johnsons get home, Marcie is caring for their cats.
4. We had better hurry, or we will miss the train.
5. I did not pass the test, which means I have to take it over.
6. Janine trained hard for the race, though she did not expect to win.
7. Last week we visited five cities in three states.
8. Because Celine was celebrating her birthday, we all brought gifts.
9. If you get an *A* on the test, you may go to the fair.
10. We should have reached Grandmother's house by now.

SPEAKING APPLICATION

With a partner, take turns discussing a movie you saw recently. Use at least two complex sentences to show the relationships between events. Your partner should listen for and identify two subordinate clauses.

PRACTICE 19.3D > Distinguishing Compound and Complex Sentences

Read the sentences. Then, label each sentence *compound* or *complex*.

EXAMPLE   When the bird landed on the branch, Shelby took a photograph.

ANSWER   *complex*

11. I went to the grocery store, and Dad went to the hardware store.
12. Cory chose to write about Australia because he wanted to learn about kangaroos.
13. If we find we are running late, we can call a taxi.
14. Loraine and Brandon enjoy basketball, and they play often.
15. While Mom and Aunt Grace fixed dinner, Dad and Uncle Sal fixed the television set.
16. Felicia is very good at math, and she wants study math in college.
17. Juwan enjoys fishing, and he often goes fishing with his brothers.
18. When I have enough money for a new bicycle, I will give you the old one.
19. Because clouds were gathering, Mom made us go inside.
20. We took photographs of the waterfall; we wanted to remember its beauty.

WRITING APPLICATION

Write a brief summary of a story you recently read. Include at least two complex sentences to show how events or actions are related.

Working with ELLs   ELL Sheltered Instruction: Cognitive

Use the prompt for the Writing Application to have students demonstrate that they understand the general meaning, main points, and important details in spoken language on topics ranging from the familiar to the unfamiliar. Describe William Shakespeare, discussing topics familiar to students, such as plays or Shakespeare's fame, and linking them to less familiar ones, such as Elizabethan England.

Beginning Ask simple questions to elicit the general meaning, main points, and important details of your description. Allow students to use illustrations or gestures to demonstrate understanding.

Intermediate Provide small groups with a main idea web. Have them record your general meaning in the center circle and add main points and important details in the outer circles. Invite groups to discuss their webs, linking familiar to unfamiliar topics.

Advanced Provide pairs with a cluster diagram in which they can record the general meaning, main points, and important details of your description. Encourage students to make connections to familiar facts about Shakespeare.

Advanced High Have students complete the Advanced activity. Then, have them use your biographical description as a model to describe a famous person to a partner.

CTICE 19.3E Combining Sentences and
Identifying the Structure

the sentences. Combine the two sentences
ch item, and write a compound or a complex
ence. Identify your sentence as compound or
▶lex.

IPLE The tickets are expensive. All of
them are sold.

VER *The tickets are expensive, yet all
of them are sold.* — compound

he television star saw the photographers.
▶e waved.

▶Ve have a dog and two kittens. We adopted
▶em from the shelter.

▶ly brother joined the Army. He is in training
▶r nine weeks.

▶icholas started telling the same old stories.
▶livia left.

▶imothy read two books by Cynthia Rylant.
▶he is his favorite writer.

▶ondra comes over every day. She must feel at
▶me here.

▶ogan's voice shook. He was cold or nervous.

▶he door slammed. There was no wind.

▶Ve lost the championship game. It was close
▶ntil the ninth inning.

▶did not go rock climbing yesterday. I did not
▶o hiking either.

PEAKING APPLICATION
▶ith a partner, talk about teachers you admire
▶ your school. Use compound and complex
▶ntences to describe them. Then, write one
▶mpound and two complex sentences about
▶other adult you respect.

PRACTICE 19.3F Writing Compound and
Complex Sentences

Read each simple sentence. Then, write a new
compound or complex sentence by adding to it.

EXAMPLE Daisy has never gotten straight A's.

ANSWER *Although Daisy has never gotten
straight A's, she could do it.*

11. The waitress took our order.
12. You can find a coupon for a free meal in the
newspaper.
13. Apples are a good buy in October.
14. Little Mikey wants to be a basketball player.
15. My ballet lesson is at 4 o'clock.
16. My grandparents are coming from Florida.
17. Our town does not have an airport.
18. Ana has read her favorite book three times.
19. Nichole swims across the lake.
20. You can visit the historic landmark.

WRITING APPLICATION
Write a short paragraph about a place. It can
be a nearby shop or a faraway spot. Use
two compound sentences and two complex
sentences. Read your paragraph to a partner,
who identifies the structures of the sentences.

Practice **431**

Extension

▶To help students synthesize and apply what
▶hey have learned about complex sentences,
▶ave students work in teams to create a
▶sentence match game. You will need six note
▶ards per team. Direct each team to write
▶hree complex sentences, using two cards for
▶ach sentence—one for the independent clause
▶nd one for the dependent clause. Have each
▶eam shuffle the cards, place them face up, and
▶hallenge another team to play the game. The
▶ther team should use the cards to form three
▶omprehensible complex sentences. For an
▶xtra challenge, have students copy, capitalize,
▶nd punctuate the sentences correctly.

SPEAKING APPLICATION
Students should identify the
independent clauses in their
sentences, and the dependent
clauses in their complex sentences.

WRITING APPLICATION
Students' paragraphs should
demonstrate that students can
write both compound and complex
sentences correctly.

PRACTICE 19.3E

Answers will vary. Sample answers:

1. The television star saw the
photographers, so he waved.—
compound
2. We have a dog and two kittens
that we adopted from the shelter.—
complex
3. My brother joined the Army, and
he is in training for nine weeks.—
compound
4. Nicholas started telling the same old
stories, so Olivia left.—compound
5. Timothy read two books by Cynthia
Rylant, who is his favorite writer.—
complex
6. Sondra comes over every day, so she
must feel at home here.—compound
7. When Logan's voice shook, he was
cold or nervous.—complex
8. The door slammed even though
there was no wind.—complex
9. We lost the championship game
even though it was close until the
ninth inning.—complex
10. I did not go rock climbing yesterday,
and I did not go hiking either.—
compound

PRACTICE 19.3F

Answers will vary. Sample answers:

11. . . . , and the food arrived ten
minutes later.
12. . . . if you buy it on Sunday.
13. . . . but we eat them all year round.
14. . . . , so he practices every day.
15. Since . . . , I have to leave school
when the bell rings.
16. . . . because my sister is graduating
from high school.
17. . . . , so we have to travel to Dallas
to fly.
18. . . . , so I am buying her another book
by that author.
19. Whenever . . . , we meet her on the
shore with towels.
20. . . . when the caretaker is at work.

T431

Test Warm-Up

1. **C** Add a comma after *yesterday*

2. **G** Add a comma after *didn't*

3. **A** I opened the front door, and there she was.

4. **J** Because I was so busy, Callie was gone for two hours before I noticed.

Reteach

If students have not mastered these skills, review the content in Section 19.3 Classifying Sentences by Structure.

1. The Complex Sentence 19.3.3

2. The Compound Sentence 19.3.2

3. The Compound Sentence 19.3.2

4. The Complex Sentence 19.3.3

Test Tip

Even though most test instructions tell students to read a passage first and then answer the questions about it, this strategy may not always be effective. Tell students that sometimes it is more effective to read the question stems (not necessarily the answer choices) before reading a passage. Then, they can search for the answers to the questions while they read the passage.

Test Warm-Up

DIRECTIONS

Read the introduction and the passage that follows. Then, answer the questions to show that you can use and understand the function of compound and complex sentences in reading and writing.

Monica wrote the following paragraph about her cat, Callie. Read the paragraph and think about the changes you would suggest as a peer editor. When you finish reading, answer the questions that follow.

Callie's Adventurous Day

(1) After getting the mail yesterday I put food in my cat's bowl. (2) Callie is always hungry, and she usually comes to gobble up food. (3) This time she didn't but I had homework and had to get back to it. (4) After a while, I checked her bowl to find it still full, and I became worried. (5) I opened the front door. (6) There she was. (7) She ran ins[ ] and dashed toward the kitchen. (8) I was so busy Callie was gone for [ ] hours before I noticed.

1 What change, if any, should be made in sentence 1?

   A Delete the word *After*

   B Add the word **and** after *yesterday*

   C Add a comma after *yesterday*

   D Make no change

2 What change should be made in sentence 3?

   F Add a comma after *time*

   G Add a comma after *didn't*

   H Add a comma after *homework*

   J Add a semicolon after *homework*

3 What is the BEST way to combine sentences 5 and 6?

   A I opened the front door, and there she was.

   B I opened the front door, there she was.

   C I opened the front door although there she was.

   D Even though I opened the front door, there she was.

4 What is the BEST way to revise sentence 8[ ]

   F I was so busy because Callie was gone two hours before I noticed.

   G That I was so busy Callie was gone for two hours before I noticed.

   H I was so busy, but Callie was gone for [ ] hours before I noticed.

   J Because I was so busy, Callie was gon[ ] for two hours before I noticed.

CHAPTER 20 LESSON PLANNER
Effective Sentences

Use the Online Lesson Planner at www.phwritingcoach.com to customize your instructional plan for an integrated Language Arts curriculum.

DAY 1 20.1 Classifying the Four Functions of a Sentence

"What Do You Notice?" **Objectives:** Identify, use, and understand the four functions of a sentence	**INSTRUCTION AND PRACTICE** Student Edition pp. 433–437

DAY 2 20.2 Combining Sentences

Objectives: Identify, use, and understand sentence-combining methods, including • combining sentence parts • joining clauses	**INSTRUCTION AND PRACTICE** Student Edition pp. 438–442

DAY 3 20.3 Varying Sentences

Objectives: Identify, use, and understand aspects of varying sentences, including • varying sentence length • varying sentence beginnings	**INSTRUCTION AND PRACTICE** Student Edition pp. 443–445

DAY 4 20.4 Avoiding Sentence Problems

Objectives: Identify, use, and understand adjectives, including • correcting sentence fragments • correcting clause fragments • recognizing run-on sentences • correcting run-on sentences	**INSTRUCTION AND PRACTICE** Student Edition pp. 446–455

Grammar Assessment

Grammar Coach:	Diagnostic Assessment	End-of-Chapter Assessment	Progress Monitoring
Personalized Instruction	Students take grammar diagnostic test online and are automatically assigned instruction and practice in areas where they need support.	Teacher uses **ExamView** to administer end-of-chapter assessment and remediation. Teachers may customize **ExamView** tests or use the ones provided.	Teachers may use the **Test Warm-Ups** and the **Cumulative Reviews** in the student book or eText to check students' mastery of grammar skills.
Teacher-Directed Instruction	Teacher administers the diagnostic test and determines focus of instruction and practice.		Students may also play **DimensionL** grammar video games to test their grammar skills.

Alternate Pacing Plans

- **Block Scheduling** Each day in the Lesson Planner represents a 40–50 minute block. Teachers using block scheduling may combine days to revise pacing to meet their classroom needs.

- **Accelerated Lesson Planning** Combine instructional days, focusing on concepts called out by students' diagnostic test results.

- **Integrated Language Arts Curriculum** Use the instruction and practice in this chapter to provide reinforcement, remediation, or extension of grammar concepts taught in your literature curriculum.

Links to Prentice Hall *LITERATURE*

- **Unit 3** Writing Workshop: Combining Sentences, p. 531
- **Unit 4** Sentence Types, p. 598; Writing Workshop: Revising for Strong, Functional Sentences, p. 617; Writing Workshop: Revising Choppy Sentences, p. 673
- **Unit 5** Writing Workshop: Combining Sentences for Variety, p. 805
- **Unit 6** Writing Workshop: Revising Sentence Fragments, p. 909

WRITING COACH
Online
www.phwritingcoach.com

Grammar Assessment and Practice

Chapter diagnostic tests assess students' skills and assign instruction and practice.

DimensionL Video Games

Fast-paced interactive video games challenge students' mastery of grammar.

Lesson Planner continues on next page

DAY 5 20.4 Avoiding Sentence Problems *(continued)*

Objectives: Identify, use, and understand methods for avoiding sentence problems, including

- recognizing run-on sentences (*continued*)
- correcting run-on sentences (*continued*)
- properly placing modifiers
- avoiding double negatives

INSTRUCTION AND PRACTICE

Student Edition pp. 451–455, 457–460

Test Warm-Up p. 456

DAY 6 20.4 Avoiding Problems *(continued)*

Objectives: Identify, use, and understand methods for avoiding common usage problems

INSTRUCTION AND PRACTICE

Student Edition pp. 461–465

DAY 8 Cumulative Review *(continued)*

Objectives: Identify, use, and understand sentence structure and style, including

- subjects and predicates
- complements
- phrases and clauses
- combining and varying sentences
- avoiding sentence problems

INSTRUCTION AND PRACTICE

Student Edition pp. 466–468

> ❝ *If we want young writers to bloom, we should spend time focusing on what good writers do before focusing on editing rules. The 'stuff' needs to get better before it gets correct. Let's start by teaching students sentence variety, and the editing will follow.* ❞
>
> **—Kelly Gallagher**

Differentiated Instruction

Differentiated Instruction Boxes in this Teacher's Edition address these student populations:

- Below-Level Students
- Above-Level Students
- Gifted and Talented Students
- Special Needs Students
- English Language Learners
- Spanish Speaking Students

In addition, for further enrichment, see the **Extension** features.

EFFECTIVE SENTENCES

Using a variety of sentences will add interest to your writing and help it flow smoothly.

WRITE GUY *Jeff Anderson, M.Ed.*

WHAT DO YOU NOTICE?

Check out different types of sentences as you zoom in on these lines from the poem "April Rain Song" by Langston Hughes.

MENTOR TEXT

Let the rain beat upon your head with silver liquid drops.
Let the rain sing you a lullaby.

The rain makes still pools on the sidewalk.
The rain makes running pools in the gutter.

Now, ask yourself the following questions:

- Which sentences give a command or an order?
- Which sentences state or declare a fact or an idea?

The first and second sentences are imperative; they command the reader to do something. The third and fourth sentences are declarative; they state a fact. Both imperative and declarative sentences usually end with a period.

Grammar for Writers Writers use different types of sentences to say what they really mean. Effective sentences give readers a strong sense of the writer's voice and message.

I look great today.

How very declarative of you to say so.

433

Grammar for Writers: Syntax

Writers can choose from among four sentence types: declarative, interrogative, imperative, and exclamatory. Each type of sentence helps writers express a different kind of meaning. By applying the rules in these lessons, students can make effective choices when they craft and punctuate sentences.

EFFECTIVE SENTENCES

As students progress in their writing skills, it will be important for them to be able to apply the rules of grammar, usage, and mechanics to their own drafts. Use the *What Do You Notice?* feature to help them see effective conventions in the work of professional writers. Encourage students to incorporate effective voice, tense, and syntax as they edit their own writing.

Read the Mentor Text aloud. Discuss how the author uses different types of sentences to create a sense of the speaker's personality. Point out that it is important to understand the structures of different sentence types in order to write clearly and smoothly.

WRITE GUY *Jeff Anderson, M. Ed.*

WHAT DO YOU NOTICE?

When students have read the Mentor Text, ask what they notice about the sentences. **Say:** Sometimes in a poem, one sentence is broken into two or more lines. There are four lines in this poem. How many sentences are there? (**Response:** There are four sentences.) Have students finish reading the page.

Say: Notice that not all of the sentences are alike. The first two sentences are commands. They tell someone to do something. The last two sentences make statements. They state facts. Different kinds of sentences help writers express different kinds of ideas.

Have students read the remainder of the page. Then, write these sentences on the board and ask volunteers to read them aloud: *That's a lullaby. THAT's a lullaby? That's a lullaby!* Ask why each sentence sounds different from the others. Point out that punctuation marks guide readers in understanding how different types of sentences should sound. Spoken questions in English end with a rising inflection. Exclamation marks add emphasis.

Lesson Objectives

1. Identify and distinguish between the four types of sentences.

2. Punctuate each type of sentence according to its purpose.

Introduce the four types of sentences—declarative, interrogative, imperative, and exclamatory—and explain that the most common type—declarative sentences—states or declares something. Discuss why writers use declarative sentences.

RULE 20.1.1 Read aloud the rule and then have students repeat the lines with you.

Say: Look at the example sentences. Notice that they all end with the same punctuation mark. **Ask:** How do sentences ending with a period sound when they are read aloud? (**Possible responses:** English speakers typically drop their voice and pause at the end of a sentence.)

Point out that the example sentences are different lengths. **Ask:** What makes all of these declarative sentences? (**Possible responses:** They all have the same purpose: to state facts, declare ideas, or share information; they all end with a period.)

Have students make up and share original declarative sentences about objects in the room or a person in the news.

20.1 Classifying the Four Functions of a Sentence

Sentences can be classified according to what they do. Some sentences present facts or information in a direct way, while others pose questions to the reader or listener. Still others present orders or directions. A fourth type of sentence expresses strong emotion.

These four types of sentences are called **declarative, interrogative, imperative,** and **exclamatory.** As well as having a different purpose, each type of sentence is constructed in a different way.

The type of sentence you are writing determines the punctuation mark you use to end the sentence. The three end marks are the **period (.),** the **question mark (?),** and the **exclamation mark (!).**

The **declarative sentence** is the most common type of sentence. It is used to state, or "declare," ideas, facts, or opinions.

> RULE 20.1.1
> A **declarative sentence** states, or declares, an idea and ends with a period.

DECLARATIVE Soccer is a team sport.

Golf is a sport that can be played throughout a lifetime.

Although most schools fund team sports, many students choose to participate in individual sports.

Interrogative means "asking." An **interrogative sentence** is a question. Interrogative sentences often begin with *who, what, when, why, how,* or *how many.* They end with a question mark.

434   **Effective Sentences**

WRITING COACH

Online

www.phwritingcoach.com

Grammar Tutorial
Brush up on your Grammar skills with these animated videos.

Grammar Practice
Practice your grammar skills with Writing Coach Online

Grammar Games
Test your knowledge of grammar in this fast-paced interactive video game.

Working with ELLs   **ELL** Sheltered Instruction: Cognitive

Give students practice speaking using a variety of sentence types by having them make statements and exclamations, give commands, and ask questions. Students should speak with increasing accuracy and ease.

Beginning Speak simple examples of each type and have students repeat, using appropriate expression and intonation. Encourage students to speak their own examples, such as asking *When is the test?* or giving a command like *Take this pen.*

Intermediate List the names of each sentence type and their end marks on the board and model examples. Have partners read the example sentences from pages 434–435. Coach them to speak with appropriate expression and intonation as partners identify the sentence type.

Advanced Have students write an example sentence using one of the four types and say it to a partner, speaking with appropriate expression and intonation. Have partners listen for and identify the sentence type.

Advanced High Challenge each student to write an example of each of the four sentence types, using correct punctuation. Then, have students read their sentences to a partner using appropriate expression. The partner should listen and identify the sentence type. Have students explain how they knew which sentence type they heard.

An **interrogative sentence** asks a question and ends with a question mark.

20.1.2 RULE

INTERROGATIVE   What is your time in the half-mile run?

Where is the county track meet being held?

Who is the fastest runner on the track team?

An **imperative sentence** gives an order, or command, or a direction and ends with either a period or an exclamation mark.

20.1.3 RULE

The word *imperative* comes from the Latin word that means "commanding." **Imperative sentences** are commands or directions. Most imperative sentences start with a verb. In this type of sentence, the subject is understood to be *you.*

IMPERATIVE   Follow my instructions carefully.

Run as hard as you can!

Notice the punctuation at the end of these examples. In the first sentence, the period suggests that a mild command is being given in an ordinary tone of voice. The exclamation mark at the end of the second sentence suggests a strong command, one given in a loud voice.

An **exclamatory sentence** conveys strong emotion and ends with an exclamation mark.

20.1.4 RULE

Exclaim means "to shout out." **Exclamatory sentences** are used to "shout out" emotions such as happiness, fear, delight, or anger.

Practice 20.1A
Practice 20.1B
Practice 20.1C
Practice 20.1D

EXCLAMATORY   She's going to crash into that hurdle!

What an outstanding runner she is!

Classifying the Four Functions of a Sentence   435

RULE 20.1.2 Read aloud the rule and then have students repeat the lines with you.

Discuss how interrogative sentences are questions that are used to find out information.

Ask volunteers to read aloud the examples of interrogative sentences. Have students listen for and explain what happens to their voices at the end of each sentence. (**Possible response:** English speakers' voices typically rise at the end of a question.)

Have students make up *What, When, Where, Who, Why,* and *How* questions about band practice or another school activity. Point out that the five W's and one H can help students gather information in and out of class.

RULE 20.1.3 Read aloud the rule and then have students repeat the lines with you.

Point out that imperative sentences give commands. Explain that even polite commands that include *please* are imperative. For example, *Please let me know when you finish* is an imperative sentence.

Explain that the subject of an imperative is always *you,* even though *you* is neither written nor spoken.

RULE 20.1.4 Read aloud the rule and then have students repeat the lines with you.

Discuss why a writer might end a sentence with an exclamation mark. Explain that exclamatory sentences should be used sparingly. If they are overused, they lose their effect.

Write these sentences on the board: *The sea was calm! The sky was a beautiful blue! Royce looked out to the horizon! Suddenly, a dark cloud appeared out of nowhere! It was a huge storm! Royce's small boat was too far out!* **Ask:** Why do exclamatory sentences lose their effect if they are used too often? (**Possible response:** any special emphasis is lost)

Work with students to decide where exclamation marks would be effective in the story of Royce and the storm.

Teacher Tip

Tell students that the name of each type of sentence gives a clue about its purpose. Ask them to identify the clues: declarative (*declare*), interrogative (*interrogate*), imperative (from the Latin *imperativus,* meaning "pertaining to a command"), and exclamatory (*exclaim*).

Quick-Write Extension

To help students synthesize and apply what they have learned about sentence types, have them work in pairs to write an advertisement for an imaginary product. Tell student pairs to use each type of sentence at least once to create varied sentence patterns that make their advertisements appealing. Have pairs exchange advertisements and identify each type of sentence used.

PRACTICE 20.1A

1. declarative
2. interrogative
3. declarative
4. exclamatory
5. imperative
6. interrogative
7. exclamatory
8. declarative
9. interrogative
10. imperative

PRACTICE 20.1B

11. Are there any peaches today?
12. He looked at the stars.
13. I can't believe you did that!
14. How will we get to school?
15. Tell us about the Arctic.
16. Is that the right answer?
17. That's terrible!
18. Don't forget your coat.
19. When will they get here?
20. I sing in the school chorus.

SPEAKING APPLICATION

Have students explain to the class how they identified each of the three types of sentences.

WRITING APPLICATION

Have students share their sentences with the class, identifying the type of each sentence.

PRACTICE 20.1A Identifying Four Types of Sentences

Read the sentences. Then, identify each type of sentence by writing *declarative*, *interrogative*, *imperative*, or *exclamatory*.

EXAMPLE   The blue whale is the largest animal on Earth.

ANSWER   *declarative*

1. Cashews originated in South America.
2. How much does an elephant eat every day?
3. Clarence Birdseye invented a method for freezing foods.
4. Jupiter is absolutely immense!
5. Put your luggage on the conveyor belt.
6. Where do birds go in the winter?
7. When the island Krakatoa exploded, it was heard more than 2,000 miles away!
8. More people drink water than drink milk.
9. When will the next storm occur?
10. Please read the sign out front.

PRACTICE 20.1B Punctuating Four Types of Sentences

Read the sentences. Then, rewrite each sentence adding the correct end punctuation.

EXAMPLE   Where is the post office

ANSWER   *Where is the post office?*

11. Are there any peaches today
12. He looked at the stars
13. I can't believe you did that
14. How will we get to school
15. Tell us about the Arctic
16. Is that the right answer
17. That's terrible
18. Don't forget your coat
19. When will they get here
20. I sing in the school chorus

SPEAKING APPLICATION

With a partner, take turns talking about something that surprised you. Include at least three different types of sentences in your discussion. Your partner should listen for and identify the three types of sentences.

WRITING APPLICATION

Write four sentences on any topics you wish. Make one declarative, one exclamatory, one interrogative, and one imperative. Be sure to punctuate them correctly.

Working with ELLs   ELL Sheltered Instruction: Cognitive

Working from the Writing Application, have students demonstrate comprehension of increasingly complex English by responding to questions.

Beginning Provide students with a brief paragraph featuring simple sentences on a subject of your choice. Preteach vocabulary, and then read the paragraph as students track. Discuss the paragraph, supporting comprehension with visuals and mime. Then, have students respond to questions about the paragraph, such as *What is the paragraph about?*

Intermediate Have partners collaborate in completing the Writing Application. Then, have pairs exchange papers and respond

to these questions: *What are the sentences about? What does the writer say about those topics?*

Advanced Have students complete the Writing Application individually. Have them exchange papers and respond to these questions: *What are the sentences about? What does the writer say about those topics? What additional information might be included? Why?*

Advanced High Have students complete the Advanced activity. Then, challenge them to offer two suggestions to improve their partner's sentences.

PRACTICE 20.1C Writing Four Types of
Sentences

Read the topics. For each topic, write the type of
sentence specified in parentheses. Be sure to use
the appropriate end punctuation.

EXAMPLE   weather (exclamatory)

ANSWER   *The weather is so cold!*

1. sun (declarative)
2. bicycle (interrogative)
3. door (imperative)
4. astronaut (declarative)
5. whales (exclamatory)
6. vacation (interrogative)
7. books (imperative)
8. forest (declarative)
9. solar eclipse (exclamatory)
10. restaurant (interrogative)

PRACTICE 20.1D Revising Four Types of
Sentences

Read the sentences. Rewrite each sentence,
changing it to the type of sentence specified in
parentheses. Be sure to use the appropriate end
punctuation.

EXAMPLE   You can watch a caterpillar.
           (interrogative)

ANSWER   *Can you watch a caterpillar?*

11. Can you go to the library? (declarative)
12. That mountain is so high! (interrogative)
13. Don't clouds sometimes look like cotton balls?
    (declarative)
14. Are elephants really big? (exclamatory)
15. Dad went to the hardware store.
    (interrogative)
16. Why don't you look where you're going?
    (imperative)
17. Those are her favorite shoes. (interrogative)
18. Would you please close the window?
    (imperative)
19. Is summer vacation starting soon?
    (declarative)
20. Is that ice dangerously thin? (exclamatory)

SPEAKING APPLICATION

With a partner, take turns giving orders, as
if you were a coach. Give at least two orders
each, using imperative sentences. Then, turn
the orders into requests, using interrogative
sentences.

WRITING APPLICATION

Write a short paragraph about something in
nature that you find interesting. Begin with
a question. Then, answer the question with
at least one declarative and one exclamatory
sentence.

Practice   437

PRACTICE 20.1C

Answers will vary. Sample answers:

1. The sun sets in the evening.
2. Do you have a bicycle?
3. Please close the door.
4. I want to be an astronaut.
5. Whales are so huge!
6. What did you do on vacation?
7. Open your books to page 10.
8. I walked through the forest.
9. A solar eclipse is an amazing thing
   to see!
10. Do you enjoy eating at a restaurant?

PRACTICE 20.1D

11. You can go to the library.
12. How high is that mountain?
13. Clouds sometimes look like cotton
    balls.
14. Elephants are really big!
15. Did Dad go to the hardware store?
16. Look where you're going.
17. Are those her favorite shoes?
18. Please close the window.
19. Summer vacation is starting soon.
20. That ice is dangerously thin!

SPEAKING APPLICATION

Have partners present their
sentences to the class. The class
should listen for and identify the
different sentence types.

WRITING APPLICATION

Have students share their
paragraphs with a partner,
explaining how to identify each
sentence type.

1. Create sentence variety by combining sentences.

2. Use conjunctions to join two main clauses.

3. Differentiate between main and subordinate clauses.

4. Combine sentences by changing one into a phrase.

Combining Sentence Parts

Discuss why skilled writers try to vary their sentences.

RULE 20.2.1 Read aloud the rule and then have students repeat the lines with you.

Use a Think Aloud as part of a gradual release progression.

Think Aloud

Say: I see that subjects, verbs, and objects can all be connected by the word *and*. So if I have two related sentences that I want to combine, I should try to connect similar parts using *and* to see if that works.

Work with students to identify the steps to follow in creating sentences with compound subjects, objects, or verbs. Write these sentences on the board: *Ali enjoys action movies. Dee enjoys action movies.* Cross out the words repeated in the second sentence (*enjoys action movies*) and insert *and Dee* after *Ali* in the first sentence to create a compound subject. Point out that this compound subject takes a plural verb, so *enjoys* becomes *enjoy*.

Then, **have students** explain how the examples on page 438 were combined to form sentences with compound verbs or objects.

Find It / FIX IT

10

Grammar Game Plan

20.2 Combining Sentences

Good writing should include sentences of varying lengths and complexity to create a flow of ideas. One way to achieve sentence variety is to combine sentences to express two or more related ideas or pieces of information in a single sentence.

Look at the example below. Then, look at how the ideas are combined in different ways.

EXAMPLE   We went to the zoo. We saw monkeys.

COMBINED   We went to the zoo and saw monkeys.

          We saw monkeys when we went to the zoo.

Combining Sentence Parts

RULE 20.2.1

> Sentences can be combined by using a **compound subject**, a **compound verb**, or a **compound object**.

EXAMPLE	Moira enjoyed watching the monkeys. Tom enjoyed watching the monkeys.
COMPOUND SUBJECT	**Moira** and **Tom** enjoyed watching the monkeys.
EXAMPLE	Lisa played the game. Lisa won a stuffed animal.
COMPOUND VERB	Lisa **played** the game and **won** a stuffed animal.
EXAMPLE	Scott rode the roller coaster. Scott rode the Ferris wheel.
COMPOUND OBJECT	Scott rode the **roller coaster** and the **Ferris wheel**.

See Practice 20.2A

438   **Effective Sentences**

Joining Clauses

A **compound sentence** consists of two or more main or independent clauses. (See Chapter 19 for more information about clauses.) Use a compound sentence when combining related ideas of equal weight.

To create a compound sentence, join two main clauses with a comma and a coordinating conjunction. Common conjunctions include *and, but, nor, for, so, or,* and *yet.* You can also link the two sentences with a semicolon (;) if they are closely related.

> Sentences can be combined by joining two main clauses to create a **compound sentence**.

20.2.2 RULE

EXAMPLE	The wind whipped against our faces.
	The screams of other riders excited us.
COMPOUND SENTENCE	The wind whipped against our faces, and the screams of other riders excited us.
EXAMPLE	The ride lasted just a few minutes.
	My stomach churned for several hours.
COMPOUND SENTENCE	The ride lasted just a few minutes, but my stomach churned for several hours.
EXAMPLE	The roller coaster is such fun.
	It's very popular.
COMPOUND SENTENCE	The roller coaster is such fun; it's very popular.
EXAMPLE	I'm so tired when I leave the amusement park.
	I can't wait to come back again.
COMPOUND SENTENCE	I'm so tired when I leave the amusement park, yet I can't wait to come back again.

e Practice 20.2B

Combining Sentences   439

Joining Clauses

Discuss how writing that contains nothing but short, simple sentences can sound choppy and repetitive. Point out that joining clauses to create compound sentences can add variety by changing the rhythm of a piece of writing.

RULE 20.2.2 Read aloud the rule and then have students repeat the lines with you.

Direct students' attention to the examples. Point out that the ideas in a compound sentence are of equal importance. Work with students to identify the coordinating conjunctions in the first two compound sentences (*and, but*). Discuss the purpose of each of these conjunctions. (**Possible responses:** *And* joins two similar things or ideas; *but* shows contrast.)

Have student pairs find examples of compound sentences in a textbook, newspaper article, or reading assignment and present those examples to the class. Students should explain how the clauses have been combined.

> *Teacher Tip*
>
> You can give students additional practice by taking a well-written paragraph and breaking it down into simple sentences. Then, have students work individually or in pairs to use sentence combining to create an improved version of the paragraph. Ask students to compare their version to the original. Remind them that the point is not to match the original exactly, but to experiment with different ways of putting sentences together.

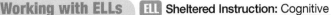

Working with ELLs   ELL Sheltered Instruction: Cognitive

As students learn about combining sentences, help them use visual support—a Venn Diagram—to enhance and confirm understanding of increasingly complex spoken language.

Beginning Say *I like peanuts. I like walnuts.* Provide pictures as support. Draw a Venn Diagram on the board, writing the two sentences in the outer circles. Then, write *I like peanuts and walnuts* in the center section and say it aloud. Discuss the meaning of the new sentence.

Intermediate Say a pair of simple sentences. Have partners record the sentences in the outer circles of a **Venn Diagram**. Then, combine the sentences. Say the new sentence aloud, and have

the students enter it in the center section. Help them understand the new sentence, referring to their diagrams.

Advanced Read the uncombined example sentences from page 438 to students. Have them record the parts of the sentences that are different in the outer circles of a **Venn Diagram**, writing common elements in the center. Then, say the combined sentences. Discuss their meaning as students refer to their diagrams.

Advanced High Have partners complete the Advanced activity, with each taking a turn in providing and combining sentences as the other listens and records.

RULE 20.2.3

RULE 20.2.3 Read aloud the rule and then have students repeat the lines with you.

Remind students of the definition of a subordinate clause. Review common subordinating conjunctions such as *because, after, although,* and *since.*

Say: Another way to combine sentences is to create a complex sentence. You can do this by changing one of the sentences into a subordinate clause. In the combined example on the page, the second sentence was changed to the subordinate clause *because the ride went so fast.* This clause is dependent on the first part of the sentence: *We were frightened.*

Work with students to write a sentence using one of the subordinating conjunctions mentioned in the first paragraph on page 440: *after, although, because, before, since,* and *unless.* Then, have student pairs write sentences for each of the remaining subordinating conjunctions.

RULE 20.2.4 Read aloud the rule and then have students repeat the lines with you.

Direct students' attention to the examples for Rule 20.2.4. Work with students to identify how sentences are combined; for example, repeated words are left out and connecting words are added when needed.

On the board, write one of the combined examples, such as *My family is leaving in the morning to go on vacation.* Work with students to show how embedded phrases can be moved to other places in a sentence without changing meaning; for example, *In the morning, my family is leaving to go on vacation.*

Teacher Tip

Post these sentences: *Because he loved mountains, Will was excited about going to Colorado. Will was excited about going to Colorado because he loved mountains.* Have students work in groups to create a poster explaining when a comma is needed in a complex sentence. Review introductory phrases before they begin.

RULE 20.2.3 Sentences can be combined by changing one of them into a **subordinate clause.**

A **complex sentence** consists of one **main** or **independent clause** and one or more **subordinate clauses.** (See Chapter 19 for more information about clauses.) Combine sentences into a complex sentence to emphasize that one of the ideas in the sentence depends on the other. A subordinating conjunction will help readers understand the relationship. Common subordinating conjunctions are *after, although, because, before, since,* and *unless.* Generally no punctuation is required when a main and a subordinate clause are combined. When the subordinate clause comes first, a comma is needed. (See Chapter 25 for more information on punctuation.)

EXAMPLE We were frightened. The ride went so fast.

COMBINED We were frightened because the ride went so fast.

See Practice 20.2C

RULE 20.2.4 Sentences can be combined by changing one of them into a **phrase.**

When combining sentences in which one of the sentences simply adds details, change one of the sentences into a **phrase.**

EXAMPLE My family is leaving to go on vacation.
We are leaving in the morning.

COMBINED My family is leaving in the morning to go on vacation.

EXAMPLE My mother packed a picnic basket.
It was filled with sandwiches.

COMBINED My mother packed a picnic basket filled with sandwiches.

See Practice 20.2D

440   Effective Sentences

Working with ELLs   **ELL** Sheltered Instruction: Cognitive

As students learn about using clauses and phrases to combine sentences, help them use contextual support to enhance and confirm their understanding of increasingly complex spoken language.

Beginning Read aloud the paired sentences in the first example on page 440. Provide context with images and gestures. Read aloud the combined sentences, and confirm understanding by asking, *What was scary?*

Intermediate Read aloud the paired sentences in the first example on page 440. Provide context by discussing various kinds of rides. Read the combined sentence, pointing out how the ideas connect. Repeat with other examples, providing context for each.

Advanced Provide context for each pair of uncombined example sentences. Have partners take turns speaking the pairs. The partner should listen, and describe how the two sentences are related. Have partners suggest a way to combine the sentences, speaking the new sentence aloud.

Advanced High Challenge students to create three sentences about the same topic and speak these sentences to a partner. Partners should use context to identify connections and suggest how two of the sentences can be combined, speaking the new sentence aloud.

PRACTICE 20.2A Combining Sentences Using Compound Subjects, Verbs, and Objects

Read the sentences. Combine the sentences in each group into a single sentence. Identify each combination as *compound subject, compound verb,* or *compound object.*

EXAMPLE Tanner went to the drugstore. Marcie went to the drugstore, too.

ANSWER *Tanner and Marcie went to the drugstore. — compound subject*

Claudio typed his report. Claudio also printed out his report.

Paul tried out for the play. Liam tried out for the play. Rubin tried out for the play.

Sari wrote a poem. Sari wrote a short story.

Yesterday my grandmother called. She invited me to visit for the weekend.

Jordan plays golf. Shelly plays golf, too.

My sister likes fruit. She also likes vegetables.

I need to paint the model cars. I need to paint the model planes, too.

The bake sale raised a lot of money. The car wash raised a lot of money, too.

My dog chased the ball. My dog caught the ball.

My mom is planning our trip to the museum. My dad is helping her.

PRACTICE 20.2B Combining Sentences Using Main Clauses

Read the sentences. Combine each pair into a compound sentence using the coordinating conjunction in parentheses. Be sure to use correct punctuation for compound sentences.

EXAMPLE Penguins look awkward on land. They are graceful in the water. (but)

ANSWER *Penguins look awkward on land, but they are graceful in the water.*

11. I went to the department store. I found the outfit I needed for band. (and)
12. We needed milk. I went to the store. (so)
13. My sister really likes math. My brother does not like math. (but)
14. In this recipe, we add peppers to the sauce. This makes the sauce spicy. (;)
15. We could go to the movies. We could go to the dance. (or)
16. A tadpole grows legs. Its tail disappears. (and)
17. We missed the bus. We took a taxi. (so)
18. My brother is feeling better. It will still be a while before he is well. (but)
19. Our class came in from recess. It was time for lunch. (;)
20. The flowers are beginning to come up. The trees are turning green. (and)

SPEAKING APPLICATION

With a partner, take turns talking about foods you like. Your partner should listen for and name three conjunctions you use.

WRITING APPLICATION

Write three sentences about the kinds of stories you most enjoy reading. Make sure your sentences combine main clauses or contain a compound verb, subject, or object.

Practice 441

PRACTICE 20.2A

1. Claudio typed and printed out his report.—compound verb
2. Paul, Liam, and Rubin tried out for the play.—compound subject
3. Sari wrote a poem and a short story.—compound object
4. Yesterday my grandmother called and invited me to visit for the weekend.—compound verb
5. Jordan and Shelly play golf.—compound subject
6. My sister likes fruit and vegetables.—compound object
7. I need to paint the model cars and planes.—compound object
8. The bake sale and car wash raised a lot of money.—compound subject
9. My dog chased and caught the ball.—compound verb
10. My mom and dad are planning our trip to the museum.—compound subject

PRACTICE 20.2B

11. I went to the department store, and I found the outfit I needed for band.
12. We needed milk, so I went to the store.
13. My sister really likes math, but my brother does not like math.
14. In this recipe, we add peppers to the sauce; this makes the sauce spicy.
15. We could go to the movies, or we could go to the dance.
16. A tadpole grows legs, and its tail disappears.
17. We missed the bus, so we took a taxi.
18. My brother is feeling better, but it will still be a while before he is well.
19. Our class came in from recess; it was time for lunch.
20. The flowers are beginning to come up, and the trees are turning green.

SPEAKING APPLICATION

Have students explain to the class how they identified the conjunctions.

WRITING APPLICATION

Have students exchange sentences and check each other's work, explaining why it is or is not correct.

PRACTICE 20.2C

Answers will vary. Sample answers:

1. I need to get the house cleaned before Mom comes home tonight. 2. Although the doctor told Rory he should not run, Rory decided to enter the race. 3. Dad went to the hardware store because we needed batteries. 4. I have to stay inside until I get my homework done. 5. When the birds start building nests, we know it's spring. 6. Liana took extra science classes so that she can get into the advanced class. 7. If you finish your chores, you may leave. 8. Stefan got an A on the test because he studied very hard. 9. While I'm baking potatoes, I'm making soup. 10. After Pedro got the soccer ball, a game of soccer started.

PRACTICE 20.2D

Answers will vary. Sample answers:

11. Ann plays the flute in the band. 12. Today, we meet Mr. Beale, the coach. 13. Jun took his model plane to the park to see it fly. 14. Frank Lloyd Wright, a famous architect, designed this house. 15. We wanted to pick the flowers covering the meadow. 16. Knowing everyone, Shelby could not go anywhere without seeing friends. 17. The dog, eager for its dinner, ran to its bowl. 18. The paper's travel section, edited by Mr. Keller, is interesting. 19. The children, laughing excitedly, played on the swings. 20. The actress walked toward the stage, followed by her costar.

SPEAKING APPLICATION

Students should explain how they identified the subordinating conjunctions.

WRITING APPLICATION

Have students explain how their phrases add details to their sentences.

PRACTICE 20.2C > **Combining Sentences Using Subordinate Clauses**

Read the sentences. Combine each pair by changing one sentence into a subordinate clause, using the subordinating conjunction in parentheses. Be sure to use the correct punctuation for complex sentences.

EXAMPLE Cleo is going to the game. Then, she is going to Sue's house. (after)

ANSWER *After Cleo goes to the game, she is going to Sue's house.*

1. I need to get the house cleaned. Mom comes home tonight. (before)
2. The doctor told Rory he should not run. Rory decided to enter the race. (although)
3. Dad went to the hardware store. We needed batteries. (because)
4. I have to stay inside. I have to get my homework done. (until)
5. The birds start building nests. We know it's spring. (when)
6. Liana took extra science classes. She can get into the advanced class. (so that)
7. You finish your chores. You may leave. (if)
8. Stefan got an *A* on the test. He studied very hard. (because)
9. I'm baking potatoes. I'm making soup. (while)
10. Pedro got the soccer ball. A game of soccer started. (after)

SPEAKING APPLICATION

With a partner, take turns talking about something you saw on television. Use at least three subordinating conjunctions. Your partner should listen for and name the conjunctions.

PRACTICE 20.2D > **Combining Sentences Using Phrases**

Read the sentences. Combine each pair of sentences by changing one into a phrase.

EXAMPLE Mrs. Shankar led the class through the museum. Mrs. Shankar is a dinosaur expert.

ANSWER *Mrs. Shankar, a dinosaur expert, led the class through the museum.*

11. Ann plays the flute. She plays in the band.
12. Today, we meet Mr. Beale. He is the coach.
13. Jun took his model plane to the park. He wanted to see it fly.
14. Frank Lloyd Wright was a famous architect. He designed this house.
15. We wanted to pick the flowers. The flowers covered the meadow.
16. Shelby knew everyone. Shelby could not go anywhere without seeing friends.
17. The dog was eager for its dinner. It ran to its bowl.
18. The paper's travel section is interesting. The section is edited by Mr. Keller.
19. The children were laughing excitedly. The children played on the swings.
20. The actress walked toward the stage. Her costar followed her.

WRITING APPLICATION

Write three sentences about a place you visited recently (a museum, park, or friend's house). In each sentence, use a phrase (any kind) to add information.

Working with ELLs   **ELL** Sheltered Instruction: Cognitive

Help students learn new language structures heard during classroom instruction by having them listen to and produce sentences with subordinate clauses and phrases.

Beginning Say and act out the following sentence: *When I come to class, I see [a book].* Have students repeat your sentence. Then, invite them to complete the sentence with something they see. Allow them to point or illustrate if necessary.

Intermediate Write this sentence on the board and read it aloud: *When I go home today, I will [eat dinner].* Point out the subordinate clause and the main clause. Then, have students supply a new main clause for the sentence.

Advanced Have partners alternate reading their combined sentences from Practice 20.2C to each other. The listener should identify the subordinate clause in each sentence.

Advanced High Challenge partners to use their sentences from Practice 20.2C to produce new sentences. Have students keep the subordinate clause but replace the main clause. Then, have them read the new sentences aloud to a partner. The partner should listen for and identify the new main clause.

20.3 Varying Sentences

When you vary the length and form of the sentences you write, you are able to create a rhythm, achieve an effect, or emphasize the connections between ideas.

There are several ways you can introduce variety into the sentences you write.

> **Varying the length of sentences makes writing lively and interesting to read.**

◁ 20.3.1 RULE

Varying Sentence Length

Reading too many long sentences in a row can be just as uninteresting as reading too many short sentences in a row. When you want to emphasize a point or surprise a reader, insert a short, direct sentence to interrupt the flow of several long sentences.

EXAMPLE   Otters are expert swimmers and divers, swimming at an average speed of seven miles per hour and staying underwater for up to two minutes. Unlike muskrats or beavers, otters barely make a ripple when swimming or a splash when diving. **Otters are even waterproof.** When they are underwater, a flap of skin covering their ears and nose closes to keep them watertight.

You can also break some longer sentences into shorter sentences. If the longer sentence contains two or more ideas, you can break up the ideas into separate sentences. However, if a longer sentence contains only one main idea, you should not break it apart.

LONGER
SENTENCE   Many animals in the world fear snakes, but the mongoose does not.

TWO
SENTENCES   Many animals in the world fear snakes. The mongoose does not.

Practice 20.3A

Varying Sentences   443

Lesson Objectives

1. Compose sentences of varying lengths.

2. Begin sentences in a variety of different ways.

Varying Sentence Length

Discuss the effect of repetitious sentence lengths.

RULE 20.3.1 Read aloud the rule and then have students repeat the lines with you.

Say: The boldfaced sentence in the example is a short sentence to emphasize how unusual otters are. **Ask:** How does the short sentence create emphasis? (**Possible responses:** It contrasts with the longer sentences; it highlights one key idea.)

On the board, write these sentences: *Fargo walked down the street. He was on his way home. He saw the streetlight was out. It was ahead of him. That made the street dark as pitch. Fargo was nervous.*

Work with students to create a paragraph that tells this story with more sentence variety.

Have student pairs write their own paragraph with varied sentence lengths.

Varying Sentence Beginnings

To introduce inverted sentences as a sentence-variety technique, point out that writers sometimes change the normal order of English sentences from subject-verb to verb-subject. Give these examples: *Soli ran* across the field. Across the field *ran Soli.*

RULE 20.3.2 Read aloud the rule and then have students repeat the lines with you.

Point to the chart titled *Ways To Vary Sentence Beginnings* on page 444. It shows the same sentence with five different beginnings. **Say:** All the sentences follow normal subject-verb order, but each sentence begins in a different way. **Help** students identify the part of speech of the word or phrase at the beginning of each sentence by examining its function or structure.

On the board, write a sentence beginning with a noun, such as *Gardens can be remarkably fun to plan.* Work with students to create four sentence variations using the sentence beginnings listed in the chart. (**Possible responses:** Gardens, remarkably, can be fun to plan. Remarkably, gardens can be fun to plan. Planning a garden can be remarkably fun. To plan a garden can be remarkably fun.)

Have student pairs create original examples that show the five ways to begin a sentence. Tell them that each sentence can be about a different subject.

Teacher Tip

Students might need to review some of the grammar terms on the chart. You can have them look up the terms or point out structural cues: adverbs often end in *-ly*; infinitives begin with *to;* gerunds end in *-ing.* You may need to remind students that gerund phrases such as *Knitting sweaters* appear to be verbs but actually function as nouns.

Varying Sentence Beginnings

Another way to create variety is by changing from the usual subject–verb order in a sentence.

RULE 20.3.2

> Sentence beginnings can also be varied by reversing the traditional subject–verb order or starting the sentence with an adverb or a phrase.

EXAMPLES

The **bus is here.**
subject verb adverb

Here is the **bus.**
adverb verb subject

The **ship sailed into the bay.**
subject verb prepositional phrase

Into the bay sailed the **ship.**
prepositional phrase verb subject

We left the **island quickly.**
subject verb direct object adverb

Quickly, we left the **island.**
adverb subject verb direct object

Another way to vary your sentences is to begin them in different ways. For instance, you can start sentences with different parts of speech.

See Practice 20.3B

WAYS TO VARY SENTENCE BEGINNINGS	
Start with a noun.	**Birdhouses,** surprisingly, are not difficult to make.
Start with an adverb.	**Surprisingly,** birdhouses are not difficult to make.
Start with an infinitive.	**To make birdhouses** is, surprisingly, not difficult.
Start with a gerund.	**Making birdhouses** is, surprisingly, not difficult.
Start with a prepositional phrase.	**For a skilled carpenter**, making birdhouses is not difficult.

444   **Effective Sentences**

Working with ELLs   **ELL** Sheltered Instruction: Cognitive

As students learn about varying sentence beginnings, help them use visual support to enhance and confirm understanding of increasingly complex spoken language.

Beginning Speak a sentence using gestures for support, such as: *I exercised this morning.* Write it on the board. Then, say your sentence with a different beginning: *This morning, I exercised,* using the same gestures. Write the new version on the board, using arrows to show how the word order changed.

Intermediate Speak a sentence featuring an adverb. Give students a flow chart and have them record your sentence in the top box. Have small groups change the sentence beginning and share their new sentences as listeners record them in their charts. Help students refer to the charts to confirm understanding.

Advanced Say a sentence with an adverb, prepositional phrase, or adverbial clause. Direct students to record it in the center of a cluster diagram. Have each student alter the beginning of the sentence and say it to a partner. Have partners record the different sentence beginnings in outer circles and discuss them.

Advanced High Challenge students to create sentences with adverbs, prepositional phrases, and adverbial clauses. Have them complete the Advanced activity using their sentences.

Varying Sentence Length

the sentences. Rewrite each long compound
nce as two or more shorter sentences.

PLE   During vacation, we went to the
       circus, and we also swam, and we
       visited a museum.

WER   *During vacation, we went to the*
       circus. We also swam, and we
       visited a museum.

Je could not stop the dripping, nor could we
rn off the water, so we put a bucket under
e leak.

ustralia has many interesting animals, such
s wombats and koalas, and they carry their
oung in pouches.

ly sister went to summer camp, and my
rother went to summer school, and I am
oing to make money mowing lawns.

n the movie, the hero captures the bad guy,
ut at the end the bad guy escapes, so I think
here will be another movie.

ethany came to the United States from
ngland, and she speaks with an English
ccent.

Varying Sentence Beginnings

Read the sentences. Rewrite each sentence,
changing the beginning as specified in
parentheses. If there are two sentences,
combine them, using one of the sentences
to help you create the specified beginning.

EXAMPLE   Repairing the bike will cost money.
           It is unfortunate. (Begin with an
           adverb)

ANSWER   *Unfortunately,* repairing the bike
           will cost money.

6. It takes a lot of practice to learn how to swim
   well. (Begin with a gerund.)

7. I found the wallet I lost during our hike. That
   was lucky. (Begin with an adverb.)

8. The film star strutted into the room. (Reverse
   the subject-verb order.)

9. Modern car engines can be confusing for
   anyone who does not know the cars. (Begin
   with a prepositional phrase.)

10. When you are planning a big project like this,
    you need lots of advice. (Begin with
    an infinitive.)

PEAKING APPLICATION

th a partner, read aloud two of the long
ntences in Practice 20.3A. Then, read the
ay you broke up the long sentences. Tell your
rtner why you think it was good to break up
e sentences.

WRITING APPLICATION

Write three sentences about people you know.
Vary the sentence beginnings, or use inverted
order. You may look at Practice 20.3B to remind
you of how sentence beginnings can be varied.

Practice   445

1. We could not stop the dripping, nor
   could we turn off the water. We put
   a bucket under the leak.

2. Australia has many interesting
   animals, such as wombats and
   koalas. They carry their young in
   pouches.

3. Sample answer: My sister went to
   summer camp. My brother went to
   summer school. I am going to make
   money mowing lawns.

4. In the movie, the hero captures the
   bad guy. At the end, the bad guy
   escapes, so I think there will be
   another movie. *or* In the movie, the
   hero captures the bad guy, but at
   the end the bad guy escapes. I think
   there will be another movie.

5. Bethany came to the United States
   from England. She speaks with an
   English accent.

6. Learning how to swim well takes a
   lot of practice.

7. Luckily, I found the wallet I lost
   during our hike.

8. Into the room strutted the film star.

9. For anyone who does not know the
   cars, modern car engines can be
   confusing.

10. To plan a big project like this, you
    need lots of advice.

SPEAKING APPLICATION

Partners should discuss the original
sentences and the revised sentences
and decide which approach is more
effective.

WRITING APPLICATION

Have students share their sentences
with the class, pointing out the
different parts of speech they used
to begin their sentences.

Lesson Objectives

1. Recognize and correct sentence fragments and run-on sentences.

2. Use a variety of complete sentences that include properly placed modifiers.

3. Compose a variety of complete sentences that include parallel structures.

4. Compose a variety of complete sentences that include consistent tenses.

Correcting Fragments

Focus on fragments as incomplete sentences that can confuse readers.

RULE 20.4.1 Read aloud the rule and then have students repeat the lines with you.

Ask: How can you tell the difference between a fragment and a sentence? (**Possible responses:** A sentence can stand alone, has a subject and a verb, and expresses a complete thought.)

Correcting Phrase Fragments

RULE 20.4.2 Read aloud the rule and then have students repeat the lines with you.

Find It / FIX IT
20
Grammar Game Plan

20.4 Avoiding Sentence Problems

Recognizing problems with sentences will help you avoid and fix any problems in your writing.

Correcting Fragments

Some groups of words—even though they have a capital letter at the beginning and a period at the end—are not complete sentences. They are **fragments.**

 RULE 20.4.1

> **A fragment** is a group of words that does not express a complete thought.

A fragment can be a group of words that includes a possible subject but no verb. A fragment could also be a group of words that includes a possible verb but no subject. It can even be a group of words that contains no subject and no verb. Fragments can be turned into complete sentences by adding a subject, a verb, or both.

FRAGMENTS	COMPLETE SENTENCES
felt happy and relaxed	**I** felt happy and relaxed. (A subject is added.)
the train around the bend	The train **was coming** around the bend. (A verb is added.)
in the early evening	The **flight arrived** in the early evening. (A subject and verb are added.)

See Practice 20.4A

Correcting Phrase Fragments A **phrase fragment** cannot stand alone because it does not have both a subject and a verb.

 RULE 20.4.2

> **A phrase fragment** should not be capitalized and punctuated as if it were a sentence.

A phrase fragment can be corrected in one of two ways: (1) by adding it to a nearby sentence or (2) by adding whatever is needed to make it a complete sentence.

446 **Effective Sentences**

Diagnostic and Instruction
Diagnostic test assesses students' instructional needs. Lessons and practice are assigned based on results.

Additional Practice
- Grammar Practice—Targeted practice addresses individual needs.
- ExamView—Teachers customize their grammar practice and tests.
- Grammar Games—Interactive video games make grammar fun.

Working with ELLs **ELL** Sheltered Instruction: Cognitive

As students learn about correcting fragments, support them in speaking using a variety of grammatical structures with increasing accuracy and ease. Focus on the idea that phrases cannot stand alone.

Beginning Ask students a simple question to elicit a phrase as an answer, such as *Where is the pencil?* (on the book). Write their responses on the board. Then, model changing the phrase into a simple sentence: *It is on the book.* Say the fragment and the complete sentence and have students echo you.

Intermediate Have students read aloud the fragments and simple sentences in the

chart. Coach them to say the sentences accurately and with correct intonation. Repeat with examples on page 448, using the grammatical structure of subordination.

Advanced Ask students questions to elicit phrases as a response, such as *What is a movie you like? Why?* Record student responses on the board. Then, have them respond orally using complete sentences. Prompt students to use subordinate clauses as appropriate.

Advanced High Have students complete the Advanced activity using simple, compound, and complex sentences.

PHRASE FRAGMENT	The travelers rode camels. **on the morning of March 4**
ADDED TO OTHER SENTENCE	The travelers rode camels **on the morning of March 4** .
PHRASE FRAGMENT	They rode the camels for hours. **parched by the hot sun**
COMPLETE SENTENCES	They rode the camels for hours. They were **parched by the hot sun** .

CHANGING PHRASE FRAGMENTS INTO SENTENCES	
PHRASE FRAGMENT	COMPLETE SENTENCE
in the ancient tomb	The treasure was found **in the ancient tomb** .
laughing at her father's jokes	Helen enjoyed **laughing at her father's jokes** .
to play soccer	Elana learned **to play soccer** .

e Practice 20.4B

Correcting Clause Fragments

All clauses have subjects and verbs, but some cannot stand alone as sentences.

> A **subordinate clause** should not be capitalized and punctuated as if it were a sentence.

20.4.3 RULE

Subordinate clauses do not express complete thoughts. Although a subordinate adjective or adverb clause has a subject and a verb, it cannot stand by itself as a sentence. (See Chapter 19 for more information about subordinate clauses and the words that begin them.)

Like phrase fragments, **clause fragments** can usually be corrected in either of two ways: (1) by attaching the fragment to a nearby sentence or (2) by adding whatever words are needed to turn the fragment into a sentence.

Avoiding Sentence Problems   447

Direct students' attention to the words highlighted in purple at the top of page 447. Point out that *on the morning of March 4* is a fragment because it lacks a subject and a verb; so does *parched by the hot sun*. Direct students' attention to the examples in the chart in the middle of the page. Ask students to identify what's missing in the fragments in the chart. (*in the ancient tomb* is a prepositional phrase, so it has neither a subject nor verb; *laughing at her father's jokes* is missing a subject and a helping verb; *to play soccer* is an infinitive phrase and is therefore missing a subject and a verb.)

Correcting Clause Fragments

Focus on subordinate, or dependent, clause fragments, which begin with subordinating conjunctions.

RULE 20.4.3 Read aloud the rule and then have students repeat the lines with you.

Point out that, unlike phrase fragments, clause fragments have a subject and a verb. However, subordinate clause fragments cannot stand on their own because they begin with a subordinating conjunction or a relative pronoun.

On the board, write several clause fragments: *after the tiger got away, if the hurricane reaches land, even though he lost his shoes, when a koala is hungry.* Have students add an independent, or main, clause to each dependent clause to correct the fragment.

(continued)

Correcting Clause Fragments
(continued)

Draw students' attention to the examples at the top of page 448. **Ask:** How can you tell that the clauses highlighted in green are fragments? (**Possible responses:** Each begins with a subordinating conjunction but is not connected to a sentence; they don't express complete thoughts; they cannot be turned into yes/no questions without adding a subject and verb.) **Ask:** How were the clause fragments in the chart corrected? (**Possible response:** The subordinate clauses were connected to an independent clause.) Have students use the clause fragments on the page to write new complete sentences.

Point out that the fragments that students inadvertently write are often clause fragments. A logical way to correct these kinds of fragments is to look at them in context to see if they belong with existing main clauses. To illustrate, write the following paragraph on the board: *We had a great time on our vacation. Mainly because we went to the beach every day and relaxed. I enjoyed lying on the warm sand. Swimming was also fun. The ocean water felt refreshing.*

Call for a volunteer to find the clause fragment. (*Mainly because we went to the beach every day and relaxed.*) Point out that even though the modifier *mainly* comes before the subordinating conjunction *because,* the group of words is still a dependent clause. Call for a volunteer to correct the fragment by joining it to an existing main clause. (*We had a great time on our vacation, mainly because we went to the beach every day and relaxed.*)

CLAUSE FRAGMENT	The audience left the concert hall. **after the band finished playing**
COMPLETE SENTENCE	**After the band finished playing**, the audience left the concert hall.
CLAUSE FRAGMENT	The class enjoyed the poem. **that I recited to them as part of my oral report on horses**
COMPLETE SENTENCE	The class enjoyed the poem **that I recited to them as part of my oral report on horses**.
CLAUSE FRAGMENT	I'll give my report today. **as long as you give yours, too**
COMPLETE SENTENCE	I'll give my report today **as long as you give yours, too**.

To change a clause fragment into a sentence by the second method, you must add an independent clause to the fragment.

CHANGING CLAUSE FRAGMENTS INTO SENTENCES	
CLAUSE FRAGMENT	COMPLETE SENTENCE
that you requested	I returned the book **that you requested**. The book **that you requested** has been returned.
when he began shouting	I looked up in surprise **when he began shouting**. **When he began shouting**, I looked up in surprise.
what she was thinking	I could not figure out **what she was thinking**.

See Practice 20.4C
See Practice 20.4D

Differentiated Instruction

RTI Strategy for Below-Level Students
Remind students that complete sentences can be turned into yes/no questions but that fragments cannot. Work with them to turn the complete sentences in the chart into questions. For example, *I returned the book that you requested* becomes *Did I return the book that you requested?* Have students apply this test to other sentences on the page and discuss their answers. Then, have students apply this test to their own writing for this or another class.

RTI Strategy for Special Needs Students
Ask students to act out the complete sentences in the chart at the bottom of page 448. Then, ask them if they can act out the fragments. Explain that, generally, the fragments will be more difficult or impossible to act out because they don't express a complete thought. On the board, copy the chart on page 448. Work with students to color code the subjects and verbs in the *Complete Sentence* column.

PRACTICE 20.4A Recognizing Fragments

Read the groups of words. Then, write whether each group of words is a *sentence* or a *fragment*.

EXAMPLE In the swimming pool.

ANSWER *fragment*

1. When you arrive.
2. Dad went to work.
3. Because of the rain.
4. A really good idea.
5. Tomorrow is a new day.
6. Mom washed the dog.
7. Cat in a tree.
8. Spring always returns.
9. Without your raincoat.
10. The car is turning.

PRACTICE 20.4B Changing Phrase Fragments Into Sentences

Read the phrase fragments. Then, use each fragment in a sentence.

EXAMPLE to the library

ANSWER *I need to go to the library.*

11. at the zoo
12. to open the box
13. around the school
14. finding my books
15. to build that model
16. after the ride
17. taking the bird food
18. in the classroom
19. to climb that tree
20. trading baseball cards

SPEAKING APPLICATION

With a partner, take turns creating phrases. Your partner should listen to the phrase and then turn the phrase into a sentence.

WRITING APPLICATION

Write three sentences about what the yard of your home or school is like and what is found there. Use at least two phrases. Underline the phrases in the sentences.

Practice   449

PRACTICE 20.4A

1. fragment
2. sentence
3. fragment
4. fragment
5. sentence
6. sentence
7. fragment
8. sentence
9. fragment
10. sentence

PRACTICE 20.4B

Answers will vary. Sample answers:

11. We saw tigers at the zoo.
12. I needed scissors to open the box.
13. We picked up trash around the school.
14. Finding my books took hours.
15. My brother needs glue to build that model.
16. We can eat lunch after the ride.
17. We saw a squirrel taking the bird food.
18. There is a globe in the classroom.
19. To climb that tree would be fun.
20. The students were trading baseball cards.

SPEAKING APPLICATION

Have students explain to the class how they turned the phrases into sentences.

WRITING APPLICATION

Have students exchange sentences and check each other's work, explaining why it is or is not correct.

Working with ELLs   **ELL** Sheltered Instruction: Metacognitive

Use the Speaking Application to have students demonstrate listening comprehension of increasingly complex spoken English by taking notes. Guide students to monitor comprehension while listening and seek clarification of spoken language as needed.

Beginning Model the Speaking Application by completing Item 1 in Practice 20.4A. Provide visuals and gestures to support student comprehension, having them raise their hands when they have trouble understanding. Write the corrected sentence on the board and have students copy it. Read it again, and have students note what is different about the corrected sentence.

Intermediate Model the Speaking Application by completing Items 1–3 in

Practice 20.4A. Have students take notes by listening for key words. Ask students if there were ideas or information they didn't understand, using their notes to ask clarifying questions.

Advanced Have partners complete the Speaking Application. While one student talks, the other should take notes. Have each student monitor comprehension and ask one question to seek clarification, such as *What did you say about X?*

Advanced High Have students complete the Advanced activity. Then, have them use their notes to summarize the sentences.

PRACTICE 20.4C

Answers will vary. Sample answers:

1. You can go out as soon as you finish your work.
2. While my little brother played, I worked on the computer.
3. John got all his work done even though he was tired.
4. We made sure our friends had a good map because they usually get lost.
5. As long as you are here, why don't you stay for dinner?
6. Mom usually gets up before the sun rises.
7. We will have to wait until Dad gets home.
8. We will play baseball unless it rains.
9. Although it seemed late, it was only 6:30.
10. We have turkey whenever Grandmother visits.

PRACTICE 20.4D

11. Sample answer: When the bell rings, the students head for the door.
12. Sample answer: Vicky went to the store to find a dress.
13. sentence
14. Sample answer: To finish the project, we will need at least three days.
15. sentence
16. Sample answer: I saw my brother eating the leftovers.
17. sentence
18. sentence
19. Sample answer: My little sister wanted to draw a picture.
20. sentence

PRACTICE 20.4C Changing Clause Fragments Into Sentences

Read the clause fragments. Then, use each fragment in a sentence.

EXAMPLE   that we bought yesterday

ANSWER   *Bring me the magazine* that we bought yesterday.

1. as soon as you finish your work
2. while my little brother played
3. even though he was tired
4. because they usually get lost
5. as long as you are here
6. before the sun rises
7. until Dad gets home
8. unless it rains
9. although it seemed late
10. whenever Grandmother visits

PRACTICE 20.4D Changing Fragments Into Sentences

Read the groups of words. If a group of words is a fragment, use it in a sentence. If a group of words is already a sentence, write *sentence*.

EXAMPLE   Looking for their dog.

ANSWER   *I saw the neighbors* looking for their dog.

11. When the bell rings.
12. To find a dress.
13. We found good seats.
14. To finish the project.
15. The snow melted.
16. Eating the leftovers.
17. The library has magazines.
18. We could go with them.
19. To draw a picture.
20. The stairs creaked.

SPEAKING APPLICATION

With a partner, take turns choosing two clause fragments from Practice 20.4D. Read the clause fragment out loud, changing one word in the fragment. Your partner should reply with a sentence using the changed fragment.

WRITING APPLICATION

Write a short paragraph about the plot or action of a movie or book you enjoyed. Include at least two clause fragments as you relate what happened. Then, exchange papers with a partner. Your partner should identify and underline the clause fragments.

SPEAKING APPLICATION

Students' revisions should demonstrate that students can correct sentence fragments.

WRITING APPLICATION

Have students share their sentences with the class, explaining how they identified the clause fragments.

Run-on Sentences

A fragment is an incomplete sentence. A **run-on**, on the other hand, is two or more complete sentences that are punctuated as though they were one sentence.

> A **run-on** is two or more complete sentences that are not properly joined or separated.

Find It/ FIX IT
15
Grammar
Game Plan

20.4.4 RULE

Find It/ FIX IT
16
Grammar
Game Plan

Run-ons are usually the result of carelessness. Check your sentences carefully to see where one sentence ends and the next one begins.

Two Kinds of Run-ons

There are two kinds of run-ons. The first one is made up of two sentences that are run together without any punctuation between them. This is called a **fused sentence.**

The second type of run-on consists of two or more sentences separated by only a comma. This type of run-on is called a **comma splice.**

FUSED SENTENCES   I flew out of my bed I ran into the hall.

The Lions ran for two touchdowns they won the game.

COMMA SPLICE   Everyone in the house was up, the smoke alarm had gone off.

The Lions have a great offensive team, they also have a great defensive team.

Practice 20.4E

A good way to distinguish between a run-on and a sentence is to read the words aloud. Your ear will tell you whether you have one or two complete thoughts and whether you need to make a complete break between the thoughts.

Run-on Sentences

Focus on what run-on sentences are and why they can be confusing to readers.

RULE 20.4.4 Read aloud the rule and then have students repeat the lines with you.

Use a Think Aloud as part of a gradual release progression.

 Think Aloud

Say: If a sentence seems to go on and on without a pause, **I might** have to take a closer look at it to judge if it is a run-on sentence. Once I notice this signal, I try to study the sentence to see if it is actually two sentences joined as one. Then, I can take the proper steps to correct it.

Write on the board *There is a great store on my corner it sells plantains and cactus.* **Work with students** to determine the correct placement of punctuation. **Ask:** Is *There is a great store* a complete thought? **(yes) Ask:** Does it make sense to put a period there? (**Possible response:** no; *On my corner it sells plantains and cactus* doesn't make as much sense as *There is a great store on my corner. It sells plantains and cactus.*) Point out that a run-on sentence is incorrect because it is unclear where one thought ends and the other begins.

Have pairs of students write three run-on sentences. Then, have them trade sentences with another pair. Pairs should correct the run-on sentences.

Two Kinds of Run-ons

Point out that there are two kinds of run-ons: fused sentences and comma splices. **Say:** So far, you have been focusing on fused sentences, or complete sentences run together. In comma splices, complete sentences are separated only by a comma.

A comma does not signal a strong enough pause to separate two complete sentences. A comma is used to indicate a pause within a sentence. It does not, on its own, signal a break between sentences.

Discuss the examples of comma splices on page 451. Call for volunteers to explain ways that the comma splices might be corrected.

As students learn about recognizing run-on sentences, help them express themselves in contexts ranging from communicating with single words to participating in extended discussions. If exact English words are unknown, help students use learning strategies, such as requesting assistance, using non-verbal cues, and using synonyms and circumlocution.

Beginning Show students pictures of different games and sports. Name and describe each one, using gestures. Elicit students' opinions, ideas, and feelings about these activities by asking *Which games or sports do you like?* Help students use non-verbal cues as necessary. Write responses on the board to illustrate complete sentences.

Intermediate List a number of games or sports on the board. Have students express opinions, ideas, and feelings about things they associate with each activity. Help students use learning strategies, like using synonyms, when necessary. Have them use phrases and complete sentences.

Advanced Prompt groups to discuss games and sports, expressing their opinions, ideas, and feelings. Have students ask peers for help when they don't know a word. Listeners should pay attention for run-on sentences.

Advanced High Have partners share their opinions, ideas, and feelings about games and sports. Ensure students use correct intonation to avoid run-on sentences and request assistance as needed.

T451

Three Ways to Correct Run-ons

Point out that run-ons can be corrected by adding proper punctuation and/or a proper conjunction.

Using End Marks

RULE 20.4.5 Read aloud the rule and then have students repeat the lines with you.

Say: Skilled writers make sure that the punctuation on the page matches the way they expect a sentence to sound when read aloud. Read the first run-on example on page 452 as punctuated. Then, ask a volunteer to read the correct version. Do the same for all the examples. **Ask:** How did using correct punctuation help the reader? (**Possible responses:** It showed how the sentence was supposed to sound; it let readers know how long to pause and whether their voices were supposed to go up or down; it broke the run-ons into chunks that made sense.)

On the board, write run-ons such as these: *Run-ons are punctuated as one sentence, they are really two. One way to correct run-ons is to use a comma with a coordinating conjunction, these conjunctions include* and, but, or, for, yet, *and* nor. Have students read each group of words with you as punctuated. Then, work with students to correct the run-ons.

Ask students to write a short paragraph summarizing what they have learned about punctuating sentences. Have them read the paragraph aloud to a partner, who should check that end punctuation matches pauses and vocal inflections. Students should then correct any run-ons in their paragraphs.

Using Commas and Coordinating Conjunctions

Explain that you can sometimes fix run-on sentences by clarifying how the two clauses are related.

> **Teacher Tip**
>
> Tell students that one way to proof for run-ons is to read their paper aloud, pausing briefly for commas and periods. Another is to find all the commas in their paper and check to see if an end mark should be used instead.

Grammar Game Plan

Three Ways to Correct Run-ons

There are three ways to correct run-on sentences. You can use end marks, commas and coordinating conjunctions, or semicolons.

Using End Marks

Periods, question marks, and exclamation marks are useful to fix run-on sentences.

RULE 20.4.5

> Use an end mark to separate a run-on sentence into two sentences.

Sometimes the best way to correct a run-on is to use an end mark to split the run-on into two shorter but complete sentences. End marks help your reader pause and group your ideas more effectively.

RUN-ON   On Saturday Jill plays softball, Luis has band practice.

CORRECTED   On Saturday Jill plays softball. Luis has band practice.

RUN-ON   Hurry up we don't want to be late.

CORRECTED   Hurry up! We don't want to be late.

RUN-ON   Are you going to the game I'll meet you there.

CORRECTED   Are you going to the game? I'll meet you there.

RUN-ON   Where have you been, I've been waiting for you for two hours!

CORRECTED   Where have you been? I've been waiting for you for two hours!

Using Commas and Coordinating Conjunctions

Sometimes the two parts of a run-on are related and should be combined into a compound sentence.

452   Effective Sentences

Working with ELLs   ELL Sheltered Instruction: Cognitive

Have students learn new language structures heard in classroom instruction, including compound sentences.

Beginning On the board, write a run-on sentence such as *I like writing, I like drawing.* Then, say the sentences as a compound sentence. Explain that this new sentence is correct; it is a compound sentence. Write it on the board, pointing out the punctuation.

Intermediate Have students work to correct the examples of run-ons under Rule 20.4.5, using a piece of paper to cover the answer while they work. Have students read aloud the run-on and the correction, as listeners discuss the differences.

Advanced Write run-on sentences on the board and have students correct the sentences using compound as well as simple sentences. Students should read their answers to a partner. Partners should listen for correct intonation to ensure the sentences are correct.

Advanced High Have students create their own run-on sentences. Have partners trade sentences and rewrite the run-ons as compound sentences. Students should read their answers to a partner as partners listen for correct intonation to ensure the sentences are correct.

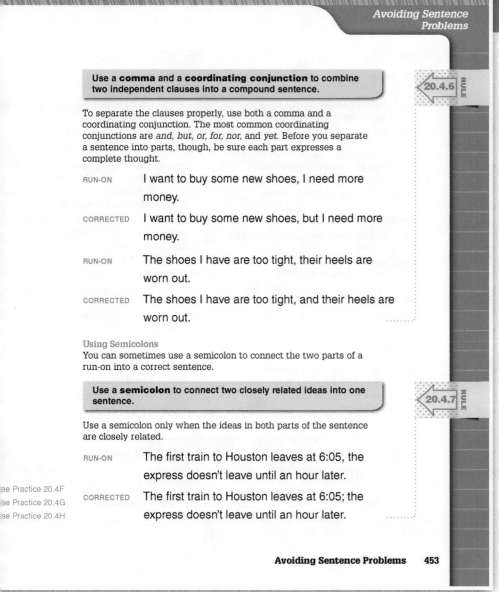

> Use a **comma** and a **coordinating conjunction** to combine two independent clauses into a compound sentence.

> 20.4.6 RULE

To separate the clauses properly, use both a comma and a coordinating conjunction. The most common coordinating conjunctions are *and, but, or, for, nor,* and *yet.* Before you separate a sentence into parts, though, be sure each part expresses a complete thought.

RUN-ON   I want to buy some new shoes, I need more money.

CORRECTED   I want to buy some new shoes, but I need more money.

RUN-ON   The shoes I have are too tight, their heels are worn out.

CORRECTED   The shoes I have are too tight, and their heels are worn out.

Using Semicolons
You can sometimes use a semicolon to connect the two parts of a run-on into a correct sentence.

> Use a **semicolon** to connect two closely related ideas into one sentence.

> 20.4.7 RULE

Use a semicolon only when the ideas in both parts of the sentence are closely related.

RUN-ON   The first train to Houston leaves at 6:05, the express doesn't leave until an hour later.

CORRECTED   The first train to Houston leaves at 6:05; the express doesn't leave until an hour later.

See Practice 20.4F
See Practice 20.4G
See Practice 20.4H

Avoiding Sentence Problems   453

RULE 20.4.6 Read aloud the rule and then have students repeat the lines with you.

Review the purpose of the common coordinating conjunctions:

and means that something is added
but, nor show contrast
or presents alternatives
for shows reason or purpose
so shows consequences
yet connects contrary ideas (People often believe. . ., yet the truth is. . .)

Have student pairs create original sentences using each of the coordinating conjunctions. Ensure that students have used the correct punctuation in their sentences.

Using Semicolons

RULE 20.4.7 Read aloud the rule and then have students repeat the lines with you.

Point out that a semicolon can be used to connect two sentences, provided that the sentences are very closely related. **Say:** One way that I can tell whether sentences are closely enough related is to see whether they are similar in structure. For example, the example sentences are closely related because they have similar subjects, *train* and *express,* and the same verb, *leave.*

Teacher Tip

Tell students that one way to remember the coordinating conjunctions is the acronym FANBOYS: *for, and, nor, but, or, yet, so.*

Extension

To help students synthesize and apply what they have learned about correcting run-on sentences, have them challenge each other to a run-on revision showdown. Working in pairs, students should write a paragraph of four or five sentences that explains how to perform a simple process, such as brushing teeth properly. In each sentence, students should omit the initial capital letter and the end mark of punctuation. Pairs should then exchange paragraphs, challenging each other to correct the run-on sentences. Pairs should check and correct each other's work.

1. run-on
2. sentence
3. run-on
4. run-on
5. sentence
6. run-on
7. sentence
8. run-on
9. run-on
10. sentence

Answers will vary. Sample answers:

11. food; it
12. *Slavery*; it
13. friends; they
14. Ecuador. It
15. station, but
16. state. Rhode
17. shipped, but
18. carnival, and
19. heroes, and
20. 1891. He

SPEAKING APPLICATION

Have students write either a run-on or a correct sentence. Then, have students share their sentences with the class, explaining why their group of words is either a run-on or a correct sentence.

WRITING APPLICATION

Have students explain how they corrected the run-on sentences in Practice 20.4F.

T454

Read the groups of words. Then, write whether each group is a *sentence* or a *run-on*.

EXAMPLE   Rachel Carson was a biologist she wrote about nature.

ANSWER   *run-on*

1. George Washington is called the Father of Our Country he was our first president.
2. Many people visit Italy because there is so much art, history, and good food there.
3. Elsa was an African lion, she became famous because of the book *Born Free*.
4. Isadora Duncan was a dancer, she danced in many countries.
5. Ruth Streeter was the first woman to hold the rank of major in the Marine Corps.
6. Squanto was a Native American who helped the Pilgrims he spoke English.
7. When Columbus first tasted hot chili peppers, he called them "violent fruit."
8. Cashews are related to poison ivy, they originally came from Brazil.
9. Benjamin Carson liked learning about science, he became a leading surgeon.
10. Grace Hopper was one of the world's first software engineers.

Read the sentences. Rewrite each run-on sentence to correct the problem.

EXAMPLE   The shepherd led the sheep he took them to a grassy field.

ANSWER   *The shepherd led the sheep. He took them to a grassy field.*

11. The herb rosemary is good in food it is also used as a symbol of remembrance.
12. Booker T. Washington wrote *Up from Slavery* it is a book about his early life.
13. Gus and Romero are good friends they go everywhere together.
14. Quito is the capital of Ecuador, it is in the northern half of the country.
15. We hurried to the train station we were late.
16. Alaska is our largest state, Rhode Island is our smallest state.
17. Bananas are green when they are shipped they turn yellow as they ripen.
18. Shandra and Lacey went to the school carnival they had a lot of fun.
19. On Memorial Day, the nation honors its heroes it recalls their bravery.
20. James Naismith invented basketball in 1891 he used peach baskets for the game.

SPEAKING APPLICATION

With a partner, take turns reading the run-ons in Practice 20.4F out loud. Talk about how speaking the run-ons out loud helps you hear where the sentences should end.

WRITING APPLICATION

Choose two run-ons from Practice 20.4F, and rewrite them. This time, feel free to reverse the order of the clauses or add more words. Be sure you don't have any run-ons when you're done.

ACTICE 20.4G Recognizing and Correcting Run-ons

d the sentences. Then, rewrite each run-on tence to correct the problem. If the sentence ot a run-on, write *correct*.

MPLE   Uncle Mike lives in Boston, he visits us often.

WER   Uncle Mike lives in Boston, *but* he visits us often.

Mom gives us oatmeal for breakfast; she says that it is good for us.

My sister likes sports my brother likes fixing things.

Aunt Grace gave us that painting she likes art.

Jose's dog is not a terrier It is a hound.

Gabriela was born in California, but now she lives in Texas.

I stumbled in the cafeteria, and my tray went flying.

Mom taught school in Dallas, Dad built roads in Austin.

The waves were rough our sailboat was tossed around.

The beach was covered with shells Diana added many to her collection.

I got a bad sunburn Diana got a deep tan.

PRACTICE 20.4H Correcting Run-ons

Read the sentences. Then, rewrite each sentence, correcting each run-on using a comma and a coordinating conjunction (e.g., *and, but, so, or, for, nor,* and *yet*).

EXAMPLE   The mail came, there was nothing for me.

ANSWER   The mail came, *but* there was nothing for me.

11. Earl has to write a paper, he has to study for a test.

12. Mr. Heriard was trying to fix the fence he ran out of wood.

13. The show must be sold out there are people standing in the back.

14. Diana woke up late she missed her plane.

15. Dad can make pizza he can make quiche.

16. Use red pens for editing use black pens for final drafts.

17. I went I didn't want to.

18. Jackson was hungry he didn't want to eat the chicken salad.

19. Mallory had to walk to school her bike has a flat tire.

20. We can leave Friday night, we can leave Saturday morning.

SPEAKING APPLICATION

Choose a paragraph from a book. Take turns with a partner. Read your paragraphs aloud without stopping for punctuation. Discuss how reading without punctuation interferes with understanding. Then, read the paragraphs correctly.

WRITING APPLICATION

Rewrite three run-ons from Practice 20.4H in another way. Remember that there are three ways to correct a run-on. Try reversing the order of the clauses and adding more words.

Practice   455

PRACTICE 20.4G

Answers will vary. Sample answers:

1. correct
2. sports, while
3. painting; she
4. terrier; rather, it
5. correct
6. correct
7. Dallas, and
8. rough. Our
9. shells; Diana
10. sunburn, but

PRACTICE 20.4H

Answers will vary. Sample answers:

11. paper, and
12. fence, but
13. out, for
14. late, so
15. pizza, and
16. editing, and
17. went, but
18. hungry, but
19. school, for
20. night, or

SPEAKING APPLICATION

Ask volunteers to read sentences from their paragraphs that caused particular confusion when read without punctuation.

WRITING APPLICATION

Have students exchange sentences, explaining why they are or are not correct.

Working with ELLs   **ELL** Sheltered Instruction: Cognitive

Help students use increasingly complex grammatical structures in their writing by using possessive case (apostrophe *s*) correctly. Use Item 4 from Practice 20.4G to model creating a possessive. Write *Ari has a report. It is Ari's report.* Point out the apostrophe and the *s*. Then:

Beginning Point to an object on a student's desk. Say: *The book belongs to [Dan]. It is [Dan]'s book.* Write the possessive *[Ana]'s pen* on the board. Have students repeat. Point to a pen on another student's desk and have students write the possessive as you write it on the board.

Intermediate On separate note cards, write students' names and an apostrophe plus s. Have students use the cards to

form the possessive. Then, have them write simple sentences using the possessives they formed.

Advanced Have partners identify three singular nouns in their corrected sentences from Practice 20.4G, form the possessive case of each, and use it in a new sentence.

Advanced High Have students complete the Advanced activity. Then, review the rules for forming possessives of plurals ending in *s* (add an apostrophe at the end), and have them revise their sentences by replacing singular with plural possessives.

Test Warm-Up

1. **C** Change the period after **Union** to a semicolon

2. **J** Make no change

3. **A** The North had advantages. More people lived there, and industry was better developed, too.

4. **G** Add a semicolon after **Gettysburg**

Reteach

If students have not mastered these skills, review the content in Section 20.4 Avoiding Sentence Problems.

1. Using Semicolons 20.4.7

2. Using Semicolons 20.4.7

3. Using End Marks 20.4.5

4. Using Semicolons 20.4.7

Test Tip

Test questions about the meaning of a word or the grammatical function of a word in a sentence often require a student to understand the context of the sentence. Suggest to students that, if a test question asks about the meaning or function of a word in a sentence, they should reread both the target sentence and the sentence before it. For example, if a question asks for the antecedent of the pronoun *it*, students should reread the prior sentence as well as the target sentence to make sure that the antecedent wasn't introduced earlier in the passage.

Test Warm-Up

DIRECTIONS
Read the introduction and the passage that follows. Then, answer the questions to show that you can recognize and correct run-on sentences in reading and writing.

David wrote this paragraph for a report about the Civil War between North (the Union) and the South (the Confederacy). Read the paragraph and think about the changes you would suggest as a peer editor. Wher finish reading, answer the questions that follow.

The Civil War

(1) Eleven states in the South withdrew from the Union. their secession led to the Civil War. (2) Confederate soldiers fired the first shots on Fort Sumter. (3) Both sides in the war had excellent general (4) Robert E. Lee led the Confederate forces; Ulysses S. Grant led the Union forces. (5) The North had advantages and more people lived th and industry was better developed, too. (6) The turning point came w the Union forces won a battle at Gettysburg the conflict lasted four y and cost many lives.

---

1 What change, if any, should be made in sentence 1?

A Add a comma after **South**

B Change the period after **Union** to a comma

C Change the period after **Union** to a semicolon

D Make no change

2 What change, if any, should be made in sentence 4?

F Add a comma after **Lee**

G Change the semicolon to a comma

H Delete the semicolon

J Make no change

3 What is the BEST way to revise sentence

A The North had advantages. More peo lived there, and industry was better developed, too.

B The North had advantages; more peo industry was better developed, too.

C The North had advantages, because n people lived there, industry was bette developed, too.

D The North had advantages, more peo lived there and industry was better developed, too.

4 What change should be made in sentence

F Add a period after **came**

G Add a semicolon after **Gettysburg**

H Add a semicolon after **won**

J Add a comma after **Gettysburg**

Properly Placing Modifiers

If a phrase or clause acting as an adjective or adverb is not placed near the word it modifies, it may seem to modify a different word. Then the sentence may seem unclear or odd.

> A **modifier** should be placed as close as possible to the word it describes.

20.4.8 RULE

A modifier placed too far away from the word it describes is called a **misplaced modifier.**

MISPLACED MODIFIER	We rented a boat at the lake **with an outboard motor**.

The misplaced phrase *with an outboard motor* makes it seem as though the lake has an outboard motor.

PROPERLY PLACED MODIFIER	At the lake, we rented a boat **with an outboard motor**.

Below is a different type of misplaced modifier that is sometimes called a **dangling modifier.** A dangling modifier at the beginning of a sentence causes the sentence to be unclear.

DANGLING MODIFIER	**Walking on the beach**, the sand felt hot under our feet.

In this sentence, *walking on the beach* should modify a person or people. Instead, it incorrectly modifies *sand.*

CORRECTED	**Walking on the beach**, we felt the hot sand under our feet.

Practice 20.4I
Practice 20.4J

Avoiding Sentence Problems   457

Properly Placing Modifiers

Discuss the importance of properly placed modifiers in complete sentences.

RULE 20.4.8 Read aloud the rule and then have students repeat the lines with you.

Say: If a modifier is misplaced, the meaning of a sentence can change, often with amusing results. What image does this sentence bring to mind? *Sapna saw a dozen squirrels walking to school.* (**Possible response:** The squirrels were walking to school.) To create the correct image, the sentence should read *Walking to school, Sapna saw a dozen squirrels.*

Work with students to review the examples on page 457 so that they understand how to recognize and correct misplaced or dangling modifiers.

Have pairs of students write sentences with misplaced or dangling modifiers. Then, have the partners rewrite the sentences so that the errors are corrected.

Teacher Tip

You can find funny examples of misplaced modifiers by checking books by grammarians like Richard Lederer or Patricia T. O'Conner. You can also search the Web using the key words *"dangling modifiers" funny.* Have students correct the funny examples.

Working with ELLs   **ELL** Sheltered Instruction: Cognitive

As students study modifiers, guide them to spell familiar words and employ English spelling rules with increasing accuracy. Teach students the spelling rule that no normal English word ends in *v.* If a word ends in /v/ sound, it is spelled *ve.*

Beginning Write the word *have* on the board. Point to the *ve* and explain that the *ve* makes a /v/ sound. Say the word *save* and have students apply the spelling rule to write it.

Intermediate Say the words *native* and *gave.* Have students apply the spelling rule to write them, then write two more words ending in *ve.*

Advanced Speak a list of words ending in *ve*, such as *brave*, and have students spell them. Then have them write each word in a sentence.

Advanced High Provide partners with lists of words ending in the *v* sound. One partner chooses a word while the other must spell the word correctly and use it in a sentence. Partners should write several sentences and check each other's work.

PRACTICE 20.4I

1. I found the book that I need for class after looking in three rooms.

2. The boy in the red shirt is my brother.

3. The shopping list that Dad wrote seemed long.

4. Eileen saw her hat crushed at the bottom of the box.

5. The bottle full of perfume fell and broke.

6. We knew the music that we liked would be played.

7. Ari's report about reptiles was fascinating.

8. We left our car with a flat tire at the shop.

9. The purse that had her wallet was lost.

10. My sister found her favorite book on the top shelf.

PRACTICE 20.4J

11. My sister found a sweater that does not belong to her in the closet.

12. Running across the yard, we felt the grass tickle our bare feet.

13. correct

14. Carlos smells the food sizzling on the grill.

15. Please discuss with your friends the information that is enclosed.

16. correct

17. My neighbors have a fence with a gate behind the house.

18. Trying three different keys, we finally unlocked the front door. *or* We tried three different keys and finally unlocked the front door.

19. correct

20. I saw a frog hopping beside the lake.

PRACTICE 20.4I Revising to Correct Misplaced Modifiers

Read the sentences. Then, rewrite each sentence to correct the underlined misplaced modifier.

EXAMPLE   A woman was walking a dog <u>in a blue dress</u>.

ANSWER   *A woman in a blue dress was walking a dog.*

1. I found the book after looking in three rooms <u>that I need for class</u>.

2. The boy is my brother <u>in the red shirt</u>.

3. The shopping list seemed long <u>that Dad wrote</u>.

4. <u>Crushed at the bottom of the box</u>, Eileen saw her hat.

5. The bottle fell and broke <u>full of perfume</u>.

6. We knew the music would be played <u>that we liked</u>.

7. Ari's report was fascinating <u>about reptiles</u>.

8. We left our car at the shop <u>with a flat tire</u>.

9. The purse was lost <u>that had her wallet</u>.

10. <u>On the top shelf</u>, my sister found her favorite book.

PRACTICE 20.4J Recognizing and Correcting Misplaced Modifiers

Read the sentences. If a sentence has a misplaced modifier, rewrite the sentence so the modifier is properly placed. If a sentence is correct, write *correct*.

EXAMPLE   Covered in flowers, Marilyn admired the hillside.

ANSWER   *Marilyn admired the hillside covered in flowers.*

11. My sister found a sweater in the closet that does not belong to her.

12. Running across the yard, the grass tickled our bare feet.

13. Carrying the luggage outside, Dad began to pack the car for our trip.

14. Sizzling on the grill, Carlos smells the food.

15. Please discuss the information that is enclosed with your friends.

16. I like the car with leather seats.

17. My neighbors have a fence behind the house with a gate.

18. Trying three different keys, the front door was finally unlocked.

19. Leaving his book unfinished, the writer decided to write a short story.

20. Hopping beside the lake I saw a frog.

SPEAKING APPLICATION

With a partner, take turns describing a place you have studied or seen in a movie. Use modifiers to add detail. Your partner should listen for and identify modifiers and what they modify.

WRITING APPLICATION

Write a short paragraph about clothes that are currently in style. Include at least two modifiers to add detail, taking care to properly place the modifiers.

458   Effective Sentences

SPEAKING APPLICATION

Have partners explain how they were able to identify modifiers and the words they modified.

WRITING APPLICATION

Students should explain how they identified the correct placement of modifiers.

Avoiding Double Negatives

Negative words, such as *nothing* and *not*, are used to deny or to say *no*. Some people mistakenly use **double negatives**—two negative words—when only one is needed.

> **Avoid writing sentences that contain double negatives.**

20.4.9 **RULE**

In the following examples, negative words are highlighted. The first sentence in each example contains double negatives. The corrected sentences show two ways to correct each double-negative sentence.

DOUBLE NEGATIVES	The lightning **didn't** damage **nothing**.
CORRECTED SENTENCES	The lightning **didn't** damage anything.
	The lightning damaged **nothing**.

DOUBLE NEGATIVES	I **haven't no** time now.
CORRECTED SENTENCES	I **haven't** any time now.
	I have **no** time now.

DOUBLE NEGATIVES	She **never** told us **nothing** about the storm.
CORRECTED SENTENCES	She **never** told us anything about the storm.
	She told us **nothing** about the storm.

DOUBLE NEGATIVES	A few clouds **don't** bother **no one**.
CORRECTED SENTENCES	A few clouds **don't** bother anyone.
	A few clouds bother **no one**.

DOUBLE NEGATIVES	Janice **didn't** invite **nobody**.
CORRECTED SENTENCES	Janice **didn't** invite anybody.
	Janice invited **nobody**.

Practice 20.4K
Practice 20.4L

Avoiding Double Negatives

Discuss how using two negative words or phrases in a sentence affects the meaning of an independent clause in English.

RULE 20.4.9 Read aloud the rule and then have students repeat the line with you.

Direct students' attention to the first example on page 459. Point out that the negative words or phrases are highlighted in blue. Ask students to count the number of negative words or phrases in *The lightning didn't damage nothing.* (two) Have students count the number of negative words or phrases in the two corrected sentences. (one) Have students skim the remaining examples. **Then, ask:** How were the examples on page 459 corrected? (**Possible response:** One of the two negative words or phrases was dropped; only one negative was used in each clause.)

Work with students to make a list of negative words or phrases, such as *no, not, cannot, none, nor, nothing, no one, nowhere, hardly, never,* and *not only.* Also consider words beginning with the prefix *un-* or *in-*, meaning "no" or "not."

Have student pairs write sentences containing double negatives. Then, have students trade sentences with a second pair. The second pair should correct the double negatives and then explain what they did to make the corrections.

Differentiated Instruction

Strategy for Spanish Speakers

Students whose home language is Spanish may mistakenly employ a double negative in English when intending a negative meaning, as this is a common structure in Spanish (*No voy nunca al cine,* literally *I am not going never to the movies*). Elicit from students words that are considered negative, such as *no, never, not, none,* and so on. On the board, write examples of sentences that show both correct use of negatives and incorrect use of double negatives. For example, write *Miguel does not like mangoes* and *Miguel does not like no mangoes.* Remind students that to convey negative meaning in an English sentence, only one negative word is needed. Point out the second negative in some of the double negative examples. Then, have students circle the negative words in each remaining sentence to help them identify the sentences that are incorrect. Finally, work with students to revise the sentences with double negatives by choosing alternative words or by changing the verb.

PRACTICE 20.4K

1. anywhere	6. is
2. has	7. anything
3. anybody	8. had
4. any	9. can
5. would	10. ever

PRACTICE 20.4L

Answers will vary. Sample answers:

11. We don't want anybody to go in there.

12. Mom can't find her rolling pin anywhere.

13. I didn't have anything to do with it.

14. My brother can never remember his password for that Web site.

15. My sister didn't take any of her books to school.

16. You haven't said anything about your band concert.

17. The movie stars didn't want to pose for any photographers.

18. We didn't tell anybody about the secret room.

19. I can't find anyone to go to the store with me.

20. She didn't go anywhere near the place.

SPEAKING APPLICATION

Have partners explain how they were able to tell when a sentence was correct and when it contained a double negative.

WRITING APPLICATION

Have students share their sentences with the class, explaining why they are correct.

PRACTICE 20.4K > Using Negatives Correctly

Read the sentences. Then, write the word in parentheses that makes each sentence negative without creating a double negative.

EXAMPLE   The coach (can, can't) find no one to be quarterback.

ANSWER   *can*

1. The new box of pencils wasn't (anywhere, nowhere) in my room.

2. Maria (has, hasn't) said nothing about her visit to her grandmother's.

3. Henry didn't know (nobody, anybody) at the party.

4. I don't like (none, any) of the television shows this season.

5. I (would, wouldn't) do nothing to hurt my little brother.

6. Our house (is, isn't) nowhere near the grocery store.

7. This magazine doesn't have (anything, nothing) about the parade.

8. We (had, hadn't) never thought that my sister would get a poem published.

9. No one (can, can't) get into our clubhouse.

10. They didn't (never, ever) go away on vacation.

SPEAKING APPLICATION

With a partner, take turns talking about things that should not happen, such as breaking rules at home or failing to take safety precautions. Your partner should listen for and identify negatives and whether they are used correctly.

PRACTICE 20.4L > Revising to Correct Double Negatives

Read the sentences. Then, rewrite each sentence to correct the double negative.

EXAMPLE   I don't have no interest in that.

ANSWER   *I have no interest in that.*

11. We don't want nobody to go in there.

12. Mom can't find her rolling pin nowhere.

13. I didn't have nothing to do with it.

14. My brother can't never remember his password for that Web site.

15. My sister didn't take none of her books to school.

16. You haven't said nothing about your band concert.

17. The movie stars didn't want to pose for no photographers.

18. We didn't tell nobody about the secret room.

19. I can't find no one to go to the store with me.

20. She didn't go nowhere near the place.

WRITING APPLICATION

Write two negative sentences about things you have seen happen—or not happen. Be sure to use the negatives correctly.

Working with ELLs   **ELL** Sheltered Instruction: Cognitive

Help students recognize and distinguish sounds in new vocabulary with increasing ease. Have them practice producing the sounds to pronounce words in an increasingly comprehensible manner and learn the relationship between the sounds and letters as they write.

Beginning Write *season* (Practice 20.4K, item 4) on the board and have students write it as you sound it out. Explain that the vowels *ea* together usually make the long e sound. Then write *hear/her* on the board. Model the difference between long and short *e,* having students repeat.

Intermediate Create note cards of words with consonant clusters from the activities, like *hurt.* Have partners sound out words and write them in sentences, then practice saying a new word featuring a consonant cluster.

Advanced Provide students with words from the activities and similar words with different vowel sounds, like *pin/pan.* Have partners write the words in sentences and then pronounce them correctly. Have them find and pronounce a new word sharing a vowel sound with one of the activity words.

Advanced High Have students complete the Advanced activity. Challenge them to find and pronounce three new words sharing a vowel sound with one of the activity words.

Avoiding Common Usage Problems

This section contains fifteen common usage problems in alphabetical order. Some are expressions that you should avoid in both your speaking and your writing. Others are words that are often confused because of similar spellings or meanings.

(1) accept, except Do not confuse the spelling of these words. *Accept*, a verb, means "to take what is offered" or "to agree to." *Except*, a preposition, means "leaving out" or "other than."

VERB	She **accepted** the gift generously.
PREPOSITION	She gave everyone a gift **except** me.

(2) advice, advise Do not confuse the spelling of these related words. *Advice*, a noun, means "an opinion." *Advise*, a verb, means "to give an opinion."

NOUN	My friend gave me **advice** about hotels in Rome.
VERB	My friend **advised** me to find a good guide.

(3) affect, effect *Affect*, a verb, means "to influence" or "to cause a change in." *Effect*, usually a noun, means "result."

VERB	The sandstorm **affected** my eyes.
NOUN	What is the **effect** of getting sand in your ears?

(4) at Do not use *at* after *where*.

INCORRECT	Do you know **where** he is **at**?
CORRECT	Do you know **where** he is?

(5) because Do not use *because* after *the reason*. Eliminate one or the other.

INCORRECT	**The reason** I am sad is **because** our trip was canceled.
CORRECT	I am sad **because** our trip was canceled.
	The **reason** I am sad is **that** our trip was canceled.

Avoiding Sentence Problems 461

Avoiding Common Usage Problems

Discuss reasons that usage errors should be avoided in writing.

Use a Think Aloud as part of a gradual release progression.

Think Aloud Say: When **I look** at this list, it seems long. So the way to handle this list is to focus on the few problems that give me trouble. One thing I need to review is the difference between *advice* and *advise*. The explanation tells me that I should use *advice* when I need a noun that means "an opinion." I should use *advise* when I need a verb that means "to give an opinion."

Work with students to complete this sentence frame: My father _____ me never to give _____ unless it was asked for.

Assign student pairs one usage problem on this page. Ask them to develop a hint or memory aid to help classmates remember the rule for correct usage. Have students share their rules.

(continued)

Teacher Tip
Have students read examples of correct usage aloud to reinforce their sense of how correct usage sounds.

Differentiated Instruction

RTI Strategy for Below-Level Students Have students work in small groups to make posters of some of the usage rules in this section, such as "Do not use *at* after *where*." If appropriate, the student groups can illustrate their posters. Otherwise, simply have them letter the rule they have chosen on the poster. Then, put the posters in a prominent place in the classroom in order to remind students of the common usage problems.

PRE-AP Enrichment for Above-Level Students Divide students into two groups. Have each member of the first group write a letter asking for advice for a simple problem. Then have them give their letters to members of the second group to respond. Each member of the second group should write an answer to the letter he or she has received. In both sets of letters, students should use correctly several of the problem words in this section.

Avoiding Common Usage Problems

(continued)

To help students understand 6) beside, besides; (7) different from, different than; and (2) advice, advise, write these sentences on the board: *I am writing to tell you how much I like your book. It was different than any other book I ever read. It was funny but sort of serious, too. Beside the story, I liked your illustrations, too. I wonder if you could give me advise about being a writer.*

Ask: What impression do you get of this person? (**Possible response:** The person seems eager and self-confident, but the number of usage errors might suggest carelessness or lack of education.)

Work with students to correct the errors: (**Possible correction:** *I am writing to tell you how much I like your book. It was different from any other book I ever read. It was funny but rather serious, too. Besides the story, I also liked your illustrations. I wonder if you could give me advice about being a writer.*)

Assign student pairs one or two of the usage errors on page 462. Have them make up original examples to illustrate correct usage for each error they are assigned.

Assign student pairs one or two of the usage errors on page 462.

Teacher Tip

Share this proofreading tip with students. They can use their word processor's Find command to check for errors they commonly make with words like *your* and *you're*. For example, if they often use *your* when they mean *you're*, they can search for *your*. Each time the word is found, they can decide whether they need a possessive pronoun or a contraction.

---

(6) beside, besides   These two prepositions have different meanings and cannot be interchanged. *Beside* means "at the side of" or "close to." *Besides* means "in addition to."

EXAMPLES   We picnicked **beside** the Mississippi River.
No one **besides** us had blankets to sit on.

(7) different from, different than   *Different from* is preferred over *different than*.

EXAMPLE   The monkeys were **different from** what I had expected.

(8) farther, further   *Farther* is used to refer to distance. *Further* means "additional" or "to a greater degree or extent."

EXAMPLES   We walked much **farther** than he did.
After he raised his voice, I listened no **further**.

(9) in, into   *In* refers to position. *Into* suggests motion.

POSITION   The tourists are **in** the history museum.
MOTION   They walked **into** the room of famous documents.

(10) kind of, sort of   Do not use *kind of* or *sort of* to mean "rather" or "somewhat."

INCORRECT   This CD of jazz music is **sort of** new.
CORRECT   This CD of jazz music is **rather** new.

(11) like   *Like*, a preposition, means "similar to" or "in the same way as." It should be followed by an object. Do not use *like* before a subject and a verb. Use *as* or *that* instead.

PREPOSITION   The pyramids looked **like** giant triangles.
INCORRECT   This stew doesn't taste **like** it should.
CORRECT   This stew doesn't taste **as** it should.

462   **Effective Sentences**

T462

(12) that, which, who   *That* and *which* refer to things. *Who* refers only to people.

THINGS	The photograph **that** I took won first prize.
PEOPLE	The dancer **who** performed is my cousin.

(13) their, there, they're   Do not confuse the spelling of these three words. *Their*, a possessive adjective, always modifies a noun. *There* is usually used as a sentence starter or as an adverb. *They're* is a contraction of *they are*.

POSSESSIVE ADJECTIVE	The tourists boarded **their** bus.
SENTENCE STARTER	**There** are many tours available.
ADVERB	The tour guide is standing over **there**.
CONTRACTION	**They're** trying to board the bus now.

(14) to, too, two   Do not confuse the spelling of these words. *To* plus a noun creates a prepositional phrase. *To* plus a verb creates an infinitive. *Too* is an adverb and modifies verbs, adjectives, and other adverbs. *Two* is a number.

PREPOSITION	**to** the house	**to** Florida
INFINITIVE	**to** meet	**to** hide
ADVERB	**too** sad	**too** quickly
NUMBER	**two** clouds	**two** dolphins

(15) when, where, why   Do not use *when*, *where*, or *why* directly after a linking verb such as *is*. Reword the sentence.

INCORRECT	To see the Alamo is **why** we came to Texas.
CORRECT	We came to Texas to see the Alamo.
INCORRECT	In the evening is **when** I walk my dog.
CORRECT	I walk my dog in the evening.

e Practice 20.4M
e Practice 20.4N
e Practice 20.4O
e Practice 20.4P

To cover the difference between **(12) that, which, who**; **(13) their, there, they're**; **(14) to, too, two**, have students pairs make up examples to illustrate correct usage of these commonly misused words. Have students read their examples aloud to the class without letting other students see what they have written. Students who listen to the examples should write the correct form of the commonly misused word in the example. After students have written their answers, write the correct answer on the board. Repeat until all students have had a chance to share an example or until you are confident that students know the usage rules.

Teacher Tip

Tell students that they will find it easier to check for usage errors if they check for one error at a time. Encourage them to pick two or three errors from the list. When they revise a paper, have them look for just one of those errors at a time. Although it sounds as if looking through the paper three times might take longer, it actually goes more quickly because students are looking for just one thing. The results are also more accurate when students focus on just one error at a time.

T463

PRACTICE 20.4M

1. their
2. advise
3. too
4. affect
5. beside
6. farther
7. who
8. into
9. except
10. two

PRACTICE 20.4N

11. from
12. advice
13. accept
14. correct
15. rather
16. as
17. correct
18. they're
19. who
20. correct

SPEAKING APPLICATION

Have partners explain to the class the differences between *affect* and *effect*, *advice* and *advise*, and *accept* and *except*, and present their sentences as examples of correct usage.

WRITING APPLICATION

Have students exchange their sentences with a partner and correct any misuse of the assigned words.

PRACTICE 20.4M Choosing the Correct Usage

Read the sentences. Then, write the word in parentheses that best completes each sentence.

EXAMPLE   When the shipment arrived, I (accepted, excepted) the package.

ANSWER   *accepted*

1. The neighbors invited us to (their, they're) house.
2. I thought Mom would be the best one to (advise, advice) me on the science project.
3. It is (to, too) cold to go out without a coat.
4. The news did not seem to (affect, effect) my sister as much as I thought it would.
5. When it is sunny, my cat loves to sleep (beside, besides) the window.
6. Our team hiked two miles (further, farther).
7. Anita is the only one (that, who) knows the combination to the lock.
8. Moisha followed Juan (into, in) the hall.
9. Everyone is here (accept, except) Lisa.
10. The football player carried the ball for only (to, two) yards.

PRACTICE 20.4N Recognizing and Correcting Usage Problems

Read the sentences. If the underlined word is used correctly, write *correct*. If the word is incorrect, write the correct word.

EXAMPLE   The moonlight had a lovely <u>affect</u> on the scene.

ANSWER   *effect*

11. The results of the experiment were different <u>than</u> what I expected.
12. I would like to have your <u>advise</u> on this issue.
13. My sister does not know how to <u>except</u> a compliment.
14. My dog loves sleeping <u>beside</u> the fireplace.
15. This food is <u>kind of</u> good.
16. The milk did not smell <u>like</u> it should.
17. I want to discuss this <u>further</u>.
18. I called Derek and Carlos, and <u>their</u> bringing food for the party.
19. This is the friend <u>that</u> went with me to the concert.
20. The stars that night looked <u>like</u> diamonds on black velvet.

SPEAKING APPLICATION

With a partner, choose four sentences from Practice 20.4M. Take turns making up new sentences that correctly use the word that *was not* the right choice in the practice. Your partner should listen and confirm that the word was used correctly.

WRITING APPLICATION

Write a short paragraph about an event in your life that was a surprise. Correctly use at least three words from Practice 20.4M and Practice 20.4N in your paragraph.

464   **Effective Sentences**

Working with ELLs   ELL Sheltered Instruction: Cognitive

Help students recognize and distinguish sounds in new vocabulary with increasing ease. Have them practice producing the sounds to pronounce words in an increasingly comprehensible manner and learn the relationship between the sounds and letters as they write.

Beginning   Write *invited* on the board, sound it out, and have students copy. Say that the first *i* is short, but the second *i* is long. Explain thatin the pattern vowel-consonant-*e*, the *e* is usually silent and makes the vowel before it long. Model long and short *i*, having students repeat.

Intermediate   Create flash cards of commonly misused words. Have partners decode the words, deciding if the vowel is short, long, or silent, then practice saying a new vocabulary word featuring one of the vowel sounds.

Advanced   Have partners read aloud their answers from Practice 20.4N, distinguishing between the sounds in similar words. Have listeners write the word they hear to check their work. Have them find and pronounce two new words that share a sound with an activity word.

Advanced High   Have students complete the Advanced activity. Challenge them to find and pronounce three new words with a sound spelled as in one of the activity words.

PRACTICE 20.4O Recognizing and Correcting Usage Problems

Read the sentences. Then, if a sentence has a usage problem, rewrite it to correct the problem. If a sentence is correct, write *correct*.

EXAMPLE   Your sandwich is different than mine.

ANSWER   *Your sandwich is different from mine.*

1. Maybe this police officer can tell us where we are at.
2. The reason I want to go is because I'll see Mark.
3. The restaurant was farther away than I thought.
4. This book is kind of interesting.
5. The costumes we rented do not fit like they should.
6. To try out for the play is why I came.
7. The woman who interviewed me is named Carlotta.
8. Five o'clock is when we are supposed to arrive.
9. Grandma and Grandpa invited me to stay at they're house.
10. I loved the special affects in that movie.

PRACTICE 20.4P Avoiding Usage Problems

Read the pairs of words. For each pair of words, write two sentences that are related in meaning.

EXAMPLE   there, their

ANSWER   *My friends invited me to their party. I put my gift over there.*

11. accept, except
12. there, they're
13. advise, advice
14. two, too
15. affect, effect
16. beside, besides
17. farther, further
18. who, that
19. into, in
20. like, as

SPEAKING APPLICATION

With a partner, talk about a place you would like to visit. Use two or three words from Practice 20.4O and Practice 20.4P to include in your discussion. Your partner should listen for the words and say whether they were used correctly.

WRITING APPLICATION

Write a very brief story (three or four sentences) about a cat or dog. Choose four "problem" words or phrases from Practice 20.4O and Practice 20.4P, and use them correctly in the story.

Practice   465

SPEAKING APPLICATION

Have partners correct the usage errors they found.

WRITING APPLICATION

Have students exchange papers with a partner and check to see that the usage is correct. Ask students to explain any problems they find.

PRACTICE 20.4O

1. Maybe this police officer can tell us where we are.
2. The reason I want to go is that I'll see Mark. *or* I want to go because I'll see Mark.
3. correct
4. This book is rather interesting.
5. The costumes we rented do not fit as they should.
6. I came to try out for the play.
7. correct
8. We are supposed to arrive at five o'clock.
9. Grandma and Grandpa invited me to stay at their house.
10. I loved the special effects in that movie.

PRACTICE 20.4P

Answers will vary. Sample answers:

11. He did not accept our packing suggestions. I remembered to pack everything except my toothbrush.
12. I have never been to a game there before. I talked to my friends, and they're coming to the game.
13. I asked my dad to advise me. I think he gave me good advice.
14. I bought two gallons of milk. Do you think that is too much?
15. Did the weather affect your weekend? The spring rain had a wonderful effect on the garden.
16. I had my photo taken beside the monument. There was no one there besides us.
17. I walked farther today than yesterday before I sat and read my book. When the hero of the story died, I could read no further.
18. There is the man who helped me with my purchase. This is the MP3 player that I bought.
19. We walked into the house. I sat in the living room.
20. That house looks just like mine. The food that we bought did not taste as it should have.

Answers will vary. Sample answers:

1. The set for the school play needs more work.
2. The marching band played three songs at halftime.
3. The substitute teacher wrote her name on the board.
4. Was the broken window hard to fix?
5. My favorite science project was making a simple battery.
6. The marathon runners ran through the streets.
7. The local library has a big book sale this month.
8. The pet monkey left an enormous mess.
9. The girl and her family traveled to the dance competition.
10. Only the best chess players competed in the tournament.

PRACTICE 2

Answers will vary. Sample answers:

1. Lions eat meat.
2. The workers are building a house.
3. On a clear night, Jill studies the stars.
4. Nick designs airplanes for a living.
5. Brianna put the leftovers in the refrigerator.
6. I asked Gina's mom for a ride home.
7. We saw acrobats at the street fair.
8. Yesterday, Dan met Darryl at the zoo.
9. Our teacher gave us a test.
10. Who put a cup of water on the chessboard?

PRACTICE 3

1. driver
2. them
3. himself
4. none
5. me

Cumulative Review Chapters 18–20

PRACTICE 1 Using Complete Subjects and Predicates

Each item below contains only a complete subject or a complete predicate. Rewrite each item, making a sentence by adding the missing part indicated in parentheses.

1. The set for the school play (add a predicate).
2. (add a subject) played three songs at halftime.
3. The substitute teacher (add a predicate).
4. Was (add a subject) hard to fix?
5. My favorite science project (add a predicate).
6. (add a subject) ran through the streets.
7. The local library (add a predicate).
8. (add a subject) left an enormous mess.
9. The girl and her family (add a predicate).
10. (add a subject) competed in the tournament.

PRACTICE 2 Using Direct Objects

Rewrite each incomplete sentence, supplying a direct object where indicated in parentheses. You may also include the article *a*, *an*, or *the* or another modifier along with the direct object.

1. Lions eat (direct object).
2. The workers are building (direct object).
3. On a clear night, Jill studies (direct object).
4. Nick designs (direct object) for a living.
5. Brianna put (direct object) in the refrigerator.
6. I asked (direct object) for a ride home.
7. We saw (direct object) at the street fair.
8. Yesterday, Dan met (direct object) at the zoo.
9. Our teacher gave us (direct object).
10. Who put (direct object) on the chessboard?

466 Phrases, Clauses, and Sentences

PRACTICE 3 Identifying Indirect Objects

Read the sentences. Then, write the indirect object in each sentence. If there is no indirect object, write *none*.

1. The police officer gave the driver a ticket.
2. I told them the story.
3. My father bought himself a new suit.
4. Nadia saved money for a new camera.
5. Please bring me a glass of water.
6. The magician showed us a new trick.
7. Miranda offered the concert tickets to Jake.
8. I wish you a happy birthday.
9. The interviewer asked Jon several questions.
10. Who gave her the new umbrella?

PRACTICE 4 Identifying Subject Complements

Read the sentences. Then, write the subject complement in each sentence. Also indicate whether it is a *predicate noun*, *predicate pronoun*, or *predicate adjective*.

1. The bus ride to the museum seemed long.
2. Maya Angelou is a famous poet.
3. The girls looked unhappy about the situation.
4. Pete will be the president of our class.
5. The person with the highest score is you.
6. She has been mayor for more than six years.
7. Of all the singers, the most talented one is you.
8. Please do not be upset with me.
9. That loud boom was not really anything.
10. Are we late for our piano lessons?

---

6. us
7. none
8. you
9. Jon
10. her

PRACTICE 4

1. long—predicate adjective
2. poet—predicate noun
3. unhappy—predicate adjective
4. president—predicate noun
5. you—predicate pronoun
6. mayor—predicate noun
7. you—predicate pronoun
8. upset— predicate adjective

9. anything—predicate pronoun
10. late—predicate adjective

ACTICE 5 Using Prepositional Phrases

ad the sentences. Then, rewrite each sentence, plying the type of prepositional phrase icated in parentheses.

The team practiced. (Add an adjectival phrase.)

Jojo flew a kite. (Add an adverbial phrase.)

The odor was strong. (Add an adjectival phrase.)

Mom baked bread. (Add an adverbial phrase.)

She twirled her baton. (Add an adverbial phrase.)

 ACTICE 6 Identifying Appositive, Participial, Gerund, and Infinitive Phrases

ad the sentences. Then, write whether e underlined phrase in each sentence is an *positive phrase*, a *participial phrase*, a *gerund rase*, or an *infinitive phrase*.

Perry loves underline{singing in the choir}.

underline{Frightened by the noise}, the bull charged.

We went to the roof underline{to gaze at the stars}.

The storm, underline{a strong hurricane}, devastated the city of Galveston.

The birds underline{flocking to the trees} were all crows.

The coach needs underline{to find another strategy}.

underline{A Missouri native}, Mark Twain in later life lived in Connecticut.

underline{Cooking Mexican food} is just one of my many interests.

underline{Running swiftly}, Jesse won the race.

Bev wants underline{to find a good hiking trail}.

PRACTICE 7 Recognizing Main and Subordinate Clauses

Read the sentences. Then, write and label the *main clause* and the *subordinate clause* in each sentence.

1. After he stayed up all night, Nick yawned all morning.
2. Nobody answered when I rang the bell at the front door.
3. Judge Levy, who lives down the road, always invites us to his annual summer barbecue.
4. Because she sews so well, Mrs. Sanchez helped with the costumes for the school play.
5. Over the winter, moths attacked the wool sweater that I bought last year.

 PRACTICE 8 Combining Sentences With Subordinate Clauses

Read the sentences. Combine each pair of sentences by turning one into a subordinate clause. Then, underline the subordinate clause, and indicate whether it is an *adjectival clause* or an *adverbial clause*.

1. My brother works late at the radio station. He gets home after midnight.
2. My sister is in the second grade. She is the youngest member of my family.
3. I searched the library shelves. I finally found an interesting book.
4. The town pool opens in June. It has a lifeguard staff of high school students.
5. My head aches. Toby is playing the trumpet again.

Continued on next page ▶

Cumulative Review   467

---

who lives down the road—subordinate clause

4. Because she sews so well—subordinate clause
Mrs. Sanchez helped with the costumes for the school play—main clause

5. Over the winter, moths attacked the wool sweater—main clause
that I bought last year—subordinate clause

PRACTICE 8

Answers will vary. Sample answers:

1. underline{When my brother works late at the radio station}, he gets home after midnight.—adverbial clause

2. My sister, underline{who is the youngest member of my family}, is in the second grade.—adjectival clause

3. I searched the library shelves underline{until I finally found an interesting book}.—adverbial clause

4. The town pool, underline{which has a lifeguard staff of high school students}, opens in June.—adjectival clause

5. My head aches underline{because Toby is playing the trumpet again}.—adverbial clause

---

PRACTICE 5

Answers will vary. Sample answers:

1. The team of baseball players practiced.
2. Jojo flew a kite in the sky.
3. The odor of lemons was strong.
4. Mom baked bread in the oven.
5. She twirled her baton in the air.

PRACTICE 6

1. gerund phrase
2. participial phrase
3. infinitive phrase
4. appositive phrase
5. participial phrase

6. infinitive phrase
7. appositive phrase
8. gerund phrase
9. participial phrase
10. infinitive phrase

PRACTICE 7

1. After he stayed up all night—subordinate clause
Nick yawned all morning—main clause

2. Nobody answered—main clause
when I rang the bell at the front door—subordinate clause

3. Judge Levy always invites us to his annual summer barbecue—main clause

Answers will vary. Sample answers:

1. The athlete worked hard at practice, and his coach was pleased.
2. A flower bloomed in the garden.
3. Tracy was tired because she coughed all night.
4. What an exciting competition!
5. Please wait for me.

1. Gregory and Mackenzie play the guitar.—compound subject
2. I add milk and fruit to my cereal.—compound object
3. Barb wanted a new bicycle for her birthday, but her mom gave her a new sweater instead.—compound sentence
4. The painter chooses and mixes his paints carefully.—compound verb
5. We may travel to Dallas by train or bus.—compound object

Answers will vary. Sample answers:

1. The bank teller was standing at her window.
2. The soup was pretty tasteless, but I ate it anyway.
3. correct
4. The color is wrong; you need a paler blue.
5. I will stop by unless you have the package delivered.

1. Everyone except Thomas went on the class trip.
2. The medical researchers studied the effects of the new treatment.
3. I thought the stars, twinkling overhead, looked awesome. *or* Twinkling overhead, the stars looked awesome I thought.
4. Many years ago, my grandmother gave me some good advice.

Cumulative Review   Chapters 18–20

 PRACTICE 9 Writing Sentences

For each item, write the indicated type of sentence, using the words provided.

1. Write a compound sentence using *the athlete* as one of the subjects.
2. Write a declarative sentence using *a flower* as the subject.
3. Write a complex sentence using *was tired* as one of the verbs.
4. Write an exclamatory sentence using the word *exciting*.
5. Write an imperative sentence using *wait* as the verb.

PRACTICE 10 Combining Sentences

Read the sentences. Combine each pair of sentences by using compound structures. Indicate whether your sentence contains a *compound subject*, a *compound verb*, or a *compound object*, or whether it is a *compound sentence*.

1. Gregory plays the guitar. Mackenzie also plays the guitar.
2. I add milk to my cereal. I add fruit to my cereal too.
3. Barb wanted a new bicycle for her birthday. Her mom gave her a new sweater instead.
4. The painter chooses his paints carefully. He mixes them carefully as well.
5. We may travel to Dallas by train. We may travel to Dallas by bus.

PRACTICE 11 Revising to Correct Fragments and Run-ons

Read each group of words. If it is a fragment, use it in a sentence. If it is a run-on, correct the run-on. If it is a sentence that needs no correction, write *correct*.

1. The bank teller standing at her window.
2. The soup was pretty tasteless, I ate it anyway.
3. Aunt Meg pays for my dance classes.
4. The color is wrong you need a paler blue.
5. Unless you have the package delivered.

PRACTICE 12 Revising to Correct Common Usage Problems

Read the sentences. Then, rewrite each sentence to correct misplaced modifiers, double negatives, and other usage problems.

1. Everyone accept Thomas went on the class trip.
2. The medical researchers studied the affects of the new treatment.
3. Twinkling overhead, I thought the stars looked awesome.
4. Many years ago, my grandmother gave me some good advise.
5. I didn't learn nothing new at the meeting.
6. The reason I am so cranky is because I had too little sleep last night.
7. Our teacher told us about earthquakes and volcanoes in our science class.
8. Their doing they're homework in the kitchen.
9. Did anyone beside you and me volunteer to help with the decorations?
10. The trees should be planted further apart.

468   **Phrases, Clauses, and Sentences**

---

5. I learned nothing new at the meeting. *or* I didn't learn anything new at the meeting.
6. The reason I am so cranky is that I had too little sleep last night. *or* I am so cranky because I had too little sleep last night.
7. In our science class, our teacher told us about earthquakes and volcanoes.
8. They're doing their homework in the kitchen.
9. Did anyone besides you and me volunteer to help with the decorations?
10. The trees should be planted farther apart.

Using Verbs

Use the Online Lesson Planner at www.phwritingcoach.com to customize your instructional plan for an integrated Language Arts curriculum.

DAY 1 21.1 Four Principal Parts of Verbs

"What Do You Notice?" **Objectives:** Identify, use, and understand the four principal parts of regular verbs	**INSTRUCTION AND PRACTICE** Student Edition pp. 469–472

DAY 2 21.1 Four Principal Parts of Verbs (continued)

Objectives: Identify, use, and understand the four principal parts of irregular verbs	**INSTRUCTION AND PRACTICE** Student Edition pp. 473–477

DAY 3 21.2 The Six Verb Tenses

Objectives: Identify, use, and understand aspects of verb tenses, including • the six verb tenses • conjugating the basic forms • conjugating be	**INSTRUCTION AND PRACTICE** Student Edition pp. 478–482

DAY 4 21.2 The Six Verb Tenses (continued)

Objectives: Identify, use, and understand aspects of verb tenses, including • the progressive tenses of verbs • the progressive tenses of *sing*	**INSTRUCTION AND PRACTICE** Student Edition pp. 483–485

Alternate Pacing Plans

- **Block Scheduling** Each day in the Lesson Planner represents a 40–50 minute block. Teachers using block scheduling may combine days to revise pacing to meet their classroom needs.

- **Accelerated Lesson Planning** Combine instructional days, focusing on concepts called out by students' diagnostic test results.

- **Integrated Language Arts Curriculum** Use the instruction and practice in this chapter to provide reinforcement, remediation, or extension of grammar concepts taught in your literature curriculum.

Links to Prentice Hall *LITERATURE*

Unit 2 Principal Parts of Verbs, p. 240; Writing Workshop: Correcting Errors With Verbs, p. 267; Simple Verb Tenses, p. 298; Perfect Tenses of Verbs, p. 330; Writing Workshop: Revising to Maintain Verb Tense, p. 359

Grammar Assessment

Grammar Coach:	Diagnostic Assessment	End-of-Chapter Assessment	Progress Monitoring
Personalized Instruction	Students take grammar diagnostic test online and are automatically assigned instruction and practice in areas where they need support.	Teacher uses **ExamView** to administer end-of-chapter assessment and remediation. Teachers may customize **ExamView** tests or use the ones provided.	Teachers may use the **Test Warm-Ups** and the **Cumulative Reviews** in the student book or eText to check students' mastery of grammar skills. Students may also play **DimensionL** grammar video games to test their grammar skills.
Teacher-Directed Instruction	Teacher administers the diagnostic test and determines focus of instruction and practice.		

WRITING COACH
Online
www.phwritingcoach.com

Grammar Assessment and Practice

Chapter diagnostic tests assess students' skills and assign instruction and practice.

DimensionL Video Games

Fast-paced interactive video games challenge students' mastery of grammar.

Lesson Planner continues on next page

DAY 5 21.2 The Six Verb Tenses *(continued)*

Objectives: Identify, use, and understand aspects of verb tenses, including ■ active and passive voice ■ moods of verbs	**INSTRUCTION AND PRACTICE** **Student Edition** pp. 486–490, 492–493 **Test Warm-Up** p. 491

DAY 6 21.3 Troublesome Verbs

Objectives: Identify, use, and understand troublesome verbs	**INSTRUCTION AND PRACTICE** **Student Edition** pp. 494–498

❝ *Since strong verbs make writing vivid, it is important that we show students how much their writing pivots on crafting the right verb. Verbs place the reader in time—past, present, or future. However, when verbs don't agree in number or person or follow the patterns of standard English, clear writing grinds to a halt.* **❞**

—Jeff Anderson

❝ Re *means 'again.'* Vision *means 'to see.'* Revision *means the paper needs to be seen again in a different light. It must move somewhere. One simple way to improve writing is to replace weak verbs with stronger verbs. Strong verbs drive strong sentences.* **❞**

—Kelly Gallagher

Differentiated Instruction

Differentiated Instruction Boxes in this Teacher's Edition address these student populations:

- Below-Level Students
- Above-Level Students
- Gifted and Talented Students
- Special Needs Students
- English Language Learners
- Spanish Speaking Students

In addition, for further enrichment, see the **Extension** features.

USING VERBS

owing how to use verb tenses will help you convey the
rrect timing of actions in your writing.

WRITE GUY *Jeff Anderson, M.Ed.*

WHAT DO YOU NOTICE?

Take a snapshot of the verbs as you zoom in on these sentences
from the story "The Circuit" by Francisco Jiménez.

MENTOR TEXT

> I was completely soaked in sweat and my mouth felt as if I had
> been chewing on a handkerchief. I walked over to the end of the
> row, picked up the jug of water we had brought, and began drinking.

Now, ask yourself the following questions:

- What about the verbs *walked* and *picked* shows that the action
  takes place in the past?
- How are the verbs *felt* and *began* different from *walked* and
  picked?

The *-ed* ending on the regular verbs *walk* and *pick* shows that
the action takes place in the past. The irregular verbs *felt* and
began also show action that takes place in the past. However,
these irregular verbs are spelled differently than their present
tenses: *feel* and *begin*.

Grammar for Writers Using carefully chosen verbs
and their correct tenses helps a writer convey
when actions happen. Be sure to use correct
tenses of regular and irregular verbs.

I felt all mixed up this morning, but now I feel fine.

And your irregular verbs are in good shape, too!

469

Grammar for Writers: Tense

Explain that learning about verb forms will
help students show clearly when the events
that they are writing about take place.

USING VERBS

As students progress in their writing skills, it
will be important for them to be able to apply
the rules of grammar, usage, and mechanics to
their own drafts. Use the *What Do You Notice?*
feature to help them see effective conventions
in the work of professional writers. Encourage
students to incorporate proper voice, tense, and
syntax as they edit their own writing.

Read the opening sentence aloud. Tell students
that verb tenses tell us not only what action
has taken place, but when that action has taken
place. In other words, verb tenses tell us about
time. Discuss how writers use different verb
tenses and forms to show when things happen.
Point out that using verb forms correctly is
necessary for clarity in writing.

WRITE GUY *Jeff Anderson, M. Ed.*

WHAT DO YOU NOTICE?

When students have read the Mentor Text,
say: Verb tenses show whether the action takes
place in the past, in the present, or in the future.
Ask: Does the Mentor Text take place in the
past, the present, or the future? (past) **Ask:** How
do you know? (**Possible response:** The verb
was in the first sentence is the past tense of
to be.) **Ask:** Does the speaker's mouth still feel
as though he is chewing on a handkerchief?
(**Possible response:** No, *had been chewing*
indicates that it happened a while ago.)

Explain that some verbs, called *regular verbs*,
can be changed into the past tense simply by
adding *-ed* or *-d* to their present tense form.
Other verbs, called irregular verbs, form the
past tense in different ways.

Ask: What are some irregular verbs used in the
Mentor Text? (*feel, begin, be*) **Ask:** What makes
these verbs irregular? (**Possible responses:**
Their past tenses aren't formed by following
a regular pattern; they don't use *-ed* or *-d* to
create the past tense.)

Lesson Objectives

1. Identify the four principal parts of verbs.

2. Distinguish between regular and irregular verbs.

3. Use the correct forms of regular and irregular verbs.

To introduce the topic of verb tense, ask a student volunteer to describe an activity (for example, studying at the library) using only present tense verbs. Then, discuss difficulties writers would face if their language had only one tense.

RULE 21.1.1 Read aloud the rule and then have students repeat the lines with you.

Say: The four principal parts of verbs shown in the chart on page 470 are used to form all the different verb tenses. The present and past forms are probably familiar, but there are two other forms which use helping verbs. The present participle **always** uses a helping verb and adds -*ing* to the end of the verb, and the past participle **always** uses a helping verb and usually adds -*d* or -*ed* to the end of the verb.

Help students think of several sentences using each principal part of common regular verbs, such as *talk* or *start*.

21.1 The Four Principal Parts of Verbs

Verbs have different tenses to express time. The tense of the verb *walk* in the sentence "They *walk* very fast" expresses action in the present. In "They *walked* too far from home," the tense of the verb shows that the action happened in the past. In "They *will walk* home from school," the verb expresses action in the future. These forms of verbs are known as **tenses**.

A verb's **tense** shows the time of the action or state of being that is being described. To use the tenses of a verb correctly, you must know the **principal parts** of the verb.

RULE 21.1.1

> A verb has four **principal parts**: the **present**, the **present participle**, the **past**, and the **past participle**.

THE FOUR PRINCIPAL PARTS OF *WALK*			
PRESENT	PRESENT PARTICIPLE	PAST	PAST PARTICIPLE
walk	(am) walking	walked	(have) walked

The first principal part, called the present, is the form of a verb that is listed in a dictionary. The present participle and the past participle must be combined with helping verbs before they can be used as verbs in sentences. The result will always be a verb phrase.

EXAMPLES   He **walks** toward us in a hurry.

June **was walking** behind us a minute ago.

They **walked** to the park.

We **have walked** three miles in the last hour.

The way the past and past participle of a verb are formed shows whether the verb is **regular** or **irregular.**

Differentiated Instruction

RTI Strategy for Below-Level Students
Students may need additional practice remembering and using the basic verb forms. Direct them to make up sentences based on the four principal parts of a regular verb. Have one student make up a sentence using the present form *walk* and share it orally. The next student should speak a sentence using the present participle with a helping verb—*am walking*. The third student should create and say a sentence using the past tense—*walked*. The fourth student should create and say aloud a sentence using a helping verb and the past participle—*have walked*.

Enrichment for Gifted/Talented Students
Challenge students to write and perform a song or a rhyme to teach the four principal parts of verbs. Student compositions should define or describe each verb form and give at least one example of each form. Have volunteers perform their pieces for the class as students listen to ensure that the rules are taught correctly.

Using Regular Verbs

Most verbs are **regular,** which means that their past and past participle forms follow a standard, predictable pattern.

> The past and past participle of a **regular verb** are formed by adding **-ed** or **-d** to the present form.

21.1.2 RULE

To form the past and past participle of a regular verb such as *chirp* or *hover,* you simply add *-ed* to the present. With regular verbs that already end in *e*—verbs such as *move* and *charge*—you simply add *-d* to the present.

PRINCIPAL PARTS OF REGULAR VERBS			
PRESENT	PRESENT PARTICIPLE	PAST	PAST PARTICIPLE
call	(am) calling	called	(have) called
change	(am) changing	changed	(have) changed
charge	(am) charging	charged	(have) charged
chirp	(am) chirping	chirped	(have) chirped
contain	(am) containing	contained	(have) contained
describe	(am) describing	described	(have) described
fix	(am) fixing	fixed	(have) fixed
hover	(am) hovering	hovered	(have) hovered
jump	(am) jumping	jumped	(have) jumped
lift	(am) lifting	lifted	(have) lifted
look	(am) looking	looked	(have) looked
move	(am) moving	moved	(have) moved
play	(am) playing	played	(have) played
save	(am) saving	saved	(have) saved
serve	(am) serving	served	(have) served
ski	(am) skiing	skied	(have) skied
talk	(am) talking	talked	(have) talked
type	(am) typing	typed	(have) typed
visit	(am) visiting	visited	(have) visited
walk	(am) walking	walked	(have) walked

Practice 21.1A
Practice 21.1B

The Four Principal Parts of Verbs   471

Using Regular Verbs

Point out that it is easy to create the principal parts of regular verbs because their past, past participle, and present participle forms follow a simple pattern.

RULE 21.1.2 Read aloud the rule and then have students repeat the lines with you.

Have students read the paragraph above the chart on page 471. Then, ask them to find other verbs on the chart that form the past and past participle by adding *-ed.* After students have shared several examples, ask them to find examples of verbs that form the past or past participle by adding *-d.*

Assign each student a regular verb. Have each student write four sentences using each of the principal parts of his or her assigned verb. Students should exchange sentences with a partner and have the partner read the sentences to check that the verbs are used correctly.

Challenge students to think of regular verbs that are not listed in the chart on page 471. Write those verbs on the board and have a volunteer use the verb in a sentence and identify which principal part of the verb they used.

Working with ELLs   **ELL** Sheltered Instruction: Social/Affective

As students read the student page, provide opportunities to use support from peers and from you to enhance and confirm understanding and to develop vocabulary needed to comprehend increasingly challenging language.

Beginning Choose a familiar verb and point to it in the chart. Then, read the words across each column as students echo you. Clarify meaning through mime and gesture, and then use the verb's various forms in sentences. Repeat with another verb, and guide students to understand that both follow a *regular,* or repeated, pattern.

Intermediate Guide students as they read the page. Have small groups use context and prior knowledge to discuss and define these words from the page: *regular* and *pattern.* Have groups present their definitions. Clarify meanings as necessary.

Advanced Present these words from the page: *regular, standard, predictable,* and *pattern.* Have partners discuss the meaning of each, consulting a dictionary and confirming understanding with you as necessary. Then, have them work together using the **KIM strategy,** writing a key word, information, and a memory clue for each word. Have partners read the page.

Advanced High Have partners complete the Advanced activity. Then, have them collaborate on a brief paragraph using all four words.

PRACTICE 21.1A

1. present
2. past participle
3. present participle
4. past
5. past participle
6. present
7. past
8. present participle
9. past participle
10. present participle

PRACTICE 21.1B

Helping verbs may vary. Parts should not.

11. drop—present
   is dropping—present participle
   dropped—past
   has dropped—past participle

12. hurry—present
   is hurrying—present participle
   hurried—past
   has hurried—past participle

13. ask—present
   is asking—present participle
   asked—past
   has asked—past participle

14. move—present
   is moving—present participle
   moved—past
   has moved—past participle

15. search—present
   is searching—present participle
   searched—past
   has searched—past participle

16. flap—present
   is flapping—present participle
   flapped—past
   has flapped—past participle

17. serve—present
   is serving—present participle
   served—past
   has served—past participle

PRACTICE 21.1A Identifying the Principal Parts of Regular Verbs

Read the sentences. Then, label each underlined verb *present*, *present participle*, *past*, or *past participle*.

EXAMPLE   I <u>enjoy</u> seeing a full moon.

ANSWER   *present*

1. When Dad has time, he <u>walks</u> to the train station.
2. My grandmother has <u>lived</u> in the same house for 70 years.
3. Our dog is <u>chasing</u> snowflakes in the backyard.
4. The teacher <u>assigned</u> three pages of homework.
5. The baseball players have <u>used</u> the same equipment for three seasons now.
6. Katrina <u>wants</u> a new microscope.
7. At a Chinese restaurant, I <u>tasted</u> shrimp for the first time.
8. Band members are <u>washing</u> cars to raise money.
9. I have never <u>climbed</u> a tree that tall.
10. My brother is always <u>looking</u> for a new hobby.

PRACTICE 21.1B Supplying the Principal Parts of Regular Verbs

Read the verbs. Write and label the four principal parts of each verb. Use a form of the helping verb *be* with the present participle and a form of the helping verb *have* with the past participle.

EXAMPLE   rely

ANSWER   *rely* — present
          is relying — present participle
          relied — past
          has relied — past participle

11. drop
12. hurry
13. ask
14. move
15. search
16. flap
17. serve
18. knock
19. close
20. divide

> **SPEAKING APPLICATION**
>
> With a partner, take turns talking about current events. Use at least three of the principal verb parts as you talk. Your partner should listen for and name the principal parts of at least three of the verbs you use.

> **WRITING APPLICATION**
>
> Write a short paragraph about friends or family members. Use all four principal verb parts in your sentences.

---

18. knock—present
   is knocking —present participle
   knocked—past
   has knocked—past participle

19. close—present
   is closing—present participle
   closed—past
   has closed—past participle

20. divide—present
   is dividing—present participle
   divided—past
   has divided—past participle

> *SPEAKING APPLICATION*
>
> **Have students explain to the class how they identified the principal parts of the verbs that their partner used.**
>
> *WRITING APPLICATION*
>
> **Have students share their paragraphs with a partner, pointing out which principal parts of verbs were used and where they were used.**

Using Irregular Verbs

While most verbs are regular, many very common verbs are **irregular**—their past and past participle forms do not follow a predictable pattern.

> The past and past participle of an **irregular verb** are not formed by adding *-ed* or *-d* to the present tense form.

21.1.3 RULE

IRREGULAR VERBS WITH THE SAME PAST AND PAST PARTICIPLE			
PRESENT	PRESENT PARTICIPLE	PAST	PAST PARTICIPLE
bring	(am) bringing	brought	(have) brought
build	(am) building	built	(have) built
buy	(am) buying	bought	(have) bought
catch	(am) catching	caught	(have) caught
fight	(am) fighting	fought	(have) fought
find	(am) finding	found	(have) found
get	(am) getting	got	(have) got *or* (have) gotten
hold	(am) holding	held	(have) held
lay	(am) laying	laid	(have) laid
lead	(am) leading	led	(have) led
lose	(am) losing	lost	(have) lost
pay	(am) paying	paid	(have) paid
say	(am) saying	said	(have) said
sit	(am) sitting	sat	(have) sat
sleep	(am) sleeping	slept	(have) slept
spin	(am) spinning	spun	(have) spun
stand	(am) standing	stood	(have) stood
stick	(am) sticking	stuck	(have) stuck
swing	(am) swinging	swung	(have) swung
teach	(am) teaching	taught	(have) taught
win	(am) winning	won	(have) won

Check a dictionary whenever you are in doubt about the correct form of an irregular verb.

Using Irregular Verbs

Point out that the past and past participle forms of irregular verbs do not follow a predictable pattern.

RULE 21.1.3 Read aloud the rule and then have students repeat the lines with you.

Ask: What is the difference between a regular and an irregular verb? (**Possible responses:** Regular verbs follow rules for forming the past tense, past participle, and present participle; irregular verbs follow no predictable pattern.)

Have students read through the principal parts of the verbs listed on the chart on page 473.

Have students close their books and, as a class, review all of the the principal parts of the irregular verbs listed in the chart on page 473. Then, challenge students to add to the list with other irregular verbs not on the list. Make sure students know the principal parts of the commonly used irregular verbs *to be, to have, to make, to take,* and *to get.*

Have student pairs choose three words from the chart and use them in at least two different forms in a story. They may retell a familiar story, tell a true story, or make up a story. After they finish writing their stories, have them make a note of the three verbs they used. Then, have them exchange their story with another pair. As the second pair reads the story, have them underline the three verbs and label the forms used.

(continued)

Working with ELLs   **ELL** Sheltered Instruction: Cognitive

Help students comprehend vocabulary used routinely in written classroom materials. Read aloud the directions for the Practice activities on page 472. Then:

Beginning Point out these routine words from the directions, and write them on the board: *read, write, label,* and *underlined.* Read them aloud with students, acting out each. Then, write a word, and have students act it out to show comprehension.

Intermediate Write vocabulary words such as *read, write, label,* and *underline* on one set of note cards. Write the four principal parts, along with examples, on another set. Provide a page of sentences featuring each principal part. Have partners take turns choosing a card from each set,

carrying out the resulting instructions (as in *label present participle*) with the page of sentences.

Advanced Provide partners with these terms from the student page: *identify, label, listen,* and *short paragraph.* Have partners find the term in the directions and read them aloud in context. Then, have them work together to write a brief explanation of each term, using a dictionary for support as necessary.

Advanced High Have partners complete the Advanced activity. Then, have them write instructions of their own for a grammar activity.

Teacher Tip

Students may struggle with the idea that past and past participle forms of irregular verbs do not follow a predictable pattern. Help students create flash cards for the past and past participle forms of the most common irregular verbs, such as *be, have, can, do, say, go,* and *get.* Routinely have student partners use the flash cards to quiz each other on the verb forms.

Using Irregular Verbs
(continued)

Ask: What do the verbs on the top chart on page 474 have in common? (**For every one of them, the present form is the same as the past and past participle form.**)

Say: When very young children first learn to speak English, they often say things like, "putted it down." When a child does that, he or she is actually following a rule for forming the past tense, but the rule doesn't work with irregular verbs. **Ask:** What is the correct way to say this sentence? (**Response:** I put it down.) **Say:** You most likely already know the principal parts of many irregular verbs. In the above example, you knew the past of *put* is also *put* rather than *putted*. Study the verbs in the first chart on page 474. Then, **ask:** Can you think of any irregular verbs not listed in the chart that have the same present, past, and past participle? (**Possible responses:** cut, quit, let)

Ask: What do the verbs on the bottom chart on page 474 have in common? (**Possible responses:** none of their forms are the same; they change in other ways than the irregular verbs in the first two charts)

Write these incomplete sentences on the board:

Last night I _____. (past)

At this moment I am _____. (present participle)

By the time _____, I _____. (past event; past participle

Model how to fill in the sentence frames using different forms of an irregular verb: *Last night I chose a book to read. At this moment I am choosing a book to read. By the time the library closed, I had chosen a book to read.*

Work with students to fill in the blanks with other irregular verbs from the second chart on page 474.

IRREGULAR VERBS WITH THE SAME PRESENT, PAST, AND PAST PARTICIPLE			
PRESENT	PRESENT PARTICIPLE	PAST	PAST PARTICIPLE
bid	(am) bidding	bid	(have) bid
burst	(am) bursting	burst	(have) burst
cost	(am) costing	cost	(have) cost
hurt	(am) hurting	hurt	(have) hurt
put	(am) putting	put	(have) put
set	(am) setting	set	(have) set

IRREGULAR VERBS THAT CHANGE IN OTHER WAYS			
PRESENT	PRESENT PARTICIPLE	PAST	PAST PARTICIPLE
arise	(am) arising	arose	(have) arisen
be, am, is, are	(am) being	was, were	(have) been
bear	(am) bearing	bore	(have) borne
beat	(am) beating	beat	(have) beaten
begin	(am) beginning	began	(have) begun
blow	(am) blowing	blew	(have) blown
break	(am) breaking	broke	(have) broken
choose	(am) choosing	chose	(have) chosen
come	(am) coming	came	(have) come
do	(am) doing	did	(have) done
draw	(am) drawing	drew	(have) drawn
drink	(am) drinking	drank	(have) drunk
drive	(am) driving	drove	(have) driven
eat	(am) eating	ate	(have) eaten
fall	(am) falling	fell	(have) fallen
fly	(am) flying	flew	(have) flown
forget	(am) forgetting	forgot	(have) forgotten
freeze	(am) freezing	froze	(have) frozen
give	(am) giving	gave	(have) given
go	(am) going	went	(have) gone

474   Using Verbs

Differentiated Instruction

RTI Strategy for Below-Level Students

Many students might continue to have difficulty remembering the four basic forms of irregular verbs. In this case it will be important to give students additional practice. Create a Bingo game to give these students the additional practice they need. To make cards, you can create a table with five columns and five rows. Ask students to fill in the cards with past participles of their choice from the charts on pages 473–475.

To play, read present participles of verbs from the charts and have students check off or place markers over any matching past participles on their card. Students may win by connecting five spaces in a row vertically, diagonally, or horizontally.

As students become more proficient, call out the present participles more quickly and begin to call out simple present and simple past forms as well. Challenge winners to create a paragraph using the irregular verbs from their winning row.

Practice 21.1C
Practice 21.1D
Practice 21.1E
Practice 21.1F

IRREGULAR VERBS THAT CHANGE IN OTHER WAYS (CONTINUED)			
PRESENT	PRESENT PARTICIPLE	PAST	PAST PARTICIPLE
grow	(am) growing	grew	(have) grown
have, has	am having	had	(have) had
know	(am) knowing	knew	(have) known
lie	(am) lying	lay	(have) lain
ride	(am) riding	rode	(have) ridden
ring	(am) ringing	rang	(have) rung
rise	(am) rising	rose	(have) risen
run	(am) running	ran	(have) run
see	(am) seeing	saw	(have) seen
shake	(am) shaking	shook	(have) shaken
sing	(am) singing	sang	(have) sung
sink	(am) sinking	sank	(have) sunk
speak	(am) speaking	spoke	(have) spoken
spring	(am) springing	sprang	(have) sprung
strive	(am) striving	strove	(have) striven
swear	(am) swearing	swore	(have) sworn
swim	(am) swimming	swam	(have) swum
take	(am) taking	took	(have) taken
tear	(am) tearing	tore	(have) torn
throw	(am) throwing	threw	(have) thrown
wear	(am) wearing	wore	(have) worn
weave	(am) weaving	wove	(have) woven
write	(am) writing	wrote	(have) written

As you can see, there are many irregular verbs. For most of these verbs, you should memorize the different forms. Whenever you are not sure of which form of an irregular verb to use, check a dictionary.

Ask students to skim the charts of irregular verbs on pages 473–475. Have them pick three verbs and use them in a paragraph. Ask students to deliberately include errors in forming past tenses. Then, have them exchange papers with a partner and correct the errors they find in verb forms. If students are not sure about the correct verb form, remind them to use the chart or a dictionary.

Challenge students to think of other irregular verbs that change in strange ways when forming the past and past participle. Examples might be *bend, dig, feed, freeze, mean, ring, spread,* and *wake.* If students are having difficulty thinking of new irregular verbs, play a challenge game instead. Call out the present form of each of the verbs listed and have students provide you with the correct present participle, past, and past participle forms.

Teacher Tip

To help students memorize irregular verb forms, revisit the charts on this page as you work through the chapter. You may want to quiz students on the principal parts of irregular verbs. Read aloud a present form of an irregular verb and have three students work together to tell you the present participle, past, and past participle forms of the verb. Ask students to use these verb forms in sentences.

Extension

To help students synthesize and apply what they have learned about irregular verbs, have them work in pairs to play a verb game. You will need four note cards per pair. Have partners use the cards to draw four boxes labeled *Present, Present Participle, Past, Past Participle.* Each student should take one card and write one of the principal parts of an irregular verb in the appropriate box. The student should then exchange cards with his or her partner, who fills in any other box. When a pair has completed its cards, it should exchange them with another pair, who checks to make sure the verb forms are correct.

PRACTICE 21.1C

Helping verbs may vary. Parts should not.
Verbs are listed in the following order:
present; present participle; past; past
participle.

1. hold; is holding; held; have held
2. spin; is spinning; spun; have spun
3. cost; is costing; cost; have cost
4. grow; is growing; grew; have grown
5. sing; is singing; sang; have sung
6. write; is writing; wrote; have written
7. bring; is bringing; brought; have brought
8. lead; is leading; led; have led
9. sit; is sitting; sat; have sat
10. swim; is swimming; swam; have swum

PRACTICE 21.1D

11. brought
12. cost
13. arisen
14. chose
15. drank
16. flown
17. built
18. known
19. sunk
20. worn

> *SPEAKING APPLICATION*
>
> Students' sentences should show
> that they can use and understand
> the function of irregular verbs.
>
> *WRITING APPLICATION*
>
> Have students identify the principal
> part of each verb they used to show
> that they can use and understand the
> function of irregular verbs.

PRACTICE 21.1C Supplying the Principal Parts
of Irregular Verbs

Read the verbs. Write and label the four principal
parts of each verb. Use a form of the helping verb
be with the present participle and a form of the
helping verb *have* with the past participle.

EXAMPLE   stick

ANSWER   *stick* — present
is sticking — present participle
stuck — past
have stuck — past participle

1. hold
2. spin
3. cost
4. grow
5. sing
6. write
7. bring
8. lead
9. sit
10. swim

> *SPEAKING APPLICATION*
>
> With a partner, choose two irregular verbs
> from Practice 21.1C. Take turns using the
> different parts of each verb in sentences. Your
> partner should listen for and name which
> principal part of the verb you have used.

PRACTICE 21.1D Choosing the Correct Form
Irregular Verbs

Read the sentences. Then, choose and write the
form of the verb in parentheses that correctly
completes each sentence.

EXAMPLE   I have (tore, torn) the paper in half

ANSWER   *torn*

11. Sheila (brung, brought) fruit to the picnic.
12. Which one (cost, costed) the most?
13. We wanted to see the sunrise, so everyone
    had (arose, arisen) while it was still dark.
14. Carlos (choosed, chose) to perform a difficu
    piece of music.
15. The water was cool, and we (drank, drunk
    our fill.
16. Celeste had never (flew, flown) in a plane
    before.
17. The town (builded, built) a new governmen
    office.
18. If we had (knew, known) then what we kne
    now, things would have been different.
19. They have (sank, sunk) the toy boats.
20. You have (wore, worn) that same shirt thre
    days in a row.

> *WRITING APPLICATION*
>
> Choose one of the irregular verbs from
> Practice 21.1C and 21.1D. Write four sentences,
> each one with a different principal part of the
> verb you selected.

Working with ELLs   **ELL** Sheltered Instruction: Cognitive

Have students write using
grade-appropriate connecting words
to combine phrases, clauses, and
sentences in increasingly accurate ways.
Provide students with these connecting
words: *and, but, for, nor, or, so, yet, after,
before, although, when,* and *while.* (See
Chapter 17.)

Beginning On the board, write: *I have a
marker, but I want a pen.* As you read the
sentence aloud, hold up each object. Point
out that the word *but* joins two groups of
words that could stand as sentences on their
own. Guide students in writing additional
completions for the cloze sentence *I have a
_____, but I want a _____.*

Intermediate Provide small groups with
three sentences using verbs from Practice

21.1C. For each sentence, have them
collaborate on an additional sentence on
the same topic. Then, have them write
using the connecting words to combine
sentence pairs.

Advanced Have partners write simple
sentences on a single topic using the verbs
in Practice 21.1C. Then, have them use the
connecting words to combine sentences.

Advanced High Have individuals complete
the Advanced activity. Then, direct them
to exchange papers and evaluate each
other's work for the appropriate choice of
conjunctions, suggesting replacements as
warranted.

PRACTICE 21.1E > Using Irregular Verbs

ad the sentences. Rewrite each sentence, using
e form of the verb in parentheses that correctly
mpletes the sentence.

AMPLE   I wish I had (know) you were
         coming.

SWER   *I wish I had known you were coming.*

. My mom (teach) math for ten years.

. It (hurt) more yesterday than it does today.

. Because the wind had (blow) all night, there
  were no leaves left on the trees.

. My great-grandfather (fly) a plane in World
  War II.

. The potted plants would have (freeze) if we
  had left them out last night.

. The carpenters (build) a stage for the spring
  play.

. What I should have (say) is, "Please."

. Grandmother had (write) a letter, and she
  wanted me to mail it for her.

. I (see) a four-leaf clover yesterday.

. My cousin had (drive) all night to join us for
  Thanksgiving dinner.

PRACTICE 21.1F > Revising for Irregular Verbs

Read the sentences. Then, if the underlined verb
is in the correct form, write *correct*. If it is not,
rewrite the sentence with the correct verb form.

EXAMPLE   We wished we could have <u>layed</u>
           there in the sun all day.

ANSWER   *We wished we could have lain there
           in the sun all day.*

11. They <u>knowed</u> I was coming.

12. My little sister has <u>grew</u> three inches since
    her last birthday.

13. When the baseball hit the window, the glass
    <u>broke</u>.

14. The bell at the fire department <u>ringed</u>.

15. We <u>ate</u> dinner at a restaurant near the park.

16. We should have <u>took</u> an extra blanket.

17. We had <u>shaken</u> all the sand out of the blanket
    before packing it.

18. My brother <u>catched</u> the fly ball.

19. My teacher had <u>spoke</u> to me about the project
    before class began.

20. My sister <u>swore</u> not to tell anyone about the
    surprise party.

SPEAKING APPLICATION

With a partner, take turns saying irregular
verbs from Practice 21.1E. Your partner should
then state one of the other principal parts of
the verb and use it in a sentence.

WRITING APPLICATION

Write three or four sentences about what last
autumn was like where you live. Use the past
and past participle of two or three irregular
verbs in your sentences. You may scan the list
of words in Practice 21.1E and 21.1F for ideas.

Practice   477

PRACTICE 21.1E >

1. My mom taught math for ten years.

2. It hurt more yesterday than it does
   today.

3. Because the wind had blown all
   night, there were no leaves left on
   the trees.

4. My great-grandfather flew a plane
   in World War II.

5. The potted plants would have frozen
   if we had left them out last night.

6. The carpenters built a stage for the
   spring play.

7. What I should have said is, "Please."

8. Grandmother had written a letter,
   and she wanted me to mail it for her.

9. I saw a four-leaf clover yesterday.

10. My cousin had driven all night to
    join us for Thanksgiving dinner.

PRACTICE 21.1F >

11. They knew I was coming.

12. My little sister has grown three
    inches since her last birthday.

13. correct

14. The bell at the fire department rang.

15. correct

16. We should have taken an extra
    blanket.

17. correct

18. My brother caught the fly ball.

19. My teacher had spoken to me about
    the project before class began.

20. correct

SPEAKING APPLICATION

**Students' sentences should
demonstrate that students can use
and understand the function of
irregular verbs in speaking.**

WRITING APPLICATION

**Students should demonstrate they
can use and understand the function
of irregular verbs in writing by
explaining how the past participle
form differs from the past form
for the verbs they used in their
sentences.**

Lesson Objectives

1. Identify the basic forms of the six tenses.

2. Use and understand the function of perfect tense and progressive tense verbs in the context of reading, writing, and speaking.

3. Use active and passive voice appropriately.

Identifying the Basic Forms of the Six Tenses

Explain that basic forms and progressive forms of verbs make it possible for writers to distinguish between actions that are completed at one specific time and actions that continue over a long period of time.

RULE 21.2.1 Read aloud the rule and then have students repeat the lines with you.

Use a Think Aloud as part of a gradual release progression.

Think Aloud

Say: The perfect tenses shown in the chart on page 478 focus on the completion of actions. Different perfect forms indicate when the action was completed. The present perfect shows actions that were completed any time right up to now. For example, *I have walked to school every day.* It can also show change over time: *You have learned so much!* The past perfect shows that one action happened before another: *She had written before she arrived.* The future perfect shows that one action will be completed before another event will take place: *We will have studied by the time we take the test.*

Draw a chart like the one on page 478 showing the six tenses of *write* on the board. **Work with students** to complete the chart with a regular verb, such as *talk.*

Draw a timeline on the board. Work with students to show how the different tenses indicate different points in time.

To challenge students, **have student pairs** work together to chart the six tenses of an irregular verb from the charts on pages 473–475. Remind them that they can use a dictionary to check their answers.

In English, verbs have six **tenses**: the **present**, the **past**, the **future**, the **present perfect**, the **past perfect**, and the **future perfect**.

RULE 21.2.1

The **tense** of a verb shows the time of the action or state of being.

Every tense has both **basic** forms and **progressive** forms.

Identifying the Basic Forms of the Six Tenses

The chart below shows the **basic** forms of the six tenses, using *begin* as an example. The first column gives the name of each tense. The second column gives the basic form of *begin* in all six tenses. The third column gives the principal part needed to form each tense. Only three of the four principal parts are used in the basic forms: the present, the past, and the past participle.

BASIC FORMS OF THE SIX TENSES OF *BEGIN*		
TENSE	BASIC FORM	PRINCIPAL PART USED
Present	I begin.	Present
Past	I began.	Past
Future	I will begin.	Present
Present Perfect	I have begun.	Past Participle
Past Perfect	I had begun.	Past Participle
Future Perfect	I will have begun.	Past Participle

Study the chart carefully. First, learn the names of the tenses. Then, learn the principal parts needed to form them. Notice also that the last four tenses need helping verbs.

As you have already learned, some verbs form their tenses in a regular, predictable pattern. Other verbs use an irregular pattern. *Begin* is an example of an irregular verb.

See Practice 21.2A

478 Using Verbs

Conjugating the Basic Forms of Verbs

A helpful way to become familiar with all the forms of a verb is by **conjugating** it.

> A **conjugation** is a list of the singular and plural forms of a verb in a particular tense.

21.2.2 RULE

Each tense in a conjugation has six forms that fit with first-, second-, and third-person forms of the personal pronouns. These forms may change for each personal pronoun, and they may change for each tense.

To conjugate any verb, begin by listing its principal parts. For example, the principal parts of the verb *go* are *go, going, went,* and *gone*. The following chart shows the conjugation of all the basic forms of *go* in all six tenses. Notice that the forms of the helping verbs may also change for each personal pronoun and tense.

CONJUGATION OF THE BASIC FORMS OF GO		
TENSE	SINGULAR	PLURAL
Present	I go. You go. He, she, or it goes.	We go. You go. They go.
Past	I went. You went. He, she, or it went.	We went. You went. They went.
Future	I will go. You will go. He, she, or it will go.	We will go. You will go. They will go.
Present Perfect	I have gone. You have gone. He, she, or it has gone.	We have gone. You have gone. They have gone.
Past Perfect	I had gone. You had gone. He, she, or it had gone.	We had gone. You had gone. They had gone.
Future Perfect	I will have gone. You will have gone. He, she, or it will have gone.	We will have gone. You will have gone. They will have gone.

Practice 21.2B

Conjugating the Basic Forms of Verbs

Tell students that conjugating verbs is a good and effective way to learn verb forms. When we conjugate a verb, we list all of the tenses for the verb, and how they are used with first, second, and third person singular and plural pronouns.

RULE 21.2.2 Read aloud the rule and then have students repeat the lines with you.

Help students understand how verbs are conjugated by working with them to convert the directions for conjugating verbs in the second paragraph on page 479 into a series of numbered steps. For example, 1. List the principal parts of the verb; 2. List the singular forms for the present tense (*I; you; he, she, or it*); 3. List the plural forms for the present tense (*we, you, they*); 4. Complete the remaining tenses: past, future, present perfect, past perfect, future perfect.

Use the directions to conjugate a regular verb, such as *stretch.*

Write on the board these sentences: *I sat. She spins. You made.* Have students rewrite the sentences in past perfect, present perfect, and future perfect tense. Have volunteers read their new sentences aloud, while the class determines the tense of the verb in each sentence.

Differentiated Instruction

RTI Strategy for Below-Level Students

Have students make a chart that shows the basic forms of the six tenses of English verbs. Have students use the chart to write the forms of additional verbs in the second column. Then, have students create a wide third column in which they write short sample sentences for each tense.

Tense	Verb
Past	try
Present	tried
Future	will try
Past Perfect	had tried
Present Perfect	have tried
Future Perfect	will have tried

Conjugating *Be*

Point out that students will need to know how to conjugate *be* when they work with progressive tenses.

Assign student pairs one tense shown on the Conjugation of the Basic Forms of *Be* chart. Have them create original complete sentences that show how to use the singular and plural forms of *be* in that tense. Students' sentences should contain a predicate nominative or a predicate adjective.

Have partners work together to write three sentences that use the three perfect tenses of the verb *be*. At least one of the sentences should use the plural form. Ask partners to share their sentences with the class.

Challenge students to memorize the full conjugation of the verb *be*. Have student pairs test each other on their memorization.

Conjugating *Be*

The verb *be* is an important verb to know how to conjugate. It is both the most common and the most irregular verb in the English language. You will use the basic forms of *be* when you conjugate the progressive forms of verbs later in this section.

PRINCIPAL PARTS OF *BE*			
PRESENT	PRESENT PARTICIPLE	PAST	PAST PARTICIPLE
be	being	was	been

Once you know the principal parts of *be*, you can conjugate all of the basic forms of *be*.

CONJUGATION OF THE BASIC FORMS OF *BE*		
TENSE	SINGULAR	PLURAL
Present	I am. You are. He, she, or it is.	We are. You are. They are.
Past	I was. You were. He, she, or it was.	We were. You were. They were.
Future	I will be. You will be. He, she, or it will be.	We will be. You will be. They will be.
Present Perfect	I have been. You have been. He, she, or it has been.	We have been. You have been. They have been.
Past Perfect	I had been. You had been. He, she, or it had been.	We had been. You had been. They had been.
Future Perfect	I will have been. You will have been. He, she, or it will have been.	We will have been. You will have been. They will have been.

See Practice 21.2C
See Practice 21.2D

PRACTICE 21.2A Identifying Present, Past, and Future Tenses of Verbs

Read the sentences. Then, label each underlined verb *present*, *past*, or *future*.

EXAMPLE   Storm clouds <u>linger</u> above the mountains.

ANSWER   *present*

1. Tomorrow we <u>will wash</u> the car.
2. My brother just <u>swept</u> the driveway yesterday.
3. I <u>check</u> my e-mail every day after school.
4. Chandra <u>touched</u> the rabbit's soft fur.
5. After this winter, we <u>will welcome</u> spring.
6. Miguel <u>brought</u> two friends to the party.
7. The bells <u>ring</u> each morning.
8. This summer I <u>will learn</u> how to swim.
9. This bucket <u>holds</u> five gallons.
10. The weather <u>will turn</u> cool this weekend.

PRACTICE 21.2B Identifying Perfect Tenses of Verbs

Read the sentences. Then, write the verb in each sentence, and label it *present perfect*, *past perfect*, or *future perfect*.

EXAMPLE   The end of summer had come so much faster than I expected.

ANSWER   *had come — past perfect*

11. I wish I had known there was a test today.
12. By this time next year, Kendra will have finished high school.
13. We have bought a copy of my favorite author's new book.
14. My mom has started a new job.
15. I had brought a salad to the luncheon.
16. Carly had planted the flowers in the window.
17. Our town has benefited from recycling.
18. By 10 P.M., the kids will have come home from the school dance.
19. The days had begun to get longer.
20. The Jacksons have built a porch on the back of their house.

SPEAKING APPLICATION

With a partner, take turns talking about school. Talk about something you did last year, something you are doing now, and something you hope to do next year. Your partner should listen for and name one past-, one present-, and one future-tense verb.

WRITING APPLICATION

Write a short paragraph about a hobby or interest you have had for a while. Write about what you have been doing with it and what you hope you will be doing in the future. Use a perfect tense verb at least once.

Practice   **481**

PRACTICE 21.2A

1. future
2. past
3. present
4. past
5. future
6. past
7. present
8. future
9. present
10. future

PRACTICE 21.2B

11. had known—past perfect
12. will have finished—future perfect
13. have bought—present perfect
14. has started—present perfect
15. had brought—past perfect
16. had planted—past perfect
17. has benefited—present perfect
18. will have come—future perfect
19. had begun—past perfect
20. have built—present perfect

PRACTICE 21.2C ▶

1. The teacher will give homework.
2. The painters have put the final coat of paint on the house.
3. We brought Aunt Shelby to every concert.
4. The Boy Scout troop will have begun the service project.
5. We had drunk the juice.
6. You ate dinner with your family.
7. Carlo will have completed the assignment.
8. They will run in a marathon.
9. Maureen had chosen a science class.
10. Some have said history repeats itself. *or* Some say history has repeated itself. *or* Some have said that history has repeated itself.

PRACTICE 21.2D ▶

11. will have completed
12. had chosen
13. will bring
14. ate
15. had drunk
16. has done
17. existed
18. writes
19. will come
20. carried

PRACTICE 21.2C ▶ Forming Verb Tenses

Read the sentences, which are all in the present tense. Then, rewrite each sentence, changing it to the tense indicated in parentheses.

EXAMPLE   My sister holds the kitten. (past perfect)

ANSWER   *My sister had held the kitten.*

1. The teacher gives homework. (future)
2. The painters put the final coat of paint on the house. (present perfect)
3. We bring Aunt Shelby to every concert. (past)
4. The Boy Scout troop begins the service project. (future perfect)
5. We drink the juice. (past perfect)
6. You eat dinner with your family. (past)
7. Carlo completes the assignment. (future perfect)
8. They run in a marathon. (future)
9. Maureen chooses a science class. (past perfect)
10. Some say history repeats itself. (present perfect)

PRACTICE 21.2D ▶ Using Verb Tenses Correctly

Read the sentences. Then, write the verb in parentheses that correctly completes each sentence.

EXAMPLE   Tomorrow (will be, was) another da

ANSWER   *will be*

11. By this time next year, Geo (will complete, will have completed) his degree.
12. Everything would change, now that Jill (chose, had chosen) to stay.
13. Rafael (will bring, will have brought) his brother to the party tonight.
14. We (ate, will eat) lunch at Grandma's yesterday.
15. They (had drunk, drink) all the milk by the time we got there.
16. The teacher said that everyone (has done, does) well this week.
17. Cooking (existed, exists) before people began recording history.
18. My mom (writes, had written) a note to my dad every morning.
19. I (will come, have come) to your party this afternoon.
20. My brother (carries, carried) the groceries in for my aunt when she came home.

Recognizing the Progressive Tense of Verbs

The six tenses of *go* and *be* in their basic forms were shown in the charts earlier in this section. Each of these tenses also has a progressive tense or form. The progressive form describes an event that is in progress. In contrast, the basic forms of a verb describe events that have a definite beginning and end.

> The **progressive tense,** or form, of a verb shows an action or condition that is ongoing.

All six of the progressive tenses of a verb are made using just one principal part: the present participle. This is the principal part that ends in *-ing.* Then, the correct form of *be* is added to create the progressive tense or form.

Progressive Tenses of *Sing*

PROGRESSIVE TENSE = be + present participle

PRESENT
I **am singing** in the chorus.
be present participle

PAST
I **was singing** in practice all last week.
be present participle

FUTURE
I **will be singing** in this weekend's concert.
be present participle

PRESENT PERFECT
I **have been singing** since I was a young child.
be present participle

PAST PERFECT
I **had been singing** only in the chorus, but now
be present participle
I also sing solos.

FUTURE PERFECT
I **will have been singing** in the chorus for ten
be present participle
years by the time I graduate.

21.2.3 RULE

Recognizing the Progressive Tense of Verbs

Write *progressive tense* on the board. Point out that the basic tenses that students have been working with show action that has a recognizable start and finish. Underline *progress* as you **say:** Progressive tenses, on the other hand, describe events that continue over a long period of time, or are still in progress.

RULE 21.2.3 Read aloud the rule and then have students repeat the lines with you.

Progressive Tenses of *Sing*

Direct students' attention to the examples showing Progressive Tenses of *Sing.* **Ask:** What do you notice about the words labeled *present participle*? (They all end in *-ing.*) Have them look at the forms of *be* in the examples. **Ask:** What does change in these examples? (**Response:** The forms of the verb *be.*)

Work with students to form the progressive tense for the verbs *work* and *leap.* Write the conjugations on the board. Have student pairs choose a progressive conjugation and use it in a sentence. Ask pairs to share their sentences with the class.

Working with ELLs **ELL** Sheltered Instruction: Cognitive

Help students acquire the basic, grade-level vocabulary words *challenge, problem, goal,* and *solution,* employing strategic learning techniques, as described below. They should use accessible language in these activities, learning the new and essential language in the process.

Beginning Echo read the words with students. Then, supply definitions using visually accessible language.

Intermediate Provide students with accessible definitions of the words.

Have them take turns testing each other by providing either a word or definition and checking their partners' response.

Advanced Have students complete compare-and-contrast charts for the words. Students can use a dictionary or thesaurus to find more information.

Advanced High Advanced High students may be familiar with the words. Review the terms, and have students create their own definitions.

Conjugating Progressive Tenses

Explain to students that, when they conjugate progressive forms of a verb, they must know the basic forms of the verb *be*.

RULE 21.2.4 Read aloud the rule and then have students repeat the lines with you.

Direct students' attention to the "Conjugation of the Progressive Forms of *Go*" chart. Ask them to skim the chart and notice what changes. Point out that the form of the main verb—*go*—does not change. Only the form of the helping verb *to be* changes. Then, have them read the paragraph directly above the chart.

Work with students to conjugate the progressive forms of *hide*. Use the present participle *hiding*.

Use the verb *sit* to guide students in using and understanding the progressive tense. **Say:** A sentence using *sit* in the present tense would be *I sit*. What is a sentence that uses *sit* in the present progressive tense? (**Response:** I am sitting.) Work with students to create more complex sentences using a progressive tense of *sit*. Work through several other examples until students are comfortable using and explaining the function of progressive tense verbs.

Have student pairs work together to choose a verb and write six sentences, one for each of the progressive tenses. Ask pairs to share their sentences with the class.

Quick-Write Extension

To help students synthesize and apply what they have learned about progressive verbs, have them describe an action-filled school scene, such as students playing on a playground or getting ready to leave at the end of the day. Direct students to use present progressive verbs to make the scene seem as if it is happening as they write; for example: *Some students are talking and laughing in the hallway. Other students are filling their backpacks with books.* Ask students to exchange descriptions and underline the progressive verbs.

Conjugating Progressive Tenses

To create the progressive tenses or forms of a verb, you must know the basic forms of *be*.

RULE 21.2.4

> To conjugate the **progressive** forms of a verb, add the present participle of the verb to a conjugation of the basic forms of *be*.

A complete conjugation of the basic forms of *be* is shown earlier in this section. Compare that conjugation with the following conjugation of the progressive forms of *go*. You will notice that, even though the present participle form of the verb does not change, the form of the helping verb does change. It is the form of *be* that tells you whether the action or condition is taking place in the past, present, or future.

CONJUGATION OF THE PROGRESSIVE FORMS OF *GO*		
TENSE	SINGULAR	PLURAL
Present Progressive	I am going. You are going. He, she, it is going.	We are going. You are going. They are going.
Past Progressive	I was going. You were going. He, she, it was going.	We were going. You were going. They were going.
Future Progressive	I will be going. You will be going. He, she, it will be going.	We will be going. You will be going. They will be going.
Present Perfect Progressive	I have been going. You have been going. He, she, it has been going.	We have been going. You have been going. They have been going.
Past Perfect Progressive	I had been going. You had been going. He, she, it had been going.	We had been going. You had been going. They had been going.
Future Perfect Progressive	I will have been going. You will have been going. He, she, it will have been going.	We will have been going. You will have been going. They will have been going.

See Practice 21.2E
See Practice 21.2F

PRACTICE 21.2E > Identifying the Progressive Tenses of Verbs

Read the sentences. Then, write whether the underlined verb tense in each sentence is *present progressive, past progressive, future progressive, present perfect progressive, past perfect progressive,* or *future perfect progressive.*

EXAMPLE   The wind was blowing across the prairie.

ANSWER   *past progressive*

The sun is rising over the ocean.

Jenny and Charlotte were watching the younger children play.

That movie will be showing at a theater next week.

I had been looking for a watch just like that.

The sky was turning from pink to orange.

I have been cooking all day.

The jet soon will be soaring high above Earth.

The students had been practicing their parts in the play for weeks.

Celia is bringing her cousin.

By next Wednesday, they will have been dancing together for two years!

PRACTICE 21.2F > Using Progressive Tenses of Verbs

Read the sentences. Then, rewrite each one as a complete sentence, using the tense of the verb in parentheses.

EXAMPLE   Candace _____ her vacation. (*plan,* present progressive)

ANSWER   Candace *is planning* her vacation.

11. Meta's story _____ more exciting. (*become,* present progressive)

12. José _____ the architecture. (*admire,* past progressive)

13. Liana _____ in New Mexico. (*live,* present perfect progressive)

14. They _____ while they study. (*eat,* future progressive)

15. Mr. Jung _____ before the alarm went off. (*sleep,* past perfect progressive)

16. I _____ for 12 hours by the time I reach China. (*fly,* future perfect progressive)

17. The author _____ her new book. (*sign,* past progressive)

18. Rosa _____ the sunshine. (*enjoy,* present progressive)

19. Dwayne _____ lawns since he was ten. (*mow,* present perfect progressive)

20. My puppy _____ on the bed. (*sleep,* past perfect progressive)

SPEAKING APPLICATION

With a partner, take turns talking about current events. Use progressive tenses of verbs. Your partner should listen for and name two progressive tense verbs.

WRITING APPLICATION

Write a brief summary of a story or book you enjoyed. Use progressive tenses of verbs in at least two sentences of the summary.

Practice   485

PRACTICE 21.2E >

1. present progressive
2. past progressive
3. future progressive
4. past perfect progressive
5. past progressive
6. present perfect progressive
7. future progressive
8. past perfect progressive
9. present progressive
10. future perfect progressive

PRACTICE 21.2F >

11. Meta's story is becoming more exciting.
12. José was admiring the architecture.
13. Liana has been living in New Mexico.
14. They will be eating while they study.
15. Mr. Jung had been sleeping before the alarm went off.
16. I will have been flying for 12 hours by the time I reach China.
17. The author was signing her new book.
18. Rosa is enjoying the sunshine.
19. Dwayne has been mowing lawns since he was ten.
20. My puppy had been sleeping on the bed.

SPEAKING APPLICATION

Students should demonstrate an understanding of the progressive tenses in their discussion.

WRITING APPLICATION

Students' summaries should demonstrate their ability to use progressive tenses in writing.

Working with ELLs   ELL Sheltered Instruction: Social/Affective

Adapt the Speaking Application, and have students take turns asking for and giving information in situations ranging from basic communication to extended speaking assignments. Students should use both high-frequency and content-based words. Have them monitor their speech and practice self-corrective techniques. For example, if listeners appear uncertain, have speakers ask *Was I being clear?* and clarify pronunciation or word choice as needed.

Beginning Have students talk with a fluent partner, asking and answering questions such as *What is your name? Where are you from?* Have them use self-corrective techniques, and support them in responding.

Intermediate Provide students with sample prompts for asking about current events, such as *What is the mayor's name?*

Have partners take turns asking and answering the questions, monitoring speech and using self-corrective techniques.

Advanced Have partners ask for and give information about current events using progressive tenses. Speakers should monitor their own speech and use self-corrective techniques. Listeners should identify two uses of a progressive tense.

Advanced High Challenge partners to complete the Speaking Application by conducting an interview about current events using progressive tenses. Have students provide thorough and extended responses to the questions. Students should monitor their speech and use self-corrective techniques.

Identifying Active and Passive Voice

Tell students that verbs can change their form to show whether or not the subject of a verb is performing an action. Write *Isaiah is being talked to by his mother.* **Say:** The subject is Isaiah, but Isaiah is not the one performing the action of "talking." Isaiah's mother is the one performing the action. This sentence is in the passive voice. To change this sentence into the active voice, rewrite the sentence so it reads, *Isaiah's mother is talking to him.* Now, the subject of the sentence is performing the action. The passive voice is useful when we know the result of an action, but not who or what did it: *The food was laid on the table.*

RULES 21.2.5, 21.2.6, 21.2.7 Read aloud the three rules and then have students repeat the lines with you.

Ask: What determines whether a sentence is in active or passive voice? (**Possible response:** whether or not the subject performs the action)

Referring to the active voice examples in the middle of the page, **ask:** Why are the sentences about Sharon and Bob in active voice? (**Possible response:** Because *Sharon* and *Bob* are the subjects of the sentences, and they are performing the action in the sentences.)

Work with students to create additional examples in the active voice.

Referring to the passive voice examples at the bottom of the page **ask:** Why might someone write these sentences about Sharon and Bob in passive voice? (**Possible response:** Because the writer wants to make the *piano* and *the debate team* the important parts of the sentences, but neither of them is performing the action of the sentences. Sharon and Bob are performing the action.)

Work with students to create additional examples of sentences in both the active and the passive voices.

Identifying Active and Passive Voice

Just as verbs change tense to show time, they may also change form to show whether or not the subject of the verb is performing an action.

> **The voice of a verb shows whether or not the subject is performing the action.**

In English, most verbs have two **voices: active,** to show that the subject is performing an action, and **passive,** to show that the subject is having an action performed on it.

> **A verb is in the active voice when its subject performs the action.**

ACTIVE VOICE

Sharon **plays** the piano.

Bob **photographed** the debate team.

In each example above, the subject performs the action, so it is said to be in the active voice.

> **A verb is in the passive voice when its subject does not perform the action.**

PASSIVE VOICE

The piano **is being played** by Sharon.

The debate team **was photographed** by Bob.

See Practice 21.2G

In each example above, the person doing the action becomes the object of the preposition *by* and is no longer the subject. Both subjects—*piano* and *team*—are receivers rather than performers of the action. When the subject is acted upon, the verb is said to be in the passive voice.

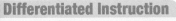

Forming the Tenses of Passive Verbs

A passive verb always has two parts.

> **A passive verb is always a verb phrase made from a form of be plus a past participle.**

21.2.8 RULE

The following chart shows a conjugation of the passive forms of the verb *report* with the pronoun *it*.

CONJUGATION OF THE PASSIVE FORMS OF *REPORT*	
TENSE	PASSIVE FORM
Present	It is reported.
Past	It was reported.
Future	It will be reported.
Present Perfect	It has been reported.
Past Perfect	It had been reported.
Future Perfect	It will have been reported.

While there are uses for the passive voice, most writing is more lively when it is in the active voice. Think about how to change each sentence below to the active voice. Follow the pattern in the first two examples.

PASSIVE   It **is decided** to bring the car.

ACTIVE   We **have decided** to bring the car.

PASSIVE   It **was decided** to bring the car.

ACTIVE   We **decided** to bring the car.

PASSIVE   It **will be decided** Tuesday if we should bring the car.

It **has been decided** to bring the car.

It **had been decided** that we will need the car.

It **will have been decided** if we need the car.

The Six Tenses of Verbs   487

Forming the Tenses of Passive Verbs

Explain to students that when they conjugate passive verbs, they will need to include two parts.

RULE 21.2.8 Read aloud the rule and then have students repeat the lines with you.

Point out the chart showing Conjugation of the Passive Forms of *Report*. Ask them to identify the forms of *be* in the second column (*is, was, will be, has been, had been, will have been*). Have them conjugate the passive forms of *tell*.

Write on the board this sentence from page 487: *It is decided to bring the car.* **Say:** Who decided it? When we don't know who performs the action of a sentence, that means the sentence is passive. Who did the "deciding" in the sentence? (**Response:** We don't know.) Cross out *It is* and write *We have* at the beginning of the sentence. **Say:** Now we know who decided to bring the car. This sentence is in the active voice.

Point out to students that the passive sentence is less lively than the active sentence. Write this sentence on the board: *The race is being run by fierce competitors.* Show students the passive voice in the sentence and have them reorder it into the active voice.

Have students write several energetic active sentences. Then have them exchange sentences with a partner. Have them rewrite the partner's sentences in the passive voice. Partners should discuss the effect this has on the meaning of their sentences.

> *Teacher Tip*
>
> To provide students with more practice with active and passive voice, write a paragraph in the passive voice and distribute copies to students. Have partners work together to rewrite the paragraph in the active voice. Encourage students to discuss which paragraph they enjoy reading more and why.

Differentiated Instruction

Strategy for Spanish Speakers

Students whose home language is Spanish may have difficulty forming the passive in English due to the multiple parts of passive sentences. Remind students that in the passive voice, the tense and person of the verb *to be* changes, but the main verb is always the past participle. Prepare one set of cards with the names of the six tenses listed on page 487. Ask students to provide several verbs (make sure they are transitive verbs) and write them on the board.

Remind students of the past participle form. Have students write the past participle of each verb. For each verb, draw a card, for example, *future*. Then have students write a passive sentence with the verb, using an appropriate subject. For example, for the verb *held* students may write a sentence such as *The auditions will be held tomorrow.* Call on volunteers to share their sentences. Have students circle the form of the verb *to be* and underline the past participle in each sentence.

Using Active and Passive Voices

Discuss with students various situations in which it might be beneficial to use the passive voice, for example, to persuade. The passive voice might also be used when the receiver of an action is more important than the performer, or when the performer of an action is unknown.

RULE 21.2.9 Read aloud the rule and then have students repeat the line with you.

Work with students to create two additional examples, using *told/was told* and *rode/was ridden*.

RULE 21.2.10 Read aloud the rule and then have students repeat the lines with you.

Ask: How does the emphasis change when the example is put into active voice? *The voters supported the candidate.* (**Possible response:** The emphasis is now on the voters who are performing the action.)

RULE 21.2.11 Read aloud the rule and then have students repeat the lines with you.

Point out that people sometimes use the passive voice to avoid taking responsibility. For example, they might say *It was written* instead of *I wrote.*

Have student pairs write two active sentences and two passive sentences. One passive sentence should be an example of the type where the receiver of the action is more important than the performer of the action. The second passive sentence should have an unknown or unnamed performer of the action. Ask pairs to share their sentences with the class.

Using Active and Passive Voices

Each of the two voices has its proper use in English.

> **Use the active voice whenever possible.**

Sentences with active verbs are less wordy and more forceful than those with passive verbs. Compare, for example, the following sentences. Notice the different number of words each sentence needs to report the same information.

ACTIVE   Students **conducted** a taste test.

PASSIVE   A taste test **was conducted** by students.

Although you should use the active voice in most of your writing, there will be times when you will need to use the passive voice.

> **Use the passive voice to emphasize the receiver of an action rather than the performer of an action.**

In the following example, the receiver of the action is the subject *candidate*. It is the *voters* (the direct object) who are actually performing the action.

EMPHASIS ON RECEIVER   The candidate **was supported** by the voters.

See Practice 21.2H
See Practice 21.2I
See Practice 21.2J

The passive voice should also be used when there is no performer of the action.

> **Use the passive voice to point out the receiver of an action when the performer is unknown or not named in the sentence.**

PERFORMER UNKNOWN   The report **was ordered** last year.

488   **Using Verbs**

Differentiated Instruction

PRE-AP **Enrichment for Above-Level Students** Sometimes, laws, rules, and other regulations are written in the passive voice, which can make the sentences harder to understand. Ask students to research state or city laws and find sentences that are written in the passive voice. Encourage students to rewrite the text in active voice for clarity.

RTI **Strategy for Special Needs Students** Remind students that most English sentences follow a pattern in which the subject performs the action of the verb and comes before the verb. Work with students to identify and practice the steps in converting a passive sentence to an active one: 1: Identify the doer of the action. 2. Drop helping verbs such as *was.* 3. Begin with the subject. 4. Continue with the action verb. 5. End with the direct object, or the receiver of the action.

PRACTICE 21.2G > Distinguishing Active and Passive Voice

Read the sentences. Then, write *AV* if the underlined verb is in active voice or *PV* if the verb is in passive voice.

EXAMPLE   The ball <u>was thrown</u> to first base.

ANSWER   *PV*

1. Sondra <u>opened</u> the door for Mrs. Santos.
2. Jason said that the book <u>was dropped</u> by Celia.
3. The event <u>is being covered</u> by a rookie reporter.
4. I <u>juggled</u> two jobs while studying for my college exams.
5. Christine <u>was awakened</u> by her alarm clock at 6:00 A.M.
6. The kitten <u>lapped</u> up the spilled milk.
7. Lexie quickly <u>drank</u> three glasses of water.
8. The results of the election <u>pleased</u> the candidate.
9. The baby <u>was comforted</u> by its mother's voice.
10. Janet <u>helped</u> her little brother with his chores.

PRACTICE 21.2H > Revising to Use Active Voice

Read the sentences. Then, rewrite each sentence that is in passive voice so that it is in active voice. If the sentence is already in active voice, write *active*. Discuss your answers with a partner to determine if they are correct.

EXAMPLE   This song was written by Jackie.

ANSWER   *Jackie wrote this song.*

11. I found a hat that I like.
12. The movie was made by a French director.
13. I went bowling yesterday.
14. The actors were applauded by the audience.
15. The snake warmed itself in the sun.
16. Sammy and Keisha were helped by Richard.
17. The show continued without further interruption.
18. The computer was fixed by the technician.
19. Ten items were scanned by the cashier.
20. Madison jogged around the park.

SPEAKING APPLICATION

With a partner, take turns saying one sentence in active voice and one sentence in passive voice. Use the sentences in Practice 21.2H as models to create your sentences. Your partner should listen to the two sentences and identify which sentence is in active voice and which is in passive voice.

WRITING APPLICATION

Write at least two sentences in passive voice about an activity you enjoy. Then, rewrite the sentences so they are in active voice.

Practice   489

PRACTICE 21.2G

1. AV
2. PV
3. PV
4. AV
5. PV
6. AV
7. AV
8. AV
9. PV
10. AV

PRACTICE 21.2H

11. active
12. A French director made the movie.
13. active
14. The audience applauded the actors.
15. active
16. Richard helped Sammy and Keisha.
17. active
18. The technician fixed the computer.
19. The cashier scanned ten items.
20. active

SPEAKING APPLICATION

Students' spoken sentences should demonstrate that they can use and understand the function of active and passive voice in the context of speaking.

WRITING APPLICATION

Students' written sentences should demonstrate that they can use and understand the function of active and passive voice in the context of writing.

PRACTICE 21.2I

1. active
2. passive—My brother returned the overdue book to the library.
3. passive—The Perrys adopted the last cat.
4. active
5. active
6. active
7. passive—My aunt made that quilt.
8. passive—Quality Construction Services is building those houses in Green Acres.
9. active
10. active

PRACTICE 21.2J

11. An expert drove the race car that came in first.
12. The trash collectors picked up the trash at 7 A.M.
13. A coyote chased our dog, Hamilton, last night.
14. I locked the door.
15. Mom made the salad, but Uncle Tony made the spaghetti.
16. Ms. Robinson wrote the play, and Mr. Jeter directed it.
17. The Internet support team solved our computer issue.
18. The twins, Jeremy and Jessica, planned the party.
19. The school board approved an increase in teachers' salaries.
20. A team of doctors has treated my grandfather for years.

SPEAKING APPLICATION

Students' discussions should demonstrate that they can use and understand the function of active and passive voice.

WRITING APPLICATION

Students' paragraphs should demonstrate that they can use and understand the function of active and passive voice in writing.

PRACTICE 21.2I Recognizing Voice

Read the sentences. Then, write whether the underlined verb is in active voice or passive voice. Rewrite the sentences that are in passive voice to ones that are in active voice. Discuss the changes that you made with a partner.

EXAMPLE   The flag <u>was carried</u> by a guard.
ANSWER   *passive — A guard carried the flag.*
EXAMPLE   The school board <u>selected</u> a new superintendent a week ago.
ANSWER   *active*

1. The instructor <u>scheduled</u> the art classes for Saturdays.
2. The overdue book <u>was returned</u> to the library by my brother.
3. The last cat <u>was adopted</u> by the Perrys.
4. Jeff <u>wears</u> those worn-out jeans with his oldest sweatshirt.
5. The class <u>elected</u> Jorge.
6. The movers <u>broke</u> the picture frame by putting a heavy box on it.
7. That quilt <u>was made</u> by my aunt.
8. Those houses in Green Acres <u>are being built</u> by Quality Construction Services.
9. The teacher <u>warned</u> you about being late.
10. The delivery service <u>brings</u> Mom's packages.

SPEAKING APPLICATION

Discuss with a partner when to use passive voice and when to use active voice. Each partner writes one sentence in active voice and one sentence in passive voice. Then, partners check each other's work.

PRACTICE 21.2J Revising Passive Voice

Read the sentences. Then, rewrite the senten in the active voice. Check your revised senten by reading them aloud to a partner.

EXAMPLE   The editorial in the school paper about traffic was written by me.
ANSWER   *I wrote the editorial in the sch paper about traffic.*

11. The race car that came in first was driven an expert.
12. The trash was picked up at 7 A.M. by the trash collectors.
13. Our dog, Hamilton, was chased by a coyo last night.
14. The door was locked by me.
15. Mom made the salad, but the spaghetti w made by Uncle Tony.
16. The play was written by Ms. Robinson, a Mr. Jeter directed it.
17. Our computer issue was solved by the Internet support team.
18. The party was planned by the twins, Jere and Jessica.
19. An increase in teachers' salaries was approved by the school board.
20. My grandfather has been treated for year a team of doctors.

WRITING APPLICATION

Write a paragraph about a sculpture or painting you have seen. Use at least one appropriate sentence in passive voice. Then, have a partner read your paragraph and identify your sentence in passive voice. Discu how active voice makes sentences stronger.

Working with ELLs   ELL Sheltered Instruction: Cognitive

As students learn about progressive tense, support them in learning the relationship between English sounds and letters and in decoding words. Write the word *making* on the board. Underline the *-ing* ending, explaining that it is commonly added to verbs. Then, point to the letters *ng* and explain that in English, these two letters work together to make one sound, /ng/. Model correct pronunciation, and have students echo. Then:

Beginning Write a sentence using the word *reading* on the board. Have students read the word aloud. Repeat with *writing*.

Intermediate Have partners scan the student page for words that end in *-ing*,

writing them on note cards. Then, have them take turns decoding the words on the cards. Monitor to ensure that students pronounce the *ng* digraph correctly.

Advanced Have partners use *-ing* words from the student page in sentences. Have them read one another's sentences aloud, decoding words that end in *-ing*.

Advanced High Have students write verbs on note cards. Have partners choose a card, add *-ing* to the verb on the card, and write a sentence featuring the new word. Partners should read each other's sentences aloud.

st Warm-Up

ECTIONS

the introduction and the passage that follows. Then, answer the
tions to show that you can use and understand the function of
e and passive voice in reading and writing.

ey wrote this paragraph about her soccer game. Read the paragraph
think about the changes you would suggest as a peer editor. When you
h reading, answer the questions that follow.

I Love Soccer!

On Saturday, I think all of us were nervous to be playing the soccer
npions from last season, but we were encouraged by our coach.
'e got the ball and dribbled down the field. (3) Kofi is good at
ping, and we hung on. (4) A great kick was made by Andra to score
nt. (5) Another point was scored by Brianna in the first half, and in
econd half the winds died down, and that calmed all of us. (6) In the
we were up 4 to 2, and a victory had been won!

---

hat change, if any, should be made in
entence 1?

A Change *were nervous* to **were being
nervous**

B Change *we were encouraged* to **we
encouraged**

C Change *we were encouraged by our
coach* to **our coach encouraged us**

D Make no change

ow should sentence 4 be revised in the
ctive voice?

F A great kick was made by Andra; a point
was scored.

G To score a point, a great kick was made.

H Andra made a great kick to score a point.

J Andra made a great kick, and a point was
scored by her.

3 What is the BEST way to revise sentence 5?

A Another point was scored by Brianna in
the first half. In the second half, we were
calmed by the winds dying down.

B Brianna scored another point in the first
half. In the second half, the winds died
down, and that calmed all of us.

C Brianna scored another point in the first
half. In the second half, the winds died
down and were calmed by all of us.

D Another point was scored by Brianna in
the first half. In the second half, dying
down were the winds that calmed all of us.

4 What change, if any, should be made in
sentence 6?

F Change *a victory had been* to **we**

G Change *were* to **had been**

H Add **by us** after *won*

J Make no change

Test Warm-Up   491

Test Warm-Up

1. **C** Change *we were encouraged
   by our coach* to **our coach
   encouraged us**

2. **H** Andra made a great kick to
   score a point.

3. **B** Brianna scored another point
   in the first half. In the second
   half, the winds died down, and
   that calmed all of us.

4. **F** Change *a victory had been*
   to **we**

Reteach

If students have not mastered these skills,
review the content in Section 21.2 Using
Active and Passive Voices.

Test Tip

Students may look for a pattern as they answer
questions in a multiple-choice test. Point out
to students that the questions on a single page
might have several different formats. Students
should approach each question individually,
rather than expecting a question to require the
same type of answer as the question before
it. For example, one question might require
students to consider a change in word choice,
while the next sentence requires them to
revise the structure of a sentence.

Moods of Verbs

The word *mood* often describes feelings. With verbs, however, it means the way in which an action takes place, or the manner of the action.

RULE 21.2.12 Read aloud the rule and then have students repeat the lines with you.

Write on the board the three moods: *indicative, subjunctive, imperative.* Have students skim page 492 to find out when each mood is used.

Ask: When is the indicative mood used? (to state something or ask questions) **Ask:** When is the subjunctive mood used? (to express a wish or state something contrary to fact)

Say: What does *contrary to fact* mean? Here's an example: *If I were a better singer, I would be an opera star.* The subjunctive mood is used in this sentence to indicate that I am not a good enough singer to sing opera, so it is not possible for me to be an opera star. The plural verb *were* is used in this sentence because the clause begins with *if.*

Ask: When is the imperative mood used? (to state a request or give a command) **Ask:** What do you notice about the tense of the verbs in the imperative examples? (All are in present tense.)

Help students understand and differentiate between the three types of sentences. Write three sentences on the board: one indicative, one subjunctive, and one imperative. Have students identify each type of sentence.

Have each student write two examples of each type of sentence and speak them aloud to a partner. Partners should identify the type of sentence.

> *Teacher Tip*
>
> Give students additional practice in using the subjunctive mood by asking them to complete sentences beginning with this prompt: *If I were able to do anything I wanted....*

Moods of Verbs

Verbs in English also use **mood** to describe the status of an action.

> There are three moods for English verbs: the **indicative mood**, the **subjunctive mood,** and the **imperative mood.**

The **indicative mood** indicates, or states, something. It is also used to ask questions. The **subjunctive mood** describes a wish or a condition that may be contrary to fact.

INDICATIVE MOOD	SUBJUNCTIVE MOOD
Melanie **is** in my class.	I wish Joanna **were** in my class.
Jared **has** a new telescope.	If he **had brought** it to camp, we could have looked at the stars.
I **would** like to be president of the debating club.	If I **were** president of the debating club, I would be fair to everyone.

The subjunctive mood can be used to describe situations that are unlikely to happen or not possible. It is often used in clauses that begin with *if* or *that.* In these cases, use the plural form of the verb.

EXAMPLES   If I **were** you, I would leave for home after the rain stops.
(I am not you, so the situation is not possible.)

Mary wishes that she **were** on vacation now.
(She is not going until next month, so the situation is not possible.)

The **imperative** mood states a request or command and always uses the present tense. A mild imperative is followed by a period; a strong imperative is followed by an exclamation point.

EXAMPLES   **Call** me after school. Please **don't** forget.
Watch out for that broken window!

See Practice 21.2K
See Practice 21.2L

Notice that the subject, *you,* is understood but omitted.

492   **Using Verbs**

Working with ELLs   **ELL** Sheltered Instruction: Cognitive

Have students use the short indicative and the longer subjunctive sentences in the examples on page 492 to practice speaking using a variety of sentence lengths with increasing accuracy and ease.

Beginning Read the sentences in the top row of the chart aloud to students, having them repeat after you. Emphasize that the first sentence says what is, and the second says what the speaker wishes for.

Intermediate Have students choral read the sentences in the second and third rows of the chart. Ask why the subjunctive sentences are longer, eliciting that they contain two ideas: a condition and its consequence. Coach them in speaking

the sentences accurately and with correct intonation.

Advanced Have partners say example sentences from the chart. Then, have students write simple indicative sentences on cards. Have partners takes turns choosing a card, saying the sentence, and then saying a longer subjunctive sentence based on the sentence. Have them correct each other as needed.

Advanced High Have students complete the Advanced activity. Extend by having them also say imperative sentences based on the sentences on the cards.

PRACTICE 21.2K > Identifying Moods of Verbs

Read the sentences. Then, write *indicative*, *subjunctive*, or *imperative* for the mood of the underlined verb in each sentence.

EXAMPLE   Please <u>close</u> the door.

ANSWER   *imperative*

1. I wish I <u>were</u> taller.
2. Lisa <u>is bringing</u> the popcorn tonight.
3. <u>Don't forget</u> your gloves.
4. If I <u>were</u> you, I would think carefully about your choice.
5. Mom and Dad <u>are going</u> out for dinner.
6. <u>Come</u> in for dinner now.
7. If it <u>were</u> up to me, we would take a different path.
8. Carla <u>has</u> a new bicycle.
9. I wish Dad <u>were</u> here now.
10. <u>Send</u> your grandmother a thank-you note.

PRACTICE 21.2L > Writing Sentences to Express Mood

Read the verbs. Then, write sentences using the different moods of verbs as indicated below.

EXAMPLE   drink (imperative)

ANSWER   *Please drink some water.*

11. were (subjunctive)
12. will bring (indicative)
13. open (imperative)
14. went (indicative)
15. had been (subjunctive)
16. put (imperative)
17. ran (indicative)
18. could hear (subjunctive)
19. are leaving (indicative)
20. finish (imperative)

SPEAKING APPLICATION

With a partner, take turns talking about what you might like to do if things were different. Your partner should confirm whether you are using the subjunctive mood correctly.

WRITING APPLICATION

Write a short paragraph about what you would like to do if you were older. Use the subjunctive mood at least twice.

Practice   493

PRACTICE 21.2K >

1. subjunctive
2. indicative
3. imperative
4. subjunctive
5. indicative
6. imperative
7. subjunctive
8. indicative
9. subjunctive
10. imperative

PRACTICE 21.2L >

Answers will vary. Sample answers:

11. If I were on vacation, I would be very happy.
12. I will bring the salad.
13. Please open a window.
14. Julia and Keisha went to the store.
15. I know we could have fixed it if Dad had been here.
16. Please put your bicycle away.
17. The dog ran into the front yard.
18. If she could hear me, she would be laughing.
19. My friends are leaving soon.
20. Finish your homework now.

SPEAKING APPLICATION

Have students explain how they formed the subjunctive mood in their sentences.

WRITING APPLICATION

Students' sentences should demonstrate that they can use the subjunctive mood in writing.

Lesson Objectives

1. Correctly use principal parts of verbs.

2. Distinguish between meanings of confusing verb pairs.

3. Avoid common mistakes in using verbs.

Discuss reasons students should master troublesome verbs.

Use a Think Aloud as part of a gradual release progression.

Say: When **I look at** this list, it seems too huge, and I don't know how I will remember every rule. Not all of these verbs give me trouble, though. So the best thing for me to do is to focus on the few verbs that I don't always use correctly. I can add them to my list of things to check when I revise my writing. One thing I need to practice is the correct use of *gone* and *went*. The explanation tells me that I should use *gone* only with a helping verb.

Ask: How can I remember to use this rule when I'm writing and speaking? **Accept all reasonable responses.**

Work with students to list strategies for improving their use of troublesome verbs. For example, students might listen for how people use these verbs, find models of good usage to imitate, and identify proofing strategies they can use to check their usage of this verb in their writing (such as highlighting places they have used *gone* and using their word processor's Find command).

Assign student pairs one usage problem on this page. Ask them to develop a hint or memory aid to help classmates remember the rule for correct usage. Have students share their rules.

21.3 Troublesome Verbs

The following verbs cause problems for many speakers and writers of English. Some of the problems involve using the principal parts of certain verbs. Others involve learning to distinguish between the meanings of certain confusing pairs of verbs.

(1) ain't *Ain't* is not considered standard English. Avoid using it in speaking and in writing.

INCORRECT   He **ain't** the first to explore this island.

CORRECT   He **isn't** the first to explore this island.

(2) did, done Remember that *done* is a past participle and can be used as a verb only with a helping verb such as *have* or *has*. Instead of using *done* without a helping verb, use *did*.

INCORRECT   I already **done** my history project.

CORRECT   I already **did** my history project.
                       I **have** already **done** my history project.

(3) dragged, drug *Drag* is a regular verb. Its principal parts are *drag, dragging, dragged,* and *dragged. Drug* is never correct as the past or past participle of *drag.*

INCORRECT   The sailor **drug** the heavy box.

CORRECT   The sailor **dragged** the heavy box.

(4) gone, went *Gone* is the past participle of *go* and can be used as a verb only with a helping verb such as *have* or *has. Went* is the past tense of *go* and is never used with a helping verb.

INCORRECT   Jean and Frank **gone** to the museum.
                       We **should have went** along with them.

CORRECT   Jean and Frank **went** (or **have gone**) to the museum.
                       We **should have gone** along with them.

See Practice 21.3A

494   Using Verbs

---

(5) *have, of* The words *have* and *of* often sound very similar. Be careful not to write *of* when you mean the helping verb *have* or its contraction *'ve*.

INCORRECT   Columbus should **of** continued on.

CORRECT   Columbus should **have** (or **should've**) continued on.

(6) *lay, lie* These verbs look and sound almost alike and have similar meanings. The first step in distinguishing between *lay* and *lie* is to memorize the principal parts of both verbs.

PRINCIPAL PARTS				
lay	laying	laid	laid
lie	lying	lay	lain

Lay usually means "to put (something) down" or "to place (something)." It is almost always followed by a direct object. *Lie* means "to rest in a reclining position" or "to be situated." This verb is used to show the position of a person, place, or thing. *Lie* is never followed by a direct object.

EXAMPLES   The captain **lays** his glasses on the desk.

                The sailors must **lie** down in bunks.

Pay special attention to the past tense of *lay* and *lie*. *Lay* is the past tense of *lie*. The past tense of *lay* is *laid*.

PRESENT TENSE OF *LAY*   I **lay** the map on the table.

PAST TENSE OF *LAY*   The sailors **laid** their uniforms on their bunks.

PAST TENSE OF *LIE*   The sailor **lay** down on his bunk.

Practice 21.3B

(7) *leave, let* *Leave* means "to allow to remain." *Let* means "to permit." Do not reverse the meanings.

INCORRECT   **Leave** me think in peace! **Let** the poor dog alone!

CORRECT   **Let** me think in peace! **Leave** the poor dog alone!

Troublesome Verbs   495

Say: I could've gone to the gym yesterday. Have students tell you whether the *uv* sound is *of* or the short form of *have*. **Say:** I thought of you today. Have students tell you whether the *uv* sound is *of* or the short form of *have*.

Write these sentences on the board:
He lays the _____ *by the door.*
He was lying _____ *by the door.*
She laid the _____ *by the door.*
She had lain _____ *by the door.*

Have students identify which of the sentences require that a word be entered in the blank space. (only the first and third) Invite students to provide nouns to fill in the blanks. Then, **ask:** What kind of word goes in the blank? If students need a review of direct objects, direct their attention to the explanation of *lie/lay* and remind them that only forms of the verb *to lay* can take a direct object.

Have students compare the sentences on the board to the examples for *lay* on page 495. Point out that *lie* never takes a direct object.

Assign student pairs to write one or more rules for using *lie/lay* correctly.

Write these sentences on the board: *Let me go! Leave the window open. Let the dog up on the couch.* Have students identify which sentences use the words *let* and *leave* correctly.

Differentiated Instruction

RTI **Strategy for Below-Level Students**
Encourage students to create a personal proofing checklist to use every time they revise their writing. Have them choose three or four verbs from those listed on pages 494–496 to add to the list.

PRE-AP **Enrichment for Above-Level Students** Encourage students to create and perform a skit that demonstrates how to use one of the troublesome verbs correctly. They might show comic misunderstandings that arise because of usage errors, present an interaction between a teacher and student(s), or act out situations that illustrate correct usage.

Have student pairs read the explanation and examples for the troublesome verbs discussed on page 496.

Use a Think Aloud as part of a gradual release progression.

Say: Of the troublesome verbs on this list, **I think** that I have had the most trouble with *raise* and *rise*. The words sound very similar. I'll need to review the meanings of each word to better understand how to use them correctly.

Lead a class discussion about the verbs listed on this page (or in this section) that students feel are the most difficult to master. Make a list on the board. **Then, guide students** in creating sentences that use each verb correctly.

Have students work in pairs to write additional examples of correct usage, using the examples on page 496 as a model. Finally, ask them to work together to write one or more rules that will help them use these troublesome verbs correctly.

---

(8) *raise, rise* *Raise* can mean "to lift (something) upward," "to build (something)," or "to increase (something)." It is usually followed by a direct object. *Rise* is not usually followed by a direct object. This verb means "to get up," "to go up," or "to be increased."

EXAMPLES   **Raise** the anchor so we can cast off.

The sailors must **rise** before five in the morning.

(9) *saw, seen* *Seen* is a past participle and can be used as a verb only with a helping verb such as *have* or *has*.

INCORRECT   I **seen** that exhibit last year.

CORRECT   I **saw** that exhibit last year.

(10) *says, said* A common mistake in reporting what someone said is to use *says* (present tense) rather than *said* (past tense).

INCORRECT   The captain **says**, "I need to sit down."

CORRECT   The captain **said**, "I need to sit down."

(11) *set, sit* The first step in learning to distinguish between *set* and *sit* is to become thoroughly familiar with their principal parts.

PRINCIPAL PARTS			
set	setting	set	set
sit	sitting	sat	sat

Set means "to put (something) in a certain place or position." It is usually followed by a direct object. *Sit* usually means "to be seated" or "to rest." It is usually not followed by a direct object.

EXAMPLES   He **set** the cup on the coaster.

We **have set** the plants safely in the cargo bay.

Mona **sat** in the captain's chair.   See Practice 21.3C

The parrot **has sat** on the perch since it ate.   See Practice 21.3D

PRACTICE 21.3A Using *Did* and *Done*

Read the sentences. Then, for each sentence, if *did* or *done* is used correctly, write *correct*. If it is not, write *incorrect*.

EXAMPLE My brother done something really dangerous.

ANSWER *incorrect*

1. We did all our homework.
2. We have did what we could to help.
3. Mom has done enough work for today.
4. I done a good job washing the car.
5. Celeste will have done everything necessary.
6. My little brother did his homework without my help.
7. Getting exercise done a lot to improve my health.
8. We have done all our shopping for the party.
9. Carmen has already did the painting.
10. We did invite Michelle and Carlos.

PRACTICE 21.3B Using *Lay* and *Lie*

Read the sentences. Then, choose and write the correct form of the verb from the pair in parentheses.

EXAMPLE Our cats love (lain, lying) near the heater.

ANSWER *lying*

11. He carefully (laid, laying) the tray on the table.
12. Why don't you (lying, lie) down for a while?
13. They were (laying, laid) out their clothes for the next day.
14. You have (lay, lain) there all day!
15. She should (lie, lay) down on the couch to rest.
16. Most chickens (laid, lay) an egg every day.
17. There is a book (lying, laid) on my desk.
18. Yesterday, I (lay, lie) on the lawn, enjoying the smell of cut grass.
19. Jamal isn't feeling well and is (lying, lain) on the bed in the nurse's office.
20. The snow (lay, laid) thick and deep on the field last week.

SPEAKING APPLICATION

With a partner, take turns talking about activities that you do around your home. Use at least two of the verbs practiced on this page. Your partner should confirm whether the verbs were used correctly.

WRITING APPLICATION

Write three sentences about chores you do around your home. In your sentences, use *did* or *done* (you may use both), as well as at least one tense of *lay*.

Practice 497

PRACTICE 21.3A

1. correct
2. incorrect
3. correct
4. incorrect
5. correct
6. correct
7. incorrect
8. correct
9. incorrect
10. correct

PRACTICE 21.3B

11. laid
12. lie
13. laying
14. lain
15. lie
16. lay
17. lying
18. lay
19. lying
20. lay

SPEAKING APPLICATION

Have students explain why they chose the verbs they used in their discussions and justify that the verbs are used correctly.

WRITING APPLICATION

Students' sentences should correctly use the verb form they have chosen.

PRACTICE 21.3C

1. set
2. sit
3. setting
4. sat
5. sitting
6. set
7. setting
8. sit
9. set
10. sat

PRACTICE 21.3D

11. correct
12. Have you done the research for your social studies project?
13. correct
14. correct
15. correct
16. The teacher gave us an assignment, and then he said it's due tomorrow.
17. Justin and Cleo went to the zoo with their friends.
18. We saw someone riding an elephant.
19. Let me sit here for a while.
20. correct

PRACTICE 21.3C Using *Set* and *Sit*

Read the sentences. Then, choose and write the correct form of the verb from the pair in parentheses.

EXAMPLE I'll just (set, sit) right here until you come back.

ANSWER *sit*

1. You can just (set, setting) it on the table.
2. If you (sat, sit) very still, you may see birds at the feeder.
3. Dad was (sitting, setting) the bags of sand in the truck when his back started to hurt.
4. The students (sat, set) in silence, waiting for the concert to begin.
5. I left the shopping list (setting, sitting) on the counter.
6. Cassie (set, sat) the books on the cart.
7. This weekend, we will be (sitting, setting) the cornerstone for the new library.
8. Our dog loves to (set, sit) on the sofa.
9. The waiter (sit, set) the bowl of soup down carefully.
10. My little brother (sit, sat) happily in the middle of the pile of toys.

PRACTICE 21.3D Using Troublesome Verbs

Read the sentences. If the underlined verb is used correctly, write *correct*. If it is not, rewrite the sentence using the correct verb.

EXAMPLE I <u>seen</u> a good place for a picnic.

ANSWER *I saw a good place for a picnic.*

11. Mom <u>dragged</u> my brother to the barber for a haircut.
12. Have you <u>did</u> the research for your social studies project?
13. My sister wants to <u>raise</u> vegetables this summer.
14. The coach should <u>have</u> sent in a different player.
15. <u>Leave</u> that cut alone, or it won't heal.
16. The teacher gave us an assignment, and then he <u>says</u> it's due tomorrow.
17. Justin and Cleo <u>gone</u> to the zoo with their friends.
18. We <u>seen</u> someone riding an elephant.
19. <u>Leave</u> me sit here for a while.
20. You should have <u>gone</u> on the class trip.

SPEAKING APPLICATION

With a partner, take turns describing an exciting event. Use at least two of the troublesome verbs. Your partner should confirm whether you are using the verbs correctly.

WRITING APPLICATION

Write a short paragraph about a visit to a zoo (real or imagined). Use at least two of the troublesome verbs in your paragraph.

498   Using Verbs

CHAPTER 22 LESSON PLANNER
Using Pronouns

Use the Online Lesson Planner at www.phwritingcoach.com to customize your instructional plan for an integrated Language Arts curriculum.

DAY 1 22.1 Case

"What Do You Notice?" Objectives: Recognize cases of personal pronouns	**INSTRUCTION AND PRACTICE** Student Edition pp. 499–501

DAY 2 22.1 Case (continued)

Objectives: Identify, use, and understand pronoun cases, including • the nominative case • the objective case	**INSTRUCTION AND PRACTICE** Student Edition pp. 502–503, 505–506 Test Warm-Up p. 508

DAY 3 22.1 Case (continued)

Objectives: Identify, use, and understand pronouns, including • the possessive case • *who* and *whom*	**INSTRUCTION AND PRACTICE** Student Edition pp. 504, 507, 509–510 Test Warm-Up p. 508

> *"Since strong verbs make writing vivid, it is important that we show students how much their writing pivots on crafting the right verb. Verbs place the reader in time—past, present, or future. However, when verbs don't agree in number or person or follow the patterns of standard English, clear writing grinds to a halt."*
>
> **—Jeff Anderson**

Grammar Assessment

Grammar Coach:	Diagnostic Assessment	End-of-Chapter Assessment	Progress Monitoring
Personalized Instruction	Students take grammar diagnostic test online and are automatically assigned instruction and practice in areas where they need support.	Teacher uses **ExamView** to administer end-of-chapter assessment and remediation. Teachers may customize **ExamView** tests or use the ones provided.	Teachers may use the **Test Warm-Ups** and the **Cumulative Reviews** in the student book or eText to check students' mastery of grammar skills. Students may also play **DimensionL** grammar video games to test their grammar skills.
Teacher-Directed Instruction	Teacher administers the diagnostic test and determines focus of instruction and practice.		

Alternate Pacing Plans

- **Block Scheduling** Each day in the Lesson Planner represents a 40–50 minute block. Teachers using block scheduling may combine days to revise pacing to meet their classroom needs.

- **Accelerated Lesson Planning** Combine instructional days, focusing on concepts called out by students' diagnostic test results.

- **Integrated Language Arts Curriculum** Use the instruction and practice in this chapter to provide reinforcement, remediation, or extension of grammar concepts taught in your literature curriculum.

Links to Prentice Hall *LITERATURE*

Unit 1 Personal and Possessive Pronouns, p. 108; Interrogative and Indefinite Pronouns, p. 130

WRITING COACH
Online
www.phwritingcoach.com

Grammar Assessment and Practice

Chapter diagnostic tests assess students' skills and assign instruction and practice.

DimensionL Video Games

Fast-paced interactive video games challenge students' mastery of grammar.

Lesson Planner continues on next page

> ❝ *Students should be taught the different cases of pronouns (nominative, objective, possessive), but they will only internalize them when they begin using them in their own writing.* ❞
>
> **—Kelly Gallagher**

Differentiated Instruction

Differentiated Instruction Boxes in this Teacher's Edition address these student populations:

- Below-Level Students
- Above-Level Students
- Gifted and Talented Students
- Special Needs Students
- English Language Learners
- Spanish Speaking Students

In addition, for further enrichment, see the **Extension** features.

Grammar Ground Rule: Keep It Simple!

Model with Students

In this chapter, keep it simple means using **pronouns**, especially **possessive pronouns**. Explain to students that a possessive pronoun such as *his* can take the place of four or five words. That makes a sentence simpler and easier to read.

Say: Suppose I want to talk about a zebra's stripes. I could say, *A zebra never changes the stripes that belong to the zebra.* Or I could say, *A zebra never changes its stripes.* The second sentence is a simpler, better sentence because of the pronoun *its.* Or consider this sentence: *Marlie is wearing the sweater of the sister of Marlie.* It's simpler and easier to say, *Marlie is wearing her sister's sweater.*

Explain that students can use possessive pronouns to make their writing simpler and clearer, but they need to be careful. **Say:** We make a noun possessive by adding an apostrophe and an –s, but you should never add that to a possessive pronoun. *Steve's hat* means "the hat of Steve." *His hat* means "the hat of him." If you add an apostrophe and an –s, you get "the hat of him of him."

Small Group Activity – Finding Pronouns

Have students form groups and find a paragraph from a short story. Have one student read the paragraph, stopping at each pronoun. The other students should then say the words that the pronoun has replaced, if they can. Sometimes an antecedent will not be in the selection. Have students discuss how the use of pronouns makes the sentences simpler and clearer. Their discussion should answer these questions:

- What kinds of words do pronouns replace?
- How do they make sentences simpler?

Have a member of each group present their conclusions to the class and give one good example of pronoun usage that follows this grammar ground rule: Keep it simple.

Grammar Ground Rules

1. Keep it clear.
2. Make them agree.
3. Make it specific.
4. Dot your *i*'s and cross your *t*'s.
5. Make it active.

USING PRONOUNS

Using the correct types of pronouns will help make your writing flow smoothly.

WRITE GUY *Jeff Anderson, M.Ed.*

WHAT DO YOU NOTICE?

Focus on the pronouns as you zoom in on these sentences from the speech "Stage Fright" by Mark Twain.

> **MENTOR TEXT**
>
> My knees were shaking so that I didn't know whether I could stand up. If there is an awful, horrible malady in the world, it is stage fright—and seasickness. They are a pair.

Now, ask yourself the following questions:

- In the first sentence, how do the pronouns *my* and *I* help you figure out whose knees were shaking?
- In the third sentence, how can you tell what the pronoun *they* refers to?

In the first sentence, the pronoun *I* shows that the text is written in the first person. Therefore, the pronoun *my* shows that the narrator is describing his own knees. The pronoun *they* in the third sentence is plural. In the previous sentence, the author says there is one horrible malady, stage fright. Then he adds seasickness. Therefore, *they* refers to both *stage fright* and *seasickness*.

Grammar for Writers Writers use pronouns to avoid awkward repetition. For example, it sounds clumsy to say, "Dave forgot Dave's homework, so Dave's mother brought it to school for Dave." Instead you could say, "Dave forgot *his* homework, so *his* mother brought it to school for *him*."

I'd like to share my pronouns with you.

Thanks! That would make them ours.

499

USING PRONOUNS

As students progress in their writing skills, it will be important for them to be able to apply the rules of grammar, usage, and mechanics to their own drafts. Use the *What Do You Notice?* feature to help them see effective conventions in the work of professional writers. Encourage students to incorporate effective voice, tense, and syntax as they edit their own writing.

Read the opening sentence aloud. Remind students that pronouns are words that take the place of nouns. Some common pronouns are *I, you, he, she, we,* and *they.* Point out that using pronouns effectively can make writing flow more smoothly.

WRITE GUY *Jeff Anderson, M. Ed.*

WHAT DO YOU NOTICE?

When students have read the Mentor Text, **say:** Is the author talking about his own feelings? How can you tell? (**Possible response:** The author uses *My* and *I* so I know he is talking about his own feelings.) Then, **say:** Notice that the Mentor Text uses the pronoun *it* to take the place of the noun *malady* after the author made it clear that he was talking about a malady, or illness. *It* replaces *malady.*

Have students finish reading the page. Remind them that pronouns can be subjects—who or what sentences are about—or objects—receivers of actions. Pronouns can also show possession.

Then, ask: What do you think would happen if a writer used only nouns? (**Possible response:** The writing would sound repetitive and boring.)

Invite students to name some pronouns in the text. **Ask:** Can you find the nouns that the pronoun *they* replaces? Guide students in understanding that readers will be confused if they cannot easily understand to which noun a pronoun refers.

Grammar for Writers: Syntax

Help students understand that using pronouns makes their writing flow smoothly by allowing them to avoid the unnecessary repetition of nouns. The rules in this chapter will help them use pronouns effectively in their writing and speaking.

Lesson Objectives

1. Identify and distinguish between various types and cases of pronouns.

2. Use and understand the difference between *who* and *whom*.

Explain that a pronoun can take different forms, such as *I* and *me,* depending on its function, or *case.*

RULE 22.1.1 Read aloud the rule and then have students repeat the lines with you.

 Think Aloud Write these sentences on the board: *(He, Him) wants to learn to cook. (She, Her) will help (he, him). He needs (his, him) cookbook.* **Say:** How can I figure out which pronoun form is right? I ask myself how the pronoun functions in the sentence. In the first sentence, I see that the pronoun is doing the action of needing. That makes the pronoun a subject. Subject pronouns are in the nominative case. By looking at the nominative case pronouns listed in the pronouns chart, I can choose the right form. **Read aloud the first row of the chart. Say:** I see that he is the correct form.

Work with students to help them figure out which pronouns to use in the other two sentences on the board.

Have pairs of students write original sentences using pronouns from each case.

22.1 Recognizing Cases of Personal Pronouns

In Chapter 1, you learned that personal pronouns can be arranged in three groups: first person, second person, and third person. Pronouns can also be grouped by their **cases.**

RULE 22.1.1

English has three cases: nominative, objective, and possessive.

The chart below shows the personal pronouns grouped according to the three cases. The case shows whether a pronoun is being used as a subject, an object, or a possessive.

THE THREE CASES OF PERSONAL PRONOUNS	
NOMINATIVE CASE	USE IN A SENTENCE
I, we, you, he, she, it, they	subject of a verb predicate pronoun
OBJECTIVE CASE	USE IN A SENTENCE
me, us, you, him, her, it, them	indirect object object of a preposition direct object
POSSESSIVE CASE	USE IN A SENTENCE
my, mine, our, ours, your, yours, his, her, hers, its, their, theirs	to show ownership

SUBJECT OF A VERB	**We** wanted badly to see the game.
PREDICATE PRONOUN	The winner is **she** .
INDIRECT OBJECT	Please give **me** the ball.
OBJECT OF A PREPOSITION	Please show the photograph to **me** .
DIRECT OBJECT	A basketball hit **him** on the head.
TO SHOW OWNERSHIP	That is **my** jacket, not **yours** .

See Practice 22.1A
See Practice 22.1B

500   Using Pronouns

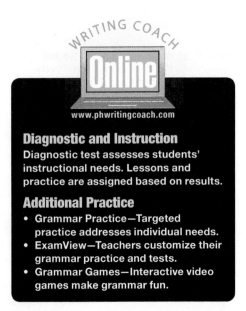
Differentiated Instruction

RTI Strategy for Below-Level Students
Some students may need a review of grammar terms such as *direct object, first person,* or *preposition.* Give students a list of terms you want them to review. Have them write a definition for each term. Collect the definitions. Then, read them aloud one at a time, asking students to name the term that matches the definition.

Enrichment for Gifted/Talented Students
Challenge students to develop a skit or multimedia presentation that might be used on a children's television program to introduce the three cases of pronouns. Ensure that students write and use several examples of sentences with the correct cases of personal pronouns.

PRACTICE 22.1A Identifying Cases of Personal Pronouns

Read the sentences. Then, identify the case of each underlined personal pronoun by writing *nominative*, *objective*, or *possessive*.

EXAMPLE   <u>They</u> wanted to go to the store.

ANSWER   *nominative*

1. Celeste offered <u>me</u> a chair.
2. Stanley made <u>his</u> way to the back of the bus.
3. <u>We</u> tried to get tickets for that concert.
4. Why did you invite <u>them</u>?
5. The person at the door announced, "It is <u>I</u>."
6. I grabbed my purse, and Mom grabbed <u>hers</u>.
7. Did you give the boxes to <u>him</u>?
8. I reminded Jena and Phil to bring <u>their</u> notebooks.
9. <u>He</u> went to the movies.
10. We can do it; just leave it to <u>us</u>.

PRACTICE 22.1B Identifying Pronoun Cases and Uses

Read the sentences. Write the case of each underlined pronoun. Then, label it *subject of a verb*, *predicate pronoun*, *direct object*, *indirect object*, or *object of a preposition*.

EXAMPLE   Ravi gave <u>her</u> the signed permission slip.

ANSWER   *objective, indirect object*

11. Carlos grabbed the ball and threw <u>it</u> to first base.
12. <u>She</u> carried the bottles to the recycling bin.
13. It was <u>they</u> who built the snow fort.
14. <u>Mine</u> was the first one picked.
15. Melanie handed the pile of papers to <u>me</u>.
16. After the tornado, <u>we</u> went outside to check for damage.
17. Chandra passed <u>him</u> the list.
18. My grocery cart ran into <u>his</u>.
19. The guide sent <u>them</u> to the information desk.
20. I wondered if it was <u>he</u> who had fixed the window.

SPEAKING APPLICATION

With a partner, take turns talking about things you do with your friends or classmates. Your partner should listen for and name at least two different cases of pronouns.

WRITING APPLICATION

Write three sentences about your family or friends. Use the nominative case in one sentence, the objective in one, and the possessive in one.

Practice   501

PRACTICE 22.1A

1. objective
2. possessive
3. nominative
4. objective
5. nominative
6. possessive
7. objective
8. possessive
9. nominative
10. objective

PRACTICE 22.1B

11. objective, direct object
12. nominative, subject of a verb
13. nominative, predicate pronoun
14. possessive, subject of a verb
15. objective, object of a preposition
16. nominative, subject of a verb
17. objective, indirect object
18. possessive, object of a preposition
19. objective, direct object
20. nominative, predicate pronoun

SPEAKING APPLICATION

Have students explain how they were able to identify pronoun cases.

WRITING APPLICATION

Have students give their sentences to partners to check. Have partners use the pronoun chart if necessary.

Working with ELLs   **ELL** Sheltered Instruction: Cognitive

As students learn about personal pronouns, have them write using newly acquired basic vocabulary, internalizing it by using and reusing it.

Beginning Hand a book to a student. Say and write on the board *I gave the book to [him/her]. Now [he/she] has it.* Use gestures to reinforce the meaning of the basic words in the sentences, including *gave, book, has,* and the pronouns. Then, have students write completions of the cloze sentence frame _____ *gave the book to* _____ . Repeat the activity with other frames, such as *I* _____ *the book to* _____, so that students may reuse the words.

Intermediate Review these basic words from page 500: *game, winner, ball,* and

jacket. Have partners write sentences for each word. Then, have them reuse the words in new sentences featuring pronouns.

Advanced Have students write definitions with example sentences for each of the basic words in the Intermediate activity, consulting a dictionary as necessary. Then, have them reuse the words in written sentences featuring pronouns.

Advanced High Have students complete the Advanced activity. Then, have them find synonyms for each of the basic words and use and reuse the synonyms correctly in written sentences.

The Nominative Case

Remind students that nominative case pronouns such as *I, he, she, we,* and *they* serve as subjects and predicate pronouns.

RULE 22.1.2 Read aloud the rule and then have students repeat the lines with you.

Remind students that a pronoun that renames a subject and is linked to it with a linking verb such as *is* should be in the nominative case. Write this example on the board: *Do you see Walter? That is (him, he).* **Say:** I see that the pronoun follows the linking verb *is.* Therefore, the pronoun is a predicate pronoun. That means I should use the nominative case pronoun *he.* Discuss the example sentences at the top of page 502.

Checking for Errors in the Nominative Case

Students often use the incorrect pronoun form in compounds such as *between you and me.* Point out that isolating pronouns in compound subjects and objects can help students decide which case to use. Write these sentences on the board: *Obed and me are working on the committee. Him and the other members have some big ideas.*

Underline the compound subjects: *Obed and me* and *him and the other members.* Have students identify the pronouns in each subject (*me, him*). Then, cross out everything in the compound subjects but the pronouns, and ask volunteers to read the sentences (*Me are working...; Him have...*). Ask students how the pronouns sound; then, have students identify the correct pronouns (I, He).

Extension

To help students synthesize and apply what they have learned about pronouns, have them play a game. On note cards, write several sentence frames that call for nominative or objective case pronouns; for example: *Please give _____ the keys. _____ will call you.* Give each student a note card on which you have written *John and I* on one side and *John and me* on the other. Have students form small groups. Give each group leader a stack of sentence frames. The leader should read aloud each frame. Group members should decide whether to use the nominative or the objective and hold up the correct side of the card.

The Nominative Case

Personal pronouns in the nominative case have two uses.

> **RULE 22.1.2**
>
> Use the **nominative** case for (1) the subject of a verb and (2) a predicate pronoun.

Note that predicate pronouns follow linking verbs. Pronouns that follow linking verbs should be in the nominative case. The linking verbs are highlighted in orange in the examples below.

SUBJECTS	**She** hopes to be on our team.
	Excitedly, **they** prepared for the game.
PREDICATE PRONOUNS	It **was I** who suggested a picnic.
	The best players **are she** and Mark.

Checking for Errors in the Nominative Case

People seldom forget to use the nominative case for a pronoun that is used by itself as a subject. Problems sometimes arise, however, when the pronoun is part of a compound subject.

| INCORRECT | John and **me** played jacks. |
| CORRECT | John and **I** played jacks. |

To make sure you are using the correct case of the pronoun in a compound subject, isolate the pronoun and the verb in the sentence. *Me played jacks* is obviously wrong, so the nominative case *I* should be used instead.

If the sentence is in verb–subject order, rearrange it into subject–verb order, and then isolate the pronoun and verb.

INCORRECT	Are you and **her** going to the dance?
REARRANGED	You and **?** are going to the dance.
CORRECT	Are you and **she** going to the dance?

See Practice 22.1C
See Practice 22.1D

Working with ELLS   **ELL** Sheltered Instruction: Cognitive

As students learn about pronouns, call on them to demonstrate their reading comprehension of increasingly complex English using retelling and summarizing techniques.

Beginning Preteach the words *hopes* and *team.* Write the example *He hopes his team will win* on the board. Read it aloud as students follow along. Help students demonstrate their comprehension by asking questions leading them to retell the sentence: for example, *What does he want?* Write students' responses on the board as they answer your questions.

Intermediate Guide students as they read page 502. Then, give them cloze prompts that they can complete to summarize the content. For example: *Predicate pronouns follow____. Pronouns that follow linking verbs should be in the____ case.* Coach students in summarizing, as needed.

Advanced Have partners reread the lesson on page 502. Have one student retell the portion of the lesson on the uses of the nominative case. Have the other retell the portion of the lesson on errors with compound subjects. Have partners correct one another's summaries.

Advanced High Have students work independently to write a summary of the page using original, creative sentences as examples. Then, have them read their summaries to the class.

The Objective Case

Personal pronouns in the objective case have three uses.

Recognizing Cases of
Personal Pronouns

22.1.3

RULE

> Use the **objective** case for (1) a direct object, (2) an indirect object, and (3) the object of a preposition.

DIRECT OBJECT	Frank's comment on the game upset **me**.
	The referee penalized **her**.
INDIRECT OBJECT	Tell **her** the good news.
	My friend gave **me** highlights of the game.
OBJECT OF PREPOSITION	Our team captain voted for **him**.
	The players swarmed around **me**.

Checking for Errors in the Objective Case

As with the nominative case, people seldom forget to use the objective case for a pronoun that is used by itself as a direct object, indirect object, or object of a preposition. Problems may arise, however, when the pronoun is part of a compound object.

INCORRECT	The players swarmed around Lucy and **I**.
CORRECT	The players swarmed around Lucy and **me**.

To make sure you are using the correct case of the pronoun in a compound object, use only the pronoun with the rest of the sentence. *The players swarmed around I* is obviously wrong, so the objective case *me* should be used instead.

If the sentence is in verb–subject order, rearrange it into subject–verb order.

INCORRECT	Did my mother give Toby and **she** a drink?
REARRANGED	My mother gave Toby and **?** a drink.
CORRECT	Did my mother give Toby and **her** a drink?

● Practice 22.1E
● Practice 22.1F

Recognizing Cases of Personal Pronouns 503

The Objective Case

Explain that people often mistakenly think that nominative case pronouns sound more "proper" than objective case pronouns.

RULE 22.1.3 Read aloud the rule and then have students repeat the lines with you.

Look at the example sentence that shows an objective case pronoun used as the direct object of the sentence. Read the sentence aloud, replacing *me* with *I*. **Say:** It sounds silly to say *Frank's comment on the play upset I*. I know that direct objects receive the action of the verb, so the pronoun following *upset* must be a direct object. I need to use an objective case pronoun as a direct object, so the correct pronoun must be *me,* which is objective case. Now look at this sentence: *Noel gave me some help.* Indirect objects name the person or character who receives the direct object. Here, *help* is the direct object, so *me* is an indirect object. I know that indirect objects take the objective case, and *me* is an objective pronoun, so *me* is correct. Objects of prepositions work the same way as direct and indirect objects, but they follow a preposition. It sounds funny to say *The birds flew over I.* So I know I need to use a pronoun from the objective case.

Checking for Errors in the Objective Case

Write these sentences on the board: *Frank's comment on the game upset Luis and I. Birds swarmed around Luis and I.* Point out that each sentence contains a compound object.

Work with students to isolate the pronouns in each sentence and replace the nominative pronouns (*I*) with the correct objective case pronouns (*me*).

Have pairs of students write their own sentences correctly using objective case pronouns. At least one sentence should contain a compound object.

> *Teacher Tip*
>
> If students have trouble recognizing prepositions, have them use the "squirrel test." Words that fit into the frame are probably prepositions:
>
> The squirrel ran ＿＿＿＿＿＿ the swing. (over, under, around, through. . .)

Differentiated Instruction

Strategy for Spanish Speakers

Students whose home language is Spanish may have difficulty using personal pronouns in the objective case because of the different pronoun types in Spanish. Remind students that in English, the pronouns *me, you, her, him, it, us, them* are used as direct objects, indirect objects, or objects of a preposition. Write an example of each type on the board, such as *My mother loves me. Alice gave me a hug. Cecelia brought a present for us.* Invite volunteers to come to the board and identify each pronoun and the way it is used in the sentence. Have students provide other examples of sentences using objective case personal pronouns. Invite volunteers to write the sentences on the board and underline the pronoun in each.

The Possessive Case

Remind students that possessive pronouns express ownership. Discuss the advantages of using pronouns such as *his*, *hers*, and *ours* instead of phrases such as *the hat that belongs to Mark*.

RULE 22.1.4 Read aloud the rule and then have students repeat the lines with you.

Say: The first example shows how possessive pronouns are usually used. Words like *its* and *my* usually show possession of nouns. In the first sentence, *its* shows possession of *game*. In the second sentence, *my* shows possession of *glove*. Some possessive pronouns, such as *mine*, *yours*, *his*, *hers*, and *theirs*, can stand alone without modifying a noun. In the third sentence, *yours* and *mine* are not followed by a noun. They stand alone.

Work with students to make a list of possessive pronouns as well as a list of possessive nouns; for example, *John's*, *Mary's*, *John and Mary's*. Write the list on the board. Help students understand that possessive pronouns replace possessive nouns.

Have pairs of students write sentences using the possessive pronouns and nouns. Have students identify the possessive noun related to each possessive pronoun.

Checking for Errors in the Possessive Case

Write these words on the board: *our's*, *their's*, *it's*. Point out that these words are spelled incorrectly because possessive pronouns do not take apostrophes.

Teacher Tip

If students have access to computers, point out that they can use their word processor's Find feature to search for apostrophes. This makes it easy to correct mistakes such as using *it's* instead of the possessive pronoun *its*.

Find It / FIX IT

14

Grammar Game Plan

RULE **22.1.4**

The Possessive Case

Personal pronouns in the possessive case show ownership of one sort or another.

> Use the **possessive** case of personal pronouns before nouns to show possession. In addition, certain personal pronouns may also be used by themselves to indicate possession.

BEFORE NOUNS	The team won **its** game.
	Chris held **my** baseball glove.
BY THEMSELVES	Is this marble **yours** or **mine**?
	Hers was the best score.

Checking for Errors in the Possessive Case

Personal pronouns in the possessive case are never written with an apostrophe because they already show ownership. Keep this in mind, especially with possessive pronouns that end in *s*.

INCORRECT	These seats are **our's**, not **their's**.
CORRECT	These seats are **ours**, not **theirs**.

When the pronoun *it* is followed by an apostrophe and an *s*, the word becomes *it's*, which is a contraction of *it is*. The possessive pronoun *its* does not have an apostrophe.

CONTRACTION	**It's** going to rain.
POSSESSIVE PRONOUN	The team loves **its** uniform.

To check if you need the contraction *it's* or the possessive pronoun *its*, substitute *it is* and reread the sentence.

INCORRECT	My sweater has lost **it's** button.
CORRECT	My sweater has lost **its** button.

See Practice 22.1G
See Practice 22.1H

Differentiated Instruction

RTI Strategy for Below-Level Students

When students edit their writing, have them highlight or circle every *it's*. Ask them if the sentence would still make sense if they substituted *it is*. If not, they should remove the apostrophe.

RTI Strategy for Special Needs Students

Have students make a four-column chart with four rows. The first column should be labeled *Person*. The rows should be labeled *first*, *second*, and *third*. The remaining columns should be labeled *Nominative*, *Objective*, and *Possessive*. Have students work with a partner to add examples of each type of pronoun to the chart.

PRACTICE 22.1C Identifying Nominative Case Pronouns

[Read] the sentences. Write the correct pronoun [from] the choices in parentheses. Then, label the [pron]oun *subject of a verb* or *predicate pronoun*.

[EXAM]PLE   It was (them, they) who brought the food.

[ANS]WER   *they — predicate pronoun*

[1.] [A]ustin and (me, I) went to the soccer game.

[2. It] was (she, her) who finished first.

[3. I] saw the twins, and (they, them) were [h]eaded for home.

[4. I] asked Pedro if it was Bill and (him, he) [w]ho found the lost dog.

[5. E]ither Tonya or (her, she) will come to [g]et you.

[6. W]eren't you and (they, them) trying out for [b]asketball?

[7. It] was (we, us) who came up with the idea.

[8. (H]e, Him) and I wanted to find a new game.

[9. T]he Steins and (us, we) are going to see [a] play.

[10. It] is (I, me) who drew the winning picture.

PRACTICE 22.1D Using Nominative Case Pronouns

Read the sentences. Write the pronoun that is in the nominative case. Then, write a new sentence using the pronoun.

EXAMPLE   Are Erin and she prepared for the test?

ANSWER   *she; Are Erin and she here in the room?*

11. Luke and I are best friends.

12. Jim and he will call us at noon.

13. We should call your friend right now.

14. The first person in line is he.

15. Angel and she are partners for today.

16. We should offer to help Ms. Roberts with her errands.

17. Will he go with me to the dentist?

18. Did they stay past your bedtime?

19. Believe it or not, the first to arrive was she.

20. Jasmine and I will co-chair the meeting.

SPEAKING APPLICATION

[W]ith a partner, take turns talking about a [m]ovie or television show you enjoyed. Your [p]artner should listen for and name at least [tw]o nominative pronouns.

WRITING APPLICATION

Write three sentences about the characters in a book you have read. Include at least two nominative case pronouns.

Practice   505

PRACTICE 22.1C

1. I—subject of a verb
2. she—predicate pronoun
3. they—subject of a verb
4. he—predicate pronoun
5. she—subject of a verb
6. they—subject of a verb
7. we—predicate pronoun
8. He—subject of a verb
9. we—subject of a verb
10. I—predicate pronoun

PRACTICE 22.1D

Answers will vary. Sample answers:

11. I; Luke and I play tennis on Sunday afternoon.
12. he; Jim and he live in Waco.
13. We; We called some of our friends yesterday.
14. he; The winner of the game is he.
15. she; Angel and she did the experiment together.
16. We; We carried her groceries up the stairs.
17. he; He went to the dentist on his own.
18. they; They left not long after supper.
19. she; The last to finish the exam was she.
20. I; Jasmine and I met a long time ago.

SPEAKING APPLICATION

Have students explain how they know that the pronouns they have named are nominative.

WRITING APPLICATION

Have students write short explanations of how they can identify nominative pronouns.

T505

PRACTICE 22.1E

Answers will vary. Sample answers:

1. her—indirect object
2. him—direct object
3. us—object of a preposition
4. her—direct object
5. us—indirect object
6. him—object of a preposition
7. me—indirect object
8. me—object of a preposition
9. us—indirect object
10. him—direct object

PRACTICE 22.1F

Answers will vary. Sample answers:

11. us; Bring us our jackets, please.
12. them; He showed them his new game.
13. her, him; We asked her and him to the play.
14. us; They took us to see the dance performance.
15. him, us; Mom gave him and us lunch.
16. them; We saw them after school.
17. us; Evie and Taylor waved at us.
18. her; I would like to get to know her.
19. me, her; My uncle lent me and her fishing rods.
20. him; Let him know we enjoyed his company!

SPEAKING APPLICATION

Have students explain how they know that the pronouns they have chosen are objective.

WRITING APPLICATION

Have students exchange sentences with a partner. Have partners check to see that the pronouns are in the correct case.

PRACTICE 22.1E Using Objective Case Pronouns

Read the sentences. Write an objective pronoun to correctly complete each sentence. Then, label each pronoun *direct object, indirect object,* or *object of a preposition.*

EXAMPLE   Jonas sat beside _____.

ANSWER   *her* — object of a preposition

1. Ali handed _____ the book.
2. The guide directed _____ to the entrance.
3. From the plane, I gazed down at the land under _____.
4. I recommended _____ for the job.
5. Dad gave _____ gift certificates.
6. I sent a letter to _____.
7. My grandmother bought _____ the book I wanted.
8. Tina got in line in front of _____.
9. Mom made _____ costumes for the play.
10. We found _____ in the basement.

PRACTICE 22.1F Writing Sentences With Objective Case Pronouns

Read the sentences. Write the pronoun or pronouns in each sentence that are in the objective case. Write your own sentence using the objective pronoun or pronouns.

EXAMPLE   Take the salad and bring some pla[ ] for us.

ANSWER   *us; Bring us some forks, also.*

11. Our warm jackets give us protection from the cold.
12. He brought them his bike to borrow for a week.
13. Are you going with her and him tonight?
14. Since we made the mistake, please forgive [ ]
15. They gave him and us their tickets.
16. When did he tell them about the mistake?
17. Evie and Taylor will be riding with us.
18. You should thank her for the gift.
19. My aunt sent me and her sweaters.
20. Will you please tell him that I am running late?

SPEAKING APPLICATION

With a partner, talk about things you and your family members do to help each other. Your partner should listen for and name three objective pronouns you used.

WRITING APPLICATION

Write three sentences. In each sentence, use compound subjects or compound objects that include only pronouns. Check to make sure that both pronouns in a compound subject or object are correct.

506   **Using Pronouns**

Working with ELLs   **ELL** Sheltered Instruction: Cognitive

Have Advanced High or native English speakers present responses to the Speaking Application prompt. As other students listen, help listeners use contextual support to enhance and confirm their understanding of increasingly complex spoken language.

Beginning Speak the sentence *I played hockey* to students, miming the words *I played*. Then, model the process of using context to confirm that *hockey* must be a game. Guide them in applying this process to the presentations, interrupting presenters as needed.

Intermediate Review the context in the presentations: things family members do to help each other. As students present, have Intermediate students raise their hand when they have difficulty understanding. Have

presenters repeat, and work with students to use context to enhance and confirm understanding.

Advanced Have students take notes on each presentation, including notes about parts they have difficulty understanding. Have them meet with partners between presentations to review their notes. Direct them to use context from the presentations to enhance and confirm understanding, writing their interpretation of difficult parts.

Advanced High Have students complete the Advanced activity. Extend by having them give presentations themselves. Coach them in including context clues in their presentations that will help other students.

PRACTICE 22.1G > Using Possessive Case Pronouns

Read the sentences. Write the correct pronoun from the choices in parentheses.

EXAMPLE   That backpack is (my, mine).

ANSWER   *mine*

1. My brother and I gathered (our, ours) books.
2. A bird builds (it's, its) nest in the spring.
3. The Corrigans invited us to (their, theirs) house.
4. Those dresses are (her's, hers).
5. It's (your, yours) turn to play.
6. Sandra brought her DVDs, and the twins brought (their, theirs).
7. The teacher pointed to (my, mine) project.
8. It turned out those shoes weren't (ours, our's).
9. I could tell the dog was friendly because it wagged (it's, its) tail.
10. My brother asked if I had seen (him, his) baseball glove.

PRACTICE 22.1H > Revising to Correct Pronoun Errors

Read the sentences. For each sentence with a pronoun error, write the incorrect pronoun. Then, rewrite the sentence with the correct pronoun. If a sentence has no pronoun error, write *correct*.

EXAMPLE   It was us who won the contest.

ANSWER   *us; It was we who won the contest.*

11. Claudia and him went to the museum.
12. A chick has to peck it's way out of the egg.
13. It was he who reached the top of the hill first.
14. Mom gave my sister and I our lunches.
15. Our class thought the prize was our's.
16. I sent you and she a letter.
17. My dad took the Johnsons and us to the movies.
18. Was it them who decorated the room?
19. I thought it was mine, but Jena said it was her.
20. John and me went to the game.

SPEAKING APPLICATION

With a partner, talk about things that belong to you or your family. Your partner should listen for and name three possessive pronouns you used.

WRITING APPLICATION

Write a paragraph about things in your home. Describe who uses them most often. Use three possessive pronouns. Read your paragraph aloud to a partner. Your partner should identify the possessive pronouns.

Practice   507

PRACTICE 22.1G

1. our
2. its
3. their
4. hers
5. your
6. theirs
7. my
8. ours
9. its
10. his

PRACTICE 22.1H

11. him; Claudia and he went to the museum.
12. it's; A chick has to peck its way out of the egg.
13. correct
14. I; Mom gave my sister and me our lunches.
15. our's; Our class thought the prize was ours.
16. she; I sent you and her a letter.
17. correct
18. them; Was it they who decorated the room?
19. her; I thought it was mine, but Jena said it was hers.
20. me; John and I went to the game.

SPEAKING APPLICATION

Have students explain how they know that the pronouns they have chosen are possessive.

WRITING APPLICATION

Have students explain how they were able to identify possessive pronouns.

Quick-Write Extension

To help students synthesize and apply what they have learned about the possessive case, have pairs of students write dialogues about who owns a luxury item such as a big screen TV. The first student begins the dialogue, which must include at least one personal pronoun. The student then gives the paper to his or her partner. The partner then writes a response that includes a personal pronoun and gives the paper back to the first student. Students should repeat the process for at least six lines. Students should then underline all pronouns in the dialogue.

Test Warm-Up

1. **B** Change *ours* to **our**
2. **F** My older brothers want a station for playing their games.
3. **B** My twin sister thinks we need a table.
4. **G** Change *mine* to **me**

Reteach

If students have not mastered these skills, review the content in Section 22.1 Recognizing Cases of Personal Pronouns.

1. The Possessive Case 22.1.4
2. The Possessive Case 22.1.4
3. The Nominative Case 22.1.2
4. The Objective Case 22.1.3

Test Tip

Tell students that most standardized tests that they will take have no penalty for wrong answers. Explain that, if students can eliminate even one possible answer from a multiple-choice question, they should make a guess from the remaining answers rather than skip the question. Often, the test administrator will include this recommendation as part of the directions. If students are unsure whether they will be penalized for wrong answers, they should ask the test administrator before beginning the test.

Test Warm-Up

DIRECTIONS
Read the introduction and the passage that follows. Then, answer the questions to show that you can use and understand the function of nominative, objective, and possessive case pronouns in reading and writing.

Cassie wrote the following paragraph about her family's ideas for using a new room. Read the paragraph and think about the changes you would suggest as a peer editor. When you finish reading, answer the questions that follow.

What Should It Be?

(1) My dad says he wants to add a room to ours house. (2) He took a survey to find out how each of us would use the space. (3) My older brothers want a station for playing them games. (4) Mom wants a corner for her craft materials. (5) My twin sister thinks us need a table. (6) We could use it for casual meals. (7) Dad wants a place for the spectacular sound system Mom gave him last year. (8) As for mine, I wonder how all of this will fit in one room.

1 What change, if any, should be made in sentence 1?

  A Add a comma after *says*

  B Change *ours* to **our**

  C Change *ours* to **our's**

  D Make no change

2 What is the BEST way to revise sentence 3?

  F My older brothers want a station for playing their games.

  G My older brothers want a station for playing them's games.

  H My older brothers want a station for playing they games.

  J My older brothers want a station for playing they's games.

3 What is the BEST way to revise sentence 5?

  A My twin sister thinks us needs a table.

  B My twin sister thinks we need a table.

  C My twin sister thinks we's need a table.

  D My twin sister thinks our need a table.

4 What change, if any, should be made in sentence 8?

  F Change *mine* to **my**

  G Change *mine* to **me**

  H Change *mine* to **you**

  J Make no change

508   **Test Warm-Up**

Cases of *Who* and *Whom* The pronouns *who* and *whom* are often confused. *Who* is a nominative case pronoun, and *whom* is an objective case pronoun. *Who* and *whom* have two common uses in sentences: They can be used in questions or to begin subordinate clauses in complex sentences.

> **Use *who* for the subject of a verb. Use *whom* for (1) the direct object of a verb and (2) the object of a preposition.**

RULE
22.1.5

You will often find *who* used as the subject of a question. *Who* may also be used as the subject of a subordinate clause in a complex sentence.

SUBJECT IN A QUESTION — **Who** hit the most home runs?

SUBJECT IN A SUBORDINATE CLAUSE — I admire the player **who** hit the most home runs.

The following examples show *whom* used in questions.

DIRECT OBJECT — **Whom** did he see at the game?

OBJECT OF PREPOSITION — From **whom** is she getting the new softball?

Questions that include *whom* are generally in inverted word order, with the verb appearing before the subject. If you reword the first example in subject–verb word order, you will see that *whom* is the direct object of the verb *did see: He did see whom?* In the second example, *whom* is the object of the preposition *from: She is getting the new softball from whom?*

Subordinate clauses that begin with *whom* can be rearranged to show that the pronoun is a direct object.

EXAMPLE — I will invite all the people **whom** he met at school.

REARRANGED SUBORDINATE CLAUSE — He met **whom** at school.

See Practice 22.1I
See Practice 22.1J

Recognizing Cases of Personal Pronouns   509

Differentiated Instruction

PRE-AP Enrichment for Above-Level Students Encourage students to develop a quiz to review personal pronoun cases using a game show format. Question categories might define terms, list pronouns, and complete rules from the chapter.

Have small groups of students write questions and answers for each category. Pool together all of the questions and answers and then play the game as a class.

Possible answers and questions for each category include: category 1—Answer: a pronoun that shows ownership/Question: What is a possessive pronoun?; category 2—Answer: *he, she,* or *I*/Question: What are nominative case pronouns?; category 3—Answer: The three cases of personal pronouns/Question: What are nominative, objective, and possessive?

Cases of *Who* and *Whom*

Explain that *whom* is the objective case form of the nominative case *who*.

RULE 22.1.5 Read aloud the rule and then have students repeat the lines with you.

Use a Think Aloud as part of a gradual release progression.

Think Aloud **Say:** To see whether I should use *who* or *whom,* I use my ear. **I try substituting** *he* or *him* in the sentence and listen to how it sounds. If *he* or another appropriate nominative case pronoun makes sense, I use *who.* If *him* or another appropriate objective case pronoun makes sense, I use *whom.* For example, suppose I have to decide whether to say, *Who is at the door?* or *Whom is at the door?* I know that questions are usually in inverted order—verb before subject—so I put the sentence in the usual subject-verb order: *Who or whom is at the door.* Then, I try inserting *he* or *him* into the sentence: *He is at the door; Him is at the door.* I hear that *Him is at the door* sounds wrong, and *He is at the door* sounds right. So I use the nominative case pronoun *who.*

Write these example sentences on the board: *Whom did you meet at the movies? From whom is she getting an invitation?* **Work with students** to reorder the sentences and substitute *he* or *him* for *whom: You did meet (he, him) at the movies. She is getting an invitation from (he, him).*

Have pairs of students write a sentence using *who* and a sentence using *whom.* Have them check to see that they have used the correct form by rewording the sentence and substituting *he* or *him.*

PRACTICE 22.1I

1. Who
2. who
3. whom
4. whom
5. Who
6. whom
7. who
8. whom
9. who
10. whom

PRACTICE 22.1J

11. May I ask who is calling?
12. correct
13. You mailed a letter to whom?
14. That is the person whom I met yesterday.
15. correct
16. Besides Mom, who else is bringing salad?
17. The teacher sent whom to the principal's office?
18. correct
19. Who is at the door?
20. The books were given to him and whom else?

SPEAKING APPLICATION

Ask partners to explain how they knew whether the pronouns were correctly used.

WRITING APPLICATION

Have students write a short explanation of why they used the pronoun they used in each sentence.

PRACTICE 22.1I > Identifying the Correct Use of *Who* and *Whom*

Read the sentences. Write the pronoun in parentheses that correctly completes each sentence.

EXAMPLE   With (who, whom) are you going?

ANSWER   *whom*

1. (Who, Whom) brought the potato salad?
2. They told me (who, whom) it was at the door.
3. Anna is the one from (who, whom) I got this book.
4. The ball rolled toward (who, whom)?
5. (Who, whom) are you?
6. I met the friend (who, whom) you brought to the party.
7. You and (who, whom) else are going tonight?
8. Jeff is the one from (who, whom) I heard the news.
9. That is the coach (who, whom) will lead us to victory.
10. The teacher introduced (who, whom) to the class?

PRACTICE 22.1J > Revising to Correct *Who* an[d] *Whom*

Read the sentences. Then, if a sentence uses *w*[ho] or *whom* incorrectly, rewrite the sentence with the correct pronoun form. If a sentence has no pronoun error, write *correct*.

EXAMPLE   I wondered to who I should give it.

ANSWER   I wondered to *whom* I should give [it].

11. May I ask whom is calling?
12. That's the aunt from whom I get my sense [of] humor.
13. You mailed a letter to who?
14. That is the person who I met yesterday.
15. If you don't come to the meeting, who will?
16. Besides Mom, whom else is bringing salad?
17. The teacher sent who to the principal's offic[e]?
18. With whom were you dancing last night?
19. Whom is at the door?
20. The books were given to him and who else?

SPEAKING APPLICATION

With a partner, take turns asking questions about giving and receiving (for example, "Who gave you that?"). Your partner should listen for and confirm whether you used *who* or *whom* correctly.

WRITING APPLICATION

Write two or three sentences about planning a party. Use *who* in one sentence and *whom* in one sentence.

510   Using Pronouns

Working with ELLs   **ELL** Sheltered Instruction: Cognitive

Use the Writing Application to give students practice with English sentence patterns. Have them write using a variety of grade-appropriate sentence patterns, including the pattern of *who/whom* questions, in increasingly accurate ways.

Beginning   Read aloud the correct responses to Practice 22.1I, items 1 and 2, having students echo you. Write the sentences on the board and have students copy. Continue modeling the sentence pattern with other examples, such as *Whom did you invite?* or *Who brought the food?* Then, guide students in writing their own *who* or *whom* questions.

Intermediate   Have partners complete the Writing Application. Coach them in locating the subject and the verb in each of their

sentences to enhance their understanding of this sentence pattern.

Advanced   Have students complete the Writing Application, writing two questions in the *who/whom* question pattern, and then exchange papers with a partner. Then, have students write answers to their partner's questions. Have partners compare the sentence patterns of questions with the patterns of answers, noting the placement of subject and verb.

Advanced High   Have students complete the Advanced activity. Challenge them to write their answers to the questions using compound and complex sentence patterns.

Use the Online Lesson Planner at www.phwritingcoach.com to customize your instructional plan for an integrated Language Arts curriculum.

DAY 1 23.1 Subject-Verb Agreement

"What Do You Notice?" **Objectives:** Identify, use, and understand aspects of subject-verb agreement, including • singular and plural subjects • singular and plural verbs • making verbs agree with singular and plural subjects	**INSTRUCTION AND PRACTICE** **Student Edition** pp. 511–518 **Test Warm-Up** p. 519

DAY 2 23.1 Subject-Verb Agreement (continued)

Objectives: Identify, use, and understand aspects of subject-verb agreement, including • making verbs agree with collective nouns • making verbs agree with compound subjects	**INSTRUCTION AND PRACTICE** **Student Edition** pp. 520–523, 525

DAY 3 23.1 Subject-Verb Agreement (continued)

Objectives: Identify, use, and understand aspects of subject-verb agreement, including • inverted sentences • indefinite pronouns	**INSTRUCTION AND PRACTICE** **Student Edition** pp. 523–524, 526–528

DAY 4 23.2 Pronoun-Antecedent Agreement

Objectives: Identify, use, and understand aspects of pronoun-antecedent agreement, including • personal pronouns • avoiding problems with number and gender • agreement between personal and indefinite pronouns	**INSTRUCTION AND PRACTICE** **Student Edition** pp. 529–532

Grammar Assessment

Grammar Coach:	Diagnostic Assessment	End-of-Chapter Assessment	Progress Monitoring
Personalized Instruction	Students take grammar diagnostic test online and are automatically assigned instruction and practice in areas where they need support.	Teacher uses **ExamView** to administer end-of-chapter assessment and remediation. Teachers may customize **ExamView** tests or use the ones provided.	Teachers may use the **Test Warm-Ups** and the **Cumulative Reviews** in the student book or eText to check students' mastery of grammar skills. Students may also play **DimensionL** grammar video games to test their grammar skills.
Teacher-Directed Instruction	Teacher administers the diagnostic test and determines focus of instruction and practice.		

Alternate Pacing Plans

- **Block Scheduling** Each day in the Lesson Planner represents a 40–50 minute block. Teachers using block scheduling may combine days to revise pacing to meet their classroom needs.

- **Accelerated Lesson Planning** Combine instructional days, focusing on concepts called out by students' diagnostic test results.

- **Integrated Language Arts Curriculum** Use the instruction and practice in this chapter to provide reinforcement, remediation, or extension of grammar concepts taught in your literature curriculum.

Links to Prentice Hall *LITERATURE*

Unit 1 Writing Workshop: Revising for Pronoun-Antecedent Agreement, p. 159

WRITING COACH

Online
www.phwritingcoach.com

Grammar Assessment and Practice
Chapter diagnostic tests assess students' skills and assign instruction and practice.

DimensionL Video Games
Fast-paced interactive video games challenge students' mastery of grammar.

Lesson Planner continues on next page

> *When our words don't match, the reader hits a snag. Making verbs agree in number simply means you need to know the difference between plural and singular. Plural nouns that end in s take no s in the verb; singular nouns need the s on the verb. Pay attention to the patterns; they exist and help you know what to do.*
>
> **—Jeff Anderson**

Differentiated Instruction

Differentiated Instruction Boxes in this Teacher's Edition address these student populations:

- Below-Level Students
- Above-Level Students
- Gifted and Talented Students
- Special Needs Students
- English Language Learners
- Spanish Speaking Students

In addition, for further enrichment, see the **Extension** features.

Grammar Ground Rule: Make Them Agree!

Model with Students

In this chapter, everything is about making them agree—pronouns and their antecedents, verbs and their subjects. Explain to students that, when it comes to agreement, nouns rule. Everything else must agree with them.

> **Say:** A noun that is the subject of a sentence or a clause can be singular or it can be plural. Whatever it is, the verb must agree with it. If I want to talk about one cat, any verb I use must be singular. *The cat sits. The cat runs. The cat walks across my computer keyboard.* If I'm talking about several cats, any verb I use must be plural. *The cats sit. The cats run. The cats knock over all my plants.*

Explain that the same thing is true for nouns and pronouns. If the noun antecedent is singular, the pronoun must be singular. Write on the board this sentence: *The cats ran for _____ food bowls.* Ask what pronoun belongs in the blank.

Small Group Activity – Finding and Describing Verbs

Have students form groups and find a simple science article. Have one student read the article, stopping at each verb. The other students should then tell whether the verb is singular or plural. Have students discuss helping verbs and the question of agreement. The discussion should answer these questions:

- In a verb phrase, does the helping verb need to agree with the subject?
- In a verb phrase, does the main verb change to agree with the subject?

Have a member of each group present their conclusions to the class and give one good example of verb usage that follows this grammar ground rule: Make them agree!

Grammar Ground Rules

1. Keep it clear.
2. Make them agree.
3. Make it specific.
4. Dot your *i*'s and cross your *t*'s.
5. Make it active.

MAKING WORDS AGREE

Making subjects agree with verbs and pronouns with the words for which they stand will help you write clear sentences.

WRITE GUY *Jeff Anderson, M.Ed.*

WHAT DO YOU NOTICE?

Pay attention to agreement as you zoom in on these lines from the poem "Wilbur Wright and Orville Wright" by Rosemary and Stephen Vincent Benét.

> **MENTOR TEXT**
>
> —And kingdoms may forget their kings
> And dogs forget their bites,
> But, not till Man forgets his wings,
> Will men forget the Wrights.

Now, ask yourself the following questions:

- How can you tell that the verb *forget* agrees with the subject *dogs* in the second line?
- Why do the poets use the pronouns *their* and *his* in the second and third lines?

Because *dogs* is a plural subject and *forget* is a plural verb, they agree with each other. While nouns ending in *-s* or *-es* are usually plural, verbs without *-s* or *-es* endings are usually plural. The poets use the plural pronoun *their* to indicate that the bites belong to the dogs. Because *dogs* is a plural noun, *their* is used instead of *its*. The poets use the singular pronoun *his* to indicate that the wings belong to Man. Because *Man* is a masculine noun, *his* is used instead of *her*.

Grammar for Writers Sentences flow smoothly when subjects and verbs agree and when pronouns match the words for which they stand.

How can you help subjects and verbs to agree?

You always give them the same number.

511

Grammar for Writers: Syntax

Explain to students that writers choose verbs that match the subjects of their sentences. When students write, they should think about the number of each subject—whether the subject is singular, plural, or compound—when they choose a verb. They should also make sure they are using pronouns that agree with the words for which they stand.

MAKING WORDS AGREE

As students progress in their writing skills, it will be important for them to be able to apply the rules of grammar, usage, and mechanics to their own drafts. Use the *What Do You Notice?* feature to help them see effective conventions in the work of professional writers. Encourage students to incorporate proper voice, tense, and syntax as they edit their own writing.

Tell students that subjects must agree with verbs and pronouns must agree with the words to which they refer. Point out that agreement avoids confusion and makes ideas clearer.

WRITE GUY *Jeff Anderson, M. Ed.*

WHAT DO YOU NOTICE?

When students have read the Mentor Text, **say:** Look at the third line. Does the verb in the third line agree with its subject? (Yes. The subject in line 3— *Man*— is singular, and the -s ending on the verb *forgets* shows that it is singular, too.) What pronoun refers to *Man*? (*His.* The pronoun agrees with *Man* because they are both singular and masculine.)

Have students finish reading the page. **Ask:** How would the Mentor Text have to be changed if the word *Man* was changed to *Men*? (The verb *forgets* would have to be changed to *forget* and the pronoun *his* would have to be changed to *their.*)

Say: Agreement between subjects and verbs is important for clear writing. If subjects do not agree with verbs, or pronouns don't agree with the words they replace, then readers will be confused by what they read.

Lesson Objectives

1. Understand and recognize subject-verb agreement in sentences.

2. Identify, use, and understand the function of prepositions and prepositional phrases and their influence on subject-verb agreement.

3. Demonstrate subject-verb agreement in speaking and writing.

Singular and Plural Subjects

Explain that the *number* of a noun, pronoun, or verb does not refer to a specific number. It means only *singular* or *plural*.

Then, tell students that subject-verb agreement is very important both in writing and speaking. Explain that the subject and verb in a sentence must agree in number.

RULE 23.1.1 Read aloud the rule and then have students repeat the line with you.

Use a Think Aloud as part of a gradual release progression.

Say: In grammar, the concept of number is simple. Words can be either singular or plural. **I think of** the word *singular* as referring to a *single* one. A plural word refers to more than one item or idea. Only nouns, pronouns, and verbs have number. Most nouns are made plural by adding *-s* or *-es* to the singular form.

For example, if I read *trees* in a sentence, I know it is plural because *-s* has been added to the singular form, *tree*. Some nouns have irregular plural forms. The plural form of *fish*, for example, is *fish*, and the plural form of *loaf* is *loaves*. If I am unsure about whether a word is singular or plural, or how to make a word plural, I look it up in a dictionary.

Work with students to determine whether each noun and pronoun in this group is singular or plural: *tables, women, jacket, we, I, lines, they.* Ask students to explain their thinking.

Have student pairs brainstorm for one sentence with a singular subject and one sentence with a plural subject. Invite partners to share their sentences with the group.

23.1 Subject-Verb Agreement

For a sentence to be correct, its subject and verb must match each other, or agree. Subject–verb agreement has one main rule.

RULE 23.1.1

> **The subject and verb in a sentence must agree in number.**

In grammar, the concept of **number** is simple. The number of a word can be either **singular** or **plural**. A singular word indicates *one*. A plural word indicates *more than one*. In English, only nouns, pronouns, and verbs have number.

Singular and Plural Subjects

Most of the time, it is easy to tell whether a simple subject, such as a noun or pronoun, is singular or plural. That is because most nouns are made plural by adding *-s* or *-es* to their singular form.

EXAMPLES

custom	custom**s**
bell	bell**s**
box	box**es**
tax	tax**es**

Some nouns form plurals in irregular ways.

EXAMPLES

knife	**knives**
mouse	**mice**
child	**children**
goose	**geese**

Pronouns also have different forms to indicate singular and plural. For example, the pronouns *I, he, she, it,* and *this* are singular. *We, they,* and *these* are plural. *You, who,* and *some* can be either singular or plural.

512   Making Words Agree

Singular and Plural Verbs

Like nouns, verbs have singular and plural forms. Problems involving number in verbs normally involve the third-person forms in the present tense (*she wants, they want*) and certain forms of the verb *be* (*I am, he is* or *was, we are* or *were*).

The chart shows all the basic forms of several different verbs in the present tense.

SINGULAR AND PLURAL VERBS IN THE PRESENT TENSE		
SINGULAR		PLURAL
First and Second Person	**Third Person**	**First, Second, and Third Person**
(I, you) send	(he, she, it) sends	(we, you, they) send
(I, you) go	(he, she, it) goes	(we, you, they) go
(I, you) look	(he, she, it) looks	(we, you, they) look
(I, you) dance	(he, she, it) dances	(we, you, they) dance
(I, you) visit	(he, she, it) visits	(we, you, they) visit
(I, you) work	(he, she, it) works	(we, you, they) work
(I, you) run	(he, she, it) runs	(we, you, they) run
(I, you) discuss	(he, she, it) discusses	(we, you, they) discuss
(I, you) vote	(he, she, it) votes	(we, you, they) vote
(I, you) choose	(he, she, it) chooses	(we, you, they) choose
(I, you) learn	(he, she, it) learns	(we, you, they) learn

Notice that the form of the verb changes only in the third-person singular, when an *-s* or *-es* is added to the verb. Unlike nouns, which usually become plural when *-s* or *-es* is added, verbs with *-s* or *-es* added to them are singular.

The helping verb *be* may also indicate whether a verb is singular or plural. The following chart shows only those forms of the verb *be* that are always singular.

FORMS OF THE HELPING VERB *BE* THAT ARE ALWAYS SINGULAR			
am	is	was	has been

Subject-Verb Agreement   **513**

Singular and Plural Verbs

Have students read the text describing singular and plural verbs. Point out that many problems distinguishing singular and plural verbs concern the third person forms.

Say: When I try to remember how to make subjects and verbs agree, I remind myself that in the third person there is a rule of opposites: If the subject has an *-s* or an *-es* then the opposite is true of the verb. For example, in the sentence, *The chickens peck in the yard,* the word *chickens* has an *-s* so I know the opposite must be true for the verb *peck.* It should not have an *-s.* Remember, though, that in the first and second person this rule does not work. In the phrase *I jump, I* is singular, but I do not add an *-s* to the verb.

Have student pairs review the sentences they crafted with their partner on page 512. The sentences with singular subjects should also have singular verbs. Similarly, the sentences with plural subjects should have plural verbs. Have students use the chart on page 513 to confirm that they have used the correct verb forms.

If necessary, review the conjugation of linking verbs, lesson 14.2, pages 319–320. Have student pairs write two additional sentences using the helping verb *to be*. One sentence should use a singular form of the verb and the other a plural.

Then, have students revise all the sentences that they wrote to make the singular subjects and verbs plural, and the plural subjects and verbs singular. Invite students to share their revised sentences with the group.

Teacher Tip

Sometimes distinguishing plural nouns and verbs from singular nouns and verbs can be confusing. Plural nouns frequently end in *-s* or *-es*, while third person singular verbs often end in *-s* or *-es*. Have students write an example sentence on a notecard. For example, *A year passes; years pass. A bird flies; birds fly.* Students can remember this formula as an aid to distinguish plural nouns and verbs from singular nouns and verbs.

Working with ELLs   **ELL** Sheltered Instruction: Cognitive

Orally present the instruction on pages 512–513, and guide students to demonstrate comprehension of general meaning, main points, and important details in contexts ranging from familiar to unfamiliar. Introduce singular and plural subjects and verbs in a familiar context—social life. A friend who says, "We should see a movie," sounds friendly—plural *we* includes both friends. A friend who says, "I should see a movie," sounds less friendly—singular *I* includes only the speaker. Then, read aloud the grammar lesson. Finally, relate the discussion to an unfamiliar context: Linguistics compares languages with many verb forms to those with fewer, such as English.

Beginning Repeat portions of your presentation, using gestures as support. Guide students in restating the general

meaning, main points, and important details using sentence frames such as *Nouns and verbs have _____ and _____ forms. _____ means "just one."*

Intermediate Have groups complete sentence frames summarizing the general meaning, main points, and important details.

Advanced Have partners create an outline summarizing general meaning, main points, and important details.

Advanced High Have partners complete the Advanced activity, and then write a brief comparison of verb forms in English and in their home language.

Making Verbs Agree With Singular and Plural Subjects

Tell students that subject-verb agreement is determined by checking the number of the subject and making sure that the verb has the same number.

As a class, read some of the students' sentences aloud. Choose sentences students wrote for exercises on pages 512 and 513. Students should listen to the sentence and then state the number of the subject. They should then determine whether the verb has the same number.

RULE 23.1.2 Read aloud the rule and then have students repeat the lines with you.

Say: Sometimes in a longer sentence it's possible to confuse the object of a prepositional phrase with the subject of the sentence. Consider this sentence: *The audience of rowdy teenagers yell loudly when the star comes out.* What is the subject of this sentence? **(audience)** What is the verb? **(yell)** Is there subject-verb agreement? **(no)** What mistake do you think this writer made? **(Possible response:** The writer thought *teenagers* was the subject of the sentence. *Teenagers* is part of a prepositional phrase.**)** What advice would you give the writer for making a revision? **(Possible response:** Change the verb from a plural form to a singular form. Then, the subject and verb will agree.**)**

Making Verbs Agree With Singular and Plural Subjects

To check subject–verb agreement, determine the number of the subject. Then, make sure the verb has the same number.

SINGULAR SUBJECT AND VERB	**Jeff enjoys** the beach.
	She was here earlier today.
PLURAL SUBJECT AND VERB	**Surfers enjoy** the beach.
	They were here earlier today.

 RULE 23.1.2

> A prepositional phrase that comes between a subject and its verb does not affect subject–verb agreement.

Often, a subject is separated from its verb by a prepositional phrase. In these cases, it is important to remember that the object of a preposition is never the subject of a sentence.

INCORRECT	The **arrival** of the firefighters **have caused** much excitement at the picnic.
CORRECT	The **arrival** of the firefighters **has caused** much excitement at the picnic.
INCORRECT	The **cheers** of the crowd **was heard** several blocks away.
CORRECT	The **cheers** of the crowd **were heard** several blocks away.

In the first example, the subject is *arrival*, not *firefighters*, which is the object of the preposition *of*. Because *arrival* is singular, the singular verb *has caused* must be used. In the second example, the subject is the plural *cheers*, not *crowd*; therefore, it takes the plural verb *were heard*.

See Practice 23.1A
See Practice 23.1B

514   Making Words Agree

Working with ELLs   ELL Sheltered Instruction: Social/Affective

As students read page 514, provide support or have them use support from peers to enhance and confirm comprehension and to develop the vocabulary needed to comprehend increasingly challenging language.

Beginning Preteach these words from page 514: *check, agreement, number, enjoy(s), beach, surfers,* and *earlier.* Then, read aloud the first part of the page (up to Rule 23.1.2) as students track in their textbooks. Review, and then guide students as they confirm comprehension by correctly completing this sentence frame: I *[enjoy/ enjoys]* _____.

Intermediate Preteach these words from page 514: *check, agreement, number, enjoy(s), separated, arrival, caused,* excitement, cheers, and crowd. Review the concept of a prepositional phrase. Then, have students working in groups take turns reading the page aloud as others follow along. Have them discuss the lesson and then confirm understanding by presenting summaries to you.

Advanced Have partners read the page, noting unfamiliar words. Have them determine the meaning of each, consulting each other, a dictionary, and you as warranted. Then, have them reread the page and collaborate on a summary of the lesson.

Advanced High Have partners complete the Advanced activity. Then, have them use each new vocabulary word in a sentence.

CTICE 23.1A Making Subjects and Verbs Agree

d the sentences. Write the verb in
ntheses that agrees with the subject. Then,
el the subject *singular* or *plural*. Be sure to
k about prepositional phrases and their
uence on subject-verb agreement.

MPLE   They (is, are) on time.

WER   *are — plural*

This tree (provides, provide) a home for birds
and squirrels.

The girls (plays, play) basketball after school.

The progress of the group of students (was,
were) slowed by the weather.

The boys (thinks, think) math is easy.

Derek (believe, believes) it is bad to litter.

Members of the band (is, are) raising money
for new uniforms.

She (meets, meet) her friends every Friday for
dinner.

The pecans in the box (is, are) ready to sell.

Twila (wants, want) to study ballet.

We (sees, see) the clouds in the distance.

PRACTICE 23.1B Revising for Subject-Verb Agreement

Read the sentences. Then, if a sentence has an
error in subject-verb agreement, rewrite the
sentence correctly. If a sentence has no error,
write *correct*.

EXAMPLE   We is excited about vacation.

ANSWER   We *are* excited about vacation.

11. They brings their lunches to school.

12. The girls in this group have decided on a
project.

13. One of the police officers have a radio.

14. The flowers in the garden is starting to
bloom.

15. My friends plans to go to college.

16. The players on that team practice every day.

17. The Smiths' dog barks at everyone.

18. I'll be happy when I gets home.

19. The cost of ten rides is fifteen dollars.

20. My sister often borrow my clothes.

PRACTICE 23.1A

1. provides—singular

2. play—plural

3. was—singular

4. think—plural

5. believes—singular

6. are—plural

7. meets—singular

8. are—plural

9. wants—singular

10. see—plural

PRACTICE 23.1B

11. They bring their lunches to school.

12. correct

13. One of the police officers has a
radio.

14. The flowers in the garden are
starting to bloom.

15. My friends plan to go to college.

16. correct

17. correct

18. I'll be happy when I get home.

19. correct

20. My sister often borrows my clothes.

Subject-Verb Agreement in Simple and Compound Sentences

Review simple and compound sentences with students. Remind students that a simple sentence has one subject and one verb.

RULE 23.1.3 Read aloud the rule and then have students repeat the lines with you.

Say: In a simple sentence the subject and verb must agree in number. A singular subject must have a singular verb, and a plural subject must have a plural verb.

Write the following sentences on the board:
Danny _____ on his cell phone all the time.
The guests _____ their hosts in the hallway.

Using the verbs *talk* and *meet*, have students complete the two sentences using the correct verb form.

Tell students that compound sentences are simply two independent clauses joined by a coordinating conjunction. Therefore, the subjects and verbs in each clause must agree.

With students, review the examples of compound sentences on page 516. Have students suggest some compound sentences. Write them on the board and as a class confirm that the subjects and verbs agree in each independent clause.

Have students work in pairs to write three compound sentences. Then have pairs exchange papers and check that the other's sentences have correct subject-verb agreement.

Subject-Verb Agreement in Simple and Compound Sentences
Both simple and compound sentences must follow the rules of subject-verb agreement.

> **In a simple sentence, the subject and verb must agree. In a compound sentence, the subject and verb in each main clause must agree.**

A simple sentence has one main clause. A main clause contains one subject and one verb and can stand alone as a sentence. A singular subject takes a singular verb. A plural subject takes a plural verb.

SIMPLE SENTENCE
Carla sends text messages every day after school.
The singular subject *Carla* takes the singular verb *sends*.

SIMPLE SENTENCE
We are not allowed to send text messages in school.
The plural subject *We* takes the plural verb *are*.

A compound sentence has two or more main clauses linked by a comma and a coordinating conjunction, such as *and, but, or, nor, for, so,* and *yet*.

You can also link the two sentences with a semicolon if they are closely related. In a compound sentence, the subject and verb in each main clause must agree.

See Practice 23.1C
See Practice 23.1D
See Practice 23.1E
See Practice 23.1F

COMPOUND SENTENCE
Carlos walks on the field, and the **fans cheer**.
In the first main clause, the singular subject *Carlos* takes the singular verb *walks*. In the second main clause, the plural subject *fans* takes the plural verb *cheer*.

COMPOUND SENTENCE
Luis leaves the game early, so **he misses** the final touchdown.
The singular subject *Luis* takes the singular verb *leaves*. The singular subject *he* takes the singular verb *misses*.

516   **Making Words Agree**

Working with ELLs   **ELL** Sheltered Instruction: Cognitive

Help students spell familiar English words using English spelling patterns with increasing accuracy. Explain that the /k/ sound at the beginning of a word can be spelled with *k* or *c*. If the next letter in the word is the vowel *i* or *e*, the word is usually spelled with a *k*. If it is not, the word usually begins with *c*. Ensure students apply the spelling pattern when writing.

Beginning Write *cup* and *kind* on the board. Have students copy, then pronounce and spell the words with you. Speak the words in sentences, emphasizing subject-verb agreement.

Intermediate Write *can* and *keep* on the board. Provide sentence frames with and

have students apply the spelling pattern to *cord* and *kit* (e.g., *The kit included batteries.*) Check subject-verb agreement.

Advanced Read aloud words that begin with /k/ (e.g., *cable, coal, king, kid*) and have students spell them correctly in sentences using parallel structure.

Advanced High Have students brainstorm for a list of words that begin with the /k/ sound. Have partners dictate their words. Partners should spell the words, paying close attention to the first letter, and write them in sentences with parallel structure.

T516

PRACTICE 23.1C ▷ Recognizing Subject-Verb Agreement

Read the sentences. Rewrite the sentences using correct subject-verb agreement, choosing the correct verb in parentheses. Then, identify the sentences as simple or compound.

EXAMPLE   The bus (stop, stops) at every corner, but often no one gets on.

ANSWER   The bus *stops* at every corner, but often no one gets on. — compound

Bethany (sing, sings) in the chorus, and she (play, plays) the piano.

Emmett (do, does) not like flying in an airplane.

The Festival of Lights (is, are) beginning on Friday.

The celebration (take, takes) place near the lake.

Mom never (ask, asks) for help, so she (has, have) to be tired.

My grandparents (travel, travels) every summer.

Aunt Kay (buy, buys) many clothes, and Uncle Joe (complain, complains).

A hero (show, shows) courage.

Drivers (was, were) honking their horns, but the truck did not move.

The rainy season (arrive, arrives) every summer in June.

PRACTICE 23.1D ▷ Revising for Subject-Verb Agreement

Read the sentences. Then, if a sentence has errors in subject-verb agreement, rewrite the sentence correctly. If the sentence has no error, write *correct*. Identify each sentence as simple or compound.

EXAMPLE   The books belongs here, and the pencils go there.

ANSWER   The books *belong* here, and the pencils go there. — compound

11. The campers was asleep by nine o'clock.

12. The sun rises in the East, and it set in the West.

13. The sky is clear, and the Big Dipper is visible.

14. My shoes is under the bed, and yours is in the closet.

15. Either your paper was finished on time, or it was not.

16. Mosquitoes are everywhere, for we has a lot of rain.

17. The new furniture is coming tomorrow.

18. You needs to put up the decorations before the party tomorrow night.

19. The new shirt is too big, and the shoes are too tight.

20. My mom bike to the park, but we likes to walk.

Practice   517

PRACTICE 23.1C ▷

1. Bethany sings in the chorus, and she plays the piano.—compound

2. Emmett does not like flying in an airplane.—simple

3. The Festival of Lights is beginning on Friday.—simple

4. The celebration takes place near the lake.—simple

5. Mom never asks for help, so she has to be tired.—compound

6. My grandparents travel every summer.—simple

7. Aunt Kay buys many clothes, and Uncle Joe complains.—compound

8. A hero shows courage.—simple

9. Drivers were honking their horns, but the truck did not move.—compound

10. The rainy season arrives every summer in June.—simple

PRACTICE 23.1D ▷

11. The campers were asleep by nine o'clock.—simple

12. The sun rises in the East, and it sets in the West.—compound

13. correct—compound

14. My shoes are under the bed, and yours are in the closet.—compound

15. correct—compound

16. Mosquitoes are everywhere, for we have a lot of rain.—compound

17. correct—simple

18. You need to put up the decorations before the party tomorrow night.—simple

19. correct—compound

20. My mom bikes to the park, but we like to walk.—compound

PRACTICE 23.1E ▶

Answers will vary. Sample answers:

1. My neighborhood is quiet, and shops are nearby.

2. The beds are in storage, and the apartment remains empty.

3. Venus shines brightly, but the moon is even brighter.

4. The boys like Connor, for he seems to be friendly.

5. The vegetables are too salty, but the meat tastes delicious.

6. This perfume smells awful, but the other bottles are fine.

7. They like push-ups, and I like aerobics.

8. Angela and Julio both paint with water colors, and Aleta uses acrylics.

9. Jake and Em exercise every day, but Lisa exercises only twice a week.

10. Carrie and Grace go skiing, but Annie prefers snowboarding.

PRACTICE 23.1F ▶

11. Shirts are on sale until Saturday, but I have no cash.

12. The performance was not sold out, so the actors were disappointed.

13. Several stores close at nine, but the mall stays open until ten.

14. The hurricane threatens Florida, yet Texas is not under a warning.

15. Baskets are on display in aisle one, and sculptures are in aisle two.

16. The rule is clear, and Bo and Max are wrong.

17. That snake is a rattlesnake, or it looks like one.

18. I choose light colors, but my best friend likes dark navy.

19. The answer was hard to find, for the problem was not clearly stated.

20. The umpire makes good calls, or the fans are unhappy.

PRACTICE 23.1E ▶ **Using Subject-Verb Agreement**

Read the sentences. Choose the correct verb for subject-verb agreement. Then, rewrite each item, adding a conjunction, to make a compound sentence.

EXAMPLE Saul and Vernon do the yard work. Brandon _____ the dishes. (do, does)

ANSWER *Saul and Vernon do the yard work, but Brandon does the dishes.*

1. My neighborhood _____ quiet. Shops are nearby. (is, are)

2. The beds _____ in storage. The apartment remains empty. (is, are)

3. Venus _____ brightly. The moon is even brighter. (shines, shine)

4. The boys like Connor. He _____ to be friendly. (seems, seem)

5. The vegetables are too salty. The meat _____ delicious. (tastes, taste)

6. This perfume _____ awful. The other bottles are fine. (smells, smell)

7. They like push-ups. I _____ aerobics. (like, likes)

8. Angela and Julio both _____ with water colors. Aleta uses acrylics. (paints, paint)

9. Jake and Em exercise every day. Lisa _____ only twice a week. (exercises, exercise)

10. Carrie and Grace go skiing. Annie _____ snowboarding. (prefers, prefer)

SPEAKING APPLICATION

In a small group, talk about healthy foods your family likes to eat. Then, write one simple sentence and two compound sentences about food. Use correct subject-verb agreement.

518 **Making Words Agree**

PRACTICE 23.1F ▶ **Using Subject-Verb Agreement in Simple and Compound Sentences**

Read the sentences. Then, rewrite each sentence using correct subject-verb agreement.

EXAMPLE The programs on television this summer are comedy reruns, or th[e] is reality shows.

ANSWER *The programs on television this summer are comedy reruns, or th[e] are reality shows.*

11. Shirts is on sale until Saturday, but I have no cash.

12. The performance was not sold out, so the actors was disappointed.

13. Several stores close at nine, but the mall s[tays] open until ten.

14. The hurricane threaten Florida, yet Texas [is] not under a warning.

15. Baskets are on display in aisle one, and sculptures is in aisle two.

16. The rule is clear, and Bo and Max is wron[g].

17. That snake is a rattlesnake, or it look like [one].

18. I choose light colors, but my best friend li[kes] dark navy.

19. The answer was hard to find, for the prob[lem] were not clearly stated.

20. The umpire makes good calls, or the fans [are] unhappy.

WRITING APPLICATION

Write simple and compound sentences of your own using correct subject-verb agreement. With a partner, identify the sentence types an[d] tell how the subjects and verbs agree.

SPEAKING APPLICATION

Students should demonstrate that they can use simple and compound sentences with correct subject-verb agreement by explaining why they chose a singular or plural verb in each sentence.

WRITING APPLICATION

Students' sentences and explanations should demonstrate that they can use simple and compound sentences with correct subject-verb agreement.

ECTIONS

 the introduction and the passage that follows. Then,
er the questions to show that you can use and understand
unction of subject-verb agreement in simple and compound
nces in reading and writing.

ndro wrote this paragraph for his report about Brazil. Read the
graph and think about the changes you would suggest as a peer
r. When you finish reading, answer the questions that follow.

Brazil

Brazil is the largest country in South America. (2) It has miles of
, and the land cover almost half of South America. (3) There are
s, mountains, and rain forests. (4) Its major river, the Amazon,
econd longest river in the world. (5) It has many kinds of wildlife.
s golden lion tamarin monkeys are most unusual animals. (7) They
anes that make them look a bit like lions. (8) They is tiny in size.

What change should be made in sentence 2?

A Change *has* to **have**

B Change *and* to **therefore**

C Change *cover* to **covers**

D Change *miles* to **mile**

3 What is the BEST way to revise sentence 4?

  A Its major river, the Amazon, is the second longest river in the world.

  B Its major river, the Amazon, are the second longest rivers in the world.

  C Their major river, the Amazon, and are the second longest river in the world.

  D Their major rivers, the Amazon, are the second longest river in the world.

What change, if any, should be made in
entence 3?

  Change *are* to **is**

  Add a comma after **are**

  Change *are* to **be**

  Make no change

4 What is the BEST way to combine sentences 7 and 8?

  F They has manes that make them look a bit like lions, but they are tiny in size.

  G They has manes that make them look a bit like lions, but they is tiny in size.

  H They have manes that make them look a bit like lions, but they are tiny in size.

  J They have manes that make them look a bit like lions, but they is tiny in size.

Test Warm-Up

1. **C** Change *cover* to **covers**

2. **J** Make no change

3. **A** Its major river, the Amazon, is the second longest river in the world.

4. **H** They have manes that make them look a bit like lions, but they are tiny in size.

Reteach

If students have not mastered these skills, review the content in Section 23.1.3 Subject-Verb Agreement in Simple and Compound Sentences

Test Tip

If students are struggling with questions about the content of passages they have read, they may want to read one or two questions, without reading the answer choices, before they read a passage. As they read the questions, have them note the key concepts and terms to which the question refers. Then, they can look for those concepts as they read the passages.

Making Verbs Agree With Collective Nouns

Tell students collective nouns name groups of people or things. Collective nouns can be tricky as subjects because they can take either singular or plural verbs. The number of the verb depends on the meaning of the collective noun in the sentence.

RULE 23.1.4 Read aloud the rule and then have students repeat the lines with you.

Use a Think Aloud as part of a gradual release progression.

Think Aloud

Say: Sometimes subject-verb agreement with collective nouns can be difficult because collective nouns can be used with either singular or plural verbs. When I want to determine what kind of verb to use with a collective noun, **I think about** whether the collective noun refers to the group as a whole or to individuals. For example, if I were thinking about this sentence: *The team wants to have an extra practice this week,* I would think to myself that *team* is a collective noun. In this sentence, the team as a single unit wants an extra practice, so *team* would use a singular verb—*wants*. Consider another sentence: *The team wear their new uniforms for games.* In this sentence, *team* refers to the individual members of the team. Each member of the team is wearing his or her new uniform. So in this second sentence the collective noun *team* uses a plural verb because the members of the team acted individually.

Work with students to brainstorm for several collective nouns. Write these words on the board. Then, ask students to describe situations where the groups identified by the nouns might act together as a group, and separately as individuals.

Have student pairs write three sentences using the collective nouns the class listed. Invite students to read them aloud. Have students state whether the collective noun refers to a single unit or individual members, and explain their thinking.

Making Verbs Agree With Collective Nouns

Collective nouns—such as *assembly, audience, class, club,* and *committee*—name groups of people or things. Collective nouns are challenging as subjects because they can take either singular or plural verbs. The number of the verb depends on the meaning of the collective noun in the sentence.

RULE 23.1.4

> Use a singular verb with a collective noun acting as a single unit. Use a plural verb when the individual members of the group are acting individually.

SINGULAR The **committee votes** on issues.

PLURAL The **committee have split** their votes.

SINGULAR The chess **club plans** a tournament.

PLURAL The chess **club were pleased** with their games.

SINGULAR The **class plants** a vegetable garden.

PLURAL The **class have divided** the responsibilities of planting among the members.

SINGULAR The scout **troop marches** in the parade.

PLURAL The scout **troop have earned** badges in many areas.

SINGULAR The **audience applauds** after the show.

PLURAL The **audience squirm** in their seats.

See Practice 23.1G
See Practice 23.1H

520   **Making Words Agree**

Teacher Tip

Making the distinction between singular and plural collective nouns can be difficult. Tell students that if they are having difficulty deciding whether a collective noun is singular or plural, they should ask themselves *Who or what is acting?* Is a group acting together as a unit, or are individuals who are part of a group acting *separately*? Explain that sometimes it can be helpful to talk with a partner in order to make this distinction.

Extension

To help students synthesize and apply what they have learned about making verbs agree with collective nouns, have students work in pairs to write sentences using collective nouns. The first student should call out a collective noun and either the word *singular* or the word *plural.* His or her partner should say a sentence that uses the noun, in the number indicated, as its subject. For example, if a student calls out "football team, singular," the partner could answer, "The football team practices after school." Have partners alternate calling words and writing sentences.

PRACTICE 23.1G Making Verbs Agree With Collective Nouns

Read the sentences. Then, write the verb in parentheses that agrees with the subject.

EXAMPLE   After a game, the team (changes, change) their clothes before going home.

ANSWER   *change*

Once the assignment is given, the class (opens, open) their books.

I read that the army (trains, train) recruits very well.

The audience (doesn't, don't) enjoy the movie.

A group of students (plans, plan) the annual bake sale.

The jury (disagrees, disagree) among themselves.

The band (travels, travel) by bus.

The cleaning crew (begins, begin) their different tasks.

A swarm of bees (is, are) moving across the field.

The family (takes, take) their places around the table.

The company (relies, rely) on the honesty of its employees.

PRACTICE 23.1H Revising for Agreement Between Verbs and Collective Nouns

Read the sentences. Then, if a sentence has an error in subject-verb agreement, rewrite the sentence correctly. If a sentence has no error, write *correct*.

EXAMPLE   The cast learns their lines for the play.

ANSWER   The cast *learn* their lines for the play.

11. Congress vote on a tax bill tomorrow.
12. The majority think their rights are protected.
13. The committee often argues among themselves.
14. The jury come to a verdict.
15. The team practice or read while they wait.
16. This bunch of bananas look good.
17. The class begins their research reports.
18. The Girl Scout troop says the Pledge of Allegiance.
19. The student council help set rules.
20. The whole herd waits at the gate.

SPEAKING APPLICATION

With a partner, take turns talking about groups you know about, such as school clubs or community groups. Your partner should listen for and name two collective nouns you used. Discuss why the noun is singular or plural.

WRITING APPLICATION

Write three sentences, in the present tense, using these collective nouns as subjects: *committee, team,* and *class*. Label the subjects *plural* or *singular*.

Practice   521

PRACTICE 23.1G

1. open
2. trains
3. doesn't
4. plans
5. disagree
6. travels
7. begin
8. is
9. take
10. relies

PRACTICE 23.1H

11. Congress votes on a tax bill tomorrow.
12. correct
13. The committee often argue among themselves.
14. The jury comes to a verdict.
15. correct
16. This bunch of bananas looks good.
17. The class begin their research reports.
18. correct
19. The student council helps set rules.
20. correct

SPEAKING APPLICATION

Have partners explain how they were able to recognize the collective nouns and whether they were plural or singular.

WRITING APPLICATION

Have students explain how they knew each noun was plural or singular.

Working with ELLs ELL Sheltered Instruction: Cognitive

Help students develop basic sight vocabulary used routinely in written classroom materials. Write these words from the directions on page 521 on the board: *write, about,* and *discuss*.

Beginning Read each basic sight word aloud as students follow along. Reread, and have students echo you. Reinforce meaning by writing each word in a simple sentence on the board, such as *Authors write books. The story was about a lion. We discussed school.* Then, read the sentences in which the words appear on the student page as students follow along. Explain the meaning of the directions.

Intermediate Read the words chorally with students. Guide students in defining or explaining them. Then, have students chorally read the sentences in which the words appear on the student page. Clarify meaning as necessary.

Advanced Have partners read the directions on page 521, locating the basic sight words. Have them write original sentences using the words and then read each other's sentences aloud. Then, have them repeat the activity for these routine words from the directions: *correct, error,* and *rewrite*.

Advanced High Have students complete the Advanced activity. Then, have them write explanations of each word in the activity.

Making Verbs Agree With Compound Subjects

Remind the class that compound subjects refer to two or more subjects that share a verb.

Say: A compound subject refers to two or more subjects that share a verb. Look at the first example sentence at the top of the page. What is the subject? (museums and historical sites) Notice the word *and*. Compound subjects are connected by conjunctions such as *and, or,* or *nor.*

Help students understand how to make verbs agree with compound subjects. **Say:** Look at the example sentences. What are some differences between the three sentences? (**Possible response:** The compound subjects are joined by different conjunctions. Some compound subjects use a plural verb, while others use a singular verb.) **Ask:** Is there a difference between what verb form is used depending upon which conjunction is used? (**Possible response:** Yes, the verbs in the sentences with *or* and *nor* are singular. The verb in the sentence with *and* is plural.)

Have students write three sentences that have a compound subject.

Compound Subjects Joined by *And*

Explain that when compound subjects are connected by *and*, the verb that follows is usually plural. Tell students that the conjunction *and* links two or more things together. Thus, a compound subject using *and* would use a plural verb.

RULE 23.1.5 Read aloud the rule and then have students repeat the line with you.

Point out the exception to this rule at the bottom of the page.

Have student pairs brainstorm for and write three compound subjects connected by *and*. Have them use one of these compound subjects in a sentence using a plural verb. Ask students to share their sentences with the class.

Making Verbs Agree With Compound Subjects

A **compound subject** refers to two or more subjects that share a verb. Compound subjects are connected by conjunctions such as *and, or,* or *nor.*

EXAMPLES
The **museums** and **historical sites** in [compound subject] Philadelphia **attract** many visitors. [plural verb]

Either **Robert** or **Jennifer** **knows** the way to the [compound subject] [singular verb] bus stop.

Neither the **Liberty Bell** nor **Independence** **Hall** **disappoints** tourists. [compound subject] [singular verb]

A number of rules can help you choose the right verb to use with a compound subject.

Compound Subjects Joined by *And*

RULE 23.1.5 → When a compound subject is connected by *and*, the verb that follows is usually plural.

EXAMPLE
Austin and **Dallas** **are** my favorite Texas cities. [compound subject] [plural verb]

There is an exception to this rule: If the parts of a compound subject are thought of as one person or thing, the subject is singular and takes a singular verb.

EXAMPLES
Spaghetti and meatballs **is** my favorite meal. [compound subject] [singular verb]

Salt and pepper **is** on the table. [compound subject] [singular verb]

Quick-Write Extension

To help students synthesize and apply what they have learned about subject-verb agreement, challenge students to use compound subjects in sentences. Working in pairs, students should list at least five compound subjects, such as *a boy and his brother, a book and a pencil,* and so on. Partners should then use each compound subject in a sentence. Call for volunteers to read their sentences to the class, which should check the subject-verb agreement of each sentence.

Compound Subjects Joined by *Or* or *Nor*

> **When two singular subjects are joined by *or* or *nor*, use a singular verb. When two plural subjects are joined by *or* or *nor*, use a plural verb.**

RULE 23.1.6

SINGULAR   A **car** or a **train** **provides** good transportation to
       compound subject   singular verb
       the city.

PLURAL   Neither **children** nor **adults** **like** to wait in line.
       compound subject   plural verb

In the first example, *or* joins two singular subjects. Although two vehicles make up the compound subject, the subject does not take a plural verb. Either a car or a train provides good transportation, not both of them.

> **When a compound subject is made up of one singular and one plural subject joined by *or* or *nor*, the verb agrees with the subject closer to it.**

RULE 23.1.7

EXAMPLES   Either the **monuments** or the **White House**
       plural subject   singular subject
       is interesting to see.
       singular verb

       Either the **White House** or the **monuments**
       singular subject   plural subject
       are interesting to see.
       plural verb

See Practice 23.1I
See Practice 23.1J

Agreement in Inverted Sentences

In most sentences, the subject comes before the verb. Sometimes, however, this order is turned around, or **inverted.** In other sentences, the helping verb comes before the subject even though the main verb follows the subject.

Subject-Verb Agreement   **523**

Differentiated Instruction

RTI Strategy for Below-Level Students
Some students may find the different rules regarding the agreement of compound subjects confusing. Have students create a two-column compound subject chart. Explain that they should list the different rules they have learned about compound subjects and verbs in the left column. They should illustrate their chart with example sentences and drawings. Encourage students to keep their charts handy and use them as needed.

PRE-AP Enrichment for Above-Level Students Tell students that they should imagine themselves as language mentors for new students. Their job is to create a role-play explaining the different rules affecting the agreement between compound subjects and verbs. Encourage students to be creative, have fun, and be informative in their role-plays.

Compound Subjects Joined by *Or* or *Nor*

Tell students that a different rule applies with the conjunctions *or* and *nor*. **Say:** When two singular subjects are connected by *or* or *nor*, the verb that follows is usually singular. When two plural subjects are joined by *or* or *nor*, the verb that follows is usually plural. **Explain** the logic of this rule by pointing out that, in the first example sentence on page 523, only one of the subjects in the sentence provides good transportation. The two possibilities are that a car provides good transportation or a train provides good transportation. In either case, the subject—*car* or *train*—is singular, so the verb should be singular, too.

RULE 23.1.6 Read aloud the rule and then have students repeat the lines with you.

Have student pairs brainstorm for several singular and plural subjects joined by *or* and several singular and plural subjects joined by *nor*. Partners should then use these compound subjects in sentences. Ask students to share their sentences with the class. Students listening should say whether the two subjects are singular or plural.

RULE 23.1.7 Read aloud the rule and then have students repeat the lines with you.

Explain to students that when a compound subject is made up of one singular and one plural subject joined by *or* or *nor*, the verb agrees with the subject closest to it.

Draw students' attention to the examples on page 523. Have students create and say aloud a sentence with a compound subject consisting of one singular and one plural noun connected by *or*. Make sure that students make the verb agree with the correct word in the subject. Then, ask another student to reverse the position of the singular and plural nouns and say the new sentence correctly.

Agreement in Inverted Sentences

Remind students that an inverted sentence is one in which the verb comes before the subject. Also, verbs are sometimes split up, such as when a helping verb comes before a subject and the main verb comes after the subject.

(continued)

Agreement in Inverted Sentences *(continued)*

RULE 23.1.8 Read aloud the rule and then have students repeat the lines with you.

Use a Think Aloud as part of a gradual release progression.

Say: In English we are used to seeing and hearing the subject come before the verb. But not all sentences follow this pattern. Sometimes sentences are inverted. The verb comes before the subject. Look at the sentence at the top of page 524. The verb *do* comes before the subject *attractions*. Questions often have inverted order. Also, sentences beginning with a prepositional phrase or the words *there* or *here* often have inverted order.

To determine the subject of an inverted sentence, **I change the order** of the sentence so that it is not inverted, then look for the word or words that perform the verb. For example, I might change the first example sentence to *The historical attractions in Boston do sound exciting to you.* Then, I look for the noun that names something that sounds exciting. That noun is *attractions,* so *attractions* must be the subject. Regardless of whether the subject comes before or after the verb, the subject and verb must *always* agree in number. This is a rule that doesn't change.

Sentences Beginning With a Prepositional Phrase

Write this sentence on the board: *Beside the bus stop was an old car.* **Work with students** to find the subject and verb and evaluate subject-verb agreement.

Sentences Beginning With *There* or *Here*

On the board write examples of sentences beginning with *here* or *there*. Walk through the example sentences in the book with students. Remind students that changing the order of sentences can help them identify the subject.

Have student pairs write four questions and underline the subject and verb in each. Invite pairs to read their sentences aloud. Challenge students to identify the subject of each sentence and state whether the subject and verb agree.

RULE 23.1.8

> When a subject comes after the verb, the subject and verb still must agree with each other in number.

EXAMPLE **Do** the historical **attractions** in Boston sound
plural verb *plural subject*
exciting to you?

Sentences Beginning With a Prepositional Phrase
In sentences that begin with a prepositional phrase, the object of the preposition may look like a subject, even though it is not.

EXAMPLE Along the shore **were** many nervous **soldiers**.
plural verb *plural subject*

In this example, the plural verb *were* agrees with the plural subject *soldiers*. The singular noun *shore* is the object of the preposition *along*.

Sentences Beginning With *There* or *Here*
Sentences beginning with *there* or *here* are almost always in inverted word order.

EXAMPLES There **were** several **books** about holidays.
plural verb *plural subject*

Here **is** the latest **book** about holidays.
singular verb *singular subject*

The contractions *there's* and *here's* both contain the singular verb *is*: *there is* and *here is*. Do not use these contractions as plural subjects.

INCORRECT Here **'s** the **keys** to the house.

CORRECT Here **are** the **keys** to the house.

Questions With Inverted Word Order
Many questions are also written in inverted word order.

EXAMPLE Where **are** the **keys** to the house?
plural verb *plural subject*

PRACTICE 23.1I › Making Verbs Agree With Compound Subjects

Read the sentences. Then, write the verb in parentheses that agrees with the subject.

EXAMPLE   Chloe and Emily (is, are) going to dance class.

ANSWER   *are*

1. Either Jason or Kevin (needs, need) to bring the basketball.
2. Weeding and watering (is, are) important parts of gardening.
3. Neither students nor teachers (enjoys, enjoy) fire drills.
4. Macaroni and cheese (is, are) easy to make.
5. My dog and the neighbor's cat (acts, act) like friends.
6. A bus or a taxi (leaves, leave) for the airport every few minutes.
7. Neither the coach nor the players (is, are) ready for this game.
8. The budding trees and the new grass (promises, promise) that spring is near.
9. Either the frills or the lace (needs, need) to be taken off the dress.
10. The canned vegetables and soup (goes, go) into the cupboard.

PRACTICE 23.1J › Revising for Agreement Between Verbs and Compound Subjects

Read the sentences. Then, if a sentence has an error in subject-verb agreement, rewrite the sentence correctly. If a sentence has no error, write *correct*.

EXAMPLE   A button or hook are needed for that skirt.

ANSWER   A button or hook *is* needed for that skirt.

11. Skiing and skating is winter sports.
12. Neither the parents nor the children wants that rule.
13. The gathering clouds and rising wind signal an approaching storm.
14. Either dirt or sand are needed for planting these seeds.
15. The eggs and milk goes into the refrigerator.
16. Neither the hippo nor the elephant seems to notice the zoo's visitors.
17. The maps and guidebook helps us find our way.
18. The museum or aquarium offer classes.
19. Peanut butter and jelly is my favorite sandwich.
20. Either the band or the chorus have a bake sale today.

SPEAKING APPLICATION

With a partner, talk about shopping for food. What sorts of things fill the shopping cart? Where are they found? Your partner should listen for and name three compound subjects and note whether the verbs agree.

WRITING APPLICATION

Write three sentences about your favorite season of the year. Use compound subjects in each sentence. Make sure the verbs agree with the subjects.

Practice   525

PRACTICE 23.1I

1. needs
2. are
3. enjoy
4. is
5. act
6. leaves
7. are
8. promise
9. needs
10. go

PRACTICE 23.1J

11. Skiing and skating are winter sports.
12. Neither the parents nor the children want that rule.
13. correct
14. Either dirt or sand is needed for planting these seeds.
15. The eggs and milk go into the refrigerator.
16. correct
17. The maps and guidebook help us find our way.
18. The museum or aquarium offers classes.
19. correct
20. Either the band or the chorus has a bake sale today.

SPEAKING APPLICATION

Have students explain how they identified the compound subjects and confirmed subject-verb agreement.

WRITING APPLICATION

Have students read one of their sentences aloud and explain their decision about subject-verb agreement.

Working with ELLs   ELL Sheltered Instruction: Cognitive

Using the Practice activities, have students use visual and contextual support as they read to enhance and confirm their understanding of grade-appropriate content-area text and to develop the grasp of language structures needed to comprehend increasingly challenging language.

Beginning Read the corrected version of Item 6 as students follow along. On the board, draw a picture of a bus and a picture of a taxi. Use these **drawings** as visual and contextual support to help students enhance and confirm their understanding of compound subjects.

Intermediate Have students read the corrected version of Item 8 chorally.

Then, coach them to use context to determine which words are in the subject: *Because the word* and *joins things together, I know both the* trees *and the* grass *are subjects.*

Advanced Have partners read and complete Item 10. Then, have them discuss how they used the context of the sentence to determine if the compound subject was singular or plural.

Advanced High Have students complete the Advanced activity. Then, have them help less fluent students complete the practice by creating illustrations for them to use as visual and contextual support.

Verb Agreement With Indefinite Pronouns

Discuss the fact that indefinite pronouns refer to people, places, or things in a general way. When indefinite pronouns are the subject of a sentence, the verb must agree in number with the pronoun.

RULE 23.1.9 Read aloud the rule and then have students repeat the lines with you.

Say: Consider this sentence: *Everyone loves puppies.* What is the verb in this sentence? (loves) What is the subject? (everyone) What kind of word is *everyone*? (singular indefinite pronoun)

When an indefinite pronoun is the subject of a sentence, the verb must agree with the pronoun in number.

Indefinite Pronouns That Are Always Singular

Point out the text stating that some indefinite pronouns are always singular. Help students understand why these indefinite pronouns are singular by reminding students that *body, one,* and *thing* are all singular nouns, so the indefinite pronouns that contain those singular nouns must also be singular.

Have student pairs make a sentence using one of the singular indefinite pronouns from the chart on page 526 as the subject. Tell students to make sure they use a singular verb to match their singular indefinite pronoun. Invite partners to read their sentences aloud. Ask students whether the subject and verb agree.

Teacher Tip

If identifying indefinite pronouns is difficult for students, explain that they can ask themselves three questions: 1. Does this word refer to people in a general way instead of a specific person or specific people? 2. Does this word refer to a place in a general way? 3. Does this word refer to a thing in a general way? If the answer to one of those questions is yes, then the word is an indefinite pronoun.

Verb Agreement With Indefinite Pronouns

Indefinite pronouns refer to people, places, or things in a general way.

When an **indefinite pronoun** is the subject of a sentence, the verb must agree in number with the pronoun.

INDEFINITE PRONOUNS				
SINGULAR			PLURAL	SINGULAR OR PLURAL
anybody	everyone	nothing	both	all
anyone	everything	one	few	any
anything	much	other	many	more
each	neither	somebody	several	most
either	nobody	someone	others	none
everybody	no one	something		some

Indefinite Pronouns That Are Always Singular

Indefinite pronouns that are always singular take singular verbs. Do not be misled by a prepositional phrase that follows an indefinite pronoun. The singular verb agrees with the indefinite pronoun, not with the object of the preposition.

EXAMPLES

Each of the basketball team banners **is** blue and white.
singular subject · singular verb

Either of the hats **is** warm.
singular subject · singular verb

Everyone in the first five rows **was** delighted by the play.
singular subject · singular verb

Each of the boys **plays** on a town team.
singular subject · singular verb

Quick-Write Extension

To help students synthesize and apply what they have learned about verb agreement with indefinite pronouns, have students write brief news reports describing a crowd of students at a school event. Students should use indefinite pronouns to tell how the parts of the crowd are alike and different in behavior, clothing, ages, and so forth. Ask students to exchange reports to check subject-verb agreement.

Indefinite Pronouns That Are Always Plural

Indefinite pronouns that are always plural are used with plural verbs.

EXAMPLE   **Both** of my suitcases **are** in the closet.
   plural subject   plural verb

     Many are waiting until it gets cooler
     plural subject   plural verb

     to go out.

     Several have not **started** their projects yet.
     plural subject   plural verb

     Few have chosen a gift yet.
     plural subject   plural verb

Indefinite Pronouns That May Be Either Singular or Plural

Many indefinite pronouns can take either a singular or a plural verb.

> **The number of the indefinite pronoun is the same as the number of its referent, or the noun to which it refers.**

⬅ 23.1.10   RULE

The indefinite pronoun is singular if the referent is singular. If the referent is plural, the indefinite pronoun is plural.

SINGULAR   **Some** of the **milk is** frozen.

PLURAL   **Some** of the **apples are** frozen, too.

In the examples above, *some* is singular when it refers to *milk*, but plural when it refers to *apples*.

SINGULAR   **All** of my **money is** gone.

PLURAL   **All** of these **presents are** for you.

See Practice 23.1K
See Practice 23.1L

In these examples, *all* is singular when it refers to *money*, but plural when it refers to *presents*.

Subject-Verb Agreement   **527**

Indefinite Pronouns That Are Always Plural

Tell students that the indefinite pronouns *both, many, several,* and *few* are always plural. Have students review the chart on page 526. When these words are used as pronouns, they always take a plural verb. Remind students that these words can also be used as adjectives. When they are used as adjectives, the nouns they modify are always plural.

Have student pairs revise the sentence they created on page 526 so that it uses a plural indefinite pronoun. Invite pairs to read their sentences aloud. Ask students whether the subject and verb agree.

Indefinite Pronouns That May Be Either Singular or Plural

Tell students that there is another category of indefinite pronouns: those that can take either a singular or plural verb. To determine whether an indefinite pronoun requires a singular or plural verb, look at the word to which the pronoun refers. If that word is plural, then the pronoun is plural. If the word is singular, then the pronoun requires a singular verb.

RULE 23.1.10 Read aloud the rule and then have students repeat the lines with you.

Review the examples of indefinite pronouns that may be singular or plural on page 526. Then, have student pairs write two sentences using those indefinite pronouns. Have partners read their sentences aloud. Ask students if the subjects and verbs agree.

Teacher Tip

Some students may have difficulty remembering the number of indefinite pronouns. To help students, provide them with a Venn diagram with the large circles labeled *Singular* and *Plural* and the center section labeled *Singular or Plural*. Work with students to fill in the Venn diagram with indefinite pronouns. Encourage students to refer to their diagrams as they complete exercises using indefinite pronouns.

Differentiated Instruction

RTI Strategy for Special Needs Students

Students may have difficulty understanding the difference in number between singular and plural indefinite pronouns. Model these sentences using common classroom items: *There are many students in this class. Some are boys and some are girls. Several sit next to the window. One sits over there by the door.* As students repeat the sentences, have them gesture or refer to the appropriate parts of the room or people in the room. **Ask:** Is this a single item or more than one? What verbs would agree with this item in number? Give students several examples of regular verbs and have them create sentences in which the subjects and verbs agree in number.

PRACTICE 23.1K

1. happens
2. are
3. like
4. gets
5. depends
6. are
7. freezes
8. knows
9. are
10. happens

PRACTICE 23.1L

11. I don't think anybody comes here now.
12. correct
13. Let me know if anything happens.
14. Others disagree with the idea.
15. correct
16. Most of the work ends today.
17. Several have already volunteered.
18. correct
19. Each of the shirts needs ironing.
20. All of the students are early.

> **SPEAKING APPLICATION**
>
> Have partners explain how they determined whether the verbs agree with the indefinite pronoun subjects of their sentences.
>
> **WRITING APPLICATION**
>
> Have students read one of their sentences aloud and explain why the subject-verb agreement is correct.

PRACTICE 23.1K **Making Verbs Agree With Indefinite Pronouns**

Read the sentences. Then, write the verb in parentheses that agrees with the subject.

EXAMPLE   Few (is, are) chosen for this honor.

ANSWER   *are*

1. Nothing (happens, happen) at school on Sundays.
2. Both (is, are) good choices.
3. Many of us (likes, like) Chinese food.
4. Each of the participants (gets, get) a certificate.
5. Everything (depends, depend) on teamwork.
6. All of the eggs (is, are) broken.
7. Most of the lake (freezes, freeze) in the winter.
8. Everyone (knows, know) what to do.
9. Several (is, are) going to appear at the event.
10. Anything (happens, happen) at these games.

PRACTICE 23.1L **Revising for Agreement Between Verbs and Indefini[te] Pronouns**

Read the sentences. Then, if a sentence has an error in subject-verb agreement, rewrite the sentence correctly. If a sentence has no error, write *correct*.

EXAMPLE   Each of the balloons float.

ANSWER   *Each of the balloons* floats.

11. I don't think anybody come here now.
12. Both of the glasses broke when shipped.
13. Let me know if anything happen.
14. Others disagrees with the idea.
15. On a good team, everyone works together.
16. Most of the work end today.
17. Several has already volunteered.
18. Nothing is on the table.
19. Each of the shirts need ironing.
20. All of the students is early.

> **SPEAKING APPLICATION**
>
> With a partner, take turns talking about events that occur in your town or school. Your partner should listen for and name two indefinite pronouns and note whether the verbs agree.

> **WRITING APPLICATION**
>
> Write three sentences using at least three of the following indefinite pronouns: *some, most, all, both, others, many, each, everyone, nothing, anybody,* and *anything*. Make sure the verbs agree with the pronouns you choose.

528   **Making Words Agree**

Working with ELLs   **EL** Sheltered Instruction: Cognitive

Using the Practice items, help students learn the relationships between English sounds and letters and practice decoding words using a combination of skills.

Beginning Write *school* on the board (Item 1). Review the sound commonly represented by *ch* (/ch/, as in *choose* or *chop*), and explain that *ch* sometimes takes a /k/ sound. Point out the double *o*, and explain that it indicates a long *u* /oo/ sound. Model the /oo/ sound and have students echo. Then, lead students in decoding the word.

Intermediate Write *Chinese* on the board (Item 3). Guide students in identifying and pronouncing the digraph *ch*. Then, review the various sounds *ch* can make (as in *cheese, chemistry, and Michigan*). Guide students in decoding the word. Discuss its meaning.

Advanced Point out the word *participants* (Item 4). Review the sound represented by *c* followed by *i* (/s/), and guide students in identifying the suffix *-ants*. Then, prompt students to sound out the word. If students have difficulty, ask them what word would make sense in context.

Advanced High Have partners collaborate in decoding the words *certificate* (Item 4), *winter* (Item 7), *volunteered* (Item 17), and *ironing* (Item 19). Provide assistance as needed. Have them contrast the *i* sound in *winter* with its sound in *ironing*.

23.2 Agreement Between Pronouns and Antecedents

An **antecedent** is the word or words for which a pronoun stands. A pronoun's antecedent may be a noun, a group of words acting as a noun, or even another pronoun. As with subjects and verbs, pronouns should agree with their antecedents.

Find It / FIX IT
17
Grammar Game Plan

Making Personal Pronouns and Antecedents Agree

Person tells whether a pronoun refers to the person speaking (first person), the person spoken to (second person), or the person, place, or thing spoken about (third person). **Number** tells whether the pronoun is singular or plural. **Gender** tells whether a third-person-singular antecedent is masculine or feminine.

> A personal pronoun must agree with its antecedent in person, number, and gender.

RULE 23.2.1

EXAMPLE   I told **David** to bring a bathing suit with **him**.

In this example, the pronoun *him* is third person and singular. It agrees with its masculine antecedent, *David*.

Avoiding Shifts in Person
A personal pronoun must have the same person as its antecedent. Otherwise, the meaning of the sentence is unclear.

INCORRECT   The **skydivers** know **we** must check the parachutes before takeoff.
(Who must check the parachutes? *We* must.)

CORRECT   The **skydivers** know **they** must check the parachutes before takeoff.
(Who must check the parachutes? *The skydivers* must.)

As you can see, a shift in the person of the personal pronoun can make it unclear who is going to check the parachutes.

Pronoun–Antecedent Agreement   529

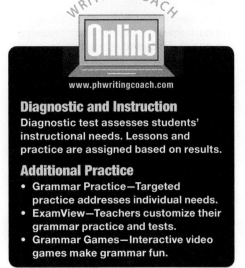

Lesson Objectives

1. Define and identify antecedents.

2. Maintain agreement between antecedents and pronouns in sentences.

3. Use a variety of complete sentences (e.g., simple, compound, complex) that include correctly identified antecedents.

Making Personal Pronouns and Antecedents Agree

Explain that an *antecedent* is a word for which a pronoun stands. For example, in the sentence *When Kathy asked, I told her the story*, the word *her* stands for *Kathy*. So *Kathy* is the antecedent of *her*. Pronouns must agree with their antecedents in person, number, and gender. Disagreement between an antecedent and a pronoun makes writing very confusing.

RULE 23.2.1 Read aloud the rule and then have students repeat the lines with you.

Avoiding Shifts in Person

Direct attention to the text warning against shifts in person. Discuss how the shift in person changes the meaning of each sentence.

Write this sentence on the board: *The Thompsons looked at pictures of their vacation.*

Work with students to analyze the use of the pronoun *their*. (The vacation was taken by all of the Thompsons so it is their vacation.) Discuss how a shift in the person of the personal pronoun would change the meaning of the sentence.

Avoiding Problems With Number and Gender

Draw students' attention to the text, and discuss how problems with number and gender often arise when collective nouns or compound nouns are used, or when the gender of the antecedent is unknown.

Making Pronouns Agree in Number With Collective Nouns

Work with students to help them understand that collective nouns can take either singular or plural pronouns. The number of the pronoun depends on the meaning of the collective noun in the sentence.

RULE 23.2.2 Read aloud the rule and then have students repeat the lines with you.

On the board, write these two sentences: *The class made its argument for a ban on pop quizzes. The class took their seats as soon as the bell rang.* Refer students to each sentence and ask whether the class is acting as one unit or as many individuals. Then, point out the pronoun in each sentence.

Have student pairs write one sentence with a singular pronoun referring to a collective noun and one sentence with a plural pronoun referring to a collective noun. Invite students to read their sentences aloud. Have student volunteers explain why the pronoun and noun agree (or don't agree).

Making Pronouns Agree in Number With Compound Nouns

Say: Adrian, Raffy, or Simone wrote the note. How many people wrote the note? (**Response:** only one) Explain that, when a subject consists of two or more singular nouns joined by *or* or *nor,* a pronoun that refers to the subject is referring to only one of the nouns. Therefore, the subject must have a singular pronoun, just as it must have a singular verb.

RULE 23.2.3 Read aloud the rule and then have students repeat the lines with you.

Have student pairs write one sentence using a compound noun joined by *or* or *nor* and one sentence with a compound noun joined by *and.* Both sentences should use a pronoun. Invite students to read their sentences aloud. Ask if the pronoun and antecedent agree.

Avoiding Problems With Number and Gender

Making pronouns and antecedents agree in number and gender can be difficult. Problems may arise when the antecedent is a collective noun, when the antecedent is a compound joined by *or* or *nor,* or when the gender of the antecedent is not known.

Making Pronouns Agree in Number With Collective Nouns
Collective nouns are challenging because they can take either singular or plural pronouns. The number of the pronoun depends on the meaning of the collective noun in the sentence.

> **Use a singular pronoun to refer to a collective noun that names a group that is acting as a single unit. Use a plural pronoun to refer to a collective noun when the members or parts of a group are acting individually.**

SINGULAR   The **class showed its** joy with a cheer.

PLURAL   The **class voted** for **their** favorite candidates.

In the first example above, the class is acting as a single unit when it shows its joy, so the singular pronoun, *its,* refers to *class.* In the second example, each member of the class is voting individually, so the plural pronoun, *their,* refers to *class.*

Making Pronouns Agree in Number With Compound Nouns

> **Use a singular personal pronoun to refer to two or more singular antecedents joined by *or* or *nor.* Use a plural pronoun with two or more singular antecedents joined by *and.***

Two or more singular antecedents joined by *or* or *nor* must have a singular pronoun, just as they must have a singular verb.

INCORRECT   **Becca** or **Megan** will take **their** backpack.

CORRECT   **Becca** or **Megan** will take **her** backpack.

CORRECT   **Becca** and **Megan** will take **their** backpacks.

530   **Making Words Agree**

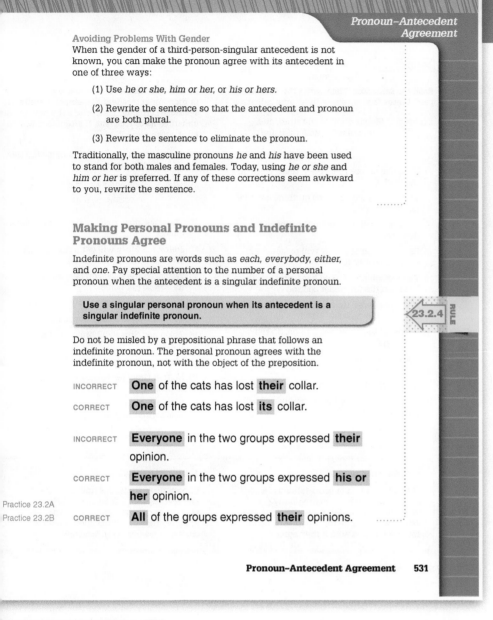

Avoiding Problems With Gender

When the gender of a third-person-singular antecedent is not known, you can make the pronoun agree with its antecedent in one of three ways:

(1) Use *he or she, him or her,* or *his or hers.*

(2) Rewrite the sentence so that the antecedent and pronoun are both plural.

(3) Rewrite the sentence to eliminate the pronoun.

Traditionally, the masculine pronouns *he* and *his* have been used to stand for both males and females. Today, using *he or she* and *him or her* is preferred. If any of these corrections seem awkward to you, rewrite the sentence.

Making Personal Pronouns and Indefinite Pronouns Agree

Indefinite pronouns are words such as *each, everybody, either,* and *one.* Pay special attention to the number of a personal pronoun when the antecedent is a singular indefinite pronoun.

> Use a singular personal pronoun when its antecedent is a singular indefinite pronoun.

23.2.4 RULE

Do not be misled by a prepositional phrase that follows an indefinite pronoun. The personal pronoun agrees with the indefinite pronoun, not with the object of the preposition.

INCORRECT **One** of the cats has lost **their** collar.

CORRECT **One** of the cats has lost **its** collar.

INCORRECT **Everyone** in the two groups expressed **their** opinion.

CORRECT **Everyone** in the two groups expressed **his or her** opinion.

Practice 23.2A
Practice 23.2B

CORRECT **All** of the groups expressed **their** opinions.

Pronoun–Antecedent Agreement 531

Avoiding Problems With Gender

Discuss with students how to avoid problems with pronoun gender using the three strategies listed.

Write this sentence on the board: *A writer works on her technique all the time.* Have students revise the sentence using one of the strategies so that it does not specify a gender.

Making Personal Pronouns and Indefinite Pronouns Agree

Remind students to pay special attention to the number of a personal pronoun when the antecedent is a singular indefinite pronoun.

RULE 23.2.4 Read aloud the rule and then have students repeat the lines with you.

Say: Indefinite pronouns are words such as *each, everybody, either,* and *one.* Indefinite pronouns are no different from any other kind of pronoun. I need to use a singular personal pronoun when its antecedent is a singular indefinite pronoun. I need to look carefully at sentences that have indefinite pronouns to make sure I do not get confused about the pronoun's antecedent. If there are other nouns in the sentence, and especially if a noun comes between the pronoun and its antecedent, I might write the sentence incorrectly.

Work with students to review the example sentences at the bottom of page 531. Have students explain why the incorrect examples are incorrect.

Have student pairs use a variety of complete sentences (e.g., simple, compound, complex) that include correctly identified antecedents. Instruct partners to write six sentences—two simple, two compound, and two complex. Students should include indefinite pronouns in at least two of their sentences. Invite students to share their sentences with the group. Have students draw an arrow from each pronoun to its antecedent and check for pronoun-antecedent agreement.

Working with ELLs **ELL** Sheltered Instruction: Cognitive

As students read the section on pronoun agreement on pages 530–531, have them demonstrate comprehension by employing basic reading skills. Expand their skills with strategies for recording and analyzing main ideas and details.

Beginning Read the first example sentence as students follow along. Use visuals to ensure comprehension. Offer a paraphrase of the rule, such as *How many? One needs one.* Have them record your paraphrase and examples in a main idea and details chart.

Intermediate Guide students as they read the example sentences aloud. Discuss the concept they illustrate. Then, read aloud the text in the green box as students follow along. Explain terms, referring to the

examples. Finally, have students work in groups to record the main idea and details in a chart.

Advanced Have partners read the section and discuss its meaning. Then, have them paraphrase the main idea and list supporting details in an outline.

Advanced High Have students read the section and record main ideas and details on cards. Have them compare results with a partner. Have them explain the connection between the details and the main idea (they are examples of the main idea).

PRACTICE 23.2A

1. his or her
2. it
3. him
4. his
5. they
6. her
7. they
8. their
9. its
10. her

PRACTICE 23.2B

11. The <u>boys</u> must wear jackets at (their) school dance.

12. <u>Juanita or Mary</u> will get a prize for (her) project.

13. correct

14. <u>Phillip and Pedro</u> said (they) would help.

15. <u>Everyone</u> took (his or her) books home.

16. correct

17. My older <u>sister</u> likes (her) job.

18. Neither <u>Gina nor Jessica</u> wanted (her) project to be late.

19. correct

20. Each <u>student</u> will read the essay (he or she) wrote.

PRACTICE 23.2A Making Pronouns and Antecedents Agree

Read the sentences. Then, write the pronoun in parentheses that agrees with its antecedent.

EXAMPLE   Marcia went to the store, and Carmine went with (him, her).

ANSWER   *her*

1. Each player took (his or her, their) place on the field.
2. This shirt is too small, so (it, they) must be returned.
3. I told my brother to bring the binoculars with (him, them).
4. Either Ramon or Danny will present (his, their) project next.
5. The firefighters worked hard, and (he, they) soon had the fire under control.
6. Marissa needed money and asked (her, his) father for ten dollars.
7. If most of the group want to go, (it, they) should go.
8. Both the builder and the designer gave (his, their) opinions.
9. Each of the dogs buried (its, their) bone.
10. Neither Sandra nor Letitia got (her, their) homework done.

SPEAKING APPLICATION

With a partner, take turns talking about places you or your family regularly goes to (for fun or errands). Your partner should listen for and name three pronouns and their antecedents and note if they agree.

PRACTICE 23.2B Revising for Pronoun-Antecedent Agreement

Read the sentences. If a sentence has an error in pronoun-antecedent agreement, rewrite the sentence correctly. Then, circle the pronoun an underline its antecedent. If a sentence has no error, write *correct*.

EXAMPLE   Each child wears a name tag they decorated.

ANSWER   Each <u>child</u> wears a name tag (he or she) decorated.

11. The boys must wear jackets at his school dance.
12. Juanita or Mary will get a prize for their project.
13. We asked the police officers if they could te us how to get home.
14. Phillip and Pedro said he would help.
15. Everyone took their books home.
16. Jason and Steve will bring their baseball mitts.
17. My older sister likes their job.
18. Neither Gina nor Jessica wanted their proje to be late.
19. Bella and I said we would happily share ou ideas with the group.
20. Each student will read the essay they wrot

WRITING APPLICATION

Choose three sentences from Practice 23.2B and rewrite each one so that a different pronoun is correct. You may change the number or gender of the antecedents or change conjunctions to accomplish this.

Working with ELLs   ELL Sheltered Instruction: Cognitive

Have students listen to, derive meaning from, and responding orally to information presented from a wide variety of print, electronic, and audiovisual media to build and reinforce language attainment. Make a recording of yourself responding to the Speaking Application prompt, and play it for students.

Beginning Pause the recording frequently and clarify as necessary. To build and reinforce language attainment, provide a small bank of words such as *fun, errands, car, plane,* and *trip*. Review the words, and have students use them in responding orally to questions about the recording. For example, ask, *What word tells how I get to the store?*

Intermediate During playback, have students raise their hands if they have difficulty understanding. Pause to clarify.

Afterward, have students respond orally to the presentation. To build language attainment, provide them with sentence frames to guide responses: for example, *One reason people go to the mall is* _____ .

Advanced Have groups discuss the presentation, offering their own views. Have them use sentence frames such as: *I agree with the point that* _____ *because* _____ . *While I agree that* _____ , *I also think that* _____ .

Advanced High Have students complete the Advanced activity. Challenge them to use at least one compound sentence in the discussion.

Use the Online Lesson Planner at www.phwritingcoach.com to customize your instructional plan for an integrated Language Arts curriculum.

DAY 1 24.1 Comparisons Using Adjectives and Adverbs

"What Do You Notice?"

Objectives: Identify, use, and understand aspects of comparison, including

- three forms of comparison
- regular modifiers with one or two syllables
- regular modifiers with three or more syllables
- adverbs ending in *–ly*
- *less* and *least*

INSTRUCTION AND PRACTICE

Student Edition pp. 533–537

DAY 2 24.1 Comparisons Using Adjectives and Adverbs *(continued)*

Objectives: Identify, use, and understand aspects of comparison, including

- irregular adjective and adverb forms
- comparative and superlative degrees

INSTRUCTION AND PRACTICE

Student Edition pp. 538–540

DAY 3 24.1 Comparisons Using Adjectives and Adverbs *(continued)*

Objectives: Identify, use, and understand aspects of making logical comparisons

INSTRUCTION AND PRACTICE

Student Edition pp. 541–543

DAY 4 24.2 Troublesome Adjectives and Adverbs

Objectives: Identify, use, and understand making clear comparisons, including using troublesome adjectives and adverbs

INSTRUCTION AND PRACTICE

Student Edition pp. 544–547
Test Warm-Up p. 548

Alternate Pacing Plans

- **Block Scheduling** Each day in the Lesson Planner represents a 40–50 minute block. Teachers using block scheduling may combine days to revise pacing to meet their classroom needs.

- **Accelerated Lesson Planning** Combine instructional days, focusing on concepts called out by students' diagnostic test results.

- **Integrated Language Arts Curriculum** Use the instruction and practice in this chapter to provide reinforcement, remediation, or extension of grammar concepts taught in your literature curriculum.

Links to Prentice Hall *LITERATURE*

Unit 3 Comparisons With Adjectives, p. 434; Writing Workshop: Revising for Correct Use of Troublesome Modifiers, p. 465

WRITING COACH

Online

www.phwritingcoach.com

Grammar Assessment and Practice

Chapter diagnostic tests assess students' skills and assign instruction and practice.

DimensionL Video Games

Fast-paced interactive video games challenge students' mastery of grammar.

Grammar Assessment

Grammar Coach:	Diagnostic Assessment	End-of-Chapter Assessment	Progress Monitoring
Personalized Instruction	Students take grammar diagnostic test online and are automatically assigned instruction and practice in areas where they need support.	Teacher uses **ExamView** to administer end-of-chapter assessment and remediation. Teachers may customize **ExamView** tests or use the ones provided.	Teachers may use the **Test Warm-Ups** and the **Cumulative Reviews** in the student book or eText to check students' mastery of grammar skills. Students may also play **DimensionL** grammar video games to test their grammar skills.
Teacher-Directed Instruction	Teacher administers the diagnostic test and determines focus of instruction and practice.		

Lesson Planner continues on next page ➤

DAY 5   Cumulative Review

Objectives: Identify, use, and understand word usage, including

- verb tenses and forms
- pronouns
- subject-verb and pronoun-antecedent agreement
- modifiers

INSTRUCTION AND PRACTICE

Student Edition pp. 549–550

> **"** *Groucho Marx once said: 'One morning I shot an elephant in my pajamas. How he got into my pajamas I'll never know!' Before teaching misplaced modifiers, give students humorous examples and have them figure out the double meanings. Let them play with misplaced modifiers before introducing the rules.* **"**
>
> **—Kelly Gallagher**

Differentiated Instruction

Differentiated Instruction Boxes in this Teacher's Edition address these student populations:
- Below-Level Students
- Gifted and Talented Students
- English Language Learners
- Above-Level Students
- Special Needs Students
- Spanish Speaking Students

In addition, for further enrichment, see the **Extension** features.

Grammar Ground Rule: Keep It Clear!

Model with Students

In this chapter, keep it clear means making your comparisons logical and balanced. Explain to students that comparisons are important in many different kinds of writing, but comparisons that don't really make sense will just confuse your reader.

Say: Suppose I want to compare two activities, to tell you which one I like better. I might say, *I like sewing my own clothes better than the piano.* But that's just confusing. You can't sew a piano, and that's what the sentences suggests. You can't compare an activity, such as sewing, with a musical instrument, such as the piano. It's much better to say, *I like sewing my own clothes better than playing the piano.* Compare things that can be compared.

Write this sentence on the board. *Riding a boogie board is easier than a surfboard.* Have students tell you what two things are being compared. (riding, surfboard) **Ask:** Does it make sense to compare these two things? How could you change the sentence so that the comparison makes sense? (*Riding a boogie board is easier than riding a surfboard.*)

Small Group Activity – Finding and Making Comparisons

Have students form groups and research or imagine two products. Have the students write a paragraph comparing the products and how they work. Have students discuss the comparisons they use in the paragraph. The discussion should answer these questions:

- What are the two things being compared?
- Does it make sense to compare these two things?

Have a member of each group present their conclusions to the class and give one good example of a comparison that follows this grammar ground rule: Keep it clear.

Grammar Ground Rules

1. Keep it clear.
2. Make them agree.
3. Make it specific.
4. Dot your *i*'s and cross your *t*'s.
5. Make it active.

SING MODIFIERS

wing how to use different forms of adjectives and adverbs to ke comparisons will enrich the descriptions in your writing.

WRITE GUY *Jeff Anderson, M.Ed.*

WHAT DO YOU NOTICE?

ok for modifiers as you zoom in on these sentences from the say "Jackie Robinson: Justice at Last" by Geoffrey C. Ward and n Burns.

MENTOR TEXT

Slowly his teammates accepted him, realizing that he was the spark that made them a winning team. No one was more daring on the base paths or better with the glove.

w, ask yourself the following questions:

In the second sentence, why do the authors use the word *more* instead of adding another ending to the adjective *daring*?

Why do the authors use the adjective *better* instead of *best* in the second sentence?

r most one- and two-syllable modifiers, you add -er or -est to ke a comparison. However, adding either ending to *daring* unds awkward; *more* or *most* is used to make the comparison stead. *Better* is used to make a comparison between two people, ile *best* is used to compare three or more people. The authors id that *no* one player on the team was more talented with e glove than Jackie Robinson, so they used *better*. If they had mpared Robinson to *all* players, they would have used *best*.

Grammar for Writers Writers can create vivid images when they use adjectives and adverbs to make comparisons. Check how many you are comparing to make sure you use the right form.

I'm the best player on the team.

Do you think of yourself as superlative, too?

533

Grammar for Writers: Voice

Help students understand that modifiers help writers compose clear descriptions. As students read about adjectives and adverbs in the lessons, they should think about how they will use these modifiers to strengthen their writing.

USING MODIFIERS

As students progress in their writing skills, it will be important for them to be able to apply the rules of grammar, usage, and mechanics to their own drafts. Use the *What Do You Notice?* feature to help them see effective conventions in the work of professional writers. Encourage students to incorporate effective voice, tense, and syntax as they edit their own writing.

Read aloud the opening sentence. Remind students that adjectives modify nouns and pronouns while adverbs modify verbs, adjectives, and other adverbs. Give examples of comparisons that contain adjectives: *The elephant is taller than the horse, but the giraffe is the tallest of all land animals.* Then, give examples of adverb comparisons: *The antelope runs faster than the lion, but the cheetah runs fastest of all three.*

WRITE GUY *Jeff Anderson, M. Ed.*

WHAT DO YOU NOTICE?

When students have read the Mentor Text, **say:** We use comparative forms of adjectives all the time when we speak and write. For example, the second sentence of the text compares Jackie Robinson to all other ball players when it says, "no one was more daring on the base paths." What other comparison does the writer make in that sentence? (**Possible response:** [no one] was better with the glove). Have students finish reading the page. How would the text change if these modifiers were not included? (**Possible response:** We wouldn't know how good Jackie Robinson was.)

Lesson Objectives

1. Recognize and use positive, comparative, and superlative forms of adjectives and adverbs.

2. Correctly use comparative and superlative forms of regular and irregular modifiers.

3. Create logical, balanced comparisons.

Three Forms of Comparison

Discuss how modifiers change form when they are used to compare things or ideas.

RULE 24.1.1 Read aloud the rule and then have students repeat the lines with you.

Review the explanation of positive degree, comparative degree, and superlative degree with students, and discuss the examples in the chart on page 534.

Use a Think Aloud as part of a gradual release progression.

Think Aloud

Say: Keeping these modifiers straight is easy, as long as I keep just one example in mind: *large, larger,* and *largest*. **I can remember** that the adjective or adverb in its regular or plain form—*large*—is the positive degree by thinking *P for plain form, P for positive form*. Then, I can think about the *-er* form—*larger*—as being the comparative degree—when only two things are being compared. The "super" degree is needed to compare three or more items, so I can remember that it is called the superlative degree.

Guide students in classifying modifiers. Draw three cluster diagrams on the board, labeling them *Positive, Comparative,* and *Superlative.*

Write these words on the board: *clear, clearest, smoother, rougher, smallest, rough, smoothest, lightest, sweeter, sweetest, light, small, clearer, smooth, lighter, sweet.* Have **students** place each modifier in the correct cluster.

Have partners use one word from each diagram in sentences.

24.1 Comparisons Using Adjectives and Adverbs

You may recall that adjectives and adverbs are **modifiers.** Adjectives can modify nouns or pronouns. Adverbs can modify verbs, adjectives, or other adverbs. You can use modifiers to make comparisons.

Three Forms of Comparison

Modifiers change their form when they show comparison. These different forms are called **forms,** or **degrees, of comparison.**

RULE 24.1.1

> Most adjectives and adverbs have three forms, or degrees, of comparison: **positive, comparative,** and **superlative.**

The **positive degree** is used when no comparison is being made. This is the form of a word that is listed in a dictionary. The **comparative degree** is used when two items are being compared. The **superlative degree** is used when three or more items are being compared. When the superlative degree is used, the article *the* is often added.

DEGREE	ADJECTIVE	ADVERB
Positive	The hermit crab moved into a **large** shell.	Sue ran **fast**.
Comparative	Soon, it will need a **larger** shell.	Sue ran **faster** than Mari.
Superlative	The crab is living in the **largest** shell it has ever had.	Of the three runners, Sue ran the **fastest**.

Like verbs, adjectives and adverbs change forms in different ways. Some adjectives and adverbs change in regular ways, or according to predictable patterns. As you can see in the chart above, *large* and *fast* form their comparative and superlative degrees regularly, by adding *-er* and *-est* to their positive form.

534 **Using Modifiers**

Teacher Tip

Some students may not have a clear understanding of what *modify* means. Explain to students that in this context, *modify* means to describe or add information to another word.

WRITING COACH

Online

www.phwritingcoach.com

Diagnostic and Instruction
Diagnostic test assesses students' instructional needs. Lessons and practice are assigned based on results.

Additional Practice
- Grammar Tutorials—Animated videos reinforce key grammar skills.
- Grammar Practice—Targeted practice addresses individual needs.
- ExamView—Teachers customize their grammar practice and tests.
- Grammar Games—Interactive video games make grammar fun.

WRITING COACH

Online

www.phwritingcoach.com

Grammar Tutorial
Brush up on your Grammar skills with these animated videos.

Grammar Practice
Practice your grammar skills with Writing Coach Online.

Grammar Games
Test your knowledge of grammar in this fast-paced interactive video game.

Regular Modifiers With One or Two Syllables

Most modifiers are **regular**—their degrees of comparison are formed in predictable ways.

> Use *-er* or *more* to form the comparative degree and use *-est* or *most* to form the superlative degree of most one- and two-syllable modifiers.

24.1.2 RULE

COMPARATIVE AND SUPERLATIVE DEGREES FORMED WITH *-ER* AND *-EST*

POSITIVE	COMPARATIVE	SUPERLATIVE
deep	deeper	deepest
fast	faster	fastest
friendly	friendlier	friendliest
narrow	narrower	narrowest
sunny	sunnier	sunniest

Use *more* to form a modifier's comparative degree when adding *-er* sounds awkward. Use *most* to form a modifier's superlative degree when adding *-est* sounds awkward.

COMPARATIVE AND SUPERLATIVE DEGREES FORMED WITH *MORE* AND *MOST*

POSITIVE	COMPARATIVE	SUPERLATIVE
careful	more careful	most careful
complete	more complete	most complete
handsome	more handsome	most handsome
often	more often	most often
quietly	more quietly	most quietly

More and *most* should not be used when the result sounds awkward, however. If you are not sure which form to use, check a dictionary. Most dictionaries list modifiers formed with *-er* and *-est*.

e Practice 24.1A

Comparisons Using Adjectives and Adverbs   535

Regular Modifiers With One or Two Syllables

Explain that it's not difficult to put most one- or two-syllable adjectives and adverbs in their comparative forms. You just apply a simple rule.

RULE 24.1.2 Read aloud the rule and then have students repeat the lines with you.

Review the first chart with students. Point out that most of the comparative degrees are formed by adding *-er* to the end of the modifier. The superlative degrees are formed by adding *-est*. Ask students what they notice about adding these endings to the adjectives and adverbs that end in *y*. (The *y* has to be changed to an *i* before adding the *-er* or *-est* ending.)

Explain that some other adjectives and adverbs don't sound right with an *-er* or *-est* ending. For these modifiers, you usually add *more* or *most* to create the comparative and superlative forms. Review the second chart with students.

Teacher Tip

If a student is unsure whether a particular adjective or adverb takes an ending or the word *more* or *most,* have him or her refer to a dictionary. Show the student how the word *heavy* becomes *heavier* and *heaviest.* Display the dictionary page with these degrees listed in the word's definition.

Working with ELLs   ELL Sheltered Instruction: Social/Affective

Help students demonstrate comprehension of increasingly complex English by participating in a shared reading of page 534.

Beginning Have fluent speakers read the first two sentences on the page as Beginning students follow along. Then, have fluent speakers choose a word from the first chart and read its degrees aloud. Pointing to the word, have the fluent speaker ask, *What makes this word comparative?* Have students complete this frame: _____ *was added to make it comparative.*

Intermediate Have students read the page in groups of three. Have them take turns reading the words in the first chart

aloud, with one student saying the word in the positive degree, one in the comparative, and one in the superlative, and review how the words change in each column.

Advanced Have partners read the page together. Have them choose a word from the first chart and write three sentences, one with each degree. Then, have partners read their sentences aloud, correcting each other as necessary.

Advanced High Have partners complete the Advanced activity. Then, challenge students to write a paragraph using one degree of each word in the first chart.

Regular Modifiers With Three or More Syllables

Explain that words with more than two syllables use *more* and *most* to form the comparative and superlative.

RULE 24.1.3 Read aloud the rule and then have students repeat the lines with you.

Use a Think Aloud as part of a gradual release progression.

Say: I know that it is sometimes automatic for me to just add an *-er* or an *-est* to form comparative words when I am speaking. But I also know that, sometimes, doing so results in a mistake. To make sure I get these forms right, I count the number of syllables a modifier has and make sure I add *more* and *most* if the modifier has more than two syllables.

Work with students to help them realize the importance of using the grammatically correct form of these words. Invite students to pronounce the three-syllable words with an incorrect *-er* and *-est* to illustrate why these are not used.

Have partners brainstorm for additional three-syllable modifiers and write sentences using the comparative and superlative forms. Have partners share their sentences with the class.

Adverbs Ending in *-ly*

RULE 24.1.4 Read aloud the rule and then have students repeat the lines with you.

Challenge the students to think of additional adverbs ending in *-ly*. (coolly, sweetly) Make a list. Ask volunteers to use each of the adverbs on the list in a sentence; then, have other students write sentences using the comparative and superlative forms of the adverbs.

Using *Less* and *Least*

RULE 24.1.5 Read aloud the rule and then have students repeat the lines with you.

Explain that *less* and *least* are opposite in meaning from *more* and *most*. Have students work with a partner to write five sentences that use *less* and *least*. Have students switch sentences with other pairs and replace *less* and *least* with *more* and *most*. Discuss the difference in meaning.

T536

Regular Modifiers With Three or More Syllables

Modifiers for words with three or more syllables follow the same rules.

RULE 24.1.3

> **Use *more* and *most* to form the comparative and superlative degrees of all modifiers of three or more syllables. Do not use *-er* or *-est* with modifiers of more than two syllables.**

DEGREES OF MODIFIERS WITH THREE OR MORE SYLLABLES		
POSTIVE	COMPARATIVE	SUPERLATIVE
expensive	more expensive	most expensive
flexible	more flexible	most flexible

Adverbs Ending in *-ly*

To modify most adverbs ending in *-ly*, use *more* or *most*.

RULE 24.1.4

> **Use *more* to form the comparative degree and *most* to form the superlative degree of most adverbs ending in *-ly*.**

EXAMPLES   quickly, more quickly, most quickly

gracefully, more gracefully, most gracefully

Using *Less* and *Least*

Less and *least* can show decreasing comparisons.

RULE 24.1.5

> **Use *less* with a modifier to form the decreasing comparative degree and *least* to form the decreasing superlative degree.**

EXAMPLES   flexible, less flexible, least flexible

quickly, less quickly, least quickly

See Practice 24.1B

536   **Using Modifiers**

Differentiated Instruction

PRE-AP Enrichment for Above-Level Students Review the lesson material. Invite students to explain why each sentence is incorrect:

He is the smallest of the two boys. (The comparative degree should be used to compare two things.) *That book is the heavier of the dozens offered.* (The superlative degree should be used to compare more than two things.) Challenge students to write incorrect sentences and ask a partner to explain why they are wrong.

RTI Strategy for Below-Level Students Students may find it helpful to circle the ending of each comparative and superlative modifier. Guide students to see that the positive degree is the word in its base word form. Discuss how the comparative ending, *-er*, is used to compare two items. The superlative ending, *-est*, is used to compare three or more items. Have students write example sentences using all three degrees of these common adjectives: *sharp, wonderful*.

PRACTICE 24.1A Forming Comparatives and Superlatives of One- and Two-Syllable Modifiers

Read the modifiers. Write the comparative and superlative forms of each modifier.

EXAMPLE   soft

ANSWER   *softer, softest*

1. cool
2. happy
3. willing
4. long
5. slowly
6. young
7. small
8. shiny
9. alert
10. straight

PRACTICE 24.1B Using Forms of Modifiers

Read the sentences. Then, write each sentence, using the form of the modifier specified in parentheses.

EXAMPLE   I am the _____ of the three children. (*old*, superlative)

ANSWER   I am the *oldest* of the three children.

11. Callie has the _____ shoe collection. (*fabulous*, superlative)
12. An apple would be a _____ choice. (*healthy*, comparative)
13. A computer is _____ than a typewriter. (*efficient*, comparative)
14. Coach was _____ than usual. (*angry*, comparative)
15. Johnny is the _____ of their children. (*young*, superlative)
16. Claire is my _____ friend. (*funny*, superlative)
17. Are there stars _____ than our sun? (*bright*, comparative)
18. The little boy ran _____ than his brother. (*slowly*, comparative)
19. I got there _____ than you. (*soon*, comparative)
20. What is the _____ way to the park? (*quick*, superlative)

SPEAKING APPLICATION

With a partner, talk about athletes you have seen or know about. Use modifiers to compare their performances or skills. Your partner should listen for and name at least two modifiers used in the comparative or superlative form.

WRITING APPLICATION

Write three or four sentences about animals you have seen or read about. Use modifiers to compare the animals' appearance, behavior, or other characteristics. Underline modifiers that are in the comparative or superlative form.

Practice   537

PRACTICE 24.1A

1. cooler, coolest
2. happier, happiest
3. more willing, most willing
4. longer, longest
5. more slowly, most slowly
6. younger, youngest
7. smaller, smallest
8. shinier, shiniest
9. more alert, most alert
10. straighter, straightest

PRACTICE 24.1B

11. Callie has the most fabulous shoe collection.
12. An apple would be a healthier choice.
13. A computer is more efficient than a typewriter.
14. Coach was angrier than usual.
15. Johnny is the youngest of their children.
16. Claire is my funniest friend.
17. Are there stars brighter than our sun?
18. The little boy ran more slowly than his brother.
19. I got there sooner than you.
20. What is the quickest way to the park?

SPEAKING APPLICATION

Have students explain how they were able to identify the comparative and superlative degrees.

WRITING APPLICATION

Have students exchange their sentences with a partner. Have partners check for correct comparative and superlative modifiers.

Irregular Adjectives and Adverbs

Tell students that there are some irregular adjectives and adverbs that do not follow the rules previously discussed.

RULE 24.1.6 Read aloud the rule and then have students repeat the lines with you.

Say: I know that not everyone uses correct grammar all the time, so I have to think of the rules as I speak and write. I know that in some cases, I have heard words said incorrectly for so long—a friend always says *beautifulest*—that they almost seem correct by now. So I really have to think about these rules, sometimes, to make sure I don't make the same error over and over again.

Work with students to help them realize that even though some modifiers are used incorrectly by some speakers, these uses are not correct grammar.

Have student pairs draw a three-panel illustration to show one of the modifier groups (for example: *many, more, most*). Tell students not to write the words they are illustrating. Have other pairs try to guess what has been illustrated.

Using Comparative and Superlative Degrees

RULE 24.1.7 Read aloud the rule and then have students repeat the lines with you.

Teacher Tip

Although students probably know the difference between adverbs and adjectives, the irregular forms may still be confusing. Display sentences using each degree of the irregular adjectives and adverbs so that students can refer to them as they strive to learn these forms.

Irregular Adjectives and Adverbs

A few adjectives and adverbs are irregular.

Memorize the comparative and superlative forms of adjectives and adverbs that have irregular spellings.

The chart lists the most common irregular modifiers.

DEGREES OF IRREGULAR ADJECTIVES AND ADVERBS		
POSITIVE	COMPARATIVE	SUPERLATIVE
bad (adjective)	worse	worst
badly (adverb)	worse	worst
far (distance)	farther	farthest
far (extent)	further	furthest
good (adjective)	better	best
well (adverb)	better	best
many	more	most
much	more	most

When you are unsure about how a modifier forms its degrees of comparison, check a dictionary.

See Practice 24.1C

Using Comparative and Superlative Degrees

Keep these rules in mind when you use the comparative and superlative degrees.

Use the comparative degree to compare *two* people, places, or things. Use the superlative degree to compare *three or more* people, places, or things.

Usually, you do not need to mention specific numbers when you are making a comparison. Other words in the sentence should help make the meaning clear whether you are comparing two items or three or more items.

538   Using Modifiers

Working with ELLs   **ELL** Sheltered Instruction: Cognitive

Help students use prereading supports to enhance comprehension of written text. Draw a concept web on the board, and model its use by writing *degrees of adjectives* in the center and writing related ideas elicited from students in the outer circles. Provide blank copies. Then:

Beginning Preteach the words *irregular, memorize, common, unsure,* and *dictionary*. Read the first section on page 538 with students, clarifying meaning. Then, have students write *irregular adjectives and adverbs* in the center of their concept webs, and guide them in filling in related ideas.

Intermediate Preteach the words *irregular, memorize,* and *modifier*. Have groups read

the first section on page 538 and then collaborate in filling in a concept web for the section. Review their webs with them.

Advanced Have partners read pages 538 and 539 and fill out two concept webs, one for each section. Review their webs with them.

Advanced High Have partners read pages 538 and 539 and fill out two concept webs, one for each section. Then, have them enter their notes in an outline to summarize the sections.

EXAMPLES   The captain felt **better** once all the
crew were safely on shore.

The rescue team completed the practice session
in their **best** time this week.

Pay particular attention to the modifiers you use when you are
comparing just two items. Do not use the superlative degree with
fewer than three items.

INCORRECT   Of their two practice runs, that one was **best**.

CORRECT   Of their two practice runs, that one was **better**.

INCORRECT   They were the **fastest** of the two teams
competing.

CORRECT   They were the **faster** of the two teams competing.

Do not make **double comparisons.** Do not use both -*er* and
more to form the comparative degree or both -*est* and *most* to
form the superlative degree. Also, be sure not to use -*er*, *more*,
and *most* with an irregular modifier.

◁ **24.1.8** RULE

INCORRECT   That student ran the **most fastest**.

CORRECT   That student ran the **fastest**.

INCORRECT   The thunderstorm was **more worse** than the one
last summer.

e Practice 24.1D

CORRECT   The thunderstorm was **worse** than the one last
summer.

Comparisons Using Adjectives and Adverbs   539

Read aloud the example sentences in the
middle of the page and explain why each
incorrect sentence is wrong. **Say:** At first this
sentence may sound okay: *Of their two practice
runs, that one was the best.* However, if I analyze
the sentence, I see that the adjective is in the
wrong form. Only two things are compared,
so I should use the comparative form *better,*
not the superlative form *best.* Similarly, in the
sentence *They were the fastest of the two teams
competing,* I should use the comparative *faster,*
not the superlative *fastest,* because only two
things are compared. Have students brainstorm
for additional examples of sentences with
comparative and superlative modifiers, and
discuss whether each modifier is presented
correctly or incorrectly and why.

Examples:
That kitten is the bigger of the large litter.
(biggest)
This is the better day of the month. (best)
Of the four brothers, he plays better. (best)
He feels worst today than last week. (worse)

Remind students that double comparisons,
such as *more stronger* and *most smartest,* are
illogical because they say the same thing twice.
More and -*er* mean the same thing. So do *most*
and -*est.* It is repetitious and incorrect to use
both.

RULE 24.1.8 Read aloud the rule and then
have students repeat the lines with you.

Read the examples together. Explain why *most
fastest,* in the first sentence, is wrong. Invite
students to tell why modifiers are not enhanced
by *more* and *most* in the other incorrect
sentences shown.

Differentiated Instruction

RTI Strategy for Below-Level Students
Review the problem of double comparisons
with students. Explain that there are three
different ways to make a comparison and
that they should always use only one.
The three ways are to add –*er,* use *more,* or
use a comparative form of an irregular verb.
Say or write on the board several sentences
that combine two of the forms, such as
Bella feels worser today and *Gigi is more
faster than Jane.* Ask students to remove
one of the comparison elements and read
the new, correct sentence.

Enrichment for Gifted/Talented Students
Have students write song lyrics to the
tune of "Oh, Susannah." Have them use a
series of the basic form of an adjective, the
comparative, and the superlative. Example:
"Fred is friendly, but Cho is friendlier. Nita
is the friendliest, and so I'll work with her."
Students may use other tunes or create
their own. Challenge students to use
interesting adjectives and adjectives with
irregular comparative forms.

Teacher Tip

Some students may have difficulty
correctly using standard irregular forms
because they are used to hearing and
using nonstandards forms. Have these
students practice using the correct
forms orally by answering questions. For
example, **ask:** Are you feeling better today?
Direct the student to use the correct form
of *bad* to answer: "No, I'm feeling worse."
Help students "hear" their errors and
correct them.

PRACTICE 24.1C

1. farther, farthest
2. worse, worst
3. more, most
4. worse, worst
5. further, furthest
6. better, best
7. more, most

PRACTICE 24.1D

8. This is the worst cold he has ever had.
9. He looks more like his father.
10. This is the best work you have done so far.
11. He played worse before he got a new coach.
12. She has the most books.
13. He did better on the test than he expected.
14. After the dog in the story died, I could not read further.
15. That is the better price.
16. Do you have more envelopes?
17. Of the two, that is the worse.

PRACTICE 24.1C Forming Comparatives and Superlatives of Irregular Adjectives and Adverbs

Read the modifiers. Write the comparative and superlative forms of each modifier.

EXAMPLE   good (adjective)
ANSWER   *better, best*

1. far (distance)
2. bad (adjective)
3. many
4. badly (adverb)
5. far (extent)
6. well (adverb)
7. much

PRACTICE 24.1D Using Comparatives and Superlatives of Irregular Adjectives and Adverbs

Read the sentences. Then, write each sentence, using the form of the modifier in parentheses.

EXAMPLE   He walked _____ than anyone else. (*far*, comparative)
ANSWER   He walked *farther* than anyone else.

8. This is the _____ cold he has ever had. (*bad*, superlative)
9. He looks _____ like his father. (*much*, comparative)
10. This is the _____ work you have done so far. (*good*, superlative)
11. He played _____ before he got a new coach. (*badly*, comparative)
12. She has the _____ books. (*many*, superlative)
13. He did _____ on the test than he expected. (*well*, comparative)
14. After the dog in the story died, I could not read _____. (*far*, comparative)
15. That is the _____ price. (*good*, comparative)
16. Do you have _____ envelopes? (*many*, comparative)
17. Of the two, that is the _____. (*bad*, comparative)

SPEAKING APPLICATION

With a partner, take turns talking about a competition (cooking, music, sports, or another) that you have seen on television. Whom did you like? Who should have won? Your partner should listen for and confirm the correct use of irregular modifiers.

WRITING APPLICATION

Write three sentences describing a place in nature you have visited or seen in pictures. Use at least two modifiers in either the comparative or superlative form. One modifier should be three or more syllables, and one should be irregular.

Working with ELLs   ELL Sheltered Instruction: Cognitive

Using the activities on the page, have students speak using a variety of sentence types with increasing accuracy and ease.

Beginning Model correct intonation as you read the answers to Practice 24.1D, items 9 and 16 (a statement and a question), aloud. Have students repeat chorally after you. Correct their intonation as necessary to foster increasing accuracy.

Intermediate Read the answers to Practice 24.1D, items 9 and 16, to students, filling in the blanks and modeling correct intonation. Have them repeat after you. Then, have students say a statement and ask a question of their own. Correct word order and intonation as necessary for increasing accuracy.

Advanced Review complex sentences with students. Then, have partners complete the Speaking Application. Direct them to use at least two complex sentences in their spoken accounts, as well as comparative and superlative degrees of modifiers.

Advanced High Review complex sentences and prepositional phrases with students. Then, have partners complete the Speaking Application. Direct them to use at least two complex sentences and one sentence beginning with a prepositional phrase, as well as comparative and superlative degrees of modifiers.

Making Logical Comparisons

In most situations, you will have no problem forming the degrees of modifiers and using them correctly in sentences. Sometimes, however, you may find that the way you have phrased a sentence makes your comparison unclear. You will then need to think about the words you have chosen and revise your sentence, making sure that your comparison is logical.

> **When you make a comparison, be sure you are comparing things that have clear similarities.**

◀ 24.1.9 RULE

Balanced Comparisons

Most comparisons make a statement or ask a question about the way in which similar things are either alike or different.

EXAMPLE Is **Chesapeake Bay deeper** than **Puget Sound**?
(Both bodies of water have depths that can be measured and compared.)

Because the sentence compares depth to depth, the comparison is balanced. Problems can occur, however, when a sentence compares dissimilar things. For example, it would be illogical to compare the depth of one bay to the shape of another bay. Depth and shape are not similar things and cannot be compared meaningfully.

ILLOGICAL The **plants in our garden** are **prettier** than **your garden**.
(*Plants* and a *garden* cannot be logically compared.)

LOGICAL The **plants in our garden** are **prettier** than the **plants in your garden**.
(Two sets of plants can be logically compared.)

> **Make sure that your sentences compare only similar items.**

◀ 24.1.10 RULE

An unbalanced comparison is usually the result of carelessness. The writer may have simply left something out. Read the following incorrect sentences carefully.

Comparisons Using Adjectives and Adverbs   541

Making Logical Comparisons

Remind students that the goal of using correct grammar in writing is to make writing clear and understandable. When a sentence is unclear, it needs to be revised. One common error is comparing two things that should not be compared. This is sometimes called "comparing apples to oranges."

RULE 24.1.9 Read aloud the rule and then have students repeat the lines with you.

Work through the explanation of the first example with students. Then, read aloud the second example.

Say: At first, this sentence may sound okay: *The plants in our garden are prettier than your garden.* When I analyze the comparison, however, I see that it is illogical. It is not logical to compare the sweetness of apples to plants in a garden to a garden. To make the comparison logical, I should compare the plants in one garden with the plants in another garden. To do that, I say: *The plants in our garden are prettier than the plants in your garden.*

Balanced Comparisons

RULE 24.1.10 Read aloud the rule and then have students repeat the line with you.

Write incorrect sentences on the board and have students revise them so that each is correct: *Painting the wall is easier than the ceiling.* (than painting the ceiling) *The number of puppies is smaller than children.* (than the number of children)

(continued)

> *Teacher Tip*
>
> If students are not able to see the weakness in the incorrect sentences, invite them to first identify and underline the complete subject. Then, have them underline what is being compared. Have them look at each underlined sentence part and ask themselves if the two parts of the sentences are aligned.

Balanced Comparisons (continued)

Read aloud the example sentences. Explain that students should ask themselves *What is being compared?* whenever they see a comparative or superlative form. In the first example on the page, *Building a ship* (an action) is being compared to *house*, a noun. You can't compare an action with a thing. So revision is necessary.

Other and *Else* in Comparisons

Explain that another kind of illogical comparison is to compare something to itself.

RULE 24.1.11 Read aloud the rule and then have students repeat the lines with you.

Use a Think Aloud as part of a gradual release progression.

 Say: I am going to make sure that when I compare part of a group with the whole group, I use the word *other* or the word *else* to make sure that I don't compare something to itself. I will reread the comparison sentences that I write and think about what I am comparing. Then, I will make sure I add the important word to make the sentence complete.

Work with students to ensure they can identify the group in each sentence and then the individual part of the group. Write these pairs of words on the board: *canoe – boat; silk – fabric; collie – dog; chair – furniture.* Have students brainstorm for sentences in which some aspect of the individual is compared with the same aspect of the group. Then, have students identify the individual and group by underlining the group and circling the individual. Call for volunteers to explain whether each comparison sentence is correct.

Have student pairs each write two sentences comparing an individual with its group. Have students exchange papers and proofread them to ensure that the comparisons are correct.

INCORRECT **Building a ship** is **harder** than a **house**.
The **number of shipwrecks** near the East Coast is **larger** than the **West Coast**.

In the first sentence, building a ship is mistakenly compared to a house. In the second sentence, events are compared to a place. Both sentences can easily be corrected to make the comparisons balanced.

CORRECT **Building a ship** is **harder** than **building a house**.
The **number of shipwrecks** near the East Coast is **larger** than the **number** near the West Coast.

See Practice 24.1E

Other and *Else* in Comparisons

Another common error in writing comparisons is to compare something to itself.

 When comparing one of a group to the rest of the group, make sure your sentence contains the word *other* or *else.*

Adding *other* or *else* can make a comparison clear. For example, in the second sentence below, because the *United States* is itself a country, it cannot logically be compared to *all countries*. It must be compared to *all other countries*.

PROBLEM SENTENCES	CORRECTED SENTENCES
A salvor is someone who returns an abandoned or sunken ship to shore before anyone.	A salvor is someone who returns an abandoned or sunken ship to shore before anyone else.
U.S. laws may allow a salvor to collect a larger reward than any country's laws do.	U.S. laws may allow a salvor to collect a larger reward than any other country's laws do.

See Practice 24.1F

542 **Using Modifiers**

Working with ELLs **ELL** Sheltered Instruction: Cognitive

Help students write using a variety of grade-appropriate sentence patterns, including balanced comparisons, in increasingly accurate ways. Review with students how to make comparisons. Then:

Beginning Read the first correct example on page 542 to students, clarifying meaning. Then, provide them with a small word bank: *running, yards, miles, eating, vegetables, easier,* and *harder*. Review the meaning of the words, and have students use them to write a balanced comparison by completing this sentence frame: _____ is _____ than _____.

Intermediate Read the first correct example on page 542 to students. Then, have partners write a new sentence

that makes a similar comparison. Coach students in identifying the subject and the verb in this simple sentence pattern.

Advanced Have partners read the correct examples on the page and identify the comparisons. Then, have each partner write five additional balanced comparisons.

Advanced High Have students complete the Advanced activity. Then, challenge them to write a compound sentence featuring two balanced comparisons.

PRACTICE 24.1E ▷ Making Balanced Comparisons

Read the sentences. Rewrite each sentence, correcting the unbalanced comparison.

EXAMPLE   My dad's car is newer than your dad.

ANSWER   *My dad's car is newer than your
dad's car.*

Our school library is bigger than their school.

The number of tigers in Asia is larger than zoos.

My brother's bicycle is faster than your brother.

The amount of money I owe is less than him.

The high school's playing field is nicer than the university.

There are fewer students in this classroom than that classroom.

Mariana's project is more complicated than Ciara.

The paint on this wall is drier than that wall.

This store's prices are lower than that store.

The distance this bus has traveled is longer than that bus.

PRACTICE 24.1F ▷ Using *Other* and *Else* to Make Comparisons

Read the sentences. Rewrite each sentence, adding *other* or *else* to make the comparisons more logical.

EXAMPLE   Russia is bigger than any country.

ANSWER   *Russia is bigger than any other
country.*

11. My brother is better at math than anyone.

12. I think the rose is lovelier than any flower.

13. My grandfather is older than anyone in our family.

14. The Pacific Ocean is bigger than any ocean.

15. Rafael studied harder than anyone in class.

16. Our park is cleaner than any park in the state.

17. This chair is more comfortable than anything.

18. She practiced longer than anyone on the team.

19. I was earlier than anyone.

20. My sister draws better than anyone in my family.

SPEAKING APPLICATION

With a partner, take turns talking about sports. Compare the sports or athletes, making sure that your comparisons are balanced and correct. Your partner should listen for and name any comparisons you might need to fix.

WRITING APPLICATION

Write three sentences comparing current clothing styles with images you have seen of past styles. One sentence should have a balanced comparison, and one should have either *else* or *other* to complete the comparison.

Practice   543

PRACTICE 24.1E

1. ... than their school library.
2. ... than the number of tigers in zoos.
3. ... than your brother's bicycle.
4. ... than the amount he owes.
5. ... than the university's playing field.
6. ... than in that classroom.
7. ... than Ciara's project.
8. ... than the paint on that wall.
9. ... than that store's prices.
10. ... than the distance that bus has traveled.

PRACTICE 24.1F

11. anyone else
12. any other
13. anyone else
14. any other
15. anyone else
16. any other
17. anything else
18. anyone else
19. anyone else
20. anyone else

SPEAKING APPLICATION

Have students explain briefly why they think their partner's comparisons need to be fixed.

WRITING APPLICATION

Have students exchange their sentences with a partner. Have partners check the comparisons and explain any problems they find.

Quick-Write Extension

To help students synthesize and apply what they have learned about making balanced comparisons, have them work in small groups to write a short TV commercial. In the commercial, students should compare different brands of a similar product, such as two similar video games, to explain why one is better than the other. The commercial must contain at least three comparison sentences. Students should then perform their commercials for the class, which listens and comments on whether comparisons are correctly formed.

Lesson Objectives

1. Identify commonly misused adjectives and adverbs.

2. Use commonly misused adjectives and adverbs correctly in both speaking and writing.

Ensure that students understand that certain verbs—*appear, feel, look,* and *sound*—can be used as either action verbs or linking verbs. Explain that when these verbs are used to tell something about the condition of the subject, they require an adjective modifier, not an adverb. Give this example: *She appeared sad.* The adjective form *sad* is correct because *appeared* is not an action verb. The subject *She* is not doing an action. In this sentence, however, *appear* is an action: *A star suddenly appeared in the sky.* The subject, *star,* is doing the appearing. Because *suddenly* is modifying an action verb, it's correct to use the adverb form *suddenly.*

Have students create sentences using *appear, feel, look,* and *sound* as linking verbs modified by adjectives. Then, discuss the sentences and identify any sentences in which students have mistakenly used adverbs instead of adjectives.

24.2 Troublesome Adjectives and Adverbs

The common adjectives and adverbs listed below often cause problems in both speaking and writing.

(1) bad and badly   *Bad* is an adjective. Use it after linking verbs, such as *are, appear, feel, look,* and *sound. Badly* is an adverb. Use it after action verbs, such as *act, behave, do,* and *perform.*

INCORRECT   Jan looked **badly** after the trip.

CORRECT   Jan looked **bad** after the trip.

INCORRECT   I did **bad** on the test.

CORRECT   I did **badly** on the test.

(2) good and well   *Good* is an adjective. *Well* can be either an adjective or an adverb, depending on its meaning. A common mistake is the use of *good* after an action verb. Use the adverb *well* instead.

INCORRECT   The children behaved **good** all day.

The apple tastes **well**.

CORRECT   The children behaved **well** all day.

The apple tastes **good**.

As adjectives, *good* and *well* have slightly different meanings, which are often confused. *Well* usually refers simply to health.

EXAMPLES   Janet felt **good** after the hike.

The fresh bread smells **good**.

That puppy is not **well**.

www.phwritingcoach.com

Diagnostic and Instruction
Diagnostic test assesses students' instructional needs. Lessons and practice are assigned based on results.

Additional Practice
- Grammar Practice—Targeted practice addresses individual needs.
- ExamView—Teachers customize their grammar practice and tests.
- Grammar Games—Interactive video games make grammar fun.

Differentiated Instruction

PRE-AP Enrichment for Above-Level Students Remind students that adverbs often modify verbs, and adjectives modify nouns and pronouns. Then, remind students that linking verbs link the subject to other information about the subject. Have students use the Internet or another resource to create a full list of verbs that can be used as either action verbs or linking verbs. (Most resources will list at least 10 linking verbs, including *appear, become, feel, grow, look, remain, seem, smell, sound, stay, taste*).

Challenge small groups to create skits in which they use several different verbs as both action verbs and linking verbs. Have volunteers perform their skits for the class. Afterward, students should list each verb they used and explain when they used it as an action verb and when they used it as a linking verb.

(3) fewer and less   Use the adjective *fewer* to answer
the question, "How many?" Use the adjective *less* to answer
the question, "How much?"

HOW MANY   **fewer** calories   **fewer** chores

HOW MUCH   **less** food   **less** work

(4) just   When used as an adverb, *just* often means "no more
than." When *just* has this meaning, place it right before the word
it logically modifies.

INCORRECT   Do you **just** want **one baked potato**?

CORRECT   Do you want **just** **one baked potato**?

(5) only   The position of *only* in a sentence sometimes affects
the sentence's entire meaning. Consider the meaning of these
sentences.

EXAMPLES   **Only** she answered that question.
            (Nobody else answered that question.)

            She **only** answered the question.
            (She did nothing else with the question.)

            She answered **only** that question.
            (She answered that question and no other question.)

Mistakes involving *only* usually occur when its placement in a
sentence makes the meaning unclear.

UNCLEAR   **Only** take advice from me.

BETTER   Take advice **only** from me.
            (not from anyone else)

Practice 24.2A
Practice 24.2B
Practice 24.2C   Take **only** advice from me.
Practice 24.2D   (nothing but advice)

Troublesome Adjectives and Adverbs   **545**

Read and discuss the sections on *fewer and
less, just,* and *only.* Explain that *fewer* should
be used with count nouns, while *less* should
be used with noncount nouns. Review the
definitions of count and noncount nouns as
necessary. (Count nouns refer to things that
can be enumerated, such as three models of
cars and two apples. Noncount nouns refer to
things that cannot be enumerated, such as rice
and water.) Invite students to write sentences
using *fewer* with count nouns and *less* with
noncount nouns.

Use a Think Aloud as part of a gradual release
progression for the study of *only.*

 Say: *Only* is another word that can
cause some confusion in our speaking
and writing. When **I write** a sentence
using *only,* I like to ask *What?* or *Who?*
after the word *only* appears in the sentence. The
response to that question tells me whether I have
placed *only* correctly in the sentence. For
example, *I have only one blue sweater.* When I
ask *What do I have?* the response is *one blue
sweater.* For the sentence *Only I have one blue
sweater,* I ask *Who has one blue sweater?* The
response to my question is *only I.* This is how I
check to make sure my sentence is written
correctly.

Work with students to ask *What?* and *Who?*
questions after the word *only* in each sample
sentence. Discuss how its placement affects the
meaning of the sentence.

Have student pairs write three new *only*
sentences and ask the *Why?* question. Then,
have students present their sentences to the
class.

> *Teacher Tip*
>
> Have students who have difficulty with
> troublesome adjectives and adverbs write
> hints and tips on note cards. Encourage
> students to refer to the cards as they
> review the chapter pages.

Extension

To help students synthesize and apply what
they have learned about the use of the word
only, have students discuss how moving *only*
to different positions in a sentence changes the
sentence's meaning. Write these sentences on
the board: *Only Joe and I know the location
of the hidden treasure. Joe and I know only
the location of the hidden treasure. Joe and I
know the location of the only hidden treasure.*
Challenge volunteers to read each sentence
aloud with proper emphasis and contrast the
meaning of the sentences.

1. badly
2. good
3. bad
4. well
5. bad
6. good
7. badly
8. well
9. badly
10. good

11. The pollution is bad in this town.
12. correct
13. These bruises still hurt badly.
14. I did well in yesterday's race.
15. correct
16. My brothers work well together.
17. This yellow dress looks bad on me.
18. correct
19. The plumber did the work badly.
20. Everything the chef made was good.

SPEAKING APPLICATION

Have students explain why they used the modifiers they used. Partners should listen to explanations and agree or disagree.

WRITING APPLICATION

Have students exchange their sentences with a partner. Have the partner explain and correct any modifier problems.

PRACTICE 24.2A Using *Bad* and *Badly*, *Good* and *Well*

Read the sentences. Write the word in parentheses that correctly completes each sentence.

EXAMPLE   I did (good, well) on the test.

ANSWER   *well*

1. He performed (bad, badly) during the concert.
2. We expected a (good, well) outcome.
3. I felt (bad, badly) about the competition results.
4. The projection equipment worked (good, well).
5. The garbage is beginning to smell (bad, badly).
6. The sets for the play look really (good, well).
7. Dad's car is running (bad, badly).
8. Did your brother finish (good, well) in the race?
9. Our dog (bad, badly) needs to be bathed.
10. The warm sunshine feels (good, well).

SPEAKING APPLICATION

With a partner, take turns talking about a movie you enjoyed. Did the actors perform well or badly? Was the story good or bad? Your partner should listen for and confirm that you have used these troublesome modifiers correctly.

546   Using Modifiers

PRACTICE 24.2B Revising for Troublesome Modifiers

Read the sentences. Rewrite the sentences that contain errors in the use of modifiers. If a sentence has no error, write *correct*.

EXAMPLE   The baking bread smells well.

ANSWER   *The baking bread smells good.*

11. The pollution is badly in this town.
12. A warm blanket feels good on a cold night.
13. These bruises still hurt bad.
14. I did good in yesterday's race.
15. Everyone felt bad about the coach leaving.
16. My brothers work good together.
17. This yellow dress looks badly on me.
18. I was sick for a while, but I'm well now.
19. The plumber did the work bad.
20. Everything the chef made was well.

WRITING APPLICATION

Write three or four sentences about characters in a story you like. What do they like? How do they do it? Use at least three of the following: *well*, *good*, *bad*, and *badly*. Be sure to use them correctly in your sentences.

Working with ELLs   **ELL** Sheltered Instruction: Metacognitive

Adapt the Speaking Application to have students demonstrate listening comprehension of increasingly complex spoken English by orally responding to questions and requests. Instruct them to monitor comprehension and seek clarification as needed.

Beginning Have students respond to two questions about a movie they have seen that they didn't like. Request that they use the words *bad* or *badly* in their answers. Provide a model: *The movie was bad.* Direct students to raise their hands to seek clarification if they do not understand something in the questions.

Intermediate Write *good, well, bad,* and *badly* on the board. Have students say each word aloud. Request that they use one of the words in answering the questions you are about to ask. Then, have students respond to two questions about a movie they have seen, directing them to ask for clarification as needed.

Advanced Have partners complete the Speaking Application. Then, have partners ask each other questions based on their respective Speaking Application responses. Have partners answer the questions, seeking clarification as needed.

Advanced High Have students complete the Advanced activity. Then, have them share with the class a tip on seeking clarification.

ACTICE 24.2C Using *Fewer* and *Less*

ad the sentences. Rewrite the sentences using
ver or *less* correctly.

AMPLE   Toddlers have (fewer, less) chores
than teenagers.

SWER   *Toddlers have fewer chores than
teenagers.*

The school can purchase (fewer, less)
equipment this year.

Shannon made (fewer, less) sandwiches than
usual.

She served (fewer, less) food to avoid leftovers
again.

Aiden has thrown (fewer, less) pitches this
season than last season.

We will face (fewer, less) opponents this year.

Right now Sophie has (fewer, less) money in
the bank.

Mom put (fewer, less) rice on my plate than
Dan's.

Diego has (fewer, less) bad habits than Adam.

My sister's high school has (fewer, less) rules
than our middle school.

I answered (fewer, less) questions correctly
on the test than Liam.

PRACTICE 24.2D Using *Just* and *Only*

Read the sentences. If the placement of *just* or
only makes sense, write *correct*. If not, rewrite
the sentence with the correct placement of
modifiers.

EXAMPLE   Do you only know one song, or can
you play many?

ANSWER   *Do you know only one song, or can
you play many?*

11. Ava just has one pencil, and it is broken.

12. Our house has only four rooms, yet it is
perfect for Dad and me.

13. There will be no test today because only the
teacher has three exam books.

14. Only two of us went to the movie, but we
both liked it.

15. I need one word only to complete this puzzle.

16. I need to find just one more item to win the
scavenger hunt.

17. One person only came to the meeting, so it
was cancelled.

18. Lila only went to Alaska with a thin coat.

19. Do you just want one egg for breakfast?

20. Did you finish just one chapter?

SPEAKING APPLICATION

With a partner, talk about a time when you did
not have enough of something. Use examples of
fewer, *less*, *just*, and *only*. Write a sentence for
each of the words and use it correctly. Discuss
your sentences with a partner.

WRITING APPLICATION

Write a paragraph about making sandwiches
without the ingredients you need. Use
examples of *fewer*, *less*, *just*, and *only*. Have
a partner check your understanding of the
words.

Practice   547

PRACTICE 24.2C

1. The school can purchase less
equipment this year.

2. Shannon made fewer sandwiches
than usual.

3. She served less food to avoid
leftovers again.

4. Aiden has thrown fewer pitches this
season than last season.

5. We will face fewer opponents this
year.

6. Right now Sophie has less money in
the bank.

7. Mom put less rice on my plate than
Dan's.

8. Diego has fewer bad habits than
Adam.

9. My sister's high school has fewer
rules than our middle school.

10. I answered fewer questions
correctly on the test than Liam.

PRACTICE 24.2D

11. Ava has just one pencil, and it is
broken.

12. correct

13. There will be no test today because
the teacher has only three exam
books.

14. correct

15. I need only one word to complete
this puzzle.

16. correct

17. Only one person came to the
meeting, so it was cancelled.

18. Lila went to Alaska with only a thin
coat.

19. Do you want just one egg for
breakfast?

20. correct

SPEAKING APPLICATION

**Have students explain why they
made the modifier choices they did.
Have partners discuss with them
whether they made the correct
choice.**

WRITING APPLICATION

**Have students write brief
explanations for why they agree or
disagree with their partner's choice
of modifiers.**

Test Warm-Up

1. **C** Move *only* to follow *need*

2. **F** Change *fewer* to *less*

3. **B** If your mixture is too thick, add just a little water.

4. **J** Try to add only a few layers at a time, so it will dry well.

Reteach

If students have not mastered these skills, review the content in Section 24.2 Troublesome Adjectives and Adverbs.

1. (5) *only*

2. (3) *fewer and less*

3. (4) *just*

4. (5) *only*

Test Tip

If students have tried all other strategies to answer a question and are still unsure about the correct answer, they should try to eliminate any answer choices that they know or suspect are not correct. They can then make a guess at a correct answer from the remaining answer choices.

Test Warm-Up

DIRECTIONS
Read the introduction and the passage that follows. Then, answer the questions to show that you can use and understand the function of troublesome adjectives and adverbs in reading and writing.

Paige wrote this paragraph for a column about crafts in the school newspaper. Read the paragraph and think about the changes you woul suggest as a peer editor. When you finish reading, answer the questions that follow.

Be a Sculptor

(1) Papier-mâché makes a great animal sculpture. (2) Besides balloons for the base, you only need water, flour, paint, and brushes. (3) Mix the fl with water to make a paste that looks like glue. (4) You will need fewer flour than water. (5) If your mixture is too thick, just add a little water. (6) Tear newspaper into strips, and soak the strips in the paste. (7) Then put them over the balloon. (8) Try only to add a few layers at a time. (9) It will dry good. (10) Once dry, paint your sculpture with whatever colors you choose.

---

1 What change, if any, should be made in sentence 2?

  A Move *only* to follow *paint*

  B Move *only* to come before *you*

  C Move *only* to follow *need*

  D Make no change

2 What change, if any, should be made in sentence 4?

  F Change *fewer* to *less*

  G Change *fewer* to *only*

  H Add *just* before *fewer*

  J Make no change

3 How should sentence 5 be revised?

  A If your mixture is just too thick, just a a little water.

  B If your mixture is too thick, add just a little water.

  C If your mixture is too thick, add a littl water, just.

  D If your only mixture is too thick, add j a little water.

4 What is the BEST way to combine sentences 8 and 9?

  F Try to add only a few layers at a time it will dry good.

  G Only try to add a few layers at a time it will dry good.

  H Only try to add a few layers at a time it will dry well.

  J Try to add only a few layers at a time, it will dry well.

nulative Review — Chapters 21–24

PRACTICE 1 — Identifying Verb Tenses

Read the sentences. For each sentence, write whether the verb is in the *present, past, future, present perfect, past perfect,* or *future perfect* tense. Also indicate if the verb is *progressive.*

1. ...ureen sings in the choir.
2. ...he new restaurant opened on Friday.
3. ...Mrs. Macy has operated a crane at a construction site before.
4. ...he secretary of state will visit India.
5. ...y noon, Samantha will have been working on the project for six hours.
6. ...My father is stuffing the turkey for our Thanksgiving dinner.
7. ...eff Jackson had once starred in a musical version of *Old Yeller.*
8. ...he Lopez family will be leaving shortly on their vacation.
9. ...lizabeth had been dancing for years.
10. ...en trumpeters were marching with the ...and.

PRACTICE 2 — Revising to Use Active Voice

Read the sentences. Then, rewrite each sentence ...assive voice so that it is in active voice. If a ...nce is already in active voice, write *active.*

1. ...he best music is played by that salsa band.
2. ...he poem was written by Emily Dickinson.
3. ...he Tremonts live in a large house by the ...ke.
4. ...his award is shared by all the people ...volved in our great film.
5. ...odd is leaving for Denver tomorrow.

PRACTICE 3 — Using Verbs Correctly

Read the sentences. Then, rewrite the sentences to correct any incorrect verb tenses. If a sentence has no errors, write *correct.*

1. A week ago, Lawrence run his best time on the track.
2. Last Saturday the phone rung all afternoon.
3. The concert has finally begun.
4. Yesterday I accidentally lay my books at the bottom of the wrong locker.
5. I always sit a vase of flowers in the center of the table.
6. Bonnie finally done her homework.
7. At the grand opening last week, Cindy says to me, "Calm down."
8. Mrs. Menendez has spoke to me about the problem with the microphones.
9. I seen the Memorial Day parade for the first time last May.
10. All day the monkeys have swinged in the trees.

PRACTICE 4 — Identifying Pronoun Cases and Uses

Read the sentences. Write whether each underlined pronoun is in the *nominative, objective,* or *possessive* case. Then, write whether it is used as a *subject,* a *predicate pronoun,* a *direct object,* an *indirect object,* or the *object of a preposition.*

1. Polly talked to <u>him</u> for two hours.
2. The teacher gave <u>her</u> a high grade.
3. <u>Mine</u> is the jacket with the fake fur trim.
4. Pedro showed <u>us</u> around the computer room.
5. The winners were Robin and <u>I</u>.

Continued on next page ▶

Cumulative Review   549

---

4. Yesterday I accidentally laid my books at the bottom of the wrong locker.
5. I always set a vase of flowers in the center of the table.
6. Bonnie finally did her homework.
7. At the grand opening last week, Cindy said to me, "Calm down."
8. Mrs. Menendez has spoken to me about the problem with the microphones.
9. I saw the Memorial Day parade for the first time last May.
10. All day the monkeys have swung in the trees.

PRACTICE 4

1. objective, object of a preposition
2. objective, indirect object
3. possessive, subject
4. objective, direct object
5. nominative, predicate pronoun

PRACTICE 1

1. present
2. past
3. present perfect
4. future
5. future perfect progressive
6. present progressive
7. past perfect
8. future progressive
9. past perfect progressive
10. past progressive

PRACTICE 2

1. That salsa band plays the best music.
2. Emily Dickinson wrote the poem.
3. active
4. All the people involved in our great film share this award.
5. active

PRACTICE 3

1. A week ago, Lawrence ran his best time on the track.
2. Last Saturday the phone rang all afternoon.
3. correct

PRACTICE 5

1. We and Roberto went to the library.
2. The shopkeeper gave Yvonne and me a discount.
3. correct
4. The cat ate its dinner.
5. The newest counselors were Sonya and I.
6. Ali is the one whom the team appointed as leader.
7. There was an agreement between Lou and her.
8. The house at the end of the street is theirs.
9. The problem worries Christine and him.
10. Young people do not know who that actor is.

PRACTICE 6

1. A book of poems sits on the shelf.
2. Each of the members belongs to other clubs too.
3. correct
4. The family sometimes argue at dinner.
5. correct
6. correct
7. The manager or her assistants greet shoppers.
8. Does Jane or Randy come here after school?
9. The committee has named her as treasurer.
10. Macaroni and cheese is my favorite dish.

PRACTICE 7

1. Each of the girls spent her money on magazines.
2. correct
3. Nate takes a class where he learns yoga.
4. Neither the dog nor the cat ate its food.
5. Back then, everyone had his or her shoes polished.
6. correct
7. Both of the horses had scars on their legs.
8. correct
9. None of the workers did their own cooking.
10. correct

PRACTICE 8

1. Fewer people visit the museum on weekdays.
2. Of the three papers, hers is the best.
3. Stuart did well in his first attempt.
4. You can walk farther in comfortable shoes.
5. Of the two villains, who is worse?
6. correct
7. Many office workers work only on weekdays.
8. The stale crackers taste really bad.
9. Most border collies are smarter than any other dogs.
10. How badly did she perform in the play?

Cumulative Review Chapters 21–24

PRACTICE 5 Using Pronouns Correctly

Read the sentences. Then, rewrite the sentences to correct any incorrect pronouns. If a sentence has no errors, write *correct*.

1. Us and Roberto went to the library.
2. The shopkeeper gave Yvonne and I a discount.
3. Whom did Anthony invite to the party?
4. The cat ate it's dinner.
5. The newest counselors were Sonya and me.
6. Ali is the one who the team appointed as leader.
7. There was an agreement between Lou and she.
8. The house at the end of the street is their's.
9. The problem worries Christine and he.
10. Young people do not know whom that actor is.

PRACTICE 6 Revising for Subject–Verb Agreement

Read the sentences. Then, rewrite the sentences to correct any errors in subject-verb agreement. If a sentence has no errors, write *correct*.

1. A book of poems sit on the shelf.
2. Each of the members belong to other clubs too.
3. Neither Miranda nor I like radio talk shows.
4. The family sometimes argues at dinner.
5. None of the triplets are in my class.
6. Cara and Leslie enjoy scuba diving.
7. The manager or her assistants greets shoppers.
8. Do Jane or Randy come here after school?
9. The committee have named her as treasurer.
10. Macaroni and cheese are my favorite dish.

PRACTICE 7 Revising for Pronoun–Antecedent Agreement

Read the sentences. Then, rewrite the sentences correct any errors in pronoun-antecedent agreeme If a sentence has no errors, write *correct*.

1. Each of the girls spent their money on magazines.
2. Several of the runners had their blisters treated.
3. Nate takes a class where you learn yoga.
4. Neither the dog nor the cat ate their food.
5. Back then, everyone had their shoes polish
6. Belle and Natalie finished their homework.
7. Both of the horses had scars on its legs.
8. Either Jane or Ann wore lip balm on her li
9. None of the workers did his or her own cook
10. Everybody remembered his or her manner

PRACTICE 8 Using Modifiers Correctly

Read the sentences. Then, rewrite the sentenc to correct any errors involving modifiers. If a sentence has no errors, write *correct*.

1. Less people visit the museum on weekday
2. Of the three papers, hers is the most good.
3. Stuart did good in his first attempt.
4. You can walk more far in comfortable shoe
5. Of the two villains, who is badder?
6. Pearl is the prettiest cat we have ever own
7. Many office workers only work on weekda
8. The stale crackers taste really badly.
9. Most border collies are smarter than any do
10. How bad did she perform in the play?

550 Cumulative Review

T550

CHAPTER 25 LESSON PLANNER
Punctuation

Use the Online Lesson Planner at www.phwritingcoach.com to customize your instructional plan for an integrated Language Arts curriculum.

DAY 1 **25.1** End Marks

"What Do You Notice?"

Objectives: Identify, use, and understand end marks, including
- periods
- question marks
- exclamation marks

INSTRUCTION AND PRACTICE

Student Edition pp. 551–555

DAYS 2–4 **25.2** Commas

Objectives: Identify and understand aspects of using commas, including
- in compound sentences
- avoiding comma splices
- in a series
- between adjectives
- after introductory material
- with parenthetical expressions
- with nonessential expressions
- with dates and geographical names
- in numbers
- with addresses and in letters
- with direct quotations

INSTRUCTION AND PRACTICE

Student Edition pp. 556–570

DAY 5 **25.3** Semicolons and Colons

Objectives: Identify and understand aspects of using semicolons and colons, including
- to join independent clauses
- to avoid confusion

INSTRUCTION AND PRACTICE

Student Edition pp. 571–574

Alternate Pacing Plans

- **Block Scheduling** Each day in the Lesson Planner represents a 40–50 minute block. Teachers using block scheduling may combine days to revise pacing to meet their classroom needs.

- **Accelerated Lesson Planning** Combine instructional days, focusing on concepts called out by students' diagnostic test results.

- **Integrated Language Arts Curriculum** Use the instruction and practice in this chapter to provide reinforcement, remediation, or extension of grammar concepts taught in your literature curriculum.

Links to Prentice Hall *LITERATURE*

- **Unit 1** Writing Workshop: Revising for Errors With Possessive Nouns, p. 89
- **Unit 6** Commas, p. 930; Semicolons and Colons, p. 954; Writing Workshop: Punctuating Citations and Titles of Reference Works, p. 993

WRITING COACH

Online

www.phwritingcoach.com

Grammar Assessment and Practice

Chapter diagnostic tests assess students' skills and assign instruction and practice.

DimensionL Video Games

Fast-paced interactive video games challenge students' mastery of grammar.

Grammar Assessment

Grammar Coach:	Diagnostic Assessment	End-of-Chapter Assessment	Progress Monitoring
Personalized Instruction	Students take grammar diagnostic test online and are automatically assigned instruction and practice in areas where they need support.	Teacher uses **ExamView** to administer end-of-chapter assessment and remediation. Teachers may customize **ExamView** tests or use the ones provided.	Teachers may use the **Test Warm-Ups** and the **Cumulative Reviews** in the student book or eText to check students' mastery of grammar skills.
Teacher-Directed Instruction	Teacher administers the diagnostic test and determines focus of instruction and practice.		Students may also play **DimensionL** grammar video games to test their grammar skills.

Lesson Planner continues on next page

DAYS 6–8 25.4 Quotation Marks, Underlining, and Italics

Objectives: Identify and understand aspects of using quotation marks including

- with quotations
- with other punctuation marks
- quotations within quotations
- explanatory material within quotations
- for dialogue
- in titles and other special words

INSTRUCTION AND PRACTICE

Student Edition pp. 575–586

DAY 9 25.5 Hyphens

Objectives: Identify and understand aspects of using hyphens, including

- in numbers
- with prefixes and suffixes
- in compound words
- with compound modifiers
- at the ends of lines
- to divide words

INSTRUCTION AND PRACTICE

Student Edition pp. 587–592

DAY 10 25.6 Apostrophes

Objectives: Identify and understand aspects of using apostrophes, including

- with possessive nouns
- with pronouns
- with contractions
- to create plurals

INSTRUCTION AND PRACTICE

Student Edition pp. 593–597

DAY 11 25.7 Parentheses and Brackets

Objectives: Identify and understand aspects of using parentheses and brackets.

INSTRUCTION AND PRACTICE

Student Edition pp. 598–600

DAY 12 25.8 Ellipses and Dashes

Objectives: Identify and understand aspects of using ellipses and dashes.

INSTRUCTION AND PRACTICE

Student Edition pp. 601–605

Test Warm-Up p. 606

Differentiated Instruction

Differentiated Instruction Boxes in this Teacher's Edition address these student populations:

- Below-Level Students
- Above-Level Students
- Gifted and Talented Students
- Special Needs Students
- English Language Learners
- Spanish Speaking Students

In addition, for further enrichment, see the **Extension** features.

PUNCTUATION

ach punctuation mark plays an important role in making your
riting understandable and unified.

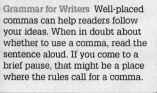

WRITE GUY *Jeff Anderson, M.Ed.*

WHAT DO YOU NOTICE?

Keep track of commas as you zoom in on these sentences from the
story "Why the Tortoise's Shell Is Not Smooth" by Chinua Achebe.

MENTOR TEXT

> When all the birds had gathered together, they set off in a
> body. Tortoise was very happy as he flew among the birds, and
> he was soon chosen as the man to speak for the party because he
> was a great orator.

Now, ask yourself the following questions:

- Why does the author use a comma after *together*?
- Why is a comma needed before *and* in the second sentence?

The first sentence begins with the subordinate clause *when all
the birds had gathered together.* Therefore, a comma is needed
after *together* to separate the subordinate clause from the main or
independent clause that follows. In the second sentence, a comma
is needed before the conjunction *and* because there are complete
thoughts on either side of it.

Grammar for Writers Well-placed
commas can help readers follow
your ideas. When in doubt about
whether to use a comma, read the
sentence aloud. If you come to a
brief pause, that might be a place
where the rules call for a comma.

Stop! I forgot a comma!

Commas are for pauses, not for stops.

551

Grammar for Writers: Syntax

Explain to students that knowing when to use
punctuation marks helps writers communicate
more effectively. The rules in the lessons will
help students to use punctuation correctly in
their writing.

PUNCTUATION

As students progress in their writing skills, it
will be important for them to be able to apply
the rules of grammar, usage, and mechanics to
their own drafts. Use the *What Do You Notice?*
feature to help them see effective conventions
in the work of professional writers. Encourage
students to incorporate proper voice, tense, and
syntax as they edit their own writing.

Remind students that it is important to
use punctuation correctly in their writing.
Misplaced punctuation can alter the meaning
of a sentence and confuse readers. Point out
that end marks, commas, semicolons, and other
punctuation marks help writers present their
ideas clearly.

WRITE GUY *Jeff Anderson, M. Ed.*

WHAT DO YOU NOTICE?

When students have read the Mentor Text, say:
You probably know that punctuation clarifies
meaning by signaling when a sentence ends,
when to pause before and after words, whether a
group of words is a quotation, and so on. You may
also know that a comma signals a brief pause,
and gives us other information about the groups
of words in sentences. For example, a comma
can tell us that there are two complete thoughts
on either side of a conjunction. It can also tell us
that a clause at the beginning of a sentence is
a subordinate clause. What punctuation marks
do you see in the Mentor Text? **(commas and
periods)**

On the board, write the Mentor Text sentences
without any punctuation. Have students read the
sentences to themselves. **Then, ask:** What was it
like to read these sentences without punctuation?
(Possible response: It was confusing because
the ideas run together and I couldn't tell where
to pause as I read.)

Incorrectly punctuate one of the sentences on
the board. For example, *When all the birds,
had gathered together. they set off in a body.*
Then, say: What effect does the incorrect
punctuation have on your understanding of the
sentence? **(Accept all reasonable responses.)**

Lesson Objectives

1. Recognize and identify end marks.

2. Correctly use and understand end marks.

Using Periods

Point out that periods are used to end sentences or abbreviations. Remind students that many types of sentences require periods. Review these types as you discuss the rules.

RULES 25.1.1, 25.1.2, 25.1.3, 25.1.4 Read aloud the rules and then have students repeat the lines with you.

Use a Think Aloud as part of a gradual release progression.

Think Aloud **Say: I keep** a few simple rules in mind when I use a period to end sentences. If the sentence makes a statement or gives a command, I end it with a period. If a sentence asks an indirect question, such as *Sara asked if I was going to school early,* I end that sentence with a period, too.

Write these sentences on the board, and **work with students to** identify why a period is (or is not) used in each case. *I like ice cream.* (A period ends a declarative statement.) *They asked me what flavor I liked.* (A period ends a sentence that contains an indirect question.) *Buy me some ice cream.* (A period ends a command.) Remind students that a period follows most abbreviations and initials. Give a few examples: *Mr.* (Use a period after an abbreviation.) *T. S. Eliot* (Use a period after initials.)

Have partners brainstorm for examples of the types of sentences described. Have partners share their examples with the class.

25.1 End Marks

End marks signal the end or conclusion of a sentence, word, or phrase. There are three end marks: the **period (.)**, the **question mark (?)**, and the **exclamation mark (!)**.

Using Periods

A **period** indicates the end of a sentence or an abbreviation.

RULE 25.1.1 Use a period to end a **declarative** sentence—a statement of fact or opinion.

DECLARATIVE SENTENCE　This is a beautiful park.

RULE 25.1.2 Use a period to end most **imperative** sentences—sentences that give directions or commands.

IMPERATIVE SENTENCE　Finish reading the chapter.

RULE 25.1.3 Use a period to end a sentence that contains an **indirect question.**

An **indirect question** restates a question in a declarative sentence. It does not give the speaker's exact words.

INDIRECT QUESTION　Mae asked me if I could stay.

RULE 25.1.4 Use a period after most **abbreviations** and **initials.**

ABBREVIATIONS　Gov.　Mrs.　Rd.　in.　Jr.

INITIALS　E. B. White　Robin F. Brancato

Note: The abbreviation for *inch, in.,* is the only measurement abbreviation that uses a period after it.

552　**Punctuation**

Quick-Write Extension

To help students synthesize and apply what they have learned about using periods, have them write short paragraphs recruiting other students to join imaginary clubs. Working in pairs, students should make up a club and create an acronym for it; for example, *Kids Always Love Sports,* or *KALS.* One student in each pair should be the president, and the other student should be the vice-president. Pairs should then write a short paragraph describing the club and asking other students to join. When they write, students should refer to themselves by their initials, for example, *P. A. Smith,* for *Peggy Ann Smith.*

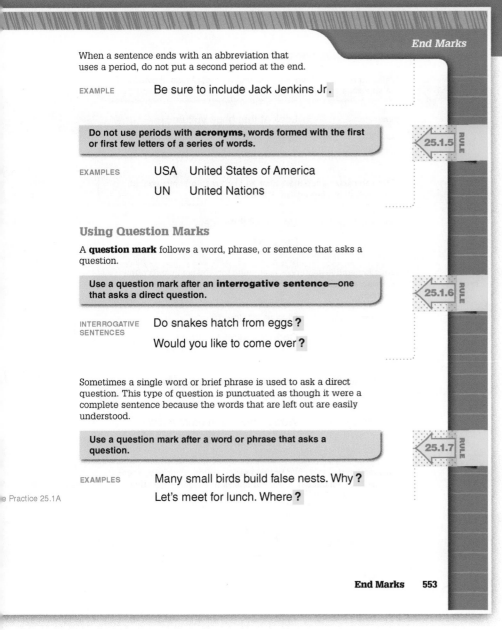

When a sentence ends with an abbreviation that uses a period, do not put a second period at the end.

EXAMPLE   Be sure to include Jack Jenkins Jr.

| Do not use periods with **acronyms**, words formed with the first or first few letters of a series of words. | **25.1.5** RULE |

EXAMPLES   USA   United States of America

UN   United Nations

Using Question Marks

A **question mark** follows a word, phrase, or sentence that asks a question.

| Use a question mark after an **interrogative sentence**—one that asks a direct question. | **25.1.6** RULE |

INTERROGATIVE SENTENCES

Do snakes hatch from eggs?

Would you like to come over?

Sometimes a single word or brief phrase is used to ask a direct question. This type of question is punctuated as though it were a complete sentence because the words that are left out are easily understood.

| Use a question mark after a word or phrase that asks a question. | **25.1.7** RULE |

EXAMPLES   Many small birds build false nests. Why?

Let's meet for lunch. Where?

e Practice 25.1A

End Marks   553

Remind students that it is generally incorrect to have two of the same marks of punctuation in a row. Thus, when a sentence ends with an abbreviation that uses a period, it is not necessary to add a second period to end the sentence. Study the example on page 553.

RULE 25.1.5 Read aloud the rule and then have students repeat the lines with you.

Remind students that acronyms—short expressions consisting of capital letters that stand for a phrase—do not have periods. Remind students that if they are unsure whether a group of letters is an acronym or what an acronym stands for, they can find the answer in an unabridged dictionary.

Using Question Marks

Point out that a question mark is used at the end of a sentence that asks a question.

RULES 25.1.6, 25.1.7 Read aloud the rules and then have students repeat the lines with you.

Work with students to identify which of these sentences and phrases require a question mark: *I studied for the test.* (This sentence requires a period. It is a statement of fact, not a question.) *When did you study for the test?* (This sentence requires a question mark. It asks a direct question.) *I asked my friend when I should study for the test.* This sentence asks an indirect question. Therefore, it does not require a question mark. *How come?* (This phrase requires a question mark. The phrase asks a question.) *What for?* (This phrase requires a question mark. The phrase asks a question.)

Teacher Tip

If students need practice identifying questions, have student pairs take turns interviewing each other about their favorite activity. For example, *What is your favorite activity? Why do you like it?* Encourage students to pepper their interviews with single-word follow-up questions, such as *Why? How? When?*

Working with ELLs   **ELL** Sheltered Instruction: Cognitive

On page 552, help students identify the difference between declarative, imperative, and interrogative sentences by distinguishing intonation patterns of English with increasing ease.

Beginning Write a declarative sentence, an imperative sentence, and an interrogative sentence on the board, and then read them aloud to students, emphasizing correct intonation (e.g., raising your pitch at the end of a yes/no question). Have students repeat the sentences after you, mimicking your intonation.

Intermediate Model correct intonation as in the Beginning activity. Then, have partners find examples of declarative, imperative, and interrogative sentences in a familiar selection. Have them read the

sentences aloud, correcting each other's intonation as needed.

Advanced Have students work individually to find examples of declarative, imperative, and interrogative sentences in a familiar selection. Then, have students read their sentences aloud to their partner without identifying the type of sentence. Ask listeners to tell the sentence type and the correct end mark, based on the partner's intonation.

Advanced High Challenge students to write their own declarative, imperative, and interrogative sentences. Have them speak these sentences to their partners, using correct intonation. Partners should copy the sentences down, using correct end punctuation.

Using Exclamation Marks

Point out that exclamation marks indicate strong emotion and forceful or urgent commands.

RULE 25.1.8 Read aloud the rule and then have students repeat the lines with you.

Explain that sentences that express surprise, anger, or other strong emotions end with an exclamation mark. Give these examples: *Oh, golly! That's amazing! Ouch! You are in so much trouble!* Call for a student volunteer to read aloud each example with feeling.

RULE 25.1.9 Read aloud the rule and then have students repeat the lines with you.

Remind students that imperative sentences give commands. Point out that in some languages, it is customary to end all or most imperative sentences with an exclamation mark. In English, however, the exclamation mark is used to end only those imperatives that give forceful or urgent commands. Discuss the examples on page 554.

RULE 25.1.10 Read aloud the rule and then have students repeat the lines with you.

Say: Overusing exclamation marks reduces their effectiveness and can even have a comic effect. Write this on the board: *Oh, dear! I forgot my umbrella! It's raining outside! I will get wet on my way to work! That will be really uncomfortable!* **Ask:** What is the effect of so many exclamation marks? (Using so many exclamation marks detracts from the sentences that really are exclamations.) Replace all of the exclamation marks except *Oh, dear!* with periods. Read the paragraph aloud, using your voice to emphasize the exclamatory statement. **Ask:** How does using fewer exclamation marks make the writing more effective? (**Possible responses:** It allows the real exclamations to stand out; it gives the writing more variety.)

Using Exclamation Marks

RULE 25.1.8 — Use an **exclamation mark** to end a word, phrase, or sentence that shows strong emotion.

EXAMPLES

Look at that huge vulture !

Watch out !

RULE 25.1.9 — Use an exclamation mark after an **imperative** sentence that gives a forceful or urgent command.

IMPERATIVE SENTENCE

Don't spill the water !

Let's go !

While imperative sentences containing forceful commands often end with an exclamation mark, mild imperatives should end with a period.

MILD IMPERATIVES

Please sit down .

Go to the store for me tomorrow .

RULE 25.1.10 — Use an exclamation mark after an **interjection** that expresses strong emotion.

INTERJECTIONS

Wow ! That was a great throw.

Oh ! Look what I found.

Exclamation marks should not be used too often. Overusing them reduces their emotional effect and makes writing less effective.

See Practice 25.1B

554   Punctuation

Working with ELLs   ELL Sheltered Instruction: Cognitive

Help students use visual and contextual support to read, to enhance and confirm understanding, and to develop vocabulary needed to comprehend increasingly challenging language.

Beginning Write the word *emotion* from rule 25.1.8 on the board. Read it aloud as students echo. Then, use facial expressions, mime, and other visual support to portray various emotions. Work with students to name each emotion. After your presentation of each, repeat the word *emotion* and guide students to understand that it names feelings generally. Then, read and discuss rule 25.1.8.

Intermediate Obtain images illustrating each of these words from page 554: *emotion, forceful, urgent,* and *mild.*

Write each word on the board. Read each aloud as students echo, and use facial expressions, mime, and the images you have provided to illustrate its meaning. Then, guide students in reading the page.

Advanced Introduce the words *emotion, forceful, urgent,* and *mild* from page 554, using visual support as in the Intermediate activity. Have students use each word in a sentence. Then, have partners read the page together, referring to the visual support to enhance and confirm meaning.

Advanced High Have students complete the Advanced activity, reading the page independently.

PRACTICE 25.1A Using Question Marks and Periods

Read the sentences. Rewrite each sentence, adding missing question marks and periods.

EXAMPLE Dr Smith checked my heart rate
ANSWER *Dr. Smith checked my heart rate.*

1. Mrs Cohen lives at 14 Maple Rd
2. Have you read anything by C S Lewis
3. Molly asked if I had 18 in of string
4. Has Mr Martinez arrived yet
5. Mrs Jones lives across the street
6. He lives at 20 Elm St
7. I need to practice before the game
8. We read about Dr Martin Luther King Jr
9. Where are they going on vacation
10. Did Mr Nguyen receive his package

PRACTICE 25.1B Using Exclamation Marks and Periods

Read the sentences. Rewrite each sentence, adding missing exclamation marks and periods.

EXAMPLE Clean your room
ANSWER *Clean your room!*

11. Please turn to page five
12. Wow That was a good catch
13. Dr Amir's house is so large
14. J R R Tolkien wrote *The Hobbit*
15. That's terrible
16. Oh I didn't know you were here
17. Watch out
18. I walked from 12 Oak St to 12 Central Rd
19. Hey I'd like some privacy, please
20. They were amazing

SPEAKING APPLICATION

With a partner, read the following sentences aloud. Use your voices to show how the different punctuation changes meaning. *Close the door. Close the door! Bring it here. Bring it here!* Discuss what the exclamation mark adds to the sentences.

WRITING APPLICATION

Write three or four sentences about working in the kitchen. Use a question mark in one, a period in another, and an exclamation mark in another.

PRACTICE 25.1A

1. Mrs. Cohen lives at 14 Maple Rd.
2. Have you read anything by C. S. Lewis?
3. Molly asked if I had 18 in. of string.
4. Has Mr. Martinez arrived yet?
5. Mrs. Jones lives across the street.
6. He lives at 20 Elm St.
7. I need to practice before the game.
8. We read about Dr. Martin Luther King Jr.
9. Where are they going on vacation?
10. Did Mr. Nguyen receive his package?

PRACTICE 25.1B

11. Please turn to page five.
12. Wow! That was a good catch.
13. Dr. Amir's house is so large!
14. J.R.R. Tolkien wrote *The Hobbit*.
15. That's terrible!
16. Oh! I didn't know you were here.
17. Watch out!
18. I walked from 12 Oak St. to 12 Central Rd.
19. Hey! I'd like some privacy, please.
20. They were amazing!

SPEAKING APPLICATION

Have students explain what they did to their voices to express an exclamation mark.

WRITING APPLICATION

Have students explain their placement of end punctuation.

Lesson Objectives

1. Use punctuation marks including commas after introductory words, phrases, and clauses.

2. Use commas correctly in writing.

Using Commas in Compound Sentences

Point out that, because misused commas can obscure meaning, it is important to learn how to use commas correctly.

RULE 25.2.1 Read aloud the rule and then have students repeat the lines with you.

Use a Think Aloud as part of a gradual release progression.

Say: I know that compound sentences consist of two or more independent clauses joined by a coordinating conjunction: *and, but, for, nor, or, so,* or *yet.* Once I identify a coordinating conjunction, I look to see if it joins two independent clauses. If it does, I put a comma before the conjunction.

Work with students to identify conjunctions. For each sentence, ask: Does this conjunction join two independent clauses? Is the comma necessary? *Max drinks skim milk, and he eats a sandwich for lunch every day.* (The comma is necessary. The conjunction, *and,* joins two independent clauses.) *Charles liked to swim, but hated the beach.* (The comma is not necessary. The conjunction, *but,* does not join two independent clauses.) *Kendra sighed but she didn't give up.* (The comma before the conjunction *but* is not necessary because the independent clauses are brief.)

Have student pairs brainstorm for compound sentences and discuss how to punctuate them.

Avoiding Comma Splices

Explain that a comma splice occurs when two sentences are joined by a comma.

Find It/ FIX IT 13 Grammar Game Plan

25.2 Commas

End marks signal a full stop. **Commas** signal a brief pause. A comma may be used to separate elements in a sentence or to set off part of a sentence. Include a comma in your writing when you want your reader to group information in your sentence.

Using Commas in Compound Sentences

A **compound sentence** consists of two or more main or independent clauses that are joined by a coordinating conjunction, such as *and, but, for, nor, or, so,* or *yet.*

RULE 25.2.1

> Use a comma before the conjunction to separate two main or independent clauses in a **compound sentence.**

COMPOUND SENTENCE

Chimpanzees are full grown at age five , but their mothers still take care of them.

Use a comma before a conjunction only when there are complete sentences on both sides of the conjunction. If the conjunction joins single words, phrases, or subordinate clauses, do not use a comma.

SINGLE WORDS
Heat and sand are common desert features.

PHRASES
Teri likes both green apples and red apples.

SUBORDINATE CLAUSES
They have decided that you should study more and that they will check on you.

See Practice 25.2A
See Practice 25.2B

In some compound sentences, the main or independent clauses are very brief, and the meaning is clear. When this occurs, the comma before the conjunction may be omitted.

EXAMPLE
Jon listened carefully but he heard nothing.

Find It/ FIX IT 16 Grammar Game Plan

Avoiding Comma Splices

A **comma splice** occurs when two or more sentences have been joined with only a comma between them.

556   Punctuation

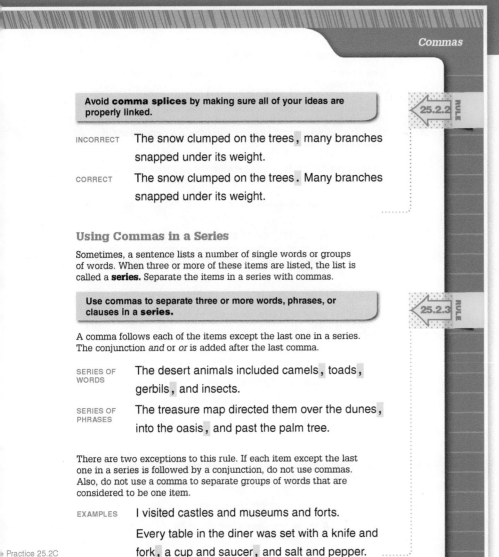

Avoid **comma splices** by making sure all of your ideas are properly linked.

25.2.2 RULE

INCORRECT The snow clumped on the trees , many branches snapped under its weight.

CORRECT The snow clumped on the trees . Many branches snapped under its weight.

Using Commas in a Series

Sometimes, a sentence lists a number of single words or groups of words. When three or more of these items are listed, the list is called a **series.** Separate the items in a series with commas.

Use commas to separate three or more words, phrases, or clauses in a **series.**

25.2.3 RULE

A comma follows each of the items except the last one in a series. The conjunction *and* or *or* is added after the last comma.

SERIES OF WORDS The desert animals included camels , toads , gerbils , and insects.

SERIES OF PHRASES The treasure map directed them over the dunes , into the oasis , and past the palm tree.

There are two exceptions to this rule. If each item except the last one in a series is followed by a conjunction, do not use commas. Also, do not use a comma to separate groups of words that are considered to be one item.

EXAMPLES I visited castles and museums and forts.

Every table in the diner was set with a knife and fork , a cup and saucer , and salt and pepper.

Practice 25.2C

Commas 557

RULE 25.2.2 Read aloud the rule and then have students repeat the lines with you.

Work with students to identify the comma splice in this sentence: *I played with the dog, I fed the cat.* Ask students how they can correct the comma splice. (Replace the comma with a period.) Then, ask them how they can turn the sentence into a compound sentence. (Insert the conjunction *and* after the comma.)

Using Commas in a Series

Explain that commas are used to separate three or more items in a row, or a series. The items may be words, phrases, or clauses.

RULE 25.2.3 Read aloud the rule and then have students repeat the lines with you.

Write this sentence on the board: *I ran to the store, bought some milk, and came quickly back home.* **Say:** When I punctuate a series, I check to see whether I have three similar items in a row. In this sentence, I see that I do. **Underline each item in the series, saying it aloud as you do.** Then, **say:** The purpose of using commas in a series is to separate the items. Therefore, I will put a comma after *ran to the store* to separate it from *bought some milk.* **Insert the comma into the sentence. Say:** I still need to separate *bought some milk* from *came quickly back home.* Therefore, I will put another comma after *bought some milk.* **Insert the comma. Say:** Notice that the series has three items and two commas. There is always one comma fewer than the number of items in the series.

Review the exceptions to the rule for punctuating series. On the board, write these sentences without commas: *I read the paper, a magazine, and a blog before starting work. Avery and Sue like to play chess.* Work with students to insert series commas where they belong.

Differentiated Instruction

RTI Strategy for Below-Level Students
On page 556, help students who are having difficulty understanding when to use commas in compound sentences. Have student pairs write several independent clauses. Work with students to identify the subject and verb in each clause. Remind students that a compound sentence is two clauses joined by a coordinating conjunction (*and, but, for, nor, or, so, yet*). Challenge student pairs to create compound sentences from their independent clauses.

PRE-AP Enrichment for Above-Level Students Remind students that a subordinate clause is not a complete sentence even though it contains a subject and a verb. A comma is not used before a subordinating conjunction, such as *after, although, until, because,* or *when.* Write this example on the board: *Georgio slept until his alarm went off.* Have students identify the subordinate clause. Challenge student pairs to learn five additional subordinating conjunctions and to use these words to make five sentences.

Using Commas Between Adjectives

Point out that commas are sometimes used between two or more adjectives in a sentence.

RULES 25.2.4, 25.2.5, 25.2.6 Read aloud the rules and then have students repeat the lines with you.

Use a Think Aloud as part of a gradual release progression.

Say: I will use a comma between adjectives if the adjectives are of equal rank; that is, if I can place *and* between them or change their order and have the sentence still make sense. Otherwise, I will not use a comma.

Write these sentences on the board without commas. *Hermon walked through the still, green forest. I will have a long restful nap this afternoon. Josie drank the cold, crisp, clear water from the stream.* **Work with students** to determine where to place commas in the sentences.

Have student pairs brainstorm for and write sentences with coordinate adjectives. Students should use the example that illustrates Rule 25.2.4 as a model. Invite students to read their sentences aloud to the group. As students listen, they should identify where the commas should be placed.

Teacher Tip

If students need more practice using commas between adjectives, have student pairs create a sentence that uses two or more adjectives to describe an item in the classroom. For example, *I am sitting on a hard, orange chair.* Use student sentences to review the rules for using commas between adjectives.

Using Commas Between Adjectives

Sometimes, two or more adjectives are placed before the noun they describe.

Use commas to separate adjectives of equal rank.

There are two ways to tell whether adjectives in a sentence are of equal rank:

- If the word *and* can be placed between the adjectives without changing the meaning, the adjectives are of equal rank.

- If the order of the adjectives can be changed, they are of equal rank.

EXAMPLE A smooth, round stone was cupped in her hand.
(*A smooth and round stone* does not change the sentence's meaning. *A round, smooth stone* also does not change the meaning.)

Do not use commas to separate adjectives that must appear in a specific order.

Do not use a comma if adding *and* or changing the order of the adjectives would result in a sentence that makes no sense.

INCORRECT It will take three and brief hours to reach the park.

INCORRECT It will take brief three hours to reach the park.

CORRECT It will take three brief hours to reach the park.

Do not use a comma to separate the last adjective in a series from the noun it modifies.

INCORRECT A large, gentle, camel stood by the road.

CORRECT A large, gentle camel stood by the road.

See Practice 25.2D

Working with ELLs **ELL** Sheltered Instruction: Cognitive

As students read page 558, enhance comprehension of written text by having them use prereading supports. Introduce the topic of adjectives of equal rank by having students generate examples in a word web. First, have students choose a favorite movie. Then:

Beginning Write on the board adjectives that might describe the movie. Guide students in filling out a word web with the adjectives. Then, have them select pairs of adjectives. For each pair, write a sentence on the board in which you use the adjectives before a noun. Then, read page 558 with students, referring to their examples.

Intermediate Guide small groups in filling out a word web with adjectives for the movie. Then, have them write sentences about the movie in which they use pairs of adjectives before a noun. Read page 558 with students, drawing on their examples.

Advanced Have partners fill out a word web with adjectives for the movie. Then, have them write sentences about the movie in which they use pairs of adjectives before a noun. Have them read the lesson and correct their sentences as needed.

Advanced High Have students complete the Advanced activity, using adjectives in a series in their sentences as well as pairs of adjectives.

PRACTICE 25.2A Using Commas in Compound Sentences

Read the sentences. Rewrite each compound sentence, adding commas where they are needed.

EXAMPLE   Julie will meet us at the field and she will bring the soccer ball.

ANSWER   *Julie will meet us at the field, and she will bring the soccer ball.*

I don't know how to skate but I can learn.

Angela wants to go to the store but she has to stay home.

Mom and Dad fixed dinner and my sister and I washed the dishes.

We will have to get up at dawn for we must start early.

Joseph won't be here Monday nor will he be here Tuesday.

Tony and Chen went to a movie but Michelle went to a concert.

You could paint the fence now or you could wait until later.

I wanted to go yet something held me back.

I have to do my work so I'll see you later.

We need to fix this bike or I won't be in the race.

PRACTICE 25.2B Writing Compound Sentences Using Commas

Read the sentences. Combine the two simple sentences to create a compound sentence. Use a comma and the coordinating conjunction in parentheses.

EXAMPLE   The dogs are playing in the yard. The cat is asleep near the fire. (and)

ANSWER   *The dogs are playing in the yard, and the cat is asleep near the fire.*

11. Zoey wanted to have pizza. Gabrielle wanted ravioli. (but)

12. Exercise is an important factor in good health. Nutrition is also important. (and)

13. Sean is quarterback on the team. His brother is the punter. (and)

14. Mrs. Spencer won't eat meat. She is a vegetarian. (for)

15. It may have been a great car once. Now it is rusty and old. (but)

16. I registered for the art class. Charlotte registered, too. (so)

17. The speaker was nervous. Maybe he was afraid. (or)

18. The mail came. I got the letter. (so)

19. Kyle skipped pracrice. He forgot to go. (or)

20. Kevin wanted to buy a computer. Something changed his mind. (yet)

PRACTICE 25.2A

1. I don't know how to skate, but I can learn.

2. Angela wants to go to the store, but she has to stay home.

3. Mom and Dad fixed dinner, and my sister and I washed the dishes.

4. We will have to get up at dawn, for we must start early.

5. Joseph won't be here Monday, nor will he be here Tuesday.

6. Tony and Chen went to a movie, but Michelle went to a concert.

7. You could paint the fence now, or you could wait until later.

8. I wanted to go, yet something held me back.

9. I have to do my work, so I'll see you later.

10. We need to fix this bike, or I won't be in the race

PRACTICE 25.2B

11. Zoey wanted to have pizza, but Gabrielle wanted ravioli.

12. Exercise is an important factor in good health, and nutrition is also important.

13. Sean is quarterback on the team, and his brother is the punter.

14. Mrs. Spencer won't eat meat, for she is a vegetarian.

15. It may have been a great car once, but now it is rusty and old.

16. I registered for the art class, so Charlotte registered, too.

17. The speaker was nervous, or maybe he was afraid.

18. The mail came, so I got the letter.

19. Kyle skipped practice, or he forgot to go.

20. Kevin wanted to buy a computer, yet something changed his mind.

PRACTICE 25.2C

1. I had a sandwich, milk, and an apple for lunch.

2. Florence, Rome, and Venice are cities in Italy.

3. At the museum I like the mummies, dinosaurs, fossils, and old jewelry.

4. I wrote the letter, folded it, and mailed it.

5. Mom could not decide whether she wanted pears, peaches, or grapes.

6. Justin prepared the soil, planted the seeds, and watered the garden.

7. The menu offered macaroni and cheese, salad, and spaghetti with meatballs.

8. Our dog ran across the lawn, through the gate, and into the street.

9. My sister used flowers, grasses, and ferns in the arrangement.

10. This year I'm taking math, Spanish, English, science, and history.

PRACTICE 25.2D

11. Rows of healthy, tall sunflowers filled the field.

12. correct

13. Australia's wild, rugged scenery is fascinating.

14. correct

15. This wet, rich land is good for growing rice.

16. correct

17. Arizona's hot, dry climate appeals to many people.

18. The sunset offered bright, beautiful colors.

19. correct

20. The deep, cold lake looked refreshing.

PRACTICE 25.2C Using Commas in a Series

Read the sentences. Rewrite each sentence, adding commas as needed.

EXAMPLE   She looked under the desk behind the dresser and in the closet.

ANSWER   *She looked under the desk, behind the dresser, and in the closet.*

1. I had a sandwich milk and an apple for lunch.

2. Florence Rome and Venice are cities in Italy.

3. At the museum I like the mummies dinosaurs fossils and old jewelry.

4. I wrote the letter folded it and mailed it.

5. Mom could not decide whether she wanted pears peaches or grapes.

6. Justin prepared the soil planted the seeds and watered the garden.

7. The menu offered macaroni and cheese salad and spaghetti with meatballs.

8. Our dog ran across the lawn through the gate and into the street.

9. My sister used flowers grasses and ferns in the arrangement.

10. This year I'm taking math Spanish English science and history.

PRACTICE 25.2D Using Commas Between Adjectives

Read the sentences. Rewrite the sentences, adding commas where necessary. If no comma is needed, write *correct*.

EXAMPLE   That large heavy book is an atlas

ANSWER   *That large, heavy book is an atlas.*

11. Rows of healthy tall sunflowers filled the field.

12. The little Boston terrier ran up to the fence.

13. Australia's wild rugged scenery is fascinating.

14. I need a small gift box.

15. This wet rich land is good for growing rice.

16. The new music teacher seems very young.

17. Arizona's hot dry climate appeals to many people.

18. The sunset offered bright beautiful colors.

19. There are just four short blocks until we reach home.

20. The deep cold lake looked refreshing.

SPEAKING APPLICATION

With a partner, pick two sentences from Practice 25.2D that needed to be fixed and two that were correct. Read the sentences aloud, reversing the order of the adjectives. Talk about how you can tell when a group of adjectives doesn't need commas.

WRITING APPLICATION

Write a brief description of someplace you have visited. Include at least two different instances in which commas are needed, such as in a compound sentence and between adjectives.

SPEAKING APPLICATION

Have students explain when a group of adjectives would need a comma and when they wouldn't.

WRITING APPLICATION

Have students explain the placement of commas in their descriptions.

Using Commas After Introductory Words, Phrases, and Clauses

When a sentence begins with an introductory word, phrase, or other structures, that word or phrase is usually separated from the rest of the sentence by a comma.

> **Use a comma after most introductory words, phrases, or dependent clauses.**

KINDS OF INTRODUCTORY MATERIAL	
Introductory Word	Hey, give me your camera quickly before the kangaroo moves.
	Pete, please bring me my shoes and socks.
	Well, I certainly didn't expect that to happen.
	Tomi, where are you?
Introductory Phrase	To conserve water, some plants drop their leaves.
	With Mark gone, Jake didn't know how he would get home.
	In the center of the city, you will see many skyscrapers.
	To visit Japan, you need a passport.
Introductory Adverbial Clause	Although the alarm had gone off, the police arrived too late.
	When the mice got into the garage, they ate the birdseed.
	When the home team entered the stadium, the crowd loudly cheered every player.

When a prepositional phrase of only two words begins a sentence, a comma is not absolutely necessary.

EXAMPLES   At night we heard the crickets.

In July we go to the lake.

For hours she patiently waited for the plane.

Practice 25.2E

Commas   561

Find It / Fix It
2
Grammar Game Plan
25.2.7
RULE

Using Commas After Introductory Words, Phrases, and Clauses

Point out that when a sentence begins with an introductory word or phrase, that word or phrase is usually followed by a comma.

RULE 25.2.7 Read aloud the rule and then have students repeat the lines with you.

Write this sentence on the board: *Before the earthquake hit, the lake was just a pond.* Read the sentence aloud, pausing for a moment after the introductory clause *Before the earthquake hit.* **Say:** When a sentence begins with an introductory word, phrase, or clause, that word, phrase, or clause is separated from the rest of the sentence by a comma. This sentence begins with an adverbial clause. I can tell because the group of words begins with a subordinating conjunction, *Before,* and contains a subject, *earthquake,* and a verb, *hit.* Underline the adverbial clause and insert a comma after *hit.*

Ask students to write three sentences that use correct punctuation marks. The first sentence should begin with an introductory word, the second with an introductory phrase, and the third with an adverbial clause. Work with students to write the first sentence, and then have students write the other sentences independently. Students should then read their sentences to a partner and discuss the effect of of correct punctuation in each sentence.

Working with ELLs   ELL Sheltered Instruction: Cognitive

On page 560, build and reinforce student attainment of concepts of comma use by having students listen to, derive meaning from, and respond orally to information presented in a wide variety of print, electronic, and audiovisual media. Make a recording of yourself reading the sentences in Practice 25.2D, pausing where commas should appear. Then:

Beginning Play the first two sentences. Repeat, having students raise their hands when they hear a pause. Explain that in writing, the pauses are represented by commas. Help students identify the words separated by pauses. Then, guide students in restating the meaning of the sentences.

Intermediate Play the first four sentences. Repeat, having students raise their hands

when they hear a pause corresponding to a comma. Discuss how the pauses help listeners follow the ideas expressed. Then, guide students in paraphrasing the sentences.

Advanced Play the recording. Repeat, having students raise their hands when they hear a pause corresponding to a comma. Discuss how the pauses help listeners follow the ideas. Then, have partners work to paraphrase the sentences.

Advanced High Have students complete the Advanced activity. Then, have students review a short video segment, noting how pauses help the speaker convey meaning.

Using Commas With Parenthetical Expressions

Remind students to use commas to set off parenthetical expressions, which are words or phrases not essential to the meaning of a sentence.

RULE 25.2.8 Read aloud the rule and then have students repeat the lines with you.

Use a Think Aloud as part of a gradual release progression.

Think Aloud

Say: Identifying a parenthetical expression in a sentence is easy. **I look for** additional information that is not essential to the meaning of the sentence. If I read aloud a sentence with a parenthetical expression, I can usually hear the pauses before and after the expression. **Write this sentence on the board:** *We all asked the new student Louis to join us for lunch.* **Read the sentence aloud, pausing before and after** *Louis.* **Say:** I know that I paused before and after *Louis.* Let me check to see whether the sentence would make sense if I omitted the word *Louis.* **Read the sentence without** *Louis.* **Say:** Yes, it does make sense. That means *Louis* is parenthetical in this sentence, and I need to set it off with commas. **Insert the commas.**

Work with students to review and understand the kinds of parenthetical expressions listed on the page.

Have student pairs generate sentences with parenthetical expressions and share their sentences with the class.

Using Commas With Nonessential Expressions

Remind students to use commas to set off words or phrases that are not essential to the meaning of a sentence.

Using Commas With Parenthetical Expressions

A **parenthetical expression** is a word or phrase that is not essential to the meaning of the sentence. These words or phrases generally add extra information to the basic sentence.

> Use commas to set off **parenthetical expressions** from the rest of the sentence.

A parenthetical expression in the middle of a sentence needs two commas. A parenthetical expression at the end of a sentence needs only one.

KINDS OF PARENTHETICAL EXPRESSIONS	
Names of People Being Addressed	Listen carefully , Lucinda , while I explain. Don't be late , Randy.
Certain Adverbs	The sand dune , therefore , is several meters higher. Your answer is incorrect , however.
Common Expressions	They believe in her ability , of course. She was not given enough credit , in my opinion.
Contrasting Expressions	The decision should be mine , not yours. These flowers , not those , are ready to be picked.

See Practice 25.2F
See Practice 25.2G

Using Commas With Nonessential Expressions

To determine when a phrase or clause should be set off with commas, decide whether the phrase or clause is **essential** or **nonessential** to the meaning of the sentence. Nonessential expressions can be left out without changing the meaning of the sentence.

562   Punctuation

> Use commas to set off **nonessential** expressions from the main clause. Do not set off **essential** material with commas.

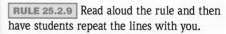

25.2.9 RULE

Appositives and Appositive Phrases

Appositives are often set off with commas, but only when their meaning is not essential to the sentence. In the first example below, the appositive *Sahara* is not set off with commas because it clarifies which movie is being discussed.

ESSENTIAL	The 1943 movie *Sahara* takes place in North Africa.
NONESSENTIAL	*Sahara*, a 1943 movie, takes place in North Africa.

Find It / FIX IT
7
Grammar
Game Plan

Participial Phrases

Like appositives, participial phrases are set off with commas when their meaning is nonessential. In the first example below, *waiting in the van* is essential because it tells which man is the guide.

ESSENTIAL	The man waiting in the van is our guide.
NONESSENTIAL	Pat, waiting in the van, asked us to hurry.

Find It / FIX IT
11
Grammar
Game Plan

Adjectival Clauses

Adjectival clauses, too, are set off with commas only if they are nonessential. In the second example below, *who could lead us to the playing field* is nonessential because it adds information about Darius. The main clause in the sentence is about people cheering, not about what Darius can do.

ESSENTIAL	We need someone who can lead us to the playing field.
NONESSENTIAL	We cheered enthusiastically for Darius, who could lead us to the playing field.

Practice 25.2H

Commas 563

RULE 25.2.9 Read aloud the rule and then have students repeat the lines with you.

Review the difference between essential and nonessential expressions and the different kinds of clauses and phrases (appositive, participial, adjectival) on the page. Point out that nonessential expressions can be left out without changing the meaning of the sentence.

Appositives and Appositive Phrases

Remind students that these phrases and clauses are essential when they are needed to identify the noun they describe. If they do not identify the noun, they are nonessential and are set off with commas.

Participial Phrases

Write this example on the board: *The woman carrying the painting ran through the museum.* Ask students whether the underlined participial phrase identifies which woman ran through the museum. Students should see that the phrase does, indeed, identify which woman. Point out that since the phrase is needed, it is essential and therefore not set off with commas.

Adjectival Clauses

Remind students that adjectival clauses are frequently introduced by the relative pronouns *who, whom, which,* or *that.* Review with students the examples of essential and nonessential adjectival clauses. Then, have students brainstorm for more examples of sentences with essential and nonessential adjectival clauses.

Have student pairs generate examples of sentences with nonessential expressions. Challenge the class to identify the appositives, participial phrases, and adjectival clauses in each sentence.

> *Teacher Tip*
>
> If students need additional practice with nonessential expressions, write a simple sentence on the board. For example, *My brother walked to the store.* Challenge students to add a nonessential expression to the sentence. For example, *My brother, who usually rides his bike, walked to the store.* Or *My brother, Jack, walked to the store.*

PRACTICE 25.2E

1. No, I do not think we have any left.

2. After you finish eating, you may go outside.

3. Jerome, are you going to the library?

4. With just two days left, we had to work faster on our project.

5. My, that was a big yawn.

6. Whether or not he is here, we are leaving.

7. Well, I'm not sure that's why he's going.

8. In the sequel to the movie, there were even more special effects.

9. Sherry, tell us about your voice lessons.

10. Even though we were late, we still got in.

PRACTICE 25.2F

When I first started this project, I thought it would last one summer. I wanted to buy beads, make necklaces, and sell them at craft fairs. Well, it was a lot of work. I bought hundreds of beads, and I began stringing them. The beads were red, blue, gold, silver, and green. Some were metal, but others were glass or stone. Although I liked all the different kinds of beads, the blue glass beads were among my favorites. I made forty necklaces that first summer, but I could have sold more. Once I started, I could not stop. It has now been three years, and I am still making and selling necklaces.

SPEAKING APPLICATION

Have students explain where they placed the comma in the example sentence and why a comma belonged there.

WRITING APPLICATION

Have students read one of their sentences aloud, pause where they placed a comma, and explain the effect of the comma on the flow and meaning of the sentence.

PRACTICE 25.2E > **Using Commas After Introductory Words, Phrases, or Clauses**

Read the sentences. Rewrite each sentence, adding the comma needed after the introductory word, phrase, or clause.

EXAMPLE   If you are done with the book put it back.

ANSWER   *If you are done with the book, put it back.*

1. No I do not think we have any left.

2. After you finish eating you may go outside.

3. Jerome are you going to the library?

4. With just two days left we had to work faster on our project.

5. My that was a big yawn.

6. Whether or not he is here we are leaving.

7. Well I'm not sure that's why he's going.

8. In the sequel to the movie there were even more special effects.

9. Sherry tell us about your voice lessons.

10. Even though we were late we still got in.

PRACTICE 25.2F > **Proofreading a Passage for Commas**

Read the paragraph. Rewrite the paragraph, adding commas where they are needed.

EXAMPLE   To earn some money during the summer I decided to make and se necklaces. Well sometimes events surprise you.

ANSWER   *To earn some money during the summer, I decided to make and necklaces. Well, sometimes eve surprise you.*

When I first started this project I thought it would last one summer. I wanted to buy bead make necklaces and sell them at craft fairs. W it was a lot of work. I bought hundreds of bea and I began stringing them. The beads were blue gold silver and green. Some were metal others were glass or stone. Although I liked a the different kinds of beads the blue glass be were among my favorites. I made forty neckla that first summer but I could have sold more. Once I started I could not stop. It has now be three years and I am still making and selling necklaces.

SPEAKING APPLICATION

With a partner, read this sentence aloud: *In the new book I found a story about spiders.* **Discuss where the comma should go and why a comma would help someone reading the sentence.**

WRITING APPLICATION

Write three sentences about activities you do in school or at home. Start each sentence with an introductory word, phrase, or clause that requires a comma.

564   Punctuation

PRACTICE 25.2G ▸ Using Commas With Parenthetical Expressions

Read the sentences. Rewrite each sentence, adding commas as needed to set off parenthetical expressions.

EXAMPLE That play will be I think a success.

ANSWER *That play will be, I think, a success.*

Do you think Tyler that you would like to go?

The information however is out of date.

I wanted red not purple.

When you arrive Manny let me know.

She thinks she is right of course.

That is a blue jay not a robin.

The outcome therefore can be predicted.

Well Anita what do you think?

I wanted fruit not yogurt.

You will need to clean up the mess however.

PRACTICE 25.2H ▸ Using Commas With Nonessential Expressions

Read the sentences. Rewrite the sentences, adding commas where necessary. If a sentence is punctuated correctly, write *correct*.

EXAMPLE My brother staring at his feet mumbled an apology.

ANSWER *My brother, staring at his feet, mumbled an apology.*

11. George Washington our first president took his oath of office on April 30, 1789.

12. The wallaby and the kangaroo carry their young in pouches.

13. Our guide standing on the hilltop waved to us to follow.

14. The phone a wonderful invention really changed communication.

15. The 1893 World's Fair was held in Chicago.

16. The Komodo dragon the world's largest lizard is found in Indonesia.

17. The man handing out papers is our teacher.

18. That table a real antique was made by my great-grandfather.

19. My sister standing on tiptoe could just reach the bottom shelf.

20. Seeing a dentist regularly is important.

SPEAKING APPLICATION

With a partner, act as if you are trying out for a play and the sentences in Practice 25.2G are your lines. Take turns reading the lines aloud. Talk about how hard it would be to read a script with no punctuation.

WRITING APPLICATION

Rewrite three of the correct sentences in Practice 25.2H so that they need commas. You may rearrange words or add words of your own so that the sentences now require commas.

Practice   565

PRACTICE 25.2G ▸

1. Do you think, Tyler, that you would like to go?

2. The information, however, is out of date.

3. I wanted red, not purple.

4. When you arrive, Manny, let me know.

5. She thinks she is right, of course.

6. That is a blue jay, not a robin.

7. The outcome, therefore, can be predicted.

8. Well, Anita, what do you think?

9. I wanted fruit, not yogurt.

10. You will need to clean up the mess, however.

PRACTICE 25.2H ▸

11. George Washington, our first president, took his oath of office on April 30, 1789.

12. correct

13. Our guide, standing on the hilltop, waved to us to follow.

14. The phone, a wonderful invention, really changed communication.

15. correct

16. The Komodo dragon, the world's largest lizard, is found in Indonesia.

17. correct

18. That table, a real antique, was made by my great-grandfather.

19. My sister, standing on tiptoe, could just reach the bottom shelf.

20. correct.

SPEAKING APPLICATION

Have students explain why lack of punctuation would make reading more difficult. What problems would they encounter?

WRITING APPLICATION

Have students read one of their sentences aloud and explain their comma placement.

Using Commas With Dates and Geographical Names

Explain to students that commas are used to separate the parts of dates that are made up of two or more parts and geographical names that are made up of two or more parts. Give this example: *My grandmother was born on Wednesday, January 14, 1895, in Lincoln, Nebraska, but she grew up in San Francisco, California.*

RULE 25.2.10 Read aloud the rule and then have students repeat the lines with you.

Use a Think Aloud as part of a gradual release progression.

 Say: When **I am writing** a date, I check to see if it has two or more parts. If the month and day come first, I put a comma before and after the year; for example, *August 17, 1954, is when my parents were married.*

Write the sentence on the board without commas. **Help students to** determine where they should insert the commas. **Ask:** Why shouldn't I put a comma between *August* and *17*? (You don't put a comma between the month and the day.)

Then, **have students write** sentences using dates with two and three parts. Have students exchange sentences with a partner and have the partner check for the correct use of commas.

RULE 25.2.11 Read aloud the rule and then have students repeat the lines with you.

Have each student use his or her address, including the name of the city and state, in a sentence. Check to make sure students have used commas correctly.

Using Commas With Dates and Geographical Names

Dates usually have several parts, including months, days, and years. Commas prevent dates from being unclear.

 RULE 25.2.10

> When a date is made up of three parts, use a comma after each item, except in the case of a month followed by a day.

Notice in the examples that commas are not used to set off a month followed by a numeral standing for a day. Commas are used when both the month and the date are used as an appositive to rename a day of the week.

EXAMPLES   On July 12 , 1979 , Aunt Mei arrived in this country with just a few possessions.

Tuesday , March 18 , was carefully circled on his calendar.

When a date contains only a month and a year, commas are unnecessary.

EXAMPLES   I will graduate in June 2010.

Most of the storms we experienced in March 2011 dropped a lot of snow.

 RULE 25.2.11

> When a geographical name is made up of a city and a state, use a comma after each item.

EXAMPLES   They lived in Marietta , Georgia , for several years and then moved to Sarasota , Florida.

Mari went to Santa Fe , New Mexico , to visit the many art galleries in the area.

See Practice 25.2I

566   Punctuation

Working with ELLs   ELL Sheltered Instruction: Cognitive

Help students demonstrate comprehension of increasingly complex English by taking notes about what they read.

Beginning Preteach these words from the student page, writing them on the board: *date, parts, item, month, year,* and *day.* Read Rule 25.2.10 aloud as students follow along. Then, read the examples for the rule with them, clarifying meaning. Read the text again, this time asking students to jot down single words and brief phrases to record the main ideas. Encourage them also to include labeled examples.

Intermediate Guide volunteers in reading aloud from the first half of page 566. Have students request clarification of unfamiliar terms or concepts. Then, have students in

small groups reread the selection, taking notes. Have students compare notes, adding to or correcting them as warranted.

Advanced Have partners read page 566 together, taking notes and asking for clarification as needed. Then, have them write sentences that tell when and where they were born, referring to their notes to ensure correct comma placement. Have partners check each other's work.

Advanced High Have students complete the Advanced activity. Then, have them write three sentences illustrating each concept on the page, referring to their notes.

Using Commas in Numbers

Numbers of one hundred or less and numbers made up of two words (for example, *three thousand*) are generally spelled out in words. Other large numbers (for example, 8,463) are written in numerals. Commas make large numbers easier to read.

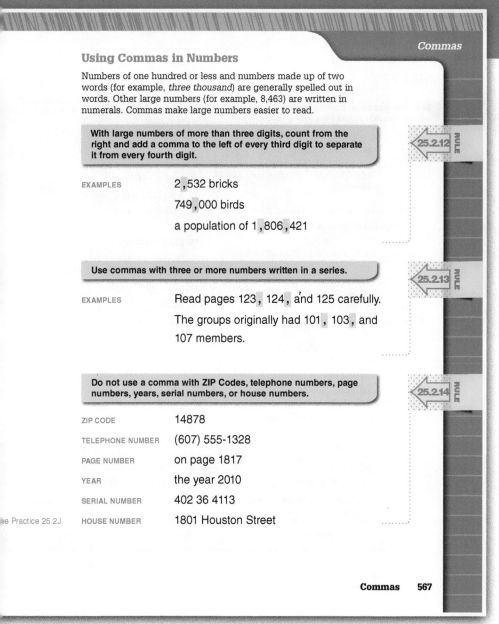

With large numbers of more than three digits, count from the right and add a comma to the left of every third digit to separate it from every fourth digit.

25.2.12 RULE

EXAMPLES

2,532 bricks

749,000 birds

a population of 1,806,421

Use commas with three or more numbers written in a series.

25.2.13 RULE

EXAMPLES

Read pages 123, 124, and 125 carefully.

The groups originally had 101, 103, and 107 members.

Do not use a comma with ZIP Codes, telephone numbers, page numbers, years, serial numbers, or house numbers.

25.2.14 RULE

ZIP CODE	14878
TELEPHONE NUMBER	(607) 555-1328
PAGE NUMBER	on page 1817
YEAR	the year 2010
SERIAL NUMBER	402 36 4113
HOUSE NUMBER	1801 Houston Street

e Practice 25.2J

Commas   567

Using Commas in Numbers

Point out that commas make large numbers easier to read, though some large numbers, such as zip codes and serial numbers, do not require commas.

RULES 25.2.12, 25.2.13, 25.2.14 Read aloud the rules and then have students repeat the lines with you.

Help the class multiply the number of students in the class by 100,000. Write this number on the board, and ask the class where to insert a comma.

Have student pairs multiply the number of students in the school by 1,000. Check to make sure they have inserted the comma(s) in the correct place. Estimate the number of students in the class, the grade, and the school. Then, write this sentence on the board, filling in the numbers that you estimated: *The number of students in the class, grade, and school is xx xx and xx.* Have students determine where the commas belong.

Review with students the types of numbers that do not require commas.

Teacher Tip

Challenge student pairs to generate a sentence that contains three or more large numbers of more than three digits each. For an extra challenge, encourage students to include at least one zip code, telephone number, page number, year, serial number, or house number in their sentence. Invite pairs to share their sentences with the class.

Differentiated Instruction

Strategy for Spanish Speakers

Students whose home language is Spanish may not know about the use of the comma in writing large numbers in English. In many Spanish-speaking countries, periods are used instead of commas. Remind students that in English, the comma is used to separate the hundreds from the thousands, the hundred thousands from the millions, and the hundred millions from the billions, and so on. Have students practice placing commas in numbers. On the board, write a series of large numbers without commas and have students copy the numbers on their own papers and insert commas where they belong. Alternately, have volunteers write large numbers on the board as they would write them in Spanish. Then, help students change the periods to commas. Have the rest of the students copy the numbers off the board.

PRACTICE 25.2I

1. Friday, March 12, is the date of our meeting.

2. St. Augustine, Florida, is the oldest city in the United States.

3. Mr. and Mrs. Sanchez were married on November 12, 1988.

4. We visited Philadelphia, Pennsylvania.

5. On July 20, 1969, American astronauts first set foot on the moon.

6. We met on Tuesday, November 5, in Boston, Massachusetts.

7. The Wright brothers made their historic flight on December 17, 1903.

8. Austin, Texas, was named for Stephen Austin.

9. On Wednesday, February 24, we will be moving to Denver, Colorado.

10. It is almost two thousand miles from Atlanta, Georgia, to Los Angeles, California.

PRACTICE 25.2J

11. 2,142 hours

12. a population of 4,709,875

13. correct

14. 1,945,580 seconds

15. correct

16. 295,943 minutes

17. 24,321 days

18. correct

19. 397,000 trees

20. correct

PRACTICE 25.2I **Using Commas in Dates and Geographical Names**

Read the sentences. Rewrite each sentence, adding commas where they are needed.

EXAMPLE   On June 21 1788 the United States Constitution went into effect.

ANSWER   *On June 21, 1788, the United States Constitution went into effect.*

1. Friday March 12 is the date of our meeting.

2. St. Augustine Florida is the oldest city in the United States.

3. Mr. and Mrs. Sanchez were married on November 12 1988.

4. We visited Philadelphia Pennsylvania.

5. On July 20 1969 American astronauts first set foot on the moon.

6. We met on Tuesday November 5 in Boston Massachusetts.

7. The Wright brothers made their historic flight on December 17 1903.

8. Austin Texas was named for Stephen Austin.

9. On Wednesday February 24 we will be moving to Denver Colorado.

10. It is almost two thousand miles from Atlanta Georgia to Los Angeles California.

WRITING APPLICATION

Write three sentences with dates and place names. You may use places or dates that have meaning for you or any dates or places. Be sure to use commas correctly.

PRACTICE 25.2J **Using Commas in Numbers**

Read the items. Rewrite each item, adding commas where needed. If no commas are needed write *correct*.

EXAMPLE   1874 miles

ANSWER   *1,874 miles*

11. 2142 hours

12. a population of 4709875

13. 1629 West Street

14. 1945580 seconds

15. ZIP Code 07960

16. 295943 minutes

17. 24321 days

18. page 1024

19. 397000 trees

20. the year 1993

WRITING APPLICATION

Write one sentence that contains a number that requires a comma. Then, write one sentence with a number that does not require a comma.

568   Punctuation

WRITING APPLICATION

Have students explain the comma placement in their sentences.

WRITING APPLICATION

Have students explain the difference between the two numbers and why they used commas differently in each.

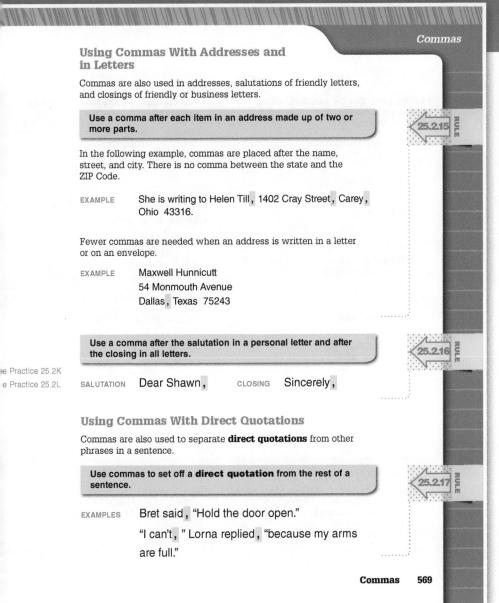

Using Commas With Addresses and in Letters

Commas are also used in addresses, salutations of friendly letters, and closings of friendly or business letters.

> **Use a comma after each item in an address made up of two or more parts.**

25.2.15 RULE

In the following example, commas are placed after the name, street, and city. There is no comma between the state and the ZIP Code.

EXAMPLE   She is writing to Helen Till , 1402 Cray Street , Carey , Ohio 43316.

Fewer commas are needed when an address is written in a letter or on an envelope.

EXAMPLE   Maxwell Hunnicutt
54 Monmouth Avenue
Dallas , Texas 75243

> **Use a comma after the salutation in a personal letter and after the closing in all letters.**

25.2.16 RULE

e Practice 25.2K
e Practice 25.2L

SALUTATION   Dear Shawn ,   CLOSING   Sincerely ,

Using Commas With Direct Quotations

Commas are also used to separate **direct quotations** from other phrases in a sentence.

> **Use commas to set off a direct quotation from the rest of a sentence.**

25.2.17 RULE

EXAMPLES   Bret said , "Hold the door open."

"I can't , " Lorna replied , "because my arms are full."

Commas   **569**

Using Commas With Addresses and in Letters

Point out that commas are used in addresses, some salutations, and the closings of letters.

RULES 25.2.15, 25.2.16 Read aloud the rules and then have students repeat the lines with you.

Say: When I write a friendly letter, I put a comma after the salutation, which is the greeting at the beginning of the letter, such as *Dear Auntie Gloria,* and after the closing. When I address the letter, I put a comma between the city and state.

Work with students to demonstrate inserting a comma after a salutation, such as *Dear Mr. Gomez,* and a closing, such as *Best regards, Nathan.*

Have student pairs write and address a letter to each other. Check to make sure the commas are correctly placed.

Using Commas With Direct Quotations

Explain that commas are used with direct quotations in a sentence to separate someone's exact words from the rest of the sentence.

RULE 25.2.17 Read aloud the rule and then have students repeat the lines with you.

Write these sentences on the board without commas. *Marissa said, "My homework was so easy, I finished it in ten minutes." "Now I know we got different assignments," DeeDee replied, "because mine took me an hour."* Work with students to insert the commas.

> *Teacher Tip*
>
> Some students may feel overwhelmed by the number of comma rules they have learned by the end of the lesson. Provide students with a Cluster Diagram with *Comma Uses* written in the center circle. Work with students to fill in the outer circles with reasons to use commas (e.g., in compound sentences, in a series, between equal adjectives). Students may create more circles as needed. Encourage students to include an example of each rule. Students should refer to this diagram as needed.

Working with ELLs   **ELL** Sheltered Instruction: Cognitive

Help students comprehend English vocabulary used routinely in written classroom materials. On the board, write these routine words from the directions on page 568: *sentences, adding, needed, if,* and *correct.* Then:

Beginning Read each word aloud as students follow along and echo. Use gestures and visuals to explain each. For example, you might draw branching paths labeled *Yes* and *No* to illustrate *if.* Then, direct students to reread each word chorally and mime its meaning or point to the correct visual. Finally, **echo-read** the sentence in which each word appears on the student page and clarify meaning.

Intermediate Present and explain each word as in the Beginning activity. Then,

have small groups read and discuss the directions. Meet with groups, and have them share their understanding of the directions as well as their questions.

Advanced Present the words, and ask volunteers to explain the meaning of each. Then, have partners read and discuss the directions. Have them present their interpretations and questions.

Advanced High Have students complete the Advanced activity. Then, challenge students to rewrite the directions for Practice 25.2l and have their partner complete the first item following the revised directions.

T569

PRACTICE 25.2K

1. correct

2. With love,

3. Dear Janice,

4. correct

5. Yours truly,

6. He is writing to Ellen Green, 1219 Main Street, Wheeling, Illinois 60090.

7. Dearest Daddy,

8. Sincerely,

9. correct

10. James Paige
    479 Ashton Court
    Richmond, VA 23173

PRACTICE 25.2L

Mr. Xavier Martinez Jr.

48 Felton Way

Houston, Texas 77020

October 16, 2010

Dear Mr. Martinez,

Thank you for the pens, markers, ribbons, and glue. They were exactly what I needed, and now I can start my project. Mr. Smith, my art teacher, loves my ideas for the project. Thanks to you, I shall be able to do it right.

Your friend,

Carlos

SPEAKING APPLICATION

Have students tell which salutations should be followed by a comma.

WRITING APPLICATION

Have students explain the difference in punctuation between an address written in a sentence and an address written on an envelope. They should also explain why different punctuation is needed in each case.

PRACTICE 25.2K ▶ **Using Commas in Addresses and Letters**

Read the items. Rewrite each item, adding commas where needed. If no commas are needed, write *correct*.

EXAMPLE Dear Grandmother

ANSWER *Dear Grandmother,*

1. 52 Hampton Road

2. With love

3. Dear Janice

4. Santa Barbara, California 93103

5. Yours truly

6. He is writing to Ellen Green 1219 Main Street Wheeling Illinois 60090.

7. Dearest Daddy

8. Sincerely

9. 846 Howland Drive

10. James Paige
    479 Ashton Court
    Richmond VA 23173

PRACTICE 25.2L ▶ **Revising a Letter by Adding Commas**

Read the letter. Rewrite the letter, adding commas where necessary.

EXAMPLE I like to use pencils pens and markers when I draw.

ANSWER *I like to use pencils, pens, and markers when I draw.*

Mr. Xavier Martinez Jr.
48 Felton Way
Houston Texas 77020

October 16 2010

Dear Mr. Martinez

Thank you for the pens markers ribbons and glue. They were exactly what I needed and now I can start my project. Mr. Smith my art teacher loves my ideas for the project. Thanks to you I shall be able to do it right.

Your friend

Carlos

SPEAKING APPLICATION

With a partner, talk about the people to whom you might write a personal letter. Look at the examples in Practice 25.2K, and come up with some salutations of your own—ones that would be followed by a comma.

WRITING APPLICATION

Write a sentence that includes your full address, using proper punctuation. Then, write your address as if you were addressing an envelope.

Working with ELLs   ELL Sheltered Instruction: Cognitive

Help students use linguistic support to enhance and confirm their understanding of increasingly complex spoken language. Present a text orally, reading aloud the letter in Practice 25.2L or a letter of your choosing. Provide linguistic support as follows.

Beginning Read each sentence aloud. Provide linguistic support by explaining unfamiliar words in simple terms. Then, repeat your reading, and guide students to summarize it.

Intermediate Provide students with vocabulary cards explaining words in the letter. Review each card. Then, read the letter aloud, pausing after each sentence featuring a vocabulary word. Ask students which word they have heard. Have them

review the appropriate card, and discuss the meaning of the sentence. Then, read the letter a second time, and guide students in summarizing it.

Advanced Read the letter aloud to students, directing them to note parts they do not understand. Discuss, identifying unfamiliar words. Have partners use the linguistic support of a dictionary to determine the meaning of each. Then, reread the letter, and have students summarize.

Advanced High Have students complete the Advanced activity. Then, have partners write and read aloud brief letters of their own. Partners should summarize.

25.3 Semicolons and Colons

The **semicolon (;)** joins related **independent clauses** and signals a longer pause than a comma. The **colon (:)** is used to introduce lists of items and in other special situations.

Using Semicolons to Join Independent Clauses

Sometimes two **independent clauses** are so closely connected in meaning that they make up a single sentence, rather than two separate sentences.

> **Use a semicolon** to join related **independent clauses** that are not joined by the conjunctions *and, or, nor, for, but, so,* or *yet.*

 25.3.1 **RULE**

INDEPENDENT CLAUSES	The fire began with a tossed match. Jamestown was burned in 1676.
CLAUSES JOINED BY SEMICOLONS	The fire began with a tossed match **;** all of Jamestown began to burn.

A semicolon should be used only when there is a close relationship between the two independent clauses. If the clauses are not very closely related, they should be written as separate sentences with a period or another end mark to separate them or joined with a coordinating conjunction.

Note that when a sentence contains three or more related independent clauses, they may still be separated with semicolons.

EXAMPLES	The birds vanished **;** the sky grew dark **;** the little pond was still. Marie won the backstroke events **;** Tamara won the freestyle events **;** Jana won the butterfly.

Semicolons and Colons　　**571**

Teacher Tip

Clip a number of individual sentences out of a magazine, snipping off the end marks. Organize students into pairs, and distribute several sentences to each pair. Have student pairs work together to brainstorm for a related independent clause for each sentence and to rewrite the independent clauses as one sentence. Have student pairs share their new sentences with the class. For each sentence, ask students to identify the independent clauses and insert the semicolon in the correct place.

Lesson Objectives

1. Use punctuation marks, including semicolons and colons, correctly in writing.

Using Semicolons to Join Independent Clauses

Point out that a semicolon looks like a comma with a period on top of it because it signals a longer pause than a comma. One use of a semicolon is to connect independent clauses when the clauses are closely related.

RULE 25.3.1 Read aloud the rule and then have students repeat the lines with you.

Use a Think Aloud as part of a gradual release progression.

Think Aloud

Say: I use a semicolon to join independent clauses, or simple sentences, that are closely related. For example, *Javier likes to read mysteries; Victor likes to read science fiction.* These independent clauses are closely related because they are about the same topic—what both Javier and Victor like to read. It is important to remember that independent clauses that are not closely related should be separated by a period. For example, *Javier likes to read mysteries; Victor goes to the movies a lot.* These independent clauses are not closely related because they are about two different topics—what Javier likes to read and what Victor does.

Write these two independent clauses on the board: *Vera likes swimming Natalie likes volleyball.* **Work with students** to use a semicolon to join these two independent clauses.

Have student pairs generate sentences that contain closely related independent clauses and correctly use semicolons to join the clauses. Invite students to share their sentences with the class.

Using Semicolons to Join Clauses Separated by Conjunctive Adverbs or Transitional Expressions

Explain to students that semicolons help writers show how their ideas connect.

RULE 25.3.2 Read aloud the rule and then have students repeat the lines with you.

Write this on the board: *I forgot to set the timer; as a result, I burned my dinner last night.*

Ask: What is the relationship between the two independent clauses? (**Response:** There is a cause-and-effect relationship. You burned your dinner because you forgot to set the timer.) **Say:** The transitional expression *as a result* connects descriptions of two events and informs us that the events have a cause-and-effect relationship. A semicolon is used before transitional expressions that show the relationship between independent clauses.

Using Semicolons to Avoid Confusion

Explain that semicolons are used to separate items in a series in order to avoid confusion.

RULE 25.3.3 Read aloud the rule and then have students repeat the lines with you.

Have student pairs use semicolons to separate items in a series that already contain commas. Students should be able to explain their reasons for using punctuation marks.

Using Semicolons to Join Clauses Separated by Conjunctive Adverbs or Transitional Expressions

Semicolons help writers show how their ideas connect.

> Use a semicolon to join independent clauses separated by either a **conjunctive adverb** or a **transitional expression**.

CONJUNCTIVE ADVERBS
also, besides, consequently, first, furthermore, however, indeed, instead, moreover, nevertheless, otherwise, second, then, therefore, thus

TRANSITIONAL EXPRESSIONS
as a result, at this time, for instance, in fact, on the other hand, that is

EXAMPLE
We were impressed with Martin's knowledge of history ; **indeed** , he was very well informed about colonization.

Remember to place a comma after the conjunctive adverb or transitional expression. The comma sets off the conjunctive adverb or transitional expression, which acts as an introductory expression to the second clause.

Using Semicolons to Avoid Confusion

Sometimes, to avoid confusion, semicolons are used to separate items in a series.

> Consider the use of semicolons to avoid confusion when items in a series already contain commas.

Place a semicolon after all but the last complete item in a series.

EXAMPLES
The fans , cheering ; the band , playing loudly ; and the cheerleaders , yelling , helped inspire the team to play well.

Three important dates in this year are April 30 , 2011 ; May 10 , 2011 ; and June 7 , 2011.

See Practice 25.3A

572   Punctuation

Working with ELLs   **ELL** Sheltered Instruction: Cognitive

Help students use contextual support to enhance and confirm their understanding of increasingly complex spoken language, including compound sentences and elaborated series.

Beginning Preteach the words *impressed, informed,* and *colonization.* Provide contextual support by talking to students about studying and learning information about a time in history. Then, read the Example sentence for Rule 25.3.2 aloud. Guide students in using the context you have given to understand and restate the sentence.

Intermediate Present context about studying and learning information about a time in history. Have volunteers discuss if they learned about a time in history that they were interested in. Then, read aloud

the Example sentence for Rule 25.3.2, and have students work in groups to restate its meaning, applying the context.

Advanced Have students complete the Intermediate activity. Then, provide context for the first example under Rule 25.3.3 by discussing what happens at a sporting event. Read the example aloud, and have partners draw on context to restate its meaning.

Advanced High Have students complete the Advanced activity. Then, have them write three sentences using series in which items contain commas. Have partners read sentences to each other. Listeners should use the context in the sentence to restate its meaning.

T572

Using Colons

The **colon (:)** is used to introduce lists of items and in certain special situations.

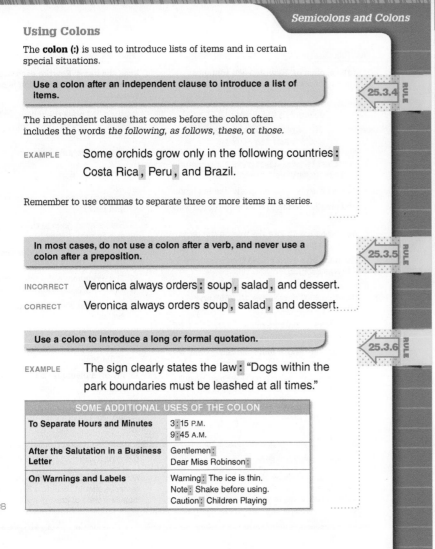

> **Use a colon after an independent clause to introduce a list of items.**
>

The independent clause that comes before the colon often includes the words *the following, as follows, these,* or *those.*

EXAMPLE   Some orchids grow only in the following countries : Costa Rica , Peru , and Brazil.

Remember to use commas to separate three or more items in a series.

> **In most cases, do not use a colon after a verb, and never use a colon after a preposition.**
>

INCORRECT   Veronica always orders : soup , salad , and dessert.

CORRECT   Veronica always orders soup , salad , and dessert.

> **Use a colon to introduce a long or formal quotation.**
>

EXAMPLE   The sign clearly states the law : "Dogs within the park boundaries must be leashed at all times."

SOME ADDITIONAL USES OF THE COLON	
To Separate Hours and Minutes	3 : 15 P.M. 9 : 45 A.M.
After the Salutation in a Business Letter	Gentlemen : Dear Miss Robinson :
On Warnings and Labels	Warning : The ice is thin. Note : Shake before using. Caution : Children Playing

Practice 25.3B

Semicolons and Colons   573

Using Colons

Explain that a colon looks like a period on top of a period. It signals a longer pause than a comma. Discuss how colons are used to introduce lists of items and to signal a longer pause to separate certain parts of a sentence.

RULES 25.3.4, 25.3.5, 25.3.6 Read aloud the rules and then have students repeat the lines with you.

Write these two sentence on the board: *The sign by the road read: "Falling rocks ahead." My alarm went off at 6:30 A.M.* Have a student come to the board and underline the colons in each sentence. **Say:** Colons are used in certain situations. Colons can be used to introduce warnings, like *"Falling rocks ahead,"* or to introduce long or formal quotations. Colons can also be used to separate hours and minutes. Write this sentence on the board: *I need to buy a few things for school: a binder, paper, and some markers.* **Say:** Colons can also be used to introduce a list of items.

Have students write three sentences demonstrating that they can use colons correctly. Each sentence should use a colon in one of the ways described on page 573. Ask students to read their sentences aloud to a partner, and then discuss the purpose of the colons in each sentence.

PRACTICE 25.3A

1. night;
2. cook;
3. tired; [and] soft;
4. tree;
5. good; [and] characters;
6. March 3, 2007; September 11, 2007;
7. movie;
8. mutt; stray;
9. television;
10. started;

PRACTICE 25.3B

11. correct
12. Here's what goes in the fruit basket: peaches, apples, and grapes.
13. correct
14. The judge made the rules clear: "You must not discuss this case with anyone."
15. correct
16. Warning: Keep away from heat.
17. Mom and Dad want to get started by 9:00 A.M.
18. correct
19. Dear Sir:
20. Put these on the shopping list: milk, carrots, lettuce, bread.

SPEAKING APPLICATION

Have students explain their placement of semicolons in their sentences.

WRITING APPLICATION

Have students explain how they knew that their partner's placement of commas was correct or incorrect.

PRACTICE 25.3A ▸ Using Semicolons

Read the sentences. Rewrite each sentence, adding any necessary semicolons.

EXAMPLE   We won the game everyone celebrated the victory.

ANSWER   *We won the game; everyone celebrated the victory.*

1. I watched television last night consequently, I did not do very well on today's test.
2. My dad is a great cook I really like his food.
3. I was really tired the bed was soft I fell asleep quickly.
4. We were sorry to lose the tree on the other hand, the garden gets more sun.
5. The book was good I liked the characters the plot was exciting.
6. There were total lunar eclipses on March 3, 2007 September 11, 2007 and February 21, 2008.
7. Dad wants to watch a movie Mom wants to watch a travel program.
8. We have one dog, a mutt one cat, a stray and two birds, a canary and a parakeet.
9. There is really nothing on television besides, I need to do some work on my project.
10. The swimming race started the swimmers dove into the pool.

WRITING APPLICATION

Write three sentences about a big event you saw or heard about. Use semicolons in at least two different ways in your description of the event.

PRACTICE 25.3B ▸ Using Colons

Read the items. Rewrite each item, adding any necessary colons. If no colon is needed, write *correct*.

EXAMPLE   I need the following for school, pencils, notebooks, paper, and a ruler.

ANSWER   *I need the following for school: pencils, notebooks, paper, and a ruler.*

11. Can you bring me some bread, peanut but and milk?
12. Here's what goes in the fruit basket, peac apples, and grapes.
13. I wrote a note to Grandmother, thanking h for my birthday present.
14. The judge made the rules clear "You must discuss this case with anyone."
15. We ordered soup, salad, chicken, and potatoes.
16. Warning Keep away from heat.
17. Mom and Dad want to get started by 900 A.M.
18. I want a bike; my brother wants a scooter.
19. Dear Sir
20. Put these on the shopping list, milk, carro lettuce, bread.

WRITING APPLICATION

Write two sentences that require colons. One sentence should include a list, and one should include a time of day.

Working with ELLs   ELL Sheltered Instruction: Cognitive

To help students write using a variety of grade-appropriate connecting words to combine sentences in increasingly accurate ways, have them practice using conjunctive adverbs to combine sentences. First, review with students the conjunctive adverbs on page 572. Then:

Beginning Write a simple sentence on the board, such as *I read a book*. Then, use yes/no questions to elicit related ideas from them, such as *Did I like the book? Did I learn anything?* List ideas on the board, writing in independent clauses. Then, list conjunctive adverbs, and work with students to choose the appropriate word to combine the simple sentence with each of the new clauses. Have students write each new sentence.

Intermediate Guide partners in writing simple related sentences and combining them with conjunctive adverbs. Then, have pairs exchange papers and underline the conjunctive adverb in each other's sentences.

Advanced Have students independently write simple related sentences and combine them with conjunctive adverbs. Have students exchange papers and identify the conjunctive adverbs in each other's work.

Advanced High Have students complete the Advanced activity. Then, have them write five simple sentences about an activity and combine them with conjunctive adverbs.

25.4 Quotation Marks, Underlining, and Italics

Quotation marks (" ") set off direct quotations, dialogue, and certain types of titles. Other types of titles may be **underlined** or set in *italics*, a slanted type style.

Find It/ FIX IT
6
Grammar
Game Plan

WRITING COACH

Online

phwritingcoach.com

Grammar Practice
ice your
mar skills with
g Coach Online.

Grammar Games
your knowledge
mmar in this
aced interactive
game.

Using Quotation Marks With Quotations

Quotation marks identify the spoken or written words of others. A **direct quotation** represents a person's exact speech or thoughts. An **indirect quotation** reports the general meaning of what a person said or thought.

Both types of quotations are acceptable when you write. Direct quotations, however, generally result in a livelier writing style.

> **Direct quotations should be enclosed in quotation marks.**

25.4.1 RULE

EXAMPLES   Kate said, "Williamsburg had the first theater."

"Where is the key?" asked Caroline.

> **Indirect quotations do not require quotation marks.**

25.4.2 RULE

EXAMPLES   Margo said that she would take the dog out.

Don wondered why the president hadn't called him with the results of the election.

Using Direct Quotations With Introductory, Concluding, and Interrupting Expressions
Commas help you set off introductory information so that your reader understands who is speaking. Writers usually identify a speaker by using words such as *he asked* or *she said* with a quotation. These expressions can introduce, conclude, or interrupt a quotation.

Find It/ FIX IT
18
Grammar
Game Plan

Differentiated Instruction

RTI Strategy for Special Needs Students
Students may have difficulty understanding the difference between direct and indirect quotations. Organize students into pairs. Give one student several index cards. On the cards are sentences such as *Hank yelled, "Ouch! That was my toe." Sophie said, "I will see you later." "Turn off the computer," my mother said.* Give the second student several index cards. On

these cards are sentences with indirect quotations that match the content of the first cards. For example: *Hank yelled when he hurt his toe. Sophie said she would see me later. My mom told me to turn off the computer.* Have students discuss which set of sentences sounds more realistic. Then, explain that the sentences with quotation marks contained direct quotations.

25.4 Quotation Marks, Underlining, and Italics

Lesson Objectives

1. Recognize and use quotation marks correctly in sentences and dialogue.

2. Use quotation marks, underlining, and italics correctly in writing.

Using Quotation Marks With Quotations

Discuss the difference between direct quotations and indirect quotations.

RULES 25.4.1, 25.4.2 Read aloud the rules and then have students repeat the lines with you.

Say: When I write, I can use direct or indirect quotations. However, direct quotations usually result in more lively writing.

Work with students to create a direct quotation set off by quotation marks in a sentence. For example, *Janis asked, "What in the world is wrong with you today?"* Then, turn the direct quotation into an indirect quotation: *Janis asked what was wrong with me.* **Ask:** What is the difference between these two sentences? (The direct quotation brings Janis to life; the indirect quotation does not.)

Using Direct Quotations . . .

Discuss the function of expressions that identify who is speaking, such as *he said.*

WRITING COACH

Online

www.phwritingcoach.com

Diagnostic and Instruction
Diagnostic test assesses students' instructional needs. Lessons and practice are assigned based on results.

Additional Practice
- Grammar Practice—Targeted practice addresses individual needs.
- ExamView—Teachers customize their grammar practice and tests.
- Grammar Games—Interactive video games make grammar fun.

Direct Quotations With Introductory Expressions

Draw students' attention to the text stating that introductory expressions often precede direct quotations and are set off by a comma.

RULE 25.4.3 Read aloud the rule and then have students repeat the lines with you.

Review the examples on the page, pointing out that a long introductory expression is set off by a colon. Point out the relationship between the long introductory clause and the quotation that follows it. The clause sums up what the quotation is about, that is, Sarah's dreams. Note also that the long introductory clause can stand alone as a complete sentence. Have students compare the clause to the introductory phrases that are punctuated with a comma rather than a colon.

Have students brainstorm for sentences with short introductory expressions and direct quotations. Write their sentences on the board. Then, have students use commas and quotation marks to punctuate the sentences.

Direct Quotations With Concluding Expressions

Explain that direct quotations can sometimes end with a concluding expression that identifies the speaker. Concluding expressions are not complete sentences.

RULE 25.4.4 Read aloud the rule and then have students repeat the lines with you.

Remind students that concluding expressions should not be capitalized. Have student pairs brainstorm for examples of direct quotations with concluding expressions. Have pairs share their examples with the group.

> *Teacher Tip*
>
> For extra practice, have student pairs work together to identify direct quotations with introductory expressions and concluding expressions in a text with which they are familiar. Invite pairs to share their findings with the group. Point out the use of commas, quotation marks, and capitalization in each example.

Direct Quotations With Introductory Expressions
Commas are also used to indicate where **introductory expressions** end.

 RULE 25.4.3

> When an **introductory expression** precedes a direct quotation, place a comma after the introductory expression, and write the quotation as a full sentence. Be sure to leave a space between the comma and the quotation mark.

EXAMPLES   The guide explained **,** **"**All historical buildings should be treated with respect.**"**

The coach warned **,** **"**If you don't show up for every practice, you won't play in the game.**"**

If an introductory expression is very long, set it off with a colon instead of a comma.

EXAMPLE   At the end of the practice, Sarah spoke of her dreams **:** **"**I hope to be able to run the final leg in the relay by my senior year.**"**

Direct Quotations With Concluding Expressions
Direct quotations may sometimes end with **concluding expressions**.

 RULE 25.4.4

> When a **concluding expression** follows a direct quotation, write the quotation as a full sentence ending with a comma, question mark, or exclamation mark inside the quotation mark. Then, write the concluding expression. Be sure to use end punctuation to close the sentence.

Concluding expressions are not complete sentences; therefore, they do not begin with capital letters. Notice also that the closing quotation marks are always placed outside the punctuation at the end of direct quotations followed by a concluding expression.

EXAMPLE   **"**Could you show us one of the houses **?** **"** interrupted Barney.

576   **Punctuation**

Direct Quotations With Interrupting Expressions

You may use an interrupting expression in a direct quotation, which is also called a **divided quotation.** Interrupting expressions help writers clarify who is speaking and can also break up a long quotation.

> When the direct quotation of one sentence is interrupted, end the first part of the direct quotation with a comma and a quotation mark. Place a comma after the **interrupting expression,** and then use a new set of quotation marks to enclose the rest of the quotation. Be sure to leave a space after the final quotation mark.

25.4.5 RULE

EXAMPLES "What would we have done," asked Corrina, "if we had lived in the path of the tornado?"

"If you get a new bicycle," my mother warned, "you'll have to remember to lock it up."

Do not capitalize the first word of the second part of the sentence.

> When two sentences in a direct quotation are separated by an **interrupting expression,** end the first quoted sentence with a comma, question mark, or exclamation mark and a quotation mark. Place a period after the interrupter, and then write the second quoted sentence as a full quotation.

25.4.6 RULE

Practice 25.4A
Practice 25.4B

EXAMPLES "Did you see those rooms?" asked Mark. "Can you imagine having such a large house?"

"I know I had my keys when I left," Jane said. "They are probably in my pocket."

Quotation Marks, Underlining, and Italics   577

Direct Quotations With Interrupting Expressions

Explain that writers sometimes use interrupting expressions to divide long quotations. Interrupting expressions can divide a single sentence or can be used between two sentences in a direct quotation.

RULES 25.4.5, 25.4.6 Read aloud the rules and then have students repeat the lines with you.

Use a Think Aloud as part of a gradual release progression.

Think Aloud

Say: I use interrupting expressions to add variety to my writing by dividing direct quotations. Using interrupting expressions is easy if I remember a few simple rules. When I use an interrupting expression, such as *she replied*, to divide a single sentence, I end the first part of the quotation with a comma and a quotation mark. Then, I place a comma after the interrupting expression and use a new set of quotation marks around the remainder of the sentence. When I divide two sentences with an interrupting expression, I end the first sentence with a comma, question mark, or exclamation mark, and I place a period after the expression. Then, I write the second sentence as a full quotation.

Work with students to create a short narrative about something that happened recently. Include examples of direct quotations divided by interrupting expressions. Help students write and punctuate the quotations on the board. Generate examples of interrupting expressions in direct quotations.

Have partners create their own dramatic narratives using extensive direct quotations. Encourage students to use interrupting expressions within single sentences and between related quotations. Invite pairs to share their examples with the group.

PRACTICE 25.4A

1. I

2. D—"We went to the movies last night," Brianna said.

3. I

4. I

5. D—"Just wait," Gail said, "and I will get it for you."

6. D—"I need help with math," my brother said.

7. I

8. D—Mrs. Johnson yelled, "Look out for that car!"

9. D—"There is room for one more," Mr. Chen said.

10. I

PRACTICE 25.4B

11. Coach said, "We will get in an extra practice this week."

12. "A tadpole grows into a frog," Miss Jenner explained.

13. "When will my car be ready?" Dad asked.

14. "Hold still," Mom said, "or your haircut will not be right."

15. The old fisherman said, "There are no trout in these waters now."

16. "I prefer country music," said Melanie.

17. The principal announced, "There will be a fire drill today."

18. "Let me go with you," my brother begged.

19. "Why," Anna asked, "would you not tell me about the party?"

20. Dad shouted, "Turn that music down."

PRACTICE 25.4A Using Quotation Marks With Direct Quotations

Read the sentences. If the sentence contains a direct quotation, write *D*. If it contains an indirect quotation, write *I*. Then, rewrite each sentence that contains a direct quotation, adding the quotation marks where needed.

EXAMPLE   Marlene said, I do not know anything about fishing.

ANSWER   *D — Marlene said, "I do not know anything about fishing."*

1. Jason asked me if I knew the answer.

2. We went to the movies last night, Brianna said.

3. Rafael told us he knew a shortcut.

4. We heard from Mr. Smith that there would be no more watermelon at the fruit stand.

5. Just wait, Gail said, and I will get it for you.

6. I need help with math, my brother said.

7. Justine shared with everyone her hope that she would get a new bike.

8. Mrs. Johnson yelled, Look out for that car!

9. There is room for one more, Mr. Chen said.

10. I was told that the Taylor twins were going to compete in the race.

PRACTICE 25.4B Punctuating With Expressions

Read the sentences. Rewrite each sentence adding commas and quotation marks where needed. Be sure to use correct spacing for quotations.

EXAMPLE   We will have a visit from a firefight the teacher announced.

ANSWER   *"We will have a visit from a firefighter," the teacher announced.*

11. Coach said We will get in an extra practic this week.

12. A tadpole grows into a frog Miss Jenner explained.

13. When will my car be ready? Dad asked.

14. Hold still Mom said or your haircut will no be right.

15. The old fisherman said There are no trout these waters now.

16. I prefer country music said Melanie.

17. The principal announced There will be a f drill today.

18. Let me go with you my brother begged.

19. Why Anna asked would you not tell me ab the party?

20. Dad shouted Turn that music down.

SPEAKING APPLICATION

With a partner, read aloud two or three of the direct quotations in Practice 25.4A and 25.4B. Only read the part that should be within quotations. Talk about why using quotation marks, proper punctuation, and spacing makes sense.

WRITING APPLICATION

Write a four-sentence conversation between two friends who are planning to go to lunch together. Vary the location of the expressions within the sentences. Make sure to use proper punctuation and spacing for quotations.

SPEAKING APPLICATION

Students should demonstrate that they can use proper punctuation and spacing for quotations by reading text with quotations and participating in a discussion on the subject.

WRITING APPLICATION

Have students demonstrate that they can use proper punctuation and spacing for quotations by using correct punctuation and spacing when writing a four-sentence conversation.

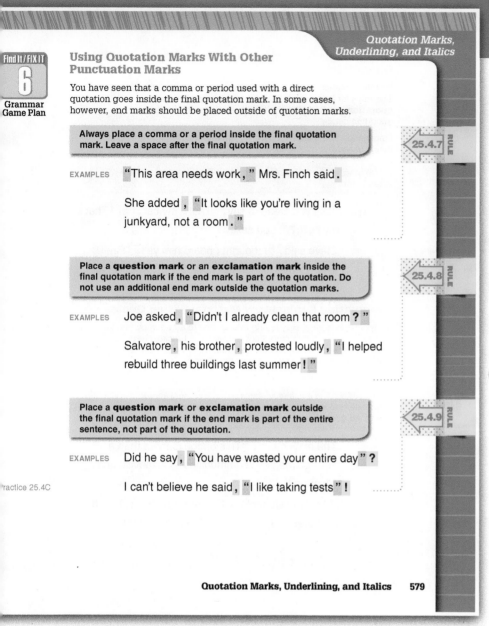

Using Quotation Marks With Other Punctuation Marks

Find It / Fix It

6

Grammar Game Plan

You have seen that a comma or period used with a direct quotation goes inside the final quotation mark. In some cases, however, end marks should be placed outside of quotation marks.

> **Always place a comma or a period inside the final quotation mark. Leave a space after the final quotation mark.**   ◄ 25.4.7 RULE

EXAMPLES   "This area needs work , " Mrs. Finch said .

She added , "It looks like you're living in a junkyard, not a room . "

> **Place a question mark or an exclamation mark inside the final quotation mark if the end mark is part of the quotation. Do not use an additional end mark outside the quotation marks.**   ◄ 25.4.8 RULE

EXAMPLES   Joe asked , "Didn't I already clean that room ? "

Salvatore , his brother , protested loudly , "I helped rebuild three buildings last summer ! "

> **Place a question mark or exclamation mark outside the final quotation mark if the end mark is part of the entire sentence, not part of the quotation.**   ◄ 25.4.9 RULE

EXAMPLES   Did he say , "You have wasted your entire day " ?

I can't believe he said , "I like taking tests " !

Practice 25.4C

Quotation Marks, Underlining, and Italics   579

Using Quotation Marks With Other Punctuation Marks

Remind students that many types of punctuation marks, such as periods or question marks, often appear inside the final quotation marks. Explain that they must be careful, however. Sometimes, other punctuation marks appear outside the final quotation mark.

RULES 25.4.7, 25.4.8, 25.4.9 Read aloud the rules and then have students repeat the lines with you.

Use a Think Aloud as part of a gradual release progression.

Think Aloud **Say:** Because **I know** how to use quotation marks with other punctuation, I am able to punctuate my writing correctly. As you know, sometimes end marks appear inside quotation marks, and sometimes they appear outside quotation marks. **Ask:** When would I place an end mark inside a quotation mark? (when the end mark is part of the quotation) **Ask:** When would I place an end mark outside a quotation mark? (when the end mark is part of the entire sentence that contains the quotation, but not part of the quotation itself)

Work with students to generate examples of sentences with end marks inside of quotation marks and examples of sentences for which the end marks belong outside of the quotation marks.

Have student pairs write and punctuate two or three sentences with quotation marks and other punctuation. Invite students to read their sentences to the group.

Using a selection featuring dialogue, such as an excerpt from a short story or a feature article, have students demonstrate comprehension of increasingly complex English by participating in **shared reading**. To facilitate, project the selection on an overhead or whiteboard.

Beginning Read the selection with students, asking simple questions and clarifying meaning as needed. Point out the punctuation of dialogue. Then, have students work in small groups with more fluent peers to write a brief summary.

Intermediate Read the selection with students, encouraging volunteers to read sections. Ask comprehension questions and clarify meaning as needed. Point out

the punctuation of dialogue. Then, have students partner with more fluent peers to write summaries.

Advanced Have students take turns reading from the selection. Ask comprehension questions and clarify meaning as needed. Then, have students write summaries. Finally, have them select an example of dialogue from the selection and explain how they can tell it is properly punctuated.

Advanced High Have students complete the Advanced activity. Then, have them write their own scenes featuring dialogue and conduct **shared readings** of them.

Using Single Quotation Marks for Quotations Within Quotations

Explain that single quotation marks are used for the inside quotation when a quotation appears within another quotation. Point out that the rules for using commas and end marks with single quotations are the same as for double quotations.

RULE 25.4.10 Read aloud the rule and then have students repeat the lines with you.

Review the examples on the page. **Ask:** When does a quotation occur within another quotation? (when the speaker reports another person's speech, word for word) Work with students to create three examples of quotations within quotations. Write the sentences on the board, and have students punctuate them.

Punctuating Explanatory Material Within Quotes

Tell students that they can use brackets to insert additional explanatory information into a quotation. Discuss situations in which students may have seen brackets used in writing.

RULE 25.4.11 Read aloud the rule and then have students repeat the lines with you.

Work with students to generate examples of explanations set off by brackets within a quotation.

Using Single Quotation Marks for Quotations Within Quotations

Double quotation marks are used to enclose the main quotation. The rules for using commas and end marks with **single quotation marks (' ')** are the same as they are with double quotation marks.

Single quotation marks are used to separate a quote that appears inside of another quotation.

> **Use single quotation marks to set off a quotation within a quotation.**

EXAMPLES "Did you mean to say, 'That's my cat,' or 'That's my hat' ? " Lori asked.

Steve said, "I thought I heard him yell, 'Fire ! ' That's why I ran out the door."

Punctuating Explanatory Material Within Quotes

Sometimes it is necessary to add information to a quotation that explains the quote more fully. In that case, brackets tell your reader which information came from the original speaker and which came from someone else. (See Section 25.7 for more information on brackets.)

> **Use brackets to enclose an explanation located within a quotation to show that the explanation is not part of the original quotation.**

EXAMPLE The mayor said, "This bridge is more than a link between two communities [Oceanville and Riverton]."

"We [the students of Center High School] wish to express our support of the student council."

See Practice 25.4D

Differentiated Instruction

RTI Strategy for Below-Level Students
Review the rules for using quotation marks. Remind students that single quotation marks follow the same rules as double quotation marks. Distribute unpunctuated dialogue that contains quotations within quotations. Have student pairs work together to insert punctuation into the passage. Invite students to share their work with the group. Challenge student partners to generate a dialogue that contains quotations within quotations.

PRE-AP Enrichment for Above-Level Students Organize students into pairs. Have students write a two-person dialogue. Encourage students to punctuate their dialogues correctly using quotation marks and single quotation marks, and enclosing any explanatory material within brackets. Invite students to read their dialogues aloud and then discuss the purpose of correct punctuation with their partner.

PRACTICE 25.4C Using Quotation Marks With Other Punctuation Marks

Read the sentences. Decide whether the missing punctuation goes inside or outside the quotation marks. Then, rewrite the sentences, using the proper punctuation and spacing for quotations.

EXAMPLE "When will he arrive" she asked.

ANSWER *"When will he arrive?" she asked.*

"Come right home afterwards" Dad instructed.

Our teacher asked, "Who knows where the equator is"

Didn't Mom say, "No television tonight"

I heard Lacie scream, "Look out"

"Do you like this bowl" the potter asked.

I can't believe you said, "No"

"Bread is easy to make" Wally stated.

Coach said, "We have a good chance of getting to the finals"

What did you mean by, "It's all over now"

"Ouch" cried Jill. "Did you have to pull the bandage off so fast"

WRITING APPLICATION

Write three sentences of a conversation you might have with someone at school. Be sure to use the proper punctuation and spacing for quotations.

PRACTICE 25.4D Punctuating Quotations Within Quotations and Explanatory Material

Read the sentences. Rewrite each sentence, using single quotation marks or brackets where needed. Be sure to use the proper punctuation and spacing.

EXAMPLE Marcia asked, "Do you remember when he said, I'll take care of it?"

ANSWER *Marcia asked, "Do you remember when he said, 'I'll take care of it'?"*

11. The teacher said, "Please say to the museum guide, Thank you for the tour."

12. "Did she say, I can help you?" Mom asked.

13. Coach shouted, "Next person who says, We can't win, does twenty push-ups."

14. "Did he say, I'm too busy?" Maria asked.

15. "He declared, It's so good to see you, when he saw me at the concert," Betsy said.

16. "Did he say, I found my keys?" Carlos asked.

17. Denise related, "Nikki asked, What am I doing here?"

18. "Which subject biology or math do you like better?" the teacher wondered.

19. Ravi reported, "My father said, You should have known better."

20. Stella demanded, "Why did she say, I wouldn't go anywhere with you?"

WRITING APPLICATION

Write an imagined conversation between two people. Each "speaker" should quote something or someone within his or her own statement. Be sure to use the proper punctuation and spacing for quotations.

Practice 581

PRACTICE 25.4C

1. "Come right home afterwards," Dad instructed.

2. Our teacher asked, "Who knows where the equator is?"

3. Didn't mom say, "No television tonight"?

4. I heard Lacie scream, "Look out!"

5. "Do you like this bowl?" the potter asked.

6. I can't believe you said, "No"!

7. "Bread is easy to make," Wally stated.

8. Coach said, "We have a good chance of getting to the finals."

9. What did you mean by, "It's all over now"?

10. "Ouch!" cried Jill. "Did you have to pull the bandage off so fast?"

PRACTICE 25.4D

11. The teacher said, "Please say to the museum guide, 'Thank you for the tour.'"

12. "Did she say, 'I can help you'?" Mom asked.

13. Coach shouted, "Next person who says, 'We can't win,' does twenty push-ups."

14. "Did he say, 'I'm too busy'?" Maria asked.

15. "He declared, 'It's so good to see you,' when he saw me at the concert," Betsy said.

16. "Did he say, 'I found my keys'?" Carlos asked.

17. Denise related, "Nikki asked, 'What am I doing here?'"

18. "Which subject [biology or math] do you like better?" the teacher wondered.

19. Ravi reported, "My father said, 'You should have known better.'"

20. Stella demanded, "Why did she say, 'I wouldn't go anywhere with you'?"

WRITING APPLICATION

Have students demonstrate that they can use proper punctuation and spacing for quotations by writing a conversation with quotations and using the proper spacing and punctuation.

WRITING APPLICATION

Have students demonstrate that they can use proper punctuation and spacing for quotations by writing a conversation that uses correct punctuation and spacing for quotations and uses correct punctuation for direct quotes within quotations.

Using Quotation Marks for Dialogue

Explain that dialogue is a conversation between two or more people. Dialogue helps to bring a scene to life. It is set off with quotation marks.

RULE 25.4.12 Read aloud the rule and then have students repeat the lines with you.

Use a Think Aloud as part of a gradual release progression.

Say: I use dialogue to bring characters to life in my writing and help my readers to experience the scene I am creating. Starting a new paragraph for each change of speaker helps my readers keep track of who is speaking.

Have two students read the example aloud, changing readers each time a paragraph ends. At the end of the example, have the class name which character each reader represented. Discuss the use of paragraph indentations, quotation marks, and information that identifies the new speaker. Have students create an original dialogue. Write the dialogue on the board, using correct paragraph structure, punctuation, and speaker identification.

Have small groups of students write short narratives with extensive dialogue between two to four characters. Students should break their paragraphs as speakers change, and use correct punctuation and speaker attribution.

Teacher Tip

Have groups of four create a passage of dialogue that includes three speakers, each of whom speaks at least twice. Have three group members assume the role of a speaker and one the role of the narrator. Ask groups to perform their passage for the class. Invite groups to share the rules they used when punctuating the dialogue.

Using Quotation Marks for Dialogue

A conversation between two or more people is called a **dialogue.** Adding dialogue makes your writing lively because it brings different points of view into your work. It makes your work sound like speech, so dialogue makes your reader feel involved in the scene you describe.

RULE 25.4.12

> When you are writing a **dialogue,** indent to begin a new paragraph with each change of speaker. Also be sure to add quotation marks around a speaker's words. When a new speaker is quoted, be sure to indicate the change to your reader by adding information that identifies the new speaker.

EXAMPLE

"Will you be going with us on the family trip again this summer ? " Noreen asked her cousin .

Gwen hesitated before answering . "I'm afraid so . My parents think I enjoy the experience of traveling with our whole family . "

"You fooled me , too , " Noreen replied . "Maybe the trip will be better this year . I think we're going to places that have large parks . If we're lucky , we might even be able to go on a few rides . "

"Well , at least it can't be any worse , " sighed Gwen . "On the last trip , we waited in line for one hour at three different historic homes in one day ! "

"I remember those lines , " said Noreen . "Didn't you get sunburned while we were waiting?"

Notice that the quotations within each sentence are properly punctuated and spaced. Also, note that paragraph spacing separates each change of speaker.

See Practice 25.4E
See Practice 25.4F

Working with ELLs   **ELL** Sheltered Instruction: Cognitive

Have students read linguistically accommodated text silently with increasing comprehension and ease for increasingly long periods and with a decreasing need for accommodation. Review the fact that English is read from left to right, top to bottom, and observe if students recognize the directionality of English reading.

Beginning Prepare linguistically accommodated, properly punctuated copies of the paragraph on page 583 in Practice 25.4E, adding simple synonyms or explanations for words such as *responded* and pictures illustrating terms such as *U.S. Constitution.* Have students read the first sentence silently to themselves. Discuss, referring to the accommodations. Repeat with subsequent sentences.

Intermediate Provide students with the text used in the Beginning activity. Have students read the entire paragraph silently. Then, discuss, referring to the accommodations.

Advanced Obtain an accommodated selection, such as a short story, that features dialogue. Have students silently read a section. Then, discuss, referring to the accommodations for support. Repeat with the remaining sections.

Advanced High Obtain an accommodated selection, such as a short story, that features dialogue. Have students silently read the selection. Then, discuss, referring to the accommodations for support.

PRACTICE 25.4E Using Quotation Marks in Dialogue

Read the dialogue. Then, rewrite the dialogue. Use proper spacing for quotations and create additional paragraphs where needed. Be sure to use quotation marks and other punctuation correctly.

EXAMPLE What do you know about the United States Constitution the teacher asked. Keisha answered, I think the U.S. Constitution explains how our government works.

ANSWER *"What do you know about the U.S. Constitution?" the teacher asked.*

Keisha answered, "I think the U.S. Constitution explains how our government works."

Attention please the teacher said. We will be starting a new project today. Will this be something we do at home Melanie asked. No the teacher responded we will be able to work on it during class time. Is it a history project asked Francisco. Yes it will be about the U.S. Constitution the teacher said. Sarah blurted out I know the opening We the people of the United States . . . Very good, Sarah the teacher said. Now turn to page 498 in your books, and let's read about the writing of the Constitution. Those writers must have been really smart Noah added.

SPEAKING APPLICATION

With a partner, take turns reading a few lines of your corrected dialogues. Talk about why you think there is a new paragraph each time the speaker changes.

PRACTICE 25.4F Revising Dialogue for Punctuation and Paragraphs

Read the dialogue. Then, rewrite the dialogue. Add quotation marks and other punctuation, and begin new paragraphs where needed.

EXAMPLE I asked my mom Is there a new museum exhibit? My mom answered Yes, there's one that just opened last week.

ANSWER *I asked my mom, "Is there a new museum exhibit?"*

My mom answered, "Yes, there's one that just opened last week."

The museum has a new exhibit the guide told us. It's on the third floor, if you'd like to see it. What is in the exhibit my brother asked. It has Egyptian mummies the guide said and wooden carvings from their tombs. There are also photographs of where the mummies were found. Great! I love anything from Egypt said my dad. So do I added my mom. I chimed in That makes three of us, so let's go. There is an elevator on the left the guide advised. Thank you for telling us about this my dad said, heading for the elevator.

WRITING APPLICATION

Write a brief dialogue between two friends planning their weekend. Write enough dialogue so that you have to start a new paragraph. Add quotation marks using the proper punctuation and spacing.

Practice   **583**

PRACTICE 25.4E

"Attention please," the teacher said. "We will be starting a new project today."

"Will this be something we do at home?" Melanie asked.

"No," the teacher responded, "we will be able to work on it during class time."

"Is it a history project?" asked Francisco.

"Yes, it will be about the U.S. Constitution," the teacher said.

Sarah blurted out, "I know the opening. 'We the people of the United States...'"

"Very good, Sarah," the teacher said. "Now turn to page 498 in your books, and let's read about the writing of the Constitution."

"Those writers must have been really smart," Noah added.

PRACTICE 25.4F

"The museum has a new exhibit," the guide told us. "It's on the third floor, if you'd like to see it."

"What is in the exhibit?" my brother asked.

"It has Egyptian mummies," the guide said, "and wooden carvings from their tombs. There are also photographs of where the mummies were found."

"Great! I love anything from Egypt," said my dad.

"So do I," added my mom.

I chimed in, "That makes three of us, so let's go."

"There is an elevator on the left," the guide advised.

"Thank you for telling us about this," my dad said, heading for the elevator.

SPEAKING APPLICATION

Have students demonstrate that they can recognize and use proper punctuation and spacing for quotations by explaining the paragraph rules for writing dialogue.

WRITING APPLICATION

Have students demonstrate that they can recognize and use proper punctuation and spacing for quotations by correctly using spacing, paragraph breaks, and punctuation.

Using Quotation Marks in Titles

Point out that quotation marks are used to identify titles of short works, such as short stories, chapters, poems, television episodes, and songs.

RULES 25.4.13, 25.4.14 Read aloud the rules and then have students repeat the lines with you.

Review with students the examples of written works and artistic works listed in the charts on page 584. For each category of work, brainstorm for a new example of a work with which students are familiar that fits into that category.

Use a Think Aloud as part of a gradual release progression.

Say: When **I refer to** a short work in my writing, I put the title of the work in quotation marks. For example, if I were to write about Robert Louis Stevenson's book *Treasure Island*, I would set the title in italics and the title of Part 1, "The Old Buccaneer," in quotes. If you were to write an article that quoted an article about the book, you would put the title of that article, "Discovering Treasure Island," in quotes.

Work with students to generate a list of short works with which they are familiar. Create and speak aloud two or three sentences that contain the names of works on the list. Then, write the sentences on the board, using quotation marks correctly.

Have partners brainstorm for several sentences that include these short works. Have partners write their example sentences, using quotation marks correctly to enclose the titles. Then, have students share their examples, including their use of quotation marks, with the class.

Using Underlining and Italics in Titles

Point out that many types of titles and special names are called out with italics or underlining when they appear in writing.

Using Quotation Marks in Titles

Quotation marks are generally used to set off the titles of shorter works.

 RULE 25.4.13

Use **quotation marks** to enclose the titles of short written works and around the title of a work that is mentioned as part of a collection.

WRITTEN WORKS THAT USE QUOTATION MARKS	
Title of a Short Story	"The Gift of the Magi"
Chapter From a Book	"The Test Is in the Tasting" from *No-Work Garden Book*
Title of a Short Poem	"Lucy"
Title of an Article	"How to Build a Birdhouse"
Title Mentioned as Part of a Collection	"Uncle Vanya" in *Eight Great Comedies*

 RULE 25.4.14

Use **quotation marks** around the titles of episodes in a television or radio series, songs, and parts of a long musical composition.

ARTISTIC WORKS THAT USE QUOTATION MARKS	
Title of an Episode	"The Nile" from *Cousteau Odyssey*
Title of a Song	"The Best Things in Life Are Free"
Title of a Part of a Long Musical Work	"The Storm" from the *William Tell Overture*

Using Underlining and Italics in Titles

Underlining and **italics** help make titles and other special words and names stand out in your writing. Underlining is used only in handwritten or typewritten material. In printed material, italic (slanted) print is used instead of underlining.

UNDERLINING The Hobbit   ITALICS *The Hobbit*

584   Punctuation

Working with ELLs   **ELL** Sheltered Instruction: Cognitive

Have students spell familiar English words by employing spelling patterns with increasing accuracy. Point out the familiar word *title* on page 584. Explain this spelling pattern to students: in many English words ending with a consonant followed by the /əl/ or /l/ sound, the sound is spelled *le*. Give them the additional examples of *table, battle,* and *apple.*

Beginning Review the model words with students. Have students copy them correctly. Then, say the words *little, able,* and *cattle.* Guide students to apply the pattern as they spell each. Review results.

Intermediate Review the model words with students. Then, have them apply the spelling pattern to spell familiar words, such as *little, able,* and *gentle,* as well as unfamiliar words, such as *cattle* and *trifle,* Review results.

Advanced Provide each partner in a pair with two different lists of familiar and unfamiliar words that follow the pattern. Then, have partners take turns reading the words as the listener writes each correctly.

Advanced High Have students complete the Advanced activity. Then, have them use a dictionary to find three new words that follow the pattern and to spell them correctly in sentences.

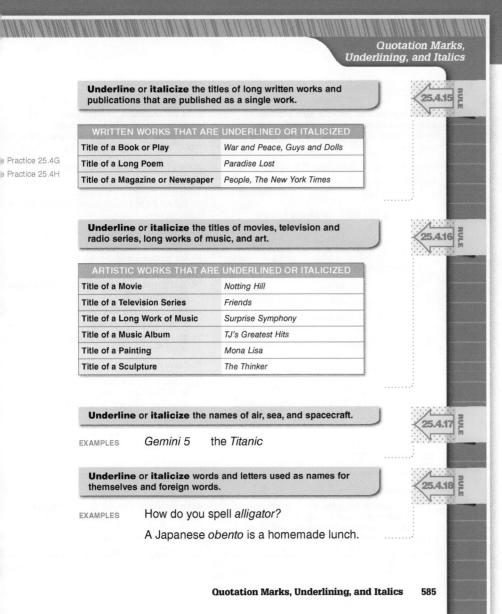

Underline or **italicize** the titles of long written works and publications that are published as a single work.

RULE 25.4.15

Practice 25.4G
Practice 25.4H

WRITTEN WORKS THAT ARE UNDERLINED OR ITALICIZED	
Title of a Book or Play	*War and Peace, Guys and Dolls*
Title of a Long Poem	*Paradise Lost*
Title of a Magazine or Newspaper	*People, The New York Times*

Underline or **italicize** the titles of movies, television and radio series, long works of music, and art.

RULE 25.4.16

ARTISTIC WORKS THAT ARE UNDERLINED OR ITALICIZED	
Title of a Movie	*Notting Hill*
Title of a Television Series	*Friends*
Title of a Long Work of Music	*Surprise Symphony*
Title of a Music Album	*TJ's Greatest Hits*
Title of a Painting	*Mona Lisa*
Title of a Sculpture	*The Thinker*

Underline or **italicize** the names of air, sea, and spacecraft.

RULE 25.4.17

EXAMPLES   *Gemini 5*   the *Titanic*

Underline or **italicize** words and letters used as names for themselves and foreign words.

RULE 25.4.18

EXAMPLES   How do you spell *alligator*?

A Japanese *obento* is a homemade lunch.

Quotation Marks, Underlining, and Italics   **585**

Explain that underlining is used to identify certain types of works with handwritten or typed writing. Italic print is used for printed material, or writing generated on a computer.

RULES 25.4.15, 25.4.16, 25.4.17 Read aloud the rules and then have students repeat the lines with you.

Talk through the charts that list written works and artistic works that are underlined or italicized. Have students create their own two-column charts that list each type of work that is underlined or italicized. Have students replace the examples in the charts with examples with which they are familiar.

Have students add one additional category to their charts: names of individual ships, planes, and spacecraft.

RULE 25.4.18 Read aloud the rule and then have students repeat the lines with you.

Explain that when you refer directly to a word as a name for itself, it should be underlined or italicized. **Say:** For example, if I want to write "I had to look up the word *perilous* the other day," I should underline or italicize *perilous*.

Have students write a paragraph in which they define several words they have made up. Remind students to italicize the words they define and to set off the definitions with quotation marks.

Differentiated Instruction

RTI Strategy for Below-Level Students
Help students understand the rules regarding the use of underlining and italics. Gather a variety of different books, magazines, and DVDs that are in the classroom. Direct attention, for example, to the title of a book. **Ask:** *If you were writing about this book, would you underline or italicize this?*

Have students raise their hands and answer the question. Ask a volunteer to write a sentence containing the book title on the board. Then, direct attention to a magazine. **Ask:** *If you were writing about this magazine, would you underline or italicize it?*

Continue the question and answer session until students have a better understanding of the rules regarding underlining and italics.

PRACTICE 25.4G ▷

1. Beauty and the Beast?
2. The Chronicles of Narnia.
3. The New York Times.
4. duplex
5. Best Westerns
6. Romeo and Juliet
7. noun *and* pronoun
8. merci is French for
9. Waltzing Australia?
10. Intrepid

PRACTICE 25.4H ▷

11. Robert Frost's short poem "Out, Out" is in this collection.
12. I read the article "The Spice Is Right" in North Shore Magazine.
13. My brother loves the short story "The Tell-Tale Heart."
14. Isn't the song "Ol' Man River" from the musical Showboat?
15. Did you see the "Live and Learn" episode of the television show Happy Days?
16. The encyclopedia has a biographical article titled "Stephen F. Austin."
17. I love the song "Yesterday."
18. "Aquarium" is my favorite part of the musical work The Carnival of the Animals.
19. Did you ever hear the song "What a Wonderful World" by Louis Armstrong?
20. I think "Just You Wait" is the funniest song in the musical My Fair Lady.

PRACTICE 25.4G ▷ Underlining Titles, Names, and Words

Read the sentences. Rewrite each sentence, underlining titles, names, and words where needed. You can use italics if you are typing your answers.

EXAMPLE   I read Charlotte's Web in fifth grade.

ANSWER   *I read Charlotte's Web in fifth grade.*

1. Have you read the book Beauty and the Beast?
2. I just read all seven books of The Chronicles of Narnia.
3. My dad reads The New York Times.
4. What does duplex mean?
5. I enjoy watching Best Westerns on television.
6. The play Romeo and Juliet always makes me cry.
7. Write noun and pronoun at the top of the page.
8. I learned that merci is French for "thank you."
9. Did you like the book Waltzing Australia?
10. The aircraft carrier Intrepid is now a floating museum.

PRACTICE 25.4H ▷ Using Underlining and Quotation Marks

Read the sentences. Rewrite each sentence, enclosing the titles in quotation marks or underlining them. You can use italics if you are typing your answers.

EXAMPLE   I read the article The Titanic.

ANSWER   *I read the article "The Titanic."*

11. Robert Frost's short poem Out, Out is in this collection.
12. I read the article The Spice Is Right in North Shore Magazine.
13. My brother loves the short story The Tell-Tale Heart.
14. Isn't the song Ol' Man River from the musical Showboat?
15. Did you see the Live and Learn episode of the television show Happy Days?
16. The encyclopedia has a biographical article titled Stephen F. Austin.
17. I love the song Yesterday.
18. Aquarium is my favorite part of the musical work The Carnival of the Animals.
19. Did you ever hear the song What a Wonderful World by Louis Armstrong?
20. I think Just You Wait is the funniest song in the musical My Fair Lady.

SPEAKING APPLICATION

With a partner, say a few sentences that need underlining or quotation marks. Discuss which seems to draw more attention to a word or title, the underlining or the quotation marks.

WRITING APPLICATION

Write three sentences recommending things a friend should read or see. Use proper mechanics, including quotation marks, and underlining or italics for book titles.

Working with ELLs   ELL Sheltered Instruction: Cognitive

Use the language in the directions for the Practice activities to help students develop basic sight vocabulary used routinely in written classroom materials. Ensure that students understand how this vocabulary will assist them as they respond to the activity. Write the words *where, answer, rewrite,* and *your* on the board.

Beginning Read each word aloud as students read with you, and discuss its meaning. Then, locate each word in the directions. Read the directions with students, clarifying meaning. Then, guide them in completing the first items in Practice 25.4G.

Intermediate Say the words aloud, and discuss their meaning. Then, direct students to read the Practice activity

directions to a partner. To ensure students understand the directions, have them summarize each set. Then, have them work in groups to complete the Practice activities.

Advanced Introduce the words, and have students locate them in the directions. Then, review these routine words: *underlining, titles,* and *quotation marks.* Have students read the directions aloud, restating their meaning. Then, have them complete the activities.

Advanced High Have students complete the Advanced activity. Then, have them write definitions or explanations of each word discussed.

25.5 Hyphens

Hyphens (-) are used to combine words and to show a connection between the syllables of words that are broken at the ends of lines.

Find It / FIX IT

19

Grammar Game Plan

WRITING COACH

Online

www.phwritingcoach.com

Grammar Practice
Practice your grammar skills with Writing Coach Online.

Grammar Games
Test your knowledge of grammar in this fast-paced interactive video game.

Using Hyphens in Numbers

Hyphens are used to join compound numbers and fractions.

> Use a **hyphen** when you write two-word numbers from twenty-one through ninety-nine.

25.5.1 RULE

EXAMPLES   seventy-eight   thirty-five

> Use a **hyphen** when you use a fraction as an adjective but not when you use a fraction as a noun.

25.5.2 RULE

ADJECTIVE   This glass is two-thirds full.

NOUN   Two thirds of the members were present.

Using Hyphens for Prefixes and Suffixes

Many words with common prefixes are no longer hyphenated. The following prefixes are often used before proper nouns: *ante-, anti-, post-, pre-, pro-,* and *un-.* Check a dictionary when you are unsure about using a hyphen.

> Use a **hyphen** after a prefix that is followed by a proper noun or adjective.

25.5.3 RULE

EXAMPLES   pre-Columbian   mid-August

> Use a **hyphen** in words with the prefixes *all-, ex-,* and *self-* and the suffix *-elect.*

25.5.4 RULE

EXAMPLES   all-American   mayor-elect

Hyphens   587

Lesson Objectives

1. Use punctuation marks, including hyphens, correctly.
2. Use hyphens correctly in writing to divide words and to form compound words.

Using Hyphens in Numbers

Point out that hyphens have many uses. They are used to represent two-word numbers, to divide a word between syllables at the end of a line, and to form compound words and compound modifiers. Hyphens signal that numbers or words are joined or divided.

RULES 25.5.1, 25.5.2 Read aloud the rules and then have students repeat the lines with you.

Say several two-word numbers to students. Have them write the numbers, using hyphens correctly. Say these two sentences aloud: One-half credit is better than none. I got nine tenths of the answers right. **Ask students to** explain which sentence should have a hyphen, and why.

Using Hyphens for Prefixes and Suffixes

Point out that, in general, hyphens are no longer used with most prefixes. Explain that there are times, however, when hyphens should be used with certain prefixes and suffixes. It is a good idea to consult a dictionary to verify whether to use a hyphen.

RULES 25.5.3, 25.5.4 Read aloud the rules and then have students repeat the lines with you.

Say: A few simple rules help me decide when to hyphenate prefixes and suffixes. If I keep in mind that many words with common prefixes are no longer hyphenated, that narrows it down a bit. But when should I use a hyphen? **Review** the rules for using hyphens with prefixes and suffixes.

Work with students to brainstorm for examples of words with prefixes or suffixes that require a hyphen. **Say:** Now, let's consult the dictionary to see if we've hyphenated our words correctly.

Have student pairs look up the words and share their findings with the class.

WRITING COACH

Online

www.phwritingcoach.com

Diagnostic and Instruction
Diagnostic test assesses students' instructional needs. Lessons and practice are assigned based on results.

Additional Practice
- Grammar Practice—Targeted practice addresses individual needs.
- ExamView—Teachers customize their grammar practice and tests.
- Grammar Games—Interactive video games make grammar fun.

Using Hyphens in Compound Words

Discuss how hyphens are used to create compound words.

RULE 25.5.5 Read aloud the rule and then have students repeat the lines with you.

Write *great-grandfather* on the board. **Say:**
A compound word is two words joined together with a hyphen to represent a single idea. Who knows what a great-grandfather is? (the father of one's grandfather) *Great-grandfather* is a compound word. It is made up by the words *great* and *grandfather*.

Write these words on the board: *brother in law, great grandfather, cousin, half brother, father.* Work with students to pick out compound words that require hyphens.

Have student pairs write the words correctly using hyphens. Repeat the exercise if necessary, using different words.

Using Hyphens With Compound Modifiers

Point out to students that hyphens help readers group information properly. Students can use a hyphen to connect a compound modifier that comes before a noun.

RULE 25.5.6 Read aloud the rule and then have students repeat the lines with you.

Discuss with students the importance of using hyphens correctly. Review the examples of compound modifiers provided on page 588.

Using Hyphens in Compound Words

Compound words are two or more words that must be read together to create a single idea.

> Use a **hyphen** to connect two or more nouns that are used as one compound word, unless the dictionary gives a different spelling.

EXAMPLES   great‑grandfather   secretary‑treasurer

Using Hyphens With Compound Modifiers

Hyphens help your reader group information properly.

> Use a hyphen to connect a **compound modifier** that comes before a noun. Do not use a hyphen with a compound modifier that includes a word ending in *-ly* or in a compound proper adjective.

EXAMPLE   Cass was a big‑hearted dog lover.

INCORRECT   clearly‑written text   West‑Indian music

CORRECT   clearly written text   West Indian music

A hyphen is not necessary when a compound modifier follows the noun it describes.

MODIFIER BEFORE NOUN   They traveled in well‑equipped wagons.

MODIFIER AFTER NOUN   They traveled in wagons that were well equipped.

However, if a dictionary spells a word with a hyphen, the word must always be hyphenated, even when it follows a noun.

EXAMPLE   The design is up‑to‑date.

See Practice 25.5A
See Practice 25.5B

PRACTICE 25.5A Using Hyphens in Numbers and Words

Read the following phrases. Then, write each phrase, adding hyphens where needed.

EXAMPLE   thirty five days

ANSWER   *thirty-five days*

1. the country's president elect
2. forty three pages
3. Mom's father in law
4. mid December party
5. three fourths full
6. seventy four miles
7. half price sale
8. self appointed leader
9. twenty one years ago
10. hard earned reward

PRACTICE 25.5B Proofreading for Hyphens

Read the sentences. Rewrite each sentence, adding hyphens where needed.

EXAMPLE   We are the all district champions.

ANSWER   *We are the all-district champions.*

11. There were thirty two sets of clearly written instructions.
12. The project is three fourths done.
13. My dad's brother in law is an ex Marine.
14. The pro freedom rally was attended by the governor elect.
15. He bought twenty eight high definition DVDs.
16. Prices are one third off at the mid June sale.
17. It was the top selling movie of the summer.
18. I inherited my great grandmother's well worn cookbook.
19. It's another forty seven miles to the highway exit.
20. Please complete the self evaluation form.

SPEAKING APPLICATION

Go through the lesson and create your own example for each rule of hyphen usage.

WRITING APPLICATION

Write three or four sentences about a trip to a store or shopping mall. Use three different applications of hyphens (numbers, compound words, compound modifiers, and so on) in your sentences.

Practice   589

PRACTICE 25.5A

1. the country's president-elect
2. forty-three pages
3. Mom's father-in-law
4. mid-December party
5. three-fourths full
6. seventy-four miles
7. half-price sale
8. self-appointed leader
9. twenty-one years ago
10. hard-earned reward

PRACTICE 25.5B

11. There were thirty-two sets of clearly written instructions.
12. The project is three-fourths done.
13. My dad's brother-in-law is an ex-Marine.
14. The pro-freedom rally was attended by the governor-elect.
15. He bought twenty-eight high-definition DVDs.
16. Prices are one-third off at the mid-June sale.
17. It was the top-selling movie of the summer.
18. I inherited my great-grandmother's well-worn cookbook.
19. It's another forty-seven miles to the highway exit.
20. Please complete the self-evaluation form.

SPEAKING APPLICATION

Have students use their examples to explain the rules of hyphen usage.

WRITING APPLICATION

Have students explain which numbers and words they hyphenated and why.

Working with ELLs   **ELL** Sheltered Instruction: Cognitive

Have students listen to, derive meaning from, and respond orally to information presented in a wide variety of print, electronic, and audiovisual media to build attainment of the concept of hyphenated words. Provide students with a print article that includes hyphenated words.

Beginning Read the article aloud as students follow along. Have students raise their hands whenever you read a hyphenated term. Discuss the reason for the use of the hyphen in each case. Ask students simple questions about the meaning of hyphenated and nonhyphenated modifiers in the article, such as, *What kind of person is the article about? How many people were at the event?*

Intermediate Have students read the article in small groups. Then, ask students

comprehension questions, such as *Where did this happen?* Finally, have them identify hyphenated words, explain the function of the hyphens, and discuss what each word contributes to the article.

Advanced Have partners read the article and discuss the text. Next, have them identify hyphenated words, explain the function of the hyphens, and explain what each word contributes to the reader's understanding or impressions.

Advanced High Have students complete the Advanced activity. Then, have them use several of the hyphenated words correctly in a paragraph of their own.

Using Hyphens at the End of Lines

Tell students that hyphens are used to divide a word between syllables at the end of a line if the entire word will not fit within the margins. Explain that this happens more often when people write with a typewriter than on a computer.

RULES 25.5.7, 25.5.8 Read aloud the rules and then have students repeat the lines with you.

Use a Think Aloud as part of a gradual release progression.

Say: While hyphens are a useful way to divide words at the end of a line, too many hyphens can make my writing choppy. If I cannot avoid dividing a word, **I will** divide it between syllables, and I will make sure the hyphen appears at the end of the first line, not at the beginning of the second line. I will also consult a dictionary to make sure I have correctly divided the word between syllables.

Work with students to find examples of hyphens used at the ends of lines in a text with which they are familiar and to share their findings with the class.

Have students write short paragraphs, correctly dividing words that don't fit on one line.

Using Hyphens Correctly to Divide Words

Point out to students that one-syllable words can never be divided at the end of a line.

RULE 25.5.9 Read aloud the rule and then have students repeat the lines with you.

Using Hyphens at the Ends of Lines

Hyphens serve a useful purpose when they are used to divide words at the ends of lines. They should not, however, be used more often than is necessary because they can make reading feel choppy.

> Avoid dividing words at the end of a line whenever possible. If a word must be divided, always divide it between syllables.

EXAMPLE   The soccer coach's pep talks are usually quite unin-
spiring and short.

Check a dictionary if you are unsure how a word is divided into syllables. Looking up the word *seriously*, for example, you would find that its syllables are *se-ri-ous-ly*.

> A hyphen used to divide a word should never be placed at the beginning of the second line. It must be placed at the end of the first line.

INCORRECT   Knock down this par
-tition.

CORRECT   Knock down this par-
tition.

Using Hyphens Correctly to Divide Words

One-syllable words cannot be divided.

> Do *not* divide one-syllable words even if they seem long or sound like words with two syllables.

INCORRECT	sch-ool	bru-ised	thro-ugh
CORRECT	school	bruised	through

590   Punctuation

Have students spell familiar English words with increasing accuracy by employing spelling rules. Point out the example word *seriously* on page 590. Explain that the word is made by adding *-ly* to *serious*. Then, review familar *-ly* words such as *quickly, tamely, happily,* and *gently*. Explain these spelling rules: When adding *-ly* or another suffix beginning with a consonant to a word ending in a consonant or silent *e*, you usually do not change the spelling of the base word. When adding *-ly* or another suffix to a word ending consonant + *y*, you usually change the *-y* to *-i*. When adding *-ly* to a word ending *-le*, such as *gentle*, you drop the *-le*.

Beginning Have students write each example word, spelling it correctly. Then, guide students as they add *-ly* to these adjectives: *kind, late, cozy,* and *noble*.

Intermediate Provide groups with lists of familiar and unfamiliar adjectives, and have them add *-ly* to each, spelling it correctly.

Advanced Provide partners with a list of familar and unfamiliar adjectives. Have them add *-ly* to each, following the rules.

Advanced High Have students complete the Advanced activity. Then, have them use a dictionary to find three new words that illustrate the rules.

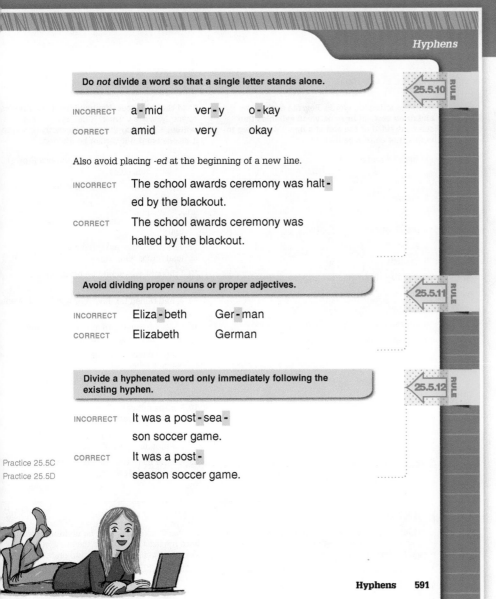

Do *not* divide a word so that a single letter stands alone.

25.5.10

INCORRECT	a-mid	ver-y	o-kay
CORRECT	amid	very	okay

Also avoid placing *-ed* at the beginning of a new line.

INCORRECT   The school awards ceremony was halted by the blackout.

CORRECT   The school awards ceremony was
halted by the blackout.

Avoid dividing proper nouns or proper adjectives.

25.5.11

INCORRECT	Eliza-beth	Ger-man
CORRECT	Elizabeth	German

Divide a hyphenated word only immediately following the existing hyphen.

25.5.12

INCORRECT   It was a post-sea-
son soccer game.

Practice 25.5C
Practice 25.5D

CORRECT   It was a post-
season soccer game.

Explain to students that hyphens help to correctly divide words between syllables.

RULES 25.5.10, 25.5.11, 25.5.12 Read aloud the rules and then have students repeat the lines with you.

Explain that proper names and proper adjectives should never be divided with a hyphen at the end of a line.

Occasionally students may need to divide a compound word at the end of a line. If the compound word has already been hyphenated, it should be divided at the existing hyphen.

Have students brainstorm for three words with three or more syllables. They should mark the syllables by drawing vertical lines. Then, have students write three sentences using the words. Each sentence should require that one of the three-syllable words be divided at the end of the line. Students should demonstrate that they can use correct punctuation, including hyphens, by correctly hyphenating the words at the line breaks. Exchange papers with a partner. Partners should proofread sentences to check for correct punctuation marks.

Teacher Tip

If students are having difficulty dividing words into syllables, have them say the words aloud and clap the syllables. Model this using the word *telescope.* Then, have students speak and clap in unison. Finally, have students speak and clap with a partner. Provide a list of multisyllabic words for additional practice.

PRACTICE 25.5C

1. in | sur | ance
2. wary
3. taste | less
4. for | ward
5. English
6. un | in | ter | est | ing
7. parted
8. Audrey
9. stunned
10. un | doubt | ed | ly

PRACTICE 25.5D

11. correct
12. The news showed the pro-American forces winning.
13. I thought you would be bringing Karen with you.
14. correct
15. Losing the game to a rival school ended our hopes of a district championship.
16. correct
17. Everyone gasped when I fell, but I was okay.
18. For the potluck, Christina had brought a casserole.
19. correct
20. On the map, we located the Russian city of Moscow.

WRITING APPLICATION

Have students explain how they can identify the syllables in a word. Have them tell you why they divided their words the way they did.

WRITING APPLICATION

Have students explain the hyphenation rule they applied to each of their sentences and the way in which they applied that rule.

PRACTICE 25.5C Using Hyphens to Divide Words

Read the following words. Rewrite each word, and draw vertical lines between syllables that can be divided at the end of a line. Do nothing to words that cannot be divided.

EXAMPLE   responsible
ANSWER   *re | spon | si | ble*

1. insurance
2. wary
3. tasteless
4. forward
5. English
6. uninteresting
7. parted
8. Audrey
9. stunned
10. undoubtedly

WRITING APPLICATION

Think of long words you know, and write them down. Then, divide them into syllables. Check a dictionary if necessary.

592   Punctuation

PRACTICE 25.5D Using Hyphens in Words in Sentences

Read the sentences. If a word has been divided correctly, write *correct*. If not, rewrite the sentence, dividing the word correctly or writing it as one word if it cannot be divided.

EXAMPLE   I was absent from today's Fre-nch class.
ANSWER   *I was absent from today's French class.*

11. The animal in that story is imaginary.
12. The news showed the pro-American forces winning.
13. I thought you would be bringing Karen with you.
14. It had rained for days, but it stopped eventually.
15. Losing the game to a rival school ended our hopes of a district championship.
16. All the musicians were on hand for the pre-concert rehearsal.
17. Everyone gasped when I fell, but I was o-kay.
18. For the potluck, Christina had brought a casserole.
19. The math book said we should multiply first, and then divide.
20. On the map, we located the Russian city of Moscow.

WRITING APPLICATION

Choose three of the rules for dividing words with hyphens. For each of the rules, write a sentence that puts the rule into practice.

Working with ELLs   **ELL** Sheltered Instruction: Cognitive

Use Practice 25.5D to help students write using increasingly complex grammatical structures, such as correct verbs and tenses. Review the past, present, and future tense, as well as the concept of correct tense.

Beginning Pair beginners with more fluent speakers. Have them complete an item from the Practice activity and then identify the verb in the sentence and its tense. Then, have them rewrite the sentence in another tense, explaining what context is appropriate for each sentence.

Intermediate Have students complete the Practice. Then, have students work in small groups to identify the verb in each sentence and its tense. Have them rewrite the sentence in another tense, explaining what context is appropriate for each sentence.

Advanced Have students complete the Practice. Then, have partners identify the verb in each sentence and its tense. Have them rewrite the sentence twice, each time in a different tense, explaining what context is appropriate for each sentence.

Advanced High Have students complete the Practice. Then, have individuals identify the verb in each sentence and its tense. Have them rewrite the sentence twice, each time in a different tense, explaining what context is appropriate for each sentence. Finally, have them exchange papers and check each other's work.

25.6 Apostrophes

The **apostrophe** (') is used to show possession or ownership. It is also used in shortened forms of words called contractions. In a contraction, the apostrophe marks the place where letters have been omitted.

Find It/ FIX IT

14

Grammar Game Plan

WRITING COACH

Online

www.phwritingcoach.com

Grammar Practice
Practice your grammar skills with Writing Coach Online.

Grammar Games
Test your knowledge of grammar in this fast-paced interactive video game.

Using Apostrophes With Possessive Nouns

Apostrophes are used with nouns to show ownership or possession.

> Add an apostrophe and *-s* to show the possessive case of most singular nouns and plural nouns that do not end in *-s* or *-es.*

 25.6.1 RULE

EXAMPLES   My dog**'**s favorite toy is a ball.

The men**'**s trek up Mt. Everest was strenuous.

Even when a singular noun already ends in *-s,* you can usually add an apostrophe and *-s* to show possession.

EXAMPLE   An iris**'**s colors are often purple and white.

In classical or ancient names that end in *-s,* it is common to omit the final *-s* to make pronunciation easier.

EXAMPLE   Odysseus**'** voyages were dangerous.

> Add an apostrophe to show the possessive case of plural nouns ending in *-s* or *-es.* Do not add an *-s.*

 25.6.2 RULE

EXAMPLE   The bears**'** den is hidden in the mountains.

Apostrophes   **593**

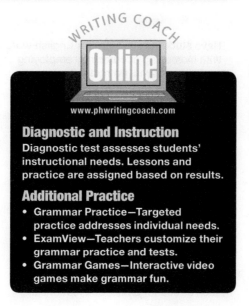
25.6 Apostrophes

Lesson Objectives

1. Use apostrophes to show ownership, make contractions, and create plural forms.

2. Use apostrophes correctly in writing.

Using Apostrophes With Possessive Nouns

Point out that apostrophes are used with nouns to show ownership or possession.

RULES 25.6.1, 25.6.2 Read aloud the rules and then have students repeat the lines with you.

Use a Think Aloud as part of a gradual release progression.

Think Aloud

Say: When **I want** to make a noun possessive in my writing, I use an apostrophe. But I keep in mind that the position of the apostrophe varies depending on whether the noun is singular or plural and whether it already ends in *-s.*

Write the words *women, teacher, glass, boys,* and *vice president* on the board. **Work with students to** form the possessive case of each word. Remind students that most nouns that don't end in *-s* or *-es* can be made possessive simply by adding *'s.* Have students form possessive nouns out of *women, teacher,* and *vice president* using this rule. For each word, **ask:** Is this a plural or singular noun?

Explain that plural nouns that end in *-s* or *-es* can be made possessive by adding an apostrophe to the end of the word. Ask students how they would form the possessive of the noun *boys.*

Have pairs of students make a list of eight additional nouns including at least two plural nouns and two nouns that end in *-s.* Have students write the possessive form of each noun.

Using Apostrophes With Possessive Nouns *(continued)*

RULE 25.6.3 Read aloud the rule and then have students repeat the lines with you.

Discuss the examples with students, and have them brainstorm for other compound nouns that would form plurals in this manner.

Using Apostrophes With Pronouns

Point out that both indefinite and personal pronouns can show possession.

RULES 25.6.4, 25.6.5 Read aloud the rules and then have students repeat the lines with you.

Review the examples on the page. Write these words on the board: *no one, our, it, your, everybody.* Work with students to form the possessive of each word. Prompt students to name whether each word is an indefinite or personal pronoun. Personal pronouns have a possessive case, as well as a nominative and objective case. Pronouns that are in the possessive case are *already possessive* without adding an apostrophe and *-s*. As a result, possessive personal pronouns never have apostrophes.

RULE 25.6.3 Add an apostrophe and *-s* (or just an apostrophe if the word is a plural ending in *-s*) to the last word of a compound noun to form the possessive.

EXAMPLES the Girl Scouts**'** cookie sale

my sister-in-law**'**s car

See Practice 25.6A

Using Apostrophes With Pronouns

Both indefinite and personal pronouns can show possession.

RULE 25.6.4 Use an apostrophe and *-s* with indefinite pronouns to show possession.

EXAMPLES another**'**s preference   nobody else**'**s business

RULE 25.6.5 Do not use an apostrophe with possessive personal pronouns.

POSSESSIVE PERSONAL PRONOUNS		
	SINGULAR	PLURAL
First Person	my, mine	our, ours
Second Person	your, yours	your, yours
Third Person	his; her, hers; its	their, theirs

Some of these pronouns act as adjectives.

EXAMPLES The spider caught a fly in its web.

Our house is for sale.

Others act as subjects, objects, and subject complements.

EXAMPLES Mine is the yellow crayon.

Someone broke yours.

See Practice 25.6B

T594

Using Apostrophes With Contractions

Contractions are used in informal speech and writing, especially in dialogue because they create the sound of speech.

> Use an **apostrophe** in a **contraction** to show where one or more letters have been omitted.

25.6.6 RULE

COMMON CONTRACTIONS		
Verb + *not*	is not = isn't	cannot = can't
Noun or Pronoun + *will*	I will = I'll	we will = we'll
Noun or Pronoun + *be*	you are = you're	Andy is = Andy's
Noun or Pronoun + *would*	she would = she'd	who would = who'd

> Avoid using contractions in formal speech and writing.

25.6.7 RULE

Contractions may be used in dialogue and in informal speech and writing, but they should be avoided in formal usage.

INFORMAL WRITING   What's the solution?

FORMAL WRITING   What is the solution?

Using Apostrophes to Create Plurals

Do not use an apostrophe to form plurals, except in specific instances.

> Use an **apostrophe** and -s to create the plural form of a letter, numeral, or a word used as a name for itself.

25.6.8 RULE

EXAMPLES   Mind your *p*'s and *q*'s.

           Remember your *please*'s, please.

Practice 25.6C
Practice 25.6D

Using Apostrophes With Contractions

Remind students that contractions are shortened words. Apostrophes indicate that letters have been omitted. Point out that writers should use contractions sparingly in formal writing.

RULES 25.6.6, 25.6.7 Read aloud the rules and then have students repeat the lines with you.

Point out that the apostrophe may substitute for one letter or it may substitute for more than one letter. It is a good idea to memorize the correct form of common contractions. Review the example contractions on page 595 with the class. Have partners generate a sentence for each common contraction on the chart. Invite pairs to share their examples with the group.

Using Apostrophes to Create Plurals

Explain that apostrophes are not always used to form plurals.

RULE 25.6.8 Read aloud the rule and then have students repeat the lines with you.

Discuss the examples on the page and work with students to brainstorm for other examples.

Teacher Tip

For extra practice using apostrophes with contractions, have students write a friendly letter to a relative or friend. Encourage students to use contractions whenever possible in their letter. Invite students to share their letters with the class. Remind students that if they were writing a formal letter, they would want to avoid contractions.

1. the shirt's collar
2. the student's project
3. the children's songs
4. the judges' decision
5. the cow's mooing
6. my mom's suggestion
7. Marcus's bicycle
8. the women's efforts
9. the sparrows' chirping
10. my great-grandfather's pocket watch

11. We respected one another's privacy.
12. correct
13. We have ours, but where are theirs?
14. correct
15. correct
16. Is this anybody's lunch?
17. correct
18. It is your turn now, but soon it will be ours.
19. Josh asked if his bicycle had been found.
20. correct

SPEAKING APPLICATION

Have students explain the difference in sound between a plural and a possessive ending and what each signifies.

WRITING APPLICATION

Have students identify and explain how they formed the possessives in each of their sentences.

PRACTICE 25.6A Using Apostrophes to Show Ownership

Read each phrase. Write the possessive form of each item.

EXAMPLE   the book of Charles

ANSWER   *Charles's book*

1. the collar of the shirt
2. the project of the student
3. the songs of the children
4. the decision of the judges
5. the mooing of the cow
6. the suggestion of my mom
7. the bicycle of Marcus
8. the efforts of the women
9. the chirping of the sparrows
10. the pocket watch of my great-grandfather

PRACTICE 25.6B Using Apostrophes With Pronouns

Read the sentences. If all pronouns in a sentence are used correctly, write *correct*. If one or more pronouns are used incorrectly, rewrite the sentence correctly.

EXAMPLE   We found everyone else's name ta but not her's.

ANSWER   *We found everyone else's name ta but not* hers.

11. We respected one anothers privacy.
12. Celeste wanted her books, not his.
13. We have ours, but where are their's?
14. This must be someone's ruler.
15. If it is not hers, whose is it?
16. Is this anybodys lunch?
17. One must be careful where one puts one's glasses.
18. It is your turn now, but soon it will be our'
19. Josh asked if his' bicycle had been found.
20. Everyone was asked if the watch was his or hers.

SPEAKING APPLICATION

With a partner, take turns reading aloud the possessive forms you wrote in Practice 25.6A. Compare the ending sound of *judges/judges'* and *Marcus/Marcus's*. Talk about how what you hear matches what you wrote.

WRITING APPLICATION

Write three or four sentences about things you and your friends or family own. Use possessive forms of a singular noun, a plural noun, and at least one pronoun.

Working with ELLs   **ELL** Sheltered Instruction: Cognitive

To help students spell familiar words with increasing accuracy, introduce this rule: *If a word ends in a silent e, you usually drop the e if you add a suffix that begins with a vowel. You usually keep the e if you add a suffix that begins with a consonant.*

Beginning Model the rule with the familiar word *use*, adding the suffixes *-ful* and *-ing* and writing *useful* and *using* on the board. Discuss meaning. Then, write a sentence for each of the words. Have students copy the sentences.

Intermediate Write the familiar words *use*, *waste*, and *hope* on the board, along with an unfamiliar word such as *force*. Then, write the suffixes *-ful*, *-ing*, and *-ed*.

Have students use the words and the suffixes to complete the Writing Application, applying the spelling rule.

Advanced Provide students with a list of familar and unfamiliar silent -e words. Have students complete the Writing Application, using words formed by adding suffixes to the words on the list. Direct students to apply the rule as they form the words.

Advanced High Have students complete the Writing Application. Direct them to include at least three words that follow the spelling rule, including two unfamiliar words from a dictionary.

PRACTICE 25.6C Using Apostrophes in Contractions

Read the sentences. Each sentence contains a word group that can be written as a contraction. Write the contractions.

EXAMPLE I cannot find my hat.

ANSWER *can't*

Who is coming to dinner?

I will get the front door.

More homework is not what I wanted.

She would like to see you.

You are welcome to come in.

Stella is planning on coming to the play.

The twins are not able to do that.

He would make a good catcher.

That will be enough.

Do not slam the door.

PRACTICE 25.6D Proofreading for Apostrophes

Read the sentences. Rewrite each sentence, adding apostrophes where needed.

EXAMPLE I cant be responsible for my youngest brothers behavior.

ANSWER *I can't be responsible for my youngest brother's behavior.*

11. Everyones supposed to bring his or her own lunch.

12. Well try to come, but its not easy to get away from work.

13. Id like to introduce you to Cindy, Bonnies cousin.

14. Theyll bring sandwiches if youll bring salad.

15. Is this someones jacket?

16. My moms new sweater isnt the right size.

17. The paint in the doctors office wasnt dry.

18. If youre in this area, stop by.

19. Hed fix Tylers bike if he could, but its too badly damaged.

20. They wont let us open Seans mail.

SPEAKING APPLICATION

With a partner, read aloud the original form of two or three sentences in Practice 25.6C. Then, say the sentence aloud, using contractions. Talk about which form sounds more like regular speech.

WRITING APPLICATION

Write two sentences about interesting people you know or have read about. Use both possessives (nouns or pronouns) and contractions in your sentences.

Practice   597

PRACTICE 25.6C

1. Who's
2. I'll
3. isn't
4. She'd
5. You're
6. Stella's
7. aren't
8. He'd
9. That'll
10. Don't

PRACTICE 25.6D

11. Everyone's supposed to bring his or her own lunch.

12. We'll try to come, but it's not easy to get away from work.

13. I'd like to introduce you to Cindy, Bonnie's cousin.

14. They'll bring sandwiches if you'll bring salad.

15. Is this someone's jacket?

16. My mom's new sweater isn't the right size.

17. The paint in the doctor's office wasn't dry.

18. If you're in this area, stop by.

19. He'd fix Tyler's bike if he could, but it's too badly damaged.

20. They won't let us open Sean's mail.

SPEAKING APPLICATION

Have students explain how they were able to form the contractions in the exercise and why the contracted form of words sounds more like regular speech.

WRITING APPLICATION

Have students identify the contractions and possessives in their sentences and explain how they were formed and why they were used.

Lesson Objectives

1. Recognize and identify parentheses and brackets.

2. Use parentheses and brackets correctly in writing.

Parentheses

Tell students that writers use parentheses to separate information from the rest of a sentence or paragraph.

RULES 25.7.1, 25.7.2, 25.7.3 Read aloud the rules and then have students repeat the lines with you.

Use a Think Aloud as part of a gradual release progression.

Say: I often see parentheses when I am reading. **I know** parentheses set off explanations or other information that is related to the rest of the sentence. I also know there are some rules I should follow when using parentheses. A parenthetical sentence within another sentence should not begin with a capital letter. Also, a parenthetical sentence within another sentence can use a question mark or an exclamation mark, but not a period.

Work with students to find examples of parentheses in books, magazines, and Web sites. Discuss the examples and have students determine whether they follow Rule 25.7.1, 25.7.2, or 25.7.3.

Have student pairs write three sentences, one simple, one compound, and one complex. Students should include a parenthetical sentence within each sentence but not mark the parentheses. Student pairs should then exchange sentences with other pairs and correctly punctuate the sentences. Invite students to read selected sentences aloud.

Extension

To help students synthesize and apply what they have learned about using parentheses, have students work in teams to research and write timelines. Select a historical event or movement and have students use library sources or the Internet to research it. In each entry on the timelines, students should use parentheses to add information. Example: May 16, 1975, Junko Tabei (of Japan) was the first woman to reach the peak of Mount Everest. Challenge students by having them write introductory paragraphs to their timelines, using a variety of sentence types and end punctuation.

Parentheses and **brackets** enclose explanations or other information that may be omitted from the rest of the sentence without changing its basic meaning or construction.

Parentheses

Parentheses are used to separate information from the rest of a sentence or paragraph.

Use parentheses to set off explanations or other information that is loosely related to the rest of the sentence.

EXAMPLE During the Civil War **(** 1861–1865 **)** he helped soldiers stay in touch with their families.

A parenthetical sentence within another sentence should not begin with a capital letter unless the parenthetical sentence begins with a word that should be capitalized.

EXAMPLE Tickets for the play **(** click here to see the schedule **)** go on sale Thursday.

A parenthetical sentence within another sentence may end with a question mark or exclamation mark if applicable, but it should not end with a period.

INCORRECT Tickets for the play **(** click here to see the schedule **.)** go on sale Thursday **.**

CORRECT Tickets for the play **(** they haven't posted the schedule yet **!)** go on sale Thursday **.**

WRITING COACH

Online

www.phwritingcoach.com

Grammar Practice
Practice your grammar skills with Writing Coach Online.

Grammar Games
Test your knowledge of grammar in this fast-paced interactive video game.

WRITING COACH

Online

www.phwritingcoach.com

Diagnostic and Instruction
Diagnostic test assesses students' instructional needs. Lessons and practice are assigned based on results.

Additional Practice
- Grammar Practice—Targeted practice addresses individual needs.
- ExamView—Teachers customize their grammar practice and tests.
- Grammar Games—Interactive video games make grammar fun.

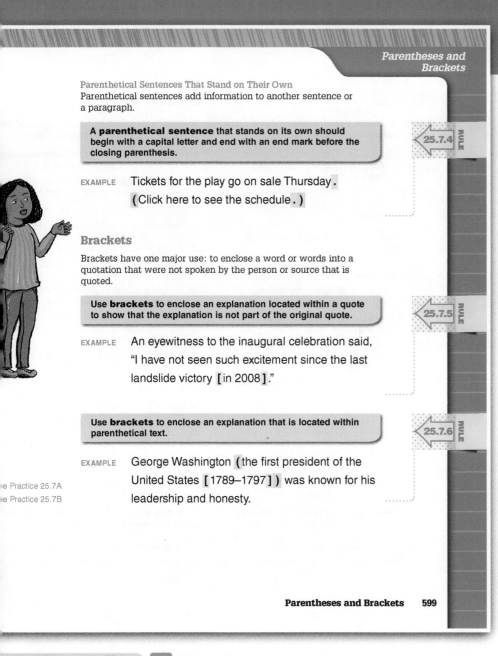

Parenthetical Sentences That Stand on Their Own

Parenthetical sentences add information to another sentence or a paragraph.

> **A parenthetical sentence** that stands on its own should begin with a capital letter and end with an end mark before the closing parenthesis.

◁ 25.7.4 RULE

EXAMPLE   Tickets for the play go on sale Thursday **.**
           (Click here to see the schedule **.)**

Brackets

Brackets have one major use: to enclose a word or words into a quotation that were not spoken by the person or source that is quoted.

> Use **brackets** to enclose an explanation located within a quote to show that the explanation is not part of the original quote.

◁ 25.7.5 RULE

EXAMPLE   An eyewitness to the inaugural celebration said, "I have not seen such excitement since the last landslide victory **[** in 2008 **]** ."

> Use **brackets** to enclose an explanation that is located within parenthetical text.

◁ 25.7.6 RULE

EXAMPLE   George Washington **(** the first president of the United States **[** 1789–1797 **])** was known for his leadership and honesty.

e Practice 25.7A
e Practice 25.7B

Parentheses and Brackets   599

Parenthetical Sentences That Stand on Their Own

Tell students that writers use parenthetical sentences to add information to another sentence or a paragraph. Parenthetical sentences are treated like other sentences— they begin with a capital letter and end with an end mark.

RULE 25.7.4   Read aloud the rule and then have students repeat the lines with you.

Have student pairs write two sentences. The second sentence should be a parenthetical sentence that adds information to the first sentence. Invite students to share their sentences with the group.

Brackets

Discuss the one major function of brackets: to show, in a quotation, that a word or words were not spoken or written by the person or source indicated. Writers use brackets to clarify quotations.

RULES 25.7.5, 25.7.6   Read aloud the rules and then have students repeat the lines with you.

Point out that the phrase *in 2008* is additional information about the last landslide victory. In the second example the years *1789–1797* provide more explanation for the parenthetical (when George Washington was president).

On page 598, help students distinguish intonation patterns of English with increasing ease. Read the example for Rule 25.7.2 aloud, modeling proper intonation for parenthetical sentences within another sentence (pausing before and after each parenthesis and, often, lowering pitch for the parenthetical sentence). Then:

Beginning   Read the example sentence aloud several times, first without the embedded parenthetical sentence, then with. Have students repeat each version after you.

Intermediate   Provide partners with three sentences with embedded parenthetical sentences. Have each student read the sentences aloud, using correct intonation. Have the listener explain how the intonation

in his or her partner's voice changed when reading the text in parentheses.

Advanced   Provide each partner with a different set of sentences with embedded parenthetical sentences. Then, have students read their sentences aloud. Ask listeners to write each sentence, following intonation to decide where to place the parentheses.

Advanced High   Challenge students to write three sentences with embedded parenthetical sentences. Have them speak these sentences to their partners, using correct intonation. Partners should copy the sentences, following their partner's intonation to decide where to place the parentheses.

Teacher Tip

If students are having difficulty distinguishing proper use of parentheses and brackets, give them this tip: brackets are used only with quotations or inside of parentheses. Parentheses are used with regular text. Provide students with additional sentences to proofread and correct for proper use of parentheses and brackets.

PRACTICE 25.7A

1. The United States entered the war (World War II) in 1941.

2. Georgia O'Keeffe (1887–1986) was an American artist.

3. My mom said, "I remember my last year of school [1989] as if it were yesterday."

4. Clara Barton's organization (the American Red Cross) was started in 1881.

5. Franklin Roosevelt was president of the United States for longer than anyone else (four terms [1933–1945]).

6. Our teacher said, "By that time [two o'clock] you should all be finished."

PRACTICE 25.7B

7. Two presidents, John Quincy Adams (1825–1829) and George W. Bush (2001–2009), were sons of earlier presidents.

8. Emily Dickinson (1830–1886) wrote, "Tell all the Truth but tell it slant."

9. Wolfgang Amadeus Mozart wrote more than 40 symphonies in his short life (36 years).

10. "The actor's [Lee Upshaw] portrayal of a loner will both move and upset you," wrote the movie reviewer.

11. Benjamin Franklin (1706–1790) offered this tip for a good life: "Early to bed and early to rise, makes a man healthy, wealthy, and wise [still good advice today]."

12. During World War II (1941–1945), many American women (Rosie the riveter, for example) took the place of men in factories.

PRACTICE 25.7A Using Parentheses and Brackets

Read the sentences. Rewrite each sentence, using parentheses or brackets where appropriate.

EXAMPLE   Alaska was once called Seward's Folly. It was bought by William Seward.

ANSWER   *Alaska was once called Seward's Folly. (It was bought by William Seward.)*

1. The United States entered the war World War II in 1941.

2. Georgia O'Keeffe 1887–1986 was an American artist.

3. My mom said, "I remember my last year of school 1989 as if it were yesterday."

4. Clara Barton's organization the American Red Cross was started in 1881.

5. Franklin Roosevelt was president of the United States for longer than anyone else four terms 1933–1945.

6. Our teacher said, "By that time two o'clock you should all be finished."

PRACTICE 25.7B Proofreading for Parentheses and Brackets

Read the sentences. Rewrite each sentence, using parentheses or brackets where appropriate.

EXAMPLE   We picked fourteen baskets of apples count them! at the orchard.

ANSWER   *We picked fourteen baskets of apples (count them!) at the orchard.*

7. Two presidents, John Quincy Adams 1825–1829 and George W. Bush 2001–2009 were sons of earlier presidents.

8. Emily Dickinson 1830–1886 wrote, "Tell all the Truth but tell it slant."

9. Wolfgang Amadeus Mozart wrote more than 40 symphonies in his short life 36 years.

10. "The actor's Lee Upshaw portrayal of a loner will both move and upset you," wrote the movie reviewer.

11. Benjamin Franklin 1706–1790 offered this tip for a good life: "Early to bed and early to rise makes a man healthy, wealthy, and wise still good advice today."

12. During World War II 1941–1945, many American women Rosie the riveter, for example took the place of men in factories.

SPEAKING APPLICATION

With a partner, take turns reading sentences in Practice 25.7B, leaving out the parts in parentheses or brackets. Discuss what taking out the information does to the sentence.

WRITING APPLICATION

Write three sentences about a period of history or a historical event that interests you. Use parentheses or brackets to add information to your sentences.

600   Punctuation

SPEAKING APPLICATION

Have students explain the use of parentheses and brackets in Practice 25.7A to show that they can recognize and use parentheses and brackets.

WRITING APPLICATION

Have students identify and explain their use of parentheses and brackets in their sentences.

25.8 Ellipses and Dashes

An **ellipsis** (. . .) shows where words have been omitted from a quoted passage. It can also mark a pause in dialogue. A **dash** (—) shows a strong, sudden break in thought or speech.

Using the Ellipsis

An **ellipsis** consists of three evenly spaced periods, or ellipsis points, in a row. There is a space before the first ellipsis point, between ellipsis points, and after the last ellipsis point. The plural form of the word *ellipsis* is *ellipses*.

> Use an **ellipsis** to show where words have been omitted from a quoted passage. Including an ellipsis shows the reader that the writer has chosen to omit some information.

25.8.1 RULE

QUOTED PASSAGE
"Four score and seven years ago our fathers brought forth on this continent a new nation conceived in liberty and dedicated to the proposition that all men are created equal." –Abraham Lincoln, *The Gettysburg Address,* November 19, 1863

QUOTED PASSAGE WITH WORDS OMITTED
"Fourscore and seven years ago our fathers brought forth . . . a new nation . . . dedicated to the proposition that all men are created equal."

Ellipses in Advertising

Ellipses are commonly used in ads for movies and other media. When you see an ellipsis in an ad, think about what might have been omitted. You might want to find the original review because the ad might be giving a different impression from what the reviewer intended.

ORIGINAL REVIEW
"It is amazing that anyone would think this was a love story."

AD WORDING
" . . . amazing . . . love story"

Ellipses and Dashes   601

@www.phwritingcoach.com

Diagnostic and Instruction

Diagnostic test assesses students' instructional needs. Lessons and practice are assigned based on results.

Additional Practice

- Grammar Tutorials—Animated videos reinforce key grammar skills.
- Grammar Practice—Targeted practice addresses individual needs.
- ExamView—Teachers customize their grammar practice and tests.
- Grammar Games—Interactive video games make grammar fun.

Lesson Objectives

1. Recognize and identify ellipses in sentences.

2. Recognize and identify dashes in sentences.

3. Use ellipses and dashes correctly in writing.

Using the Ellipsis

Tell students that an ellipsis consists of three evenly spaced periods in a row.

RULE 25.8.1 Read aloud the rule and then have students repeat the lines with you.

Use a Think Aloud as part of a gradual release progression.

Think Aloud

Say: When I am reading and I come across an ellipsis, **I know** that the writer has omitted some words from a quoted passage. Writers use ellipses to show that information has been omitted from the quoted passage. In regular writing, writers use ellipses to omit unnecessary words and information. In advertising, however, sometimes ellipses can be used in tricky ways. Look at the example sentences at the bottom of page 601. If I read only the ad wording, I would think this movie was a good one to see. But when I read the original review, I learned that the reviewer had a very different impression.

Distribute magazines and newspapers. Have students access the Internet, if possible. **Work with students** to find examples of ellipses in advertising. Lead a discussion about the uses of ellipses in advertising.

Have student pairs take one of the examples of ellipses in advertising. Students should rewrite the example by removing the ellipses and use their imaginations to fill in the missing words and information. Invite students to share their sentences aloud.

(continued)

Using the Ellipsis
(continued)

Tell students that several rules guide the use of ellipses.

RULES 25.8.2, 25.8.3, 25.8.4, 25.8.5 Read aloud the rules and then have students repeat the lines with you.

Hand out a lengthy quotation from a book or an article with which students are already familiar. Have students use ellipses to remove unnecessary words and information. Tell students that ellipses can be used to mark a pause in a dialogue or speech. Ask students to indicate whether their ellipses are omitting information or marking a pause. Invite students to read aloud their quotations.

RULE 25.8.2 Use an **ellipsis** to mark a pause in a dialogue or speech.

EXAMPLE   "But, in a larger sense, we can not dedicate **. . .** we can not consecrate **. . .** we can not hallow **. . .** this ground."

RULE 25.8.3 It is not necessary to use an **ellipsis** to show an omission at the beginning of material you are quoting. However, if you choose to omit any words *within* material you quote, you must use an ellipsis to show where information has been omitted.

UNNECESSARY   " **. . .** Now we are engaged in a great civil war, testing whether that nation, or any nation, so conceived and so dedicated, can long endure."

CORRECT   "Now we are engaged in a great civil war, testing whether that nation, or any nation so conceived and so dedicated, can long endure."

RULE 25.8.4 Use an **ellipsis** in the middle of the sentence to show an omission, pause, interruption, or incomplete statement.

EXAMPLE   "But, in a larger sense, we cannot dedicate **. . .** this ground."

RULE 25.8.5 Use an **ellipsis** and an end mark at the end of the sentence to show an omission, pause, or incomplete statement.

EXAMPLE   "I wonder how we are ever going to finish this project. Maybe we could. **. . .** "

If you omit words from a source you are quoting, omit the punctuation that accompanies the words unless it is correct in your sentence.

Working with ELLs   **ELL** Sheltered Instruction: Cognitive

Help students use linguistic support to enhance and confirm their understanding of increasingly complex spoken language.

Beginning Provide linguistic support by writing these words on the board: *ellipsis, pause, speech,* and *interruption.* Say each aloud, and review its meaning. Then, read aloud Rules 25.8.2 and 25.8.4 as students listen. Repeat, and then guide students in confirming understanding by reviewing the examples on the student page.

Intermediate Provide linguistic support by writing these words on the board: *ellipsis, pause, speech, omission, omit, quoting,* and *interruption.* Say each aloud, and review its meaning. Then, read aloud each of the rules

as students listen. Repeat your reading. Then, have students meet in small groups to summarize what they have learned, drawing on the linguistic support you have provided.

Advanced Have students use the linguistic support of a dictionary to look up each of the words listed for the Intermediate activity. Read aloud each of the rules, and have partners discuss what they have learned.

Advanced High Have students complete the Advanced activity. Then, have them apply what they have learned by writing three sentences with ellipses.

Dashes

Like commas and parentheses, **dashes** separate certain words, phrases, or clauses from the rest of the sentence or paragraph. Dashes, however, signal a stronger, more sudden interruption in thought or speech than commas or parentheses. A dash may also take the place of certain words before an explanation.

> **Use a dash to show a strong, sudden break in thought or speech.**

25.8.6 RULE

EXAMPLE   I can't believe how many free throws my brother missed — I don't even want to think about it!

If the interrupting expression is in the middle of the sentence, use a dash on either side of it to set it off from the rest of the sentence.

EXAMPLE   I read an article — I forget who wrote it — about renewable energy sources.

> **Use a dash in place of *in other words*, *namely*, or *that is* before an explanation.**

25.8.7 RULE

EXAMPLES   Ruth plays ball for one purpose — to win.

To see his jersey hanging from the rafters — this was his greatest dream.

Dashes can also be used to set off nonessential appositives or modifiers.

EXAMPLE   The selfish player — a "star" who is concerned mainly with his own glory — will not pass the ball.

See Practice 25.8D

Dashes

Point out that dashes are similar to commas and parentheses. All three types of punctuation separate words, phrases, or clauses from the rest of the sentence or paragraph. Dashes are distinctive because they signal a stronger, more sudden interruption in thought or speech. Writers use dashes to show a strong, sudden break in thought or speech.

RULES 25.8.6, 25.8.7 Read aloud the rules and then have students repeat the lines with you.

Use a Think Aloud as part of a gradual release progression.

Think Aloud **Say:** When **I see** dashes in a book or article, I know the writer is showing a sudden, strong break in thought or speech. Dashes can also be used in place of certain words, such as *namely*, *that is*, or *in other words*. When I am writing, sometimes I might use dashes. Dashes can make writing energetic. However, overusing dashes can make writing seem disconnected and hard to understand.

Work with students to find examples of dashes in books, articles, or Web sites.

Have student pairs write three sentences using dashes. Students should not include the dashes in the sentences. Then, each pair should exchange sentences with another pair. Student pairs should then insert dashes in the correct places in the sentences. Invite students to read selected sentences aloud to the group.

> *Teacher Tip*
>
> If students find ellipses and dashes confusing, remind them that ellipses are usually used with quoted material. Ellipses indicate omitted information. Dashes, on the other hand, show stronger, sudden interruptions in thought or speech. Read aloud several sentences. Some sentences use commas, others use ellipses, and still others use dashes. Indicate with your phrasing the differences between pauses for commas, ellipses, and dashes. Have students read with you, and then have students read aloud to a partner.

1. pause
2. omission
3. omission
4. pause
5. pause

6. omission
7. interruption
8. omission
9. omission
10. pause

11. Jada spoke hesitantly, "Well . . . I guess . . . what if?"

12. My favorite Emily Dickinson poem begins, "I dwell in Possibility . . ."

13. MARSHA (to *FAITH*): It's time to . . . FAITH (*breaking* in): You're wrong!

14. "What is your point . . . please . . . say something," Millie begged.

15. "We shall pay any price, bear any burden . . ." comes from John F. Kennedy's Inaugural Address.

16. "That's one small step . . ." was the beginning of Neil Armstrong's message to America when he stepped on the moon.

17. "Oh no . . . you can't come?"

18. "Oops . . . there goes the glass of water."

19. Let me think . . . did you notice anything unusual?"

20. Superb handling . . . Roomy trunk . . . Fuel economy . . . What more could you want?

Read the sentences. For each sentence, tell whether ellipses (or ellipses points) are used to indicate a *pause*, an *interruption*, or an *omission*.

EXAMPLE   Mom said, "Don't go . . . ," but I didn't hear the rest.

ANSWER   *omission*

1. I'm not sure . . . perhaps we should wait.

2. "We hold these truths to be self-evident . . . endowed . . . with certain . . . rights . . . ."

3. "I pledge allegiance to the flag . . . and to the republic . . . ."

4. Gosh . . . I . . . uh . . . I'm not sure.

5. This is important . . . really important . . . maybe the most important thing I've ever done.

6. I love the song that begins, "O beautiful for spacious skies . . . ."

7. Wait . . . please . . . I can't do this alone.

8. I heard, "Read page 280 through . . . ," but I didn't catch the final page number.

9. "We the people of the United States . . . do ordain and establish this Constitution . . . ."

10. I was slowing down . . . and I wasn't sure . . . I would make it.

WRITING APPLICATION

Write three sentences using ellipses to indicate omissions, interruptions, or incomplete statements. Explain the purpose of the ellipses in each sentence.

604   Punctuation

Read the sentences. Identify where the ellipses belong in the sentences. Rewrite the sentences using ellipses to show the pause, the interruption, or the omission.

EXAMPLE   "Huh what are you trying to say?" asked Zach.

ANSWER   *"Huh . . . what are you trying to say?" asked Zach.*

11. Jada spoke hesitantly, "Well I guess what if

12. My favorite Emily Dickinson poem begins, "I dwell in Possibility."

13. MARSHA (to *FAITH*): It's time to FAITH (*breaking in*): You're wrong!

14. "What is your point please say something," Millie begged.

15. "we shall pay any price, bear any burden" comes from John F. Kennedy's Inaugural Address.

16. "That's one small step" was the beginning Neil Armstrong's message to America when he stepped on the moon.

17. "Oh no you can't come?"

18. "Oops there goes the glass of water."

19. "Let me think did you notice anything unusual?"

20. Superb handling Roomy trunk Fuel economy What more could you want?

WRITING APPLICATION

Write a short dialogue between characters in a story or play. Use ellipses to show pauses, interruptions, or omissions in the conversation. Read the dialogue aloud with a partner, paying attention to the ellipses.

SPEAKING APPLICATION

Students' sentences should demonstrate that they can recognize and use punctuation marks including ellipses to indicate omissions and interruptions or incomplete statements.

WRITING APPLICATION

Have students demonstrate that they can recognize and use punctuation marks including ellipses to indicate omissions and interruptions or incomplete statements by identifying and explaining the ellipses in their dialogues.

Working with ELLs   **ELL** Sheltered Instruction: Cognitive

Using the long and short sentences in Practice 25.8B, have students speak using a variety of sentence lengths with increasing accuracy and ease.

Beginning Pair fluent speakers with Beginning students. Have fluent partners read aloud sentence 17, pausing to indicate the ellipses in the sentence. Have the Beginning students echo their partners. Repeat with other short sentences in the exercise. Finally, provide practice with longer sentences by having partners repeat the exercise, adding "he said" or "she said" to the beginning of each sentence.

Intermediate Have partners take turns reading each sentence in Practice 25.8B aloud, indicating with pauses where the ellipses appear. Coach students as they encounter sentences with increasing lengths.

Advanced Have partners read the sentences in Practice 25.8B aloud, pausing to indicate ellipses. Have each partner choose three sentences to copy, adding information to increase the length of the sentence. Partners should exchange papers and read the sentences aloud.

Advanced High Have partners complete the Advanced activity. As they create longer sentences, challenge them to use compound and complex sentences.

PRACTICE 25.8C ▷ Using Ellipses

[Rea]d each statement. Then, rewrite each [sen]tence adding ellipses where appropriate. [Sta]te whether the ellipses indicate an omission, [an] interruption, or an incomplete statement.

EXAMPLE That outfit looks too What would you call it?

ANSWER *That outfit looks too . . . What would you call it?—incomplete statement or omission*

Stop I can't understand what you're saying.

This motor is I know what's wrong.

We can't present the award without see if you can find him.

Your term paper is good, but it needs

Love is special. Love is

I'm not sure Could you say that again?

Jason where do I know him from?

Wait until I OK, I'm finished.

I wonder if we could

Look over there quick!

PRACTICE 25.8D ▷ Using Dashes

Read the sentences. Rewrite each sentence, adding dashes where they are needed.

EXAMPLE It was important so important, in fact, I couldn't let anything stop me.

ANSWER *It was important—so important, in fact, I couldn't let anything stop me.*

11. The United States had a mission to be the first to the moon.

12. I would like to show you my collection of hey, what was that?

13. We went to a store I don't remember which one to look for a dress.

14. I have one purpose in life to become a scientist.

15. See you tomorrow oh, don't forget to take the handouts.

16. He needed a job even a part-time one for the money.

17. We saw a movie I don't remember the title on Saturday.

18. We'll talk after class you do have time, don't you? about our plans.

19. She came for a reason to clean up this place.

20. When we go and we will go you can come with us.

SPEAKING APPLICATION

[W]ith a partner, take terms reading the new [s]entences created in Practice 25.8C. Discuss [w]hether your new sentences show omissions, [i]nterruptions, or incomplete statements. Then, [p]ractice reading sentences containing ellipses [w]ith proper expression.

WRITING APPLICATION

Write two sentences about your weekend. In each sentence, use a dash to show a sudden break in thought or speech or to replace *in other words, namely,* or *that is* before an explanation.

Practice   605

PRACTICE 25.8C

1. Stop . . . I can't understand what you're saying.—interruption

2. This motor is . . . I know what's wrong.—incomplete statement or omission

3. We can't present the award without . . . see if you can find him.—incomplete statement or omission

4. Your term paper is good, but it needs . . .—incomplete statement or omission

5. Love is special. Love is . . .—incomplete statement

6. I'm not sure . . . Could you say that again?—incomplete statement or omission

7. Jason . . . where do I know him from?—interruption

8. Wait until I . . . OK, I'm finished.—incomplete statement or omission

9. I wonder if we could . . .—incomplete statement or omission

10. Look over there . . . quick!—interruption

PRACTICE 25.8D

11. The United States had a mission—to be the first to the moon.

12. I would like to show you my collection of—hey, what was that?

13. We went to a store—I don't remember which one—to look for a dress.

14. I have one purpose in life—to become a scientist.

15. See you tomorrow—oh, don't forget to take the handouts.

16. He needed a job—even a part-time one—for the money.

17. We saw a movie—I don't remember the title—on Saturday.

18. We'll talk after class—you do have time, don't you?—about our plans.

19. She came for a reason—to clean up this place.

20. When we go—and we will go—you can come with us.

SPEAKING APPLICATION

Students should demonstrate that they can recognize and use punctuation marks including ellipses to indicate omissions and interruptions or incomplete statements by explaining the results of their discussions with partners.

WRITING APPLICATION

Students should demonstrate that they can recognize and use dashes to show a sudden break in thought or speech or to replace certain words by identifying and explaining the dashes in their sentences.

Test Warm-Up

1. **D** "You will be home—my decision is final—every day by four o'clock.

2. **H** Add ellipses after *Mom*

3. **D** "No . . . it's time—way past time—for you to get serious about school."

4. **G** Add ellipses after *but*

Reteach

If students have not mastered these skills, review the content in Section 25.8 Ellipses and Dashes.

1. Dashes 25.8.6

2. Using the Ellipsis 25.8.5

3. Dashes 25.8.6

4. Using the Ellipsis 25.8.5

Test Tip

If time remains after students have finished answering questions for a test, encourage them to look over their answer sheets for errors in recording their answers. Students should first make sure that their answer sheets were correctly aligned with their test booklets so that each of their answer choices is applied to the correct question. Then, students should look over their answer sheets and erase random marks that might be misinterpreted as answers by a test grader. Finally, students should make sure that each question has been answered only once.

Test Warm-Up

DIRECTIONS

Read the introduction and the passage that follows. Then, answer the questions to show that you can recognize and use punctuation marks, including ellipses, to indicate omissions and interruptions or incomplete statements.

Erin wrote this dialogue about Ashley and her mother for a class play. Read the paragraph and think about the changes you would suggest as a peer editor. When you finish reading, answer the questions that follow.

Getting Serious About Grades

(1) Ashley and her mother, Mrs. Holland, are discussing new rules. (2) Mrs. Holland is unhappy about Ashley's grades, and Ashley doesn't think the rules are fair. (3) "You must be home my decision is final every day by four o'clock. (4) You cannot text or watch television until your homework is done. (5) Is that clear?" said Mrs. Holland. (6) "But . . . Mom" (7) "No . . . it's time way past time for you to get serious about school." (8) Ashley spoke quietly, "Well . . . I see your point but." (9) "No more buts . . . ." replied Mrs. Holland, leaving the room.

1 What is the BEST way to revise sentence 3?

  A "You must be home . . . my decision is final every day by four o'clock.

  B "You must be home my decision is final every . . . day by four o'clock.

  C "You must be—home my decision is final every day and by four o'clock.

  D "You will be home—my decision is final—every day by four o'clock.

2 What change, if any, should be made in sentence 6?

  F Delete the ellipsis

  G Use a lowercase *M* on *Mom*

  H Add ellipses after *Mom*

  J Make no change

3 What is the BEST way to revise sentence 7?

  A "No. It's time, way past time, for you to get serious about school."

  B "No . . . it's time—way past time for you to get serious about school."

  C "No . . . it's time—way—past time—for you to get serious about school."

  D "No . . . it's time—way past time—for you to get serious about school."

4 What change should be made in sentence 8?

  F Add a comma after *well*

  G Add ellipses after *but*

  H Add ellipses after *see*

  J Add a dash after *point*

CHAPTER 26 LESSON PLANNER
Capitalization

Use the Online Lesson Planner at www.phwritingcoach.com to customize your instructional plan for an integrated Language Arts curriculum.

DAY 1 26.1 Capitalization

"What Do You Notice?" **Objectives:** Identify, use, and understand capitalization, including • with the word *I* • in sentences • in quotations • for proper nouns	**INSTRUCTION AND PRACTICE** **Student Edition** pp. 607–618

DAY 2 26.1 Capitalization

Objectives: Identify, use, and understand capitalization, including • for proper adjectives • for titles of people • for titles of works • in letters • in abbreviations, acronyms, and initials	**INSTRUCTION AND PRACTICE** **Student Edition** pp. 619–627 **Test Warm-Up** p. 628

DAY 3 Cumulative Review

Objectives: Identify, use, and understand mechanics, including • punctuation • capitalization	**INSTRUCTION AND PRACTICE** **Student Edition** pp. 629–630

Alternate Pacing Plans

- **Block Scheduling** Each day in the Lesson Planner represents a 40–50 minute block. Teachers using block scheduling may combine days to revise pacing to meet their classroom needs.

- **Accelerated Lesson Planning** Combine instructional days, focusing on concepts called out by students' diagnostic test results.

- **Integrated Language Arts Curriculum** Use the instruction and practice in this chapter to provide reinforcement, remediation, or extension of grammar concepts taught in your literature curriculum.

WRITING COACH

Online

www.phwritingcoach.com

Grammar Assessment and Practice

Chapter diagnostic tests assess students' skills and assign instruction and practice.

DimensionL Video Games

Fast-paced interactive video games challenge students' mastery of grammar.

Grammar Assessment

Grammar Coach:	Diagnostic Assessment	End-of-Chapter Assessment	Progress Monitoring
Personalized Instruction	Students take grammar diagnostic test online and are automatically assigned instruction and practice in areas where they need support.	Teacher uses **ExamView** to administer end-of-chapter assessment and remediation. Teachers may customize **ExamView** tests or use the ones provided.	Teachers may use the **Test Warm-Ups** and the **Cumulative Reviews** in the student book or eText to check students' mastery of grammar skills.
Teacher-Directed Instruction	Teacher administers the diagnostic test and determines focus of instruction and practice.		Students may also play **DimensionL** grammar video games to test their grammar skills.

Lesson Planner continues on next page

> *With apologies to e.e. cummings, capitalization needs to be addressed more vigorously in our classrooms. This is especially true in the age of text-messaging, instant messaging, and social Web site posts.*
>
> **—Kelly Gallagher**

Differentiated Instruction

Differentiated Instruction Boxes in this Teacher's Edition address these student populations:

- Below-Level Students
- Above-Level Students
- Gifted and Talented Students
- Special Needs Students
- English Language Learners
- Spanish Speaking Students

In addition, for further enrichment, see the **Extension** features.

Grammar Ground Rule: Dot Your *i*'s and Cross Your *t*'s!

Model with Students

In this chapter, dotting your *i*'s and crossing your *t*'s means being careful to use the right capitalization. Explain to students that, when almost everything was written by hand, dotting your *i*'s and crossing your *t*'s was very important.

Say: An undotted *i* could look like an *e,* and an uncrossed *t* could look like an *i.* So the last thing a writer did was to go over what he or she had written to make sure that these letters were dotted and crossed. Today, we use this phrase to mean "make sure you've got the details right." In other words, you need to edit your writing. I don't like to worry about all the details of capitalization when I'm writing my first draft. I like to let the ideas flow. That's why I make sure that I always edit what I've written.

Write this sentence on the board, incorrect capitalization and all: *when mr. thomas went to houston, he took the Train.* Have students work with you to edit and revise the sentence. As they make suggestions for capitalizing, have them explain why they think the word in question should be capitalized or lower case.

Small Group Activity – Editing and Revising

Have students form groups to find an article about a vacation area. Have the students rewrite a paragraph from the article, changing the capitalization so that it is incorrect. Then have the groups exchange articles and edit the paragraphs. As they do their revisions, have the groups discuss the changes they are making. The discussions should answer these questions:

- Why should this particular word be capitalized?
- Why should this other word *not* be capitalized?

Have a member of each group present their conclusions to the class and give one good example of a sentence that follows this grammar ground rule: Dot your *i*'s and cross your *t*'s.

Grammar Ground Rules

1. Keep it clear.
2. Make them agree.
3. Make it specific.
4. Dot your *i*'s and cross your *t*'s.
5. Make it active.

CAPITALIZATION

owing which words to capitalize will make the content of
ur writing clearer and easier to read.

WRITE GUY *Jeff Anderson, M.Ed.*

WHAT DO YOU NOTICE?

earch for examples of capitalization as you zoom in on sentences
om the story "Stray" by Cynthia Rylant.

MENTOR TEXT

> In January, a puppy wandered onto the property of
> Mr. Amos Lacey and his wife, Mamie, and their daughter, Doris.

ow, ask yourself the following questions:

Why is the word *January* capitalized?

Why does the abbreviation *Mr.* begin with a capital letter?

he word *January* is capitalized because it names a specific period
f time. The abbreviation *Mr.* begins with a capital letter because
stands for *Mister*, which is part of Amos Lacey's name. *Mamie*
nd *Doris* are capitalized because they are also proper nouns that
ame specific people.

rammar for Writers Knowing the rules of capitalization helps
writer signal the start of a new sentence and present specific
eople, places, things, and events accurately. Be sure to check
our writing for words that need to be capitalized.

607

CHAPTER 26

CAPITALIZATION

As students progress in their writing skills, it will be important for them to be able to apply the rules of grammar, usage, and mechanics to their own drafts. Use the *What Do You Notice?* feature to help them see effective conventions in the work of professional writers. Encourage students to incorporate proper voice, tense, and syntax as they edit their own writing.

Read the opening sentence aloud. Remind students that capitalization plays a very important role in crafting well-written sentences. Point out that capitalization applies to the written word rather than the spoken word. Used correctly, it tells the reader which words are proper nouns or when a new sentence or dialogue begins.

WRITE GUY *Jeff Anderson, M.Ed.*

WHAT DO YOU NOTICE?

When students have read the Mentor Text, **say:** Why are so many words in this sentence capitalized? What does the capital letter at the beginning of a word tell us about the word? (**Possible response:** There are a lot of names in the sentence. Many of the capital letters indicate proper nouns. One of them indicates the start of a sentence.) **Say:** What feeling do you get from all the capital letters, as well as the word *Mr.?* (**Possible response:** The sentence is dealing with very specific people. It seems like we will get to know a lot more about Mr. and Mrs. Lacey and Doris in the story. **Say:** Why aren't the words *wife* and *daughter* capitalized? (**Response:** They are not proper nouns.)

Explain that capitalization is one important way writers relay information to readers. Without it, ideas would not be accurately expressed. Capitalization helps writers be precise.

Grammar for Writers: Syntax

Remind students that a writer's use of capitalization shows how well he or she understands his or her subject matter. The rules and activities that follow will help them use capitalization correctly.

T607

Lesson Objectives

1. Use conventions of capitalization correctly.

2. Proofread for capitalization.

The Word *I*

Tell students that the pronoun *I* always represents a specific person. For that reason, it is always capitalized.

RULE 26.1.1 Read aloud the rule and then have students repeat the line with you.

Write on the board several sentences using the pronoun *I,* but do not capitalize *I.* Ask students to come to the board and correct the errors in capitalization.

Sentences

Give students a strategy for remembering to capitalize the beginning of every sentence. Tell them that all sentences should "introduce" themselves. Explain that a capital letter introduces the words and ideas that make up a sentence.

RULE 26.1.2 Read aloud the rule and then have students repeat the lines with you.

Write on the board these scrambled sentences. Have students unscramble each and then apply the capitalization rules for sentences.

1. is chocolate flavor my favorite. (Chocolate is my favorite flavor.)

2. evening she's asleep since been yesterday! (She's been asleep since yesterday evening!)

3. outside clean room your before you go. (Clean your room before you go outside.)

4. sandwich a wants who? (Who wants a sandwich?)

Have students brainstorm for and write four sentences (declarative, interrogative, imperative, exclamatory) that apply the rules of capitalization. Tell students to include one sentence in which the missing parts are understood. Make sure that students begin each sentence with a capital letter.

Find It / FIX IT

8

Grammar Game Plan

26.1 Using Capitalization

Capital letters are used for the first words in all sentences and in many quotations. They are also used for the word *I*, no matter what its position is in a sentence.

The Word *I*

RULE 26.1.1

> **The pronoun *I* is always capitalized.**

EXAMPLE | **I** worked for two years as a clerk before **I** received a promotion.

Sentences

One of the most common uses of a capital letter is to signal the beginning of a sentence. The first word in a sentence must begin with a capital letter.

RULE 26.1.2

> **Capitalize the first word in declarative, interrogative, imperative, and exclamatory sentences.**

DECLARATIVE | **S**trong gusts of wind made it dangerous to drive on the bridge.

INTERROGATIVE | **W**ho found the clue leading to the suspect's arrest?

IMPERATIVE | **T**hink carefully before you decide.

EXCLAMATORY | **W**hat an amazing coincidence this is!

Sometimes only part of a sentence is written. The rest of the sentence is understood. In these cases, a capital is still needed for the first word.

EXAMPLES | **W**hen?   **W**hy not?   **C**ertainly!

608   Capitalization

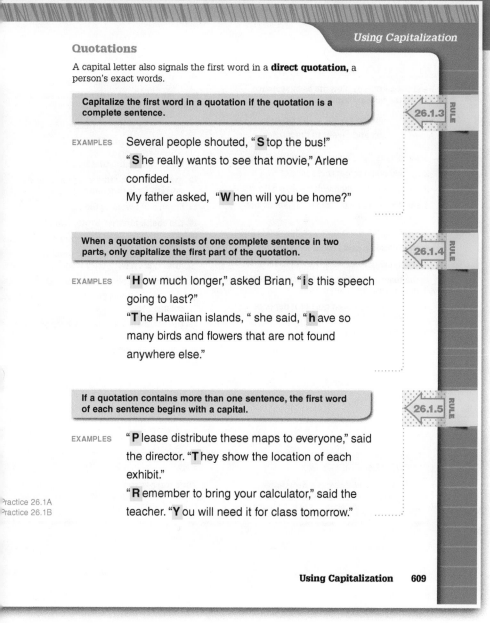

Quotations

A capital letter also signals the first word in a **direct quotation,** a person's exact words.

> **Capitalize the first word in a quotation if the quotation is a complete sentence.**

RULE 26.1.3

EXAMPLES   Several people shouted, "**S**top the bus!"

"**S**he really wants to see that movie," Arlene confided.

My father asked, "**W**hen will you be home?"

> **When a quotation consists of one complete sentence in two parts, only capitalize the first part of the quotation.**

RULE 26.1.4

EXAMPLES   "**H**ow much longer," asked Brian, "**i**s this speech going to last?"

"**T**he Hawaiian islands, " she said, "**h**ave so many birds and flowers that are not found anywhere else."

> **If a quotation contains more than one sentence, the first word of each sentence begins with a capital.**

RULE 26.1.5

EXAMPLES   "**P**lease distribute these maps to everyone," said the director. "**T**hey show the location of each exhibit."

"**R**emember to bring your calculator," said the teacher. "**Y**ou will need it for class tomorrow."

Practice 26.1A
Practice 26.1B

Quotations

Remind students that, when we use a direct quotation, we repeat the exact words of another person. One convention of capitalization is to place a capital letter right after a quotation mark if the quoted sentence is complete.

RULES 26.1.3, 26.1.4, 26.1.5 Read aloud the rules and then have students repeat the lines with you.

Say: Writers often split direct quotations. They may interrupt a quotation to clarify who is speaking or to make a comment. If a sentence in a quotation is split apart by a phrase like *she said,* or *Khanh replied,* capitalize only the first word of each complete sentence in the quotation.

When a direct quotation consists of several complete sentences, the first word of each sentence begins with a capital letter.

Have partners look in one of their English or social studies books. Have them identify an example of each of the three types of direct quotations. They should copy each quotation, underline the first word of each complete sentence, and note whether the quotation is a complete sentence, a split quotation, or more than one complete sentence.

Working with ELLs   ELL Sheltered Instruction: Cognitive

Have students demonstrate reading comprehension and expand reading skills by employing inferential skills, such as making predictions. Choose a selection that students are reading in class. Review the portion of the selection that students have already read. Then:

Beginning Guide students in mapping possible outcomes based on what they have read so far. Then, with students, preview the illustrations for the next part. Guide students in using simple terms and, if needed, **drawings** to express predictions about what will happen next.

Intermediate Have students work in small groups to map possible outcomes based on what they have read so far. Have them preview illustrations for the next part. Then,

have groups make a prediction about what will happen next. Have them record part of their discussion using this frame: _____ said, " _____."

Advanced Have partners review what they have read, preview the next part, and predict what will happen next. Have them record predictions, stating one as a direct quotation.

Advanced High Have partners complete the Advanced activity. Then, have them write a dialogue based on their discussion using direct quotations.

PRACTICE 26.1A

1. You
2. Are
3. When
4. The; Do; Do
5. Who; What; When
6. The; I
7. When; I; I
8. The; There
9. We
10. My; If; I; I

PRACTICE 26.1B

11. When
12. The; This; Everything
13. I
14. The; Avoid
15. Mom; Could
16. When; I
17. Steel
18. When; I'm; I
19. The; Please
20. What

WRITING APPLICATION

Have students exchange their papers with partners and check their partners' capitalization.

WRITING APPLICATION

Have students dictate their sentences to a partner, then check to see if their partner has capitalized correctly.

PRACTICE 26.1A Supplying Capitalization

Read the sentences. Rewrite each sentence, adding the missing capitals.

EXAMPLE   he and i went to the movies.

ANSWER   *He* and *I* went to the movies.

1. Mom said, "you need to finish that."
2. are we going to get there soon?
3. Jason asked, "when will we arrive?"
4. the container read, "do not shake. do not place near heat."
5. who? what? when was this decided?
6. the Schmidts said i could use their pool.
7. when i was younger, i wanted to be a doctor.
8. the teacher announced, "there will be no test next week."
9. Dad said, "we might go, but it depends on the weather."
10. my sister warned, "if i were you, i would keep quiet."

PRACTICE 26.1B Proofreading for Capitalization

Read the sentences. Rewrite each sentence, adding the missing capitals.

EXAMPLE   "is it true?" i asked.

ANSWER   *"Is it true?" I* asked.

11. when was your father born?
12. the coach said, "this is a new season. everything is different."
13. Sarah and i went to the park.
14. the health reporter wrote, "avoid sugar."
15. mom asked, "could you bring me two eggs
16. "when i was young," my grandma said, "we didn't have a television."
17. steel made it possible to build skyscrapers
18. Greg said, "when i'm older, i want to go to college."
19. the librarian said, "please keep your voices down."
20. "what is that?" he wondered.

WRITING APPLICATION

Write three sentences: one declarative, one interrogative, and one exclamatory. Use capitalization correctly in each sentence.

WRITING APPLICATION

Write three sentences about your family or friends. Include a quotation in each sentence. Use capitalization correctly.

Working with ELLs   ELL Sheltered Instruction: Metacognitive

Using the Writing Application for Practice 26.1B on page 610, have students demonstrate listening comprehension of increasingly complex spoken English by taking notes. Instruct students to monitor comprehension and seek clarification as needed.

Beginning Write a conversation, and read the conversation aloud, sharing roles with a fluent speaker. Remind students to monitor understanding, asking for clarification as needed. Then, ask students comprehension questions such as *Whom was I speaking to? What were we talking about?* Write their responses on the board, and have students copy the responses as notes.

Intermediate Read aloud a model conversation as students take notes. Have students monitor understanding by using their notes to retell the conversation, asking for clarification as needed.

Advanced Have partners each write a conversation and then take turns reading their conversations aloud as the listening partner takes notes. Have students monitor understanding and seek clarification by asking their partner questions based on their notes.

Advanced High Have partners each write a conversation and then take turns reading their conversations aloud as the listening partner takes notes. Have students write a summary based on their notes, asking for clarification as needed.

Using Capitalization for Proper Nouns

An important use of capital letters is to show that a word is a **proper noun.** Proper nouns name specific people, places, or things.

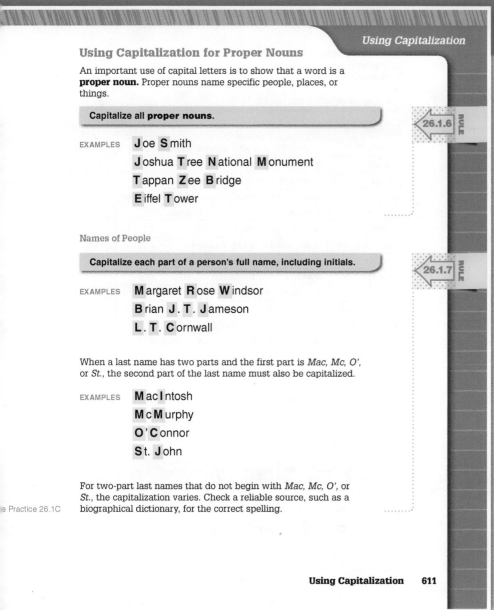

| Capitalize all **proper nouns.** | | RULE **26.1.6** |

EXAMPLES **J**oe **S**mith

Joshua **T**ree **N**ational **M**onument

Tappan **Z**ee **B**ridge

Eiffel **T**ower

Names of People

| Capitalize each part of a person's full name, including initials. | | RULE **26.1.7** |

EXAMPLES **M**argaret **R**ose **W**indsor

Brian **J**. **T**. **J**ameson

L. **T**. **C**ornwall

When a last name has two parts and the first part is *Mac, Mc, O',* or *St.,* the second part of the last name must also be capitalized.

EXAMPLES **M**ac**I**ntosh

Mc**M**urphy

O'**C**onnor

St. **J**ohn

For two-part last names that do not begin with *Mac, Mc, O',* or *St.,* the capitalization varies. Check a reliable source, such as a biographical dictionary, for the correct spelling.

e Practice 26.1C

Using Capitalization **611**

Using Capitalization for Proper Nouns

Point out that capitalization helps to distinguish proper nouns from common nouns. Specific persons, places, and things are easily identified when they're capitalized. Say the names of a student, the county, and the state as examples of proper nouns.

RULE 26.1.6 Read aloud the rule and then have students repeat the line with you.

Have students brainstorm for a list of proper nouns. Then, direct students to capitalize and use each proper noun correctly in a sentence.

Names of People

Clarify for students the importance of capitalizing each part of a person's full name. Because an initial stands in place of a name, it is also capitalized.

RULE 26.1.7 Read aloud the rule and then have students repeat the line with you.

Use a Think Aloud as part of a gradual release progression.

Think Aloud **Say: I know** that nouns referring to general types of persons, places, or things should not be capitalized. **Recite** this sentence: *The U.S. Constitution is one of our nation's most important documents.* **Ask:** In that sentence, which words refer to the U. S. Constitution? (*U.S. Constitution, one,* and *documents*) And which of those words are capitalized? (U.S. Constitution) Why? (because they name a specific document) Why isn't the word *documents* capitalized? (It names a general type of object.)

Work with students to use conventions of capitalization to capitalize the names of several students and teachers.

Have student pairs brainstorm for and write the names of five family members and friends. Remind students that the names must use conventions of capitalization. Have students post their names around the room. Then, have students walk around and critique the capitalization of their classmates' names.

Differentiated Instruction

RTI Strategy for Below-Level Students
In order for students to apply the conventions of capitalization to proper nouns, they must understand what distinguishes proper nouns from common nouns. Provide practice in distinguishing between the two. Give students several pairs of related words written on small slips of paper. In each pair, there should be a common and a proper noun. Do not capitalize either word. Some examples include: *woman, dr. maldonado; city, los angeles; store, betty's boutique.*

Have students use the conventions of capitalization to write the correctly capitalized words in a T-chart labeled *Common Nouns* and *Proper Nouns.* (**Answers:** Common Nouns: woman, city, store. Proper Nouns: Dr. Maldonado, Los Angeles, Betty's Boutique.)

Geographical Places

Remind students that the names of geographical places often include words that can function as common nouns. For example, the name *Lake Michigan* includes the common noun *lake.* Because *Lake* is a part of Lake Michigan's name, it is capitalized.

RULE 26.1.8 Read aloud the rule and then have students repeat the line with you.

Remind students that names of specific geographical places, such as those that would be found on a map, are always capitalized. Have students write a sentence correctly capitalizing the name of a place they would like to visit.

Regions and Map Directions

To help students differentiate between regions and directions, tell them that a region can be visited but a map direction cannot be visited. It indicates a direction, not a specific place.

RULE 26.1.9 Read aloud the rule and then have students repeat the lines with you.

Say: Specific geographic places are just like all other specific places—they must be capitalized. What should be capitalized in these sentences? *I grew up south of here, in North Carolina. I really like it in the East.* (*North Carolina* and *East.* The word *south* is not capitalized because it is used as a direction.)

As a class, discuss specific geographic locations students have visited or read about. Work with students to help them understand the difference between proper and common nouns.

Have students write a paragraph about a specific geographic place. Tell students to include these elements: 1. the name of the particular geographic place; 2. the name of a geographic region; 3. at least one map direction.

Teacher Tip

Have a wall map or globe handy for students unable to think of a specific geographic place. Allow students to use the map to brainstorm for ideas. It may also be helpful to draw and post the compass points.

Geographical Places
Any specific geographical location listed on a map should be capitalized.

RULE 26.1.8

> **Capitalize geographical names.**

GEOGRAPHICAL NAMES	
Streets	Warren Street, Carlton Avenue, Interstate 10
Cities	Baltimore, London, Memphis, Tokyo
States	Arizona, Florida, Hawaii, Idaho
Nations	Italy, Canada, Kenya, France, Peru, South Korea
Continents	North America, Asia, Africa, Antarctica
Deserts	Sahara, Negev, Mojave
Mountains	Mount Everest, Rocky Mountains
Regions	Great Plains, Appalachian Highlands, Northwest
Islands	Canary Islands, Fiji Islands
Rivers	Mississippi River, Amazon River
Lakes	Lake Michigan, Great Salt Lake, Lake Erie
Bays	Hudson Bay, Baffin Bay, Biscayne Bay
Seas	Black Sea, Mediterranean Sea, North Sea
Oceans	Atlantic Ocean, Arctic Ocean

Regions and Map Directions
Names of regions, such as the South and the Northeast, are capitalized because they refer to a specific geographical location. Map directions that do not refer to a specific geographical location are not capitalized.

RULE 26.1.9

> **Do not capitalize compass points, such as north, southwest, or east, when they simply refer to direction.**

REGION   We spent our vacation in the Southeast.

DIRECTION   Our boat headed north on the river.

Working with ELLs   **ELL** Sheltered Instruction: Cognitive

Help students comprehend language structures used routinely in written classroom materials, including correctly capitalized geographical names and other proper nouns. Provide students with copies of a simple historical map labeled with names of places, people, and events. Then:

Beginning Review entries on the map. Guide students in identifying words spelled with capital letters. Clarify the meaning of each, identifying the language structure it represents (personal name, place name, and so on).

Intermediate Have students work in groups to list terms on the map that are capitalized and to identify the language structure that each represents (personal

name, place name, and so on). Have them seek clarification as needed. Then, guide them to restate in writing two facts that they learn from the map, capitalizing terms correctly.

Advanced Have partners list capitalized terms on the map and identify the language structure that each represents. Have them list four facts represented on the map and draw a conclusion about geography or history based on those facts.

Advanced High Have partners complete the Advanced activity. Then, have them compare the map to a current map of the region and write a brief comparison.

		RULE 26.1.10

Capitalize the names of specific events, periods of time, and documents.

The following chart contains examples of events, periods of time, and documents that require capitalization.

SPECIFIC EVENTS AND TIMES	
Historical Periods	Age of Enlightenment, Middle Ages, the Renaissance
Historical Events	World War II, Boston Tea Party, Battle of Lexington
Documents	Bill of Rights, Treaty of Paris, Declaration of Independence
Days	Wednesday, Saturday
Months	December, October
Holidays	Thanksgiving, Labor Day
Religious Days	Christmas, Passover, Ramadan
Special Events	Fiddlers' Convention, Boston Marathon, Super Bowl

Names of Seasons
The names of the seasons are an exception to this rule. Even though they name a specific period of time, the seasons of the year are not capitalized unless they are part of a title or an event name.

SEASONS   The most popular color this **f**all is rust.

The students traveled in the **s**ummer.

TITLE   During a hot **s**ummer, I read *The Long **W**inter*.

EVENT   It was so cold at the **M**ontana **S**pring Festival that it felt like **w**inter.

See Practice 26.1D

Using Capitalization   613

Specific Events and Time Periods

Explain to students that specific events, time periods, and documents are capitalized as a way to express their importance.

RULE 26.1.10 Read aloud the rule and then have students repeat the lines with you.

Discuss the chart of specific events and times on page 613 with students. Explain that the names of historical periods, events, and documents are capitalized only if many different people would recognize the specific event, time period, or document from the name. If the name could mean different things to different people, it is probably not capitalized. Have students identify specific events and time periods in a newspaper. Encourage students to identify specific documents in the newspaper as well. Don't forget to point out the newspaper itself as a specific document.

Names of Seasons

Have students practice distinguishing between seasons used as names of specific time periods and seasons that are used as part of an event name or a title. Say aloud the names of the four seasons (winter, autumn, summer, spring) and two event titles (Winter Fest, Spring Spectacular). Ask students to write one sentence using each. Tell students they must use conventions of capitalization in their sentences.

Differentiated Instruction

Strategy for Spanish Speakers
Students whose home language is Spanish may find it difficult to use proper capitalization because far fewer words are capitalized in Spanish than in English. Remind students that capitalization is used much more frequently in English. Review the chart on page 613. Put students in pairs or small groups. Provide each group with a blank copy of the chart with enough space to write in each category. Have the groups provide as many answers in as many categories as they can in five minutes. Remind students to capitalize where necessary. Time the students and then see which group came up with the most examples. Have students share their answers and fill in a master chart on the board for the whole class to see.

PRACTICE 26.1C ▷

1. Ulysses S. Grant
2. Cyrus McCormick
3. J.R.R. Tolkien
4. Orville and Wilbur Wright
5. Sandra Day O'Connor
6. Colin Powell
7. Ronald Reagan
8. Harriet Beecher Stowe
9. A. A. Milne
10. Pocahontas, John Rolfe

PRACTICE 26.1D ▷

11. London, England
12. South America
13. Blue Ridge Mountains
14. Nile River, Egypt
15. Northeast
16. Renaissance
17. Pacific Ocean
18. Pennsylvania, Ohio, Indiana
19. Gobi Desert, Mongolia
20. World Series

WRITING APPLICATION

Have students exchange sentences and check each other's work for correct capitalization.

WRITING APPLICATION

Have students dictate their sentences to a partner. Then, have them check to see if the capitalization matches.

PRACTICE 26.1C ▷ Using Capitalization for Names of People

Read the sentences. Write each name, adding the missing capitals.

EXAMPLE Our third president was thomas jefferson.

ANSWER *Thomas Jefferson*

1. ulysses s. grant was a general during the Civil War.
2. The inventor who perfected a machine to cut wheat was cyrus mccormick.
3. Do you like the writing of j.r.r. tolkien?
4. orville and wilbur wright built and flew the first successful airplane.
5. sandra day o'connor was the first woman appointed to the Supreme Court.
6. The first African American secretary of state was colin powell.
7. President ronald reagan helped bring the Cold War to an end.
8. harriet beecher stowe wrote a book that helped Americans realize the cruelty of slavery.
9. *Winnie the Pooh* was written by a. a. milne.
10. When pocahontas married john rolfe, it helped create peace in Jamestown.

WRITING APPLICATION

Write three sentences about people who played a part in the history of the United States. Be sure to capitalize the names correctly.

PRACTICE 26.1D ▷ Using Capitalization for Geographical Places, Specif Events, and Time Periods

Read the sentences. Write the name of each geographical place, specific event, and time period, adding the missing capitals.

EXAMPLE The mississippi river is the longest river in the united states.

ANSWER *Mississippi River, United States*

11. My aunt visited london, england, in June.
12. We are studying about south america.
13. Have you ever visited the blue ridge mountains?
14. The nile river flows through egypt.
15. The weather in the northeast can be cold.
16. I enjoyed studying renaissance paintings at the museum.
17. The pacific ocean is the largest ocean.
18. We drove across pennsylvania, ohio, and indiana.
19. The gobi desert covers the southern part of mongolia.
20. Last year, my favorite baseball team won th world series.

WRITING APPLICATION

Write three sentences about places you have studied or would like to visit. Be sure to capitalize geographical names correctly.

Working with ELLs **ELL** Sheltered Instruction: Social/Affective

As students work through Practice 26.1D, have them use support from peers and from you to read, to enhance and confirm understanding, and to develop background knowledge needed to comprehend increasingly challenging language.

Beginning Choose a sentence from Practice 26.1D, and have students read it with you. Help students share their background knowledge about geography to enhance understanding, and develop background by locating the places named on a map or by sharing their history. Then, guide students in completing the item.

Intermediate Have groups read the items in the Practice, sharing geographical and historical background knowledge to enhance

and confirm understanding. Circulate, and provide additional background as needed. Have groups complete the Practice.

Advanced Have partners read and discuss the items in the Practice, sharing geographical and historical background knowledge to enhance and confirm understanding and asking for additional background from you as needed. Then, partners should complete the Practice.

Advanced High Have partners complete the Advanced activity. Then, have them use library or Internet resources to acquire additional background about three of the places named in the Practice. Have them share their findings with the class.

Specific Groups

Proper nouns that name specific groups also require capitalization.

> **Capitalize the names of various organizations, government bodies, political parties, and nationalities, as well as the languages spoken by different groups.**

26.1.11 RULE

EXAMPLES   The ambassadors attended the first session of the **A**ustrian **P**arliament.

She delivered a brief address in **J**apanese and received warm applause.

Three **E**agle **S**couts demonstrated search and rescue techniques.

The proper nouns shown in the chart are groups with which many people are familiar. All specific groups, however, must be capitalized, even if they are not well known.

Practice 26.1E

SPECIFIC GROUPS	
Clubs	**K**iwanis **C**lub **R**otary **C**lub
Organizations	**N**ational **G**overnors **A**ssociation **N**ational **O**rganization for **W**omen
Institutions	**M**assachusetts **I**nstitute of **T**echnology **S**mithsonian **I**nstitution
Businesses	**S**imon **C**hemical **C**orporation **F**ido's **F**avorite **P**et **F**oods
Government Bodies	**U**nited **S**tates **C**ongress **S**upreme **C**ourt
Political Parties	**D**emocrats **R**epublican **P**arty
Nationalities	**C**hinese, **G**erman **N**igerian, **I**ranian
Languages	**E**nglish, **S**panish **K**orean, **S**wahili

Specific Groups

The names of specific groups are capitalized because they represent a particular body of people. Remind students that each part of a group's name must be capitalized.

RULE 26.1.11 Read aloud the rule and then have students repeat the lines with you.

With students, read through and discuss the examples for Rule 26.1.11 and the examples in the chart on page 615.

Say: What are some of the clubs to which you or your family and friends belong? How should they be capitalized? **(Accept all correct answers.)** What are the names of some businesses you saw on your way to school today? List a few examples if students can't think of any. **(Accept all correct answers.)** And what did you notice about the names of the businesses? Were they capitalized? Discuss the appearances of the names, noting the conventions of capitalization.

Work with students to list the names of familiar institutions, government bodies, nationalities, languages, and other specific groups using conventions of capitalization. As students identify groups, write them on the board. Define and discuss the groups if necessary. **Say:** When you write, always be sure to capitalize the names of specific groups.

Have students select five of the specific groups you've listed. Pair students and have them write a paragraph using the group names. Tell students they can write about anything they'd like. Remind students to use the conventions of capitalization.

Teacher Tip

It may be helpful to give students visual examples of specific groups. Photographs of signs that show a business's name written using the conventions of capitalization or a pamphlet with the name of a college or neighborhood club may help them understand how a specific group's name is written.

Religious References

Discuss the importance of capitalizing the names of religions, deities, and religious scriptures. Note that religious references are proper nouns because they name specific people, places, and things.

RULE 26.1.12 Read aloud the rule and then have students repeat the lines with you.

Say: Religions and religious references are always capitalized. It may be helpful for you to think of religions in the same way you do abstract nouns—those nouns that you can't access through the senses. Though you can't see, hear, taste, touch, or smell a religion, you can think and write about it. Allow students to ask any questions they may have.

With students, walk through the chart on page 616 of specific religious references that are capitalized. Remind students the words *god* and *goddess* are not capitalized when they refer to deities in Greek mythology. The individual names of ancient Greek gods and goddesses, however, are proper nouns and should always be capitalized.

Write on the board these sentence pairs. Have students select and copy the sentences that use the conventions of capitalization. Discuss students' answers.

1. The Quran contains Islamic laws and scripture.

2. The quran contains islamic laws and scripture.

3. The old testament is part of the bible.

4. The Old Testament is part of the Bible.
   (Correct answers: 1 and 4).

Religious References
Use capitals for the names of the religions of the world and certain other words related to religion.

Capitalize references to religions, deities, and religious scriptures.

The following chart presents words related to five of the world's major religions. Next to each religion are examples of some of the related religious words that must be capitalized. Note that the name of each religion is also capitalized.

RELIGIOUS REFERENCES	
Christianity	**G**od, **L**ord, **F**ather, **H**oly **S**pirit, **B**ible, books of the **B**ible (**G**enesis, **D**euteronomy, **P**salms, and so on)
Judaism	**L**ord, **F**ather, **P**rophets, **T**orah, **T**almud, **M**idrash
Islam	**A**llah, **P**rophet, **M**ohammed, **Q**ur'an
Hinduism	**B**rahma, **B**hagavad **G**ita, **V**edas
Buddhism	**B**uddha, **M**ahayana, **H**inayana

Note in the following examples, however, that the words *god* and *goddess* in references to mythology are not capitalized. A god's or goddess's name, however, is capitalized.

EXAMPLES   In Roman mythology, the supreme **g**od was **J**upiter.

The **g**oddess **J**uno was the wife of **J**upiter and was the **g**oddess of women.

616   Capitalization

Differentiated Instruction

RTI Strategy for Below-Level Students

In order to apply the conventions of capitalization to religious references, students must understand what qualifies as a religious reference. Students may fail to capitalize religious references because they don't recognize them. To help students avoid making errors, teach them how to find information about unfamiliar words using printed reference works and online sources. Show students how to use reputable online references to define unfamiliar words. Once students know a word's part of speech and definition, they can correctly apply capitalization conventions.

Enrichment for Gifted/Talented Students

Have students use reliable online sources to research a world religion of their choice. Students should create a chart of common religious references used in the religion. Have students explain their charts to the class.

Specific Places and Items

Monuments, memorials, buildings, celestial bodies, awards, the names of specific vehicles, and trademarked products should be capitalized.

> **Capitalize the names of specific places and items.**

26.1.13 RULE

OTHER SPECIAL PLACES AND ITEMS	
Monuments	Statue of Liberty Washington Monument
Memorials	Winston Churchill Memorial Vietnam Veterans Memorial
Buildings	Houston Museum of Fine Arts Empire State Building the Capitol Building (in Washington, D.C.)
Celestial Bodies (except the moon and sun)	Earth, Milky Way Jupiter, Aries
Awards	Newbery Medal Nobel Peace Prize
Air, Sea, and Space Craft	Spirit of St. Louis Monitor Voyager 2 Metroliner
Trademarked Brands	Krazy Korn Eco-Friendly Cleanser
Names	Zenox Kermit the Frog the Great Houdini

> **Capitalize the names of awards.**

26.1.14 RULE

Notice that *the* is not capitalized in these examples.

EXAMPLES   the **A**cademy **A**wards

the **F**ulbright **S**cholarship

the **P**ulitzer **P**rize

the **M**edal of **H**onor

See Practice 26.1F

Specific Places and Items

Explain that certain types of specific places, items, and awards require capitalization.

RULES 26.1.13, 26.1.14 Read aloud the rules and then have students repeat the lines with you.

Read aloud the examples of names that are capitalized in the chart on page 617. With students, discuss why each name is capitalized.

Provide students with a copy of this paragraph. Have students correct capitalization errors.

I was traveling far from earth, somewhere in the milky way. I was in a space ship called the new adventurer. Suddenly, I landed on a planet called aka. As I stepped onto its surface, I saw familiar sights. There was a replica of the brooklyn bridge and the lincoln memorial. The sign on a small building said "pete's hot dogs." When george washington stepped around a rock, I knew I was dreaming. (**Correct answers:** Earth, Milky Way, New Adventurer, Aka, Brooklyn Bridge, Lincoln Memorial, Pete's Hot Dogs, George Washington)

Teacher Tip

Point out context clues in the paragraph to help students identify specific places or things that require capitalization as proper nouns. *I was travelling far from* and *a sign on a small building said* may signal proper nouns.

PRACTICE 26.1E

1. American Medical Association
2. Congress
3. Capital Airlines
4. Democrats, Republicans
5. North Central High School
6. Midwest Writers Association
7. Girl Scouts, Boy Scouts
8. Cuban, Russian, Indian
9. House of Representatives, House of Commons
10. English, Spanish

PRACTICE 26.1F

11. Washington Monument
12. Genesis, Bible
13. Museum of Science and Industry
14. Islam, Qur'an
15. Jupiter
16. Pulitzer Prize
17. Jewish, Torah, Christian, Bible
18. Holocaust Memorial
19. Apollo
20. Hindu, Buddhist

WRITING APPLICATION

Students' sentences should demonstrate that students can correctly use capitalization, including capitalization for organizations.

WRITING APPLICATION

Students' descriptions of the organization should demonstrate that they can use capitalization, including capitalization for organizations.

PRACTICE 26.1E Using Capitalization for Groups and Organizations

Read the sentences. Write each group or organization, adding the missing capitals.

EXAMPLE   My brother joined the boy scouts.

ANSWER   *Boy Scouts*

1. My dad is a member of the american medical association.
2. Do you know who represents you in congress?
3. We flew on capital airlines to California.
4. Our state is divided between democrats and republicans.
5. The north central high school basketball team is one of the best teams in the state.
6. The midwest writers association held a meeting on Tuesday.
7. Both girl scouts and boy scouts were in the parade.
8. He has cuban, russian, and indian neighbors.
9. Instead of a house of representatives, England has a house of commons.
10. Mariano speaks both english and spanish.

PRACTICE 26.1F Using Capitalization for Religious References and Specific Items and Places

Read the sentences. Write each term that should be capitalized, adding the missing capitals.

EXAMPLE   A planet close to earth is mars.

ANSWER   *Earth, Mars*

11. I wanted to visit the washington monument.
12. genesis is the first book in the bible.
13. The museum of science and industry has wonderful displays.
14. In islam, people read the qur'an.
15. The largest of the planets is jupiter.
16. The pulitzer prize is awarded for great writing.
17. The jewish torah makes up part of the christian bible.
18. The holocaust memorial attracts many visitors.
19. The apollo 11 spacecraft landed on the moon on July 20, 1969.
20. In India, there are more hindu temples than buddhist temples.

WRITING APPLICATION

Write two sentences about organizations to which you, friends, or family members belong, including clubs, businesses, and schools. Be sure to use the correct capitalization for the names of the organizations.

WRITING APPLICATION

Choose an organization that you would like to join, either now or in the future. Write three sentences about why you would like to be a member. Be careful to use the correct capitalization of the organization.

618   Capitalization

Working with ELLs   ELL Sheltered Instruction: Cognitive

Have students read linguistically accommodated text silently with increasing ease and comprehension for longer periods of time and with a decreasing need for accommodation. Monitor to ensure all students are able to recognize directionality of English reading, reading left to right. Create a handout of Practice 26.1F, simplifying the language as much as possible and providing explanatory glosses of vocabulary. Then:

Beginning Have students silently read the directions on your handout. Then, read the directions aloud as they follow along. Clarify meaning, and repeat with the Example.

Intermediate Have students silently read the directions, Example, and first two items on your handout. Then, discuss the text,

clarifying meaning. Repeat with the next four items, and then with the final four.

Advanced Have partners silently read the handout. Discuss their questions about the text. Then, have them complete the Practice.

Advanced High Have partners silently read the handout. Discuss their questions about the text. Then, have them turn back to the student page and complete the original Practice.

Using Capitalization for Proper Adjectives

When a proper noun or a form of a proper noun is used to describe another noun, it is called a **proper adjective.** Proper adjectives usually need a capital letter.

Capitalize most **proper adjectives.**

26.1.15 RULE

In the following examples, notice that both proper nouns and proper adjectives are capitalized. Common nouns that are modified by proper adjectives, however, are not capitalized.

PROPER NOUNS	W orld W ar I
	C anada
PROPER ADJECTIVES	a W orld W ar I b attle
	a C anadian f lag

The names of some countries and states must be modified to be used as proper adjectives. For example, something from Kenya is Kenyan, someone from Texas is a Texan, a chair from Spain is a Spanish chair, and a building in France is a French building.

Brand Names as Adjectives

Trademarked brand names are considered to be proper nouns. If you use a brand name to describe a common noun, the brand name becomes a proper adjective. In this case, capitalize only the proper adjective and not the common noun.

Capitalize brand names used as adjectives.

26.1.16 RULE

| PROPER NOUN | H ealthy G rains |
| PROPER ADJECTIVE | H ealthy G rains c ereal |

Notice that only the proper adjective *Healthy Grains* is capitalized. The word *cereal* is not capitalized because it is a common noun; it is not part of the trademarked name.

Practice 26.1G

Using Capitalization for Proper Adjectives

Remind students that proper adjectives are adjectives that are formed from proper nouns. For example, in the sentence *I like Thai food,* the word *Thai* is a proper adjective that is formed from the proper noun *Thailand.*

RULE 26.1.15 Read aloud the rule and then have students repeat the line with you.

Discuss the examples of proper nouns and proper adjectives listed for rule 26.1.15 listed on page 619. Focus on the fact that proper adjectives should be capitalized. Have students use these proper adjectives in five original sentences: *Oklahoma, Polish, Sci-Fi Expo, Mars, Saturday.* Students should convert these words into proper adjectives and write sentences using the proper adjectives with correct capitalization.

Brand Names as Adjectives

Explain that a brand name is the name of a specific product or group of products that is sold or made by a specific company. Other companies might make or sell a similar product, but their products would have different brand names. As a class, list and discuss several brand names.

RULE 26.1.16 Read aloud the rule and then have students repeat the line with you.

Play a game with students to strengthen their capitalization skills. Tell students that they will have 60 seconds to write as many brand names beginning with the capital letter *T* as they can. The student who writes the longest list of brand names that are accurately capitalized is the winner. Write on the board the brand names students listed. Then, brainstorm with students for sentences that use the brand names as proper adjectives. Write several of the sentences on the board, capitalizing the proper adjectives correctly.

Using Capitalization for Titles of People

Explain that a person's title shows his or her relationship to other people.

Social and Professional Titles

RULE 26.1.17 Read aloud the rule and then have students repeat the lines with you.

Review the examples for rule 26.1.17 with students. Explain that *Detective* and *Doctor* are capitalized because they are directly followed by the person's name. *Sergeant* is capitalized because it is a title used as a noun of direct address.

Point out that whether or not to capitalize a person's title depends on how it is used in a sentence.

Use a Think Aloud as part of a gradual release progression.

Say: I know that a title that is immediately followed by a person's name should be capitalized. Also, I know that if a person's name can be substituted for a title, the title should be capitalized. If the person's name cannot be substituted, the title should not be capitalized. I can use this rule to determine whether to capitalize *nurse* in the sentence *I saw Nurse Reyes today.* The title *nurse* is directly followed by a proper name, so it must be capitalized.

On the board, write several titles followed by specific names. Some examples include *Governor Gill* and *Miss Drabicki.* Have students generate a few examples of their own.

On the board, write these examples and **work with students** to capitalize titles:

1. He asked, "Rabbi, will you help me?" (Point out that if *Rabbi* were replaced with *Sam* the sentence would still make sense, so *Rabbi* should be capitalized.)

2. The governor held a press conference. (Point out that if *governor* were replaced with *James* the sentence would not make sense, so *governor* should not be capitalized.)

On the board, write these sentences. **Have students work in pairs to** fill in the blanks using the conventions of capitalization.

1. The (title) will be in shortly.

2. (title) (proper name) is expected any moment.

(**Possible answers:** 1. doctor; 2. Ms. Nelson)

T620

Using Capitalization for Titles of People

A person's title shows his or her relationship to other people. Whether a title is capitalized often depends on how it is used in a sentence.

Social and Professional Titles
Social and professional titles may be written before a person's name or used alone in place of a person's name.

> Capitalize the title of a person when the title is followed by the person's name or when it is used in place of a person's name in direct address.

BEFORE A NAME
Detective O'Toole and **D**octor Perkins have arrived.

IN DIRECT ADDRESS
Look, **S**ergeant, the fingerprints match!

TITLES OF PEOPLE	
Social	**M**ister, **M**adam or **M**adame, **M**iss, **M**s., **S**ir
Business	**D**octor, **P**rofessor, **S**uperintendent
Religious	**R**everend, **F**ather, **R**abbi, **B**ishop, **S**ister
Military	**P**rivate, **E**nsign, **C**aptain, **G**eneral, **A**dmiral
Government	**P**resident, **S**enator, **R**epresentative, **G**overnor, **M**ayor, **P**rince, **Q**ueen, **K**ing

In most cases, do not capitalize titles that are used alone or that follow a person's name—especially if the title is preceded by the articles *a, an,* or *the.*

EXAMPLES
Samantha Rodgers, the **d**octor on call, will be able to see you.

Tell your **s**enator how you feel about the issue.

My cousin Ralph, who is a **p**rivate in the army, will be home on leave soon.

Differentiated Instruction

RTI Strategy for Special Needs Students
Students will benefit from repetition of instruction. Each time they review a concept, they gain a bit more confidence. Over the course of a few days, review the rules for capitalizing the titles of people. Each time, allow students to exercise more independence. During the first review, use specific sentence starters to provide students with structured practice.

For example: *I'm waiting for my (lowercase title of person who helps people) to assist me.*

During the second review, delete sentence starters and allow students to rely on their knowledge: *I'm waiting for my _____ to assist me.*

Government Officials

Government Officials

> **Capitalize the titles of government officials when they immediately precede the name of specific officials. If no person is named, these titles should be written in lowercase.**

26.1.18 RULE

EXAMPLES

President **O**bama will answer questions from reporters after the speech.

The club **p**resident will answer questions after the speech.

Mayor **W**alker will speak to the people about conserving energy.

The **m**ayor of a large city is responsible for energy conservation and planning.

Note: Certain honorary titles are always capitalized, even if the title is not used with a proper name or direct address. These titles include the First Lady of the United States, Speaker of the House of Representatives, Queen Mother of England, and the Prince of Wales.

Titles for Family Relationships

> **Capitalize titles showing family relationships when the title is used with the person's name or as the person's name—except when the title comes after a possessive noun or pronoun.**

26.1.19 RULE

BEFORE A NAME

We respect **U**ncle Frank's opinion.

IN PLACE OF A NAME

Is **G**randmother going?

AFTER POSSESSIVES

Alan's **f**ather is the team captain.

Notice that the family title *father* used in the last example is not capitalized because it is used after the possessive word *Alan's*.

Practice 26.1H

Using Capitalization 621

Government Officials

Point out that the capitalization conventions for titles of government officials are similar to the capitalization conventions for the titles of people.

RULE 26.1.18 Read aloud the rule and then have students repeat the lines with you.

Review the examples for rule 26.1.18 with students. For each example, have students explain why the title is capitalized or is not capitalized.

Titles for Family Relationships

Explain that how a family title is used in a sentence determines whether or not it is capitalized.

RULE 26.1.19 Read aloud the rule and then have students repeat the lines with you.

On the board, write these sentences. For each, ask students to highlight the title and/or proper name and then explain why the title is capitalized or not capitalized.

1. His uncle promised to help him get a job.

2. I think Aunt Julia will be making lemon bars.

3. Last week, Grandmother King took the kids to the fair.

4. Elena's mother found what she wanted at the market.

(1. The word *uncle* is not used with the person's name or as the person's name, so it is not capitalized. 2. The word *Aunt* is used with the person's name, so it must be capitalized. 3. Because *Grandmother* is immediately followed by the person's proper name, it should be capitalized. 4. Because *mother* comes after a possessive noun or pronoun, it should not be capitalized.)

Teacher Tip

Provide a word bank of common government titles so that students focus on using capitalization conventions rather than on identifying titles.

PRACTICE 26.1G

1. American
2. Vietnam War
3. Spanish-language
4. Krazy Corn
5. Russian
6. World War
7. Japanese-influenced
8. Chinese
9. Newbery
10. German

PRACTICE 26.1H

11. Queen
12. correct
13. Miss, Mister
14. Doctor
15. correct
16. General, Admiral
17. correct
18. Reverend
19. correct
20. Private

WRITING APPLICATION

Have students trade papers with a partner. Then, have students check each other's capitalization of proper adjectives.

WRITING APPLICATION

Have students exchange papers and check each other's capitalization of names and titles.

PRACTICE 26.1G Using Capitalization for Proper Adjectives

Read the sentences. Write the proper adjectives, adding the correct capitalization.

EXAMPLE   Have you ever been to a french restaurant?

ANSWER   *French*

1. Each morning, they raise the american flag.
2. The soldier talked about a vietnam war battle he fought in.
3. We watched a spanish-language film.
4. I prefer the krazy corn brand of chips.
5. The conference was in the russian capital.
6. He was a world war II hero.
7. The japanese-influenced architecture was lovely.
8. I like chinese food.
9. That book won the newbery medal.
10. Were you on time for your german class?

PRACTICE 26.1H Using Capitalization for Titles of People

Read the sentences. If the title in each sentence is correctly capitalized, write *correct*. If it is no rewrite the title correctly.

EXAMPLE   I met representative Dan Rutherfor at the rally.

ANSWER   *Representative*

11. In England, queen Elizabeth has reigned fo more than fifty years.
12. There is a sergeant on duty now.
13. He was talking with miss Jenner and mister Chen.
14. When she fell, we had to rush Juanita to doctor Pradesh's office.
15. We wondered what it was like to be a professor at that college.
16. Both general Patton and admiral Nimitz wo important battles during World War II.
17. Look, Senator, they have begun the session
18. The reverend Joel Sarnoff officiated at the wedding ceremony.
19. The sign on the door said Governor David Johnson.
20. Straighten up, private; no slouching on duty

WRITING APPLICATION

Write two sentences about places or events in your social studies book. Include in each sentence something that can be modified by a proper adjective.

WRITING APPLICATION

Think of everyone you know at school, at home, and anywhere else. Write people's names with their titles. Be careful to capitalize titles correctly.

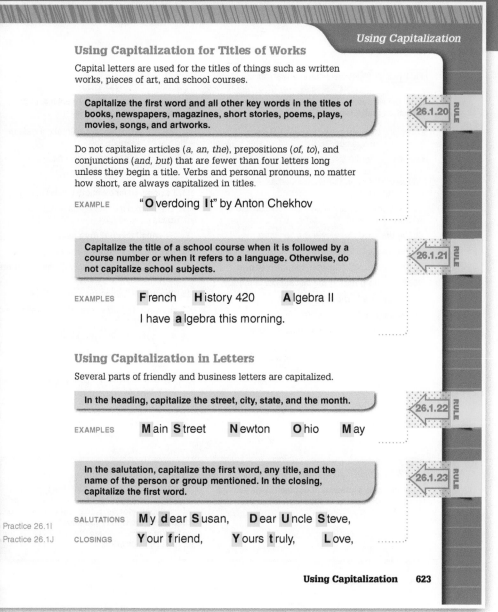

Using Capitalization for Titles of Works

Capital letters are used for the titles of things such as written works, pieces of art, and school courses.

> **Capitalize the first word and all other key words in the titles of books, newspapers, magazines, short stories, poems, plays, movies, songs, and artworks.**
>
> RULE 26.1.20

Do not capitalize articles (*a, an, the*), prepositions (*of, to*), and conjunctions (*and, but*) that are fewer than four letters long unless they begin a title. Verbs and personal pronouns, no matter how short, are always capitalized in titles.

EXAMPLE   "**O**verdoing **I**t" by Anton Chekhov

> **Capitalize the title of a school course when it is followed by a course number or when it refers to a language. Otherwise, do not capitalize school subjects.**
>
> RULE 26.1.21

EXAMPLES   **F**rench   **H**istory 420   **A**lgebra II

I have **a**lgebra this morning.

Using Capitalization in Letters

Several parts of friendly and business letters are capitalized.

> **In the heading, capitalize the street, city, state, and the month.**
>
> RULE 26.1.22

EXAMPLES   **M**ain **S**treet   **N**ewton   **O**hio   **M**ay

> **In the salutation, capitalize the first word, any title, and the name of the person or group mentioned. In the closing, capitalize the first word.**
>
> RULE 26.1.23

Practice 26.1I
Practice 26.1J

SALUTATIONS   **M**y **d**ear **S**usan,   **D**ear **U**ncle **S**teve,

CLOSINGS   **Y**our **f**riend,   **Y**ours **t**ruly,   **L**ove,

Using Capitalization   **623**

Using Capitalization for Titles of Works

Explain that the formal titles of publications and published works or works that could reasonably be published (such as poems and short stories), are capitalized.

RULES 26.1.20, 26.1.21 Read aloud the rules and then have students repeat the lines with you.

Ask students to create a chart with these headings: *Books, Poems, Movies, Songs*.

Have students write, in each column, two of their favorite works. Remind students that articles, prepositions, and short conjunctions are not capitalized unless they begin the title. Once students have completed their charts, have them share them with a partner. Ask partners to check the charts for correct use of capitalization. Allow students to discuss their favorite works with their partners.

Write on the board a list of courses offered by your school. Omit all capitalization. Have students copy the course names, correcting their capitalization.

Using Capitalization in Letters

Identify the parts of a letter that are commonly capitalized, and discuss how capitalization rules are applied to salutations and closings.

RULES 26.1.22, 26.1.23 Read aloud the rules and then have students repeat the lines with you.

Have students write a friendly letter to a friend or relative. Students may write about anything they like, but in their letters they should correctly apply conventions of capitalization.

Working with ELLs   **ELL** Sheltered Instruction: Social/Affective

As students learn about capitalization, help them demonstrate comprehension of increasingly complex English by participating in a **shared reading**. Write a sample letter in which the writer names works she is reading for her classes. Provide students with a copy.

Beginning Pair students with fluent speakers, and have the fluent speaker read as the Beginning student follows along. Then, have pairs repeat the reading, stopping after each sentence or item that contains capital letters and discussing its meaning, as well as the reasons for capitalizing the terms.

Intermediate Have students working in small groups read the letter, with each student taking a turn reading aloud as the others follow along. Then, have groups repeat the reading, pausing to discuss the meaning of each section and the capitalization rules it illustrates.

Advanced Have students complete the Intermediate activity. Then, have them write their own letters modeled on yours.

Advanced High Have students write their own letters based on your model, mentioning titles of works and courses and following proper letter format. Have them conduct **shared readings** of one another's letters, correcting capitalization as needed.

PRACTICE 26.1I

Accept italics or underlining.

1. Encyclopedia International
2. "The Tortoise and the Hare"
3. The Lion King
4. The Good Earth
5. "The Star-Spangled Banner"
6. The Last Supper
7. The Daily Express
8. History 101
9. The Merchant of Venice
10. "The Man From Snowy River"

PRACTICE 26.1J

Accept italics or underlining.

11. I signed up for an English class.
12. The Phantom of the Opera is a popular musical.
13. He sang "Pennies From Heaven."
14. Did you see the movie Cinderella Story?
15. Mark Twain is the author of The Adventures of Tom Sawyer.
16. She will be taking German.
17. Rudyard Kipling wrote "The Sing-Song of Old Man Kangaroo."
18. The Daily Herald is our local paper.
19. Have you ever seen the painting The Potato Eaters?
20. My dad read me the poem "The Charge of the Light Brigade."

WRITING APPLICATION

Have students dictate their sentences to a partner after they have written them. Have partners compare the way they capitalized the titles.

WRITING APPLICATION

Have students explain which words in their paragraphs required capitalization and why.

PRACTICE 26.1I **Using Capitalization for Titles of Things**

Read the sentences. Write the titles, adding the correct capitalization.

EXAMPLE   We subscribe to *national geographic* magazine.

ANSWER   *National Geographic*

1. I looked it up in the *encyclopedia international*.
2. Have you read the story "the tortoise and the hare"?
3. We watched the movie *the lion king*.
4. Pearl S. Buck wrote *the good earth*.
5. She performed "the star-spangled banner."
6. Da Vinci's painting *the last supper* is in Italy.
7. My dad reads *the daily express*.
8. I signed up for history 101.
9. My parents saw the play *the merchant of venice*.
10. I like the poem "the man from snowy river."

WRITING APPLICATION

Write three sentences about the things you like to read. Be careful to capitalize titles correctly.

---

624   **Capitalization**

PRACTICE 26.1J **Using Capitalization for Titles of Things**

Read the sentences. Rewrite each sentence, adding the missing capitals.

EXAMPLE   After lunch, I will take a quiz in spanish.

ANSWER   *After lunch, I will take a quiz in Spanish.*

11. I signed up for an english class.
12. *The phantom of the opera* is a popular musical.
13. He sang "pennies from heaven."
14. Did you see the movie *cinderella story*?
15. Mark Twain is the author of *the adventures of tom sawyer*.
16. She will be taking german.
17. Rudyard Kipling wrote "the sing-song of old man kangaroo."
18. The *daily herald* is our local paper.
19. Have you ever seen the painting *the potato eaters*?
20. My dad read me the poem "the charge of the light brigade."

WRITING APPLICATION

Write a brief paragraph about the types of entertainment available in your area. Think of museums, movies, plays, and concerts, and then name the things you might see in these places or at these events. Be sure to check for correct capitalization.

Working with ELLs **ELL** Sheltered Instruction: Cognitive

The Writing Application for 26.1J on page 624 provides students an opportunity to write using a variety of grade-appropriate sentence lengths in increasingly accurate ways. Read the directions aloud. Then:

Beginning Pair students with more fluent speakers. Have partners brainstorm for a movie, book, or television program they have enjoyed, with fluent speakers prompting Beginning students by asking simple questions. Then, have partners choose adjectives to describe the work. Next, have the fluent speaker compose a sentence about the work using one of the adjectives. Have the Beginning student copy the sentence. Finally, have partners write a longer sentence by adding another adjective to their original.

Intermediate Have partners complete the Writing Application. Then, have them write longer sentences by adding descriptive words or phrases to their sentences.

Advanced Have students complete the Writing Application. Then, have them write longer sentences by adding clauses to their statements, forming compound or complex sentences.

Advanced High Have students write a one-paragraph review of a book, article, movie, or television program, capitalizing titles correctly. Have them reread their drafts and revise to ensure that they have used a variety of sentence lengths.

Using Capitalization in Abbreviations, Acronyms, and Initials

An **abbreviation** is a shortened form of a word or phrase. An **acronym** is an abbreviation of a phrase that takes one or more letters from each word in the phrase being abbreviated.

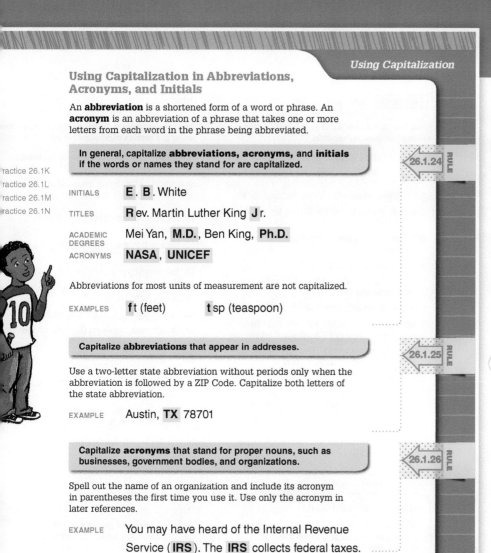

> In general, capitalize **abbreviations**, **acronyms**, and **initials** if the words or names they stand for are capitalized.

26.1.24 RULE

INITIALS	**E . B** . White
TITLES	**R** ev. Martin Luther King **J** r.
ACADEMIC DEGREES	Mei Yan, **M.D.** , Ben King, **Ph.D.**
ACRONYMS	**NASA** , **UNICEF**

Abbreviations for most units of measurement are not capitalized.

EXAMPLES	**f** t (feet) **t** sp (teaspoon)

> Capitalize **abbreviations** that appear in addresses.

26.1.25 RULE

Use a two-letter state abbreviation without periods only when the abbreviation is followed by a ZIP Code. Capitalize both letters of the state abbreviation.

EXAMPLE	Austin, **TX** 78701

> Capitalize **acronyms** that stand for proper nouns, such as businesses, government bodies, and organizations.

26.1.26 RULE

Spell out the name of an organization and include its acronym in parentheses the first time you use it. Use only the acronym in later references.

EXAMPLE	You may have heard of the Internal Revenue Service (**IRS**). The **IRS** collects federal taxes.

Using Capitalization   625

Practice 26.1K
Practice 26.1L
Practice 26.1M
Practice 26.1N

Quick-Write Extension

To help students synthesize and apply what they have learned about using capitalization in abbreviations, acronyms, and initials, have them write brief entries for an encyclopedia of not-for-profit organizations. Direct students to choose familiar organizations and write everything they know or can quickly research. Have students exercise care in the capitalization in their entries and exchange the entries with their partners to be checked for correctness.

Using Capitalization in Abbreviations, Acronyms, and Initials

Point out to students that conventions of capitalization apply to abbreviations, acronyms, and initials because they often stand for words that are capitalized.

RULES 26.1.24, 26.1.25, 26.1.26 Read aloud the rules and then have students repeat the lines with you.

Use a Think Aloud as part of a gradual release progression.

Think Aloud

Say: Even when I abbreviate a word or write an acronym or set of initials, **I must use** conventions of capitalization. To remember the importance of capitalizing in these cases, I remind myself that abbreviations, acronyms, and initials may represent proper nouns or academic degrees. Tell students to write their names and their initials using conventions of capitalization.

Write the following on the board:

1. (the initials of someone famous)
2. Mister Ricardo O'Reilly
3. Bachelor of Arts degree
4. National Endowment for the Arts
5. 12 feet
6. Tulsa, Oklahoma

Work with students to use the conventions of capitalization to write the abbreviation, acronym, or initials on the board. Then, **have students** complete the rest of the list on their own.

Responses:

1. Accept all answers that correctly represent a person's initials. **2.** Mr. Ricardo O'Reilly **3.** B. A. **4.** NEA **5.** 12 ft **6.** Tulsa, OK

PRACTICE 26.1K

1. Mr.

2. Dr.

3. Jr.

4. St.

5. M.D.

6. MA

7. Rev.

8. Ft.

9. CA

10. Ph.D.

PRACTICE 26.1L

11. My appointment next week is with Lucia Martinez, M.D.

12. My teacher, Ms. Collins, is working on her Ed.D. in educational administration.

13. The seat of our government is Washington, D.C.

14. My letter is addressed to Mr. James Peabody in San Antonio, TX.

15. The recipe calls for 8 oz. of milk.

16. On all major holidays, the NYSE closes, and no stocks are traded.

17. Mr. Calvin Percy Jr. has been appointed president of GWC Industries.

18. Send the check to Chicago, IL, and not Phoenix, AZ.

19. My baby brother has this long name: Elijah Thomas Welby Jr.

20. My aunt lives at 2350 Park NW, in St. Petersburg.

PRACTICE 26.1K > Using Capitalization for Abbreviations

Read the sentences. Write each abbreviation, adding the missing capitals.

EXAMPLE   Have you seen mt. Rushmore?

ANSWER   *Mt.*

1. I addressed the letter to mr. William Park.

2. Did dr. Hill examine Mark's leg for any broken bones?

3. Benjamin O. Davis jr. organized the Tuskegee Airmen.

4. We visited st. Augustine, Florida.

5. Ben Carson, m.d., is one of the country's leading surgeons.

6. Her address is Cambridge, Ma 01773.

7. According to a Gallup poll, rev. Billy Graham is one of the country's most admired people.

8. The flag that inspired "The Star-Spangled Banner" flew over ft. McHenry.

9. His new address is Los Angeles, ca 90001.

10. Karen Phillips, ph.d., is the new professor in the economics department.

PRACTICE 26.1L > Using Capitalization for Abbreviations

Read the sentences. Then, rewrite each senten using the correct capitalization for abbreviatic

EXAMPLE   After being away for six months, lt. Inez Ray wanted to see her frien

ANSWER   *After being away for six months, Lt. Inez Ray wanted to see her frien*

11. My appointment next week is with Lucia Martinez, m.d.

12. My teacher, ms. Collins, is working on her ed.d. in educational administration.

13. The seat of our government is Washington,

14. My letter is addressed to mr. James Peabo in San Antonio, tx.

15. The recipe calls for 8 Oz. of milk.

16. On all major holidays, the nyse closes, and stocks are traded.

17. Mr. Calvin Percy jr. has been appointed president of gwc Industries.

18. Send the check to Chicago, il, and not Phoenix, az.

19. My baby brother has this long name: Elijah Thomas Welby jr.

20. My aunt lives at 2350 Park, nw, in St. Petersburg.

WRITING APPLICATION

Write a complete address, real or imagined. Include at least three abbreviations in the address. Make sure abbreviations are capitalized correctly.

WRITING APPLICATION

Write the names of people and companies— real or imagined—using the following abbreviations: *Mr., Co., Hon., Inc.,* and *Rev.* Write at least three sentences using the names

626   Capitalization

WRITING APPLICATION

Students should demonstrate that they can correctly use capitalization for abbreviations by explaining what they capitalized in the addresses they have written, and why.

WRITING APPLICATION

Students' sentences should demonstrate that they can correctly use capitalization for abbreviations.

PRACTICE 26.1M Using Capitalization for Initials and Acronyms

Read the sentences. Write the initials and acronyms, adding the missing capitals.

EXAMPLE   The central intelligence agency (cia) gathers and analyzes information.

ANSWER   *Central Intelligence Agency (CIA)*

Some great science fiction stories were written by h. g. Wells.

I need a map of the usa.

He's a member of the cap (civil air patrol).

nasa (national aeronautics and space administration) is the government agency for space exploration.

The Chicago transit authority (cta) is a city government department.

The women's army corps (wac) was active during World War II.

The spca (society for the prevention of cruelty to animals) has an important job protecting animals.

Many drivers are members of the American automobile association (aaa).

Madame c. j. Walker was the first African American woman to become a millionaire.

The environmental protection agency (epa) monitors pollution levels.

WRITING APPLICATION

Use initials that stand for words to make up names for three organizations or companies. Then write three sentences with the new names. Use sentence context to help readers understand what the initials mean.

PRACTICE 26.1N Using Capitalization for Initials and Acronyms

Read the sentences. Rewrite each sentence using the correct capitalization for the initial or the acronym.

EXAMPLE   Harry Potter's creator is j. k. Rowling.

ANSWER   *Harry Potter's creator is J. K. Rowling.*

11. My dad is going to school at night to get his mba.

12. Mr. j. m. Smith was once a coach for an nba team.

13. Another ufo was sighted over Texas last month.

14. The United States and Canada are members of nato.

15. My mom is in charge of r&d for the Belmont Corp.

16. My best friend is named Kathryn Christine, but her dad calls her k. c.

17. The ceo, Charles s. Grayson, signed the letter.

18. My aunt's favorite mystery writer is p. d. James.

19. Grandfather likes to watch the news on the bbc.

20. We used to belong to an hmo for our healthcare.

WRITING APPLICATION

Look up the following acronyms: HUD, VFW, USMC. Write the full names of the organizations.

PRACTICE 26.1M

1. H. G.

2. USA

3. CAP (Civil Air Patrol)

4. NASA (National Aeronautics and Space Administration)

5. Chicago Transit Authority (CTA)

6. Women's Army Corp (WAC)

7. SPCA (Society for the Prevention of Cruelty to Animals)

8. American Automobile Association (AAA)

9. C. J.

10. Environmental Protection Agency (EPA)

PRACTICE 26.1N

11. My dad is going to school at night to get his MBA.

12. Mr. J. M. Smith was once a coach for an NBA team.

13. Another UFO was sighted over Texas last month.

14. The United States and Canada are members of NATO.

15. My mom is in charge of R&D for the Belmont Corp.

16. My best friend is named Kathryn Christine, but her dad calls her K. C.

17. The CEO, Charles S. Grayson, signed the letter.

18. My aunt's favorite mystery writer is P. D. James.

19. Grandfather likes to watch the news on the BBC.

20. We used to belong to an HMO for our healthcare.

WRITING APPLICATION

Students should explain to a partner what they capitalized in their sentences and why to demonstrate that they can use capitalization correctly for abbreviations, initials, and acronyms.

WRITING APPLICATION

Have students work together to find the names represented by the acronyms to show that they can use capitalization correctly for abbreviations, initials, and acronyms.

Test Warm-Up

1. **B** Change *ms* to **Ms**.

2. **H** I am interested in space exploration, so I went to the NASA Internet site.

3. **C** Capitalize the initials *l.b.*

4. **J** I will mail my letter to NASA Johnson Space Center, 2101 NASA Pkwy. 1, Houston, TX 77058.

Reteach

If students have not mastered these skills, review the content in Section 26.1.24 Using Capitalization in Abbreviations, Acronyms, and Initials.

Test Tip

Students may have trouble clarifying what a test or a test item asks them to do. Remind them to read all the directions carefully. Then, as they read each question stem, suggest that they mentally paraphrase the question to make sure they understand what it is asking. Students can check their understanding of a question by making sure that the answer choices make sense with their paraphrased version of the question.

Test Warm-Up

DIRECTIONS
Read the introduction and the passage that follows. Then, answer the questions to show that you can use and understand the function of capitalization for abbreviations, initials, and acronyms in reading and writing.

Noah wrote this paragraph about his plan to write a letter. Read the paragraph and think about the changes you would suggest as a peer editor. When you finish reading, answer the questions that follow.

Spacesuits and Photos From Space

(1) My homework assignment in ms Russell's class is to write a letter to request information. (2) I am interested in space exploration. (3) I went to the nasa Internet site. (4) It's amazing! (5) The public can borrow real spacesuits, scale models of space shuttles, and photos of Earth from space. (6) We have an annual science fair at l.b. Johnson High School, and I am going to write a letter to see how I can plan an exhibit. (7) My letter will be mailed to NASA Johnson Space Center, 2101 NASA pkwy. 1, Houston, Tx 77058.

---

1 What change, if any, should be made in sentence 1?

A Change *ms* to **MS**

B Change *ms* to **Ms**.

C Capitalize the word *class*

D Make no change

2 What is the BEST way to combine sentences 2 and 3?

F I am interested in space exploration, so I went to the nasa Internet site.

G I am interested in space exploration, so I went to the Nasa Internet site.

H I am interested in space exploration, so I went to the NASA Internet site.

J I am interested in space exploration, so I went to the nasa Internets Site.

3 How should sentence 6 be revised?

A Change *Johnson* to **johnson**

B Capitalize the word *exhibit*

C Capitalize the initials *l.b.*

D Capitalize the words *science fair*

4 What is the BEST way to revise sentence 7?

F I will mail my letter to NASA Johnson Space Center, 2101 NASA Pkwy. 1, Houston, tx 77058.

G My letter should be mailed to nasa Johnson Space Center, 2101 nasa Pkwy. 1, Houston, tx 77058.

H My letter should be mailed to NASA Johnson Space Center, 2101 NASA pkwy. 1 Houston, TX 77058.

J I will mail my letter to NASA Johnson Space Center, 2101 NASA Pkwy. 1, Houston, TX 77058.

PRACTICE 1 Using Periods, Question Marks, and Exclamation Marks

Read the sentences. Then, rewrite the sentences, adding periods, question marks, and exclamation marks where needed.

1. Are you going to the dog show
2. Please help me with the dishes
3. What a wonderful teacher she is
4. Mr Wu lives in Richmond
5. He asked if he could borrow the lawn mower
6. Many people visit the UN each year
7. Keep your hands away from the hot stove
8. Sabrina hopes to make the team Can she
9. Wow How magnificent the eagle looked
10. Will you be joining the book club

PRACTICE 2 Using Commas Correctly

Read the sentences. Then, rewrite the sentences, adding commas where needed. If a sentence is correct as is, write *correct*.

1. Those pants cost a lot but this shirt costs more.
2. Dirt got on my face in my shoe and on the floor.
3. The thick jagged object was a piece of glass.
4. To prevent snoring breathe through your nose.
5. Jack said "Tell me sir what is the problem?"
6. Exactly 3421 people visited on May 3 2009.
7. The manatee a sea mammal swam nearby.
8. Two white pillars held up the porch roof.
9. I first visited Austin Texas in March 2007.
10. "It must be finished soon of course" said Amy.

PRACTICE 3 Using Colons, Semicolons, and Quotation Marks

Read the sentences. Rewrite the sentences, using colons, semicolons, and quotation marks where needed. If a sentence is correct as is, write *correct*.

1. We moved last year, we love our new home.
2. Who said, Give me liberty, or give me death?
3. Bring these items a comb, a brush, and tissues.
4. I'm sorry, said Rose, but I must leave by 430.
5. He won a trophy, however, he soon broke it.
6. How I love the poem Birches!
7. Warning Keep out of the hands of children.
8. Luis likes chicken, rice, and corn.
9. Mia asked, When will this difficult day be over?
10. Native to the Americas are the turkey, a bird, the chipmunk, a rodent, and the tomato, a plant.

PRACTICE 4 Using Apostrophes Correctly

Read the sentences. Then, rewrite the sentences, adding or removing apostrophes as needed. If a sentence is correct as is, write *correct*.

1. Mom is deaf and cant hear Mels voice.
2. The horse stays in it's stall when its raining.
3. Silas's bags got mixed up with someone elses.
4. The five top students grades were all As.
5. The myth described the god Zeus' thunderbolts.
6. Donalds prized possession is an 08 yearbook.
7. I'm amazed that you dont tell him hes too loud.
8. Theirs is the best restaurant in town.
9. She couldn't make other plans on Tuesdays.
10. Its hard to tell whats hers and whats yours.

Continued on next page ▶

Cumulative Review 629

PRACTICE 1

1. Are you going to the dog show?
2. Please help me with the dishes.
3. What a wonderful teacher she is!
4. Mr. Wu lives in Richmond.
5. He asked if he could borrow the lawn mower.
6. Many people visit the UN each year.
7. Keep your hands away from the hot stove.
8. Sabrina hopes to make the team. Can she?
9. Wow! How magnificent the eagle looked!
10. Will you be joining the book club?

PRACTICE 2

1. Those pants cost a lot, but this shirt costs more.
2. Dirt got on my face, in my shoe, and on the floor.
3. The thick, jagged object was a piece of glass.
4. To prevent snoring, breathe through your nose.
5. Jack said, "Tell me, sir, what is the problem?"
6. Exactly 3,421 people visited on May 3, 2009.
7. The manatee, a sea mammal, swam nearby.
8. correct

9. I first visited Austin, Texas, in March 2007.
10. "It must be finished soon, of course," said Amy.

PRACTICE 3

1. We moved last year; we love our new home.
2. Who said, "Give me liberty, or give me death"?
3. Bring these items: a comb, a brush, and tissues.
4. "I'm sorry," said Rose, "but I must leave by 4:30."
5. He won a trophy; however, he soon broke it.
6. How I love the poem "Birches"!
7. Warning: Keep out of the hands of children.
8. correct
9. Mia asked, "When will this difficult day be over?"
10. Native to the Americas are the turkey, a bird; the chipmunk, a rodent; and the tomato, a plant.

PRACTICE 4

1. Mom is deaf and can't hear Mel's voice.
2. The horse stays in its stall when it's raining.
3. Silas's bags got mixed up with someone else's.
4. The five top students' grades were all A's.
5. correct
6. Donald's prized possession is an '08 yearbook.
7. I'm amazed that you don't tell him he's too loud.
8. correct
9. correct
10. It's hard to tell what's hers and what's yours.

1. Who wrote the novel <u>The Yearling</u>? *or* Who wrote the novel *The Yearling*?

2. My sister-in-law is a happy-go-lucky person.

3. I asked Bridget—she is our new neighbor—to be sure to join us at our block party.

4. The film is set during World War II (1939–1945).

5. correct

6. Today in court, one person shouted, "She [meaning Mrs. Gibbs] is guilty!"

7. correct

8. The Supreme Court ruled on the case. (See page 4 for the actual ruling [column 2].)

9. The team's goal—to win the championship—finally seemed within reach.

10. The Pilgrims sailed here on the <u>Mayflower</u>. *or* The Pilgrims sailed here on the *Mayflower*.

1. Touring the Southwest, we saw the Grand Canyon.

2. On Sunday, Reverend Sykes gave a fine sermon.

3. The Treaty of Versailles ended World War I.

4. Lewis Carroll, a British author, wrote "The Walrus and the Carpenter."

5. Every morning Grandma eats Tasty Choice cereal.

6. Former Vice President Al Gore Jr. was awarded the Nobel Prize.

7. The planet Jupiter is named for a Roman god.

8. "I met Mr. Kim," said Jo, "when I visited Ohio."

9. The Norton Museum of Art is on South Olive Avenue in West Palm Beach, Florida.

10. The Republican Party met just north of Houston.

Cumulative Review Chapters 25–26

PRACTICE 5 Using Underlining (or Italics), Hyphens, Dashes, Parentheses, Brackets, and Ellipses

Read the sentences. Then, rewrite the sentences, adding underlining (or italics if you type your answers on a computer), hyphens, dashes, brackets, parentheses, or ellipses. If a sentence is correct as is, write *correct*.

1. Who wrote the novel The Yearling?

2. My sister in law is a happy go lucky person.

3. I asked Bridget she is our new neighbor to be sure to join us at our block party.

4. The film is set during World War II 1939–1945.

5. This is a nicely written essay.

6. Today in court, one person shouted, "She meaning Mrs. Gibbs is guilty!"

7. Americans "pledge allegiance to the flag . . . with liberty and justice for all."

8. The Supreme Court ruled on the case. See page 4 for the actual ruling column 2.

9. The team's goal to win the championship finally seemed within reach.

10. The Pilgrims sailed here on the Mayflower.

PRACTICE 6 Using Correct Capitalization

Read the sentences. Then, rewrite each sentence, using capital letters where they are needed.

1. touring the southwest, we saw the grand canyon.

2. on sunday, reverend sykes gave a fine sermon.

3. the treaty of versailles ended world war I.

4. lewis carroll, a british author, wrote "the walrus and the carpenter."

5. every morning, grandma eats tasty choice cereal.

6. former vice president al gore jr. was awarded the nobel prize.

7. the planet jupiter is named for a roman god

8. "i met mr. kim," said jo, "when i visited ohi

9. the norton museum of art is on south olive avenue in west palm beach, florida.

10. the republican party met just north of houston.

11. my sister takes history 101 at yale universit

12. our family visited the lincoln memorial in washington, D.C.

13. "i believe doctor patel is from india," greta said. "he came to the united states in marc of 2003."

14. the bible is sacred to christians.

15. was aunt meg in the girl scouts of america?

PRACTICE 7 Writing Sentences With Correct Capitalization

Write a sentence about each of the following people, places, or things. Be sure to use correct capitalization.

1. the governor of your state

2. a local museum or tourist attraction

3. your favorite vacation spot

4. your favorite television show

5. a book that you have enjoyed

---

11. My sister takes History 101 at Yale University.

12. Our family visited the Lincoln Memorial in Washington, D.C.

13. "I believe Doctor Patel is from India," Greta said. "He came to the United States in March of 2003."

14. The Bible is sacred to Christians.

15. Was Aunt Meg in the Girl Scouts of America?

Answers will vary. Sample answers:

1. Governor Hutchinson was elected last November.

2. I like to go to the Houston Museum of Natural Science to learn about dinosaurs and space exploration.

3. The best place I ever visited was Yellowstone National Park near Jackson, Wyoming.

4. When I was much younger, my favorite television show was <u>Sesame Street</u>. *or* When I was much younger, my favorite television show was *Sesame Street*.

5. I really enjoyed reading <u>The Lion, the Witch, and the Wardrobe</u> by C. S. Lewis. *or* I really enjoyed reading *The Lion, the Witch, and the Wardrobe* by C. S. Lewis.

RESOURCES FOR Writing COACH

R1

WRITING IN THE
Content Areas

Writing in the content areas—math, social studies, science, the arts, and various career and technical studies—is an important tool for learning. The following pages give examples of content area writing along with strategies.

FORMS OF MATH WRITING

Written Estimate An estimate, or informed idea, of the size, cost, time, or other measure of a thing, based on given information.

Analysis of a Problem A description of a problem, such as figuring out how long a trip will take, along with an explanation of the mathematical formulas or equations you can use to solve the problem.

Response to an Open-Ended Math Prompt A response to a question or writing assignment involving math, such as a word problem or a question about a graph or a mathematical concept.

Writing in Math

Prewriting

- **Choosing a Topic** If you have a choice of topics, review your textbook and class notes for ideas, and choose one that interests you.

- **Responding to a Prompt** If you are responding to a prompt, read and then reread the instructions, ensuring that you understand all of the requirements of the assignment.

Drafting

- **State Problems Clearly** Be clear, complete, and accurate in your description of the problem you are analyzing or reporting on. Make sure that you have used technical terms, such as *ratio*, *area*, and *factor*, accurately.

- **Explain Your Solution** Tell readers exactly which mathematical rules or formulas you use in your analysis and why they apply. Clearly spell out each step you take in your reasoning.

- **Use Graphics** By presenting quantitative information in a graph, table, or chart, you make it easier for readers to absorb information. Choose the format appropriate to the material, as follows:

  ✓ **Line Graphs** Use a line graph to show the relationship between two variables, such as time and speed in a problem about a moving object. Clearly label the x- and y-axis with the variable each represents and with the units you are using. Choose units appropriately to make the graph manageable. For example, do not try to represent time in years if you are plotting changes for an entire century; instead, use units of ten years each.

  ✓ **Other Graphs** Use a pie chart to analyze facts about a group, such as the percentage of students who walk to school, the percentage who drive, and the percentage who take the bus. Use a bar graph to compare two or more things at different times or in different categories. Assign a single color to each thing, and use that color consistently for all the bars representing data about that thing.

  ✓ **Tables** Use a table to help readers look up specific values quickly, such as the time the sun sets in each month of the year. Label each column and row with terms that clearly identify the data you are presenting, including the units you are using.

Revising

- **Ensure Accuracy** For accuracy, double-check the formulas you use and the calculations you make.

- **Revise for Traits of Good Writing** Ask yourself the following questions: *How well have I applied mathematical ideas? Does my organizational plan help readers follow my reasoning? Is my voice suitable to my audience and purpose? Have I chosen precise words and used mathematical terms accurately? Are my sentences well constructed and varied? Have I made any errors in grammar, usage, mechanics, and spelling?* Use your answers to help you revise and edit your work.

Writing in Science

Prewriting

- **Choosing a Topic** If you have a choice of topics, look through class notes and your textbook, or conduct a "media flip-through," browsing online articles, or watching television news and documentaries to find a science-related topic.

- **Responding to a Prompt** If you are responding to a prompt, read the instructions carefully, analyzing the requirements and parts of the assignment. Identify key direction words in the prompt or assignment, such as *explain* and *predict*.

- **Gathering Details**
  - ✔ If your assignment requires you to conduct research, search for credible and current sources. Examples of strong sources may include articles in recent issues of science magazines or recently published books. Confirm key facts in more than one source.
  - ✔ If your assignment requires you to conduct an experiment, make sure you follow the guidelines for the experiment accurately. Carefully record the steps you take and the observations you make, and date your notes. Repeat the experiment to confirm results.

Drafting

- **Focus and Elaborate** In your introduction, clearly state your topic. Make sure you tell readers why your topic matters. As you draft, give sufficient details, including background, facts, and examples, to help your readers understand your topic. Summarize your findings and insights in your conclusion.

- **Organize** As you draft, follow a suitable organizational pattern. If you are telling the story of an important scientific breakthrough, consider telling events in chronological order. If you are explaining a natural process, consider discussing causes and the effects that follow from them. If you are defending a solution to a problem, you might give pros and cons, answering each counterargument in turn.

- **Present Data Visually** Consider presenting quantitative information, such as statistics or measurements, in a graph, table, or chart. Choose the format appropriate to the material. (Consult the guidance on visual displays of data under "Use Graphics" on page R2.)

Revising

- **Meet Your Audience's Needs** Identify places in your draft where your audience may need more information, such as additional background, more explanation, or the definition of a technical term. Add the information required.

- **Revise for Traits of Good Writing** Ask yourself the following questions: *How clearly have I presented scientific ideas? Will my organization help a reader see the connections I am making? Is my voice suitable to my audience and purpose? Have I chosen precise words and used technical terms accurately? Are my sentences well constructed and varied? Have I made any errors in grammar, usage, mechanics, and spelling?* Use your answers to revise and edit your work.

FORMS OF SCIENCE WRITING

Lab Report A firsthand report of a scientific experiment, following an appropriate format. A standard lab report includes a statement of the hypothesis, or prediction, that the experiment is designed to test; a list of the materials used; an account of the steps performed; a report of the results observed; and the experimenter's conclusions.

Cause-and-Effect Essay A scientific explanation of the causes and effects involved in natural or technical phenomena, such as solar flares, the digestion of food, or the response of metal to stress.

Technical Procedure Document A step-by-step guide to performing a scientific experiment or performing a technical task involving science. A well-written technical procedure document presents the steps of the procedure in clear order. It breaks steps into substeps and prepares readers by explaining what materials they will need and the time they can expect each step to take.

Response to an Open-Ended Science Prompt A response to a question or writing assignment about science.

Summary of a Science-Related Article A retelling of the main ideas in an article that concerns science or technology, such as an article on a new medical procedure.

Writing in Social Studies

FORMS OF SOCIAL STUDIES WRITING

Social Studies Research Report
An informative paper, based on research, about a historical period or event or about a specific place or culture. A well-written research report draws on a variety of sources to develop and support a thoughtful point of view on the topic. It cites those sources accurately, following an accepted format.

Biographical Essay An overview of the life of a historically important person. A well-written biographical essay reports the life of its subject accurately and clearly explains the importance of his or her contributions.

Historical Overview A survey, or general picture, of a historical period or development, such as the struggle for women's right to vote. A successful historical overview presents the "big picture," covering major events and important aspects of the topic without getting lost in details.

Historical Cause-and-Effect Essay An analysis of the causes and effects of a historical event. A well-written historical explanation makes clear connections between events to help readers follow the explanation.

Prewriting

- **Choosing a Topic** If you have a choice of topics, find a suitable topic by looking through class notes and your textbook. Make a quick list of topics in history, politics, or geography that interest you and choose a topic based on your list.

- **Responding to a Prompt** If you are responding to a prompt, read the instructions carefully, analyzing the requirements and parts of the assignment. Identify key direction words in the prompt or assignment, such as *compare*, *describe*, and *argue*.

- **Gathering Details** If your assignment requires you to conduct research, consult a variety of credible sources. For in-depth research, review both primary sources (documents from the time you are investigating) and secondary sources (accounts by those who analyze or report on the information). If you find contradictions, evaluate the likely reasons for the differences.

Drafting

- **Establish a Thesis or Theme** If you are writing a research report or other informative piece, state your main point about your topic in a thesis statement. Include your thesis statement in your introduction. If you are writing a creative piece, such as a historical skit or short story, identify the theme, or main message, you wish to convey.

- **Support Your Thesis or Theme** Organize your work around your main idea.

  ✔ In a research report, support and develop your thesis with well-chosen, relevant details. First, provide background information your readers will need, and then discuss different subtopics in different sections of the body of your report. Clearly connect each subtopic to your main thesis.

  ✔ In a creative work, develop your theme through the conflict between characters. For example, a conflict between two brothers during the Civil War over which side to fight on might dramatize the theme of divided loyalties. Organize events to build to a climax, or point of greatest excitement, that clearly conveys your message.

Revising

- **Sharpen Your Focus** Review your draft for sections that do not clearly support your thesis or theme, and consider eliminating them. Revise unnecessary repetition of ideas. Ensure that the sequence of ideas or events will help reader comprehension.

- **Revise for Traits of Good Writing** Ask yourself the following questions: *How clearly have I developed my thesis or my theme? Will my organization help a reader follow my development of my thesis or theme? Is my voice suitable to my audience and purpose? Have I chosen precise and vivid words, accurately using terms from the period or place about which I am writing? Are my sentences well constructed and varied? Have I made any errors in grammar, usage, mechanics, and spelling?* Use your answers to revise and edit your work.

Writing About the Arts

Prewriting

Experience the Work Take notes on the subject of each work you will discuss. Consider its mood, or general feeling, and its theme, or insight into life.

✔ For visual arts, consider the use of color, light, line (sharp or smooth, smudged or definite), mass (heavy or light), and composition (the arrangement and balance of forms).

✔ For music, consider the use of melody, rhythm, harmony, and instrumentation. Also, consider the performers' interpretation of the work.

Drafting

Develop Your Ideas As you draft, support your main ideas, including your insights into or feelings about a work, with relevant details.

Revising

Revise for Traits of Good Writing Ask yourself the following questions: *How clearly do I present my ideas? Will my organization help a reader follow my points? Is my voice suitable to my audience and purpose? Have I chosen precise and vivid words, to describe the works? Are my sentences varied? Have I made any errors in grammar, usage, and mechanics?* Use your answers to revise and edit your work.

Writing in Career and Technical Studies

Prewriting

Choosing a Topic If you have a choice of topics, find a suitable one by looking through class notes and your textbook or by listing your own related projects or experiences.

Drafting

Organize Information As you draft, follow a logical organization. If you are explaining a procedure, list steps in the order that your readers should follow. If they need information about the materials and preparation required, provide that information first. Use formatting (such as headings, numbered steps, and bullet points), graphics (such as diagrams), and transitional words and phrases (such as *first, next,* and *if... then*).

Revising

Revise for Traits of Good Writing Ask yourself the following questions: *Have I given readers all the information they will need? Will my organization help a reader follow my points? Is my voice suitable to my audience and purpose? Have I chosen precise words, using technical terms accurately? Are my sentences well constructed? Have I made errors in grammar, usage, and mechanics?* Use your answers to revise and edit your work.

FORMS OF WRITING ABOUT THE ARTS

Research Report on a Trend or Style in Art An informative paper, based on research, about a specific group of artists or trend in the arts.

Biographical Essay An overview of the life of an artist or performer.

Analysis of a Work A detailed description of a work offering insights into its meaning and importance.

Review of a Performance or Exhibit An evaluation of an artistic performance or exhibit.

FORMS OF CAREER AND TECHNICAL WRITING

Technical Procedure Document A step-by-step guide to performing a specialized task, such as wiring a circuit or providing first aid.

Response to an Open-Ended Practical Studies Prompt A response to a question or writing assignment about a task or concept in a specialized field.

Technical Research Report An informative paper, based on research, about a specific topic in a practical field, such as a report on balanced diet in the field of health.

Analysis of a Career An informative paper explaining the requirements for a particular job, along with the responsibilities, salary, benefits, and job opportunities.

New technology has created many new ways to communicate. Today, it is easy to contribute information to the Internet and send a variety of messages to friends far and near. You can also share your ideas through photos, illustrations, video, and sound recordings.

Writing for Media gives you an overview of some ways you can use today's technology to create, share, and find information. **Here are the topics you will find in this section:**

- **Blogs**
- **Social Networking**
- **Widgets and Feeds**
- **Multimedia Elements**
- **Podcasts**
- **Wikis**

Blogs

A **blog** is a common form of online writing. The word *blog* is a contraction of *Web log*. Most blogs include a series of entries known as posts. The posts appear in a single column and are displayed in reverse chronological order. That means that the most recent post is at the top of the page. As you scroll down, you will find earlier posts.

Blogs have become increasingly popular. Researchers estimate that 75,000 new blogs are launched every day. Blog authors are often called bloggers. They can use their personal sites to share ideas, songs, videos, photos, and other media. People who read blogs can often post their responses with a comments feature found in each new post.

Because blogs are designed so that they are easy to update, bloggers can post new messages as often as they like, often daily. For some people blogs become a public journal or diary in which they share their thoughts about daily events.

Types of Blogs

Not all blogs are the same. Many blogs have a single author, but others are group projects. These are some common types of blog:

- **Personal blogs** often have a general focus. Bloggers post their thoughts on any topic they find interesting in their daily lives.

- **Topical blogs** focus on a specific theme, such as movie reviews, political news, class assignments, or health-care opportunities.

 WEB SAFETY Using the Internet safely means keeping personal information personal. Never include your address (e-mail or physical), last name, or telephone numbers. Avoid mentioning places you go to often.

Never give out passwords you use to access other Web sites and do not respond to e-mails from people you do not know.

Anatomy of a Blog

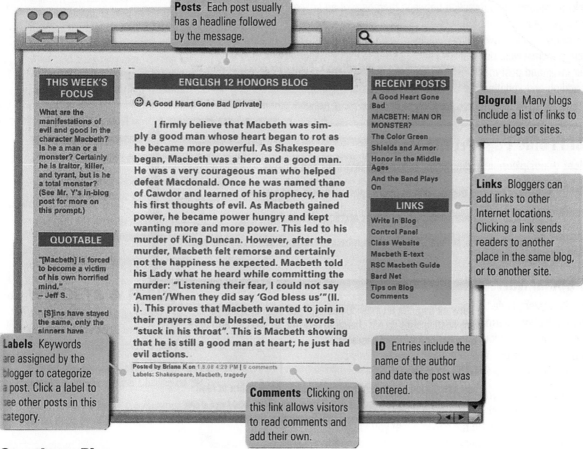

Posts Each post usually has a headline followed by the message.

THIS WEEK'S FOCUS

What are the manifestations of evil and good in the character Macbeth? Is he a man or a monster? Certainly he is traitor, killer, and tyrant, but is he a total monster? (See Mr. Y's in-blog post for more on this prompt.)

QUOTABLE

"[Macbeth] is forced to become a victim of his own horrified mind."
– Jeff S.

"[S]ins have stayed the same, only the sinners have

ENGLISH 12 HONORS BLOG

☺ A Good Heart Gone Bad [private]

I firmly believe that Macbeth was simply a good man whose heart began to rot as he became more powerful. As Shakespeare began, Macbeth was a hero and a good man. He was a very courageous man who helped defeat Macdonald. Once he was named thane of Cawdor and learned of his prophecy, he had his first thoughts of evil. As Macbeth gained power, he became power hungry and kept wanting more and more power. This led to his murder of King Duncan. However, after the murder, Macbeth felt remorse and certainly not the happiness he expected. Macbeth told his Lady what he heard while committing the murder: "Listening their fear, I could not say 'Amen'/When they did say 'God bless us'" (II. i). This proves that Macbeth wanted to join in their prayers and be blessed, but the words "stuck in his throat". This is Macbeth showing that he is still a good man at heart; he just had evil actions.

Posted by Briana K on 1.8.08 4:29 PM | 8 comments
Labels: Shakespeare, Macbeth, tragedy

RECENT POSTS

A Good Heart Gone Bad
MACBETH: MAN OR MONSTER?
The Color Green
Shields and Armor
Honor in the Middle Ages
And the Band Plays On

LINKS

Write In Blog
Control Panel
Class Website
Macbeth E-text
RSC Macbeth Guide
Bard Net
Tips on Blog Comments

Blogroll Many blogs include a list of links to other blogs or sites.

Links Bloggers can add links to other Internet locations. Clicking a link sends readers to another place in the same blog, or to another site.

ID Entries include the name of the author and date the post was entered.

Labels Keywords are assigned by the blogger to categorize a post. Click a label to see other posts in this category.

Comments Clicking on this link allows visitors to read comments and add their own.

Creating a Blog

Keep these hints and strategies in mind to help you create an interesting and fair blog:

- Focus each blog entry on a single topic.

- Vary the length of your posts. Sometimes, all you need is a line or two to share a quick thought. Other posts will be much longer.

- Choose font colors and styles that can be read easily.

- Many people scan blogs rather than read them closely. You can make your main ideas pop out by using clear or clever headlines and boldfacing key terms.

- Give credit to other people's work and ideas. State the names of people whose ideas you are quoting or add a link to take readers to that person's blog or site.

- If you post comments, try to make them brief and polite.

Social Networking

Social networking means any interaction between members of an online community. People can exchange many different kinds of information, from text and voice messages to video images. Many social network communities allow users to create permanent pages that describe themselves. Users create home pages to express themselves, share ideas about their lives, and post messages to other members in the network. Each user is responsible for adding and updating the content on his or her profile page.

Here are some features you are likely to find on a social network profile:

Features of Profile Pages

- A **biographical description**, including photographs and artwork
- **Lists of favorite things**, such as books, movies, music, and fashions
- **Playable media** elements such as videos and sound recordings
- **Message boards**, or "walls," on which members of the community can exchange messages

Privacy in Social Networks

Social networks allow users to decide how open their profiles will be. Be sure to read introductory information carefully before you register at a new site. Once you have a personal profile page, monitor your privacy settings regularly. Remember that any information you post will be available to anyone in your network.

Users often post messages anonymously or using false names, or pseudonyms. People can also post using someone else's name. Judge all information on the net critically. Do not assume that you know who posted some information simply because you recognize the name of the post author. The rapid speed of communication on the Internet can make it easy to jump to conclusions—be careful to avoid this trap.

You can create a social network page for an individual or a group, such as a school or special interest club. Many hosting sites do not charge to register, so you can also have fun by creating a page for a pet or a fictional character.

Tips for Sending Effective Messages

Technology makes it easy to share ideas quickly, but writing for the Internet poses some special challenges. The writing style for blogs and social networks is often very conversational. In blog posts and comments, instant messages, and e-mails, writers often express themselves very quickly, using relaxed language, short sentences, and abbreviations. However in a face-to-face conversation, we get a lot of information from a speaker's tone of voice and body language. On the Internet, those clues are missing. As a result, Internet writers often use italics or bracketed labels to indicate emotions. Another alternative is using emoticons—strings of characters that give visual clues to indicate emotion.

:-) **smile** *(happy)*   :-(**frown** *(unhappy)*   ;-) **wink** *(light sarcasm)*

> *Use these strategies to communicate effectively when using technology:*
>
> ✔ *Before you click Send, **reread your message** to make sure that your tone is clear.*
>
> ✔ ***Do not jump to conclusions**—ask for clarification first. Make sure you really understand what someone is saying before you respond.*
>
> ✔ ***Use abbreviations** your reader will understand.*

Widgets and Feeds

A **widget** is a small application that performs a specific task. You might find widgets that give weather predictions, offer dictionary definitions or translations, provide entertainment such as games, or present a daily word, photograph, or quotation.

A **feed** is a special kind of widget. It displays headlines taken from the latest content on a specific media source. Clicking on the headline will take you to the full article. Many social network communities and other Web sites allow you to personalize your home page by adding widgets and feeds.

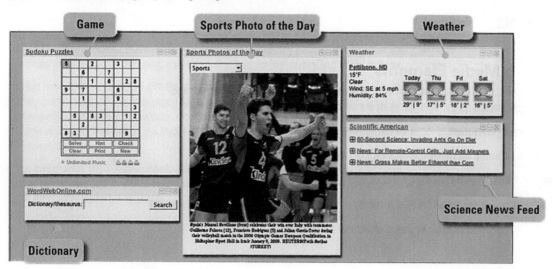

Game · Sports Photo of the Day · Weather · Science News Feed · Dictionary

Multimedia Elements

One of the great advantages of communicating on the Internet is that you are not limited to using text only. When you create a Web profile or blog, you can share your ideas using a wide variety of media. In addition to widgets and feeds (see page R9), these media elements can make your Internet communication more entertaining and useful.

GRAPHICS	
Photographs	You can post photographs taken by digital cameras or scanned as files.
Illustrations	Artwork can be created using computer software. You can also use a scanner to post a digital image of a drawing or sketch.
Charts, Graphs, and Maps	Charts and graphs can make statistical information clear. Use spreadsheet software to create these elements. Use Internet sites to find maps of specific places.

VIDEO		AUDIO	
Live Action	Digital video can be recorded by a camera or recorded from another media source.	**Music**	Many social network communities make it easy to share your favorite music with people who visit your page.
Animation	Animated videos can also be created using software.	**Voice**	Use a microphone to add your own voice to your Web page.

Editing Media Elements

You can use software to customize media elements. Open source software is free and available to anyone on the Internet. Here are some things you can do with software:

- **Crop** a photograph to focus on the subject or brighten an image that is too dark.

- **Transform** a drawing's appearance from flat to three-dimensional.

- **Insert** a "You Are Here" arrow on a map.

- **Edit** a video or sound file to shorten its running time.

- **Add** background music or sound effects to a video.

Podcasts

A **podcast** is a digital audio or video recording of a program that is made available on the Internet. Users can replay the podcast on a computer, or download it and replay it on a personal audio player. You might think of podcasts as radio or television programs that you create yourself. They can be embedded on a Web site or fed to a Web page through a podcast widget.

Creating an Effective Podcast

To make a podcast, you will need a recording device, such as a microphone or digital video camera, as well as editing software. Open source editing software is widely available and free of charge. Most audio podcasts are converted into the MP3 format. Here are some tips for creating a podcast that is clear and entertaining:

- **Listen to several podcasts by different authors** to get a feeling for the medium.

- **Make a list** of features and styles you like and also those you want to avoid.

- **Test your microphone** to find the best recording distance. Stand close enough to the microphone so that your voice sounds full, but not so close that you create an echo.

- **Create an outline** that shows your estimated timing for each element.

- **Be prepared** before you record. Rehearse, but do not create a script. Podcasts are best when they have a natural, easy flow.

- **Talk directly to your listeners**. Slow down enough so they can understand you.

- Use software to **edit your podcast before publishing it**. You can edit out mistakes or add additional elements.

You can change the information on a wiki, but be sure your information is correct and clear before you add it. Wikis keep track of all changes, so your work will be recorded and can be evaluated by other users.

Wikis

A **wiki** is a collaborative Web site that lets visitors create, add, remove, and edit content. The term comes from the Hawaiian phrase *wikiwiki*, which means "quick." Web users of a wiki are both the readers and the writers of the site. Some wikis are open to contributions from anyone. Others require visitors to register before they can edit the content. All of the text in these collaborative Web sites was written by people who use the site. Articles are constantly changing, as visitors find and correct errors and improve texts.

Wikis have both advantages and disadvantages as sources of information. They are valuable open forums for the exchange of ideas. The unique collaborative writing process allows entries to change over time. However, entries can also be modified incorrectly. Careless or malicious users can delete good content and add inappropriate or inaccurate information. Wikis may be useful for gathering background information, but should not be used as research resources.

WRITING FOR THE
Workplace

Writing is something many people do every day at work, school, or home. They write letters and reports, do research, plan meetings, and keep track of information in notes.

Writing for the Workplace shows you some models of the following forms of writing:

- **Note Cards**
- **Meeting Agenda**
- **Business Letter**
- **Friendly Letter**

Creating Note Cards

Whether you are working on a research report or gathering information for another purpose, it is helpful to keep your notes on individual cards or in note files on a computer. You will need to make sure that you note your sources on your cards. You can organize information many different ways, but it is most helpful to keep notes of one kind together.

> You can name the **source**, as shown here, or refer to the source by number (e.g., Source 3) if you are using source cards.

> The **topic** is the main focus of the notes.

Topic: Octopus
Source: PBS Web site Accessed 10/15/2010
http://www.pbs.org/wnet/nature/episodes/ the-octopus-show/
a-legend-of-the-deep/2014/

- Acrobatic and shy animals
- Can squeeze into very small spaces to hide or catch food
- Talented swimmers
- Can change color
- Live in all kinds of environments

> *In the notes section focus on the ideas that are most important to your research. Note that these ideas may not always be the main ideas of the selection you are reading. You do not need to write in full sentences. However, you may want to use bullets to make your notes easier to read.*

Writing a Meeting Agenda

When you have a meeting, it is helpful to use an agenda. An agenda tells what will be discussed in the meeting. It tells who is responsible for which topic. It also provides a guide for the amount of time to be spent on each topic.

Book Drive Project Meeting

Saturday, February 6, 2010 2:00 P.M.–6:00 P.M.

Called by Daphne Farkis

Attendees: Bill Aldridge, Erika Cruz, Alexis Chang, Daphne Farkis, Alex Guitierrez, Tiffany Hopper, John Robinson, Sylvie Snopes

Time	Item	Owner
2:00 P.M.–2:30 P.M.	Welcome and introduction	Daphne
2:30 P.M.–3:30 P.M.	Overview of book drive process	Daphne
3:30 P.M.–4:00 P.M.	Discuss roles and responsibilities	Alexis, All
4:00 P.M.–4:30 P.M.	Break	All
4:30 P.M.–5:00 P.M.	Brainstorm session for flyer ideas	Erika, All
5:00 P.M.–5:30 P.M.	Next steps and deadlines	Daphne, All
5:30 P.M.–6:00 P.M.	Recap and adjournment	Daphne

Your meeting will need a **title** that explains the purpose of the meeting.

You should also include the **date** and **time**.

This is the person who **called** the meeting. The person often, but not always, leads parts of the meeting.

The **attendees** are all the people invited to the meeting.

The **time** provides a guide for how long a topic should be discussed.

This is the **item**, or **topic**, to be discussed.

The **owner** is the person who will lead each section of the meeting.

Writing Business Letters

Business letters are often formal in tone and written for a specific business purpose. They generally follow one of several acceptable formats. In block format, all parts of the letter are at the left margin. All business letters, however, have the same parts: heading, inside address, salutation, body, closing, and signature.

The **heading** shows the writer's address and organization (if any).

The **inside address** indicates where the letter will be sent and the date.

A **salutation**, or **greeting,** is punctuated by a colon. When the specific addressee is not known, use a general greeting such as "To Whom It May Concern."

The **body** of the letter states the writer's purpose. In this case, the writer requests that the class participate in the book drive.

The **closing**, "Sincerely," is common, as are "Best regards," "Yours truly," and "Respectfully yours."

Oscar Diego
Community Book Drive
P.O. Box 34535
Middletown, NY 10941

February 10, 2010
Yin Wallenez
English Teacher
Marsden School
1515 Main River Drive
Middletown, NY 10940

Dear Ms. Wallenez:

We are writing to you to encourage you and your class to join in this year's Community Book Drive. We really appreciated your participation last year and hope you will join us again. As you know, the Community Book Drive gathers books for hundreds of children who otherwise could not afford them. Last year we gathered more than 1,500 books!

Participating this year is simple. Just nominate two members of your class to serve as the book drive leaders. They will post flyers about the book drive around the school and other community areas. They will also be responsible for letting the book drive team leaders know when the drop boxes at your school are getting full.

Please let me know if you are interested. I sure hope that your class will be able to make this year's drive as much of a success as the last! Thanks for your time and consideration.

Sincerely,

Oscar Diego

Oscar Diego • Co-Coordinator, Community Book Drive

Writing Friendly Letters

Friendly letters are less formal than business letters. You can use this form to write to a friend, a family member, or anyone with whom you'd like to communicate in a personal, friendly way. Like business letters, friendly letters have the following parts: heading, inside address, salutation, body, closing, and signature. The purpose of a friendly letter might be:

- to share news and feelings
- to send or answer an invitation
- to express thanks

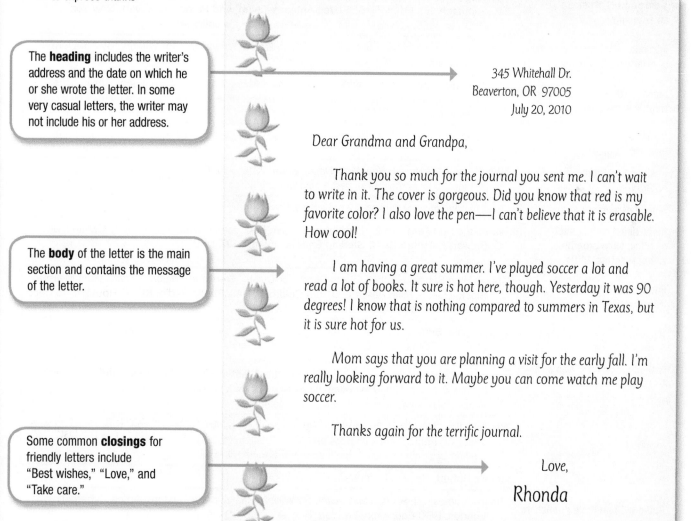

The **heading** includes the writer's address and the date on which he or she wrote the letter. In some very casual letters, the writer may not include his or her address.

The **body** of the letter is the main section and contains the message of the letter.

Some common **closings** for friendly letters include "Best wishes," "Love," and "Take care."

345 Whitehall Dr.
Beaverton, OR 97005
July 20, 2010

Dear Grandma and Grandpa,

Thank you so much for the journal you sent me. I can't wait to write in it. The cover is gorgeous. Did you know that red is my favorite color? I also love the pen—I can't believe that it is erasable. How cool!

I am having a great summer. I've played soccer a lot and read a lot of books. It sure is hot here, though. Yesterday it was 90 degrees! I know that is nothing compared to summers in Texas, but it is sure hot for us.

Mom says that you are planning a visit for the early fall. I'm really looking forward to it. Maybe you can come watch me play soccer.

Thanks again for the terrific journal.

Love,

Rhonda

MLA Style for Listing Sources

Book with one author	London, Jack. *White Fang.* Clayton: Prestwick, 2007. Print.
Book with two or three authors	Veit, Richard, and Christopher Gould. *Writing, Reading, and Research.* 8th ed. Boston: Wadsworth-Cengage Learning, 2009. Print.
Book prepared by an editor	Twain, Mark. *The Complete Essays of Mark Twain.* Ed. Charles Neider. New York: Da Capo, 2000. Print.
Book with more than three authors or editors	Donald, Robert B., et al. *Writing Clear Essays.* 3rd ed. Upper Saddle River: Prentice, 1996. Print.
A single work from an anthology	Poe, Edgar Allan. "The Fall of the House of Usher." *American Literature: A Chronological Approach.* Ed. Edgar H. Schuster, Anthony Tovatt, and Patricia O. Tovatt. New York: McGraw, 1985. 233–247. Print. [Indicate pages for the entire selection.]
Introduction, foreward, preface, or afterward in a book	Vidal, Gore. Introduction. *Abraham Lincoln: Selected Speeches and Writings.* By Abraham Lincoln. New York: Vintage, 1992. xxi–xxvii. Print.
Signed article in a weekly magazine	Walsh, Brian. "Greening This Old House." *Time* 4 May 2009: 45–47. Print. [For a multi-page article that does not appear on consecutive pages, write only the first page number on which it appears, followed by a plus sign.]
Signed article in a monthly magazine	Fischman, Josh. "A Better Life with Bionics." *National Geographic* Jan. 2010: 34–53. Print.
Unsigned editorial or story	"Wind Power." Editorial. *New York Times* 9 Jan. 2010: A18. Print. [If the editorial or story is signed, begin with the author's name.]
Signed pamphlet	[Treat the pamphlet as though it were a book.]
Audiovisual media, such as films, slide programs, videocassettes, DVDs	*Where the Red Fern Grows.* Dir. Norman Toker. Perf. James Whitmore, Beverly Garland, and Stewart Peterson. 1974. Sterling Entertainment, 1997. DVD.
Radio or TV broadcast transcript	"Texas High School Football Titans Ready for Clash." *Weekend Edition Sunday.* Host Melissa Block. Guests Mike Pesca and Tom Goldman. Natl. Public Radio. KUHF, Houston, 18 Dec. 2009. Print. Transcript.
A single page on a Web site	U.S. Census Bureau: Customer Liaison and Marketing Services Office. "State Facts for Students: Texas." *U.S. Census Bureau.* U.S. Census Bureau, 15 Oct. 2009. Web. 1 Nov. 2009. [Indicate the date of last update if known or use "n.d." if not known. After the medium of publication, include the date you accessed the information. You do not need the URL unless it is the only way to find the page. If needed, include it in angled brackets at the end, i.e. <http://www.census.gov/schools/facts/texas.html >.]
Newspaper	Yardley, Jim. "Hurricane Sweeps into Rural Texas; Cities Are Spared." *New York Times* 23 Aug. 1999: A1. Print. [For a multipage article that does not appear on consecutive pages, write only the first page number on which it appears, followed by a plus sign.]
Personal interview	Jones, Robert. Personal interview. 4 Sept. 2006.
Audio with multiple publishers	Simms, James, ed. *Romeo and Juliet.* By William Shakespeare. Oxford: Attica Cybernetics; London: BBC Education; London: Harper, 1995. CD-ROM.
Signed article from an encyclopedia	Askeland, Donald R. "Welding." *World Book Encyclopedia.* 1991 ed. Print. [For a well known reference, you do not need to include the publisher information, only the edition and year, followed by the medium used.]

R16   MLA Style for Listing Sources

Commonly Misspelled Words

The list on this page presents words that cause problems for many people. Some of these words are spelled according to set rules, but others follow no specific rules. As you review this list, check to see how many of the words give you trouble in your own writing.

absence	benefit	conscience	excellent	library	prejudice
absolutely	bicycle	conscientious	exercise	license	previous
accidentally	bought	conscious	experience	lightning	probably
accurate	brief	continuous	explanation	likable	procedure
achievement	brilliant	convenience	extension	literature	proceed
affect	bulletin	coolly	extraordinary	mathematics	pronunciation
agreeable	bury	cooperate	familiar	maximum	realize
aisle	buses	correspondence	fascinating	minimum	really
all right	business	courageous	February	misspell	receipt
allowance	cafeteria	courteous	fiery	naturally	receive
analysis	calendar	criticism	financial	necessary	recognize
analyze	campaign	curiosity	foreign	neighbor	recommend
ancient	canceled	deceive	fourth	niece	rehearse
anniversary	candidate	decision	generally	ninety	repetition
answer	capital	defendant	genuine	noticeable	restaurant
anticipate	capitol	definitely	government	occasion	rhythm
anxiety	career	dependent	grammar	occasionally	sandwich
apologize	cashier	description	guidance	occur	schedule
appearance	category	desert	height	occurred	scissors
appreciate	ceiling	dessert	humorous	occurrence	theater
appropriate	certain	dining	immediately	opinion	truly
argument	changeable	disappointed	immigrant	opportunity	usage
athletic	characteristic	distinguish	independence	parallel	valuable
attendance	clothes	effect	independent	particularly	various
awkward	colonel	eighth	individual	personally	vegetable
bargain	column	embarrass	intelligence	persuade	weight
battery	commercial	enthusiastic	judgment	physician	weird
beautiful	commitment	envelope	knowledge	possibility	whale
beginning	condemn	environment	lawyer	precede	yield
believe	congratulate	especially	legible	preferable	

English Glossary

A

accuracy (ak´yər ə sē) *n.* the state of being without error

alliteration (ə lit´ər ā´shən) *n.* the repetition of beginning sounds in words that are next to or near each other

alternative (ôl tur´nə tiv) *n.* another possibility

analysis (ə nal´ə sis) *n.* the process of looking at something closely to understand its meaning, structure, or parts

analyze (an´ə līz) *v.* to look at something carefully to understand its meaning or structure

audience (ô´dē əns) *n.* all the readers of a book or other piece of writing; a group of listeners or viewers

B

believe (bə lēv´) *v.* to accept as true

C

character (kar´ik tər) *n.* a person (or animal) who plays a part in the action of a story, play, or movie

chronological (krän ə läj´i kəl) *adj.* described or arranged in the order of time, starting with what happened first

citations (sī tā´shənz) *n.* references to sources of information

communicate (kə myü´ni kāt´) *v.* to exchange information

community (kə myü´nə tē) *n.* a group of people who live in the same area or are alike in some way

compare (kəm par´) *v.* to examine the differences and similarities between things

conclusion (kən klü´zhən) *n.* the end of a piece of writing that sums up the main points

consequence (kän´si kwens´) *n.* the result of an action

contrast (kən trast´) *v.* to compare in a way that shows differences

counter-argument (kount´ər är´gyü mənt) *n.* a reason against the original argument

D

demonstrate (dem´ən strāt´) *v.* to make a fact clear by giving proof or evidence

describe (di skrīb´) *v.* to say what something is like

detail (dē´tāl´) *n.* a specific fact or piece of information about something

develop (di vel´əp) *v.* to explain or build an idea or example bit by bit

dialogue (dī´ə lôg´) *n.* a conversation between two or more people in a book, play, or movie

document (däk´yü mənt) *n.* anything printed or written that gives information; *v.* to support ideas with information from sources

E

effect (e fekt´) *n.* the way that something changes because of a separate action

element (el´ə mənt) *n.* one of several parts that make up a whole

evaluate (ē val´yü āt´) *v.* to look into something carefully to assess and judge it

event (ē vent´) *n.* something that happens

evidence (ev´ə dəns) *n.* anything that gives proof or shows something to be true

example (eg zam´pəl) *n.* something typical of a particular group which can be used to represent or help explain

experience (ek spir´ē əns) *n.* the knowledge gained by doing a job or living through a situation; something a person has encountered firsthand; *v.* to have an event or feeling happen to you or to be affected by it

explain (ek splān´) *v.* to make something clear by describing it or giving important details

express (ek spres´) *v.* to say or show thoughts, feelings, or ideas

F

fact (fakt) *n.* a piece of information that can be shown to be true

focus (fō´kəs) *n.* the main topic or most important point; the center of attention

formal (fôr´məl) *adj.* reflecting language that is traditional and correct, not casual

formatting (fôr´mat´ing) *adj.* related to the arrangement of text, images, and graphics on a page

G

genre (zhän´rə) *n.* a type of writing that contains certain features

I

image (im´ij) *n.* a word or phrase in a poem or other kind of writing which appeals to one or more of the five senses

inform (in fôrm´) *v.* to give facts and information

insight (in´sīt´) *n.* a useful, important, deep understanding about a topic

instructions (in struk´shənz) *n.* steps to be followed to accomplish something

interpret (in tʉr´prət) *v.* to decide on and explain the meaning of something

introduction (in´trə duk´shən) *n.* the part at the beginning of a piece of writing which often tells what the rest will be about

J

judgment (juj´mənt) *n.* an opinion or conclusion formed after careful thought and evaluation

L

logical (läj´i kəl) *adj.* clear and reasonable; based on logic

M

metaphor (met´ə fôr´) *n.* a figure of speech in which something is described as if it were another thing

meter (mēt´ər) *n.* a poem's rhythmic pattern, made by the number of beats in each line

N

narrative (nar´ə tiv) *n.* a story, either fiction or nonfiction

O

onomatopoeia (än´ō mät´ō pē´ə) *n.* the use of words that imitate the sounds they describe

opinion (ə pin´yən) *n.* a belief or view that is not necessarily based on facts

organized (ôr´gə nīzd´) *adj.* the state of being in order

P

plot (plät) *n.* the sequence of events in a story

point of view (point uv vyü) *n.* the perspective from which a story is told; an attitude, position, standpoint, or way of looking at a situation; an opinion

position (pə zish´ən) *n.* a point of view or attitude toward something

purpose (pur´pəs) *n.* the reason that something exists or is done

R

reader-friendly (rēd´ər frend´lē) *adj.* easy for an audience to read and understand

reasoning (rē´zən ing) *n.* the process of reaching a conclusion by looking at the facts

relate (ri lāt´) *v.* to tell, as in to tell a story; to be connected to; to be concerned with

relationship (ri lā´shən ship´) *n.* the way two or more things are connected

relevant (rel´ə vənt) *adj.* closely connected, important, or significant to the matter at hand

reliable (ri lī´ə bəl) *adj.* able to be depended upon

resolution (rez´ə lü´shən) *n.* what happens to resolve the conflict in the plot of a story

respond (ri spänd´) *v.* to say or do something in response; to make an answer

rhyme (rīme) *n.* the repetition of the same sounds at the ends of words, especially in poetry

S

sense (sens) *n.* one of the five abilities of sight, touch, taste, hearing, and smell

sensible (sen´sə bəl) *adj.* having, showing, or a product of good sense and reason

sensory (sen´sər ē) *adj.* of or relating to the five senses

sequence (sē´kwəns) *n.* when a series of things follows each other in a particular order

setting (set´ing) *n.* the time and place of the action in a story or other piece of writing

similar (sim´ə lər) *adj.* alike but not exactly the same

simile (sim´ə lē´) *n.* a sentence or phrase that compares one thing to another, using the words *like* or *as*

standard (stan´dərd) *adj.* used as a basis for comparison

structure (struk´chər) *n.* the way something is organized and put together; *v.* to put together according to a pattern or plan

style (stīl) *n.* a way of doing something; a way of writing

summarize (sum´ə rīz´) *v.* to briefly state the main points or main ideas

suspense (sə spens´) *n.* a feeling of anxiety and uncertainty about what will happen in a story or other piece of writing

T

thesis (thē´sis) *n.* an idea or theory that is stated and then discussed in a logical way

technical (tek´ni kəl) *adj.* related to technology, computers, or applied sciences

topic (täp´ik) *n.* a subject that is written about or discussed

transition (tran zish´ən) *n.* the change from one part, place, or idea to another; in writing, the change between sentences, paragraphs, and ideas

U

understand (un´dər stand´) *v.* to know the meaning of something; to know how someone feels; to know why or how something happens

urgent (ʉr´jənt) *adj.* needing immediate action or attention

V

valid (val´id) *adj.* reasonable and logical, and therefore worth taking seriously; acceptable as true and correct

Spanish Glossary

A

accuracy / exactidud *s.* el estado de no tener errores

alliteration / aliteración *s.* la repetición de los sonidos iniciales de palabras seguidas o cercanas.

alternative / alternativa *s.* otra posibilidad u opción

analysis / análisis *s.* el proceso de examinar algo detenidamente para entender su significado, su estructura o sus partes

analyze / analizar *v.* examinar algo detenidamente para entender su significado o estructura

audience / audiencia, público *s.* los lectores de un libro u otra obra escrita; un grupo de oyentes o espectadores

B

believe / creer *v.* aceptar como la verdad

C

character / personaje *s.* un individuo (humano o animal) que tiene un papel en la acción de un cuento, una obra de teatro o una película

chronological / cronológico *adj.* descrito o arreglado en el orden temporal, empezando con el evento que ocurrió primero

citations / citas *s.* referencias a fuentes de información

communicate / comunicar *v.* intercambiar información

community / comunidad *s.* un grupo de personas que viven en la misma zona o tienen algunas cosas o atributos en común

compare / comparar *v.* examinar las diferencias y semejanzas entre cosas

conclusion / conclusión *s.* el final de una obra escrita que resume las ideas centrales

consequence / consecuencia *s.* el resultado de una acción

contrast / contrastar *v.* comparar dos o más cosas para señalar las diferencias entre ellas

counter-argument / contraargumento *s.* una razón contra el argumento original

D

demonstrate / demostrar *v.* aclarar un hecho por dar pruebas o evidencia

describe / describir *v.* decir cómo es algo

detail / detalle *s.* un dato específico o información específica de algo

develop / desarrollar *v.* explicar o exponer poco a poco una idea o ejemplo

dialogue / diálogo *s.* una conversación entre dos personajes o más en un libro, obra de teatro o película

document / documento *s.* cualquier cosa impresa o escrita que aporta información; documentar *v.* apoyar las ideas con información de fuentes

E

effect / efecto *s.* la manera en la que algo cambia a causa de una acción separada

element / elemento *s.* una de varias partes que forman una totalidad

evaluate / evaluar *v.* investigar algo cuidadosamente para analizarlo y valorarlo

event / evento *s.* algo que ocurre

evidence / pruebas *s.* cualquier cosa que demuestre o indique que algo es cierto

example / ejemplo *s.* algo típico de un grupo particular que se puede usar para representar o aclarar

experience / experiencia *s.* el conocimiento adquirido por hacer un trabajo o sobrevivr una situación; algo que una persona encuentra directamente experimentar *v.* pasar por un evento o sentimiento o ser afectado por un evento o sentimiento

explain / explicar *v.* aclarar algo describiéndolo o dando detalles importantes

express / expresar *v.* decir or mostrar los pensamientos, sentimientos o ideas

F

fact / hecho *s.* un dato que se puede verificar

focus / foco, idea central *s.* el tema principal o la idea más importante; el centro de atención

formal / formal *adj.* que refleja lenguaje tradicional y correcto, no informal

formatting / formateo *s.* la colocación de texto, imágenes y gráficos en una página

G

genre / género *s.* una clase de escritura que tiene características específicas

I

image / imagen *s.* una palabra o frase en un poema u otra clase de escritura que atrae uno o más de los cinco sentidos

inform / informar *v.* dar datos e información

insight / perspicacia *s.* el profundo entendimiento útil e importante de un tema

instructions / instrucciones *s.* los pasos que hay que seguir para realizar algo

interpret / interpretar *v.* determinar y explicar el significado de algo

introduction / introducción *s.* la parte inicial de una obra escrita que muchas veces cuenta de qué se trata el resto de la obra

J

judgment / juicio *s.* una opinión o conclusión formada después de una consideración y evaluación cuidadosa

L

logical / lógico *adj.* claro y razonable; basado en la lógica

M

metaphor / metáfora *s.* una figura retórica que describe algo como si fuera otra cosa

meter / métrica *s.* el patrón rítmico de un poema, marcado por el tiempo y ritmo de cada verso

N

narrative / narrativa *s.* un cuento de ficción o no ficción

O

onomatopoeia / onomatopeya *s.* el uso de palabras que imitan los sonidos que describen

opinion / opinión *s.* una creencia o perspectiva que no es necesariamente basada en los hechos

organized / organizado *adj.* que está ordenado

P

plot / argumento *s.* la secuencia de eventos en una historia

point of view / punto de vista *s.* la perspectiva de la cual se cuenta una historia

position / postura *s.* el punto de vista o la actitud hacia algo

purpose / propósito *s.* la razón por la cual algo existe o se hace

R

reader-friendly / fácil de leer *adj.* no complicado, fácil de entender y leer

reasoning / razonamiento *s.* el proceso de llegar a una conclusión por examinar los hechos

relate / relatar, relacionar *v.* contar, como contar un cuento; estar conectado con; tratarse de

relationship / relación *s.* la manera en la que dos cosas o más están conectadas

relevant / relevante *adj.* conectado estrechamente, importante o significativo al asunto en cuestión

reliable / fiable *adj.* que se puede fiar de la información

resolution / resolución *s.* lo que ocurre para resolver el conflicto en el argumento de una historia

respond / responder *v.* decir o hacer algo como respuesta; contestar

rhyme / rima *s.* la repetición de los mismos sonidos al final de las palabras, especialmente en la poesía

S

sense / sentido *s.* una de las cinco habilidades de visión, tacto, gusto, audición y olfato

sensible / sensato *adj.* tener, demostrar o ser un producto de buen sentido y razonamiento

sensory / sensorial *adj.* perteneciente o relativo a los cinco sentidos

sequence / secuencia *s.* cuando una serie de eventos ocurre en un orden determinado

setting / escenario *s.* el lugar y el momento de la acción en un cuento u otra obra escrita

similar / similar *adj.* semejante pero no exactamente igual

simile / simil *s.* una oración o frase que compara una cosa con otra, usando la palabra como (en inglés like o as)

standard / estándar *adj.* usado como base de comparación

structure / estructura *s.* la manera en la que algo está organizado o compuesto; estructurar *v.* organizar o componer según un patrón o plan

style / estilo *s.* una manera de hacer algo; una manera de escribir

summarize / resumir *v.* exponer de una manera breve los puntos o ideas principales

suspense / suspenso *s.* una sensación de ansiedad e incertidumbre sobre lo que va a pasar en una historia u otra obra escrita

T

technical / técnico *adj.* perteneciente o relativo a la tecnología, la informática o las ciencias aplicadas

thesis / tesis *s.* una idea o teoría que se expone y que se discute de una manera lógica

topic / tema *s.* una idea de la cual se escribe y que se discute

transition / transición *s.* el cambio entre partes, lugares y conceptos; en la escritura, el cambio entre oraciones, párrafos e ideas

U

understand / entender *v.* saber el significado de algo; saber cómo se siente alguien; comprender por qué o cómo ocurre algo

urgent / urgente *adj.* requiriendo acción o atención inmediata

V

valid / válido *adj.* razonable y lógico y por lo tanto vale la pena tomarlo en serio; aceptable como verdadero y correcto

Meeting Agenda

Meeting Title: _____

Date: _____

Time: _____

Called by: _____

Attendees: _____
_____

Time	Item	Owner

Cause and Effect Chart

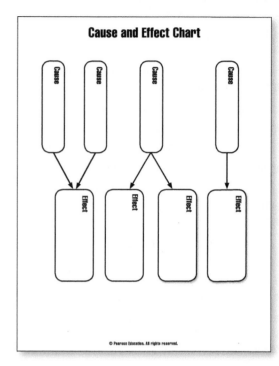

Cluster Diagram

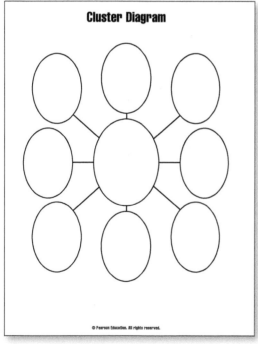

Five Ws Chart

Use these questions as you read, and write important details. Remember, you may not need to answer every question.

Who?

What?

When?

Where?

Why?

KWL Chart

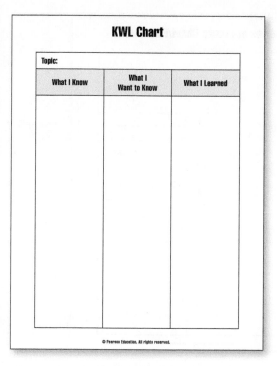

Main Idea and Details Web

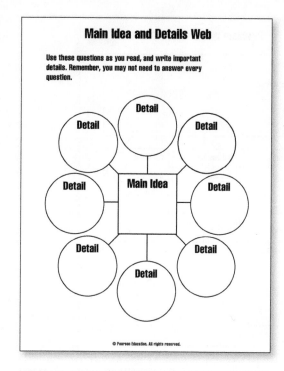

Meeting Notes

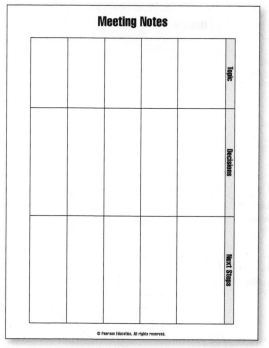

Note Card

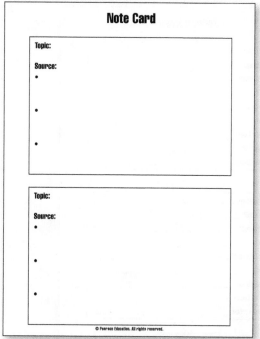

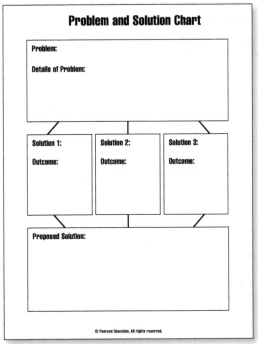

Problem and Solution Chart

Problem:

Details of Problem:

Solution 1:

Outcome:

Solution 2:

Outcome:

Solution 3:

Outcome:

Proposed Solution:

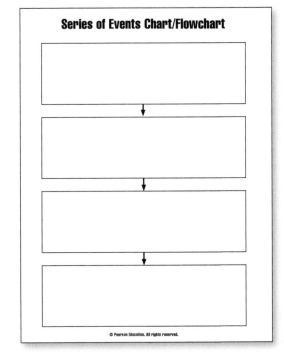

Series of Events Chart/Flowchart

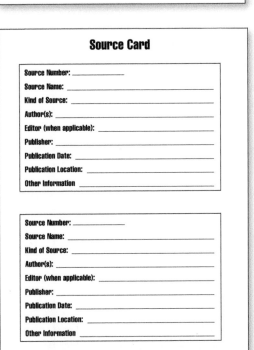

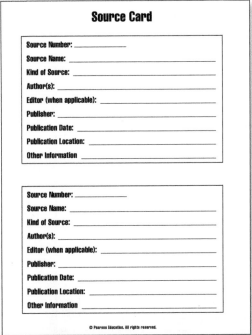

Source Card

Source Number: _____

Source Name: _____

Kind of Source: _____

Author(s): _____

Editor (when applicable): _____

Publisher: _____

Publication Date: _____

Publication Location: _____

Other Information _____

Source Number: _____

Source Name: _____

Kind of Source: _____

Author(s): _____

Editor (when applicable): _____

Publisher: _____

Publication Date: _____

Publication Location: _____

Other Information _____

Outline

Topic   I. _____
  Subtopic   A. _____
    Supporting   1. _____
    details   2. _____
              3. _____
              4. _____
  Subtopic   B. _____
    Supporting   1. _____
    details   2. _____
              3. _____
              4. _____
Topic   II. _____
  Subtopic   A. _____
    Supporting   1. _____
    details   2. _____
              3. _____
              4. _____
  Subtopic   B. _____
    Supporting   1. _____
    details   2. _____
              3. _____
              4. _____

R26   Graphic Organizer Handbook

Steps in a Process Chart

Steps	Details
Step 1:	
Step 2:	
Step 3:	
Step 4:	
Step 5:	

Storyboard

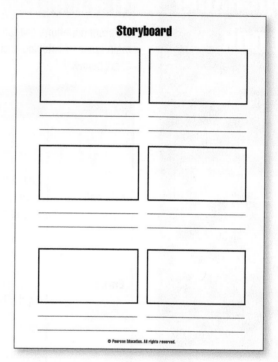

Timeline

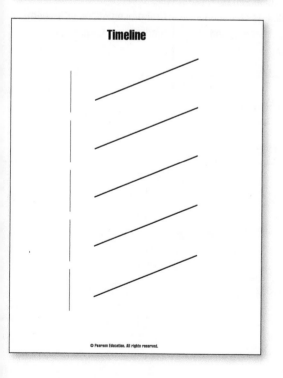

Venn Diagram

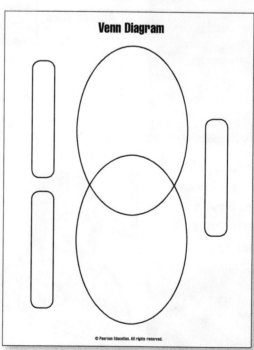

Listening and Speaking Handbook

Communication travels between people in many forms. You receive information by listening to others, and you convey information through speaking. The more developed these skills are, the more you will be able to communicate your ideas, as well as to comprehend the ideas of others.

If you improve your listening skills, it will become easier to focus your attention on classroom discussions and to identify important information more accurately. If you develop good speaking skills, you will be better prepared to contribute effectively in group discussions, to give formal presentations with more confidence, and to communicate your feelings and ideas to others more easily.

This handbook will help you increase your ability in these two key areas of communication.

Listening

Different situations call for different types of listening. Learn more about the four main types of listening—critical, empathic, appreciative, and reflective—in the chart below.

Types of Listening		
Type	**How to Listen**	**Situations**
Critical	Listen for facts and supporting details to understand and evaluate the speaker's message.	Informative or persuasive speeches, class discussions, announcements
Empathic	Imagine yourself in the other person's position, and try to understand what he or she is thinking.	Conversations with friends or family
Appreciative	Identify and analyze aesthetic or artistic elements, such as character development, rhyme, imagery, and descriptive language.	Oral presentations of a poem, dramatic performances
Reflective	Ask questions to get information, and use the speaker's responses to form new questions.	Class or group discussions

Using Different Types of Questions

A speaker's ideas may not always be clear to you. You may need to ask questions to clarify your understanding. If you understand the different types of questions, you will be able to get the information you need.

- An **open-ended question** does not lead to a single, specific response. Use this question to open up a discussion: "What did you think of the piano recital?"

- A **closed question** leads to a specific response and must be answered with a yes or no: "Did you play a piece by Chopin at your recital?"

- A **factual question** is aimed at getting a particular piece of information and must be answered with facts: "How many years have you been playing the piano?"

Participating in a Group Discussion

In a group discussion, you openly discuss ideas and topics in an informal setting. The group discussions in which you participate will involve, for the most part, your classmates and focus on the subjects you are studying. To get the most out of a group discussion, you need to participate in it.

Use group discussions to express and to listen to ideas in an informal setting.

Communicate Effectively Think about the points you want to make, the order in which you want to make them, the words you will use to express them, and the examples that will support these points before you speak.

Ask Questions Asking questions can help you improve your comprehension of another speaker's ideas. It may also call attention to possible errors in another speaker's points.

Make Relevant Contributions Stay focused on the topic being discussed. Relate comments to your own experience and knowledge, and clearly connect them to your topic. It is important to listen to the points others make so you can build off their ideas. Work to share the connections you see. For example, say whether you agree or disagree, or tell the goup how your ideas connect.

Speaking

Giving a presentation or speech before an audience is generally recognized as public speaking. Effective speakers are well prepared and deliver speeches smoothly and with confidence.

Recognizing Different Kinds of Speeches

There are four main kinds of speeches: informative speeches, persuasive speeches, entertaining speeches, and extemporaneous speeches.

Consider the purpose and audience of your speech before deciding what kind of speech you will give.

- Give an **informative speech** to explain an idea, a process, an object, or an event.

- Give a **persuasive speech** to get your listeners to agree with your position or to take some action. Use formal English when speaking.

- Give an **entertaining speech** to offer your listeners something to enjoy or to amuse them. Use both informal and formal language.

- Give an **extemporaneous speech** when an impromptu occasion arises. It is an informal speech because you do not have a prepared manuscript.

Preparing and Presenting a Speech

If you are asked to deliver a speech, begin choosing a topic that you like or know well. Then, prepare your speech for your audience.

To prepare your speech, research your topic. Make an outline, and use numbered note cards.

Gather Information Use the library and other resources to gather reliable information and to find examples to support your ideas.

Organizing Information Organize your information by writing an outline of main ideas and major details. Then, when you deliver your speech, write the main ideas, major details, quotations, and facts on note cards.

When presenting your speech, use rhetorical forms of language and verbal and nonverbal strategies.

Use Rhetorical Language Repeat key words and phrases to identify your key points. Use active verbs and colorful adjectives to keep your speech interesting. Use parallel phrases to insert a sense of rhythm.

Use Verbal and Nonverbal Strategies Vary the pitch and tone of your voice, and the rate at which you speak. Speak loudly and emphasize key words or phrases. Avoid consistently reading your speech from you notes. Work to maintain eye contact with the audience. As you speak, connect with the audience by using gestures and facial expressions to emphasize key points.

R30   Listening and Speaking Handbook

Evaluating a Speech

Evaluating a speech gives you the chance to judge another speaker's skills. It also gives you the opportunity to review and improve your own methods for preparing and presenting a speech.

When you evaluate a speech, you help the speaker and yourself to learn from experience. Listed below are some questions you might ask yourself while evaluating another person's speech or one of your own speeches.

- Did the speaker introduce the topic clearly, develop it well, and conclude it effectively?

- Did the speaker support each main idea with appropriate details?

- Did the speaker approach the platform confidently and establish eye contact with the audience?

- Did the speaker's facial expressions, gestures, and movements appropriately reinforce the words spoken?

- Did the speaker vary the pitch of his or her voice and the rate of his or her speaking?

- Did the speaker enunciate all words clearly?

Listening Critically to a Speech

Hearing happens naturally as sounds reach your ears. Listening, or critical listening, requires that you understand and interpret these sounds.

Critical listening requires preparation, active involvement, and self-evaluation from the listener.

Learning the Listening Process Listening is interactive; the more you involve yourself in the listening process, the more you will understand.

Focus Your Attention Focus your attention on the speaker and block out all distractions—people, noises, and objects. Find out more about the subject that will be discussed beforehand.

Interpret the Information To interpret a speaker's message successfully, you need to identify and understand important information. You might consider listening for repeated words or phrases, pausing momentarily to memorize and/or write key statements, watching non-verbal signals, and combining this new information with what you already know.

Respond to the Speaker's Message Respond to the information you have heard by identifying the larger message of the speech, its most useful points, and your position on the topic.

Index

Note: Page numbers in **boldface** refer to pages where terms are defined; *italicized* page numbers refer to writing applications.

reader's, 7
See also Blogs

K

KWL chart, R25

L

Lab reports, 21

Label warnings, colons in, 573

Language(s)
names of, 615
polite/professional, 198, 257
powerful, 172
rhetorical, R30
See also Figurative language; Vivid images/language

Leader (in collaborative group), 6

Learning log, 4

Legends/myths, 12, 93

Legible writing, 25, 84, 85, 138, 139, 165, 190, 191, 248

Letters
alphabet, capitalization of, 623
written messages
body of, R14, R15
business, 22, 260, 262, R14
closing for, 22, 198, 258, 260, 262, R14, R15
to editors, 19, 173
friendly, 22, 257, 258–259, 262–263, R15
greeting/salutation, 22, 198, 260, 263, R14
informal, 257, 260, 261, 262, 263, 266, 267
punctuation in, 569, 570, 573
thank-you letters, 260–261

Letters to authors, 20, 198–221
analysis and, 198, 203, 208, 210, 212, 215, 220, 221
audience and, 199, 201, 205, 210, 211, 212, 213, 216, 217, 219, 221
characteristics of, 198
characters and, 199, 204, 207, 218, 221
conventions and, 214, 215
drafting and, 208–209
editing and, 214–215
evidence and, 198, 202, 203, 206, 207, 208, 209, 210, 211, 212, 215, 218, 219, 220, 221
examples, 200–201, 202–203
focus and, 204, 205, 208, 209, 211, 213, 214, 215
graphic organizers and, 205, 206, 207, 209, 219, 220
insights and, 198, 211, 212, 218, 219, 221
organization and, 208, 209, 215
plot and, 198, 199, 200, 204
prewriting and, 204–207
publishing and, 216
purpose and, 199, 201, 205, 210, 211, 212, 213, 216, 217, 219, 221
revising and, 210–213
rubric for, 215
setting and, 198
sharing, with school community, 217
thesis statements and, 198, 203, 206, 207, 208, 209, 210, 211, 212, 220, 221
topics and, 204, 205, 216, 217
See also Interpretative response essays

Lines, 120
See also Poetry

Linking verbs, 136, 319–320, *321, 322, 323*
predicate pronouns following, 502
subject complement following, 396
See also Action verbs

Listening
listener (in collaborative group), 6
Listening and Speaking, *25, 85, 113, 139, 165, 191, 217, 249, 265*
Listening and Speaking Handbook, R28–R31
types of, R29

Literary elements, 198
See also Characters; Plot; Settings

Literary strategies, 11

Literary/rhetorical devices, 54–55
See also Narrative devices

Literature responses, *See* Interpretative response essays

Lyric poems, 121

M

Magazines
articles, 17, 147
covers, 192–193
/eZines, informational research reports and, 249

Main clauses
combining sentences using, 427, 439–440, *441*
commas and, 285, 563
in sentence structure, 417, 418, *419*
See also Independent clauses

Main idea, *See* Ideas

Main verbs, 324–325, *326*

Map directions, 612

Maps, 241, 266, 614, R10

Meaning
sentence meaning, 562–563
word meaning, 199, 273
See also Thoughts, complete/incomplete

modifiers with three or more, 535, 540

Symbolism, 55, 129

T

Tab key, 52

Tall tales, 12

Tautology. *See* Repetition

Teacher/family feedback. *See* Feedback

Technology
collaboration and, 7
science fiction and, 12, 93
sharing letters with, 217
spelling/grammar check tools and, 43
tab key and, 52
thesaurus tool and, 39, 55

Television series titles. *See* Titles

Tense, 470, 478

Test prompts (writing to test prompts), 17
compare-and-contrast essays and, *168–169*
interpretative response essays and, *220–221*
I-Search reports and, *254–255*
personal narratives and, *88–89*
persuasive essays and, *194–195*
poetry and, *142–143*
procedural writing and, *268–269*
short stories and, *116–117*
See also ABCDs of On-Demand Writing

Thank-you letters, 260–261

Thank-you notes, 3, 22

Themes, 24
See also Controlling idea

Thesaurus, 39, 55, 273

Thesaurus tool, 39, 55

Thesis statements, 20
compare-and-contrast essays and, 15, 146, 148, 149, 151, 154, 155, 156, 157, 160
drafting and, 30, 35, 141
informational research report and, 224, 237, 238, 239, 244, 247, 264, 265
interpretative response essays and, 20
introduction and, 53
letters to authors and, 198, 203, 206, 207, 208, 209, 210, 211, 212, 220, 221
persuasive essays and, 18, 172, 174, 177, 179, 180, 181, 182, 183, 184, 185, 186, 195
research writing and, 21
See also Controlling idea; Topic sentences

Things. *See* Nouns

Thoughts, complete/incomplete
to show sudden break in, 603
using clauses, 417–418, 419
using complements, 387–388, 389
using subjects/verbs, 292, 369, 370, 373, 374
See also Expressions; Fragments

Time (hours of day), 573

Time periods, 613

Timeline, R27

Timetable
informational research reports and, 237
writing and, 5

Titles
of people, capitalization of, 620–621, *622*
of works

capitalization of, 280, 623, 625
quotation marks in, 584, 586
underlining/italics in, 584–585, 586

Topic sentences, 50, 224, 226, 229, 238, 239, 240, 241, 242, 243, 244, 252, 264, 265
See also Informational research reports; Thesis statements

Topics (writing topics)
choosing, 32–33
compare-and-contrast essays and, 152–153
friendly letters and, 263
information gathering for, 34, 223
informational research reports, 230–231
letters to authors and, 204, 205, 216, 217
narrowing, 33–34, 73, 101, 127, 153, 179, 205, 231
personal narratives and, 72–73
persuasive essays and, 178–179, 181, 182, 190, 191, 193
poetry and, 126–127
short stories and, 100, 101, 105, 117
workplace writing and, 259

Tracking writing ideas, 4

Traits, writing. *See* Writing traits

Transitional expressions, 572

Transitions, 360, *365, 366*
commas and, 360
prepositional phrases and, 110, 111
sentences linked with, 109, 146, 157, 160, 161, 169, 213

Transitive verbs, 316, 318

Travel essays, 14

short story and, 111
See also Active voice; Passive voice

Vowel sound, 331

W

Watching, 3

Web
voice on Web page, R10

Web safety, R7

White space, 54

Widgets, R9

Wikis, R11

Word choice
poetry and, 120
as writing trait, 27, 28, 48, 58, 63
compare-and-contrast essays and, 163
letters to an author and, 215
personal narratives and, 83
persuasive essays and, 189
poetry and, 137
research reports and, 247
short stories and, 111
wrong, 273

Word order
agreement in inverted, 523–524, 525
normal/inverted, 381–382, 383
reversing, for variety, 444, *445*
rewording inverted
to identify pronoun case, 509, 510
to identify subject, 382–385, *386*

Words
commonly misspelled, R17
missing, 281
root words, 199
single, commas separating, 285
word meaning, 199, 273
See also specific types of words

Workplace writing, 22–23, 256–269
characteristics of, 257
example of, 258
forms of, 257
purpose and, 257
reader-friendly formatting techniques and, 22, 257, 259, 261, 263, 267
topics and, 259

Works Cited list, 228, 229, 234, 236, 237, 244, 275

Writing
budgeting time for, 5
building blocks of, 48–52
collaborative, 6, 7
comfortable environment for, 5
cooperative, 6
emotions/feelings and, 87, 91, 119
figurative, 55
finished, 7
free writing versus, 4
genres, 8–25
groups and, 6
ideas. *See* Ideas
legible, 84, 138, 139, 165, 190
materials for, 5
for media. *See* Multimedia projects
motivations for, 2
paragraphs and, 50–52

portfolios and, 7, 84, 112, 138, 164, 248
reflecting on, 7, 25, 47, 84, 112, 138, 248
sentences and, 48–49
topics. *See* Topics
types of, 8–25
ways of, 3
workplace, 22–23, 256–269
See also ABCDs of On-Demand Writing; Compositions; Descriptive essays; Essays; Expository writing; Fiction narration; Interpretative response essays; Nonfiction narration; Persuasive essays; Poetry; Procedural writing; Research writing; Test prompts

Writing process, 30–47
biographical narratives and, 87
diagram of, 30
reasons for using, 31
rubrics and, 28–29
stages in, 30
tips for, 31
See also Drafting; Editing; Prewriting; Publishing; Revising

Writing traits, *26–27, 56–59*
See also Conventions; Ideas; Organization; Sentence fluency; Voice; Word choice

Writing conventions. *See* Conventions

Index of Authors and Titles

Acknowledgments

Grateful acknowledgment is made to the following for copyrighted material:

Brandt & Hochman Literary Agents, Inc.

"Wilbur Wright and Orville Wright" by Stephen Vincent Benet, from *A Book of Americans* by Rosemary and Stephen Vincent Benet. Copyright © 1933 by Rosemary and Stephen Vincent Benet. Copyright renewed © 1961 by Rosemary Carr Benet. Used by permission of Brandt & Hochman Literary Agents, Inc.

Jenny Darling & Associates Pty Ltd.

"A Gentleman's Agreement" by Elizabeth Jolley from *Stories*. Copyright © 1976 Elizabeth Jolley. Used by permission.

Alfred A. Knopf, Inc., A Division of Random House, Inc.

"April Rain Song" from *The Collected Poems of Langston Hughes* by Langston Hughes, edited by Arnold Rampersad with David Roessel, Associate Editor, copyright © 1994 by The Estate of Langston Hughes. Used by permission of Alfred A. Knopf, a division of Random House, Inc.

Neal Levin

"Baby Ate a Microchip" by Neal Levin previously published in *Rolling in the Aisles* (Meadowbrook Press). Copyright © 2004 Neal Levin. Used by permission.

Longman Publishing Group, A Division of Pearson Education, Inc.

Writing in a Second Language" from *Writing: A Guide for College and Beyond (2nd Edition)* by Lester Faigley. Copyright © 2010 by Pearson Education. Used by permission.

National Council of Teachers of English (NCTE)

"Mistakes are a fact of Life: A National Comparative Study" by Andrea A. Lunsford and Karen J. Lunsford translated from *bcs. bedfordstmartins.com/lunsford/PDF/Lunsford_article_Mistakes. pdf*. Copyright © NCTE. Used by permission of National Council of Teachers of English (NCTE).

Harold Ober Associates Incorporated

"April Rain Song" from *The Collected Poems of Langston Hughes* by Langston Hughes, copyright © 1994 by The Estate of Langston Hughes. Used by permission of Harold Ober Associates Incorporated.

Philadelphia Inquirer c/o The YGS Group

"Search for boy and giant chicken will charm young and old" by Sandy Bauers from *Philadelphia Inquirer 9/15/2004, Book Review, Page H.15*. Copyright © 2004 Philadelphia Inquirer. Used by permission.

St. Louis Post-Dispatch

"Individuals Can Make a Difference and Little Things Can Have a Big Impact" by Martha M. Everett. From *St. Louis Post-Dispatch, 6/9/2008*. Copyright © 2008 St. Louis Post-Dispatch. Used by permission.

Viking Penguin, Inc., A division of Penguin Group (USA), Inc.

"Roommates" by Jon Scieszka from *Knucklehead*. Copyright © 2005, 2008 by Jon Scieszka. Used by permission of Viking Children's Books, A Division of Penguin Young Readers Group, A Member of Penguin Group (USA) Inc., 345 Hudson Street, NY, NY 10014. All rights reserved.

Weekly Reader Publishing Group

"Profiles in Caring: Volunteering Provides Teens with Great Experience in Work and in Life" by Kirsten Weir from *Career World, Feb–Mar 2009*. Copyright © Weekly Reader. Used by permission.

Note: Every effort has been made to locate the copyright owner of material reproduced in this component. Omissions brought to our attention will be corrected in subsequent editions.

Image Credits

Illustrations
    Robert Neubecker

All interior photos provided by Jupiter Images. Except

    118: © Corbis/age fotostock; 196: © Stockbroker/age fotostock.

Sentence Diagraming Workshop

Sentence diagraming is one of many useful tools for teaching the elements of English grammar. Sentence diagrams are particularly helpful to visual learners, but they can encourage all students to build their knowledge of sentence structure, placing each new concept logically on those that precede it. As you use this workshop, point out to students how diagraming clearly illustrates the relationship of one word to another in a sentence.

> **"** *Every English poet should master the rules of grammar before he attempts to bend or break them.* **"**
> **—Robert Graves**

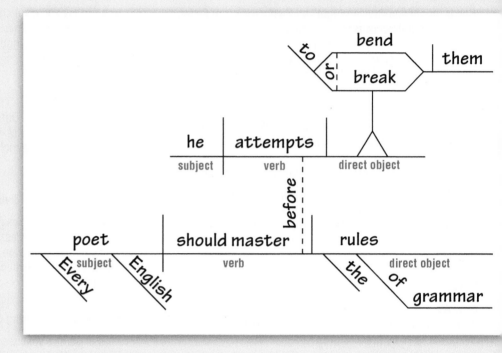

The Basics of Diagraming

This Sentence Diagraming workshop provides instruction that you can use with the downloadable practice pages you will find online, covering the basics of diagraming step by step.

- Sentence Forms and Modifiers
- Compound Sentence Elements
- Complements
- Prepositional Phrases and Appositive Phrases
- Participles and Participial Phrases
- Gerund Phrases
- Infinitives and Infinitive Phrases
- Compound Sentences
- Complex Sentences
- Compound-Complex Sentences

Each step of the process is accompanied by example sentences for you to use in the classroom, with diagrams and, in some cases, italics that will help you identify sentence parts. The practice pages allow you to give your students further diagraming work to hone their skills. You can download copies of the Practice Dages in the Teacher Center at www.phwritingcoach.com and distribute them to students. Practice page answers are included in this workshop.

Sentence Forms and Modifiers

Have students look at the most basic skeleton of a sentence by diagraming sentences with a variety of subject/verb orders. Emphasize these points.

Declarative Sentences

The basic diagram is a horizontal line, intersected by a vertical line.

- Place the simple subject to the left of the vertical line.
- Place the simple verb to the right of the vertical line.

EXAMPLE: Kathleen laughed.

Adding Modifiers

Explain that, to show how the words relate, place modifiers on slanted lines *directly below* the words they modify.

EXAMPLE: Quite hesitant, my sister did not answer quickly.

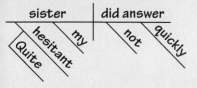

Imperative Sentences

The subject of an imperative sentence is understood to be *you*. To show this, place *(you)* in the usual place for the subject.

EXAMPLE: Stand up.

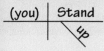

Interrogative Sentences

Inverted sentences follow the usual subject-verb order in a diagram. This is useful for locating the subject and verb in a sentence.

EXAMPLE: How are you?

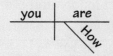

Name _____ Date _____

1 DIAGRAMING: SENTENCE FORMS AND MODIFIERS

Diagram the following sentences. See the example below.

Example: Where do you really live?

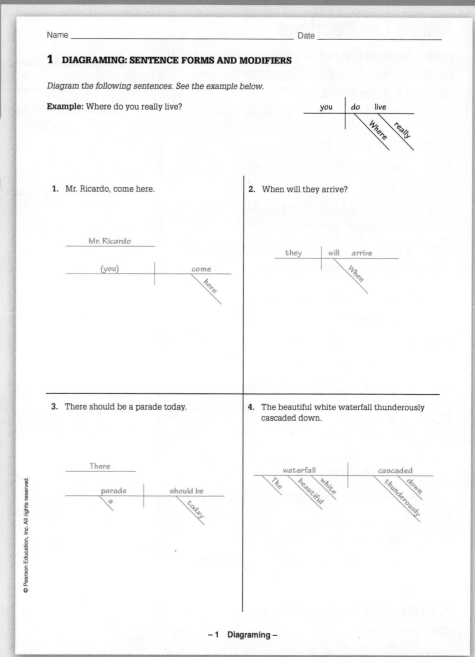

1. Mr. Ricardo, come here.

2. When will they arrive?

3. There should be a parade today.

4. The beautiful white waterfall thunderously cascaded down.

– 1 Diagraming –

Diagraming Practice
You can download copies of the Practice pages in the Teacher Center at www.phwritingcoach.com and distribute them to students.

Sentence Diagraming Workshop

Adding Conjunctions

Explain how the diagram emphasizes the parallel nature of compound sentence elements. Emphasize these points.

Compound Subjects

Split the horizontal line to the left of the diagram and place one subject on each line.

- Connect the subjects with a dotted line and write the conjunction next to it.
- Place two-word correlative conjunctions on either side of the dotted line.

EXAMPLE: Neither Amanda nor Lisa lived near the school.

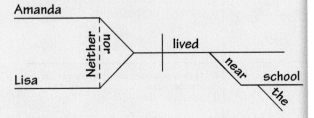

Compound Predicates

Split the horizontal line on the right side of the diagram.

- Place each verb on its own line.
- Place the conjunction on a dotted line between the two verbs.

EXAMPLE: Felicia walked into the room and sat down.

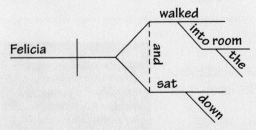

Note: When an adjective or adverb modifies both parts of a compound sentence element, place it on the main line.

Name _____   Date _____

2 DIAGRAMING: COMPOUND SENTENCE ELEMENTS

Diagram the following sentences. See the example below.

Example: The cat purred happily and stretched.

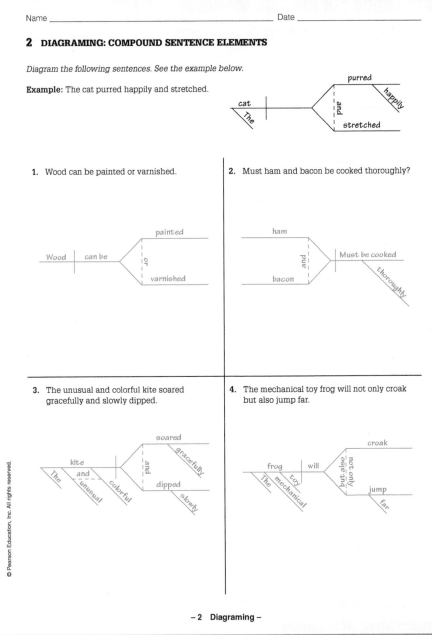

1. Wood can be painted or varnished.

2. Must ham and bacon be cooked thoroughly?

3. The unusual and colorful kite soared gracefully and slowly dipped.

4. The mechanical toy frog will not only croak but also jump far.

Compound Modifiers

Draw a dotted line between modifiers that a conjunction connects and write the conjunction on that line.

EXAMPLE: The small but fierce dog barked loudly and steadily.

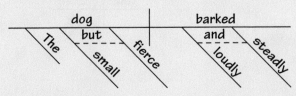

Diagraming Practice
You can download copies of the Practice pages in the Teacher Center at www.phwritingcoach.com and distribute them to students.

Complements

Help students recognize the relationship of a complement to the word it works with in the diagram. Emphasize these points.

Direct Objects and Indirect Objects

When diagraming a direct object, draw a vertical, upright line after the verb.

- Place the direct object to the right of that line.
- Place the indirect object, if any, on a horizontal line extended from a slanted line directly below the verb.

EXAMPLE: I gave Ted advice.

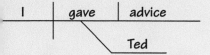

Objective Complement

Draw a line that slants to the left after the direct object and place the objective complement to the right of that line.

EXAMPLE: The President named him Chief of Staff.

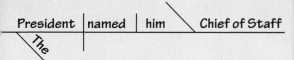

Predicate Nominatives and Predicate Adjectives

Draw a line that slants to the left after the verb and place the predicate nominative or the predicate adjective to the right of the line.

EXAMPLE: My dog is a spaniel.

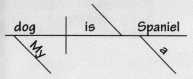

EXAMPLE: We felt grouchy.

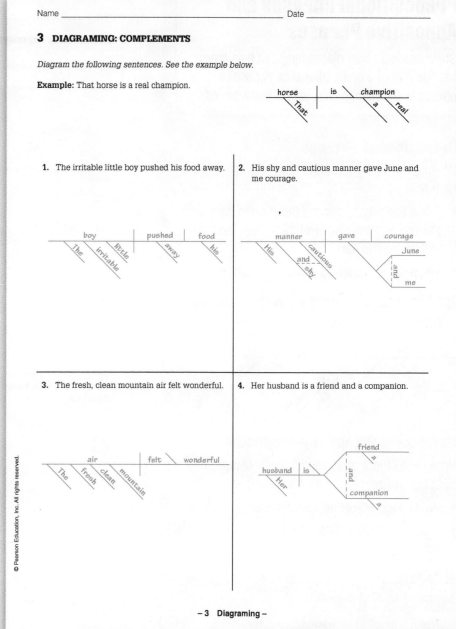

Name _____ Date _____

3 DIAGRAMING: COMPLEMENTS

Diagram the following sentences. See the example below.

Example: That horse is a real champion.

1. The irritable little boy pushed his food away.

2. His shy and cautious manner gave June and me courage.

3. The fresh, clean mountain air felt wonderful.

4. Her husband is a friend and a companion.

– 3 Diagraming –

Diagraming Practice
You can download copies of the Practice pages in the Teacher Center at www.phwritingcoach.com and distribute them to students.

Prepositional Phrases and Appositive Phrases

Show students how diagraming can help them see the role of a prepositional or appositive phrase in a sentence. Emphasize these points.

Prepositional Phrases

When diagraming a prepositional phrase, draw a bent line.

- Place the preposition on the slanted part of the line and the object of the preposition on the horizontal part.
- Place the phrase below the word modified.

EXAMPLE: The child *with the red ball* skipped *up the hill.*

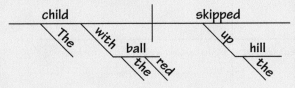

Compound Object of a Preposition

When the object of a preposition is compound, split the horizontal line for the object.

- Write each object on its own line.
- Place the conjunction on a dotted line between the two object lines.

EXAMPLE: We need a house *with three bedrooms and a den.*

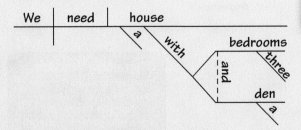

Appositives and Appositive Phrases

Place an appositive in parentheses just to the right of the noun or pronoun it identifies, renames, or explains. Place any modifiers of the appositive directly below it.

EXAMPLE: Harriet Danby, *her friend,* is a lawyer.

Harriet Danby (friend) | is \ lawyer
her / a

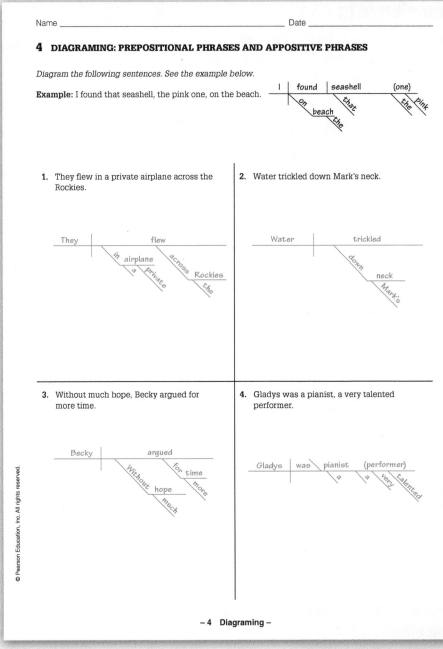

Name _____ Date _____

4 DIAGRAMING: PREPOSITIONAL PHRASES AND APPOSITIVE PHRASES

Diagram the following sentences. See the example below.

Example: I found that seashell, the pink one, on the beach.

1. They flew in a private airplane across the Rockies.

2. Water trickled down Mark's neck.

3. Without much hope, Becky argued for more time.

4. Gladys was a pianist, a very talented performer.

– 4 Diagraming –

Diagraming Practice
You can download copies of the Practice pages in the Teacher Center at www.phwritingcoach.com and distribute them to students.

Participles and Participial Phrases

Help students see how a diagram helps them understand the role a participle plays in a sentence. Emphasize these points.

Participial Phrase

Place a participial phrase on a bent line, like that of a prepositional phrase. Explain that the form of the diagram helps us see that the phrase is a modifier.

- Write the participle in a curve along the line.
- As an adjective, a participle or participial phrase is placed directly below the noun or pronoun it modifies.

EXAMPLE: *Stopping suddenly,* I almost fell.

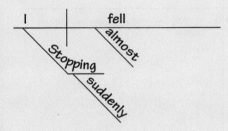

Participle With a Complement

A participial phrase may have a complement, just like a sentence or a prepositional phrase, and it is diagramed in a similar way.

- When a participle has a direct object, place the object after a vertical line.
- When a participle has a predicate adjective or predicate nominative, place that complement after a line that slants to the left.

EXAMPLE: *Carefully reviewing books for children,* Russell stays busy.

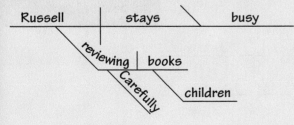

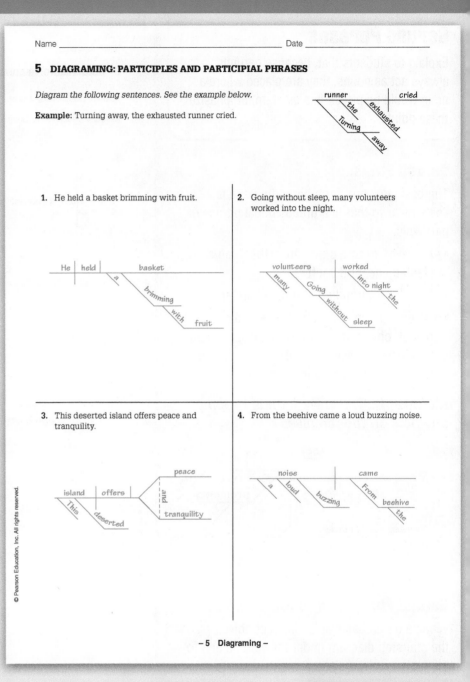

Name _____ Date _____

5 DIAGRAMING: PARTICIPLES AND PARTICIPIAL PHRASES

Diagram the following sentences. See the example below.

Example: Turning away, the exhausted runner cried.

1. He held a basket brimming with fruit.

2. Going without sleep, many volunteers worked into the night.

3. This deserted island offers peace and tranquility.

4. From the beehive came a loud buzzing noise.

– 5 Diagraming –

Diagraming Practice
You can download copies of the Practice pages in the Teacher Center at www.phwritingcoach.com and distribute them to students.

SD5

Sentence Diagraming Workshop

Gerund Phrases

Explain to students that, because gerunds always act as nouns, they are placed where a noun would be placed in a diagram. Emphasize these points.

Gerund Phrases

The basic diagram for a gerund phrase is a line similar to that of a prepositional phrase or participle.

- However, draw a stairstep, rather than a slanted line, at the left side.
- Curve the gerund around the stairstep.
- When a gerund acts as a subject, direct object, object of a preposition, or predicate nominative, place the stairstep on a pedestal wherever it would go if it were simply a noun.

EXAMPLE: The lease forbids *keeping any pets on the premises.*

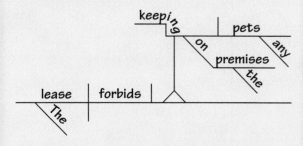

Gerund Phrases as Indirect Objects

When a gerund acts as an indirect object, place the stairstep diagram under the verb, joined to the main line by a slanted line.

EXAMPLE: His lecture gave *traveling to South America* new dimensions.

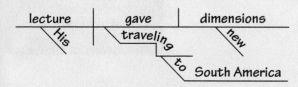

Gerund Phrases as Appositives

When a gerund or gerund phrase acts as an appositive, place it on a pedestal to the right of

the noun or pronoun it identifies, renames, or explains. Place parentheses around the bottom of the pedestal.

EXAMPLE: We mastered one sport, *playing tennis.*

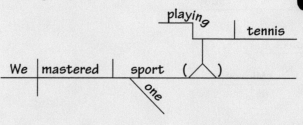

Name _____   Date _____

6 DIAGRAMING: GERUND PHRASES

Diagram the following sentences. See the example below.

Example: Paul loved working in the garden.

1. His favorite activity was hiking through the woods.

2. Achieving the position of senator will be very difficult.

3. Clark's fear, injuring his elbow, kept him on the bench.

4. All of Jill's friends like helping her with her projects.

– 6 Diagraming –

Infinitives and Infinitive Phrases

Explain to students that diagraming can help them see how an infinitive functions in a sentence, as a noun or as a modifier. Emphasize these points.

Infinitive Phrases as Nouns

When an infinitive phrase is used as a noun, place it on a bent line, like that of a prepositional phrase.

- Place the phrase diagram on a pedestal like that of a gerund.
- Place the object of an infinitive to the right of a vertical line on the horizontal line.
- Place the pedestal wherever it would go if the phrase were simply a noun.

EXAMPLE: She wanted *to show us her stamp collection.*

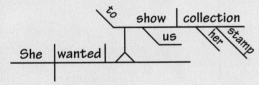

Infinitive Phrases With Subjects

When an infinitive phrase has a subject, place it on a horizontal line extending to the left from the diagram for the infinitive.

EXAMPLE: We asked *her* to stay.

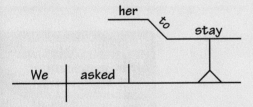

Infinitives as Modifiers

When an infinitive is used as an adjective or adverb, diagram it as you would a prepositional phrase.

Name _____ Date _____

7 DIAGRAMING: INFINITIVES AND INFINITIVE PHRASES

Diagram the following sentences. See the example below.

Example: Kendra began to study in the evening.

1. Joey's greatest joy is to go down the slide.

2. Her mother let Susan go to the movies.

3. To focus on just one problem would be advisable.

4. Her inclination was to tell him the truth about his idea.

– 7 Diagraming –

EXAMPLE: Beth was proud *to try.*

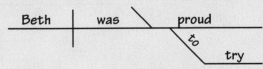

Note: When an infinitive does not include the word *to*, add that word to the diagram in parentheses.

Diagraming Practice
You can download copies of the Practice pages in the Teacher Center at www.phwritingcoach.com and distribute them to students.

SD7

Sentence Diagraming Workshop

Compound Sentences

Point out to students how diagraming makes clear the parallel nature of clauses in compound sentences. Emphasize these points.

Compound Sentences With Conjunctions

In a compound sentence joined by a conjunction, diagram each clause separately, one under the other.

- Join the two clauses with a stairstep dotted line between the two verbs.
- Write the conjunction on the horizontal part of the dotted line.
- Check to see whether the two clauses both have subjects and verbs.

EXAMPLE: A gentle breeze blew across the lake, and the raft floated inland.

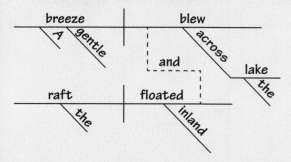

Compound Sentences With Semicolons

In a compound sentence joined by a semicolon, diagram each clause separately, one under the other.

- Join the two clauses with a stairstep dotted line between the two verbs.
- Write the semicolon on the horizontal part of the dotted line.

EXAMPLE: The book fell from the shelf; it was too close to the edge.

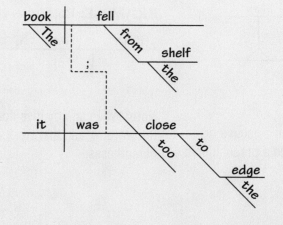

Name _____ Date _____

8 DIAGRAMING: COMPOUND SENTENCES

Diagram the following sentences. See the example below.

Example: I have two tennis rackets, but we need four.

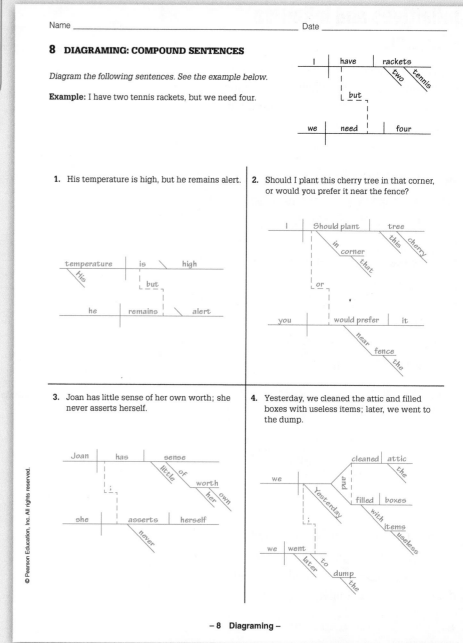

1. His temperature is high, but he remains alert.

2. Should I plant this cherry tree in that corner, or would you prefer it near the fence?

3. Joan has little sense of her own worth; she never asserts herself.

4. Yesterday, we cleaned the attic and filled boxes with useless items; later, we went to the dump.

– 8 Diagraming –

Diagraming Practice
You can download copies of the Practice pages in the Teacher Center at www.phwritingcoach.com and distribute them to students.

SD8

Complex Sentences

Explain to students how diagraming a complex sentence can help them see how a subordinate clause functions. Emphasize these points.

Adjective Clauses

When diagraming a complex sentence with an adjective clause, diagram the main clause first.

- Below it, diagram the adjective clause.
- Connect the clauses with a dotted line extending from the modified noun or pronoun to the relative pronoun in the adjective clause.

EXAMPLE: My friend *whom you met* just called.

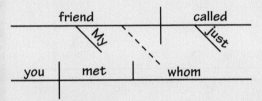

Adverb Clauses

When diagraming a complex sentence with an adverb clause, diagram the main clause first.

- Below it, diagram the adverb clause.
- Connect the clauses with a dotted line extending from the modified verb to the verb in the adverb clause.
- Write the subordinating conjunction that joins them on the dotted line.

EXAMPLE: She looks *before she leaps*.

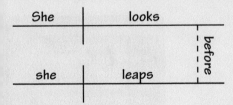

Noun Clauses

When diagraming a complex sentence with a noun clause, diagram the main clause first.

- Diagram the noun clause separately, on a pedestal that extends upward from the position the noun clause fills in the sentence.

- The pedestal should meet the noun clause diagram at the verb.

EXAMPLE: *Whatever you decide* is fine.

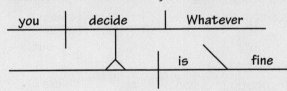

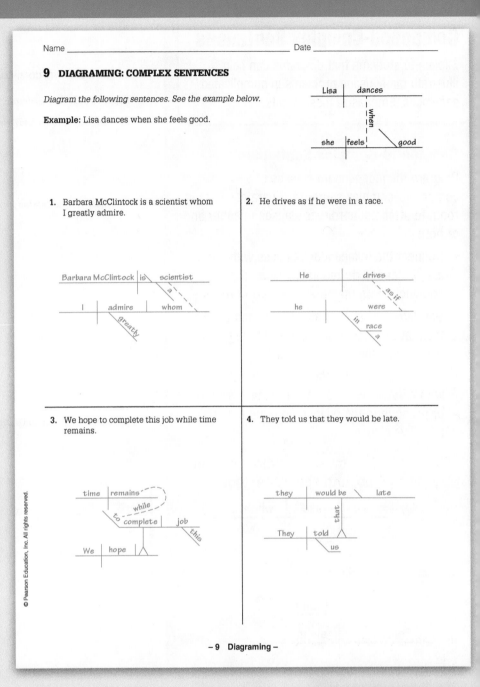

Compound-Complex Sentences

Explain to students that diagrams can help illustrate many usage problems in complicated sentences. Emphasize these points.

Compound-Complex Sentences

Diagram the independent clauses of a compound-complex sentence separately, leaving room to attach subordinate clauses to either and/or both.

- Connect the independent clauses with a stairstepped dotted line, placing the conjunction on the horizontal part of the line.

- Diagram the subordinate clauses and connect them at the appropriate places to their respective independent clauses.

- An adjective clause should be connected with a dotted line from the modified noun or pronoun to the relative pronoun in the adjective clause.

EXAMPLE: The musician whom we like plays the piano, and she sings, too.

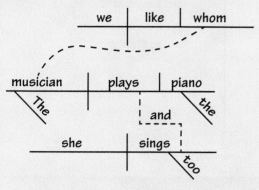

- An adverb clause should be connected with a dotted line extending from the modified verb to the verb in the adverb clause.

- A noun clause should sit on a pedestal that extends upward from the position the noun would occupy in the sentence.

EXAMPLE: Before he leaves, he will sweep, but he thinks that mopping is too hard.

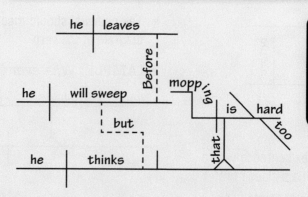

Name _____ Date _____

10 DIAGRAMING: COMPOUND-COMPLEX SENTENCES

Diagram the following sentences. See the example below.

Example: When you are ready, we can leave, but don't hurry.

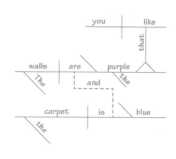

Example: The walls are the purple that you like and the carpet is blue.

Example: When Luis arrives, Rosa will bring out the cake, and Anita will give us the signal.

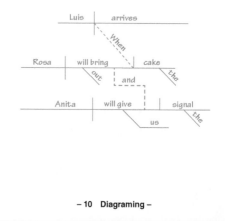

– 10 Diagraming –

Diagraming Practice
You can download copies of the Practice pages in the Teacher Center at www.phwritingcoach.com and distribute them to students.